1 MONTH OF FREE READING

at
www.ForgottenBooks.com

By purchasing this book you are eligible for one month membership to ForgottenBooks.com, giving you unlimited access to our entire collection of over 1,000,000 titles via our web site and mobile apps.

To claim your free month visit:
www.forgottenbooks.com/free1042091

ISBN 978-0-331-24434-2
PIBN 11042091

THE STATE OF OHIO

LEGISLATIVE ACTS

PASSED

AND

JOINT RESOLUTIONS

Adopted

BY THE

EIGHTY-THIRD GENERAL ASSEMBLY

At Its Regular Session

WHICH BEGAN JANUARY 7, 1919.

VOLUME CVIII

Springfield, Ohio:
The Springfield Publishing Company,
State Printers.
1919.
Bound at the State Bindery.

277331

GENERAL LAWS

[House Bill No. 45.]

To make supplementary appropriations for the General Assembly

AN ACT

Be it enacted by the General Assembly of the State of Ohio:

SECTION 1. The sums set forth in section 2 herein for the purposes specified, are hereby appropriated out of any monies in the state treasury to the credit of the General Revenue Fund, not otherwise appropriated.

SECTION 2. The following sums shall not be expended to pay liabilities incurred subsequent to June 30, 1919.

Appropriations.

HOUSE OF REPRESENTATIVES.

Personal Service—

A 1. Salaries—

124 members $124,000 000

Maintenance—

F Contract and Open Order Service—

F. 8. Contingencies 1,000 00

SENATE.

Personal Service—

A 1. Salaries—

33 members $33,000 00

A 2. Wages—

6 Clerks	4,500 00
3 Sergeants-at-arms	2,250 00
5 Pages	2,250 00
1 Custodian	750 00
2 Doorkeepers	1,500 00
2 Custodians of cloak room.........	1,500 00
2 Telephone attendants	1,500 00
10 Stenographers	7,500 00
1 Assistant postmaster.............	750 00
1 Assistant bill clerk..............	750 00
3 Committee room attendants.......	2,250 00
7 Porters	4,200 00

SECTION 3. The following items in H. B. 584, approved March 31, 1917 (107 O. L. 314), are hereby repealed:

Appropriations.

A 2. Wages—

5 Clerks	$3,000	00
4 Assistant sergeant-at-arms	2,400	00
3 Doorkeepers	1,260	00
4 Committee room attendants	1,680	00
2 Custodians of cloak room	840	00
2 Telephone attendants	840	00
Assistant postmaster	600	00
Assistant bill clerk	600	00
7 Stenographers	4,200	00
4 Pages	1,200	00
2 Porters	840	00
	$17,460	00

This act is not of a general and permanent nature, and requires no sectional number. JOHN G. PRICE, Attorney General.

CARL R. KIMBALL,
Speaker of the House of Representatives.
CLARENCE J. BROWN,
President of the Senate.

Passed January 15, 1919.
Approved January 21, 1919.

JAMES M. COX,
Governor.

Filed in the office of the Secretary of State at Columbus, Ohio, on the 22nd day of January, A. D. 1919.
1G.

[House Bill No. 147.]

AN ACT

To amend section 13560 of the General Code, relative to the persons who may have access to grand juries.

Be it enacted by the General Assembly of the State of Ohio:
SECTION 1. That section 13560 of the General Code be amended to read as follows:

Who may have access to grand jury.

Sec. 13560. The prosecuting attorney or assistant prosecuting attorney shall be allowed at all times to appear before the grand jury for the purpose of giving information relative to a matter cognizable by it or advise upon a legal matter when required. Such attorney may interrogate witnesses before such jury when it or he deems it necessary, but no other person shall be permitted to remain in the room with the jury while the jurors are expressing their views or giving their votes on a matter before them. In a matter or case which the attorney-general is required to investigate or prosecute by the governor or general assembly, he, and any attorney or attorneys at law selected by him for that purpose, shall have all the rights, privileges and powers conferred by this section and the next succeeding section, upon prosecuting attorneys.

SECTION 2. That original section 13560 of the General Code be and the same is hereby repealed. _{Repeal.}

SECTION 3. This act is hereby declared to be an emergency act necessary for the immediate preservation of the public peace and safety. Such necessity exists because of the reason that an epidemic of crime prevails in some parts of the state resulting in the loss of life and property to many citizens, and it is essential that the attorney-general, as the chief law officer of the state, should be clothed with power sufficient to enable him to initiate at once all investigations and prosecutions necessary for the punishment of criminals and the termination of lawlessness. _{Emergency act.}

The sectional number in this act is in conformity to the General Code.
JOHN G. PRICE,
Attorney General.

CARL R. KIMBALL,
Speaker of the House of Representatives.
CLARENCE J. BROWN,
President of the Senate.

Passed January 31, 1919.
Approved February 4, 1919.

JAMES M. COX,
Governor.

Filed in the office of the Secretary of State at Columbus, Ohio, on the 4th day of February, A. D. 1919.

2G.

[House Bill No. 83.]

AN ACT

To appropriate the sum of one thousand dollars for the use of Mrs. James W. Neiswonger.

Be it enacted by the General Assembly of the State of Ohio:

SECTION 1. That the sum of one thousand dollars be, and the same is hereby appropriated out of any monies in the state treasury to the credit of the general revenue fund not otherwise appropriated, for the use of Mrs. Laura Neiswonger, of Beallsville, Ohio, being the unpaid salary of her husband, J. W. Neiswonger, a member in the 82nd general assembly of Ohio. The auditor of state is hereby authorized and directed to issue said Mrs. Laura Neiswonger, upon the order of the speaker of the house of representatives of _{Appropriation for use of Mrs. James W. Neiswonger.}

the 83rd general assembly, a warrant on the treasurer of the state for the sum herein appropriated.

This act is not of a general and permanent nature, and requires no sectional number. JOHN G. PRICE, Attorney General.

CARL R. KIMBALL,
Speaker of the House of Representatives.
CLARENCE J. BROWN,
President of the Senate.

Passed February 7, 1919.
Approved February 19, 1919.

JAMES M. COX,
Governor.

Filed in the office of the Secretary of State at Columbus, Ohio, on the 19th day of February, A. D. 1919.

3L.

[House Bill No. 95.]

AN ACT

To appropriate the sum of one thousand dollars for the use of Mrs. W. S. Hoy.

Be it enacted by the General Assembly of the State of Ohio:

Appropriation for use of Mrs. W. S. Hoy.

SECTION 1. That the sum of one thousand dollars be, and the same is hereby appropriated out of any monies in the state treasury to the credit of the general revenue fund not otherwise appropriated, for the use of Mrs. W. S. Hoy, of Wellston, Ohio, being the unpaid salary of her husband Dr. W. S. Hoy, a member of the 82nd general assembly of Ohio. The auditor of state is hereby authorized and directed to issue to said Mrs. W. S. Hoy, upon the order of the speaker of the house of representatives of the 83rd general assembly, a warrant on the treasurer of the state for the sum herein appropriated.

This act is not of a general and permanent nature, and requires no sectional number. JOHN G. PRICE, Attorney General.

CARL R. KIMBALL,
Speaker of the House of Representatives.
CLARENCE J. BROWN,
President of the Senate.

Passed February 7, 1919.
Approved February 19, 1919.

JAMES M. COX,
Governor.

Filed in the office of the Secretary of State at Columbus, Ohio, on the 19th day of February, A. D. 1919.

4L.

7

AN ACT

To amend section 4, and to re-enact section 6, of an act entitled "An act to provide for the appointment of a commission to carry out the recommendations made by the committee under House Joint Resolution No. 11 of the general assembly, viz., to purchase a site and erect thereon a proper building to be used · as a home for future governors of the state, and to provide by appropriation the necessary funds therefor."

Be it enacted by the General Assembly of the State of Ohio:

SECTION 1. That section 4 of an act entitled "An act to provide for the appointment of a commission to carry out the recommendations made by the committee under House Joint Resolution No. 11 of the general assembly, viz.: to purchase a site and erect thereon a proper building to be used as a home for the future governors of the state, and to provide by appropriation the necessary funds therefor," be amended to read as follows:

Sec. 4. The board is authorized and empowered to pur- chase a dwelling in the city of Columbus, with the grounds pertaining thereto, for use as a home for the governors of this state; to purchase other grounds adjacent to such dwelling; to remove any of the buildings thereon; to alter or repair said dwelling; to further improve and embellish said grounds; to fully furnish and equip said dwelling for residence purposes; to make expenditures for any other purposes which the board shall find necessary or proper in furtherance of the end in view; and to exchange the present site intended for an executive mansion (heretofore pur- chased by said board) in part payment for the dwelling above stated. In event of such exchange, the governor of state is hereby empowered and authorized to execute a deed on behalf of the state, conveying the intended site above mentioned. Such deed shall contain a restriction and covenants that on the ninety-four feet front and rear of ground, the east end of said premises so conveyed, there shall never be erected any structures or buildings except a dwelling for a single family and outbuildings necessary for the use of such family only. The expenditures authorized by this section shall be exempted from the provisions of chapter 1, title IX, part first of the General Code. *(margin: Authority to purchase home for future governors.)*

SECTION 2. That said original section 6 of the act hereinbefore referred to be, and the same is hereby re-en- acted, and shall read as follows: *(margin: Re-enactment.)*

Sec. 6. For the purpose of providing a fund for car- rying this act into effect there is hereby appropriated from the money in the state treasury, not otherwise appropriated, the sum of seventy-five thousand six hundred and thirty- two and sixty-nine one-hundredths dollars. *(margin: Appropriation.)*

SECTION 3. That said original sections 4 and 6 of the *(margin: Repeals.)*

8

act hereinbefore referred to be, and the same are hereby repealed.

CARL R. KIMBALL,
Speaker of the House of Representatives.
CLARENCE J. BROWN,
President of the Senate.

Passed February 5, 1919.
Approved February 26, 1919.

JAMES M. COX,
Governor.

Filed in the office of the Secretary of State at Columbus, Ohio, this 27th day of February, A. D. 1919.
5L.

[House Bill No. 113.]

AN ACT

For the relief of Bernice Auch, Teacher.

Be it enacted by the General Assembly of the State of Ohio:

SECTION 1. That the board of education of West Alexandria village school district, Preble county, Ohio, be, and it is hereby authorized to pay Bernice Auch for services rendered as teacher in such school district, out of any funds under the control of said board of education, not otherwise appropriated, the sum of sixty dollars in full payment for her services as such teacher for the time from May 4, 1918, to May 31, 1918, as aforesaid, being payment in full at the rate agreed upon at the time she was employed, such payment to be made in the usual manner of paying teachers in said district.

CARL R. KIMBALL,
Speaker of the House of Representatives.
CLARENCE J. BROWN,
President of the Senate.

Passed February 13, 1919.
Approved February 28, 1919.

JAMES M. COX,
Governor.

Filed in the office of the Secretary of State at Columbus, Ohio, on the 28th day of February, A. D. 1919.
6L.

[Senate Bill No. 25.]

AN ACT

To authorize the appointment of soldiers' memorial commission to erect a tablet in memory of the "Andrews" Raiders, led by Captain James J. Andrews in the civil war.

Be it enacted by the General Assembly of the State of Ohio:

SECTION 1. That the governor of the state of Ohio be, and he hereby is authorized to appoint a soldiers' and sailors' commission of three members, each of whom served in the civil war. Such commission shall have authority to erect a suitable tablet or memorial in the rotunda of the capitol, in the state of Ohio, with the names of those participating in what is known as the "Andrews Raid" from Big Shanty, Georgia, north until captured in said state, their company and regiment, and a short sketch of said raid, and to do all other things necessary to carry out the purpose of this act. As soon as possible after being appointed, the members of the commission shall meet and organize by choosing a chairman and secretary.

Commission to erect tablet in memory of "Andrews" raiders.

SECTION 2. No member of such commission shall receive any compensation for his services in connection therewith.

No compensation.

SECTION 3. For the purpose of paying the cost of erecting such tablet or memorial, there is hereby appropriated, out of any funds in the state treasury to the credit of the general revenue fund, not otherwise appropriated, the sum of five hundred dollars, which shall be available on and after July 1, 1919.

Appropriation.

This act is not of a general and permanent nature, and requires no sectional number.
JOHN G. PRICE.
Attorney General.

CARL R. KIMBALL,
Speaker of the House of Representatives.
CLARENCE J. BROWN,
President of the Senate.

Passed February 13, 1919.
Approved February 28, 1919.

JAMES M. COX,
Governor.

Filed in the office of the Secretary of State at Columbus, Ohio, on the 28th day of February, A. D. 1919.
7G.

10

AN ACT

To amend sections 11710 and 11711 of the General Code, relating to the number of times premises being sold under execution should be offered for sale before reappraisement or sale by the court.

Be it enacted by the General Assembly of the State of Ohio:

SECTION 1. That sections 11710 and 11711 of the General Code be amended to read as follows:

New appraisement, when.

Sec. 11710. When real estate taken on execution and appraised, and advertised and offered for sale, is unsold for want of bidders, the court from which the execution issued, on motion of the plaintiff, shall set aside such appraisement, and order a new appraisement to be made, or set aside the levy and appraisement, and award a new execution to issue, as the case requires. When such real estate or a part of it has been two times appraised and thereafter advertised and offered for sale, and is unsold for want of bidders, the court may direct the amount for which it shall be sold.

New appraisement; terms of sale.

Sec. 11711. When premises are ordered to be sold, and having been advertised and offered for sale, remain unsold for want of bidders, the court from which the order of sale issued, on motion of the plaintiff or defendant, shall order a new appraisement, and also may order that the land be sold as follows: One-third cash in hand, one-third in nine months from the day of sale, and the remaining third in eighteen months from the day of sale, the deferred payments to draw six per cent interest, and be secured by mortgage on the premises.

Repeals.

SECTION 2. That said original sections 11710 and 11711 of the General Code be and the same are hereby repealed.

CARL R. KIMBALL,
Speaker of the House of Representatives.
CLARENCE J. BROWN,
President of the Senate.

The sectional numbers in this act are in conformity to the General Code. JOHN G. PRICE, *Attorney General.*

Passed February 18, 1919.
Approved February 28, 1919.

JAMES M. COX,
Governor.

Filed in the office of the Secretary of State at Columbus, Ohio, on the 28th day of February, A. D. 1919.

8G.

11

[House Bill No. 31.]

AN ACT

To amend section 4411 of the General Code, relating to employes of the local boards of health.

Be it enacted by the General Assembly of the State of Ohio:

SECTION 1. That section 4411 of the General Code be amended to read as follows:

Sec. 4411. The board may also appoint as many persons for sanitary duty as in its opinion the public health and sanitary conditions of the corporation require, and such persons shall have general police powers and be known as sanitary police. The board may also appoint as many persons for public health nurse duty as in its opinion the public health and sanitary conditions of the corporation require, and such persons shall be registered nurses and shall be known as public health nurses; provided, however, that where registered nurses are not available the board may appoint other suitable persons as public health nurses. *(margin: Appointment of sanitary officers and public health nurses.)*

The council may determine the maximum number of sanitary police and public health nurses so to be appointed. *(margin: Maximum number determined.)*

SECTION 2. That said original section 4411 of the General Code be, and the same is hereby repealed. *(margin: Repeal.)*

SECTION 3. That this act be and is hereby declared to be an emergency measure; that the emergency therefor being the prevalence in the state of Ohio of the Spanish influenza in malignant form and other contagious and infectious diseases demanding immediate and vigorous attention in order that the health and safety of the citizens of said state may be properly protected and preserved. *(margin: Emergency act.)*

CARL R. KIMBALL,
Speaker of the House of Representatives.
CLARENCE J. BROWN,
President of the Senate.

Passed February 13, 1919.
Approved February 28, 1919.

JAMES M. COX,
Governor.

Filed in the office of the Secretary of State at Columbus, Ohio, on the 28th day of February, A. D. 1919.

9G.

[House Bill No. 58.]

AN ACT

To validate all marriages of soldiers in this state solmenized since the declaration of war against Germany under any license issued by military authorities, and to amend section 11186 of the General Code so as to except soldiers' and sailors' brides from residence requirement.

Be it enacted by the General Assembly of the State of Ohio:

Section 11198-1.

Validating marriages of soldiers licensed by military authorities.

SECTION 1. That all the marriages heretofore performed in this state since the declaration of the war against Germany of soldiers of the United States then stationed at military camps in this state, under a marriage license issued by their commanding officers or other military authority, be, and the same are, hereby declared valid and binding marriages as though solemnized under a marriage license issued by the probate judge of the county where the prospective bride had her place of residence and it shall be the duty of the probate judge of the county in which such marriages were solemnized to record on his marriage records the certificate of such marriages which may hereafter be filed with him upon the payment of a fee of fifty cents for each certificate.

The sectional number on the margin hereof is designated as provided by law. JOHN G. PRICE, *Attorney General.*

SECTION 2. That section 11186 of the General Code be amended to read as follows:

Publication of bans before marriage; how.

License to be procured, when and where.

The sectional numbers in this act are in conformity to the General Code. JOHN G. PRICE, *Attorney General.*

Sec. 11186. Previous to persons being joined in marriage, notice thereof shall be published in the presence of the congregation on two different days of public worship; the first publication to be at least ten days before the marriage, within the county where the female resides; or, a license must be obtained for that purpose from the probate judge in the county where such female resides, provided that until the demobilization of the armies assembled in the present war against the central powers of Europe it shall be the duty of the probate judge of any county to issue such license to any soldier or sailor of the United States who may be stationed for duty in his county, and to the prospective bride of any such soldier or sailor regardless of the fact of the non-residence of said bride.

Repeal.

SECTION 3. That said original section 11186 of the General Code be, and the same is, hereby repealed.

CARL R. KIMBALL,
Speaker of the House of Representatives.
CLARENCE J. BROWN,
President of the Senate.

Passed February 18, 1919.
Approved February 28, 1919.

JAMES M. COX,
Governor.

Filed in the office of the Secretary of State at Columbus, Ohio, on the 28th day of February, A. D. 1919.

10G.

[Amended Senate Bill No. 8.]

AN ACT

To require husband and wife to join in the execution of chattel mortgages, etc., given upon personal household property owned by either or both of them.

Be it enacted by the General Assembly of the State of Ohio:

Sec. 8565-1.

SECTION 1. It shall be unlawful for either husband or wife (where that relation exists) to create any lien by chattel mortgage or otherwise upon any personal household property owned by either or both of them, without the joint consent of both husband and wife, and from and after the time this act shall take effect, no such mortgage of such personal household property shall be valid unless executed by both husband and wife. *Husband and wife must join in chattel mortgage on household property.*

Sec. 8565-2.

SECTION 2. The provisions of the act shall not apply to any mortgage on personal household property now in force, nor to any mortgage or lien for the purchase price of such property, nor in any manner affect any lien upon any personal property whatsoever now existing. *Not applicable to existing mortgage or lien.*

The sectional numbers on the margin hereof are designated as provided by law. JOHN G. PRICE, *Attorney General.*

CLARENCE J. BROWN,
President of the Senate.
CARL R. KIMBALL,
Speaker of the House of Representatives.

Passed February 19, 1919.
Approved March 7, 1919.

JAMES M. COX,
Governor.

Filed in the office of the Secretary of State at Columbus, Ohio, on the 7th day of March, A. D. 1919.

11G.

[House Bill No. 135.]

AN ACT

To reimburse Harry D. Knox for monies expended on state property.

Be it enacted by the General Assembly of the State of Ohio:

SECTION 1. That the sum of three hundred and fifty dollars together with interest for two years at six per cent. be paid Harry D. Knox as a reimbursement for monies paid in settlement of contracts for filling, grading, building cement drives and walks, placing ornamental gate posts and shrubbery on state armory lot at Marietta, Ohio. *Reimburse Harry D. Knox.*

SECTION 2. Said reimbursement to be paid from funds received and set apart for military purposes. The auditor of state is hereby authorized and directed to issue to said Harry D. Knox a warrant on the treasurer of state for the sum herein appropriated.

CARL R. KIMBALL,
Speaker of the House of Representatives.
CLARENCE J. BROWN,
President of the Senate.

This act is not of a general or permanent nature, and requires no sectional number.
JOHN G. PRICE, *Attorney General.*

Passed February 20, 1919.
Approved March 7, 1919.

JAMES M. COX,
Governor.

Filed in the office of the Secretary of State at Columbus, Ohio, on the 7th day of March, A. D. 1919.   12L.

[House Bill No. 124.]

To enact supplementary sections 1306-1 and 1306-2 to aid the re-establishment of pharmacists and assistant pharmacists who during the war have served in the army or navy of the United States.

Be it enacted by the General Assembly of the State of Ohio:

Pharmacists and assistants who served in army or navy permitted to practice for six months; issue of permits.

Sec. 1306-1. That every person registered as a pharmacist or as an assistant pharmacist or under a corresponding title in any other state or territory of the United States of America, or in the District of Columbia, who has served in the army or navy of the United States while at war with Austria-Hungary and Germany, and who has been honorably discharged from the service of the United States army or navy shall be permitted within six months after such honorable discharge, upon proof thereof, and upon proof of such registration above mentioned, to the satisfaction of the state board of pharmacy, to practice the profession as a pharmacist or assistant pharmacist, as the case may be, within the state for a period not to exceed six months. The state board of pharmacy shall issue a permit to that effect to all persons applying therefor and complying with the requirements of this section.

When and how pharmacists and assistants holding permits may register.

Sec. 1306-2. Any person who under the provision of section 1306-1, has received such permission for the period of six months to practice the profession as a pharmacist or assistant pharmacist, after having resided within this state for not less than three months, who upon oath declares an intention to permanently reside therein, may apply to the state board of pharmacy for registration as a pharmacist or assistant pharmacist, as the case may be, under the laws of this state, upon payment of the fees provided for in section 1311 of the General Code for issuing a certificate to a pharmacist or assistant pharmacist and proof of good character and reputation, subject to the rules and regulations for that purpose prescribed by the state board of pharmacy, and said board upon such application, satisfactory proof and payment of fees, shall issue a certificate of registration as pharmacist or assistant pharmacist, as the case may be, to such a person without requiring him to meet other provisions of law which may otherwise prevail for reciprocal registration within this state, subject, however, after registration, to all the other provisions of law which govern those who are registered within the state as pharmacist or assistant pharmacist.

CARL R. KIMBALL,
Speaker of the House of Representatives.
CLARENCE J. BROWN,
President of the Senate.

Passed February 20, 1919.
Approved March 7, 1919.

JAMES M. COX,
Governor.

Filed in the office of the Secretary of State at Columbus, Ohio, on the 7th day of March, A. D. 1919.   13G.

[Amended Senate Bill No. 36.]

AN ACT

To amend sections 5777, 5778 and 5784 of the General Code, relating to the ninth United States pharmacopoeia, and the fourth edition of the national formulary.

Be it enacted by the General Assembly of the State of Ohio:
SECTION 1. That sections 5777, 5778 and 5784 of the General Code be amended to read as follows:

Sec. 5777. A drug is adulterated within the meaning of this chapter (1) if, when sold under or by a name recognized in the * * * ninth decennial revision of the United States Pharmacopoeia, or in the * * * fourth edition of the National Formulary, it differs from the standard of strength, quality or purity laid down therein; (2) if, when sold under or by a name not recognized in the * * * ninth decennial revision of the United States Pharmacopoeia, or the * * * fourth edition of the National Formulary, but which is found in some other pharmacopoeia, or other standard work on materia medica, it differs materially from the standard strength, quality or purity laid down in such work; (3) if its strength, quality or purity falls below the professed standard under which it is sold; (4) if it is an imitation of, or offered for sale under the name of another article; (5) if the contents of the package as originally put up shall have been removed, in whole or in part, and other contents shall have been placed

What is adulteration of drugs.

in such package; (6) if it contains any methyl or wood alcohol. (100 v. 105 sec. 3.)

What is adulteration as to food, drink, confectionery, etc.

Sec. 5778. Food, drink, confectionery or condiments are adulterated within the meaning of this chapter (1) if any substance or substances have been mixed with it, so as to lower or depreciate or injuriously affect its quality, strength or purity; (2) if any inferior or cheaper substance or substances have been substituted wholly, or in part, for it; (3) if any valuable or necessary constituent or ingredient has been wholly, or in part, abstracted from it; (4) if it is an imitation of, or is sold under the name of another article; (5) if it consists wholly, or in part, of a diseased, decomposed, putrid, infected, tainted or rotten animal or vegetable substance or article, whether manufactured or not or, in the case of milk, if it is the product of a diseased animal; (6) if it is colored, coated, polished or powdered, whereby damage or inferiority is concealed, or if by any means it is made to appear better or of greater value than it really is; (7) if it contains any added substance or ingredient which is poisonous or injurious to health; (8) if, when sold under or by a name recognized in the * * * ninth decennial revision of the United States Pharmacopoeia, or the * * * fourth edition of the National Formulary, it differs from the standard of strength, quality or purity laid down therein; (9) if, when sold under or by a name not recognized in the * * * ninth decennial revision of the United States Pharmacopoeia, or the * * fourth edition of the National Formulary, but if found in some other pharmacopoeia, or other standard work on materia medica, it differs materially from the standard of strength, quality or purity laid down in such work; (10) if the strength, quality or purity falls below the professed standard under which it is sold; (11) if it contains any methyl or wood alcohol. (100 v. 105 sec. 3.)

What is misbranding of drugs.

Sec. 5784. A drug shall be misbranded within the meaning of this chapter: (1) if the package fails to bear a statement on the label of the quantity or proportion of grain or ethyl alcohol, morphine, opium, cocaine, heroin, alpha or beta eucaine, chloroform, cannabis, chloral hydrate, acetanilid or any derivative or preparation of such substances contained therein, provided, that the provisions of this section shall not apply to the prescriptions of regular licensed physicians, dentists and doctors of veterinary medicine, nor to such drugs and preparations as are officially recognized in the * * * ninth decennial revision of the United States Pharmacopoeia, or the * * * fourth edition of the National Formulary, and which are sold under the name by which they are so recognized; (2) if the package containing it or any label thereon bears a statement, design or device regarding it or the ingredients or substances contained therein, which is false or misleading in any particular; (3) if the package containing it or any label thereon bears or contains any statement, design or device regarding the curative or the therapeutic effect of such article or any of the ingredients or substances contained therein, which is false and fraudulent. (103 v. 137.)

SECTION 2. That said original sections 5777, 5778 and 5784 of the General Code be, and the same are hereby repealed.

Repeals.

CARL R. KIMBALL,
Speaker of the House of Representatives.
CLARENCE J. BROWN,
President of the Senate.

Passed February 27, 1919.
Approved March 13, 1919.

JAMES M. COX,
Governor.

Filed in the office of the Secretary of State at Columbus, Ohio, on the 14th day of March, A. D. 1919.
14 G.

[House Bill No. 66.]

AN ACT

Permitting the city of Elyria, Ohio, to pay a cost bill in the sum of $552.36 to The Schafer-Suhr Coal Company of Cleveland, Ohio.

Be it enacted by the General Assembly of the State of Ohio:

SECTION 1. That the city of Elyria be, and hereby is, authorized to pay out of funds not otherwise appropriated the sum of five hundred and fifty-two dollars and thirty-six cents, the same being the purchase price of coal bought of The Schafer-Suhr Coal Company, Cleveland, by the service director of Elyria in November, 1909, said amount being payment in full for the indebtedness of the city of Elyria to said The Schafer-Suhr Coal Company for said coal.

Elyria authorized to pay Schafer-Suhr Coal Company.

CARL R. KIMBALL,
Speaker of the House of Representatives.
CLARENCE J. BROWN,
President of the Senate.

Passed February 27, 1919.
Approved March 13, 1919.

JAMES M. COX,
Governor.

Filed in the office of the Secretary of State at Columbus, Ohio, on the 14th day of March, A. D. 1919.
15 L.

[House Bill No. 106.]

AN ACT

To amend sections 13698, 13700, 13702 and 13703 of the General Code, relating to suspension of sentence in criminal cases during the pendency of proceedings in error.

Be it enacted by the General Assembly of the State of Ohio:

SECTION 1. That sections 13698, 13700, 13702 and 13703 of the General Code be amended as follows:

When and how sentence may be suspended after conviction; recognizance.

Sec. 13698. When a person has been convicted of any bailable offense, including the violation of an ordinance of a municipal corporation, in the court of common pleas, or by any magistrate, mayor or officer inferior to the court of common pleas, and gives notice in writing to the trial court or magistrate of his intention to file, or apply for leave to file, a petition in error, such court, magistrate, mayor, or other officer may, and, if such person so convicted is not confined in prison, shall, suspend execution of the sentence or judgment for such fixed period as will give the accused time to prepare and file, or to apply for leave to file, a petition in error, and such suspension shall be upon condition that the accused enter into a recognizance with sureties to be approved by the court, magistrate, mayor or other officer by whom the sentence or judgment was pronounced, conditioned that the accused will prosecute such error proceedings without delay, and abide the judgment or sentence of the court.

When recognizance may be increased or reduced.

Sec. 13700. No further recognizance shall be required of the accused during the pendency of the proceedings in error, unless it be made to appear to the trial court, magistrate, mayor or other officer, or to the court in which error is being prosecuted, that there is good cause to reduce or increase said recognizance. In the event such court in which error is being prosecuted finds there is good cause to reduce or increase the amount of such recognizance it shall so order. Such new recognizance shall be in the amount so ordered but otherwise to the approval of and filed with the clerk of the court in which error is being prosecuted.

Sentence shall be executed, when.

Sec. 13702. If no petition in error is filed, or leave to file a petition in error is refused, or the judgment of the trial court is affirmed, such trial court, magistrate, mayor or other officer, shall carry into execution the sentence or judgment which had been pronounced against the accused.

Recapture after escape.

Sec. 13703. If a person escape after sentence and before confinement in the penitentiary, the clerk of the court, upon application of the prosecuting attorney, shall issue a warrant stating such conviction and sentence, and commanding the sheriff to pursue such person into any county of the state.

SECTION 2. That said original sections 13698, 13700, Repeals. 13702 and 13703 of the General Code be, and the same are hereby repealed.

CARL R. KIMBALL,
Speaker of the House of Representatives.
CLARENCE J. BROWN,
President of the Senate.

Passed February 25, 1919.
Approved March 13, 1919.

JAMES M. COX,
Governor.

Filed in the office of the Secretary of State at Columbus, Ohio, on the 14th day of March, A. D. 1919.

16 G.

[House Bill No. 116.]

AN ACT

Authorizing county commissioners to invest sinking funds in bonds of the United States, the state of Ohio, or of any municipal corporation, school, township or county bonds, in such state.

Be it enacted by the General Assembly of the State of Ohio:

Sec. 2614-1.

SECTION 1. That the commissioners of any county, when they are of the opinion that it will be for the best financial interest of the county, may invest sinking funds in bonds of the United States, the state of Ohio, or of any municipal corporation, school, township or county bonds, in such state, subject to the approval of the prosecuting attorney and a judge of the common pleas court of the county. Before any such investment is made by the county commissioners, they shall pass and enter of record on their journal a resolution that they deem it will be for the best financial interest of the county to purchase certain bonds and embody a description of such bonds in the entry and thereupon submit the proposal in writing to the prosecuting attorney and a judge of the court of common pleas of their county and if such prosecuting attorney and judge, after investigation, shall approve in writing of the investment of such bonds, the county commissioners shall enter such approval on their journal and shall thereupon be authorized to proceed with the investment in such bonds.

Commissioners may invest sinking funds in bonds; approval of prosecuting attorney and common pleas court.

CARL R. KIMBALL,
Speaker of the House of Representatives.
CLARENCE J. BROWN,
President of the Senate.

Passed February 27, 1919.
Approved March 14, 1919.

JAMES M. COX,
Governor.

Filed in the office of the Secretary of State at Columbus, Ohio, on the 14th day of March, A. D. 1919.

17 G.

[House Bill No. 137.]

AN ACT

To amend section 7604 of the General Code, relative to a deposit of school funds and limitation of the amount a bank may receive.

Be it enacted by the General Assembly of the State of Ohio:

SECTION 1. That section 7604 of the General Code be amended to read as follows:

Depositing of school funds upon competitive bidding.

·Sec. 7604. That within thirty days after the first Monday of January, 1916, and every two years thereafter, the board of education of any school district by resolution shall provide for the deposit of any or all moneys coming into the hands of its treasurer. But no bank shall receive a deposit larger than the amount of its paid in capital stock, and in no event to exceed one million dollars.

SECTION 2. That original section 7604 of the General Code be, and the same is hereby repealed.

The sectional number in this act is in conformity to the General Code. JOHN G. PRICE, *Attorney General.*

CARL R. KIMBALL,
Speaker of the House of Representatives.
CLARENCE J. BROWN,
President of the Senate.

Passed February 26, 1919.
Approved March 13, 1919.

JAMES M. COX,
Governor.

Filed in the office of the Secertary of State at Columbus, Ohio, on the 14th day of March, A. D. 1919.

18 G.

[House Bill No. 276.]

AN ACT

To make sundry and supplementary appropriations for the remainder of the current fiscal year.

Be it enacted by the General Assembly of the State of Ohio:

Sundry and supplementary appropriations.

SECTION 1. The sums set forth in sections 2 and 3 of this act, in the columns therein designated "Appropriations" are hereby appropriated out of any monies in the state treasury not otherwise appropriated. Appropriations made in sections 2 and 3 herein for the highway department are hereby made from special funds provided by law to maintain such department; and, in the event that monies now to the credit of such special funds, or which may be credited thereto prior to June 30, 1919, are not adequate to meet such appropriations, only the amount of such special funds is hereby appropriated to such department. The appropriation to the rotary fund of such department shall be made from monies provided by section 6294 et seq. of the General Code, and monies appropriated for main market roads are hereby authorized to be expended in the construction of such roads, section 1221 of the General Code to the contrary notwithstanding.

Appropriations herein made to the automobile department shall be paid from funds derived from the registration of automobiles, and all other appropriations made in sections 2 and 3 herein are hereby made out of any monies in the state treasury to the credit of the general revenue fund.

SECTION 2. The following sums shall not be expended to pay liabilities incurred subsequent to June 30, 1919:

ADJUTANT GENERAL.

Maintenance—	Items.	Appropriations.
F Contract and Open Order Service—		
F 9. General Plant—		
Inaugural expenses		$1,792 37

OHIO BOARD OF ADMINISTRATION.

Maintenance—

C Supplies—

C 1.	Food	$500,000 00
C 2.	Forage	25,000 00
C 3.	Fuel	155,000 00
C 5.	Medical	3,000 00
C 6.	Laundry, c l e a n-	
	ing, etc	5,000 00
C 11.	General plant	15,000 00
	Total	$703,000 00

D Materials—

D 2.	Building	$10,000 00
D 3.	General plant	90,000 00
	Total	$100,000 00

E Equipment—

E 2.	Household	$10,000 00
E 4.	Live stock	2,500 00
E 7.	Wearing apparel.	33,000 00
	Total	$45,500 00

F Contract and Open Order Service—

F 1.	General repairs	$8,000 00
F 3.	Water	5,000 00
	Total	$13,000 00
	Total maintenance	$861,000 00

DEPARTMENT OF AGRICULTURE.

	Items.	Appropriations.

Maintenance—
  C Supplies—
    C 11. General Plant—
      Pigs for serum................ $20,000 00
  H Fixed Charges and Contributions—
    H 8. Contributions—
      Compensation due owners of
      tubercular cattle and glan-
      dered horses killed accord-
      ing to law................ 50,000 00

OHIO COMMISSION FOR BLIND.

Personal Service—
  A 1. Salaries—
    Seven Home Teachers............. $260 00

BOARD OF STATE CHARITIES.

Personal Service—
  A 3. Unclassified $600 00
Maintenance—
  C Supplies—
    C 4. Office $625 00
    C 5. Medical 200 00
    C 11. General plant.... 750 00
      Total $1,575 00
  F Contract and Open Order
    Service—
    F 7. Communication .. 75 00
  H Fixed Charges and Con-
    tributions—
    H 6. Rent 250 00
      Total maintenance............. 1,900 00
      Total $2,500 00

HIGHWAY DEPARTMENT.

Maintenance—
  F Contract and Open Order Service—
    F 1. Repairs—
      To police, patrol and maintain
      highways as provided in
      Sec. 6309 of the General
      Code $800,000 00
    I Rotary 200,000 00

INDUSTRIAL COMMISSION OF OHIO.

	Items.	Appropriations.

Maintenance—
C Supplies—
   C 4. Office $17,000 00
F Contract and Open Order Service—
   F 6. Transportation .. 16,000 00

     Total $33,000 00
H Fixed Charges and Contributions—
  H 7. Insurance—
    To be credited to state insurance fund according to provisions of Sec. 1465-64 of the General Code 15,000 00

INSURANCE DEPARTMENT.

Maintenance—
F Contract and Open Order Service—
  F 6. Transportation $2,000 00

DEPARTMENT OF PUBLIC INSTRUCTION.

Personal Service—
A 1. Salaries—
   Inspector of teacher training....... $625 00

INSPECTOR OF OILS.

Personal Service—
A 1. Salaries $1,200 00
Maintenance—
F Contract and Open Order Service—
  F 6. Transportation 5,000 00

STATE BINDERY.

Personal Service—
A 1. Salaries $1,306 11

AUTOMOBILE DEPARTMENT.

Personal Service—
A 2. Wages—
   Extra help $2,000 00
Maintenance—
C Supplies—
  C 11. General Plant—
    Automobile and motor cycle tags 20,000 00

PURCHASING AGENT.

	Items.	Appropriations.
Personal Service—		
A. 1. Salaries	....	$2,940 00
Maintenance—		
I Rotary	....	25,000 00

COMMON SCHOOLS.

Maintenance—
H   Fixed Charges and Contributions—
   H 8.   Contributions $80,000 00

STATE AID TO WEAK SCHOOLS.

Maintenance—
H   Fixed Charges and Contributions—
   H 8.   Contributions $225,000 00

DEPARTMENT OF SECURITIES.

Maintenance—
H · Fixed Charges and Contributions—
   H 6.   Rent $540 00

OHIO SOLDIERS' AND SAILORS' ORPHANS' HOME.

Maintenance—
C   Supplies—

C 1.	Food	....	$10,000 00
C 2.	Forage	....	2,000 00
C 3.	Fuel	....	5,000 00
C 6.	Cleaning	....	1,200 00
C 11.	General plant...		2,000 00

      Total $20,200 00

D   Materials—
   D 3   General plant.... 8,000 00

E   Equipment—
   E 9.   General plant... 1,000 00

F   Contract and Open Order
   Service—
   F 6.   Transportation .. 1,000 00
   F 9.   General plant... 500 00

      Total $1,500 00
      Total $30,700 00

TREASURER OF STATE.

	Items.	Appropriations.

Personal Service—
A 1. Salaries .... $60 00 Sundry and supplementary appropriations.
Maintenance—
C Supplies—
C 4. Office 1,500 00

PUBLIC UTILITIES COMMISSION OF OHIO.

Maintenance—
F Contract and Open Order Service—
F 6. Transportation $5,000 00

DEPARTMENT OF PUBLIC WORKS.

Personal Service—
A 2. Wages—
Laborers, Miami & Erie Canal...... $4,000 00
Maintenance—
F Contract and Open Order Service—
F 9. General Plant—
To survey and set markers along
the south side of Loramie
reservoir 2,000 00

KENT STATE NORMAL SCHOOL.

Maintenance—
C Supplies—
C 3. Fuel $6,830 56

F Contract and Open Order
Service—
F. 3. Water 510 56
F 4. Light, heat and
power 800 00

Total $1,310 56
Total $8,141 12

OHIO UNIVERSITY.

Maintenance—
C Supplies—
C 3. Fuel $7,000 00

COMBINED NORMAL AND INDUSTRIAL DEPARTMENT OF WILBERFORCE UNIVERSITY.

Maintenance—
F Contract and Open Order Service—
F 1. Repairs—
To restore and repair gymnasium $3,000 00

JAMES K. MERCER.

Items.	Appropriations.

For preparation and publication of "Ohio Legislative History," Vol. II as per H. J. R. No. 38 (107 O. L. 770)..... **$3,800 00**

Charles Reed and Frederick W. Green for legal services rendered to the special joint taxation committee of the 82nd general assembly $1,800.00 each..... **3,600 00**

SECTION 3. The following sums shall not be expended to pay liabilities incurred subsequent to June 30, 1919:

OHIO BOARD OF ADMINISTRATION.

G Additions and Betterments—
  G 2. Buildings—
    To supplement appropriations made in H. B. 584 (107 O. L., 341) for "5 cottages—300 patients, $142,000.00" and 6 cottages—350 patients.......$108,000 00 **$50,000 00**
  G 3. Non-structural Improvements—
    To supplement appropriations made in H. B. 584 (107 O. L., 343) for "New brick stack—Columbus institution ....$6,500 00" **1,000 00**

STATE HOUSE AND GROUNDS.

G 2. Buildings—
  Women's Comfort station......... **$6,500 00**

HIGHWAY DEPARTMENT.

G 3. Non-structural Improvements—
  To construct, improve, maintain and repair main market roads........... **$500,000 00**

MIAMI UNIVERSITY.

G 3. Non-structural Improvements—
  To supplement appropriations made in H. B. 584 (107 O. L., 349) "125 K. V. A. engine generator $6,000.00"... **$2,600 00**

OHIO UNIVERSITY

G 2. Buildings—
  Hospital **$5,000 00**

27

OHIO STATE UNIVERSITY.

Items.	Appropriations.

G 2. Buildings—
To supplement appropriation made
in H. B. 452 (107 O. L., 51) for
women's building $150,000.00... $90,000 00

Sundry and supplementary appropriations.

SECTION 4. Sections 4, 5, 6, 7 and 8 of a law entitled
"An act to make general appropriations (107 O. L., H. B.
584) passed by the 82nd general assembly and filed in the
office of the secretary of state March 31, 1917, shall apply
to and govern the apporpriations made in sections 2 and 3
herein with the same force and effect as to the appropriations made in said original act hereinbefore cited.

CARL R. KIMBALL,
Speaker of the House of Representatives.
CLARENCE J. BROWN,
President of the Senate.

Passed March 12, 1919.
Approved March 19, 1919.

JAMES M. COX,
Governor.

Filed in the office of the Secretary of State at Columbus,
Ohio, on the 20th day of March, A. D. 1919.

19 G.

[House Bill No. 28.]

AN ACT

Making appropriations in full settlement for damage resulting from
destruction of tubercular cattle and glandered horses by order
of the state board of agriculture.

Be it enacted by the General Assembly of the State of Ohio:

SECTION 1. The following sums for the purposes and
to the persons herein specified are hereby appropriated out
of any monies in the state treasury to the credit of the
general revenue fund and not otherwise appropriated:

Appropriation to pay damage for destroyed tubercular cattle and glandered horses.

In full settlement for damage resulting from destruction of tubercular cattle by order of the State Board of
Agriculture.

Abbott, A. G., Wadsworth....................	$90 00
Adams, L. W., Columbia Station.............	117 50
Amstutz, D. N., Orrville....................	417 50
Andrews Institute, Willoughby..............	177 50
Baer, E. E., Marshallville..................	382 50
Bailey, Allen, Barnesville..................	347 50
Bailey, L. P., Tacoma......................	4,177 50
Baldwin, J. E., Hilliard....................	105 00

Ballard, A. O., McClure....................	37 50
Ballou, H. W., Columbus...................	562 50
Beck, J. L., Newton Falls..................	107 50
Belle Vernon Co., Novelty.................	95 00
Betz, Clarence, East Rochester.............	37 50
Bishop, C. E., Peninsula....................	37 50
Bishop, Geo. S., Poland....................	150 00
Bishop, Geo., Milford Center...............	30 00
Bixler, D. D., Seville......................	400 00
Black, B. H. & Son, Freeport..............	573 75
Black, F. B., Mansfield....................	100 00
Blackburn, I. Robert, Dayton..............	987 50
Boerger, C. J., Irwin......................	75 00
Braley, Levva, Langsville..................	15 00
Brantingham, Joshua, Winona..............	36 25
Brantingham, J. & J. C., Winona...........	75 00
Brooks & Barker, Salem....................	75 00
Brown, W. P., Greenwich..................	280 00
Buehler, Gottlieb, Alliance................	45 00
Bundy, D. C., Barnesville..................	120 00
Burns, Mrs. Fred, Plain City..............	150 00
Boyle, F. V., Malvern.....................	721 25
Carlton, M. A., Medina....................	140 00
Campbell, E. H., Salem....................	100 00
Case, Nelson, Hudson.....................	550 00
Carpenter & Rose, Mansfield...............	2,050 00
Chambers, M. E., Grove City..............	530 00
Climo, A. H., Mentor......................	107 50
Condit, L. S., Condit......................	137 50
Coppock, F. C. & Son, Salem..............	27 50
Curren, P. J., Sabina......................	35 00
Dempsey, Thomas, Westerville..............	75 00
Denkhaus, Lewis, Lisbon...................	150 00
Derrer, M. & Son, Camp Chase.............	2,480 00
Dieke, Godfrey, Brooklyn Station...........	167 50
Doner, P. W., Sandusky...................	150 00
Douglas, George, Camden..................	135 00
Dunham, Charles, Richfield................	195 00
Edde, C. W.............................	100 00
Edgerton, Walter G., Hanoverton..........	82 50
Enlow, D. S., East Akron..................	37 50
Epworth League Camp, Painesville.........	37 50
Eyster, R. S., Beloit......................	299 00
Fairmont Children's Home, Alliance........	397 50
Farriss, W. J., South Akron...............	227 50
Figley, Chance, Lisbon....................	52 50
Finney, E. E., Cedarville..................	25 00
Folk, H. C., Louisville....................	1,050 00
Foss, R. H. & W. F., Springfield............	625 00
Fraley Bros., Hannibal....................	732 50
Frank, C. W., Fairlawn...................	475 00
Frederick, R. E., Poland..................	682 50
French, B. J., Garfield...................	917 50

Frey, Benjamin, Plain City.................	878 50	Appropriation to pay damage for destroyed tubercular cattle and glandered horses.
Frizzell, Mary, Barnesville..................	25 00	
Gallagher & Wells, Cadiz....................	215 00	
Gardner, V. A., Powell.....................	170 00	
Garrow, J. A., Morenci, Mich...............	300 00	
Gerst, William, Cincinnati..................	1,570 00	
Gest, Chas., Grafton........................	36 25	
Glass, Bert, Paris..........................	31 00	
Good Hold Farm Co., Mentor...............	1,127 50	
Gooding, Dr. H. B., Tiffin..................	100 00	
Green, Perry, Hiram........................	412 50	
Greendale Co., Hiram.......................	100 00	
Greenwalt, William, Sebring................	265 00	
Grundhauser, Anton, Mt. Carmel............	137 50	
Halfred Farms, Chagrin Falls...............	300 00	
Hall, Mansel, Quaker City..................	70 00	
Hartsell, J. C., Sebring.....................	92 50	
Hartenstein, Jacob, Alliance................	125 00	
Hawley, T. E., Sullivan.....................	100 00	
Hay, Charles E., Findlay....................	23 75	
Hazen, A. F., Alliance......................	622 50	
Hibbard, Earl, Novelty......................	107 50	
Higley, Charles, Leipsic.....................	35 00	
Hill, C. O., Napoleon.......................	125 00	
Hinde, John, Huron.........................	262 50	
Hoff, Rollo D., Beloit.......................	55 00	
Homegardner, Geo., Sandusky...............	100 00	
Houston, Foster B., South Charleston........	885 00	
Jackson, L. V., Delaware....................	65 00	
Jasbring, John, Collinsville.................	608 50	
Johnson, Thomas, Columbus................	850 00	
Joy, E. B., Cuyahoga Falls..................	310 00	
Kahler, F. J., Plain City....................	400 00	
Kelly, J. E., Xenia.........................	700 00	
Kelley, J. J., Kensington....................	205 00	
Kerr, John E., Monclova....................	75 00	
Keyes, B. W., Woodstock....................	645 00	
Keys, Samuel, Jr., Dresden..................	43 75	
Kimmel, J. & Son, Freeport.................	285 00	
Kimball, C. R., Madison....................	487 50	
King, E. A., Vanlue........................	509 00	
King, S. S., Orrville........................	100 00	
Kintner, Peter, Defiance....................	50 00	
Klingel, Ed., Marion........................	82 50	
Knudson Brothers, Millbury.................	739 00	
Koerber, Chas., North Eaton................	727 50	
Kovacs, M., Grafton........................	467 75	
Lampman, J. C., Chardon...................	187 50	
Lanman, Miss C. T., Columbus..............	375 00	
Lashly, Arnold J., Columbus................	782 50	
Lehnert, Fred J., Galloway.................	355 00	
Lippincott, E. F., East Rochester...........	75 00	
Long, E. E., Upper Sandusky...............	21 25	

Lunn, D. B., Reynoldsburg	305	00
Luther, E. W., Peninsula	380	00
Luthey, Fannie, Delta	150	00
McClelland, T. W., Williamsfield	92	50
McColloch, James, Homesville	195	00
McGregor, David, Springfield	295	00
Mangold, H. A., Sonora	492	50
Marks, A. H., Akron	325	00
Martig, Christ, Sr., Beloit	692	50
Martig, Christ, Jr., Beloit	2,635	00
Martin, Geo., Garrettsville	1,492	50
Mayer, G. J., Grove City	297	50
Melick Bros., Mt. Perry	530	00
Merwine, Norman, Westerville	193	75
Methodist Children's Home, Worthington	70	00
Michaels, B. A., Tiffin	37	50
Mills, A. L., West Dover	75	00
Minser, E. K. & Son, Salem	90	00
Moomaw, R. M., Wooster	902	50
Moore, P. T. & Son, Mechanicsburg	185	00
Morris, Jas., Peninsula	275	00
Morley, T. D., Mentor	100	00
Morrow County Infirmary, Mt. Gilead	57	50
Nail, E. S., Mansfield	75	00
National Fireproofing Co., Haydenville	270	00
National Orphans' Home, Tiffin	72	50
Nelson, Thomas, Hillsboro	2,937	50
Nichols, H. C., Garrettsville	1,600	00
Nichols, L. W., Garrettsville	200	00
Paumier, Lawrence, Louisville	1,182	50
Penrose, Chas. S., Fairview	103	75
Pottorf, J. C., Salem	681	25
Price, Harry J., Mesopotamia	3,155	00
Quaintance, I. E., Bucyrus	100	00
Rausch, Leo P., Marysville	400	00
Rehm, J. F., Orrville	255	00
Rice, Harry, Homerville	225	00
Richardson, Mrs. G. G., Glendale	1,235	00
Riggle, M. E., Pt. Washington	32	50
Robinson, J. T., Marysville	112	50
Romp, L. F. & Son, West Dover	542	50
Ross & Spahr, Springfield	137	50
Rudebaugh, W. F., Lisbon	1,142	50
Ruhlen, Frank, Plain City	217	50
Rupprecht, Frank M., Marysville	300	00
Sackett, Francis, Tallmadge	886	25
Sackett, Frank H., Tallmadge	550	00
Sater, Martin, Harrison	37	50
Schlegel, Charles H., Wauseon	307	50
Schoepf, W. K., Glendale	100	00
Scott, John, Pomeroy	67	50
Scott, L. H., Alexandria	37	50
Scott, Seth P., Lisbon	150	00

Seeman, Preston, Hartsville................. 705 00 Appropriation to pay damage for destroyed tubercular cattle and glandered horses.
Sevits, Irvin, Danville..................... 25 00
Shaffer, Elsa, St. Marys.................... 380 00
Shipley, Wm. G., Fairview.................. 57 50
Sidner, D. R., West Jefferson............... 422 50
Siermans, H. W., Grove City............... 150 00
Sites, Clark, Camp Chase................... 30 00
Slagle, Homer B. & Son, Poland............. 626 25
Smith, C. C. & Son, Parkman............... 3,607 50
Snider, D. D., Pataskala.................... 252 50
Spence, E. E., Chillicothe.................. 2,412 50
St. John, J. O., Xenia...................... 100 00
Standish, W. H., Lyons..................... 600 00
Steiner, Fred, Massillon.................... 1,550 00
Steiner, G. C., Orrville.................... 175 00
Steiner, Wm., Massillon.................... 187 50
Stern, Edwin H., Massillon................. 405 00
Stratton, W. B., Winona................... 120 00
Stillson Brothers, Kent..................... 572 50
Stocker, Bart, Alliance..................... 788 00
Stout, Frank, Sandusky.................... 212 50
Swigart, W. W., Sharon Center............. 500 00
Taylor, Marion, Beloit..................... 400 00
Taylor, U. F., Marysville.................. 430 00
Telling, Belle-Vernon Co., Cleveland......... 832 50
Thomas, C. E., Peninsula................... 300 00
Treap, Geo. W., Peninsula.................. 95 00
Tritton, Samuel, Lisbon.................... 1,041 50
VanShoyck, Wm., Reynoldsburg............. 200 00
Wakefield, W. H., Bedford.................. 1,308 75
Wagner, A. W., Williamsfield............... 73 75
Wales, H. W., Massillon.................... 1,650 00
Warrick, Mrs. Adda, Barnesville............ 90 00
Warren, Jacob, Alliance.................... 308 75
Watson, J. A., Youngstown................. 445 00
Watson, J. A. & W. W., Youngstown......... 447 50
Watson, W. W., Youngstown................ 2,995 00
Wedemeyer, Gust., Westerville.............. 165 00
Welday, J. L., Smithfield................... 75 00
Wenger, Albert, Clayton.................... 425 00
West, C. P. & Son, Bloomingburg............ 702 50
Westover, Allen, Poland.................... 75 00
Werren, Samuel, North Benton.............. 7,775 00
Whinery, O. E., Salem...................... 362 50
Whinery, Guy, Salem....................... 100 00
Whinery, Willis, Salem..................... 37 50
White, E. W., Galena....................... 42 50
Wilkinson, W. G., Berea.................... 300 00
Williams, S. P., Degraff.................... 150 00
Williamson, Ray R., Pataskala.............. 187 50
Willing, H. C., Grove City.................. 75 00
Wing, Charles B., Mechanicsburg............ 35 00
Winzenreid, Christ, Blaine................. 435 00

Wright, Alfred, Sandusky....................	112 50
Woodin, F. N., Chardon.....................	100 00
Zehring, E. L., Germantown.................	800 00
Zehring, O. O., Germantown.................	275 00

HORSES DESTROYED ON ACCOUNT OF GLANDERS.

Adams Express Co., Cincinnati..............	$4,975 00
American Express Co., Cleveland............	160 00
Barclay, Ora, Batavia......................	60 00
Bell, Archie W., Cincinnati.................	90 00
Bell, C. L., Cincinnati.....................	125 00
Bricketto, L., Cincinnati...................	85 00
Burger, Wm., Madisonville..................	75 00
Burkhead, W. H., Kirkersville...............	787 50
Carey, E. D., Bedford......................	250 00
Carey, H. J., Bedford......................	800 00
Carey, H. J., & Bros., Bedford..............	500 00
Comer & Jordan, Cincinnati.................	100 00
Cone, Addie, Ross..........................	65 00
Conkling, L. W., Terrace Park..............	55 00
Cramer, Moses, Xenia......................	125 00
Edlean, I., Cincinnati......................	60 00
Electric Package Co., Cleveland.............	450 00
Emrich, J. M., Cleveland...................	2,785 00
Folck, E. H., Osborn.......................	150 00
Garrison, T. H., Cozaddale.................	75 00
Gillette, R. B., Tippecanoe City.............	562 50
Heffner, Jacob A., Tippecanoe City.........	120 00
Henderson, John, Elk Lick (Cincinnati).....	50 00
Hill, Harry A., Fayetteville.................	200 00
Jewel Tea Company, Cleveland..............	150 00
Kelley, Frank W., Plainville................	75 00
Kline, Joseph, Hamilton...................	30 00
Kohli, Jarvis F., Cleveland.................	240 00
Kramer, W. H., Evanston...................	85 00
McRitchie, J. H., Port Clinton..............	75 00
Merwine, E. A., Columbus..................	80 00
Miller, J. C., Osborne......................	100 00
Pavey & Schneck, Columbus.................	285 00
Radford, Doc., Pomeroy....................	75 00
Robbins, David, Covington..................	100 00
Rogers, John, Hamilton....................	30 00
Root, L. P., Somerville.....................	112 50
Schuster, Joseph, Cincinnati................	100 00
Slone, J. S., Norwood......................	1,775 00
Smith, L. M., Norwood.....................	300 00
Smith, Matthew, Cleveland.................	90 00
Van Camp Brothers, Cincinnati.............	1,107 50
Wallace Transfer Co., Cincinnati............	2,225 00
Weiss, John J., Cincinnati..................	350 00
Williams, Geo., Cincinnati.................	35 00
Wilson, R. A., New Carlisle.................	177 50

33

Woolley, D. P., Cincinnati	125 00
Workman, Alonzo, Perintown	80 00
Union Reduction Co., Cincinnati	50 00

Appropriation to pay damage for destroyed tubercular cattle and glandered horses.

SECTION 2. The moneys herein appropriated shall be paid upon the approval of a special auditing committee consisting of the major appointee authorized by section 270-5 of the General Code, commonly known as the budget commissioner, the attorney general, the auditor of the state, the chairman of the finance committee of the senate and the chairman of the finance committee of the house of representatives. Such auditing committee is hereby authorized and directed to make careful inquiry as to the validity of each and every claim herein made and pay only so much thereof as may be found to be correct and just. *Payment shall be made upon approval of auditing committee.*

SECTION 3. This bill. is hereby declared to be an emergency bill. That its enactment into law is necessary for the preservation of the public peace, safety and welfare of the inhabitants of the state of Ohio, and that the provisions of this bill shall be enacted into law and become effective at the earliest possible time, and shall take effect and be in full force from and after its passage and approval by the governor. The necessity therefor lies in the fact that the claimants have already waited an unreasonable time for their money and the committee is of the opinion that it should be paid at once. *Emergency act.*

CARL R. KIMBALL,
Speaker of the House of Representatives.
CLARENCE J. BROWN,
President of the Senate.

Passed March 6, 1919.
Approved March 18, 1919.

JAMES M. COX,
Governor.
Filed in the office of the Secretary of State at Columbus, Ohio, on the 20th day of March, A. D. 1919.
20 G.

[House Bill No. 3.]

AN ACT

To repeal sections 6253, 11683 and 11684 of the General Code, relating to the publication of election notices in the German language.

Be it enacted by the General Assembly of the State of Ohio:

Repeals.

SECTION 1. That sections 6253, 11683 and 11684 of the General Code be and the same are hereby repealed.

This act does not require a General Code number.
JOHN G. PRICE, *Attorney General.*

CARL R. KIMBALL,
Speaker of the House of Representatives.
CLARENCE J. BROWN,
President of the Senate.

Passed March 4, 1919.
Approved March 17, 1919.

JAMES M. COX,
Governor.

Filed in the office of the Secretary of State at Columbus, Ohio, on this 20th day of March, A. D. 1919.

21 G.

[House Bill No. 8.]

AN ACT

To amend section 2950 of the General Code, relative to the burial of soldiers.

Be it enacted by the General Assembly of the State of Ohio:

SECTION 1. That section 2950 of the General Code be amended to read as follows:

Burial of soldiers; how undertaker selected.

Sec. 2950. The county commissioners of each county shall appoint two suitable persons in each township and ward in the county, other than those prescribed by law for the care of paupers and the custody of criminals, who shall contract, at a cost not to exceed one hundred dollars, with the undertaker selected by the friends of the deceased, and cause to be interred in a decent and respectable manner, the body of any honorably discharged soldier, sailor or marine having at any time served in the army or navy of the United States, or the mother, wife or widow of any such soldier, sailor or marine, or any army nurse who did service at any time in the army of the United States, who dies, not having the means to defray the necessary funeral expenses. Such burial may be made in any cemetery or burial ground within the state, other than those used exclusively for the burial of paupers and criminals.

SECTION 2. That said original section 2950 of the General Code be, and the same is hereby repealed. Repeal.

CARL R. KIMBALL,
Speaker of the House of Representatives.
CLARENCE J. BROWN,
President of the Senate.

Passed March 6, 1919.
Approved March 19, 1919.

JAMES M. COX,·
Governor.

Filed in the office of the Secretary of State at Columbus, Ohio, on the 20th day of March, A. D. 1919.

22 G.

[House Bill No. 146.]

AN ACT

To appropriate the sum of one thousand dollars for the use of the children of John H. Brown.

Be it enacted by the General Assembly of the State of Ohio:

SECTION 1. That the sum of one thousand dollars be, and the same is hereby appropriated out of any moneys in the state treasury to the credit of the general revenue fund not otherwise appropriated for the use of the children of John H. Brown deceased, said sum being the unpaid salary of John H. Brown, a member of the 82nd general assembly of Ohio. The auditor of state is hereby authorized and directed to issue to the administrator of the estate of John H. Brown deceased, upon the order of the speaker of the house of representatives of the 83rd general assembly, a warrant on the treasurer of the state for the sum herein appropriated. Appropriation to pay John H. Brown.

CARL R. KIMBALL,
Speaker of the House of Representatives.
CLARENCE J. BROWN,
President of the Senate.

Passed March 7, 1919.
Approved March 19, 1919.

JAMES M. COX,
Governor.

Filed in the office of the Secretary of State at Columbus, Ohio, on the 20th day of March, A. D. 1919.

23 L.

[House Bill No. 87.]

AN ACT

To amend section 13755 of the General Code, relating to what judgments may be rendered on petitions in error in criminal cases.

Be it enacted by the General Assembly of the State of Ohio:

SECTION 1. That section 13755 of the General Code be amended to read as follows:

What judgment may be rendered on petitions in error; costs on reversal.

Sec. 13755. Upon the hearing of a petition in error, the court may affirm the judgment or reverse it, in whole or in part, and order the accused to be discharged or grant a new trial. If the judgment be reversed, the plaintiff in error shall recover from the defendant in error all court costs incurred to secure such reversal, including the cost of bills of exceptions and transcripts. In capital cases, when the judgment is affirmed, and the day fixed for the execution of the sentence is passed, the court shall appoint a day therefor, and the clerk thereof shall issue a warrant, under the seal of such court, to the sheriff of the proper county, commanding him to carry the sentence into execution at the day so appointed. Such sheriff shall execute and return such warrant, and such clerk shall record such warrant and return as provided in this title.

Repeal.

SECTION 2. That said original section 13755 of the General Code be and the same is hereby repealed.

CARL R. KIMBALL,
Speaker of the House of Representatives.
CLARENCE J. BROWN,
President of the Senate.

The sectional number in this act is in conformity to the General Code. JOHN G. PRICE, *Attorney General.*

Passed March 7, 1919.
Approved March 19, 1919.

JAMES M. COX,
Governor.

Filed in the office of the Secretary of State at Columbus, Ohio, on the 20th day of March, A. D. 1919.

24 G.

[House Bill No. 40.]

AN ACT

To amend an act entitled: ''An act to incorporate the Society of St. John's Church in Worthington and parts adjacent,'' passed January 27, 1807, 5 Ohio Laws, page 56, to authorize said society to affiliate with the Protestant Episcopal Church in the United States of America and the diocese thereof having jurisdiction of Franklin county, and to authorize said society to conform in the conduct and management of its affairs to the canons of said church and diocese.

Amendment to act incorporating St. John's Church of Worthington.

Be it enacted by the General Assembly of the State of Ohio:

SECTION 1. That sections 4, 5, 6, 7, 8 and 9 of an act entitled: ''An act to incorporate the society of St. John's

Church in Worthington and parts adjacent," passed January 27, 1807, 5 Ohio Laws, page 56, be amended; and that sections 3 and 9 of said act be supplemented by sections 3-A and 9-A, respectively, to read as follows:

Sec. 3-A. Said society may by a majority vote of the members thereof present at any annual meeting, or meeting called for that purpose, become affiliated with the Protestant Episcopal church in the United States of America and the diocese of said church having jurisdiction in Franklin county, and subject itself to the canons, discipline, rules and regulations of said church and diocese which may from time to time be·in force and effect. *Affiliation with Methodist Protestant Chnch authorized.*

Sec. 4. Be it further enacted, that for the better regulating and governing said society, and managing the affairs thereof, there shall be a meeting of the corporation at said Worthington, on the first Monday after Easter Sunday, annually, at one o'clock p. m., and being so met, they shall first appoint in such a manner as they may think proper, a moderator, who shall preside in said meetings and cause due order to be observed. They shall then proceed to elect three trustees, a treasurer, a clerk and a collector and such other officers as the corporation may find necessary, who shall hold their offices one year and until their successors shall be elected and duly qualified; provided, that if by any neglect or casualty, an election of the officers should not be made on the day appointed for the annual meeting, or in the event of a vacancy in any office, by death, removal or otherwise, the society may elect their officers, or supply such vacancy at any meeting of the corporation duly appointed. Provided further, that said society having become affiliated with the Protestant Episcopal church in the United States of America, it may hold its annual and other meetings at such times and elect for its governing body such officers, bearing such titles and having such qualifications as may be prescribed by the canons of said church and the diocese thereof having jurisdiction of said society. *Meeting for election of trustees; time and place.*

Sec. 5. Be it further enacted, that all elections of the corporation shall be by ballot, and the person having the majority of all the ballots given for any office, shall be considered duly elected; and all votes in society matters, shall be determined by a majority of the members acting in any meeting of the corporation duly assembled. Provided, that said society having become affiliated with the Protestant Episcopal church in the United States of America, elections of officers and votes of the society on other matters shall be had, conducted and determined in manner provided by the canons of said church and the diocese thereof having jurisdiction of said society. *Elections shall be by ballot.*

Sec. 6. Be it further enacted, that all meetings of the corporation, either for the election of officers or for the transaction of the other business of the society, shall be called by the trustees, or a majority of them, who shall cause notifications in writing to be posted up in three public *Meetings shall be called by trustees; notice.*

places in said Worthington, at least fifteen days previous thereto, mentioning the time, place and object of such meeting. Provided, that said society having become affiliated with the Protestant Episcopal church in the United States of America, such meetings shall be called and notice thereof given in the manner provided by the canons of said church and the diócese thereof having jurisdiction of said society.

Authority to make contracts; rules and regulations. Sec. 7. Be it further enacted that the trustees, or a major part of them, shall have power and authority to make all contracts in behalf of the corporation, which shall be necessary to carry into effect and accomplish the objects of the institution, and manage all pecuniary and prudential matters and other concerns, which pertain to the good order, interest and welfare of the society, and make such rules, regulations and by-laws for the government of the society and for regulating and conducting the affairs of the same, as shall from time to time be deemed necessary and expedient; provided, that such rules, regulations and by-laws be not inconsistent with the laws of the United States, or this state, and that the same, before they have effect, be approved by the corporation; provided, also, that all moneys **Application of moneys.** which constitute the funds of the society, shall be applied to such purposes only for which they have been appropriated by the corporation, or specifically given by the donor or devisor. Provided further, that said society having become affiliated with the Protestant Episcopal church in the United States of America, the officers of said society elected according to the canons of said church and the diocese thereof having jurisdiction of said society, shall have and may exercise all powers herein granted to the trustees of said society, and such other and further powers as may be prescribed by the canons of said church and diocese, and that all by-laws, rules and regulations adopted by such officers shall become effective in manner provided by the canons of said church and diocese.

How membership obtained; withdrawal; certificate. Sec. 8. Be it further enacted, that whenever any person shall wish to become a member of said society, he shall have the right so to do, by applying to the clerk and subscribing his name to the by-laws and ordinances adopted for the government of the corporation, and thereupon he shall become a member, fully entitled to a participation of all the privileges and immunities, and subject to all the rules and determinations of the corporation, in common with the original subscribers, so long as he shall continue a member; and furthermore, whenever any person that now is or that shall hereafter become a member of said society, shall wish to withdraw himself from the corporation, he shall have full right and power so to do by lodging a certificate, under his hand and seal, with the clerk, stating such his wish, and that he is not therefore to be considered as a member; and the clerk immediately, on the receipt of such certificate, shall endorse thereon the date when received, and record as soon as convenient, both the certificate and endorsement at length, in a book provided for that purpose by the corporation. And the clerk (if required) shall give to any person withdrawing from the society as aforesaid, a writing under his hand and seal, acknowledging the receipt of such certificate, and that without any fee or reward from such applicant. Provided, that said society having become affiliated with the Protestant Episcopal church in the United States of America, the right of admission to membership in said society and the right to withdraw therefrom shall be governed by the canons of said church and the diocese thereof having jurisdiction of said society.

Sec. 9. Be it further enacted, that the treasurer shall give bond with sufficient surety, to the trustees and their successors in office, in such sum as the trustees shall deem sufficient, conditioned for the faithful performance of those duties that may appertain to his office, by the rules, regulations and by-laws of the corporation. Provided, that said society having become affiliated with the Protestant Episcopal church in the United States of America, the treasurer and other officers shall give such bonds as may be required by the rules of the society and the canons of said church and the diocese thereof having jurisdiction of said society. *Bond of treasurer.*

Section 9-A. Said society shall be subject to all laws of the state of Ohio relating to actions by and against corporations not for profit. *Society subject to state laws.*

Section 2. That said original sections of said act, numbered 4, 5, 6, 7, 8 and 9, be and the same are hereby repealed. *Repeals.*

Carl R. Kimball,
Speaker of the House of Representatives.
Clarence J. Brown,
President of the Senate.

Passed March 6, 1919.
Approved March 19, 1919.

James M. Cox,
Governor.

Filed in the office of the Secretary of State at Columbus, Ohio, on the 20th day of March, A. D. 1919.

25 L.

act is not general and ment na- and re- be no sec- member. G. Price. Attorney General.

[House Bill No. 90.]

AN ACT

To amend section 2508 of the General Code, relating to the publication of the report of the county auditor.

Be it enacted by the General Assembly of the State of Ohio:
SECTION 1. That section 2508 of the General Code be amended to read as follows:

Submission of report to common pleas judge; publication of report.

Sec. 2508. Upon completing said report the county auditor shall submit the same to a judge of the court of common pleas for said county who shall determine whether said report is in conformity to this act, and if not said judge shall direct the said auditor to make specified changes therein so as to make it conform herewith. If the judge certifies that said report is in compliance herewith or after the auditor shall make changes therein as directed by the judge, said auditor shall cause an exact copy of said report to be immediately published one time in one English newspaper of the political party casting the largest vote in the state at the last general election, and in one English newspaper of the political party casting the second largest vote in the state at the last general election, published in the county and of general circulation in said county; if there are two such papers published; if not, then a publication in one newspaper only is required, provided, however, such report shall be published only in the English language.

Repeal.

SECTION 2. That said original section 2508 of the Genearl Code be and the same is hereby repealed.

The sectional number in this act is in conformity to the General Code.
JOHN G. PRICE,
Attorney
General.

CARL R. KIMBALL,
Speaker of the House of Representatives.
CLARENCE J. BROWN,
President of the Senate.

Passed March 4, 1919.
Approved March 17, 1919.

JAMES M. COX,
Governor.

Filed in the office of the Secretary of State at Columbus, Ohio, on the 20th day of March, A. D. 1919.

26 G.

[House Bill No. 176.]

AN ACT

To amend sections 12694 and 13423 of the General Code, relative to the illegal practice of medicine and surgery, or any of its branches, and the enforcement of penalties therefor.

Be it enacted by the General Assembly of the State of Ohio:
SECTION 1. That sections 12694 and 13423 of the General Code be amended to read as follows:

Sec. 12694. Whoever practices medicine or surgery, or any of its branches before obtaining a certificate from the state medical board in the manner required by law, or whoever advertises or announces himself as a practitioner of medicine or surgery, or any of its branches, before obtaining a certificate from the state medical board in the manner required by law; or whoever opens or conducts an office or other place for such practice before obtaining a certificate from the state medical board in the manner required by law; or whoever not being a licensee conducts an office in the name of some person who has a certificate to practice medicine or surgery, or any of its branches; or whoever practices medicine or surgery, or any of its branches, after a certificate has been duly revoked, or, if suspended, during the time of such suspension, shall, for the first offense be fined not less than twenty-five dollars nor more than five hundred dollars, and for each subsequent offense be fined not less than fifty dollars nor more than five hundred dollars, or imprisoned in the county jail or workhouse not less than thirty days nor more than one year, or both. *Practice of medicine or surgery without certificate, unlawful; penalty.*

A certificate signed by the secretary of the state medical board, to which is affixed the official seal of the said state medical board to the effect that it appears from the records of the state medical board that no such certificate to practice medicine or surgery, or any of its branches, in the state of Ohio has been issued to any such person or persons specified therein, or that a certificate, if issued, has been revoked or suspended, shall be received as prima facie evidence of the record of such board in any court or before any officer of this state. *Certificate prima facie evidence.*

Sec. 13423. Justices of the peace, police judges and mayors of cities and villages shall have jurisdiction, within their respective counties, in all cases of violation of any law relating to: *Special jurisdiction of police judges, mayors and justices.*

1. Adulteration or deception in the sale of dairy products and other food, drink, drugs and medicines.

2. The prevention of cruelty to animals and children.

3. The abandonment, non-support or ill treatment of a child by its parent.

4. The abandonment or ill treatment of a child under sixteen years of age by its guardian.

5. The employment of a child under fourteen years of age in public exhibitions or vocations injurious to health, life, morals, or which will cause or permit it to suffer unnecessary physical or mental pain.

6. The regulation, restriction or prohibition of the employment of minors.

7. The torturing, unlawfully punishing, ill treating, or depriving anyone of necessary food, clothing or shelter.

8. The selling, giving away or furnishing of intoxicating liquors as a beverage, or keeping a place where such liquor is sold, given away or furnished, in violation of any

law prohibiting such acts within the limits of a township and without the limits of a municipal corporation.

9. The shipping, selling, using, permitting the use of, branding or having unlawful quantities of illuminating oil for or in a mine.

10. The sale, shipment or adulteration of commercial feed stuffs.

11. The use of dust creating machinery in workshops and factories.

12. The conducting of a pharmacy, or retail drug or chemical store, or the dispensing or selling of drugs, chemicals, poisons or pharmaceutical preparations therein.

13. The failure to place and keep in a sanitary condition a bakery, confectionery, creamery, dairy, dairy barn, milk depot, laboratory, hotel, restaurant, eating-house, packing house, slaughter-house, ice cream factory, or place where a food product is manufactured, packed, stored, deposited, collected, prepared, produced or sold for any purpose.

14. Offenses for violation of laws in relation to inspection of steam boilers, and of laws licensing steam engineers and boiler operators.

15. The prevention of short weighing and measuring and all violations of the weights and measures laws.

16. The violation of any law in relation to the practice of medicine or surgery, or any of its branches.

Repeals. SECTION 2. That original sections 12694 and 13423 of the General Code be, and the same are hereby repealed.

CARL R. KIMBALL,
Speaker of the House of Representatives.
CLARENCE J. BROWN,
President of the Senate.

The sectional numbers in this act are in conformity to the General Code. JOHN G. PRICE, Attorney General.

Passed March 11, 1919.
Approved March 18, 1919.

JAMES M. COX,
Governor.

Filed in the office of the Secretary of State at Columbus, Ohio, on the 20th day of March, A. D. 1919.

27 G.

[House Bill No. 198.]

AN ACT

To amend section 13555 of the General Code, relative to the number of persons necessary to constitute a grand jury.

Be it enacted by the General Assembly of the State of Ohio:

SECTION 1. That section 13555 of the General Code be amended to read as follows:

Number constituting grand jury; appointment of foreman. Sec. 13555. A grand jury shall consist of fifteen persons, resident electors of the county, having the qualifications of jurors. When a grand jury is impaneled in the manner provided by law, the court shall appoint one of the members thereof as foreman.

SECTION 2. That original section 13555 of the General Code be and the same is hereby repealed.

CARL R. KIMBALL,
Speaker of the House of Representatives.
CLARENCE J. BROWN,
President of the Senate.

Passed March 6, 1919.
Approved March 17, 1919.

JAMES M. COX,
Governor.

Filed in the office of the Secretary of State at Columbus, Ohio, on the 20th day of March, A. D. 1919.

28 G.

[House Bill No. 48.]

AN ACT

To amend section 4228 of the General Code, relating to the publication of ordinances, resolutions, etc., of municipalities which are required to be published by law.

Be it enacted by the General Assembly of the State of Ohio:

SECTION 1. That section 4228 of the General Code be amended to read as follows:

Sec. 4228. Unless otherwise specifically directed by statute, all municipal ordinances, resolutions, statements, orders, proclamations, notices and reports, required by law or ordinance to be published, shall be published as follows: In two English newspapers of opposite politics printed and of general circulation in such municipality, if there be such newspapers; if two English newspapers of opposite politics are not printed and of general circulation in such municipality, then in any English newspaper printed and of general circulation therein; if no English newspaper is printed and of general circulation in such municipality, then in any English newspaper of general circulation therein or by posting as provided in section forty-two hundred thirty-two of the General Code, at the option of council. Proof of the place of printing and required circulation of any newspaper used as a medium of publication hereunder shall be made by affidavit of the proprietor of either of such newspapers, and shall be filed with the clerk of council.

SECTION 2. That original section 4228 of the General Code be and the same is hereby repealed.

marginaliaThe sectional number in this act is in conformity to the General Code. JOHN G. PRICE, *Attorney General.*

CARL R. KIMBALL,
Speaker of the House of Representatives.
CLARENCE J. BROWN,
President of the Senate.

Passed March 4, 1919.
Approved March 17, 1919.

JAMES M. COX,
Governor.

Filed in the office of the Secretary of State at Columbus, Ohio, on the 20th day of March, A. D. 1919.

29 G.

[House Bill No. 55.]

AN ACT

To prescribe a rule of evidence, relating to corporations not organized under the laws of this state.

Be it enacted by the General Assembly of the State of Ohio:

marginaliaSec. 190-1.

.Certificate of compliance with laws prima facie evidence of incorporation.

SECTION 1. The certificate of compliance with the laws of this state issued to a corporation, not organized under the laws of this state, or a copy of such certificate duly certified to by the state officer issuing same, or his successors in office, shall be prima facie evidence of the due incorporation and existence of the corporation therein named. All officers authorized to issue certificates of compliance with the laws of this state, to corporations not organized under the laws of this state, shall keep a record of such certificates issued by them.

marginaliaThe sectional number on the margin hereof is designated as provided by law. JOHN G. PRICE, *Attorney General.*

CARL R. KIMBALL,
Speaker of the House of Representatives.
CLARENCE J. BROWN,
President of the Senate.

Passed March 6, 1919.
Approved March 20, 1919.

JAMES M. COX,
Governor.

Filed in the office of the Secretary of State at Columbus, Ohio, on the 21st day of March, A. D. 1919.

30 G.

45

[House Bill No. 438.]

AN ACT

To make an appropriation for maintaining certain state-city free
employment offices for the remainder of the fiscal year.

Be it enacted by the General Assembly of the State of Ohio:
SECTION 1. The following sum is hereby appropriated Appropriation to maintain state-city free employment offices.
out of any monies in the state treasury to the credit of the
general revenue fund, not otherwise appropriated:

INDUSTRIAL COMMISSION OF OHIO.

A· Personal Service—
A3. Unclassified—
To maintain certain state-city free employment offices
which have been largely financed by the federal government, but which in consequence of the failure of the general deficiency bill to pass congress before the end of the
session, must be closed, unless the state provides funds to
continue same in operation.................. $18,000 00

CARL R. KIMBALL,
Speaker of the House of Representatives.
CLARENCE J. BROWN,
President of the Senate.

Passed March 20, 1919.
Approved March 21, 1919.

JAMES M. COX,
Governor.

Filed in the office of the Secretary of State at Columbus,
Ohio, on the 21st day of March, A. D. 1919.

31 G.

This act is not
of a general and
permanent na-
ture and re-
quires no sec-
tional number.
JOHN G. PRICE,
*Attorney
General.*

[House Bill No. 17.]

AN ACT

To amend section 4250 of the General Code permitting the merging
of the departments of public service and public safety in cities
under fifty thousand.

Be it enacted by the General Assembly of the State of Ohio:
SECTION 1. That section 4250 of the General Code be
amended to read as follows:
Sec. 4250. The mayor shall be the chief conservator General powers of mayor; merger of certain departments permitted.
of peace within the corporation. He shall have power to
appoint, and have power to remove, the director of public
service, the director of public safety, and the heads of the
sub-departments of public service and public safety, and
shall have such other powers and shall perform such other
duties as are conferred and required by law. In cities hav-

46

ing a population of less than fifty thousand, the council
may by a majority vote merge the office of director of public safety with that of public service, one director to be
appointed for the merged department.

Repeal.

SECTION 2. That said original section 4250 of the General Code be and the same is hereby repealed.

The sectional
number in this
act is in con-
formity to the
General Code.
JOHN G. PRICE,
Attorney
General.

CARL R. KIMBALL,
Speaker of the House of Representatives.
F. E. WHITTEMORE,
President Pro Tem. of the Senate.

Passed March 18, 1919.
Approved March 27, 1919.

JAMES M. COX,
Governor.

Filed in the office of the Secretary of State at Columbus,
Ohio, on the 27th day of March, A. D. 1919.

32 G.

[Senate Bill No. 15.]

AN ACT

To amend sections 1352, 6259 and 6262, to add supplementary section 1236-6 and to repeal sections 6257 and 6258 of the General
Code relative to classification and inspection of hospitals.

Be it enacted by the General Assembly of the State of Ohio:

SECTION 1. That sections 1352, 6259 and 6262 be
amended and supplementary section 1236-6 of the General
Code be added to read as follows:

Hospitals and
dispensaries shall
register with and
report to state
department of
health.

Sec. 1236-6. The commissioner of health shall have
power to define and classify hospitals and dispensaries.
Within thirty days after the taking effect of this act, and
annually thereafter, every hospital and dispensary, public
or private, shall register with, and report to, the state department of health, on forms furnished by the commissioner
of health, such information as he may prescribe.

Duties of the
board.

Sec. 1352. The board of state charities shall investigate by correspondence and inspection the system, condition
and management of the public and private benevolent and
correctional institutions of the state and county, and municipal jails, workhouses, infirmaries and children's homes as
well as all institutions whether incorporated, private, or
otherwise, which receive and care for children. Officers in
charge of such institutions or responsible for the administration of public funds used for the relief and maintenance of the poor shall furnish the board or its secretary
such information as it requires. The board may prescribe
such forms of report and registration as it deems necessary.

Employment of
visitors.

For the purpose of such investigation and to carry out the
provisions of this chapter it shall employ such visitors as

may be necessary, who shall, in addition to other duties, investigate the care and disposition of children made by institutions for receiving children, and by all institutions including within their objects the placing of children in private homes, and, when they deem it desirable they shall visit such children in such homes, and report the result of such inspection to the board. The members of the board and such of its executive force as it shall designate may attend state and national conferences for the discussion of questions pertinent to their duties. The actual traveling expense so incurred by the members and such of its executive force as it shall designate shall be paid as provided by section 1351 of the General Code. *Attending national conferences.*

Sec. 6259. The commissioner of health may grant licenses to maintain maternity hospitals or homes, lying-in hospitals, or places where women are received and cared for during parturition. An application therefor shall first be approved by the board of health of the city, village or township in which such maternity hospital or home, lying-in hospital, or place where women are received and cared for during parturition is to be maintained. A record of the license so issued shall be kept by the state department of health, which shall forthwith give notice to the board of health of the city, village or township, in which the licensee resides, of the granting of such license and of the terms thereof. *Licenses granted; applications must be approved; record and notice.*

Sec. 6262. The commissioner of health and the boards of health of cities, villages or townships shall annually, and may, at any time, visit and inspect, or designate a person to visit and inspect the system, condition and management of the institutions and premises so licensed. *Visitation and inspection.*

SECTION 2. That original sections 1352, 6259 and 6262 and sections 6257 and 6258 of the General Code be, and the same are hereby repealed. *Repeals.*

CARL R. KIMBALL,
Speaker of the House of Representatives.
CLARENCE J. BROWN,
President of the Senate.

The sectional numbers in this act are in conformity to the General Code.
JOHN G. PRICE,
Attorney General.

Passed March 11, 1919.
Approved March 27, 1919.

JAMES M. COX,
Governor.

Filed in the office of the Secretary of State at Columbus, Ohio, on the 27th day of March, A. D. 1919.

33 G.

[House Bill No. 145.]

AN ACT

To amend sections 1295-5 and 1295-6 of the General Code, relative
to the registration of nurses.

Be it enacted by the General Assembly of the State of Ohio.
SECTION 1. That sections 1295-5 and 1295-6 of the
General Code be amended to read as follows:

Qualifications
and procedure
required to en-
title graduate
applicant to cer-
tificate.

Sec. 1295-5. On and after January 1, 1916, no person
shall practice nursing as a registered nurse in this state
without first complying with the requirements of this act.
All graduates in nursing shall either personally or by letter
or proxy, present their diplomas to the nurses' examining
committee for verification. Accompanying such diploma
the applicant shall file an affidavit, duly attested, stating
that the applicant is the person named in the diploma and
is the lawful posesssor of the same. The applicant shall
state date of birth and the actual time spent in the study of
nursing. If the committee shall find the diploma to be genuine and from a nurses' training school in good standing,
as defined by the state medical board, and connected with
a hospital or sanatorium, and the person named therein to
be the person holding and presenting the same, and that
said person has paid the fee as hereinafter provided for
the examination of applicants, the committee shall issue a
certificate to that effect signed by its secretary and chief
examiner; such certificate, when left with the probate judge
for record as hereinafter required, shall be conclusive evidence that its owner is entitled to practice nursing as a
registered nurse in this state.

Record of certifi-
cate.

All other persons desiring to engage in such practice in
this state, shall apply to the nurses' examining committee
for a certificate, and submit to the examination hereinafter
provided, except that all students who were on May 1, 1915,
matriculated in a training school for nurses located in the
state of Ohio, recognized by the state medical board of
Ohio, and who shall have graduated subsequent to May
1, 1915, and who shall file their diploma for registration
prior to June 1, 1918, shall receive certificate as heretofore
provided. The applicant shall file with secretary a written
application, under oath, on a form prescribed by the state
medical board, and provide proof that said applicant is
more than twenty-one years of age and of good moral character. The applicant shall file documentary evidence that
before matriculating in a training school for nurses, said
applicant received an education equivalent to that required
for completion of the first year of high school course of the
first grade in this state, of four units of high school work,
as defined in the school laws of Ohio, and evaluated by the
entrance examiner of the state medical board in the same
manner as provided in section 1270 of the General Code
of Ohio, and a diploma of graduation from a training school

Examination of
applicants other
than graduates.

in good standing, as defined by the state medical board and connected with a hospital or sanatorium. At the time of application the applicant shall present such diploma with the affidavit that said applicant is the person named therein and is the lawful possessor thereof, stating date of birth, residence, the training school or schools at which said applicant obtained education and training in nursing, the time spent in each, the time spent in the study and training of nursing, and such other facts as the state medical board required. If engaged in the practice of nursing, the affidavit shall state the period during which and the place where said nurse has been so engaged.

Sec. 1295-6. If the committee finds the applicant possesses the credentials necessary for admission to the examination, that the diploma is genuine and was granted by a training school for nurses in good standing, as defined by the state medical board and connected with a hospital or sanatorium and that the person named in the diploma is the person holding and presenting it and is of good moral character, the committee shall admit the applicant to an examination. *When applicant shall be admitted to examination.*

SECTION 2. That said original sections 1295-5 and 1295-6 of the General Code be, and the same are hereby repealed. ' *Repeals.*

sectional bers in this are in con- ity to the mal Code. 2s G. PRICE, wracy General.

CARL R. KIMBALL,
Speaker of the House of Representatives.
CLARENCE J. BROWN,
President of the Senate.

Passed March 6, 1919.
Approved March 27, 1919.

JAMES M. COX,
Governor.

Filed in the office of the Secretary of State at Columbus, Ohio, on the 27th day of March, A. D. 1919.

34 G.

[Amended Senate Bill No. 12.]

AN ACT

To amend section 11273 of the General Code, relating to venue of actions.

Be it enacted by the General Assembly of the State of Ohio:
SECTION 1. That section 11273 of the General Code be amended to read as follows:

"Sec. 11273. An action against the owner or lessee of a line of mail stages or other coaches, a railroad company, interurban railroad company, suburban railroad company or street railroad company owning or operating a railroad, interurban railroad or street railroad within the state, or against a transportation company owning or operating an *Action against railroad company, interurban, suburban or street railroad, and stage companies, where brought.*

electric traction road located upon either bank of a canal belonging to the state, may be brought in any county through or into which such line, railroad, interurban railroad, street railroad or electric traction road, passes or extends; provided that all actions against interurban, suburban or street railroad companies for injuries to person or property, or for wrongful death must be brought in the county in which the cause of action.or some part thereof, arose, or in the county in which the claimant for injuries to person or property or one whose wrongful death was caused, resided at the time when the cause of action arose, if the road or line of such companies or any part thereof be located in such county.'' If no part of such electric line or road be located in such county, then such actions may be brought in the county in which any part of such road or line is located, nearest the place where the claimant for injuries to person or property or the one whose wrongful death was caused, so resided.

Repeal.

SECTION 2. That said original section 11273 be, and the same hereby is repealed.

The sectional number in this act is in conformity to the General Code. JOHN G. PRICE, Attorney General.

CARL R. KIMBALL,
Speaker of the House of Representatives.
CLARENCE J. BROWN,
President of the Senate.

Passed March 6, 1919.

This bill was presented to the Governor on March 17, 1919, and was not signed or returned to the house wherein it originated within ten days after being so presented, exclusive of Sundays and the day said bill was presented and was filed in the office of the Secretary of State on the 29th day of March, 1919.

ROBERT T. CREW,
Veto Clerk.

Filed in the office of the Secretary of State at Columbus, Ohio, on the 29th day of March, A. D. 1919.

35 G.

[House Bill No. 50.]

AN ACT

To amend section 5704 of the General Code, relating to the publication of lists of lands on which the taxes have become delinquent.

Be it enacted by the General Assembly of the State of Ohio:

SECTION 1. That section 5704 of the General Code be amended to read as follows:

Publication of list of delinquent lands in two English newspapers.

Sec. 5704. Each county auditor shall cause a list of delinquent lands in his county to be published once a week for two consecutive weeks, between the twentieth day of December and the second Thursday in February, next ensuing, in one daily newspaper in the English language of the political party casting the largest vote in the state at the last general election, and in one daily English newspaper of the political party casting the next largest vote in the state at the same election, both published in the county and of general circulation therein. If there be no such daily newspaper published in the county then in two weekly English newspapers published and circulated therein, if there are two such papers published; if not then in one such weekly English newspaper will be sufficient. There shall be attached to the list a notice that the delinquent lands will be certified to the auditor of state as delinquent, as provided by law.

The sectional number in this act is in conformity to the General Code.
John G. Price, Attorney General.

SECTION 2. That original section 5704 of the General Repeal. Code be and the same is hereby repealed.

CARL R. KIMBALL,
Speaker of the House of Representatives.
F. E. WHITTEMORE,
President Pro Tem. of the Senate.

Passed March 18, 1919.
Approved April 4, 1919.

JAMES M. COX,
Governor.

Filed in the office of the Secretary of State at Columbus, Ohio, on the 7th day of April, A. D. 1919.

36 G.

[House Bill No. 246.]

AN ACT

To amend section 3092 of the General Code, relating to care of dependent children by county commissioners.

Be it enacted by the General Assembly of the State of Ohio:

SECTION 1. That section 3092 of the General Code be amended to read as follows:

Sec. 3092. In any county where such home has not already been provided the board of county commissioners may enter into a contract for the care of its neglected or dependent children with a county children's home, or with any institution or association in the state which has for one of its objects the care of dependent or neglected children, provided such institution or association has been duly certified by the board of state charities; or the board of county commissioners may pay reasonable board and provide suitable clothing and personal necessities as well as medical, dental and optical examination and treatment of dependent or neglected children who may be placed in the care of private families within the county. Provided that

Commissioners may contract for care of dependent children in certain institutions, when.

in any such case such dependent or neglected children shall
be duly committed to the aforesaid institution or association or placed in the care of a private family by the juvenile
court as provided by law.

Repeal.

SECTION 2.   That said original section 3092 of the General Code be, and the same is hereby repealed.

The sectional
number in this
act is in con-
formity to the
General Code.
JOHN G. PRICE,
*Attorney
        General.*

CARL R. KIMBALL,
Speaker of the House of Representatives.
F. E. WHITTEMORE,
President Pro Tem. of the Senate.

Passed March 18, 1919.
Approved April 4, 1919.

JAMES M. COX,
Governor.

Filed in the office of the Secretary of State at Columbus,
Ohio, on the 7th day of April, A. D. 1919.

37 G.

[Amended Senate Bill No. 11.]

AN ACT

To regulate the selling, offering or exposing for sale of agricultural
seeds, and to repeal sections 5805-1 to 5805-12 inclusive of the
General Code.

Be it enacted by the General Assembly of the State of Ohio:

Sec. 5805-1.

"Agricultural
seeds" defined.

SECTION 1.   The term "agricultural seeds" or "agricultural seed" as used in this act, shall be defined as brome
grass, Kentucky blue grass, Canada blue grass, fescues,
Italian rye grass, timothy, alfalfa, alsike clover, crimson
clover, red clover, white clover, sweet clover, Canada field
peas, cowpeas, soybeans, vetches, barley, corn of all kinds,
oats, rye, wheat, buckwheat, flax, kaffir corn, millets, sor-
ghum, cabbage and all other grasses, legumes, cereals and
forage plants which are sold, offered or exposed for sale
within this state for seeding purposes within this state.

Sec. 5805-2.

Statement on
each lot of seeds;
what it shall
contain.

SECTION 2.   Every lot of agricultural seeds, as defined
in section one of this act, except as herein otherwise provided, when in quantities of ten pounds or more, except in
case of rape when one pound or more shall be the quantity
requiring a label, shall have affixed thereto in a conspicuous
place on the exterior of each container of such agricultural
seeds, a plainly written or printed tag or label in the English language stating:

(a)   Commonly accepted name of such agricultural
seeds.

(b)   The approximate percentage by weight of pure
seed present, meaning the freedom of such agricultural
seeds from inert matter and from other seeds distinguish-
able by their appearance.

(c)   The approximate total percentage of weight of

weed seed; the term "weed seeds" as herein used being
defined as the noxious weed seeds listed in section three and
all seeds not listed in section one as agricultural seeds.

(d) The name of each kind of seed or bulblets of the
noxious weeds named in section three which are present
singly or collectively as follows: (1) in excess of one seed
or bulblet in each five grams of timothy, red top, orchard
grass, Kentucky blue grass, Canada blue grass, fescues,
brome grasses, perennial and Italian rye grass, crimson
clover, red clover, white clover, alsike clover, sweet clover,
alfalfa, and all other grasses and clovers not classified:
(2) one in twenty-five grams of millet, rape, flax, and other
seeds not specified in one or three of this sub-section: (3)
one in one hundred grams of wheat, oats, rye, barley, buckwheat, vetches, and other seeds as large or larger than
wheat.

(e) The approximate percentage of germination of
such agricultural seed together with the month and year
such seed was tested, provided, however, that this statement
shall not be a basis for prosecution under this act.

(f) The full name and address of the vendor of such
agricultural seed.

SECTION 3. The term "noxious weeds" as used in this
act shall include Canada thistle (Cirsium arvense), wild
onion (Allium vineale), quack grass (Agropyron repens),
dodders (Cuscuta species), plantains (Plantago species),
wild carrot (Daucus carota), oxeyedaisy (Chrysanthemum
leucanthemum), corn cockle (Agrostemma githargo), docks
(Rumex species), chicory (Chichorium intybus,) and such
other weeds as the secretary of agriculture, the director of
the Ohio state agricultural experiment station and the dean
of the college of agriculture of Ohio State University may
determine to be noxious and a menace in Ohio provided,
however, that prior to the promulgation of the order defining that any weed seed or seeds are noxious within the
definition of this act, a public hearing upon due notice
thereof shall be given and to persons affected by such order, at which hearing such person may appear in person or
by attorney, and provided further that said order determining that any weed seed or seeds shall be deemed to
be noxious, shall not be effective until six months after the
promulgation and publication of said order of the secretary
of agriculture, the director of the Ohio agricultural experiment station and the dean of the college of agriculture of
Ohio State University.

SECTION 4. Mixtures shall consist of two or more
kinds of agricultural seeds which are grown together and
sold, or are prepared and sold for general agricultural field
purposes, each present in excess of five per cent. by weight
of the total mixture, when sold, offered or exposed for sale
in lots of ten- pounds or more such mixtures shall have
affixed thereto in a conspicuous place on the exterior of the

container of such mixture a plainly written or printed tag or label in the English language stating:

(a) That such seed is a mixture.

(b) The name and approximate percentage by weight of each kind of agricultural seed present in such mixtures in excess of five per cent. by weight of the total mixture.

(c) The approximate percentage by weight of weed seed as defined in section two, sub-section (c) of this act.

(d) The name of each kind of seed or bulblet of the noxious weeds listed in section three which are present singly or collectively in excess of one seed or bulblet in each fifteen grams of such mixture.

(e) The approximate percentage of germination of each kind of agricultural seed present in such mixture in excess of five per cent. by weight of the entire mixture, together with the month and year said seed was tested, provided, however, that this statement shall not be a basis for prosecution under this act.

(f) Full name and address of the vendor of such mixture.

Sec. 5805-5.

Special mixtures; statement on each package or container required.

SECTION 5. Special mixtures shall consist of all mixtures of agricultural seeds which are prepared and sold for special purposes, including lawn mixtures and golf mixtures. When sold, offered, or exposed for sale as mixtures in bulk, packages, or other containers of eight ounces or more special mixtures shall have affixed thereto in a conspicuous place on the exterior of the container of such mixture a plainly written tag or label in the English language stating:

(a) That such seed is a mixture.

(b) The name of each kind of agricultural seed which is present in proportion of five per cent. or more of the total mixture.

(c) The approximate total percentage by weight of weed seeds as defined in section two, sub-section (c) of this act.

(d) Approximate percentage by weight of inert matter.

(e) The name of each kind of seed or bulblet of noxious weeds listed in section three of this act, which are present, singly or collectively, in excess of one seed or bulblet in each fifteen grams of such mixture.

(f) The full name and address of the vendor of such mixture.

Sec. 5805-6.

When seeds or mixtures are exempt from provisions of law.

SECTION 6. Agricultural seeds or mixtures of the same shall be exempt from the provisions of this act.

(a) When possessed, exposed for sale, or sold for food purposes only.

(b) When sold direct to seed merchants or shipped to a general market to be cleaned or graded before being offered or exposed for sale for seeding purposes.

(c) When in store for the purpose of recleaning, or not possessed, sold, or offered for sale for seeding purposes within the state.

(d) When such seed is grown, sold and delivered by any producer on his premises for seeding purposes by the purchaser himself, unless the purchaser of said seeds demands and receives from the seller at the time of the sale a certificate that said seed is subject to the provisions of this act. If, however, said seed be advertised for sale through the medium of the public press or by circular letter or for delivery through a common carrier said producer shall be considered a vendor, and said seed must be labeled in accordance with the provisions of this act.

106-7. SECTION 7. The secretary of agriculture shall receive sample or samples of seeds from any grower, seedman, person, firm or corporation who shall send such sample to him for examination; and said secretary shall have sample or samples of seeds examined and analyzed in conformity with the provisions of this act and the standards fixed by the regulations provided for herein. Said examination and analysis shall be made free of charge to residents of Ohio and· a report submitted showing the condition of the same with respect to percentage of purity together with the percentage and kind of noxious weed seeds· and other impurities, as well as statement of percentage of germination, to the sender within a reasonable time after the sample is received.

Samples of seeds shall be examined and analyzed free; statement of result.

105-8. SECTION 8. It shall be the duty of the said secretary, either by himself or his duly authorized agents, to inspect, examine and make analysis of and test any agricultural seeds sold, offered or exposed for sale within this state for seeding purposes within this state, at such time and place, and to such extent as he may determine. The secretary of agriculture, or his agents, shall have free access at all reasonable hours to any premises or structures to make examination of any such agricultural seeds, whether such seeds are upon the premises of the owner or consignee of such seeds or on the premises or in possession of any warehouse, elevator, railway or steamship company, and he is hereby given authority in person or by his agents upon notice to the dealer, his agents or the representative of any warehouse, elevator, railway or steamship company, if present, to take for analysis sample of such agricultural seeds. Said sample shall be thoroughly mixed and two official samples taken therefrom, each official sample shall be securely sealed. One of these official samples shall be furnished to the vendor or party in interest in person, if present, and if not present shall be promptly forwarded to the shipper or owner and the other retained by the secretary of agriculture or agent for analysis. In case a sample drawn as provided herein upon test or analysis is found to fall below the statement on the tag or label attached to the lot from which said sample was secured, or to violate

Seeds sold, offered or exposed for sale shall be examined and analyzed; right of entry provided to take samples.

Notice to vendor when test is found below statement.

any of the provisions of this act, the vendor or consignee of said lot of seed shall be notified and a copy of said notice mailed to the person, firm or corporation whose tag or label was found affixed thereto.

Sec. 5805-9.

Enforcement of law; rules and regulations; publication of examinations; seizure of seeds.

SECTION 9. The secretary of agriculture shall enforce the provisions of this act and shall be empowered to adopt such reasonable rules and regulations as may be deemed necessary in order to secure its efficient enforcement. It shall be the duty of the secretary of agriculture in his discretion to publish or cause to be published the results of the examinations, analyses and tests of any and all samples of agricultural seeds or mixture of such seeds drawn as provided for in section eight, together with the dates such tests were made. The secretary of agriculture is empowered to seize any seed sold in or offered for sale in Ohio which is not properly labeled and hold same until proper labeling is effected by the shipper or seller of such seed.

Sec. 5805-10.

Laboratory equipment; appointment of assistants; compensation.

SECTION 10. The secretary of agriculture shall maintain a laboratory with necessary equipment, and may appoint such analysts, inspectors, and assistants as may be necessary for the enforcement of the provisions of this act. He shall fix the compensation for such analysts, inspectors, and assistants who shall be paid their actual and necessary expenses incurred when traveling in the discharge of their duties. All such expense vouchers shall be approved by the secretary of agriculture.

Sec. 5805-11.

Violations a misdemeanor; penalty.

Interference with duties a misdemeanor.

SECTION 11. Every violation of the provisions of this act, relating to failure to label, or false labeling, shall be deemed a misdemeanor, punishable by a fine of not more than one hundred dollars. Whoever interferes with the secretary of agriculture, or any of his duly authorized agents, when in the discharge of the duties herein enjoined, or refuses such persons the privilege of entering any room, building or other place where the seeds herein named are kept for sale for seeding purposes, within this state, shall be guilty of a misdemeanor, and upon conviction shall be fined not less than fifty dollars, nor more than one hundred dollars, and shall pay the cost of prosecution.

Sec. 5805-12.

Application of fees, fines, etc.

SECTION 12. All moneys received from license fees, fines and costs imposed and recovered under the provisions of this act, shall be paid to the secretary of agriculture or his agents and by him paid into the state treasury to the credit of the general revenue fund.

Sec. 5805-13.

Annual license fee; certificate.

SECTION 13. For the purpose of defraying the costs of inspection and analyses of agricultural seeds under the provisions of this act it is hereby further provided that before any person, firm, company or corporation shall sell, offer for sale, or expose for sale in this state any of the agricultural seeds, except as provided in section 6, subsection (d) of this act, he or they shall pay each year a license fee to the secretary of agriculture of five dollars, and shall receive from said secretary of agriculture a certificate to sell agricultural seed until the first day of January next following.

Sec. 5805-14. SECTION 14. It shall be the duty of the secretary of agriculture or his representatives to bring prosecution for all violations under the provisions of this act before justice of peace, police judge, mayor or other court of competent jurisdiction. *(Courts having jurisdiction.)*

SECTION 15. This law shall be effective on and after September first, nineteen hundred and nineteen. *(When act shall take effect.)*

SECTION 16. That sections 5805-1 to 5805-12 of the General Code be, and the same are hereby repealed. *(Repeals.)*

F. E. WHITTEMORE,
President Pro Tem. of the Senate.
CARL R. KIMBALL,
Speaker of the House of Representatives.

The sectional numbers on the margin hereof are designated as provided by law. JOHN G. PRICE, Attorney General.

Passed March 13, 1919.
Approved April 4, 1919.

JAMES M. COX,
Governor.

Filed in the office of the Secretary of State at Columbus, Ohio, on the 7th day of April, A. D. 1919.

38 G.

[Amended Senate Bill No. 26.]

AN ACT

Relating to the carrying and displaying of certain flags.

Be it enacted by the General Assembly of the State of Ohio:

Sec. 13398-1. SECTION 1. That no red or black flag, nor any banner, ensign or sign having upon it any inscription opposed to organized government or which is sacrilegious or which may be derogatory to public morals shall be carried in parade within this state or displayed upon any street or building therein; and it shall be unlawful to display the flag of any anarchistic society upon any public or private building or to carry or display such flag in any street procession or parade within this state. Nothing in this act shall apply to the pennants of any university, college or other recognized institution of learning. *(Carrying and displaying certain flags prohibited.)*

Sec. 13398-2. SECTION 2. Whoever violates any provision of this act may be arrested without a warrant and shall be punished *(Penalty.)*

for each offense by a fine of not more than one hundred dollars.

F. E. WHITTEMORE,
President Pro Tem. of the Senate.
CARL R. KIMBALL,
Speaker of the House of Representatives.

The sectional numbers on the margin hereof are designated as provided by law.
JOHN G. PRICE,
Attorney
General.

Passed March 18, 1919.
Approved April 4, 1919.

JAMES M. COX,
Governor.

Filed in the office of the Secretary of State at Columbus, Ohio, on the 7th day of April, A. D. 1919.

39 G.

[Amended Senate Bill No. 74.]

AN ACT

To amend section 871-1 of the General Code, relative to the Industrial Commission of Ohio.

Be it enacted by the General Assembly of the State of Ohio:

SECTION 1. That section 871-1 of the General Code, be amended as follows:

Appointment of members; confirmation, qualification, term.

Sec. 871-1. The industrial commission of Ohio, heretofore created shall be composed of three members to be appointed by the governor, with the advice and consent of the senate. Such appointment shall be made to take effect upon the expiration of the present term of each member, and each of such appointments hereafter made shall be for the term of six years. Not more than one of the appointees to such commission shall be a person who, on account of his previous vocation, employment or affiliations, can be classed as a representative of employers, and not more than one of such appointees shall be a person who, on account of his previous vocation, employment or affiliations can be classed as a representative of employes; not more than two of the members of said commission shall belong to the same political party.

Repeal.

SECTION 2. That said original section 871-1 of the General Code be, and the same is hereby repealed.

CARL R. KIMBALL,
Speaker of the House of Representatives.
CLARENCE J. BROWN,
President of the Senate.

The sectional number in this act is in conformity to the General Code.
JOHN G. PRICE,
Attorney
General.

Passed March 13, 1919.

To the General Assembly:

I respectfully return to you, amended Senate Bill No. 74, entitled, "An act to amend section 871-1 of the Gen-

eral Code relative to the industrial commission of Ohio,''
with my disapproval.

The circumstances attendant upon the adoption of this
bill and the principle upon which it is based, are both, I
think, lacking in the elements which make for public confidence. Whenever a measure is passed through the assembly without a committee hearing being given in either
branch, after it is requested, the natural assumption is that
an emergency is involved, or the details and probable con-
sequences of the measure are not intended to be subjected
to the illumination of open discussion. No one will con-
tend that an emergency exists.

The authorized representatives of both employers and
employes in this state requested a hearing and there was
no concealment of their unreserved opposition to the bill.
It is therefore fair to assume that the two most directly
interested elements approve the present status quo which
this bill disturbs and the reasons for it can best be stated
by recounting certain developments since the existing industrial act was passed.

In the public hearing which was had during the month
of January, 1913, those who opposed the bill then pending,
advanced two pleas, first that the expense of administration
would be more than the state could bear, and second that
the efficiency required would be impossible under governmental direction because administrative policy might be
tinctured with politics. The first contention has disap-
peared through the simple demonstration, through experience, of its unsoundness. The interest on the fund now held
by the industrial commission is more than sufficient to
pay the cost of administration.

When the principle of workmen's compensation under
government control was first carried into legislative expres-
sion, under the limitations of the old constitution, senatorial
confirmation of the appointment of administrative officers
was not provided for, for the very definite reason that the
whole structure and plan were to be left as far removed
from political disputation as was possible under a democ-
racy in government. I need not remind your honorable
body that mature thought inspired this original provision,
because the interests opposed to the basic scheme of com-
pensating the injured workmen and the dependents of those
who lost their lives, were able and ingenious. At the out-
set, they aroused some degree of uncertainty in the public
mind so that every official step was carefully taken.

The bill that you now propose is a departure from the
very precaution exercised by those who framed the laws
under both the old and new constitution. The administration of the workmen's compensation law is a specialized
business, and a tenure both determined and guaranteed by
statutory act is most necessary, not only for the purpose of
procuring capable men, but of familiarizing them with the
intricate details of the task, as well.

The state of Ohio is the custodian of almost eighteen millions of dollars, part of which belongs to crippled workmen, while another part forms the means of supporting the widows and orphans of those who have lost their lives. In the face of doubt and specious antagonism, the fund has grown and lives now as a stable institution. Why interfere with it? This is no time, gentlemen, to disturb the confidence of labor. World-wide conditions bring to us all, a responsibility which should strip us of every consideration save that for the public weal. Lives and resource have been given to stabilize the affairs of civilization, and in these days of reconstruction, every man in official station must raise himself to a higher moral outlook. Labor does not want this bill—it opposes it; capital does not want this bill—it opposed it. If you can justify it then name the interests in Ohio which ask its passage. If the voice of a single manufacturer, a single workingman, a widow or an orphan has been raised in support of it, I have not heard it.

JAMES M. COX,
Governor.

March 21, 1919.

Passed in the house of representatives, notwithstanding the objections of the governor, having received a constitutional majority.

CARL R. KIMBALL,
Speaker of the House of Representatives.

Passed in the senate, notwithstanding the objections of the governor, having received a constitutional majority.

CLARENCE J. BROWN,
President of the Senate.

Filed in the office of the Secretary of State at Columbus, Ohio, on the 8th day of April, A. D. 1919.

40 G.

[House Bill No. 27.]

AN ACT·

To supplement section 934 of the General Code by the enactment of section 934-1, requiring washrooms to be provided and maintained at coal mines for the use of employes.

Be it enacted by the General Assembly of the State of Ohio:

SECTION 1. That section 934 of the General Code be supplemented by the enactment of section 934-1 of the General Code, to read as follows:

Wash room required at mine.

Sec. 934-1. Every owner, operator, lessee or agent of a coal mine, where five or more persons are employed, shall provide and keep in repair a wash room, convenient to the principal mine entrance, adequate for the accommodation of the employes, for the purpose of washing and changing their clothes when entering and returning from the mine. Such wash room shall be properly lighted and heated, supplied with warm and cold water and adequate and proper facilities for washing purposes.

SECTION 2. This act shall take effect and be in force **Repeal.** from and after April 30, 1920.

CARL R. KIMBALL,
Speaker of the House of Representatives.
CLARENCE J. BROWN,
President of the Senate.

The sectional number in this act is in conformity to the General Code.
JOHN G. PRICE, *Attorney General.*

Passed March 26, 1919.
Approved April 18, 1919.

JAMES M. COX,
Governor.

Filed in the office of the Secretary of State at Columbus, Ohio, on the 9th day of April, A. D. 1919.

41 G.

[House Bill No. 47.]

AN ACT

Requiring sheriffs to investigate shanty boats and to report to the prosecuting attorney persons living in or operating the same without license.

Be it enacted by the General Assembly of the State of Ohio:

See. 13403-1.

SECTION 1. The sheriff of each county, which borders on a navigable stream or lake, shall, at least once in each sixty days, make investigation of all boats or watercraft, not propelled by steam, used as places of residence or abode, or, which engage in business, trade or traffic, found in such county, for the purpose of ascertaining whether the person living in or occupying such boats or watercraft, or engaging in business, trade or traffic therein or thereby, has duly obtained a license from the probate court of such county therefor; and such sheriff shall make report to the prosecuting attorney of the county of all such persons as may be found without such license. The prosecuting attorney shall thereupon, without delay, proceed to prosecute such offenders in the manner provided by law for such offense.

Investigation of shanty boats; prosecution for failure to obtain license.

CARL R. KIMBALL,
Speaker of the House of Representatives.
CLARENCE J. BROWN,
President of the Senate.

The sectional number on the margin hereof is designated as provided by law. JOHN G. PRICE, *Attorney General.*

Passed March 25, 1919.
Approved April 8, 1919.

JAMES M. COX,
Governor.

Filed in the office of the Secretary of State at Columbus, Ohio, on the 9th day of April, A. D. 1919.

42 G.

62

[House Bill No. 65.]

AN ACT

To amend section 3138-1 and to repeal section 2502 of the General Code, relating to contracts between county commissioners and hospitals organized for charitable purposes.

Be it enacted by the General Assembly of the State of Ohio:
SECTION 1. That section 3138-1 of the General Code be amended to read as follows:

Commissioners may contract with corporation or association for certain indigent sick; payment.

Sec. 3138-1. That the board of county commissioners of any county may enter an agreement with one or more corporations or associations, organized for charitable purposes, or with one or more corporations or associations organized for the purpose of maintaining and operating a hospital in any county where such hospital has been established, for the care of the indigent sick and disabled, excepting persons afflicted with pulmonary tuberculosis, upon such terms and conditions as may be agreed upon between said commissioners, and such corporations or associations, and said commissioners, shall provide for the payment of the amount agreed upon, either in one payment, or in installments, or so much from year to year as the parties stipulate. Nothing herein shall authorize the payment of public funds to a sectarian institution.

Repeal.

SECTION 2. That said original section 3138-1 and section 2502 of the General Code be, and the same are hereby repealed.

The sectional number in this act is in conformity to the General Code. JOHN G. PRICE, Attorney General.

CARL R. KIMBALL,
Speaker of the House of Representatives.
CLARENCE J. BROWN,
President of the Senate.

Passed March 27, 1919.
Approved April 8, 1919.

JAMES M. COX,
Governor.

Filed in the office of the Secretary of State at Columbus, Ohio, on the 9th day of April, A. D. 1919.

43 G.

———

[House Bill No. 229.]

AN ACT

To amend section 2980-1 of the General Code, relating to additional allowance for the deputies in the various county offices; how obtained.

Be it enacted by the General Assembly of the State of Ohio:
SECTION 1. That section 2980-1 of the General Code be amended to read as follows:

63

Sec. 2980-1. The aggregate sum so fixed by the county commissioners to be expended in any year for the compensation of such deputies, assistants, bookkeepers, clerks or other employes except court constables, shall not exceed for any county auditor's office, county treasurer's office, probate judge's office, county recorder's office, sheriff's office, or office of the clerk of the courts, an aggregate amount to be ascertained by computing forty per cent, on the first two thousand dollars or fractional part thereof, sixty per cent, on the next eight thousand dollars or fractional part thereof and eighty-five per cent, on all over ten thousand dollars, of the fees, costs, percentages, penalties, allowances and other perquisites collected for the use of the county in any such office for official services during the year ending September thirtieth next preceding the time of fixing such aggregate sum; provided, however, that if at any time any one of such officers require additional allowance in order to carry on the business of his office, said officer may make application to a judge of the court of common pleas, of the county wherein such officer was elected; and thereupon such judge shall hear said application and if, upon hearing the same said judge shall find that such necessity exists, he may allow such a sum of money as he deems necessary to pay the salary of such deputy, deputies, assistants, bookkeepers, clerks or other employes as may be required, and thereupon the board of county commissioners shall transfer from the general county fund, to such officers' fee fund, such sum of money as may be necessary to pay said salary or salaries.

Notice in writing of such application and the time fixed by such judge for the hearing thereof shall be served by the applicant, five days before said hearing upon the board of county commissioners of such county. And said board shall file in said proceeding their approval or disapproval of the allowance asked for and shall have the right to appear at such hearing and be heard thereon; and evidence may be offered.

When the term of an incumbent of any such office shall expire within the year for which such an aggregate sum is to be fixed, the county commissioners at the time of fixing the same, shall designate the amount of such aggregate sum which may be expended by the incumbent and the amount of such aggregate sum which may be expended by his successor for the fractional parts of such year.

Repeal.

SECTION 2. That said original section 2980-1 of the General Code be and the same is hereby repealed.

CARL R. KIMBALL,
Speaker of the House of Representatives.
CLARENCE J. BROWN,
President of the Senate.

The sectional number in this act is in conformity to the General Code. JOHN G. PRICE, *Attorney General.*

Passed March 20, 1919.
Approved April 8, 1919.

JAMES M. COX,
Governor.

Filed in the office of the Secretary of State, at Columbus, Ohio, on the 9th day of April, A. D. 1919.

44 G.

[House Bill No. 111.]

AN ACT

For the protection by law of badge, button, insignia or emblem used by the United Veterans of the Republic, a war veteran organization legally incorporated within the state of Ohio.

Be it enacted by the General Assembly of the State of Ohio:

Sec. 13163-1.

SECTION 1. It shall be a misdemeanor punishable by fine or imprisonment, or both, for any person, not a member of the United Veterans of the Republic, to wear, display or use for advertising purposes, any badge, button, insignia or emblem used by United Veterans of the Republic, a war veteran organization legally incorporated under the laws of Ohio. Any one violating this act shall be fined not more than one hundred dollars or imprisoned for not more than six months, or both, in the discretion of the court.

Wearing or displaying badge of United Veterans of Republic not being a member, prohibited; penalty.

CARL R. KIMBALL,
Speaker of the House of Representatives.
CLARENCE J. BROWN,
President of the Senate.

The sectional number on the margin hereof is designated as provided by law. JOHN G. PRICE, *Attorney General.*

Passed March 25, 1919.
Approved April 8, 1919.

JAMES M. COX,
Governor.

Filed in the office of the Secretary of State at Columbus, Ohio, on the 9th day of April, A. D. 1919.

45 G.

[House Bill No. 130.]

AN ACT

To amend section 7491 of the General Code, relating to watering places on public highways.

Be it enacted by the General Assembly of the State of Ohio:

SECTION 1. That section 7491 of the General Code be amended to read as follows:

Sec. 7491. The township trustees may provide and, when provided, shall maintain suitable watering places for procuring water for persons and animals on the public highways in their township, and the trustees of two or more townships may join in providing and maintaining such watering place where it is located on or near the township line, or on a road leading from one township into another; provided that such trustees may by resolution abandon any such watering places when the necessity therefor ceases to exist. *(Provide watering places on public highways.)*

SECTION 2. That said original section 7491 of the General Code be, and the same is hereby repealed. *(Repeal.)*

(The sectional number in this act is in conformity to the General Code. JOHN G. PRICE, Attorney General.)

CARL R. KIMBALL,
Speaker of the House of Representatives.
F. E. WHITTEMORE,
President Pro Tem. of the Senate.

Passed March 18, 1919.

This bill was presented to the governor on March 27, 1919, and was not signed or returned to the house wherein it originated within ten days after being so presented, exclusive of Sudnays and the day said bill was presented, and was filed in the office of the Secretary of State on the 9th day of April, A. D. 1919.

ROBERT T. CREW,
Veto Clerk.

Filed in the office of the Secretary of State at Columbus, Ohio, on the 9th day of April, A. D. 1919.

46 G.

[House Bill No. 93.]

AN ACT

To amend section 7817 of the General Code, relative to the number of meetings held each year by the county board of school examiners for the examination of applicants for teachers' certificates.

Be it enacted by the General Assembly of the State of Ohio:

SECTION 1.   That section 7817 of the General Code be amended to read as follows:

Meetings each year for examination of applicants. No private examinations nor antedating certificates.

Sec. 7817.   Each board shall hold public meetings for the examination of applicants for county teachers' certificates on the first Saturday of September, May, and July and on the last Friday of August of each year unless any such day falls on a legal holiday, in which case it shall be held on the corresponding day of the succeeding week, at such place within the county as, in the opinion of the board, best will accommodate the greatest number of applicants. In no case shall the board hold any private examinations or antedate any certificate.

Repeal.

SECTION 2.   That original section 7817 of the General Code be, and the same is hereby repealed.

CARL R. KIMBALL,
Speaker of the House of Representatives.
CLARENCE J. BROWN,
President of the Senate.

The sectional number in this act is in conformity to the General Code.
JOHN G. PRICE,
..*l* *rey*
General.

Passed March 25, 1919.
Approved April 9, 1919.

JAMES M. COX,
Governor.

Filed in the office of the Secretary of State at Columbus, Ohio, on the 10th day of April, A. D. 1919.

47 G.

[House Bill No. 455.]

AN ACT

To give certain credits on the required three years' study of law to certain members of the army, navy and marine corps of the United States.

Be it enacted by the General Assembly of the State of Ohio:

Sec. 1701-1.

SECTION 1. Any person who is or was a member of the army, navy or marine corps of the United States of America in the present world war and is in good standing or has been honorably discharged from the service and who at the time he entered the service was engaged in the study of law shall be entitled, upon the presentation of proper credentials to the supreme court of Ohio, to a credit for the time that he was in the service, not exceeding one year, however, on the three years' period of study that is required as a condition precedent to the taking of the bar examination.

Credits to certain members of army, navy and marine corps.

The sectional number on the margin hereof is designated as provided by law. JOHN G. PRICE, *Attorney General.*

CARL R. KIMBALL,
Speaker of the House of Representatives.
CLARENCE J. BROWN,
President of the Senate.

Passed March 27, 1919.
Approved April 9, 1919.

JAMES M. COX,
Governor.

Filed in the office of the Secretary of State at Columbus, Ohio, on the 10th day of April, A. D. 1919.

48 G.

68

[House Bill No. 155.]

AN ACT

Providing for changing the name of "County Infirmary" to "County Home."

Be it enacted by the General Assembly of the State of Ohio:

Sec. 2419-3.

Change of name from "county infirmary" to "county home."

SECTION 1. The institutions known as "county infirmaries" of the various counties of the state shall be known hereafter as "county homes." The words "infirmary" or "county infirmary" whenever they occur in the General Code of Ohio shall be construed to read "county home." The county commissioners of each county shall within sixty days after the taking effect of this act, provide a suitable sign or placard bearing the name "County Home" and place such sign on the building or grounds of such institution, displacing the original placard or sign.

The sectional number on the margin hereof is designated as provided by law. JOHN G. PRICE, *Attorney General.*

CARL R. KIMBALL,
Speaker of the House of Representatives.
CLARENCE J. BROWN,
President of the Senate.

Passed March 25, 1919.
Approved April 9, 1919.

JAMES M. COX,
Governor.

Filed in the office of the Secretary of State at Columbus, Ohio, on the 10th day of April, A. D. 1919.

49 G.

69

[House Bill No. 228.]

AN ACT

To amend section 8574 of the General Code, relative to the order of descent of property acquired by purchase.

Be it enacted by the General Assembly of the State of Ohio:
SECTION 1. That section 8574 of the General Code be amended to read as follows:

Sec. 8574. If the estate came not by descent, devise, or deed of gift, it shall descend and pass as follows: *(Order of descent when estate acquired by purchase.)*

1. To the children of the intestate and their legal representatives.

2. If there are no children, or their legal representatives, the estate shall pass to and be vested in the husband or wife, relict of such intestate.

3. If such intestate leaves no husband or wife, relict to himself or herself, the estate shall pass to the brothers and sisters of the intestate of the whole blood, and their legal representatives.

4. If there are no brothers or sisters of the intestate of the whole blood, or their legal representatives, the estate shall pass to the brothers and sisters of the half blood, and their legal representatives.

5. If there are no brothers or sisters of the intestate of the half-blood, or their legal representatives, the estate shall ascend to the father and mother equally; if one of them be dead, then to the other.

6. If the father and mother are dead, the estate shall pass to the next of kin, and their legal representatives, to and of the blood of the intestate.

SECTION 2. That original section 8574 of the General Code be, and the same is hereby repealed. *(Repeal.)*

The sectional number in this act is in conformity to the General Code. JOHN G. PRICE, Attorney General.

CARL R. KIMBALL,
Speaker of the House of Representatives.
CLARENCE J. BROWN,
President of the Senate.

Passed March 25, 1919.
Approved April 9, 1919.

JAMES M. COX,
Governor.

Filed in the office of the Secretary of State at Columbus, Ohio, on the 10th day of April, A. D. 1919.

50 G.

70

[House Bill No. 35.]

AN ACT

To amend section 3061 of the General Code, relating to memorial buildings.

Be it enacted by the General Assembly of the State of Ohio:
SECTION 1. That section 3061 of the General Code be amended to read as follows:

Question to be submitted to vote at regular or special election.

Sec. 3061. Immediately upon the appointment and organization of such board of trustees, they shall certify to the deputy state supervisors of elections of the county, the fact of their appointment and organization, and direct the submission to popular vote at the next regular election, or at a special election called by such deputy state supervisors of elections for that purpose, of the question of the issue of bonds in the amount so named in the original resolution, and of the erection and maintenance of the memorial building contemplated. Such deputy state supervisors shall submit the question to popular vote at the next regular election, or such special election, with such forms of ballot as the deputy state supervisors prescribe, and shall certify the result of such election to the board of trustees. If a majority of the votes cast upon the question is in favor of the issuance of such bonds and the construction and maintenance of such memorial building, the board of trustees shall proceed as hereinafter authorized.

Repeal.

SECTION 2. That said original section 3061 of the General Code be, and the same is hereby repealed.

CARL R. KIMBALL,
Speaker of the House of Representatives.
CLARENCE J. BROWN,
President of the Senate.

The sectional number in this act is in conformity to the General Code.
JOHN G. PRICE,
Attorney General.

Passed April 2, 1919.
Approved April 9, 1919.

JAMES M. COX,
Governor.

Filed in the office of the Secretary of State at Columbus, Ohio, on the 10th day of April, A. D. 1919.

51 G.

71

[House Bill No. 314.]

AN ACT

To supplement section 218 by the enactment of section 218-1 of the General Code, relative to the registration of births or deaths of residents of Ohio occurring outside the state.

Be it enacted by the General Assembly of the State of Ohio:

SECTION 1. That section 218 of the General Code be supplemented by the enactment of section 218-1 to read as follows:

Sec. 218-1. Births of children whose mothers are residents of the state of Ohio, while such mothers are temporarily absent therefrom, and deaths of residents of the state of Ohio, while temporarily absent therefrom, shall be registered in accordance with the provisions of this chapter, except that in lieu of the certificates herein provided, the local registrar may accept a certified copy of the certificate filed in the place where such birth or death occurred, if in accordance with the laws of such place and not materially different from the certificates herein provided. Such births or deaths occurring before the enactment of this section may be registered in accordance with its provisions on payment to the local registrar of a fee of fifty cents for each birth or death.

Registration of births and deaths occurring outside the state.

CARL R. KIMBALL,
Speaker of the House of Representatives.
CLARENCE J. BROWN,
President of the Senate.

Passed April 1, 1919.
Approved April 10, 1919.

JAMES M. COX,
Governor.

Filed in the office of the Secretary of State at Columbus, Ohio, on the 11th day of April, A. D. 1919.

52 G.

[House Bill No. 190.]

AN ACT

To amend section 9618 of the General Code, relating to liabilities of mutual live stock insurance associations.

Be it enacted by the General Assembly of the State of Ohio:

SECTION 1. That section 9618 of the General Code be amended to read as follows:

When charter shall be forfeited. Sec. 9618. Should the amount at risk in such company be reduced below fifty thousand dollars, it shall issue no more certificates or policies of insurance until bona fide applications, sufficient to restore the insurance to such amount have been secured, and a sworn statement of that fact is filed with and approved by the superintendent of insurance, and by him certified to the company. If such company fails to restore such amount, for the period of six months, it shall forfeit its right to do business. When its liabilities exceed seven per cent of the amount of risk in force, as determined by the last preceding assessment, such company shall be deemed to be insolvent, and to have forfeited its charter. Such forfeiture shall be enforced by the superintendent of insurance by proceedings in quo warranto.

Repeal. SECTION 2. That said original section 9618 of the General Code be, and the same is hereby repealed.

CARL R. KIMBALL,
Speaker of the House of Representatives.
CLARENCE J. BROWN,
President of the Senate.

The sectional number in this act is in conformity to the General Code. JOHN G. PRICE, Attorney General.

Passed March 27, 1919.
Approved April 10, 1919.

JAMES M. COX,
Governor.

Filed in the office of the Secretary of State at Columbus, Ohio, on the 11th day of April, A. D. 1919.

53 G.

[House Bill No. 240.]

AN ACT

Defining optometry, providing a state board of optometry, providing for the licensing of persons to practice optometry and for the revocation and suspension of such licenses, and providing penalties for violations.

Be it enacted by the General Assembly of the State of Ohio:

SECTION 1. The practice of optometry is defined to be the application of optical principles, through technical methods and devices in the examination of human eyes for the purpose of ascertaining departures from the normal, measuring their functional powers and adapting optical accessories for the aid thereof.

Practice of optometry defined.

SECTION 2. That on and after January 1st, 1920, it shall not be lawful for any person in this state to engage in the practice of optometry or to hold himself out as a practitioner of optometry, or attempt to determine by an examination of the eyes the kind of glasses needed by any person, or to hold himself out as a licensed optometrist when not so licensed, or to hold himself out as able to examine the eyes of any person for the purpose of fitting the same with glasses, excepting those hereinafter exempted, unless he has first fulfilled the requirements of this act and has received a certificate of licensure from the state board of optometry created by this act, nor shall it be lawful for any person in this state to represent that he is the lawful holder of a certificate of licensure such as is provided for in this act, when in fact he is not such lawful holder or to impersonate any licensed practitioner of optometry or to fail to register the certificate as provided in section nine of this act.

Practice without license unlawful.

Any person violating the provisions of this section shall be guilty of a misdemeanor and, upon conviction, for his first offense shall be fined not more than five hundred dollars at the discretion of the court and upon conviction for a second or later offense shall be fined not less than five hundred dollars, nor more than one thousand dollars or imprisoned not less than six months nor more than one year at the discretion of the court.

Penalty.

SECTION 3. The governor, with the advice and consent of the senate, shall appoint a state board of optometry consisting of five persons, citizens of Ohio, each of whom shall be a non-medical man or woman, actually engaged in the practice of optometry as defined in section 1, of this act, for five years next preceding his appointment.

State board of optometry; appointment, qualifications, vacancy.

Said board shall be so appointed within thirty days after the taking effect of this act, one for the term of one year, one for the term of two years, one for the term of three years, one for the term of four years and one for the term of five years, who shall hold said office until their successors are appointed and qualified.

Thereafter, one member of said board shall be appointed each year for the term of five years, and shall hold said office until his successor is appointed and qualified.

No person so appointed shall be a stockholder in or member of the faculty, or of the board of trustees of any school of optometry, or serve to exceed two terms.

Vacancies on said board shall be filled by appointment by the governor in the manner hereinbefore provided.

Sec. 1395-24.

Organization of board; meetings; quorum; rules and regulations.

SECTION 4. The state board of optometry shall organize by the election from its members of a president and a secretary, who shall hold their respective offices for one year.

It shall hold regular meetings for examination, beginning on the second Tuesday of June and November of each year, and additional meetings at such times and places as it shall determine, not to exceed one every three months, but the November meeting shall be held in the city of Columbus.

A majority of the board shall constitute a quorum, but a less number may adjourn from time to time.

The board shall make such rules and regulations as may be necessary to carry out the provisions of this act; provided, however, that it shall require the concurrence of a majority of the members of the board to grant or to revoke a license.

Sec. 1395-25.

Bond and oath of office.

SECTION 5. Before entering upon the discharge of the duties of his office the secretary of the state board of optometry shall give a bond to the state, to be approved by the board, in the sum of two thousand dollars conditioned for the faithful discharge of the duties of his office. The premium for such bond to be paid from the funds paid into the state treasury by the secretary of the board.

Such bond, with the approval of the board and oath of office indorsed thereon, shall be deposited with the secretary of state and kept in his office. Each month all moneys received by the secretary shall be paid by him into the state treasury to the credit of a fund for the use of the state board of optometry.

Sec. 1395-26.

Compensation of members and secretary.

SECTION 6. Each member of the state board of optometry shall receive ten dollars for each day actually employed in the discharge of his official duties, and his necessary expenses incurred.

The secretary shall receive an annual salary to be fixed by the board, and his necessary expenses incurred in the discharge of his official duties.

The compensation and expenses of the secretary and members of the board, and the expenses of the board necessary in carrying out the provisions of this act, shall be paid from the fund in the state treasury for use of the board on the requisition signed by the president and the secretary of the board and the warrant of the auditor of the state; provided, however, that said compensation and expenses shall not exceed the amount paid into the state treasury under the provisions of this act.

Sec. 1295-27.

SECTION 7. The state board of optometry shall have an official seal and shall keep a record of its proceedings, a register of persons registered as optometrists and register of licenses by it revoked.

Official seal; record of proceedings; proof of records.

Its record shall be open to public inspection, and it shall keep on file all examination papers for a period of ninety days after each examination. A transcript of an entry in such records, certified by the secretary under the seal of the board, shall be evidence of the facts therein stated. The board shall annually, on or before the first day of January make a report to the governor of all its official acts during the preceding year, and of its receipts and disbursements, and a full and complete report of the conditions of optometry in this state.

Sec. 1295-28.

SECTION 8. Every person desiring to commence the practice of optometry, or if now in practice, to continue the practice thereof after January 1, 1920, except as herein otherwise provided, shall take the examination provided in this act and fulfill the other requirements hereof as herein provided. Any person who has been engaged in the practice of optometry in this state for two full years immediately prior to the passage of this act or for one year in this and for the year preceding it in another state, and is of good character shall be entitled to take a limited examination covering the following only:

Examination required by practitioners.

    (a) The limitations of the sphere of optometry.

    (b) The necessary scientific instruments used.

    (c) The form and power of lenses used.

    (d) A correct method of measuring presbyopia, hypermetropia, myopia and astigmatism.

    (e) The writing of formulae or prescriptions for the adoption of lenses in aid of vision.

Any person serving in the military or naval forces of the United States who was engaged in the practice of optometry previous to his entering such service shall be deemed as being engaged in the practice of optometry during the time he is in such service.

Any person over the age of 21 years, of good moral character, who has had a preliminary education equivalent to two years of the course in a first grade high school, which shall be ascertained by examination or by acceptable certificate as to credentials for work done in such approved institution, and has graduated from a school or college of optometry in good standing, as determined by the board, which maintains a course in optometry of not less than two years shall be entitled to take a standard examination. Said standard examination shall consist of tests in practical, theoretical and physiological optics, in theoretical and practical optometry and in the anatomy and physiology of the eye and in pathology as applied to optometry. Provided that any person not less than twenty-one years of age who is actually engaged in the practice of optometry at the time of the passage of this act shall be entitled to take the

Standard examination; who may take.

standard examination merely upon proof to the board that he is of good moral character, and is not addicted to the intemperate use of alcohol or narcotic drugs.

Sec. 1295-29.

Application for examination; re-examination at expiration of six months.

SECTION 9. Every person desiring to be licensed as in this act provided, shall file with the secretary of said board upon appropriate blank to be furnished by said secretary an application, verified by oath, setting forth the facts which entitle the applicant to examination and licensure under the provisions of this act. The said board shall hold at least two examinations each year. In case of failure at any standard examination the applicant, after the expiration of six months and within two years, shall have the privilege of a second examination by the board without the payment of an additional fee. In case of failure at any limited examination the applicant shall have the privilege of continuing the practice of optometry and of taking a second examination without the payment of an additional fee. But in the event of his failure to pass a second examination on or before July 1st, 1920, he shall thereafter cease to practice optometry in this state. Every applicant who shall pass the standard examination, or the limited examination as the case may be, and who shall otherwise comply with the provisions of this act, shall receive from the said board under its seal a certificate of licensure entitling him to practice optometry in this state, which certificate shall be duly registered in a record book to be properly kept by the secretary of the board for that purpose, which shall be open to public inspection, and a duly certified copy of said record shall be received as evidence in all courts of this state in the trial of any case. Each person to whom a certificate shall be issued by said board shall keep said certificate displayed in a conspicuous place in office or place of business wherein said person shall practice optometry, together with the photograph of said person attached to the lower right-hand corner of said certificate and shall whenever required exhibit the said certificate to any member or agent of said board.

License, registration of; display of certificate.

Peddling prohibited.

Peddling from door to door, or the establishment of temporary offices is specifically forbidden under penalty of revocation of said certificate by said board. Whenever any person shall practice optometry outside of or away from his office or place of business he shall deliver to each person, fitted with glasses by him, a certificate signed by him wherein he shall set forth the amounts charged, his post-office address and the number of his certificate. Each person to whom a certificate has been issued by said board shall, before practicing under the same register said certificate in the office of the clerk of the court of common pleas in each county wherein he proposes to practice optometry, and shall pay therefor such fee as may be lawfully chargeable for such registry. The clerk of the court of common pleas in each county shall keep a certificate registration book wherein he shall promptly register each certificate for which the fee is paid.

Certificate must be registered in office of clerk of court.

1395-30. SECTION 10. Said board shall charge the following fees for examinations, registrations and renewals of certificates. The sum of twenty-five dollars for a standard examination, and ten dollars for a limited examination. Every registered optometrist who desires to continue the practice of optometry shall, annually, on or before the first day of January, pay to the secretary of the board a renewal registration fee of two dollars, for which he shall receive a renewal of his certificate. *Examination, registration and renewal fees.*

In case of neglect to pay the renewal registration fee herein specified, the board may revoke such certificate and the holder thereof may be re-instated by complying with the conditions specified in this act. But no certificate or permit shall be revoked without giving sixty days' notice to the delinquent, who, within such period shall have the right of renewal of such certificate on payment of the renewal fee with a penalty of five dollars provided that retirement from practice for a period not exceeding five years shall not deprive the holder of said certificate of the right to renew his certificate on the payment of all lapsed fees. *Revocation on failure to pay fees; notice.*

The board shall adopt a seal and certificate of suitable design and shall have an office at Columbus in this state, where examinations may be held and where all its permanent records shall be kept, which records shall be open to public inspection. It shall have power to make requisition upon the proper state officials for office rooms and supplies, including stationery and furniture. All printing and binding necessary for the work of the said board shall be done by the state printer upon an order issued by said board through its president and secretary to the supervisor of public printing. *Seal; place of office; equipment.*

1395-31. SECTION 11. The board shall refuse to grant a certificate of licensure to any applicant and may cancel, revoke or suspend the operation of any certificate by it granted for any or all of the following reasons, to-wit: The conviction of a crime involving moral turpitude, habitual intemperance in the use of ardent spirits or stimulants, narcotics or any other substance which impairs the intellect and judgment to such an extent as to incapacitate for the performance of the duties of an optometrist. The certificate of licensure of any person convicted of a violation of section two of this act shall be ipso facto revoked. *Refusal, cancellation and revocation of certificates; grounds for.*

Any person who is the holder of a certificate of licensure or who is an applicant for examination for a certificate of licensure, against whom is preferred any charges, shall be furnished by the board with a copy of the complaint and shall have a hearing before the board, at which hearing he may be represented by counsel. At such hearing witnesses may be examined for and against the accused respecting the said charges, which examination shall be conducted in the manner usually followed in the taking of testimony before commissions in this state. The suspension of a certificate of licensure, by reason of the use of stimu- *Copy of complaint furnished applicant for or holder of certificate.*

lants or narcotics may be removed when the holder thereof shall have been adjudged by the said board to be cured and capable of practicing optometry.

Sec. 1295-32.

Reciprocity with other states; fee.

SECTION 12. An applicant for a certificate of licensure who has been examined by the state board of another state which, through reciprocity, similarly accredits the holder of a certificate issued by the board of this state to the full privileges of practice within such state shall, on the payment of a fee of twenty-five dollars to the said board and on filing in the office of the board a true and attested copy of the said license, certified by the president or secretary of the state board issuing the same, and showing also that the standard of requirements adopted and enforced by said board is equal to that provided for by this act shall, without further examination, receive a certificate of licensure provided that such applicant has not previously failed at an examination held by the board of this state.

Sec. 1295-33.

Title of doctor, oculist, etc., prohibited.

SECTION 13. Nothing in this act shall be construed as conferring on the holder of any certificate of licensure issued by said board the title of doctor, oculist, ophthalmologist, or any other word or abbreviation indicating that he is engaged in the practice of medicine or surgery, or the treatment or the diagnosis of diseases of, or injuries to the human eye, or the right to use drugs or medicines in any form for the treatment or examination of the human eye.

Sec. 1295-34.

To whom act does not apply.

SECTION 14. The provision of this act shall not apply (a) to physicians or surgeons practicing under authority of licenses issued under the laws of this state for the practice of medicine or surgery, or (b) to persons selling spectacles and eye-glasses but who do not assume directly or indirectly to adapt them to the eye, or neither practice nor profess to practice optometry.

Sec. 1295-35.

Number and gender; interpretation.

SECTION 15. Wherever in this act the singular number is used it shall be interpreted as meaning both singular and plural if compatible with the sense of the language used, and vice versa, and, wherever in this act the masculine gender is used it shall be construed as comprehending also the feminine gender.

The sectional numbers on the margin hereof are designated as provided by law. JOHN G. PRICE, Attorney General.

CARL R. KIMBALL,
Speaker of the House of Representatives.
CLARENCE J. BROWN,
President of the Senate.

Passed March 20, 1919.
Approved April 10, 1919.

JAMES M. COX,
Governor

Filed in the office of the Secretary of State at Columbus, Ohio, on the 11th day of April, A. D. 1919.

54 G.

79

[House Bill No. 238.]

AN ACT

To supplement sections 3082 and 3107 of the General Code by the enactment of sections 3082-1 and 3107-1 relating to county children's homes.

Be it enacted by the General Assembly of the State of Ohio:

SECTION 1. That sections 3082 and 3107 of the General Code be supplemented by sections 3082-1 and 3107-1, to read as follows:

Sec. 3082-1. Such board of trustees shall hold a meeting once each month at which time they shall examine all accounts presented for payment and order the payment of such accounts as a majority of the members may approve. Such board shall also examine into the conditions of the property, carefully observe the manner of care afforded the wards of such boards whether inmates of the home or residing in foster families, and shall file with the state board of charities annually, or oftener if required, a detailed account, giving the whereabouts of each child and the moral and physical condition of each child. Called or adjourned meetings of the board may be held at any time as the members may provide. Failure of a trustee to attend three consecutive regular meetings of the board, unless for reasons beyond his control, shall be sufficient cause for removal.

Meeting each month to examine accounts, condition of property and care of wards or inmates.

Sec. 3107-1. At the request of the superintendent the board of trustees may issue an order upon the county auditor for the payment to such superintendent a sum not exceeding at any time two hundred dollars to be known and designated as a reserve fund to be used by such superintendent for payment of emergency accounts. He shall keep an itemized account of such expenditures and when such fund is about exhausted submit an itemized statement of expenditures therefrom to the county auditor before he shall honor another such order issued by the board of trustees. The amounts so paid in any fiscal year shall not exceed twenty per cent of the total expenditures for such home during the preceding year.

Reserve fund for payment of emergency accounts; maximum expenditure.

CARL R. KIMBALL,
Speaker of the House of Representatives.
CLARENCE J. BROWN,
President of the Senate.

Passed March 28, 1919.
Approved April 10, 1919.

JAMES M. COX,
Governor.

Filed in the office of the Secretary of State at Columbus, Ohio, on the 11th day of April, A. D. 1919.

55 G.

[House Bill No. 200.]

AN ACT

Revising and codifying the laws relating to the organization of banks and the inspection thereof.

Be it enacted by the General Assembly of the State of Ohio:

Sec. 710-1.

Definitions of terms.

SECTION 1. The following definitions shall be applied to the terms used in this act:

The term "surplus" means a fund created pursuant to the provisions of section 130 of this act by a bank or trust company from its net earnings or undivided profits, which to the amount specified and any additions thereto set apart and designated as such is not available for the payment of dividends and cannot be used for the payment of expenses or losses so long as such bank or trust company has undivided profits.

The term "undivided profits" means the credit balance of the profit and loss account of any bank or trust company.

The term "net earnings" means the excess of the gross earnings of any bank or trust company over expenses and losses chargeable against such earnings during any dividend period.

The term "time deposits" means all deposits the payment of which cannot legally be required within thirty days.

The term "demand deposits" means all deposits the payment of which can legally be required within thirty days.

The term "unincorporated bank" shall include every unincorporated person, firm or association transacting banking business in this state; and the term "board of directors" shall include the owner or owners of such banks.

Sec. 710-2.

What the term "bank" shall include.

SECTION 2. The term "bank" shall include any person, firm, association, or corporation soliciting, receiving or accepting money, or its equivalent, on deposit as a business, whether such deposit is made subject to check or is evidenced by a certificate of deposit, a passbook, a note, a receipt, or other writing, and unless the context otherwise requires as used in this act includes commercial banks, savings banks, trust companies and unincorporated banks; provided that nothing herein shall apply to or include money left with an agent pending investment in real estate or securities for or on account of his principal; nor to building and loan associations or title guarantee and trust companies incorporated under the laws of this state. All

All banks subject to examination and regulation.

banks, including the trust department of any bank, organized and existing under laws of the United States, shall be subject to inspection, examination and regulation as provided by law.

SECTION 3. The use of the words "bank," "banker" or "banking," or "trust," or words of similar meaning in any foreign language, as a designation or name, or part of a designation or name, under which business is or may be conducted in this state, is restricted to banks as defined in the preceding section. All other persons, firms or corporations are prohibited from soliciting, accepting or receiving deposits, as defined in section 2 of this act and from using the word "bank," "banker," "banking," or "trust," or words of similar meaning in any foreign language, as a designation or name, or part of a designation or name, under which business may be conducted in this state. Any violation of this prohibition, after the day when this act becomes effective, shall subject the party chargeable therewith, to a penalty of $100.00 for each day during which it is committeed or repeated. Such penalty shall be recovered by the superintendent of banks by an action instituted for that purpose, and in addition to said penalty, such violation may be enjoined and the injunction enforced as in other cases.

Provided, however, that any corporation now incorporated under a name which includes the word "trust," and which is qualified to transact a trust business, may continue the use of such word so long as it complies with the requirements of this act; provided, that every corporation incorporated under a name which includes the word "trust" and is not qualified to transact a trust business is required to change its name so as to eliminate the word "trust" therefrom within two years from the date when this act becomes effective during which period such company shall not be subject to the penalty of this section.

SECTION 4. Wherever the term "Federal Reserve Act" is used in this act the same shall be held to mean the act of the 63rd congress of the United States, entitled "An act to provide for the establishment of federal reserve banks, to furnish an elastic currency, to afford means of rediscounting commercial paper, to establish a more effective supervision of banking in the United States, and for other purposes," approved by the President of the United States on December 23rd, 1913, and subsequent amendments thereto; and wherever the terms "Federal Land Banks" and "Joint Stock Land Banks" are used in this act the same shall be held to mean banks organized under the act of the 64th congress of the United States approved by the president July 17, 1916, and known by the short title of "The Federal Farm Loan Act," and subsequent amendments thereto.

SECTION 5. Every bank, in addition to the powers, rights and privileges possessed by it under the laws of Ohio shall have the right and power to become a member bank under the federal reserve act upon the terms and conditions set forth in said federal reserve act, or hereafter provided by law. Every bank which becomes a member

Side notes:
28-3.

Use of words "bank," "banker," etc., in foreign language restricted to preceding definition.

Persons and firms prohibited from using terms "bank," "banker," etc.; penalty.

When and how long the word "trust" may be used.

28-4.

"Federal Reserve Act," "Federal Land Banks" and "Joint Stock Land Banks" defined.

28-5.

Every bank may become member under Federal Reserve Act; rights and powers of member banks.

bank shall have the right and power to do everything required of or granted by said federal reserve act to member banks which are organized under state laws; and compliance by banks with the reserve requirements of said federal reserve act, shall be accepted in lieu of the reserve requirements provided by the laws of Ohio. Any such bank or trust company shall continue to be subject to the supervision and examinations required by the laws of this state, except that the federal reserve board shall have the right, if it deems necessary, to make examinations; and the authorities of this state having supervision over such bank or trust company may disclose to the federal reserve board, or to examiners duly appointed by it, all information in reference to the affairs of any bank or trust company which has become, or desires to become, a member of a federal reserve bank. Nothing contained in this section shall in any way or manner affect or have reference to banks which do not become member banks under said federal reserve act except as provided in this act.

Sec. 710-6.

SECTION 6. The governor, with the advice and consent of the senate, shall appoint a superintendent of banks, who shall hold his office for the term of four years and until his successor is appointed and qualified. The superintendent may be removed by the governor, at any time, for inefficiency, neglect of duty, malfeasance in office, or any misconduct involving moral turpitude. In case of removal, the governor shall file in the office of the secretary of state a complete statement of the specific acts or omissions for which such removal is made. The superintendent of banks shall execute the laws in relation to banks.

Sec. 710-7.

SECTION 7. The superintendent of banks may employ from time to time necessary deputies, assistants, clerks and examiners to assist in the discharge of the duties imposed upon him by law. He may remove any such deputies, assistants, clerks or examiners. He shall summarily remove any such deputy, assistant, clerk or examiner upon the violation by any such deputy, assistant, clerk or examiner of any of the provisions of section 11 of this act.

Sec. 710-8.

SECTION 8. The superintendent of banks shall fix the salaries of the deputies, assistants, clerks and examiners. Upon vouchers approved by the superintendent of banks, such salaries shall be paid semi-monthly by the treasurer of state upon the warrant of the auditor of state.

All expenses incurred by the superintendent of banks in the performance of the duties imposed upon him by law, including the salary of such superintendent, his deputies, assistants, clerks and examiners, shall be paid from funds appropriated therefor.

Sec. 710-9.

SECTION 9. The actual and necessary traveling expenses, within or without the state, of the superintendent of banks and of the deputies, assistants, clerks and examiners incurred in the discharge of their official duty or in the interest of the department, shall be paid by the treas-

Subject to state supervision and examination of Federal Reserve Board.

Superintendent of banks; appointment, term, removal.

Employment of deputies, assistants, clerks, etc.; removal.

Salaries of deputies, clerks, etc.

Expenses, how paid.

Traveling expenses, how paid.

urer of state upon the warrant of the auditor of state. Provided, however, that the superintendent of banks or any employe of the department shall not attend, at state expense, outside of the state, a meeting or conference of any society, convention or association, except as provided by section 2313-3 of the General Code. Vouchers therefor shall be fully itemized, approved by the superintendent of banks and countersigned by the auditor of state.

10-10.   SECTION 10. Before entering upon the discharge of his duties, the superintendent of banks shall give bond to the state in the sum of fifty thousand dollars with sureties approved by the governor, conditioned for the faithful discharge of his official duties. Such bond, with the approval of the governor and the oath of office indorsed thereon, shall be filed with the secretary of state and kept in his office. The superintendent of banks shall require all deputies, assistants, clerks and examiners heretofore mentioned to give bond in such amount and with sureties to be approved by him and conditioned on the faithful performance of the duties of their office or employment. If the surety be a qualified surety company, the premium on such bond or bonds, including the bond of the superintendent of banks, shall be paid out of any fund or funds provided for the contingent expenses of the department. *Bond of superintendent, deputies, assistants, etc.*

10-11.   SECTION 11. Neither the superintendent of banks, nor any deputy, assistant, clerk, examiner or employe appointed by him, shall be interested, directly or indirectly, in any national bank or in any bank under his supervision, or be engaged in the business of banking, or directly or indirectly borrow money from any bank or person under his supervision. *Superintedent nor employee shall be interested in nor borrow from banks.*

10-12.   SECTION 12. The superintendent of banks shall be furnished by the state suitable rooms for conducting the business of his office at the seat of government and in any other city of the state where it is necessary to keep an examiner constantly. *Office of superintendent.*

10-13.   SECTION 13. The seal of the superintendent of banks shall be one and three-fourth inches in diameter and shall be surrounded by the words: "The superintendent of banks of the state of Ohio." *Seal of superintendent.*

10-14.   SECTION 14. All suits or proceedings brought by the superintendent of banks under authority of law, or to collect any penalty or forfeiture, shall be brought in the name of the state upon his relation, and shall be conducted under the direction and supervision of the attorney general. Such suit or proceeding may be prosecuted in the common pleas court of Franklin county, or of any other county in which the defendant or one or more of the defendants reside or may be found. In all suits or proceedings instituted by the superintendent of banks the writ may be sent by mail to the sheriff of any county, and returned by him in like manner. For such service the sheriff shall be allowed the same mileage and fees as if the writ had been issued from *How and by whom proceedings shall be brought.*

the common pleas court of his county and made returnable thereto.

SECTION 15. The salary of the superintendent of banks shall be seventy-five hundred dollars per annum.

Sec. 710-16.
Copies of rec-
ords and papers,
under seal, evi-
dence.

· SECTION 16. Copies of all certificates, records and papers in the office of the superintendent of banks, duly certified by him and authenticated by his seal of office, shall be evidence in all courts of this state, of every matter which could be proved by the production of the original.

Sec. 710-17.
Schedule of fees;
time of payment.

SECTION 17. That for the purpose of maintaining the department of the superintendent of banks and the payment of expenses incident thereto, and especially the expenses of inspection and examination, the following fees shall be paid to the superintendent of banks of Ohio:

(a) Each bank, which under the laws of Ohio is subject to inspection and examination by the superintendent of banks and is authorized to do business, or is in process of voluntary liquidation on the day preceding the first Monday in May in each year, shall pay to the superintendent of banks on or before the fifteenth day of July, 1919, and thereafter on or before the 15th day of June in each year, the sum of twenty dollars, and in addition thereto one one-ninetieth of one per cent of the total aggregate resources of such bank in excess of fifty thousand dollars as shown by the report of the condition of each such bank, made upon call by the superintendent of banks last before such day preceding the first Monday in May of such year; provided however, that in no event shall such total fee exceed the sum of two thousand dollars in any one year, and that at the time of payment on the fifteenth day of July, 1919, payment of eight-twelfths of such fee only shall be made; provided, also, that in addition to the fees prescribed herein, the actual cost of the examination of the trust department of a bank, or of any bank organized under the laws of the United States, as fixed by the superintendent of banks, shall be paid by such bank.

(b) Each bank, company, corporation, person, association and co-partnership desiring and intending to transact business in this state, which will be subject to inspection and examination by the superintendent of banks, shall pay to the superintendent of banks for the preliminary examination required by law to be made by the superintendent of banks a fee of seventy-five dollars, such fee to be paid prior to the consideration of such application as provided in sections 42 et seq. of this act. ·

(c) Each foreign trust company desiring and intending to do business in this state shall annually pay to the superintendent of banks a fee of one hundred dollars for issuance to it of a certificate authorizing it to transact business in this state, and such fees shall be paid before such certificate is issued.

(d) Every railroad, steamship or express company transacting business in this state under section 181 of this act shall pay to the superintendent of banks on or before the fifteenth day of June in each year a fee of two hundred and fifty dollars.

(e) All fees, charges and penalties required by law to be paid to the superintendent of banks, and collected by him, shall be paid by him into the state treasury to the credit of a fund for the use of the department of banks, and shall be used upon the order of the superintendent of banks, but shall not be used or paid out or appropriated for any other purpose.

In any year when such fund is sufficient for maintaining the department of banks for the ensuing year then the assessment provided for in paragraph (a) hereof shall be omitted for such year. *When assessment omitted.*

SECTION 18. At the end of each fiscal year, the superintendent of banks shall make an annual report to the governor, which report shall exhibit: *Annual report to governor; contents of report.*

(a) A summary of the state and condition of every bank from which reports have been received during the year, with an abstract of the whole amount of capital returned by them, the whole amount of their debts and liabilities, the total amount of means and resources, separating the reports of the various kinds of banks, and specifying the amount of lawful money held by them at the time of their several returns, a list of the officers and directors of each bank, and such other information in relation to such banks, as in his judgment may be required;

(b) A statement of the banks, whose business has been closed during the year, the amount of their resources and liabilities, and the amount paid to the creditors thereof;

(c) The names and compensation of the deputies, assistants, clerks and examiners employed or appointed by him, and the whole amount of expenses of the banking department during the year;

(d) The amount of fees and charges received from such banks, and penalties collected and paid into the state treasury.

(e) A statement of the banks, liquidated or in process of liquidation by the superintendent of banks, and the status of affairs of each of said banks, at the time of said report, including the amount of their resources and liabilities and the nature of the same and the amounts paid the creditors.

SECTION 19. At least once each year and as often as the superintendent of banks may deem necessary, the superintendent of banks or an examiner appointed for that purpose shall thoroughly examine the cash, bills, collaterals, securities, books of account and affairs of each bank. He shall also ascertain if such bank is conducting its business in the manner perscribed by law and at the place designated in its articles of incorporation, if incorporated, and if unincorporated, then at the place authorized. *Examination of banks, when.*

Sec. 710-20.

Doubtful or disputed assets; appraisement of.

SECTION 20. If any assets of a bank are of doubtful or disputed value an appraisement of such assets may be had for which purpose one appraiser shall be chosen by the bank, one by the superintendent of banks, and the two so chosen shall choose the third. The valuation as fixed by two appraisers shall be accepted as the probable value of such assets for the purposes of such examination. No appraiser shall be in any way interested in such bank or be connected with the banking department. All expenses of such appraisement shall be paid by such bank.

Sec. 710-21.

Examination upon written request.

SECTION 21. When requested in writing upon the authority of the board of directors or stockholders of any bank to make an examination of such bank, the superintendent of banks shall do so.

Sec. 710-22.

Expense of special examination.

SECTION 22. Whenever the superintendent of banks makes a special examination of any bank at the request of the directors or stockholders, or upon his own determination, the expense thereof shall be paid by the bank. Such expenses shall be collected by the superintendent of banks and paid into the state treasury as provided by law.

Sec. 710-23.

Special examination defined.

SECTION 23. Any examination made by the superintendent of banks otherwise than in the ordinary routine of the department and because in his opinion the condition of the bank requires such examination, and every examination made at the request of the board of directors or stockholders of any bank, shall be deemed a special examination within the meaning of the preceding section.

Sec. 710-24.

Power to administer oaths.

SECTION 24. For the purpose of such examination, the superintendent of banks or such examiner may administer oaths to and examine any officer, agent, clerk, customer, depositor, shareholder of such bank or other person touching its affairs and business.

Sec. 710-25.

Authority to summon officer, agent, clerk, etc.

SECTION 25. The superintendent of banks may summon in writing under his seal any such officer, agent, clerk, customer, depositor, shareholder or any person resident of the state to appear before him or a deputy or examiner and testify in relation thereto. If a person so summoned to appear and give testimony, fails to appear or neglects or refuses to answer any pertinent or legal question that may be put to him by the superintendent of banks or such examiner or deputy, touching the matter under examination, the superintendent shall apply to the probate court of the county in which such inquiry is conducted to issue a subpoena to such person to appear before him.

Sec. 710-26.

Probate judge shall issue subpoena, when.

SECTION 26. Upon such application, the probate judge shall issue a subpoena for the appearance forthwith of such person or persons before him to give testimony. Whoever, being so subpoenaed, fails to appear, or appearing, refuses to testify, shall be subject to like proceedings and penalties for contempt as witnesses in actions pending in the probate court.

87

1-27. SECTION 27. Each witness who appears before the superintendent of banks, or before such deputy or examiner, by order of the superintendent of banks, shall receive for his attendance, the fees and mileage provided for witnesses in civil cases in the common pleas court, which shall be audited and paid by the state out of moneys appropriated for the department of banks for the purpose of transportation, upon the presentation of proper voucher, sworn to by such witness and approved by the superintendent of banks. *Witness fees and mileage.*

1-28. SECTION 28. The officers of every bank shall submit its books, assets, papers and concerns to the inspection and examination of the superintendent of banks or any deputy, or duly appointed examiner, and on refusal so to do or to be examined on oath touching the affairs of such bank, the superintendent of banks may forthwith take possession of the property and business of such bank and liquidate its affairs and remain in possession of its property and business until its affairs be finally liquidated, as hereinafter provided. *Books, assets, papers, etc., shall be submitted; possession taken of bank on refusal.*

1-29. SECTION 29. All examinations required to be made by the superintendent of banks under the provisions of this act shall be made without previous notice to the bank, to be examined. *Examinations made without previous notice.*

1-30. SECTION 30. Every bank whose capital stock has not been paid in as required by law, and every bank whose capital shall have become impaired by losses or otherwise, shall within three months after receiving notice from the superintendent of banks, cause the deficiency in such capital to be paid in by assessemnt upon the stockholders pro rata for the amount of capital stock held by each. If any stockholder of such bank neglects or refuses to pay such assessment as herein provided, it shall be the duty of the board of directors to cause a sufficient amount of the capital stock of such stockholder or stockholders to be sold at public auction, upon thirty days' notice given by posting such notice of ·sale in the office of the bank and by publishing such notice in a newspaper in the place where ·the bank is located, and if none, then in a newspaper published nearest thereto, to make good the deficiency, and the balance, if any, shall be returned to such delinquent shareholder or shareholders. If any bank shall fail to cause to be paid in such deficiency in its capital stock for three months after receiving such notice from the superintendent of banks, the superintendent of banks may forthwith take possession of the property and business of such bank until its affairs be finally liquidated as provided by law. *Assessments to pay deficiencies in capital. Sale of stock at auction, on refusal. Possession taken on failure to pay deficiency within three months.*

A sale of stock as provided in this section, shall effect an absolute cancellation of the outstanding certificate, or certificates, evidencing the stock so sold, and shall make said certificate null and void, and a new certificate shall be issued by the bank to the purchaser of such stock. *Sale shall effect cancellation.*

Sec. 710-31.

Number of reports required yearly to superintendent; what reports shall exhibit; publication of summary.

SECTION 31. Every bank shall make to the superintendent of banks four, and if the superintendent of banks so orders, then five reports during each calendar year, according to and in the form which may be prescribed by him, verified by the oath or affirmation of the president, vice-president, cashier, secretary or treasurer of such bank. Each such report shall exhibit in detail and under appropriate heads, the resources, assets and liabilities of such bank at the close of business on any past day by the superintendent of banks specified, and shall be transmitted to the superintendent of banks within ten days after the receipt of a request or requisition therefor, from him; and in the form prescribed by the superintendent of banks, a summary of such report shall be published in a newspaper published in the place where such bank is established, or if there is no newspaper in the place, then in the one published nearest thereto in the same county, at the expense of such bank; and such proof of such publication shall be furnished the superintendent of banks as may be required by him. So far as possible the day specified by the superintendent of banks, shall be the same as that specified by the comptroller of the currency for reports from national banking associations.

Sec. 710-32.

Special report may be required.

SECTION 32. The superintendent of banks may call for a special report whenever in his judgment it is necessary to inform him fully of the condition of any bank; which report shall be in and according to the form prescribed by the superintendent of banks, shall be transmitted to him within five days after the receipt of a requisition therefor from him, shall be verified as provided in the last preceding section, and shall be published as therein provided if required by the superintendent of banks.

Sec. 710-33.

Penalty for failure to make or publish reports.

SECTION 33. Every bank failing to make and transmit to the superintendent of banks any of the reports required by this act and in and according to the form prescribed by the superintendent of banks therefor, or failing to publish the reports as required by law, shall forthwith be notified by the superintendent, and, if such failure continues for five days after receipt of such notice, such delinquent bank shall be subject to a penalty of one hundred dollars for each day thereafter that such failure continues, such penalty to be recovered by the superintendent of banks and paid into the fund provided for by section 17 of this act.

Sec. 710-34.

Official communication submitted to board of directors; record; certification.

SECTION 34. Each official communication directed by the superintendent of banks or one of his deputies to a bank or to any officer thereof, relating to an examination or investigation conducted by the banking department or containing suggestions or recommendations as to the conduct of the business of the bank, shall if required by the superintendent of banks be submitted by the officer receiving it to the executive committee or board of directors of such bank, and duly noted in the minutes of such meeting. The receipt and submission of such notice to the executive committee or board of directors shall be certified within five

89

days thereafter to the superintendent of banks by three members of such committee or board.

§ 35. SECTION 35. Whoever, being the superintendent of banks, a deputy, assistant, clerk in his employ or an examiner, fails to keep secret the facts and information obtained in the course of an examination, except when the public duty of such officer requires him to report upon or take official action regarding the affairs of the person, partnership, corporation, company, society or association so examined, or wilfully makes a false official report as to the condition of such person, partnership, corporation, company, society or association, shall be fined not more than five hundred dollars or imprisoned in the penitentiary not less than one year nor more than five years, or both. Nothing in this section shall prevent the proper exchange of information relating to banks and the business thereof, with the representatives of the banking departments of other states, with the national bank authorities, or with clearing house association examiners. *(margin: Facts and information obtained in examination kept secret; penalty for violation.)*

Any official, violating any provision of this section, in addition to the penalties therein provided shall be removed from office and be liable, with his bondsmen, in damages to the person or corporation injured by the disclosure of such secrets. *(margin: Removal.)*

§ 36. SECTION 36. In proceedings connected with any authority exercised under this act, all accounts and other papers may be signed and sworn to in behalf of such bank by any officer thereof duly authorized by it. The answers and examinations under oath, of such officer, shall be received as the answers and examinations of the bank. A court may order and compel any officers of such bank to answer and attend such examination the same as if they, instead of the bank, were parties to the proceedings or inquiry. *(margin: Signing and verifying papers in proceedings.)*

§ 37. SECTION 37. The capital of a commercial or savings bank or a combination of both shall be not less than twenty-five thousand dollars; provided that in cities the population of which exceeds ten thousand such capital shall be not less than fifty thousand dollars. *(margin: Minimum capital of commercial or savings banks and trust corporations.)*

The capital of a corporation transacting a trust business shall be not less than one hundred thousand dollars and if such business is combined with that of a commercial or savings bank, or a combination of both, such capital shall be in addition to the capital required for such commercial or savings bank, or a combination of both, as provided herein.

§ 38. SECTION 38. Every incorporated bank now having a lesser capital than that required by section 37, except societies for savings and savings societies heretofore chartered and incorporated under a special act, shall within three years from the enactment of this act cause the amount of its capital to be increased and paid up to the amount of said minimum capital prescribed in said section. *(margin: Existing banks must increase capital within three years.)*

Sec. 710-39.

When articles of incorporation may be filed and recorded.

SECTION 39. All corporations hereafter incorporated as commercial banks, savings banks, trust companies, or a corporation having departments for two or more, or all such classes of business, shall be incorporated and organized with a capital stock, and under the provisions of this act. The secretary of state shall not file or record articles of incorporation for any such proposed corporation, unless in accordance therewith, and only upon certificate of the superintendent of banks, as provided in sections 44 and 46 of this act.

Sec. 710-40.

Foreign bank prohibited from doing other than loan business.

SECTION 40. No bank or banking institution incorporated under the laws of any other state shall be permitted to receive deposits or transact any banking business of any kind in this state, except to lend money, or as otherwise provided by law in relation to trust companies.

Sec. 710-41.

Number and qualifications of persons required to establish bank.

SECTION 41. Any number of persons, not less than five, a majority of whom are citizens of this state, may associate and become incorporated to establish a commercial bank, a savings bank, a trust company, or to establish a bank having departments for two or more or all of such classes of business, upon the terms and conditions and subject to the limitations hereinafter and by law prescribed.

Requisites of articles of incorporation.

Such persons shall subscribe and acknowledge before an officer authorized to take acknowledgment of deeds, articles of incorporation, the form of which shall be prescribed by the secretary of state, which must contain:

a. The name by which such corporation is to be known, which shall begin with the word "The" and end with the word "bank" or "company."

b. The place where its business is to be transacted, designating the particular city, village or township.

c. The purpose for which it is formed, whether that of a commercial bank, savings bank, trust company, or a combination of two or more or all, of such classes of business, or a special plan bank, as provided in section 180 of this act.

d. The amount of its capital, which shall be divided into shares of one hundred dollars each.

Sec. 710-42.

Certificate of clerk of court.

Authority of superintendent required before record of articles.

SECTION 42. The official character of the officer before whom the acknowledgment of articles of incorporation is made, shall be certified by the clerk of courts of common pleas of the county in which the acknowledgment is taken and the articles shall be filed in the office of the secretary of state. The secretary of state shall forthwith transmit to the superintendent of banks a copy of such articles of incorporation and shall not record the same until duly authorized so to do by the superintendent of banks as hereinafter provided.

Sec. 710-43.

Publication of notice of proposed bank.

SECTION 43. Such persons shall, at or before the time such articles of incorporation are forwarded to the secretary of state, cause notice to be published in a newspaper published in the place where such bank is to be located, and if no newspaper is published in such place, then in one published nearest thereto. Such notice shall specify the name of the proposed bank, its location, the amount of its proposed capital and the names of the persons who propose to incorporate the same. Such notice shall be published for two weeks and a certified copy thereof furnished to the superintendent of banks.

§ 44.   SECTION 44.   Upon receipt of a copy of the articles of incorporation of such proposed bank, the superintendent of banks shall at once examine into all the facts connected with the formation of such proposed corporation including its location and proposed stockholders and if it appears that such corporation, if formed, will be lawfully entitled to commence the business of banking, the superintendent of banks shall so certify to the secretary of state, who shall thereupon record such articles of incorporation. But the superintendent of banks may refuse to so certify to the secretary of state, if upon such examination and investigation he has reason to believe that the proposed corporation is to be formed for any other than legitimate banking business, or that the character and general fitness of the persons proposed as stockholders in such corporation, are not such as to command the confidence of the community in which such bank is proposed to be located or that the public convenience and advantage will not be promoted by its establishment, or that the name of the proposed corporation is likely to mislead the public as to its character or purpose; or if the proposed name is the same as one already adopted, or appropriated by an existing bank in this state, or so similar thereto as to be likely to mislead the public, unless the place of business of such proposed corporation is to be located in a county other than the one in which the corporation bearing such similar name is then doing business and the corporation so adopting such name adds thereto the words "of ―――――."   (Indicating thereby the name of the city, village or township in which its place of business is situated.)

Duties of superintendent relative to proposed bank.

§ 45.   SECTION 45.   If the superintendent of banks withholds such certificate an appeal may be made to a board composed of the governor, superintendent of banks and the attorney general. The decision of such board in the matter shall be final. Such board shall prescribe the rules and procedure under which all appeals shall be heard, and may from time to time amend the same. Upon its order, the superintendent of banks shall summon in writing, under his seal, any person resident of this state, to appear before such board and testify in relation to any such appeal, and in the event of the failure of any person summoned to appear before such board and to testify as herein provided, such board shall proceed in all respects as provided in sections 25, 26 and 27 of this act.

Appeal when certificate withheld; hearing.

§ 46.   SECTION 46.   Upon receipt of such certificate from the superintendent of banks the secretary of state shall record said articles of incorporation; one copy thereof, duly cer-

Duties of secretary of state.

tified by the seroetary of state shall thereupon be furnished
to the incorporators of such corporation, and one copy to
the superintendent of banks, to be by him filed in his office.
All certificates thereafter filed in the office of the secretary
of state relating to such corporation shall be recorded, and
a certified copy thereof forthwith furnished to the superintendent of banks and filed in his office.

Sec. 710-47.

Enumeration of
powers.

SECTION 47. When such articles of incorporation are
so recorded, the persons who subscribe them, their associates, successors and assigns, by the name designated
therein, shall become a body corporate with succession, and,
as such, shall have power:

(a)   To adopt and use a corporate seal, and to alter
it at will;

(b)   To contract and be contracted with;

(c)   To sue and be sued;

(d)   To adopt regulations for the government of the
corporation, not inconsistent with the constitution and laws
of this state;

(e)   To do all needful acts, to carry into effect the
objects for which it was created.

Sec. 710-48.

Opening books
of subscription.

SECTION 48. The persons named in the articles of incorporation of any such company, or a majority of them,
shall order books to be opened for subscription to the capital stock of the company in the manner provided for other
corporations. An installment of ten per cent. on each
share of stock shall be payable at the time of making the
subscription, and the balance shall be payable as soon thereafter as may be required by the board of directors.

Sec. 710-49.

Certificate of
subscripition;
choosing direc-
tors.

SECTION 49. As soon as the capital stock of such corporation is fully subscribed, the subscribers of the articles
of incorporatioñ, or a majority of them, shall so certify in
writing to the secretary of state, who shall transmit a copy
thereof to the superintendent of banks, and such subscribers shall thereupon give notice to the stockholders, in
the manner provided for other corporations, to meet for
the purpose of choosing not less than five nor more than
thirty directors, who shall continue in office until the time
fixed for the annual election, and until their successors are
elected and qualified. But if all subscribers are present in
person or by proxy, such notice may be waived in writing.

Sec. 710-50.

Regulations, how
adopted or
changed.

SECTION 50. Regulations of the corporation may be
adopted or changed by the assent thereto, in writing, of
two-thirds of the stockholders in number and amount; or
by a majority of the stockholders in number and amount,
at a meeting held for that purpose, notice of which has
been giveñ for that purpose by the president or secretary
or any two directors personally or by written notice to
each stockholder, and by publication, for thirty days, in
some newspaper of general circulation in the county in
which the corporation is located.

151. SECTION 51. The fiscal year of each bank shall end on the 31st day of December in each year, and unless the regulations of the corporation otherwise provide the annual meeting for the election of directors of every such bank shall be held on the second Wednesday of January in each year.

Fiscal year; annual meeting for election of directors.

152. SECTION 52. Such corporation shall be created, organized, governed and conducted, and directors shall be chosen in all respects in the same manner as provided by law for corporations organized under the general incorporation laws of this state, in so far as the same shall not be inconsistent with the provisions of this act.

General provisions applicable, when.

153. SECTION 53. When a stockholder or his assigns fails to pay an installment on his stock, as required by the board of directors, the directors for such company may sell his stock at public sale for not less than the amount due thereon, including cost incurred, to the person who will pay the highest price therefor, having first given the delinquent stockholder five days' notice of such sale personally, or if no personal notice can be given, then by mail at his last known address as appears from the corporate record, and having advertised the sale for a like period in a paper of general circulation within the county in which the corporation is located. If no bidder can be found who will pay for such stock the amount due thereon, with costs incurred, such stock shall be sold as the directors may order, for not less than the amount then due thereon with all costs of sale.

Failure to pay installment; sale of stock.

154. SECTION 54. The stock sold by any bank in process of organization or for an increase of capital stock shall be accounted for to the bank in the full amount paid for the same. No commission or fee shall be paid to any person, association or corporation for selling such stock. The superintendent of banks shall refuse authority to commence business to any bank, if commissions or fees have been paid, or have been contracted to be paid, directly or indirectly by the bank, or by anyone in its behalf, to any person, association or corporation for securing subscriptions for or selling stock in such bank.

No commission for sale of stock allowed.

155. SECTION 55. When a certificate is transmitted to the superintendent of banks, signed by the president, secretary or treasurer of such corporation, notifying him that the entire capital stock of such corporation is subscribed, and paid in, and that such corporation has complied with all the provisions of law required to be done before it can be authorized to commence business, the superintendent of banks shall examine into its affairs, ascertain especially the amount of money paid in on account of its capital, the name and place of residence of each director, the amount of capital stock of which each is the owner in good faith, and whether such corporation has complied with all the provisions of law required to entitle it to engage in business.

Examination on certificate of notification of compliance with law.

SECTION 56. If upon such examination of the facts referred to in section 55, and of any other facts which may come to the knowledge of the superintendent of banks, he finds that such corporation is lawfully entitled to commence business, he shall give it a certificate under his hand and official seal that it has complied with all the provisions required by law and is authorized to commence business.

SECTION 57. The corporation shall cause such certificate to be published in some newspaper printed in the city, village or county where it is located, once a week for four successive weeks or if no newspaper is published in such county, then in a newspaper published at the nearest county seat.

SECTION 58. No such corporation shall transact business except such as is incidental and necessarily preliminary to its organization, until it has been authorized by the superintendent of banks.

SECTION 59. A corporation doing business under the provisions of this act, may increase its capital stock as provided by law for other corporations. Such increase in the capital stock of any bank shall be fully paid in within six months from the date when such increase is authorized.

SECTION 60. Such a corporation may reduce its capital stock in the manner provided for other corporations, but notice of such reduction shall be published in a newspaper of general circulation in the city, village or county, in which it is doing business. No reduction shall be made to an amount less than the minimum amount of capital stock required for such bank by law, nor shall such reduction be valid or warrant the cancellation of stock certificates until it has been approved by the superintendent of banks. Such approval shall not be given except upon a finding by him that the security of existing creditors of the corporation will not be impaired.

SECTION 61. The corporate powers, business and property of banks formed under this chapter, shall be exercised, conducted and controlled by the board of directors, which shall meet at least once each month. Such board shall consist of not less than five nor more than thirty directors, to be chosen by the stockholders, who shall hold office for one year and until their successors are elected and qualified.

SECTION 62. The board of directors may appoint an executive committee to consist of at least three of its members, with such duties and powers as are defined by the regulations or by-laws, who shall serve until their successors are appointed. Such executive committee shall meet as often as the board of directors require, which shall not be less frequently than once each month, and approve or disapprove all loans and investments. All loans and investments shall be made under such rules and regulations as the board of directors prescribe.

95

SECTION 63. Minutes shall be kept of all meetings of the board of directors and of the executive committee, and the same shall be recorded in a book which shall be kept on file in the bank. Such minutes shall show a record of the action of the board of directors or executive committee on all loans, discounts and investments made or authorized, and the minutes of the executive committee shall be submitted to the board of directors for approval at each meeting of the board. *Minutes of meetings; what record shall show.*

SECTION 64. In elections of directors, and in deciding questions at meetings of stockholders, each stockholder shall be entitled to one vote for each share of stock held by him. Any stockholder also may vote by proxy duly authorized in writing. *Elections; proxy.*

SECTION 65. Every director of a bank shall be the owner and holder of shares of stock in the bank having a par value of at least $500.00, and every such director shall hold such shares in his own name unpledged and unincumbered in any way. Any director at any time violating any of the provisions of this section shall be removed from office by the board of directors or by the superintendent of banks. At least three-fourths of the directors of every bank shall be residents of this state. *Qualifications of a director.*

SECTION 66. Every director shall within thirty days after his election, take and subscribe in duplicate, an oath that he will diligently and honestly perform his duties in such office, not knowingly violate, or permit to be violated, any provisions of this act, and that he is the owner in good faith of the shares of stock of the company required to qualify him for such office, standing in his own name, on its books, and one of such oaths shall be forthwith filed with the superintendent of banks. *Oath of director.*

SECTION 67. Any director of a bank who shall knowingly violate, or who shall knowingly permit any of the officers, agents or employees of a bank to violate any of the provisions of this act shall be held liable in his personal and individual capacity for all damages which the bank, its stockholders, or any other person shall have sustained in consequence of such violation. *Liability of director for violations.*

SECTION 68. The officers of such bank, before entering upon the discharge of their duties, shall give bond to the bank in the amount required by the directors and to the satisfaction of the superintendent of banks and with surety to be approved by them, for the faithful performance of their duties as such officers. The superintendent of banks or directors may require an increase of the amount of such bonds whenever they deem it necessary. The directors as such shall not be required to give bond. *Bond of officers.*

SECTION 69. A committee of at least three directors or stockholders annually shall be appointed by the board of directors to examine, or to superintend the examination of, the assets and liabilities of the bank and to report to the board of directors the result of such examination, and *Annual examination; report to superintendent.*

the board of directors may provide for such examination by a certified public accountant, or a clearing house examiner in any city where such examination is provided by the rules of such clearing house association. A copy of such report attested and verified under oath by the signatures of at least three members of such committee, shall be forthwith filed with the superintendent of banks.

Sec. 710-70.
Record of stock; transfers.

SECTION 70. A book shall be provided and kept by every such bank, in which shall be entered the name and residence of each stockholder, the number of shares held by each, the time when each person became a stockholder; together with all transfers of stock, stating the time when made, the number of shares and by whom transferred, which book shall be subject to the inspection of the directors, officers and stockholders of the bank at all times during the usual hours of transacting business.

Sec. 710-71.
Books and accounts; form prescribed by superintendent.

SECTION 71. The superintendent of banks may prescribe the manner and form of keeping the books and accounts of banks, so that the books and accounts of banks of the same class may be as nearly uniform as circumstances permit. All entries in all books of banks and in pass books of depositors shall be made in ink.

Sec. 710-72.
Fee, gift, etc., prohibited; penalty.

SECTION 72. No gift, fee, commission or brokerage charge shall be received directly or indirectly by any officer, director or employee of a bank, on account of any transaction to which the bank is a party unless duly authorized by the directors. Whoever violates this provision shall be subject to a penalty of $100 for each violation to be recovered by the superintendent of banks, and shall be and thereafter remain ineligible as an officer, director or employee of such bank.

Sec. 710-73.
Books and records shall be kept in bank and open to inspection of stockholder.

SECTION 73. The books and records, except books and records of deposit and trust, of every bank, at all reasonable times shall be open to the inspection of every stockholder. All books and records of the bank shall be kept at all times in the bank. No branch bank shall be established until the consent and the approval of the superintendent of banks has been first obtained, and no bank shall establish a branch bank in any place other than that designated in its articles of incorporation, except in a city or village contiguous thereto. If such consent and approval is refused, an appeal may be taken therefrom in the same manner as is provided in section 45 of this act.

Sec. 710-74.
Penalty for failure to comply with order or requisition.

SECTION 74. Any bank which fails or neglects to comply with any lawful order or requisition of the superintendent of banks within the time specified by him in such order or requisition, if no penalty has been specifically provided, shall be subject to a penalty of $100, for each day after the expiration of five days from said date so specified by the superintendent of banks, that it fails or neglects to comply with such order or requisition; such penalty to be recovered by the superintendent of banks, by suit against such bank.

§-75.   SECTION 75.   Stockholders of banks shall be held in- Individual lia-
bility of stock-
holders.
dividually responsible, equally and ratably, and not one for
another, for all contracts, debts and engagements of such
bank, to the extent of the amount of their stock therein,
at the par value thereof, in addition to the amount invested
in such shares.   The stockholders in any bank who shall
have transferred their shares or registered the transfer
thereof within sixty days next before the failure of such
bank to meet its obligations, or with knowledge of such
impending failure, shall be liable to the same extent as if
they had made no such transfer, to the extent that the subsequent transferee fails to meet such liability; but this
provision shall not be construed to affect in any way recourse which such stockholders might otherwise have against
those in whose names such shares are registered at the
time of such failure.   At any time after taking possession
of a bank for the purpose of liquidation when the superintendent of banks ascertains that the assets of such bank
will be insufficient to pay its debts and liabilities he may
enforce the individual liability of the stockholders.

§-76.   SECTION 76.   No authority to transact a banking busi- Duly organized
corporation only
shall transact
banking business.
ness in this state shall be granted, except to a corporation
duly organized and qualified for that purpose.   Unincorporated banks now authorized to transact and actually
transacting a banking business may continue such banking
business in the city, village, or township in which they are
now located so long as they comply with the provisions of
this act.

§-77.   SECTION 77.   Every unincorporated bank now transac- Unincorporated
banks; detailed
statement by, re-
quired.
ing a banking business in this state, shall, under oath file
with the superintendent of banks, a full, complete detailed
statement of,

1.   Name of the bank.

2.   A copy of the articles of co-partnership or agreement, under which the business of the bank is being conducted, which shall be executed and acknowledged by all
of the parties interested therein, and at least one of whom
shall be at all times a resident of the state of Ohio.   If the
banking business is being transacted or carried on by an
individual, such individual shall at all times, while engaged in such banking business, be a resident of the state
of Ohio.

3.   The county and city or village in which the bank
is located, and the business carried on.

4.   The amount of permanent capital actually paid in
and remaining in its possession, bona fide, as its property,
for the sole purposes of the bank.

5.   A statement of the responsibility and the net worth
of the individual members of such unincorporated bank.

6..   If not disclosed in the articles of co-partnership or
agreement, then the name of the officers, agents or employes
in active charge of the management of the business of the
bank.

Every such unincorporated bank shall on or before January 1, 1920, and annually thereafter, file with the superintendent of banks a detailed statement as provided herein.

Sec. 710-78.
Minimum of capital stock of unincorporated banks.

SECTION 78. Every unincorporated bank transacting a banking business in this state shall have a capital actually paid in and remaining in its possession, bona fide, as the property of such bank and to be used for its sole purposes and for the security of its creditors, of not less than $10,-000.00; in villages, and cities the population of which exceeds two thousand and does not exceed ten thousand, such paid in capital shall be not less than twenty-five thousand dollars; in cities, the population of which exceeds ten thousand, such paid in capital shall be not less than fifty thousand dollars.

Segregated capital and unimpaired security.

Such capital shall at all times be segregated from all other property or business of the owner or owners of such bank, and shall be kept and maintained unimpaired for the security of the creditors of such bank.

All such unincorporated banks shall comply with the provisions of this section within one year from the day this act goes into effect.

Sec. 710-79.
Property of bank shall be held, how; assets subject to execution, when.

SECTION 79. All property, real or personal, owned by an unincorporated bank, shall be held in the designated name of such bank or in the name of an individual as trustee therefor and not in the name of the owner or owners of such bank. All the assets of such bank shall be exempt from attachment or execution by any creditor of such owner or owners until all the liabilities of such bank shall have been paid in full. No person, firm or association owning or conducting an unincorporated bank shall use any of the funds of such bank for his or their private business, except as a borrower in due course of business.

Sec. 710-80.
Depositors have first lien on assets.

SECTION 80. The depositors in any unincorporated bank shall have first lien on the assets of such bank, in case it is wound up, to the amount of their several deposits, and for any balance remaining unpaid, such depositors shall share in the general assets of the owner or owners alike with the general creditors.

Sec. 710-81.
List of owners and persons interested must be posted conspicuously.

SECTION 81. Every such unincorporated bank shall post in the room in which it transacts its business, and in plain view of its customers a printed list of all the owners of, and parties interested in, such bank, and a statement that the bank is an unincorporated bank. Should the interests of any members of such bank, or, of an individual doing a banking business under the provisions of this act, change either by death, devise, sale or otherwise, then and in that case the superintendent of banks of the State of Ohio shall be notified of such change and printed notice shall be posted in the room of any such bank. No such bank shall advertise by newspaper, letterhead, or in any other way, a larger capital than has been actually paid in.

SECTION 82. Every unincorporated bank shall have printed on all its advertising matter and business stationery, the word "unincorporated" immediately following the name of the firm or business title.

"Unincorporated" must be printed on advertising and stationery.

SECTION 83. All reports received from unincorporated banks shall be kept on file in the office of the superintendent of banks, and open to the inspection of all persons, at the discretion of the superintendent of banks. The provision of section 31 of this act as to publication of reports of banks shall apply to unincorporated banks.

Reports shall be kept on file and open for inspection.

SECTION 84. Whenever any of the funds of the state, or any of the political subdivisions of the state, shall be deposited under any of the depositary laws of the state, every unincorporated bank shall be permitted to bid upon and be designated as depository of such funds, upon furnishing such surety or securities therefor as is prescribed by the law.

Permitted to bid upon public funds.

SECTION 85. A bank may go into liquidation and be closed by the vote of its stockholders owning two-thirds of its stock, in number and amount. When a vote to go into liquidation is so taken, the board of directors shall cause notice of such fact to be certified under seal of the bank, by its president or vice president and secretary, treasurer or cashier, to the superintendent of banks, together with certified copies of all proceedings had by directors and stockholders of such bank, which such stockholders' proceedings shall set forth that stockholders owning at least two-thirds of the capital stock voted in favor of placing the bank in liquidation and shall also set forth the reasons for placing the bank in liquidation. After such certified copies have been filed with the superintendent of banks, he shall make an examination of the bank, to determine whether or not the interests of its depositors and creditors will suffer by such liquidation and his consent to or rejection of such liquidation shall be based thereon and no such liquidation shall be made without the consent of the superintendent of banks. The expenses of such examination shall be paid by such bank. In case the superintendent of banks consents to such liquidation, such bank shall make a report to the superintendent of banks, at least once each thirty days from and after the date when the bank ceased to transact business as such, which report shall give a list of assets wholly or partially realized upon, together with the amount of each so remaining uncollected, and also a list of the liabilities retired by application of such amount so realized. The superintendent of banks shall have power to examine into the affairs of the bank so liquidated, at any time, to determine whether the rights of creditors and depositors are being protected, and if at any time he finds that such liquidation is being improperly conducted, or that the interests of the depositors and creditors are not being properly protected, he may forthwith take possession of the property and business of such bank and complete the liqui-

When and how bank may go into liquidation.

dation thereof in the same manner as is provided in other cases. All unclaimed deposits and dividends remaining in the hands of such bank, shall be subject to the provisions of sections 9864, 9866, 9868 and 9869 of the General Code of Ohio, except that the time of the payment to the treasurer of the county shall be subject to the order of the superintendent of banks. When the superintendent of banks consents to such liquidation, such bank shall immediately publish notice thereof in a newspaper published in the place in which such bank is located, and if none is there published, then in the place nearest thereto, that it is closing up its affairs and notifying creditors to present their claims against the bank for payment. Such notice shall be published for four consecutive weeks.

Sec. 710-86.

Consolidation with or transfer of assets to another bank; procedure.

SECTION 86. A bank may consolidate with or transfer its assets and liabilities to another bank. Before such consolidation or transfer shall become effective, each bank concerned in such consolidation or transfer, shall file, or cause to be filed, with the superintendent of banks, certified copies of all proceedings had by its directors and stockholders which such stockholders' proceedings shall set forth that holders of at least two-thirds of the stock, voted in the affirmative on the proposition of consolidation or transfer. Such stockholders' proceedings shall also contain a complete copy of the agreement made and entered into between said banks, with reference to such consolidation or transfer. Upon the filing of such stockholders' and directors' proceedings as aforesaid the superintendent of banks shall cause to be made an examination of each bank to determine whether the interests of the depositors and creditors and stockholders of each bank are protected and that such consolidation or transfer is made for legitimate purposes, and his consent to or rejection of such consolidation or transfer shall be based upon such examination. No such consolidation or transfer shall be made without the consent of the superintendent of banks. If such consent is refused, an appeal may be taken therefrom in the same manner as is provided in section 45 of this act. The expenses of such examination shall be paid by such banks. Notice of such consolidation or transfer, shall be published for four weeks, before or after the same is to become effective, at the discretion of the superintendent of banks, in a newspaper published in a city, village or county, in which each of such banks is located, and a certified copy thereof shall be filed with the superintendent of banks.

Sec. 710-87.

Rights of creditors protected.

SECTION 87. In case of either transfer or consolidation, the rights of creditors shall be preserved unimpaired and the respective companies deemed to be in existence, to preserve such rights.

Sec. 710-88.

Certified copy of approval of consolidation filed with secretary of state.

SECTION 88. In case of consolidation, when the agreement of consolidation is made and a duly certified copy thereof is filed in the office of the secretary of state, together with a certified copy of the approval of the superintendent of banks to such consolidation; the banks, parties thereto, shall be held to be one company possessed of the rights, privileges, powers and franchises of the several companies, but subject to all the provisions of law relating to the different departments of its business. The directors and other officers named in the agreement of consolidation shall serve until the first annual election, the date for which shall be named in the agreement. On filing such agreement all and singular the property and rights of every kind of the several companies shall thereby be transferred to and vested in such new company, and be as fully its property as they were of the companies parties to such agreement.

SECTION 89. The superintendent of banks may forthwith take possession of the business and property of any bank to which this act is applicable, whenever it shall appear that such bank: *Superintendent may take possession of bank, when.*

1—Has violated its charter or any law applicable thereto;

2—Is conducting its business in an unauthorized or unsafe manner;

3—Is in an unsound or unsafe condition to transact its business;

4—Has an impairment of its capital for a period of ninety days;

5—Has refused to pay its depositors in accordance with the terms on which such deposits were received;

6—Has become otherwise insolvent;

7—Has neglected or refused to comply with the terms of a duly issued order of the superintendent of banks;

8—Has refused, upon proper demand, to submit its records and affairs for inspection to an examiner of the banking department; or

9—Its officers have refused to be examined upon oath regarding its affairs.

Such bank may with the consent of the superintendent of banks, resume business upon such conditions as may be approved by him.

SECTION 90. Upon taking possession of the property and business of any such bank, the superintendent of banks shall forthwith give written notice of such fact to all banks, companies, associations and individuals holding or in possession of any assets of such bank. The superintendent of banks shall cause notice to be given by advertisement in such newspapers as he may direct weekly for four consecutive weeks, calling on all persons who may have claims against such bank to present the same to the superintendent of banks, and to make legal proof thereof at a place and within a time not later than the last day therein specified. The superintendent of banks shall mail a similar notice to all persons whose names appear as creditors upon the books of said bank. *Notice of taking possession of bank.*

Sec. 710-91.

Rights and lia-
bilities after pos-
session taken.

SECTION 91. No bank, trust company, corporation, firm, association or individual knowing that the superintendent of banks has taken possession of such bank, shall have a lien or charge for any payment advanced or any clearance thereafter made, or liability thereafter incurred against any of the assets of the bank of whose property and business the superintendent of banks shall have taken possession.

Sec. 710-92.

Adjustment of claims.

SECTION 92. If the superintendent of banks doubts the justice and validity of any claim, he may reject the same and serve notice of such rejection upon the claimant, either by mail or personally, an affidavit of the service of such notice, which shall be prima facie evidence thereof, shall be filed in his office. An action upon a claim so rejected must be brought within six months after such service. Claims presented and allowed after the expiration of the time fixed in the notice to creditors, shall be entitled to be paid the amount of all prior dividends thereon if there be funds sufficient therefor and share in the distribution of the remaining assets in the hands of the superintendent of banks equitably applicable thereto.

Sec. 710-93.

Inventory of as-
sets; filing copies.

Duties of auditor
of state.

List of claims;
supplemental
lists; filing of
same.

Book of de-
positors and
other creditors;
final distribu-
tion.

SECTION 93. Upon taking possession of the property and assets of such bank the superintendent of banks shall make an inventory of the assets of such bank in triplicate, one copy to be filed in the office of the superintendent of banks, one in the office of the clerk of the county in which the office of such bank was located, and one with the auditor of state. It shall be the duty of the auditor of state to have such inventory immediately verified by comparison with the current books of the bank. Upon the expiration of the time fixed for the presentation of claims, the superintendent of banks shall make in triplicate a full and complete list of the claims presented, including and specifying such claims as have been rejected by him, of which one copy shall be filed in the office of the superintendent of banks, one in the office of the clerk of the county in which the office of such bank was located, and one with the auditor of state. And the superintendent of banks shall in like manner make and file supplemental lists showing all claims presented subsequent to the filing of the first list, such supplemental lists to be filed at least fifteen days before the declaration of any dividend, and in any event such supplemental lists shall be filed at intervals of not exceeding six months. The superintendent of banks shall cause to be entered in a book prepared for that purpose, the names of all depositors and other creditors of such bank, together with the amount due each as shown by the books of such bank, said book to be one of the permanent records of such liquidation. At the time of the order for final distribution of any such bank, the superintendent of banks shall make a detailed report in triplicate of its liquidation, showing the disposition of each asset and acquired asset, one copy to be filed in the office of the superintendent of banks, one in the office of the clerk of the county in which such bank was located, and one with the auditor of state. Such report, inventory and list of claims shall be open at all reasonable times for inspection.

SECTION 94. The superintendent of banks may under his hand and official seal appoint one or more special deputy superintendents of banks as agent or agents to assist him in the duty of liquidation and distribution, a certificate of such appointment to be filed in the office of the superintendent of banks and a certified copy in the office of the clerk of the county in which the office of such bank was located. The superintendent of banks shall require from such agent or agents such surety for the faithful discharge of their duties as he may deem proper. All bonds given shall be deposited with the superintendent of banks and kept in his office. *Special deputy superintendents; appointment of.*

SECTION 95. Upon taking possession of the property and business of such bank, the superintendent of banks is authorized to collect money due to such bank, and to do such other acts as are necessary to preserve its assets and business, and shall proceed to liquidate the affairs thereof, as hereinafter provided. The superintendent of banks shall collect all debts due and claims belonging to it, and upon the order of the common pleas court in and for the county in which the office of such bank was located, may sell or compound all bad or doubtful debts, and on like order may sell the real estate and personal property of such bank, on such terms as the court shall direct. The superintendent of banks shall give notice to such bank of the time and place of making application to said court for such order. The superintendent of banks upon the terms of sale or compromise directed by the court, shall execute and deliver to the purchaser of such real and personal property such deeds or instruments as shall be necessary to evidence the passing of the title; and if said real estate is situated outside the county in which the office of the bank was located, a certified copy of such order authorizing and ratifying said sale shall be filed in the office of the recorder of the county within which said property is situated; and may, if necessary to pay the debts of such bank, enforce the individual liability of the stockholders. *Powers and duties after taking possession.*

SECTION 96. The moneys collected in process of such liquidation by the superintendent of banks shall be from time to time deposited in one or more banks organized under the laws of this state, subject to his order as herein provided. *Disposition of moneys on liquidation.*

SECTION 97. The expenses incurred by the superintendent of banks in the liquidation of any bank in accordance with the provisions of this act, shall include the expenses of deputies or assistants, clerks and examiners employed in such liquidation, together with reasonable attorney fees for counsel employed by said superintendent of banks in the course of such liquidation. Such compensation of *Expenses of liquidation; how paid.*

counsel, deputies, assistants, clerks and examiners in the liquidation of any such bank, and all expenses of supervision and liquidation shall be fixed by the superintendent of banks, subject to the approval of the common pleas court of the county in which the office of such bank was located, on notice to such bank. The expense of such liquidation shall be paid out of the property of such bank in the hands of said superintendent of banks, and such expenses shall be a valid charge against the property in the hands of said superintendent of banks and shall be paid first in the order of priority; provided, however, that no such expense shall be paid out of the property of such bank until an account of such expense shall have been filed with and approved by the common pleas court of the county in which such bank is located, and the superintendent of banks shall give notice, by publication of the application for the approval of such expense account, in a newspaper of general circulation in the community in which such bank is located at least ten days before such court shall pass upon such application.

Sec. 710-98.

Dividends, when and how paid; unclaimed deposits.

SECTION 98. At any time after the expiration of the date fixed for the presentation of claims, the superintendent of banks may, out of the funds remaining in his hands after the payment of expenses, declare one or more dividends, and after the expiration of one year from the first publication of notice to creditors, he may declare a final dividend, such dividends to be paid to such persons and in such amounts and upon such notice as may be directed by the common pleas court of the county in which the office of such bank was located. Dividends due to stockholders on claims as depositors or otherwise, to the extent of the individual liability of such stockholders shall be withheld by the superintendent of banks until it is ascertained that it will not be necessary to enforce their individual stock liability. The court shall make proper provision for unproved and unclaimed deposits.

Sec. 710-99.

Objections to claims; how made; hearing.

SECTION 99. Objection to any claim not rejected by the superintendent of banks may be made by any party interested by filing a copy of such objection with the superintendent of banks, who shall present the same to the common pleas court of the county in which the office of such bank was located, upon written notice to claimant and to the party filing the same, said notice setting forth the time and place of the presentation. The court upon return day of said notice shall hear the objections raised to said claim, or refer the determination of said objections to a referee for report, or upon demand of either the superintendent of banks or the party filing the objections may direct that the issues be tried before a jury.

Sec. 710-100.

Application for injunction; proceedings; hearing.

SECTION 100. Whenever any such bank of whose property and business the superintendent of banks has taken possession, as aforesaid, deems itself aggrieved thereby, it may at any time within thirty days after taking such possession apply to the common pleas court of the county in which the office of such bank was located, to enjoin further proceedings in liquidation, and said court, after citing the superintendent of banks to show cause why further proceedings should not be enjoined and hearing the allegation and proofs of the parties and determining the facts, may dismiss such application or enjoin the superintendent of banks from further proceedings, and direct him to surrender such business and property to such person, partnership, corporation, company, society or association.

101.
SECTION 101. No receiver shall be appointed by any court, nor shall any deed of assignment for the benefit of creditors be filed in any probate court or court of insolvency within this state for any bank except upon notice to the superintendent of banks, unless in case of urgent necessity it becomes in the judgment of the court necessary so to do in order to preserve the assets of such bank. The superintendent of banks may within five days after the service of such notice upon him take possession of such bank, in which case no further proceedings shall be had upon such application for the appointment of receiver or under such deed of assignment, or, if a receiver has been appointed or such assignee shall have entered upon the administration of his trust, such appointment shall be vacated or such assignee shall be removed upon application of the superintendent of banks to the proper court therefor, and the superintendent of banks shall proceed in all such cases to administer the assets of such bank, as herein provided.

Notice to superintendent before appointment of receiver or deed of assignment filed.

102.
SECTION 102. Whenever the superintendent of banks shall have paid to each depositor and creditor of such bank, not including stockholders, whose claim or claims as such depositor or creditor shall have been duly proved and allowed, the full amount of such claims, and shall have made proper provision for unclaimed or unpaid deposits or dividends, and shall have paid all the expenses of the liquidation, the superintendent of banks shall call a meeting of the stockholders of such bank, by giving notice thereof for four consecutive weeks in one or more newspapers published in the county wherein the office of such bank was located. At such meeting the stockholders shall determine whether the superintendent of banks shall continue to administer its assets and wind up the affairs of such bank, or whether an agent or agents shall be elected for that purpose; and in so determining the said stockholders shall vote by ballot in person, or by proxy, each share entitling the holder to one vote and the majority of the stock shall be necessary to a determination.

Superintendent shall call meeting of stockholders; notice of meeting.

When superintendent shall continue to administer assets.

103.
SECTION 103. In case it is determined to continue the liquidation under the superintendent of banks, he shall complete the liquidation of the affairs of such bank, and after paying the expenses thereof shall distribute the proceeds among the stockholders in proportion to the several holdings of stock, in such manner and upon such notice as may be directed by the common pleas court of the county in which

Distribution upon completion of liquidation.

106

the office of such bank was located. In case it is determined to appoint an agent or agents to liquidate, the stockholders shall thereupon select such agent or agents by ballot, a majority of the stock present and voting, in person or by proxy, being necessary to a choice. Such agent or agents shall file with the superintendent of banks a bond to the state of Ohio in such amount and with such sureties as shall be approved by the superintendent of banks for the faithful performance of all the duties of his or their trust, and thereupon the superintendent of banks shall transfer to such agent or agents all the undivided or uncollected or other assets of such bank then remaining in his hands; and upon such transfer and delivery the said superintendent of banks shall be discharged from all further liability to such bank and its creditors.

Sec. 710-104.

Conversion of assets before distribution.

SECTION 104. Such agent or agents shall convert the assets coming into his or their possession into cash, and shall account for and make distribution of the property of such bank as herein provided in the case of distribution by the superintendent of banks, except that the expenses thereof shall be subject to the direction and control of the common pleas court of the county in which the office of such bank was located.

Sec. 710-105.

Successor in case of death or removal of agent.

SECTION 105. In case of death or removal or refusal to act of any such agent, or agents, the stockholders may elect a successor as hereinbefore provided who shall have the same powers and be subject to the same liabilities and duties as the agent, or agents, originally elected.

Sec. 710-106.

Deposit of dividends and unclaimed deposits with treasurer of state.

SECTION 106. Dividends and unclaimed deposits remaining in the hands of the superintendent of banks for six months after the order for final distribution shall be by him deposited with the treasurer of state who shall hold such funds as custodian, subject to the order of the superintendent of banks and without the necessity of appropriation by the general assembly. The superintendent of banks may pay over the moneys so held by the treasurer of state to the persons respectively entitled thereto, upon being furnished satisfactory evidence of their right to the same. In

Doubtful or conflicting claims.

case of doubt or conflicting claims he may apply to the common pleas court of the county in which the office of such bank was located for an order authorizing and directing the payment thereof. All unclaimed deposits and uncalled for dividends for which no claim has been made within a period of five years, after the order of final distribution, shall be paid into the state treasury upon the warrant of the auditor of state.

Sec. 710-107.

Books and papers deposited with clerk of courts after liquidation.

SECTION 107. All books, papers and records of a bank which has been finally liquidated by the superintendent of banks, shall be deposited by the superintendent of banks in the office of the clerk of courts for the county in which the office of such bank was located, such books, papers and records to be held by the clerk of courts of such county subject to the order of the court of common pleas for such county.

Agent may be appointed to liquidate.

§-108.   SECTION 108. A bank may purchase, lease, hold and convey real estate only as follows: *(Real estate bank may purchase, lease, hold or convey.)*

(a) A building or quarters therein, or lands whereon is erected or may be erected a building or buildings useful for the transaction of its business and from portions of which, not required for its use, a revenue may be derived; but the cost of such building or buildings and the lands whereon they are erected, in no case shall exceed sixty per cent of its paid-in capital and surplus;

(b) Such as is mortgaged or conveyed to it in good faith by way of security for loans made by or money due to such corporation;

(c) Such as has been purchased by it at sales upon the foreclosure of mortgages owned by it, or on judgments or decrees obtained or rendered for debts due to it, or in settlements effected to secure such debts. All real property referred to in this paragraph shall be sold by such bank within five years after it is vested therein, unless upon application by the board of directors, the superintendent of banks extends the time within which such sales shall be made.

§-109.   SECTION 109. A bank may provide fire and burglar proof safes and vaults in its banking premises and let out safety deposit boxes and other receptacles therein for the uses, purposes and benefits of depositors. *(Fire and burglar proof safes; safety deposit boxes.)*

§-110.   SECTION 110. A bank may receive on deposit for safe keeping in its vaults and safes, securities, stocks, bonds, coins, plate, jewelry, books, papers, documents and other valuable papers and property, upon such terms and conditions as it may prescribe. *(Property bank may receive for safe keeping.)*

§-111.   SECTION 111. A bank may invest its capital, surplus, undivided profits and deposits in the following securities: *(Securities designated in which investment may be made.)*

(a) Bonds or other interest bearing obligations of the United States, the Philippines, Hawaii, Porto Rico, and the District of Columbia, or those for which the faith of the United States is pledged to provide payment of the interest and principal, and in farm loan bonds issued by federal land banks and joint stock land banks.

(b) Bonds or other interest-bearing obligations of any foreign government not at war with the United States since 1900, and of the Dominion of Canada and New Foundland, which has not defaulted in the payment of principal or interest on its bonds or obligations within the period of twenty years last prior thereto.

(c) Bonds or other interest-bearing obligations of any state or territory of the United States.

(d) Bonds or other interest-bearing obligations of any county, town, township, city, school district, improvement district or sewer district, or other organized or political sub-division in this state.

(e) Bonds or other interest bearing obligations of any city, town, county or other legally constituted political or taxing subdivision situated in one of the states of the

Securities desig-
nated in which
investment may
be made.

United States, or any cities of the Philippines, Hawaii or
Porto Rico, which city, town, county or taxing subdivision
has been in existence ten years and which for a period of
ten years previously has not defaulted for a period of
more than ninety days in the payment of any part of either
principal or interest of any debt contracted by it and whose
net indebtedness after deducting the amount of its water
bonds and bonds issued for other self sustaining public
utilities and the amount of sinking funds which are available for the payment of its bonds or interest bearing obligations other than water bonds and self sustaining public
utilities, does not exceed ten per cent. of the value of taxable property in such city, town, county or political or taxing subdivision to be ascertained by the valuation of property therein for the assessment of taxes next preceding such
investment; provided, that no bonds or other interest bearing obligations of any such county shall be eligible for investment unless such county has a population of not less
than ten thousand inhabitants, and, provided, that no bonds
or other interest bearing obligations of any such city, town
or political or taxing subdivision shall be eligible for investment unless such city, town or political or taxing subdivision has a population of not less than one thousand inhabitants as ascertained by United States or state census
or by any municipal census taken by authority of the state
next preceding such investment, and, provided, further,
that there shall be eligible hereunder the bonds or other
interest bearing obligations of a political or taxing subdivision which has not been in existence for ten years, but
which is erected out of another eligible subdivision or com-
prises in whole or in part another eligible subdivision or
subdivisions or parts of eligible subdivisions if such subdivision shall comply with the other requirements of this
paragraph.

But nothing herein contained shall authorize the investment of funds in any special assessment or improvement bonds or other bonds or other interest bearing obligations which are not the direct obligations of the district
issuing same and for which the full faith and credit of the
entire district are not pledged.

(f) Bonds or debentures of any Province of the
Dominion of Canada.

Bonds or debentures of any city or town or district
except school district in the Dominion of Canada having a
population of not less than ten thousand inhabitants, as ascertained by official census next preceding such investment
and which has not since 1900 defaulted for more than
ninety days in the payment of any part of principal or interest of any debt authorized to be contracted by it and
which has a net indebtedness exclusive of water debt and
bonds issued for other self sustaining public utilities and
the amount of sinking funds available for the payment of
its bonds other than water bonds and bonds issued for pub-

lic utilities, which net indebtedness does not exceed seven per cent of the last valuation of its taxable property for the assessment of taxes preceding such investment, and in all other respects such bonds shall conform to the requirements of clause E of this section; and in the bonds or obligations of any city, town or district therein unconditionally guaranteed as to payment of principal and interest by the Dominion of Canada or any province thereof.

Securities designated in which investment may be made.

(g) Bonds of cities of foreign countries that have not been at war with the United States since 1900, having a population of more than one hundred thousand inhabitants, whose net indebtedness does not exceed seven per cent. of the last valuation of its taxable property for the assessment of taxes preceding such investment, exclusive of bonds issued for public utilities and sinking funds other than for public utilities and which have not defaulted for more than ninety days on any installment of any part of principal or interest of any debt authorized to be contracted by it for twenty-five years preceding such investment.

(h) Bankers acceptances of the kind and maturity made eligible by law for re-discount with federal reserve banks, provided the same are accepted by a bank incorporated under the laws of this state or any member bank of the federal reserve system.

(i) Mortgage bonds, collateral trust bonds, debenture bonds or notes of any regularly incorporated company which, or the constituent companies comprising which for four years (4) prior to the date of purchase has earned over and above all fixed charges other than interest on indebtedness, an amount equal to at least double the interest charges which it will be required to pay upon its outstanding obligations; or mortgage bonds, collateral trust bonds, debenture bonds or notes of any regularly incorporated company, which bonds or notes plus all prior incumbrances are outstanding in an amount not in excess of 50% of the actual value of the property securing said bonds or notes.

j) Railroad equipment bonds or car trust certificates issued in the United States or Canada, and bonds secured by first mortgage on steel steamships, in an amount not exceeding 50% of the value of such vessels.

(k) Bonds or notes secured by first mortgage on improved real estate as defined in section 113 hereof of not more than 60% of the value thereof.

All securities as enumerated above, having a fixed maturity shall be charged and entered upon the books of the bank at their cost to the bank, and when a premium is paid therefor an annual amortization charge shall be made thereon so as to bring the cost of same to the face value of said bonds at maturity. The superintendent of banks shall have the power to require any security to be charged down to such sum as in his judgment represents its value. The superintendent of banks may order any securities which he deems undesirable removed from the assets of a bank.

Securities shall be charged on books at cost.

Sec. 710-112.

Loans upon
mortgage; limitations.

SECTION 112. Loans by banks upon mortgage notes shall be made upon first mortgage upon real estate situated in this state, or in states contiguous thereto, and shall not exceed forty per cent (40%) of the value of such real estate if unimproved, and sixty per cent (60%) of such value if improved, and the improvements shall be kept adequately insured. In the case of commercial banks not more than fifty per cent (50%) and in the case of savings banks and trust companies, not more than sixty per cent (60%) of the amount of the paid in capital, surplus and deposits of such bank or trust company at any time shall be invested in such real estate securities. Loans on collateral enumerated in clauses (i), (j) and (k) of section 111 of this act, shall not exceed eighty per cent. of the value of such collateral.

Sec. 710-113.

"Improved" real estate defined.

SECTION 113. The term "improved" real estate as used in this act shall be held to mean land upon which buildings have been erected suitable and intended to be used for residence, business or other purposes and fit for use and occupancy, or under construction for such purposes; and in the case of farm property shall mean tillable land with farm buildings thereon and actually under use for farm purposes, and when so used the same may include pasture and wood lands.

Sec. 710-114.

Loans may not be made upon shares of its capital stock; sale of pledged stock, when.

SECTION 114. No bank shall loan money on the security or pledge of the shares of its capital stock; nor be the purchaser or holder of any such shares, unless such security or purchase be necessary to prevent loss upon debt previously contracted in good faith. Stock so acquired shall, within six months from the time of its purchase, be sold or disposed of at public sale on thirty days' notice from the superintendent of banks, and in default thereof the superintendent of banks may forthwith take possession of the property and business of such bank until its affairs be finally liquidated, as herein provided.

Sec. 710-115.

Loans to officer, director, etc., prohibited, unless authorized.

SECTION 115. No loan shall be made, directly or indirectly to any officer, director or member of the executive committee of any bank unless duly authorized or approved by the directors. Such authorization or approval shall be recorded in the records of their proceedings, and all loans when so authorized and made to officers, directors or members of the executive committee shall be made and secured in the same manner as loans to other persons.

Sec. 710-116.

Separate books shall be kept, when.

SECTION 116. A corporation formed to combine two or more classes of business under this act, shall keep separate books of accounts for each class. Receipts, investments and transactions relating to each of such classes of business shall be governed by the provisions and restrictions herein specifically provided therefor.

Sec. 710-117.

How deposits shall be entered.

SECTION 117. All deposits of money, or its equivalent. made with a bank shall be entered on its books, in terms of lawful money of the United States, and in no other way, and shall be payable at the authorized place of business of such bank.

§-118.   Section 118. Every bank shall preserve all of its records, including cards used under a card system, and deposit tickets, for at least six years from the time of making same, and from the date of the last entry thereon. Records preserved six years.

§-119.   Section 119. When an account is opened in any bank by or in the name of a minor it shall be payable to such minor, and such payment shall be as valid as if such minor were of legal age. • Accounts in name of minors.

§-120.   Section 120. When a deposit has been made, or shall hereafter be made in any bank or trust company transacting business in this state in the name of two or more persons, payable to either, or the survivor, such deposit or any part thereof, or any interest or dividend thereon, may be paid to either of said persons whether the other be living or not; and the receipt or acquittance of the person so paid shall be a valid and sufficient release and discharge to the bank for any payments so made. Deposits in name of two or more persons.

§-121.   Section 121. Not more than twenty per cent of the capital and surplus of a bank doing business under this chapter shall be invested in any one stock or security unless it be in bonds or other interest bearing obligations enumerated in paragraphs a, b, c, d, e and h of section 111 of this act; or in the stock of a corporation owning the land, building or buildings occupied by such bank for its banking quarters, and then not exceeding sixty per cent of its capital and surplus shall be so invested, which shall be carried on the books of the bank as an investment or equity in real estate. Limitation of investment in securities and stocks.

§-122.   Section 122. A bank shall not lend, including overdrafts, to any one person, company, corporation or firm, more than twenty per cent of its paid-in capital and surplus, unless such loan be secured by first mortgage upon improved farm property in a sum not to exceed sixty per cent of its value. Limitation of loans to company, firm or corporation.

    The total liabilities, including overdrafts, of any one person, company, corporation or firm, to any bank, either as principal debtor or as security or indorser for others, for money borrowed, except as additional security for a liability previously incurred, at no time shall exceed twenty per cent of its paid-in capital stock and surplus; provided, however, that (1) the discount of bills of exchange drawn in good faith against actually existing values, (2) the discount of trade-acceptances or other commercial and business paper actually owned by the person, company, corporation or firm, negotiating the same, and (3) the purchase or discount of any note or notes secured by not less than a like face amount of bonds of the United States, or certificates of indebtedness of the United States, shall not be considered as money borrowed within the meaning of this section.

§§-123.   Section 123. The limitations provided in section 122 shall not be applicable to loans made by unincorporated banks for agricultural, industrial or commercial purposes Loans to which limitations not applicable.

or the proceeds of which have been used or are to be used for such purposes; but such loans shall not include notes, drafts or bills of exchange issued or drawn for the purpose of carrying or trading in stocks, bonds or other investments, except bonds and notes of the United States; provided, the total liabilities, including overdrafts of a person, company, corporation or firm to any unincorporated bank, either as principal debtor or as security or indorser for others, for money borrowed, except as additional security for a liability previously incurred, at no time shall exceed twenty per cent of the net worth of the owners of such bank, as shown by the report last filed in accordance with section 77 of this act.

Sec. 710-124.

"Commercial or business paper" and "trade acceptance" defined.

SECTION 124. As used in this act the term "commercial or business paper" is hereby defined to mean a promissory note, and the term "trade acceptance" to mean a draft or bill of exchange issued or drawn for agricultural, industrial or commercial purposes, or the proceeds of which have been used or are to be used for such purposes, but such definition shall not include notes, drafts or bills of exchange covering merely investments, or issued or drawn for the purpose of carrying or trading in stocks, bonds or other investment securities, except bonds and notes of the government of the United States. Such notes, drafts and bills of exchange shall have a maturity at the time of discount of not more than ninety days except when drawn or issued for agricultural purposes or based on live stock, when such maturities shall not exceed six months from the date thereof.

Sec. 710-125.

Unauthorized deposits deemed loans.

SECTION 125. The deposit of funds by any bank in another bank or trust company, not duly designated as a depository by its board of directors as hereinafter provided, shall be held to be a loan within the meaning of section 122 of this act.

Sec. 710-126.

Borrowing of money and securities limited.

SECTION 126. No bank may borrow money, bonds or other securities in any sum exceeding the amount of its capital stock and surplus, except with the written consent of the superintendent of banks, provided that the rediscount of notes, bills of exchange and acceptances shall not be considered money borrowed. Every such re-discount shall be entered upon the books of the bank, and the total amount thereof shall appear as a contingent liability upon every report of condition made to the superintendent of banks or published by said bank.

Sec. 710-127.

Reserve banks may be designated; resolution certified to superintendent.

SECTION 127. A bank may by resolution of its board of directors designate other banks organized under the law of this state, or of another state, or of the national banking act of the United States, as reserve banks in which such part of its reserve not required to be kept by it may be deposited, subject to payment upon demand. A copy of such resolution shall upon its adoption be forthwith certified to the superintendent of banks and the depositary so designated shall be subject to the approval of the superintendent of banks.

§-128. SECTION 128. No bank shall deposit as a reserve or otherwise in any other bank or national bank an amount in excess of 50% of the capital stock and surplus of such depositary bank; nor shall any two banks be reciprocal depositaries each for the other. Deposit in other bank as reserve, etc., limited.

§-129. SECTION 129. When the reserve of a bank falls below the amount required by law, it shall not make new loans or discounts, otherwise than by discounting or purchasing bills of exchange, payable at sight or on demand, nor make dividends of its profits, until the reserve required by law is restored. The superintendent of banks shall require any bank whose reserve falls below the amount required, immediately to make such reserve good. In case the bank fails for thirty days thereafter to make good its reserve, the superintendent of banks may forthwith take possession of the property and business of such bank until its affairs be adjusted or finally liquidated, as provided by law. Loans, discounts or dividends of profits, prohibited, when.

§-130. SECTION 130. The board of directors of any bank may declare a dividend of so much of its undivided profits as they deem expedient. Before such dividend is declared, not less than one-tenth of the net earnings of the company for the preceding half-year, or for such period as is covered by the dividend, shall be carried to surplus until such surplus amounts to fifty per cent of its capital stock. Dividend of undivided profits may be declared, when.

In order to ascertain the undivided profits from which such a dividend may be made, in the account of profit and loss there shall be charged and deducted from the actual profits: Undivided profits, how ascertained.

(1) All ordinary and extraordinary expenses, paid or incurred, in managing the affairs and transacting the business of the bank,

(2) Interest paid or then due, on debts which it owes,

(3) All taxes due,

(4) All losses sustained by the corporation. In computing its losses, debts owing to it which have become due and which are not in process of collection and on which interest for one year or more is due and unpaid, unless same are well secured, and debts upon which final judgment has been recovered, but has been for more than one year unsatisfied, and on which also for said period of one year, no interest was paid, unless same are well secured, shall be included.

§-131. SECTION 131. Whenever any deposit shall be made in a bank by any person in trust for another, and no other or further notice of the existence and terms of a legal and valid trust shall have been given in writing to the bank, in the event of the death of the trustee, the same, or any part thereof, together with the dividends or interest thereon, may be paid to the person for whom said deposit was made. Deposits in trust for another; to whom paid.

Sec. 710-132.

Non-payment of
check through
error or mistake,
bank not liable
to depositor,
when.

SECTION 132. No bank shall be liable to a depositor because of the non-payment through mistake or error and without malice of a check which should have been paid unless the depositor shall allege and prove actual damage by reason of such non-payment and in such event the liability shall not exceed the amount of damage so proved.

Sec. 710-133.

What deemed
due diligence in
forwarding check,
notes, etc., for
collection.

SECTION 133. Any bank, banker or trust company, organized under the laws of or doing business in this state, receiving for collection or deposit, any check, note or other negotiable instrument drawn upon or payable at any other bank, located within or without this state, may forward such instrument for collection direct to the bank on which it is drawn or at which it is made payable and such method of forwarding direct to the payor, shall be deemed due diligence and the failure of such payor bank, because of its insolvency or other default, to account for the proceeds thereof, shall not render the forwarding bank liable therefor, provided, however, such forwarding bank shall have used due diligence in other respects in connection with the collection of such instrument.

Sec. 710-134.

When and how
surplus of bank
may be used.

SECTION 134. The surplus of any bank shall not be used for the payment of dividends nor shall the same be used for the payment of expenses or losses until the credit to undivided profits on the books of the bank has been exhausted. But any portion of such surplus may be converted into capital stock and distributed to stocksolders by way of a stock dividend provided that such surplus shall not thereby be reduced below twenty per cent of the aggregate capital stock of said bank issued and outstanding after the payment of such dividend.

Sec. 710-135.

Accounts sub-
ject to check
may be received.

SECTION 135. Commercial banks may receive deposits of funds subject to withdrawal or to be paid upon check of the depositor. All deposits in such banks shall be payable on demand without notice except when the contract of deposit shall otherwise provide.

Sec. 710-136.

Loans and dis-
counts may be
made.

SECTION 136. Commercial banks may loan money upon personal or collateral security, discount, buy, sell or assign promissory notes, drafts, bills of exchange, trade and bank acceptances, and other evidences of debt and buy and sell exchange, coin and bullion.

Sec. 710-137.

Drafts, bills of
exchange of
future date may
be accepted.

Letters of credit
may be issued,
when.

SECTION 137. A commercial bank may accept for payment at a future date, drafts or bills of exchange having not more than six months sight to run, drawn upon it by its customers under acceptance agreements and which grow out of transactions involving the importation or exportation of goods; and issue letters of credit authorizing the holders thereof to draw upon it or its correspondents, provided that there is a definite bona fide contract for the shipment of goods within a specified reasonable time and the existence of such contract is certified in the acceptance agreement; or which grow out of transactions involving the domestic shipment of goods, provided that shipping documents conveying or securing to the accepting bank title to readily marketable goods, are attached or in the hands of an agent of the accepting bank, independent of the drawer, for its account, at the time of acceptance or which are secured at the time of acceptance, by warehouse receipts or other such documents conveying or securing to the accepting bank title to readily marketable goods fully covered by insurance, the warehouse receipts or other such documents to be those of a responsible warehouse independent of the drawer, the acceptor to remain so secured during the life of the acceptance unless other suitable security of the same character, or cash, be substituted; and, provided that no commercial bank shall accept drafts or bills under this section, to an aggregate amount at any time more than equal to the sum of its paid up and unimpaired capital stock and surplus; and provided further that no commercial bank shall accept whether in a foreign or domestic transaction, for any one person, firm or corporation, to an amount equal at any time to more than twenty per centum of its paid up and unimpaired capital stock and surplus, unless the accepting bank is secured either by the attached documents or those held for its account by its agent independent of the drawer, or by some other actual security of the same character. Should the accepting bank purchase or discount its own acceptances, such acceptances will be considered as a direct loan to the drawer and be subject to the limitation of section 122 of this act. The superintendent of banks may issue such further regulations as to such acceptances as he may deem necessary in conformity with this act. *Limitation of amount of accepted drafts or bills.*

As used herein, the word "goods" shall be construed to include goods, wares, merchandise or agricultural products, including live stock. *Word "goods" defined.*

§9-138. SECTION 138. Commercial banks shall keep as reserve at least fifteen per cent of their total deposits; at least four per cent of that part of such deposits which is payable on demand, and at least two per cent of that part of such deposits which are time deposits shall be kept in the vaults of the bank in lawful money, national bank notes, federal reserve notes, federal reserve bank notes, or bills, notes and gold and silver certificates issued by the United States. *Percentage of deposits kept as reserve.*

§9-139. SECTION 139. A savings bank may invest its funds in or loan money on, discount, buy, sell or assign promissory notes, drafts, bills of exchange, trade and bank acceptances and other evidences of debts; but all such investments or loans made except those secured by mortgages on real estate or pledge of collateral security shall be upon notes, drafts, bills of exchange, trade or bank acceptances, or other evidences of debt payable at a time not exceeding six months from the date thereof, but not more than thirty per cent. of the capital, surplus and deposits of such bank shall be so invested. *Investments and loans by savings banks; enumeration of evidences of debt.*

Sec. 710-140.

Investment of funds by savings bank; securities enumerated.

SECTION 140. A savings bank may invest its funds in:

(a) The securities mentioned in section 111 of this act subject to the limitations and restrictions therein contained; except that investments in real estate securities shall be subject to the restrictions contained in section 112 of this act.

(b) Stocks of companies, upon which or the constituent companies comprising the same, dividends have been earned and paid for five consecutive years next prior to the investment; provided, every such investment shall be authorized by an affirmative vote of a majority of the board of directors of such savings bank.

No purchase or investment shall be made in the stock of any other corporation organized or doing business under the provisions of this act or of the national banking act of the United States.

(c) Promissory notes of individuals, firms or corporations when secured by a sufficient pledge of collateral approved by the executive committee or board of directors.

(d) Ground rents or certificates of participation or beneficial ownership in improved lands under lease for a period of not less than twenty-five years from the date thereof, and conditioned that the lessee shall pay all taxes and assessments thereon and keep and maintain said premises in full and complete repair, with insurance in an amount equal to the insurable value of the improvements thereon, provided that the aggregate par amount of such rents or certificates shall not exceed the value of the land nor sixty per cent of the total value of the land and improvements. But nothing in this section contained shall prevent the investment in such rents or certificates in unimproved lands, where by the terms of the lease thereof the construction of a new building thereon is provided for and funds have been deposited or will be deposited from the proceeds of the sale of such rents or certificates sufficient for the cost of such construction, and conditioned that such construction shall begin within six months thereafter and that the funds so deposited shall be paid out to meet the cost of such construction as the work progresses and for no other purpose.

Sec. 710-141.

Savings banks may receive deposits from whom.

SECTION 141. A savings bank may receive on deposit any sum of money offered for that purpose by any person, firm, society or corporation, or by any municipal corporation, township, school district, taxing district, county or state, or other body politic, or which is ordered to be deposited by any court of this or any other state, or of the United States, having custody of money, and make investment or loans thereof in the manner provided herein. It also may credit and pay such rates of interest thereon as may be agreed upon.

SECTION 142. The board of directors of a savings bank shall prescribe the terms upon which deposits shall be received and paid out and a pass book shall be issued to each savings depositor, containing the rules and regulations adopted by the board of directors governing such deposits, in which shall be entered each deposit made, the interest allowed thereon, and each payment made to such depositor. By accepting such book the depositor assents and agrees to the rules and regulations therein contained,

Terms upon which deposits received prescribed by directors.

SECTION 143. No payment or check against any savings bank account shall be made or paid unless accompanied by and entered in the pass book issued therefor, except for good cause and on assurance satisfactory to the officers of the bank; but nothing herein shall prevent savings banks issuing time certificates of deposit or certificates for deposit specially issued according to the rules and regulations governing savings deposits.

Check against account may be paid, when and how.

SECTION 144. Savings banks shall keep as reserve at least ten per cent of their time deposits, and at least fifteen per cent of their demand deposits; at least four per cent of that part of such deposits which is payable on demand, and at least two per cent of that part of such deposits which are time deposits shall be kept in the vaults of the bank in lawful money, national bank or federal reserve notes, federal reserve bank notes, or bills, notes, and gold and silver certificates issued by the United States.

Percentage of deposits required as reserve.

SECTION 145. Associations incorporated under the act entitled "an act to incorporate savings societies," passed April 16, 1867, and the act passed March 19, 1868, entitled "an act to amend an act entitled, 'an act to incorporate savings societies,' passed April 16, 1867," may continue their business under such acts, and without prejudice to any rights acquired. Such institutions and other savings and loan institutions organized under the laws of this state, if they so elect may continue their business under this act, by signifying such election, under their seal, to the secretary of state, and conforming their action thereto. The secretary of state shall record it, and his certificate be evidence thereof.

Associations and societies formerly incorporated, may continue; election.

SECTION 146. Savings societies organized and doing business under the acts named in the preceding section, in addition to the investments authorized in such acts, may invest their funds in the bonds of a county or municipal corporation issued pursuant to any law of this state, and charge interest on loans of not more than eight per cent per annum payable semi-annually.

Investment of funds of such societies.

SECTION 147. Societies for savings, duly incorporated by the general assembly, and doing business under their respective acts of incorporation, may invest in land, and in the erection of buildings thereon, for the purpose of their own business, such sum as the trustees thereof deem necessary, not to exceed five per cent of the amount of deposits

Investment of societies incorporated by general assembly.

held by them and also rent any part of such buildings not needed for their own use.

Sec. 710-148.

Dividends may be paid, when.

SECTION 148. Before a dividend, or interest on deposits, is paid by such societies, they shall have a surplus fund equal to not less than five per cent of the whole amount of deposits, and gradually increase such fund to an amount equal to ten per cent of the amount of deposits.

Sec. 710-149.

Societies whose charters are subject to alteration or repeal.

SECTION 149. All "societies for savings" and "savings societies" now doing business, whose charters are subject to alteration or repeal, may continue their business under their respective charters, after the expiration thereof, subject, however, to the repeal of any such charter, and to such amendments, alterations, rules and regulations as may be prescribed, from time to time, by any laws of the state.

Sec. 710-150.

Trust companies may accept trusts, when; capital; deposit with treasurer of state.

SECTION 150. No trust company, or corporation, either foreign or domestic, doing a trust business shall accept trusts which may be vested in, transferred or committed to it by a person, firm, association, corporation, court or other authority, of property within this state, until its paid in capital is at least one hundred thousand dollars, and until such corporation has deposited with the treasurer of state in cash the sum of one hundred thousand dollars, except that the full amount of such deposit by such corporation may be in bonds of the United States, or of this state or any municipality or county therein, or of any other state or any municipality or county therein, or in the first mortgage bonds of any railroad corporation that for five years last past has earned at least five per cent net on its issued and outstanding capital stock, which securities and the sufficiency thereof shall be approved by the superintendent of banks. From time to time said treasurer shall, with the approval of the superintendent of banks, permit withdrawals of such securities or cash, or part thereof, upon deposit with him and approval of the superintendent of banks, of cash or other securities of the kind heretofore named, so as to maintain the value of such deposits as herein provided, and so long as it continues solvent he shall permit it to collect the interest on its securities so deposited.

Sec. 710-151.

Foreign trust company may do business in this state, when; deposit; license fee.

SECTION 151. Every foreign trust company shall, upon being admitted to do business within this state as otherwise provided by law, file a certified copy of its certificate of admission with the superintendent of banks, together with a certified copy of the last published statement made by it and filed with the proper department of the state in which it is organized and doing business, and upon approval thereof and of the funds and securities to be deposited as in the preceding section provided, he shall certify that fact to the treasurer of state, and upon deposit of such funds and securities with the treasurer of state the superintendent of banks shall thereupon, and upon the payment of a license fee of one hundred dollars therefor, license said trust company to transact business within this state for the period of one year thereafter.

16-152.   SECTION 152. Every foreign trust company doing a trust business in this state shall annually within thirty days after complying with all the provisions of law in relation to foreign corporations transacting business within this state, file with the superintendent of banks a certificate of the tax commission of Ohio as to such compliance together with a copy of the last published statement of said corporation, and if such trust company is not in default as to any trust matter or estate within this state, the superintendent of banks shall thereupon, and upon payment of a fee of one hundred dollars therefor, license said corporation to transact business within this state for a further period of one year.

Certificate of tax commission filed annually with superintendent.

10-153.   SECTION 153. The superintendent of banks shall have the right to examine, by any deputy, examiner or person especially appointed for that purpose, the books or affairs of any foreign trust company, or any corporation doing a trust business, as to any and all matters relating to any trust, estate or property within this state and concerning which such trust company is acting in a trust or representative capacity, the expense of which shall be charged to and paid by such trust company.

Examination of trust company; expense.

10-154.   SECTION 154. No such trust company, foreign or domestic, authorized to accept and execute trusts, either directly or indirectly through any officer, agent or employe thereof, shall certify to any bond, note or other obligation to evidence debt, secured by any trust deed or mortgage upon or accept any trust concerning property located wholly or in part in this state, without complying with the provisions of sections 150, 151 and 152 of this act. But nothing herein contained shall prevent a foreign corporation from qualifying as executor or administrator of property in this state, after appointment as executor or administrator by the courts of any other state as provided by law, when the decedent was a resident of such state at the time of his death, or from acquiring, holding or transferring title to lands or other property within this state as trustee to secure any bond, note or other obligation aforesaid, or from certifying thereto, but provided always, that by the laws of such other state a trust company organized and doing business under the laws of this state shall have equal privileges as to any similar estate, deed or trust of property in such other state.

Compliance with law required before acceptance or execution of any trust; qualifying as executor or administrator.

710-155.   SECTION 155. Upon the retirement from this state of any foreign trust company, notice of such proposed retirement shall be published once each week for four consecutive weeks in a newspaper of general circulation in the city or village in which the principal place of buisness of such company is located within this state and proof of such publication shall be filed with the superintendent of banks. Such company shall within thirty days after the expiration of the period provided for in such notice, file its application in the court of common pleas of the county in which its

Retirement from state; notice; application to court for authority.

principal place of business is located within the state, for authority to withdraw from the treasurer of state the securities or fund deposited with him under the provisions of section 150 of this act; and said court, if satisfied that such company has fulfilled and met all of its obligations may so find and may authorize the withdrawal of such securities by such trust company; and upon receipt of a certified copy of such order, the superintendent of banks shall so certify to the treasurer of state and thereupon such treasurer of state shall deliver and surrender to such trust company the securities or funds heretofore deposited with him for the faithful performance of the trusts assumed by such trust company.

Sec. 710-156.

How and from whom moneys may be received and held.

SECTION 156. A trust company may receive and hold moneys, or property in trust, or on deposit from executors, administrators, assignees, guardians, trustees, corporations or individuals upon such terms and conditions as may be agreed upon between the parties.

Sec. 710-157.

Courts may order moneys deposited with trust companies.

SECTION 157. Any court in this state, including probate courts, may by order, decree or otherwise, direct moneys or property under its control, or paid into court by parties to an action or legal proceedings, or which are brought into court by reason of an order, judgment or decree, in equity or otherwise, to be deposited with a trust company, by such court designated upon such terms and subject to such instructions as are expedient.

Sec. 710-158.

Empowered to act as agents relative to evidences of indebtedness.

SECTION 158. A trust company may act as agent or trustee for the purpose of registering, countersigning or transferring the certificates of stock, bonds, or other evidences of indebtedness of a corporation, association, municipality, state or public authority, upon such terms as may be agreed upon, and act as trustee under any mortgage or deed of trust to secure bonds issued by any corporation, association, municipality or body politic, and may accept and execute any other corporate or municipal trusts not inconsistent with the laws of the state.

Sec. 710-159.

Management and disposition of property; may accept and execute all trusts.

SECTION 159. A trust company may act as agent, and take, accept and execute any and all trusts, duties and powers in regard to the holding, management and disposition of any property or estate, real or personal, which may be committed or transferred to, or vested in said trust estate, and the rents and profits thereof or the sale thereof, as may be granted or confided to it by any person, association, corporation, municipal or other authority; and may act as trustee under any will or deed or other instrument creating a trust for the care and management of property under the same circumstances and in the same manner, and subject to the same control by the court having jurisdiction of the same as in the case of a legally qualified person.

Sec. 710-160.

Trusts of fiduciary character; may accept and execute on order of court.

SECTION 160. A trust company may take, accept and execute all such trusts which may be committed to it by order of any court of record or probate court of this or any other state or of the United States, to act as executor, administrator, assignee, guardian, receiver, or trustee, or in any other trust capacity, and receive and take title to any real estate which may be the subject of any such trust; and such courts of record and probate courts may appoint such trust company to act as executor, administrator, assignee, guardian, receiver, trustee or in any other trust capacity, provided that any such appointment as guardian shall apply to the estate only and not to the person. But no such trust company shall be required to assume or execute a trust without its consent thereto.

9-161. SECTION 161. The capital stock of such trust company, with the liabilities of the stockholders existing thereunder, and the fund deposited with the treasurer of state as provided by law shall be held as security for the faithful discharge of the duties undertaken by such trust company in respect to any trust, and no bond or other security, except as hereinafter provided, shall be required from any such trust company for or in respect to any trust, nor when appointed executor, administrator, guardian, trustee, receiver, assignee, or depositary; except that the court or officer making such appointment may, upon proper application, require any trust company which shall have been so appointed to give such security for the faithful performance of its duties as to the court or officer shall seem proper, and upon failure of such trust company to give security as required may remove such trust company and revoke such appointment. *Capital and deposits with state treasurer held as security.*

10-162. SECTION 162. Any judge of a court in which such trust company is acting in such trust capacity, if he deems it necessary, or upon the written application of any party interested in the estate which it holds in a trust capacity, at any time, may appoint a suitable person or persons, who shall investigate the affairs and management of such trust company concerning such trust and make sworn report to the court of such investigation. The expense thereof shall be taxed as costs against the party asking for such examination, or the trust fund of such trust company as the court decrees. Such court at any time may examine any officers of such trust company, under oath or affirmation, as to its trust matters in the court, or as to its affairs and management while considering its appointment in such capacity; and for any cause, applicable to natural persons in the same capacity, order that such trust company forthwith settle its trust. *Court may order investigation of company, when; expense.*

10-163. SECTION 163. In proceedings in the probate court or any court of record, connected with any authority exercised under this act, all accounts, returns and other papers may be signed and sworn to in behalf of such trust company by a duly authorized officer thereof. The examination and answers of such officer under oath shall be received as the examination and answers of the trust company. The court may order and compel any of its officers to attend such examinations and to answer such questions as may be put to *Officer empowered to sign and swear to accounts, papers, etc.*

him relating to any such proceeding, in all respects as
otherwise provided by law.

SECTION 164. In the management of money and property held by it as trustee, such trust company may invest
such money and property in a general trust fund of the
trust company. But it shall be competent for the authority
making the appointment to direct whether such money and
property shall be held separately or any part thereof invested in a general trust fund of the trust company. The
trust company always shall follow and be entirely governed by the directions contained in any will or instrument
under which it acts.

SECTION 165. No property or securities received or
held by any trust company in trust shall be mingled with
the investments of the capital stock or other properties belonging to such trust company or be liable for its debts or
obligations. Moneys pending distribution or investment
may be treated as a deposit in the trust department, or
may be deposited in any other department of the bank,
subject in other respects to the provisions of law relating
to deposit of trust funds by trustees and others.

SECTION 166. A trust company may invest in or loan
its trust funds upon the securities, bonds and other interest-
bearing obligations enumerated in sections 111, 112 and 140
of this act, but subject to all limitations as to the amount of
the investment or loan therein or thereon as provided by
law, and in stocks and bonds of corporations when authorized by the affirmative vote of the board of directors, or of
the executive committee of such trust company.

SECTION 167. A trust company shall keep the same
reserve as is required of savings banks, and shall be governed by the same provisions of law in all respects relating
thereto, but shall not be required to keep a reserve on trust
funds or property held in trust.

SECTION 168. A title guaranty and trust company
heretofore organized and now existing may be granted the
power to establish a commercial or a savings bank or a combination of both in the manner provided in this act for the
organization, conduct and supervision of commercial and
savings banks; provided, that such title guaranty and trust
company shall, in addition to its present capital, establish
and maintain the capital required for a commercial or a
savings bank or a combination of both as prescribed in section 37 of this act; provided, such capital and all other
assets of the commercial savings bank or both of such title
guaranty and trust company, shall be held solely for the
repayment of the depositors of said bank and shall not be
liable for or be pledged or used to pay any other obligation
or liability of such title guaranty and trust company until
provision has been made for payment in full of all of the
depositors of said bank; provided, further, that said commercial or savings bank or both shall be governed by all
of the provisions of law applicable to commercial and sav-

ings banks; but nothing in this act shall limit the powers now granted by law to title guaranty and trust companies.

}-169. SECTION 169. When a title guaranty and trust company has complied with the provisions of this act and acquired banking powers herein granted, such company as to business transacted under powers heretofore granted to such title guaranty and trust company, shall thereafter make its report to and be examined by the superintendent of banks, who shall inspect and supervise such company according to the provisions of sections 9850, 9851, 9852 and 9855 of the General Code; and as to the banking powers granted herein, it shall be subject to all requirements of this act as to commercial and savings banks. A title guaranty and trust company accepting the provisions of this act shall not be subject to the limitations prescribed by section 9853 of the General Code. *Subject to supervision and inspection laws.*

}-170. SECTION 170. A title guaranty and trust company heretofore organized and now existing may accept the provisions of this act and be granted trust company powers provided that it shall qualify and comply with all the requirements herein provided for the organization, conduct and supervision of trust companies; provided also that upon the acceptance of the powers granted under this act, all trust powers heretofore granted to title guaranty and trust companies are thereby revoked. *May have trust company powers when qualified.*

0-171. SECTION 171. Title guaranty and trust companies shall make such reports to the auditor of state as are required to be made by trust companies to the superintendent of banks, and shall be subject to like examination, penalties and fees; such examination to be made by and such fees and penalties assessed by and paid to the auditor of state. *Reports to auditor of state and superintendent.*

Fees so received by the auditor of state and by him paid into the state treasury to the credit of the general revenue fund are hereby appropriated for the express purpose of paying the cost of such examinations. *Application of fees.*

}6-172. SECTION 172. Whoever being an officer, employe, agent or director of a bank, embezzles, abstracts, or wilfully misapplies any of the money, funds, credit or property of such bank whether owned by it or held in trust, or wilfully and fraudulently issues or puts forth a certificate of deposit, draws an order or bill of exchange, makes an acceptance, assigns a note, bond, draft, bill of exchange, mortgage, judgment or decree, or makes a false entry in a book, report or statement of such bank, or makes a false statement or certificate as to a trust deposit, fund or contract, for or under which such bank is acting as trustee, or fictitiously borrows or solicits, obtains or receives money for the bank not in good faith intended to become and be the property of the bank, with intent to defraud or injure the bank or another person or corporation, or to deceive an officer of the bank or an agent appointed to examine the affairs of such bank, or publishes a false statement or report relating to the financial condition of the bank with intent to defraud *Embezzlement, misapplication, etc., of funds, unlawful; penalty.*

or injure it or another person or corporation, shall be fined not more than ten thousand dollars, or imprisoned in the penitentiary not more than thirty years, or both.

Sec. 710-173.
Wrongful charge on account or certifying checks; penalty.

SECTION 173. Whoever being an officer, employe, agent or director of a bank, wilfully certifies a check drawn on such bank and fails forthwith to charge the amount thereof against the account of the drawer thereof, or wilfully certifies a check drawn upon the bank unless the drawer of such check has on deposit with the bank an amount of money subject to the payment of such check and equal to the amount specified therein, shall be fined not more than five thousand dollars or imprisoned not less than one year nor more than five years, or both.

Sec. 710-174.
Receiving money, etc., when insolvent; penalty.

SECTION 174. Whoever, being an officer or employe of a bank, receives or, being an officer thereof, permits an employe to receive money, checks, drafts or other property as a deposit therein when he has acknowledged that it is insolvent, shall be fined not more than five thousand dollars or imprisoned in the penitentiary not more than five years, or both.

Sec. 710-175.
Receiving fictitious obligation, etc.; penalty.

SECTION 175. Whoever, being an officer or employe of a bank, resorts to a device, or receives a fictitious obligation in order to evade the provisions of this section and the next two preceding sections, or certifies a check unless there has been regulalry entered to the credit of the drawer thereof upon the books of such bank, an amount at least equal to the amount of such check, shall be fined not more than five thousand dollars or imprisoned not less than one year nor more than five years, or both.

Sec. 710-176.
Drawing check, draft, etc., without credit; penalty.

SECTION 176. Any person who, with intent to defraud, shall make or draw or utter or deliver any check, draft or order for the payment of money upon any bank or other depository, who, at the time thereof, has insufficient funds or credit with such bank or depositary, shall be guilty of a felony, and upon conviction thereof shall be fined not less than fifty dollars and not more than two hundred dollars, or imprisoned in the Ohio state penitentiary for not less than one year nor more than three years or both.

Prima facie evidence of intent to defraud.

As against the maker or drawer thereof, the making, drawing, uttering or delivering of a check, draft or order, payment of which is refused by the drawee, shall be prima facie evidence of intent to defraud, and knowledge of insufficient funds in, or credit with, such bank or other depository. The word "credit" as used herein shall be construed to mean any contract or agreement with the bank or depositary for the payment of such check, draft or order, when presented.

Sec. 710-177.
False advertising of capital; penalty.

SECTION 177. It shall be unlawful for a bank to advertise by newspaper, letter head, or in any other way, a larger capital than actually has been paid in.

A bank violating this provision shall forfeit and pay to the state of Ohio five hundred dollars for each and every such offense, to be recovered with costs of suit in an action, to be prosecuted by the superintendent of banks, before any court of competent jurisdiction in the county wherein it is located. Two or more violations of the provisions of this section may be joined in the same prosecution.

Sec. 710-178. SECTION 178. It shall be unlawful for any bank not organized or transacting business under the provisions of the laws of this state and for all persons, corporations, firms or partnerships doing the business of bankers, brokers or savings institutions, not organized or transacting business under the provisions of this act, to use the word "State" as a portion of the name or title of such bank, corporation, firm or partnership. *Use of word "State" prohibited to unorganized banks; penalty.*

Any violation of the foregoing provisions shall subject the party chargeable therewith to a penalty of fifty dollars for each day during which it is committed or repeated, to be recovered with costs of suit in an action, to be prosecuted by the superintendent of banks, before any court having jurisdiction of such bank or of such person, corporation, firm or partnership.

Sec. 710-179. SECTION 179. Every bank now existing, or which may hereafter become incorporated, shall be subject to the provisions of this act. Nothing in this act shall affect the legality of corporations heretofore organized or investments or loans heretofore made, or of transactions heretofore had, but the superintendent of banks may require the change of investments or loans for those named herein, as it can be done by the sale or redemption of securities so invested in or loaned upon, in such manner as to prevent loss or injury to the bank. No renewal or extension of such a loan or investment shall be made by such a bank unless it be approved by the superintendent of banks. *Banks subject to this act.*

Sec. 710-180. SECTION 180. Any bank organized and doing business as a special plan bank, and which by the terms of its contract with its depositors provides for the receipt of deposits which are not payable unconditionally upon demand or at a fixed time, may in the case of any loan made upon the security of the character and earning capacity of the borrower and of the co-makers or endorsers on the borrower's note evidencing the loan, in addition to discounting interest at the rate allowed by law, require such borrowers as additional security for such loan to make equal periodical deposits in such bank during the period of the loan, with or without an allowance of interest on such deposits, and such transaction shall not be deemed usurious. A special plan bank shall keep only the same reserve as is required of savings banks against all deposits which by the contract with the depositor are not to be paid upon demand or at a fixed time, and no reserve shall be required against deposits hypothecated to secure indebtedness of the depositor to the bank. *Special plan banks; reserve required.*

Banks, railroad, steamship and express companies only may receive and transmit money to foreign countries.

SECTION 181. No person, firm or corporation, except banks and duly incorporated and qualified railroad, steamship and express companies, shall engage in this state in the business of receiving money for the purpose of transmitting the same, or the equivalent thereof, to foreign countries. Every such company transacting or intending to transact such business shall have an amount of paid in capital not less than the amount required for an incorporated bank in the largest place where such company has an office or agency for the transaction of business in this state. Every such company shall, within thirty days after the date this act goes into effect, and thereafter on or before the first day of January and first day of July in each year file with the superintendent of banks a certificate specifying each place in this state where such company maintains its own office where money is or will be received for transmission to foreign countries, and the person or persons in such office authorized to receive money for such purpose; and shall also, within thirty days after this act goes into effect file with the superintendent of banks a certificate specifying the name and business address of every person, not regularly employed by it in its own office, who is authorized to receive money for the purpose of transmitting the same, or the equivalent thereof, to foreign countries; and each person specified in such certificates shall be the designated agent of the company making the certificate for all purposes connected with or incident to the receipt and transmission of money or its equivalent to foreign countries.

Filing certificate with superintendent by company intending to transact business; contents.

Notice when additional agent employed or change made.

Whenever any such agent who is not regularly employed by any such company in its own office is replaced, or an additional agent, who is not so employed by any such company, is authorized to receive money for the purpose of transmitting same, or the equivalent thereof as aforesaid, notice of such fact and of the name of the person replacing the original agent, or the name of such additional agent, shall be certified forthwith to the superintendent of banks; and such person shall thenceforth be the designated agent of such company as aforesaid, until notice of the termination of such agency is filed with the superintendent of banks. The deposit hereinafter required shall be in addition to and not in lieu of the primary liability of any such company for the acts of its designated agents.

Cash or security deposit with state treasurer, additional to capital; bond in lieu thereof.

At the time of filing the certificate first herein required, and before any agent of any such company is authorized to transact any business hereunder, the company filing such certificate shall deposit with the treasurer of state, the sum of fifty thousand dollars in cash, or in the securities specified in section 150 of this act; in case such deposit is in securities, the company making the same shall have the privilege of withdrawal, substitution and collection of interest provided in said section; or in lieu thereof such company shall execute and deliver to the superintendent of banks, who shall deposit it with the treasurer of state, a bond in the sum of fifty thousand dollars to cover money received by any and all its agents in this state for the purpose of transmission to foreign countries; such bond to be conditioned upon the faithful holding and transmission of money, or the equivalent thereof, which shall be delivered to or deposited with any such agent for transmission to a foreign country, for the benefit of such persons as shall deliver to or deposit money with any such agent of such company for such purpose. Such bond shall be executed by such company with a corporate surety company, acceptable to the superintendent of banks, as surety. Such moneys or securities deposited with the treasurer of state and the money which in case of default shall be paid on such bond, shall constitute a trust fund for the benefit of such persons as shall deliver to or deposit with any such designated agent of such company money for transmission to foreign countries as aforesaid; suit to recover on any such bond may be brought by or upon the relation of any party aggrieved, in the common pleas court of any county in which such company has an agent; and service of summons on any agent of such company shall be sufficient. All moneys received for transmission to a foreign country by a railroad, steamship or express company shall be forwarded to the person to whom the same is directed to be transmitted within ten days after the receipt thereof. The receipt given by any such company by its agent or agents, for deposits of money received for transmission to a foreign country shall be on a form or forms certified copies of which have first been filed with the superintendent of banks; in case of use by any such company of a form or forms for this purpose certified copies of which have not been filed with the superintendent of banks, whether the use of such receipts is authorized or not, shall not relieve such company of its liability for the acts of such agent hereunder and such company shall be subject to a penalty of fifty dollars for every such violation. *Moneys transmitted within ten days.* *Form of receipt.*

Every agent of any such company not regularly employed in its own office shall be subject to inspection and examination by the superintendent of banks in order to ascertain that such business is being lawfully conducted, and that all moneys received are properly accounted for; for which purpose the superintendent of banks may also prescribe the manner and form of keeping the books and accounts of such agent as provided in section 71 of this act as to banks. *Agent not regularly employed subject to examination.*

Whenever the superintendent of banks upon his own determination makes an examination of any such agent transacting or about to transact business under the provisions of this section, the expenses thereof shall be paid by the company represented by such agent. *Expense paid by company.*

Every railroad, steamship and express company transacting business in this state under this section shall annually, on or before the 15th day of March, file with the *Report by railroad, steamship and express companies.*

superintendent of banks its duly verified report, in the form prescribed by the superintendent of banks, showing in such detail as may be required by him, its business and transactions during the preceding calendar year relative to the receipts and transmission of money to foreign countries. The superintendent of banks shall have the power to revoke the authority to transact such business in this state of any railroad, steamship or express company which fails to make and file such annual report as herein provided.

Transmission of money by telegraph; act does not apply.

This section shall not apply to the receipt of money for immediate transmission by telegraph by the duly authorized agent of any duly incorporated telegraph company, at any regularly established office of such company.

Sec. 710-182.

False representation as officer or agent, unlawful; penalty.

SECTION 182. Whoever, not being an authorized officer or employe of a bank, or the duly designated agent for that purpose of a railroad, steamship or express company, holds himself out as authorized to receive, or solicits, or receives money for the purpose of transmitting the same, or the equivalent thereof, to foreign countries, shall, upon conviction, be fined not more than five thousand dollars or imprisoned in the penitentiary not more than ten years, or both.

Sec. 710-183.

Certificate of auditor of state before engaging in business.

SECTION 183. No person, firm or corporation shall engage in selling steamship or railroad tickets for transportation to or from foreign countries, until they shall have obtained from the auditor of state a certificate of compliance with the provisions of the two sections next following. The certificate shall be conspicuously displayed in the place of business of such person, firm or corporation.

Sec. 710-184.

Bond.

SECTION 184. Such person, firm or corporation shall make, execute and deliver a bond to the state of Ohio in the sum of five thousand dollars, conditioned for the selling of genuine and valid steamship or railroad tickets for transportation to or from foreign countries.

Sec. 710-185.

Security required; approval of bond.

SECTION 185. Such bond shall be executed by such person, firm or corporation as principal, with at least two good and sufficient sureties, who shall be responsible and owners of real estate within the state. The bond of a surety company may be received, if approved, or cash, or the securities enumerated in section 150 of this act, may be accepted surety. Such bond shall be approved by the auditor of state, and filed in his office. Upon the relation of any party aggrieved, a suit to recover on such bond may be brought in a court of competent jurisdiction.

Sec. 710-186.

"Bond book" kept by auditor of state.

SECTION 186. The auditor of state shall keep a book to be known as a "bond book" wherein he shall place in alphabetical order all such bonds received by him, the date of receipt, the name or names of the principals and place or places of residence, and place or places for transacting their business, the names of surety upon the bond, and the name of the officer before whom the bond was executed or acknowledged. Such record shall be open to public inspection. The auditor of state shall collect a fee of five dollars for each bond so filed.

·187.   SECTION 187. A person, firm or corporation which engages in such business, contrary to the provisions of the four preceding sections, shall be fined not more than five hundred dollars or imprisoned not more than six months, or both. Violations of act; penalty.

But nothing in the said sections shall apply to national banks, duly incorporated and qualified railroad, steamship, express companies, banks or trust companies. To what companies act does not apply.

188.   SECTION 188. That sections 290, 291, 292, 293, 294, 295, 710, 711, 712, 713, 714, 715, 716, 717, 718, 719, 720, 721, · 722, 723, 724, 725, 726, 727, 728, 729, 730, 731, 732, 733, 734, 735, 736, 736-1, 736-2, 737, 738, 739, 740, 741, 742, 742-1, 742-2, 742-3, 742-4, 742-5, 742-6, 742-7, 742-8, 742-9, 742-10, 742-11, 742-12, 742-13, 742-14, 742-15, 742-16, 743, 744-1, 744-2, 744-3, 744-4, 744-5, 744-6, 744-7, 744-8, 744-9, 744-10, 744-11, 744-12, 744-13, 9676, 9677, 9678, 9679, 9680, 9681, 9682, 9683, 9684, 9685, 9686, 9687, 9688, 9689, 9690, 9691, 9692, 9693, 9694, 9695, 9696, 9697, 9698, 9699, 9700, 9701, 9702, 9703, 9704, 9705, 9706, 9707, 9708, 9709, 9710, 9711, 9712, 9713, 9714, 9715, 9716, 9717, 9718, 9719, 9720, 9721, 9722, 9723, 9724, 9725, 9726, 9727, 9728, 9729, 9730, 9731, 9732, 9733, 9734, 9735, 9736, 9737, 9738, 9739, 9740, 9741, 9742, 9743, 9744, 9745, 9746, 9747, 9748, 9749, 9750, 9752, 9752-1, 9752-2, 9753, 9754, 9755, 9756, 9757, 9758, 9759, 9760, 9761, 9762, 9763, 9764, 9765, 9766, 9767, 9768, 9769, 9770, 9771, 9772, 9773, 9774, 9775, 9776, 9777, 9778, 9779, 9780, 9781, 9782, 9783, 9784, 9785, 9786, 9787, 9788, 9789, 9790, 9790-1, 9791, 9792, 9793, 9794, 9795, 9796, 9796-1, 9796-2, 9796-3, 9797, 9798, 9799, 9800, 9801, 9802, 9803, 9804, 9805, 9806, 9807, 9808, 9809, 9810, 9811, 9812, 9813, 9814, 9815, 9816, 9817, 9818, 9819, 9820, 9821, 9822, 9823, 9824, 9825, 9826, 9827, 9828, 9829, 9830, 9831, 9832, 9833, 9834, 9835, 9836, 9837, 9838, 9839, 9840, 9841, 9842, 9843, 9844, 9845, 9846, 9847, 9848, 9849, 9856, 12473, 12898, 12899, 13182, 13183, 13184, 13185, 13186, 13187 and 13193-1 of the General Code of Ohio and all acts or parts of acts inconsistent herewith be and the same are hereby repealed. Repeals.

189.   SECTION 189: Nothing in this act contained repealing any law for the regulation or conduct of banking, shall be construed to relieve any person from punishment for any acts heretofore committed violating said law or laws, nor effect in any manner an existing indictment or prosecution by reason of such repeal; and for that purpose such law or Repeals do not relieve punishment under former laws.

9 L. A.

laws shall continue in full force and effect notwithstanding such repeal.

The sectional numbers on the margin hereof are designated as provided by law. JOHN G. PRICE, Attorney General.

CARL R. KIMBALL,
Speaker of the House of Representatives.
CLARENCE J. BROWN,
President of the Senate.

Passed April 4, 1919.
Approved April 11, 1919.

JAMES M. COX,
Governor.

Filed in the office of the Secretary of State at Columbus, Ohio, on the 12th day of April, A. D. 1919.

56 G.

[House Bill No. 12.[

AN ACT

To amend section 5243 of the General Code, relating to the use or occupancy of armories.

Be it enacted by the General Assembly of the State of Ohio:

SECTION 1. That section 5243 of the General Code be amended to read as follows:

Sec. 5243. The armories erected, constructed, owned or leased by virtue of this chapter, shall be for the use and benefit of the permanent organized militia quartered therein; but in each of such armories there shall at all times be provided and maintained a suitable room or rooms for the free use and occupancy of the organizations known as the Grand Army of the Republic, Sons of Veterans, Sons of Veterans Auxiliary, Daughters of Veterans, United Spanish War Veterans, Veterans of the World War of 1917 and 1918, Union Veteran Legion, Army and Navy Union of the United States of America and honorably retired officers of the Ohio National Guard, unless such room or rooms are already provided by the erection of a county memorial building or otherwise by the state, or by a county, township or municipality. Provided that this section shall not be construed to require a separate room to be maintained for each organization.

SECTION 2. That said original section 5243 of the General Code be, and the same is hereby repealed.

CARL R. KIMBALL,
Speaker of the House of Representatives.
CLARENCE J. BROWN,
President of the Senate.

Passed April 2, 1919.
Approved April 10, 1919.

JAMES M. COX,
Governor.

Filed in the office of the Secretary of State at Columbus, Ohio, on the 11th day of April, A. D. 1919.

57 G.

[House Bill No. 314.]

AN ACT

To supplement section 1286 of the General Code by adding section 1286-2, providing for the administration of anaesthetics by registered nurses.

Be it enacted by the General Assembly of the State of Ohio:

SECTION 1. That section 1286 of the General Code be supplemented by the addition of section 1286-2 as follows:

Sec. 1286-2. Nothing in this chapter shall be construed to apply to or prohibit in any way the administration of an anaesthetic by a registered nurse under the direction of and in the immediate presence of a licensed physician, provided such nurse has taken a prescribed course in anaesthesia, at a hospital in good standing.

Registered nurse may administer anaesthetic.

CARL R. KIMBALL,
Speaker of the House of Representatives.
CLARENCE J. BROWN,
President of the Senate.

The sectional number in this act is in conformity to the General Code. JOHN G. PRICE, *Attorney General.*

Passed March 20, 1919.
Approved April 14, 1919.

JAMES M. COX,
Governor.

Filed in the office of the Secretary of State at Columbus, Ohio, on the 14th day of April, A. D. 1919.

58 G.

[Senate Bill No. 84]

AN ACT

To amend section 5366-1 and to supplement section 5404 of the General Code, by the enactment of a supplemental section to be known as section 5404-1, providing for the time when personal property shall be listed for taxation.

Be it enacted by the General Assembly of the State of Ohio:

SECTION 1. That section 5366-1 of the General Code be amended and that section 5404 be supplemented by the addition of section 5404-1, to read as follows:

Sec. 5366-1. The listing of all personal property, moneys, credits, investments in bonds, stocks, joint stock companies, or otherwise, except in stock in trade of transient persons, shall be made between the second Monday of April and the first Monday of June, annually.

When personal property shall be listed for taxation.

The listing and valuation of all such property for taxation shall be made as of the day preceding the second Monday of April, annually, and all personal property, moneys, credits and investments except as otherwise provided in this act shall be listed and valued with respect to

Valuation shall be made as of second Monday of April.

the ownership thereof on said date and in the place where then taxable, provided that the provisions of this section shall not apply to the return of the resources and liabilities of incorporated and unincorporated banks, nor the returns made by incorporated companies, nor in any case where property is required to be returned for taxation, or to be valued, by the tax commission of Ohio; nor in any case where the liability of any person or of any property to taxation is required to be originally determined by the tax commission of Ohio.

Property of companies, stocks of merchandise and materials shall be valued as of Jan. 1st.

Sec. 5404-1. All the listing and valuation of the personal property, moneys, credits, investments in stocks, bonds, joint stock companies, or otherwise, of incorporated companies, and all the averages of the stocks of merchandise and material used as a manufacturer, of such incorporated companies, shall be listed, valued and ascertained as of the first day of January, annually.

Repeal.

SECTION 2. That said original section 5366-1 of the General Code be and the same is hereby repealed.

The sectional numbers in this act are in conformity to the General Code. JOHN G. PRICE, Attorney General.

CARL R. KIMBALL,
Speaker of the House of Representatives.
CLARENCE J. BROWN,
President of the Senate.

Passed March 26, 1919.
Approved April 14, 1919.

JAMES M. COX,
Governor.

Filed in the office of the Secretary of State at Columbus, Ohio, on the 15th day of April, A. D. 1919.

59 G.

[Am. Senate Bill No. 61.]

AN ACT

To amend section 8301 of the General Code, making the twelfth day of February, known as Lincoln's birthday, a legal holiday.

Be it enacted by the General Assembly of the State of Ohio:
SECTION 1. That section 8301 of the General Code be amended to read as follows:
Sec. 8301. The following days, viz.:

Legal holidays.

1. The first day of January, known as New Year's day;

2. The twenty-second day of February, known as Washington's birthday;

3. The thirtieth day of May, known as Decoration or Memorial day;

4. The fourth day of July, known as Independence day;

5. The first Monday of September, known as Labor day;

6. The twelfth day of October, known as Columbus Discovery day;

7. The twenty-fifth day of December, known as Christmas day;

8. Any day appointed and recommended by the governor of this state or the president of the United States as a day of fast or thanksgiving;

9. The twelfth day of February, known as Lincoln's birthday; and

10. Any day which may hereafter be made a legal holiday, shall for the purpose of this division, be holidays. But if the first day of January, the twenty-second day of February, the thirtieth day of May, the fourth of July, or the twenty-fifth day of December be the first day of the week, known as Sunday, the next succeeding secular or business day shall be a holiday.

SECTION 2. That said original section 8301 be and the same is hereby repealed. Repeal.

CARL R. KIMBALL,
Speaker of the House of Representatives.
CLARENCE J. BROWN,
President of the Senate.

Passed March 27, 1919.
Approved April 14, 1919.

JAMES M. COX,
Governor.

Filed in the office of the Secretary of State at Columbus, Ohio, on the 15th day of April, A. D. 1919.

60 G.

[House Bill No. 5.]

AN ACT

To amend section 7621 and to enact supplementary sections 7621-1 and 12906-1 of the General Code, relative to displaying the national flag over or within school buildings.

Be it enacted by the General Assembly of the State of Ohio:

SECTION 1. That section 7621 be amended and supplementary sections 7621-1 and 12906-1 of the General Code be enacted to read as follows:

Sec. 7621. All boards of education, all proprietors or principals of private schools and all authorities in control of parochial schools or other educational institutions shall display the United States national flag, not less than five feet in length, over or within all school houses under their control, during each day such schools are in session. In all public schools the boards of education shall make all rules and necessary regulations for the care and keeping of such flags, the expense thereof to be paid out of their contingent fund.

Duty of county superintendent; report to prosecuting attorney; prosecution.

Sec. 7621-1. It shall be the special duty of the county superintendent of schools to see that the provisions of section 7621 of the General Code are enforced, and he shall promptly report all violations thereof to the prosecuting attorney of the county, whose duty it shall be to institute prosecutions against all persons violating the provisions of section 7621 of the General Code in his respective county.

Failure to comply with law a misdemeanor; penalty.

Sec. 12906-1. Whoever, having control of any school house or other educational institution either as an individual or in connection with any person or persons, neglects or refuses to carry out the provisions of section 7621 of the General Code, shall be deemed guilty of a misdemeanor, and upon conviction thereof shall for the first offense be fined not less than five dollars, nor more than twenty-five dollars, and for each subsequent offense shall be fined not less than twenty-five dollars, nor more than one hundred dollars. Each day of such refusal or neglect shall be held to constitute a separate offense.

Repeal.

SECTION 2. That original section 7621 of the General Code be, and the same is hereby repealed.

CARL R. KIMBALL,
Speaker of the House of Representatives.
CLARENCE J. BROWN,
President of the Senate.

The sectional numbers in this act are in conformity to the General Code. JOHN G. PRICE, Attorney General.

Passed March 25, 1919.
Approved April 14, 1919.

JAMES M. COX,
Governor.

Filed in the office of the Secretary of State at Columbus, Ohio, on the 15th day of April, A. D. 1919.

61 G.

[House Bill No. 156.]

AN ACT

To provide medical and surgical treatment of crippled children, by the enactment of sections 1352-8 to 1352-11 inclusive of the General Code.

Be it enacted by the General Assembly of the State of Ohio:

SECTION 1. That section 1352 of the General Code be supplemented by the enactment of supplemental sections to be known as sections 1352-8, 1352-9, 1352-10 and 1352-11 to read as follows:

When board shall provide treatment for crippled children; application to juvenile court; copy of decree; notice to court.

Sec. 1352-8. In order to provide suitable medical and surgical treatment of crippled children whose parents or guardians fail or are financially unable to provide such treatment, the board of state charities is authorized and empowered to receive into its custody such children. Application for such care and treatment shall first be made to the juvenile court by a parent, guardian or some interested person. If such court is of the opinion that such child is in need of such treatment, and finds that the parent or guardian fails to provide it, he may make an order to that end; or if the parent or guardian is financially unable to pay all or a part of the expense of such treatment, the court shall make a porper finding and decree. In either case the court shall at once forward a copy of the decree and a statement of facts to the board of state charities, and such board shall, when able to do so under this act, accept such child for care as hereinbefore provided. Upon receipt of notice from such board that such child can be given treatment in a suitable institution, the court shall then commit such child to such board and provide for its conveyance in charge of a suitable person to the place designated by such board for treatment. The expenses for conveyance shall be paid by the county or by the parent or guardian as the court may direct. Such commitment shall be only for the period necessary for the treatment of such child.

Sec. 1352-9. The board of state charities shall by contract arrange for treatment of crippled children in any public or private hospital which in its judgment is equipped to give adequate medical, surgical and educational attention to such cases. Compensation for such service, including all surgical and other professional attention, shall be allowed by the board of state charities upon such terms and conditions as may be agreed upon between said board and the hospital admitting such crippled children as herein provided and shall be paid from fund appropriated for such purpose upon vouchers approved by the secretary of said board. Necessary clothing shall be furnished by the board of state charities, but such board may require parents or guardians to pay the state for such expenses when in its judgment such action is just. Such board shall exercise close supervision over such crippled children while patients in such hospitals and may at any time terminate any contracts so made when in its judgment such action should be taken. Each hospital caring for crippled children under this act shall be visited at least once each calendar month by a representative of such board who shall prepare and present to the board a written report concerning the progress of each patient who is being treated in accordance with this act.

Sec. 1352-10. Whenever it appears that a crippled child has been successfully treated, or that it can not be further benefited by such treatment, the board shall order its discharge and thereupon its guardianship and responsibility shall cease. After such a child has been a patient in a hospital in accordance with this act for more than one year the parent or guardian, with the approval of the juvenile court, may cause its release from the hospital and the supervision of the board of state charities.

When contracts of board may be terminated. Sec. 1352-11. After the Ohio institution for the treatment and education of deformed and crippled children is established and ready for the treatment of such children the board of state charities may terminate all contracts made under this act and transfer such children under its care to such institution, unless such institution cannot care for all such children who are eligible for admission.

CARL R. KIMBALL,
Speaker of the House of Representatives.
CLARENCE J. BROWN,
President of the Senate.

The sectional numbers in this act are in conformity to the General Code. JOHN G. PRICE, Attorney General.

Passed March 25, 1919.
Approved April 14, 1919.

JAMES M. COX,
Governor.

Filed in the office of the Secretary of State at Columbus, Ohio, on the 15th day of April, A. D. 1919.

62 G.

[House Bill No. 44.]

AN ACT

To amend sections 12815 and 9156 of the General Code, relative to disorderly conduct in or about railway stations.

Be it enacted by the General Assembly of the State of Ohio:
SECTION 1. That sections 12815 and 9156 of the General Code be amended to read as follows:

Disorderly conduct on trains or about railway stations. Sec. 12815. Whoever wilfully disturbs, by disorderly conduct or obscene language, or unlawfully interferes with the peace and comfort of any passenger or other person upon a passenger train, or in and about a railway station, shall be fined not more than twenty-five dollars, or imprisoned not more than ten days, or both.

When conductor, ticket agent and special policeman are police officers. Sec. 9156. The conductor of every train carrying passengers, and the ticket agent and special policemen employed in or about an interurban or steam railway station are hereby invested with the powers, duties and responsibilities of police officers while on duty on such train, or on such car or cars, or in or about such interurban or steam railway station, and may wear the badge of a special policeman.

137

SECTION 2. That original sections 12815 and 9156 of ^{Repeals.} the General Code be, and the same are hereby repealed.

The sectional member in this act is in conformity to the General Code. JOHN G. PRICE, Attorney General.

CARL R. KIMBALL,
Speaker of the House of Representatives.
CLARENCE J. BROWN,
President of the Senate.

Passed April 2, 1919.
Approved April 14, 1919.

JAMES M. COX,
Governor.

Filed in the office of the Secretary of State at Columbus, Ohio, on the 15th day of April, A. D. 1919.

63 G.

[House Bill No. 164.]

AN ACT

To amend rule 3 of section 1 of an act, entitled, ''An act to provide for the control and management of the public parks of the state; to define the duties of police patrolmen and to establish rules for the navigation of state reservoirs by power or sail boats, and all other watercraft located or operated thereon, etc.'' (Sec. 479 General Code.)

Be it enacted by the General Assembly of the State of Ohio:

SECTION 1. That rule 3 of section 479 of the General Code be amended to read as follows:

Sec. 479. Rule 3. The superintendent of public works is hereby authorized to employ one police patrolman at each reservoir park, at a salary of not to exceed twelve hundred dollars per year, two assistant police patrolmen at each state reservoir for three and one-half months prior to and including Labor day, at the rate of seventy-five dollars per month, and may expend for special patrolmen at each state reservoir during the summer months, a sum not exceeding ninety dollars, at the rate of $3.00 per day for each patrolman employed, all of which expenses shall be paid from the receipts from leases, boat permits and sale of special privileges to be derived from each of the state reservoir parks or funds appropriated for such purposes, but no funds shall be expended for this purpose upon any reservoir in excess of its own earnings, except from funds specially appropriated for such purposes.

SECTION 2. That said original rule 3 of section 479 of the General Code be, and the same is hereby repealed.

CARL R. KIMBALL,
Speaker of the House of Representatives.
CLARENCE J. BROWN,
President of the Senate.

Passed March 20, 1919.

This bill was presented to the Governor on April 2, 1919, and was not signed or returned to the house wherein it originated within ten days after being so presented, exclusive of Sundays and the day said bill was presented and was filed in the office of the Secretary of State on the fifteenth day of April, 1919.

ROBERT T. CREW,
Veto Clerk.

Filed in the office of the Secretary of State at Columbus, Ohio, on the 15th day of April, A. D. 1919.

64 G.

[Amended Senate Bill No. 72.]

AN ACT

To amend section 5366 of the General Code, relative to the listing of personal property.

Be it enacted by the General Assembly of the State of Ohio:

SECTION 1. That section 5366 of the General Code be amended to read as follows:

Sec. 5366. In order to facilitate the listing of personal property, moneys, credits, investments in bonds, stocks, joint stock companies or otherwise, in the sub-divisions mentioned in section 3349 of the General Code, each person required by law to list the same shall make a return thereof under oath to the county auditor on the second Monday in April, or within fifteen days thereafter, of any year, the same to be made on the blanks furnished, by order of the state tax commission for such purposes, which the auditor shall have supplied at his office for use of persons required to list such property of any character. The county auditor may mail or distribute such blanks prior to the second Monday in April to the persons required to list such property, or may place listing blanks at convenient places in each taxing subdivision, and give notice thereof in one newspaper of general circulation in the county. Each person required by law shall correctly list all such property on such blanks giving the true value thereof in money, and, answer all questions correctly, and give all information, asked and required by the printed forms contained on such blanks. The person making such return for taxation shall subscribe and make oath to the correctness of all matters

contained therein, and such oath may be administered by
any assessor, assistant assessor, county auditor, deputy
county auditor, mayor, justice of the peace, township clerk
or notary public, after which the same shall be delivered
.in person or by mail to the county auditor, on or before the
first day of May. Any person required by law to list such
property for taxation, who fails or neglects to file with the
county auditor, as required by this act, a true list and valuation of his property, shall not be entitled to any exemption as provided by section 5360 of the General Code.

Failure to list
property forfeits
exemption.

The county auditor shall examine such returns and
after giving notice to the person making oath thereto, may
make corrections thereof and may go over the same together
with the assessor of the same taxing sub-division, and if
they believe any property is omitted from any returns, or
that the value is incorrect, the assessor shall call upon the
person listing such property and upon actual view list and
assess such property at its true value in money. The county
auditor shall deliver to the assessors of the respective subdivisions at the time of their meeting for instructions, a list
of all persons and property so returned for taxation, and
may deliver the original returns to such assessor for his
use, and such assessor shall inspect the returns made and
cause to be listed and returned for taxation as provided in
this act, all such property not at that time listed and returned to the county auditor. No assessor or assistant assessor shall be paid any per diem for administering an oath
as herein provided where returns are being made to the
county auditor, but they shall administer all oaths to persons making returns as herein provided to the county auditor, without charge to such person, but shall be paid the
sums of ten cents for each person so sworn to his return
prior to May first, of any year, on the warrant of the
county auditor, at the time of payment of his per diem
services.

Examination of
returns; omis-
sions assessed;
lists delivered to
assessors; pay
for administering
oath.

For the purpose of carrying out the provisions of this
act and the provisions of sections 2583, 5366 and 5612 of
the General Code, each county auditor shall appoint such
number of experts, deputies, clerks and employes as may
from time to time be prescribed for him by the tax commission of Ohio. Such experts, deputies, clerks and employes shall hold their employment for such time as may be
prescribed by the tax commission of Ohio. The compensation of such experts, deputies, clerks and employes shall
be fixed by the county auditor subject to the approval of
the tax commission of Ohio, and shall be paid monthly out
of the general county fund upon warrant of the county
auditor. Such compensation shall constitute a charge
against the county, regardless of the amount of money in
the county treasury appropriated for such purposes and
notwithstanding any failure of the county commissioners
to levy or appropriate funds therefor. On the first day of
January, annually, any amount in the fee fund of the

Appointment of
experts, deputies,
etc.; term of em-
ployment; com-
pensation, how
fixed.

county auditor in excess of that necessary to pay the one-sixth of the aggregate compensation of the deputies, assistants, clerks and other employes of such auditor as fixed under section 2980-1 of the General Code, but not in excess of the amount paid out of the general county fund under the provisions of this section, shall be transferred to the general county fund without action by the county.

Act does not apply to public utilities or banks.

Provided, however, that the provisions of this section shall not apply to public utilities, banks and bankers, the listing and return of the property of which is otherwise provided by law.

Repeal.

SECTION 2. That original section 5366 of the General Code be, and the same is hereby repealed.

The sectional numbers in this act are in conformity to the General Code. JOHN G. PRICE, Attorney General.

CARL R. KIMBALL,
Speaker of the House of Representatives.
CLARENCE J. BROWN,
President of the Senate.

Passed March 26, 1919.
Approved April 15, 1919.

JAMES M. COX,
Governor.

Filed in the office of the Secretary of State at Columbus, Ohio on the 16th day of April, A. D. 1919.

65 G.

[House Bill No. 285.]

AN ACT

To supplement section 1352 of the General Code, by the enactment of supplemental section to be known and designated as section 1352-6, relating to institutions caring for children.

Be it enacted by the General Assembly of the State of Ohio:

SECTION 1. That section 1352 of the General Code be supplemented by section 1352-6 to read as follows:

"Institution" and "association" defined with relation to institutions caring for children.

Sec. 1352-6. For the purpose of this chapter the words "institution" and "association" shall include any incorporated or unincorporated organization, society, association or agency, public or private, which may receive or care for children; any individual not connected with any organization, society, association or agency, who, for hire, gain, or reward, receives or cares for dependent, neglected or delinquent children, or who in any manner becomes a party to the placing of such in foster homes, unless he is related by blood or marriage.

CARL R. KIMBALL,
Speaker of the House of Representatives.
CLARENCE J. BROWN,
President of the Senate.

Passed April 1, 1919.
Approved April 15, 1919.

JAMES M. COX,
Governor.

Filed in the office of the Secretary of State at Columbus, Ohio, on the 16th day of April, A. D. 1919.

66 G.

[Amended Senate Bill No. 89.]

AN ACT

To amend sections 5449, 5450, 5451, 5458, 5470, 5473-1 and 5474 of the General Code, relating to reports to the tax commission by express, telegraph and telephone companies and changing the date of ascertaining and assessing the value of the property of express companies by the tax commission of Ohio and the date of certifying by the tax commission of Ohio to the county auditor the amount apportioned to his county and to each city, village, township or other taxing district therein and to repeal original sections 5449, 5450, 5451, 5458, 5470, 5473-1 and 5474 of the General Code.

Be it enacted by the General Assembly of the State of Ohio:

SECTION 1. That sections 5449, 5450, 5451, 5458, 5470, 5473-1 and 5474 of the General Code be amended to read as follows:

Sec. 5449. On or before the first day of March, annually, every express, telegraph and telephone company, doing business in this state, under the oath of the person constituting such company, if a person, or under the oath of the president, secretary, treasurer, superintendent or chief officer in this state of such association or corporation, if an association or corporation, shall make and file with the commission a statement in such form as the commission may prescribe. *Annual statement to tax commission.*

Sec. 5450. Such statement shall contain: *Contents of statement.*

1. The name of the company.

2. The nature of the company, whether a person or persons, or association or corporation, and under the laws of what state or county organized.

3. The location of its principal office.

4. The name and postoffice address of the president, secretary, auditor, treasurer and superintendent or general manager.

5. The name and postoffice address of the chief officer or managing agent of the company in this state.

6. The number of shares of the capital stock.

7. The par value and market value, or if there is no market value, the actual value of its shares of stock on the thirty-first day of the month of December, next preceding and the amount of its capital stock subscribed and the amount thereof actually paid in.

8. A detailed statement of the real estate owned by the company in this state, where situated, and the value thereof as assessed for taxation.

9. A full and correct inventory of the personal property, including moneys and credits, owned by the company in this state on the thirty-first day of the month of December next preceding, where situated, and the value thereof.

10. The total value of the real estate owned by the company and situated outside of this state.

11. The total value of the personal property owned by the company and situated outside of this state.

12. The total amount of bonded indebtedness and of indebtedness not bonded; the gross receipts from whatever source derived for business wherever done, for the year ending on the thirty-first day of December next preceding; and the total gross expenditures for such year.

13. In the case of telegraph and telephone companies, such statement shall also set forth, the whole length of their lines, and the length of so much of their lines as is without and is within this state, which shall include the lines such telegraph and telephone companies control and use under lease or otherwise and the miles of wire in each taxing district in this state.

16. In the case of express companies, the gross receipts for the year ending on the thirty-first day of December, from whatever source derived, of each office within this state, giving the name of each office in this state.

17. In the case of express companies, such statement shall also contain the whole length of the lines of rail and water routes, over which the company did business on the thirty-first day of December and the length of so much of such lines of land and water transportation as is without and within this state, naming the lines within this state.

When value of property shall be ascertained.

Sec. 5451. On the first Monday in July of each year, the commission shall ascertain and assess the value of the property of the express, telegraph and telephone companies in this state.

When apportionment certified to subdivisions.

Sec. 5458. On the second Monday in July, the commission shall certify to the county auditor the amount apportioned to his county and to each city, village, township or other taxing district therein.

Public utility shall file statement, when.

Sec. 5470. Each public utility except street, suburban and interurban railroad and railroad companies, doing business in this state, shall, annually, on or before the first day of August, and each street, suburban and interurban railroad and railroad company, shall, annually, on or before the first day of September, under the oath of the person constituting such company, if a person, or under the oath of the president, secretary, treasurer, superintendent or chief officer in this state, of such association or corporation, if an association or corporation, make and file with the commission a statement in such form as the commission may prescribe.

Sec. 5474. In the case of all such public utilities except railroad, street, suburban and interurban railroad companies and express, telegraph and telephone companies, such statement shall also contain the entire gross receipts of the company, including all sums earned or charged, whether actually received or not, from whatever source derived, for business done within this state for the near next preceding the first day of May, including the company's proportion of gross receipts for business done by it within this state in connection with other companies, firms, corporations, persons or associations, but this shall not apply to receipts from interstate business, or business done for the federal government. Such statement shall also contain the total gross receipts of such company for such period in this state from business done within the state. **Contents of statement.**

Sec. 5473-1. In the case of telegraph and telephone companies, such statement shall also contain the entire gross receipts, including all sums earned or charged, whether actually received or not, for the year ending the thirtieth day of June, from whatever source derived, whether messages, telephone tolls, rentals, or otherwise, for business done within this state, including the company's proportion of gross receipts for business done by it within this state in connection with other companies, firms, corporations, persons or associations excluding therefrom all receipts derived wholly from interstate business or business done for the federal government. Such statement shall also contain the total gross receipts of such company, for such period, from business done within this state. **Statement of telegraph and telephone companies.**

In the case of express companies, such statement shall also contain the entire receipts including all sums earned or charged, whether actually received or not, from whatever source derived, for business done within this state, for the year ending the thirtieth day of June, for and on account of such company, including the company's proportion of gross receipts for business done by it within this state in connection with other companies, firms, corporations, persons, or associations, excluding therefrom all receipts derived wholly from interstate business or business done for the federal government. Such statement shall also contain the total gross receipts of such company, for such period, from business done within this state. **Statement of express companies.**

SECTION 2. That original sections 5449, 5450, 5451, **Repeals.**

144

5458, 5470, 5473-1 and 5474 of the General Code be, and the same are hereby repealed.

The sectional numbers in this act are in conformity to the General Code.
JOHN G. PRICE, Attorney General.

CARL R. KIMBALL,
Speaker of the House of Representatives.
CLARENCE J. BROWN,
President of the Senate.

Passed March 26, 1919.
Approved April 15, 1919.

JAMES M. COX,
Governor.

Filed in the office of the Secretary of State at Columbus, Ohio, on the 16th day of April, A. D. 1919.

67 G.

[House Bill No. 204.]

AN ACT

To amend section 13706 of the General Code, relating to probation of persons convicted of crimes.

Be it enacted by the General Assembly of the State of Ohio:

SECTION 1. That section 13706 of the General Code be amended to read as follows:

What prisoners may be put upon probation.

Sec. 13706. In prosecutions for crime, except as hereinafter provided, where the defendant has pleaded or been found guilty, and the court or magistrate has power to sentence such defendant to be confined in or committed to the penitentiary, the reformatory, a jail, workhouse, or correctional institution, and the defendant has never before been imprisoned for crime, either in this state or elsewhere, and it appears to the satisfaction of the court or magistrate that the character of the defendant and circumstances of the case are such that he is not likely again to engage in an offensive course of conduct, and that the public good does not demand or require that he shall suffer the penalty imposed by law, such court or magistrate may suspend the execution of the sentence, at any time before such sentence is carried into execution, and place the defendant on probation in the manner provided by law.

SECTION 2. That said original section 13706 of the General Code be, and the same is hereby repealed.

The sectional number in this act is in conformity to the General Code.
JOHN G. PRICE, Attorney General.

CARL R. KIMBALL,
Speaker of the House of Representatives.
CLARENCE J. BROWN,
President of the Senate.

Passed March 28, 1919.
Approved April 16, 1919.

JAMES M. COX,
Governor.

Filed in the office of the Secretary of State at Columbus, Ohio, on the 17th day of April, A. D. 1919.

68 G.

145

AN ACT

To amend sections 11, 12, 13, 14, and 15 of an act entitled "An act to provide for the appointment of a commission to acquire a site, and to prepare and adopt plans for the erection thereon of a new penitentiary," passed April 19th, 1913, and approved May 2nd, 1913. (103 Ohio Laws, pp. 247-250).

Be it enacted by the General Assembly of the State of Ohio:
SECTION 1. That sections 11, 12, 13, 14 and 15 of an act entitled "An act to provide for the appointment of a commission to acquire a site, and to prepare and adopt plans for the erection thereon of a new penitentiary," passed April 19th, 1913, and approved May 2nd, 1913, (103 Ohio Laws, pp. 247-250), be amended to read as follows:

Sec. 11. Such commission shall prepare ground plans of and plans for the erection of a new penitentiary in its entirety, or for any building, groups of buildings, or any parts or units of the new penitentiary, upon the site so purchased or appropriated by the state; it shall, by visitation or otherwise, secure information, employ a competent architect, and do whatever else may be necessary and essential to obtain the best possible plans for this purpose. The compensation of such architect shall be fixed by the commission, and shall, together with other expenses incident to the preparation of such plans, be paid in the same manner as other expenses of the commission. The employment and compensation of such architect shall be subject to the approval of the governor. *Duties of commission as to plans.* *Employment of architect; approval.*

Sec. 12. Before any ground plans or plans for the erection of a new penitentiary, or of any building, or groups of buildings or any parts or units of the new penitentiary, are finally approved and adopted by the commission, such plans shall be exhibited in the state house for not less than fifteen days, and any criticism of the same shall be considered by such commission in determining whether such plans shall be finally adopted. *Exhibition of plans in state house..*

Sec. 13. Such commission shall determine what ground plans and plans for the erection of the new penitentiary in its entirety, or for any building, groups of buildings, or any parts or units of the new penitentiary shall be adopted by formal vote of the commission at a public meeting. The plans adopted by the commission shall thereupon be submitted to the governor for his approval; if approved by him such plans shall be the final plans for the erection of the new penitentiary in its entirety, or for any building, groups of buildings, or any parts or units of the new penitentiary, and thereafter shall not be changed except when necessary, and then upon the consent of the governor, the penitentiary commission and the board of administration. *Adoption of plans; approval by governor; change of plans.*

Ohio Board of Administration empowered to construct penitentiary.

·Sec. 14. Upon the final approval of such final plans, or upon the final approval of the final plans of any building or groups of buildings or any parts or units of the new penitentiary, the Ohio board of administration is' authorized and empowered to construct such building or groups of buildings or any parts or units of such new penitentiary, or such new penitentiary in its entirety, upon said site so purchased or appropriated by the state, out of funds to be appropriated for that purpose by the General Assembly, such construction in all things to conform to and be governed by the plans approved as provided by this act. After the final approval of such plans in whole or in part as herein provided, and during the period of construction of any building or groups of buildings or any parts or units of said new penitentiary, and until such new penitentiary is wholly completed, the penitentiary commission, in addition to the performance and execution of other duties and powers in this act conferred upon it shall, until relieved by the governor, act in an advisory capacity to the board of administration; such construction, including the preparation and grading and laying out of said site, shall be done, so far as possible, by prisoners of the penitentiary or the prisoners of any other penal or reformatory institution of the state of Ohio. Before the board of administration shall proceed to do any work other than by the direct labor of prisoners, the·approval of the governor shall be first secured.

Commission to act in advisory capacity until relieved.

Work which cannot be performed by prisoners to be let by contract.

Sec. 15. Work on said site and buildings which cannot be performed by the direct labor of prisoners, the board of administration shall award by contract. In letting such contracts and in erecting said buildings the board of administration shall be governed in all things by the provisions of sections 2314 to 2332, inclusive, of the General Code of Ohio governing the erection, alteration and improvement of state buildings; except that it may accept the bid of any contractor as to all or a part of the work and may do a part of the work by direct labor of the prisoners in the penitentiary. Before any contract is entered into by the board of administration it shall be submitted to the governor who shall hear any complaints against the same, and at his discretion may order the board to readvertise. The board of administration may adopt such other provisions as to the terms of such bids and in the letting of contracts as it may deem necessary.

Repeals.

SECTION 2. That said original sections 11, 12, 13, 14 and 15 of said act be and the same are hereby repealed.

Emergency act.

SECTION 3. This act is hereby declared to be an emergency law necessary for the immediate preservation of the public peace, health and safety. Such necessity arises from the fact that the state is in immediate need of a new penitentiary in which to confine persons convicted and sentenced for felonies, and also because the state has acquired the necessary land for which a large sum of money has been

appropriated and paid, and has in course of construction
thereon the new penitentiary, but by reason of ambiguity
in the present law such construction work has been suspended and is being delayed, thereby endangering the
public peace, health and safety.

act is not
general and
ad re-
no sec-
number.
G. PRICE,
Attorney
General.

> CLARENCE J. BROWN,
> *President of the Senate.*
> CARL R. KIMBALL,
> *Speaker of the House of Representatives.*

Passed April 8, 1919.
Approved April 17, 1919.

> JAMES M. COX,
> *Governor.*

Filed in the office of the Secretary of State at Columbus,
Ohio, on the 17th day of April, A. D. 1919.

69 L.

[House Bill No. 309.]

AN ACT

To authorize the board of education of Madison township school district of Butler county, Ohio, to pay Mary Williamson, the sum
of four hundred and thirteen dollars.

Be it enacted by the General Assembly of the State of Ohio:

SECTION 1. That the board of education of Madison
township school district of Butler county, Ohio, be and it
is hereby authorized to allow and pay to Mary Williamson,
out of any funds under its control and not otherwise appropriated, the sum of four hundred and thirteen dollars,
being the amount of her salary for a period from September
3, 1917, to February 23, 1918. Upon the order of the
board of education, the clerk of such board is hereby authorized to issue his duplicate warrant in favor of Mary Williamson for the above amount upon receipt of the original
warrants illegally issued for the amount covered by such
warrants.

Board of educa-
tion authorized
to pay Mary
Williamson.

act is not
general or
na-
re-
no sec-
nber.
PRICE,
General.

> CARL R. KIMBALL,
> *Speaker of the House of Representatives.*
> CLARENCE J. BROWN,
> *President of the Senate.*

Passed April 8, 1919.
Approved April 17, 1919.

> JAMES M. COX,
> *Governor.*

Filed in the office of the Secretary of State at Columbus,
Ohio, on the 17th day of April, A. D. 1919.

70 L.

[Senate Bill No. 121.]

AN ACT

To provide a seal for the state department of health for the authentication of records and to authorize the administering of oaths.

Be it enacted by the General Assembly of the State of Ohio:

Section 1232-1.

Seal of "The State Department of Health."

SECTION 1. The state department of health shall have a seal bearing the following inscription: "The State Department of Health of Ohio." The seal shall be affixed to all writs, orders and authentications of copies of records and to such other instruments as the commissioner of health or public health council shall direct. All courts shall take judicial notice of said seal.

Section 1233-1.

Transcript of journal under seal accepted in court.

SECTION 2. The commisioner of health shall keep a journal in which entry shall be made of all official acts performed by him. A certified transcript of an entry in such journal or certified transcript of a recorded action of the public health council when impressed with the seal of the state department of health shall be accepted in court in lieu of the original journal entry or of the record of the public health council.

Section 1234-1.

Power to administer oaths.

SECTION 3. The commissioner of health and the secretary of the public health council shall have power to administer oaths in all parts of the state so far as the exercise of such power is incidental to the performance of the duties of the commissioner of health or the public health council.

The sectional numbers on the margin hereof are designated as provided by law. JOHN G. PRICE, Attorney General.

CLARENCE J. BROWN,
President of the Senate.
CARL R. KIMBALL,
Speaker of the House of Representatives.

Passed April 9, 1919.
Approved April 17, 1919.

JAMES M. COX,
Governor.

Filed in the office of the Secretary of State at Columbus, Ohio, on the 17th day of April, A. D. 1919.

71 G.

149

AN ACT

To amend sections 1579-91, 1579-92, 1579-93, 1579-97, 1579-102, 1579-111a, 1579-119 and to add supplemental sections 1579-92a, 1579-92b, 1579-92c and 1579-126a of the General Code, relating to the municipal court of Hamilton, Butler county.

Be it enacted by the General Assembly of the State of Ohio:
SECTION 1. That sections 1579-91, 1579-92, 1579-93, 1579-97, 1579-102, 1579-111a and 1579-119 of the General Code be amended, and supplemental sections 1579-92a, 1579-92b, 1579-92c and 1579-126a be added, to read as follows:

Sec. 1579-91. Said municipal court shall be presided over by one judge, designated as a "Municipal Judge," whose term of office shall be for a period of four years, beginning on the first day of January after his election, and shall hold office until his successor is duly elected and qualified. Such municipal judge shall receive such compensation payable out of the treasury of the city of Hamilton, Ohio, not less than two thousand dollars per annum, payable monthly, as the council may prescribe, and such further compensation payable out of the treasury of Butler county, Ohio, not less than one thousand dollars per annum, payable monthly, as the county commissioners may prescribe. Said municipal judge at the time of his election or appointment shall be a qualified elector and resident of the city of Hamilton, Ohio, and have been admitted to the practice of law in the state of Ohio for not less than five years. The present incumbent of said office of municipal judge or his successor for the unexpired term in case of a vacancy, shall serve out his present term which expires the first day of January, 1922 and until his successor is duly elected and qualified. A municipal judge of said court shall be elected at the regular municipal election in November, 1921 and in every fourth year thereafter.

Sec. 1579-92. Said municipal court herein established shall have the same jurisdiction in criminal matters and prosecutions for misdemeanors, or violations of ordinances as heretofore had by the mayor of Hamilton and any justice of the peace, and in addition thereto shall have ordinary civil jurisdiction within the limits of said city of Hamilton in the following cases:

1. In all actions and proceedings of which justices of the peace have or may be given jurisdiction.

2. In all actions and porceedings at law for the recovery of money or personal property of which the courts of common pleas have, or may be given jurisdiction, when the amount claimed by any party, or the appraised value of the personal property, sought to be recovered, does not exceed one thousand dollars, and in such actions judgment may be rendered for over one thousand dollars when the

excess over one thousand dollars shall consist of interest and damages, or costs accrued after the commencement of the action.

3. In all actions on contracts expressed or implied by law or in fact, when the amount claimed by the plaintiff does not exceed one thousand dollars, and in such action judgment may be rendered for over one thousand dollars when the excess over one thousand dollars shall consist of interest or damages, or costs accrued after commencement of the action. When a cause rising out of a contract is pending in the municipal court and when the ends of justice demand that an account be taken or that the contract or contracts be reformed or cancelled, the municipal court shall have jurisdiction to decree such accounting, reformation or cancellation.

4. In all actions and proceedings whether legal or equitable, to enforce the collection of its own judgments.

5. In all actions and proceedings for the sale of personal property under a chattel mortgage, lien or other charge or encumbrance, irrespective of amount, and for the foreclosure and marshaling of all liens thereon and the rendering of personal judgment therein, irrespective of amount, in favor of any party.

6. In all actions and proceedings for the sale of real property under the lien of a judgment of a municipal court, or the lien thereon for machinery, material or fuel furnished or labor performed irrespective of amount, and in such cases the court may proceed to foreclose and marshal all liens thereon, and all rights, vested or contingent therein, and to render personal judgment, irrespective of amount, in favor of any party.

7. In all actions and proceedings in the nature of creditor's bills and in aid of execution, to subject the interest of a judgment debtor in real or personal property to the payment of a judgment of the municipal court.

8. In all actions and proceedings in the nature of interpleader.

Jurisdiction within limits of Butler county. Sec. 1579-92a. The municipal court shall have jurisdiction within the limits of the county of Butler:

1. To compel attendance of witnesses in any pending action or proceeding.

2. To issue execution on its own judgments.

3. In all actions and proceedings whether legal or equitable, to enforce the collection of its own judgments.

4. In all actions and proceedings in the nature of creditor's bills, and in aid of execution to subject the interest of a judgment debtor in real or personal property to the payment of a judgment of the municipal court and in such cases the court may proceed to marshal and foreclose liens thereon, irrespective of amount, and all rights, vested or contingent, therein.

5. In all actions and proceedings where one or more

defendants resides or is served with summons in the city of Hamilton.

Sec. 1579-92b. In any action or proceeding of which the municipal court has jurisdiction of the subject matter, when the defendant, or some one of the defendants, resides or is served with summons in the city of Hamilton, the municipal court shall have jurisdiction, and summons, writs and process may be issued to the sheriff of any county against one or more of the defendants.

When summons, writs and process shall issue to sheriffs.

Sec. 1579-92c. Whenever an action or proceeding is properly brought in the municipal court, the court shall have the jurisdiction to determine, preserve and enforce all rights involved therein and to afford all legal and equitable remedies therefor.

Empowered to afford complete remedies.

Sec. 1579-93. In all causes the municipal court shall have jurisdiction in every ancillary and supplemental proceeding before and after judgment, including attachment of person or property, arrest before judgment, interpleader, aid of execution, trial of the right of property, revivor of judgment, and the appointment of a receiver, for which authority is now, or may hereafter be conferred upon the court of common pleas, or a judge thereof, or upon justices of the peace; and in all cases wherein the justices of the peace are given or may hereafter be given jurisdiction in this state the procedure in such ancillary and supplemental proceeding shall be the same as is now, or may hereafter be provided for similar proceedings in the courts of the justices of the peace, and in all other causes the proceedings shall be the same as are now or may hereafter be provided for similar proceedings in the court of common pleas.

Jurisdiction in ancillary and supplemental proceedings.

Sec. 1579-97. Whenever the appraised value of property sought to be recovered or sold (save in the excepted instances heretofore set forth) in any action in the municipal court exceeds $1,000.00, the judge of the municipal court shall certify the proceedings in the case to the court of common pleas of Butler county and thereupon the clerk of the municipal court shall file the original papers and pleadings, together with a certified transcript of the docket and journal entries in the case, in the office of the clerk of said common pleas court. The bailiff shall turn over the property in his possession to the sheriff of Butler county, to be by him held as in like cases originating in the court of common pleas. The case must then proceed as if it had been commenced there.

When proceedings certified to common pleas court.

Sec. 1579-102. In all civil actions and proceedings the cost of summoning jurors and the fees of jurors shall be taxed as part of the costs and such costs may be required in advance from the party demanding the jury, or said party may, in lieu thereof, file an affidavit of inability to make such advance deposit.

Cost of summoning and juror fees may be required in advance.

Sec. 1579-111a. In all cases not otherwise specially provided by law, either party may appeal from the final judgment of the municipal court to the court of common

Appeal to court of common pleas.

pleas of Butler county in the same manner and under the same conditions as is now provided or which may hereafter be provided for appeal from a court of a justice of the peace to the court of common pleas except as otherwise provided for in this act. Appeals in the following cases shall not be allowed:

1. On judgments rendered on confessions.

2. Cases tried by a jury.

3. In an action for the forcible entry and detention or forcible detention of real property.

4. In an action where neither party claims in his statement of claim a sum larger than $100.00.

5. In trials for the right of property under the statutes, either levied upon by execution or attached.

Sec. 1579-119. Except as otherwise provided for in this act, in all actions and porceedings wherein a court of a justice of the peace is given jurisdiction, the fees and costs may be the same and taxed in the same manner as is now, or may hereafter be provided for actions and proceedings heard and determined in a court of a justice of the peace. In other actions and proceedings the fees and costs may be the same, and taxed in the same manner, as is now, or may hereafter be, provided for actions and proceedings heard and determined in the court of common pleas. In criminal proceedings all fees and costs may be the same as is now, or may hereafter be fixed in police courts of the state of Ohio. Provided, however, that the municipal court, in lieu of the aforesaid methods of taxing costs, by rule of court may establish a schedule of fees and costs to be taxed in all actions and proceedings, in no case to exceed fees and costs provided for like actions and proceedings by a general law.

Sec. 1579-126a. No justice of the peace in any township in Butler county, or mayor of any village, in any proceeding, whether civil or criminal, in which any warrant, order of arrest, summons, order of attachment or garnishment or other process except subpoenas for witnesses, shall have been served upon a citizen or resident of Hamilton or a corporation having its principal office in Hamilton shall have jurisdiction, unless such service be actually made by a personal service within the township or village in which said proceeding may have been instituted or in a criminal matter, unless the offenes charged in any warrant or order of arrest shall be alleged to have been committed within said township or village.

SECTION 2. That original sections 1579-91, 1579-92, 1579-93, 1579-97, 1579-102, 1579-111a and 1579-119 of the General Code be, and the same are hereby repealed. Repeals.

CARL R. KIMBALL,
Speaker of the House of Representatives.
CLARENCE J. BROWN,
President of the Senate.

Passed April 3, 1919.
Approved April 17, 1919.

JAMES M. COX,
Governor.

Filed in the office of the Secretary of State at Columbus, Ohio, on the 18th day of April, A. D. 1919.

72 G.

[House Bill No. 347.]

AN ACT

To amend sections 1579-197, 1579-198, 1579-204, 1579-207, 1579-220, 1579-224, 1579-226, 1579-229 of the General Code, enlarging the jurisdiction of the municipal court of Alliance, Ohio, providing for certain officers thereof, and defining their powers and duties.

Be it enacted by the General Assembly of the State of Ohio:
SECTION 1. That sections 1579-197, 1579-198, 1579-204, 1579-207, 1579-220, 1579-224, 1579-226, 1579-229 of the General Code be amended to read as follows:
Sec. 1579-197. Said municipal court herein established shall have the same jurisdiction in criminal matters and prosecutions for misdemeanors, for violations of ordinances as mayor of cities and any justice of the peace, and in addition thereto shall have ordinary civil jurisdiction within the limits of said city of Alliance and townships of Lexington and Washington, in the county of Stark and state of Ohio, in the following cases: Jurisdiction in criminal and civil proceedings.
(1) In all actions and proceedings of which justices of the peace, or such courts as may succeed justice of the peace courts, have or may be given jurisdiction.
(2) In all actions and proceedings at law for the recovery of money and of personal proerty of which the court of common pleas has or may be given jurisdiction, when the amount claimed by any party, or the appraised value of the personal property sought to be recovered does not exceed one thousand dollars, and in such actions, judgment may be rendered for over one thousand dollars, when the amount over one thousand dollars shall consist of interest or damages, or costs accrued after the commencement of the action.
(3). All actions on contracts express or implied, when the amount claimed by the plaintiff, exclusive of all costs,

does not exceed one thousand dollars. When a cause arising out of a contract is pending in the municipal court and when the ends of justice demand that the contract or contracts be reformed or rescinded, the municipal court shall have jurisdiction to decree such reformation or recession.

(4). All actions or proceedings, whether legal or equitable to enforce the collection of its own judgments.

(5). All actions for the sale of personal property under chattel mortgage, lien or other charge or incumbrance upon personal property, and for marshalling of all liens thereon when the appraised value of such property shall not exceed one thousand dollars.

(6). All actions and proceedings for the sale of personal property under lien of judgment of the municipal court or lien for material or fuel furnished or labor performed and for the marshalling of all liens thereon.

(7). All actions and proceedings in the nature of creditors' bills in aid of execution, to subject the interest of a debtor in real or personal property to the payment of a judgment of the municipal court.

(8). All actions and proceedings in the nature of interpleader and involving one thousand dollars or less, but parties may interplead as to larger amounts in any action originally instituted, involving one thousand dollars or less.

(9). Whenever an action or proceeding is properly brought in the municipal court, the court shall have jurisdiction to determine, preserve, and enforce all rights involved therein and to afford all legal and equitable remedies therefor.

Jurisdiction within Stark county; to compel attendance of witnesses from certain townships outside Stark county.

Sec. 1579-198. The municipal court shall have jurisdiction within the limits of Stark county.

(1). To compel attendance of witnesses in any pending action or proceeding; also to compel the attendance of witnesses from the township of Knox, Columbiana county, the township of Smith, Mahoning county, and the townships of Deerfield and Atwater, Portage county, state of Ohio.

(2). To issue execution on its own judgments.

(3). In all actions and proceedings whether legal or equitable to enforce the collection of its own judgments.

(4). In all actions and proceedings where one or more defendants resides or is served with summons in the townships of Lexington or Washington, county of Stark and state of Ohio; and, in all actions or proceedings of which the municipal court has jurisdiction of the subject matter when the defendant, or some one of the defendants, resides or is served with summons in the townhsips of Lexington or Washington, county of Stark and state of Ohio, the municipal court shall have jurisdiction, and summons, writs and process may be issued to the sheriff of any county against one or more of the defendants and in any action or proceeding of which the municipal court has jurisdiction of the subject-matter, when one or more of the defendants may, under the laws of Ohio, be summoned from any county of the state into the county of Stark in which the municipal court of Alliance is located.

Sec. 1579-204. Civil actions and proceedings in the municipal court shall be commenced as in the common pleas court, and action shall be deemed pending so as to carry notice thereof to third persons from the delivery of the summons or writ by the clerk to the bailiff for service. *Commencement of actions.*

(1). All writs and process in the municipal court shall be served and returned by the bailiff if service is to be made within Stark county, Ohio, or by publication, in the same manner as is now, or may hereafter be provided by law for the service and return of writs and process in the court of common pleas. Where the manner of service is not so provided for, service and return may be made in the same manner provided by law for the service and return of process and writs issued by a police court or mayor or a justice of the peace, or by the common pleas court. *Service of writs and process.*

(2). The return day shall be fixed by rule of court and the summons or writs shall, unless accompanied with an order to arrest, be served at least three days before the return day of the summons, writ or process. *Return day.*

(3). In all civil cases in the municipal court, the plaintiff before issuing a summons, shall file a petition setting out his statement of claim, and the defendant shall file an answer setting out a statement of any set-off, counter-claim or defense which he may desire to assert or make. The statement of answer containing a statement of defense shall be filed in such cases, and within such time as may be required by rule of court. In such cases where an answer is required, the summons shall set forth the date when such answer shall be filed, as fixed by rule of court, which shall be not less than seven days, after the return day of the summons, but the court may grant leave for further time to file such answer on good cause shown. The statement shall set forth in plain, direct language the facts constituting the cause of action, set-off, counter-claim or defense. *Filing of petition and answer.*

(4). To expedite the business and promote the ends of justice, said judge may from time to time, adopt, publish and revise rules relating to the matters of practice and procedure, classify the causes of action in the court, and prescribe with reference to each class the degree of particularity with which a cause of action, set-off, counter-claim or defense shall be set up. Until otherwise provided by rule of court and except as herein provided, the practice as to pleadings and procedure shall be governed by the civil code of procedure provided for the common pleas court of the state. *Rules of practice and procedure.*

Sec. 1579-207. All causes in the municipal court both civil and criminal, shall be tried to the court unless, in civil cases, before the day assigned for trial of a cause upon *When cause shall be tried by jury.*

the merits of the cause, a jury shall be demanded in writing by either party to the action, and unless in criminal cases a demand for a jury trial is made by the accused before the court shall proceed to inquire into the merits of the cause, otherwise a jury shall be deemed to be waived. In all civil actions where a jury shall be demanded, except as hereinafter provided, it shall be composed of six men, having qualifications of electors unless the parties agree on a less number; provided, however, that when the amount claimed by any party or the appraised value of the personal property sought to be recovered exceeds the sum of two hundred dollars, either party may demand a jury of twelve men by specifying that number in said written demand. In all actions and proceedings in said municipal court, of which police courts in cities have or may hereafter be given jurisdiction, where a jury may be and is demanded, it shall be composed of twelve men having the qualifications of electors. In all civil actions a jury shall render a verdict upon the concurrence of three-fourths or more of their number.

Election of clerk; term, compensation and bond.

Sec. 1579-220. A clerk for said municipal court shall be elected at the next regular municipal election after the going into effect of this act for a term of four years, commencing on the first day of January next after said election, and shall hold said office until his successor is duly elected and qualified and shall receive such compensation payable out of the treasury of the city of Alliance not less than twelve hundred dollars per annum, payable in monthly installments, as the city council may prescribe. Before entering upon the duties of his office, the clerk of the municipal court shalll give a bond to the city of Alliance in the sum of five thousand dollars ($5,000.00), with surety to the approval of the municipal judge conditioned upon the faithful performance of his duties as such clerk. The said bond shall be given for the benefit of the city of Alliance, and for the benefit of any person who may suffer loss by reason of a default in any of the conditions of said bond. Deputies to the clerk shall be designated as hereinafter provided in this act.

Designation of bailiff; compensation; bond.

Sec. 1579-224. One bailiff shall be designated as hereinafter provided for in this act. He shall perform for the municipal court, services similar to those usually performed by the sheriff for courts of common pleas and by the constable of courts of justices of the peace. Such bailiff shall receive such compensation not less than six hundred dollars per annum payable out of the treasury of the city of Alliance in monthly installments as the council may prescribe. Before entering upon his duties, said bailiff shall make and file in the office of the clerk of the city of Alliance, a bond in the amount of not less than two thousand dollars. The terms and sufficiency of said bond shall be subject to the approval of the judge of the court. The said bond shall be given for the benefit of the city of Alliance and of any person who shall suffer loss by reason of the default of any of the conditions of said bond. The bailiff or deputy bailiff shall receive from the treasury of the city of Alliance, in addition to his compensation his actual expenses in serving process of the court and in transporting prisoners under his control, payable upon the order of the municipal judge.

Sec. 1579-226. The council of the city of Alliance shall provide suitable accommodations for the municipal court and its officers, including a private room for said judge and sufficient jury room. The council shall also provide for the use of the court complete sets of the reports of the supreme and inferior courts of Ohio and such other authorities as it shall be deemed necessary and shall provide for the court room the latest edition of the General Code of Ohio and necessary supplies, including telephone, stationery, furniture, heat and janitor services; and council shall provide for such other ordinary or extraordinary expense as it may deem advisable or necessary for the proper operation or administration of said court. *Accommodations and equipment.*

Sec. 1579-229. Whenever the incumbent of any office created by this act, excepting the municipal judge shall die, resign, be temporarily absent or incapacitated from acting, the judge shall appoint a substitute who shall have all the qualifications required of the incumbent of the office. Such appointee shall serve until the return of the regular incumbent, or until his incapacity ceases, or in case of death or resignation until a successor is elected or appointed and qualified. In case said judge shall be incapacitated from sitting in any case, or by reason of absence or inability be unable to attend sessions of said court, the mayor of the city of Alliance may appoint some attorney having the qualifications required by this act, to act in his stead until said judge is able to resume his said position. Such appointments shall be certified by the court or mayor as the case may be and entered upon the record, provided, however, that in the event an attorney at law receives the appointment, nothing contained in this act nor in other laws of Ohio, shall prevent the acting municipal judge from practicing as an attorney and counselor at law, in any other court in said state, in any and all matters of business not originated or pending in said municipal court. *Substitute when officer incapacitated, absent, dies or resigns.*

SECTION 2. That the said original sections 1579-197, 1579-198, 1579-204, 1579-207, 1579-220, 1579-224, 1579-226, *Repeals.*

and 1579-229 of the General Code be, and the same are hereby repealed.

CARL R. KIMBALL,
Speaker of the House of Representatives.
CLARENCE J. BROWN,
President of the Senate.

Passed March 26, 1919.

This bill was presented to Governor Cox on April 8th, 1919, and was not signed or returned to the house wherein it originated within ten days after being so presented, exclusive of Sundays and the day said bill was presented and was filed in the office of the Secretary of State, April 21st, 1919.

ROBERT T. CREW,
Veto Clerk.

Filed in the office of the Secretary of State at Columbus, Ohio, on the 21st day of April, A. D. 1919.

73 G.

[House Bill No. 581.]

AN ACT

To amend section 13560 of the General Code, relative to proceedings before grand juries, as amended on the fourth day of February, 1919.

Be it enacted by the General Assembly of the State of Ohio:

SECTION 1. That section 13560 of the General Code be amended to read as follows:

Sec. 13560. The prosecuting attorney or assistant prosecuting attorney,. except as hereinafter provided, shall be * * * authorized at all times to appear before the grand jury for the purpose of giving information relative to a matter cognizable by it or advise upon a legal matter when required. Such attorney may interrogate witnesses before such jury when it or he deems it necessary, but no other person shall be permitted to remain in the room with the jury while the jurors are expressing their views or giving their votes on a matter before them. In * * * matters or cases which the attorney general is required to investigate or prosecute by the governor or general assembly, he * * * shall have and exercise any or all the rights, privileges and powers conferred by * * * law upon prosecuting attorneys, and any assistants or special counsel designated by him for that purpose shall have full power and authority to act for and on behalf of the attorney general in any matter or case in which he is authorized to act, and any stenographer designated by him for that purpose shall have the same privileges and authority in relation to the proceedings conducted by him as are provided in case of the official stenographer of the county acting at the request of the prosecuting attorney and shall make disclosure of testimony taken or heard only to such grand jury or the attorney general and such assistants or special counsel, and all proceedings in relation to such matters or cases shall be under the exclusive supervision and control of the attorney general; and for the purpose of any investigation or prosecution conducted by the attorney general pursuant to direction by the governor or general assembly, the court of common pleas of any county or a judge thereof, on written request of the attorney general, shall order the sheriff to call together a special grand jury from the bystanders or neighboring citizens of fifteen good and lawful men having the qualifications of grand jurors, who shall be returned and sworn, and shall proceed in the manner provided by the laws relating to grand juries. Such special grand jury may be called and discharge its duties either before, during or after any session of the regular grand jury, and its proceedings shall be independent of the proceedings of the regular grand jury, but of the same force and effect.

SECTION 2. That original section 13560 of the General Code, as amended on the fourth day of February, 1919, be and the same is hereby repealed.

SECTION 3. This act is hereby declared to be an emergency act necessary for the immediate preservation of the public peace and safety. Such necessity exists because of the reason that an epidemic of crime prevails in some parts of the state resulting in the loss of life and property to many citizens, and it is essential that the attorney general, as the chief law officer of the state, and the courts of the state should be clothed with power sufficient to authorize the immediate institution of all investigations and prosecutions and the calling of special grand juries, appropriate for the speedy punishment of criminals and the termination of lawlessness.

CARL R. KIMBALL,
Speaker of the House of Representatives.
CLARENCE J. BROWN,
President of the Senate.

Passed April 17, 1919.
Approved April 21, 1919.

JAMES M. COX,
Governor.

Filed in the office of the Secretary of State at Columbus, Ohio, on the 21st day of April, A. D. 1919.

74 G.

[Amended Senate Bill No. 77.]

AN ACT

To amend section 1288 of the General Code and to grant osteopathic physicians an examination in surgery by the state medical board.

Be it enacted by the General Assembly of the State of Ohio:

SECTION 1. That section 1288 of the General Code be amended to read as follows:

Sec. 1288. The provisions of this chapter shall not apply to an osteopathic physician who passes an examination before the state medical board in the subjects of anatomy, physiology, obstetrics, surgery and diagnosis in the manner required by the board, receives a certificate from such board, and deposits it with the probate judge as required by law in the case of other certificates. Such certificate shall authorize the holder thereof to practice osteopathy and surgery in the state, but shall not permit him to prescribe or administer drugs, except anesthetics and antiseptics. No osteopathic physician holding a license to practice osteopathy at the time of the passage of this act, shall be permitted to practice major surgery, which shall be defined to mean the performance of those surgical operations attended by mortality from the use of the knife or other surgical instruments, until he shall have passed the examination in surgery given by the state medical board, but he may practice minor and orthopedic surgery, not in conflict with the definition of major surgery in this act. The certificate of an osteopathic physician may be refused, revoked or suspended as provided in section 1275 of the General Code of Ohio.

SECTION 2. That original section 1288 of the General Code be, and the same is, hereby repealed.

CLARENCE J. BROWN,
President of the Senate.
CARL R. KIMBALL,
Speaker of the House of Representatives.

Passed April 8, 1919.
Approved April 22, 1919.

JAMES M. COX,
Governor.

Filed in the office of the Secretary of State at Columbus, Ohio, on the 23rd day of April, A. D. 1919.

75 G.

Marginal notes:

Requirements to practice osteopathy.

May practice major surgery only after passing examination.

Refusal, revocation and suspension of certificate.

Repeal.

The sectional number in this act is in conformity to the General Code.
JOHN G. PRICE,
Attorney General.

[House Bill No. 174.]

AN ACT

To amend section 12788 of the General Code, relating to the protection of motormen and conductors.

Be it enacted by the General Assembly of the State of Ohio:
SECTION 1. That section 12788 of the General Code be amended to read as follows:

Sec. 12788. Whoever, being an officer, agent, or employee in authority, of a corporation, individual, or association, directs or permits to be operated an electric car, other than a trail car (whether such electric car be a passenger car, a freight car, a sweeper or other car), unprovided at the forward end with a screen of glass or other material sufficient to completely protect from dust, wind and storm the motorman or other person or persons stationed there for guiding or operating such car, or who fails to maintain during the entire period succeeding October 31st of each year and ending on each succeeding April 15th, within any electric car so being operated, whether a passenger car, a trail car, or other car (except in freight cars) and (excepting in trail cars) within the space behind any such screen, a temperature at all times of not less than sixty degrees Fahrenheit, shall be fined not less than twenty-five dollars nor more than one hundred dollars, for each day during which at any time such a car is operated while so unprovided, or while such temperature is not so maintained. It shall be the duty of the prosecuting attorneys of the various counties of the state of Ohio to enforce the provisions of this act.

SECTION 2. That original section 12788 of the General Code be, and the same is hereby repealed.

CARL R. KIMBALL,
Speaker of the House of Representatives.
CLARENCE J. BROWN,
President of the Senate.

Passed April 3, 1919.
Approved April 22, 1919.

JAMES M. COX,
Governor.

Filed in the office of the Secretary of State at Columbus, Ohio, on the 23rd day of April, A. D. 1919.

76 G.

Screen for protection of motormen and conductors required.

Temperature of 60° to be maintained.

Repeal.

The sectional number in this act is in conformity to the General Code. JOHN G. PRICE, Attorney General.

162

AN ACT

To amend secfion 1693 of the General Code, relating to the compensation of court constables.

Be it enacted by the General Assembly of the State of Ohio:
SECTION 1.   That section 1693 of the General Code be amended to read as follows:

Compensation of court constables.

Sec. 1693.   Each constable shall receive the compensation fixed by the judge or judges of the court making the appointment.   In counties where four or more judges regularly hold court, said compensation shall not exceed eighteen hundred and twenty dollars each year, in counties where two judges and not more than three judges hold court at the same time, not to exceed twelve hundred and fifty dollars each year, and in counties where only one judge holds court, such amount, not to exceed one thousand dollars each year, as may be fixed by the court, and shall be paid monthly from the county treasury on the order of the court.   Such court constable or constables when placed

Additional compensation.

by the court in charge of the assignment of cases, may be allowed further compensation not to exceed one thousand five hundred dollars per year, as the court by its order entered on the journal determines.   In counties where only one judge holds court the constable provided for herein, when not attending the common pleas court, shall upon the order of the judge of such common pleas court, and without additional compensation, attend the probate court and the court of appeals of said county.

Repeal.

SECTION 2.   That said original section 1693 of the General Code as amended in 107 Ohio Laws page 689, be and the same is hereby repealed.

CLARENCE J. BROWN,
President of the Senate.
CARL R. KIMBALL,
Speaker of the House of Representatives.

The sectional number in this act is in conformity to the General Code. JOHN G. PRICE, *Attorney General.*

Passed April 15, 1919.
Approved April 22, 1919.

JAMES M. COX,
Governor.

Filed in the office of the Secretary of State at Columbus, Ohio, on the 23rd day of April, A. D. 1919.

77 G.

[House Bill No. 290.]

AN ACT

To supplement section 2766 of the General Code of Ohio, by the enactment of supplemental section 2766-1, providing for plats, records and documents for use of county and municipal authorities.

Be it enacted by the General Assembly of the State of Ohio:

SECTION 1. That section 2766 of the General Code be supplemented by the enactment of supplemental section 2766-1, to read as follows:

Sec. 2766-1. Whenever the county recorder, county auditor and county treasurer or a majority of them, determine to provide, for the convenience of the various county officials and the more efficient performance of their duties, including the duties perscribed by section 8572-1 to section 8572-118, General Code of Ohio, plats, records, abstracts, books, copies of records, abstracts of records, existing or destroyed by fire or otherwise, or other documents or instruments affecting the title of any lands, tenements or hereditaments within the county, they may acquire the same by purchase, lease or rental; when so acquired, the same shall be kept up and maintained in the office of the county recorder or county auditor, as said officials shall determine, and the same shall be at all times subject to the use, examination, and inspection of the public and all officials of the county and the municipalities therein, and of their subordinates.

Plats, records and documents for use of county and municipal authorities.

CARL R. KIMBALL,
Speaker of the House of Representatives.
CLARENCE J. BROWN,
President of the Senate.

The sectional number in this act is in conformity to the General Code. JOHN G. PRICE, Attorney General.

Passed April 4, 1919.
Approved April 22, 1919.

JAMES M. COX,
Governor.

Filed in the office of the Secretary of State at Columbus, Ohio, on the 23rd day of April, A. D. 1919.
78 G.

164

[House Bill No. 99.]

AN ACT

To prevent the spread of hog cholera and other diseases, regulating
the business of disposing of the bodies of dead animals by the
process of burying, burning, or cooking; providing for the issuance of licenses to persons, firms or corporations, permitting
them to follow such business; providing for the inspection of
plants where such business is carried on; providing for the violation of any of its provisions.

Be it enacted by the General Assembly of the State of Ohio:

Sec. 1177-60.

License required to dispose of bodies of dead animals.

SECTION 1. That any person, firm or corporation desiring to engage in the business of disposing of the bodies
of dead animals, by burying, burning, or cooking; and any
person, firm or corporation in such business and desiring
to continue same, shall first procure from the secretary of
agriculture a license to do so, which license shall be for a
period of one year and no longer. No license shall be
required under the provisions of this act prior to January
1, 1920.

Sec. 1177-61.

Who deemed en-
gaged in the
business.

SECTION 2. Any person, firm or corporation who shall
obtain from any other person, firm or corporation, by purchase or otherwise, the body of an animal for the purpose
of obtaining the hide, skin or grease from such dead animal or for the purpose of disposing of the carcass of such
dead animal in any way whatsoever, shall be deemed to
have engaged in the business of disposing of the bodies of
dead animals and shall be subject to all the provisions and
penalties of this act. This act shall not apply to any person, firm or corporation engaged in the business of gathering up and disposing of the bodies of dead fowls, cats,
dogs, and other small animals in cities and villages under
contract with such cities and villages to dispose of such
dead bodies as garbage, nor to any person in such city or
village who may employ another person to lawfully and
legally dispose of the body of any animal which may have
died in such city or village. Nothing in this act shall apply
to the original owner disposing of carcasses of dead animals
on his own premises.

**To whom act
does not apply.**

Sec. 1177-62.

Application for
license; fee.

SECTION 3. Any person, firm or corporation desiring
a license to engage in such business shall file an application
for such license with the secretary of agriculture. Such
applicant, at the time he files such application shall pay
to the secretary of agriculture a fee of $50.00. In case
more than one inspection of the premises of said applicant
is necessary as hereinafter provided the applicant shall
pay a further fee of $25.00 for each such inspection before
the licenses shall be issued.

Sec. 1177-63.

Inspection of
premises of ap-
plicant before
license issued.

SECTION 4. Immediately after the filing of said application the secretary of agriculture shall cause the premises,
where such applicant desires to conduct such business, to
be inspected. If the secretary of agriculture shall find that

such applicant is a responsible person, firm or corporation, and that the rules and regulations of the secretary of agriculture as hereinafter provided have been complied with, he shall issue a license to such applicant.

If said secretary of agriculture shall find that such rules and regulations have not been complied with; he shall notify the applicant of that fact and shall specify in writing the changes that must be made before such license will be issued.

Upon request of the applicant and payment by him of the additional fee provided for in section 3 the secretary of agriculture shall cause a second inspection to be made and such proceedings shall be had as in the case of the first inspection. Second inspection.

1177-64.

SECTION 5. The secretary of agriculture shall make and cause to be printed such reasonable rules and regulations for the carrying on of such business, for the physical and sanitary conditions of the premises and equipment as may seem to him to be necessary and proper. He shall furnish copies of such rules and regulations to any person who shall apply for them. Publication of rules and regulations.

1177-65.

SECTION 6. The secretary of agriculture, in person or by deputy, shall inspect or cause to be inspected each place licensed under this act at least once each year, and as often as the secretary of agriculture may require, and shall see that the licensee conducts the business in conformity to this act and to the rules and regulations made and established by the secretary of agriculture. For failure or refusal to obey the provisions of this act or said rules and regulations by any licensee, the secretary of agriculture may suspend or revoke the license held by such licensee. Annual inspection; revocation of license.

.1177-66.

SECTION 7. Proper blank applications for licenses shall be provided and furnished free to the applicant by the secretary of agriculture. Blank applications furnished.

1177-67.

SECTION 8. Any person, firm or corporation holding license under the provisions of this act may haul and transport hogs which are afflicted with and carcasses of hogs that have died of disease in a covered wagon bed or tank which is water tight and is so constructed that no drippings or seepage can escape from such wagon bed or tank. Provided, however, such wagon bed or tank shall be so constructed as to conform to the rules and regulations that may be established by the secretary of agriculture and said carcasses shall not be moved from said wagon bed or tank except at the place of final disposal. Transportation of animals; regulations.

1177-68.

SECTION 9. Any person, firm or corporation violating any of the provisions of this act, shall be deemed guilty of a misdemeanor, and upon conviction shall be fined not less than fifty dollars nor more than two hundred dollars; such fines and penalties to be collected in the name of the state of Ohio. All moneys received for fines and license fees under this act shall be paid to the secretary of agriculture and by him paid into the state treasury. Penalty for violations; application of fines and fees.

Sec. 1177-69.
Prosecution.

SECTION 10. It shall be the duty of the attorney general or any county prosecuting attorney to prosecute all violations of this act when so requested by the secretary of agriculture.

Sec. 1177-70.
Courts having jurisdiction.

SECTION 11. A justice of the peace, mayor or police judge shall have final jurisdiction within his county in prosecutions relating to violations of the provisions of the law relating to the business of disposing of the bodies of dead animals and of transporting hogs afflicted with disease.

**The sectional numbers on the margin hereof are designated as provided by law.
JOHN G. PRICE, Attorney General.**

CARL R. KIMBALL,
Speaker of the House of Representatives.
CLARENCE J. BROWN,
President of the Senate.

Passed April 8, 1919.
Approved April 22, 1919.

JAMES M. COX,
Governor.

Filed in the office of the Secretary of State at Columbus, Ohio, on the 24th day of April, A. D. 1919.

79 G.

[House Bill No. 254.]

AN ACT

To amend sections 1579-6, 1579-8, 1579-16, 1579-20, 1579-26, 1579-36 and 1579-39 of the General Code, relating to the municipal court of Cleveland and enlarging its jurisdiction.

Be it enacted by the General Assembly of the State of Ohio:

SECTION 1. That sections 1579-6, 1579-8, 1579-16, 1579-20, 1579-26, 1579-36 and 1579-39 of the General Code be amended to read as follows:

Civil jurisdiction in Cleveland.

Sec. 1579-6. The municipal court shall have original civil jurisdiction within the limits of the city of Cleveland in the following cases:

1. In all actions and proceedings of which justices of the peace have or may be given jurisdiction.

Recovery of money or personal property.

2. In all actions and proceedings at law for the recovery of money or personal property of which the courts of common pleas of the county of Cuyahoga have or may be given jurisdiction, when the amount claimed by any party, or the appraised value of the personal property sought to be recovered, does not exceed twenty-five hundred dollars, and in such actions judgment may be rendered for an amount over twenty-five hundred dollars when the excess over twenty-five hundred dollars shall consist of interest or damages, or costs accrued after the commencement of the action.

Action on contract when amount does not exceed $2,500.

3. In all actions on contracts, express or implied in law or in fact, when the amount claimed by the plaintiff does not exceed twenty-five hundred dollars, and in such

actions judgment may be rendered for over twenty-five hundred dollars when the excess over twenty-five hundred dollars shall consist of interest or damages or costs accrued after commencement of the action. When a cause rising out of contract is pending in the municipal court and the ends of justice demand that an account be taken or that the contract or contracts, be reformed or cancelled, the municipal court shall have jurisdiction to decree such accounting, reformation, or cancellation.

4. In all actions and proceedings, whether legal or equitable, to enforce the collection of its own judgments. *Collection of judgments.*

5. In all actions and proceedings for the sale of personal property under a chattel mortgage, lien or other charge or encumbrance, irrespective of amount, and for the foreclosure and marshaling of all liens thereon, and the rendering of personal judgment therein, irrespective of amount, in favor of any party. *Sale under chattel mortgage, lien etc.*

6. In all actions and proceedings for the sale of real property under the lien of a judgment of a municipal court, or the lien thereon for machinery, material or fuel furnished or labor performed irrespective of amount, and in such cases the court may proceed to foreclose and marshal all liens thereon, and all rights vested or contingent, therein, and to render personal judgment irrespective of amount in favor of any party. *Sale of real property under lien.*

7. In all actions and proceedings in the nature of creditor's bills, and in aid of execution to subject the interest of a judgment debtor in real or personal property to the payment of a judgment of the municipal court. *Creditor's bills or in aid of execution.*

8. In all actions and proceedings in the nature of interpleader. *Interpleader.*

9. In any action for the foreclosure of a mortgage on real property given to secure the payment of money, the enforcement of a specific lien for money or other incumbrance or charge on real property, when the amount claimed by the plaintiff does not exceed twenty-five hundred dollars and the real porperty is situated within the limits of the city of Cleveland, and in such cases the court may proceed to foreclose all liens thereon and all rights vested and contingent therein and proceed to render such judgments, and make such findings and orders, between the parties, in the same manner and to the same extent as in like cases in the court of common pleas. *Foreclosure of mortgage.*

Sec. 1579-8. In any action or proceeding of which the municipal court has jurisdiction of the subject matter, when the defendant or some one of the defendants resides or is served with summons in the city of Cleveland, the municipal court shall have jurisdiction, and summons, writs and mesne and final process, including executions, may be issued to the sheriff of any county against one or more of the parties. *When summons, writs, etc., shall issue to sheriff.*

Proceedings certified to common pleas court, when.

Sec. 1579-16. Whenever the appraised value of property sought to be recovered in any action in the municipal court exceeds twenty-five hundred dollars, the judge of the municipal court shall certify the proceedings in the case to the court of common pleas of Cuyahoga county, and thereupon the clerk of the municipal court shall file the original papers and pleadings, together with a certified transcript of the docket and journal entries in the case, in the office of the clerk of said court of common pleas. The bailiff shall deliver the property in his possession to the sheriff of Cuyahoga county, to be by him held as in like cases originating in the court of common pleas, and the case shall then be proceeded with in said court as though originating therein.

All appraisal of property sought to be recovered in any action in the municipal court shall be made in the manner hereinafter provided.

Practice and procedure in criminal cases.

Sec. 1579-20. In all criminal cases and proceedings, the practice and procedure and mode of bringing and conducting prosecutions for offenses, and the powers of the court in relation thereto, shall be the same as those which are now, or may hereafter be, possessed by police courts in municipalities.

Approval of surety.

All recognizances for the appearance of a defendant, charged with an offense, when the offense is bailable, shall be entered into before the clerk and approved by him; and the surety or sureties therein shall be qualified by the clerk as provided by law.

Qualifications of surety.

One surety in every such bond must be a resident within the jurisdiction of the court, and the sureties must own property worth double the sum to be secured, and must have real estate within the county of Cuyahoga liable to execution of a value equal to the sum to be secured; and when two or more sureties are offered to the same bond or recognizance, they must have in the aggregate the qualification prescribed herein. The recognizance shall require the prisoner to appear before the court to answer the charge against him or before the court of common pleas, when the defendant is held to the grand jury as provided by law.

What recognizance shall disclose.

The recognizance shall clearly disclose the full name of the surety or sureties, together with the residence address, and there shall be endorsed thereon, a brief but pertinent description of the real estate owned by such surety or sureties.

When bond a lien.

When the recognizance or bond shall be thus entered into, approved and accepted, the same shall become a subsisting lien on the real estate of the surety or sureties therein, upon which they have qualified, until the recognizance shall have been exonerated or discharged.

Certified copy of bond filed with recorder; fee.

A copy of every such bond or recognizance, duly certified under the seal of the court by the clerk, as a true copy, shall be filed by him with the recorder of Cuyahoga county forthwith, unless in the meantime the defendant shall have been acquitted or discharged by the court. The said recorder shall provide a suitable record book, properly indexed, in which he shall record all recognizances certified to him as herein provided. The recorder shall be entitled to receive from the clerk, such fees and record charges as are now authorized by law for recording deeds and mortgages; and such fees and charges shall be taxed by the clerk in the costs of the respective cases, and shall be paid to the recorder by the clerk from funds in his hands upon certified vouchers or bills rendered by said recorder.

The clerk shall transmit to the recorder each day a certified list under the seal of the court, of all bonds or recognizances which have been exonerated or discharged, and the recorder shall note on the margin of the record of each recognizance the discharge or satisfaction of the same, and the lien on the real estate of the surety or sureties in such recognizance or bond shall thereby be cancelled and discharged. *List of discharged bonds filed with recorder.*

The clerk shall not approve nor accept as surety or sureties on any such recognizance any person who is then liable on any recognizance or bond theretofore executed in the municipal court, unless it shall appear to the satisfaction of the clerk, that the person offering himself as surety has sufficient equity in his real estate over and above his liability thereon, to justify the subsequent bond or bonds as herein provided, or unless said prior bond or bonds shall have been exonerated and discharged. *Clerk shall not approve surety, when.*

The clerk shall be entitled to tax in the costs of the case, such fee or fees for making the copies and certificates herein required as the court may by rule provide. *What fees taxed in costs.*

Provided, however, that in all misdemeanor cases, the clerk, in lieu of the surety or sureties herein required, may accept a deposit of money, in United States legal tender, in an amount equal to the penal sum stipulated in the bond or recognizance, and in any felony case a judge of the municipal court may direct the clerk to accept such a deposit in an amount fixed by the judge, which amount shall be the sum stipulated in the recognizance or bond, and such deposit shall be retained by the clerk as security thereon until the recognizance or bond shall have been exonerated and discharged; and in the event of the forfeiture of any such bond or recognizance, the clerk shall apply the money so deposited in satisfaction of any judgment that may be rendered on the recognizance and the depositor of such fund shall surrender and forfeit all right in and to the same to the extent of such judgment. *Deposit of money in lieu of bond.*

Sec. 1579-26. In all civil cases when a jury trial is demanded the party making such demand may, by rule of court, be required to make an advance deposit of ten dollars for a jury of six men and twenty dollars for a jury of twelve men; provided, however, the party making such demand may by leave of court, file in lieu of such deposit *Deposit when jury demanded.*

of ten dollars, an affidavit of inability to make such advance deposit when a jury of six men is demanded.

Sec. 1579-36. Proceedings in error may be taken to the court of appeals of Cuyahoga county from a judgment or final order of the municipal court in the same manner and under the same conditions as are provided by law for proceedings in error from the court of common pleas to the court of appeals; provided, however, no proceedings to reverse, vacate or modify, such a judgment or final order shall be commenced unless within sixty days after the overruling of the motion for a new trial, or the entry of the judgment or final order complained of, when the motion for a new trial is not filed; or in case the person entitled to such proceedings is an infant, a person of unsound mind, or imprisoned within forty days, exclusive of the time of such disability. And provided further:—

Proceedings in error taken to court of appeals; limitations.

That in actions in forcible entry and detention the party objecting to the finding of the court on questions of law and evidence shall reduce his objections to writing and present same to the trial court not more than ten days after the overruling of a motion for a new trial of said action, and no petition in error to reverse, modify or vacate the judgment or final order in such cases shall be filed in the court of appeals except upon leave of said court of appeals or a judge thereof, and upon notice of such application being first given to the opposite party.

And provided further that in all criminal actions and proceedings of which the municipal court has final jurisdiction, if the defendant shall deem himself aggrieved by a decision of the court he may present his bill of exceptions thereto, within ten days from the overruling of a motion for a new trial, or from the date the decision, judgment or sentence of the court is entered, which bill of exceptions the court shall allow and sign if the same be correct, and it shall be made a part of the record, and the taking of all bills of exceptions shall be governed by the rules established in civil cases and shall have like force and effect. For good cause shown, the time for signing and allowing a bill of exceptions in any criminal case may be extended a further period not exceeding ten days, by the judge with whom it is filed, and in which event the extension must be endorsed on the bill by such judge.

And provided further, that in all proceedings in error relating to judgments or orders of the municipal court, the reviewing courts shall take judicial notice of all rules relating to pleading, practice or procedure of the municipal court.

When any error proceedings has been determined or dismissed by the court of appeals, the clerk of such court shall immediately after the time allowed by law for the commencement of proceedings to review the judgment of said court of appeals, if such proceedings have not been commenced, transmit to the clerk of the municipal court all of the original papers and pleadings in such case.

Sec. 1579-39.   Stay of execution on the following judgments shall not be allowed: Stay of execution not allowed on certain judgments.

1.   Judgments against sureties or bail for the stay of execution.

2.   Judgments rendered in favor of sureties or bail who have been compelled by judgment to pay money on account of their principal.

3.   Judgments rendered against a surety on a bond or undertaking given in any action or proceeding in any court.

4.   Judgments for an amount not exceeding $100.00 rendered in favor of any person for wages due for manual labor by him performed.

5.   Judgments and decrees in actions of foreclosure of mortgages, mechanics' liens and in proceedings to subject real property to the payment of judgments and marshaling of liens.

SECTION 2.   That said original sections 1579-6, 1579-8, 1579-16, 1579-20, 1579-26, 1579-36, and 1579-39 of the General Code be, and the same are hereby repealed. Repeals.

CARL R. KIMBALL,
Speaker of the House of Representatives.
CLARENCE J. BROWN,
President of the Senate.

The sectional numbers in this act are in conformity to the General Code. JOHN G. PRICE, Attorney General.

Passed April 4, 1919.
Approved April 24, 1919.

JAMES M. COX,
Governor.

Filed in the office of the Secretary of State at Columbus, Ohio, on the 25th day of April, A. D. 1919.

80 G.

[House Bill No. 261.]

AN ACT

To establish a municipal court for the city of Newark, Licking county, Ohio, and fixing the jurisdiction thereof, and providing for a judge thereof, and other necessary officers, and defining their powers and duties.

Be it enacted by the General Assembly of the State of Ohio:

Sec. 1579-367.   SECTION 1.   That there be and hereby is created a court of record for the city of Newark, and the township of Newark, in the county of Licking, state of Ohio, to be styled "The Municipal Court of Newark, Ohio," the jurisdiction thereof to be as herein and hereinafter fixed and determined. Municipal court of Newark, Ohio.

Sec. 1579-368.

Municipal judge; qualifications, election, term and compensation.

SECTION 2. Said municipal court shall be presided over by one judge, to be designated herein as "Municipal Judge," which office is hereby created, and whose term of office shall be for a period of four years, and said judge shall receive such compensation, payable out of the treasury of Licking county, not more than eight hundred dollars, per annum, payable monthly, as the county commissioners may prescribe, and out of the treasury of Newark township, Licking county, Ohio, not more than two hundred dollars per annum payable monthly, as the township trustees may prescribe, and such further compensation, not more than two thousand dollars per annum, payable monthly out of the treasury of the city of Newark, Ohio, as the council of said city or other legislative authority may prescribe. Said municipal judge at the time of his election or appointment, and during the continuance of his office shall be a qualified elector and resident of either the township of Newark, or the city of Newark, Ohio, and have been admitted to the practice of law in the state of Ohio for a period of not less than three years. Said judge shall be elected at the next regular municipal and township election after the going into effect of this act, for a term of four years, commencing on the first day of January next, after said election, and shall hold said office until his successor is elected or appointed and duly qualified. Said judge shall be nominated and elected under the same general laws and statutes providing for the nomination and election of other judges.

Sec. 1579-369.

Removal; vacancy.

SECTION 3. The judge of the municipal court shall be subject to the same disabilities and may be removed from office for the same causes as the judge of the court of common pleas. The vacancy arising from any cause excepting as herein provided shall be filled by appointment by the governor of the state of Ohio.

Sec. 1579-370.

Judge may not practice law; employes shall not practice before court.

SECTION 4. The judge of the municipal court shall be disqualified from the practice of the law during the term of his office. Neither the judge, nor clerk, nor other employee of said court shall take or prosecute any claim or claims, or any cause of action whatsoever, nor defend the same, and neither he nor they shall accept any fee or gratuity whatsoever on account of services rendered or to be rendered in said court. The judge so doing shall be subject to impeachment, and the employees' summary dismissal.

Sec. 1579-371.

Acting judge; appointment, when.

SECTION 5. In case the judge of the municipal court shall be incapacitated from sitting in any case, or by reason of absence or illness be unable to attend sessions of said court, the mayor of the city of Newark, Ohio, may appoint some attorney having the qualifications required by this act. Such appointee shall serve until the return of the regular incumbent of the office and shall have the jurisdiction and powers conferred upon the judge of the municipal court herein, and be styled "Acting Judge" of the municipal court, and as such sign all process and records during the time he shall serve and perform all other acts pertaining to the office. All courts shall take judicial notice of the actions and powers of such persons.

Provided, however, that nothing contained in this act nor any other laws of Ohio, shall prevent the acting municipal judge from practicing as an attorney and counselor at law, in any other court in said state, or in any matter of business in said municipal court in which he is not engaged as attorney or counselor, in such cases in which he is engaged as attorney or counselor he shall be disqualified to perform any judicial functions.

Sec. 1579-372.

SECTION 6. In addition to the exercise of all powers of a judge of said court, he shall render a complete annual report to the council of the city of Newark, covering the preceding year, which report shall show the work performed by the court, a summary of all expenses of the civil and criminal branches of the court respectively, a statement of receipts and expenditures, the number of cases heard, decided and settled by the court, and the number of decisions of the municipal court reversed or affirmed by a reviewing court, and such data as the council may require. The conduct of the criminal branch shall be arranged by said judge. The judge of the municipal court may summon and impanel jurors, tax costs, preserve order, punish for contempt, and may exercise all powers in such matters which are now, or may hereafter be conferred upon the court of common pleas, or the judge thereof. *Annual report to council.*

Sec. 1579-373.

SECTION 7. The judge of the municipal court shall have jurisdiction and the authority to perform any and all acts conferred upon justices of the peace under the general laws of the state of Ohio, and such jurisdiction and authority to perform acts as by law may be hereafter created for such justice of the peace courts or justices of the peace. *Jurisdiction.*

Sec. 1579-374.

SECTION 8. To expedite the business of said court and promote the ends of justice, said judge may from time to time adopt, publish and revise rules relating to matters of practice in said court, not inconsistent with the provisions of this act. *Rules of practice.*

Sec. 1579-375.

SECTION 9. A clerk for said municipal court shall be appointed by the judge, who shall hold office until his successor is duly appointed and qualified, and shall receive such compensation payable out of the treasury of the city of Newark, Ohio, not more than fifteen hundred dollars per annum, payable monthly, as the council may prescribe. *Appointment of clerk; compensation.*

Sec. 1579-376.

SECTION 9-a. The clerk of the municipal court shall keep at least seven books, to be called the appearance docket, trial docket, journal, complete record, execution docket, city criminal record, and state criminal record. He shall keep a direct index to the trial docket, journal, city criminal record and state criminal record and shall keep a direct and reverse index to the appearance docket, complete record, and execution docket. Such records, and such other records as *Duties of clerk.*

shall be approved by the court shall be furnished said court by the city of Newark, Ohio.

Sec. 1579-377.

Powers of the clerk and further duties.

SECTION 10. The clerk of the municipal court shall have power to administer oaths, and take affidavits, and acknowledgments, and to issue executions upon any judgment rendered in the municipal court, including a judgment for unpaid costs; he shall have power to issue and sign all writs, processes and papers issuing out of the court, and to attach the seal of the court thereto; shall have power to approve all bonds, recognizances and undertakings, fixed by any judge of the court or by law; shall file and safely keep all journals, dockets, records, books and papers belonging to or appertaining to the court, record its proceedings and perform all other duties which the judge of the court shall prescribe. He shall pay over to the proper parties all monies received by him as clerk; he shall receive and collect all costs, fines and penalties, and shall pay the same monthly to the treasurer of the city of Newark, and the treasurer of the county of Licking, as is by law provided, and take their receipt therefor. He shall keep a record showing all receipts and disbursements, which shall be open for public inspection at all times, and he shall on the first Monday of each term make to the city auditor a report of all receipts and disbursements for the preceding term.

Sec. 1579-378.

Bond of clerk.

SECTION 11. Before entering upon the duties of his office, the clerk of the municipal court shall give a bond to the city of Newark, Ohio, in the sum of two thousand dollars, with surety to the approval of the judge of said court, conditioned upon the faithful performance of his duties as such clerk. The bond shall be given for the benefit of the city of Newark, Ohio, and the township of Newark, Licking county, Ohio, and for the benefit of any person who may suffer loss by reason of a default in any of the conditions of said bond.

Sec. 1579-379.

Deputy clerk; compensation, powers and duties.

SECTION 12. There shall also be appointed by the judge one deputy clerk who shall hold office until a successor has been appointed and qualified, and who shall receive such compensation payable out of the treasury of the city of Newark, Ohio, not more than nine hundred dollars per annum, payable monthly, as the city council may prescribe. Such deputy clerk shall have the power to administer oaths, take affidavits, issue process and perform any and all of the duties of the clerk herein prescribed.

Sec. 1579-380.

Bond of deputy clerk.

SECTION 13. Before entering upon the duties of office, the deputy clerk of the municipal court shall give a bond to the city of Newark, Ohio, in the sum of one thousand dollars, with surety to the approval of the judge of said court, conditioned upon the faithful performance of the duties as deputy clerk. The bond shall be given for the benefit of the city of Newark, and the township of Newark, Licking county, Ohio, and for the benefit of any person who may suffer loss by reason of a default in any of the conditions of said bond.

Sec. 1579-381 SECTION 14. One bailiff shall be appointed by the judge of the municipal court. He shall perform for the municipal court, services similar to those usually performed by the bailiff, and sheriff for the court of common pleas, and by the constable of the courts of justice of the peace. Such bailiffs shall receive such compensation not more than one thousand dollars per annum, payable monthly, out of the treasury of the city of Newark, Ohio, as the council of the city of Newark, Ohio, may prescribe, and such additional compensation for costs and expenses as will not exceed two hundred and fifty dollars yearly as the city council or county commissioners may allow. *Bailiff; compensation.*

Sec. 1579-382 SECTION 15. Before entering on his duties, said bailiff shall make and file in the office of the clerk of the city of Newark, Ohio, a bond in the amount of not less than two thousand dollars. Said bond shall be given for the faithful performance of his duties as bailiff, and shall be given for the benefit of the city of Newark, Ohio, and the township of Newark, Licking county, Ohio, and of any person who shall suffer loss by reason of the default of any of the conditions of said bond. *Bond of bailiff.*

Sec. 1579-383. SECTION 16. Every police officer of the city of Newark, Ohio, shall be ex officio a deputy bailiff of the municipal court, and the chief of police shall assign one or more such police officers from time to time to perform such duties in respect to cases within the jurisdiction of said court as may be required of them by said court or the clerk. Such deputy bailiff shall have the same power and authority as is conferred upon the bailiff under the terms of this act. *Ex officio bailiffs.*

Sec. 1579-384. SECTION 17. The court shall appoint an official stenographer who shall serve until his successor is appointed. The stenographer shall be entitled to a per diem compensation of five dollars to be charged as costs in such cases as his services may be required in a civil action upon request of either party. The party requesting such service shall in any event be liable for such services, if the opposing party is insolvent, and the costs of said service cannot be collected. The court may regulate the charge for transcripts of testimony, which in no event shall be more than that charged in the common pleas court of said county for similar work, and the cost thereof shall be paid to the clerk and by him accounted for. *Court stenographer; compensation.*

Sec. 1579-385. SECTION 18. The solicitor for the city of Newark, Ohio, shall also be prosecuting attorney of the municipal court. He may designate such number of assistant prosecutors as the council of the city of Newark, Ohio, may authorize. The persons thus appointed shall receive for their services in city cases such salary as the council may prescribe. The prosecuting attorney of the municipal court shall prosecute all cases of a criminal nature brought before such court and perform the same duties, so far as they *Solicitor shall be prosecuting attorney of the court.*

are applicable thereto, as are required of the prosecuting attorney of the county.

Sec. 1579-386.

Accommodations and equipment.

SECTION 19. The council of the city of Newark, Ohio, shall provide suitable accommodations for the municipal court and its officers, including a private room for said judge and a sufficient jury room. Council shall also provide the necessary supplies, including telephones, stationery, furniture, heat, light and janitor services.

Sec. 1579-387.

Seal of the court.

SECTION 20. The said municipal court shall have a seal which shall have engraved thereon the coat of arms of the state, and shall be approximately one inch in diameter and shall be surrounded by these words, "The Municipal Court of Newark, Ohio," and shall have no other words or device engraved thereon.

Sec. 1579-388.

Criminal and civil jurisdiction.

SECTION 21. Said municipal court herein established shall have the same jurisdiction in criminal matters and prosecutions for misdemeanors and felonies, for violations of ordinances and the criminal laws of the state, as mayors of cities and justices of the peace, and in addition thereto shall have civil jurisdiction within the said city of Newark, and Newark township in Licking county, in the state of Ohio, in the following cases:

(1) In all actions and proceedings of which justices of the peace, or such courts as may succeed justices of the peace, have or may be given jurisdiction.

(2) In all actions and proceedings at law for the recovery of money and of personal property of which the court of common pleas has or may be given jurisdiction, when the amount claimed by any party, or the appraised value of the personal property sought to be recovered does not exceed one thousand dollars, and in such actions judgment may be rendered for over one thousand dollars, when the amount over one thousand dollars, shall consist of interest or damages, or costs accrued after the commencement of the action.

(3) All actions for money only on contracts express or implied, when the amount claimed by the plaintiff, exclusive of costs and interest accrued after the commencement of an action, does not exceed one thousand dollars. When a cause arising out of a contract is pending in the municipal court and when the ends of justice demand that the contract or contracts be reformed or rescinded, the municipal court shall have jurisdiction to decree such reformation or recision.

Sub-division (4). In all actions and proceedings where one or more defendants resides or is served with summons in the township of Newark, or the city of Newark, Ohio, and, in all actions or proceedings of which the municipal court has jurisdiction of the subject matter when the defendant, or some of the defendants resides or is served with summons in the township of Newark, or the city of Newark, Ohio, the municipal court shall have jurisdiction, and summons, writs and process may be issued to the sheriff of any county in the state of Ohio, against one or more defendants, and in any action or proceeding of which the municipal court has jurisdiction of the subject matter, when one or more of the defendants may, under the laws of the state of Ohio, be summoned from any county of the state into the county of Licking in which the municipal court of Newark is located.

Sub-division (5). And generally, such civil, criminal and quasi-criminal jurisdiction as is now or hereafter may be conferred by general statutes upon police courts, justices of the peace courts or mayor's courts.

(6) All actions and proceedings for the sale of personal property under a lien of judgment of the municipal court or lien for material furnished or labor performed, and for the marshalling of all liens thereon.

(7) All actions and proceedings in the nature of creditor's bills in aid of execution, to subject the interest of a debtor in personal property to the payment of a judgment of the municipal court.

Sec. 1579-389.

SECTION 22. The municipal court of Newark, Ohio, shall have jurisdiction within the limits of Licking county:—

(1) To compel the attendance of witnesses in any pending action or proceeding.

(2) To issue execution on its own judgments.

(3) In all actions and proceedings, excepting to create liens upon or to sell real estate, whether the same be equitable or legal, to enforce the collection of its own judgments.

(4) In all actions and proceedings where one or more defendants resides in or is served with summons in the city of Newark or Newark township, Licking county, Ohio.

(5) And generally, such civil and criminal jurisdiction as is now or hereafter may be conferred by general statutes upon justices of the peace or mayor's courts.

Sec. 1579-390.

SECTION 23. Civil actions for money only and replevin in the municipal courts shall be commenced and deemed pending as in the common pleas court, and shall proceed· as to pleadings and otherwise as provided by the code of civil procedure excepting as herein specifically otherwise provided. All other actions shall be commenced and deemed pending, and shall proceed in the manner now or that may hereafter be provided for justices of the peace. *Commencement of actions; procedure.*

Sec. 1579-391.

SECTION 24. All writs and process in actions for money only and replevin in the municipal court shall be served and returned by the bailiff or a deputy, if service is to be made within Licking county, Ohio, or by publication, in the same manner as is now or may hereafter be provided for the service and return of writs and process in the court of common pleas, excepting as herein otherwise provided. In all other civil actions service and return shall be made in the same manner as is now or may hereafter be *Service of writs and process.*

provided by law for the service and return of process and writs issued by justice of the peace courts.

SECTION 25. In civil actions for money only and replevin, the return day of all writs shall be the third day after the issuance thereof and the defendant shall be required to plead within ten days from the return day of the writ unless such time is extended by leave of court, and the defendant shall plead to the answer within ten days after the same is filed, unless such time is extended by leave of court. All other civil actions shall follow the practice and procedure as is now or hereafter may be conferred by general statutes upon justice of the peace courts.

SECTION 26. In actions for money only predicated upon either a written contract, promissory note, book account, or other written evidence of debt, where the amount claimed by the plaintiff is fifty dollars or less, a copy of such instrument may be filed, and no other or future pleading is required to be filed by said plaintiff than a statement of what is claimed to be due thereon. The defendant need file no pleading unless a set-off or counter-claim is interposed, and if either or both be interposed a statement of the same must be filed setting forth the same in an informal way on or before the answer day herein provided. A defendant may urge any other defense without specially pleading the same. Summons must issue in such cases in the manner provided herein for other actions.

SECTION 27. All civil actions in the municipal court shall be tried to the court unless, before the day assigned for trial, a jury shall be demanded in writing by either party to the action. In all civil actions where a jury shall be demanded, it shall be composed of six men having the qualifications of electors of Newark township or the city of Newark, Ohio; in all criminal actions and proceedings in said municipal court, of which police or mayors' courts have or may hereafter be given jurisdiction, where a jury may be and is demanded, it shall be composed of twelve men having the qualifications of electors of Newark township or the city of Newark. In all civil actions a jury shall render a verdict upon the concurrence of three-fourths or more of their number.

SECTION 28. In all civil actions and proceedings, when the amount claimed by any party or the appraised value of the personal property sought to be recovered does not exceed three hundred dollars, the cost of summoning the jurors and the fees of the jurors shall be taxed as part of the costs, and such costs must be deposited or secured in advance by the party demanding a jury. In all civil actions and proceedings where the amount claimed by any party or the appraised value of the personal property sought to be recovered is in excess of three hundred dollars, the cost of summoning jurors and the fees of jurors shall be paid out of the treasury of Licking county, Ohio, and charged to the appropriate fund for the payment of jurors serving in

Sec. 1579-392.

Return day; practice and procedure.

Sec. 1579-393.

Pleadings when amount $50 or less.

Sec. 1579-394.

Jury trial may be had, when.

Sec. 1579-395.

Assessment and collection of jurors' fees and costs in civil actions.

the common pleas court, and shall be collected from the county and distributed by the clerk of the municipal court; provided, however, that when the amount claimed by any plaintiff, or by any defendant by way of counter-claim or set-off, shall exceed the sum of three hundred dollars, and in such case such claimant shall demand a jury and shall thereafter recover a verdict on his claim of less than fifty dollars, the fees of the jurors shall be taxed against such party so demanding such jury as a part of the costs, and when collected such jury fees shall be paid to the county and credited to the appropriate fund for the payment of jurors serving in the common pleas court.

Sec. 1579-396. SECTION 29. All jurors shall have the qualification of an elector of the township or city of Newark. Jurors in civil cases shall be summoned, impaneled and sworn in the manner provided by law for jurors in civil cases in the justice of the peace courts, and shall receive the same compensation as provided for jurors in justice of the peace courts. No juror shall serve more than once as juror in three months. Jurors in criminal cases shall be summoned, impaneled and sworn and receive such compensation as is provided for jurors in the mayors' courts in cities. *Qualifications of jurors.*

Sec. 1579-397. SECTION 30. Costs shall be taxed the same as in the common pleas court, excepting in such special proceedings where the practice and procedure of the justice of the peace courts is provided, and in such proceedings costs shall be taxed the same as in the justice of the peace court. All costs shall be taxed as herein specified, excepting as herein otherwise provided, and the judge of the municipal court may by rule provide for all cases not covered by this act a standard of fees and costs, not in excess of those provided by general laws. All payments and deposits of costs and jury fees shall be refunded when the same shall have been paid by the losing party. *Taxing costs; rules.*

Sec. 1579-398. SECTION 31. In all criminal cases and proceedings the practice and procedure and the mode of bringing and conducting the procedure of defenses and the powers of the court in relation thereto, shall be the same as those which are now, or may hereafter be possessed by the police courts, mayors' courts and justices of the peace courts, unless otherwise provided herein. And the municipal court shall exercise such jurisdiction as is now, or may hereafter be granted to such courts, in criminal matters. *Rules of practice and procedure.*

Sec. 1579-399. SECTION 32. Whenever the appraised value of the personal property sought to be recovered or sold (save in the excepted instances herein set forth) in any action in the municipal court, or in cases in which an interpleader is filed, exceeds one thousand dollars, the judge of the municipal court shall certify the proceedings in the case to the court of common pleas of Licking county, and thereupon the clerk of the municipal court shall file the original papers and pleadings together with a certified transcript of the docket and journal entries in the case, in the office *When appraised value exceeds $1,000, proceedings certified to common pleas court.*

of the clerk of the common pleas court. The bailiff shall turn over the property in his possession to the sheriff of Licking county, to be held by him as in like cases originating in the court of common pleas. The case shall then proceed as if it had been originally commenced in said common pleas court, without new service of porcess.

Sec. 1579-400.

Excess may be remitted, when amount exceeds jurisdiction.

SECTION 33. When the amount claimed by the defendant exceeds the sum for which the municipal court is authorized to render judgment, he may remit the excess, and judgment may be rendered for the residue. A defendant having a counter-claim or set-off which is in excess of such sum, may assert the same, and the municipal court shall have jurisdiction to hear and determine such counter-claim or set-off, and render judgment thereon to the amount of one thousand dollars, but such defendant shall not be thereby precluded from setting up the residue of his claim in a separate action. And, such defendant may, at his option, withhold setting up such counter-claim or set-off and may make the same the subject of a separate action.

Sec. 1579-401.

Ancillary and supplemental proceedings, jurisdiction in.

SECTION 34. In all causes the municipal court shall have jurisdiction in every ancillary and supplemental proceeding, before and after judgment including attachment of person or property, arrest before judgment, aid of execution, for which authority is now, or may hereafter be conferred upon the court of common pleas, or judge thereof, or upon justices of the peace, and the procedure may be the same as is provided by general statutes for either of such courts.

Sec. 1579-402.

Appointment of trustee to receive portion of personal earnings; distribution.

SECTION 35. The municipal court shall have jurisdiction upon the application of the debtor to appoint a trustee to receive that portion of the personal earnings of the debtor, which as against claims for necessaries is not exempt from execution, attachment, or proceedings in aid of execution, and such additional sums as the debtor may voluntarily pay or assign to said trustee, and to distribute the money pro rata among creditors having claims for necessaries against the debtor at the time of the application. When a trustee shall be so appointed, no proceedings in the attachment, aid of execution or otherwise to subject the personal earnings of the debtor to the payment of claims for necessaries shall be brought or maintained by any creditor having a claim against such debtor at the time of the application herein, before any justice of the peace or in any court, so long as at least fifteen per cent of the personal earnings of such debtor is paid to the trustee at regular intervals, as fixed by the court, provided, however, that this provision shall not be construed to prohibit creditors from recovering judgments against the debtor nor to prohibit the levy, under a writ of attachment or execution, upon any other property which is not exempt from execution. The maintaining of a proceeding in attachment, aid of execution or otherwise, in violation of the foregoing provisions, may be prevented by a writ of prohibition, in addition to all other remedies provided by law. The municipal court may provide by rule, for notice to creditors, the authentication and adjudication of claims, the time and manner of payments by the debtor, the distribution of the fund, and for all other matters necessary or proper to carry into effect the jurisdiction conferred by this section. The clerk of the municipal court, unless the order of appointment otherwise specifies, shall act as trustee, without additional compensation and his official bond shall be construed as conditional upon the fulfillment of the trust, and no additional bond shall be required. Clerk of court as trustee.

Sec. 1579-403.   SECTION 36. Where an order of attachment has been issued from the municipal court, and it appears from the return of the bailiff, or from the examination of a garnishee, that no property, moneys, rights, credits or effects of the defendant have been taken under the attachment, but that the defendant is the owner of an interest in real estate in the county, the judge of the municipal court, before whom the action is pending, must at the request of the plaintiff, forthwith certify his proceedings to the court of common pleas of Licking county, and thereupon the clerk of said court shall docket the cause, and the action shall be proceeded with in all respects as if the same had originated there. Proceedings certified to common pleas court, when.

Sec. 1579-404.   SECTION 37. All moneys deposited as security for costs, and all other moneys, other than costs, paid into the municipal court, shall be noted on the record of the case in which they are paid, and they shall be deposited by the clerk in such banking institutions as shall be designated under the city depository act, there to abide the order of the court. On the first Monday in January of each year the clerk shall make a list of the titles of all causes in the municipal court which were fully determined more than one year past, in which there remains unclaimed in the possession of the clerk any such funds, or any part of a deposit for security for costs not consumed by the costs in the case. The clerk shall give notice of the same to the parties entitled to said moneys, or to their attorneys of record. All such moneys remaining unclaimed on the first day of April of each year shall be paid by the clerk to the city treasurer, provided, however, that any part of such moneys shall be paid by such treasurer at any time to the court. Record of moneys. Unclaimed costs; notice.

Sec. 1579-405.   SECTION 38. The court at any time before trial may order any case which it deems peculiarly fit to be tried by a jury, to be so tried. It shall not be necessary for the court to charge the jury generally in matters submitted to it, but either party may present written instructions to the court on matters of law, and request them to be given to the jury, in the manner provided by the code of civil procedure. Court may order trial by jury.

Sec. 1579-406.

Laws governing courts of common pleas shall apply.

SECTION 39. The laws governing the court of common pleas as to security for costs, except as herein otherwise provided for, pleadings and procedure, motions for new trial, vacation or modification of judgments before and after terms, referring of matters to a referee, the issuing of execution, attachment, garnishment, order of arrest in civil cases, and the taking of depositions shall be held to

Stay of execution; bond.

apply so far as applicable to the municipal court. Provided, that a person against whom a judgment has been rendered in the municipal court may stay execution thereon by entering into a bond to the adverse party within ten days after the rendition of such judgment, with sufficient surety, who shall be a freeholder owning real property situated in the county of Licking, in the state of Ohio, or a corporation authorized to execute surety bonds in this state, approved by the clerk of the court, and conditioned for the payment of the amount of such judgment, interest and costs. Such bond shall be entered on the docket of the clerk of court and shall be signed by such surety. The giving of such bond shall in no manner impair any lien had against any property of said judgment debtor.

The stay of execution hereby authorized shall be graduated as follows:

(1) On a judgment of fifty dollars and under, for thirty days.

(2) On a judgment exceeding fifty dollars, but not exceeding five hundred dollars, for ninety days.

(3) On a judgment exceeding five hundred dollars, for one hundred and twenty days.

Sec. 1579-407.

Appeal shall not be taken; proceedings in error may be taken to court of appeals and court of common pleas.

SECTION 40. No appeal shall be taken from the judgment of the municipal court. Proceedings in error may be taken to the court of appeals of Licking county from a final judgment, order or decree of the municipal court, where the amount involved is three hundred dollars or more, in the same manner and under the same conditions as to time and otherwise as is now or may hereafter be provided by law for proceedings in error from the court of common pleas to the court of appeals. Where the amount involved is less than three hundred dollars proceedings in error may be had in such cases to the court of common pleas, in the same manner and under the same conditions as to time and otherwise as is now or may hereafter be provided for proceedings in error from the common pleas court to the court of appeals.

Sec. 1579-408.

Proof of records.

SECTION 41. The records of the municipal court may be proved by the production of the original records, or by a transcript thereof certified by the clerk of said court under its seal.

Sec. 1579-409.

Setting aside verdict or judgment.

SECTION 42. In all cases the municipal court shall have the same authority to set aside a verdict or judgment, as is now, or may hereafter be conferred upon courts of common pleas.

188

Sec. 1579-410.   SECTION 43. The party in whose favor a judgment is rendered by the municipal court may file a transcript of such judgment in the office of the clerk of common pleas, in the same manner and under the same conditions as are now, or may hereafter be provided for filing of transcripts of judgments rendered by justices of the peace; all provisions relative to transcripts of judgments and liens of judgments rendered by justices of the peace, shall so far as applicable, be applied to transcripts of judgments and liens of judgments rendered by the municipal court. *(Transcripts of proceedings.)*

Sec. 1579-411.   SECTION 44. The lien of judgment of the municipal court may be enforced in the courts of common pleas in the same manner as the lien of a judgment rendered by the court of common pleas. Execution may be issued on such judgments at any time after a transcript thereof has been filed, as if the judgment had been rendered by the court of common pleas, but all liens shall remain as provided by this act. *(Enforcement of liens.)*

Sec. 1579-412.   SECTION 45. The calendar of the municipal court shall be divided into four terms of three months each, beginning respectively, on the first day of January, April, July and October, of each year. The judge of the municipal court may continue the session of any terms of said court beyond the time fixed for the commencement of the next term, when such continuance is necessary to finish the trial of any cause, or to receive the verdict or pronounce judgment in any cause, the trial of which has been commenced during the term. *(Court calendar.)*

Sec. 1579-413.   SECTION 46. No justice of the peace in any township in Licking county, or mayor in any village, in any proceeding, whether civil or criminal, in which any warrant, order of arrest, summons, order of attachment, garnishment or replevin or other process, except subpoena for witnesses, shall have juirsdiction, either criminal or civil over a citizen or resident of the city of Newark and Newark township or a corporation or firm having its principal office therein, unless service be actually made by personal service within the township or village in which said proceedings may have been instituted, or a criminal matter, unless the offense charged in any warrant or order of arrest shall be alleged to have been committed within said township or village. *(Jurisdiction of justices and mayors; limitation in Newark and Newark township.)*

Sec. 1579-414.   SECTION 47. All proceedings, judgments, executions, dockets, papers, money, property and persons subject to the jurisdiction of the mayor's court of the city of Newark, and the courts of the justices of the peace of Newark township, in Licking county in December 31st, 1919, shall be turned over to the municipal court herein created, whereupon such courts shall cease and be abolished. Thereafter such causes shall proceed in the municipal court as if originally instituted therein, the parties making such amendments to their pleadings as the court may require to conform the same to the rules of the court herein established. *(All proceedings dockets, papers, etc., turned over to municipal court.)*

Sec. 1579-415.

Section or part held void shall not affect others.

SECTION 48. Each section and each subdivision of any section of this act is hereby declared to be independent, and the finding or holding of any section or subdivision of any section thereof to be invalid or void shall not be deemed or held to affect the validity of any other section or subdivision.

CARL R. KIMBALL,
Speaker of the House of Representatives.
CLARENCE J. BROWN,
President of the Senate.

The sectional numbers on the margin hereof are designated as provided by law.
JOHN G. PRICE,
Attorney General.

Passed April 8, 1919.

This bill was presented to the Governor April 16th, 1919, and was not signed or returned to the house wherein it originated within ten days after being so presented exclusive of Sundays and the day said bill was presented, and was filed in the office of the Secretary of State, April 29th, 1919.

ROBERT T. CREW,
Veto Clerk.

Filed in the office of the Secretary of State at Columbus, Ohio, on the 29th day of April, A. D. 1919.

81 G.

[House Bill No. 310.]

AN ACT

To amend section 3618-1 of the General Code, relating to the power of municipal corporations owning a municipal gas plant or system of gas distribution to purchase gas without advertisement or competitive bidding.

Be it enacted by the General Assembly of the State of Ohio:
SECTION 1. That section 3618-1 of the General Code be amended to read as follows:

When municipality may purchase gas without advertisement or competitive bidding.

Sec. 3618-1. That any municipal corporation owning a municipal gas plant or system of gas distribution shall have the power to purchase gas, natural or artificial, and to furnish the same to said municipality and the inhabitants thereof for the purposes of light, power and heat. To carry out the power herein conferred, any such municipality is hereby authorized to make and execute a contract to purchase such gas through its appropriate boards or officers for any period not exceeding ten years, upon the council of such municipality authorizing and directing such contract to be made; and such board or officer may enter into such contract for the purchase of such gas after being so authorized by such council, without advertisement or competitive bidding, irrespective of the amount of money to be expended. Any such municipality may furnish and supply to its inhabitants any gas, natural or artificial, so purchased, on such terms and under such regulations as may be determined by the proper officers and authorities of said municipality.

SECTION 2. That original section 3618-1 of the General Code be, and the same is hereby repealed. Repeal.

The sectional number in this act is in conformity to the General Code.
JOHN G. PRICE, Attorney General.

CARL R. KIMBALL,
Speaker of the House of Representatives.
CLARENCE J. BROWN,
President of the Senate.

Passed April 3, 1919.

This bill was presented to the Governor April 16th, 1919, and not signed or returned to the house wherein it originated within ten days after being so presented, exclusive of Sundays and the day said bill was presented and was filed in the office of the Secretary of State, April 29th, 1919.

ROBERT T. CREW,
Veto Clerk.

Filed in the office of the Secretary of State at Columbus, Ohio, on the 29th day of April, A. D. 1919.

82 G.

[Am. Senate Bill No. 87.]

AN ACT

To authorize and empower the commissioners of Franklin county to sell and convey the Franklin county children's home and to purchase grounds and erect a children's home for Franklin county.

WHEREAS, Prior to the year 1878 the board of county commissioners of Franklin county, Ohio, pursuant to law erected a children's home for said Franklin county, and have since and are still maintaining and using said home as a children's home for said county; and

WHEREAS, By reason of the increase of population in said Franklin county, said children's home is not of sufficient size nor suitable to accommodate and care for the children entitled to its care under the law; and

WHEREAS, By reason of the growth of the city of Columbus and the extension of its corporate limits, said city has grown to and around and wholly encloses said children's home, thereby rendering it unsuitable for the purposes of a children's home; and

WHEREAS, By reason of the growth of said city of Columbus, the price of adjoining and contiguous lands has increased in value until it is impracticable to purchase lands suitable for the enlargement of said present children's home, now therefore,

Be it enacted by the General Assembly of the State of Ohio:

Authority to sell Franklin County Children's Home; notice of sale. SECTION 1. The board of county commissioners of Franklin county, Ohio, are hereby authorized and empowered to sell and convey the present Franklin county children's home. Said sale shall be made after four weeks' advertisement in two newspapers of general circulation in Franklin county, Ohio, and that said sale shall be made to the highest and best bidders, and said board of county commissioners may at said bidding, reject any and all bids and readvertise the same, as herein provided for the sale of said premises.

Proceeds to purchase land and erect buildings for children's home; tax levy. SECTION 2. The commissioners of said county are hereby authorized and directed to use the amount of money derived from the sale of the present children's home in the purchase of farm lands and the erection thereon of suitable buildings and equipment for said children's home. The commissioners are hereby also authorized and directed to cause estimates to be made of the probable cost thereof and in order to defray the expenses of the same, the commissioners are authorized and directed to cause to be levied a tax upon all the taxable property in said county, and to issue the notes or bonds of the county in anticipation of the collection of the same for a sum of money not exceeding two hundred and fifty thousand dollars; that the county auditor and county treasurer be, and they are hereby authorized and directed to place said tax upon the duplicate of the taxable property of Franklin county for the purpose of the redemption of said notes or bonds of the county, as issued by said commissioners, and for the maintenance of the said institution as now provided by law. Said notes or bonds may be issued when, and in such amounts, as may be needed, and be redeemable at such period, as may be decided upon by said county commissioners; but in no case shall said bonds or notes be payable at a period longer than ten years from date of issue, and at a rate of interest no greater than six per centum per annum.

This act is not of a general and permanent nature and requires no sectional number. JOHN G. PRICE, Attorney General.

CLARENCE J. BROWN,
President of the Senate.

CARL R. KIMBALL,
Speaker of the House of Representatives.

Passed April 9, 1919.
Apporved May 6, 1919.

JAMES M. COX,
Governor.

Filed in the office of the Secretary of State at Columbus, Ohio, on the 6th day of May, A. D. 1919.

83 L.

[Senate Bill No. 43.]

AN ACT

To amend section 7620 of the General Code, relating to the powers
and duties of boards of education.

Be it enacted by the General Assembly of the State of Ohio:

SECTION 1. That section 7620 of the General Code, be
amended to read as follows:

Sec. 7620. The board of education of a district may   Powers and duties of boards.
build, enlarge, repair and furnish the necessary school
houses, purchase or lease sites therefor, or rights of way
thereto, or purchase or lease real estate to be used as play-
grounds for children or rent suitable schoolrooms, either
within or without the district, and provide the necessary
apparatus and make all other necessary provisions for the
schools under its control. It also, shall provide fuel for
schools, build and keep in good repair fences enclosing such
school houses, when deemed desirable plant shade and ornamental trees on the school grounds, and make all other pro- .
visions necessary for the convenience and prosperity of the
schools within the subdistricts.

SECTION 2. That original section 7620 of the General   Repeal.
Code be, and the same is hereby repealed.

The sectional
number in this
act is in con-
formity to the
General Code.
JOHN G. PRICE,
Attorney
General.

CLARENCE J. BROWN,
President of the Senate.
CARL R. KIMBALL,
Speaker of the House of Representatives.

Passed April 4, 1919.
Approved May 7, 1919.

JAMES M. COX,
Governor.

Filed in the office of the Secretary of State at Columbus,
Ohio, on the 7th day of May, A. D. 1919.

84 G.

[Senate Bill No. 49.]

AN ACT

To supplement section 12512 of the General Code by the enactment
of section 12512-1 to make it unlawful to tamper with fire
hydrants, pipes, mains, meters and other water works property.

Be it enacted by the General Assembly of the State of Ohio:

SECTION 1. That section 12512 be supplemented by the
enactment of section 12512-1 to read as follows:

Sec. 12512-1. Whoever, not the agent or employee for   Unlawful to tamper with hydrant, pipe, meter, etc.; penalty.
that purpose of the owner or operator thereof, maliciously
opens, closes, adjusts or interferes with a fire hydrant,
valve, regulator, gauge, gate, disc, curb-cock, stock cock,

meter or other regulator, operating or measuring device or appliance in or attached to the wells, tanks, reservoirs, conduits, pipes, mains, service pipes, house pipes or other pipes or apparatus of a water company or furnisher of water, with intent to cause the escape of water or to injure or destroy such property, or taps, severs, opens or makes unauthorized connections with a main or pipe used or intended for the transmission of water, shall be fined not less than twenty-five dollars nor more than three hundred dollars or imprisoned not more than thirty days or both; provided that nothing herein contained shall apply to anything done by or under authority of any regularly constituted fire department.

The sectional number in this act is in conformity to the General Code. JOHN G. PRICE, *Attorney General*.

CLARENCE J. BROWN,
President of the Senate.
CARL R. KIMBALL,
Speaker of the House of Representatives.
Passed April 15, 1919.
Approved May 7, 1919.

JAMES M. COX,
Governor.

Filed in the office of the Secretary of State at Columbus, Ohio, on the 7th day of May, A. D. 1919.

85 G.

[Substitute Senate Bill No. 96.]

AN ACT

To amend section 2252-1 of the General Code, relative to extra compensation of judges where probate and common pleas courts have been combined.

Be it enacted by the General Assembly of the State of Ohio:

Additional salary when probate and common pleas courts combined.

Sec. 2251-1. When in any county, having a population of less than sixty thousand, as ascertained by the federal census next preceding such election, by a vote of the electors thereof, the probate court shall be combined with the court of common pleas, the resident judge of the court of common pleas with which such probate court has been so combined shall, after such office has been so combined, receive, in addition to the salary provided for in sections 2251 and 2252, an annual salary of five hundred dollars. Such additional salary shall be paid quarterly from the treasury of such county upon the warrant of the county auditor.

SECTION 2. That original section 2252-1 of the General Code, be, and the same is hereby repealed. ~ ^{Repeals.}

The sectional number in this act is in conformity to the General Code. JOHN G. PRICE, Attorney General.

CLARENCE J. BROWN,
President of the Senate.
CARL R. KIMBALL,
Speaker of the House of Representatives.
Passed April 17, 1919.
Approved May 7, 1919.

JAMES M. COX,
Governor.

Filed in the office of the Secretary of State at Columbus, Ohio, on the 7th day of May, A. D. 1919.

86 G.

[House Bill No. 477.]

AN ACT

Defining the crime of criminal syndicalism and prescribing punishment therefor.

Be it enacted by the General Assembly of the State of Ohio:

Sec. 13421-23.

SECTION 1. That criminal syndicalism is the doctrine which advocates crime, sabotage, which is defined as the malicious injury or destruction of the property of another, violence, or unlawful methods of terrorism as a means of accomplishing industrial or political reform. The advocacy of such doctrine, whether by word of mouth or writing, is a felony, punishable as is in this act provided. ^{Criminal syndicalism defined.}

Sec. 13421-24.

SECTION 2. Any person who by word of mouth or writing, advocates or teaches the duty, necessity or propriety of crime, sabotage, violence or unlawful methods of terrorism as a means of accomplishing industrial or political reform; or prints, publishes, edits, issues or knowingly circulates, sells, distributes or publicly displays, any book, paper, document, or written matter in any form, containing or advocating, advising or teaching the doctrine that industrial or political reform should be brought about by crime, sabotage, violence or unlawful methods of terrorism; or openly, wilfully, and deliberately justifies, by word of mouth or writiing, the commission or the attempt to commit crime, sabotage, violence or unlawful methods of terrorism with intent to exemplify, spread or advocate the propriety of the doctrines of criminal syndicalism; or organizes or helps to organize or become a member of, or voluntarily assembles with any society, group or assemblage of persons formed to teach or advocate the doctrines of criminal syndicalism; is guilty of a felony and punishable by imprisonment in the state penitentiary for not more than ^{Penalty for advocating, teaching, editing, publishing, distributing, etc.}

ten years, or by a fine of not more than five thousand dollars, or both.

SECTION 3. Whenever two or more persons assemble for the purpose of advocating or teaching the doctrines of criminal syndicalism as defined in this act, such an assemblage is unlawful, and every person voluntarily participating therein by his presence, aid or instigation is guilty of a felony and punishable by imprisonment in the state penitentiary for not more than ten years, or by a fine of not more than five thousand dollars, or both.

SECTION 4. The owner, agent, superintendent, janitor, caretaker, or occupant of any place, building or room, who wilfully and knowingly permits therein any assemblage of persons prohibited by the provisions of section 3 of this act, or who, after notification that the premises are so used, knowingly permits such use to be continued, is guilty of a misdemeanor and punishable by imprisonment in the county jail for not more than one year or by a fine of not more than five hundred dollars, or both.

SECTION 5. This act is hereby declared to be an emergency act necessary for the immediate preservation of the public peace and safety. The emergency necessitating the enactment of this act arises out of the fact that there are persons in, and also persons threatening to enter, the state for the purpose of teaching the doctrine of criminal syndicalism as defined in this act, and advocating such doctrine . and the commission of the other acts and practices declared by this act to be unlawful, the tendency of which will be to destroy our institutions and government, and put the people into a condition of unrest and terror.

CARL R. KIMBALL,
Speaker of the House of Representatives.
CLARENCE J. BROWN,
President of the Senate.

Passed April 15, 1919.
Approved May 7, 1919.

JAMES M. COX,
Governor.

Filed in the office of the Secretary of State at Columbus, Ohio, on 7th day May, A. D. 1919.

87 G.

[Amended Senate Bill No. 63.]

AN ACT

Providing for the publication and distribution of the roster of Ohio soldiers, sailors and marines engaged in the war with the Central Powers of Europe.

Be it enacted by the General Assembly of the State of Ohio:

SECTION 1. The governor, secretary of state and adjutant general are hereby authorized to prepare and secure the publication in book form of a complete roster of all Ohio soldiers, sailors and marines who entered the service of the United States in the war of 1917-19 with the Central Powers of Europe. The preparation of such roster shall be under the direction and supervision of the adjutant general who shall employ such assistants and incur such expenses as may be necessary and the compensation of such assistants and such expenses shall be paid out of the state treasury on the warrant of the auditor of state upon the presentation of vouchers signed by the adjutant general. *(margin: Roster of Ohio soldiers, sailors and marines who served in war with Central Powers, authorized.)*

SECTION 2. Such roster shall contain the principal items of the record of each soldier, sailor or marine as shown by the rolls in the office of the adjutant general of Ohio and in the war and navy departments of the United States. In the preparation of such roster all names shall be arranged in alphabetical order if possible, or in such a manner as to render all information contained therein readily accessible. Preparation of the roster shall begin as soon as possible and continue until the work is completed. *(margin: Contents and arrangement.)*

SECTION 3. The contract for the printing of the roster shall be let to the lowest and best bidder, and such contract may be let for the entire roster or bids may be taken for the printing of each volume as completed. The binding shall be done at the state bindery under the direction of the supervisor of public printing and the general assembly shall make proper appropriations therefor. Not more than ten thousand copies or sets of such roster shall be printed and when completed shall be delivered to the secretary of state. *(margin: Printing and binding; number of copies.)*

SECTION 4. The distribution of said volumes shall be under the direction of the secretary of state and shall be as follows: To each member of the general assembly, ten copies or sets; to the adjutant general, for distribution to the adjutants general of each state and territory, and proper officials of the navy and war departments of the United States, one hundred copies or sets; to each elective state officer of Ohio, to be kept as a part of the official records of his office, one copy; to the state library, one hundred copies for exchange and ten copies to be retained permanently therein; to the Ohio Archaeological and Historical society, twenty-five copies; to each public library of the state, one copy; to each college or university library, one copy; to each county recorder, to be kept by him in his office and *(margin: Distribution and sale.)*

transferred to his successor as other public records, one copy. The remainder of said copies after such distribution shall be placed on sale by the secretary of state at a price to be fixed by the commissioners of public printing. The secretary of state shall keep a record of such sales and shall in the manner provided by law, pay into the state treasury weekly the amounts so collected by him, until all of said volumes are sold.

Appropriation.

SECTION 5. For the preparation and printing of the roster as provided for in this act there is hereby appropriated out of any moneys in the state treasury to the credit of the general revenue fund and not otherwise appropriated, the sum of fifty thousand dollars, and the general assembly may from time to time appropriate such other sums as may be necessary to carry out the purpose of this act.

This act is not of a general and permanent nature and requires no sectional number. JOHN G. PRICE, Attorney General.

CLARENCE J. BROWN,
President of the Senate.
CARL R. KIMBALL,
Speaker of the House of Representatives.
Passed April 17, 1919.
Approved May 7, 1919.

JAMES M. COX,
Governor.

Filed in the office of the Secretary of State at Columbus, Ohio, on the 8th day of May, A. D. 1919.

88 G.

[House Bill No. 25.]

AN ACT

To amend sections 4698, 4699 and 4701 of the General Code, relating to city school districts.

Be it enacted by the General Assembly of the State of Ohio:
SECTION 1. That sections 4698, 4699 and 4701 of the General Code be amended to read as follows:

Board in districts less than 50,000 population.

Sec. 4698. In city school districts containing according to the last federal census a population of less than 50,000 persons, the board of education shall consist of not less than three members nor more than five members elected at large by the qualified electors of such district.

In districts more than 50,000 and less than 150,000.

In city school districts containing according to the last federal census a population of 50,000 persons or more, but less than 150,000 persons, the board of education shall consist of not less than two members nor more than seven members elected at large or not less than two members nor more than seven members elected at large and not more than two members elected from subdistricts by the qualified electors of their respective subdistricts. The office of sub-

district member in boards of education in all such city
school districts having more than two subdistrict members
is hereby abolished and the terms of members elected from
such subdistricts shall terminate on the day preceding the
first Monday in January, 1920.

In city school districts containing according to the
last federal census a population of 150,000 persons or more,
the board of education shall consist of not less than five nor
more than seven members elected at large by the qualified
electors of such district; the office of subdistrict member
in boards of education in all such city school districts is
hereby abolished and the terms of members elected from
subdistricts shall terminate on the day preceding the first
Monday in January, 1920.

In districts more than 150,000.

Sec. 4699. Within thirty days after this act shall
take effect, the board of education of each and every city
school district in which the number of members does not
conform to the provisions of section 4698 shall by resolution
determine within the limits prescribed by said sections the
number of members of said board of education. Said resolution shall provide for the classification of the terms of
members so that they will conform to the provisions of
section 4702, General Code, taking into consideration the
terms of office of the existing members whose terms do not
expire or terminate on the day preceding the first Monday
in·January, 1920.

Boards must conform to the law within 30 days; resolution.

At the same time such boards of education in city
school districts containing according to the federal census
a population of 50,000 persons or over, but less than 150,000
persons, and electing to have subdistricts, shall subdivide
such city school district into subdivisions equal in number
to the number of members of the board of education in the
district, who are to be elected from subdistricts therein so
established. Such subdistricts shall be bounded, as far as
practicable, by corporation lines, streets, alleys, avenues,
public grounds, canals, watercourses, ward boundaries, voting precinct boundaries, or present school district boundaries, and shall be as nearly equal in population as possible and be composed of adjacent and as compact territory
as practicable. Such subdivision shall be numbered from
one up consecutively and the lines thereof so fixed shall not
be changed until after each succeeding federal census.
Within three months after the official announcement of the
result of each succeeding federal census, the board of education of each city school district which according to such
census shall have a population of 50,000 persons or over and
less than 150,000 persons, and shall elect to have subdistricts, shall redistrict such district into subdistricts in accordance with the provisions of this chapter. If the board
of education of any such district fails to district or redistrict such city school district, as herein required then
the state superintendent of public instruction shall forth-

Division into subdistricts; numbering.

with district or redistrict such city school district, subject to the requirements of this chapter.

Sec. 4701. Whenever the number of members of the board of education of a city school district is so fixed in the resolution provided for in section 4699, that the number of members of said board to be elected in the year 1921 in order to comply with the provisions of section 4702, exceeds the number of members whose terms expire on the day preceding the first Monday in January, 1922, such excess number of members of such school board shall be elected at the general school election in the year 1919 for such terms of two years necessary to comply with the provisions of sections 4698 and 4702.

Whenever the number of members of any such board of education is so fixed as provided in this act, that the number of members of said board to be elected in the year 1921, in order to comply with the provisions of section 4702, is less than the number of members whose terms expire or terminate on the day preceding the first Monday in January, 1922, the member or members to retire, so that there will be a compliance with sections 4698 and 4702, shall be determined by lot from among those whose terms would expire on the day preceding the first Monday in January, 1922, the terms of office of those on whom the lot falls shall expire on the day preceding the first Monday in January, 1920.

SECTION 2. That said original sections 4698, 4699 and 4701 of the General Code be, and the same are hereby repealed.

CARL R. KIMBALL,
Speaker of the House of Representatives.
CLARENCE J. BROWN,
President of the Senate.

Passed April 16, 1919.
Approved May 8, 1919.

JAMES M. COX,
Governor.

Filed in the office of the Secretary of State at Columbus, Ohio, on the 9th day of May, A. D. 1919.

89 G.

[House Bill No. 359.]

AN ACT

To provide a state-wide retirement system for teachers in schools supported wholly or in part by public funds.

Be it enacted by the General Assembly of the State of Ohio:

Sec. 7896-1.

SECTION 1. That the following words and phrases as used in this act, unless a different meaning is plainly required by the context, shall have the following meanings:

Definition of words and phrases.

"Retirement System" shall mean the "State Teachers' Retirement System" provided for in this act.

"Retirement Board" shall mean the board provided for in this act to administer said retirement system.

"Employer" shall mean the board of education, school district or other agency within the state of Ohio by which a teacher is employed or paid.

"Teacher" shall mean any teacher or other person regularly employed in the public schools of the state of Ohio, who is required by law to have a teachers' certificate; and any teacher in any school or college or other institution wholly controlled and managed, and wholly or partly supported by the state or any subdivision thereof, the board of trustees or other managing body of which shall accept the requirements and obligations of this act.

"Present-teacher" shall mean any person who was a teacher, as defined by this act, before the first day of September, nineteen hundred and twenty; whose membership in the retirement system has been continuous; and,

(a) who became a member on said date, or on the date of his first service as a teacher after said date and within one year after his last day of service previous to said first day of September, nineteen hundred and twenty; or,

(b) who was a teacher of a school or college or other institution on said date, or on a subsequent date within one year after his last day of service as such teacher previous to said first day of September, nineteen hundred and twenty, and who continued thereafter to be a teacher thereof until he, with the teaching staff of such school or college or other institution, became a member of the retirement system as provided in this-act; or,

(c) who was a member of a local district pension system on said date, or on the date of his first eligibility to such membership after said date and within one year after his last day of membership therein previous to said first day of September, nineteen hundred and twenty, and who continued thereafter to be a member until he, with the membership of such local district pension system, became a member of the retirement system.

"New-entrant" shall mean any teacher who is a member except a present-teacher.

"Prior-service" shall mean all service as a teacher, as

defined by this act, rendered before the first day of September, nineteen hundred and twenty, by a present-teacher and similar service in another state credit for which was procured by a present-teacher as provided by this act.

"Total-service" shall mean all service of a member of the retirement system since last becoming a member and, in addition thereto, all his prior-service, computed as provided in this act.

"Member" shall mean any person included in the membership of the retirement system as provided in this act.

"Contributor" shall mean any person who has an account in the teachers' savings fund.

"Beneficiary" shall mean any person in receipt of a retirement allowance or other benefit provided by this act.

"Regular interest" shall mean interest at four per centum per annum, compounded annually.

"Accumulated contributions" shall mean the sum of all amounts deducted from the compensation of a member and credited to his individual account in the teachers' savings fund together with regular interest thereon.

"Final average salary" shall mean the average annual compensation, not exceeding two thousand dollars, earnable as a teacher by a member during the ten years immediately preceding his date of retirement.

"Annuity" shall mean payments for life derived from contributions made by a contirbutor and paid from the annuity and pension reserve fund as provided in this act. All annuities shall be paid in twelve equal monthly installments.

"Pension" shall mean annual payments for life derived from appropriations made by an employer and paid from the employers' accumulation fund or the annuity and pension reserve fund as provided in this act. All pensions shall be paid in twelve equal monthly installments.

"Retirement allowance" shall mean the pension plus the annuity.

"Annuity reserve" shall mean the present value, computed upon the basis of such mortality tables as shall be adopted by the retirement board with regular interest, of all payments to be made on account of any annuity, or benefit in lieu of any annuity, granted to a member under the provisions of this act.

"Pension reserve" shall mean the present value computed upon the basis of such mortality tables as shall be adopted by the retirement board with regular interest, of all payments to be made on account of any pension, or benefit in lieu of any pension, granted to a member under the provisions of this act.

The year for the administration of this act shall mean the school year and shall begin September first and end with August thirty-first next following.

"Local district pension system" shall mean any school

teachers' pension fund created in any school district of the state of Ohio in accordance with the laws of such state prior to the first day of September, nineteen hundred and twenty.

Sec. 7896-2.

SECTION 2. A state teachers' retirement system is hereby established for the teachers of the public schools of the state of Ohio which shall include the several funds created and placed under the management of a "Retirement Board" for the payment of retirement allowances and other benefits under the provisions of this act. The retirement board herein created shall have the right to sue and be sued, plead and be impleaded, contract and be contracted with and do all things necessary to carry out the provisions of this act and by such name all of its business shall be transacted, all of its funds invested, all warrants for money drawn and payments made, and all of its cash and securities and other property shall be held. *Teachers' retirement system established; rights of retirement board.*

Sec. 7896-3.

SECTION 3. The general administration and the management of the state teachers' retirement system and the making effective the provisions of this act are hereby vested in the retirement board which shall have authority to make all necessary rules and regulations, not inconsistent with the provisions of this act, to carry into effect the provisions thereof. *Administration and management vested in board.*

Sec. 7896-4.

SECTION 4. The retirement board shall consist of five members as follows: (a) the superintendent of public instruction; (b) the auditor of state; (c) the attorney general, two other members known as teacher members, who shall be members of the retirement system and who shall be elected by ballot by the members of the retirement system. *Membership of board.*

Sec. 7896-5.

SECTION 5. The first election of teacher members of the retirement board shall be conducted by and under the supervision of the superintendent of public instruction within sixty days after the first day of September next succeeding the passage of this act. At the first election each teacher shall be deemed to be a member of the retirement system and shall have the right to vote for two candidates for membership in the retirement board, provided, that any teacher in a local district pension system who exercises such right to vote shall be deemed to have petitioned for a merger with the state teacher's retirement system as provided in this act and his name shall be deemed to have been duly signed to any such petition subsequently circulated in such local district pension system. The candidate receiving the highest number of votes shall be elected to serve for a period ending on the second thirty-first of August following the election; the candidate receiving the second highest number of votes shall be elected to serve for a period ending on the thirty-first of August following the election. *Election of teacher members.*

Sec. 7896-6.

SECTION 6. Annually after the first election a member of the retirement system shall be elected by ballot to mem- *Annual election; filling vacancies.*

bership in the retirement board to serve for a term of two years beginning on the first day of September following the election. Vacancies occurring in the terms of teacher members of the board shall be filled by the remaining members of the board by election for the unexpired terms. Teacher members of the retirement board who fail to attend the meetings of the board for four months or longer, without being excused, shall be considered as having resigned and successors shall be elected for their unexpired terms.

Sec. 7896-7.
Time of election;
who eligible.

SECTION 7. All elections for members of the retirement board after the first election shall be held on the first Monday of May of each year under the direction of the retirement board. Any member of the retirement system shall be eligible for election as a member of the retirement board and the name of any member who shall be nominated by a petition signed by at least one hundred members of the retirement system shall be placed upon the ballots by the retirement board as a regular candidate. Other names of eligible candidates may at any election be substituted for the regular candidates by writing such names upon the ballots. The candidate receiving the highest number of votes for any term as member of the retirement board shall be elected a member of the retirement board for such term.

Sec. 7896-8.
Acting board
until first election.

SECTION 8. Until the first election shall have been held and the teacher-members elected thereat duly installed, the ex officio members of the retirement board shall constitute an acting retirement board.

Sec. 7896-9.
Oath of office.

SECTION 9. Each member of the retirement board created by this act upon appointment or election shall take an oath of office that he will support the constitution of the United States, the constitution of the state of Ohio, and that he will diligently and honestly administer the affairs of the said board and that he will not knowingly violate or wilfully permit to be violated any of the provisions of law applicable to this act. Such oath shall be subscribed to by the member making it, and certified by the officer before whom it is taken, and shall be immediately filed in the office of the secretary of state.

Sec. 7896-10.
Quorum.

SECTION 10. A majority of the members of the retirement board shall constitute a quorum for the transaction of any business.

Sec. 7896-11.
No compensation; expenses.

SECTION 11. The members of the retirement board shall serve without compensation, but they shall be reimbursed from the expense fund for all actual necessary expenses and for any loss of salary or wages they may suffer through serving on the retirement board.

Sec. 7896-12.
Chairman.

SECTION 12. The retirement board shall elect from its membership a chairman.

Sec. 7896-13.
Custodian of funds.

SECTION 13. The treasurer of the state of Ohio shall be the custodian of the funds of the retirement system, and all disbursements therefrom shall be paid by him only upon vouchers duly authorized by the retirement board and bearing the signatures of said board; or, such vouchers may bear the fac-similie signatures of the board members printed thereon and the signatures of the president and secretary of said board.

The treasurer of state shall give a separate and additional bond in such amount as may be fixed by the governor, but not less than the amount of money in all of the funds of the retirement system at the time such bond is fixed and with sureties to the approval of the governor, conditioned for the faithful performance of the duties of such treasurer as custodian of the funds of the retirement system provided for herein. Such bond shall be deposited with the secretary of state and kept in his office. The governor may from time to time require the treasurer of state to give other and additional bonds, as the funds of said retirement system increase, in such amounts and at such times as may be fixed by the governor which additional bonds shall be conditioned and filed as is provided for the original bond of the state treasurer covering the funds of the retirement system. *Additional bond; where deposited.*

The treasurer of state is hereby authorized and directed to deposit any portion of the funds of the retirement system not needed for immediate use in the same manner and subject to all the provisions of law with respect to the deposit of state funds by such treasurer, and all interest earned by such portion of the said retirement funds as may be deposited by the state treasurer in pursuance of authority herewith given shall be collected by him and placed to the credit of such fund or funds. *Deposit of funds.*

Sec. 7896-14.

SECTION 14. The attorney general of the state of Ohio shall be the legal adviser of the retirement board. *Legal adviser.*

Sec. 7896-15.

SECTION 15. The retirement board shall have power to employ a secretary and to secure the service of such technical and administrative employees as may be necessary for the transaction of the business of the retirement system. The compensation of all persons engaged by the retirement board and all other expenses of the board necessary for the proper operation of the retirement system shall be paid at such rates and in such amounts as the retirement board shall approve. The retirement board shall receive and act upon all applications for retirement under the provisions of this act and shall provide for the payment of all retirement allowances and other benefits and shall make such other necessary expenditures as are required or authorized by the provisions of this act. *Employment of secretary, etc.; compensation.* *Action upon applications.*

Sec. 7896-16.

SECTION 16. The members of the retirement board shall be the trustees of the several funds created by this act and said board shall have full power to invest same in bonds of the United States, the state of Ohio or of any county, city, village or school district of the state of Ohio at current market prices for such bonds; provided that such purchase be authorized by a resolution adopted by the board; and all such bonds so purchased, forthwith, shall *Members of board shall be trustees of the funds; investment; collection of interest.*

be placed in the hands of the treasurer of state, who is hereby designated as custodian thereof, and it shall be his duty to collect the interest thereon as the same becomes due and payable and also the principal thereof and place the same when so collected into the retirement funds herein provided for. The treasurer of state shall honor and pay all vouchers drawn on the retirement funds for the payment of such bonds upon delivery of said bonds to him when there is attached to such vouchers a certified copy of such resolution of the board authorizing the purchase of such bonds; and the board may sell any of said bonds upon like resolution, and the proceeds thereof shall be paid by the purchaser to the treasurer of state upon delivery to him of said bonds by the treasurer.

Sec. 7896-17.

Apportionment of interest.

SECTION 17. All interest earned upon the entire amount of money belonging to said retirement system shall be divided among the various funds thereof proportionately, except that no interest shall be credited to the guarantee and expense funds herein provided for.

Sec. 7896-18.

Trustee or employe shall have no interest in profits nor borrow funds.

SECTION 18. Except as herein provided, no trustee and no employee of the retirement board shall have any interest direct or indirect in the gains or profits of any investment made by the board nor as such directly or indirectly receive any pay or emolument for his services. And no trustee or employee of the said board directly or indirectly, for himself or as an agent or partner of others, shall borrow any of its funds or deposits or in any manner use the same except to make such current and necessary payments as are authorized by the board; nor shall any member or employee of said board become an endorser or surety or become in any manner an obligor for moneys loaned by or borrowed of the board.

Sec. 7896-19.

Individual accounts shall be kept; other data.

SECTION 19. The retirement board shall provide for the maintenance of an individual account with each member showing the amount of the member's contributions and the interest accumulations thereon. It shall collect and keep in convenient form such data as shall be necessary for the preparation of the required mortality and service tables, and for the compilation of such other information as shall be required for the actuarial valuation of the assets and liabilities of the various funds created by this act. Upon the basis of the mortality and service experience of the members and beneficiaries of the system, the retirement board from time to time shall adopt the tables to be used for valuation purposes and for determining the amount of annuities to be allowed on the basis of the contributions of members.

Sec. 7896-20.

Report showing assets and liabilities of the various funds, etc.

SECTION 20. At such times as the retirement board may deem it necessary and at least once within the first three years of the operation of this act, and once in each quinquennial period thereafter the retirement board shall have prepared by a competent actuary familiar with retirement systems, a report showing a complete valuation of the present and prospective assets and liabilities of the various funds created by this act with the exception of the guarantee fund and the expense fund. The actuary shall make an investigation of the mortality and service experience of the members of the system and shall report fully upon the condition of the retirement system together with such recommendations as he shall deem advisable for the information of the retirement board in the proper operation of the retirement system.

Sec. 7896-21.

SECTION 21. The custodian shall furnish annually to the retirement board a sworn statement of the amount of the funds in his custody belonging to the retirement system. The records of the retirement board shall be open to public inspection and any member of the retirement system shall be furnished with a statement of the amount to the credit of his individual account upon written request by such member, provided that the retirement board shall not be required to answer more than one such request of a member in any one year. *Annual statement of amount of funds.*

Sec. 7896-22.

SECTION 22. The membership of the retirement system shall consist of the following: *Membership of the retirement system.*

(a) All teachers in service on the first day of September, nineteen hundred and twenty, except teachers who have filed with their employer a statement in writing requesting exemption from membership or teachers who are excluded by the provisions of this act.

(b) All teachers who became teachers or who were reappointed as teachers after the first day of September, nineteen hundred and twenty, except teachers who are excluded by the provisions of this act.

(c) The teachers in any school or college or other institution supported in whole or in part by the state or any subdivision thereof and wholly controlled and managed by the state or any subdivision thereof shall become members on the same terms and conditions as the teachers in the public schools, provided that the board of trustees or other managing body of such school, college or other institution, if such institution is now in existence or if in existence on said date, shall agree by formal resolution adopted before September first, nineteen hundred twenty-one, to accept all the requirements and obligations imposed by this act upon employers of members. Any institution which comes into existence as such thereafter shall have ninety days in which to accept said requirements and obligations. A certified copy of said resolution shall be filed with the retirement board. When such resolution shall have been adopted and a copy of it filed with the retirement board, it shall not later be subject to rescindment or abrogation. Service in such schools, colleges or other institutions shall be then considered in every way the same as service in the public schools so far as the purposes of this act are concerned, and

(d) All other teachers who become contributors under the provisions of this act.

SECTION 23. Members of a local district pension system maintained under the laws of the state of Ohio from appropriations or contributions made wholly or in part by any employer and existing at the time this bill becomes a law are hereby excluded from membership in this retirement system. But should a majority of all the teachers participating in any such local district pension system apply for membership in the retirement system created by

this act by a petition duly signed and verified, approved by their employer, and filed with the retirement board, all the teachers included in the membership of such local district pension system shall become members of the retirement system created by this act at such time within three months after the filing of such petition and the compliance with the other provisions of this act relative to the dissolution and discontinuance of such local district pension system as the retirement board shall designate.

SECTION 24. The retirement board, notwithstanding the foregoing provisions, may deny the right to become members to any class of teachers, whose compensation is only partly paid by the state, or who are not serving on a per annum basis, or who are on a temporary basis, or who are not required to have a teacher's certificate, and it may also, in its discretion, make optional with teachers in any such class their individual entrance into membership.

SECTION 25. The membership of any person in the retirement system shall cease if he withdraw his accumulated deductions or if he retire on a pension as provided in this act, or if he die, or if, in any four-year period after he last became a member, he shall render less than two years of service as a teacher.

SECTION 26. Each teacher, upon becoming a member, shall file a detailed statement of all his previous service as a teacher and shall furnish such other facts as the retirement board may require for the proper operation of the retirement system.

SECTION 27. To the extent to which it is used in determining the liability of any fund created by this act, the retirement board shall verify such statement by the best evidence it shall be able to obtain. If official records are not available as to the length of service, salary or other information required for the administration of this act, the board is hereby empowered to use its discretion as to the evidence to be accepted.

SECTION 28. The retirement board shall credit a year of service to any teacher who is employed in a school district for the number of months the regular day schools of such district were or shall be in session in said district within any year beginning on or about the first day of September and ending on or about the first day of August following, and shall fix and determine by appropriate rules and regulations how much credit shall be given for parts thereof, but in computing such service, or in computing final compensation, it shall credit no time during which a member was absent without pay, and it shall credit not more than one year for all service rendered in any school year.

Sec. 7896-29.

SECTION 29. Subject to the above restrictions, and to such other rules and regulations as the retirement board shall adopt, said board shall issue to each present-teacher a certificate certifying to the aggregate length of all his prior-service as a teacher as defined in this act. — *Certificate of prior service.*

Sec. 7896-30.

SECTION 30. Any present-teacher or new entrant, in addition to service as a teacher as defined in this act, may claim credit for similar service as a teacher in the public day schools of another state of the United States or of any territory or possession of the United States and such service shall be treated by the retirement board and included in his prior-service certificate as if it were service in the state of Ohio provided the teacher shall pay into the employers' accumulation fund an amount equal to the additional liability assumed by such fund on account of the crediting of such years of service rendered outside of the state. The retirement board shall have final authority to determine and fix the amount that any teacher shall pay on account of such service outside of the state in the case of any present-teacher or new entrant, who desires to claim outside service and make such payment. — *Additional credits.*

Sec. 7896-31.

SECTION 31. So long as membership continues, a prior-service certificate shall be final and conclusive for retirement purposes as to such service, unless modified by the retirement board upon application made by the member or upon its own initiative within one year after the date of its issuance or modification, or in case a mistake is found therein within one year of the time such mistake is so found. — *When prior service certificate shall be conclusive.*

Sec. 7896-32.

SECTION 32. When a present-teacher ceases to be a member his prior-service certificate shall be void and not renewable. — *When certificate void.*

Sec. 7896-33.

SECTION 33. At retirement the total service credited a teacher shall consist of all his service as teacher since he last became a member and, if he has a prior-service certificate which is in full force and effect, all service certified on such prior-service certificate. — *Total service credited at retirement.*

Sec. 7896-34.

SECTION 34. Any teacher, except a new-entrant with less than five years of service, who has attained sixty years of age may retire, if a member, by filing with the retirement board an application for retirement. The filing of such application shall retire such member as of the end of the school year then current. At the end of the school year in which they become members, the retirement board shall retire all teachers who were over seventy years of age at the time they became members and shall automatically re- — *Who eligible to retire.*

tire all other teachers who are members at the end of the school year in which age seventy is attained.

Sec. 7896.35.

Allowance upon superannuation retirement.

SECTION 35. Upon superannuation retirement, a teacher shall be granted a retirement allowance consisting of:

(a) An annuity having a reserve equal to the amount of the teacher's accumulated contributions at that time, and

(b) A pension of equivalent amount; and

(c) An additional pension, if such teacher is a present-teacher, equal to one and one-third percentum of his average final salary multiplied by the number of years of service certified in his prior-service certificate.

Sec. 7896-36.

Commuted super-annuation allow-ance.

SECTION 36. Any teacher who has completed thirty-six years of total service may retire, if a member, on a commuted superannuation allowance by filing with the retirement board an application for such form of allowance. The filing of such application shall retire such member as of the end of the school year then current. Upon retirement on a commuted superannuation allowance, a teacher shall be granted a retirement allowance consisting of:

(a) an annuity having a reserve equal to the amount of the teacher's accumulated contributions at that time; and

(b) a pension, having a reserve equal to the amount of the total liability of the employers' accumulation fund for the payment upon superannuation retirement of a pension equal to the annuity which the teacher's accumulations would purchase provided such teacher made no further payments; and

(c) an additional pension, if such teacher is a present-teacher, having a reserve equal to the amount of the total liability of the employers' accumulation fund for the payment of the pension allowable on superannuation retirement by reason of prior-service as certified in such teacher's prior-service certificate. Provided, however, that no teacher retiring after thirty-six years of service shall receive less than twenty-five dollars per month as a total retirement allowance.

Sec. 7896-37.

Medical exam-ination for dis-ability.

SECTION 37. Medical examination of a member for disability shall be made upon the application of the employer or upon the application of the member or of a person acting in his behalf stating that said member is physically or mentally incapacitated for the performance of duty and ought to be retired, provided that the said member was a teacher as defined in this act for not less than ten years preceding his retirement and was a member in each of such ten years which were subsequent to the year nineteen hundred and twenty. If such medical examination, conducted by a competent disinterested physician, or physicians, selected by the retirement board shows that the said member is physically or mentally incapacitated for the performance of duty and ought to be retired, the examining physician, or physicians, shall so report and the retirement board shall retire the said member for disability forthwith.

Sec. 7896-38.

SECTION 38. Upon disability retirement, a member shall receive a retirement allowance which shall consist of: *Allowance upon disability retirement.*

(a) an annuity having a reserve equal to the amount of the teacher's accumulated contributions at that time; and

(b) a pension which, together with his annuity, shall provide a retirement allowance of one and one-fifth per centum of his final average salary multiplied by the number of his years of total-service, but not less than thirty per centum of said final average salary, with the exception that in no case shall the rate per centum of final average salary to which said retirement allowance amounts exceed nine-tenths of the rate per centum of final average salary to which he probably would have been entitled had retirement been deferred to the age of sixty.

Sec. 7896-39.

SECTION 39. A disability beneficiary, notwithstanding the provisions of this act, shall be considered on leave of absence during his first five years on the retired list and shall retain his membership in the retirement system. Once each year during said period, the retirement board shall require any disability beneficiary under the minimum age for superannuation retirement to undergo medical examination, said examination to be made at the place of residence of said beneficiary or other place mutually agreed upon. Upon completion of such examination by an examining physician, or physicians, selected by the retirement board, the examiner shall report and certify to the board whether said beneficiary is physically and mentally capable of resuming service similar to that from which he was retired. If the retirement board concur in a report by the examining physician or physicians that the said disability beneficiary is capable of resuming service similar to that from which he was retired, the board shall so certify to his last employer before retirement and said employer by the first day of the next succeeding school year shall restore said beneficiary to his previous position and salary or to a position and salary similar thereto. Should any disability beneficiary die during such leave of absence aforesaid his estate shall be paid the balance which remains to his credit in the retirement fund at his death. Should a disability beneficiary be restored to active service his retirement allowance shall cease and the annuity and pension reserves on his allowance at that time in the annuity and pension reserve fund shall be transferred from the annuity and pension reserve fund to the teachers' savings fund and the employers' accumulation fund respectively. Should any disability beneficiary, during his first five years on the retired list and while under the age of sixty years, refuse to submit to a medical examination as required by this act, his retirement allowance shall be discontinued until his withdrawal of such refusal, and should such refusal continue for one year, all his rights in and to such retirement allowance shall be forfeited. After a disability beneficiary

Disability beneficiary considered on leave of absence; annual examination of beneficiary.

Restoration to position and salary, when.

Allowance ceases on restoration to active service.

Effect of refusal to submit to medical examination.

has been on the retired list for a period of five years he shall not be required to submit to further disability examination.

Sec. 7896-40.

Contributor who ceases to teach entitled to balance; limitation.

SECTION 40. A contributor who ceases to be a teacher for any cause other than death or retirement, upon demand, within ten years after such cessation of service, shall be paid the accumulated contributions standing to the credit of his individual account in the teachers' savings fund. Ten years after such cessation of service, if no previous demand has been made, any accumulated contributions of a contributor shall be returned to him or to his legal representative. If the contributor or his legal representatives cannot then be found, his accumulated contributions shall be forfeited to the retirement system and credited to the guarantee fund.

Sec. 7896-41.

Payment on death of contributor.

SECTION 41. Should a contributor die before retirement, his accumulated contributions shall be paid to his estate or to such person as he shall have nominated by written designation duly executed and filed with the retirement board. If no legal representatives can be found, his accumulated contributions shall be forfeited to the retirement system and credited to the guarantee fund.

Sec. 7896-42.

Election by beneficiary; options.

SECTION 42. Until the first payment on account of any benefit is made, the beneficiary may elect to receive such benefit in a retirement allowance payable throughout life, or the beneficiary may then elect to receive the actuarial equivalent at that time of his annuity, his pension, or his retirement allowance, in a lesser annuity, or a lesser pension, or a lesser retirement allowance, payable throughout life with the provision that,

Option 1—If he die before he has received in payments the present value of his annuity, his pension, or his retirement allowance, as it was at the time of his retirement, the balance shall be paid to his legal representatives or to such person, having an insurable interest in his life, as he shall nominate by written designation duly acknowledged and filed with the retirement board.

Option 2—Upon his death, his annuity, his pension, or his retirement allowance, shall be continued throughout the life of and paid to such person having an insurable interest in his life, as he shall nominate by written designation duly acknowledged and filed with the retirement board at the time of his retirement.

Option 3—Upon his death, one-half of his annuity, his pension, or his retirement allowance, shall be continued throughout the life of such person, having an insurable interest in his life as he shall nominate by written designation duly acknowledged and filed with the retirement board at the time of his retirement.

Option 4—Some other benefit or benefits shall be paid either to the beneficiary or to such other person or persons as he shall nominate provided such other benefit or benefits, together with such lesser annuity, or lesser pension, or lesser retirement allowance shall be certified by the actuary engaged by the retirement board to be of equivalent actuarial value to his annuity, his pension or his retirement allowance, and shall be approved by the retirement board.

Sec. 7896-43.

SECTION 43. Each teacher who is a member of the retirement system shall contribute four per centum of his earnable compensation not exceeding two thousand dollars per annum, to the teachers' savings fund. Each employer shall deduct from the compensation of each contributor on each and every payroll of such contributor for each and every payroll period subsequent to the date upon which such contributor for each and every payroll period subsequent to the date upon which such contributor became a member an amount equal to four per centum of such contributor's earnable compensation provided that the amount of a contributor's earnable compensation in excess of two thousand dollars per annum shall not be considered. In determining the amount earnable by a contributor in a payroll period, the retirement board and the employer may consider the rate of compensation payable to such contributor on the first day of the payroll period as continuing throughout such payroll period and deductions may be omitted from compensation for any period less than a full payroll period, if a teacher was not a contributor on the first day of the payroll period; and to facilitate the making of deductions, the deduction required of any contributor may be modified in any payroll period by an amount not exceeding ten cents. The deductions provided herein shall be made notwithstanding that the minimum compensation provided for by law for any member shall be reduced thereby. Every member shall be deemed to consent and agree to the deductions made and provided for herein and shall receipt in full for his salary or compensation, and payment less said deductions shall be a full and complete discharge and acquittance of all claims and demands whatsoever for the services rendered by such person during the period covered by such payment. Each teacher shall pay with the first payment to the teachers' savings fund each year, and in addition thereto a sum to be determined by the retirement board, but not to exceed one dollar, which amount shall be credited to the expense fund. Said payments for the expense fund shall be made to the retirement board in the same way as payments to the teachers' savings fund shall be made.

Per centum of compensation as contribution required; deductions by employer.

Payment to expense account.

Sec. 7896-44.

SECTION 44. Each employer of a teacher who is a member of the retirement system shall pay to the employers' accumulation fund a certain per centum of the earnable compensation of each such teacher to be known as the "normal contribution" and a further per centum of the earnable compensation of each such teacher to be known as the "deficiency contribution." The amount paid by an employer on account of the deficiency contribution shall after the first payment be at least three per centum greater

Payment to "normal contribution" and "deficiency contribution" funds; rates, how fixed.

than the amount paid by him during the preceding year. The rates per centum of such contributions shall be fixed on the basis of the liabilities of the retirement system and shall be certified to the employers by the retirement board after each actuarial valuation. Until the first such certification, the normal contribution shall be two and eight-tenths per centum of the members' salaries and the deficiency contributions shall be two and seventy-seven hundredths per centum of the members' salaries.

Sec. 7896-45.
How "normal contribution" rate determined.

SECTION 45. On the basis of regular interest and of such mortality and other tables as shall be adopted by the retirement board, the actuary engaged by the retirement board to make each valuation required by this act during the period over which the deficiency contribution is payable, immediately after making such valuation, shall determine the uniform and constant percentage of the earnable compensation of the average new entrant, who is a contributor, which, if contributed on the basis of the compensation of such contributor throughout his entire period of active service, would be sufficient to provide at the time of his retirement the total amount of his pension reserve. The rate per centum so determined shall be known as the "Normal contribution" rate. After the deficiency contribution has ceased to be payable, the normal contribution shall be the rate per centum of the earnable salary of all contributors obtained by deducting from the total liabilities of the employers' accumulation fund of the amount of the funds in hand to the credit of that fund and dividing the remainder by one per centum of the present value of the prospective future salary of all contributors as computed on the basis of the mortality and service tables adopted by the retirement board and on regular interest. The normal rate of contribution shall be determined by the actuary after each valuation, and shall be certified to the employers by the retirement board and shall continue in force until a new valuation and certification.

Sec. 7896-46.
How "deficiency contribution" rate determined.

SECTION 46. Immediately succeeding the first valuation, the actuary engaged by the retirement board shall compute the percentage of the total compensation of all contributors during the preceding school year which is equivalent to four per centum of the amount of the total pension liability to all contributors not dischargable during the remainder of the active service of all contributors by the aforesaid normal contribution. The contribution derived by deductions at the rate per centum so determined shall be known as the "deficiency contribution."

Sec. 7896-47.
Monthly payments into employers' accumulation fund.

SECTION 47. Each employer shall pay annually into the employers' accumulation fund, in such monthly or less frequent installments as the retirement board shall require, an amount certified by the retirement board which shall equal the per centum of the total compensation, earnable by all contributors during the preceding school year, which is the sum of the two rates per centum hereinbefore described and required to be computed, to wit, the sum of the normal contribution rate plus the deficiency contribution rate. The aggregate of all such payments by employers shall be sufficient, when combined with the amounts in the employers' accumulation fund, to provide the pensions payable out of the fund during the year then current, and if not, the additional amount so required shall be collected by means of an increased rate per centum of the deficiency contribution which shall be certified to the employers by the retirement board and shall continue in force for the period of one year.

Sec. 7896-48.

SECTION 48. The beforementioned deficiency contribution contributable by the employers shall be discontinued as soon as the accumulated reserve in the employers' accumulation fund shall equal the present value, as actuarially computed, and approved by the retirement board, of the total liability of such fund for the payment of pensions less the present value, computed on the basis of the normal contribution rate then in force, of the normal contributions to be received on account of teachers who are at that time contributors. *When deficiency contribution shall be discontinued.*

Sec. 7896-49.

SECTION 49. Each employer, before employing any teacher to whom this act may apply, shall notify such person of his duties and obligations under this act as a condition of his employment. *Notification before employment.*

Any such appointment or reappointment of any teacher in the public day schools of the state on or after the first day of September, nineteen hundred and twenty, or service upon indefinite tenure after that date shall be conditioned upon the teacher's acceptance of the provisions of this act, as a part of the contract. *Provisions of act part of contract.*

Sec. 7896-50.

SECTION 50. During September of each year, or at such other time as the retirement board shall approve, each employer shall certify to the retirement board the names of all teachers to whom this act applies. *Names of teachers certified to board.*

Sec. 7896-51.

SECTION 51. Each employer shall on the first day of each calendar month, or at such less frequent intervals as the retirement board may approve, notify the retirement board of the employment of new teachers, removals, withdrawals and changes in salary of teachers that shall have occurred during the month preceding or the period since the period covered by the last notification. *Notification of changes, monthly.*

Sec. 7896-52.

SECTION 52. Each employer shall cause to be deducted on each and every payroll of a contributor for each and every payroll period, subsequent to the first day of September, nineteen hundred and twenty, the contribution payable by such contributor as provided in this act. Each employer shall certify to the treasurer of said employer on each and every payroll a statement as voucher for the amounts so deducted and for the amount of the normal contribution and the deficiency contribution payable by the employer as provided in this act. Each employer shall *Deductions by employer certified to treasurer; duplicate to secretary of board.*

send a duplicate of such statement to the secretary of the retirement board.

Sec. 7896-53.

Transmittal monthly of payments to board.

SECTION 53. The treasurer of each employer on receipt from the employer of the voucher for deductions from the salaries of teachers and for the contributions of the employer as provided in this act shall transmit monthly or at such times as the retirement board shall designate the amounts specified in such voucher to the secretary of the retirement board. The secretary of the retirement board after making a record of all such receipts shall pay them to the treasurer of the state of Ohio for use according to the provisions of this act.

Sec. 7896-54.

Employer shall keep records.

SECTION 54. Each employer shall keep such records and shall furnish such information and assistance to the retirement board as it may require in the discharge of its duties.

Sec. 7896-55.

Preference of tax levy.

SECTION 55. Employers who obtain funds directly by taxation are hereby authorized and directed to levy annually such additional taxes as are required to provide the additional funds necessary to meet the financial requirements imposed upon them by this act, and said tax shall be placed before and in preference to all other items except for sinking fund or interest purposes.

Sec. 7896-56.

Various funds created; their uses and purposes.

SECTION 56. The funds hereby created are the teachers' savings fund, the employers' accumulation fund, the annuity and pension reserve fund, the guarantee fund and the expense fund.

(a) The teachers' savings fund shall be the fund in which shall be accumulated contributions from the compensation of contributors for the purchase of annuities.

The accumulated contributions of a contributor returned to him upon his withdrawal, or paid to his estate or designated beneficiary in the event of his death as provided in this act shall be paid from the teachers' savings fund. Any accumulated contributions forfeited by a failure of a teacher or his estate to claim the same as provided in this act shall be transferred from the teachers' savings fund to the guarantee fund. The accumulated contributions of a contributor shall be transferred from the teachers' savings fund to the annuity and pension reserve fund in the event of his retirement.

(b) The employers' accumulation fund shall be the fund in which shall be accumulated the reserves for the payment of all pensions payable as provided by this act. The amounts paid by employers on account of their normal contributions and their deficiency contributions shall be credited to the employers' accumulation fund.

Until the deficiency contribution shall have been discontinued, upon the retirement of a contributor, an amount equal to his annuity reserve shall be transferred from the employers' accumulation fund to the annuity and pension reserve fund and a pension equal to his annuity shall be paid therefrom. The remainder of any pension granted to him shall be paid directly from the employers' accumulation fund until the pension reserve thereon shall have been fully accumulated and the deficiency contribution shall have been discontinued. Thereupon, the full reserve on all pensions theretofore payable from the employers' accumulation fund shall be transferred from said fund to the annuity and pension reserve fund and said pensions shall thereafter be paid from the annuity and pension reserve fund. Upon the retirement of a contributor thereafter, the full amount of his pension reserve shall be transferred from the employers' accumulation fund to the annuity and pension reserve fund.

(c) The annuity and pension reserve fund shall be the fund from which shall be paid all pensions and annuities, or benefits in lieu thereof, on account of which reserves have been transferred from the teachers' savings fund or the employers' accumulation fund as provided in this act.

When the deficiency contributions have ceased to be payable, the full amount of the pension reserves on the pensions then directly payable from the employers' accumulation fund shall be transferred from said fund to the annuity and pension reserve fund. The annuity and pension reserve fund then and thereafter shall be the fund from which shall be paid all annuities and all pensions, and all benefits in lieu thereof, which are payable as provided in this act. Upon the retirement of a contributor, then and thereafter, his accumulated deductions shall be transferred from the teachers' savings fund to the annuity and pension reserve fund, and an amount equal to his full pension reserve shall be transferred from the employers' accumulation fund to the annuity and pension reserve fund.

Any teacher at the time of retirement shall be permitted to deposit in the annuity and pension reserve fund such amounts in multiples of one hundred dollars as such teacher shall desire and such teacher shall receive in return therefor an annuity having a reserve equal to the amount deposited, provided, that in no case shall a teacher have the right to purchase an annuity which together with the retirement allowance otherwise provided under the provisions of this act shall exceed such teacher's final average salary.

(d) A guarantee fund is hereby created to facilitate the crediting of uniform interest on the amounts in the various other funds with the exception of the expense fund, and to provide a contingent fund out of which special requirements of any of the other funds may be covered. All income, interest and dividends derived from the deposits and investments authorized by this act shall be paid into the guarantee fund.

The retirement board is hereby authorized to accept gifts and bequests. Any funds that may come into possession of the retirement system in this manner or which may be transferred from the teachers' savings fund by reason of lack of claimant or because of a surplus in any fund created by this act or any other moneys whose disposition is not otherwise provided for herein shall be credited to the guarantee fund.

The interest allowed by the retirement board to each of the funds as provided in this act shall be paid to such funds from the guarantee fund. Any deficit occurring in any fund which would not be automatically covered by the payments to that fund as otherwise provided by this act shall be met by payments from the guarantee fund to such fund. Should the amount in this fund in any year be insufficient to meet the amounts payable therefrom the amount of such deficiency with regular interest added thereto, shall be assessed by the retirement board in the succeeding years among the employers on the basis of the amount of the normal contributions paid by them, and the amounts so asessed shall be payable by such employers in the same manner and out of the same funds as their normal contributions are made and shall be credited to the guarantee fund.

(e) The expense fund shall be the fund from which shall be paid the expense of the administration of this act, exclusive of amounts payable as retirement allowances and as other benefits as provided in this act.

Sec. 7896-57.

Annual estimate to defray expense.

SECTION 57. The retirement board shall estimate annually the amount required to defray such expense in the ensuing year. The retirement board shall apportion the amount of the expense so estimated in equal amounts among the contributors, provided that the amount so apportioned in any year shall not exceed one dollar per contributor. If the amount estimated to be required to meet the expenses of the retirement board is in excess of one dollar per contributor for the year, the amount of suoh excess shall be paid from the guarantee fund. If in the judgment of the retirement board, as evidenced by a resolution of that board recorded in its minutes, the amount in the guarantee fund exceeds the amount necessary to cover the ordinary requirement of that fund for a period of five years in the future, the board may transfer to the expense fund such excess amount not exceeding the entire amount required to cover the expenses as estimated for the year and the retirement board may then apportion the remaining amount required for the expense fund, if any, among the contributors as before mentioned.

Sec. 7896-58.

Appropriation for establishment of system.

SECTION 58. The sum of ten thousand dollars is hereby appropriated from the moneys in the general revenue fund of the state of Ohio, not otherwise appropriated, for the expense of establishing, organizing and starting the operations of the retirement system and of establishing an office therefor. This sum shall be credited to the expense fund and expended only on order of the retirement board.

Sec. 7896-59. SECTION 59. If a local district pension system votes to merge with the retirement system as provided in this act, the retirement board created by this act shall employ an actuary to value the assets and liabilities which will be taken over by the retirement system hereby created in the event of such merger. The actuary so employed shall be an actuary also approved by the employer in whose district the local district pension system is operated, and the expense of the valuation shall be paid by such employer. The actuary shall compute the present value of the liabilities on account of teachers in service in the local district pension system and on account of pensioners in the rolls of such local district pension system. He shall also compute the present value of the prospective amount to be received by reason of the payment of the normal contributions by the employer on behalf of the active teachers of such local system in the event of the contemplated merger. From the present value of the total liability for pensions on account of teachers in service in the local district pension system as previously determined, the actuary shall deduct the present value of the normal contributions. The amount remaining, together with the excess, if any, of the present value of all payments, necessary to continue the pensions of the pensioners of the local district pension system, over and above the amount of the moneys and securities of such system, shall be known as the "accrued liability." Provided that no teacher, a member of a local district pension system at the time of the passage of this act, shall receive a lesser total retirement allowance upon retirement after merger of the local system with the state system than said teacher would have received upon retirement under the provisions of the local system.

Merger of local system with retirement; procedure.

Sec. 7896-60. SECTION 60. The actuary shall then determine the amount of a deficiency contribution which payable annually without regard to the payroll of contributors and increasing by three per centum of itself each year, until the year in which the deficiency contribution payable by other employers who had no local pension system may be expected to be discontinued, shall have a present value equal to this accrued liability.

Deficiency contribution determined.

Sec. 7896-61. SECTION 61. The increasing contribution so determined by the actuary shall be paid by the employer instead of the deficiency contribution computed as otherwise provided by this act, anything to the contrary notwithstanding. In the event of merger, the moneys and securities to the credit of the local district pension system, not exceeding an aggregate amount equal to the present value of the payments to be made on account of all pensions to the pensioners on the rolls of the local district pension system, shall be transferred to the employers' accumulation fund and the pensions then payable by the local district pension system shall thereafter be paid from the employers' accumulation fund until the reserves on these pensions with

Transfer of moneys, credits, etc., in event of merger.

the other pensions payable from the employers' accumulation fund shall have been accumulated and shall be transferred to the annuity and pension reserve fund, from which fund they shall thereafter be payable. The pensions of the active members of the local district pension system and of the new-entrants shall thereafter be payable as are the pensions of other members of the retirement system hereby created. The amount of the excess of the moneys and securities of the local district pension system over and above the present value of the payments to be made on account of all pensions to the pensioners of the rolls of the local district pension system shall be transferred to the teachers' savings fund and shall be credited pro rata to the active teachers of such local district pension system on the basis of the amounts of their previous contributions to the local district pension system, provided, however, that in case such method of distribution shall not be found practicable by the retirement board, the board may use such other method of apportionment as may seem fair and equitable to such board. The amount so credited in any case shall be considered as a part of the teacher's accumulated contributions for all purposes except in the case of retirement in which it shall be considered as an amount in excess of the teacher's accumulated contributions and shall be used in purchasing from the annuity and pension reserve fund an annuity, in addition to any other annuity or pension benefit otherwise provided by this act.

After the moneys and securities of any local district pension system shall have been transferred to the employers' accumulation fund or to the teachers' savings fund as hereinbefore provided, such local district pension system shall cease to exist.

Sec. 7896-62.

Exemption of allowances from tax, execution, etc.

SECTION 62. The right of a person to a pension, an annuity, or retirement allowance itself, any optional benefit, any other right accrued or accruing to any person under the provisions of this act, the various funds created by this act and all moneys and investments and income thereof, are hereby exempt from any state, county, municipal or other local tax, and shall not be subject to execution, garnishment, attachment, the operation of bankruptcy or insolvency laws or any other process of law whatsoever, and shall be unassignable except as in this act specifically provided.

Sec. 7896-63.

Penalty for false statement, record, etc.

SECTION 63. Any person who shall knowingly make any false statement, or shall falsify or permit to be falsified any record or records of this retirement system in any attempt to defraud such system as a result of such act, shall be guilty of a misdemeanor and shall upon conviction thereof be fined not less than ten nor more than one thousand dollars.

The sectional numbers on the margin hereof are as designated as provided by law.
JOHN G. PRICE,
Attorney
General.

CARL R. KIMBALL,
Speaker of the House of Representatives.
CLARENCE J. BROWN,
President of the Senate.

Passed April 16, 1919.
Approved May 9, 1919.

JAMES M. COX,
Governor.

Field in the office of the Secretary of State at Columbus, Ohio, on the 9th day of May, A. D. 1919.

90 G.

[Amended Senate Bill No. 130.]

AN ACT

To prevent the frequent tearing up and obstruction of streets and other public thoroughfares by authorizing the council of municipalities to require defective and worn out rails, ties, roadbeds, and tracks of street railway companies existing in streets and other public thoroughfares proposed to be improved, paved, or repaved, surfaced, or resurfaced, to be renewed, replaced, repaired or reconstructed at the time at which such improvement is made; authorizing municipalities to make such renewals, replacements, repairs or reconstructions upon the failure of the street railway company so to do, and assess the cost thereof against such street railway company, and authorizing the issuance of bonds in anticipation of the collection of such assessments.

Be it enacted by the General Assembly of the State of Ohio:

SECTION 1. That section 3812 of the General Code, be and the same is hereby supplemented by the enactment of supplementary sections 3812-2 and 3812-3 of the General Code, which shall read as follows:

Sec. 3812-2. At the time of, or subsequent to the adoption by council of a municipality of a resolution declaring it necessary to improve, pave, repave, surface or resurface a street or other public thoroughfare, wherein are located rails, ties, roadbed or tracks owned or operated by a street railway company or companies, which have become worn out or defective, the council of such municipality may by resolution declare the necessity of requiring said street railway company or companies, at the time such street or other public thoroughfare is torn up for said street improvement, paving or repaving, surfacing or resurfacing, to renew, replace, repair or reconstruct the rails, ties, roadbed, and tracks in said street or thoroughfare in accordance with the plans and specifications prepared by the chief engineer of such municipality, which plans and specifications together with the engineer's estimate of the cost of the labor and materials necessary for such renewal, re-

Resolution requiring company to improve at the time municipality authorizes improvement.

placement, reconstruction or repair shall be on file and open to public inspection in the office of such chief engineer, and shall conform to the usual methods of such construction, reconstruction or repair.

Copy of resolution and notice given company; service.

A certified copy of such resolution, together with a written notice setting forth the time and place at which a hearing will be given said company or companies and at which it or they may be present to make any objections to said resolution, shall be sent by registered mail to the street railway company or companies owning or operating such rails, ties, roadbed and tracks.

Ordinance for improvement; notice of modifications.

After holding such hearing council may by ordinance order and require that at the time at which such street, or other public thoroughfare is torn up for such improvement, paving or repaving, surfacing or resurfacing, the street railway or companies owning or operating such rails, ties, roadbed and tracks shall renew, replace, reconstruct or repair the same in accordance with said plans and specifications, and any modifications or corrections thereof that may be made by council, and a certified copy of such ordinance shall be sent to said street railway company or companies by registered mail.

Appeal to Public Utilities Commission of Ohio.

Unless, if the said street railway company or companies are dissatisfied with such ordinance of council requiring such renewal, replacement, repair or reconstruction, it or they may, within ten days after the passage of said ordinance, file a written complaint or appeal with the public utilities commission of Ohio. Notice of the time fixed by said commission for the hearing of said appeal

Notice to solicitor of hearing.

shall be given to the solicitor of said city or village, and it shall be the duty of said commission, within thirty days after the filing of said appeal to hear and determine the same and approve, revise, modify or reverse the action of council and substitute its finding on such ordinance. Unless within twenty (20) days after the mailing of such certified copy of the ordinance such street railway company or companies shall notify council in writing that it or they will so renew, replace, repair or reconstruct such rails, ties, roadbed and tracks in accordance with said plans and specifications, and any such modification or corrections thereof or that said company has appealed to the public utilities commission, the council may by ordinance authorize the

When bids for improvement may be authorized.

director of public service in cities, and the council in villages, to receive bids and enter into contracts for the furnishing of the necessary material and labor for such renewal, replacement, repair, or reconstruction of such rails, ties, roadbed and tracks, all of which work shall be done at the time that such street or other public thoroughfare is torn up for the making of such street improvement, paving or repaving, surfacing or resurfacing.

When municipality may make improvement on the part of company.

In the event that such street railway company or companies notify council that it or they will so renew, replace, repair or reconstruct such rails, ties, roadbed or tracks, but fail at the time of making of such street improvement, paving or repaving, surfacing or resurfacing, to renew, replace, repair or reconstruct such rails, ties, roadbed or tracks, the council may by ordinance authorize the director of public service in cities, and the council in villages, to receive bids and enter into contracts for the furnishing of the necessary material and labor for such renewal, replacement, repair or reconstruction, and said work shall be done at the time such street or other public thoroughfare is torn up for the making of such street improvement, paving or repaving, surfacing or resurfacing; and said contract or contracts shall be awarded to the lowest bidder.

Sec. 3812-3. Council shall by ordinance assess the entire cost and expense of the labor and materials required for such renewal, replacement, repair or reconstruction, against such street railway company or companies, and upon its or their failure to pay such assessment in cash, or by assessment as hereinafter provided the same shall be a lien upon all of the property of such company or companies, located in said city or village. Said assessing ordinance may provide for the payment of said assessments in not to exceed ten (10) equal annual installments with interest thereon until paid at not to exceed six (6) per cent per annum; provided, however, the company or companies shall not be liable for the installment or installments of said assessments due after the expiration of the company or companies' franchise unless the use of said track or tracks is continued thereafter by said company or companies. Upon the non-payment of such installments as the same severally become due, the auditor in cities, and the clerk in villages, shall certify the same to the auditor of the county in which the municipality is situated, who shall place the same upon the tax duplicate of said county and add the amount thereof to the tax bills of said street railway company or companies and shall collect such assessments including interest in the same manner provided by law for the collection of taxes levied against real estate. If the entire amount of the cost and expense of such renewal, replacement, repair or reconstruction be not paid in cash at the time specified in such assessing ordinance, council may by ordinance provide for the payment of the cost and expense of such renewal, replacement, repair or reconstruction, including interest on such installments of assessments, by the issuance of bonds in anticipation of the collection of such assessments, which bonds shall bear interest at not to exceed six (6) per cent. per annum.

The assessment herein provided for shall not be subject to any other statute of the state of Ohio limiting or restrict-

Assessment of cost and expense against company.

What ordinance may provide.

Certification to auditor on non-payment; collection.

Bond issue in case of non-payment.

Not subject to other statutes of limitations.

ing the power of levying and collecting special assessments.

CLARENCE J. BROWN,
President of the Senate.
CARL R. KIMBALL,
Speaker of the House of Representatives.

Passed April 17, 1919.
Approved May 9, 1919.

JAMES M. COX,
Governor.

Filed in the office of the Secretary of State at Columbus, Ohio, on the 12th day of May, A. D. 1919.

91 G.

The sectional numbers in this act are in conformity to the General Code. JOHN G. PRICE. Attorney General.

[House Bill No. 484.]

AN ACT

To amend section 5966 of the General Code, relating to actions at law in betting.

Be it enacted by the General Assembly of the State of Ohio:

SECTION 1. That section 5966 of the General Code be amended to read as follows:

Money, etc., lost at games may be recovered; exceptions.

Sec. 5966. If a person, by playing a game, or by a bet or wager, loses to another money or other thing of value, and pays or delivers it or a part thereof, to the winner thereof, such person so losing and paying or delivering, within six months after such loss and payment or delivery, may sue for and recover such money or thing of value or part thereof. from the winner thereof, with costs of suit.

Provided however, that neither this section, nor section 5969 of the General Code, shall apply to any business transacted upon a regularly established stock exchange or board of trade through a member thereof whose relation to the transaction is that of broker only, and who actually delivers or receives the securities or other commodity bought or sold in accordance with the rules and regulations of said stock exchange or board of trade.

Repeal.

SECTION 2. That said original section 5966 of the General Code be, and the same is hereby repealed.

The sectional number in this act is in conformity to the General Code. JOHN G. PRICE. Attorney General.

CARL R. KIMBALL,
Speaker of the House of Representatives.
CLARENCE J. BROWN,
President of the Senate.

Passed April 16, 1919.
Approved May 10, 1919.

JAMES M. COX,
Governor.

Filed in the office of the Secretary of State at Columbus, Ohio, on the 12th day of May, A. D. 1919.

92 G.

[House Bill No. 313.]

AN ACT

To supplement section 412 of the General Code, by adding thereto
sections 412-1, 412-2, 412-3, 412-4, 412-5, 412-6, 412-7, 412-8,
412-9, 412-10, 412-11, 412-12, 412-13, 412-14 and 412-15 relative
to preventing destructive floods and conserving and preventing
waste of the waters of the streams, lakes and public waters
of the state of Ohio, and to provide for the sale or lease to the
public of such water for agricultural, commercial, manufacturing and other public purposes.

Be it enacted by the General Assembly of the State of Ohio:

SECTION 1. That section 412 of the General Code be
supplemented by sections 412-1, 412-2, 412-3, 412-4, 412-5,
412-6, 412-7, 412-8, 412-9, 412-10, 412-11, 412-12, 412-13,
412-14 and 412-15, to read as follows:

Sec. 412-1. That, in addition to all other powers
granted to and duties devolving upon the superintendent
of public works, as provided by law, when in his judgment
he deems it for the public welfare and the best interests of
the citizens of the state, that the surplus, flood and other
waters of any of the water-sheds, rivers, streams, water
courses or public waters should be conserved, impounded
and stored in order to insure and promote the public health,
welfare and safety, and to encourage and promote agriculture, commerce, manufacturing and other public purposes,
he shall proceed as provided by law, and in furtherance of
the purposes of this act and the preservation of the use of
such waters for navigation in case the same shall be required
therefor, to construct such reservoirs, dams, storage basins,
dikes, canals, raceways and other improvements as may be
necessary for such purposes, or he may make additions to,
enlarge and make alterations in and upon such reservoirs,
dams, storage basins, dikes, canals, raceways, and other improvements, then in existence and constituting a part of
the public works, as may be necessary for such purposes;
but no rights or privileges herein granted shall in any wise
interfere with the control and maintenance of the state
reservoirs or public parks which have been dedicated to the
public for purposes of recreation and pleasure.

(margin note: Construction of reservoirs, dams, etc., to prevent floods, preserve waste waters, authorized.)

Said superintendent may, subject to the written approval of the governor of the state, acquire by gift, purchase
or by appropriation proceedings, in the name of and on
behalf of the state of Ohio, such real and personal property, rights, privileges and appurtenances as may be necessary in his judgment for the construction of such reservoirs, dams, storage basins, dikes, canals, raceways and
other improvements, or for the alteration, enlargement or
maintenance of such existing reservoirs, dams and other
improvements, together with such rights of way, drives and
roadways as may be necessary for convenient access thereto.

(margin note: Acquisition of property on approval of governor.)

Before proceeding to purchase or appropriate any such
property or rights for the construction of any such im-

(margin note: Plans and estimates when cost exceeds $1,000.)

provements, or for making additions to, enlargements of, or alterations in any of those already in existence, the cost of which, together with the land or real estate necessary upon which to locate and construct the same, including damages to remaining property, shall be in excess of one thousand dollars, the superintendent shall prepare or cause to be prepared plans, specifications and estimates of such cost, including all material and labor therefor, together with the cost of such land or real estate and damages, and shall thereupon submit such plans, specifications and estimates to the governor for his approval.

Publication of notice of improvement; objections; hearing.

The governor shall thereupon cause written notice to be published once a week for two consecutive weeks in a newspaper printed and of general circulation in the county or counties where any such improvements are proposed to be constructed, setting forth the location and character of the proposed improvements, that the plans, specifications and estimates therefor are on file in his office, and that objections thereto, if any, will be heard by him on a day to be named in said notice, which day shall be not less than ten nor more than twenty days after the first publication thereof. Within thirty days after the date fixed for said hearing, the governor shall return such plans, specifications and estimates to the superintendent of public works, with his written approval or rejection thereof endorsed thereon.

Construction after approval; bonds authorized.

Sec. 412-2. If the governor approve said plans, specifications and estimates, the superintendent of public works shall thereupon proceed, as hereinafter provided, to construct such improvements or to make alterations in or to enlarge those already existing, in manner and form as shown by such plans and specifications, and in order to provide the funds for such construction, alteration or enlargement, he shall proceed, in manner and form as hereinafter provided, to issue and sell bonds of the state of Ohio, not in excess of the estimated cost of such improvements. Said bonds shall be issued in denominations of not less than one hundred ($100.00) dollars payable as a whole or in series on or before twenty-five (25) years from the date thereof, with interest not to exceed six per cent per annum, payable either annually or semi-annually, and the date of maturity of none of said bonds shall be more than twenty-five (25) years from the date of the issue thereof.

Bonds not a state debt; how paid.

Said bonds shall show, on their face, the purpose for which issued and shall create no liability upon, nor in any wise be considered an indebtedness of the state of Ohio, but shall be paid, both principal and interest, solely out of the proceeds arising from the sale or lease of the water impounded and conserved or the power generated by the improvements constructed, altered or enlarged by said superintendent of public works, in accordance with the terms and provisions of this act, or from the proceeds of the sale on foreclosure, of the lien securing said bonds on such improvement or such part thereof as may be constructed from the money realized from the sale of said bonds, as hereinafter provided.

The form of said bonds shall be approved by the attorney general, and they shall be signed by the governor of the state of Ohio, and attested by the superintendent of public works. Said bonds may be issued as coupon bonds, payable to bearer only, or upon demand of the owner or holder thereof, as registered bonds. *Approval of bonds.*

The treasurer of the state of Ohio shall be the treasurer of the fund realized from the sale of said bonds and he shall hold said fund as trustee for the holder or holders of said bonds and for all persons performing labor or furnishing material for the construction, alteration or enlargement of any improvements made under the provisions of this act. Said fund shall not be turned into the state treasury, but shall be deposited and disbursed by said treasurer in manner and form as provided in this act. The interest coupons attached to said bonds shall bear the signature of said treasurer, executed either by himself or printed or lithographed thereon. Said bonds, both interest and principal, shall be made payable at the office of said treasurer in the city of Columbus, Ohio, and shall be paid by him, without warrant or other authority from the auditor of said fund, to the owner or holder thereof, upon presentation by him of matured interest coupons or bonds. *State treasurer shall hold fund as trustee.* *When bonds payable.*

They shall be sold by the superintendent of public works to the highest bidder therefor but for not less than the par value thereof, with accrued interest thereon, after thirty days' notice in at least two newspapers of general circulation in the county where such improvements are to be constructed, setting forth the nature, amount, rate of interest and length of time said bonds have to run, with the time and place of sale. *Sale of bonds.*

The proceeds of the sale of said bonds shall be turned over to said treasurer and by him deposited in a solvent bank, located either in the city of Columbus, or in the county in which such improvement or improvements, constructed or enlarged, are located, and shall be kept by such bank in a fund to be known as the "Water Conservation Improvement Fund," which fund shall be used to acquire the necessary real estate and to construct such new improvements or to alter or enlarge such existing improvements and for no other purpose, except that the treasurer of said water conservation improvement fund is hereby authorized to pay the interest on said bonds during the period of condemnation and the construction of such improvements out of the proceeds arising from the sale of said bonds for a term not exceeding three years from the date at which said bonds are issued. *Proceeds of sale known as "Water Conservation Improvement Fund."*

Said bank shall give bond to the state of Ohio in such amount as said treasurer may deem advisable, and with surety to his satisfaction, for the benefit of the holder or holders of said bonds, and for the benefit of any contractor *Depositary shall give bond.*

or contractors performing labor or furnishing material for
the construction of such improvements, as provided by law,
conditioned that it will safely keep said money and will
make no payments or disbursements therefrom except as
herein provided.

Contract for improvement, how made. Sec. 412-3. Immediately after the sale of said bonds
and the payment of the proceeds thereof to said treasurer
as herein provided, the superintendent of public works shall
proceed to make a written contract for the construction of
such improvements or the making of additions to or alterations in such existing improvements with the lowest and
best bidder, after advertisement once a week, for four consecutive weeks, in one newspaper in each of the cities of
Columbus, Cleveland and Cincinnati, having a general circulation therein, and one trade paper, having a circulation
among contractors engaged in the construction of public
improvement work of like character, and two newspapers
having a general circulation within the county in which
said dam, reservoir, storage basin or other improvement is
then or is thereafter to be located.

Award of contract. All bids shall be filed with the superintendent of public works at his office in the city of Columbus, Ohio, within
the time fixed for the filing thereof in said advertisement.
The bids shall be opened at twelve o'clock noon on the last
day for filing the same, by the superintendent of public
works, and publicly read by him. Each bid shall contain
the full names of every person or company interested in it
and shall separately state the price of both the labor and
material to be furnished under it and shall be accompanied
by a sufficient bond or certified check on a solvent bank
that, if the bid is accepted a contract will be entered into
by the bidders, and the performance of it properly secured.

Performance shall be guaranteed. When entered into, the performance of such contract
shall be guaranteed by a bond in manner and form as pro-
vided in sections 2365-1, 2365-2, 2365-3 and 2365-4 of the
General Code of the state of Ohio.

Bids may be rejected; re-advertisement. The superintendent may reject any or all bids. If he
reject all bids, he shall, within sixty days thereafter, pro-
ceed to readvertise for bids for the construction of such
improvements, as above provided, and may continue to readvertise for bids every sixty days until a bid or bids are
received, made to his satisfaction and in conformity to the
provisions of this act.

Separate contracts for each part may be awarded. The superintendent may award separate contracts to
bidders for each part of the labor to be done or material to
be furnished for the construction of such improvements;
provided, however, that the amount of the contract, if
awarded as a whole, or the aggregate of said several contracts, if awarded separately, shall not, together with the
cost of the land or real estate necessary for such improvements and the estimated damages to remaining property,
be in excess of the estimated cost of the construction thereof, including such land or real estate and damages; and

provided further that such contract or contracts shall provide that all payments thereunder shall be made from the proceeds of the sale of the bonds issued for the construction of such improvements and not otherwise, and that no contractor or contractors shall be entitled to receive payment· for any work or labor performed or material furnished for such improvements, unless the contract therefor was, at the time of its execution, approved by the governor by his written endorsement thereon.

Sec. 412-4. The auditor of the state of Ohio shall be the auditor of said fund. Upon the making of a contract or contracts, by the superintendent for the construction of such improvements, in manner and form as herein provided, a copy of such contract, duly certified by such superintendent, shall be delivered both to the said treasurer and to said auditor, and upon presentation to the auditor, from time to time, of estimates or statements for either material theretofore furnished or labor theretofore performed under said contract by said contractor, duly certified as to the correctness thereof, under oath by him or his authorized agent, and approved in writing by the superintendent of public works, he shall draw a voucher or warrant, payable to the order of such contractor, for the amount of such estimates or statements, and said treasurer shall, upon presentation thereof, pay the same by check signed by him as treasurer of said fund, realized from the sale of said bonds, and payable therefrom. *Auditor of fund*

Certified copy of contracts delivered to auditor and treasurer of state.

Sec. 412-5. The superintendent of public works shall, by contract, in writing, sell or lease, to be used for agricultural, commercial, manufacturing or other lawful purposes, for any term not exceeding twenty-five years, the water or any part thereof, conserved and stored by such improvement or improvements then existing, or that will be conserved and stored by any such improvements thereafter to be constructed by him, as shown by the plans and specifications prepared by him therefor, and approved by the governor of the state, as herein provided, for a certain price or rental for the water furnished to or used by such grantees, lessees or their assigns, to be paid quarterly, semi-annually or annually as he may deem advisable. *Sale or lease of water authorized.*

Said superintendent of public works may, for a term not exceeding twenty-five years, sell or lease power generated by any head of water raised or maintained by any such improvements, or he may sell or lease the right to use such head of water for generating power or other hydraulic purposes. All such contracts of sale or lease, whether for water or power, shall contain such reservations or restrictions as the superintendent of public works may deem necessary and proper, in furtherance of the purposes of this act and the preservation of the use of such waters for navigation in case the same shall be required therefor. *Sale or lease of power.*

As to their general form and legality, such contracts or leases must be approved by the attorney general and, be- *Contracts or leases approved by attorney general.*

fore becoming binding obligations on the state of Ohio they shall be approved by the governor, by his written endorsement thereon.

Tentative agreements for sale or lease may be made.

Sec. 412-6. In order to ascertain whether the public interest and welfare reasonably require such improvements in the locality where it is proposed to construct the same, and whether the revenues which the state may derive from the leasing and sale of the waters which are estimated will be conserved, impounded and stored, or the power generated thereby, will be sufficient to pay the interest on the bonds to be issued, to create a sinking fund to retire said bonds at their maturity, and to maintain and keep said improvements in repair, the superintendent of public works may before selling such bonds or receiving bids for such construction enter into tentative agreements for the sale or lease of such water, or power, the performance and carrying out of which shall be conditional upon the ability of such superintendent to sell said proposed bonds at not less than par and accrued interest and to secure bids for the furnishing of all the labor and material necessary in the construction of such improvements, including all real estate required, and damages incurred, at such a price that the rentals or compensation to be paid for such water, or power, will provide during the term or terms of such contracts or leases sufficient to pay said interest, retire said bonds and to maintain and keep said improvements in repair.

Treasurer of fund; deposit and disbursement of "Water Conservation Fund."

Sec. 412-7. The treasurer of the state of Ohio shall be treasurer of all moneys derived from the sale or lease of the water conserved and stored, or of the power generated by any such improvements and he shall hold said moneys as trustee for the maintenance of any improvements constructed under this act and for the holder or holders of any of said bonds. Said moneys shall not be turned into the state treasury, but shall be deposited and disbursed by said treasurer in manner and form as provided in this act. All such moneys shall be collected by said treasurer on statements to be furnished by the superintendent of public works and when so collected, shall be deposited in solvent banks in the state of Ohio upon the same terms as state funds are now loaned and said funds shall be kept by such banks in a fund known as the "Water Conservation Fund" and shall be used, first, to maintain and keep in repair such dams, reservoirs, storage basins and other improvements, and second, to pay the interest upon and principal of the bonds issued and sold pursuant to the terms hereof, as such interest falls due or the principal of said bonds mature.

Banks in which funds shall be deposited; distribution of deposits.

The bank or banks in which said treasurer deposits any of the moneys belonging either to said "Water Improvement Conservation Fund" or said "Water Conservation Fund" as herein provided shall be state depository banks as provided for in sections 321 to 330-12 inclusive of the General Code. Not to exceed fifty thousand ($50,000) dollars of the amount of money on deposit at any one time

in said "Water Conservation Improvement Fund," and
not to exceed ten thousand ($10,000) dollars in said
"Water Conservation Fund," shall be held by any of said
banks as an active deposit, and said bank or banks, shall
pay the said treasurer on such deposits, both active and in-
active, the same rate of interest then being paid by it or
them upon the funds of the state of Ohio, then deposited
with it or them by the treasurer of said state. All such
payments of interest shall be credited to the respective
funds upon which such interest is paid.

Sec. 412-8. When the cost of any repairs to such improvements does not exceed the sum of one thousand ($1,-
000.00) dollars, the superintendent of public works may
make such repairs himself or let a contract therefor, without advertising for bids for the making of the same. If the
cost of any such repairs shall be in excess of the sum of one
thousand ($1,000.00) dollars, the superintendent of public
works shall advertise for bids for the making of the same
and let a contract or contracts therefor in like manner as
herein provided for the letting of contracts for the original
construction of any such improvements, or the making of
alterations in or additions to any existing improvements.

Sec. 412-9. The auditor of the state of Ohio shall be
the auditor of said "Water Conservation Fund" and, upon
the presentation to him of itemized statements, showing the
amount of labor performed and material furnished in the
making of such repairs, duly verified by the person making
the same, and approved in writing by the superintendent
of public works, he shall draw a voucher or warrant for
the amount of such statement, payable to the order of the
person making such repairs and, upon presentation thereof
to him, the said treasurer shall pay the same by check,
signed by him, as treasurer of said "Water Conservation
Fund" and payable therefrom.

Sec. 412-10. If such reservoir, dam, storage basin or
other improvement, so constructed or enlarged by the superintendent of public works as herein provided, shall constitute a part of the "canal system" of the state of Ohio,
or shall be located upon any river, stream, or body of water
therefore used as a feeder for said canal system, no water,
shall be sold or leased therefrom by the superintendent of
public works, except that stored or conserved by such improvement in excess of the quantity which may at all times
be required for navigation purposes.

Sec. 412-11. The funds derived from the sale or lease
of the water impounded and conserved or the power generated by said improvements are hereby expressly pledged
for the purpose of maintaining and keeping in repair said
improvements and for the payment of the interest and principal of said bonds, as the same fall due and mature, and,
in addition thereto, the owner or owners of such bonds are
hereby given a lien for the payment thereof, both principal
and interest, upon any such dam, reservoir, storage basin,

Contracts when cost not in excess of $1,000.

Auditor of "Water Conservation Fund."

Sale when improvement part of "canal system."

Application of funds derived from sales and leases.

or other improvement or any part thereof, with the appurtenances thereunto belonging, constructed by the superintendent of public works, with the funds derived from the
sale of such bonds and, if default be made in the payment
of the interest on any of said bonds for three (3) or more
successive years, or, if bonds, aggregating in par value not
less than ten per cent of the total amount of such bonds
then outstanding be not paid at maturity, then all of said
bonds, both principal and interest, shall become due and
payable, and the owner or owners of any of said bonds,
aggregating in par value not less than ten per cent of the
total amount of such bonds then outstanding, may institute
proceedings against the state of Ohio in the court of common pleas of the county in which is located any of said
improvements, constructed, altered or enlarged, out of the
proceeds of the sale of such bonds, to foreclose such lien,
and said court shall have jurisdiction of such action with
full power to foreclose such lien, and to make an order to
the sheriff of said county, acting as a master commissioner,
directing him to make a sale of such improvements or part
thereof at not less than two-thirds of the appraised value
thereof, and upon such terms and in manner and form as
provided for in said order, and to pay the proceeds of such
sale to the clerk of said court, and upon motion of the purchaser of such improvements at such sale, the court shall,
if the same be found to be regular in all respects and according to law, confirm the same and order the sheriff to
execute a deed to such purchaser and his assigns, conveying to him all the right, title and interest of the holders of
said bonds and each of them in and to said improvements,
and all the right, title and interest of the state of Ohio,
for a period of twenty-five (25) years, from the date of
such conveyance, in and to the same, with full right and
franchise, for said period of twenty-five (25) years, to
operate said improvements and dispose of the water conserved, or the power generated thereby, with the further
right, for said period of twenty-five (25) years, to flow,
transport and convey said water from said improvements,
or to conduct and transmit power generated thereby,
through, over and upon any of the lands of the state or
channels or beds of any of its reservoirs, lakes, canals, races,
aqueducts or water courses; provided, however, that, in the
exercise of such rights, such purchaser or his assigns shall
at all times during the term of said grant keep and maintain the improvements so conveyed to him or them in a good
state of repair and shall in no wise interfere with the navigation of the canals of the state nor the control and maintenance thereof, nor the sale of water by the state from its
dams, reservoirs, and improvements other than those so
constructed, nor shall the state be held to incur any liability
on its part by reason of such sale and the rights granted
thereunder, to continue to maintain such canals, races, chan-
nals or water courses, or to continue the use thereof, and

227

such conveyance or grant by the sheriff as such master commissioner shall contain a clause, giving the superintendent of public works such control of waste gates and wickets, as to regulate the flow of water in the state reservoirs, or canals, in such manner as to maintain the proper level of the state's reservoirs, and canals and to prevent the flowing into such reservoirs and canals of such quantities of water as might impair any of the property of the state or its lessees.

Upon the foreclosure of said lien and the sale of said improvement or improvements as herein provided, all contracts or leases for the sale or lease of water or power then outstanding shall become null and void, and the rights both of the state of Ohio and the several lessees thereunder, shall cease and determine.

Contract or lease void, when.

Upon the making of an order by the court for the sale of such improvements as herein provided, and before the same shall be offered for sale by the sheriff, the court shall appoint three disinterested appraisers, one of whom shall be a water works or hydraulic engineer, with at least five years' experience in the practise of his profession, and two of whom shall be freeholders, residing in the county in which any of such improvements are located. Said appraisers shall proceed to appraise said improvements and shall, within the time fixed by the court, file such appraisal in writing with the clerk thereof. In the event that the lien herein given as security for the payment of said bonds, covers a part only of said improvements, said appraisers shall appraise said improvements as an entirety, and shall also appraise separately the part constructed from the proceeds of the sale of said bonds, the lien of which is being foreclosed in such proceeding.

Appointment of appraisers; filing of appraisement.

In making such appraisal and fixing the value of said improvements or of such part thereof, said appraisers shall have access to all papers and documents on file in the office of the superintendent of public works relating to such improvements including the plans and specifications therefor, and the bids made and contracts entered into for the construction thereof, and all leases and contracts for the sale of water impounded therein and power generated thereby. The order of the court shall direct the sale only of such part of said improvements as shall have been constructed from the proceeds of the sale of said bonds, and the purchaser at such sale shall, in the operation of such improvements during the term of the franchise herein granted to him, draw from the dam or reservoir impounding such water only such portion thereof as the appraised value of that part of such improvements, constructed from the proceeds of the sale of such bonds, and sold to him under the order of the court, bears to the entire appraised value of such improvements. If, at any time during the term of the franchise granted to the purchaser of such improvements at such foreclosure sale, any controversy shall arise between

Access to papers and documents in appraisement.

Application to court in case of controversy.

him or his assigns and the superintendent of public works as to the operation of such improvements, or as to the amount of water which said purchaser or his assigns are drawing or are entitled to draw therefrom, either said purchaser or his assigns or said superintendent of public works may file a petition in said court of common pleas, setting forth the facts connected with such controversy.

Notice of filing petition; answer. Notice in writing of the filing of such petition shall be given to the opposite party to said controversy within thirty days from the date of the filing thereof, either by serving the same personally upon such opposite party by the sheriff of such county or by the clerk of the court mailing the same to the name and address which the purchaser shall file with said clerk at the time of the delivery to him by the sheriff of the deed herein provided. Within thirty days from the serving or mailing of such notice as herein provided, the opposite party to said controversy shall file his answer in said court, and thereupon the court shall hear and determine said controversy, and make such order in regard to the same as it may deem just and proper, which order shall be binding upon all the parties to said controversy.

When rights and privileges granted, shall cease. At the termination of said period of twenty-five (25) years, all of the rights and privileges conveyed to said purchaser by the deed and grant of such sheriff as master commissioner shall cease and determine and said improvements, with all the appurtenances thereunto belonging, shall revert to and become the property of the state of Ohio, free and clear of any and all claims of whatsoever kind or nature against the same.

Distribution of money received by master commissioner. The clerk of said court shall distribute and pay the money received by him from the sheriff as such master commissioner, from the sale of such improvements, to the holders of said bonds pro rata, and upon such payment to any of said bondholders, they shall surrender to the said clerk their bonds, with all unpaid interest coupons thereon, belonging thereto, and the clerk shall thereupon cancel the same, and deliver them, so cancelled, to the treasurer of said water conservation improvement fund.

Appropriation of property, how made. Sec. 412-12. All appropriations of property made by the superintendent of public works in the carrying out of any of the provisions of this act shall be made in accordance with sections 442 to 454 inclusive, of the General Code of Ohio, provided, however, that possession of any property so appropriated shall not be taken by the state of Ohio or the superintendent of public works before the compensation and damages, if any, awarded therefor in such appropriation proceedings, shall have been paid into court.

Impairment of quantity or quality of water prohibited. Sec. 412-13. Nothing in this act shall be construed to authorize any reduction in the quantity, or any impairment in the quality of the water in any water-shed, stream or basin, developed or undeveloped, from which water-shed, stream or basin any municipality or other political subdivision of the state is at the time said superintendent of public works proposes and is proceeding to construct in such water-shed, stream or basin any of the improvements herein provided, taking water for the use of itself or its inhabitants, or has plans under way, or has made or begun appropriation of any property or rights in such water-shed, stream or basin for the purpose of acquiring a water supply for itself or its inhabitants for either domestic, industrial or other uses and purposes; nor shall anything herein contained be so construed as to authorize the superintendent of public works to sell or lease the right to use water at any time for any purpose or to such an extent as to preju- dice, abrogate or supersede any of the water rights hereto- fore granted by the state to the city of Akron by an act entitled "An act to provide for the granting to the city of Akron the right to use and occupy certain waters and lands of the state for water works and park purposes" as con- tained in sections 14203-1, 14203-2 and 14203-3 of the Gen- eral Code of the state of Ohio.

Rights heretofore granted not ab- rogated.

Sec. 412-14. If, by reason of severe drought or other causes, the water supply of any municipality or other polit- ical subdivision of the state be, in the judgment of the su- perintendent of public works at any time so reduced or impaired as to endanger the property of such municipality or political subdivision, or the health, safety or property of the inhabitants thereof, then the superintendent of public works may, under such regulations as he may prescribe, grant to such municipality the right, during the continuance of such emergency, to draw or take such quantity of water as may be necessary to protect the property of such munic- ipality or political subdivision and the health, safety or property of its inhabitants from any improvement con- structed under the provisions of this act, before any of the lessees or grantees of the state, using the water for indus- trial purposes, shall take water therefrom. Such municipal- ity or other political subdivision shall pay for the water so taken by it such price per thousand gallons as may be fixed or determined by the superintendent of public works and the governor of the state; provided that price so fixed shall not exceed the maximum price then being paid for water to the state by any of its lessees or grantees; and provided further that such grant by the superintendent of public works to such municipality or political subdivision shall in no wise modify the terms or impair the validity of any leases then existing between the state and other persons, firms or corporations, except as herein expressly provided.

Emergency of municipality or political subdivi- sion paramount to industrial needs.

Sec. 412-15. This act shall take effect and be in force at the earliest date allowed by law.

CARL R. KIMBALL,
Speaker of the House of Representatives.
CLARENCE J. BROWN,
President of the Senate.

Passed April 10, 1919.
Approved May 9, 1919.

JAMES M. COX,
Governor.

Filed in the office of the Secretary of State at Columbus, Ohio, on the 12th day of May, A. D. 1919.

93 G.

[House Bill No. 403.]

AN ACT

To supplement section 3141 of the General Code by the enactment of section 3141-1 and to amend sections 3147, 3153-1, 3153-2, 3153-3 and 3153-6 of the General Code, relating to hospitals for tuberculosis.

Be it enacted by the General Assembly of the State of Ohio:

SECTION 1. That section 3141 of the General Code be supplemented by the enactment of section 3141-1 and that sections 3147, 3153-1, 3153-2, 3153-3 and 3153-6 of the General Code be amended to read as follows:

When county having joined in erection of tuberculosis hospital may erect and maintain a hospital; tax levy.

SECTION 3141-1. In any county which has joined in the erection of a district tuberculosis hospital and in which such hospital has not capacity to afford suitable accommodation for all cases of tuberculosis that should be admitted to such institution, and where the trustees of such district tuberculosis hospital or the joint board of county commissioners fail or refuse to provide additional accommodation in such hospital, the county commissioners may, with the consent of the state department of health, erect and maintain a county tuberculosis hospital. For the purpose of constructing and maintaining such county hospital the county commissioners may issue bonds and shall annually levy a tax and set aside the funds necessary for such maintenance. Such funds shall not be used for any other purpose. When it shall become necessary to enlarge, repair, or improve such county hospital for tuberculosis, the county commissioners shall proceed in the same manner as provided for other county buildings. Plans and estimates of cost for all additions to hospitals for tuberculosis shall be submitted to and approved by the state department of health and the board of state charities.

Supervision by state health department.

Sec. 3147. The state department of health shall have general supervision of all hospitals for tuberculosis and shall prescribe and may enforce such rules and regulations for their government as it deems necessary. All persons in charge of or employed at such hospital or residents thereof, shall faithfully obey and comply with all such rules and regulations. The location, plans and estimates of cost for all district hospitals for tuberculosis or additions thereto shall be submitted to and approved by the state department of health, and the board of state charities.

Sec. 3153-1. The county commissioners may appoint one or more instructing and visiting nurses who may visit any home or place in the county wherein there is a case of tuberculosis, but such appointments shall be subject to the approval of the state department of health. *Appointment of instructing and visiting nurses.*

Sec. 3153-2. Where such appointments are made by the board of county commissioners, such nurses shall be subject to the supervision of the county commissioners, and the state department of health, and may be detailed for service under any local board of health or health department having jurisdiction. *Supervision of nurses.*

Sec. 3153-3. The board of county commissioners appointing such instructing and visiting nurses shall fix the compensation of such nurses, and may authorize such nurses to attend conferences where the care, treatment or prevention of tuberculosis, public health or nursing are subjects for consideration. Such compensation and the necessary expenses incurred by such nurses shall be paid from the poor fund of the county, or from the funds provided for the hospital for tuberculosis. *Compensation of nurses.*

Sec. 3153-6. In such counties as have not constructed a county hospital for tuberculosis, or have not contracted with a municipal tuberculosis hospital, or in such counties as have joined in the construction of a district tuberculosis hospital and in which the joint board of county commissioners of such district shall fail or refuse to maintain tuberculosis dispensaries as herein provided, the county commissioners may establish and maintain one or more tuberculosis dispensaries in the county and may employ physicians, public health nurses and other persons for the operation of such dispensaries or of other means provided for the prevention, care and treatment of cases of tuberculosis and may provide by tax levies or otherwise the necessary funds for their establishment and maintenance. *When tuberculosis dispensaries may be established.*

SECTION 2. That original sections 3147, 3153-1, 3153-2, 3153-3 and 3153-6 of the General Code be and the same are hereby repealed. *Repeals.*

The sectional numbers in this act are in conformity to the General Code. JOHN G. PRICE, Attorney General.

CARL R. KIMBALL,
Speaker of the House of Representatives.
CLARENCE J. BROWN,
President of the Senate.

Passed April 4, 1919.
Approved May 9, 1919.

JAMES M. COX,
Governor.

Filed in the office of the Secretary of State at Columbus, Ohio, on the 12th day of May, A. D. 1919.

94 G.

[House Bill No. 218.]

AN ACT

To re-enact sections 7146, 7150, 7151, 7152 and 7153 of the General Code relating to destruction of Canada or Russian thistles, wild parsnip, wild carrot, oxeye daisy or wild mustard.

Be it enacted by the General Assembly of the State of Ohio:

SECTION 1. That sections 7146, 7150, 7151, 7152 and 7153 of the General Code be re-enacted to read as follows:

Destruction of brush, briars, weeds, etc., on highways.

Sec. 7146. Township trustees or street commissioners having control of and being charged with the duty of repairing macadamized, graveled or improved roads and turnpikes, and road superintendents of county and township roads and the street commissioners of each city or village, between the first and twentieth days of June, and between the first and twentieth days of August, and, if necessary, between the first and twentieth days of September of each year, shall destroy or cause it to be done, all brush, briars, burrs, vines, Russian and Canadian or common thistles, or other noxious weeds, growing or being within the limits of a county or township road, turnpike, improved, graveled or macadamized road, street, or alley within their jurisdiction.

Notice to destroy weeds, etc., to land owner.

Sec. 7150. Upon written information that Canada or Russian thistles, wild parsnip, wild carrot, oxeye daisy or wild mustard are growing on lands in a township, and are about to spread or mature seeds, the trustees of the township shall cause a written notice to be served upon the owner, lessee, agent or tenant having charge of such land notifying him that said noxious weeds are growing on such lands and that they must be cut and destroyed within five days after the service of such notice.

Fees for serving notice.

Sec. 7151. A constable or a marshal of a city or village, or his deputy, may make service and return of the notice provided for in the next preceding section and the fees therefor shall be the same as are allowed for service and return of summons in civil cases before a magistrate.

Effect of non-compliance with notice.

Sec. 7152. If the owner, lessee, agent or tenant having charge of the lands mentioned in section seventy-one hundred and fifty, fails to comply with such notice, the township trustees shall cause said noxious weeds to be cut and destroyed and may employ the necessary labor to carry out the provisions of this section. All expenses incurred shall, when approved by the township trustees, be paid out of any money in the treasury of the township not otherwise appropriated.

Expense a lien upon land.

Sec. 7153. The township trustees shall make a written return to the board of commissioners of their county of their action under the next three preceding sections with a statement of the charges for their services, the amount paid for the performing of such labor and the fees of the officers who made the service of the notice and return and a proper description of the premises. Such amounts, when allowed, shall be entered upon the tax duplicate and be a lien upon such lands from and after the date of the entry and be collected as other taxes and returned to the township with the general fund.

CARL R. KIMBALL,
Speaker of the House of Representatives.
CLARENCE J. BROWN,
President of the Senate.

Passed April 17, 1919.
Approved May 9, 1919.

JAMES M. COX,
Governor.

Filed in the office of the Secretary of State at Columbus, Ohio, on the 12th day of May, A. D. 1919.

95 G.

———

[House Bill No. 182.]

AN ACT

To amend sections 4744-2, 7654-1, 7654-2, 7654-3, 7654-4 and 7654-5 of the General Code, relative to county normal schools.

Be it enacted by the General Assembly of the State of Ohio:

SECTION 1. That sections 4744-2, 7654-1, 7654-2, 7654-3, 7654-4 and 7654-5 of the General Code, be amended to read as follows:

Sec. 4744-2. On or before the first day of August of each year the county board of education shall certify to the county auditor the number of teachers to be employed for the ensuing year in the various rural and village school districts within the county school district, and also the number of district superintendents employed and their compensation and the compensation of the county superintendent; and such board of education shall also certify to the county auditor the amounts to be apportioned to each district for the payment of its share of the salaries of the county and district superintendents and of the local expense of the normal school in the county.

Number of teachers to be employed certified to county auditor; districts; apportionment.

Sec. 7654-1. County boards of education may establish county normal schools in districts maintaining first grade high schools for the training of teachers for village and rural schools. Not more than one such normal school shall be established in any county school district. Counties desiring such normal schools shall make application therefor to the superintendent of public instruction through the county board of education. The superintendent of public instruction shall examine all applications and shall designate the location of such normal school.

County normal schools may be established; location of school; rooms and furniture; expense.

.Two or more county boards of education may unite to form a joint county normal school and when such is formed it shall be under the direct control of the superintendent of the county in which the normal school is located. The support for such normal school shall be apportioned equally among the counties thus uniting.

The board of education of the district in which the normal school is located shall furnish suitable room or rooms and provide such furniture as may be required by the superintendent of public instruction. The county board of education shall furnish such other equipment as may be necessary. The local expense of maintaining the normal school in each county shall be paid by the county board of education from its contingent fund.

Course; entrance requirements. Sec. 7654-2. Each county normal school shall offer at least a one-year course for the training of teachers. The entrance requirements to such schools shall be fixed by the superintendent of public instruction. Such schools may offer short courses during the school year but shall not offer summer courses unless practice departments are maintained during such courses.

Director and instructors. Sec. 7654-3. Each normal school shall employ a director and such other instructors as the superintendent of public instruction may prescribe. Such director shall be employed by the county board of education on the nomination of the county superintendent.

Practice division. Sec. 7654-4. Each normal school may maintain a practice division and shall be authorized to arrange with different boards of education for observation and practice teaching privilege in the rural schools under their control.

Salaries of director and instructors. Sec. 7654-5. The county board of education of any county school district that maintains a county normal school approved by the superintendent of public instruction shall fix the salary of the director and other instructors and shall receive from the state one thousand dollars to be applied to the payment of the salary of the director and five hundred dollars to be applied to the payment of the salary of each additional instructor. Such amount shall be allowed by the auditor of state upon the approval of the superintendent of public instruction. All expense in excess thereof shall be paid by the county board of education from its contingent fund.

Repeals. SECTION 2. That original sections 4744-2, 7654-1, 7654-2, 7654-3, 7654-4 and 7654-5 of the General Code be, and the same are hereby repealed.

CARL R. KIMBALL,
Speaker of the House of Representatives.
CLARENCE J. BROWN,
President of the Senate.

The sectional numbers in this act are in conformity to the General Code. JOHN G. PRICE, Attorney General.

Passed April 10, 1919.
Approved May 9, 1919.

JAMES M. COX,
Governor.

Filed in the office of the Secretary of State at Columbus, Ohio, on the 12th day of May, A. D. 1919.

96 G.

[House Bill No. 163.]

AN ACT

To amend section 4727 of the General Code, providing for the transfer of territory to or from a centralized school district.

Be it enacted by the General Assembly of the State of Ohio:
SECTION 1. That section 4727 of the General Code be amended to read as follows:

Sec. 4727. When the schools of a rural school district have been centralized such centralization shall not be discontinued within three years, and then only by petition and election, as provided in section 4726. If at such election more votes are cast against centralization than for it, the division into subdistricts as they existed prior to centralization shall thereby be re-established. Nothing in this or the foregoing sections, namely, sections 4726 and 4726-1, shall prevent a county board of education upon the petition of two-thirds of the qualified electors of the territory petitioning for transfer, from transferring territory to or from a centralized school district, the same as to or from a district not centralized.

Submission of question of decentralization.

Transfer of territory authorized.

SECTION 2. That said original section 4727 of the General Code be, and the same is hereby repealed.

The sectional number in this act is in conformity to the General Code. JOHN G. PRICE, Attorney General.

CARL R. KIMBALL,
Speaker of the House of Representatives.
CLARENCE J. BROWN,
President of the Senate.

Passed April 16, 1919.
Approved May 9, 1919.

JAMES M. COX,
Governor.

Filed in the office of the Secretary of State at Columbus, Ohio, on the 12th day of May, A. D. 1919.

97 G.

[House Bill No. 311.]

AN ACT

To create municipal and general health districts for purposes of local health administration; and to amend sections 1245, 1246, 4404, 4405, 4408, 4409, 4410, 4413, 4429, 4430, 4436, 4437, 4476 and 12785 of the General Code relating to the powers and duties of boards of health and to repeal original sections 1245, 1246, 3391, 3392, 3393, 3394, 4404, 4405, 4408, 4409, 4410, 4413, 4429, 4430, 4436, 4437, 4476 and 12785 of the General Code.

Be it enacted by the General Assembly of the State of Ohio:

Sec. 1261-16.
Health districts.

SECTION 1. For purposes of local health administration the state shall be divided into health districts. Each city having at the last preceding federal census a population of twenty-five thousand or more shall constitute a health district and for the purpose of this act shall be known as and hereinafter be referred to as a municipal health district. The townships and municipalities in each county, exclusive of any city having twenty-five thousand population or more at the last preceding federal census, shall constitute a health district and for the purposes of this act shall be known as and hereinafter be referred to as a general health district. Provided, that where any municipality having less than twenty-five thousand population at the last preceding federal census is located in more than one county it shall be included for the purposes of this act, in the county in which the largest part of the area of such municipality is located. As hereinafter provided, there may be a union of two general health districts or a union of a general health district and a municipal health district located within such district.

When present district may constitute separate municipal health district.

Provided, that when any municipality of not less than ten thousand nor more than twenty-five thousand population at the last preceding federal census maintains at the time of the passage of this act a board of health or health department furnishing, in the opinion of the state department of health, a sanitary administration equal to that to be provided in the district under the provisions of this act, the state commissioner of health shall declare such a municipality a separate municipal health district and from and after the beginning of the next fiscal year after such action, such municipality shall be and constitute a separate municipal health district within the meaning of this act. Should the state department of health, after investigation, subsequently find that such municipality does not maintain a sanitary administration equal to that provided in the general health district in which such municipality is located, the state department of health may, after notice to the mayor of the municipality, declare such municipality a part of the general health district and from the beginning of the next fiscal year thereafter the municipality shall be a part of the general health district as provided in this act.

Sec. 1261-17.

SECTION 2. In each general health district, except in a district formed by the union of a general health district and a municipal health district, there shall be a district board of health consisting of five members to be appointed as hereinafter provided and as provided in section 4406 of the General Code. The members of the board of health of a general health district shall receive no compensation for their services but shall be reimbursed for all necessary and lawful expenses incurred in attending meetings of the board. A vacancy in the membership of the board of health of a general health district shall be filled in like manner as an original appointment· and shall be for the unexpired term. Provided, that when a vacancy shall occur more than ninety days prior to the annual meeting of the district advisory council the remaining members of the district board of health may select a resident of the district to fill such vacancy until such meeting. A majority of the members of the district board of health shall constitute a quorum.

District boards of health; filling of vacancy; quorum.

Sec. 1261-18.

SECTION 3. Within sixty days after this act shall take effect the mayor of each municipality not constituting a municipal health district and the chairman of the trustees of each township in a general health district shall meet at the county seat and shall organize by selecting a chairman and a secretary. Such organization shall be known as the district advisory council. The district advisory council shall proceed to select and appoint a district board of health as hereinbefore provided, having due regard to the equal representation of all parts of the district. Where the population of any municipality represented on such district advisory board exceeds one-fifth of the total population of the district, as determined by the last preceding federal census, such municipality shall be entitled to one representative on the district board of health for each fifth of the population of the district represented by the population of such municipality. Of the members of the district board of health, one shall be a farmer, two shall be physicians, and one shall be an attorney-at-law. Annually thereafter the district advisory council shall meet on the first Monday in February for the purpose of electing its officers and a member of the district board of health and shall also receive and consider the annual or special reports of the district board of health and make recommendations to the district board of health or to the state department of health in regard to matters for the betterment of health and sanitation within the district or for needed legislation. It shall be the duty of the secretary of the district advisory board to notify the district health commissioner and the state commissioner of health of the proceedings of such meeting. Special meetings of the district advisory council shall be held on request of the district board of health or on the order of the state commissioner of health. On certification of the chairman and secretary the necessary expenses of

District advisory council; organization; appointment of members of district board.

Annual meeting of advisory council; duties; special meetings.

238

each delegate to an annual or special meeting shall be paid by the city, village or township he represents.

The district health commissioner shall attend all meetings of the district advisory council.

Sec. 1261-19.

Organization of district board; appointment of health commissioner; duties.

SECTION 4. Within thirty days after the appointment of the members of the district board of health in a general district, they shall organize by selecting one of their members as president and another member as president pro tempore. The district board of health shall appoint a district health commissioner, who shall be secretary of the board and who shall give his entire time to the duties of his office and shall not engage in any other business. The health commissioner shall be appointed from an eligible list certified by the state civil service commission of Ohio, as hereinafter provided, and said appointee shall not be removed except it be for good cause and by a majority vote of the membership of the district board of health. In the absence of an eligible list, a temporary appointment may be made, but no such appointment shall be made without the approval of the state commissioner of health. A health commissioner who has been removed from office may appeal to the public health council. Upon notice of such appeal the district board of health shall prefer charges against the health commissioner and a hearing shall be given at which the district board of health and the health commissioner may be present. After such hearing the public health council shall render a decision and such decision shall be a final determination of the case. The hearing may be held within the general health district or at the city of Columbus. The district health commissioner shall be the executive officer of the district board of health and shall carry out all orders of the district board of health and of the state department of health. He shall be charged with the enforcement of all sanitary laws and regulations in the district, and shall have within the general health district all the powers now conferred by law upon health officers of municipalities. It shall be the duty of the district health commissioner to keep the public informed in regard to all matters affecting the health of the district.

Removal of commissioner; appeal; hearing.

Sec. 1261-20.

Union of municipal with general health districts; vote on question.

SECTION 5. When it is proposed that a municipal health district unite with a general health district in the formation of a single district, the district advisory council of the general health district shall meet and vote on the question of union and it shall require a majority vote of the total number of townships, villages and cities entitled to representation voting affirmatively to carry the question. The council or body performing the duties of council of the municipality shall likewise vote on the question and a majority voting affirmatively shall be required for approval. When the majority of the district advisory council and council of the municipality have voted affirmatively, the chairman of the district advisory council and the mayor or chief executive officer of the municipality shall enter into a contract subject to the approval of the state commissioner of health, for the administration of health affairs in the combined district. Such contract shall state the proportion of the expenses of the board of health or health department of the combined district to be paid by the municipality and by that part of the district lying outside such municipality; shall provide for the amount and character of sanitary service to be rendered in the parts of the district lying outside such municipality and the date on which the board of health or health department of the municipality shall take over the administration of the combined health district. After such union is completed the board of health or health department of the municipal health district shall have within the combined district all the powers herein or hereafter granted to and perform all the duties herein or hereafter required of the board of health of a general health district.

Contract for administration of health affairs.

Sec. 1261-21.

SECTION 6. Where it is proposed that two general health districts shall unite in the formation of one general health district, the district advisory council of each general health district shall meet and vote on the question of union and an affirmative majority vote of the total number of townships, villages and cities entitled to representation on the district advisory council shall be required for approval. When the two district advisory councils have voted affirmatively on the question, they shall meet in joint session and shall elect a district board of health for the combined districts, and not more than three members shall be from any one original district. When such union is completed such districts shall constitute a general health district and shall be governed in the manner herein provided for general health districts. Where two general health districts unite to form one district, the office of the district board of health shall be located at the county seat of the most populous county, except that for good cause such office may, with the approval of the state commissioner of health, be located in the municipality most accessible by usual means of transportation to the whole of the district.

Union of general health districts; procedure.

Locaton of office.

Sec. 1261-22.

SECTION 7. In any general health district the district board of health shall upon the recommendation of the health commissioner appoint for whole-time service a public health nurse and a clerk and such additional public health nurses, physicians and other persons, within the classes to be fixed by the state civil service commission of Ohio as hereinafter provided, as may be necessary for the proper conduct of its work. Such number of public health nurses shall be employed as is necessary to provide adequate public health nursing service to all parts of the district. The board of health of each district shall provide such infant welfare stations, prenatal clinics and other measures for the protection of children as it may deem necessary. It shall also provide for the prevention and treatment of trachoma and

Appointment of nurse, nurses, clerk, physicians and others.

Infant welfare stations, prenatal clinics, etc.

may establish clinics or detention hospitals and provide the necessary medical and nursing service therefor.

Sec. 1261-23.
Sanitary administration in municipalities of district.

SECTION 8. The board of health of any general health district shall make adequate provision for the sanitary administration of any municipalities forming part of such district. It shall establish an office in each city, in rooms which the council of such city shall provide for that purpose and shall designate for duty therein a deputy health officer and such inspectors and nurses as may be necessary properly to administer sanitary affairs of such city. The amount and quality of sanitary service to be furnished in any such municipality shall in no case be less than that in effect in such city at the time this act shall take effect.

Sec. 1261-24.
Appointment of board by state commissioner, when.

SECTION 9. If in any general health district the district advisory council shall fail to meet or to select a district board of health, within ninety days after this act shall take effect, the state commissioner of health may, with the consent of the public health council, appoint a district board of health for such district which shall have and exercise all powers conferred by this act on district boards of health.

Sec. 1261-25.
Preferment of charges on failure or neglect of duty.

SECTION 10. If the state commissioner of health shall find that the members of the board of health of a general or municipal health district, or any member thereof, has failed to perform any or all the duties required by this act, he shall prefer charges against such members of the board or such member before the public health council and shall notify the members of such board or such member as to the time and place at which such charges will be heard. If the public health council shall, after hearing, find the members of such board or such member guilty of the charge

Removal of members; vacancies.

or charges, it may remove such members of the board or such member from office. When all, or a majority of the members of the board of health of a general or municipal health district be so removed from office, the district advisory council or the mayor of the municipality, upon notice of such removal, shall within thirty days after receipt of such notice select a new board of health or members to fill the vacancies caused by removal, and if the district advisory council or mayor fails within sixty days, to select such board or such member or members, the state commissioner of health, with the approval of the public health council, may appoint a board of health for such general or municipal health district or fill the vacancies caused by removal.

Sec. 1261-26.
Duties of district board.

SECTION 11. In addition to the duties now required of boards of health it shall be the duty of each district board of health to study and record the prevalence of disease within its district; to provide for the prompt diagnosis and control of communicable diseases; to provide for the medical and dental supervision of school children; to provide for the free treatment of cases of venereal diseases; to provide for the inspection of schools, public institutions, jails, workhouses, children's homes, infirmaries and other charitable, benevolent, correctional and penal institutions; to provide for the inspection of dairies, stores, restaurants, hotels and other places where food is manufactured, handled, stored, sold or offered for sale, and for the medical inspection of persons employed therein; to provide for the inspection and abatement of nuisances dangerous to public health or comfort; and to take all steps necessary to protect the public health and to prevent disease.

Provided that in the medical supervision of school children as herein provided, no medical or surgical treatment shall be administered to any minor school child except upon the written request of the parent or guardian of such child; and provided further, that any information regarding any diseased condition or defect found as a result of any medical school examination shall be communicated only to the parent or guardian of such child and if in writing shall be in a sealed envelope addressed to such parent or guardian.

Sec. 1361-27. SECTION 12. Each district board of health shall provide for the carrying on of such laboratory work as is necessary for the proper conduct of its work. It may establish a district laboratory or may contract with any existing laboratory within or convenient to the district for the performance of such work or may unite with another district in the establishment of a joint laboratory. It shall be the duty of all state institutions supported in whole or in part by public funds to furnish such laboratory service as may be required by any district board of health under terms to be agreed upon. Any contract for the furnishing of laboratory service to a district board of health and any proposal for the establishment of a joint laboratory, shall be subject to the approval of the state commissioner of health. In the operation of such laboratories standard methods approved by the state commissioner of health shall be used. *Provisions for laboratory work.*

Sec. 1361-28. SECTION 13. Each district board of health shall provide for the free treatment of cases of gonorrhea, syphilis and chancroid. It may establish and maintain one or more clinics for such purpose and may provide for the necessary medical and nursing service therefor. The district board of health shall provide for the quarantine of such carriers of syphilis, gonorrhea or chancroid as the state commissioner of health shall order to be quarantined. It shall use due diligence in the prevention of such veneral diseases and shall carry out all orders and regulations of the state department of health in connection therewith. *Free treatment for venereal diseases.*

Sec. 1361-29. SECTION 14. Each district board of health shall provide for the free distribution of antitoxin for the treatment of cases of diphtheria and shall establish sufficient distributing stations to render such antitoxin readily available in all parts of the district. *Free distribution of antitoxin.*

Sec. 1361-30. SECTION 15. The district board of health hereby created shall exercise all the powers and perform all the *Supersedes existing board of health.*

duties now conferred and imposed by law upon the board of health of a municipality, and all such powers, duties, procedure and penalties for violation of the sanitary regulations of a board of health shall be construed to have been transferred to the district board of health by this act. The district board of health shall exercise such further powers and perform such other duties as are herein conferred or imposed.

Sec. 1261-31.

Inspections of county institutions.

SECTION 16. The district health commissioner shall make or cause to be made frequent inspections of all county infirmaries, children's homes, workhouses, jails or other charitable, benevolent, correctional or penal institutions in the district, including physical examinations of the inmates whenever necessary, and shall make or cause to be made such laboratory examinations of such inmates as may be requested by any state or county official having jurisdiction over such institution.

Sec. 1261-32.

District commissioner shall be deputy registrar of vital statistics; reports.

SECTION 17. The district health commissioner shall be a deputy of the state registrar of vital statistics and shall under his direction enforce all laws governing the registration of births and deaths. Each local registrar of vital statistics shall on or before the fifth day of each month transmit to the health commissioner of the district having jurisdiction all certificates of birth or deaths received by such registrar during the preceding month. The health commissioner shall within five days transmit such certificates to the state registrar of vital statistics. When any registrar shall receive any certificate of a death from any contagious or communicable disease, he shall within twenty-four hours after receipt of such certificate notify the health commissioner of the district having jurisdiction of such death on a form to be furnished by the district board of health.

Sec. 1261-33.

Detention hospitals may be established; cost of care, etc.

SECTION 18. The district board of health may establish detention hospitals for cases of communicable diseases and provide for the support and maintenance thereof. It may collect from persons committed to such hospitals the cost of the care and treatment of such persons while inmates therein. The expenses of such indigent persons as are committed to such detention hospitals shall be a proper charge against and shall be collected from the township or municipality from which such person was sent to the hospital.

Sec. 1261-34.

Survey of boards by civil service commission; examinations for employes.

SECTION 19. The state civil service commission of Ohio, shall upon recommendation of the state commissioner of health, survey the duties of employes necessary for efficient operation of district boards of health and shall classify such employes in so far as is practicable, determine the qualifications of, and fix a standard rate of compensation for each class. Such classification shall also include positions to be filled on a part-time basis. The state civil service commission shall hold examinations in various parts of the state and prepare lists of eligibles for the classes of employes so fixed. Such examinations shall be open to suitably qualified persons without restriction as to residence. The state civil service commission shall, upon request of any district board of health, certify lists of eligibles for appointment, giving preference in each case to eligibles resident in the district.

Sec. 1261-35.

SECTION 20. All appointments by boards of health of general health districts shall be from the list of eligibles certified by the state civil service commission, except that where no list of eligibles is furnished, temporary appointments for a period not to exceed ninety days may be made with the approval of the state civil service commission, and the rate of compensation of persons so appointed shall be that fixed by the state civil service commission for that class. In grave emergency, and to prevent or combat serious epidemics, the state commissioner of health may authorize the temporary employment of physicians, nurses and other necessary persons for periods not to exceed ninety days. Appointments to positions on a part-time basis shall be from lists certified by the civil service commission for part-time employment and the compensation paid any part-time employe shall not in any one year exceed one-half the compensation fixed by the civil service commission for whole-time service in the same class. Persons appointed for whole-time service shall give their entire time to the duties of such position and shall not engage in any other business.

Appointments from eligible lists.

Sec. 1261-36.

SECTION 21. It shall be the duty of the county commissioners or of the city council to furnish suitable quarters for any board of health or health department having jurisdiction over all or a major part of such county or municipality in accordance with the provisions of this act.

Suitable quarters furnished.

Sec. 1261-37.

SECTION 22. In general health districts the prosecuting attorney of the county constituting all or a major part of such district shall act as the legal advisor of the district board of health. In a proceeding in which the board of health of any general health district is a party the prosecuting attorney of the county in which such proceeding is instituted shall act as the legal representative of the district board of health.

Legal adviser of district board.

Sec. 1261-38.

SECTION 23. The treasurer of a city which constitutes a separate health district shall be the custodian of the health fund of such municipal health district. The county treasurer of a county which constitutes all or the major portion of a general health district shall be the custodian of the health fund of that health district. The auditor of a county which constitutes all or a major portion of a general health district shall act as the auditor of the general health district. The auditor of a municipality which constitutes a municipal health district shall act as the auditor of the municipal health district. Expenses of the district board of health of a general health district shall be paid on the warrant of the county auditor issued on vouchers ap-

Custodian of health fund.

Auditor of health district.

proved by the district board of health and signed by the
district health commissioner. Expenses of the board of
health or health department of a municipal health district
shall be paid on the warrant of the auditor of the municipality issued on vouchers approved by the board of health
or health department of the municipal health district and
signed by the municipal health commissioner.

SECTION 24. When any general or municipal health
district has been duly organized as provided by this act
and has employed for whole-time service a health commissioner, a public health nurse and a clerk, the chairman of
the board of health, or the principal executive officer of the
department of health as the case may be shall semi-annually
upon the first day of January and of July certify such fact
to the state commissioner of health, stating the salaries paid
such health commissioner, public health nurse and clerk
during the preceding six months. If such board of health
or health department has complied with the orders and regulations of the state department of health and has truly
and faithfully complied with the provisions of this act, the
state commissioner of health shall endorse such facts on
the certificate and shall transmit the certificate to the auditor of state, who shall thereupon draw a voucher on the
treasurer of state to the order of the custodian of the funds
of such health district, payable out of the general revenue
fund, in amount equal to one-half of the amount paid by
the district board of health or health department to such
health commissioner, public health nurse and clerk, during
such semi-annual period. Provided, that if the amount paid
by such district board of health or health department during any six months is in excess of two thousand dollars,
the amount to be paid by the auditor of state shall be one
thousand dollars and no more, and no payment shall be
made unless the certificate of the district board of health
or health department shall have been endorsed by the state
commissioner of health as herein provided.

SECTION 25. The board of health of a general health
district shall annually, on or before August first, estimate
in itemized form the amounts needed for the current expenses of such district for the fiscal year beginning on the
first day of January next ensuing. Such estimate shall be
certified to the county auditor and by him submitted to
the district advisory council at a meeting held at his office
on the second Monday of September. The district advisory
council may reduce any item or items in such estimate but
may not increase any item or the aggregate of all items.
The aggregate amount as fixed by the district advisory
council shall be apportioned by the county auditor among
the townships and municipalities composing the health district on the basis of population as shown by the last preceding federal census. The district board of health shall

certify to the county auditor the amount due from the
state as its share of the salaries of the district health com-

missioner, public health nurse and clerk for the next fiscal year which shall be deducted from the total of such estimate before an apportionment is made. The county auditor, when making his semi-annual apportionments of funds shall retain at each such semi-annual apportionment, one-half of the amount so apportioned to each township and municipality. Such moneys shall be placed in a separate fund, to be known as the "district health fund." When a general health district is composed of townships and municipalities in two or more counties, the county auditor making the original apportionment shall certify to the auditor of each county concerned the amount apportioned to each township and municipality in such county. Each auditor shall withhold from the semi-annual apportionment to each such township or municipality the amount so certified, and shall pay the amounts so withheld to the custodian of the funds of the health district concerned, to be credited to the district health fund. Where any general health district has been united with a municipal health district located therein, the mayor of the municipality shall annually on or before the first day of August certify to the county auditor the total amount due for the ensuing fiscal year from the municipalities and townships in the district as provided in the contract between such municipality and the district advisory council of the original health district. The county auditor shall thereupon apportion the amount so certified to the townships and municipalities, and withhold the sums so apportioned as herein provided.

SECTION 26. In case of epidemic or threatened epidemic or during the unusual prevalence of a dangerous communicable disease, if the moneys in the district health fund of a general health district are not sufficient, in the judgment of the board of health of such district, to defray the expenses necessary to prevent the spread of such disease, such board of health shall estimate the amount required for such purpose and apportion it among the townships and municipalities in which the condition herein described exists, on the basis provided for in section 25 of this act. Such estimate and apportionment shall be certified to the county auditor of the proper county or counties, who shall draw an order on the clerk, auditor or other similar officer of each township or municipality affected thereby, for the amount to it apportioned. Such clerk, auditor or other similar officer shall forthwith draw his warrant on the treasurer of such township or municipality for the amount of such certification, which shall be honored by the treasurer from any general treasury balances subject to his control, regardless of funds. The clerk, auditor or other similar officer shall thereupon set up an account to be designated "emergency health account," showing a deficit therein, and certify the action taken to the trustees or council or other body having the power to borrow money. Thereupon the trustees or council or other similar body may exercise the powers provided for in sections 4450 and 4451 of the General Code. Tax levies made for the purpose set forth in this section shall be subject to the provisions of section 5649-4 of the General Code. Moneys raised under the authority herein conferred shall be placed in the treasury of the borrowing subdivision and credited to the "emergency health account," which shall thereupon be closed; so that the moneys taken from general cash balances shall be restored thereto and the regular funds of the subdivision shall be restored thereby.

Power to borrow money.

If there is not sufficient money in the general cash balances of such subdivisions to satisfy the warrant so drawn by the clerk, auditor or other similar officer, the treasurer thereof shall honor the same to the extent of the cash in such treasury and the balance shall be certified by the clerk, auditor or other officer and the treasurer, jointly, to the trustees, council or other borrowing authority, which shall immediately exercise the powers provided for in this section, to raise the amount of the warrant. The proceeds of such action shall be paid into the general cash balance in the treasury of the subdivision, and the balance due on the warrant shall then be paid.

Separate account of expenditures.

The warrants provided for in this section shall be drawn in favor of the county treasurer, as treasurer of the district health fund, and the proceeds shall go into such fund. A separate account shall be kept of expenditures under this section. If a greater amount is expended in any township or municipality than the amount drawn therefrom by action hereunder, the execss shall be charged against such subdivision at the next annual apportionment in addition to the amount apportionable to such subdivision under section 25 of this act. If the amount drawn under this section is not wholly expended in any subdivision, the unexpended remainder shall be credited to the next annual apportionment to such subdivision.

Enforcement of official duties.

Performance of the official duties by this section imposed on officers, boards and legislative bodies, may be enforced by mandamus on the relation of the district board of health, which is hereby given special capacity to sue in such action. In any such case the return day of the alternative writ shall not be more than three days after the filing of the petition.

Sec. 1261-42.

Orders and regulations for board and for general public; publication.

SECTION 27. The board of health of a general health district may make such orders and regulations as it deems necessary for its own government, for the public health, the prevention or restriction of disease, and the prevention, abatement or suppression of nuisances. All orders and regulations not for the government of the board, but intended for the general public, shall be adopted, recorded and certified as are ordinances of municipalities and record thereof shall be given in all courts of the state the same force and effect as is given such ordinances, but the advertisements of such orders and regulations shall be by publication in one newspaper published and of general circulation within the general health district. Publication shall be made once a week for two consecutive weeks and such orders and regulations shall take effect and be in force ten days from date of first publication. Provided, however, that in cases of emergency caused by epidemics of contagious or infectious diseases, or conditions or events endangering the public health, such boards may declare such orders and regulations to be emergency measures, and such orders and regulations shall become immediately effective without such advertising, recording and certifying.

Sec. 1261-43.

The sectional numbers on the margin hereof are designated as provided by law.
John G. Price, Attorney General.

SECTION 28. In case any section or sections or part of any section or sections of this act shall be found unconstitutional, the remainder of the act shall not thereby be invalidated, but shall remain in full force and effect.

Section or part held void shall not affect others.

Sec. 1245. The state department of health shall make provision for annual conferences of district health commissioners for the consideration of the cause and prevention of dangerous communicable diseases and other measures to protect and improve the public health. Each board of health or other body or person appointed or acting in place of a board of health shall appoint its health commissioner or health officer a delegate to such annual conferences. The district board of health shall pay the necessary expenses of such delegate upon presentation of a certificate from the state commissioner of health that the delegate attended the sessions of such conference.

Annual conference; expenses.

Sec. 1246. The state commissioner of health may require any district health commissioner to attend immediately after his appointment, a school of instruction to be conducted by the state department of health at Columbus. The course at such school of instruction shall not exceed four weeks in duration, and the necessary expenses of the district health commissioner in attending such school shall be paid by the district board of health upon certification from the state commissioner of health that such officer has attended the school of instruction.

District commissioner may be required to attend school of instruction.

Sec. 4404. The council of each municipality constituting a municipal health district, shall establish a board of health, composed of five members to be appointed by the mayor and confirmed by the council who shall serve without compensation and a majority of whom shall be a quorum. The mayor shall be president by virtue of his office. Provided that nothing in this act contained shall be construed as interfering with the authority of a municipality constituting a municipal health district, making provision by charter for health administration other than as in this section provided.

Municipality shall establish a board of health; appointment.

Sec. 4405. If any such municipality fails or refuses to establish a board of health the state commissioner of health, with the approval of the public health council, may appoint a health commissioner therefor and fix his salary and term of office. Such health commissioner shall have

When state commissioner may appoint officer for municipality; salary.

the same powers and perform the duties granted to or imposed upon boards of health, except that rules, regulations or orders of a general character and required to be published made by such health commissioner shall be approved by the state commissioner of health. The salary of the health commissioner so appointed, and all necessary expenses incurred by him in performing the duties of the board shall be paid by and be a valid claim against such municipality.

Board shall appoint commissioner, nurse, clerk, physician, etc.

Sec. 4408. In any municipal health district, the board of health or person or persons performing the duties of a board of health shall appoint within the classes fixed by the state civil service commission of Ohio for whole-time service, a health commissioner, a public health nurse and a clerk. It may also appoint physicians, public health nurses and other persons, within the classes fixed by the state civil service commission of Ohio. Where the municipal civil service commission has held examinations for appointment within the classes so fixed, and has certified lists of eligibles for the classes from which appointment is to be made, such appointments shall be made from the lists so certified, but if the municipal civil service commission has not held examinations in accord with the classification made by the state civil service commission, or cannot furnish lists of eligibles for such classes, appointment shall be made from lists of eligibles furnished by the state civil service commission as hereinbefore provided. Where no list of eligibles is furnished by the municipal or state civil service commission, temporary appointments may be made for periods not to exceed ninety days with the consent of the state civil service commission. Provided that the status of persons employed at the time this act shall take effect by a board of health or health department under the provisions of municipal civil service for whole-time service shall not be affected by the passage of this act.

Record of proceedings and record of diseases.

Sec. 4409. The secretary of the board shall keep a full and accurate record of the proceedings of the board together with a record of diseases reported to the health commissioner and on termination of his office shall turn over to his successor, books, records, papers and other matter belonging to the board. Each board of health, or person or persons performing the duties of the board of health shall procure suitable books, blanks, and other things necessary to the transaction of its business. Such records shall be kept as are required by the state commissioner of health and such forms shall be used as he may prescribe.

Care of sick poor and quarantined persons.

Sec. 4410. The board of health shall care for the sick poor and each person quarantined when such person is unable to pay for care and treatment, and for all persons sent to the municipal detention hospital when such persons are unable to pay for care and treatment.

Orders and regulations of municipal board.

Sec. 4413. The board of health of a municipality may make such orders and regulations as it deems necessary for its own government, for the public health, the prevention or restriction of disease, and the prevention, abatement or suppression of nuisance. Orders and regulations not for the government of the board, but intended for the general public, shall be adopted, advertised, recorded and certified as are ordinances of municipalities, and the record thereof shall be given, in all courts of the state, the same force and effect as is given such ordinances. Provided, however, that in cases of emergency caused by epidemic of contagious or infectious diseases, or conditions or events endangering the public health, such boards may declare such orders and regulations to be emergency measures, and such orders and regulations shall become immediately effective without such advertising, recording and certifying.

Sec. 4429. When a case of smallpox, cholera, plague, *Quarantine of persons having or exposed to contagious disease.* yellow fever, typhus fever, diphtheria, membranous croup, scarlet fever or other communicable diseases declared by the board of health or state department of health to be quarantinable is reported within its jurisdiction, the board of health shall at once cause to be placed in a conspicuous position on the house wherein such disease occurs a quarantine card having printed on it in large letters the name of the disease within, and prohibit entrance to or exit from such house without written permission from the board of health, or shall enforce such restrictive measures as may be prescribed by the state department of health. No person shall remove, mar, deface, or destroy such quarantine card. which shall remain in place until after the patient has been removed from such house, or has recovered and is no longer capable of communicating the disease, and the house and the contents thereof have been properly purified and disinfected by the board of health or treated in such manner as may be prescribed by the state department of health.

Sec. 4430. Each physician attending a person affected *Duration of quarantine.* with any such disease shall use such precautionary measures to prevent the spread of the disease as is required by the board of health. No person quarantined by a board of health on account of having a contagious disease or for having been exposed thereto, shall leave such quarantined house or place without the written permission of the board of health, and where other inmates of such house have been exposed to and are liable to become ill of any such diseases, for such period thereafter as may be prescribed in the rules and regulations of the state department of health.

Sec. 4436. When a house or other place is quaran- *Maintenance of person confined in quarantined house.* tined on account of contagious diseases, the board of health having jurisdiction shall provide for all persons confined in such house or place, food, fuel and all other necessaries of life, including medical attendance, medicine and nurses when necessary. The expenses so incurred, except those for disinfection, quarantine or other measures strictly for the protection of the public health, when properly certified by the president and clerk of the board of health, or health officer where there is no board of health, shall be paid by the persons or persons quarantined, when able to make such payment, and when not, by the municipality or townships in which quarantined.

When person residing in quarantined house may attend public gathering. Sec. 4437. No person residing in or occupying a house in which a person is suffering from smallpox, cholera, plague, typhus fever, diphtheria, membranous croup, scarlet fever or other dangerous contagious disease, shall be permitted to attend any public, private or parochial school or college or Sunday school, or any other public gathering, until the quarantine provided in such diseases has been removed by the board of health. All school principals, Sunday school superintendents, or other persons in charge of such schools, are hereby required to exclude any and all such persons until they present a written permit of the board of health to attend or re-enter such schools.

Annual reports. Sec. 4476. On or before the fifteenth day of January of each year, the board of health or health department shall make a report in writing for the preceding calendar year to the council of the municipality and to the state commissioner of health. Such report shall be on the sanitary condition and prospects of such municipality, and shall contain the statistics of deaths, the action of the board and its officers and agents and the names thereof. It shall contain other useful information, and the board shall suggest therein any further legislative action deemed proper for the better protection of life and health. Such board of health and health departments shall promptly furnish any special report called for by the state commissioner of health.

Exposure in public having contagious disease; giving or selling articles in charge of such person; penalty. Sec. 12785. Whoever, while suffering from smallpox, cholera, plague, yellow fever, diphtheria, membranous croup, scarlet fever or other dangerous contagious disease, wilfully or unlawfully exposes himself in a street, shop, inn, theater or other public place or public conveyance, or, being in charge of a person so suffering, so exposes such sufferer, or gives, lends, sells, transmits or exposes without previous disinfection by the board of health bedding, clothing, rags, or other thing, which has been exposed to infection from such disease, or knowingly lets for hire a house, room or part of a house in which a person has been suffering from such disease, prior to the disinfection thereof by the board of health, shall be fined not more than one hundred dollars or imprisoned not more than ninety days, or both.

Repeals. SECTION 29. That said original sections 1245, 1246, 3391, 3392, 3393, 3394, 4404, 4405, 4408, 4409, 4410, 4413,

4429, 4430, 4436, 4437, 4476 and 12785 of the General Code be and the same are hereby repealed, but this section shall not go into effect until January 1, 1920.

CARL R. KIMBALL,
Speaker of the House of Representatives.
CLARENCE J. BROWN,
President of the Senate.

The sectional numbers in this act are in conformity to the General Code. Attorney General, JOHN G. PRICE.

Passed April 17, 1919.
Approved May 9, 1919.

JAMES M. COX,
Governor.

Filed in the office of the Secretary of State at Columbus, Ohio, on the 12th day of May, A. D. 1919.

98 G.

[House Bill No. 299.]

AN ACT

To amend section 2412 of the General Code, relating to the employment of legal counsel, for county boards and officers.

Be it enacted by the General Assembly of the State of Ohio:

SECTION 1. That section 2412 of the General Code be amended to read as follows:

Sec. 2412. If it deems it for the best interests of the county, the common pleas court, upon the application of the prosecuting attorney and the board of county commissioners, may authorize the board of county commissioners to employ legal counsel temporarily to assist the prosecuting attorney, the board of county commissioners or any other county board or officer, in any matter of public business coming before such board or officer, and in the prosecution or defense of any action or proceeding in which such county board or officer is a party or has an interest, in its official capacity.

Employment of legal counsel; duties.

SECTION 2. That said original section 2412 of the General Code be, and the same is hereby repealed.

The sectional number in this act is in conformity to the General Code. JOHN G. PRICE, Attorney General.

CARL R. KIMBALL,
Speaker of the House of Representatives.
CLARENCE J. BROWN,
President of the Senate.

Passed April 16, 1919.
Approved May 9, 1919.

JAMES M. COX,
Governor.

Filed in the office of the Secretary of State at Columbus, Ohio, on the 12th day of May, A. D. 1919.

99 G.

[House Bill No. 388.]

AN ACT

To amend section 3148 of the General Code of Ohio, relating to county and district hospitals for tuberculosis.

Be it enacted by the General Assembly of the State of Ohio:

SECTION 1.   That section 3148 of the General Code be amended to read as follows:

Commissioners of two or more counties may establish district tuberculosis hospital.

Sec. 3148.   The commissioners of any two or more counties not to exceed ten, may form themselves into a joint board for the purpose of establishing and maintaining a district hospital, provided there is no municipal tuberculosis hospital therein for care and treatment of persons suffering from tuberculosis, and may provide the necessary funds for the purchase of a site, which site shall be separate and apart from the infirmary boundaries in any county and also may provide for the erection of the necessary buildings thereon; and provided further that where any number of counties have already constructed and are operating a district tuberculosis hospital, counties may

Counties may join or withdraw.

join such counties for enlargement and use of such hospital, and providing further that the county commissioners of any county within a district which desires to withdraw from said district, may dispose of its interest in said district hospital by selling same to any county or counties in said district and subject to the approval of the state board

Approval by state department required.

of health.   Any new district or addition to a district shall be approved by the state board of health.   Such necessary expenses as may be incurred by the county commissioners in meeting with the commissioners of other counties for consideration of the proposal to establish a district tuberculosis hospital shall be paid from the general fund of the county.   After the organization of the joint board such expenses shall be paid from the fund provided for the erection and maintenance of such hospital.

SECTION 2.   That said original section 3148 of the General Code be, and the same is hereby repealed.

The sectional number in this act is in conformity to the General Code. JOHN G. PRICE, *Attorney General.*

CARL R. KIMBALL,
Speaker of the House of Representatives.
CLARENCE J. BROWN,
President of the Senate.

Passed April 17, 1919.
Approved May 9, 1919.

JAMES M. COX,
Governor.

Filed in the office of the Secretary of State at Columbus, Ohio, on the 12th day of May, A. D. 1919.
100 G.

[House Bill No. 404.]

AN ACT

To supplement section 3148 of the General Code, by adding sections 3148-1, 3148-2 and 3148-3, relating to county and district hospitals for tuberculosis.

Be it enacted by the General Assembly of the State of Ohio:

SECTION 1. That section 3148 of the General Code of Ohio, be supplemented by the addition of the following:

Sec. 3148-1. The county commissioners of any county wherein is located a municipal tuberculosis hospital, may provide the necessary funds for the purchase or lease of a site, and the erection or lease of the necessary buildings thereon, for the operation and maintenance of a county hospital for the treatment of persons suffering from tuberculosis. Any municipality within said county at present maintaining and operating a hospital for the treatment of tuberculosis may continue to maintain said hospital as a municipal hospital, or may lease or sell the same to the county. *[County may build or purchase or lease municipal tuberculosis hospital.]*

Sec. 3148-2. The management and control of such tuberculosis hospital shall be vested in a board of trustees, which board of trustees, shall have all the powers conferred by law upon the board of trustees of district hospitals for the care of persons suffering from tuberculosis, and all laws applicable to the levy of taxes for the erection, maintenance and operation of said district hospitals shall apply to the leasing, erection, operation and maintenance of said county hospital for the treatment of persons suffering from tuberculosis. *[Control vested in board of trustees.]*

Sec. 3148-3. The county commissioners shall constitute the board of trustees of such hospital. *[Commissioners shall constitute board.]*

The sectional number in this act is in conformity to the General Code. JOHN G. PRICE, Attorney General.

CLARENCE J. BROWN,
President of the Senate.
CARL R. KIMBALL,
Speaker of the House of Representatives.
Passed April 17, 1919.
Approved May 9, 1919.

JAMES M. COX,
Governor.

Filed in the office of the Secretary of State at Columbus, Ohio, on the 12th day of May, A. D. 1919.

101 G.

[House Bill No. 311.]

AN ACT

To amend sections 1302, 1303 and 1303-1 of the General Code, relating to the requirements for examination as a pharmacist or assistant pharmacist.

Be it enacted by the General Assembly of the State of Ohio:

SECTION 1. That sections 1302, 1303 and 1303-1 of the General Code be amended to read as follows:

Qualifications of pharmacists.

Sec. 1302. An applicant for certificate as pharmacist shall be a citizen of the United States, shall be not less than twenty-one years of age, shall be a graduate from a school of pharmacy in good standing as defined in section 1303-2 of the General Code, shall have completed at least a two-years' course in such school as defined in section 1303-2 of the General Code and shall have had at least two years of practical experience in a drug store in charge of a registered pharmacist where physicians' prescriptions are compounded; provided, however, that if the applicant has taken a longer course in a school of pharmacy in good standing, each additional year successfully passed shall be counted as one year of practical experience.

Qualifications of assistant pharmacists.

Sec. 1303. An applicant for certificate as assistant pharmacist shall be a citizen of the United States, shall be not less than eighteen years of age, shall be a graduate from a two-years' course in pharmacy from a school in good standing as defined in section 1303-2 of the General Code, or shall have had at least one year of practical experience in a drug store in charge of a registered pharmacist in which physicians' prescriptions are compounded and one year successfully passed in a school of pharmacy in good standing as defined in section 1303-2 of the General Code.

Entrance examiner; qualifications; duties.

Sec. 1303-1. The state board of pharmacy shall appoint an entrance examiner who shall not be directly or indirectly connected with a school of pharmacy and who shall have received the degree of B. A. or B. Sc., and who shall determine the sufficiency of the preliminary education of the applicants for admission to a school of pharmacy in good standing as defined in section 1303-2 of the General Code, and to whom all applicants shall submit credentials.

Preliminary education of applicants.

The following preliminary educational credentials shall be sufficient: The equivalent of eight units as given in a high school of the state of Ohio and on and after January 1, 1920, a diploma from a legally constituted high school, normal school or academy, issued after at least four years of study; provided, however, that in the absence of the foregoing qualifications, the entrance examiner shall examine the applicant in such branches as are required to obtain them. Applicants desiring to enter a school of pharmacy in good standing as defined in section 1303-2 of the General Code must submit certificates to the entrance examiner from their school authorities describing in full the work completed: Provided, that in the absence of all or any part of the foregoing qualifications, the applicant must present himself before the entrance examiner for the scheduled examinations: Provided further, that the applicants upon presentation of certificates from their school authorities or in case of examination, must pay in advance to the board of pharmacy a fee of three dollars. If the entrance examiner finds that the preliminary education of the applicant is sufficient, he shall issue to the applicant a certificate therefor which shall be attested by the secretary of the state board of pharmacy. The compensation of the entrance examiner shall be fixed by the state board of pharmacy.

Examination fee.

SECTION 2. That said original sections 1302, 1303 and 1303-1 of the General Code be, and the same are hereby repealed. Repeals.

The sectional numbers in this act are in conformity to the General Code.
JOHN G. PRICE,
Attorney General.

. CARL R. KIMBALL,
Speaker of the House of Representatives.
CLARENCE J. BROWN,
President of the Senate.

Passed April 14, 1919.
Approved May 9, 1919.

JAMES M. COX,
Governor.

Filed in the office of the Secretary of State at Columbus, Ohio, on the 12th day of May, A. D. 1919.

102 G.

---

*[House Bill No. 305.]

AN ACT

To amend sections 3128, 3130, 3131, 3132, 3133, 3134, 3136 and 3137 of the General Code, relative to the erection and maintenance of county hospitals.

Be it enacted by the General Assembly of the State of Ohio:
SECTION 1. That sections 3128, 3130, 3131, 3132, 3133, 3134, 3136 and 3137 of the General Code be amended to read as follows:

. Sec. 3128. The petitions thus filed with the county commissioners shall stipulate the maximum amount of money to be expended in purchasing or building such hospital, and it shall be published with notices of the election in at least two newspapers of opposite politics of general circulation in the county, at least one time, twenty or more days prior to the election. Filing of petition; notice of election.

And when a majority of the taxpayers signing the petitions submitted to the county commissioners under the preceding section, shall state therein that it is desired by them that such hospital be designated as a memorial to May be designated as a memorial, when; equipment.

commemorate the services of the soldiers, sailors, marines and pioneers of the county, then such hospital, if erected in accordance with the provisions of this act, shall be known and designated as a county memorial hospital; and such plates, tablets, busts, statues and other memorials and equipment as the board of county hospital trustees hereinafter provided for shall deem fit to properly accomplish and preserve the memorial feature in such hospital, shall be incorporated in its construction. And if the memorial feature be thus incorporated, this fact shall be mentioned in the published notices hereinbefore required.

Issue of bonds.

Sec. 3130. If a majority of the electors of the county voting at such election are in favor of the issuance of bonds, the commissioners shall provide for the issuing and sale thereof according to law and in conformity to the provisions of this chapter.

Result certified to governor; appointment of trustees.

Sec. 3131. If a majority of the electors of the county voting at such election are in favor of the issuance of bonds, the deputy state supervisors of elections for such county shall certify the result of such election to the governor of the state; whereupon the governor shall, within ten days after the receipt of such certification, appoint a board of county hospital trustees, composed of four freeholders of such county.

Notification of appointment.

Such board shall be bipartisan, with two members from each of the two political parties casting the highest number of votes in such county for their respective candidates for governor at the next preceding gubernatorial election. And the governor shall forthwith notify the persons so selected of their appointment as such trustees, by mail, and fix a date not more than ten days later when such trutsees shall meet at the county seat of such county to organize such board.

Organization of board; vacancies; meetings; account.

On the date thus fixed such trustees shall meet and organize such board by electing one of their number as chairman and another as secretary. The county commissioners shall fill all vacancies which may occur in such board of trustees, as well as in the board of hospital trustees hereinafter provided for, which may result from death, resignation or removal from office. Such board of trustees shall hold such meetings as the performance of its duties may require and shall keep a record of its proceedings and a strict account of all its receipts, disbursements and expenditures; and upon completion of their duties as herein provided, they shall file such account with the board of county commissioners and make final settlement with such board.

Such hospital trustees shall serve until such hospital be fully completed and sufficiently equipped for occupancy, whereupon their successors shall be appointed as hereinafter provided.

Powers and duties of trustees; bonds.

Sec. 3132. Such board of trustees shall have full charge and control of the selection and purchase of a site for such hospital (taking title thereto in the name of the

257

county), the selection of plans and specifications, the determination and erection of all necessary buildings thereon, and of the selection and installation of all necessary and proper furniture, fixtures and equipment therefor.

Such hospital trustees and their successors herein provided for may receive and hold in trust for the use of the hospital any grant or devise of land or any gift or bequest of money or other personal property that may be given for the erection or support of the hospital.

The trustees shall serve without compensation, but shall be allowed their necessary and reasonable expenses incurred in the performance of their duties, the same to be paid out of the funds provided for such hospital. They may employ such help as they shall deem necessary to perform their clerical work and to superintend properly the construction of such hospital, and pay the expenses thereof out of the funds provided for such hospital.

Each trustee shall give bond for the proper performance of his duties in such sum as the board of county commissioners may require, with sureties to its approval.

Sec. 3133. Upon the certificate of such trustees, stating the amount necessary, the county commissioners shall issue and sell the bonds of the county in the amount so certified but not in excess of the amount named in said petitions. Said bonds shall be sold in anticipation of taxes to be levied as hereinafter provided; they shall bear interest at a rate not exceeding six per cent per annum, payable semi-annually, and the proceeds thereof shall be used for the purpose of purchasing a site and erecting hospital buildings, or of purchasing a site with buildings already erected thereon and for equipping and maintaining the same. *Sale of bonds.*

Annually thereafter the commissioners shall levy, in addition to all other levies authorized by law, an amount sufficient to properly maintain and conduct said hospital and furnish such extensions and further equipment thereof as may be necessary; and also to provide a sufficient sinking fund for the ultimate payment of such bonds and interest as the same shall mature. *Tax levy.*

Sec. 3134. The fund arising from the sale of such bonds shall be placed in the county treasury to the credit of a fund to be known as the "county hospital fund." And such fund shall be paid out on the order of said board of county hospital trustees, certified by the chairman and secretary thereof. *"County Hospital Fund."*

If, upon the final completion of such county hospital, an unexpended balance of the fund remains in the county treasury, such balance shall be placed and kept to the credit of the sinking fund herein provided for.

Sec. 3136. When said hospital shall have been fully completed and sufficiently equipped for occupancy as hereinbefore provided, the county commissioners shall appoint a board of four trustees as follows: one for one year, one *Hospital trustees; appointment; vacancies.*

9—C. & L. A.

for two years, one for three years and one for four years from the first Monday of March thereafter. Not more than two of such trustees shall be of the same political party. Annually thereafter on the first Monday of March, the county commissioners shall appoint one such trustee, who shall hold his office for the term of four years and until his successor be appointed and qualified.

The commissioners shall immediately fill any vacancy in such board which may be caused by death, resignation or removal, by appointment for the unexpired term. They may remove any trustee appointed by such board of commissioners for cause impairing faithful, efficient and intelligent administration, or for conduct unbecoming to such office, after an opportunity be given to be heard upon written charges; but no removal shall be made for political reasons.

Organization of trustees. Sec. 3137. Upon the appointment and qualification of such trustees as herein provided, they shall organize by the election of one of their members as president and another as clerk.

Such board shall hold meetings at least once a month, and shall adopt necessary rules for the regulation of its business, and keep a complete record of its proceedings. Three members of such board shall constitute a quorum.

Control of property. Such board shall assume and continue the operation of such hospital. It shall have the entire management and control of the hospital and shall establish such rules for the government thereof and the admission of persons thereto as it deems expedient; it shall have control of the property of the hospital and deposit all monies thereof with the county treasurer to the credit of the hospital fund; and the same shall be paid out only for the maintenance and operation of such hospital, on the warrant of the county auditor, issued pursuant to the orders of the trustees.

Employment of superintendent. Such board shall employ a superintendent, and, upon the nomination by such superintendent, shall confirm the employment of such physicians, nurses and other employes as may be necessary for the proper care, control and management of such hospital and its inmates; and shall fix their respective salaries and compensation; and any such person may be removed by such trustees at any time when, in their judgment, the welfare of such institution may so warrant.

Fixing compensation for treatment. Such trustees may determine whether patients presented at the hospital for treatment are subjects for charity, and shall fix the compensation to be paid by patients other than those unable to assist themselves. They may provide for the free treatment in such hospital of soldiers, sailors and marines of the county, under such conditions and regulations as they shall prescribe.

Bond. The hospital superintendent herein provided for shall give such bond for the faithful performance of his duties as such trustees may require and with sureties to their approval.

The trustees shall annually on the first day of March file with the county commissioners a statement of their receipts and expenditures for the preceding year and shall submit to such commissioners an estimate of the financial requirements of such hospital for the ensuing year. **Annual statement to commissioners.**

SECTION 2. That original sections 3128, 3130, 3131, 3132, 3133, 3134, 3136 and 3137 of the General Code be, and the same are hereby repealed. **Repeals.**

CARL R. KIMBALL,
Speaker of the House of Representatives.
CLARENCE J. BROWN,
President of the Senate.

Passed April 16, 1919.
Approved May 9, 1919.

JAMES M. COX,
Governor.

Filed in the office of the Secretary of State at Columbus, Ohio, on the 12th day of May, A. D. 1919.

103 G.

[House Bill No. 61.]

AN ACT

To supplement section 2421 of the General Code, by the addition of supplemental section 2421-1, empowering the board of county commissioners to turn over to a municipality part of the county bridge fund levied upon property within said municipality.

Be it enacted by the General Assembly of the State of Ohio:

SECTION 1. That section 2421 of the General Code be supplemented by the addition of section 2421-1 to read as follows:

Sec. 2421-1. When the council of any city having a population not exceeding fifteen thousand or of a village shall cause to be filed in the office of the county auditor of the county in which such corporation is situated in whole or in part a certified copy of a resolution of such council demanding some portion of the county bridge fund levied upon property within such corporation, the county commissioners of such county may, by resolution, authorize the county auditor to draw his warrant upon the county treasurer in favor of such corporation for not to exceed sixty per cent of the county bridge fund then levied or collected, or in process of collection, upon the property in such corporation. Such fund so received by such corporation shall **County's portion of bridge may be turned over to municipality; procedure.**

be used by it for the construction, repair and maintenance of any bridges and viaducts within such corporation.

CARL R. KIMBALL,
Speaker of the House of Representatives.
CLARENCE J. BROWN,
President of the Senate.

Passed April 16, 1919.
Approved May 9, 1919.

JAMES M. COX,
Governor.

Filed in the office of the Secretary of State at Columbus, Ohio, on the 12th day of May, A. D. 1919.

104 G.

[House Bill No. 345.]

AN ACT

To amend sections 1643, 1672 and 3093 of the General Code, relative to guardianship of children.

Be it enacted by the General Assembly of the State of Ohio:
SECTION 1. That sections 1643, 1672 and 3093 of the General Code be amended so as to read as follows:

When jurisdiction terminates.

Sec. 1643. When a child under the age of eighteen years comes into the custody of the court under the provisions of this chapter, such child shall continue for all necessary purposes of discipline and protection, a ward of the court, until he or she attain the age of twenty-one years. The power of the court over such child shall continue until the child attains such age. Provided, in case such child is committed to the permanent care and guardianship of the Ohio board of administration, or the board of state charities, or of an institution or association, certified by the board of state charities, with permission and power to place such child in a foster home, with the probability of adoption, such jurisdiction shall cease at the time of commitment.

When writ of habeas corpus may issue.

No court shall issue a writ of habeas corpus against any parties holding a child by reason of a commitment of the juvenile court before such parties have been heard by the court to which application has been made for such writ and their rights to hold such child have been finally determined by the proper court.

When child is in temporary or permanent care and custody.

Sec. 1672. If the court awards a child to the care of an institution, association, or a state board in accordance with the provisions of this and other chapters, the judge shall in the award or commitment designate whether it is for temporary or permanent care and custody. If for temporary care, the award or commitment shall not be for more than twelve months, and before the expiration of such period the court shall make other disposition of the matter, or recommit the child in the same manner. During such period of temporary care the institution, association or state board to which such child is committed shall not place it in a permanent foster home, but shall keep it in readiness for return to parents or guardian whenever the court shall so direct. At any time during such temporary custody the institution or board to whom such child is committed, may, whenever there is an opportunity to place such child in a foster home by adoption, request the court to determine whether such commitment should be modified to include permanent care and custody. Whenever a child is committed to the permanent care of an institution, association or a state board, it shall ipso facto come under the sole and exclusive guardianship of such institution, association or state board, whereupon the jurisdiction of the court shall cease and determine, except that such institution, association or board, to which such child is permanently committed may petition said court to make other disposition of such child because of physical, mental or moral defects. Such institution, association or state board may place such child in a foster family home and shall be made a party to any proceedings for the legal adoption of the child. Assent on the part of such institution, association or state board shall be sufficient to authorize the judge to enter the proper order or decree of adoption. In a similar manner the court may award a child to the care or guardianship of an individual, but such individual shall not place such child in the care of another person or assent to adoption except upon order of said juvenile court; such guardianship shall not include the guardianship of any estate of the child. For the purpose of information and co-operative supervision the juvenile court shall report monthly to the board of state charities the names of children committed to institutions and individuals; provided that such report shall not include a child coming under the supervision and custody of the court but permitted to remain with parents or guardian. The board of state charities shall prepare and furnish suitable blanks for such reports. **Procedure in adoption.**

Monthly report by juvenile court to board of state charities.

Sec. 3093. All wards of a county or district children's home, or of any other accredited institution or agency caring for dependent children who by reason of abandonment, neglect or dependence have been committed by the juvenile court to the permanent care of such home, or who have been by the parent or guardian voluntarily surrendered to such an institution or agency, shall be under the sole and exclusive guardianship and control of the trustees until they become of lawful age. The board of trustees may by contract or otherwise provide suitable accommodations outside of the home and may provide for the care of any child under its control by payment of a suitable amount of board, **Guardianship and control of inmates.**

to a competent person, whenever the interests of such child
require such an arrangement. Children committed for temporary care or received by arrangement with parent or
guardian shall be considered under the custody and control
of the trustees only during the period of such temporary
care, except as hereinafter provided. Whenever a child
has been received upon agreement of parent to pay a stip-
ulated- sum for his support and such parent is in arrears
for a period of six months or more, the trustees may institute proceedings in the juvenile court to ascertain whether
such child has been abandoned. The judge of the juvenile
court shall after hearing the case make such order for the
future care of the child as in his judgment is just and
proper for the best interest of the child.

"Juvenile Court" defined.

SECTION 2. The term "juvenile court" as used in this
act shall be construed as applying to such courts as are
created by section 1639 and all other courts now or hereafter created to administer the provisions of law relating to
dependent, delinquent and neglected children.

Repeals.

SECTION 3. That said original sections 1643, 1672 and
3093 of the General Code be, and the same are hereby repealed.

The sectional numbers in this act are in con-
formity to the General Code.
JOHN G. PRICE,
Attorney
General.

CARL R. KIMBALL,
Speaker of the House of Representatives.
CLARENCE J. BROWN,
President of the Senate.

Passed April 17, 1919.
Approved May 9, 1919.

JAMES M. COX,
Governor.

Filed in the office of the Secretary of State at Columbus,
Ohio, on the 12th day of May, A. D. 1919.

105 G.

[House Bill No. 143.]

AN ACT

To amend sections 50, 276 and 1981 of the General Code, relative
to transportation expenses of public officials.

Be it enacted by the General Assembly of the State of Ohio:
SECTION 1. That sections 50, 276 and 1981 of the General Code be amended to read as follows:

Salary; pay-
ment monthly;
mileage.

Sec. 50. Every member of the general assembly shall
receive as compensation a salary of one thousand dollars a
year during his term of office. Such salary for such term
shall be paid in the following manner:—two hundred dollars in monthly installments during the first session of such

term and the balance of such salary for such term at the end of such session.

Each member shall receive the legal rate of railroad transportation each way for mileage once a week during the session from and to his place of residence, by the most direct route of public travel to and from the seat of government, to be paid at the end of each regular or special session. If a member is absent without leave, or is not excused on his return, there shall be deducted from his compensation the sum of ten dollars for each day's absence.

Sec. 276. The chief inspector and supervisor shall appoint such assistants as he deems necessary, who shall be known as state examiners, and such other assistants as he deems necessary, who shall be known as assistant state examiners. State examiners and assistant state examiners shall receive the following compensation for each day necessarily employed by them in the discharge of such duties as may be assigned to them: each state examiner assigned to examine county or city offices or institution, ten dollars; each state examiner assigned to examine offices or institutions of other taxing districts, eight dollars; each assistant state examiner, not more than five dollars. In addition thereto, each state examiner and assistant state examiner shall be allowed mileage at the legal rate of railroad transportation on official business under orders of the chief inspector and supervisor or the deputy inspectors and supervisors. Should any such examiner or assistant be called upon to testify in any legal proceeding in regard to any official matters, they shall be entitled to the compensation and expense herein provided, to be paid in the same manner, but shall not be entitled to witness fees.

Appointment of examiners; compensation and mileage.

Sec. 1981. The probate judge shall make a complete record of all proceedings in lunacy. The costs and expenses, other than the fees of the probate judge and sheriff, to be paid under the provisions of this chapter, shall be as follows: To each of the two physicians designated by the court to make examination and certificate, five dollars, and witness fees as allowed in the court of common pleas; to witnesses the same fees as are allowed in the court of common pleas; to the person other than the sheriff or deputy sheriff making the arrest, the actual and necessary expense thereof and such fees as are allowed by law to sheriffs for making arrests in criminal cases; to the person other than the sheriff, deputy sheriff or assistant, for taking any insane person to state hospital or removing one therefrom upon the warrant of the probate judge, mileage at the rate of five cents per mile, going and returning; and for the transportation of each patient to or from the hospital mileage at the legal rate of railroad transportation; to one assistant to convey to the hospital, when authorized by the probate judge, two dollars and mileage at the legal rate of railroad transportation; all mileage allowed herein shall be for the distance actually and necessarily traveled.

Fees, costs and expenses in lunacy cases.

SECTION 2. That original sections 50, 276 and 1981 of the General Code be, and the same are hereby repealed.

CARL R. KIMBALL,
Speaker of the House of Representatives.
CLARENCE J. BROWN,
President of the Senate.

Passed April 15, 1919.
Approved May 9, 1919.

JAMES M. COX,
Governor.

Filed in the office of the Secretary of State at Columbus, Ohio, on the 12th day of May, A. D. 1919.

106 G.

[House Bill No. 539.]

AN ACT

To make sundry and supplementary appropriations for the remainder of the current fiscal year.

Be it enacted by the General Assembly of the State of Ohio:
SECTION 1. The sums set forth in section 2 of this act, in the columns therein designated "Appropriations" are hereby appropriated out of any monies in the state treasury not otherwise appropriated,
SECTION 2. The following sums shall be expended to pay liabilities incurred prior to June 30, 1919:

OHIO BOARD OF ADMINISTRATION.

			Items	Appropriations
Maintenance—				
C Supplies—				
C	2	Forage	$22,200 00	
C	3	Fuel	50,000 00	
C	5	Medical	1,800 00	
C	6	Cleaning	8,000 00	
C	9	Agricultural ...	4,700 00	
C	11	General plant...	2,500 00	
		Total		$89,200 00
E Equipment—				
E	2	Household	$15,000 00	
E	3	Medical	1,000 00	
E	7	Wearing apparel.	42,000 00	
		Total		58,000 00

	Items	Appropriations	Sundry and supplementary appropriations.
F Contract and Open Order Service—			
F 1 Repairs	$9,000 00		
F 7 Communication .	900 00		
F 9 General Plant....	4,000 00		
Total		13,900 00	
Total maintenance............		$161,100 00	

HOUSE OF REPRESENTATIVES.

Personal Service—
A 2 Wages—

	Items	Appropriations
10 Assistant clerks....	$1,400 00	
11 Stenographers	1,430 00	
4 Sergeants-at-arms ..	570 00	
1 Assistant postmaster	130 00	
2 Telephone attendants	354 00	
2 Cloak room attendants	328 00	
5 Doorkeepers	740 00	
5 Porters	1,076 00	
5 Committee room attendants	220 00	
10 Pages	1,000 00	
Total		$7,248 00

Maintenance—
C Supplies—

	Items	Appropriations
C 6 Cleaning	$100 00	
F Contract and Open Order Service—		
F 6 Traveling expense	$3,000 00	
F 9 General plant....	2,000 00	
Total	$5,000 00	
H Fixed Charges and Contributions—		
H 6 Rent	$150 00	
Total maintenance............		5,250 00
Total		$11,498 00

STATE BOARD OF CHARITIES.

Maintenance—

	Appropriations
I Rotary	$1,500 00

COMBINED NORMAL AND INDUSTRIAL DEPARTMENT OF WILBERFORCE UNIVERSITY.

<table>
<tr><td></td><td>Items</td><td>Appropriations</td></tr>
</table>

Sundry and supplementary appropriations. Maintenance—

    C Supplies—

        C 3   Fuel $880 00

    F Contract and Open Order Service—

        F 6   Traveling expense $270 00

            Total $1,150 00

SECTION 3. Sections 4, 5, 6, 7 and 8 of a law entitled "an act to make general appropriations" (107 O. L., H. B. 584), passed by the 82d General Assembly and filed in the office of the secretary of state March 31, 1917, shall apply to and govern the appropriations made in section 2 herein with the same force and effect as to the appropriations made in said original act hereinbefore cited.

This act is not of a general and permanent nature and requires no sectional number. JOHN G. PRICE, Attorney General.

                          CARL R. KIMBALL,
        Speaker of the House of Representatives.
                      CLARENCE J. BROWN,
                    President of the Senate.

Passed May 8, 1919.
Approved May 15, 1919.

                JAMES M. COX,
                      Governor.

Filed in the office of the Secretary of State at Columbus, Ohio, on the 15th day of May, A. D. 1919.

                      107 G.

[House Bill No. 150.]

AN ACT

To amend sections 2394, 2522, 2523, 2526, 2528, 2532, 2535, 2542, 2544, 2546, 2548, 2549, 2550, 2553, 2554, 2555, 2556, 2572, 3476, 3479, 3481, 3482, 3483, 3484, 3492, 3493 3994 and 3495, and to repeal sections 2533, 2534, 2551, 2552, 2545, 2557 and 3002 of the General Code, relating to county infirmaries and poor relief.

Be it enacted by the General Assembly of the State of Ohio:
    SECTION 1. That sections 2394, 2522, 2523, 2526, 2528, 2532, 2535, 2542, 2544, 2546, 2548, 2549, 2550, 2553, 2554, 2555, 2556, 2572, 3476, 3479, 3481, 3482, 3483, 3484, 3492, 3493, 3494 and 3495 of the General Code be amended to read as follows:

Sec. 2394. If the plans, drawings, representations, bills of material and specifications of work and estimates of the cost thereof relate to the building, addition to, or alteration of an infirmary, they shall be submitted to the county commissioners. If approved by a majority of them, a copy thereof shall be deposited in the office of the auditor and kept for the inspection and use of parties interested. Plans, drawings, bills of materials, etc., shall be submitted to commissioners.

Sec. 2522. The board of county commissioners shall make all contracts for new buildings and for additions to and repairs of existing buildings necessary for the county infirmary and shall prescribe such rules and regulations as it deems proper for its management and good government, and to promote sobriety, morality and industry among inmates. The superintendent may employ a matron and such labor from time to time, at rates of wages to be fixed by the county commissioners, as may not be found available on the part of the inmates of the institution. The superintendent and matron shall be removed if they or either of them, require or permit inmates or employes to render services for the private interests of the superintendent, matron or member of the board of county commissioners, or any private interest. At least once a month the board of county commissioners shall make a complete inspection of the physical and sanitary conditions of the infirmary buildings and grounds and an examination into the care and treatment of the inmates thereof, unaccompanied by the superintendent or matron. The commissioners shall keep a separate book in which the clerk, or if there be no commissioners' clerk, the county auditor, shall keep a separate record of their transactions respecting the county infirmary, which book shall be known as the infirmary journal, and shall be kept in the manner provided by sections 2406 and 2407 of the General Code of Ohio, and said book shall at all reasonable times be open to public inspection. Powers and duties of commissioners.
Removal of superintendent and matron; inspection monthly.
Records and accounts.

Sec. 2523. The county commissioners shall appoint a superintendent, who shall reside in some apartment of the infirmary or other buildings contiguous thereto, and shall receive such compensation for his services as they may determine. The superintendent and matron shall each be allowed their actual necessary expenses incurred in the discharge of their official duties. The superintendent shall perform such duties as the commissioners impose upon him, and be governed in all respects by their rules and regulations. He shall not be removed by them except for good and sufficient cause. The commissioners may by resolution provide for the appointment by the superintendent of an assistant superintendent who shall perform such duties at the infirmary or elsewhere as may be prescribed by such superintendent. The commissioners shall not appoint one of their own number superintendent, nor shall any commissioner be eligible to any other office in the infirmary or receive any compensation as phyiscian, or otherwise, di- Appointment of superintendent; salary and expenses.

rectly or indirectly, wherein the appointing power is vested in such board.

Labor by inmates; purchase of supplies; sale of products.

Sec. 2526. The superintendent and matron of the infirmary shall require all persons received therein to perform such reasonable and moderate labor, without compensation, as is suited to their age and bodily strength. The superintendent and matron shall make such purchases as may be authorized by the rules prescribed by the county commissioners. As far as practicable, all supplies shall be purchased on competitive bids, except those ordered from the state as required by law, and all supplies of whatever kind purchased and delivered to the superintendent, or to the infirmary, shall be accompanied by itemized bills, showing quantities, qualities and price, which shall be checked by the superintendent as having been received, and the correctness of the bill or claim shall be duly certified by him before the same may be allowed by the commissioners. The superintendent, under the direction of the commissioners, shall sell all products of the infirmary farm not necessary for the use of the infirmary, and pay all moneys arising therefrom into the county treasury, at least monthly, to the credit of the county poor fund. The superintendent shall have full authority to discharge inmates from the infirmary.

Reserve fund for emergency; account.

Sec. 2528. At the request of the superintendent, the county commissioners shall set apart from the poor fund a reserve fund not to exceed at any time $200.00, which upon their order shall be paid to the superintendent and expended by him as needed for emergency supplies and expenses. The superintendent shall keep an accurate account of such funds in a book to be provided at the expense of the county for that purpose and all expenditures therefrom shall be audited by the board and the poor fund shall be reimbursed by the superintendent in full for any and all items by him expended from such fund which are not allowed by the board. When, and as often as such amount is entirely disbursed, on the order of the commissioners, the county auditor shall pay to the superintendent the amount so appropriated.

Monthly examination of condition.

Sec. 2532. Once each month the county commissioners shall carefully examine the condition of the infirmary and the inmates, the manner in which they are fed, clothed and otherwise provided for and treated. They shall ascertain what labor the inmates are required to perform and shall inspect the books and accounts of the superintendent.

Daily papers.

The county commissioners shall subscribe for at least two daily papers of opposite politics for the use of the inmates of the county infirmary.

Statistical information; contents of report; examination.

Sec. 2535. On or before the third Monday of September of each year the superintendent of the infirmary shall submit to the county commissioners a report giving all statistical information for the year preceding the first day of the month shown by the record of inmates of the infirmary required herein to be kept by the superintendent. The report shall show the whole number of inmates at the beginning of such year, the number received during the year, the number born in the infirmary, the total number of inmates for the year, the number discharged; the number of deaths, the number removed to other counties, states and institutions during the year and the number remaining; the daily average; the whole number of children under sixteen years of age, number placed in homes and otherwise released or discharged, the number remaining......boys, ...girls, the number of other inmates remaining; how many of sound mind; how many helplessly crippled; how many insane......males, ...females; how many epileptics......males, ...females; how many idiotic...... males, ...females; total current expense of infirmary, exclusive of farm products for the year; total value of farm products for the year; total amount paid in county for outdoor relief during the year; amount of salaries paid during the year to superintendent and matron and amount of wages paid other employes. This report shall contain such other information as the commissioners may require and an account of all moneys received by him for the sale of farm products, or from any other sources, and by him paid into the county treasury to the credit of the poor fund, said account to be properly itemized, showing dates of receipts, from whom and for what purpose, and dates of payment of same into the county treasury. Said report shall be examined by the commissioners, and if found correct, be accepted, and such acceptance entered in the minutes of their proceedings. Such report shall then be filed in the auditor's office and by him safely preserved.

Sec. 2542. Unless the approval of the court exercising the powers and jurisdiction of the juvenile court is first obtained, no child under the age of one year shall be separated from its mother, if such mother is an inmate of a county infirmary. *When child shall not be separated from mother.*

Sec. 2544. In any county having an infirmary, when the trustees of a township or the proper officers of a corporation, after making the inquiry provided by law, are of the opinion that the person complained of is entitled to admission to the county infirmary, they shall forthwith transmit a statement of the facts to the superintendent of the infirmary, and if it appears that such person is legally settled in the township or has no legal settlement in this state, or that such settlement is unknown, and the superintendent of the infirmary is satisfied that such person should become a county charge he shall account such person as a county charge and shall receive and provide for him in such institution forthwith or as soon as his physical condition will so permit. The county shall not be liable for any relief furnished, or expenses incurred by the township trustees. *Admission through township trustees.*

Sec. 2546. The county commissioners may contract with one or more competent physicians to furnish medical *Employment of physicians; quarterly report.*

relief and medicines necessary for the inmates of the infirmary, but no contract shall extend beyond one year. Medical statistics shall be kept by said physician, who shall report same to the county commissioners quarterly showing the nature and extent of the services rendered, to whom, and the character of the diseases treated. The commissioners may discharge any such physician for proper cause. No medical relief for persons in their homes shall be furnished by the county, except for persons who are not residents of the state or county for one year, or residents of a township or city for three months, and except under provisions of section 2544.

When county charge is owner of property. Sec. 2548. When a person becomes a county charge or an inmate of a city infirmary and is possessed of or is the owner of property, real or personal, or has an interest in remainder, or in any manner legally entitled to a gift, legacy or bequest, whatever, the county commissioners or the proper officers of the city infirmary shall seek to secure possession of such property by filing a petition in the probate court of the county in which such property is located, and the proceedings therefor, sale, confirmation of sale and execution of deed by such county commissioners or officer of the city infirmary shall in all respects be conducted as for the sale of real estate by guardians. The net proceeds thereof shall be applied in whole or in part, under the special direction of the county commissioners or the proper city officer as is deemed best, to the maintenance of such person, so long as he remains a county charge or an inmate of a city infirmary.

Proceeds of sale credited to person. Sec. 2549. The net proceeds arising from the sale of such property shall be paid to the county or city treasurer, and by him placed to the credit of such person to be paid out on the warrant of the county auditor, upon the order of the county commissioners, or by the city auditor upon the order of the proper officer of the infirmary. The superintendent shall open an account with the person and charge him with board at a reasonable rate and items furnished for his exclusive use, which account shall be approved by the county commissioners or by the proper city officer at the close of each month.

Distribution of balance on death or discharge. Sec. 2550. Upon the death of such person or when he lawfully ceases to be a county charge or is lawfully discharged from a city infirmary, whose property or effects have been so disposed of, and the avails thereof so applied, any balance due and in favor of such person on the books of the institution shall be paid by the superintendent of the infirmary to him, or in case of his death to his legal representative. When any such fund has become exhausted or any balance paid in manner described above, the superintendent shall file with the proper probate court a complete statement showing receipts, itemized expenditures and balance, if any, and such court shall file such report with the records relating to the original order of sale of such person.

Sec. 2553. County commissioners or officers of a city infirmary shall not seek to take charge of property in manner described in section 2548 if the guardian, husband, wife, heirs, or persons entitled to the residuary interest in property give bond to such county commissioners or officers to their satisfaction and, at such times as they require, pay into the hands of the superintendent of the county or city infirmary, an amount sufficient to support the person while he remains a county charge or an inmate of the city infirmary. The probate court at time of hearing a petition for sale may, in lieu of an order for sale, order the guardian, husband, wife, heirs or persons entitled to a residuary interest in the property of such person, to make payments to the superintendent of the infirmary for the maintenance of such person and failure so to do shall make any person so ordered punishable by the court as for contempt. *Effect of bond for support by relatives.*

Sec. 2554. No county commissioners shall directly or indirectly sell or supply an article, to a superintendent or other person, for the relief of the poor, and no order shall be made by a county commissioner for the payment of supplies so sold or furnished nor shall an order for the payment of money for supplies sold or furnished be paid to any such commissioner or assignee or holder thereof. No county commissioner or employe shall be sold or given any article belonging to, grown or produced at a county infirmary or other public institution. A superintendent, commissioner, trustee or other officer, who certifies to, allows or draws an order for the payment of an account or bill, knowing it to be false or fraudulent, in whole or in part, shall forfeit and pay not less than five hundred dollars nor more than three thousand dollars for each offense, and shall be liable to criminal prosecution, as provided by law. *Commissioners shall not sell nor supply; false account or bill.*

Sec. 2555. If a person transports, removes, or brings, or causes to be transported, removed or brought a poor or indigent person into a city, township, or county in this state, without lawful authority, and there leaves such poor or indigent person, knowing that such city, township, or county will probably become chargeable with his support, the person so offending shall forfeit and pay the sum of fifty dollars for each such offense, for the use of the poor of the city, township or county in which the indigent person is left, to be recovered by civil action, in the name of the state, before any court of competent jurisdiction. When a public official furnishes transportation to an indigent person, it shall be done only after investigation and satisfaction that such transportation will make it possible for such person to be cared for by responsible persons; and the transportation furnished shall be to final destination in this state or elsewhere. *Penalty for bringing into city, township or county.*

Sec. 2556. The board of county commissioners shall provide for holding religious services on Sunday in the infirmary at least once a month, and upon request, shall provide for the conduct of funeral services over deceased *Religious services.*

inmates. Such services shall be conducted by clergymen employed by the board for that purpose but the total compensation paid to such clergymen in any one year shall not exceed the sum of $300.00.

Bills and vouchers shall be filed and recorded.

Sec. 2572. A bill or voucher for payment of money from any fund controlled by the commissioners must be filed with the county auditor and entered in a book for that purpose at least five days before its approval for payment by the commissioners. When approved, the date thereof shall be entered on such book opposite the claim, and payment thereof shall not be made until after the expiration of five days after the approval has been so entered.

Trustees and municipal officers shall afford relief.

Sec. 3476. Subject to the conditions, provisions and limitations herein, the trustees of each township or the proper officers of each city therein, respectively, shall afford at the expense of such township or municipal corporation public support or relief to all persons therein who are in condition requiring it. It is the intent of this act that townships and cities shall furnish relief in their homes to all persons needing temporary or partial relief who are residents of the state, county and township or city as described in sections 3477 and 3479. Relief to be granted by the county shall be given to those persons who do not have the necessary residence requirements, and to those who are permanently disabled or have become paupers and to such other persons whose peculiar condition is such they cannot be satisfactorily cared for except at the county infirmary or under county control. When a city is located within one or more townships, such temporary relief shall be given only by the proper municipal officers, and in such cases the jurisdiction of the township trustees shall be limited to persons who reside outside of such a city.

Who considered having legal settlement.

Sec. 3479. A person having a legal settlement in any county in the state shall be considered as having a legal settlement in the township, or municipal corporation therein, in which he has last resided continuously and supported himself for three consecutive months without relief, under the provisions of law for the relief of the poor. When a person has for a period of more than one year not secured a legal settlement in any county, township or city in the state, he shall be deemed to have a legal settlement in the county, township or city where he last has such settlement.

Proper officers shall visit persons requiring relief; examination and report.

Sec. 3481. When complaint is made to the township trustees or to the proper officers of the municipal corporation that a person therein requires public relief or support, one or more of such officers, or some other duly authorized person, shall visit the person needing relief, forthwith, to ascertain his name, age, sex, color, nativity, length of residence in the county, previous habits and present condition and in what township and county in this state he is legally settled. The information so ascertained shall be transmitted to the township clerk, or proper officer of the municipal corporation, and recorded on the proper records. No relief or support shall be given to a person without such visitation or investigation, except that within counties, where there is maintained a public charity organization, or other benevolent association, which investigates and keeps a record of facts relating to persons who receive or apply for relief, the infirmary superintendents, township trustees or officers of a city shall accept such investigation and information and may grant relief upon the approval and recommendation of such organization. Every reasonable effort shall be made by the township trustees and municipal officers to secure aid from relatives and interested organizations before granting relief from public funds.

Sec. 3482. When it has been so ascertained that a person requiring relief has a legal settlement in some other county of the state, such trustees or officers shall immediately notify the infirmary superintendent of the county in which the person is found, who, if his health permits, shall immediately remove the person to the infirmary of the county of his legal settlement. If such person refuses to be removed, on the complaint being made by the infirmary superintendent, the probate judge of the county in which the person is found shall issue a warrant for such removal, and the county wherein the legal settlement of the person is, shall pay all expenses of such removal and the necessary charges for relief and in case of death the expense of burial if a written notice is given the county commissioners thereof within twenty days after such legal settlement has been ascertained. *Removal of foreign paupers to their own county; removal expenses.*

Sec. 3483. Upon refusal or failure to pay such expenses, such board of county commissioners may be compelled so to do by a civil action against them by the board of county commissioners of the county from which such person is removed, in the court of common pleas of the county to which such removal is made. If such notice is not given within twenty days after such board of county commissioners ascertain such person's residence, and within ninety days after such relief has been afforded, the board of county commissioners where such person belongs shall not be liable for charges or expenditures accruing prior to such notice. *Notice to other county; action for recovery.*

Sec. 3484. When the trustees of a township in a county in the state in which there is no county infirmary ascertain that any person in such township has a legal settlement in another county of the state, they shall immediately notify the board of county commissioners thereof to remove such person to the infirmary of such county. Should his health permit, such board of county commissioners shall immediately remove such person to their infirmary, and, if within twenty days after such legal settlement is ascertained, a written notice is given them, to pay all expenses theretofore incurred for his relief in the township in which such person is found. Upon their refusal or failure to so remove such person, the trustees of such township may furnish him the necessary relief and collect the amount *Removal of indigent persons to their own counties.*

thereof from such board of county commissioners by a civil action, in the name of such township trustees, in the court of common pleas of the county in which such infirmary is situated.

Non-liability after contract.
Sec. 3492. When the township trustees or the officers of a municipal corporation enter into such contract, such township or municipality shall not be liable for any relief thereafter otherwise furnished such person, so long as such contract remains in force.

Performance of labor by recipient of public relief.
Sec. 3493. When public relief, not in a county or city infirmary is applied for, or afforded by the infirmary officials of any county or the trustees of a township or officers of a municipal corporation, and the applicant or recipient is able to do manual labor, such officers, shall require a male applicant or recipient to perform labor to the value of the relief afforded, at any time, upon any free public park, public highway, or other public property or public contract therein, under the direction of the proper authorities having charge or control thereof. If relief has been afforded and such recipient refuses to perform the labor provided, record of the fact shall be made, all relief or support thereafter refused him, and he may be proceeded against as a vagrant.

Control of paupers property by commissioners and trustees.
Sec. 3494. The commissioners of counties having no infirmary, the trustees of a township or the proper officer of a municipal corporation therein, shall have and may exercise the same rights, powers, and duties with reference to the property of persons coming under their charge under the poor laws of the state, as are conferred upon and exercised by infirmary officials in counties having infirmaries.

Burial of dead in certain cases.
Sec. 3495. When the dead body of a person is found in a township or municipal corporation, and such person was not an inmate of a penal, reformatory, benevolent or charitable institution, in this state, and whose body is not claimed by any person for private interment at his own expense, or delivered for the purpose of medical or surgical study or dissection in accordance with the provisions of section 9984, it shall be disposed of as follows: If he were a legal resident of the county, the proper officers of the township or corporation in which his body was found shall cause it to be buried at the expense of the township or corporation in which he had a legal residence at the time of his death; if he had a legal residence in any other county of the state at the time of his death, the infirmary superintendent of the county in which his dead body was found shall cause it to be buried at the expense of the township or corporation in which he had a legal residence at the time of his death, but if he had no legal residence in the state, or his legal residence is unknown, such infirmary superintendent shall cause him to be buried at the expense of the county.

Marker at grave.
It shall be the duty of such officials to provide at the grave of such person, a stone or concrete marker on which

shall be inscribed the name and age of such person, if known, and the date of death.

SECTION 2. That said original sections 2394, 2522, 2523, 2526, 2528, 2532, 2533, 2534, 2535, 2542, 2544, 2545, 2546, 2548, 2549, 2550, 2551, 2552, 2553, 2554, 2555, 2556, 2557, 2572, 3002, 3476, 3479, 3481, 3482, 3483, 3484, 3492, 3493, 3494 and 3495 of the General Code be, and the same are hereby repealed. *Repeals.*

The sectional numbers in this act are in conformity to the General Code. JOHN G. PRICE, *Attorney General.*

CARL R. KIMBALL,
Speaker of the House of Representatives.
CLARENCE J. BROWN,
President of the Senate.

Passed April 17, 1919.
Approved May 10, 1919.

JAMES M. COX,
Governor.

Filed in the office of the Secretary of State at Columbus, Ohio, on the 16th day of May, A. D. 1919.

108 G.

[Amended Senate Bill No. 113.]

AN ACT

To amend section 10605 of the General Code, relating to when and to whom letters testamentary to issue.

Be it enacted by the General Assembly of the State of Ohio:

SECTION 1. That section 10605 of the General Code be amended to read as follows:

Sec. 10605. When a will is duly approved and allowed, the probate court shall issue letters testamentary thereon to the executor, if any be named therein, if he is legally competent, and accepts the trust and gives bond, if that be required. Provided, however, if the executor named in a will be a non-resident of this state, the court may refuse to issue letters testamentary to such person named therein. Otherwise, the court shall grant letters of administration on the estate as hereinafter provided. *When letters testamentary shall issue.*

SECTION 2. That said original section 10605 of the General Code be, and the same is hereby repealed.

The sectional number in this act is in conformity to the General Code. JOHN G. PRICE, *Attorney General.*

CLARENCE J. BROWN,
President of the Senate.
CARL R. KIMBALL,
Speaker of the House of Representatives.

Passed April 17, 1919.
Approved May 10, 1919.

JAMES M. COX,
Governor.

Filed in the office of the Secretary of State at Columbus, Ohio, on the 16th day of May, A. D. 1919.

109 G.

[House Bill No. 282.]

AN ACT

To amend sections 1483, 1488 and 1520 of the General Code, to provide for the reporting of cases in the courts of appeals and the publication of official court reports.

Be it enacted by the General Assembly of the State of Ohio:

SECTION 1. That sections 1483, 1488 and 1520 of the General Code be amended to read as follows:

Reporter shall attend sessions of court; publication of court reports.

Sec. 1483. When requested by the supreme court, the reporter shall attend its sessions and consultations and under its direction he shall report and prepare its decisions for publication. He shall also prepare for publication and edit, tabulate and index such opinions and decisions of any court of appeals as any such court may designate and furnish him for publication, and such opinions and decisions of any of the inferior courts of the state, as may be designated by him and approved by the chief justice of the supreme court. Such official reporter may, with the approval

Assistants to reporter.

and consent of the supreme court, appoint such assistant or assistants as may be necessary to carry on the work of his office, whose compensation shall not exceed two thousand dollars a year for each person so employed, to be paid out of the state treasury upon the warrant of the state auditor. No case in the courts of appeals shall be reported for publication except such as may be selected by the several courts of appeals, or by a majority of the judges thereof. When-

Cases reported; preparation of syllabus.

ever it has been thus decided to report a case for publication the syllabus thereof shall be prepared by the judge delivering the opinion, and approved by a majority of the members of the court; and the report may be per curiam, or if an opinion be reported, the same shall be written in as brief and concise form as may be consistent with a clear presentation of the law of the case. Opinions for permanent publiaction in book form shall be furnished to the reporter of the supreme court and to no other person. Only such cases as are hereafter reported in accordance with the provisions of this section shall be recognized by and receive the official sanction of any court within the state.

Contract for printing and binding reports.

Sec. 1488. With the approval and under the direction of the supreme court, the reporter may contract with a responsible person, firm or corporation, resident of and doing business in the state of Ohio, to furnish materials, print and bind the reports of the supreme court, courts of appeals and such of the inferior courts of the state as are designated by the reporter, with the approval of the chief justice of the supreme court. Such contract shall provide for the delivery to the clerk of the supreme court of three hundred and fifty copies of each volume of reports without expense to the state. The said contract shall also provide for the furnishing of an additional number of copies of each volume sufficient to supply the demand of the citizens of the state to be sold by the contractor to persons or companies in this state at not exceeding two dollars and fifty cents per volume. No such contract shall be for a period greater than two years. The contractor shall have the exclusive right to publish such reports during the term of the contract.

Sec. 1520. Each court of appeals may appoint one or more official stenographers. They shall take an oath of office, serve at the pleasure of the court, perform such duties as the court directs, and have such powers as are vested in official stenographers of the common pleas court. Provided, however, that whenever an opinion, per curiam or report of a case has been prepared in accordance with section 1483 of the General Code as herein amended, it shall be the duty of the official stenographer to immediately forward one copy of such opinion, per curiam or report to the reporter of the supreme court, without cost or expense to the supreme court reporter.

SECTION 2. That original sections 1483, 1488 and 1520 of the General Code be, and the same are hereby repealed.

CARL R..KIMBALL,
Speaker of the House of Representatives.
CLARENCE J. BROWN,
President of the Senate.

The sectional numbers in this act are in conformity to the General Code, JOHN G. PRICE, Attorney General.

Passed April 16, 1919.
Approved May 10, 1919.

JAMES M. COX,
Governor.

Filed in the office of the Secretary of State at Columbus, Ohio, on the 16th day of May, A. D. 1919.

110 G.

[Senate Bill No. 139.]

AN ACT

To supplement section 1465-58 of the General Code by the enactment of section 1465-58a of the General Code, relating to the investment of the surplus or reserve of the state insurance fund.

Be it enacted by the General Assembly of the State of Ohio:

SECTION 1. That section 1465-58 of the General Code be supplemented by the enactment of section 1465-58a of the General Code to read as follows:

Sec. 1465-58a. All bonds of any taxing district of Ohio purchased by the industrial commission shall be printed or lithographed upon paper of the size and the interest coupons shall be attached thereto in the manner required by the industrial commission. The principal and interest of such bonds shall be payable at the office of the treasurer of the state of Ohio. Such bonds shall be of the denomination required by the industrial commission in its resolution to purchase, and the proper officers of each taxing district issuing such bonds are hereby authorized and required without additional procedure or legislation on their part to comply with the provisions of this act. Provided, however, that the industrial commission shall not be authorized to change the date of maturity of any bond nor shall it require a bond of any issue to be of larger denomination than the aggregate amount of such issue falling due at any date.

The sectional number in this act is in conformity to the General Code. JOHN G. PRICE, *Attorney General.*

CLARENCE J. BROWN,
President of the Senate.
CARL R. KIMBALL,
Speaker of the House of Representatives.

Passed April 16, 1919.
Approved May 10, 1919.

JAMES M. COX,
Governor.

Filed in the office of the Secretary of State at Columbus, Ohio, on the 16th day of May, A. D. 1919.

111 G.

[House Bill No. 428.]

AN ACT

To authorize and empower the township trustees of the township of LaGrange, Lorain county, Ohio, to use certain funds for road improvement in said township.

Be it enacted by the General Assembly of the State of Ohio:

LaGrange township, Lorain county authorized to use certain funds for roads.

SECTION 1. That the trustees of the township of La-Grange, Lorain county, Ohio, are hereby authorized and empowered to use for road improvement within said township, the funds realized and remaining to the credit of such township from the bonds approved by the voters of said township at a special election in 1915 for the improvement of a certain highway. Such funds are to be used in accordance with law for the improvement of roads under the direction of township trustees.

This act is not of a general and permanent nature and requires no code numbers. JOHN G. PRICE, *Attorney General.*

CARL R. KIMBALL,
Speaker of the House of Representatives.
CLARENCE J. BROWN,
President of the Senate.

Passed April 17, 1919.
Approved May 10, 1919.

JAMES M. COX,
Governor.

Filed in the office of the Secretary of State at Columbus, Ohio, on the 16th day of May, A. D. 1919.

112 L.

[House Bill No. 420.]

AN ACT

To authorize the superintendent of public works to lease, subject to the approval of the governor and attorney general, certain state lands in the city of Defiance, Ohio, to the owners of existing leases thereon.

Be it enacted by the General Assembly of the State of Ohio:

SECTION 1. That the superintendent of public works, subject to the approval of the governor and attorney general, be, and he is hereby authorized to lease to the owners of existing state leases, for the term of ninety-nine years, renewable forever, on an appraisement to be determined by said superintendent and at an annual rental of six per cent. on such appraisement, payable semi-annually in advance on the first day of May and November of each and every year during the full term of said lease and the renewals thereof the following described property : *Lease of certain lands to city of Defiance.*

To The Defiance Machine Works, lots Nos. 114 and 115, as shown on the original plat of the city of Defiance, Defiance county, Ohio; *Description.*

To C. P. Harley, all of lot No. 113, as shown on the recorded plat of said city of Defiance, except 5 feet off the south side of said lot;

To The Farmers Co-operative Company, all of lot No. 112 and 5 feet off the southside of lot No. 113, as shown on the recorded plat of said city of Defiance.

SECTION 2. Said leases shall contain a clause providing for the re-appraisement of the real estate described therein at the end of each fifteen year period during the full term of such leases. *Reappraisement at end of term.*

SECTION 3. As soon as any lease is approved by the governor, the superintendent of public works is hereby authorized and directed to cancel the existing lease therefor. *Cancellation of existing lease.*

CARL R. KIMBALL,
Speaker of the House of Representatives.
CLARENCE J. BROWN,
President of the Senate.

This act is not of a general and permanent nature and requires no sectional number.
JOHN G. PRICE,
Attorney General.

Passed May 5, 1919.
Approved May 10, 1919.

JAMES M. COX,
Governor.

Filed in the office of the Secretary of State at Columbus, Ohio, on the 16th day of May, A. D. 1919.

113 L.

[House Bill No. 393.]

AN ACT

To authorize the governor, attorney general and the superintendent of public works to sell at private sale, to the abutting landowners, a certain portion of the berme embankment of the Ohio canal, in the city of Massillon, Stark county, Ohio.

Be it enacted by the General Assembly of the State of Ohio:

SECTION 1. That authority be and is hereby granted to the governor, attorney general, and the superintendent of public works to sell, at private sale to the abutting landowners, the following described canal lands, situate in the city of Massillon, Stark county, Ohio, to-wit: Being the berme embankment of the Ohio canal, commencing at a line drawn parallel to and fifty (50) feet south of the southerly line of West Main street in the city of Massillon, Stark county, Ohio, and extending thence southerly over and along the berme embankment of the Ohio canal including the full width thereof of about twelve (12) feet, two hundred fifty (250) feet more or less to the northerly line of West Charles street in said city, providing application is made by the abutting landowners within two years from the passage of this act.

SECTION 2. As a preliminary to such sale, the superintendent of public works shall appraise said land in accordance with the provisions of section 13971 of the General Code, taking into consideration, however, the benefits that will accrue to the state by reason of the construction of the retaining wall hereinafter required.

SECTION 3. If such appraisement is satisfactory to the governor and attorney general, the governor, upon payment of the purchase money into the general revenue fund in the state treasury, shall execute a deed therefor to the purchaser, reserving, however, to the state an easement in such land for embankment purposes for restraining the water of the canal within its proper channel, and also requiring the purchaser to construct and maintain, so long as the canal exists, either a stone or concrete retaining wall along the westerly line of the land herein described, which wall shall be satisfactory to the superintendent of public works. On the consummation of the sale, and the execution of a deed for the lands herein described, the superintendent of public works is hereby authorized to cancel any existing leases for said lands.

Authority to sell portion of canal lands in Massillon; description.

Appraisement.

Purchase money paid into state treasury; reservation.

CARL R. KIMBALL,
Speaker of the House of Representatives.
CLARENCE J. BROWN,
President of the Senate.

This act is not of a general and permanent nature and requires no sectional number.
JOHN G. PRICE,
Attorney General.

Passed April 17, 1919.
Approved May 10, 1919.

JAMES M. COX,
Governor.

Filed in the office of the Secretary of State at Columbus, Ohio, on the 16th day of May, A. D. 1919.

114 L.

[House Bill No. 366.]

AN ACT

To supplement section 3285 of the General Code by the enactment of section 3285-1, authorizing township trustees of a township composed in whole or in part of islands to purchase and operate a scow or lighter.

Be it enacted by the General Assembly of the State of Ohio:

SECTION 1. That section 3285 of the General Code be supplemented by the enactment of section 3285-1, to read as follows:

Sec. 3285-1. The trustees of a township which is composed in whole or in part of islands, accessible from the main land only by water craft, may purchase and operate, and may let for hire, a scow or lighter of sufficient tonnage to carry stone and other road building material, equipped with or without a proper crane or loading device, and for such purpose may levy a tax upon all the taxable property in the township, in such amount as they may determine. The question of levying such tax, and the amount thereof, shall be separately submitted to the qualified electors of the township at a general election. Twenty days' notice thereof shall be previously given by posting in at least three public places in the township. Such notice shall state specifically the amount to be raised and the purpose thereof. If a majority of all the votes cast at such election upon the proposition are in favor thereof, the tax provided for shall be considered authorized.

When trustees authorized to operate scow or lighter.

CARL R. KIMBALL,
Speaker of the House of Representatives.
CLARENCE J. BROWN,
President of the Senate.

The sectional number in this act is in conformity to the General Code.
JOHN G. PRICE,
Attorney General.

Passed April 17, 1919.
Approved May 10, 1919.

JAMES M. COX,
Governor.

Filed in the office of the Secretary of State at Columbus, Ohio, on the 16th day of May, A. D. 1919.

115 G.

[House Bill No. 161.]

AN ACT

To amend sections 2573 and 2768 of the General Code, relating to conveyances of property to name of purchaser, and the transfer of same by county auditor before record.

Be it enacted by the General Assembly of the State of Ohio:

SECTION 1. That sections 2573 and 2768 of the General Code be amended to read as follows:

Transfer of property to name of purchaser before record.

Sec. 2573. On application and presentation of title, with the affidavits required by law, or the proper order of a court, the county auditor shall transfer any land or town lot or part thereof or minerals therein or mineral rights thereto, charged with taxes on the tax list from the name in which it stands into the name of the owner, when rendered necessary by a conveyance, partition, devise, descent or otherwise. If by reason of the conveyance or otherwise, a part only of a tract or lot, or minerals therein or mineral rights thereto, as charged in the tax list is to be transferred, the person desiring the transfer shall make satisfactory proof of the value of such part compared with the value of the whole, as charged on the tax list, before the transfer is made. The auditor shall indorse on the deed or other evidences of title presented to him that the proper transfer of the real estate therein described has been made in his office or that it is not entered for taxation, and sign his name thereto.

Deed shall not be recorded before transfer unless endorsed "transfer not necessary."

Sec. 2768. The county recorder shall not record any deed of absolute conveyance of land or any conveyance, absolute or otherwise, of minerals or mineral rights until it has been presented to the county auditor, and by him indorsed "transferred," or "transfer not necessary." Before any real estate the title to which shall have passed under the laws of descent shall be transferred, as above provided, from the name of the ancestor to the heir at law or next of kin of such ancestor, or to any grantee of such heir at law or next of kin; and before any deed or conveyance of real estate made by any such heir at law or next

Affidavit, when title passes by law of descent, presented to auditor before transfer.

of kin shall be presented to or filed for record by the recorder of any county, such heir at law or next of kin, or his or their grantee, his agent or attorney, shall present to such auditor the affidavit of such heir or heirs at law or next of kin, or of two persons resident of the state of Ohio, each of whom has personal knowledge of the facts, which affidavit shall set forth the date of such ancestor's death, and the place of residence at the time of his or her death; the fact that he or she died intestate; the names, ages, and addresses, so far as the ages and addresses are known and can be ascertained of each of such ancestor's heirs at law and next of kin, who by his death inherited such real estate and the relationship of each to such ancestor and the part or portion of such real estate inherited by each, which such transfers shall be made by the auditor in accordance with the statement contained in such affidavit, and such auditor shall indorse upon such deed or conveyance the fact that such transfer was made by affidavit. Such affidavit shall be filed with the recorder of the county in which such real estate is situated at or before the time when such deed or conveyance shall be filed with such recorder for record and shall be by him recorded in the record of deeds, and such affidavit of descent shall be by him indexed in the general index of deeds, in his office, in the name of such ancestor as grantor and in the name of each of such heirs at law or next of kin as grantees in the same manner as if such names occurred in a deed of conveyance from such ancestor to said heirs at law and for such indexing and recording the recorder shall receive the same fees as are provided by law for the indexing and recording of deeds.

The said record of the affidavit above mentioned, shall, in the trial of any cause, so far as competent, be prima facie evidence with foregoing provision of this act, but the truth of such statements may be rebutted or overcome by any competent evidence. *Record of affidavit prima facie evidence.*

Any person or persons who shall, wilfully and fraudulently make affidavit to any statement above mentioned, which shall be false, knowing the same to be false or who shall, for the purpose above mentioned, deliver to any county auditor for the purpose of obtaining any such transfer, or deliver to the county recorder, for the purpose of having the same recorded, any such affidavit containing any such false statements, knowing the same to be a false statement, shall be guilty of a misdemeanor and on conviction thereof, be fined in any sum not exceeding five hundred dollars and be imprisoned in the county jail not to exceed six months, or both, and in addition, be liable in damages to any person who may be injured by the making, filing, recording or use as aforesaid of such affidavit. *Penalty for false affidavit.*

SECTION 2. That said original sections 2573 and 2768 of the General Code be, and the same are hereby repealed. *Repeals.*

CARL R. KIMBALL,
Speaker of the House of Representatives.
CLARENCE J. BROWN,
President of the Senate.

The sectional numbers in this act are in conformity to the General Code.
JOHN G. PRICE, Attorney General.

Passed April 17, 1919.
Approved May 10, 1919.

JAMES M. COX,
Governor.

Filed in the office of the Secretary of State at Columbus, Ohio, on the 16th day of May, A. D. 1919.

116 G.

[House Bill No. 488.]

AN ACT

To provide for the acquisition of the land upon which the tomb of William H. Harrison is situate and to establish a commission to care for same.

Be it enacted by the General Assembly of the State of Ohio:

Sec. 15301-1.

William Henry Harrison Memorial Commission.

SECTION 1. That the governor of Ohio shall appoint three commissioners to serve as a committee to be called the William Henry Harrison Memorial Commission.

Sec. 15301-2.

Powers of commission.

SECTION 2. That said commission is hereby empowered to receive deeds for the property upon which the present tomb of William Henry Harrison is now situate in Hamilton county, state of Ohio, and all other adjacent ground which may be granted, or acquired in fee simple in the name of the state of Ohio for the purpose of creating a state public park upon said property.

Sec. 15301-3.

Park created.

SECTION 3. That such created park shall hereafter be known as the William Henry Harrison Memorial Park.

Sec. 15301-4.

Powers of commission.

SECTION 4. That said commission be, and the same is hereby empowered to draw upon the general revenue funds of the state, not otherwise appropriated, a sum sufficient to place said granted lands in suitable condition for park purposes.

Sec. 15301-5.

Powers of commission.

SECTION 5. That said commission be, and the same is, hereby empowered to draw upon the general revenue funds of the state, not otherwise appropriated, a sum sufficient for the purpose of placing the tomb and ground upon which the tomb of William Henry Harrison is located in a suitable and decent condition in order that the memory of Ohio's first present and gallant soldier, William Henry Harrison, may be fittingly commemorated.

Sec. 15301-6.

Powers of commission.

SECTION 6. That said commission and all succeeding commissioners be and the same are hereby empowered to contract for the upkeep and repairs of said Harrison memorial park tomb and memorial, said expense not to exceed in any one year more than $600.00 and to draw upon the general revenue funds of the state, not heretofore appropriated, for this purpose except that the first commission shall not draw any funds whatsoever except as provided in this act.

Sec. 15301-7.

Appointment of commission.

SECTION 7. That said commission shall be appointed every two years hereafter upon the inauguration of the governor of Ohio as prescribed by law.

Sec. 15301-8.

Salary.

SECTION 8. Said commission hereby appointed and all succeeding commissions shall receive no salary and shall render to the auditor of state at the expiration of each year a complete record of their transactions with receipts for all monies expended during the year.

Sec. 15301-9.

Appropriation.

SECTION 9. That there shall be appropriated out of any monies in the state treasury to the credit of the general revenue fund, not otherwise appropriated, the sum of $10,-

000.00 to the use of said commission for the purpose of carrying out the provisions of this act and that said commissioners furnish the auditor of said state with a bond for the faithful performance of their respective duties as he may direct, each bond not to exceed in amount $10,000.00.

CARL R. KIMBALL,
Speaker of the House of Representatives.
CLARENCE J. BROWN,
President of the Senate.

Passed April 10, 1919.
Approved May 9, 1919.

JAMES M. COX,
Governor.

Filed in the office of the Secretary of State at Columbus, Ohio, on the 16th day of May, A. D. 1919.

117 G.

[House Bill No. 104.]

AN ACT

Providing for the granting of badges of honor to the Ohio soldiers and sailors who served in the world war of 1917-1919, the Spanish-American War of 1898 and 1899, and surviving soldiers and sailors who served in the armies of the United States in the Civil War.

Be it enacted by the General Assembly of the State of Ohio:

SECTION 1. The adjutant general of the state of Ohio is hereby authorized and directed to procure and furnish to each officer, enlisted and selective service man, and proper mementoes to the parents or next of kin of those killed in action, or who died while in the service, residing in Ohio at the time of his entering the service, and who has served under the call of the president of the United States in the World War of 1917 and 1918, the Spanish-American war of 1898-1899, and all surviving soldiers and sailors who served in the army and navy of the United States in the Civil War a badge of honor emblematic of such service, and as a mark of appreciation of the people of Ohio.

SECTION 2. The adjutant general of the state of Ohio is hereby authorized and directed to distribute said badges in the manner deemed by him most efficient, to soldiers and sailors honorably discharged from the service of the United States, and such soldiers and sailors as are now in service when any shall apply to the adjutant general of Ohio for one of such badges of honor; and any soldier or sailor now in service who has theretofore received such badge, and who may be thereafter dishonorably discharged shall return said badge forthwith to said adjutant general of Ohio.

Margin notes:

The sectional numbers on the margin hereof are designated as provided by law. JOHN G. PRICE, Attorney General.

Sec. 14867-2.

Badge of honor for soldiers and sailors who served the United States in war.

Sec. 14867-3.

Distribution by adjutant general.

Sec. 14867-4.
Badges not
awarded to
conscientious
objectors.

SECTION 3. Said badges of honor and gratitude are in no wise to be awarded to conscientious objectors.

Sec. 14867-5.
Design of
badges; committee to
award contract.

SECTION 4. Said badges are to be designed so as to express in appropriate form Ohio's sentiment for the service of her sons in the World War, the Spanish-American War and surviving soldiers and sailors of the Civil War.

The design shall be selected by a committee of three, consisting of one member appointed by the governor, one member appointed by the president of the senate, and one member appointed by the speaker of the house of representatives. This committee shall award the contract of manufacturing such badges to the lowest and best bidder and shall receive no compensation for their services.

Sec. 14867-6.
Appropriation.

SECTION 5. There is hereby appropriated out of any moneys in the state treasury to the credit of the general revenue fund not otherwise appropriated, the sum of seventy-five thousand dollars, or as much thereof as may be necessary to the use of the adjutant general for the purpose of carrying out the provisions of this act.

Sec. 14867-7.
Penalty for unlawfully wearing badge.

SECTION 6. Any person unlawfully wearing such badge shall be guilty of a misdemeanor, and shall be subject to a fine of not more than one hundred dollars.

Sec. 14867-8.
Courts having
jurisdiction.

SECTION 7. Mayors, justices of peace, municipal and police court judges shall have final jurisdiction in all cases involving the violation of this act.

The sectional
numbers on the
margin hereof
are designated
as provided by
law.
JOHN G. PRICE,
Attorney
General.

CARL R. KIMBALL,
Speaker of the House of Representatives.
CLARENCE J. BROWN,
President of the Senate.

Passed April 16, 1919.
Approved May 10, 1919.

JAMES M. COX,
Governor.

Filed in the office of the Secretary of State at Columbus, Ohio, on the 16th day of May, A. D. 1919.

118 G.

[House Bill No. 419.]

AN ACT

Providing certain regulations with respect to the sale of feed stuffs.

Be it enacted by the General Assembly of the State of Ohio:

Sec. 1141.

SECTION 1. Whoever sells or offers for sale within this state any feed stuffs or condimental stock or poultry feeds, animal or poultry regulators, conditioners, tonics, or similar articles, for any of which any food value is claimed in any manner by the manufacturer or seller thereof, in carload lots or in bulk packages thereof, shall furnish with each carload or quantity in bulk or package thereof or affix to each bag, barrel or other package thereof, in a conspicuous place on the outside thereof, a plainly printed certificate, which shall state the number of net pounds in each car or quantity in bulk or in each package, the name, brand, or trade-mark, under which it is sold or offered for sale, the name and postoffice address of the manufacturer, shipper or vendor, and the names of each and all ingredients of which the article is composed. Such certificate shall contain also, a chemical analysis of the product to be sold which shall state the minimum percentage of crude protein, allowing one per cent. of nitrogen to equal six and one-fourth per cent. of protein or crude fat and crude fibre, also the maximum percentage of crude fibre of the product to be sold.

Printed statement on outside of package, etc.; contents of statement.

The sectional number on the margin hereof is designated as provided by law. JOHN G. PRICE, *Attorney General.*

CARL R. KIMBALL,
Speaker of the House of Representatives.
CLARENCE J. BROWN,
President of the Senate.

Passed April 14, 1919.
Approved May 10, 1919.

JAMES M. COX,
Governor.

Filed in the office of the Secretary of State at Columbus, Ohio, on the 16th day of May, A. D. 1919.

119 G.

[Amended Senate Bill No. 14.]

AN ACT

To create a hotel division in the office of the state fire marshal; to provide for the administration of each division and prescribe its duties and powers; to amend section 840 of the General Code relative to salaries of the state fire marshal and the first deputy fire marshal.

Be it enacted by the General Assembly of the State of Ohio:

Sec. 843.

Hotel division in department of state fire marshal; rules; deputies; bond.

SECTION 1. There is hereby created in the department of the state fire marshal of the state of Ohio a division of said department to be known as the hotel division, and to be administered as hereinafter set forth. The state fire marshal is hereby authorized and required to make such rules and regulations as are necessary to carry out the provisions of this act. With his deputies and assistants he shall enforce the provisions herein set forth. He shall give a bond to the state in such amount as may be fixed by the governor.

Sec. 843-1.

What deemed to be a hotel.

SECTION 2. Every building or other structure kept, used, maintained, advertised or held out to the public to be a place where food is served and sleeping accommodations are offered for pay to transient guests, in which five or more rooms are used for the accommodation of such guests, and having one or more dining rooms or cafes where meals or lunches are served to such transient guests, such sleeping accommodations and dining rooms being conducted in the same building or in buildings in connection therewith, and every building or other structure kept, used, maintained, advertised or held out to the public to be a place where sleeping accommodations are offered for pay to transient guests, in which five or more rooms are used for the accommodation of such guests, shall, for the purposes of this act, be deemed a hotel.

Sec. 843-2.

Term restaurant defined.

SECTION 3. Every building or other structure kept, used, maintained, advertised or held out to the public to be a place where meals or lunches are served for consideration, without sleeping accommodations, shall, for the purpose of this act, be defined to be a restaurant.

Sec. 843-3.

Who shall procure license.

SECTION 4. On or before January first, nineteen hundred and twenty, and each year thereafter, every person, firm or corporation now engaged in the business of conducting a hotel or restaurant, or both, in all cities of the state and all villages of more than two thousand five hundred population and every person, firm or corporation who shall hereafter engage in conducting such business, in such cities and villages, shall procure a license for each hotel or restaurant so conducted or proposed to be conducted; provided, that one license shall be sufficient for each combined hotel and restaurant where both are conducted in the same building and under the same management. No hotel or restaurant shall be maintained and conducted in any city or village of more than two thousand five hundred population in this state after the taking effect of this act without a license therefor. No license shall be transferable without the consent of the state fire marshal.

License not transferrable.

Provided, however, that a license to maintain and operate a hotel shall not be issued to the keeper, owner or lessee of any hotel, nor the keeper or owner of a rooming or boarding house, where accommodations for assignation purposes are furnished, nor to any keeper, owner, or lessee who has been convicted of keeping a place in violation of the law relating to houses of assignation or places of public nuisance.

What places shall not be licensed.

Sec. 843-4.

SECTION 5. The annual fee for a license to conduct a hotel, rooming house or restaurant in any city or village of more than two thousand five hundred inhabitants in this state shall be as follows:

Schedule of license fees.

For hotel, dining room and restaurant combined, or hotel without a restaurant, containing less than fifteen sleeping rooms, five dollars; for all hotels containing fifteen or more and less than fifty sleeping rooms, ten dollars; for all hotels containing more than fifty and less than two hundred sleeping rooms, fifteen dollars; for all hotels containing more than two hundred and less than four hundred sleeping rooms, twenty dollars; for all hotels containing more than four hundred sleeping rooms, twenty-five dollars; for all restaurants in any city or village of more than two thousand five hundred inhabitants where no hotel license is granted, and where said restaurant is separate from the management of a hotel and has a seating capacity of less than twenty-five persons, three dollars; and when such restaurant has a seating capacity of over twenty-five persons, five dollars.

Each fee must be paid to the state fire marshal before such license is issued and such fee shall be paid into the state treasury and placed to the credit of the special fund for maintenance of the office of the state fire marshal.

Where a license has been issued to a hotel or restaurant the same shall be kept in the office of such hotel or restaurant or displayed in a conspicuous and public manner therein. Such license may be cancelled by the state fire marshal at any time when for violation of any law or regulation of a board of health.

Display of license.

Sec. 843-5.

SECTION 6. In every hotel or restaurant the person, firm or corporation operating which is required to have a license by the provisions of this act, the kitchen, dining room, cellar, office, ice boxes, refrigerators and all places where foods are prepared, kept or stored, shall be kept clean and in a sanitary condition. The toilets and outclosets shall, at all times be kept in a clean and sanitary condition in such restaurants and hotels. All garbage, tin cans and kitchen refuse must be kept in a tight, metal can with a lid encircling the top of the can and said contents must be removed once daily. The dining rooms, kitchens and pantries where food is kept, stored or served, must be

Sanitary provisions.

10 C. & L. A.

thoroughly screened from flies and insects. Serving tables, trucks, trays, boxes, buckets, knives, saws, cleavers and other utensils and machinery used in moving, handling, cutting, chopping, mixing or serving foods are required to be thoroughly sterilized daily by hot water or steam, and thoroughly cleaned and the clothes and hands of cooks, stewards, waiters and persons handling food must be clean and sanitary.

In all restaurants and hotels where food is on display the same shall have full protection from dust, dirt, flies and vermin by being kept under a glass case.

Sec. 843-6.

Employee must be free from certain diseases.

SECTION 7.   No person suffering from or afflicted with tuberculosis, a venereal or a contagious disease shall be employed in or about any part of a restaurant or its kitchen, or handle food stuffs or products used therein, and the state fire marshal or his deputies shall have the power to compel a person handling food stuffs in any restaurant or hotel to present a certificate from a reputable physician showing him or her to be free from any infectious or contagious disease.

Sec. 843-7.

Duties of fire marshal, owner, proprietor or agent.

SECTION 8.   It is hereby made a duty of the state fire marshal to inspect or cause to be inspected, at least once annually, every hotel and restaurant which comes within the provision of this act, and for that purpose he shall have the right of entry thereto at any reasonable time. Whenever, upon such inspection, it shall be found that such business and property so inspected is not being conducted, or is not equipped in the manner and condition required by the provisions of this act or the health laws of this state, it shall thereupon be the duty of the state fire marshal to notify the owner, proprietor or agent in charge of such business, or the owner or agent of the building so occupied, of such changes or alterations as may be necessary to effect a complete compliance with the provisions of this act, or the health laws of the state. It shall therefore be the duty of such owner, proprietor or agent in charge of such business to make such alterations or changes as may be necessary and put such building and premises in such condition that will fully comply with the requirements of this act within thirty days after being notified by the state fire marshal.

Sec. 843-8.

Cumulative penalties for violations.

SECTION 9.   Whoever shall fail or refuse to comply with the provisions of this act shall be deemed guilty of a misdemeanor and shall be subject to a fine of ten dollars for each day that such violation is continued. If any such violation continue for more than thirty days, the building and premises involved may be closed for use as such hotel or restaurant until all the provisions of this act shall be complied with to the satisfaction of the state fire marshal.

Sec. 843-9.

Plumbing, lighting and ventilation.

SECTION 10.   Every hotel and restaurant in this state shall have proper plumbing, lighting and ventilation which shall conform to the provisions of the building code so far as they apply.

Sec. 843-10.

SECTION 11. In all cities and villages where a system of waterworks and sewerage is maintained for public use, every hotel and restaurant coming under this act shall within six motnhs after the taking effect of this act be equipped with a sufficient number of suitable water-closets for the accommodation of its guests, which water-closets shall be ventilated and connected by proper plumbing with such sewerage system. All lavatories, bathtubs, sinks, drains, closets and urinals in such hotels or restaurants shall be properly constructed and shall be kept clean and well ventilated at all times. Separate apartments shall be furnished for different sexes, each being properly designated. *Lavatories, sinks, drains, closets, etc.*

Sec. 843-11.

SECTION 12. All hotels shall provide each bed, bunk, cot or other sleeping place for the use of guests with pillow slips and under and top sheets. Such top sheets shall be at least ninety inches in length. Such sheets and pillow slips shall be made of white cotton or linen, and all such sheets and pillow slips, after being used by one guest, shall be washed and ironed before being used by another guest. *Beds and bedding.*

Sec. 843-12.

SECTION 13. All bedding, including mattresses, quilts, blankets, pillows, sheets and comforts used in any hotel or rooming house in this state must be thoroughly aired, disinfected and kept clean; and no bedding which is infested with vermin or bedbugs shall be used on any bed in any hotel or rooming house. All floors, carpets and equipment in hotels and restaurants, and all walls and ceilings shall be kept in a clean and sanitary condition at all times. *Bedding, floors, carpets, etc., must be kept sanitary.*

Sec. 843-13.

SECTION 14. When any room has been occupied by a person having an infectious or contagious disease, such room shall not be used again until thoroughly fumigated and the bedding and pillows therein disinfected. *When fumigation required.*

Sec. 843-14.

SECTION 15. No cot, bed or bunk may be kept or used for sleeping purposes in any room in which foodstuffs are prepared or cooked. *Bed in cook room prohibited.*

All notices to be served by the state fire marshal, provided for in this act, shall be in writing and shall be either delivered personally or by United States mail addressed to the owner, agent, lessee or manager of such building and premises, or the owner, lessee, agent or manager of such hotel or restaurant. *Notice, how served.*

Sec. 843-15.

SECTION 16. The prosecuting attorney of each county is hereby authorized and required upon complaint of the state fire marshal or other person representing him, to prosecute to termination before any court of competent jurisdiction, a proper action or proceeding against any person or persons violating any provisions of this act. *Enforcement of law.*

Sec. 843-16.

SECTION 17. The state fire marshal, his deputies and assistants shall accept no gift or gratuity in any form from any hotel or restaurant under penalty of summary dismissal. *Gifts to officers prohibited.*

Sec. 843-17.

Villages not exempt from law.

SECTION 18. Nothing in this act shall release villages of two thousand five hundred population or less from the sanitary and health provisions herein required of such villages.

Sec. 843-19.

Posting of hotel rates; diagram filed with fire marshal.

SECTION 19. The owner or manager of each hotel shall post in a conspicuous place in each room thereof a card or sign stating the price per day of such room, and shall file with the state fire marshal a diagram or list showing the price of each room in said hotel and no advances shall be made in this schedule, without twenty days' written notice to the state fire marshal.

SECTION 20. That section 840 of the General Code be amended to read as follows:

Salaries of state fire marshal and deputies.

Sec. 840. The state fire marshal shall receive an annual salary of four thousand five hundred dollars; the first deputy fire marshal two thousand five hundred dollars, and the second deputy fire marshal fifteen hundred dollars. Such salaries, compensation of clerks and assistants and all other expenses of the department of the state fire marshal necessary in the performance of the duties imposed upon him by law, shall not exceed in any year the amount paid into the state treasury for that year by fire insurance companies as provided in the next following section, and by the state fire marshal as provided in this act.

SECTION 21. That original section 840 of the General Code be and the same is hereby repealed.

The sectional numbers on the margin hereof are designated as provided by law.
JOHN G. PRICE,
Attorney General.

CLARENCE J. BROWN,
President of the Senate.
CARL R. KIMBALL,
Speaker of the House of Representatives.
Passed April 9, 1919.
Approved May 10, 1919.

JAMES M. COX,
Governor.

Filed in the office of the Secretary of State at Columbus, Ohio, on the 16th day of May, A. D. 1919.

120 G.

[House Bill No. 378.]

AN ACT

To fix standards for Climax baskets, small fruit baskets, hampers and round stave baskets for fruits and vegetables and to repeal section 13108 of General Code.

Be it enacted by the General Assembly of the State of Ohio:

Sec. 6422-1.

Standards for Climax baskets, for fruits and vegetables.

SECTION 1. That standards for Climax baskets for grapes and other fruits and vegetables shall be the two-quart basket, four-quart basket and twelve-quart basket respectively:

293

(a) The standard two-quart Climax basket shall be
of the following dimensions: Length of bottom piece, nine
and one-half inches; width of bottom piece, three and one-
half inches; thickness of bottom piece, three-eights of an
inch; height of basket, three and seven-eighths inches, outside
measurement; top of basket, length eleven inches and width
five inches outside measurement. Basket to have a cover of
five by eleven inches, when a cover is used.

(b) The standard four-quart Climax basket shall be
of the following dimensions: Length of bottom piece,
twelve inches; width of bottom piece, four and one-half
inches; thickness of bottom piece, three-eighths of an inch;
height of basket, four and eleven-sixteenths inches, outside
measurement; top of basket, length fourteen inches, width
six and one-fourth inches, outside measurement. Basket to
have cover six and one-fourth inches by fourteen inches,
when cover is used.

(c) The standard twelve-quart Climax basket shall
be of the following dimensions: Length of bottom piece,
sixteen inches; width of bottom piece, six and one-half
inches; thickness of bottom piece, seven-sixteenths of an
inch; height of basket, seven and one-sixteenth inches, outside measurement; top of basket, length nineteen inches,
width nine inches, outside measurement. Basket to have
cover nine inches by nineteen inches, when cover is used.

Sec. 6422-2.
SECTION 2. That standard basket or other container
for small fruits, berries and vegetables shall be of the following capacities: namely, dry one-half pint, dry pint, dry
quart, or multiples of the dry quart.

Standard for small fruits and vegetables.

(a) The dry half-pint shall contain sixteen and eight-
tenths cubic inches.

(b) The dry pint shall contain thirty-three and six-
tenths cubic inches. .

(c) The dry quart shall contain sixty-seven and two-
tenths cubic inches.

The dimensions of the one-quart box used in the sale
of berries or other small fruits shall be as follows: Five
and one-tenth inches square on top, four and three-tenths
inches square on the bottom and three inches in depth.

Sec. 6423-3.
SECTION 3. That the standard hampers for fruits and
vegetables shall be the one peck hamper, one-half bushel
hamper, one bushel hamper, and one and one-half bushel
hamper respectively.

Standard hampers for fruits and vegetables.

(a) The standard one peck hamper shall contain five
hundred thirty-seven and six-tenths cubic inches, and conform to the following specifications: The inside diameter
between staves at upper edge of the top inside hoop shall
be ten and three-eighths inches; the inside diameter of the
bottom shall be six and one-half inches; the inside length of
the staves shall be nine and five-eighths inches; the inside
top hoop shall be one-tenth inch thick and set with its upper edge even with the upper ends of the staves; there
shall be ten staves, each not less than one-tenth inch thick

and ten and one-eighth inches long; and the bottom piece shall be one-half inch thick.

(b) The standard one-half bushel hamper shall contain one thousand, seventy-five and twenty-one one-hundredths cubic inches, and conform to the following specifications: The inside diameter between staves at upper edge of the top inside hoop shall be thirteen inches; the inside diameter of the bottom shall be eight inches; the inside length of staves shall be twelve and one-half inches; the inside top hoop shall be one-ninth of an inch thick and set with its upper edge even with the upper ends of the staves; there shall be ten staves, each not less than one-tenth of an inch thick and thirteen and one-eighth inches long; and the bottom piece shall be five-eighths of an inch thick.

(c) The standard one bushel hamper shall contain two thousand, one hundred fifty and forty-two one-hundredths cubic inches, and conform to the following specifications: The inside diameter between staves at upper edge of the top inside hoop shall be fifteen and one-eighth inches; the inside diameter of the bottom shall be nine inches; the inside length of the staves to the upper edge of the top inside hoop shall be nineteen inches; the inside top hoop shall be one-eighth of an inch thick and set with its upper edge three-eighths of an inch below the upper ends of the staves; there shall be either ten or twelve staves, each not less than one-eighth of an inch thick and twenty inches long; and the bottom piece shall be five-eighths of an inch thick.

(d) The standard one and one-half bushel hamper shall contain three thousand, two hundred twenty-five and sixty-three one-hundredths cubic inches, and conform to either of the following specifications:

(1) The inside diameter between staves at upper edge of the top inside hoop shall be sixteen and one-fourth inches; the inside diameter of the bottom shall be nine inches; the inside length of the staves to the upper edge of the top inside hoop shall be twenty-five and thirteen-sixteenths inches; the inside top hoop shall be one-eighth of an inch thick and set with its upper edge three-eighths of an inch below the upper ends of the staves; there shall be ten staves, each not less than one-sixth of an inch thick and twenty-seven inches long; and the bottom piece shall be five-eighths of an inch thick.

(2) The inside diameter between staves at upper edge of the top inside hoop shall be sixteen and three-fourths inches; the inside diameter of the bottom shall be ten inches; the inside length of the staves to the upper edge of the top inside hoop shall be twenty-three inches; the inside top hoop shall be one-eighth of an inch thick and set with its upper edge three-eighths of an inch below the upper ends of the staves; there shall be ten staves, each not less than one-eighth of an inch thick and twenty-four inches long,

and the bottom piece shall be five-eighths of an inch thick.

Sec. 6422-4. SECTION 4. That the standard round stave baskets for *Standard round stave baskets for fruits and vegetables.* fruits and vegetables shall be one-half bushel basket, one bushel basket, one and one-half bushel basket and two bushel basket respectively.

(a) The one-half bushel round stave basket shall contain one thousand seventy-five and twenty one-hundredths cubic inches, and conform to the following specifications: The inside diameter at the upper inner edge of the top inside hoop shall be thirteen and one-half inches; the average inside depth shall be not less than eight and one-half inches; the web shall consist of twenty intersecting staves, each not less than one-eighteenth of an inch thick and of such length that they will form the sides and bottom of a basket which shall contain sixteen quarts, standard dry measure.

(b) The one bushel round stave basket shall contain two thousand, one-hundred fifty and forty-two one-hundredths cubic inches, and conform to the following specifications: The inside diameter at upper inner edge of the top inside hoop shall be seventeen inches; the average inside depth shall be not less than ten and three-fourths inches; the web shall consist of twenty intersecting staves, each not less than one-eighteenth of an inch thick and of such length that they will form the sides and bottom of a basket which shall contain thirty-two quarts standard dry measure.

(c.) The one and one-half bushel round stave basket shall contain three thousand, two hundred and twenty-five and sixty-three one-hundredths cubic inches, and conform to the following specifications: The inside diameter at upper inner edge of the top inside hoop shall be nineteen inches; the average inside depth shall be not less than twelve and three--fourth inches; the web shall consist of twenty-four intersecting staves, each not less than one-sixteenth of an inch thick and of such length that they will form the sides and bottom of a basket which shall contain forty-eight quarts standard dry measure.

(d) The two bushel round stave basket shall contain four thousand, three hundred, and eighty-four one-hundredths cubic inches, and conform to the following specifications: The inside diameter at upper inner edge of the top inside hoop shall be twenty and three-fourths inches; the average inside depth shall be not less than thirteen and three-fourths inches; the web shall consist of twenty-four intersecting staves, each not less than one-sixteenth of an inch thick and of such length that they will form the sides and bottom of a basket which shall contain sixty-four quarts, standard dry measure.

Sec. 6432-5. SECTION 5. That it shall be unlawful to ship or deliver for shipment within the state of Ohio, Climax baskets, *Penalty for violations of law.* small fruit baskets, hampers, or round stave baskets, for fruits or vegetables, either filled or unfilled or parts of such Climax baskets, small fruit baskets, hampers or round stave baskets, that do not comply with this act; or fruits or vegetables in Climax baskets, small fruit baskets, hampers or round stave baskets, that at the time of such shipment, delivery for shipment, or offer for sale, are not filled to the full capacity thereof, stricken measure. Any individual, partnership, association or corporation, that wilfully violates this section shall be deemed guilty of a misdemeanor and upon conviction thereof shall be punished by a fine of not exceeding $100.00 or imprisonment not exceeding sixty days or both.

Sec. 6422-6.

Rules and regulations; examinations and tests.

SECTION 6. That the secretary of agriculture is authorized to prescribe such regulations as he may find necessary for carrying into effect the provisions of this act, and to cause such examinations and tests to be made as may be necessary in order to determine whether Climax baskets, small fruit baskets, hampers and round stave baskets or parts thereof subject to this act, meet its requirements. For said purpose the authorized officers and agents of the secretary of agriculture may visit factories, stock rooms, and other places of business where such hampers or baskets or parts thereof are manufactured or held for sale or shipment or offered for sale, may enter cars, vessels, other vehicles and places under the control of carriers engaged in the transportation of such hampers or baskets or parts thereof, and may take samples of such hampers or baskets or parts, the cost of which samples, upon request, shall be paid to the person entitled thereto.

Sec. 6422-7.

Enforcement of law and rules.

SECTION 7. It shall be the duty of the secretary of agriculture to enforce all the provisions of this act, and to prescribe such rules and regulations not otherwise herein provided, as he may deem necessary, for the efficient execution of the provisions of the same, including the amount of tolerance necessary in the enforcement of this act, because of the impossibility of perfect scientific exactitude in the manufacture of such Climax baskets, small fruit baskets, hampers and round stave baskets; and which regulations and tolerances shall be in conformity with those from time to time promulgated by the United States department of agriculture.

Sec. 6422-8.

Different forms of baskets may be permitted.

SECTION 8. The secretary of agriculture for good and sufficient reasons may permit the use of Climax baskets, small fruit baskets, hampers and round stave baskets of a different form from the baskets prescribed in this act but of the same capacity.

Sec. 6422-9.

When dealer shall not be prosecuted.

SECTION 9. That no dealer shall be prosecuted under the provisions of this act when he can establish a guaranty signed by the manufacturer, wholesaler, jobber, or other party residing within the United States from whom such Climax basket, baskets, or other containers as defined in this act, were purchased, to the effect that said Climax basket, baskets, or other containers are correct within the meaning of this act. Said guaranty, to afford protection, shall contain the name and address of the party or parties making the sale of Climax basket, baskets, or other containers, hampers or round stave baskets, to such dealer, and in such case said guarantor shall be amenable to the prosecutions, fines and other penalties which would attach in due course to the dealer under the provisions of this act.

Sec. 6422-10.

SECTION 10. That this act shall be in force and effect from and after the first day of November, nineteen hundred and twenty.

When act to take effect.

SECTION 11. Section 13108 of the General Code be, and the same is hereby repealed.

The sectional numbers on the margin hereof are designated as provided by law.
JOHN G. PRICE, Attorney General.

CARL R. KIMBALL,
Speaker of the House of Representatives.
CLARENCE J. BROWN,
President of the Senate.

Passed April 17, 1919.
Approved May 10, 1919.

JAMES M. COX,
Governor.

Filed in the office of the Secretary of State at Columbus, Ohio, on the 16th day of May, A. D. 1919.

121 G.

[Senate Bill No. 127.]

AN ACT

To amend sections 1249, 1250, 1251, 1252, 1253, 1254, 1255, 1256, 1257, 1258, 1259, 1259-1, 1260 and 1261 of the General Code; to add supplemental sections 1258-1, 1258-2,1258-3, 1258-4, 1285-5, 1285-6, 1258-7, 1258-8, relating to the pollution of streams and the protection of public water supplies; and to repeal original sections 1249, 1250, 1251, 1252, 1253, ·1254, 1255, 1256, 1257, 1258, 1259, 1259-1, 1260 and 1261, General Code.

Be it enacted by the General Assembly of the State of Ohio:
SECTION 1. That sections 1249, 1250, 1251, 1252, 1253, 1254, 1255, 1256, 1257, 1258, 1259, 1259-1, 1260 and 1261 be amended to read as follows and that section 1258 be supplemented by the addition of sections 1258-1, 1258-2, 1258-3, 1258-4, 1258-5, 1258-6, 1258-7, 1258-8.

Sec. 1249. Whenever the council or board of health, or the officer or officers performing the duties of a council or board of health, of a city or village, the commissioners of a county, the trustees of a township or fifty of the qualified electors of any city, village or township, or the managing officer or officers of a public institution set forth in writing to the state department of health that a city, village, public institution, corporation, partnership or person is discharging or is permitting to be discharged sewage or other wastes into a stream, water course, canal, lake or pond, and is hereby creating a public nuisance detrimental to

Investigation by state department of health on written complaint.

health or comfort, or is polluting the source of any public water supply; the commissioner of health shall forthwith inquire into and investigate the conditions complained of.

Notice of findings and hearing, how given.

Sec. 1250. If the commissioner of health finds that the discharge of sewage or other wastes from a city, village or public institution, or by a corporation, partnership or person, has so corrupted a stream, water course, canal, lake or pond, as to give rise to foul and noxious odors or to conditions detrimental to health or comfort, the source of public water supply of a city, village, community or public institution is subject to contamination, or has been rendered impure by such discharge of sewage or other wastes, he shall notify the mayor or managing officer or officers of such city, village, public institution or corporation, partnership or person of his findings and of the time and place when and where a hearing may be had before the public health council. The notice herein provided shall be by personal service or by registered letter.

Order by commissioner to make improvement; approval by council.

Sec. 1251. After such hearing if the public health council shall determine that improvements or changes are necessary and should be made, the commissioner of health shall notify the mayor or managing officer or officers of such city, village, public institution, or corporation, partnership or person to install works or means, satisfactory to the commissioner of health, for purifying or otherwise disposing of such sewage or other wastes, or to change or enlarge existing works, in a manner satisfactory to the commissioner of health. Such works or means must be completed and put into operation within the time fixed in the order. The order of the commissioner of health and the time fixed for making the improvements or changes shall be approved by the public health council, and notification shall be had by personal service upon or by registered letter to the mayor or managing officer or officers of the city, village, public institution or corporation, partnership or person to whom said order shall apply. But no city or village discharging sewage into a river which separates the state of Ohio from another state shall be required to install sewage purification works so long as the unpurified sewage of cities or villages of another state is discharged into such river above such city or village of this state.

Complaint of impure water supply; investigation.

Sec. 1252. Whenever the board of health, or officer or officers performing the duties of a board of health of a city or village or ten per cent of the electors thereof or the managing officer or officers of a public institution, shall file with the state department of health a complaint, in writing, setting forth that it is believed that the public water supply of such city or village, or public institution, is impure and dangerous to health, the state commissioner of health shall forthwith inquire into and investigate the conditions complained of.

Sec. 1253. If the commissioner of health finds that Notice of findings and time and place of hearing. the public water supply of a city, village or public institution is impure and dangerous to health and that it is not practicable to sufficiently improve the character of such supply by removing the source or sources of pollution affecting it, or if the commissioner of health finds that such water supply is being rendered impure and dangerous to health by reason of improper construction or inadequate size of existing water purification works, he shall notify such city, village, or public institution, corporation, partnership or person owning or operating such water supply or water works of his findings and of the time and place when and where a hearing may be had before the public health council. Such notice shall be by personal service or shall be sent by registered letter to the mayor or managing officer or officers of the city, village, public institution, or corporation, partnership or person owning or operating such water supply or water works.

Sec. 1254. After such hearing, if the public health Changes may be required on approval of public health council. council shall determine that improvements or changes are necessary and should be made, the commissioner of health shall notify the mayor or managing officer or officers of the city, village, public institution or corporation, partnership or person owning or operating such water supply or water works to change the source of supply or to install and place in operation water purification works or device satisfactory to the commissioner of health, or to change or enlarge existing water purification works in a manner satisfactory to said commissioner. The order of the commissioner of health and the time fixed for making the improvements or changes shall be approved by the public health council and notification shall be had by personal service upon or by registered letter to the mayor or managing officer or officers of the city, village, public institution or corporation, partnership or person to whom said order shall apply.

Sec. 1255. When the commissioner of health finds Order for improvement of water works. upon investigation, that any water purification or sewage treatment works, on account of incompetent supervision or inefficient operation is not producing an effluent of such quality as might be reasonably obtained from such water purification or sewage treatment works, and by reason of such neglect the public water supply has become impure and dangerous to health, or that a stream, water course, canal, lake, pond, or body of water has become offensively polluted or has become a public nuisance or that a public water supply taken from such stream, water course, canal, lake, pond or body of water has been rendered impure and dangerous to health, the commissioner of health shall issue an order to the mayor or managing officer or officers of the city, village, public institution, or corporation, partnership or person having charge of or owning such water purification or sewage treatment works, to secure an effluent of such quality as might be reasonably expected from such works and satisfactory to the commissioner of health.

Order to appoint and pay competent person on failure to comply. Sec. 1256. If the managing officer or officers of such city, village, public institution, or corporation, partnership or person fails, for a period of five days after receiving such order, to secure an effluent satisfactory to the commissioner of health, the commissioner of health shall report the fact to the public health council and upon its approval may order such managing officer or officers or person owning such works to appoint within ten days, and pay the salary of a competent person to be approved by the commissioner of health, to take charge of and operate such works as to secure the results demanded by the commissioner of health.

Right of appeal; procedure. Sec. 1257. If the findings or order of the commissioner of health, when approved by the public health council and made in pursuance of the provisions of this chapter relating to stream pollution and public water supply, are not acceptable to any city, village, public institution, corporation or owner effected thereby, such city, village, public institution, corporation or owner shall have the right of appeal as follows: Two reputable and experienced sanitary engineers shall be chosen, one by the city, village, public institution, corporation or owner and the other by the commissioner of health, who shall not be a regular employe of the state department of health. Such persons shall act as referees. If the referees so chosen are unable to agree, they shall choose a third engineer of like standing and the vote of the majority shall be final. As soon as such referees are chosen, the commissioners of health shall file with them a certified copy of the complaint and the findings and order of the state department of health, and it shall be the duty of such referees to investigate the conditions complained of and to determine if such findings are correct and if the order provides a proper remedy for such conditions. The appeal provided for in this section shall be made within thirty days from the date of service of the order upon the mayor or managing officer or officers of the city, village, public institution or corporation or owner, and notice thereof in writing, shall be served upon the commissioner of health by personal service for which there shall be acknowledgment, or sent by registered letter.

Powers of referees; fees and expenses, how paid. Sec. 1258. Such referees may affirm or reject the findings or order of the commissioner of health or may modify such order as to the time within which improvements or changes shall be made, and their decision, which must be in writing and be made within a reasonable time, shall be reported to the commissioner of health and to the city, village, public institution, corporation or owner and shall be final except as hereinafter provided. If said findings and order shall be approved or modified by said referees, the order shall be enforced by the commissioner of health in the manner provided for in this chapter. The fees and expenses of the referee appointed by the commissioner of health shall be paid from funds appropriated to the state department of health for such purpose. The fees and expenses of the referee appointed by the city, village, public institution, corporation or owner shall be paid by the city, village, public institution, corporation or owner making such appeal. The fees and expenses of the third referee shall be equally divided between the state department of health and the city, village, public institution, corporation or owner making appeal.

Sec. 1258-1. Where an order of the commissioner of health to a corporation, partnership or person owning and operating a water works is approved or modified by the referees provided for in sections 1257 and 1258 of the General Code, or if such corporation, partnership or person shall accept such order without appeal to such referees and it shall be claimed by such corporation, partnership or person that the revenues derived from the operation of such water works are not sufficient to warrant the expense of making the improvements or changes so ordered, an application may be made to the public utilities commission of Ohio for authority to make and collect additional charges from the water consumers and user of the utility's service. Upon the filing of such application the commission shall fix a time for the hearing thereof and give notice thereof to the mayor of the municipality and the state commissioner of health and if upon hearing the public utilities commission shall determine and find that the rates theretofore authorized to be charged will not provide revenue sufficient to operate said water works and make a reasonable return upon the investment after such improvements and changes are made, it shall by order authorize the collection of such additional charges and compensation as may under all the circumstances be just and reasonable. *When and how additional charges for supply obtained.*

Sec. 1258-2. An order as made by the commissioner of health or as approved or modified by the referees as herein provided, shall be reversed, vacated or modified by the supreme court on a petition of error, if upon consideration of the record such court is of the opinion that such order was unlawful and unreasonable. *Vacating or modifying order.*

Sec. 1258-3. The proceeding to obtain such reversal, vacation or modification shall be by petition in error, filed in the supreme court by the municipal corporation, managing board or officer of a public institution, corporation, partnership or person to which such order of the commissioner of health shall apply, setting forth the errors complained of; thereupon, unless the same is duly waived, a summons shall issue and be served, as in other cases, upon the commissioner of health, or in his absence by leaving a copy at his office at the city of Columbus. *Proceeding by petition in error; service of summons; waiver.*

Sec. 1258-4. Upon service or waiver of summons in error the commissioner of health shall forthwith transmit to the clerk of the supreme court a transcript of his journal entries, original papers or transcripts thereof and a certi- *Transcript to supreme court.*

fied copy of all evidence adduced upon the hearing before the public health council in the proceeding complained of, which shall be filed in said court.

When proceeding ' med commenced.

Sec. 1258-5. No proceeding to reverse, vacate or modify an order of the commissioner of health shall be deemed commenced unless the petition therefor is filed within thirty days after service of the order upon the mayor or managing officer or officers of the municipal corporation, public institution, or corporation, partnership or person to whom such order shall apply. Or if there has been an appeal to referees then such petition shall be filed within two weeks after the determination of such appeal and due notice thereof. A proceeding to reverse, vacate or modify an order of the commissioner of health shall operate to stay execution thereof until the supreme court shall render a decision thereon.

Supreme court only has power to suspend order.

Sec. 1258-6. No court other than the supreme court shall have the power to review, suspend or delay any order of the commissioner of health, or enjoin, restrain or interfere with the commissioner of health or public health council in the performance of official duties required or power exercised under the provisions of this act.

Former orders shall continue in full force.

Sec. 1258-7. All orders heretofore issued or promulgated by the state board of health or by the state department of health shall continue in full force and have the same effect as though they had been lawfully made, issued or promulgated under the provisions of this act.

Section or part held void does not affect others.

Sec. 1258-8. Each section of this act and every part thereof is hereby declared to be an independent section, and part of a section, and the holding of a section or part of a section thereof to be void or ineffective for any cause shall not be deemed to affect any other section or part thereof.

How funds provided.

Sec. 1259. Each municipal council, department or officer having jurisdiction to provide for the raising of revenues by tax levies, sale of bonds, or otherwise shall take all steps necessary to secure the funds for any such purpose or purposes. When the funds are so secured, or the bonds therefor have been authorized by the proper municipal authority, such funds shall be considered as in the treasury and appropriated for such particular purpose or purposes, and shall not be used for any other purpose. The bonds authorized to be issued for any such purpose or purposes shall not exceed three per cent of the total value of all property in any city or village, as listed and assessed for taxation, and may be in addition to the total bonded indebtedness of such city or village otherwise permitted by law. The question of the issuance of such bonds shall not be required to be submitted to a vote of the electors.

Levies exempt from all limitations.

Sec. 1259-1. Interest and sinking fund levies on account of bonds issued under section 1259 of the General Code, in compliance with orders of the state commissioner of health, shall be exempt from all the limitations on tax levies provided by sections 5649-2 and 5649-3a of the General Code. Such levies shall also be exempt from the limitations provided by section 5649-5b of the General Code, if the question of making such additional levy shall be submitted to the electors of the municipality issuing, or proceeding to issue, such bonds in the manner provided in sections 5649-5 and 5649-5a of the General Code, and the same is approved by a majority of the electors voting on such question; and the proper legislative authorities of any such municipal corporation are hereby authorized to submit such question in the manner provided in said sections of the General Code at any regular election or at a special election. The number of years for which such levy shall be authorized shall not be required to be printed on the ballot, and the approval of the electors shall constitute sufficient authority for the making of such additional levy annually, during the time for which the bonds are to run, or until the same are redeemed, or the redemption thereof with interest is fully provided for.

Sec. 1260. If a council, department or officer of a municipality, or person, partnership or private corporation fails or refuses for a period of thirty days, after notice given him or them by the commissioner of health of his findings and order and the approval thereof by the public health council, to perform any act or acts required of him or them by this chapter relating to stream pollution and public water supply, the members of such council or department, or such officer or officers, person, partnership or private corporation shall be personally liable for such default, and shall forfeit and pay to the state of Ohio five hundred dollars to be paid into the state treasury to the credit of the general revenue fund. · *For forfeiture for failure to obey orders.*

Sec. 1261. An action may be begun for the recovery of such penalty by the prosecuting attorney of a county in the name of the state in the court of common pleas of such county having jurisdiction of any such party or parties, or it may be begun by the attorney general in such county or the county of Franklin, as provided by law. The court of common pleas, upon good cause shown, may, at its discretion, remit such penalty or any part thereof. *Action for recovery.*

SECTION 2. That said original sections 1249, 1250, 1251, 1252, 1253, 1254, 1255, 1256, 1257, 1258, 1259, 1259-1, 1260 and 1261 of the General Code be and the same are hereby repealed. *Repeals.*

CLARENCE J. BROWN,
President of the Senate.
CARL R. KIMBALL,
Speaker of the House of Representatives.

Passed April 17, 1919.
Approved May 10, 1919.

The sectional numbers in this act are in conformity to the General Code. JOHN G. PRICE, *Attorney General.*

JAMES M. COX,
Governor.

Filed in the office of the Secretary of State at Columbus, Ohio, on the 16th day of May, A. D. 1919.

122 G.

[House Bill No. 326.]

AN ACT

To provide for the appointment by county commissioners of section men to repair improved county roads.

Be it enacted by the General Assembly of the State of Ohio:

Sec. 6957.

Section men to repair improved county roads.

SECTION 1. In any county in which on the first day of November, 1919, the aggregate of the tax duplicate for real estate and personal property is twenty-one million dollars or less, and in which county there are at least twenty-five miles of improved county roads, the county commissioners prior to the first Monday of January, 1920, shall divide into convenient sections all improved county roads and shall employ yearly a patrol or section man for each section to keep the same in repair for the year ending on the first Monday of February thereafter. In the event the repair and maintenance fund for county roads in any year is insufficient in any county having such a tax duplicate to employ section men on all such roads, then the provisions of this act shall apply to such improved county roads as are most heavily traveled and are in need of the most repair and attention.

Sec. 6958.

Materials for repair.

SECTION 2. The county commissioners shall provide and furnish the materials for repair and may require the section men to quarry and haul stone, gravel and other material to places where needed on such highways within the limits of their sections.

Sec. 6959.

Tools and equipment.

SECTION 3. Each section man shall provide himself at his own expense, with the following tools and equipment: Pick, mattock, shovel, sledge hammer, knapping hammer, axe, one strong horse and harness therefor, one large two-wheeled cart with bed arranged for quick dumping and with a capacity of at least one-half a cubic yard of crushed stone or gravel. Provided that the tools and equipment aforementioned shall be subject to the approval of the county commissioners and they may, if they deem it best, require any one or more of such section men to furnish and use a wagon and two horses for hauling materials, and may require them to provide themselves with a folding tent for protection while breaking and knapping stone during inclement weather, and may if they so desire furnish plows, scrapers and other tools for the use of such section men. If additional tools and equipment are required of such section men, the number and kind shall be fully stated in the advertisement for bids hereinafter provided for.

Sec. 6960.

Qualifications and duties of section men.

SECTION 4. Each section man employed must be physically strong, healthy and inured to manual labor and it shall be his duty to patrol his section and care for the drainage; promptly to patch holes as they may appear on such highways within his section; to place at convenient points broken rock, gravel and suitable materials for repair along his section and have the same in readiness for immediate use when needed; to remove weeds and bushes growing thereon; to spend on his section eight hours of actual and faithful labor each day; and to keep his section in as good condition for travel as his opportunities will permit subject to the rules and regulations made by the county commissioners, the provisions of law herein and under the supervision of the county surveyor. No section' man shall substitute the work of another man on his section, in the event of his disability or otherwise, without the consent in writing of the county commissioners. On Monday of each week where they are employed for full time, the section men shall mail to the county auditor on blanks furnished by the county commissioners, a detailed report in writing, stating the nature and extent of their work and hours of service on each day of the previous week and any other information deemed of importance to the county commissioners. When they are not employed for full time, such section men shall make reports at such times as the county commissioners may require.

Sec. 6961. SECTION 5. Before the employment of such section men, the county commissioners shall name, number and describe the various sections and enter the same on their journal. They shall adopt rules and regulations subject to the approval of the county surveyor to govern the section men and record the same on their journal and file a copy thereof with the county auditor. Prior to the first Monday of February each year they shall give notice in two newspapers in the county, of opposite politics, of general circulation and printed in the English language, for two successive weeks that they will receive sealed bids until noon on the first Monday of February for section men for each of the sections named in the notice, subject to the rules and regulations adopted by the county commissioners and on file in the auditor's office and subject to the provisions of law. If there be not two such newspapers printed in the county, one newspaper of general circulation printed in the English language shall be sufficient. If there be no such newspaper printed in the county, then printed notices shall be posted in each township, precinct and municipality in the county. The commissioners may reject any bid that in their opinion is too high or does not meet the requirements herein and if two or more bids are the same they are authorized to make choice. Upon the acceptance of any bid and the giving of a proper bond by the bidder the commissioners shall enter into a written contract with the bidder.

Name and number of sections; rules and regulations.

When and how contracts shall be let.

Sec. 6962. SECTION 6. Each section man before entering upon the discharge of his duties shall give a bond in the sum of $500.00 conditioned for the faithful discharge of his duties to be approved by the county commissioners. The forms for such bond and contract shall be prepared by the prosecuting attorney and furnished to the successful bidders by the county commissioners.

Bond of section men.

Sec. 6963.
Compensation
paid monthly.

SECTION 7. The compensation of such section men shall be allowed and paid monthly upon bills presented therefor. If any of such section men fail to comply with the terms of their contract or neglect, fail or refuse to abide by the law or the rules and instructions of the county commissioners, and county surveyor, the county commissioners shall allow only such sum as they deem them to be entitled to for their services, and may terminate the contract upon giving thirty days' notice to any of such section men.

Sec. 6964.

Part time when
fund insufficient.

SECTION 8. In the event the repair and maintenance fund is insufficient in any year to employ such section men for full time or for other good reasons, they may be employed for a part of the time, but their employment shall be so arranged that the time on duty and off duty shall alternate by the week or month as the county commissioners may think best and the same shall be so stated in the advertisement for bids. If a vacancy should occur by resignation, death, removal or other cause of a section man less than six months before the first Monday of February, the county commissioners may employ for the remainder of the year, without giving notice in a newspaper, otherwise they shall advertise for sealed bids.

Filling vacancies.

The sectional
numbers on the
margin hereof
are designated
as provided by
law.
JOHN G. PRICE,
Attorney
General.

CARL R. KIMBALL,
Speaker of the House of Representatives.
CLARENCE J. BROWN,
President of the Senate.

Passed April 17, 1919.
Approved May 10, 1919.

JAMES M. COX,
Governor.

Filed in the office of the Secretary of State at Columbus, Ohio, on the 16th day of May, A. D. 1919.

123 G.

[House Bill No. 259.]

AN ACT

Providing for the construction, maintenance and inspection by the state fire marshal of dry cleaning and dry dyeing buildings and establishments, and providing a penalty for the violation thereof.

Be it enacted by the General Assembly of the State of Ohio:

Sec. 843-19.

Dry cleaning or
dry dyeing defined.

SECTION 1. For the purpose of this act a dry cleaning or dry dyeing business is defined to be the business of cleaning or dyeing cloth, clothing, feathers, or any sort of fabrics or textiles by the use of carbon bi-sulphide, gasoline, naphtha, benzine, benzol, or other light petroleum or coal tar products or inflammable liquid, or cleaning or dyeing by processes known as dry cleaning and dry dyeing where inflammable volatile substances are used.

Sec. 843-20.

SECTION 2. No building or establishment shall be used for the business of dry cleaning or dry dyeing as above defined, or for the storage of inflammable or volatile substances for use in such business until an application for permission to do so shall have been filed with and approved by the state fire marshal of the state of Ohio, and on blanks provided by him for that purpose.

Permission required; application.

Sec. 843-21.

SECTION 3. Upon the filing of every such application, the applicant shall pay to the state fire marshal a filing and inspection fee of ten ($10.00) dollars.

Filing and inspection fee

Sec. 843-22.

SECTION 4. When any application is filed with the state fire marshal and the fee paid as above mentioned the state fire marshal by himself, his deputies or assistants shall make an inspection of such building, buildings or establishments, and if the same conforms to the requirements of law and rules which may be prescribed by the state fire marshal for such places, then the state fire marshal shall issue a permit to the applicant for the conduct of such business, which permit shall extend until the first day of January next after the date of the issuing of same.

When permit shall issue; term of permit.

Sec. 843-23.

SECTION 5. The permits may be renewed at any time within thirty days after the termination thereof, by the filing of an application for such renewal and the payment of a fee of five dollars therefor, provided the applicant for such renewal permit has complied with the provisions of this act, and with the laws of the state of Ohio, and the ordinances of the municipality where the business or establishment is located.

When permits renewed; fee.

Sec. 843 24.

SECTION 6. All permits must be exhibited for inspection to the state fire marshal or any of his deputies or assistants whenever the same are requested, and no one except the person to whom the same are issued shall have the right to operate a business or establishment under any permit.

Exhibition of permits.

Sec. 843-25.

SECTION 7. Permits may be refused, suspended, or revoked by the state fire marshal, for fraud in procuring the same, a vioaltion of any law of the state of Ohio, or ordinance of the municipality in which the business is located, or a violation of any rule or regulation lawfully provided for the conduct of any such business or establishment.

Refusal, suspension and revocation of permits; causes.

Sec. 843-26.

SECTION 8. All buildings or establishments used or to be used for the purpose of the business of dry cleaning or dry dyeing as above defined, shall be of fire-resistive design and construction, and not exceed one story in height, and shall be without basement, cellar or open space below the ground floor.

Character of buildings that may be used.

Sec. 843-27.

SECTION 9. All walls of such dry cleaning and dry dyeing buildings or establishments shall be of brick laid in cement mortar, or of reinforced concrete not less than twelve inches in thickness, or of stone, laid in cement mortar not less than sixteen inches in thickness, or of other non-combustible and fire-resistive material constructed of a thickness of not less than twelve inches. The roof of such building shall be of fire-resistive construction.

Specifications for walls and roof of buildings.

Sec. 843-28.

Sewer connections specified.

SECTION 10. There shall be no sewer connection with such dry cleaning and dry dyeing building or establishment, and the floor of the same shall be of concrete construction laid not lower than the surface of the earth surrounding the wall, and be pitched at such grade from all of its walls as to secure perfect drainage, flow of all liquids to an underground, cement line pit or well on the outside of said building, and of sufficient capacity below the level of the floor of said building to hold twice the quantity of liquids that may be used or kept in said building at any one time, the top of said pit or well to extend not less than twelve inches above the level of the floor of said building, and to be provided with a tight fitting cover, and kept locked when not in use.

Sec. 843-29.

Ventilating apertures and coverings.

SECTION 11. Ventilating aperatures of size not less than sixty square inches in area shall be placed in the walls of such dry cleaning and dry dyeing building at or near the level of the floor, and spaced not over six feet apart from center to center; such openings shall be covered with 2x2 wire mesh, number sixteen galvanized wire web or its equal, and shall be kept clear of all obstructions and such ventilating apertures shall be so arranged as to completely change the air volume every five minutes while the plant is in operation. Other ventilating systems may be substituted for the above, which will completely change the air every five minutes while the plant is in operation provided same are approved before constructed by the state fire marshal.

Sec. 843-30.

Skylights and windows.

SECTION 12. Skylights and windows must be of wired glass and metal frames, and provided with fusible link connecting to an automatic closing device, and shall be covered with 12x12 mesh, or equivalent brass wire screen to prevent spark or other fire entrance.

Sec. 843-31.

Fire extinguishment provisions.

SECTION 13. As a means of fire extinguishment in any such buildings, the same shall be equipped with not less than two inch steam pipes, to be so connected as to give as nearly as possible an equal distribution of steam, and to be so placed that the steam when turned in will immediately fill the entire room; such steam pipes shall be provided with perforations or jets of one-quarter of one inch in diameter, equally spaced, so that there is one opening to each twenty-five square feet of floor space; a quick acting lever valve shall be placed in the steam service line or lines connected to this perforated steam pipe outside of the building, and to be accessible for operation in case of fire. The steam supply for such pipes shall be continually available for service while the plant is in operation, and shall be sufficient to completely fill the room space in less than one minute.

Sec. 843-32.

Protection of steam or hot water pipes, windows, doors, etc., required.

SECTION 14. All steam or hot water pipes must be protected by wire screen or otherwise so as to prevent contact of pipes and inflammable goods. All windows, doors or other openings in the dry cleaning building or drying rooms within one hundred feet of exposed openings or combustible structures or materials shall be provided with wired glass in metal frames, or fireproof shutters, doors or covers. All doors shall be arranged for ready opening from either side in case of emergency.

Sec. 843-33. SECTION 15. One approved hand chemical extinguisher, especially efficient for such conditions shall be provided for each five hundred feet of floor space. *Fire extinguishers required.*

Sec. 843-34. SECTION 16. All dry cleaning, washing, extracting and redistilling shall be carried on in closed machines which shall be fluid tight; washers shall have hinged doors and shall be arranged so that in case of an explosion the door will automatically close. The transfer of all liquids shall be through continuous piping, and all outlet or drain lines shall be drained by gravity to settling or storage tanks. No dry cleaning liquid shall be settled in any open or unprotected vessels or, tanks. All piping and all metallic parts of each machine shall be properly grounded by at least number ten copper insulated wire to a water pipe or other grounded device. Scrubbing and brushing may be performed in the dry cleaning room, but not more than one gallon of volatile fluid shall be used in any one container, and shall be so used in a metallic pan or container, and such volatile substance shall be returned to the settling or storage tanks as soon as the brushing or cleaning operation is completed. *Operations carried on in closed fluid tight machines. Transferring and storing liquids; scrubbing and brushing.*

Sec. 843-35. SECTION 17. Settling tanks shall be constructed, located and vented essentially as given for the storage tanks. At the close of the day's operations all liquid contained in washers, extractors, stills or otherwise shall be returned to the stock or settling tanks. The location of all tanks, buried or otherwise, and their contents and hazards shall be plainly marked by signs as approved by the state fire marshal. *Settling tanks; location and construction.*

Sec. 843-36. SECTION 18. No gas or gasoline engine, steam generator or heating device nor any electrical dynamo or motor shall be located, maintained or used inside of nor within a distance of ten feet of any building used for the business of dry cleaning and dry dyeing as above defined, except that an electrical motor may be placed within such ten feet but without a solid fireproof wall. *Location of engine or heating device.*

Sec. 843-37. SECTION 19. The lighting of such buildings shall be secured only by keyless socket incandescent electric lights with globe or bulbs in vaporproof receptacles, and all switches, cut-offs or fuses used in the installation or operation of such lights shall be located and operated from the outside of such building. The interior electrical equipment must conform with the most advanced stage of the art at the time of installation. *Lighting of buildings.*

Sec. 843-38. SECTION 20. The heating of such buildings shall be secured only by the use of steam or hot water systems. *Heating of buildings.*

Sec. 843-39. SECTION 21. Drying rooms if under the same roof as the dry cleaning and dry dyeing rooms must be separated from such rooms by a fire-resistive wall, the entrance of such drying room shall conform to the conditions provided *Drying rooms; separation from others; ventilation.*

with standard, self-closing fire doors. Means for the ventilation of such drying room shall conform to the conditions provided in relation to dry cleaning and dry dyeing buildings, and the provision for the presence of steam jets for fire extinguishment must be complied with. If the drying room be a separate building, it must conform in all respects of construction and equipment to the conditions named relative to dry cleaning and dry dyeing buildings as above described.

Sec. 843-40.

Storing volatile substances.

SECTION 22. All volatile substances received for use in the business of dry cleaning and dry dyeing as above defined shall be stored in steel tanks, the shell of which may not be less than three sixteenths of an inch thick, the exterior of such tank to be coated with an approved rust preventative, and all joints in same shall be calked in an approved manner.

Sec. 843-41.

Location of storage tanks.

SECTION 23. No storage tank shall be placed, constructed or maintained under a public sidewalk or in a sidewalk area.

Sec. 843-42.

Underground tanks; depth.

SECTION 24. All such tanks shall be buried underground to such a depth as to secure a covering of earth of at least three feet above the top of the tank at the surface level of the ground.

Sec. 843-43.

Vent pipe specifications.

SECTION 25. All such tanks shall be provided with a vent pipe not less than one inch in diameter, extending from the top of the tank to the outer air, and discharging at a point not less than two feet above the roof of said dry cleaning and dry dyeing building, and also be provided at the discharge end with an inverted "U" cap or gooseneck.

Sec. 843-44.

Filling pipe specifications.

SECTION 26. All such tanks must be provided with a filling pipe of not less than one inch in diameter, extending from the top of the tank shell to within one inch of the bottom of the tank. Such filling pipe must be laid with inclination toward the tank to secure proper drainage; the intake end of said filling pipe shall be fitted with a controlling feed cock or valve which shall be kept closed except while in use, and the intake end of the pipe above such cock or valve shall be provided with a screw cap secured in place by an iron or other metal chain; such screw cap to be securely screwed on the feed pipe inlet when the same is not in use. Both the controlling cock or valve and the feed pipe inlet must be enclosed in an iron box or hood set level or above the surface of the ground, and be kept securely locked when not in use; such feed pipe inlet and controlling cock or valve shall in no case be located inside of any building.

Sec. 843-45.

Pipe connection specifications.

SECTION 27. All pipes connected to the said storage tanks used in said dry cleaning and dry dyeing business must enter or be attached to same at their tops; service pipes carrying volatile substances from the storage tanks to the dry cleaning and dry dyeing machines or apparatus shall extend from the top of the tank shell, and the controlling cock or valve in said service pipes shall be kept closed when not in use.

Sec. 843-46.

SECTION 28. No volatile substances shall be carried or converted into the dry cleaning and dry dyeing building or any of its machines or apparatus, or be returned to the storage tanks from such devices except through service pipes as above described; the movement or transmission of such volatiles through such service pipes shall be secured by pumps or syphon only; such device to be so located as to insure the return of all volatile substances remaining in the service pipes when delivery is shut off to the storage tanks by gravity. *Carrying and returning volatile substances to storage tanks.*

Sec. 843-47.

SECTION 29. No carbon bi-sulphide, gasoline, naphtha, benzol or light petroleum or coal tar product used in the dry cleaning and dry dyeing business shall be distilled or redistilled in connection with the said dry cleaning or dry dyeing business except in a building of fireproof construction, which building must be located more than twenty-five feet from any other building or lot occupied for business, dwelling, manufacturing or storage purposes, except the buildings used in said dry cleaning and dry dyeing business. *Requirements as to distilling products used.*

Sec. 843-48.

SECTION 30. The provisions of this act shall not be held to apply to any building, business or establishment now in use, so as to cause the same to be rebuilt, remodeled, or repaired so as to conform to the provisions hereof, but should any building or establishment, or part thereof, be reconstructed, rebuilt or repaired, the same shall be so constructed, built or repaired in conformity to the provisions hereof. Nothing in this act shall be held to in any manner limit the laws which provide against fire hazards in this state. Nothing in this section shall permit any person to operate a business or establishment mentioned in this act without first securing a license as provided herein, for so doing, but the provisions of this section shall be given full consideration by the state fire marshal in issuing licenses to persons now engaged in said business. *To what building or business act does not apply.*

Sec. 843-49.

SECTION 31. Should any building, business or establishment of dry cleaning or dry dyeing as herein defined, be discontinued or not carried on in any building which does not conform to the provisions herein set forth, for a period of three months, such business shall be considered as having been abandoned, and before the same can again be carried on in such building, the said building must be so constructed, repaired or rebuilt as to conform to the provisions of this act. *When business considered abandoned.*

Sec. 843-50.

SECTION 32. All buildings, structures, pipes, storage tanks, electrical wiring, connections and apparatus constructed and used in said dry cleaning and dry dyeing business shall be inspected and approved by the state fire marshal or a deputy or assistant before being used in said dry cleaning and dry dyeing business. *Inspection and approval.*

Sec. 843-51.

SECTION 33. Any person or persons being the owner, occupant, lessee or agent, who shall violate any of the provisions of this act or fail to comply therewith, or who shall *Penalty for violation of law or rules.*

violate or fail to comply with any order or regulation made
thereunder, within ten days, or who shall build in violation
of any detailed statement of specifications or plans submitted and approved thereunder, or any certificate or permit issued thereunder shall severally for each and every
such violation and noncompliance respectively be guilty of
a misdemeanor, and upon conviction thereof shall be fined
for the first offense not less than ten dollars, nor more than
two hundred dollars, and for the second offense shall be
fined not less than fifty dollars, nor more than five hundred dollars, and imprisoned in a county jail or workhouse
not to exceed six months.

Sec. 843-52.

Enforcement of
law.

SECTION 34. It shall be the duty of the state fire
marshal, his deputies and assistants, to enforce the provisions of this act, and he shall have the same power and
authority in the enforcement of the provisions hereof as
are given to the state fire marshal under the provisions of
the state fire marshal law, namely section 820, et seq. of
the General Code of Ohio.

Sec. 843-53.

Application of
fees and pen-
alties.

SECTION 35. All fees, penalties or forfeitures collected
by the state fire marshal, his deputies or assistants under
the provisions of this act, shall when paid into the state
treasury be credited to the special fund for the maintenance
of the office of the state fire marshal and shall be disbursed
in the same manner as other moneys which come into said
fund are disbursed.

The sectional
numbers on the
margin hereof
are designated
as provided by
law.
JOHN G. PRICE,
Attorney
General.

CARL R. KIMBALL,
Speaker of the House of Representatives.
CLARENCE J. BROWN,
President of the Senate.

Passed April 14, 1919.
Approved May 10, 1919.

JAMES M. COX,
Governor.

Filed in the office of the Secretary of State at Columbus,
Ohio, on the 16th day of May, A. D. 1919.

124 G.

[House Bill No. 424.]

AN ACT

To amend sections 1465-45, 1465-47, 1465-48, 1465-49, 1465-53,
1465-54, 1465-55, 1465-60, 1465-61, 1465-69, 1465-79, 1465-80,
1465-82, 1465-83, 1465-90, 1465-93, 1465-94, 1465-95, and to
supplement section 1465-72, of the General Code of Ohio, by the
enactment of section 1465-72a, relating to workmen's compensation.

Be it enacted by the General Assembly of the State of Ohio:
SECTION 1. That sections 1465-45, 1465-47, 1465-48,
1465-49, 1465-53, 1465-54, 1465-55, 1465-60, 1465-61, 1465-
69, 1465-79, 1465-80, 1465-82, 1465-83, 1465-90, 1465-93,
1465-94, 1465-95 of the General Code of Ohio be amended,
and section 1465-72 be supplemented by the enactment of
section 1465-72a, to read as follows:

Sec. 1465-45. Every employer shall furnish the industrial commission of Ohio upon request, all information required by it to carry out the purpose of this act. In the month of January of each year, every employer of the state, employing five or more employes regularly in the same business, or in or about the same establishment, shall prepare and mail to the commission at its main office in the city of Columbus, Ohio, a statement containing the following information, viz.: the number of employes employed during the preceding year from January 1st to December 31st inclusive; the number of such employes employed at each kind of employment and the aggregate amount of wages paid to such employes, which information shall be furnished on a blank or blanks to be prepared by the commission; and it shall be the duty of the commission to furnish such blanks to employers free of charge upon request therefor. Every employer receiving from the commission any blank, with directions to fill out the same, shall cause the same to be properly filled out so as to answer fully and correctly all questions therein propounded, and to give all the information therein sought, or if unable to do so, he shall give to the commission in writing good and sufficient reasons for such failure. The commission may require that the information herein required to be furnished be verified under oath and returned to the commission within the period fixed by it or by law. The commission or any member thereof, or any person employed by the commission for that purpose, shall have the right to examine, under oath, any employer, or the officer, agent or employe thereof for the purpose of ascertaining any information which such employer is required by this act to furnish to the commission.

Statement by employer required annually; blank form furnished.

Examinations under oath.

Any employer who shall fail or refuse to furnish to the commission the annual statement herein required, or who shall fail or refuse to furnish such other information as may be required by the commission under authority of

Penalty for failure or refusal to make statement.

this section, shall be liable to a penalty of five hundred dollars, to be collected in a civil action brought against said employer in the name of the state; all such penalties, when collected, shall be paid into the state insurance fund and become a part thereof. .

Who may administer oaths and certify official acts.

Sec. 1465-47. Each member of the industrial commission of Ohio, its secretary, director of claims, all inspectors, examiners and claims referees appointed by the commission shall, for the purposes contemplated by this act, have power to administer oaths, certify to official acts, take depositions, issue subpoenaes, compel the attendance of witnesses and the production of books, accounts, papers, records, documents and testimony.

Attachment proceeding to compel obedience.

Sec. 1465-48. In case of disobedience of any person to comply with the order of the industrial commission of Ohio or subpoena issued by the commission, its secretary, director of claims or any of its inspectors, examiners, or claims referees, or on the refusal of a witness to testify to any matter regarding which he may be lawfully interrogated, or refuse to permit an inspection as aforesaid, the probate judge of the county in which the person resides, on application of any member of the commission, its secretary, director of claim, any inspector, examiner, or claims referee appointed by it, shall compel obedience by attachment proceedings as for contempt, as in the case of disobedience of the requirements of subpoena issued from such court on a refusal to testify therein.

Fees of officers and witnesses.

Sec. 1465-49. Each officer who serves such subpoena, shall receive the same fees as a sheriff, and each witness who appears, in obedience to a subpoena, before the industrial commission of Ohio, its secretary, director of claims, inspector, examiner or claims referee shall receive for his attendance the fees and mileage provided for witnesses in civil cases in courts of common pleas, which shall be audited and paid from the state treasury in the same manner as other expenses are audited and paid, upon the presentation of proper vouchers, approved by any two members of the commission. No witness subpoenaed at the instance of a party other than the commission, its secretary, director of claims, inspector, examiner, or claims referee shall be entitled to compensation from the state treasury unless the commission shall certify that his testimony was material to the matter investigated.

Classification of occupations or industries.

Sec. 1465-53. The industrial commission of Ohio shall classify occupations or industries with respect to their degree of hazard, and determine the risks of the different classes and fix the rates of premium of the risks of the same, based upon the total payroll in each of said classes of occupation or industry sufficiently large to provide an adequate fund for the compensation provided for in this act, and to maintain a state insurance fund from year to year.

Sec. 1465-54. It shall be the duty of the industrial commission of Ohio, in the exercise of the powers and discretion conferred upon it in the preceding section, ultimately to fix and maintain, for each class of occupation, or industry, the lowest possible rates of premium consistent with the maintenance of a solvent state insurance fund and the creation and maintenance of a reasonable surplus, after the payment of legitimate claims for injury and death that it may authorize to be paid from the state insurance fund for the benefit of injured and the dependents of killed employes; and, in order that said object may be accomplished, said commission shall observe the following requirements in classifying occupations or industries and fixing the rates of premium for the risks of the same: *Fixing premium rates and maintaining surplus.*

1. It shall keep an accurate account of the money paid in premiums by each of the several classes of occupations or industries, and the losses on account of injuries and death of employes thereof, and it shall also keep an account of the money received from each individual employer and the amount of losses incurred against the state insurance fund on account of injuries and death of the employes of such employer. *Requirements in classifying occupations.*

2. Ten per cent. of the money that has heretofore been paid into the state insurance fund and ten per cent. of all that may hereafter be paid into such fund shall be set aside for the creation of a surplus until such surplus shall amount to the sum of one hundred thousand dollars ($100,-000.00) after which time, whenever necessary in the judgment of the industrial commission to guarantee a solvent state insurance fund, a sum not exceeding five per cent. of all the money paid into the state insurance fund shall be credited to such surplus fund. On the first day of July, 1917, and annually thereafter a revision of rates shall be made in accordance with the experience of said commission in the administration of the law as shown by the accounts kept as provided herein; and said commission shall adopt rules governing said rate revisions, the object of which shall be to make an equitable distribution of losses among the several classes of occupation or industry, which rules shall be general in their application.

4. The industrial commission of Ohio shall have the power to apply that form of rating system which, in its judgment, is best calculated to merit or individually rate the risk most equitably, predicated upon the basis of its individual industrial accident experience, and to encourage and stimulate accident prevention; shall develop fixed and equitable rules controlling the same, which rules, however, shall conserve to each risk the basic principles of workmen's compensation insurance.

Sec. 1465-55. The industrial commission of Ohio shall adopt rules and regulations with respect to the collection, maintenance and disbursements of the state insurance fund; one of which rules shall provide that in the event there is *Adoption of rules for collection maintenance and disbursement of fund.*

developed as of any given rate revision date a surplus of
earned premium over all losses which, in the judgment of
the commission, is larger than is necessary adequately to
safeguard the solvency of the fund, the commission may
return such excess surplus to the subscriber to the fund in
either the form of cash refunders or credit premiums; another of which rules shall provide that in the event the
amount of premiums collected from any employer at the
beginning of any period of six months is ascertained and
calculated by using the estimated expenditure of wages
for the period of time covered by such premium payments
as a basis, that an adjustment of the amount of such premium shall be made at the end of such six months' period
and the actual amount of such premium shall be determined in accordance with the amount of the actual expen- ·
diture of wages for said period; and, in the event such
wage expenditure for said period is less than the amount on
which such estimated premium was collected, then such employer shall be entitled to receive a refunder from the state
insurance fund of the difference between the amount so
paid by him and the amount so found to be actually due,
or to have the amount of such difference, credited on succeeding premium payments at his option, and should such
actual premium, when ascertained as aforesaid exceed in
amount the premium so paid by such employer at the beginning of such six months' period, such employer shall
immediately upon being advised of the true amount of such
premium due, forthwith pay to the treasurer of state an
amount equal to the difference between the amount actually
found to be due and the amount paid by him at the beginning of said six months' period.

Employers sub-
ject to law.   Sec. 1465-60.   The following shall constitute employers subject to the provisions of this act:

1.   The state and each county, city, township, incorporated village and school district therein.

2.   Every person, firm and private corporation, including any public service corporation, that has in service
five or more workmen or operatives regularly in the same
business, or in or about the same establishment under any
contract or hire, express or implied, oral or written.

Definition of
terms.   Sec. 1465-61.   The terms "employe," "workman"
and "operative" as used in this act, shall be construed to
mean:

1.   Every person in the service of the state, or of any
county, city, township, incorporated village or school district therein, including regular members of lawfully constituted police and fire departments of cities and villages,
under any appointment or contract of hire, express or implied, oral or written, except any official of the state, or of
any county, city, township, incorporated village or school
district therein.   Provided that nothing in this act shall
apply to police or firemen in cities where the injured policemen or firemen are eligible to participate in any policemen's

or firemen's pension funds which are now or hereafter may be established and maintained by municipal authority under existing laws.

2. Every person in the service of any person, firm or private corporation, including any public service corporation, employing five or more workmen or operatives regularly in the same business, or in or about the same establishment under any contract of hire, express or implied, oral or written, including aliens and minors, but not including any person whose employment is but casual and not in the usual course of trade, business, profession or occupation of his employer.

3. Every person in the service of any independent contractor or sub-contractor who has failed to pay into the state insurance fund the amount of premium determined and fixed by the industrial commission of Ohio for his employment or occupation, or to elect to pay compensation direct to his injured and to the dependents of his killed employes, as provided in section 1465-69, General Code, shall be considered as the employe of the person who has entered into a contract, whether written or verbal, with such independent contractor unless such employes, or their legal representatives or beneficiaries elect, after injury or death, to regard such independent contractor as the employer.

Sec. 1465-69. Except as hereinafter provided, every employer mentioned in sub-division 2 of section 1465-60, General Code, shall, in the month of January, 1914, and semi-annually thereafter, pay into the state insurance fund the amount of premium determined and fixed by the industrial commission of Ohio for the employment or occupation of such employer the amount of which premium to be so paid by each such employer to be determined by the classifications, rules and rates made and published by said commission; and such employer shall semi-annually thereafter pay such further sum of money into the state insurance fund as may be ascertained to be due from him by applying the rules of said commission, and a receipt or certificate certifying that such payment has been made shall immediately be mailed to such employer by the industrial commission of Ohio, which receipt or certificate, attested by the seal of said commission shall be prima facie evidence of the payment of such premium. *Payments semiannually by employer to state insurance fund.*

Provided, however, that as to all employers who were subscribers to the state insurance fund prior to January 1st, 1914, or who may first become subscribers to said fund in any other months than January or July, the foregoing provisions for the payments of such premiums in the month of January, 1914, and semi-annually thereafter shall not apply, but such semi-annual premiums shall be paid by such employers from time to time upon the expiration of the repsective periods for which payments into the fund have been made by them. And provided further, that such employers who will abide by the rules of the industrial commission of Ohio and as may be of sufficient financial ability to render certain the payment of compensation to injured employes or the dependents of killed employes, and the furnishing of medical, surgical, nursing and hospital attention and services and medicines, and funeral expenses equal to or greater than is provided for in sections 1465-78 to 1465-89, General Code, and who do not desire to insure the payment thereof or indemnity themselves against loss sustained by the direct payment thereof, may, upon a finding of such fact by the industrial commission of Ohio, elect to pay individually such compensation, and furnish such medical, surgical, nursing and hospital services and attention and funeral expenses directly to such injured or the dependents of such killed employes; and the industrial commission of Ohio may require such security or bond from said employers as it may deem proper, adequate and sufficient to compel, or secure to such injured employes, or to the dependents of such employes as may be killed, the payment of the compensation and expenses herein provided for, which shall in no event be less than that paid or furnished out of the state insurance fund, in similar cases, to injured employes or to dependents of killed employes, whose employers contribute to said fund, except when an employe of such employer, who has suffered the loss of a hand, arm, foot, leg, or eye, prior to the injury for which compensation is to be paid, and thereafter suffers the loss of any other of said members as the result of an injury sustained in the course and arising out of his employment, the compensation to be paid by such employer shall be limited to the disability suffered in the subsequent injury, additional compensation, if any, to be paid by the industrial commission of Ohio, out of the surplus created by section 1465-54 of the General Code. Should municipal or other bonds be accepted by said commission as security for said payments, such bonds shall be deposited with the treasurer of state whose duty it shall be to have custody thereof and to retain the same in his possession according to the conditions prescribed by the order of said commission accepting the same as security, and said treasurer shall retain possession of said bonds until such time as he may be directed by said commission as to the mode and manner of his disposition of the same; and said commission shall make and publish rules and regulations governing the mode and manner of making application and the nature and extent of the proof required to justify such finding of fact by said commission as to permit such election by such employers, which rules and regulations shall be general in their application, one of which rules shall provide that all employers, electing directly to compensate their injured and the dependents of their killed employes as hereinbefore provided, shall pay into the state insurance fund such amount or amounts as are required to be credited to the surplus in paragraph 2 of section 1465-54,

Deposit of securities with treasurer of state.

General Code. The industrial commission of Ohio may at any time change or modify its findings of fact herein provided for, if in its judgment such action is necessary or desirable to secure or assure a strict compliance with all the provisions of the law in reference to the payment of compensation and the furnishing of medical, nurse, and hospital services and medicines and funeral expenses to injured and the dependents of killed employes.

Sec. 1465-72a. In all cases of injury or death, claims for compensation shall be forever barred, unless, within two years after the injury or death, application shall have been made to the industrial commission of Ohio or to the employer in the event such employer has elected to pay compensation direct. *Claims barred after two years.*

Sec. 1465-79. In case of temporary disability, the employe shall receive sixty-six and two-thirds per cent. of his average weekly wages so long as such disability is total, not to exceed a maximum of fifteen dollars per week, and not less than a minimum of five dollars per week, unless the employes wages shall be less than five dollars per week, in which event he shall receive compensation equal to his full wages; but in no case to continue for more than six years from the date of the injury, nor to exceed three thousand, seven hundred and fifty dollars. *Percentum in case of temporary disability.*

Sec. 1465-80. In case of injury resulting in partial disability, the employe shall receive sixty-six and two-thirds per cent, of the impairment of his earning capacity during the continuance thereof, not to exceed a maximum of twelve dollars per week, nor a greater sum in the aggregate than thirty-seven hundred and fifty dollars, and such compensation shall be in addition to the compensation allowed to the claimant for the period of temporary total disability resulting from such injury. In cases included in the following schedule, the disability in each case shall be deemed to continue for the period specified and the compensation so paid for such injury shall be specified herein, and shall be in addition to the compensation allowed to the claimant for the period of temporary total disability resulting from such injury, to-wit: *Compensation in case of partial disability.*

For the loss of a thumb, 66 2/3% of the average weekly wages during sixty weeks. *Schedule of disability and compensation.*

For the loss of a first finger, commonly called index finger, 66 2/3% of the average weekly wages during thirty-five weeks.

For the loss of a second finger, 66 2/3% of the average weekly wages during thirty weeks.

For the loss of a third finger, 66 2/3% of the average weekly wages during twenty weeks.

For the loss of a fourth finger, commonly known as the little finger, 66 2/3% of the average weekly wages during fifteen weeks.

The loss of the second, or distal phalange, of the thumb shall be considered to be equal to the loss of one-half of such thumb; the loss of more than one-half of such thumb shall be considered to be equal to the loss of the whole thumb.

The loss of the third, or distal phalange, of any finger shall be considered to be equal to the loss of one-third of such finger.

The loss of the middle, or second phalange, of any finger, shall be considered to be equal to the loss of two-thirds of such finger.

The loss of more than the middle and distal phalanges of any finger shall be considered to be equal to the loss of the whole finger; provided, however, that in no case will the amount received for more than one finger exceed the amount provided in this schedule for the loss of a hand.

For the loss of the metacarpal bone (bones of palm) for the corresponding thumb, finger, or fingers as above, add ten weeks to the number of weeks as above.

For ankylosis (total stiffness of) or contractures (due to scars or injuries) which makes any of the fingers, thumbs or parts of either more than useless, the same number of weeks apply to such members or parts thereof as given above.

For the loss of a hand, 66 2/3% of the average weekly wages during one hundred and fifty weeks.

For the loss of an arm, 66 2/3% of the average weekly wages during two hundred weeks.

For the loss of a great toe, 66 2/3% of the average weekly wages during thirty weeks.

For the loss of one of the toes other than the great toe, 66 2/3% of the average weekly wages during ten weeks.

The loss of more than two-thirds of any toe shall be considered to be equal to the loss of the whole toe.

The loss of less than two-thirds of any toe shall be considered to be no loss.

For the loss of a foot, 66 2/3% of the average weekly wages during one hundred and twenty-five weeks.

For the loss of a leg, 66 2/3% of the average weekly wages during one hundred and seventy-five weeks.

For the loss of an eye, 66 2/3% of the average weekly wages during one hundred weeks.

For the permanent partial loss of sight of an eye, 66 2/3% of the average weekly wages for such portion of one hundred weeks as the commission may, in each case, determine, based upon the percentage of vision actually lost as a result of the casualty, but in no case shall an award of compensation be made for less than a 25 per cent. loss of vision.

The amounts specified in this clause are all subject to the limitation as to the maximum weekly amount payable as hereinbefore specified in this section.

Benefits in case of death.   Sec. 1465-82. In case the injury causes death within the period of two years, the benefits shall be in the amount and to the persons following:

1. If there be no dependents, the disbursements from the state insurance fund shall be limited to the expenses provided for in section forty-two hereof.

2. If there are wholly dependent persons at the time of the death, the payment shall be sixty-six and two-thirds per cent. of the average weekly wages, not to exceed fifteen dollars per week in any case and to continue for the remainder of the period between the date of the death and eight years after the date of the injury, and not to amount to more than a maximum of five thousand dollars, nor less than a minimum of two thousand dollars.

3. If there are partly dependent persons at the time of the death, the payment shall be sixty-six and two-thirds per cent. of the average weekly wages, not to exceed fifteen dollars per week in any case, and to continue for all or such portion of the period of eight years after the date of the injury, as the commission in each case may determine, and not to amount to more than a maximum of five thousand dollars.

4. In cases in which compensation on account of the injury has been continuous to the time of the death of the injured person, and the death is the result of such original injury, compensation shall be paid for such death as though same had occurred within the two years hereinbefore provided, deducting from the final award therefor the total amount theretofore paid on account of total or partial disability on account of such injury.

5. The following persons shall be presumed to be wholly dependent for support upon a deceased employe:

(A) A wife upon a husband with whom she lives at the time of his death.

(B) A child or children under the age of sixteen years (or over said age if physically or mentally incapacitated from earning) upon the parent with whom he is living at the time of the death of such parent.

In all other cases, the question of dependency, in whole or in part, shall be determined in accordance with the facts in each particular case existing at the time of the injury resulting in the death of such employe, but no person shall be considered as dependent unless a member of the family of the deceased employe, or bears to him the relation of husband, or widow, lineal descendant, ancestor or brother or sister. The word "child" as used in this act shall include a posthumous child, and a child legally adopted prior to the injury.

Sec. 1465-83. The benefits in case of death, shall be paid to such one or more of the dependents of the decedent, for the benefit of all the dependents as may be determined by the industrial commission of Ohio, which may apportion the benefits among the dependents in such manner as it may deem just and equitable. Payment to a dependent subsequent in right may be made, if the commission deems it proper, and shall operate to discharge all other claims

To whom benefits paid.

therefor. The dependents or person to whom benefits are paid shall apply the same to the use of the several beneficiaries thereof according to their respective claims upon the decedent for support, in compliance with the finding and direction of the commission.

In all cases of death where the dependents are a widow and one or more minor children, it shall be sufficient for the widow to make application to the commission on behalf of herself and minor children; and in cases where all of the dependents are minors, the application shall be made by the guardian or next friend of such minor dependents.

In all cases of death from causes other than the injury for which award had theretofore been made on account of temporary, or permanent partial, or total disability, in which there remains an unpaid balance, representing payments accrued and due decedent at the time of his death, the commission may at its discretion, after satisfactory proof has been made warranting such action, award or pay any unpaid balance of such award to such of the dependents of the decedent, or for services rendered on account of the last illness or death of such decedent, as the commission shall determine in accordance with the circumstances in each such case.

Power of commission to hear and determine questions; appeal in certain cases.

Sec. 1465-90. The commission shall have full power and authority to hear and determine all questions within its jurisdiction, and its decision thereon shall be final. Provided, however, in case the final action of such commission denies the right of the claimant to participate at all or to continue to participate in such fund on the ground that the injury was self-inflicted or on the ground that the accident did not arise in the course of employment, or upon any other ground going to the basis of the claimant's right, then the claimant, within thirty (30) days after the notice of the final action of such commission, may, by filing his appeal in the common pleas court of the county wherein the injury was inflicted or in the common pleas court of the county wherein the contract of employment was made, in case where the injury occurs outside of the state of Ohio. be entitled to a trial in the ordinary way, and be entitled to a jury if he demands it. In such a proceeding, the prosecuting attorney of the county, unless he represents the appellant, shall represent the industrial commission of Ohio, without additional compensation, and he shall be notified by the clerk forthwith of the filing of such appeal, but if said prosecuting attorney represents the appellant. the industrial commission of Ohio shall be notified by said clerk forthwith of the filing of said appeal.

Petition and further pleadings.

Within thirty days after filing his appeal, the appellant shall file a petition in the ordinary form against such commission as defendant, and further pleadings shall be had in said cause, according to the rules of civil procedure, and the court, or the jury, under the instructions of the court, if a jury is demanded, shall determine the right of the claimant; and

323

if they determine the right in his favor, shall fix his compensation within the limits under the rules prescribed in this act; and any final judgment so obtained shall be paid by the industrial commission of Ohio out of the state insurance fund in the same manner as such awards are paid by such commission. In claims for compensation, medical, hospital and nursing services and medicines and funeral expenses brought before said commission, by an injured employe or by his dependents in the event of his death as the result of injury sustained in the course of employment, in which said commission denies the right of claimant or claimants to receive or to continue to receive compensation from an employer who has duly elected to pay compensation, medical, hospital and nursing services, and medicines and funeral expenses direct to his injured and the dependents of his killed employes on the ground that the injury was self-inflicted, or on the ground that the injury did not arise in the course of employment, or upon any other ground going to the basis of the claimant's right, the claimant or claimants shall have the right to appeal to the common pleas court of the county wherein the injury was inflicted, or to the common pleas court of the county wherein the contract of employment was made, in cases where the injury occurs outside of the state of Ohio, in the same manner as in claims against the state insurance fund and as heretofore prescribed in this section, except that the employer shall be the defendant in such proceedings; and if a verdict is rendered in favor of the claimant or claimants, compensation shall be fixed within the limits under the rules prescribed in this act; and any final judgment so obtained shall be paid by the employer. Such judgment shall have the same preference against the assets of the employer in favor of the claimant or claimants as is now, or may hereafter be, allowed by law on judgment rendered for claims for taxes. Any claims for compensation, medical, hospital and nursing services, and medicines and funeral expenses brought before said commission by an injured employe, or by his dependents in the event of his death as a result of injury sustained in the course of employment in which said commission denies the right of claimant or claimants to receive or to continue to receive compensation from an employer who has failed or neglected, either to contribute to the state insurance fund or to elect to pay compensation, medical, hospital or nursing services, and medicines and funeral expenses direct to his injured, or the dependents of his killed employes, on the ground that the injury was self-inflicted or on the ground that the injury did not arise in the course of employment, or upon any other ground going to the basis of the claimant's right, the claimant or claimants have the right to appeal to the common pleas court of the county wherein the injury was inflicted, or to the common pleas court of the county wherein the contract of employment was made, in cases where the injury occurs out-

Claims for compensation, medical, hospital, funeral, etc., expenses.

Preference of judgment.

Appeal to common pleas court.

side of the state of Ohio, in the same manner as in claims against the state insurance fund and as heretofore prescribed in this section; except that the employer shall be the defendant in such proceedings; and if a verdict is rendered in favor of the claimant or claimants, compensation shall be fixed within the limits under the rules prescribed in this act; and any final judgment so obtained shall be paid by the employer. Such judgment shall have the same preference against the assets of the employer in favor of the claimant or claimants as is now, or may hereafter be, allowed by law on judgment rendered for taxes. The cost of such proceeding, including a reasonable attorney's fee to the claimant's attorney to be fixed by the trial judge,

Right to prosecute error. shall be taxed against the unsuccessful party. Either party shall have the right to prosecute error as in the ordinary civil cases.

Minor deemed sui juris. Sec. 1465-93. A minor shall be deemed sui juris for the purposes of this act, and no other person shall have any cause of action or right to compensation for an injury to such minor workman, but in the event of the award of a lump sum of compensation to such minor employe, such sum shall be paid only to the legally appointed guardian of such minor.

Agreement to waive rights void. Sec. 1465-94. No agreement by an employe to waive his rights to compensation under this act shall be valid, except that an employe who is blind may waive the compensation that may become due him for injury or disability in cases where such injury or disability may be directly caused by or due to his blindness. The industrial commission of Ohio may adopt and enforce rules governing the employment of such persons and the inspection of their places of employment. No agreement by an employe to pay any portion of the premium paid by his employer into

Deduction of portion of premium from wages unlawful. the state insurance fund shall be valid, and any employer who deducts any portion of such premium from the wages or salary of any employe entitled to the benefits of this act shall be guilty of a misdemeanor, and upon conviction thereof shall be fined not more than one hundred dollars for each such offense.

Claimant must submit to medical examination. Sec. 1465-95. Any employe claiming the right to receive compensation under this act may be required by the industrial commission of Ohio to submit himself for medical examination at any time and from time to time at a place reasonably convenient for such employe, and as may be provided by the rules of the commission. Such employe or claimant so required by the commission to submit himself or herself for such medical examination, at a point outside of the place of permanent or temporary residence of such claimant, as herein provided for, shall be entitled to have paid to him by the commission the necessary and actual expenses on account of such attendance for such medical examination after approval of such expense statement by the commission or its duly appointed representative for that purpose. If such employe refuses to submit to any such examination or obstructs the same, his right to have his claim for compensation considered, if his claim be pending before the commission, or to receive any payment for compensation theretofore granted shall be suspended during the period of such refusal or obstruction.

SECTION 2. Sec. 1465-45, sub-division 2 of Sec. 1465-60 and sub-division 2 of Sec. 1465-61, shall become effective July 1, 1920. [margin: Time of taking effect of certain sections.]

SECTION 3. That said original sections, 1465-45, 1465-47, 1465-48, 1465-49, 1465-53, 1465-54, 1465-55, 1465-60, 1465-61, 1465-69, 1465-79, 1465-80, 1465-82, 1465-83, 1465-90, 1465-93, 1465-94, 1465-95 of the General Code be, and the same are hereby repealed. [margin: Repeals.]

The repeal of section 1465-45, sub-division 2 of section 1465-60 and sub-division 2 of section 1465-61, shall take effect on July 1, 1920. [margin: When certain repealed sections take effect.]

[margin: The sectional numbers in this act are in conformity to the General Code. JOHN G. PRICE, Attorney General.]

CARL R. KIMBALL,
Speaker of the House of Representatives.
CLARENCE J. BROWN,
President of the Senate.

Passed April 17, 1919.
Approved, May 10, 1919.

JAMES M. COX,
Governor.

Filed in the office of the Secretary of State at Columbus, Ohio, on the 16th day of May, A. D. 1919.

125 G.

[House Bill No. 398.]

AN ACT

To regulate the manufacture and sale of soft drinks and non-alcoholic beverages in bottles.

Be it enacted by the General Assembly of the State of Ohio

[margin: Sec. 1089-3.]

SECTION 1. The term "soft drinks" as used in this act shall be held to mean and include any carbonated soda water, artificial or natural mineral water, and all other similar non-alcoholic carbonated or non-carbonated beverages. [margin: Term "soft drinks" defined.]

No person, firm or corporation shall manufacture and bottle for sale within this state any such soft drink without a license issued by the secretary of agriculture of Ohio. [margin: License required.]

Such license shall beissued only on written application stating the location at which such manufacture is to be conducted, and the applicant shall furnish the secretary of agriculture with a sample of each such soft drink so proposed to be manufactured. Upon receipt of the application [margin: Application; examination; fee; inspection.]

the secretary of agriculture shall cause an examination to
be made into the sanitary conditions of such place of manufacture, and may also cause an analysis to be made of
such samples, or any of them. If the buildings so to be
used be found by the secretary of agriculture in a sanitary
condition, and if the analysis of said samples show the
same to be unadulterated and free from harmful drugs and
other ingredients injurious to health, the secretary of agriculture, upon the payment of a license fee of fifty dollars
($50.00), shall cause a license to be issued authorizing the
applicant to manufacture any such soft drinks as hereinafter provided. Said license shall run one year unless
sooner revoked as herein provided, and shall be renewed
annually thereafter upon the payment of the same fee and
compliance with the same conditions.

All such soft drinks and places of manufacture of same
shall be subject to inspection as hereinafter provided.

Sec. 1089-4.

Soft drinks
from outside the
state, subject to
inspection; reg-
istration; fee.

SECTION 2. No such bottled soft drink that is manufactured out of the state of Ohio shall be sold or offered
for sale within this state unless the same is first inspected
and analyzed and approved as above by the secretary of
agriculture, and registered by him, which shall be upon a
like application as above provided, and a fee af fifty dollars
($50.00) shall be paid therefor. Like samples for such in-
spection and anlysis shall be furnished as above provided.
Such registration shall be renewed annually upon the same
terms and conditions and subsequent inspections and analysis may be made by the secretary of agriculture at any time
in his discretion for the purpose of ascertaining whether
or not the standard and quality of such soft drinks is being
maintained.

Sec. 1089-5.

Retailer must
register all soft
drinks in pos-
session; license
fee.

SECTION 3. No person, firm or corporation shall sell
or offer for sale, or have in his possession with intent to sell,
any soda water syrup or extract, or soft drink syrup, to be
used in making, drawing or dispensing soda water or other
soft drinks, without first registering his name and address
and the name and address of the manufacturer thereof, and
the number and variety of such syrups or extracts so intended to be sold, the trade name or brand thereof, if any
be adopted, with the secretary of agriculture, together with
such samples of the same as the secretary of agriculture may
from time to time request for the purposes of analysis. He
shall also pay into the state treasury at the time of making
such registration a license fee of five dollars ($5.00) and said
license shall not be granted by the secretary of agriculture
unless he determine that said syrup or extract is free from
all harmful drugs and other ingredients injurious to health.
Said registration shall be renewed annually upon like terms;
provided that whenever any manufacturer, agent or seller
shall have paid his fee, his agent or seller using the same
shall not be required to do so.

The provisions of this section shall not apply to local
sellers of soft drinks as to such syrups and extracts made
by themselves for their own use exclusively.

All moneys collected by the secretary of agriculture under the provisions of this act shall be paid into the state treasury.

Sec. 1089-6. SECTION 4. The secretary of agriculture is authorized to appoint an inspector, in addition to those already employed in his department, whose duty shall be to represent and assist him in the enforcement of the provisions of this act. *Appointment of inspector; revocation of license.*

The secretary of agriculture shall have the power to revoke any license issued under the provisions of this act whenever he shall determine that any provisions of this act have been violated. Any person, firm or corporation whose license has been so revoked shall discontinue the manufacture and sale of soft drinks, syrups and extracts, until the provisions of this act have been complied with and a new license issued.

The secretary of agriculture may revoke such license temporarily until there is a compliance with such conditions as he may prescribe, or permanently for the unexpired term of such license.

Sec. 1089-7. SECTION 5. Before revoking any license the secretary of agriculture shall give written notice to the licensee affected, stating that he contemplates the revocation of the same and giving his reasons therfor. Said notice shall appoint a time of hearing before said secretary and may be sent by registered mail to the licensee. On the day of hearing, the licensee may present such evidence to the secretary as he deems fit, and after hearing all the testimony, the secretary shall decide the question in such manner as to him appears just and right. *Notice of revocation; hearing.*

Sec. 1089-8. SECTION 6. Any such person whose license has been revoked or registration cancelled, as above provided, who feels aggrieved at the decision of the secretary of agriculture, may appeal from said decision within ten days to the common pleas court of Franklin county, or of the county in which such manufactory or the principal place of business of such seller of syrups and extracts is located, and issue shall be made up in said court upon said appeal, and the same shall be tried and disposed of therein. *Appeal to common pleas court.*

Sec. 1089-9. SECTION 7. For the purpose of this act a bottled soft drink, except pure non-alcoholic fruit juices, shall consist of a beverage made from pure cane or beet sugar syrup containing pure flavoring materials with or without added fruit acid, with or without added color, and shall contain in the finished product not less than 7% sugar, provided that nothing in this act shall prohibit the use of any other harmless ingredient in the manufacture of such soft drinks, but any substitute for sugar used in such manufacture shall be equal in sweetening power to 7% cane or beet sugar, and the use of saccharin is prohibited. And provided further that, whenever artificial coal-tar colors are used, nothing but the certified colors as approved by the federal government are permissible. The provisions of this section shall not apply to retailers who do not bottle soft drinks, except as to *Bottled soft drink defined.*

saccharin; and all bottled soft drinks not in compliance with the standards established by this act shall be deemed to be adulterated. All adulterations of any of the drinks, extracts or other articles mentioned in this act shall be unlawful.

Sec. 1089-10.

When soft drinks shall be labeled "Artificially Colored and Flavored," etc.

SECTION 8. Whenever artificial colors and artificial flavors are used in the manufacture of soft drinks to imitate a natural product, the bottle or other container shall be distinctly labeled "Artifically Colored and Flavored" by a printed label upon the side thereof, or said words may be upon the metal crown or cap thereof. All other non-alcoholic . ciders, fruitades, fruit juices, or other similar drinks that are made in imitation of the natural product shall be properly and distinctly labeled in the manner above provided with the word "Imitation" followed by the name of the beverage. If the drinks and beverages above mentioned and containing artificial coloring or artificial flavoring of any character are sold in bulk, label or sign containing the word "Artificially Colored, Artificially Flavored", or "ArtificiallyColored, Imitation Flavor", and printed or painted in letters not less than one inch long and of appropriate comparative width shall be displayed in a conspicuous place on the counters or shelves, or on all stands, booths or other places where such drinks or beverages are sold or dispensed. When such drinks or beverages contain artificial color and natural fruit flavor, it shall be sufficient to label the same "Artificially Colored". When they contain artificial flavors and no artificial color they may be labeled "Artificial Flavor" or "Imitation Flavor."

Sec. 1089-11.

When manufactured waters shall be labeled.

SECTION 9 All manufactured waters, whether compounded and made in imitation of specified natural water or not, shall be labeled either as "Artificial" or "Imitation". The word "Artificial" or "Imitation" shall be placed at the top of the label, and shall be in letters of a size equal to or greater than any other wording on the label, and equally as prominent, and the label shall have a uniform background.

All natural waters which have anything added to them or abstracted from them shall be labeled in the same manner with either of said words, and the manner in which the same has been so altered shall be clearly stated on the label.

Waters made in imitation of any natural spring water or mineral water, and bearing the name of such spring water or mineral water, as provided above, shall contain the same chemical ingredients and composition as the natural water after which they are so named.

All mineral waters whether of natural or artificial origin sold or offered for sale must be of good quality when judged by the results of the sanitary chemical analysis, special significance being attributed to the presence of nitrite, to free ammonia in excess of 0.05 miligram per liter, and to an undue amount of organic matter, if not so found, they shall be deemed to be adulterated.

Sec. 1089-12.

SECTION 10. All bottles except siphons used in the manufacture of soft drinks, before being filled, shall be sterilized by soaking in a hot caustic solution of not less temperature than one hundred and twenty degrees Fahrenheit, that shall contain not less than three per cent, caustic or alkali expressed in terms of sodium hydrate for a period of not less than five minutes, then thoroughly rinsed in clean water until free from alkali or sodium hydrate. Each and every bottle so sterilized, when filled with a soft drink, must be distinctly labeled with the true name thereof in the manner above provided.

Sterilizing containers and apparatus.

Sec. 1089-13.

SECTION 11. All buildings, stores, factories or other places where such soft drinks are manufactured or bottled shall be well lighted and ventilated and shall be kept at all times in a clean and sanitary condition. All machines, bottles, jars or other utensils used in the manufacture of soft drinks shall be kept at all times in a clean and sanitary place and in a sanitary condition.

Ventilation of building.

Sec. 1089-14.

SECTION 12. No bottles shall be used in the manufacture of soft drinks in which the metal or rubber part of the stopper comes in contact with the beverage.

The provisions of this section shall not apply to carbonated water put up in "siphons".

Provision as to rubber stopper.

Sec. 1089-15.

SECTION 13. The secretary of agriculture shall enforce the provisions of this act and shall make suitable rules and regulations for carrying out its provisions.

Enforcement of law.

Sec. 1089-16.

SECTION 14. Any person, firm or corporation who shall do any of the acts or things prohibited, or neglect or refuse to do any of the acts or things required by this act, or in any way violates any of its provisions, or who neglects or refuses to comply with any order of the secretary of agriculture, or in any manner obstructs or resists him in the performance of his duties, shall be deemed guilty of a misdemeanor and fined not more than one hundred dollars ($100); and for the second or subsequent offense may be fined a like sum or imprisoned in the county jail for a period of not more than ninety days, or both, at the discretion of the court.

Penalty for violations.

CARL R. KIMBALL,
Speaker of the House of Representatives.
CLARENCE J. BROWN,
President of the Senate.

Passed April 17, 1919.
Approved May 10, 1919.

JAMES M. COX,
Governor.

Filed in the office of the Secretary of State at Columbus, Ohio, on the 16th day of May, A. D., 1919.

126 G.

The sectional numbers on the margin hereof are designated as provided by law.
JOHN G. PRICE,
Attorney General.

[House Bill No. 490.]

AN ACT

To provide for the inspection, license and sanitary regulation of commercial canneries and for the publication of reports of same.

Be it enacted by the General Assembly of the State of Ohio:

Sec. 1090.

Commercial canneries under the supervision of state secretary; inspection.

SECTION 1. All commercial vegetable and fruit canneries located within the state of Ohio shall be under the supervision and subject to the regulations of the secretary of agriculture. For the purpose of this act a commercial cannery is hereby defined to be a place or building where fruits or vegetables are packed in hermetically sealed containers and sterilized, and the products of which are placed on the market for general consumption as human food; but shall not be held to include private homes where farmers or others pack such fruits and vegetables for their own use and make occasional sales of a surplus thereof. At such times as the secretary of agriculture may deem proper he shall cause to be inspected all such canneries where fruits or vegetables are packed and preserved, and shall require the correction of all insanitary conditions, and may enter and search all places in or about the premises of any such cannery for the purposes of such inspection and investigation.

Sec. 1090-1.

Inspectors of canneries; duties.

SECTION 2. The secretary of agriculture shall appoint and assign, upon the passage of this act, an efficient and experienced inspector of canneries who has a thorough knowledge of the canning business, who shall have charge of such inspection, and whose duties it shall be to visit and inspect commercial fruit and vegetable canneries as often as may be required; see that such canneries and the operation thereof shall comply with the provisions of this act and with the regulations made by the secretary of agriculture hereunder; superintend the work of special inspectors stationed at canneries; and make reports thereof to the secretary of agriculture.

Sec. 1090-2.

Special inspector; duties.

SECTION 3. The secretary of agriculture shall, whenever he deems it necessary, furnish an efficient special inspector to be stationed at a commercial cannery or group of canneries while in operation, who shall see that such canneries and the operation thereof shall at all times comply with the provisions of this act and with such regulations made by the secretary of agriculture and that none but fit, wholesome and sound raw material is used in the preparation of such canned food products.

Sec. 1090-3.

When fruit shall be condemned.

SECTION 4. Fruits or vegetables unfit for human food shall not be packed at any cannery, and shall be condemned as being unfit for such use by the inspector of canneries or by such special inspector.

331

Sec. 1090-4.	SECTION 5. Any person, firm or corporation owning or operating such cannery where fruits or vegetables are packed, canned or preserved in hermetically sealed containers to be sold as food, may label and sell the same as having been packed in compliance with the laws of Ohio and the regulations of the secretary of agriculture, provided the person, firm or corporation packs, cans or preserves a product which is made from sound, fit and wholesome raw materials and which is absolutely free from chemical coloring matter and adulterants of any kind and whose canneries and cannery operations comply with the provisions of this act and the regulations of the secretary of agriculture. The secretary of agriculture shall furnish to each cannery that shall have fully complied with the provisions of this act and with such regulations, a certificate of inspection that such cannery has been inspected and has complied with all such laws and regulations. The secretary of agriculture may authorize the owner, owners or operators of such canneries to use a label or certificate on his products to read substantially as follows: "Packed and inspected in compliance with the laws of Ohio and regulations of the department of agriculture," or such other device or certificate with the words "Inspected and Approved" thereon, as the secretary of agriculture may from time to time designate by published regulations.
	When canned fruits, vegetables, etc., may be labeled and sold; certificate of inspection.
	Certain label may be authorized.
Sec. 1090-5.	SECTION 6. No commercial cannery shall be located in an insanitary place or one which cannot be made sanitary or maintained in a sanitary condition, or where it is impossible to receive the raw material in a cleanly manner without danger of damage or contamination; or where sewage, garbage and other refuse can not be quickly and effectively removed.
	Location must be in sanitary place.
Sec. 1090-6.	SECTION 7. All garbage and waste material shall be removed daily to a distance of not less than one hundred feet from any building used in preparing or handling fruits and vegetables intended for canning, provided, however, that this section does not apply to the storage upon the premises of a cannery of by-products in silos or other structures or containers or in stacks, if such storage is made in an approved manner and is not a direct menace to proper sanitation.
	Removal of garbage and waste daily.
Sec. 1090-7.	SECTION 8. Horses, cattle or other live-stock shall not be kept or fed within seventy-five feet of any building, shed, room or place while used for the preparation of canned fruits or vegetables or for the storage of raw materials intended for canning.
	Keeping live stock near cannery.
Sec. 1090-8.	SECTION 9. Any building used in the preparation or handling of fruits or vegetables intended for canning shall be suitably ventilated and lighted either by artificial or natural means. All floors in such buildings shall be so constructed as to permit proper washing or cleaning, and sufficient drains, gutters or sewers provided to insure the proper removal of water and liquid waste. First floors shall be
	Ventilation and light; floor construction.

waterproofed in such manner as will prevent the ground below from becoming wet, sloppy or insanitary.

Sec. 1090-9.

Provisions as to toilets.

SECTION 10. Separate toilet rooms for each sex shall be provided upon the premises of all canneries, said toilets to be completely separated from work rooms by tight partitions and properly lighted and having an opening to the outside air. When out-door toilets without modern plumbing and sewerage systems are used, such toilets shall be located at least 75 feet from any building, room or place used in the preparation or canning of fruits and vegetables. All doors, windows and other openings in toilets, whether same be located within buildings or out of doors shall be screened against flies.

Sec. 1090-10.

Wash rooms, lavatories, etc.

SECTION 11. Wash rooms, wash stations or lavatories for employes shall be provided in or adjacent to rooms or places used for the preparation or canning of fruits and vegetables, and such rooms or stations must be properly lighted and ventilated and provided with facilities necessary for keeping them in a sanitary condition.

Sec. 1090-11.

Smoking or spitting.

SECTION 12. It shall be unlawful for any person to smoke or to spit on floors or walls in any room or building where fruit or vegetables intended for canning are being prepared or handled.

Sec. 1090-12.

Employment of diseased person prohibited.

SECTION 13. Persons affected with tuberculosis or other communicable or infectious disease shall not be employed in or about any commercial cannery.

Sec. 1090-13.

Clean garments.

SECTION 14. All employes who assist in preparing or handling fruit and vegetables intended for canning shall wear clean garments of washable fabrics and all female employes engaged in the same work shall wear clean washable caps covering the hair.

Sec. 1090-14.

Utensils and equipment must be kept in sanitary condition.

SECTION 15. All machinery, belts, chains, conveyors, utensils, and other equipment used in the preparation or handling of food or materials intended for food in commercial canneries shall be thoroughly cleaned daily and kept in a clean and sanitary condition. All cans and other containers intended for the hermetic sealing of such food products shall be washed, steamed or sterilized before filling.

Sec. 1090-15.

Fruits, etc., must be washed and cleaned.

SECTION 16. All fruits and vegetables in preparation for canning shall be thoroughly washed or cleaned before being scalded, blanched, cooked or filled into containers.

Sec. 1090-16.

Syrups, brine, etc.

SECTION 17. Only potable water shall be used for making syrups or brine for canned fruits or vegetables or for washing equipment coming in contact with such material intended for canning.

Sec. 1090-17.

License required.

SECTION 18. No person, firm or corporation shall engage in the business of operating a commercial cannery without first obtaining a license for the operation of each such cannery from the secretary of agriculture.

In order to obtain such license an application shall be made, for which the secretary of agriculture may prescribe the form and which shall be accompanied by a fee of fifteen dollars. The secretary of agriculture shall thereupon cause an investigation to be made, and if it be found that the applicant is supplied with the facilities necessary for complying with this act, and that such commercial cannery is in sanitary condition, such license shall be issued and shall run for one year and shall be thereafter renewed upon the same conditions and payment. Application; investigation; fee.

The secretary of agriculture may suspend any such license temporarily for failure to comply with the provisions of this act or any regulation or order made by him hereunder, and shall have the power finally to revoke the same for such cause. Suspension or surrender of license.

Before any such suspension or revocation of a license is made the secretary of agriculture shall give written notice to the licensee that he contemplates the suspension or revocation of the same and giving his reasons therefor. Such notice shall appoint a time for hearing before said secretary of agriculture and may be sent by registered mail to the licensee. On the day of the hearing the licensee may present such evidence as he desires and after hearing the evidence the secretary of agriculture shall decide the matter in such manner as to him appears just and right. Notice; hearing; evidence.

A licensee shall have the right to appeal to the board of agriculture from any such decision of the secretary of agriculture suspending or revoking his license, within three days from the time of receiving notification of such suspension or revocation, and such appeal shall stay the enforcement of such suspension or revocation until the decision of the board of agriculture. The board of agriculture shall fix a time for hearing such appeal and give such licensee opportunity to be heard and to produce evidence, and after hearing such evidence the board of agriculture shall either affirm or disaffirm or modify said decision of the secretary of agriculture. Appeal to board; hearing.

Sec. 1090-18. SECTION 19. At such times as the secretary of agriculture may deem proper he shall issue public bulletins of information, report and publish the conditions found in canneries, furnish and disseminate information regarding the canning industry and for that purpose may arrange for educational exhibits, demonstrations, public meetings, and give instructions to processors, superintendents, and managers of canneries as to the meaning and interpretation of this act and the regulations made by him hereunder. Such information shall be available to any person who is a resident of this state, and those now engaged in the business of canning, and to those who may hereafter engage therein, who may properly apply therefor. Publication of bulletins of information.

Sec. 1090-19. SECTION 20. The secretary of agriculture is hereby authorized to use funds available from the appropriations Funds authorized.

made for the general use of his department to enable him to carry this act into effect.

Sec. 1090-20.
Enforcement of law.

SECTION 21. The secretary of agriculture shall enforce the provisions of this act and shall make suitable rules and regulations for carrying out its provisions.

Sec. 1090-21.
Penalty for violations of law.

SECTION 22. Whoever, shall, without authorization by the secretary of agriculture, and without inspection by the inspector of canneries or special inspectors appointed by the secretary of agriculture, use the certificate or label as provided for in section 4 of this act, or any other device authorized by the secretary of agriculture, or who shall use any raw materials, articles, or substances forbidden to be used in canning, or who shall violate any of the provisions of this act shall be guilty of a misdemeanor and shall upon conviction for the first offense be fined not less than' fifty dollars nor more than two hundred dollars, and for the second offense shall be fined not less than one hundred dollars nor more than five hundred dollars, or imprisoned in the county jail for not less than ten days nor more than sixty days, or both.

SECTION 23. This act shall take effect and be in force from and after the earliest period allowed by law.

The sectional numbers on the margin hereof are designated as provided by law.
JOHN G. PRICE,
Attorney General.

CLARENCE J. BROWN,
President of the Senate.
CARL R. KIMBALL,
Speaker of the House of Representatives.

Passed April 17, 1919.
Approved May 10, 1919.

JAMES M. COX,
Governor.

Filed in the office of the Secretary of State at Columbus, Ohio, on the 16th day of May, A. D., 1919.

127 G.

[Amended Senate Bill No. 122.]

AN ACT

An act relating to the manufacture, keeping, storage, transportation and sale of explosives, and providing penalties for any violation of this act.

Be it enacted by the General Assembly of the State of Ohio:

DEFINITIONS.

Sec. 5903-1.
Definitions of terms.

SECTION 1. The term "explosive" or "explosives" whenever used in this act shall be held to mean and include any chemical compound or mechanical mixture that is intended for the purpose of producing an explosion, that contains any oxidizing and combustible units, or other ingre-

dients, in such proportions, quantities or packing that an Definitions of terms.
ignition by fire, friction, by concussion, by percussion, or by
detonator of any part of the compound or mixture may
cause such a sudden generation of highly heated gases that
the resultant gaseous pressures are capable of producing
destructive effects on contiguous objects, or of destroying
life or limb.

For the purpose of this act manufactured articles shall
not be held to be explosives when the individual units contain explosives in such limited quantities, of such nature,
or in such packing, that it is impossible to procure a simul-
taneous or a destructive explosion of such units, to the injury of life, limb or property by fire, by friction, by concussion, by percussion, or by detonator, such as fixed ammuni-
tion for small arms, firecrackers, safety fuse matches, et
cetera.

The term "magazine" as used herein means any building or other structure used for the storage of explosives.

The term "building" or "buildings" as used herein
shall be held to mean and include only a building or buildings occupied in whole or in part as a habitation for human
beings, or any church, school house, railway station or other
building where people are accustomed to assemble, but not
including the buildings of a manufacturing plant where the
business of manufacturing explosives is carried on.

The term "factory building" as used herein shall be
held to mean any building or other structure (including rest
and blending houses) in which explosives are manufactured
or handled, excepting magazines.

The term "railway" or "railroad" as used herein shall
be held to mean and include any steam, electric or other
railroad which carries passengers for hire, but shall not include auxiliary tracks, spurs and sidings installed and primarily used in serving any mine, quarry or plant.

The term "highway" as used herein shall be held to
mean and include only any public street, alley or public
road, legally established.

The term "efficient artificial barricade" as used herein
shall be held to mean an artificial mound or properly rev-
etted wall of earth of a minimum thickness of not less than
three feet or an equivalent artificial protection.

The term "person" as used herein shall be held to
mean and include firms, partnerships, corporations and
jointstock association, as well as natural persons.

The term "agricultural purposes" as used herein means
explosives used by agriculturists on their own farms for
tree planting, subsoiling, ditching, bowlder breaking, or
other purposes exclusively agricultural, but not for quar-
rying or mining.

Words used in the singular number shall include the
plural and the plural the singular.

PROHIBITIONS AND EXCEPTIONS.

Sec. 5903-2.

Prohibitions and exceptions.

SECTION 2. No person shall manufacture, have, keep or store explosives in this state, except in compliance with this act, except that explosives may be manufactured without compliance with this act in experimental and analytical laboratories, permission for which has been obtained in writing from the industrial commission, or its authorized representative, in the laboratories of schools, colleges and similar institutions for the purpose of instruction and investigation.

It shall be unlawful to sell, give away or otherwise dispose of or deliver to any person under sixteen years of age any explosives, whether said person is acting for himself or for any other person.

QUANTITY AND DISTANCE TABLE.

Sec. 5903-3.

Quantity permitted and distance from building, railway, etc.

SECTION 3. All factory buildings and magazines in which explosives are had, kept or stored must be located at distances from buildings, railroads and highways in conformity with the following quantity and distance table, and this table shall be the basis on which applications for certificate of compliance, as provided in section 10 hereof, shall be made and the certificates of compliance issued; provided, that the quantity and distance table may be disregarded and a certificate of compliance may be issued for two second-class magazines (see section 8) in any building not otherwise prohibited by law, if the contents and location of the magazine are as follows: (a) one second-class magazine containing not more than fifty (50) pounds of explosives may be allowed if the second-class magazine is placed on wheels and located not more than ten feet from and on the same floor with and directly opposite to the entrance on the floor nearest the street level; (b) one second-class magazine containing not more than five thousand (5000) blasting caps may be allowed if the said second-class magazine is placed on wheels and located on the floor nearest street level.

QUANTITY AND DISTANCE TABLE.

Column 1				Column 2	Column 3	Column 4
Quantity that may be kept or stored from nearest building, highway or railway				Distance from nearest building	Distance from nearest railway	Distance from nearest highway
Blasting and Electric Blasting Caps		Other Explosives				
Number over	Number not over	Pounds over	Pounds not over	Feet	Feet	Feet
1,000	5,000	------	------	30	20	10
5,000	10,000	------	------	60	40	20
10,000	20,000	------	------	120	70	35
20,000	25,000	------	50	145	90	45
25,000	50,000	50	100	240	140	70
50,000	100,000	100	200	360	220	110
100,000	150,000	200	300	520	310	150
150,000	200,000	300	400	640	380	190
200,000	250,000	400	500	720	430	220
250,000	300,000	500	600	800	480	240
300,000	350,000	600	700	860	520	260
350,000	400,000	700	800	920	550	280
400,000	450,000	800	900	980	590	300
450,000	500,000	900	1,000	1,020	610	310
500,000	750,000	1,000	1,500	1,060	640	320
750,000	1,000,000	1,500	2,000	1,200	720	360
1,000,000	1,500,000	2,000	3,000	1,300	780	390
1,500,000	2,000,000	3,000	4,000	1,420	850	420
2,000,000	2,500,000	4,000	5,000	1,500	900	450
2,500,000	3,000,000	5,000	6,000	1,560	940	470
3,000,000	3,500,000	6,000	7,000	1,610	970	490
3,500,000	4,000,000	7,000	8,000	1,660	1,000	500
4,000,000	4,500,000	8,000	9,000	1,700	1,020	510
4,500,000	5,000,000	9,000	10,000	1,740	1,040	520
5,000,000	7,500,000	10,000	15,000	1,780	1,070	530
7,500,000	10,000,000	15,000	20,000	1,950	1,170	580
10,000,000	12,500,000	20,000	25,000	2,110	1,270	630
12,500,000	15,000,000	25,000	30,000	2,260	1,360	680
15,000,000	17,500,000	30,000	35,000	2,410	1,450	720
17,500,000	20,000,000	35,000	40,000	2,550	1,530	760
		40,000	45,000	2,680	1,610	800
		45,000	50,000	2,800	1,680	840
		50,000	55,000	2,920	1,750	880
		55,000	60,000	3,030	1,820	910
		60,000	65,000	3,130	1,880	940
		65,000	70,000	3,220	1,940	970
		70,000	75,000	3,310	1,990	1,000
		75,000	80,000	3,390	2,040	1,020
		80,000	85,000	3,460	2,080	1,040
		85,000	90,000	3,520	2,120	1,060
		90,000	95,000	3,580	2,150	1,080
		95,000	100,000	3,630	2,180	1,090
		100,000	125,000	3,670	2,200	1,100
		125,000	150,000	3,800	2,280	1,140
		150,000	175,000	3,930	2,360	1,180
		175,000	200,000	4,060	2,440	1,220
		200,000	225,000	4,190	2,520	1,260
		225,000	250,000	4,310	2,590	1,300
		250,000	275,000	4,430	2,660	1,340
		275,000	300,000	4,550	2,730	1,380

REDUCTION OF DISTANCE.

Sec. 5903-4.

When distance may be reduced.

SECTION 4. Whenever the building, railroad or highway to be protected is effectually screened from the factory building or magazine where explosives are had, kept or stored either by natural features of the ground or by efficient artificial barricade of such height that any straight line drawn from the top of any side wall of the factory building or magazine to any part of the building to be protected will pass through such intervening natural or efficient artificial barricade, and any straight line drawn from the top of any side wall of the factory building or magazine to any point twelve feet above the center of the railroad or highway to be protected will pass through such intervening natural or efficient artificial barricade, the applicable distances given in columns two, three and four of the quantity and distance table may be reduced one-half; provided, however, when the physical conditions and surroundings warrant, the industrial commission, in its discretion, may reduce the barricaded distances to less than one-half the applicable distances given in columns two, three and four of the quantity and distance table.

DISTANCE OF MAGAZINE AND FACTORY BUILDINGS FROM OTHER EXPOSURES.

Sec. 5903-5.

Distance factory buildings located from another and magazine from other exposures.

SECTION 5. The distance at which factory buildings may be located one from another, the distance at which magazines may be located with relation to factory buildings and the distance at which magazines and factory buildings may be located from structures, other exposures or places frequented by persons, not mentioned in section three of this act shall be determined and regulated by the industrial commission, provided, however, that any person interested either because of ownership in or occupation of any property affected by any order, ruling or otherwise, made by the industrial commission, may petition the commission for a hearing on the reasonableness and lawfulness of any such order or ruling in the manner provided in sections 871-27 and 871-29 of the Ohio General Code.

MAXIMUM ALLOWED.

Sec. 5903-6.

Maximum amount that may be kept or stored.

SECTION 6. No quantity in excess of three hundred thousand (300,000) pounds, or in the case of blasting caps no number in excess of twenty million (20,000,000) caps, shall be had, kept or stored in any factory building or magazine in this state.

CONTAINERS.

Sec. 5903-7.

Containers required; particles not allowed to remain outside.

SECTION 7. Except only at a factory building, and except while being used, no person shall have, keep or store explosives at any place within this state unless such explosives are completely enclosed or encased in tight metallic, wooden or fibre containers, and, except while being transported, or used, or in the custody of a common carrier awaiting shipment or pending delivery to consignee during the time permitted by federal law, explosives shall be kept and stored in a magazine constructed and operated as provided in section eight of this act, and no person having explosives in his possession or control shall, under any circumstances, permit or allow any grains or particles to be or remain on the outside or about the containers in which such explosives are held. All containers in which explosives are held shall be plainly marked with the name of the explosive contained therein.

MAGAZINES.

Sec. 5903-8.

SECTION 8. Magazines in which explosives may lawfully be kept or stored shall be of two classes, as follows: Classes of magazines; specifications

(a) Magazines of the first class shall be constructed of brick, concrete, iron or wood covered with iron, and shall have no openings except for ventilation and entrance. The doors of such magazine must at all times be kept closed and locked, except when necessarily opened for the purpose of storing or removing explosives therein or therfrom, by persons lawfully entitled to enter the same. Every such magazine shall have sufficient openings for ventilation thereof, which must be screened in such manner as to prevent the entrance of sparks of fire through the same. No matches or fire or other flame producing device of any kind, except electric incandescent flash lights, shall at any time be permitted in any such magazine. No package of explosives shall at any time be opened in or within fifty feet of any magazine, nor shall any open package of explosive be kept therein except in the original containers. Magazines in which more than fifty pounds of explosives are kept and stored must be detached from other structures, and magazines where more than five thousand pounds of explosives are kept and stored must be located at least two hundred feet from any other magazine, and magazines where explosives over twenty-five thousand pounds are kept and stored must have an increase over two hundred feet of two and two-thirds (2 2-3) feet for each one thousand pounds of explosives in excess of twenty-five thousand pounds stored therein; provided, that where magazines are protected one from the other by approved natural or efficient artificial barricades, the distances above required may be reduced one-half. The premises on which such magazines are located must be conspicuously defined and marked by signs containing the words "Explosives—Keep Off" legibly printed thereon in letters not less than three inches high. Such signs must not be placed on the magazine and must be so located that a bullet passing through the face of such sign at right angles will not strike the magazine. Except that nothing contained in this section shall prohibit the installation and operation of suitable heating apparatus in magazines used exclusively for the storage of liquid nitroglycerin, for the purpose of preventing liquid nitroglycerin from freezing; provided that such heating apparatus must be entirely enclosed in fire proof material properly vented to the outside air and equipped with proper regulators or devices as will prevent such heating apparatus from creating a temperature in the magazines in excess of one hundred degrees Fahrenheit and nothing but oil or gas shall be used as fuel for such heating.

(b) Magazines of the second class shall be constructed of fireproof material or wood with outside covering of iron, and not more than fifty pounds of explosives or five thousand blasting caps shall at any time be kept or stored therein, and, except when necessarily opened for use by authorized persons shall at all times be kept securely locked. Upon each such magazine there shall at all times be kept conspicuously posted a sign, with words "Magazine-Explosives-Dangerous" legibly printed thereon, and not more than two such magazines shall be had or kept in any building.

BLASTING CAPS.

Sec. 5903-9.

Caps shall not be stored with other explosives.

SECTION 9. No blasting caps, or other detonating or fulminating caps or detonators, shall be kept or stored in any magazine in which other explosives are kept or stored. Blasting caps, detonating or fulminating caps or detonators, in quantities of one thousand or over, must be kept in a separate magazine constructed in accordance with the provisions of section eight, and certificate of compliance must be obtained from the industrial commission.

REPORTS AND CERTIFICATE OF COMPLIANCE.

Sec. 5903-10.

Report to industrial commission; statements required.

SECTION 10. All persons engaged in keeping or storing explosives on the date when this act takes effect shall within sixty (60) days thereafter, and all persons engaged in keeping or storing explosives after this act takes effect shall before engaging in the keeping or storing of explosives make a report in writing, subscribed to by such person or his agent, to the industrial commission on blanks to be furnished by the commission stating:

(1) The location of the magazine, if then existing, or in case of a new magazine, or a removal of any existing magazine, the proposed location of such magazine.

(2) The kind of explosives that are kept or stored, or intended to be kept or stored, and the maximum quantity that is intended to be kept or stored thereat.

(3) The distance that such magazine is located, or intended to be located, from the nearest buildings, railways and highways.

Certificate of compliance.

The industrial commission shall, as soon as may be after receiving such report, cause an inspection to be made of the magazine, if then constructed; and in the case of a new magazine or the removal of an existing magazine, as soon as may be after the same is constructed or moved to a new location. If upon such inspection the magazine is found to be constructed in accordance with the specifications provided in section eight of this act the industrial commission shall determine the amount of explosives that may be kept or stored in such magazine by reference to the quantity and distance table set forth in section three of this act, and shall issue a certificate to the person applying therefor, showing compliance with the provisions of this act, which certificate shall set forth the maximum quantity of explosives that may be had, kept or stored in said magazine. Except in the case of an existing magazine which has previously been inspected by an inspector or authorized representative of the industrial commission and for which a certificate has been issued as provided in section fifty-nine hundred and four of the Ohio General Code, now repealed, the industrial commission shall, provided no changes have been made or taken place in the physical conditions surrounding said existing magazine as set forth in paragraphs "A", "B" and "C" of this section, issue a certificate with or without making another inspection of such existing magazine. Such certificate of compliance shall be valid until cancelled for cause as hereinafter provided. Whenever by reason of change in the physical conditions surrounding any magazine after the issuance of the certificate of compliance therefor, such as:

Grounds for cancellation of certificate; notice.

    (a)   The erection of buildings near said magazine.

    (b)   The construction of railways nearer said magazine, or

    (c)   The opening for public travel of highways nearer said magazine; then the owner or operator of such magazine shall immediately notify the industrial commission and the commission shall modify or cancel such certificate in accordance with the changed conditions. Whenever any person to whom a certificate of compliance has been issued by the industrial commission keeps or stores in the magazine covered by such certificate of compliance any quantity of explosives in excess of the maximum amount set forth in said certificate of compliance, or whenever any person fails for thirty days to pay the annual license fee hereinafter provided after the same becomes due or otherwise violates any of the provisions of this act, the industrial commission is authorized to cancel such certificate of compliance. Whenever a certificate of compliance is cancelled by the industrial commission for any cause hereinbefore specified, the industrial commission shall notify in writing the person to whom such certificate of compliance is issued of the fact of such cancellation, and shall in said notice direct the removal of all explosives stored in said magazine within ten days from the giving of said notice. Failure to remove the explosives stored in said magazine within the time specified in said notice, shall constitute a violation of this act.

LICENSE.

Sec. 5903-11.

Schedule of annual license fees.

SECTION 11. Every person engaged in the keeping or storing of explosives shall pay an annual license fee for each magazine maintained. Such license fee shall be as shown in the following graduated schedules:

(Schedule of annual license fees for magazines containing explosives other than blasting and electric blasting caps or other detonators):

Second class magazines, containing not over fifty pounds ....$ 1 00

First class magazine, grade A, containing over fifty pounds and not over 500 pounds.............. 2 50

First class magazines, grade B, containing over 500 pounds and not over 5,000 pounds............ 5 00

First class magazines, grade C, containing over 5,000 pounds and not over 15,000 pounds............ 10 00

First class magazines, grade D, containing over 15,000 pounds and not over 25,000 pounds..... 15 00

First class magazines, grade E, containing over 25,000 pounds and not over 150,000 pounds.... 20 00

First class magazines, grade F, containing over 150,000 pounds and not over 300,000 pounds.... 25 00

(Schedule of annual license fees for magazines containing blasting caps or other detonating or fulminating caps or detonators):

Second class magazines, containing not over 5,000 caps ....$ 1 00

First class magazines, containing not over 35,000 caps 1 00

First class magazines, containing over 35,000 caps... 5 00

Said annual license fees shall be payable in advance to the industrial commission and by the commission paid to the state treasurer.

BOND REQUIRED.

Sec. 5903-12.

Bond required.

SECTION 12. The owner or operator of every factory in which explosives are manufactured or handled, within sixty days after demand therefor in writing by the industrial commission upon such owner or operator, unless exempted therefrom as hereinafter provided, shall file and keep on file with the state department of insurance an indemnity bond payable to the state in such sums as may be determined by the industrial commission and set forth in such demand, not in excess of two hundred and fifty thousand dollars nor less than ten thousand dollars, with surety or sureties satisfactory to said department, conditioned for the payment of all final judgments that may be rendered against said owner or operator for damages caused to persons and of property by reason of any explosion at said factory of the explosives there manufactured or handled. Any such owner or operator desiring to be exempted from filing such bond shall make application to the said state department of insurance showing his financial ability to discharge all such judgments to the amount of said bond required by said industrial commission that may be entered against him, whereupon said department, if satisfied of such financial ability of the applicant, shall by written order exempt such applicant from the filing of such bond; and said department of insurance may from time to time require further statements from the applicant showing his financial ability aforesaid, and if dissatisfied therewith, may in its discretion revoke such exemption and require the filing of such bond.

WHO MAY ENTER.

Sec. 5903-13.

SECTION 13. No person, except an official as authorized herein or a person authorized to do so by the owner thereof, or his agent, shall enter any factory building, magazine or railway car containing explosives in this state.

Who may enter factory, building, etc.

TRANSPORTATION.

Sec. 5903-14.

SECTION 14. Every vehicle while carrying explosives upon the public highway shall display upon an erect pole at the front end of such vehicle and at such height that it shall be visible from all directions, a red flag with the word "Danger" printed, stamped or sewed thereon, in white letters at least three inches in height, or in lieu of such flag the words "Explosives, Dangerous", must be painted or attached to the ends and each side of such vehicle in white letters on proper background at least three inches in height. It shall be unlawful for any person in charge of a vehicle containing explosives to smoke in, upon or near such vehicle, to drive the vehicle while intoxicated, to drive the vehicle in a careless or reckless manner, or to load or unload such vehicle in a careless or reckless manner, or to make unnecessary stops. It shall be unlawful for any person to place or carry, or cause to be placed or carried, any metal tool or other similar piece of metal in the bed or body of the vehicle containing explosives, unless contained in a box or other container approved by the industrial commission or its authorized representative. It shall be unlawful for any person to place or carry, or cause to be placed or carried, in the bed or body of a vehicle containing explosives, any exploders, detonators, blasting caps or other similar explosive material, or to carry in or upon such vehicle any matches or any other flame-producing device. Vehicles used for transportation of explosives shall not be driven at a rate of speed exceeding fifteen miles per hour. Nothing contained in this section shall prohibit the transportation of explosives in motor-driven vehicles.

Red flag with words of warning displayed on vehicle transporting explosives.

FIREARMS.

Sec. 5903-15.

SECTION 15. No person shall discharge any firearm at or against or within five hundred feet (500) of any magazine, factory building or explosive sign. Except that the

Discharge of firearms at or near magazine, etc., prohibited.

provisions of this section shall not apply to the testing of firearms or explosives in or upon the premises of any manufacturing plant engaged in the manufacture of firearms or explosives nor in guarding any magazine or factory building. The method of testing all firearms in any manufacturing plant engaged in the business of manufacturing firearms shall be subject to the approval of the industrial commission.

EXEMPTIONS.

Sec. 5903-16.

Exemptions from provisions of law.

SECTION 16. Nothing contained in this act shall apply to explosives while being transported upon vessels or railroad cars in conformity with the regulations adopted by the interstate commerce commission; nor to the transportation or use of blasting explosives for agricultural purposes in quantity not exceeding two hundred (200) pounds at any one time; nor to any explosives in quantities not exceeding five (5) pounds at any one time. Nothing contained in this act shall be deemed to include gasoline, kerosene, naphtha, turpentine or benzine. Nothing in this section shall be construed as conflicting with or cancelling in any manner whatever the effectiveness of section nineteen of this act.

EXISTING ORDINANCES NOT AFFECTED.

Sec. 5903-17.

Existing ordinances and regulations not affected.

SECTION 17. Nothing contained in this act shall affect any existing ordinances, rule or regulation of any city or municipality not less restrictive than this act governing the manufacture, storage, sale, use or transportation of explosives, or affect, modify or limit the power of cities or municipalities in this state to make ordinances, rules or regulations not less restrictive than this act, governing the manufacture, storage, sale, use or transportation of explosives within their respective corporate limits.

LIQUOR AND MATCHES.

Sec. 5903-18.

Entry of plant with matches, etc., or while intoxicated prohibited.

SECTION 18. No employe or other person shall enter or attempt to enter any explosive plant with matches or other flame-producing devices, except electric incandescent flashlights nor shall any employe or other person enter or attempt to enter such premises with narcotics in his or her possession or control, or while under the influence of liquor or narcotics, or to partake of intoxicants or narcotics while within the plant nor shall any person smoke in a factory building or upon the premises thereof except at such places as shall be designated by the owner or his authorized representative, under penalty of misdemeanor.

The superintendent may authorize in writing any employe or other person to have approved safety matches in his possession or to depart from the other provisions of this section.

It shall be the duty of the superintendent or other person in charge of all plants included within this act to provide safety containers for matches at all entrances to said plants.

UNLAWFUL POSSESSION OR USE OF EXPLOSIVES A FELONY.

Sec. 5903-19.

SECTION 19. Any person who shall have in his possession or control any cartridge, shell, bomb or similar device, charged or filled with one or more explosives, intending to use the same or cause the same to be used for an unlawful purpose, or attempts to use it to the injury of persons or property, or places or deposits it upon or about the premises of another without his consent, shall be deemed guilty of a felony, and upon conviction shall be punished by imprisonment in a state prison for a term of not less than one year nor more than twenty years. The possession or control by any person of any such device so charged or filled, shall be deemed prima facie evidence of an intent to use the same, or cause the same to be used, for an unlawful purpose.

Unlawful possession a felony.

RECEPTACLE WHICH CONTAINS OR HAS CONTAINED NITROGLYCERIN.

Sec. 5903-20.

SECTION 20. It shall be unlawful for any person to leave unguarded or unprotected a can, shell or receptacle which contains or has contained liquid nitroglycerin, at any place other than a stock wagon, shooter's wagon, factory building or magazine where liquid nitroglycerin is manufactured or stored.

Unguarded explosive receptacle unlawful.

REPORT TO BE MADE TO THE INDUSTRIAL COMMISSION OF ANY FIRE OR EXPLOSION INVOLVING LOSS OF LIFE OR DAMAGE TO PROPERTY.

Sec. 5903-21.

SECTION 21. All persons handling explosives shall report to the industrial commission any fire or explosion occurring in the manufacture, transportation or storage involving loss of life or causing damage to property in excess of five hundred dollars ($500.00). Such report to be made on the same day that the fire or explosion takes place and shall be transmitted to the industrial commission by telephone or telegraph if practicable. If not practical to make such report by telephone or telegraph, a written report shall be made. The expense of transmitting such reports to be borne by the person making the same.

Report of fire or explosion to industrial commission.

EXCEPTION COVERING CONSTRUCTION AND LO-
CATION OF MAGAZINES AND FACTORY BUILD-
INGS, CONSTRUCTED AND IN OPERA-
TION AT THE TIME THIS ACT BE-
COMES EFFECTIVE.

Sec. 5903-22.

Exception as to construction and location of magazines, etc.

SECTION 22. Those provisions of sections three and eight of this act relating to the construction of magazines and the location of magazines and factory buildings, shall not apply to magazines and factory buildings constructed and in operation and for which a certificate has been issued as provided in section five thousand nine hundred and four of the Ohio General Code, now repealed, at the time this act becomes effective. Except as provided in section ten of this act where the physical conditions surrounding such magazines and factory buildings shall have changed after the issuance of the certificate of compliance as therein described and excepting that, the industrial commission, in accordance with the provisions of sections 871-22 to 871-44 inclusive of the Ohio General Code, may issue such general and special orders affecting the location and construction of such existing magazines and factory buildings as it may deem necessary for the safety of employes and the public.

PENALTIES.

Sec. 5903-23.

Penalties for violations of law.

SECTION 23. Whoever fails to comply with or violates any of the provisions of this act shall be guilty of a misdemeanor, and upon conviction shall be punished by a fine of not less than tyenty-five ($25.00) dollars nor more than five hundred ($500.00) dollars, and whoever, after receiving written notice from the industrial commission or its authorized representative, directing compliance with specified provisions of the act, fails to comply with the provisions of the act specified in said notice shall be guilty of a misdemeanor, and upon conviction shall be punished by fine not less than fifty dollars ($50.00) nor more than five thousand dollars ($5000.00), or by imprisonment for not exceeding one year, or by both such fine and imprisonment, in the discretion of the court.

DUTIES OF DISTRICT INSPECTOR ASSIGNED TO
INSPECTION OF EXPLOSIVES.

Sec. 5903-24.

Duties of district inspector.

SECTION 24. The district inspector of the industrial commission assigned to the inspection of factory buildings wherein explosives are manufactured, shall inspect all manufacturing establishments in the state wherein powder, dynamite, nitroglycerin, compounds, fuses or other explosives are manufactured, all magazines or storehouses wherein such explosives are stored and perform such other duties connected with the work as the industrial commission directs.

INSPECTION OF MANUFACTURE AND STORAGE
OF EXPLOSIVES.

Sec. 5903-25.

SECTION 25. The district inspector of the industrial commission assigned to the inspection of factory buildings and magazines shall inspect the process of manufacture and the handling and storing of explosives and in consequence of such inspection the industrial commission may order such changes or additions in or about such factory buildings or magazines as it deems necessary for the safety of the employes and the public. The industrial commission may render such general and special orders and provide such rules and regulations as it deems necessary, which, with the laws relating thereto, and the duties of the inspector shall be applicable to the places of manufacturing, sale and storage of explosives, provided any person interested either because of ownership in or occupation of any property affected by any such order, or otherwise, may petition the industrial commission for a hearing on the reasonableness and lawfulness of any such order in the manner provided in sections 871-27 and 871-29 of the Ohio General Code.

Inspection of factories and magazines.

CONSTITUTIONALITY OF ACT.

Sec. 5903-26.

SECTION 26. In case any provisions of this act shall be adjudged unconstitutional or void for any reason, such adjudication shall not affect any of the other provisions of this act.

Any provision held void shall not affect others.

SECTION 27. Sections 991, 992, 5903, 5904, 5905, 5906, 5907, 12533, 12534, 12535, 12536, 12537, 12537-1, 12538, 12539, 12540, and 12541 of the General Code of Ohio, as well as all acts and parts of acts inconsistent with the provisions of this act, are hereby repealed.

Repeals.

CLARENCE J. BROWN,
President of the Senate.
CARL R. KIMBALL,
Speaker of the House of Representatives.
Passed April 16, 1919.
Approved May 10, 1919.

The sectional numbers on the margin hereof are designated as provided by aw.
JOHN G. PRICE, Attorney General.

JAMES M. COX,
Governor.

Filed in the office of the Secretary of State at Columbus, Ohio, on the 16th day of May, A. D., 1919.

128 G.

[House Bill No. 511.]

AN ACT

To accord special recognition to officers and enlisted men receiving awards for gallantry and to acquaint citizens and soldiers of the state with the appearance and comparative rank of American decorations awarded them for distinguished gallantry and heroism, and to establish a special state roll of honor.

Be it enacted by the General Assembly of the State of Ohio:

Sec. 14867-9.

Governor authorized to request citizens to report names and address of soldiers, sailors, etc., who have received medal of honor, etc.

SECTION 1. That the governor or his representative is hereby authorized and directed to request citizens of the state of Ohio, to voluntarily, and without cost to the state, ascertain and report the name and address of each soldier, sailor, marine or aviator in their vicinity (or former address if dead), who has been awarded the Medal of Honor or Distinguished Service Cross or the Silver Citation Star, by the United States of America, for most distinguished gallantry, to the adjutant general or other authorized official, who shall request satisfactory evidence as to authentic official possession of the said decoration.

Sec. 14867-10.

Complimentary commissions authorized.

SECTION 2. The governor shall then direct that if the soldier, sailor, marine or aviator is shown to have been awarded the Medal of Honor (the highest decoration) he shall receive a complimentary commission of Brevet Major (without compensation) and if he has been shown to have been awarded the Distinguished Service Cross, he shall receive a complimentary commission of Brevet Captain (without compensation), and if shown to have been awarded the Silver Citation Star, he shall receive a complimentary commission of Brevet First Lieutenant (without compensation). His higher or lower rank in the national or state service to be disregarded, and not in any manner affected thereby.

Sec. 14867-11.

Recognition by the state; date of performance and deed of gallantry.

SECTION 3. The said complimentary commission to be exclusively an official recognition by the state of Ohio, of the particular deed of most distinguished gallantry for which the decoration was awarded by the United States of America, and to bear date corresponding to the date of performance of the deed of gallantry mentioned in said award.

Sec. 14867-12.

Recital of commission.

SECTION 4. Each commission shall recite therein the national award of the herein mentioned decoration for most distinguished gallantry, as the special reason for this honorary recognition by the state of Ohio, somewhat as follows:

Name of recipient .... having been officially awarded the Medal of Honor, or Distinguished Service Cross, or the Silver Citation Star, by the United States of America, for most distinguished gallantry on the .... day of .... at ....: in the war of .... (past, present or future war) is hereby commissioned under the provisions of the laws of the state of Ohio, Brevent .... and the herein mentioned deed of most distinguished gallantry, has been duly recorded in detail in the archives of the state of Ohio, as a Special State Roll of Honor.

Sec. 14867-12. SECTION 5. The said commission shall be entirely distinct from, and shall not affect any award of service or other medals, that the soldier, sailor, marine or aviator may receive from the nation, state or other source, for foreign or other service, or wounds, and shall be brevet, without compensation or authority, and carry no right to wear a national or state uniform or insignia not sanctioned by law, and shall not conflict with any national or state military regulations. *Commisison distinct from other award or medal.*

Sec. 14867-14. SECTION 6. That the adjutant general of the state is authorized to secure for future consideration by the general assembly an estimate of the cost of erecting at an appropriate place in the state house a suitable tablet on which shall be inscribed the names of all soldiers composing the Special State Roll of Honor, with the proper letters after each name to signify the award (M. H., D. S. C., S. S.). *Estimate of cost for memorial tablet in state house.*

Sec. 14867-15. SECTION 7. That a sufficient sum of money, not to exceed a total of fifteen hundred dollars, is hereby appropriated from the funds of the state treasury, not otherwise appropriated, to carry into effect the provisions of this act. *Appropriation.*

The sectional numbers on the margin hereof are designated as provided by law. JOHN G. PRICE, *Attorney General.*

CARL R. KIMBALL,
Speaker of the House of Representatives.
CLARENCE J. BROWN,
President of the Senate.

Passed April 16, 1919.
Approved May 10, 1919.

JAMES M. COX,
Governor.

Filed in the office of the Secretary of State at Columbus, Ohio, on the 16th day of May, A. D. 1919.
129 G.

[Amended Senate Bill No. 58.]

AN ACT

To regulate private employment agencies and to repeal sections 886, 887, 888, 889, 890, 891, 892, 893, 894, 895 and 896 of the General Code.

Be it enacted by the General Assembly of the State of Ohio:

Sec. 886. SECTION 1. No person, firm, association of persons or corporation shall engage in the business of an employment agency, for hire, within the state of Ohio, without first obtaining a license so to do from the industrial commission of Ohio, and paying to said industrial commission an annual *License required to engage in business of employment agency.*

license fee of one hundred dollars and executing and filing with the said industrial commission a bond as provided in section 6 of this act.

Sec. 887.

What deemed an employment agency.

SECTION 2. A person, firm, association of persons, or corporation who secures, or, by any form of representation or by means of signs, bulletins, circulars, cards, writings, or advertisements, offers or agrees to secure or furnish employment, engagements of help, or information or service of any character concerning or intended or purporting to promote, lead to or consummate employment, shall be deemed an employment agency, and subject to this act governing such agencies.

Sec. 888.

The term "hire" defined.

SECTION 3. The term "hire," as used in this act, shall be deemed to mean and include any charge, fee, compensation, service or benefit exacted, demanded or accepted, or any gratuity received, for or in connection with any act, service or transaction comprehended by the term "employment agency," or for or in connection with any transaction or representation which includes matters comprehended by the term "employment agency."

Sec. 889.

The term "employment" defined.

SECTION 4. The term "employment," as used in this act shall be deemed to mean and include every character of service rendered or to be rendered and every engagement undertaken, for wages, salary commission or other form of remuneration whatsoever.

Sec. 890.

Organizations not subject to these provisions.

SECTION 5. Bona fide educational, religious, charitable, fraternal, and benevolent organizations in which no fee, commission, or other charge is made for services rendered other than the ordinary membership dues; bona fide labor organizations undertaking to secure, or securing work for their own members; and bona fide employers' organizations undertaking to secure, or securing help for their own members shall not be subject to the provisions of this act.

Sec. 891.

Granting of license; fee; bond.

SECTION 6. Licenses shall be granted only upon written application which shall be upon blanks prescribed and furnished by the industrial commission of Ohio. The application shall be accompanied by the annual license fee of one hundred dollars payable to the industrial commission and by a sufficient bond payable to the state of Ohio, in the penal sum of one thousand dollars ($1,000.00), to the satisfaction of the industrial commission, conditioned for the observance of the provisions of this act and of the lawful orders of the industrial commission issued thereunder, and an action may be brought thereon by the industrial commission for violation of the provisions of this act or lawful orders issued thereunder. And such bond shall be liable for all injuries accruing to any person or persons on account of the violation of the provisions of this act, or lawful orders of the industrial commission by such licensee or his representatives, and an action may be brought thereon by the party injured in his own name for such recovery.

Sec. 892.

SECTION 7. Upon approval of the application for license and bond by the industrial commission, a license which shall be effective for one year from the date thereof, unless revoked as provided herein, shall be issued by the industrial commission. The license shall contain the name or names of the applicant, location of office, name of person who is to have general management of the business, name under which business is to be carried on, the number of the license, and the date of issuance and date of expiration of the license.

Term of license; revocation; contents of license.

Sec. 893.

SECTION 8. The industrial commission of Ohio may refuse to issue a license to an applicant, if, in its judgment, such applicant or its officials or members are not of good moral character or have violated the laws or orders of the industrial commission of Ohio relating to employment agencies, or have violated laws of Ohio or ordinances of any city or village thereof, which in the judgment of the industrial commission, renders such persons improper persons for such license. If the industrial commission refuses to grant a license the license fee and bond shall be returned to the applicant by the said industrial commission.

License may be refused, when.

Sec. 894.

SECTION 9. If the industrial commission of Ohio as herein provided, shall find a licensee, or representative, partner or employee of such licensee has been convicted in any court of the state of Ohio of violating any of the provisions of this act or orders of the industrial commission, or if such licensee, or representative, partner, or employee of such licensee has been guilty of violating any of the provisions of this act or orders of the commission or is found by the industrial commission to be not of good moral character, said industrial commission may revoke said license which shall thereupon become null and void and said industrial commission shall immediately notify such licensee of such revocation whereupon such licensee may within ten days after the issuance of such notice petition the industrial commission of Ohio for a hearing in the same manner as is provided for employers or other persons specified in section 27 of the industrial commission act, approved March 18, 1913 (103 O. L., 95).

Grounds for revocation.

Sec. 895.

SECTION 10. Each license shall become void upon the date of its expiration as set forth in the license and it shall be returned immediately to the industrial commission of Ohio.

When license void.

Sec. 896.

SECTION 11. No licensee shall change the location of his business to any place other than that specified in the license without first obtaining the written consent of the industrial commission and no license shall be effective for any place of business other than that designed therein.

Written consent to change location.

Sec. 896.1.

SECTION 12. Each licensee shall post his license in a conspicuous place in his waiting room and a copy of the law and the orders relating to its enforcement adopted by the industrial commission of Ohio in each room used for business purposes.

Posting license conspicuously.

Sec. 896-2.

Record of transactions required.

SECTION 13. Every licensee shall keep a true and correct record in the English language of the business transactions of his office upon such forms only as are prescribed or approved by the industrial commission of Ohio. Such records shall be open at all reasonable hours to the inspection of the industrial commission of Ohio, or any of its authorized representatives. On or before the fifth day of each month, every employment agency shall mail to the industrial commission of Ohio upon a form prescribed and furnished by said industrial commission, a report covering the work of the preceding calendar month.

Sec. 896-3.

Restrictions on operation of agencies.

SECTION 14. The following restrictions are placed on the operations of licensed employment agencies:

(a) No applicant for employment shall be sent to a house of ill-repute, or other place resorted to for prostitution or gambling.

(b) No prostitute, gambler, intoxicated person, procurer or other bad character shall be allowed to remain in the office or place of business.

(c) No applicant for employment shall be sent or directed to any fictitious job or position and no employment agency shall knowingly or negligently make any false representation concerning any matter within the scope of the business of the employment agency and the non-existence of any such job or position or the falsity of any such representation, shall constitute prima facie evidence of the violation of this section.

(d) No employment agency shall knowingly or negligently send an applicant to any place where a strike or lockout exists or is impending without notifying the applicant of such condition in writing and the existence of a strike or lockout, shall constitute prima facie evidence of the violation of this section.

(e) No person conducting an employment agency shall connive with any employer or his agents or employees to secure the discharge of an employee; nor shall an employer or any one in his employ or representing it, give or receive any gratuity, divide, or offer to divide, or share directly or indirectly, any fee, charge or compensation received from any applicant for employment.

(f) No person conducting an employment agency shall circulate any false information by advertisements, signs, letters, posters, cards, or in any other way; or make any false statements or misrepresentations to any person seeking employment, or to any employer seeking an employee.

(g) No person conducting an employment agency shall make any false entry or statement in any record or in any receipt or other document used in his business.

(h) No person conducting an employment agency shall use any name or designation in his business unless such name has been approved by the industrial commission of Ohio.

(i) No employment agency shall be conducted in connection with any place in which intoxicating liquors are sold in or in any room adjacent thereto.

Sec. 896 4.
SECTION 15. Employment agencies may charge such registration fees as shall be fixed by the industrial commission of Ohio. The schedule of maximum fees, charges, and commissions for actually securing employment or help shall be fixed by the industrial commission of Ohio and such fees shall be graded according to nature of business, length of employment, and wages. These schedules of registration fees and of other fees, charges and commissions shall be posted in a conspicuous place in every room in which business is conducted by the employment agency. *Schedule of fees shall be fixed by commission.*

Sec. 896-5.
SECTION 16. The industrial commission of Ohio shall enact regulations providing conditions under which the licensee shall refund registration fees, and other fees, charges and commissions, and under which the licensee shall pay expenses incurred when applicants are sent outside the city in which the employment agency is located to alleged jobs or positions which did not exist or to jobs or positions where conditions were misrepresented. *Commission shall enact regulations.*

Sec. 896-6.
SECTION 17. A receipt, in such form as the industrial commission of Ohio shall prescribe or approve shall be given to every person paying a fee or other commission to an employment agency. *Receipt for fee.*

Sec. 896-7.
SECTION 18. Whoever violates section 1 of this act shall be guilty of a misdemeanor and shall be fined for the first offense not less than one hundred dollars ($100.00) nor more than five hundred dollars ($500.00) and costs of prosecution; and for the second or any subsequent offense, he shall be fined not less than two hundred dollars ($200.00) nor more than one thousand dollars ($1,000.00) and costs of prosecution. *Penalty for violations.*

Sec. 896-8.
SECTION 19. Whoever violates any provision of this act relating to employment agencies or orders of the industrial commission of Ohio, issued thereunder, except as otherwise provided in section 18 shall be fined for the first offense not less than twenty-five dollars ($25.00) nor more than five hundred dollars ($500.00) and costs of prosecution; and for the second or any subsequent offense, he shall be fined not less than one hundred dollars ($100.00) nor more than five hundred dollars ($500.00) and costs of prosecution. *Other violations; penalty.*

Sec. 896-9.
SECTION 20. All fines collected under the provisions of this act shall be paid, one-half to the county in which the prosecution is had and one-half to the industrial commission of Ohio, and all money received by the industrial commission from license fees, bonds recovered, or fines as provided by this act, shall be paid by the industrial commission into the state treasury. *Disposition of fines and penalties.*

Sec. 896-10.
SECTION 21. The industrial commission of Ohio shall have full power, exclusive supervisory jurisdiction and authority to administer the provisions of this act, as pro- *Enforcement of law.*

vided in section 22, sub-section 9, of the industrial commission act, approved March 18, 1913 (103 O. L., 95); and to issue all necessary orders for carrying into effect this act, as provided in sections 25 and 41 of the industrial commission act.

Sec. 896-11.
What prima facie evidence.

SECTION 22. At all trials for offenses against the provisions of this act and orders of the industrial commission issued thereunder, a certificate of the custodian of the records of the industrial commission of Ohio attested by the secretary of said industrial commission, to the effect that the records do not disclose that the defendant in such proceeding was the holder of a license at the time of the commission of the offense charged, shall constitute prima facie evidence in said case that the defendant was not authorized to engage in the business of an employment agency.

Sec. 896-12.
What considered competent evidence.

SECTION 23. In the prosecution for conducting an employment agency for hire without being licensed, it shall be competent to allege and prove any number of transactions or particulars coming within the scope of the term "employment agency," but a single transaction shall be deemed engaging in the business of an employment agency.

Sec. 896-13.
Who liable for violations of law.

SECTION 24. The owner or manager or other person in control of an employment agency shall be liable for all violation of laws or lawful orders of the industrial commission of Ohio committed by any agent, representative, or employee of said agency within the scope of the business of the agency, as well as all parties personally participating in such violations.

Sec. 896-14.
Courts of jurisdiction.

SECTION 25. Justices of the peace, police judges, judges of municipal courts, and mayors of cities and villages shall have final jurisdiction co-extensive with the county in all cases for violation of provisions of this act or of orders of the industrial commission issued thereunder and the procedure provided by law for such courts shall extend to all such cases.

Sec. 896-15.
Prosecution not required to advance or secure costs.

SECTION 26. A person authorized by law to prosecute a case under the provisions of this act shall not be required to advance or secure costs therein. If the defendant be acquitted or discharged from custody, or if he be convicted and committed in default of payment of fine and cost, such cost shall be certified under oath by the justice of the peace, police judge, judge of municipal court, or mayor to the county auditor who shall correct all errors therein and issue his warrant on the county treasurer payable to the person or persons entitled thereto.

Sec. 896-16.
Section or part held void shall not affect others.

SECTION 27. The sections of this act and every part of such sections are hereby declared to be independent sections and parts of sections and the holding of any section or part thereof to be void or ineffective shall not affect any other section or part thereof.

SECTION 28. That sections 886, 887, 888, 889, 890, 891, 892, 893, 894, 895 and 896 of the General Code be, and the same are hereby repealed.

Repeals.

The sectional numbers on the margin hereof are designated as provided by law. JOHN G. PRICE, *Attorney General.*

CLARENCE J. BROWN,
President of the Senate.
CARL R. KIMBALL,
Speaker of the House of Representatives.
Passed April 16, 1919.
Approved May 15, 1919.

JAMES M. COX,
Governor.

Filed in the office of the Secretary of State at Columbus, Ohio, on the 17th day of May, A. D. 1919.

130 G.

[House Bill No. 323.]

AN ACT

Granting permission to The Massillon Electric and Gas Company to construct a transmission line across state property, being part of sections 19, 20, 21, 22, 27, 28, 29 and 30, in Perry township, Stark county, Ohio.

Be it enacted by the General Assembly of the State of Ohio:

SECTION 1. That the Massillon Electric and Gas Company, its successors and assigns, be given the right to enter in and upon such part or parts of sections number nineteen (19), twenty (20), twenty-one (21), twenty-two (22), twenty-seven (27), twenty-eight (28), twenty-nine (29) and thirty (30) of Perry township, Stark county, Ohio, and to construct, maintain and operate thereon an electrical transmission line consisting of towers, poles, wires, cross arms, insulators, and other proper material and equipment, that it be used for a transmission line only, and that the same be located as may be agreed upon by the Ohio board of administration, upon the payment to the state of such sums of money as may be agreed upon by said state board of administration and said the Massillon Electric and Gas Company.

Massillon permitted to construct transmission line across state property; description.

SECTION 2. The Ohio board of administration is also hereby empowered and authorized to convey such right or rights to said the Massillon Electric and Gas Company, its successors and assigns, by deed or lease, or other proper instrument of writing such conveyance to be made in the name of the state by said Ohio board of administration; provided, however, that such instrument shall contain a condition that the state of Ohio shall not be liable to any person for any injury that may result from the construc-

Authority to convey other rights.

tion, maintenance or operation of said transmission line across said premises.

CARL R. KIMBALL,
Speaker of the House of Representatives.
CLARENCE J. BROWN,
President of the Senate.

Passed April 16, 1919.
Approved May 15, 1919.

JAMES M. COX,
Governor.

Filed in the office of the Secretary of State, at Columbus, Ohio, on the 17th day of May, A. D. 1919.

131 L.

[House Bill No. 397.]

AN ACT

To amend sections 367-2, 367-5 and 367-6 of the General Code, relative to the powers and duties of the state board of education relative to vocational education.

Be it enacted by the General Assembly of the State of Ohio:

SECTION 1. That sections 367-2, 367-5 and 367-6 of the General Code be amended to read as follows:

Sec. 367-2. The benefits of all funds appropriated under the provisions of said act are hereby accepted as to:

(a) Appropriations for the salaries of teachers, supervisors and directors of agricultural subjects.

(b) Appropriations for salaries of teachers of trade, home economics and industrial subjects.

(c) Appropriations for the preparation of teachers, supervisors and directors of agricultural subjects and teachers of trade, and industrial, and home economics subjects.

Sec. 367-5. The state board of education shall have all necessary authority to co-operate with the federal board for vocational education in the administration of said act of congress and of any legislation pursuant thereto enacted by the state of Ohio, and in the administration of the funds provided by the federal government and the state of Ohio under the provisions of this act, for the promotion of vocational education in agriculture, commercial, industrial, trade, and home economics subjects. The board shall have authority to appoint such directors, supervisors and other assistants as may be necessary to carry out the provisions of this act, and fix their compensation; such appointments to be made upon the nomination of the secretary of the board. The salaries and traveling expenses of such directors, supervisors and assistants, and such other expenses as may be necessary to carry out the provisions of this act, shall be paid upon the approval of the board. They shall

Subjects for which funds are accepted.

Co-operation of state board with federal board.

Directors, supervisors and assistants; compensation and expenses; authority granted.

have full authority to formulate plans for the promotion of vocational education in such subjects as an essential and integral part of the public school system of education in Ohio; and to provide for the preparation of teachers of such subjects, and to expend federal and state funds appropriated under the provisions of this act for any purposes approved by the federal board for vocational education. They shall have authority to make studies and investigations relating to prevocational and vocational education in such subjects; to promote and aid in the establishment by local communities of schools, departments and classes, giving training in such subjects; to co-operate with local communities in the maintenance of such schools, departments and classes; to establish standards for the teachers, supervisors and directors of such subjects; and to co-operate in the maintenance of schools, departments, or classes supported and controlled by the public for the preparation of teachers, supervisors and directors of such subjects.

Sec. 367-6. Any school, department, or class giving instruction in agricultural, commercial, industrial, trade and home economics subjects approved by the state board of education and any school or college so approved, training teachers of such subjects, which receives the benefit of federal moneys as herein provided, shall be entitled also to receive for the salaries of teachers of said subjects an allotment of state money equal in amount to the amount of federal money which it receives, as herein provided, for the same year. The state board of education shall recommend to each session of the general assembly the amount of money which will need to be appropriated by the state for such allotments and for such other expenditures as may be necessary for the administration of this act, during the succeeding biennial period. The state board shall also recommend such additional legislation as may be necessary for the promotion and administration of vocational education in the state.

Approved schools shall receive state money equal in amount to federal money.

SECTION 2. That original sections 367-2, 367-5 and 367-6 of the General Code be, and the same are hereby repealed.

CARL R. KIMBALL,
Speaker of the House of Representatives.
CLARENCE J. BROWN,
President of the Senate.

*The sectional numbers in this act are in conformity to the General Code.
JOHN G. PRICE,
Attorney General.*

Passed April 17, 1919.
Approved May 15, 1919.

JAMES M. COX,
Governor.

Filed in the office of the Secretary of State at Columbus, Ohio, on the 17th day of May, A. D. 1919.

132 G.

[H. B. No. 396.]

AN ACT

To provide for the protection of agriculture and horticulture; to prevent the introduction into and the dissemination within the state of insect and disease pests injurious or harmful to plants or plant products; providing for inspection of nurseries; providing for quarantines necessary to the enforcement of this act; imposing penalties; and repealing original sections 1122, 1123, 1124, 1125, 1126, 1127, 1128, 1129, 1130, 1131, 1132, 1133, 1134, 1135, 1136, 1136-1, 1137, 1138, 1139 and 1140 of the General Code.

Be it enacted by the General Assembly of the State of Ohio:

Sec. 1122.

Definition of terms.

SECTION 1. For the purposes of this act, the following terms shall be construed, respectively to mean

(1) The singular and plural forms of any word or term in this act shall be interchangeable and equivalent within the meaning of this act.

(2) The word "person" shall include corporations, companies, societies, associations, partnerships, or any individual or combination of individuals. When construing and enforcing the provisions of this act, the act, omission or failure of any officer, agent, servant, or other individual acting for or employed by any person as above defined within the scope of his employment or office, shall in every case be deemed to be the act, omission or failure of such person, as well as that of the officer, agent, servant, or other employee.

(3) The term "insects," "insect pests," "diseases," or "plant diseases" mentioned in this act are defined as those insect pests and diseases injurious and harmful to plants and plant products of this state, including any of the stages of development of such pests or diseases.

(4) The term "nursery stock" shall include all field-grown florists' stock, trees, shrubs, vines, cuttings, grafts, scions, buds, fruit pits and other seeds of fruit and ornamental trees and shrubs, and other plants and plant products for propagation, except field, vegetable and flower seeds, bedding plants, and other herbaceous plants, bulbs and roots.

(5) The term "nursery" shall be construed to mean any grounds or premises on or in which nursery stock is propagated and grown for sale, or any grounds or premises on or in which nursery stock is being fumigated, treated, packed or stored.

(6) The term "nurseryman" shall mean the person who owns, leases, manages, or is in charge of a nursery.

(7) The term "dealer" shall be construed to apply to any person not a grower of nursery stock who buys nursery stock for the purpose of reselling or reshipping, independently of any control of a nursery.

(8) The term "agent" shall be construed as applying to any person soliciting orders for, or selling nursery

stock, under the partial or full control of a nurseryman, or of a dealer or other agent. This term shall also apply to any person engaged with a nurseryman, dealer, or agent in handling nursery stock on a co-operative basis.

(9) The term "landscape gardener" shall be construed to mean any person who plans or executes ornamental planting for others. He may prepare and transmit an order for nursery stock needed for such planting, provided that the payment for such stock shall be direct from the owner of the property on which the planting is made to the nurseryman, dealer or agent, and that no part of the remuneration of the landscape gardener shall be for nursery stock furnished or secured by him.

Sec. 1123. SECTION 2. The secretary of agriculture shall appoint a compentent entomologist as chief of the bureau of horticulture who shall be ex officio chief inspector, hereinafter called the "inspector," who shall be charged with the enforcement of the provisions of this act. Chief of bureau known as inspector.

Sec. 1124. SECTION 3. The secretary of agriculture is hereby authorized to appoint deputy inspectors who shall carry out the instructions of the inspector in the enforcement of the provisions of this act. Such deputy inspectors are hereby invested with the same police power as the inspector and shall be furnished with official badges or other insignia of authority, which shall be carried while on duty. Deputy inspectors; powers.

Sec. 1125. SECTION 4. The secretary of agriculture shall have the power to prescribe, modify, and enforce such rules, regulations, and orders as may be needed to carry out the provisions of this act, and may publish an annual report describing various phases of the inspection, or may publish such other information as may seem desirable, concerning the inspection and such insects and diseases as are covered by this act. Such rules and regulations shall be printed from time to time and furnished free to interested persons. Enforcement of rules and orders.

Sec. 1126. SECTION 5. The secretary of agriculture through the inspector or deputies shall at least once each year inspect all nurseries and other places in which nursery stock is stored or kept for sale. For this purpose such inspector or deputies shall have free access, within reasonable hours, to any field, orchard, garden, packing ground, building, cellar, freight or express office, warehouse, car, vessel, or other place, which it may be necessary or desirable for him to enter in carrying out the provisions of this act. It shall be unlawful to deny such access to the inspector or deputies or to hinder, thwart, or defeat such inspection by misrepresentation or concealment of facts or conditions or otherwise. Annual inspection of nurseries and nursery stock.

Sec. 1127. SECTION 6. The secretary of agriculture through the inspector or deputies shall have the authority to inspect any field or farm crop, orchard, fruit or garden plantation, park, cemetery, private premises, public place, and any place which might become infested or infected with dangerous or harmful insects or plant diseases. He shall also Inspection of farm crops, orchards, gardens, etc.

360

have the authority to inspect or reinspect at any time or place any nursery stock shipped in or into the state and to treat it as hereinafter provided in sections 11 and 12 respectively.

Sec. 1128. *Investigation of insect or plant diseases.*

SECTION 7. The secretary of agriculture through the inspector and deputies is hereby empowered to investigate outbreaks of dangerous insect or plant diseases occurring within the state and to prescribe and enforce such preventive and remedial measures as he may deem necessary to the control or eradication of such outbreaks, and for such purposes shall have free access to any property or premises within the state.

Sec. 1129. *Power to prevent shipping certain nursery stock or quarry products.*

SECTION 8. The secretary of agriculture is hereby empowered to prohibit and prevent the removal or shipment or transportation of nursery stock or any class of stone or quarry products, or any other article of any character whatsoever capable of carrying any injurious or harmful insect pest or plant disease from any private or public property, or property held or controlled by the state or any section of the state, which in the judgment of the secretary of agriculture may be dangerously infested or infected with insect pests or plant diseases, for such periods and under such conditions as, in the judgment of the secretary of agriculture seems necessary in order to prevent the further spread of the infestation or infection, giving such notice thereof as may be prescribed by the secretary of agriculture and during the existence of such order no person shall remove or ship from such area any such material whatever except by special permission or order of the secretary of agriculture, provided, however, that before the secretary of agriculture shall promulgate the order of quarantine as provided in this section, that the secretary of agriculture shall after due notice to interested persons, give a public hearing under such rules and regulations as the secretary of agriculture shall prescribe, at which hearing any interested person may appear and be heard, either in person or by attorney.

Sec. 1130. *Unlawful to permit insect or plant disease on premises.*

SECTION 9. It shall be unlawful for any person in this state knowingly to permit any destructive or dangerously harmful insect or plant disease to exist in or on his premises. It shall also be unlawful knowingly to sell or offer for sale any nursery stock infested or infected with such insect or disease.

Sec. 1131. *Notice when disease found; withholding certificate.*

SECTION 10. In case the inspector or deputy shall find present in or on any nurseryman or dealer's premises or any packing ground or in any cellar or building used for storage or sale of nursery stock, any injurious insect or plant disease, he shall notify the owner or person having charge of the premises in writing, to that effect, and the secretary of agriculture shall withhold his certificate hereinafter provided for, until the premises are freed from such injurious insect or plant disease, as hereinafter provided. It shall be unlawful for any person after receiving such notice to ship or deliver or cause to be shipped or delivered any nursery stock from such aforesaid premises.

Sec. 1132. SECTION 11. (1) If the inspector or deputy shall find on examination any nursery, field or farm crop, orchard, small fruit plantation, park, cemetery, or any private or public premises infested or infected with injurious insects or plant disease, he shall notify the owner or person having charge of such premises to that effect, and the owner or person having charge of the premises shall within ten days after such notice cause the removal and destruction of such trees, plants, shrubs or other plant material if incapable of successful treatment; otherwise cause them to be treated as the secretary of agriculture may direct. No damages shall be awarded to the owner for the loss or destruction of infested trees, plants, shrubs, or other plant material under this act. Such infested or infected trees, plants, shrubs, or other plant material shall be deemed to be a public nuisance. *[Disease or infection must be removed within ten days; damages.]*

(2) In case the owner or person in charge of such premises shall refuse or neglect to carry out the orders of the secretary of agriculture within ten days after receiving written notice, the secretary of agriculture may proceed to treat or destroy the infested or infected plants or plant material. The expense thereof shall be assessed, collected and enforced as taxes are assessed, collected and enforced against the premises upon which such expense was incurred. The amount of such expense when collected shall be paid to the secretary of agriculture and by him deposited with the state treasurer. *[When expense charged against premises.]*

Sec. 1133. SECTION 12. Nurserymen, dealers, and agents selling or delivering nursery stock in this state except as herein otherwise provided, shall make application in writing before June fifteenth of each year to the secretary of agriculture for inspection of their nursery stock growing in this state, or failing to give such notice, such nurserymen, dealers, or agents shall be liable for the additional expense of the inspector for the inspection of the nursery stock. *[Dealers shall apply for inspection before delivery.]*

Sec. 1134. SECTION 13. Every person receiving directly or indirectly any nursery stock from foreign countries shall notify the secretary of agriculture of the arrival of such shipment, the contents thereof, and the name of the consignor; and shall hold such shipment unopened until duly inspected or released by the secretary of agriculture. In case any infested or infected stock is discovered in such shipment, the shipment shall be subject to the provisions of section 22. *[Notice when stock is received from foreign countries.]*

Sec. 1135. SECTION 14. (1) The secretary of agriculture shall cause to be issued to each nurseryman in this state, after the nursery stock in his nursery has been officially inspected as provided in this act and found to be apparently free from injurious or harmful insects or plant disease, a certificate signed by the inspector setting forth the fact of such inspection. Said certificate shall be valid not to exceed one year from September fifteenth. *[Certificate of inspection.]*

(2) It shall be unlawful for any person to sell or offer for sale or to remove or ship from a nursery or other premises any nursery stock unless such stock has been officially inspected and a certificate or permit signed by the inspector has been granted by the secretary of agriculture.

Sec. 1136.

Nurserymen outside the state may obtain certificate.

SECTION 15. Nurserymen, residing or doing business outside the state desiring to solicit orders for nursery stock in the state shall upon filing a certified copy of their original state certificate with the secretary of agriculture, obtain a certificate permitting such persons to solicit orders for nursery stock in the state.

Sec. 1137.

All dealers must obtain certificate.

SECTION 16. Each dealer within the meaning of this act, located either within or without the state, engaged in selling nursery stock in the state or soliciting orders for nursery stock within this state, shall secure annually a dealer's certificate by furnishing a sworn affidavit that he will buy and sell only stock which has been duly inspected and certified by an official state or federal inspector; and that he will maintain with the secretary of agriculture a list of all sources from which he secures his stock. Such affidavit shall be accompanied by a fee of five dollars ($5.00).

Sec. 1138.

Agent's certificate required.

SECTION 17. All agents within the meaning of this act selling nursery stock or soliciting orders for nursery stock within the state for any nurseryman or dealer located within the state or outside the state shall file annually with the secretary of agriculture a sworn statement that he will sell only stock that has been duly inspected by an official state or federal inspector, accompanying such statement with a fee of one dollar, and shall secure and carry an agent's certificate and a copy of the certificate held by his principal. Said agent's certificate shall be issued only by the secretary of agriculture to agents authorized by their principal or upon request of their principal. Names and addresses of such agents shall not be divulged by the inspector nor the secretary of agriculture.

Sec. 1139.

Sworn statement by landscape gardener required.

SECTION 18. Each landscape gardener. within the meaning of this act, located either within or without the state, who shall practice his profession within the state, shall file annually with the secretary of agriculture a sworn statement that he will use and recommend only such nursery stock as shall have been duly inspected and certified by an official state or federal inspector, and that he will maintain with the secretary of agriculture a list of all sources from which he secures his stock.

Sec. 1140.

Revocation of certificate.

SECTION 19. The secretary of agriculture shall at any time have the power to revoke any certificate for sufficient cause, including any violation of this act, or non-conformity with any rule or regulation promulgated under this act.

Sec. 1140-1.

False declaration or concealment.

SECTION 20. (1) It shall be unlawful for any person to make a false declaration of acreage or to cause any concealment of nursery stock from inspection.

(2) Each person selling nursery stock in the state, shall if requested, furnish the secretary of agriculture with copies of his order forms, contracts and agreements with his customers which are furnished for the use of agents or customers, or both. *Copies of orders, etc., shall be furnished on request.*

Sec. 1140-2. SECTION 21. Each person who shall sell and deliver nursery stock in the state is hereby required to attach on the outside of each package, box, bale or carload lot sold or delivered a tag or poster on which shall appear an exact copy of his valid certificate. The use of tags or posters bearing an invalid or altered certificate, and the misuse of any valid certificate tag is hereby prohibited. *Poster on outside car, package, etc.*

Sec. 1140-3. SECTION 22. Except as herein otherwise provided, it shall be unlawful for any person to accept for transportation any nursery stock without a valid certificate plainly affixed on the outside of the package, box, bale or car containing the same, showing that the contents have been duly inspected by an official state or federal inspector, or without a valid certificate of inspection, or copy thereof, as provided in section 14. If nursery stock is shipped into this state from another state, country or province without having attached thereto the valid certificate of inspection of an official state or federal inspector, such failure must be promptly reported to the secretary of agriculture by the person transporting the same into this state, stating the names and addresses of the consignor and consignee and the nature of the shipment, and such nursery stock shall not be delivered to the consignee unless and until the inspector shall inspect and, finding such nursery stock apparently free from insect pests and plant diseases, shall release such nursery stock for delivery to consignee. If such stock be found to be infested or infected with insect pests or plant diseases it shall be seized and the shipper thereof notified to remove it from the state. If it be not removed from the state within ten days it may be destroyed. *Unlawful to accept for transportation without certificate.* *Seizure of stock, when.*

Sec. 1140-4. SECTION 23. (1) Any person in interest or affected by any order of the secretary of agriculture or inspector may appeal therefrom to the board of agriculture of Ohio within five days of the service of such order upon him setting forth in writing specifically and in full detail the order on which a hearing is desired, and every reason why such order is deemed to be unreasonable. *Appeal to secretary.*

(2) On receipt of such appeal the board of agriculture of Ohio shall with reasonable promptness order a hearing thereon and consider and determine the matters in question. Notice of the time and place of hearing shall be given to the petitioner and to such other persons as the board of agriculture of Ohio may direct. Such appeal shall suspend the operation of the order appealed from except as to the orders of the secretary of agriculture promulgating a quarantine as provided in section eight hereof. All hearings of the board of agriculture of Ohio shall be *Notice; hearing.*

open to the public. The appellant shall have the right to be represented by attorney.

SECTION 24. Any person violating any of the provisions of this act or any rule or regulation of the secretary of agriculture promulgated under this act shall be guilty of a misdemeanor and on conviction thereof shall be fined not exceeding the sum of of one hundred dollars ($100).

Sec. 1140-6.
Courts having jurisdiction.

SECTION 25. The probate court of each county shall have original and final jurisdiction in prosecutions under the provisions of this act. Such court shall be opened at all times for such purposes regardless of the terms fixed therein for the trial of criminal cases, and the complainant shall not be required to give security for costs. The prosecuting attorney of each county, or the attorney general, shall conduct such prosecutions and all fines recovered shall be paid to the secretary of agriculture.

SECTION 26. This act shall take effect and be in force from and after its passage and approval.

Repeals.

SECTION 27. Orginial sections 1122, 1123, 1124, 1125, 1126, 1127, 1128, 1129, 1130, 1131, 1132, 1133, 1134, 1135, 1136, 1136-1, 1137, 1138, 1139 and 1140 of the General Code of Ohio be and are hereby repealed.

CARL R. KIMBALL,
Speaker of the House of Representatives.
CLARENCE J. BROWN,
President of the Senate.

The sectional numbers on the margin hereof are designated as provided by law.
JOHN G. PRICE,
Attorney General.

Passed April 17, 1919.
Approved May 15, 1919.

JAMES M. COX,
Governor.

Filed in the office of the Secretary of State at Columbus, Ohio, on the 17th day of May, A. D. 1919.

133 G.

[House Bill No. 257.]

AN ACT

To further supplement section 9921 by the addition of supplementary section 9921-6 of the General Code, authorizing the employment of home demonstration agents in the several counties of the state, and providing for the further development of agriculture.

Be it enacted by the General Assembly of the State of Ohio:

SECTION 1. That section 9921 be further supplemented by adding supplementary section 9921-6 of the General Code to read as follows:

Appropriation for home demonstration agent; duties of agent.

Sec. 9921-6. The county commissioners of each and every county of the state in addition to the powers conferred in section 9921-4 of the General Code are herby authorized and empowered to make additional appropriations annually to further the development of agriculture and country life in the county including the employment of a home demonstration agent and the county commissioners of said county or counties are authorized to set apart and appropriate said sum of money and transmit the same to the state treasurer who shall place it to the credit of the agricultural extension fund to be paid for the purpose aforesaid by warrant issued by the auditor of state on voucher approved by the Ohio state university. If for any reason it shall not be used as contemplated in this act, it shall revert to the county from which it came. The home demonstration agent shall acquaint herself with conditions in the county to which she is assigned, and as far as practicable, respond to invitations with reference to the selection and preparation of foods for persons both in health and sickness, the feeding of infants, the preservation and storage of foods, the choice of fabrics and making of garments, the arrangement and installation of household mechanical devices, and the choice and repair of household furnishings and decorations. She shall cooperate with the United States department of agriculture, the Ohio agricultural experiment station, and other public agencies to the end that the women of the county may have at hand the services of these agencies. She shall have an office in which bulletins and other printed matter and records of value to housewives may be consulted and through which the agent may at all times be reached as she travels from home to home in the discharge of her duties. After having appropriated under this section and a home demonstration agent having been employed for the county, the county commissioners shall appropriate under this section in each succeeding year for five years not less than one thousand dollars.

The sectional number in this act is in conformity to the General Code.
JOHN G. PRICE, Attorney General.

CARL R. KIMBALL,
Speaker of the House of Representatives.
CLARENCE J. BROWN,
President of the Senate.

Passed April 10, 1919.
Approved May 15, 1919.

JAMES M. COX,
Governor.

Filed in the office of the Secretary of State at Columbus, Ohio, on the 17th day of May, A. D. 1919.

134 G.

Repeal.

SECTION 2. That said original section 10933 of the
General Code, as amended, March 21st, 1917, Volume 107,
Ohio Laws, page 404, be and the same is hereby repealed.

CARL R. KIMBALL,
Speaker of the House of Representatives.
CLARENCE J. BROWN,
President of the Senate.

The sectional
number in this
act is in con-
formity to the
General Code.
JOHN G. PRICE,
*Attorney
General.*

Passed April 16, 1919.
Approved May 15, 1919.

JAMES M. COX,
Governor.

Filed in the office of the Secretary of State at Columbus,
Ohio, on the 17th day of May, A. D. 1919.

135 G.

[House Bill No. 281.]

AN ACT

To amend sections 6602-1, 6602-4, 6602-8b, and 6602-8h of the
General Code, relative to county sewer districts.

Be it enacted by the General Assembly of the State of Ohio:
SECTION 1. That sections 6602-1, 6602-4, 6602-8b, and
6602-8h of the General Code, be amended to read as follows:

Sewers outside
of municipalities;
name, number,
outlet.

Sec. 6602-1. For the purpose of preserving and pro-
moting the public health and welfare, the boards of county
commissioners of the several counties of this state may, by
resolution, lay out, establish and maintain one or more sewer
districts within their respective counties, outside of incorporated municipalities. Each district shall be designated
by an appropriate name or number. Any board of county
commissioners may acquire, construct, maintain and operate
such main, branch, intercepting, or local sewer or sewers
within any such sewer district, and such outlet sewer or sewers and sewage treatment or disposal works within or without such sewer district, as may be necessary to care for and
conduct the sewage or surface water from any or all parts
of such sewer district to a proper outlet, so as to properly
treat or dispose of same. Any such board of county com-

Employment of
sanitary engi-
neer.

missioners may employ a competent sanitary engineer for
such time or times and on such terms as they deem best; and,
in any county having a population exceeding 100,000, the
board of county commissioners may create and maintain a
sanitary engineering department, to be under their supervision and in charge of a competent sanitary engineer, to be appointed by such board of county commissioners, for the purpose of aiding them in the performance of their duties under
this act or their other duties regarding sanitation provided
by law; and said board shall provide suitable rooms for the
use of such department and shall provide for and pay the

compensation of such engineer and all necessary expenses of such engineer and department which may be authorized by such board. Any such sanitary engineer in charge of such sanitary engineering department, so appointed by such board of county commissioners, may, with the approval of such board, appoint necessary assistants and clerks and the compensation of any such assistants and clerks shall be fixed and paid by such board. The board of county commissioners may make, publish and enforce rules and regulations for the construction, maintenance, protection and use of sewers and sewer improvements in their respective counties outside of incorporated municipalities, including the establishment of connections. Such rules and regulations shall not be inconsistent with the laws of the state of Ohio or the rules and regulations of the state board of health. No sewers or sewage treatment works shall be constructed in any county outside of incorporated municipalities by any person, firm, or corporation, until the plans and specifications for the same shall have been approved by the board of county commissioners, and any such construction shall be done under the supervision of the county sanitary engineer, and any person, firm, or corporation, proposing or constructing such improvements, shall pay to the county all expenses incurred by the commissioners in connection therewith. The sanitary engineer shall have the right to enter upon any public or private property for the purpose of making surveys or examinations necessary for the laying out of sewer districts or designing or examining sewers or treatment works, and to make such surveys and examinations. No person, firm, or corporation shall forbid or interfere with the sanitary engineer or his duly authorized assistants entering upon such property for such purpose or making such surveys or examinations. If, however, actual damage is done to property by the making of such surveys and examinations, the commissioners shall pay the reasonable value of such damage to the owner of the property damaged, and such cost shall be included in the assessment upon the property benefited by the improvement for which such surveys and examinations are made. Any person or persons violating any provisions of this act or any rules or regulations herein provided for shall be liable to a fine not exceeding one hundred ($100.00) dollars to be paid on conviction of such violation. All fines imposed and collected shall be paid to the county treasurer and credited to any county sewer improvement or maintenance fund as the county commissioners shall direct.

Sec. 6602-4. For the purpose of paying a part or the whole of the cost of construction, maintenance, repair or operation of any improvement provided for in this act or for paying the sanitary engineer provided for under the provisions of this act, and for paying for his assistants and all his other necessary expenses, the board of county commissioners may borrow money at a rate of not exceeding six

[marginal notes: Appointment of assistants. Rules and regulations. Plans and specifications. Interference with engineer prohibited. Payment of damages. Penalty for violations. Authority to borrow money to construct or maintain.]

(6%) per cent per annum on certificates of indebtedness to be signed by its president and clerk; such certificates of indebtedness shall be made payable at a time not more than five (5) years from their date, or, for such purposes, the board of county commissioners may issue bonds as herein provided, or may appropriate money from any funds in the county treasury available. After the adoption of the improvement resolution, to provide means to pay the cost of any such improvement, the board of county commissioners shall, by resolution of said board, appropriate any funds in the county treasury available for that purpose or, when necessary, may authorize the issue of bonds of the county in an amount not exceeding the estimated cost thereof by more than ten per cent, plus such amount as shall be necessary to pay the installments of interest on such bonds or on certificates of indebtedness to accrue before the first installment of taxes and assessments hereinafter provided for shall be collected. Such bonds shall state the particular improvement or improvements on account of which they are issued and the date of resolution or order of the board directing their issuance. Such bonds may bear interest at a rate not exceeding six (6%) per cent per annum, payable semi-annually, may be of such denominations and payable at such time and place as the board of county commissioners shall provide and may be issued from time to time as the work progresses and advertised and sold as other county bonds are required to be advertised and sold.

Resolution appropriating funds; bonds. *(margin note)*

Sec. 6602-8b. The county sanitary engineer, upon the completion of any such improvement, shall prepare and present to the board an estimated assessment, in proportion as nearly as may be, to the benefits resulting from such improvement or improvements to such lots and lands respectively. The board of county commissioners shall cause notice to be published once a week for two consecutive weeks in a newspaper published and of general circulation within the county, that such estimated assessment has been made and is on file in the office of such board and that the same may be examined by all persons interested. Such notice shall contain a description of the lots or parcels of land within said district to be assessed, and shall designate a time and place, to be fixed by such board, when and where objections to the apportionment made in such estimated assessment will be heard by the board. Any such objections shall be in writing and shall be filed within ten (10) days after the date of the last publication of such notice. At the time and place designated for such hearing, or at other time or times to which such hearing may be adjourned, the board shall consider any such objections and hear and consider any competent evidence concerning any such objections, and shall determine any questions involved and may, if deemed proper, amend such estimated assessment and shall approve and confirm the same as made or as so amended, and, when so confirmed, the same shall be final and conclusive. The

Estimated assessment filed with board; publication of estimates. *(margin note)*

Written objections, when filed; hearing. *(margin note)*

board of county commissioners may, from time to time and at such intervals as they may deem expedient, assess the lots and parcels of land specified in said notice of assessment and levy taxes upon the taxable property of the district so improved, to pay the cost of the maintenance and operation of any such improvement or improvements, including disposal of sewage, after completion thereof, and no notice shall be necessary of such maintenance, repair or operation assessment unless the amount thereof shall exceed ten per cent of the original cost of the construction. If such maintenance, repair and operation assessment shall exceed ten per cent of the original cost of the construction, the method and manner of making said assessment, together with the notice thereof, shall be the same as provided herein for the original assessment. Assessments and tax levies for maintenance and repair.

Sec. 6602-h. At any time after the formation of any sewer district, the board of county commissioners, when deemed expedient, may, on application by a corporation, individual or public institution outside of any sewer district, contract with such corporation, individual or public institution for depositing sewage from premises outside such district in the sewers constructed or to be constructed to serve such district and for the treatment or disposal thereof, on such terms and conditions as shall be by such board of county commissioners deemed equitable, but the amount to be paid shall in no case be less than the original assessment for similar property within the district, and such board of county commissioners, in any such case, shall appropriate any monies received for such service to and for the use and benefit of such sewer district; provided, however, that whenever the board of county commissioners deem it necessary to contract with a corporation, individual or public institution for depositing sewage from premises outside such sewer district in the sewers constructed or to be constructed to serve such district, they shall so determine by resolution, and may collect said amount in cash, or the same may be assessed against said lots or parcels of land, and the method and manner of making said assessment, together with the notice thereof, shall be the same as provided herein for the original assessment. May contract for depositing or disposing of sewage, in certain cases.

Whenever a sewer or sewers have been constructed by a corporation, individual or public institution at their own cost and expense for the purpose of supplying sanitary drainage to any allotment, development, subdivision or similar enterprise, or to any institution, and it is deemed expedient by the board of county commissioners to acquire said sewer or sewers or any part thereof for the purpose of supplying sanitary drainage to territory outside the allotment, subdivision, development or other such enterprise for which such sewer or sewers were constructed, the sanitary engineer shall examine said sewer or sewers and, if he finds the same properly designed and constructed, he shall make an appraisal of the present value of said sewer or sewers Acquisition of sewers already constructed; appraisement; resolution to purchase; assessment of cost.

or parts thereof to the district as a means of supplying sanitary drainage to territory outside the allotment, subdivision, development or similar enterprise for which it was originally constructed and shall certify same to the board of county commissioners. In such appraisal no allowance shall be made for the value of such sewer or sewers to the territory for the service of which it was originally constructed. The board of county commissioners, by resolution, may determine to purchase said sewer or sewers at a cost not to exceed the present value of said sewer or sewers as certified by the sanitary engineer. For the purpose of paying for said sewer or sewers and the maintenance thereof, the board of county commissioners may issue bonds and assess the cost against the benefited property in the same method and manner as provided herein for the construction of an original sewer.

Repeals. SECTION 2. That said original sections 6602-1, 6602-4, 6602-8b and 6602-8h of the General Code be, and the same are hereby repealed.

The sectional numbers in this act are in conformity to the General Code. JOHN G. PRICE, Attorney General.

CARL R. KIMBALL,
Speaker of the House of Representatives.
CLARENCE J. BROWN,
President of the Senate.

Passed April 10, 1919.
Approved May 16, 1919.

JAMES M. COX,
Governor.

Filed in the office of the Secretary of State at Columbus, Ohio, on the 17th day of May, A. D. 1919.

136 G.

[House Bill No. 29.]

AN ACT

To amend sections 504-2 and 504-3 of the General Code, enlarging the powers and duties of the public utilities commission with reference to the abandonment of service and facilities by railroad and public utilities.

Be it enacted by the General Assembly of the State of Ohio:

SECTION 1. That sections 504-2 and 504-3 of the General Code be amended to read as follows:

Abandonment of track, depot, line, pumping stations, etc.; forfeiture. Sec. 504-2. No railroad as defined in section 501 of the General Code, operating any railroad in the state of Ohio, and no public utility as defined in section 614-2a of the General Code furnishing service or facilities within the state of Ohio, shall abandon or be required to abandon or withdraw any main track or tracks or depot of a railroad or main pipe line, gas line, telegraph line or telephone toll line, electric light line, water line or steam pipe line, or any portion thereof, pumping station, generating plant, power

373

station, or service station of a public utility, or the service
rendered thereby, which has once been laid, constructed,
opened and used for public business, nor shall be closed for
traffic or service thereon, therein or thereover except as provided in section 504-3. Any railroad or public utility violating the provisions of this section shall forfeit and pay
into the state treasury not less than one hundred ($100.00)
dollars, nor more than one thousand ($1,000.00) dollars, and
shall be subject to all other legal and equitable remedies for
the enforcement of the provisions of this act.

Sec. 504-3. Any such railroad or any political subdivision desiring to abandon, close, or have abandoned, withdrawn or closed for traffic or service all or any part of such
main track or tracks, or depot, and any such public utility,
or political subdivision desiring to abandon or close, or have
abandoned, withdrawn or closed for traffic or service all or
any part of such line or lines, pumping station, generating
plant, power station or service station, shall first make application to the public utilities commission in writing who
shall thereupon cause reasonable notice thereof to be given,
stating the time and place fixed by the commission for the
hearing of said application. Upon the hearing of said application said commission shall ascertain the facts, and make
its finding thereon, and if such facts satisfy the commission that the proposed abandonment, withdrawal or closing
for traffic or service is reasonable, having due regard for
the welfare of the public and the cost of operating the
service or facility, they may allow the same; otherwise it
shall be denied, or if the facts warrant, the application may
be granted in a modified form. Provided, however, that
should the application ask for the abandonment or withdrawal of any main track, main pipe line, gas line, telegraph line or telephone toll line, electric light line, water
line or steam pipe line, pumping station, generating plant,
power station, service station, or the service rendered thereby, in such manner as can result in the permanent abandonment of service between any two points on such railroad, or
of service and facilities of any such public utility, no application shall be granted unless the company or public utility
shall have operated said track, pipe line, gas line, telegraph
line or telephone toll line, electric light line, water line, or
steam pipe line, pumping station, generating plant, power
station or service station for a period of at least five years,
and such notice shall be given by publication in a newspaper
of general circulation throughout any county or municipality which may have granted a franchise to said company
or public utility, under which said track, pipe line, gas line,
telegraph line or telephone toll line, electric light line, water
line or steam pipe line, pumping station, generating plant,
power station or service station is operated or in which the
same is located, once a week for four consecutive weeks before the hearing of said application, and notice of said hearing shall be given such county, municipality or public utility

Application to commission for abandonment.

Hearing upon abandonment.

in the manner provided for the service of orders of the commission in section 614-71 of the General Code, and except that the provisions of section 504-2 and 504-3 shall not apply to a gas company when removing or exchanging abandoned field lines.

To what provisions apply.

The provisions of this section shall apply to all such service now rendered and facilities furnished or hereafter built and operated, and an order of the commission authorizing the abandonment or withdrawal of any such service or facility shall not affect rights and obligations of a railroad or public utility beyond the scope of said order, anything in its franchise to the contrary notwithstanding.

Repeals.

SECTION 2. That said original sections 504-2 and 504-3 of the General Code be, and the same are hereby repealed.

The sectional numbers in this act are in conformity to the General Code. JOHN G. PRICE, Attorney General.

CARL R. KIMBALL,
Speaker of the House of Representatives.
CLARENCE J. BROWN,
President of the Senate.

Passed April 15, 1919.
Approved May 16, 1919.

JAMES M. COX,
Governor.

Filed in the office of the Secretary of State at Columbus, Ohio, on the 17th day of May, A. D. 1919.

137 G.

]House Bill No. 20.[

AN ACT

To amend section 2253 of the General Code as amended 104 O. L. 250, relating to expenses of judges incurred while holding court in a county where he does not reside.

Be it enacted by the General Assembly of the State of Ohio:

SECTION 1. That section 2253 of the General Code be amended to read as follows:

Additional allowance when holding court outside the county of residence.

Sec. 2253. In addition to the annual salary and expenses provided for in sections 1529, 2251, 2252-1, each judge of the court of common pleas and of the court of appeals, shall receive his actual and necessary expenses, not exceeding three hundred dollars in any one year for a judge of the court of common pleas and not exceeding six hundred dollars in any one year for a judge of the court of appeals, incurred while holding court in a county in which he does not reside, to be paid from the state treasury upon the warrant of the auditor of state, issued to such judge; each judge of the court of common pleas who is assigned by the chief justice by virtue of section 1469, to aid in disposing of business of some county other than that in which he resides, shall receive ten dollars per day for each day of such as-

signment, and his actual and necessary expenses incurred in
holding court under such assignment, to be paid from the
treasury of the county to which he is so assigned upon the
warrant of the auditor of such county, and the amount allowed herein for actual and necessary expenses shall not
exceed three hundred dollars in any one year for a judge
of the court of common pleas nor six hundred dollars for a
judge of the court of appeals.

SECTION 2. That said original section 2253 of the
General Code be and the same is hereby repealed.

CARL R. KIMBALL,
Speaker of the House of Representatives.
CLARENCE J. BROWN,
President of the Senate.

Passed April 17, 1919.
Approved May 15, 1919.

JAMES M. COX,
Governor.

Filed in the office of the Secretary of State at Columbus,
Ohio, on the 17th day of May, A. D. 1919.

. 138 G.

The sectional number in this act is in conformity to the General Code. JOHN G. PRICE, *Attorney General.*

[House Bill No. 280.]

AN ACT

To amend sections 6602-17, 6602-20, 6602-26 and 6602-32 of the General Code, relative to water supply and waterworks systems in county sewer districts.

Be it enacted by the General Assembly of the State of Ohio:

SECTION 1. That sections 6602-17, 6602-20, 6602-26
and 6602-32 of the General Code be amended to read as
follows:

Sec. 6602-17. For the purpose of preserving and pro-
moting the public health and welfare, and providing fire
protection, the boards of county commissioners of the several counties of this state may by resolution, acquire, construct, maintain and operate any public water supply or
waterworks system within their respective counties, not outside of any established sewer district. In this act "public
water supply" shall mean any or all of the following:
Wells, springs, streams or other source of water supply,
pumping equipment, treatment or purification plants, distributing mains, cisterns, reservoirs, necessary equipment
for fire protection, other equipment, and lands, rights-of-
way and easements, necessary for the proper development
and distribution of the supply. Any board of county commissioners may acquire, construct, maintain and operate
such public water supply and may provide for the protection thereof and prevent the pollution and unnecessary

Commissioners may construct and maintain water supply system not outside sewer districts.

waste thereof. By contract with any municipal corporation, or any person, firm or private corporation furnishing
a public water supply within or without their county, they
may provide such supply of water to such sewer district or
districts from the waterworks of such municipality, person, firm or private corporation. The sanitary engineer, if
any, or sanitary engineering department, if any, of such
county shall, in addition to other duties assigned to such
engineer or department assist the commissioners in the performance of their duties under this act, and shall be charged
with such other duties and services in relation thereto as
the commissioners may prescribe. The board of county
commissioners may make, publish and enforce rules and
regulations for the construction, maintenance, protection
and use of public water supplies in their respective counties
outside of incorporated municipalities, including the establishment of connections. Such rules and regulations shall
not be inconsistent with the laws of the state of Ohio or the
rules and regulations of the state board of health. No public water supplies or water pipes or mains shall be constructed in any county outside of incorporated municipalities by any person, firm or corporation, except for the purpose of supplying water to such incorporated municipalities, until the plans and specifications for the same shall
have been approved by the board of county commissioners,
and any such construction shall be done under the supervision of the county sanitary engineer, and any person, firm
or corporation, proposing or constructing such improvements, shall pay to the county all expense incurred by the
commissioners in connection therewith. The sanitary engineer shall have the right to enter upon any public or
private property for the purpose of making surveys and
examinations necessary for the design or examination of
public water supplies, and to make such surveys and examinations. No person, firm, or corporation shall forbid or
interfere with the sanitary engineer, or his duly authorized
assistants entering upon such property for such purpose, or
making such surveys or examinations. If, however, actual
damage is done to property by the making of such surveys
and examinations, the commissioners shall pay the reasonable value of such damage to the owner of the property
damaged and such cost shall be included in the assessment
upon the property benefited by the improvement for which
such surveys and examinations are made. Any person or
persons violating any provision of this act or any rules or
regulations herein provided for shall be liable to a fine not
exceeding one hundred ($100.00) dollars to be paid on con-
viction of such violation. All fines imposed and collected
shall be paid to the county treasurer and credited to such
fund as the commissioners may determine. The commissioners may fix reasonable rates to be charged for water,
when the source of supply or distributing pipes are owned

Rules and regu-
lations.

Costs and dam-
ages; assess-
ment; fines.

by the county or district. When the source of supply is owned by a municipal corporation, or any person, firm or private corporation, the schedule of rates to be charged by such municipal corporation, person, firm or private corporation shall be ratified by the board of county commissioners at the time any contract is entered into for the use of water from such municipal corporation, person, firm or private corporation. All money collected as rents or for waterworks purposes from any district shall be paid to the county treasurer and kept in a separate and distinct fund to the credit of such district. Such fund shall be applied first to the conduct, management and operation of such water supply or waterworks system, and any surplus thereafter remaining shall be applied to the enlargement or extension thereof, to the payment of interest or principal of any loan, indebtedness or liability incurred in connection therewith, or for the creation of a sinking fund for the liquidation of any debt created in connection therewith; but in no case shall money so collected be expended otherwise than for the use and benefit of such district.

Sec. 6602-20. For the purpose of paying a part or the whole of the cost of construction, maintenance, repair or operation of any improvement provided for in this act or for paying the sanitary engineer and for paying for his assistants and all his other necessary expenses, the board of county commissioners may borrow money at the rate of not exceeding six (6%) per cent per annum on certificates of indebtedness to be signed by its president and clerk; such certificates of indebtedness shall be made payable at a time not more than five (5) years from their date, or for such purposes the board of county commissioners may issue bonds as herein provided, or may appropriate money from any funds in the county treasury available. After the adoption of the improvement resolution, to provide means to pay the cost of any such improvement, the board of county commissioners shall, by resolution of said board, appropriate money from any funds in the county treasury available for that purpose or, when necessary, may authorize the issue of bonds of the county in an amount not exceeding the estimated cost thereof by more than ten per cent, plus such amount as shall be necessary to pay the installments of interest, on such bonds or on certificates of indebtedness to accrue before the first installment of taxes and assessments hereinafter provided for shall be collected. Such bonds shall state the particular improvement or improvements on account of which they are issued and the date of resolution or order of the board directing their issuance. Such bonds may bear interest at a rate not exceeding six (6) per cent per annum, payable semi-annually, may be of such denominations and payable at such time and place as the board of county commissioners shall provide, and may be issued from time to time as the work progresses and advertised and sold as other county bonds are required to be advertised and sold.

Publication of estimated assessments.

Sec. 6602-26. The county sanitary engineer, upon the completion of any improvement, shall prepare and present to the board, an estimated assessment in proportion, as nearly as may be, to the benefits resulting from such improvement or improvements to such lots and lands respectively. The board of county commissioners shall cause notice to be published once a week for two consecutive weeks in a newspaper published and of general circulation within the county, that such estimated assessment has been made and is on file in the office of such board and that the same may be examined by all persons interested. Such notice

Written objections; hearing; tax levy for maintenance.

shall contain a description of the lots or parcels of land within said district to be assessed, and shall designate a time and place, to be fixed by such board, when and where objections to the apportionment made in such estimated assessment will be heard by the board. Any such objections shall be in writing and shall be filed within ten days after the date of the last publication of such notice. At the time and place designated for such hearing, or at any other time or times to which such hearing may be adjourned, the board shall consider any such objections and hear and consider any competent evidence concerning any such objections and shall determine any questions involved and may, if deemed proper, amend such estimated assessment and shall approve and confirm the same as made or as so amended, and, when so confirmed, the same shall be final and conclusive. The board of county commissioners may, from time to time and at such intervals as they may deem expedient, assess the lots and parcels of land specified in said notice of assessment and levy taxes upon the taxable property of the district so improved, to pay the cost of the maintenance and operation of any such improvement or improvements, after completion thereof, and no further notice shall be necessary of such maintenance, repair or operation assessment unless the amount thereof shall exceed ten per cent of the original cost of the construction. If such maintenance, repair or operation assessment shall exceed ten per cent of the original cost of the construction, the method and manner of making such assessment, together with the notice thereof, shall be the same as provided herein for the original assessment.

May contract to supply water outside sewer district.

Sec. 6602-32. At any time after the formation of any sewer district, the board of county commissioners, when deemed expedient, may, on application by a corporation, individual or public institution, outside of any sewer district, contract with such corporation, individual or public institution for supplying water to their premises on such terms and conditions as shall be by such board of county commissioners deemed equitable, but the amount to be paid shall in no case be less than the original assessment for similar property within the district, and such board of county commissioners, in any such case, shall appropriate any moneys received for such service to and for the use and benefit of such sewer district; provided, however, that when-

ever the board of county commissioners deem it necessary
to contract with a corporation, individual or public institution outside of any sewer district for supplying water to
their premises from water supply lines constructed or to be
constructed to serve such district, they shall so determine
by resolution and may collect said amount in cash, or the
same may be assessed against said lots or parcels of land,
and the method and manner of making said assessment, together with the notice thereof, shall be the same as provided
herein for the original assessment.

Whenever a water supply line or lines have been con- *May acquire water supply lines, how.*
structed by a corporation, individual or public institution
at their own cost and expense for the purpose of supplying
water to any allotment, development, subdivision or similar
enterprise, or to any institution, and it is deemed expedient
by the board of county commissioners to acquire said water
supply line or lines or any part thereof for the purpose of
supplying water to territory outside the allotment, subdivision, development or other such enterprise for which such
line or lines were constructed, the sanitary engineer shall
examine said water supply line or lines and if he finds the
same properly designed and constructed, he shall make an
appraisal of the present value of said water supply line or
lines or parts thereof to the district as a means of supplying
water to territory outside the allotment, subdivision, development or similar enterprise for which it was originally constructed and shall certify same to the board of county commissioners. In such appraisal no allowance shall be made
for the value of such water supply line or lines to the territory for the service of which it was originally constructed.

The board of county commissioners, by resolution, may *Resolution to purchase; bond issue.*
determine to purchase said water supply line or lines at a
cost not to exceed the present value of said water supply line
or lines as certified by the sanitary engineer. For the purpose of paying for said water supply line or lines and the
maintenance thereof, the board of county commissioners
may issue bonds and assess the cost against the benefited
property in the same method and manner as provided herein
for the construction of an original water supply line or
lines.

SECTION 2. That said original sections 6602-17, 6602- *Repeals.*
20, 6602-26, and 6602-32 of the General Code be, and the
same are hereby repealed.

The sectional numbers in this act are in con-formity to the General Code. JOHN G. PRICE, Attorney General.

CARL R. KIMBALL,
Speaker of the House of Representatives.
CLARENCE J. BROWN,
President of the Senate.

Passed April 10, 1919.
Approved May 16, 1919.

JAMES M. COX,
Governor.

Filed in the office of the Secretary of State at Columbus,
Ohio, on the 17th day of May, A. D. 1919.

139 G.

[House Bill No. 460.]

AN ACT

Providing for the transfer of former road district funds to the county road fund and making provision for the payment of interest and principal of outstanding road district bonds.

Be it enacted by the General Assembly of the State of Ohio:

Authority to transfer funds of road districts and to provide for their application.

SECTION 1. Funds of road districts which were in existence at the time of the taking effect of the act passed May 17, 1915, approved June 2, 1915, entitled "an act to provide a system of highway laws for the state of Ohio, and to repeal all sections of the General Code, and acts, inconsistent herewith," shall be transferred to the road fund of the county, and the same shall be under the control of the county commissioners. Interest upon outstanding and unpaid bonds duly issued to meet the expense of the improvement of a road or roads in any road district, prior to the passage of said act, shall be paid from funds so transferred, and the county commissioners shall, annually make such tax levies upon the property comprised within such road districts as may be necessary to pay the interest upon such bonds and provide a sinking fund for their redemption at maturity. Whenever the same may become necessary, the county commissioners may refund such bonds in the manner provided by law for refunding of other bonds of the county.

This act is not of a general or permanent nature and requires no sectional number. JOHN G. PRICE, Attorney General.

CARL R. KIMBALL,
Speaker of the House of Representatives.
CLARENCE J. BROWN,
President of the Senate.

Passed May 6, 1919.
Approved May 15, 1919.

JAMES M. COX,
Governor.

Filed in the office of the Secretary of State at Columbus, Ohio, on the 17th day of May, A. D. 1919.

140 L.

[House Bill No. 292.]

AN ACT

To repeal sections 1683-12, 1683-13, 1683-14, 1683-15, 1683-16, 1683-17, 1683-18 and 1683-19 of the General Code, providing for a court of domestic relations for Lucas county, Ohio, and prescribing the jurisdiction of said court.

Be it enacted by the General Assembly of the State of Ohio:

Court of domestic relations, Lucas county.

SECTION 1. That the act of the General Assembly of the state of Ohio entitled an act to provide a court of domestic relations for Lucas county, Ohio, and prescribing the jurisdiction of said court, passed March 21st, 1917, also designated as sections 1683-12, 1683-13, 1683-14, 1683-15, 1683-16, 1683-17, 1683-18 and 1683-19 of the General Code of Ohio, be and the same is hereby repealed.

SECTION 2. All cases, matters and proceedings pending Jurisdiction. in the said court of domestic relations of Lucas county, Ohio, at the time this repealing act takes effect, of which the court of common pleas of Lucas county, Ohio, has or may have jurisdiction, shall be transferred to said court of common pleas and shall proceed to final adjudication therein. All other cases, matters or proceedings pending in said court of domestic relations at the time of the taking effect of this act shall be transferred to the proper court having jurisdiction thereof located in Lucas county, Ohio.

SECTION 3. Nothing in this act shall effect any judg- Former judgments, decrees or orders not affected. ments, decrees or orders rendered or made in said court of domestic relations, and the same shall remain in full force and effect and may be carried into execution by the proper officers or by further proceedings in any court in Lucas county, Ohio, which would hereafter have jurisdiction in like cases.

This act is not of a general or permanent nature and requires no sectional number.
JOHN G. PRICE,
Attorney General.

CARL R. KIMBALL,
Speaker of the House of Representatives.
CLARENCE J. BROWN,
President of the Senate.

Passed April 9, 1919.
Approved May 15, 1919.

JAMES M. COX,
Governor.

Filed in the office of the Secretary of State at Columbus, Ohio, on the 17th day of May, A. D. 1919.

141 G.

[House Bill No. 474.]

AN ACT

To amend sections 9880, 9880-1, 9881, 9882, 9884, 9894 and 9899 and to add supplementary sections 9884-1 to 9884-4 inclusive, and to repeal sections 9880-1, 9883, 9911, 9914 and 9915 of the General Code, relative to county agricultural societies.

Be it enacted by the General Assembly of the State of Ohio:

SECTION 1. That sections 9880, 9880-1, 9881, 9882, 9884, 9894 and 9899 be amended and supplementary sections 9884-1 to 9884-4, inclusive, of the General Code be added, to read as follows:

Sec. 9880. When thirty or more persons, residents of Organization of societies. a county organize themselves into a county agricultural society, which adopts a constitution and by-laws, selects the usual and proper officers, and otherwise conducts its affairs in conformity to law, and the rules of the state board of agriculture, and when such county society has held an annual exhibition in accordance with sections 9881, 9882 and 9884 of the General Code, and made proper report to the state board, then upon presentation to the county auditor, of a certificate from the president of the state board attested by the secretary thereof, that the laws of the state and the rules of the board have been complied with, the county auditor of each county wherein such agricultural societies are organized, annually shall draw an order on the treasurer of the county in favor of the president of the county agricultural society for a sum equal to two cents to each inhabitant thereof, on the basis of the last previous national census. The total amount of such order, shall not exceed one hundred per cent of the amount paid in regular class premiums, and shall not in any county exceed two cents for each inhabitant as aforesaid or the sum of eight hundred dollars, and the treasurer of the county shall pay it.

Independent societies, organization of. Sec. 9880-1. When thirty or more persons of a county or of contiguous counties, not to exceed three shall have been organized into an independent agricultural society and has held an annual exhibit for three years previous to January 1st, 1919, in a county wherein is located a county agricultural society, and when such independent society has held an annual exhibition, in accordance with the three following sections and made proper report to the state board, then, upon the presentation to the county auditor of a certificate from the president of the state board attested by the secretary thereof, that the laws of Ohio and the rules of the board have been complied with, the county auditor of the county, if the fair board be residents of one county, shall draw an order on the treasurer of the county in favor of the president of the independent association for a sum equal to one hundred per cent of the amount paid in regular class premiums, as calculated in section 9880 herein and the treasurer shall pay said order.

Payment of class premiums. If the fair board be residents of more than one county the auditor of such counties shall draw orders on their respective treasurers for the proportionate share of an amount equal to an average amount paid to the several county fair boards to be divided according to population of the counties according to the last federal census, but shall not exceed more than one hundred per cent of the amount paid in regular class premiums, nor the amount of two cents for each inhabitant of the county in which such independent fair is held and the treasurer or treasurers shall pay such order or orders from the county funds.

Premiums offered Sec. 9881. The several societies formed under the provisions of the preceding sections, annually shall offer and award premiums for the improvement of grains, fruit, vegetables, live stock, articles of domestic industry, public school displays, and such other articles, productions and improvements, as they deem proper, and may perform all acts that are best calculated to promote the agricultural and household manufacturing interests of the county or counties, and of the state. They shall regulate the amount of premiums, and their different grades, so that all may have an opportunity to compete therefor.

Sec. 9882. Persons offering to compete for premiums on improved methods of production of crops or other articles, before such premium is adjudged, shall deliver to the awarding committee if required, a full and correct statement of the process of the method of production, and the expense and value thereof, with a view of showing accurately the profits derived or expected to be derived therefrom.

Duties of persons offering to compete therefor.

Sec. 9884. County societies shall publish annually an abstract of the treasurer's account, in a newspaper of the county, and make a report of their proceedings during the year. Also make a synopsis of the awards for improvement in agriculture and household manufactures which shall be made in accordance with the rules and regulations of the state board of agriculture, and be forwarded to the secretary of agriculture on or before the first Thursday after the second Monday in January of each year. No subsequent payment shall be made from the county treasury unless a certificate be presented to the county auditor, from the secretary of agriculture showing that such reports have been made.

Publication of treasurer's account and list of awards.

Sec. 9884-1. Members of county agricultural societies must be residents of the county in which the county agricultural society is organized. The annual membership fee shall be fixed by each society or its board of directors and paid to the secretary or treasurer as its by-laws may direct. A printed certificate of membership shall be issued to each member who pays the required fee, and said certificates shall be issued from a book in which duplicate stubs of same shall be properly filled out and preserved. All certificates shall be numbered consecutively. No person shall pay or secure more than one membership, and that for himself or herself. The secretary of each society shall send the name and address of each member of the board of directors to the secretary of the state board of agriculture within ten days after the election. A list of the members shall be kept in the office of the secretary of each society and open to public inspection at all times so as to afford convenient information to any resident of the county.

Who may be members; certificate; fee.

List of members sent to state secretary and kept in local office.

Sec. 9884-2. The board of directors shall consist of at least eight members, and the county agent and county school superintendent may be members ex-officio. The terms of office shall be determined by the rules of the state board of agriculture. Any vacancy, caused by death, resignation, refusal to qualify, removal from county, or other cause, may be filled by the board until the next annual election when a director shall be elected for the unexpired term. The annual election of the directors shall be by ballot at time and place fixed by the board; provided, however, that this election shall not be held later than the first Saturday in December. The secretary shall give notice of the director's

Board of directors; term of office; election; vacancy.

election for three weeks prior to the holding thereof, in at least two newspapers of opposite politics and of general circulation in the county, or by letter mailed to each member. Only persons holding membership certificates at the close of the fair, or at least fifteen calendar days before the date of election, as may be fixed by the board of directors, shall be entitled to vote, unless such election is held during the time of the holding of the annual county fair. If the said election is held on the fairgrounds during the continuance of the county fair, then all persons holding membership certificates of the date and hour of the election shall be entitled to vote. When the election is to be held during the continuance of the annual county fair, notice of such election must be prominently mentioned in the premium list, in addition to the notice required in newspapers. The terms of office of the retiring directors shall expire, and that of the directors-elect shall begin not later than the first Saturday in January of each year.

Annual meeting; organization of board; oath.

Sec. 9884-3. The board of directors shall annually meet not later than the first Saturday of January, and elect a president, vice-president, treasurer, secretary, and such other officers as it may deem proper; the president, vice president and treasurer to serve one and the secretary not to exceed three years, as the board of directors may determine and until their successors are elected and qualified. The president and vice-president shall be directors. The secretary and treasurer may or may not be directors. Before election of officers the newly elected directors shall qualify by taking oath (or affirmation) before a competent authority; and the board of directors shall conform to the rules and regulations of the state board of agriculture.

Permit shall not be issued to sell, etc., liquors; immoral shows.

Sec. 9884-4. County agricultural societies shall not sell or grant to any person or persons, or permit in any manner, the privilege of selling, dealing, or bartering in spirituous, vinous or malt liquors, allow, or tolerate immoral shows, lottery devices, games of chance, or gambling of any kind, including pool selling and paddle wheels, in or about any building or anywhere on its fairgrounds, at any time.

When aid of state withheld.

If it be shown from the report of any county agricultural society, from witnesses or otherwise, that the annual exhibition held by such society was not conducted along moral or agricultural lines or was not of sufficient educational value to justify the expenditure of the per capita tax as provided by section 9880 of the General Code, the certificate for such financial aid may be withheld by the state board of agriculture.

One-tenth mill levy for use of society.

Sec. 9894. When a county or a county agricultural society, owns or holds under a lease, real estate used as a site whereon to hold fairs, and the county agricultural society therein has the control and management of such lands and buildings, for the purpose of encouraging agricultural fairs, the county commissioners shall on the request of the agricultural society annually levy taxes of not exceeding a tenth of one mill upon all taxable property of the county, but in no event to exceed the sum of two thousand dollars, or be less than fifteen hundred dollars, which sum shall be paid by the treasurer of the county to the treasurer of the agricultural society, upon an order from the county auditor duly issued therefor. Such commissioners shall pay out of the treasury any sum from money in the general fund not otherwise appropriated, in anticipation of such levy.

Sec. 9899. The county commissioners of a county shall insure the buildings on the grounds of the county agricultural society for the benefit of such society. **Insurance on buildings.**

SECTION 2. That original sections 9880, 9880-1, 9881, 9882, 9884, 9894 and 9899 and sections 9883, 9911, 9914 and 9915 of the General Code be, and the same are hereby repealed. **Repeals.**

CARL R. KIMBALL,
Speaker of the House of Representatives.
CLARENCE J. BROWN,
President of the Senate.

The sectional numbers on the margin hereof are designated as provided by law. JOHN G. PRICE, *Attorney General.*

Passed April 17, 1919.
Approved May 15, 1919.

JAMES M. COX,
Governor.

Filed in the office of the Secretary of State at Columbus, Ohio, on the 17th day of May, A. D. 1919.

142 G.

[Senate Bill No. 91.]

AN ACT

To regulate the payment of losses under contracts for casualty insurance.

Be it enacted by the General Assembly of the State of Ohio:

Sec. 9510-3.

SECTION 1. In respect to every contract of insurance made between an insurance company and any person, firm or corporation by which such person, firm or corporation is insured against loss or damage on account of the bodily injury or death by accident of any person for which loss or damage such person, firm or corporation is responsible. whenever a loss or damage occurs on account of a casualty covered by such contract of insurance, the liability of the insurance company shall become absolute, and the payment of said loss shall not depend upon the satisfaction by the assured of a final judgment against him for loss, or damage or death occasioned by such casualty. No such contract of insurance shall be cancelled or annulled by any agreement between the insurance company and the assured, after the said assured has become responsible for such loss or damage or death, and any such cancellation or annullment shall be void. **Liability of insurance company for bodily injury or death.**

Cancellation or annulment void.

19—G. & L. A.

Sec. 9510-4.

When judgment creditor entitled to have insurance money applied to judgment.

SECTION 2. Upon the recovery of a final judgment against any firm, person or corporation by any person, including administrators and executors, for loss or damage on account of bodily injury or death, if the defendant in such action was insured against loss or damage at the time when the right of action arose, the judgment creditor shall be entitled to have the insurance money provided for in the contract of insurance between the insurance company and the defendant applied to the satisfaction of the judgment, and if the judgment is not satisfied within thirty days after the date when it is rendered, the judgment creditor may proceed in a legal action against the defendant and the insurance company to reach and apply the insurance money to the satisfaction of the judgment.

The sectional numbers on the margin hereof are in conformity to the General Code. JOHN G. PRICE, Attorney General.

CLARENCE J. BROWN,
President of the Senate.
CARL R. KIMBALL,
Speaker of the House of Representatives.

Passed May 7, 1919.
Approved May 15, 1919.

JAMES M. COX,
Governor.

Filed in the office of the Secretary of State at Columbus, Ohio, on the 17th day of May, A. D. 1919.

143 G.

[House Bill No. 356.]

AN ACT

To reimburse Bessie G. Lyle for money loaned to Company F, Seventh Infantry, Ohio National Guards.

Be it enacted by the General Assembly of the State of Ohio:

Reimbursement of Bessie G. Lyle for money loaned Co. F, 7th Inf., O. N. G.

SECTION 1. That the sum of two hundred and eighty dollars be paid to Bessie G. Lyle as a reimbursement for money loan by the said Bessie G. Lyle to Company F, Seventh Infantry, Ohio National Guards, for the purpose of altering a building at Gallipolis, state of Ohio, for armory purposes, in this to wit: installing lockers, suitable shower baths, interior decorating and partitioning off certain rooms.

SECTION 2. Said reimbursement to be paid from funds received and set apart for military purposes.

This act is not of a general or permanent nature and requires no sectional number. JOHN G. PRICE, Attorney General.

CARL R. KIMBALL,
Speaker of the House of Representatives.
CLARENCE J. BROWN,
President of the Senate.

Passed April 17, 1919.
Approved May 15, 1919.

JAMES M. COX,
Governor.

Filed in the office of the Secretary of State at Columbus, Ohio, on the 17th day of May, A. D. 1919.

144 L.

[House Bill No. 524.]

AN ACT

To amend section 2419 of the General Code, authorizing the county commissioners to expend funds for the establishment, equipment and maintenance of public offices.

Be it enacted by the General Assembly of the State of Ohio:

SECTION 1. That section 2419 of the General Code be and the same is hereby amended to read as follows:

Sec. 2419. A court house, jail, public comfort station, offices for county officers and an infirmary shall be provided by the commissioners when in their judgment they or any of them are needed. Such buildings and offices shall be of such style, dimensions and expense as the commissioners determine. They shall also provide all the equipment, stationery and postage, as the county commissioners may deem necessary for the proper and convenient conduct of such offices, and such facilities as will result in expeditious and economical administration of the said county offices. They shall provide all room, fire and burglar-proof vaults and safes and other means of security in the office of the county treasurer, necessary for the protection of public moneys and property therein.

SECTION 2. That original section 2419 of the General Code be, and the same is hereby repealed.

Buildings, vaults, comfort stations, safes for county purposes; equipment.

CARL R. KIMBALL,
Speaker of the House of Representatives.
CLARENCE J. BROWN,
President of the Senate

The sectional number in this act is in conformity to the General Code. JOHN G. PRICE, Attorney General.

Passed April 17, 1919.
Approved May 15, 1919.

JAMES M. COX,
Governor.

Filed in the office of the Secretary of State at Columbus, Ohio, on the 17th day of May, A. D. 1919.

145 G.

[Senate Bill No. 115.]

AN ACT

To amend section 10989 of the General Code, relating to lunatics, idiots and imbeciles.

Be it enacted by the General Assembly of the State of Ohio:

SECTION 1. That section 10989 of the General Code be amended to read as follows:

Sec. 10989. Upon satisfactory proof that a person resident of the county, or having legal settlement in any township thereof, is an idiot or imbecile, or lunatic, or an in-

Guardians for idiots, imbeciles or lunatics, when and how appointed.

competent by reason of advanced age or mental or physical disability or infirmity, the probate court shall appoint a guardian for such person, who by virtue of such appointment shall be the guardian of the minor children of his ward, unless the court appoints some other person as their guardian. No such guardian shall be appointed until at least three days after the personal service of a written notice setting forth the time and place of the hearing shall have been served upon the person for whom such appointment is sought; and also until at least three days after written notice has been served upon the persons next of kin of such person for whom appointment is sought, resident in the county in which application is made, to attend such hearing at the same time and place; which notice shall be served by delivering a copy of it to each person named therein or by leaving such copy at his or her usual place of residence.

SECTION 2. That said original section 10989 of the General Code be and the same is hereby repealed.

The sectional number in this act is in conformity to the General Code. JOHN G. PRICE, Attorney General.

CLARENCE J. BROWN,
President of the Senate.
CARL R. KIMBALL,
Speaker of the House of Representatives.
Passed April 17, 1919.
Approved May 15, 1919.

JAMES M. COX,
Governor.

Filed in the office of the Secretary of State at Columbus, Ohio, on the 17th day of May, A. D. 1919.

146 G.

[House Bill No. 24.]

AN ACT

To prohibit the liquor traffic and to provide for the enforcement of such prohibition, and to repeal all sections of the General Code, and acts inconsistent herewith.

Be it enacted by the General Assembly of the State of Ohio:

Sec. 6212-13.

Act deemed an exercise of the police power of the state.

SECTION 1. This entire act shall be deemed to be an exercise of the power granted in article XV, section 9, of the constitution of Ohio, and of the police power of the state for the protection of the public welfare, health, peace, safety and morals of the people of the state of Ohio, and all of its provisions shall be liberally construed for the accomplishment of these purposes.

Sec. 6212-14.

Interpretation; definition of words and phrases.

SECTION 2. In the interpretation of this act the following words shall be held and construed to be respectively as follows: Words of the singular number to include their plurals, and vice versa; words of the masculine gender to

include the feminine or neuter, as the case may be, and vice
versa; words of the present tense to include the future tense
and vice versa; "person" to mean and include any natural
person, firm, corporation, and any association or combination of persons, whether acting by themselves or by a servant, agent, or employe; "commissioner" to mean commissioner of prohibition of Ohio; "retail" and "wholesale" quantities to mean respectively less than one gallon
and one gallon or more; "permit" to mean a permit granted
by the commissioner; "alcohol" to mean ethyl alcohol;
"conviction" to include "plea of guilty."

Sec. 6212-15.

SECTION 3. Except as herein provided, the word
"liquor," or the phrase "intoxicating liquors," wherever
used in this act, shall be construed to include any distilled,
malt, spirituous, vinous, fermented or alcoholic liquor, and
also any alcoholic liquid or compound whether or not the
same is medicated, proprietary, or patented, which liquid
or compound is potable or capable of being used as a beverage.

"Intoxicating liquors" defined.

Sec. 6212-16.

SECTION 4. Except as herein provided, it shall be unlawful on and after the 27th day of May, 1919, for any
person, directly or indirectly, to manufacture, sell, barter,
receive, possess, transport, export, deliver, furnish or give
away intoxicating liquors, or possess any equipment used
or to be used after the aforesaid date for the manufacture
of intoxicating liquor.

Manufacture, sale, etc., un-lawful after May 27, 1919.

Sec. 6212-17.

SECTION 5. As herein provided the following are permitted: (1) manufacturers of alcohol or wine having permits may manufacture and possess such liquors, and possess and use such equipment for making the same, and sell
such liquors to wholesale and retail druggists; (2) manufacturers of alcohol or wine having permits and wholesale
druggists may possess such liquors and sell the same to the
following: (a) retail druggists, (b) other persons having
permits only to possess alcohol or wine in wholesale quantities, and (c) manufacturers (having permits) of such
patent or proprietary medicines or preparations, or of such
toilet, medical and antiseptic preparations and solutions,
or of such flavoring extracts, or of such chemicals, dyes and
other preparations, as are recited in section 7 of this act;
(3) retail druggists may possess alcohol and wine and, by
a registered pharmacist sell the same in retail quantities
upon prescription or affidavit; (4) registered pharmacists
may sell alcohol and wine in retail quantities upon prescription or affidavit at the drug store of a retail druggist;
(5) common carriers may receive alcohol or wine from any
manufacturer of such alcohol or wine having a permit, or
from any wholesale druggist, and transport such liquor
and deliver the same to any manufacturer having a permit
or to any other person having a permit to possess or permitted to receive alcohol or wine in wholesale quantities;
(6) persons may receive from a retail druggist alcohol or
wine upon affidavit or prescription; (7) the foregoing may

Exceptions from provisions of act.

390

be done only when the wine is for sacramental, medicinal or pharmaceutical purposes and the alcohol for medicinal, chemical, pharmaceutical, scientific, mechanical or industrial purposes, as the case may be; (8) a clergyman, minister or priest may purchase and possess, and receive from a common carrier, wine for sacramental purposes in wholesale or retail quantities, and manufacturers and wholesalers of wines for sacramental purposes, who have permits, may sell wine for such purposes in wholesale quantities to such persons upon their affidavit; (9) educational and scientific institutions may purchase and possess pure, unmedicated ethyl alcohol and medicated or denatured alcohol and may dispense same in retail quantities to scientific workers and properly enrolled students for use in scientific experiments, under such restrictions as may be formulated by the commissioner.

Sec. 6212-18.

Package or container must have prescription or affidavit attached.

SECTION 6. Whoever has in his possession the following: (1) alcohol for medical purposes or wine for sacramental purposes or alcohol for mechanical, scientific, industrial or other permitted purposes, shall have pasted or permanently attached to the container, a copy of the required prescription or affidavit, as the case may be, upon which authority it was purchased, as herein provided; (2) alcohol or wine received from a common carrier, must have pasted or permanently attached to the container a copy of the consignee's affidavit filed with such carrier, and must have in his possession a verified copy of his permit or of his affidavit to the seller as herein provided.

Sec. 6212-19.

Certain fruit juices and preparations excepted from provisions of law.

SECTION 7. The provisions of this act shall not be construed (1) to prevent the manufacture, sale and keeping of cider and fruit juices for the purpose of making vinegar, or the manufacture for use or sale, or the sale and keeping and storing for use or sale, of non-intoxicating cider and fruit juices or other non-alcoholic beverages that are not subject to the payment of the United States retail liquor dealer's tax; or (2) to prevent the manufacture, sale and keeping and storing for sale of (a) any alcoholic medical preparation manufactured in accordance with formulas prescribed by the United States Pharmacopoeia or National Formulary, or by any other pharmacopoeia or other standard work on materia medica, or any alcoholic medicinal or pharmaceutical preparations, or any alcoholic patent or proprietary preparations in conformity with the Ohio laws, unless such medical preparations are suitable for use as a beverage; (b) alcoholic toilet, medical, antiseptic, chemical and other similar preparations and solutions which are not suitable for beverage purposes; or (c) food products containing alcohol and known as flavoring extracts which shall be manufactured or sold for cooking, flavoring and culinary purposes only, and which contain no more alcohol than is necessary for the purpose of extraction, solution or preservation; or (3) to prevent (a) the possession and use, in chemical, or other scientific laboratories, or in plants not manufacturing intoxicating liquors for beverage purposes, but manufacturing dye, chemicals and other similar preparations, of any equipment usually pertaining to such laboratories or plants; or (b) the possession of equipment necessary for the manufacture of any cider or fruit juices permitted herein, provided that persons manufacturing such cider or fruit juices for sale or charge for making, shall be required to obtain a permit from the commissioner to possess and use such equipment; or (4) the manufacturer of such preparations as are recited in section 7 (2) of this act, from purchasing, possessing, storing, and transporting only such alcohol or wine as is necessary for, and as is uesd in, the manufacture of said articles, provided that the manufacturer of such articles shall secure a permit from the commissioner and otherwise comply with the requirements herein, and provided, further, that upon the outside of each bottle, package, or box of any of the aforesaid preparations, solutions or extracts there is printed in English, conspicuously, legibly, and clearly the quantity by volume of alcohol in said preparations, solutions or extracts and the name and address of the manufacturer thereof, provided that nothing herein shall be construed to require the label on toilet, antiseptic and chemical preparations, not intended for internal use, to show the quantity of alcohol contained therein.

Nothing in this act shall have any application to denatured alcohol or denatured rum intended for use only in the industrial or mechanical arts, nor shall anything herein prevent the storage in the United States bonded warehouses or bonded wineries or wine storehouses in the custody or under the supervision and control of the United States collector of internal revenue, of all liquors manufactured prior to May 27th, 1919, or to prevent the transportation of such liquors for purposes not prohibited at the point of destination, providing the tax is paid thereon, from such warehouses or wineries or wine storehouses to points outside of the state, where the sale of such liquors is not prohibited.

The commissioner is hereby authorized to issue additional rules and regulations not inconsistent herewith relating to the manufacture, possession and sale of alcohol, wine and preparations listed by the commissioner, and any violation of such rules and regulations shall be deemed a violation of this act. *Additional regulations; violations.*

Whenever the commissioner is informed and has reason to believe that an alcoholic preparation is suitable for, and is being used as a beverage in this state, he shall cause an analysis of said preparation to be made by the state chemist, and if upon analysis, the commissioner shall find that said preparation is not a legitimate preparation within the meaning of this section and is suitable for beverage purposes, he shall give ten days' notice in writing sent by registered mail to the person, firm or corporation who is the manufacturer thereof to show cause why said preparation *Analysis of preparations authorized.*

should not be listed as an intoxicating beverage and its sale forbidden in this state.

When sale of preparation forbidden; petition to common pleas court for review.

If the manufacturer of said preparation shall not be able to show to the satisfaction of the commissioner that the preparation in question is unsuitable for beverage purposes and is a legitimate alcoholic preparation, as defined in this section, then the commissioner shall list said preparation as one, the sale of which is forbidden in this state; provided that said manufacturer may file his petition within thirty days in the court of common pleas of Franklin county, asking that the action of the commissioner, placing said preparation on said list be reviewed, and the said common pleas court, or a judge thereof, shall proceed to hear said case de novo, and shall make such order or reversal, modification, or confirmation of the decision of the commissioner as the facts and the law of the case demand. During the pendency of such review in the courts, the sale of such preparation shall be suspended and enjoined until the question is finally decided. From the decision of the common pleas court either party shall have the right to prosecute error. The commissioner is hereby authorized to file with the clerk of the common pleas court of each county at such time, or times, as he shall deem proper, the names of those preparations, with the name and address of the manufacturer thereof, which are listed by him under the provisions of this section. He shall also supply such information to the press.

Sec. 6212-20.

Issue of permits; expiration.

SECTION 8. The commissioner shall issue all permits, and any permit granted hereunder shall expire on the 31st day of December of each year, or at the death of the grantee, if such death occurs prior to said date. Each permit shall be issued in duplicate, giving the serial number thereof, the name and address of the grantee, location of place where such permit is to be used, and a brief statement as to the conditions under which the privileges granted thereunder are to be exercised.

Application for permit; proof required; revocation.

An application for a permit shall be signed by the applicant under oath and be filed with the commissioner or any of his deputies. Such applicant shall present such proof as is required by the commissioner or any of his deputies, to sustain such application, but before the commissioner, or any deputy, or inspector named by the commissioner to hear the applicant, shall grant any such permit, he shall be satisfied from the contents of the application and the proof made that there is a necessity existing for the granting of such permit, and that the applicant will observe all the laws of the state of Ohio and of the United States relating to the liquor traffic. Such permit grants the privileges only to the person named therein and only at the place named therein and only for the purposes named therein, and such permit is not transferable either as to person or place, nor assignable or subject to process of execution.

Any such permit may be revoked by the commissioner for good cause shown.

Sec. 6212-21. SECTION 9. For good cause shown by the applicant, permits hereunder shall be granted for permitted purposes to the following: (1) manufacturers of alcohol and wine; (2) manufacturers of such preparations as are included in section 7 (2) of this act; (3) persons making potable alcohol from denatured alcohol; (4) manufacturers of cider and fruit juices for sale, if manufactured and sold in such quantities as the commissioner may see fit to require a permit. Provided, that nothing herein shall require a permit of a druggist who prepares alcoholic medicinal or pharmaceutical compounds in the usual course of his business. *(Purposes for which permits granted.)*

Sec. 6212-22. SECTION 10. The commissioner shall keep a special permit record arranged alphabetically by counties, showing for each county (1) the names of the grantees of permits alphabetically arranged; (2) the address of each grantee; (3) the date when granted; (4) the nature of the place for which each permit is granted; and (5) the street or building location of such place. Such record also shall show the convictions of grantees, if any, and the revocations, cancellations, and lapses of permits by death, together with the date of each of such revocations, cancellations and lapses. Said commissioner shall not later than the first day of July, 1919, provide each prosecuting attorney with a copy of that part of such record applying to his county, and on the first day and the fifteenth day of each succeeding calendar month thereafter, the commissioner shall send to each prosecuting attorney a copy of additions to such permit record for his county, including convictions and revocations, cancellations and lapses of permits by death. *(Record by counties arranged alphabetically shall be kept.)*

Forms for applications for permits shall be provided by the commissioner in such form as he shall deem proper, not inconsistent with the provisions of this act, making such changes as the privileges and limitations under the particular permit and qualifications required of the applicant demand. *(Forms furnished.)*

Sec. 6212-23. SECTION 12. Before any permit hereunder is granted, the applicant shall pay to the commissioner the following respective amounts: (1) Manufacturers of alcohol, from $25 to $100; (2) manufacturers of wine, from $10 to $50; (3) manufacturers of alcoholic preparations, except druggists and pharmacists making alcoholic medicinal and pharmaceutical compounds in the usual course of their business, from $10 to $100. *(Schedule of fees.)*

All other persons required to hold permits, from $2.00 to $10.00, the amount to be determined by the commissioner.

All moneys received by the commissioner under this section, shall be paid monthly into the state treasury, accompanied with a report to the state treasurer showing the amounts received and the persons from whom received. Such moneys shall be credited to the general revenue fund of the state. *(Monthly payment into state treasury.)*

Sec. 6212-24.
Retail quantities
may be sold in
following cases.

. SECTION 13. Every registered pharmacist, or retail druggist, may by himself, if a registered pharmacist, or by his clerk, if such clerk is a registered pharmacist sell in retail quantities in the following cases:

(a) Alcohol or wine upon a written prescription issued and signed in good faith by a physician of good standing in his profession who is lawfully and regularly engaged in the practice of his profession where the sale is made.

(b) Alcohol for medicinal, chemical, mechanical, scientific, industrial, or other well known non-beverage purposes, on the affidavit of the superintendent or of the person in charge, of any hospital, laboratory, manufactory, educational or eleemosynary institution, where such liquors are needed only for such aforesaid purposes.

(c) Wine for sacramental purposes to any clergyman, minister, or priest, having charge of, or recognized officer of, a church, upon the affidavit of such clergyman, minister, or priest, or recognized officer of such church when personally presented.

(d) Alcohol for art, scientific, mechanical, chemical or pharmaceutical purposes, upon the affidavit of the purchaser.

(e) Alcohol upon a personally presented affidavit by a licensed physician, licensed dentist, licensed veterinarian or licensed osteopathic physician for only professional purposes.

Alcohol sold for external medicinal purposes as provided in this section must be alcohol medicated in conformity with the laws and regulations of the federal government.

Sec. 6212-25.
Record by retail
druggist of sales
required.

SECTION 14. A retail druggist shall keep a public record of all sales of liquor mentioned herein as follows:

RETAIL DRUGGIST'S RECORD.

Name 'of doctor issuing the prescription, or person securing liquor by affidavit. Kind of liquor. If alcohol state if medicated or non-medicated. Amount. Purposes. Date of sale. Sales on previous prescriptions or affidavits to such person for liquor within six months. Purchaser. Signatures of purchaser and of individual making sale. Prescription or affidavit.

No retail druggist shall fill a prescription for alcohol or make a sale thereon except such prescription be given on blanks provided by the commissioner, and when such prescription has been filled or sale made thereon, it shall be marked "cancelled" and be pasted on, or attached to, the end of the record of such transaction in the space provided.

When alcohol or wine is sold on affidavit the following form of affidavit shall be sufficient.

State of Ohio,
County of ....
............being duly sworn, deposes and says: I

am more than 21 years of age and am not of intemperate habits, and have not been convicted of violating any law relating to the prohibition of the liquor traffic within......
years. I need............... amount of alcohol (wine) for............ purposes and will not use any part of said alcohol (wine) for any other purposes or allow others to so use it. I have not received or possessed any alcohol (wine) within the last (30) days except............ and I do not have any alcohol (wine) in my possession or control except............

Sworn to before me this........ day of........ 19..
and subscribed in my presence.

....

Any registered pharmacist may administer the oath provided herein. The affidavit must be permanently attached to or pasted on the end of the record of such sale in the space provided, and on the copy of such affidavit or prescription placed on the container of the liquor sold there shall be endorsed by the seller, the date of sale, the word "cancelled" and his signature.

A retail druggist shall not keep alcohol and wine in his place of business in an amount that represents more than two per cent. of the value of the stock of goods on hand in his drug store, and a wholesale druggist shall not keep alcohol and wine in his place of business in an amount that represents more than four per cent. of the value of the stock of goods on hand in his drug store.

Sec. 6312-36.   SECTION 15. Sales of alcohol or wine made by a manufacturer of such or by a wholesale druggist must be made upon affidavits similar to that used in case of a sale by a retail druggist upon an affidavit and the record to be kept of such sales shall be made as that in case of sale by a retail druggist except as to signature of purchaser. Persons making potable alcohol from denatured alcohol shall be subject to the same regulations as to sale, records and reports as the manufacturer of alcohol. *(Record by manufacturer and wholesale druggist.)*

Sec. 6312-37.   SECTION 16. Every physician who issues a prescription for alcohol or wine shall not issue such except on blanks furnished by the commissioner and shall keep a record alphabetically arranged in a separate book provided by the commissioner, which record shall show: *(Record of prescriptions by physician.)*
Date. Kind of liquor. Amount. To whom issued. Disease or malady for which issued. Result of personal investigation. Directions for use, giving amount and frequency of the dose. Number of prescriptions issued to such person for alcohol within four months prior thereto.

Sec. 6312-38.   SECTION 17. All persons required to keep a record by the provisions of this act, and all manufacturers required to have a permit by the provisions of this act, shall file with the commissioner a semi-annual report on blanks furnished by said commissioner, setting forth the facts upon which a report is required. *(Semi-annual report to commissioner.)*

Sec. 6212-29.

Forms of prescriptions and affidavits furnished.

SECTION 18. The commissioner shall provide forms of prescriptions and affidavits for alcohol or wine as herein provided, and shall furnish the same only to persons needing the same as manifest from a written request therefor. The prescriptions and affidavits for alcohol or wine which are filed with the person from whom such alcohol or wine is purchased shall be provided in book form, numbering in duplicate each affidavit or prescription, as the case may be, with a duplicate consecutive serial number from one to one hundred, and each affidavit book shall be given a number as shall also each prescription book, and a stub in each book shall carry the same number as the affidavit or prescription, as the case may be, which shows the copy of the record of such sale. The stub and the affidavit in the affidavit book shall show the same data as is required to be kept by a retail druggist, and. the stub and the prescription in the prescription book shall show the same data as a physician is required to keep in his alphabetical record. The book containing such stubs shall be returned to the commissioner when the affidavits or prescriptions, as the case may be, are used, or when the holder thereof discontinues business. All unused, mutilated or defaced blanks shall be returned with the book. No sale of alcohol or wine herein permitted to be made on affidavit or prescription, nor delivery of such liquors by a common carrier permitted to be made to the consignee upon presentation of such consignee's affidavit shall be made except such affidavit or prescription be on blanks as herein provided. The commissioner shall provide also application blanks for permits, blanks for reports required herein, and blank forms of consignee's affidavits to the carrier, the last to be prepared in triplicate and numbered consecutively. All record books, affidavit and prescription forms, and blanks for reports required by this act shall be furnished by the commissioner at actual cost.

Sec. 6212-30.

Complaint under oath; revocation of permit; hearing.

SECTION 19. If at any time there shall be filed with the prohibition commissioner a complaint under oath by at least two persons setting forth that any person who has a permit is not in good faith conforming to the provisions of this act, or is guilty of violating any of the laws of the state of Ohio, or the laws of the United States, relating to the liquor traffic, or that said person is in the habit of using intoxicating liquor as a beverage, such commissioner shall immediately issue an order citing such person to appear before the commissioner, on a day named not more than thirty (30) days from the issuing of such order, at which time the question of cancellation of such permit shall be heard. If it be found that such person is guilty of violating any of the laws of the state of Ohio, or of the United States, relating to the liquor traffic, or is in the habit of using intoxicating liquors as a beverage, such permit shall be revoked, and no permit shall be granted to such person for two (2) years thereafter; provided, that nothing herein shall prevent the commissioner from revoking a permit for any other good cause shown.

In the hearing provided for in this section, and in all other hearings provided for in this act before the commissioner, the defending party may be represented by counsel. Witnesses may be had either for or against such party, but no witness shall be entitled to compensation from the state for attendance, or travel, unless the commissioner certifies that his testimony was material to the inquiry. The commissioner shall have authority to subpoena witnesses to appear at such hearings and to bring with them papers, books and documents as may be pertinent to the inquiry, and to punish as for contempt a person who being duly summoned refuses to appear or produce such papers, books, or documents. Such witnesses shall receive such fees and mileage as are allowed witnesses in the court of common ·pleas which fees and mileage shall be audited and paid, as other expenses are audited and paid, upon the presentation of proper vouchers sworn to by such witnesses and approved by the commissioner. *(Defendant may be represented by counsel; witnesses; fees.)*

Sec. 6212-31. SECTION 20. Any officer or court before whom any person holding a permit, has been convicted of an offense under this act, and such conviction is not subject to further review, shall certify the fact of such conviction to the commissioner, which certificate shall be forthwith made a matter of public record by the commissioner whereupon the commissioner may revoke such permit without a hearing, and no new permit shall be granted to the same person for one (1) year. *(Revocation of permit on conviction; certification to commissioner.)*

Any registered pharmacist or retail druggist or any retail druggist's employe who has been convicted of violating any of the provisions of this act, as disclosed by the records of the commissioner's office, shall be reported by the commissioner to the state board of pharmacy upon forms presented and supplied by the said state board of pharmacy. Upon receipt of the report from the commissioner, the state board of pharmacy may cite such person so reported to appear before the board and may, after due notice and hearing refuse to grant a renewal of certificate, or may revoke or suspend a certificate of such person, if registered as a pharmacist, assistant pharmacist or apprentice. If such person as reported is neither registered as a pharmacist, assistant pharmacist or apprentice, but subsequently makes application for registration as such, the state board of pharmacy may refuse to grant such registration until the time when said board is satisfied the applicant is entitled to such registration. *(Violation by druggist, etc., reported to board of pharmacy; hearing.)*

Sec. 6212-32. SECTION 21. Persons who are permitted to manufacture or possess alcohol or wine in wholesale quantities, may receive the same from a common carrier upon the presentation of a verified copy of the permit or of the affidavit to the seller, and, in either instance, an affidavit by the consignee to the carrier that such alcohol or wine was sent to *(Who may receive alcohol or wine from common carrier; affidavit; identification.)*

the purchaser or person receiving such liquor on his affidavit to the seller, which stated the purpose for which the liquor was ordered and declared that the alcohol or wine would not be used in violation of law. If the person receiving the liquor is not known to the agent of the carrier, then such person must be identified by two other responsible persons. If identification is made by the agent he must sign the record as such agent under "Identified by" in the record as provided in the following section. If identification is made by persons other than the agent of the common carrier, then such persons must each sign such record giving his address.

Sec. 6212-33.
Record by common carrier.

SECTION 22. The record to be kept in the office of delivery by the common carrier shall show:

Consignor and address. Consignee and address. Kind and quantity of liquor. Date received. Date and place of delivery. Date of last delivery to consignee. Consignee's permit number. Consignee's signature. Identified by....
.... and ....
(name) (address)   (name) (address)
Attach affidavit here.

The address required in the above record shall include the post office and the street or building number, if any.

The affidavit of consignee to be attached to the above record shall be as follows:

State of Ohio,
⎱ ss.
County of............⎰

..............being duly sworn, deposes and says that my address is..................(or other definite description giving street number or hotel); that I am not a minor nor of intemperate habits; that I am the owner of a package in the office of a common carrier, to wit..........; that it contains.................(giving amount and kind of liquor) which I ordered in writing on the............ day of............19..., upon the authority of Permit No. ....; that the purpose for which I ordered such liquor is............; that I have not received from any carrier or any person, nor have I had in my control at any place, or places, more than............(amount) of alcohol and............(amount) of wine within the last three months preceding this date, and I do not have any liquor on hand except............; that I will not use any such liquor, nor allow any one else to use such liquor for beverage purposes or for purposes other than herein stated; and that such liquor was obtained from....
....upon an affi-
(address)   (address)
davit stating that said liquor was for the following purposes.............................and declaring that such liquor would not be used in violation of law,

....

Sworn to and subscribed in my presence this........
day of....................,19...

....

(Agent of carrier.)

The agent of the common carrier is hereby authorized to administer the oath to the foregoing consignee, but not before identification as aforesaid.

Agent may administer oath.

Such affidavit shall be pasted or permanently attached at the bottom of the record mentioned herein and a copy attached permanently to the bottle or container of such liquor. If such bottle or container is enclosed in a package with other material, then such copy shall be attached to such package or pasted on the bottle or container when it is taken from such package and before the liquor is delivered.

Attachment of affidavit to container.

SECTION 23. It shall be the duty of the common carrier to keep in the office of delivery in a legible hand or typewriting, an accurate permanent record of such alcohol or wine delivered, arranged alphabetically as to the consignees, which record shall be an abstract of the record required in the preceding section to be kept. Not later than the tenth day of each month duplicate copies of the record mentioned in this section, for the calendar month preceding, shall be made, one to be sent to the commissioner and the other to be sent to the clerk of the court of the county where such delivery was made. Nothing herein shall be construed to authorize the transportation of liquor for other than permitted purposes, nor the carriage of alcohol and wine by any other than a common carrier, except by any person who has sold or obtained such liquor on an affidavit or prescription as herein provided.

Sec. 6318-34.

Alphabetically arranged record by carrier; monthly report to commissioner.

SECTION 24. Within ten (10) days after the date when this act shall become operative, every person except those persons permitted herein legally to possess liquor, shall remove or cause to be removed all intoxicating liquors in his possession, provided, that each of the aforesaid excepted persons shall report to the commissioner and to the clerk of the court of his county within said ten (10) days' period the kinds and amount of intoxicating liquor on hand. All signs whether printed or otherwise, relating to intoxicating liquors, or to the manufacture thereof, shall be permanently removed and obliterated within five days after this act becomes operative. Within the same time limits all screen, stained glass, or other obstructions, which prevent a clear view of the interior of any room or place where intoxicating liquors were sold within one year before this act became operative, shall be removed or so changed as to give a permanent unobstructed view of the interior of said room or place.

Sec. 6312-35.

Removal of liquors in possession; removal of signs, screens, etc.

SECTION 25. It shall be unlawful:

(1) To advertise anywhere, on land, or water, or in

Sec. 6312-36.

Unlawful advertisement of alcohol, wine, etc.

air, upon or in any place, or object, stationary or movable, or by any medium, means or method, intoxicating liquors, or to advertise the manufacture, sale, keeping for sale or furnishing of the same, or where, how, from whom and at which price the same may be obtained; provided, that the manufacturer of alcohol or wine and wholesale druggists having a permit under this act shall be allowed to send price lists to those to whom they are permitted to sell alcohol or wine under this act;

(2) To permit any sign or billboard, containing such prohibited advertisement to remain upon one's premises, or to circulate any prohibited price list, order blank or other matter designed to induce or secure orders for such intoxicating liquors. The commissioner or any other officer charged with the enforcement of this act, is authorized to remove, paint over or otherwise obliterate any such advertisement from any sign, billboard, or other public place when it comes to his notice, and shall do so upon demand of any citizen. Any advertisement or notice containing the picture of a brewery, distillery, bottle, keg, barrel, or box or other receptable representing as containing intoxicating liquors, or designed to serve as an advertisement thereof, shall be within the inhibition of this section.

(3) For any newspaper or periodical to print in its columns statements concerning the liquor traffic, directly or indirectly, for which said newspaper or periodical receives compensation of any kind, without giving the names of the persons paying for the same and without printing at the beginning and at the close of said advertisements in type of the same sized used in the body of the said article the following statement, ''Printed as paid advertisement.''

Sec. 6212-37.

Advertisement, sale, etc., of compound, tablet, etc., unlawful.

SECTION 26. It shall be unlawful to advertise, sell, deliver, furnish or possess any preparation, compound, or tablet, from which an intoxicating liquor capable of being used as a beverage is made, or equipment, recipe, or directions for making such intoxicating liquors, provided, that this section shall not apply to alcohol or wine for permitted purposes.

Sec. 6212-38.

Soliciting, purchasing or receiving orders.

SECTION 27. It shall be unlawful for any person to solicit any orders for, or purchases of, intoxicating liquors, or to take or receive any such orders, from any person in this state, or give any information how such prohibited liquors may be obtained or where such liquors are, or to send for such liquors. This section shall not apply to the soliciting and taking or receiving orders for alcohol or wine for permitted purposes by persons permitted to manufacture, possess, or sell the same.

Sec. 6212-39.

Procuring by hotel proprietor or employe.

SECTION 28. Any proprietor of any hotel or house of public or private entertainment who shall permit any employe, or other person, to, or who shall himself, procure intoxicating liquors for, or give directions or information by which intoxicating liquors can be secured by, any guest, patron or other person, or keeps in his employ any person, after he knows such employe has been violating any of the provisions of this act, shall be deemed guilty of a misde-meanor.

SECTION 29. It shall be unlawful for any person to cause, or induce any common carrier or any servant, agent or employe thereof, or any person, to carry, transport, or ship any container having therein any liquors without notifying the carrier, its servants or agent, or any person who carries the same, of the true nature and character of the thing to be carried, shipped, or transported. But failure to notify the carrier thereof shall not be a defense for illegal transportation.   *Shipping or procuring transportation without notice.*

SECTION 30. It shall be unlawful for any person for whom liquor is consigned, whether consigned to the party by the right name or by a fictitious name, to give to any other person an order for such liquor to any common carrier, or to any officer, agent or employe thereof, or to any other person, where the purpose of such order is to enable such person to whom the order is given to obtain or receive such liquor for himself, or for any other person than the consignee.   *Consignment in right or fictitious name.*

SECTION 31. It shall be unlawful for any person to deliver to, to receive or possess any liquors from, a common carrier, or to transport such liquors, unless there appears in a conspicuous place on the outside of the package containing such liquors in letters at least one-fourth inch high in the English language, the following information: *Delivering or receiving without certain information on package.*

Name and address of the consignor or seller; name and address of the consignee, or person receiving the liquor; kind and quantity of liquor contained therein. Any consignor delivering, or consignee accepting or receiving any package containing any such liquors upon which appears a false statement, or any person consigning, shipping, transporting or delivering any such package, knowing that such statement appearing on the outside is false, shall be deemed guilty of violating the provisions of this section.

SECTION 32. Any person who in this state, with knowledge, or who, without knowledge, negligently consigns, ships, carries, conveys, transports, delivers, or receives, or accepts for such shipment or carriage, or accepts or receives from any common carrier, any intoxicating liquors, the containers of which are covered over with, hidden or secreted in or among, or mixed or confused with, any other articles or substances, shall be guilty of a misdemeanor.   *Negligent shipments, consignments, etc., a misdemeanor.*

SECTION 33. It shall be unlawful for any person not being a physician, to issue a prescription for intoxicating liquors. It shall likewise be unlawful for any physician to issue prescriptions if he is addicted to the use of any narcotic drug, or to fail to comply with the regulations in this act; or to give a prescription for or including intoxicating liquors to any person for the purpose of enabling or assisting such person to evade the provisions of this act or to obtain liquor for use as a beverage, or for sale or dis-   *Who may not issue prescriptions.*

posal in any manner in violation of this act; or to give a prescription to any person without making a careful personal examination of the person for whom alcohol is prescribed, or to any person who he has reason to believe will use such alcohol for beverage purposes or who does not need such alcohol for medicinal purposes. Any shift or device by which intoxicating liquors may be improperly prescribed shall constitute a violation of this section. In addition to the penalty prescribed for a conviction of a physician of a second offense under this act, the right of such physician to issue prescriptions shall be deemed revoked forthwith.

Sec. 6212-45.
Changing or extracting prohibited.

SECTION 34. It shall be unlawful for any person to change, or extract from, denatured alcohol or denatured rum or any other liquid or compound containing non-potable alcohol or rum, any part of it so as to make it, or the residue capable of being used as a beverage, without first obtaining a permit to manufacture alcohol and thereafter complying with all the provisions hereof applicable to such manufacture.

Sec. 6212-46.
Information to prevent apprehension of offender, a misdemeanor.

SECTION 35. Any person who gives such information to an offender under this act as will prevent or tend to prevent such offender from being apprehended in his violation shall be guilty of a misdemeanor.

Sec. 6212-47.
Term "bootlegger" defined; injunction.

SECTION 36. Except as herein provided, any person who shall by himself, or his employe, servant, or agent, for himself or any other person, keep or carry around on his person, or in a vehicle, or leave in a place for another to secure, any intoxicating liquor, or sell or dispose of the same by gift or otherwise, or who shall in any manner, directly or indirectly, solicit, take or accept any order for the sale, shipment, or delivery of intoxicating liquor in violation of law, shall be termed a "bootlegger," and shall be guilty of a misdemeanor. Every such "bootlegger" may be restrained by injunction from committing any of the offenses prohibited by this act, and, so far as applicable, all of the provisions for abatement of a nuisance as herein defined, by proceedings in equity herein, shall be applicable to such injunction proceedings against such person, and the fact that an offender has no known or permanent place of business or base of supplies, or quits the business after the commencement of the action, or within thirty (30) days before the commencement of the action, shall not prevent a temporary or permanent injunction, as the case may be, from issuing, and any injunction granted shall be binding throughout the state.

Sec. 6212-48.
Maintaining or keeping a nuisance; penalty.

SECTION 37. Whoever shall keep or use any building, erection, thing or place, whether stationary or movable, where any offense herein prohibited is committed, is guilty of maintaining or keeping a nuisance, and upon conviction thereof shall pay a fine of not less than three hundred ($300.00) dollars nor more than one thousand ($1,000.00)

dollars, and cost of prosecution, and shall stand committed
to the county jail or workhouse until such fines and costs
are paid, or are secured to be paid, or he is otherwise discharged according to law; and the building, erection, thing
or place, or the ground itself, in or upon which the unlawful act is committed, and also the furniture, vessels,
fixtures and contents, are declared a nuisance, and in addition to the penalties hereinbefore defined shall be abated
as herein provided. And if it shall be proven that the
owner of any building, erection, place, thing or premises
has knowingly or negligently suffered the same to be used
or occupied for violating any of the provisions of this act,
judgment for fine and costs shall be a lien upon such building, erection, thing, place, or premises, and such building,
erection, thing, place, or premises may be sold to pay all
fines, costs, and forfeited bonds assessed against the occupant of the building, erection, thing, place or premises for
any violation of this act; and such lien may be enforced by
the commissioner, attorney general, prosecuting attorney,
or municipal law officer, in any court having jurisdiction.

Sec. 6312-49.

SECTION 38. The commissioner, his agents and deputies, or any officer of the state, prosecuting attorney or
municipal law officer, or any resident of the state in any
county where such a nuisance, as is defined in the preceding section, exists, or is kept or maintained, may prosecute
a suit in equity to abate and perpetually enjoin the same.
Upon the presentation of a complaint alleging that such a
nuisance exists and is being made to appear by affidavit,
or otherwise to the satisfaction of the court, or a judge in
vacation, that the nuisance complained of exists, a temporary order of injunction and abatement shall forthwith
be granted. When a temporary injunction is granted, the
court may issue an order restraining the defendant, and all
other persons from removing, or in any way interfering
with, the liquor or fixtures or other things used in connection with such alleged violations of this act constituting
such nuisance. When an injunction has been granted, it
shall be binding throughout the state and any violation of
its provisions shall be contempt.

The hearing for the permanent injunction shall be triable at or before the first term of the court after due notice
of the temporary injunction has been given. Evidence of
the general reputation of the place shall be admissible for
the purpose of proving the existence of the nuisance, and
evidence for the granting of the temporary order shall be
prima facie evidence for the purpose of proving knowledge
on the part of the owner, lessor or person having charge
as agent or otherwise, or having any interest in the building, erection, thing, place or premises where such nuisance
exists. No bond or security for costs shall be required by
the court if the action is instituted by the commissioner,
his deputies, attorney general, prosecuting attorney, municipal law officer or any officer of the law. It shall not

be necessary for the court to find the building, erection, thing, place or premises involved were being unlawfully used as aforesaid at the time of the hearing, but on finding that the material allegations of the petition, are true, the court shall order that the nuisance shall be abated and that no liquor shall be sold, manufactured, bartered, given away, distributed, dispensed, possessed, stored, solicited for or bootlegged, nor this act in any other way be violated on or in such building, erection, thing, place or premises, or in any part thereof. In case of a drug store, such order for abatement shall, in the discretion of the court, be binding for a period not exceeding one year from and after such finding; in all other cases such order for abatement shall be perpetual. But in any case the order may be made not only against the defendant named in the action, but in general terms against occupants, grantees, assignees, heirs, administrators, executors, trustees, or other classes including persons who have or may have an interest or estate in such place against which the order is made. And upon judgment of the court ordering such nuisance to be abated the court may order that said room, building, structure, erection, thing, premises, or place of any kind shall be closed for one year, or until the owner, lessee, tenant, or occupant thereof shall give bond with sufficient surety, to be approved by the court making the order, in the penal sum of not less than five hundred ($500.00) dollars, nor more than five thousand ($5,000.00) dollars, payable to the state of Ohio and conditioned that intoxicating liquors will not thereafter be manufactured, sold, bartered, given away or furnished or otherwise disposed of or possessed or kept, nor this act in any other way violated therein or thereon, and that he will pay all fines, forfeited bonds, costs, and damages that may be assessed for any violation of this act upon said premises.

Sec. 6212-50.

Enforcement of law against place where liquor is sold; abatement of nuisance; fees.

SECTION 39. In case the existence of a place where liquor is sold in violation of law appears in any criminal proceedings under this act, it shall be the duty of the prosecuting attorney, municipal law officer, attorney general or commissioner to proceed promptly in an action in a court of equity to enforce the provisions of this act against such place as a nuisance, and the finding of the defendant guilty in such criminal proceedings, unless reversed, shall be conclusive against such defendant as to the existence of the nuisance. For removing and selling property in connection with the abatement of such a nuisance, the officer performing that duty shall be entitled to charge and receive the same fees as the sheriff of the county would receive for levying upon and selling property on execution, and for closing the premises and keeping them closed, a reasonable sum shall be allowed by the court.

Sec. 6212-51.

SECTION 40. Any person violating the terms of the injunction and order of abatement as provided for in this act shall be tried, and, if found guilty, be punished for contempt by a fine of not less than five hundred ($500.00) dollars nor more than one thousand ($1,000.00) dollars, and by imprisonment of not less than thirty (30) days nor more than twelve (12) months; and, in addition to the provisions herein, the court shall have the power to enforce such injunction by such measures and means as in the judgment of the court may be necessary.

Penalty for violation of injunction or order of abatement.

In contempt proceedings arising out of the violation of any injunction granted under the provisions of this act, the court, or in vacation a judge thereof, shall have the power to try summarily and punish the party guilty as required by law. Process shall issue in the name of the state of Ohio. The affidavit upon which the attachment for contempt issues shall make a prima facie case for the state. The accused may plead in the same manner as to an information, or indictment, in so far as the same is applicable. Evidence may be oral or in the form of affidavits, or both. The defendant may be required to make answer to interrogatories, either written or oral, as in the discretion of the court or judge may seem proper. The defendant shall not necessarily be discharged upon his denial of the facts stated in the affidavit or information. The clerk of the court shall, upon the application of either party, issue subpoenas for witnesses, and, except as above set forth, the practice in such contempt proceedings shall conform as nearly as may be to the procedure and practice of courts of equity in this state.

Proceedings on contempt.

Sec. 6212-52.

SECTION 41. Any violation of this act by the lessee or occupant of any premises shall, at the option of the lessor, work a forfeiture of the lease.

Forfeiture of lease.

Sec. 6212-53.

SECTION 42. A husband, wife, child, parent, guardian, employer, or other person injured in person, property, home, care, means of support, or parental or marital relation, or otherwise, which injury is caused, or contributed to, by an intoxicated person, or in consequence of the intoxication of a person, shall have a right of action in his or her name, severally or jointly, against any person who unlawfully sold, furnished or gave away intoxicating liquor to such intoxicated person in violation of the laws of the state of Ohio, or of the United States, relating to the liquor traffic, or who assisted or aided in, or contributed to, such unlawful selling, furnishing, or giving such intoxicated person such intoxicating liquor which caused, or contributed to, the intoxication of such intoxicated person, in which action exemplary as well as any damages resulting from such injury may be awarded. The owner of a building or premises, and the person renting or leasing the same, who, having knowledge, or who having leased the same for other purposes, knowingly permits intoxicating liquors to be manufactured, sold, kept or stored in or on such building or

Right of action for injury to person or property by one intoxicated.

Who liable for damages.

premises, wherein or whereon was sold, furnished or given the liquor, which caused, or contributed to, the intoxication of such intoxicated person hereinbefore described in this section, shall be liable severally or jointly with any and all persons liable hereunder for such aforesaid damages sustained as well as exemplary damages. Such damages, together with costs of suit, shall be recoverable in an action before any court of competent jurisdiction, and where the owner of such building or premises is held liable for such damages, such damages and costs shall be a lien on such building or premises.

Who may sue for recovery.

In any case where parents shall be entitled to such damages, either the father or mother may sue alone therefor, but recovery by one of such parties shall be a bar to suit brought by the other. All damages recovered by a minor under this section shall be paid either to such minor, or to his parent, guardian or next friend, as the court shall direct. In case of the death of either the party injured, or the party liable for such injury, the action, or right of action given by this section, shall survive to or against, as the case may be, the executor or administrator.

SEARCH AND SEIZURE.

Sec. 6212-54.

Search and seizure without warrant and affidavit.

SECTION 43. All intoxicating liquors unlawfully manufactured, possessed, transported, labeled, or stored are contraband, and any officer whose duty it is to enforce the law, may, except in a private dwelling not subject to search as provided in section 50 of this act, without a search warrant and affidavit therefor being filed, seize such liquors and the receptacles and instruments or equipment used in such unlawful acts, and such liquors, receptacles, instruments and equipment used in such unlawful acts, and such liquors, receptacles, instruments and equipment shall be free from replevin or other process as provided in this act.

Filing of affidavit; disposition of liquors and containers.

The officer or person seizing such liquor shall file a proper affidavit forthwith with a magistrate, judge or court, having jurisdiction herein, and if such liquors are held to be manufactured, sold, possessed, labeled, transported or stored in violation of law, they, the containers thereof, and other said equipment and instruments shall be forthwith destroyed, or otherwise disposed of according to law. No officer or person who destroys contraband liquor or, containers or equipment for the unlawful use thereof, shall be held liable for any damages for such act.

Sec. 6212-55.

Search and seizure upon complaint or affidavit; duties of officers.

SECTION 44. If any person makes a sworn complaint or affidavit before any magistrate, judge or court, having jurisdiction under this act, that he has reason to believe and does believe that any intoxicating liquors are being manufactured, sold, furnished, given away, or possessed, or orders for liquors are received or solicited contrary to law, in or on any building, erection, thing or place, stationary or movable, whether on land, in or on water, or in the air, or that any such liquors are stored or kept temporarily or otherwise in any depot, freight house, express office, or in any other building or place contrary to the provisions of this act, such magistrate, judge or court shall immediately issue his warrant to any officer whom the complainant may designate, having power to serve criminal process, commanding him to search the premises, object, place or thing described and designated in such complaint and warrant, and if such liquors are there found, to seize the same together with the vessels in which they are contained, and all the stills, implements, furniture, records, order books, advertising matter and all paraphernalia used and kept for such illegal manufacturing, selling, furnishing, giving away, possessing, keeping, storing, or soliciting or receiving orders for such liquors, and them safely keep and make immediate return on said warrant; and to arrest all parties found at such place or thing, the principals, aiders and abetters to be charged with an offense as hereinafter provided and the others to be held as witnesses either on their own or others' recognizance, as the magistrate, judge or court may direct. The names and addresses of all such parties shall be noted by the officer in his return. Such liquors, stills, furniture, vessels, implements and all paraphernalia used in such manufacturing, possessing, keeping, storing, or soliciting or receiving orders or selling shall be held subject to the order of such magistrate, judge or court, to be used in evidence in the prosecution of any case for a violation of this act.

Sec. 6212-56.

SECTION 45. When such intoxicating liquors or stills, implements, vessels, records or order books, blanks or advertising matter, or furniture are seized, as hereinbefore provided, the officer serving the warrant shall forthwith file a complaint in writing and on oath, charging the violation of the law which the evidence in the case justifies. If such officer refuses or neglects to file such complaint, then the person filing the affidavit for a search warrant, or any other person, may file such complaint, but nothing herein contained shall prevent any person or officer from filing such complaint before the search warrant is issued or served, and all intoxicating liquors, stills, furniture, vessels, implements, order books and all paraphernalia hereinbefore recited, so seized, may be used as evidence at the trial or hearing, based upon such complaint charging the violation of this act.

Filing verified complaint in writing by officer or other person; evidence.

Sec. 6212-57.

SECTION 46. No warrant for search shall be issued until there has been filed with such magistrate, judge or court an affidavit describing the building, place, premises, or object to be searched, the things to be searched for, and alleging substantially the offense in relation thereto, and that the affiant believes or has good cause to believe that such liquor is there concealed. Provided, however, that any description that will enable the officer to find the building, premises, place, or object to be searched shall be deemed

When search warrant shall issue; form of warrant.

to be sufficient. The warrant for search shall be directed to the proper officer and shall show by a copy of the affidavit inserted therein or annexed and referred to, or shall recite, all of the material facts alleged in the affidavit, and shall describe the things to be searched for and the building, place, premises or object to be searched. A warrant for search and seizure substantially in the following form shall be sufficient:

County of ⁝ .... ⎫
⎬ ss.
State of Ohio .... ⎭

To .... Greetings:
Whereas there has been filed with the undersigned an affidavit of which the following is a true copy: (Here copy of affidavit.)

These are, therefore, to command you in the name of the people of the state of Ohio, together with the necessary and proper assistance to enter (here describe the building or place, premises or object designated in the affidavit) of the said .... situated in the .... of .... in the county aforesaid, and there diligently search for the said intoxicating liquors, implements, records, order blanks, and other paraphernalia, to wit: (here describe the articles in affidavit) and that you bring the same or any part thereof found in such search forthwith before me to be disposed of and dealt with according to law; and that you arrest all persons found therein or thereat and bring them before me to be dealt with according to law.

Given under my hand this .... day of ...., A. D. 19...

....
(Official Title.)

Sec. 6212-58.
Fluids secreted or poured out, prima facie evidence.

SECTION 47. If fluids be poured out, secreted or otherwise destroyed by the owner or occupant of the buildings, premises, place or thing, or by the tenant, assistant or other person, when the building, premises, place or thing are searched or to be searched, manifestly for the purpose of preventing their seizure by officers authorized to make search and seizure, such fluids shall be held to be prima facie intoxicating liquor.

Sec. 6212-59.
Statement by officer making seizure; disposition of property seized.

SECTION 48. When liquors, stills, records or order books, vessels, furniture and other paraphernalia are seized as provided in the preceding sections, the officer who made such seizure shall, in his return upon the warrant, make a statement, setting forth their seizure by him and their place of detention, and they shall be held by said officer subject to order of the court. Upon final judgment of the magistrate, judge or court upon the complaint provided for herein, such intoxicating liquors, receptacles, records and other paraphernalia, shall be returned to their lawful owner in case of acquittal, or destroyed or otherwise disposed of according to the order of the court in case of conviction. When liquors, stills, vessels or furniture and other paraphernalia hereinbefore recited shall have been seized by virtue of such warrant, said warrant shall not be held void, nor such liquors, stills, vessels or furniture or other paraphernalia returned to any person claiming the same, by reason of any alleged insufficiency of the description in the complaint or warrant, provided, that a new complaint or warrant shall issue within twenty-four hours.

Sec. 6212-60.

SECTION 49. If no one is found in possession of the premises or object where such liquors are kept or stored, the officer taking the same shall post in a conspicuous place on said object, building, place or premises, a copy of the warrant and take posession of such liquors, stills, vessels, furniture and other paraphernalia hereinbefore recited and hold them subject to the order of the magistrate, judge or court issuing the warrant and make return of his action thereon. Whereupon it shall be the duty of the magistrate, judge or court to fix a time for hearing and determining the purpose for which such liquors are kept, and issue notice thereof to the officer who shall post a copy thereof on the building, premises, place or object where the liquors were found. If at the time for said hearing no person appears, nor within thirty (30) days thereafter, to claim such liquors, vessels, furniture or other said paraphernalia, the magistrate or court or judge shall order the same destroyed, or otherwise disposed of according to law.

Posting copy of warrant on vacant premises; seizure of property; hearing.

Sec. 6212-61.

SECTION 50. No warrant shall be issued to search a private dwelling occupied as such unless some part of it is used as a store or shop, hotel or boarding house, or for any other purpose than a private residence, or unless such residence is a place of public resort for drinking liquors, or intoxicating liquor is manufactured, sold or furnished therein in violation of the law. Provided, that the word "possess" as used in this act in reference to intoxicating liquors shall not apply to intoxicating liquors in a bona fide private residence.

Private residence not subject to search.

Sec. 6212-62.

SECTION 51. The person making the affidavit for the warrant to search any place may, personally or by agent, accompany the officer who serves the warrant and enter the place with such officer and give information and assistance, if required, to such officer in searching such place for such intoxicating liquors as hereinbefore described.

Person making affidavit may accompany officer.

Sec. 6212-63.

SECTION 52. Liquors, stills, vessels, furniture and other paraphernalia seized, as hereinbefore provided, shall not be taken from the custody of the officer by a writ of replevin or other process while the proceedings herein provided are pending. Final judgment of conviction in such proceedings is in all cases a bar to all suits for the recovery of liquors, stills, vessels, furniture and other said paraphernalia seized of their value or for damages alleged to arise by seizure and detention thereof.

Writ of replevin shall not issue pending proceedings.

Sec. 6212-64.

Search of wagon, buggy, automobile, etc., seizure of vehicle and arrest of person.

SECTION 53. When the commissioner, his deputies, inspectors, or any sheriff, constable, police or other officer, shall have reason to suspect that intoxicating liquors are being transported in any wagon, buggy or automobile or other vehicle, or conveyance by land, air, or water contrary to law, it shall be his duty to search such wagon, buggy, automobile, or other vehicle or conveyance and to seize any and all intoxicating liquors found therein which is being transported contrary to law. Whenever any intoxicating liquors which are being transported illegally or are being transported for an illegal use, shall be seized by an officer of the state of Ohio, he shall take possession of the vehicle, and team or automobile or boat, or land, air or water craft, or any other conveyance owned and used by any railroad, steamboat, or express company, or by any other person, in which liquor shall be found, and shall also arrest any person in charge of such team, vehicle, or other said conveyance. Such officer shall at once proceed against the person arrested under the provisions of this act before any magistrate, judge or court having competent jurisdiction.

Sale of seized property; proceeds of sale.

The magistrate or judge before who, or the court wherein, conviction is made, shall, unless the owner clearly proves that he did not know, nor negligently permit the person convicted to be in possession of such team, vehicle, automobile or other conveyance, order a sale by public auction of the property seized, and the officer making the sale, after deducting the expenses of keeping the animals and vehicles or automobiles or other conveyance, the costs of the sale and the fee for seizure, shall pay the proceeds to the officer authorized to receive the fine. In the event that the proceeds of the sale shall exceed the amount of the fines and the cost above mentioned, the balance remaining after the fines and costs have been paid shall be paid to the owner of the vehicle, team, automobile or other conveyance. If, however, no one shall be found in charge of the team, vehicle, automobile, or other conveyance, and no claimant shall establish his ownership in such team, vehicle, automobile or other conveyance within thirty days after seizure, thereof, such team, vehicle, automobile, or other conveyance, as the case may be, shall be sold and the proceeds after deducting the costs of the case and the expense of keeping and selling the said team, vehicle, automobile or other conveyance, shall be paid and disposed of as are fines imposed under this act. In any case the intoxicating liquors seized shall be destroyed or otherwise disposed of according to law and the containers shall be sold or destroyed.

Sec. 6212-65.

Sale of liquid after removal of alcohol; disposition of proceeds.

SECTION 54. The commissioner is authorized, at his discretion, to have the alcohol contained in all seized and confiscated liquors separated and removed therefrom and to sell such alcohol at the same price at which, to the persons to whom, and under the same regulations under which, the manufacturer of alcohol sells the same. After all necessary expenses are defrayed the disposition of the net proceeds from each such sale shall follow the provisions herein as to disposition of fines. Any magistrate, judge or court having in custody seized and confiscated liquor, shall, except in cases of acquittal, notify the commissioner before final disposition thereof.

The commissioner shall make to the clerk of the court of the county wherein were seized the liquors from which the alcohol was separated or removed, a report such as is required in section 17 of this act, and in addition thereto a report of the gross and net receipts from the sale of alcohol separated or removed from the liquors seized and confiscated in such county. The commissioner shall also keep on file in his office, a record by counties, showing the title of each case wherein such liquor was seized, the trial officer or court, the amount of liquor in such seizure from which alcohol was obtained, the amount of alcohol obtained therefrom, the gross receipts and expenses and net receipts. *Report to clerk of court.*

Sec. 6319-66. SECTION 55. Whenever complaint shall be made by any person on oath before any magistrate, judge or court, having jurisdiction, that any person is found intoxicated, or has been intoxicated, or that liquor is being kept in any hotel, store, public building, street, alley, highway, or other public place, it shall be the duty of such magistrate, judge or court, to issue subpoena to compel the attendance of such person found intoxicated or other person suspected of having knowledge of the presence of liquor at the place aforesaid, to appear before the magistrate, judge or court issuing the same, to testify in regard to the person or persons of whom, the time when, the place where and the manner in which the liquor producing his intoxication was procured, or as to other violations complained of, and if such person when subpoenaed shall neglect or refuse to obey such writ, the said magistrate, judge or court who issued the same shall have the power and authority to compel the attendance of the person so subpoenaed and to enforce obedience to such writ, just as is done in instance of a like writ in any case not an ex parte proceeding. Whenever the person so subpoenaed shall appear before the magistrate, judge or court to testify as aforesaid, he shall be required to answer on oath. And if such person shall refuse to answer fully and fairly such questions on oath, he shall be punished and dealt with in the same manner as for contempt of court as in other cases, or fined from seventy-five to one hundred dollars. If it shall appear from the testimony of such person that any of the offenses specified in this act have been committed, such magistrate, judge or court before whom such testimony is given, shall make a true record of the same and cause it to be subscribed by such witnesses; and the said testimony or answers, when subscribed as aforesaid, shall be deemed sufficient complaint to authorize the issuing of a warrant to arrest any person who may appear from said complaint to be guilty of *Examination of person found intoxicated; refusal to testify contempt; record of cause subscribed by witnesses.*

having violated any of the provisions of this act. Any person arrested on a warrant issued pursuant to the provisions of this section, shall be brought before the magistrate, judge or court issuing the same, and all subsequent proceedings in such suit or prosecution shall be governed by rules of the law applicable thereto as in other cases under this act. Provided, that the person so testifying under the provisions of this section shall not be held or prosecuted for the intoxication or other violations of law concerning which such testimony shall be given; provided, further, that nothing contained herein shall be so construed as to prevent the prosecution of persons for being drunk or intoxicated, when the testimony of said person is not sought under the provisions of this act.

Sec. 6212-67.

Authority of conductor, etc., to arrest violators of act.

SECTION 56. Any conductor or person in charge of any car, train, boat, or other public coach, automobile, or other public conveyance, shall have authority to arrest any person who is a passenger, or is being conveyed by such car, coach, automobile, or other conveyance, for violating any of the provisions of this act, and to turn him over to any sheriff, constable, police officer, to be proceeded against by law; and any carrier or agent thereof, may without being subject to civil or criminal action, refuse passage to a person intoxicated or in any way violating the provisions of this act.

Sec. 6212-68.

Device to evade law punishable.

SECTION 57. Any shift or device, whatever, to evade the provisions of this act, shall be deemed unlawful, and shall be punished as a violation of this act.

Sec. 6212-69.

Separate offenses may be united in separate counts.

SECTION 58. In any affidavit, information or indictment for a violation of this act, separate offenses may be united in separate counts and the defendant may be tried on all of the separate offenses at one trial and the cumulative penalty for all offenses charged may be imposed by the magistrate, judge or court. It shall not be necessary in any affidavit, information or indictment to include the names of persons with whom the illegal transaction took place or any defensive negative averments, but shall be sufficient to state that the act complained of was then and there prohibited and unlawful.

Sec. 6212-70.

Security of costs not required of officer.

SECTION 59. Whenever complaint is made by any officer of the law for any violation of this act, the officer before whom such complaint is made shall not require security for costs to be given.

Sec. 6212-71.

Incrimination no excuse from testifying.

SECTION 60. No person shall be excused from testifying against persons who have violated any provisions of this act for the reason that such testimony will tend to incriminate him, but no person required so to testify shall be punished for acts disclosed by such testimony.

Sec. 6212-72.

Penalty for manufacture or sale.

SECTION 61. Any person who manufactures intoxicating liquor, or any wholesale or retail druggist, or pharmacist, who sells such liquor in violation of this act, for a first offense shall be fined not less than two hundred ($200.00) dollars, nor more than one thousand ($1,000.00) dollars; .

for a second offense he shall be fined not less than five hundred ($500.00) dollars, nor more than two thousand ($2,-000.00) dollars, and be imprisoned not less than ninety (90) days, nor more than six (6) months; and for a third and each subsequent offense he shall be fined not less than one thousand ($1,000.00) dollars, and be imprisoned in the state penitentiary not less than one (1) year.

Any other person violating, or failing to comply with any of the provisions of this act, for which a penalty is not herein prescribed, for a first offense shall be fined not less than one hundred ($100.00) dollars, nor more than five hundred ($500.00) dollars; for a second offense he shall be fined not less than two hundred ($200.00) dollars, nor more than one thousand ($1,000.00) dollars, and be imprisoned not less than thirty (30) days, nor more than ninety (90) days; and for a third and each subsequent offense he shall be fined not less than five hundred ($500.00) dollars, and be imprisoned in the state penitentiary not less than six (6) months. It shall be unlawful for any magistrate, judge or court to suspend any sentence imposed or remit any part of fines assessed, except upon the recommendation of the commissioner, nor shall the superintendent or board of directors of any workhouse release any one from confinement resulting from a violation of this act unless upon the recommendation of the commissioner.

Sec. 6312-73.

SECTION 62. In addition to the penalties imposed by this act for the violation of any of its provisions, the magistrate, judge or court may, in its discretion, after conviction, require the defendant to execute a bond with approved security, in a penalty of not less than five hundred ($500.00) dollars, nor more than five thousand ($5,000.00) dollars, conditioned that the said defendant will not violate any of the provisions of this act for the term of one year. And if said bond shall not be given, the defendant shall be committed to jail until it shall be given or until he shall be discharged by the magistrate, judge or court, provided that he shall not be confined a longer period than six months. *Bond against future violations.*

Sec. 6212-74.

SECTION 63. Any hearing on either an affidavit, information or indictment, charging a violation of this act, shall be held within thirty (30) days after the filing of the affidavit or information or the finding of an indictment by the grand jury, unless the magistrate, judge or court hearing the matter is satisfied that good reasons exist for a longer period, but then, in any event, not more than thirty (30) additional days shall be granted. *Limitation within which hearing shall be had.*

Cases arising under this act shall be advanced on the docket when such is necessary to have a hearing thereon within the first said thirty-day period, and when in any county it appears that the crowded condition of the docket may prevent such hearing within the full sixty-day period, then, upon application made by the commissioner, prosecuting attorney or attorney general, the chief justice of the state supreme court shall assign judges from other coun- *Advancement of cases.*

ties to hear cases in any county named in such application by the commissioner, prosecuting attorney or attorney general.

Sec, 6212-75.
Proceedings in error.

SECTION 64. Error may be prosecuted to a judgment of conviction rendered by any officer or court having jurisdiction hereunder, by filing a petition in error, accompanied by a bill of exceptions and a transcript of the docket of the trial officer or court, but before such petition in error can be filed, a motion for leave to file such petition in error must be granted by the reviewing court, of which motion reasonable notice of the time and place of hearing must have been given counsel for the complainant in the original case. Such motion and petition in error must be filed in the court of common pleas except when a judgment of such court or of a judge thereof is to be reviewed, and in such instance such motion must be made and petition in error be filed in the court of appeals, but in any instance such petition in error, if allowed to be filed, must be filed within not more than thirty (30) days after the rendition of the judgment complained of, and the case shall be heard by such reviewing court within thirty (30) days after the filing of such petition in error. When a reviewing court is not in session in the district within the time provided, the motion for leave to file petition in error and the petition in error may be filed with, and shall be heard by, such reviewing court within ten (10) days after such court is in session in such district.

Error to the judgment of the common pleas court affirming a judgment of conviction may be prosecuted in the same manner, under the same conditions and subject to the same limitations, as is error to a judgment of conviction of the common pleas court as herein provided.

Sec. 6212-76.
Division of fines and forfeited recognizances.

SECTION 65. Money arising from fines and forfeited and violated bonds shall be paid one-half into the state treasury and one-half into the treasury of the political subdivision where the prosecution is held.

Sec. 6212-77.
Fines, costs and forfeited bonds a lien.

SECTION 66. All premises, places, objects or things are subject to liens for fines and costs and for violated or forfeited bonds, resulting from offenses committed in, at, on, or about such premises, places, objects or things, if the owner thereof had knowledge of such offenses, or if, without knowledge, he negligently permitted such offenses to be committed. Such lien may be enforced by a civil action brought in any court having jurisdiction by the commissioner, and any of his deputies, attorney general, prosecuting attorney or municipal law officer, and such premises, place, object or thing may be ordered sold to satisfy such lien. Any of such officers shall also have authority to bring suit on a forfeited or violated bond against the principal and sureties therein.

SECTION 67. The attorney general, prohibition commissioner and the several prosecuting attorneys and other officers whose duty it is to enforce this act, are herein authorized to secure from the federal internal revenue collectors, a certified copy of the names of all persons and their places of business who have paid to the federal government special taxes imposed upon them for manufacturing, selling, or rectifying intoxicating liquors within their respective counties after July 1, 1919, and to pay the internal revenue collector the fee prescribed by the statutes of the United States, and each month thereafter such prosecuting attorneys and commissioners shall revise such lists if there be any changes in the names of such lists in the internal revenue collector's records. When such statement is received, each prosecuting attorney shall file the same with the clerk of the court of his county and the commissioner shall file the same in his office, each of whom shall record the same in a book kept therefor. *Certified copy of names and places from internal revenue collector obtained and filed with clerk of courts.*

SECTION 68. It shall be the duty of the county clerk and commissioner immediately upon receipt of any statements or lists provided herein to be filed with such officials, to file such statements and lists as a part of the files of his respective office in a permanent record alphabetically arranged, or separate book or docket, and to permit any and all persons desiring to do so to inspect the said statements and lists, or record thereof, at any time during the office hours. It shall be the further duty of the said county clerk or commissioner to furnish certified copies of such statements or lists, or record thereof, to any person requesting the same, upon payment of the lawful fees therefor, and the said original statements or lists, or certified copies thereof, or of the record thereof, shall be competent evidence upon the trial of any cause whatever and in any of the courts of this state, in which the same may be relevant. All records required by this act to be kept, except in the instance of the commissioner and the clerk of the court in each county, shall be subject to inspection at any reasonable hours by any of the officers authorized to enforce this act, or by any magistrate or any judge of any court, or by any person having an order from any such officer, magistrate or judge, to be permitted to make such inspection, and any such person shall be permitted to make copies from such records. In case of the commissioner and the clerk of the court of each county, the records required to be kept and reports required to be filed by such officers shall be open to public inspection during office hours. *Filing and recording statements and lists.* *Records subject to inspection.*

SECTION 69. Every clerk of a court or officer having jurisdiction to try cases for violating the provisions of this act shall send a report once a quarter to the commissioner, showing the number of arrests and convictions for drunkenness, the number of fines assessed and the amount of fines collected, and such other matter as said commissioner may require relating thereto, during such quarter, and similar *Quarterly report by clerk to commissioner.*

data as to the corresponding quarter of the year before. After the first year the statement of arrests and convictions for the previous year shall be omitted.

Sec. 6212-81.

Courts having final jurisdiction.

SECTION 70. Any justice of the peace, mayor, municipal court, police court, probate court, court of common pleas, judge of any such courts or any other judge or court within the county with whom an affidavit is filed charging the violation of any of the provisions of this act, when the offense is alleged to have been committed in the county in which such mayor, justice of the peace, or judge or court may be sitting, shall have final jurisdiction to try such cases upon such affidavit without a jury, unless imprisonment is a part of the penalty, but error may be prosecuted to the judgment of such mayor, justice of the peace, judge, or court as herein provided. And in any such case where imprisonment is not a part of the penalty, the defendant cannot waive examination nor can said mayor, justice of the peace, judge, or court recognize such defendant to the grand jury; nor shall it be necessary that any information be filed by the prosecuting attorney or an indictment shall be found by the grand jury. Any such trial magistrate, judge, or court shall have authority to issue a capias. The purpose of this section is to enlarge the jurisdiction of the aforesaid officers in addition to jurisdiction now given and provided by law in the prosecution of criminal cases.

Sec. 6212-82.

Duties of certain officers.

SECTION 71. It shall be the duty (a) of the commissioner and any of his deputies and inspectors; (b) of sheriffs, deputy sheriffs and prosecuting attorneys of any county; (c) of the mayor, manager or other executive authority, municipal law officer, chief of police, police officer or patrolman, or marshal or deputy marshal of any municipality; (d) of any constable or deputy constable of any township, to investigate alleged violations of, and to enforce and co-operate with officers in enforcing, the provisions of this act. No such officer shall be liable, either civilly or criminally for any act performed by him in good faith in enforcing or attempting to enforce or carry out any of the provisions of this act, and it shall be a good defense to any civil suit or criminal prosecution against any officer that the acts complained of were committed by him while acting in good faith, either with or without process of law, in enforcing or attempting to enforce or carry out the provisions of this act; but any wilful or negligent failure or refusal on the part of any such officer to perform any of the duties and obligations imposed upon him by any of the provisions of this act within the political subdivision in which he was elected, for which he was appointed, or by which he is employed, shall work a forfeiture of his office for which he is removable from office by any method herein or elsewhere provided by law.

Sec. 6212-82. SECTION 72. In addition to any other provision made for such removal, an action in quo warranto may be brought against any such officer by the commissioner, attorney general, prosecuting attorney, municipal law officer or any resident of the subdivision in which it was such officer's duty to enforce the provisions of this act. *Quo warranto proceedings in removal of officers.*

The mayor, manager, or other executive authority of a municipality shall remove any police, police officer, patrolman, marshal or deputy marshal who fails or refuses to perform any of the duties and obligations imposed upon him herein or elsewhere by law. Proceedings for such removal shall be begun by filing with the executive authority of the municipality a complaint, setting forth the causes why such officer should be removed, and a copy of such complaint shall be served upon such officer against whom the complaint is filed, at least ten days before the hearing of said complaint. The complaint may be filed by the commissioner or any of his deputies, or by the law officer or any resident of the municipality, or by the executive himself. Pending such investigation the executive, in his discretion, may suspend for a period of not to exceed twenty days the officer complained against. Such removal proceedings shall be public and the decision of the mayor, manager, or other executive authority shall be final. *Removal of police officer.*

In case of failure of the commissioner, or a mayor, manager, or other executive authority, or the law officer of a municipality, or of the sheriff or the prosecuting attorney of a county, to perform any of the duties and obligations imposed upon him herein or elsewhere by law, the governor of the state shall remove such incumbent from office, and the proceedings for such removal shall be the same as provided in sections 4268 and 4269, General Code. *Removal of commissioner, mayor, etc.*

The provisions herein are not intended to take away any other remedies already provided by law for removal of officers, and resort to any one remedy shall not preclude the use of any other remedy for such removal, provided that no more than one removal proceeding against any official shall be pending at the same time, and that removal under one proceeding shall be a bar to another proceeding against the same officer.

Sec. 6212-84. SECTION 73. All suits or actions pending when this act becomes operative under any law inconsistent with this act, whether on behalf of the state or of any person, may be prosecuted to final judgment, and such judgment be enforced in like manner and with the same effect as though this act were not passed, and all rights of action accrued to said state or to any person under any existing law when this act became effective, are hereby preserved and saved and excepted from the operation and effect of this act, and the same may be prosecuted and sued to recovery in like manner, and to the same extent, as might have been done if this act had not been passed. *Pending actions.*

SECTION 74. If any section, subsection, sentence, clause or phrase of this act is for any reason held to be unconstitutional, such decision shall not affect the validity of the remaining portions of this act. The general assembly hereby declares it would have passed the act and each section, subsection, sentence, clause and phrase thereof, irrespective of the fact that any one or more sections, subsections, sentences, clauses, or phrases be declared unconstitutional.

Sec. 6212-85.

Section or part held void shall not affect others.

Repeals.

SECTION 75. The provisions of an act to provide for license to traffic in intoxicating liquors, as found in volume 103, Ohio Laws, at pages 216-243, known as sections 1261-16, 1261-17, 1261-18, 1261-19, 1261-20, 1261-21, 1261-22, 1261-23, 1261-24, 1261-25, 1261-26, 1261-27, 1261-28, 1261-29, 1261-30, 1261-31, 1261-32, 1261-33, 1261-34, 1261-35, 1261-36, 1261-37, 1261-38, 1261-39, 1261-40, 1261-41, 1261-42, 1261-43, 1261-44, 1261-45, 1261-46, 1261-47, 1261-48, 1261-49, 1261-50, 1261-51, 1261-52, 1261-53, 1261-54, 1261-55, 1261-56, 1261-57, 1261-58, 1261-59, 1261-60, 1261-61, 1261-62, 1261-63, 1261-64, 1261-65, 1261-66, 1261-67, 1261-68, 1261-69, 1261-70, 1261-71, 1261-72, 1261-73 and amendments thereto, and sections 6064, 6065, 6066, 6070, 6083, 6084, 6087, 6088, 6089, 6091, 6102, 6103, 6104, 6105, 6106, 6108, 6109, 6110, 6111, 6112, 6113, 6114, 6115, 6116, 6117, 6118, 6119, 6120, 6122, 6125, 6127, 6128, 6130, 6132, 6134, 6135, 6136, 6137, 6138, 6140, 6142, 6143, 6144, 6145, 6146, 6147, 6148, 6149, 6150, 6151, 6152, 6155, 6156, 6157, 6159, 6161, 6162, 6163, 6164, 6165, 6166, 6167, 6168, 6187, 6188, 6189, 6190, 6191, 6192, of the General Code, and all laws or parts of laws inconsistent with this act but to the extent only of such inconsistency, are hereby repealed.

When act takes effect.

SECTION 76. The provisions of this act shall take effect and be in force on and after May twenty-seven (27), nineteen hundred nineteen (1919).

The sectional numbers on the margin hereof are designated as provided by law. JOHN G. PRICE, *Attorney General.*

CARL R. KIMBALL,
Speaker of the House of Representatives.
CLARENCE J. BROWN,
President of the Senate.

Passed April 17, 1919.
Approved May 16, 1919.

JAMES M. COX,
Governor.

Filed in the office of the Secretary of State at Columbus, Ohio, on the 19th day of May, A. D. 1919.

147 G.

[House Bill No. 346.]

AN ACT

To provide penalties for the use of salamanders or other coke-burners giving off obnoxious or injurious gases in enclosures where persons work or are employed.

Be it enacted by the General Assembly of the State of Ohio:

Sec. 12798-6.

The sectional numbers on the margin hereof is in conformity to the General Code. JOHN G. PRICE, *Attorney General.*

SECTION 1. Whoever uses or causes or permits to be used an open salamander or coke burner or other outfit or receptacle of any kind in which charcoal, coke, coal, or any other fuel or combustible substance is burned or in process of combustion so as to give off obnoxious gases or gases detrimental to health, in any enclosed residence or enclosed building under construction while a person or persons work or are employed therein without providing a proper pipe, chimney or enclosure to carry said gases from said open salamander, coke burner, outfit or receptacle to the outside of said enclosed building or residence, shall be guilty of a misdemeanor, and on conviction for the first offense shall be fined not more than one hundred dollars, and for a second or subsequent offense shall be fined not less than one hundred dollars nor more than two hundred dollars, and in each case he shall stand committed until such fine and the costs are paid or until he is otherwise discharged by due process of law.

Unlawful to use burners giving off obnoxious gases, when; penalty.

CARL R. KIMBALL,
Speaker of the House of Representatives.
CLARENCE J. BROWN,
President of the Senate.

Passed April 17, 1919.
Approved May 19, 1919.

JAMES M. COX,
Governor.

Filed in the office of the Secretary of State at Columbus, Ohio, on the 19th day of May, A. D. 1919.

148 G.

[House Bill No. 440.]

AN ACT

To amend section 660 of the General Code, relating to the licensing of solicitors and adjusters of insurance companies not authorized to transact business in the state of Ohio.

Be it enacted by the General Assembly of the State of Ohio:

SECTION 1.   That section 660 of the General Code be amended to read as follows:

License to solicit certain insurance.

Sec. 660.   The superintendent of insurance may issue licenses to citizens of this state, subject to revocation at any time, permitting the person named therein to solicit and issue fire, lightning, tornado, explosion, automobile or marine insurance on property in this state in insurance companies not authorized to transact business in this state.   Each such license shall expire on the thirty-first day of March next after the year in which it is issued, and may be then renewed;

Penalty for unauthorized company, agent, etc., doing business.

Provided, however, any officer, agent, solicitor, broker, inspector, adjuster, or employee of any unauthorized insurance company not licensed under section 660, or any agent, broker or other representative of the owner of property in this state, or any adjuster, agent or person who shall take or receive any application for insurance upon property in this state, or receive or collect a premium or any part thereof for any unauthorized insurance company, or adjust any loss thereon, or make any inspection thereof, or shall attempt or assist in any such act, or perform any act in this state relating to or concerning any policy or contract of insurance of any unauthorized insurance company, shall be punished by a fine of not less than $25.00 nor more than $500.00 or by imprisonment in the state penitentiary for not exceeding one year, or by both such fine and imprisonment.

Repeal.

SECTION 2.   That said original section 660 of the General Code be, and the same is hereby repealed.

CARL R. KIMBALL,
Speaker of the House of Representatives.
CLARENCE J. BROWN,
President of the Senate.

**The sectional number in this act is in conformity to the General Code.
JOHN G. PRICE,
Attorney General.**

Passed April 17, 1919.
Approved May 19, 1919.

JAMES M. COX,
Governor.

Filed in the office of the Secretary of State at Columbus, Ohio, on the 19th day of May, A. D. 1919.

149 G.

[House Bill No. 29.]

AN ACT

To amend section 2967 and 2968 of the General Code, relative to increasing the amount that may be allowed for the relief of the needy blind.

Be it enacted by the General Assembly of the State of Ohio:

SECTION 1.   That sections 2967 and 2968 of the General Code be amended to read as follows:

Sec. 2967.   At least ten days prior to action on any claim for relief hereunder, the person claiming shall file with the board of county commissioners a duly verified statement of the facts bringing him within these provisions. The list of claims shall be filed in a book kept for that purpose in the order of filing, which record shall be open to the public. No certificate for qualification of drawing money hereunder shall be granted until the board of county commissioners shall be satisfied from the evidence of at least two reputable residents of the county, one of whom shall be a registered physician, that they know the applicant to be blind and that he has the residential qualifications to entitle him to the relief asked. Such evidence shall be in writing, subscribed to by such witnesses, and be subject to the right of cross-examination by the board of county commissioners or other person. If the board of county commissioners be satisfied that the applicant is entitled to relief hereunder, said board shall issue an order therefor in such sum as said board finds needed, not to exceed two hundred dollars per annum, to be paid quarterly from the funds herein provided on the warrant of the county auditor, and such relief shall be in place of all other relief of a public nature; provided, however, that where a husband and wife are both blind, and both have made application for blind relief as herein provided, the total relief given by said county commissioners to such husband and wife shall not exceed three hundred dollars per annum, and such relief shall be in place of all other relief of a public nature, to which such husband and wife, or either of them, might be entitled as a blind person. *(Verified statement; order for relief.)*

Sec. 2968.   At least once a year, and oftener if it deems necessary, the board of county commissioners shall make examination as to the qualifications, disability and needs of any or all persons on the blind list, and said board may at any time increase or decrease the amount of such relief, within the limits fixed by law. If not satisfied that any person on the blind list is qualified to draw his money, said board shall remove such person from the list, and shall forthwith notify the county auditor of such action. The board of county commissioners may in their discretion appoint such clerks as they deem necessary for the purpose of investigating the qualifications, disability and needs of any person who has theretofore been placed on the blind list, or who has made an application to be placed on such list. *(Increase or decrease of allowance.)* *("Blind relief clerks;" duties; compensation.)*

Said clerks shall be known as "blind relief clerks" and shall serve for such length of time only as said county commissioners prescribe and may be discharged by said commissioners at any time. The county commissioners shall fix the compensation of such clerks, which compensation, after being fixed, shall be paid monthly from the general fund of the county upon the warrant of the county auditor.

In addition to their compensation, said clerks shall be allowed monthly, their actual and necessary expenses incurred in the discharge of their official duties; but no such expenses shall be allowed or paid until an itemized statement of the same, duly verified, shall first have been filed by said clerks with said county commissioners. When so allowed, said expenses shall also be paid from the general fund of the county, upon the warrant of the county auditor.

Medical evidence may be required. If, upon the examination of the application of a person for blind relief, said county commissioners desire medical evidence of the blindness of said applicant, additional to that furnished by the evidence of the physician subscribing to said application, said commissioners shall have the right to employ another registered physician who, if said applicant is willing, shall examine the eye condition of said applicant and make written report to said commissioners concerning the same. Said county commissioners shall have the right to pay said physician making such examination and furnishing such additional evidence as aforesaid, a fee not to exceed the sum of ten dollars, which, when allowed by said county commissioners, shall be paid out of the general county fund upon the warrant of the county auditor.

Repeals. SECTION 2. That said original sections 2967 and 2968 of the General Code be, and the same are hereby repealed.

CARL R. KIMBALL,
Speaker of the House of Representatives.
CLARENCE J. BROWN,
President of the Senate.

The sectional numbers in this act are in conformity to the General Code. JOHN G. PRICE, Attorney General.

Passed April 17, 1919.
Approved May 19, 1919.

JAMES M. COX,
Governor.

Filed in the office of the Secretary of State at Columbus, Ohio, on the 19th day of May, A. D. 1919.

150 G.

[House Bill No. 478.]

AN ACT

Relative to authorizing the Dayton, Springfield and Xenia Southern Railway Company to extend its line over a part of the grounds of the Ohio Soldiers'' and Sailors' Orphans' Home.

Be it enacted by the General Assembly of the State of Ohio:

SECTION 1. The board of trustees of the Ohio Soldiers' and Sailors' Orphans' Home is hereby empowered to enter into a contract with the Dayton, Springfield and Xenia Southern Railway Company, an Ohio corporation having its principal office in Dayton, whereunder the railway company may be authorized to extend in an easterly direction from its present terminus near the western boundary line of the home grounds, its single track electric railroad over and upon a strip of ground not to exceed 15 feet in width and 700 feet in length, which strip of ground shall at all points be located north of the driveway along the northern portion of the artificial body of water known as "McDowell Lake." .

Said contract shall be prepared by the attorney general and shall contain such provisions as he may deem necessary to protect and safeguard the interests of the state and the children of the home, and it shall not become effective until written approval of the governor and attorney general is indorsed thereon, and until it is recorded in the minutes of the board of trustees and in the office of the recorder of Greene county, and filed in the office of the governor.

Extension of line over part of ground of O. S. and S. O. Home, authorized.

Contract and approval.

CARL R. KIMBALL,
Speaker of the House of Representatives.
CLARENCE J. BROWN,
President of the Senate.

This act is not of a general or permanent nature and requires no sectional number.
JOHN G. PRICE, *Attorney General.*

Passed April 17, 1919.
Approved May 19, 1919.

JAMES M. COX,
Governor.

Filed in the office of the Secretary of State at Columbus, Ohio, on the 19th day of May, A. D. 1919.

151 L.

[House Bill No. 178.]

AN ACT

Releasing the city of Cincinnati from payment of rental provided for in leases of part of the Miami and Erie canal executed under authority of the act passed May 15th, 1911 (102 Ohio Laws 168), and the act passed May 17, 1915 (106 Ohio Laws 293) from March 31, 1919, to March 31, 1925.

Be it enacted by the General Assembly of the State of Ohio:

Release from rental on part of Miami and Erie canal for certain period.

SECTION 1. That for and during the period between March 31, 1919, and March 31, 1925, the city of Cincinnati is hereby released from all its covenants, obligations and agreements for the payment of rent for that portion of the Miami and Erie canal leased by the state of Ohio to the city of Cincinnati by the lease dated August 29, 1912, executed under authority of the act passed May 15, 1911, (102 Ohio Laws 168) and by the amended lease dated January 6, 1917, executed under authority of the act passed May 17, 1915, (106 Ohio Laws 293) and for and during said period no rent or installment thereof shall be or become due or payable from said city to said state, all provisions in said lease and amended lease, and in said acts of May 15, 1911, and May 17, 1915, to the contrary notwithstanding.

Lease valid and in full force.

SECTION 2. Said lease and amended lease, and all the terms, conditions, covenants and agreements therein contained as modified in section 1 of this act, are hereby declared to be valid and in full force and effect and are hereby ratified and confirmed.

Stipulation as to rental of other portion of canal.

SECTION 3. That whenever the city of Cincinnati shall determine to lease the portion of the canal extending from a point three hundred feet north of Mitchell avenue to a point in the city of St. Bernard one thousand feet beyond the crossing of the canal by the tracks of the Baltimore and Ohio Southwestern Railroad, including the width thereof. in accordance with sections 1, 2, 3 and 4 of the act passed April 18, 1913 (103 Ohio Laws 720), it shall be provided in said lease that the rental therein stipulated shall not be due or payable for the period between March 31, 1919, and March 31, 1925, anything in the act passed May 15, 1911 (102 Ohio Laws 168), the act passed April 18, 1913 (103 Ohio Laws 720), or in the act passed May 17, 1915 (106 Ohio Laws 293), to the contrary notwithstanding.

CARL R. KIMBALL,
Speaker of the House of Representatives.

CLARENCE J. BROWN,
President of the Senate.

This act is not of a general and permanent nature and requires no sectional number.
JOHN G. PRICE, *Attorney General.*

Passed April 11, 1919.
Approved May 19, 1919.

JAMES M. COX,
Governor.

Filed in the office of the Secretary of State at Columbus, Ohio, on the 19th day of May, A. D. 1919.

182 6.

[House Bill No. 315.]

AN ACT

To authorize the governor to convey to the village of Hicksville, Defiance county, Ohio, certain land located therein.

Be it enacted by the General Assembly of the State of Ohio:

SECTION 1.   That the governor of the state of Ohio be and he is hereby authorized and directed on behalf of the state of Ohio to execute and deliver to the village of Hicksville, Defiance county, Ohio, a deed in such form as the attorney general of Ohio in conjunction with the auditor of state may prescribe, conveying to the said vilage of Hicksville certain land located therein which was acquired as a site for an armory but which will not be used for that purpose and which is described as follows: Governor authorized to convey certain land to Hicksville.

"Situated in the village of Hicksville, county of Defiance, and in the state of Ohio, and known as the whole of lots Nos. 145 and 146, and a part of lots Nos. 147 and 148 of the original plat of the village of Hicksville, Defiance county, Ohio; also a part of lots Nos. 143½ and 144½ of the vacated streets of said village of Hicksville as numbered on the auditor's plat thereof; also a part of lots Nos. 14, 15 and 16 of the first addition of said village of Hicksville, and which said entire premises are described by metes and bounds as follows, to-wit: Description of land.

"Commencing at a point on the northwesterly line of High street in said village of Hicksville, 23 feet distant northeasterly from the most southerly point of lot No. 147 of the original plat of said village and which point is 27 feet southwesterly from the most northerly point of said lot on said street; thence from said point of beginning, northeasterly along the northwesterly line of said High street, 127 feet to a point 10 feet southwesterly from the most northerly point on said street of said lot No. 143½ of the vacated streets, aforesaid; thence northwesterly at right angles with High street and on a line parallel with the northeasterly line of lots Nos. 143½ and 144½ of said vacated streets, and in continuation thereof, 260 feet; thence southwesterly and parallel with High street 127 feet; thence, southeasterly and in a direct line, 260 feet to the place of beginning.   Said premises being 27 feet off from the northeasterly sides of lots Nos. 147 and 148, the whole of lots Nos. 145 and 146, and 50 feet off from the southwesterly sides of said lots Nos. 143½ and 144½ of the vacated streets of said village, and sufficient off from the rear ends of lots Nos. 14, 15 and 16 of said first addition to make the entire premises herein conveyed 127 feet frontage on High street by 260 feet back therefrom northwesterly at right angles."

SECTION 2.   Such deed after being signed by the governor shall be countersigned by the secretary of state and   Signing and sealing.

sealed with the great seal of the state and shall be recorded in the office of the auditor of state before being deliverd.

This act is not of a general and permanent nature and requires no sectional number. JOHN G. PRICE, *Attorney General.*

CARL R. KIMBALL,
Speaker of the House of Representatives.
CLARENCE J. BROWN,
President of the Senate.

Passed April 14, 1919.
Approved May 19, 1919.

JAMES M. COX,
Governor.

Filed in the office of the Secretary of State at Columbus, Ohio, on the 19th day of May, A. D. 1919.

153 L.

[House Bill No. 512.]

AN ACT

To designate certain portions of Route No. VIII of the main market roads of Ohio as "The Scioto Trail."

Be it enacted by the General Assembly of the State of Ohio:

Sec. 6859-3a.

Part of Route No. VIII designated as "Scioto Trail."

SECTION 1. That part of Route No. VIII of the main market roads of Ohio commencing at Sandusky and extending, by way of Attica, Bucyrus, Marion, Prospect and Delaware to Columbus, and thence on the line of the former Columbus and Portsmouth turnpike by way of Circleville, Chillicothe, Waverly and Piketon, to Portsmouth shall be known and designated as "The Scioto Trail."

The sectional number on the margin hereof is designated as provided by law. JOHN G. PRICE, *Attorney General.*

CARL R. KIMBALL,
Speaker of the House of Representatives.
CLARENCE J. BROWN,
President of the Senate.

Passed April 17, 1919.
Approved May 19, 1919.

JAMES M. COX,
Governor.

Filed in the office of the Secretary of State at Columbus, Ohio, on the 19th day of May, A. D. 1919.

154 G.

[House Bill No. 532.]

AN ACT

To amend section 1207 of the General Code, relative to penalties for violations of the pharmacy laws.

Be it enacted by the General Assembly of the State of Ohio:

SECTION 1. That section 12708 of the General Code be amended to read as follows:

Sec. 12708. Sections twelve thousand seven hundred and five and twelve thousand seven hundred and six shall not prohibit a person from selling Paris green and other materials or compounds used exclusively for spraying and disinfecting when put up in bottles or boxes, bearing the name of a legally registered pharmacist or wholesale dealer, and labeled as required by law, or apply to or interfere with the exclusively wholesale business of a dealer.

Certain preceding sections do not prohibit sale of Paris green, etc., when.

SECTION 2. That original section 12708 of the General Code be and the same is hereby repealed.

CARL R. KIMBALL,
Speaker of the House of Representatives.
CLARENCE J. BROWN,
President of the Senate.

The sectional number in this act is in conformity to the General Code. JOHN G. PRICE, Attorney General.

Passed April 17, 1919.
Approved May 19, 1919.

JAMES M. COX,
Governor.

Filed in the office of the Secretary of State at Columbus, Ohio, on the 19th day of May, A. D. 1919.

155 G.

[Am. Senate Bill No. 124.]

AN ACT

To amend sections 1356 and 1357 of the General Code, relating to duties of the board of state charities.

Be it enacted by the General Assembly of the State of Ohio:

SECTION 1. That sections 1356 and 1357 of the General Code be amended so as to read as follows:

Sec. 1356. The board of state charities may call an annual conference, of the officials specified in section 1357 and representatives of the various social agencies in the state, to be known as the Ohio welfare conference. The purpose of the conference shall be to facilitate discussion of the problems and methods of practical human improvement, to increase the efficiency of agencies and institutions devoted to this cause; to disseminate information and to consider such other subjects of general social importance as may be determined upon by the conference itself. For this pur-

Board may call conferences, other officials and agencies.

Ohio welfare conference.

pose the conference shall organize by the elction of officers, the appointment of the proper committees, and the adoption of rules and regulations. The board may also call other conferences at any time or place for the consideration of problems relating to any particular group of institutions and agencies.

Expenses of attending conferences, how paid.

Sec. 1357. The necessary expenses of such officers of the state, county and municipal boards, benevolent and correctional institutions, and officials responsible for the administration of public funds used for the relief and maintenance of the poor and members of boards of county visitors as are invited by the board of state charities to the conferences provided for in section 1356 shall be paid from any fund available for their respective boards and institutions, provided they first procure a certificate from the secretary of the board of state charities as evidence that they were invited to and were in attendance at the sessions of such confernces.

SECTION 2. That original sections 1356 and 1357 of the General Code be and the same are hereby repealed.

The sectional numbers in this act are in conformity to the General Code. JOHN G. PRICE, Attorney General.

CLARENCE J. BROWN,
President of the Senate.
CARL R. KIMBALL,
Speaker of the House of Representatives.

Passed April 17, 1919.
Approved May 19, 1919.

JAMES M. COX,
Governor.

Filed in the office of the Secretary of State at Columbus, Ohio, on the 19th day of May, A. D. 1919.

156 G.

[Amended Senate Bill No. 107.]

AN ACT

To amend section 614-44 of the General Code, relative rates to be charged by certain public utilities.

Be it enacted by the General Assembly of the State of Ohio:

SECTION 1. That section 614-44 of the General Code be amended to read as follows:

Power of municipality to fix rate, price, charge, etc.

Sec. 614-44. Any municipal corporation in which any public utility is established may, by ordinance, at any time within one year before the expiration of any contract entered into under the provisions of sections 3644, 3982 and 3983 of the General Code between the municipality and such public utility with respect to the rate, price, charge, toll, or rental to be made, charged, demanded, collected, or exacted, for any commodity, utility or service by such public utility, or at any other time authorized by law proceed to fix the price, rate, charge, toll or rental that such public utility may charge, demand, exact or collect therefor for an ensuing period as provided in sections 3644, 3982 and 3983 of the General Code. Thereupon, the commission, upon complaint in writing, of such public utility, or upon complaint of one per centum of the electors of such municipal corporation, which complaints shall be filed within sixty days after the passage of such ordinance, shall give thirty days' notice of the filing and pendency of such complaint to the public utility and the mayor of such municipality, of the time and place of the hearing thereof, and which shall plainly state the matters and things complained of. Written complaint; hearing.

Provided, however, if the council of any municipality fails by ordinance to regulate the rates to be charged by any utility engaged in business of supplying water for public or private consumption within sixty days after the expiration of any unlawful rate, such water company or one per centum of qualified electors of the municipality may petition the public utilities commission to fix the just and reasonable rates for the furnishing of such services, and the public utilities commission may thereupon proceed to fix the just and reasonable rates, tolls and charges for such services which may be charged for a period of two years from the date of the filing of such petition and .thereafter until changed, altered or modified by the council of such municipality or further order of the commission upon like application. When commission shall fix rates.

If any public utility shall have accepted any rate, price, charge, toll, or rental fixed by ordinance of such municipality, the same shall become operative, unless within sixty days after such acceptance there shall have been filed with the commission, a complaint signed by not less than three per centum of the qualified electors of such municipality. Upon such filing, the commission shall forthwith give notice of the filing and pendency of such complaint to the mayor of such municipality and fix a time and place for the hearing thereof. The commission shall, at such time and place, proceed to hear such complaint, and may adjourn the hearing thereof from day to day. Hearing upon accepted rates; procedure.

The filing of a complaint by a public utility, as herein provided, shall be taken and held to be the consent of such public utility to continue to furnish its product or service, and devote its property engaged therein to such public use during the term so fixed by ordinance or by the provisions of this act. Parties thereto shall be entitled to be heard, represented by counsel, and to have process to force the attendance of witnesses.

SECTION 2. That original section 614-44 of the General Code be, and the same is hereby repealed.

The sectional number in this act is in conformity to the General Code.
JOHN G. PRICE, Attorney General.

CLARENCE J. BROWN,
President of the Senate.
CARL R. KIMBALL,
Speaker of the House of Representatives.

Passed April 17, 1919.
Approved May 19, 1919.

JAMES M. COX,
Governor.

Filed in the office of the Secretary of State at Columbus, Ohio, on the 19th day of May, A. D. 1919.

157 G.

[House Bill No. 358.]

AN ACT

To provide an additional institution for the custody and care of the feeble-minded and to make appropriation therefor.

Be it enacted by the General Assembly of the State of Ohio:

Sec. 1904-1.

Additional institution for feeble-minded; location by Ohio board of administration.

SECTION 1. In addition to the institution for feeble-minded, an additional institution of the state for the custody, supervision, control, care, maintenance and training of feeble-minded persons committed to the custody and care of the Ohio board of administration shall be established and located, in the northern or in the southern part of the state, at such point as the Ohio board of administration may determine to be most suitable therefor and best adapted to the public convenience and welfare, having regard to the location of the present institution for feeble-minded, the centers of population in the northern and southern parts of the state, respectively, the availability of land suitable for such institution, and due economy in the acquisition of desirable site, provided, however, that nothing herein contained shall prevent the Ohio board of administration in its discretion from receiving in any of the institutions for feeble-minded. feeble-minded persons committed to its custody and care from any county in the state.

Sec. 1904-2.

Acquisition of land and construction of buildings authorized.

SECTION 2. The Ohio board of administration shall proceed forthwith to acquire by purchase, gift, lease, or appropriation the necessary real estate for the said institution and thereon to establish, construct, furnish and equip such building or buildings and such other improvements and facilities as it may deem necessary and proper for the custody and care of the feeble-minded. In the procuring of plans and specifications and in the letting of contracts for the construction, equipment and furnishing of said building or buildings and of the said improvements and facilities, as well as in the supervision of the construction, equipment and furnishing of the same and in the disbursement of the funds hereinafter appropriated therefor, the Ohio board of administration shall observe and be governed by all and singular the provisions of law relative and pertinent to the purchase and acquisition of land, the construction, equipment and furnishing of such building or buildings, and the disbursement of funds therefor by said board; provided, however, that the Ohio board of administration with the unanimous approval of the state building commission and whenever said commission may deem it more economical so to do, may construct, in whole or in part, any of such buildings or other improvements, and may purchase or furnish such materials, supplies, and labor for the construction, equipment, and furnishing of said buildings, improvements, and facilities as it may deem necessary or advisable, in which event the provisions of section 2314 to 2330 of the General Code, both inclusive, shall not apply.

Sec. 1904-3. SECTION 3. The sum of six hundred and fifty thousand Appropriation. dollars is hereby appropriated out of any moneys in the state treasury to the credit of the general revenue fund, not otherwise appropriated, to be used and disbursed by said Ohio board of administration for the purchase of land for the site of said additional institution for the feeble-minded, the making of the necessary improvements thereon, and the construction, equipment and furnishing of such suitable building or buildings as the Ohio board of administration may find necessary.

The sectional numbers on the margin hereof are designated as provided by law. JOHN G. PRICE, Attorney General.

CARL R. KIMBALL,
Speaker of the House of Representatives.
CLARENCE J. BROWN,
President of the Senate.

Passed April 17, 1919.
Approved May 19, 1919.

JAMES M. COX,
Governor.

Filed in the office of the Secretary of State at Columbus, Ohio, on the 19th day of May, A. D. 1919.

158 G.

[House Bill No. 406.]

AN ACT

To amend sections 7730, 7595-1 and 7595-2 of the General Code and to supplement the same with sections 7594-1, 7595-3, 7595-4 and 7595-5 of the General Code, relating to state aid to weak school districts.

Be it enacted by the General Assembly of the State of Ohio:
SECTION 1. That sections 7730, 7595-1 and 7595-2 of the General Code be amended and that sections 7594-1,

7595-3, 7595-4 and 7595-5 of the General Code be enacted supplementary to section 7594 so as to read as follows:

Adjustment by budget commission. Sec. 7594-1. Whenever the board of education of a school district attaches to its budget a certification that it intends to make application for state aid pursuant to sections 7595-1 and 7595-2 of the General Code, and that it is entitled thereto, the budget commission shall proceed to make adjustments in accordance with the provisions of section 5649-3c, but shall lay such adjustment aside and thereupon proceed to make an adjustment which shall allow to such school district a levy of not less than four mills exclusive of the levy necessary to provide for indebtedness incurred prior to 1911 or incurred by a vote of the people. This last adjustment shall be certified by the budget commission pursuant to section 5649-3c. If it should thereafter appear that such school district did not so apply for such state aid or was not entitled thereto, then the adjustment first made and laid aside as above provided shall be deemed to be the final adjustment and the county auditor shall distribute, or redistribute the proceeds of tax collections in accordance with such first adjustment, or if such school district has received its distribution of the tax collections, the county auditor shall deduct from the sum due such school district on the distribution of the tax collections next following, the sum necessary to make such redistribution of tax collections.

Application for state aid; conditions first to be complied with. Sec. 7595-1. A school district may make application for state aid to cover deficiencies in its tuition fund by filing with the auditor of state an application therefor in such form as the auditor of state shall prescribe, and by first complying and showing compliance with the following conditions:

1. It shall place in the tuition fund at least two-thirds of the proceeds of the levy as adjusted by the budget commission pursuant to section 7594-1.

2. It shall place in the tuition fund the whole sum of the state common school fund and interest on the common school fund received by the district.

3. It shall pay its teachers neither more nor less than the following salaries: In elementary schools, teachers without having less than one year's professional training or less than three years' teaching experience in the state, sixty dollars per month; teachers having at least one year professional training or three years' teaching experience in the state, sixty-five dollars a month; teachers having completed the full two years' course in any normal school, teachers' college or university approved by the superintendent of public instruction, or who have had five years' teaching experience in the state, seventy-five dollars a month. In high schools, inclusive of joint high school districts, an average of ninety dollars a month in each high school. Such salaries shall be for full time and in high schools if any teacher be not employed full time, then, in computing the average, the

salary for each hour of service paid such part time teacher shall, for the purposes of the calculation, be multiplied by the number of full time hours in each month, and the sum so ascertained shall be assumed to be the salary paid such part time teacher. In no case shall a teacher be employed at less than sixty dollars per month for full time, or at the rate of sixty dollars per month for part time.

4. It shall maintain its schools for eight months in each year.

5. It shall not transfer or cause to be transferred to any other fund any moneys that may be in the tuition fund. Nor shall it expend any moneys that may be in the tuition fund except for the following purposes:

(a) Payment of salaries of teachers.

(b) Payment of expenses for attending institute.

(c) Payment of temporary loans incurred to meet current expenses in anticipation of revenue which would accrue to the tuition fund.

(d) That part of tuition payable to other school districts which represent the expense of teachers' salaries as computed pursuant to section 7736.

(e) Salaries of principals or superintendents, or additional salaries paid teachers as compensation for duties performed as principals or superintendents. Provided, however, that, if additional salaries are paid as compensation for duties performed by teachers as principals or superintendents, the state superintendent of public instruction shall. first certify that such additional duties are required and performed.

6. The county auditor in making his deductions pursuant to section 4744-3 of the General Code shall deduct two-thirds of the total sum from the two-thirds yield of the tax levy which is distributable to the tuition fund pursuant to this section, and the remaining one-third from the remaining part of the yield of such tax levy.

Sec. 7595-2. The application to the state auditor for state aid shall be filed between the first day of September and the first day of October for the then current school year, and upon demand of the state auditor the books or any records of the school district shall be transmitted to the auditor of state. The application shall be accompanied by the copy of the distribution of the county auditor made on the preceding August settlement, and an estimate of the county auditor showing the probable yield and distribution of the taxes, state common school fund and interest on the common school fund to be distributed to such district on the February settlement next following, together with a copy of his balance sheet as the same appears on his school fund distribution record for the school year for which such application is made. *When and how application made.*

Sec. 7595-3. Upon receipt by the auditor of state of such application, and satisfying himself in all things essential to his proper determination of the right of such district *When warrant for aid shall be issued.*

to have aid from the state he shall determine the probable
deficiency that will exist in the tuition fund of such school
district. Should there be ascertained to be a probable deficiency therein the state auditor shall issue his voucher for
the issuance of a warrant on the treasurer of state in favor
of such school district for the sum of such probable deficiency, against any funds appropriated for such purposes
then being in the state treasury. Should the fund available
for the payment of such state aid be insufficient to pay the
total sums so found due the several districts making application for and entitled to such aid, the auditor of state shall
apportion the whole available fund among the districts entitled to such aid.

Application by joint high school district. Sec. 7595-4. Whenever two or more school districts
have joined pursuant to section 7669 to establish a joint high
school, and one or more of such school districts makes application for such state aid to cover a probable deficiency
in the tuition fund, then a condition precedent to the determination and rendering of such state aid the high school
committee shall place in the tuition fund that part of tuition
received from other districts which represents the expense
for salaries of teachers as computed pursuant to section
7736. And the school district applying for such aid shall,
in placing in a separate fund its contribution to the high
school committee pursuant to section 7671, pay out of its
tuition fund only that part of the total contribution which
represents the needs of the high school committee for salaries of the high school teachers. And such high school committee in its disbursements of moneys from the tuition fund
shall be governed by the limitations of section 7595-1 of the
General Code.

When deficiency or balance occurs. Sec. 7595-5. If it should appear in any year, after
state aid is paid pursuant to the sections preceding, that
either a deficiency or a balance exists in the tuition fund, the
auditor of state in making his calculation pursuant to section 7595-3 shall credit the district with such deficiency and
charge the district with such balance.

Power of board to suspend rural or village school; notice. Sec. 7730. The board of education of any rural or village school district may suspend temporarily or perma-
nently any or all schools in such village or rural district because of disadvantageous location or any other cause.
Whenever the average daily attendance of any school in the
school district for the preceding year has been below ten the
county board of education shall direct the suspension, and
thereupon the board of education of the village or rural district shall suspend such school. Whenever any school is suspended the board of education of the district shall provide
for the transfer of the pupils residing within the territory
of the suspended school to other schools. If the suspended
school be in a village school district the board of education
of the district may, or if in a rural school district shall provide for the pupils of legal school age who reside in the territory of the suspended school conveyance to a public school

within such school district or in an adjoining school district. Notice of such suspension shall be posted in five conspicuous places within such village or rural school district by the board of education within ten days after the resolution providing for such suspension is adopted. Wherever such suspension is had on the direction of the county board of education, then upon the direction of such county board, and in other cases upon the finding of the board of education ordering such suspension that such school ought to be re-established, such school shall be re-established. If at any time it appears that the average daily attendance of enrolled pupils residing within the territory of the suspended schools as it was prior to such suspension is twelve or more then, upon a petition asking for re-establishment signed by a majority of the voters of the said territory, the board of education shall re-establish such school. *May be re-established, when.*

Whenever, after March 21, 1915, a school or schools have been or hereafter shall be suspended pursuant to this section, or have been or shall be consolidated, and such suspended schools not re-established, and the transportation of the pupils thereof to other schools within such school district provided for, then the auditor of state shall ascertain the number of teachers and total salaries paid such teachers for the entire district in the year preceding such suspension or consolidation, and the number of teachers and the total salaries paid them for the entire district in the year in which such suspension or consolidation is had, and the difference shall be held to be the savings in teachers and in salaries resulting from such suspension or consolidation. *Savings in teachers and salaries ascertained by auditor of state.*

Whenever at any time thereafter such school district shall apply for state aid pursuant to section 7595-1 and such suspended school or schools have not been re-established, the sum of saving in salaries so ascertained shall be included as an expenditure in calculating the sum of state aid pursuant to section 7595-1, and if it then be determined that a deficiency exists, the sum of such deficiency shall be apportioned among the whole number of teachers actually employed in such district plus the number of teachers dispensed with, and the sum so ascertained shall be multiplied by the number of teachers so dispensed with and applied to the transportation of pupils of such suspended schools. *When savings shall be included as expenditure; apportionment of deficiency.*

SECTION 2. That original sections 7730, 7595-1 and 7595-2 of the General Code be, and the same are hereby repealed. *Repeals.*

CARL R. KIMBALL,
Speaker of the House of Representatives.
CLARENCE J. BROWN,
President of the Senate.

Passed April 17, 1919.
Approved May 19, 1919.

JAMES M. COX,
Governor.

Filed in the office of the Secretary of State at Columbus, Ohio, on the 19th day of May, A. D. 1919.

159 G.

AN ACT

To amend sections 1579-282, 1579-286, 1579-288, 15799-293, 1579-295, 1579-296, 1597-297, 1579-301, 1579-307, 1579-308, 1579-311, 1579-312, 1579-313, 1579-314, 1579-318, 1579-319, 1579-320, 1579-321, 1579-322, 1579-324, and 1579-326 of the General Code (107 O. L. 704) relating to the establishment of a municipal court in the city of Toledo.

Be it enacted by the General Assembly of the State of Ohio:

SECTION 1. That sections 1579-282, 1579-286, 1579-288, 1579-293, 1579-295, 1579-296, 1579-297, 1579-301, 1579-307, 1579-308, 1579-311, 1579-312, 1579-313, 1579-314, 1579-318, 1579-319, 1579-320, 1579-321, 1579-322, 1579-324 and 1579-326 of the General Code be amended to read as follows:

Election of presiding judge.

Sec. 1579-282. One of the judges of the municipal court, who is not holding office by appointment or election to fill a vacancy, shall be elected by the judges to act as presiding judge for such period as may be designated by them at the time of the election, and in case of absence or disability of the presiding judge his place shall be temporarily filled by one of the other judges not holding office by appointment or election to fill a vacancy to be designated by the presiding judge.

Original jurisdiction in city of Toledo.

Sec. 1579-286. The municipal court shall have and exercise original jurisdiction within the limits of the city of Toledo as follows:

1. In all actions and proceedings of which justices of the peace have or may be given jurisdiction.

2. In all civil actions and proceedings at law for the recovery of money or personal property of which the courts of common pleas have, or may be given jurisdiction, when the amount claimed by any party, or the appraised value of the personal property sought to be recovered, does not exceed seven hundred and fifty dollars; and in such actions judgment may be rendered for an amount over seven hundred and fifty dollars when the excess over seven hundred and fifty dollars shall consist of interest, damages, or costs accrued after the commencement of the action.

3. In all actions on contracts, express or implied, when the amount claimed by the plaintiff, exclusive of all costs, does not exceed seven hundred and fifty dollars. When a cause arising out of contract is pending in the municipal court and the ends of justice demand that an account be taken or that the contract or contracts be reformed or cancelled, the municipal court shall have jurisdiction to decree such accounting, reformation or cancellation.

4. In all actions and proceedings at law to enforce the collection of its own judgments or the judgment or revivor of judgment heretofore rendered by justices of the peace in Port Lawrence township, Lucas county, or rendered by the city and justice court of the city of Toledo and Port

Lawrence township, Lucas county, hereinafter referred to as its own judgments.

5. In all actions and proceedings for the sale of personal property under a chattel mortgage, lien or other charge or encumbrance upon personal property, and for the marshalling of all liens thereon, when the amount sought to be recovered does not exceed seven hundred and fifty dollars.

6. In all actions and proceedings in the nature of creditors' bills in aid of execution to subject the interest of a judgment debtor in any property to the payment of a judgment enforceable by the municipal court.

7. In all actions and proceedings in the nature of interpleader involving amounts not in excess of seven hundred and fifty dollars.

8. In all actions in forcible entry and detention of real property.

9. The right to hear and determine questions of exemptions, upon execution or attachment, upon the application or motion of any officer of the municipal court or of any party to a cause pending or adjudicated in said municipal court.

10. The right to distribute and control all property levied upon or seized by any legal process issuing from said municipal court, or the proceeds thereof, which may come into the hands of its officers, and to order the immediate sale of any property of a perishable nature which may come into the hands of an officer of this court upon any process issuing from said court, and the money realized therefrom shall be held and retained by the officer until distributed by order of court as herein provided.

11. The right to examine a judgment debtor as provided by sections 11768, 11769, 11770 and 11771 of the General Code, and to enjoin the judgment debtor and the judgment debtor's debtors from disposing of or encumbering any property which he may own or which they may have in their possession.

12. The right to perform marriage ceremonies; take acknowledgments of deeds and other instruments, administer oaths, and perform any other duty now given or that may be conferred upon justices of the peace. All fees, including marriage fees, earned by a municipal judge by virtue of this subsection, when not connected with any cause or proceeding pending in the municipal court, shall be collected by and belong to the judge so earning said fees.

13. Within the jurisdiction of this court, the right to make any person a defendant who has or claims an interest in the controversy adverse to the plaintiff, or who is a necessary party to a complete determination or settlement of a question involved therein.

14. Within the jurisdiction of this court, the right to determine any controversy between parties before it, when it can be done without prejudice to the rights of others, or by saving their rights. When such determination cannot

be had without the presence of other parties the court may order them to be brought in, or dismiss the action without prejudice.

Jurisdiction in ancillary and supplemental proceedings.

Sec. 1579-288. In all causes the municipal court shall have jurisdiction in the following ancillary and supplemental proceedings before and after judgment, to-wit: Attachment of person or property; arrest before or after judgment; interpleader; aid of execution; trial of the right of property; revivor of judgment. In addition the plaintiff shall have an order of attachment against the property of the defendant in any civil action of which the municipal court has jurisdiction for the grounds enumerated in section 10253 and shall have service by publication in the manner provided by section 10263 of the General Code, and kindred sections. Service by publication may be further made in those cases coming within section 11292 of the General Code in which the municipal court has jurisdiction, and said service by publication shall be made in the same manner and form as provided by sections 11293 to 11299, inclusive, of the General Code.

Limitation of jurisdiction of mayors and justices in Lucas county.

Sec. 1579-293. No justice of the peace in any township in Lucas county, or mayor of any village in Lucas county, in any proceedings whether civil or criminal, in which any warrant, order of arrest, summons, order of attachment or garnishment or other process, except subpoena for witnesses, shall have been served upon a citizen or resident of Toledo or a corporation having its principal office in Toledo, shall have jurisdiction, unless such service be actually made by personal service within the township or village in which said proceedings may have been instituted, or in a criminal matter, unless the offense charged in any warrant or order of arrest shall be alleged to have been committed within said township or village; and any such justice of the peace or mayor knowingly assuming jurisdiction in any civil or criminal case contrary to the foregoing provision shall be deemed guilty of a misdemeanor and shall be fined not more than one hundred dollars or imprisoned in the county jail not more than thirty days, or both, and upon conviction thereof shall forfeit his office.

When proceedings certified to common pleas court.

Sec. 1579-295. Whenever the appraised value of property sought to be recovered in any action in the municipal court exceeds seven hundred and fifty dollars, the judge of the municipal court shall forthwith certify the proceedings in the case to the court of common pleas of Lucas county, and the clerk of the municipal court shall forthwith file the original papers and pleadings together with a certified transcript of the docket and journal entries in the case with the clerk of the common pleas court. The marshal shall forthwith turn over the property in his possession to the sheriff of Lucas county, to be by him held as in like cases originating in the court of common pleas. The case must then proceed as if it had been commenced in the court of common pleas.

Sec. 1579-296. Civil actions and proceedings in the municipal court shall be commenced by filing a complaint or statement of claim, as hereinafter provided, upon which summons or writ shall be issued by the clerk. The form of summons or writ shall be prescribed by rule of court, except as hereinafter otherwise provided. In attachment and garnishment proceedings, a true copy of the affidavit shall be served with the summons and order of attachment or garnishment.

1. All writs and process in the municipal court shall be served and returned by the marshal, or by publication, in the same manner as is now, or may hereafter be provided by law for service and return of writs and process of a justice of the peace, unless otherwise provided herein.

2. The return day shall be fixed by a rule of court not later than seven days after issuance, and the summons or writ shall, unless accompanied with an order of arrest, be served at least three days before the time of appearance.

3. In all civil cases in the municipal court, except conciliation cases, the plaintiff shall file a statement of claim, and the defendant shall file a like statement of the set-off or counterclaim he may desire to assert. A statement of defense shall be filed in such cases and within such time as may be required by rule of court. In cases where a statement of defense is required the summons shall set forth the date when such statement shall be filed, as fixed by rule of court, which shall be not less than five days after the return day of the summons. Except as herein otherwise provided, the form and requisite of the statement of claim and other pleadings shall be prescribed by rule of court.

4. In actions of forcible entry and detention, and replevin, the landlord's complaint and affidavit in replevin as prescribed by sections 10452 and 10462 of the General Code may be made the statement of claim by rule of court, and no other pleading need be filed by plaintiff or defendant unless required by rule of court.

5. To expedite the business of the court and promote the ends of justice the judges from time to time shall adopt, publish and revise rules relating to the matters of practice and procedure, classifying the causes of action in the court, and, except as herein otherwise provided, prescribe with reference to each class, the degree of particularity with which a cause of action, set-off, counterclaim or defense shall be stated.

6. The laws relating to practice and procedure in actions in the court of common pleas, and before justices of the peace and police courts, defining the rights and obligations of the parties and prescribing the powers and duties of the officers thereof, shall apply to like proceedings in the municipal court in so far as consistent with the provisions of this act and of other laws relating to said municipal court.

Sec. 1579-297. In all actions for the recovery of money only, the summons shall be served by mail, unless a precipe be filed by the party requesting that service be made by the marshal, or unless the summons is accompanied by an order of attachment, in which cases service shall be made by the marshal or sheriff, in the manner hereinbefore otherwise provided. In all cases of service by mail the writ shall be enclosed in a sealed envelope bearing proper postage for and be sent by mail, and such envelope shall be addressed to the party to be served at his correct residence address. The envelope shall bear a request for a return of the envelope after three days to the marshal, in case of non-delivery. There shall be printed on the outside of the envelope, in red ink, the following words:

"This envelope contains a legal writ from the municipal court of Toledo." The return of the marshal shall show the address to which the writ was mailed. In case of the return of an envelope containing a writ undelivered, the envelope and writ shall be placed in the files of the cause and the marshal shall immediately notify the clerk, who shall forthwith issue a new summons to the marshal or other proper officer, to be served in the manner hereinbefore otherwise provided. Upon the return day, if it shall appear that the envelope containing the summons has not been returned to the files in any cause as undelivered, it will be presumed that the same has been delivered to the defendant, and the cause shall thereupon proceed to judgment in the absence of the defendant as upon default. In the case of a corporation, domestic or foreign, or a partnership, a return of the marshal or sheriff that a true copy of the writ or process was deposited in the mail, enclosed in an envelope addressed to the corporation or partnership at its office or place where it regularly receives mail, in the city of Toledo, or when the court has jurisdiction, elsewhere in Lucas county or the state of Ohio, shall be proof of service, provided that such address be the office of the corporation, or partnership, or the place where the corporation or partnership regularly receives mail, and that such envelope be not returned by the postal authorities as undelivered; and provided further that, in any case, any person requesting service by marshal or sheriff shall be entitled thereto. Postage shall be taxed as a part of the costs in the action. In all actions in the municipal court subpoenas shall be served by mail unless otherwise directed by precipe of a party or order of the court, and all provisions relative to the service and return of summons by mail shall apply to such service of subpoenas.

Summoning and impaneling jury. Sec. 1579-301. Jurors in the municipal court shall be chosen and summoned in accordance with a rule of said court. Jurors of the municipal court shall be impaneled in the same manner and challenged for the same causes and receive the same fees as jurors in the court of common pleas. Their fees shall be paid out of the treasury of the city of Toledo. In all civil actions and proceedings the fees of jurors shall be taxed and collected as part of the costs.

Sec. 1579-307. Proceedings in error in both civil and criminal cases may be prosecuted to the court of common pleas of Lucas county from a judgment or final order of the municipal court in the same manner and under the same conditions, including proceedings for stay of execution, as provided by law for proceedings in error from the court of common pleas to the court of appeals. In such case the clerk and the marshal of the municipal court shall turn over any moneys or property held by either of them in the action, to the clerk and the sheriff respectively of Lucas county, to be by them held as in like cases originating in the court of common pleas. Provided, however, that the bill of exceptions shall be filed with the clerk of the municipal court within fifteen days after the rendition of the judgment or the making of the order complained of. After the filing of said bill of exceptions, the opposing attorney shall have ten days in which to file his objections to said bill of exceptions. The trial judge shall thereafter have five days in which to examine and approve or disapprove of said bill of exceptions. Thereupon the clerk of the municipal court shall forthwith transmit said bill of exceptions to the clerk of the court of common pleas. The petition in error shall be filed in the court of common pleas within thirty days from the date of said judgment or order. *Proceedings in error to the common pleas court.*

Sec. 1579-308. In all civil cases not otherwise specially provided by law, either party may appeal from the final judgment of the municipal court to the court of common pleas of Lucas county. Appeals in the following cases shall not be allowed: *Appeal to court of common pleas.*

1. On judgments rendered on confession of the parties or party.

2. In cases where neither party claims in his statement of claim a sum exceeding one hundred dollars.

3. In an action for forcible entry and detention, or forcible detention of real property.

4. In trials for the right of property under the statutes, either levied upon by execution or attached.

5. Upon exemptions determined or fixed by the trial judge of said court.

Sec. 1579-311. The financial responsibility of proposed sureties upon all bonds in both civil and criminal proceedings shall be the subject of careful inquiry before they are permitted to sign any bond. Sureties owning less property than required by law, and all sureties then or thereafter more than thirty days in default for the payment of a liquidated sum due upon any bond given in the municipal court, shall not be accepted as sureties or if accepted, shall not be continued as sureties upon such bonds, and all persons offering themselves as sureties on any bond may be required by affidavit or otherwise to make oath to any and all facts affecting his qualifications as such surety. Additional security may be required at any time upon motion of a *Responsibility of surety; additional surety.*

party to any civil or criminal action or proceeding, or at the discretion of the court.

Who admitted to bail.

In all criminal cases the clerk of the municipal court shall admit to bail any person accused of a felony, misdemeanor or violation of an ordinance of the city of Toledo for his apearance at the next sitting of the criminal branch of said court, as provided by rule of court. When a person is accused of a misdemeanor or violation of an ordinance of the city of Toledo, the judges by rule of court may provide for the admission of such person to bail by receiving money in lieu thereof. The manner of receiving and the amounts to be received in each class of offenses shall be fixed by rule of court. The bail so given or the money so deposited shall continue until the case is finally disposed of.

Transcript; appeal bond.

Sec. 1579-312. The clerk of the municipal court shall make and certify a transcript of the proceedings, including a transcript of the appeal bond, and on demand, after being paid the legal fee therefor, shall deliver the same to the appellant, or his agent, who shall deliver the same to the clerk of the common pleas of Lucas county, on or before the thirtieth day from the rendition of the judgment appealed from. The clerk of the municipal court shall also deliver or transmit the statement or statements of claim or claims, the depositions, evidence, and all other original papers, if any, used on the trial in the municipal court, to such clerk on or before the thirtieth day from the judgment; and all further proceedings of the municipal court in that case shall cease and be stayed from the time of entering into the undertaking. In such case the clerk and the marshal of the municipal court shall turn over any moneys or property held by them in the action, to the clerk and sheriff, respectively, of Lucas county, to be by them held as in like cases originating in the court of common pleas. If for any reason the cause is not heard and determined by the appellate court, or if the appeal is dismissed by the appellate court, or judgment is entered against the appellant, the surety on the appeal undertaking shall be liable to the appellee for the whole amount of the debts, costs and damages recovered against the appellant not to exceed the amount of the bond.

Election of clerk; term, salary.

Sec. 1579-313. There shall be a clerk of the municipal court, who shall be nominated and elected for a term of four years, in the same manner as is now or may be provided by charter of the city of Toledo for the nomination and election of city officials. The first election of clerk shall be held at the regular municipal election in the year one thousand nine hundred and seventeen, and every four years thereafter a successor shall be elected for a like term. The clerk shall have such power and shall perform such duties as are herein given and required. He shall receive an annual salary of three thousand dollars, two thousand dollars of which shall be paid out of the treasury of the city of Toledo in monthly installments, and one thousand dollars shall be paid out of the treasury of Lucas county, in monthly installments. The

term of office of the clerk shall commence on the first day
of January next after his election and he shall hold office
until his successor is elected and qualified. The said clerk
shall appoint such deputy clerks as the court shall approve,
each of whom shall be an elector of the city of Toledo and
shall receive such compensation as is fixed by the court, not
exceeding two thousand dollars per annum, payable in
monthly installments out of the treasury of the city of
Toledo. At least two of such deputy clerks shall be stenographers.

Sec. 1579-314. The clerk shall perform such duties as **Powers and duties of clerk.**
may be directed and required by the court. The clerk shall
have general power to administer oaths and take affidavits,
and to issue executions upon judgments rendered in the
municipal court, including a judgment for unpaid costs; the
clerk shall have power to issue and sign all writs, process and
papers issuing out of such court, and to attach the seal of
the court thereto; to approve all bonds, recognizances, and
undertakings required or fixed by any judge of the court
or by law. in civil cases, except as herein otherwise provided; he shall file and safely keep all journals, records,
books and papers belonging or appertaining to the court,
including all records of its proceedings and he shall perform all other duties which the judges of said court shall by
rule of court prescribe. He shall pay over to the proper
parties all moneys received by him as clerk; he shall receive and collect all costs, fees, fines and penalties and shall
pay the same monthly into the treasury of the city of Toledo
and take a receipt therefor, except as otherwise provided
by law; but money deposited as security for costs shall be
retained by him pending litigation. He shall keep a book
showing all receipts and disbursements, which shall be open
for public inspection at all times. He shall succeed to and
have all the powers and perform all the duties of police
clerks, except as herein otherwise provided.

Sec. 1579-318. All cases involving an amount of thir- **Conciliation department; en-tries; hearing.**
ty-five dollars or less, shall be entered by the clerk upon a
separate docket to be known as the conciliation docket of the
municipal court. Cases in the conciliation department of
the municipal court shall be commenced by filing a complaint upon which summons or writ shall be issued by the
clerk and service by mail or as otherwise herein provided
shall thereupon be made upon the defendant. The cases
upon the conciliation docket shall be heard by a judge of
the municipal court to be designated by the presiding judge,
but no one judge shall have said docket for more than three
months during any one year, which judge shall endeavor to
effect an amicable adjustment of the differences between
the parties in the case. If an agreement between the parties
effected, judgment by confession shall be entered, or such
other entry shall be made as the court may deem proper. If
an agreement between the parties cannot be effected, the
court shall proceed at its earliest convenience to hear and de-

termine the case and to enter judgment therein. The form
and requisites of the complaint shall be prescribed by rule
of court. No further pleading shall be required, however,
that the defendant may assert a counterclaim or set-off as
provided by rule of court. A filing fee of fifty cents shall
be paid by the plaintiff in all cases provided for in this
section, before a complaint is filed or summons or writ shall
issue, unless otherwise ordered by a judge of the municipal
court upon good cause shown.

Appointment of marshals and deputies; salary; bond. Sec. 1579-319. The judges, or a majority of them,
shall appoint a marshal and not to exceed four deputy mar-
shals, to be known as service marshals, unless a larger number of deputies shall be authorized by the council of the
city of Toledo, who shall be electors of the city of Toledo.
Such marshal shall serve as assignment clerk, and with the
deputy marshals, shall in addition to other duties perform
for the municipal court, services similar to those usually
performed by the sheriff and his deputies for the court of
common pleas and by constables for justices of the peace,
with all the powers of such officers, and shall perform such
other duties as may be required by rule of court. The marshal shall receive as compensation the sum of eighteen hundred dollars per annum, the deputy (service) marshals each
the sum of one thousand two hundred dollars per annum,
which compensation of the marshal and deputy marshals
shall be payable in monthly installments out of the treasury
of the city of Toledo. Before entering upon the duties of
their office, the marshal and deputy marshals shall each give
bond to the city of Toledo, the marshal in the sum of three
thousand dollars and the deputies each in the sum of two
thousand dollars, with surety to the approval of the presiding judge, for the benefit of the city of Toledo and of any
person who shall suffer by reason of any default in any of
the conditions of such bond, conditioned that they shall pay
to the parties entitled thereto all moneys received by them
and otherwise faithfully and fully discharge the duties of
their office as marshal and deputy marshals, respectively.
Whenever the marshal or deputy marshals shall give a
surety or bonding company bond the premium thereon shall
be paid out of the treasury of the city of Toledo.

Execution marshals; duties. In addition to the deputy marshals above provided for,
the judges, or a majority of them, may appoint not to ex-
ceed two deputy marshals to be known as execution marshals, who shall have the same qualifications and be dismissed in the same manner prescribed for deputy marshals
and shall have the same powers and give the same bond as
other deputy marshals. Their sole duty, unless otherwise
directed by the marshal or by rule of court, shall be to collect judgments on execution. They shall receive as compensation the sum of fifteen hundred dollars per annum
payable in monthly installments out of the treasury of the
city of Toledo.

Sec. 1579-320. Each deputy marshal and each execu- Compensation of deputy marshals. tion marshal hereinbefore provided for shall receive from the treasury of the city of Toledo, in addition to his compensation, his actual expenses in serving process of the court, not to exceed the sum of twenty-five dollars per month, payable upon the order of the presiding judge.

Sec. 1579-321. All deputy clerks, the marshal and Term of office. deputy marshals, shall hold their offices during the pleasure of the appointing power.

Sec. 1579-322. Every police officer of the city of To- Ex-officio deputy marshals. ledo shall be ex officio a deputy marshal of the municipal court and shall perform from time to time such duties as may be required by the court or any judge thereof, without additional compensation.

Sec. 1579-324. One probation officer may be appointed Probation officers; compensation. by the judges of the municipal court who shall serve at the pleasure of the court. Additional probation officers may be appointed by the judges of the municipal court when in their judgment the same are necessary, but such additional appointments can only be made by and with the consent of the council of the city of Toledo. The compensation of each probation officer shall be one thousand dollars per annum, payable out of the treasury of the city of Toledo in monthly installments. If a member of the police department is appointed probation officer, he shall have the privilege of returning at any time to active service in the department and to the same rank and standing as he had at the time of appointment as probation officer.

Sec. 1579-326. Except as otherwise provided in this Taxing costs; schedule of fees. act, in all civil actions where the municipal court has jurisdiction, the same as the jurisdiction of the court of common pleas, the fees and costs may be fixed in the same manner and taxed in the same amounts as is now or may hereafter be provided for such actions in the court of common pleas. In all other civil actions the fees and costs may be fixed in the same manner and taxed in the same amounts as is now or may hereafter be provided for such actions before a justice of the peace. In all criminal actions the fees and costs may be fixed in the same manner and taxed in the same amounts as is now or may hereafter be provided for police courts of municipalities. Provided, however, that the municipal court, in lieu of the aforesaid methods of taxing costs, by rule of court may establish a schedule of fees and costs to be taxed in all actions and proceedings, in no case to exceed fees and costs provided for like actions and proceedings by general law. And, provided further, that where the jurisdiction of the municipal court is the same as the exclusive jurisdiction of a justice of the peace, not to exceed the amounts set forth in the following table shall be collected in any civil action or proceedings as fees and costs due the court for services performed by the judges, the clerks or the marshals of said court, viz.:

In each action for the recovery of money only, up to and including the entry of judgment...........$3 00

In each action for the recovery of money only, when the summons is accompanied by an order of attachment or garnishment, up to and including the entry of judgment........................... 5 00

In each action in replevin, up to and including the entry of judgment........................... 5 00

In each action in forcible entry and detention, up to and including the entry of judgment........... 2 00

Upon each writ of restitution...................... 1 00

Upon each execution or order of sale, poundage and not to exceed the additional sum of............. 2 00

In each proceedings in aid of execution............. 2 00

In each order of arrest before or after judgment..... 1 00

In each proceedings for the trial of the right of property 2 00

Upon each determination of exemptions............ 1 00

For each transcript............................. 1 25

For each trustee service........................ 2 00

But none of the items in the above table shall be construed to include any fees or costs due for services rendered by some person other than the services rendered by the judges, the clerks or the marshals of the municipal court in any civil action or proceedings.

Advance payment in civil actions.

Fifty cents shall be payable in advance upon the institution of any civil action in the municipal court, unless the party instituting said action shall be allowed by one of the judges of the municipal court, for good cause shown, to institute said action without such advance payment. Said fifty cents shall in all cases be applied to the payment of costs due the court or its officers. In all civil and criminal actions witnesses' fees shall be fixed in the same manner and taxed in the same amounts as is now or may hereafter be provided for witnesses' fees in the court of common pleas. Nothing in this section shall be construed so as to prevent a party in any cause from demanding security for costs in a proper case or to prevent the clerk or a judge of the municipal court from requiring a deposit of money or bond for security for costs in a proper case.

Repeals.

SECTION 2. That said original sections 1579-282, 1579-286, 1579-288, 1579-293, 1579-295, 1579-296, 1579-297, 1579-301, 1579-307, 1579-308, 1579-311, 1579-312, 1579-313, 1579-314, 1579-318, 1579-319, 1579-320, 1579-321, 1579-322, 1579-

324 and 1579-326, of the General Code be, and the same are hereby repealed.

Be sectional numbers in this
id are in con-
fmity to the
neral Code.
BEN G. PRICE,
Attorney
General.

CARL R. KIMBALL,
Speaker of the House of Representatives.
CLARENCE J. BROWN,
President of the Senate.

Passed April 8, 1919.

This bill was presented to the Governor May 7th, 1919, and was not signed or returned to the house in which it originated within ten days after being so presented, exclusive of Sundays and the day said bill was presented and was filed in the office of the Secretary of State May 20, 1919.

ROBERT T. CREW,
Veto Clerk.

Filed in the office of the Secretary of State at Columbus, Ohio, on the 20th day of May, A. D. 1919.

160 G.

[House Bill No. 510.]

AN ACT

To establish a municipal court for the city of Massillon, Stark county, Ohio, and fixing the jurisdiction thereof, and providing for a judge thereof, and other necessary officers, and defining their powers and duties.

Be it enacted by the General Assembly of the State of Ohio:

Sec. 1579-416

SECTION 1. That there be and hereby is created a court of record in and for the city of Massillon and the townships of Perry and Tuscarawas, in the county of Stark and state of Ohio, to be styled "The Municipal Court of Massillon, Ohio" (the jurisdiction thereof, to be as herein and hereinafter fixed and determined). "The municipal court of Massillon, Ohio," established.

Sec. 1579-417.

SECTION 2. Said municipal court shall be presided over by one judge, to be designated herein as a "municipal judge," which office is hereby created, and whose term of office shall be for a period of four years, and said judge shall receive such compensation, payable out of the treasury of Stark county not less than twelve hundred dollars per annum, payable monthly, as the county commissioners may prescribe, and out of the treasury of Perry township, Stark county, Ohio, not less than three hundred dollars per annum, payable monthly as the township trustees may prescribe, and out of the treasury of Tuscarawas township, Stark county, Ohio, not less than two hundred dollars per annum, payable monthly as the township trustees may prescribe, and such further compensation, not less than fifteen hundred dollars per annum, payable in monthly installments out of the treasury of the city of Massillon, Ohio, as the council or legislative authority may prescribe, provided the salary at no time shall exceed four thousand dollars. Municipal judge; election, qualification, term, salary.

Said municipal judge at the time of his election or appointment, and during the continuance of his office shall be a qualified elector and resident of either the township of Perry or the township of Tuscarawas, county of Stark, and state of Ohio, and have been admitted to the practice of law in the state of Ohio for not less than five years. Said judge shall be elected at the next regular municipal election after the going into effect of this act, for a term of four years, commencing on the first day of January next, after said election and shall hold said office until his successor is elected and duly qualified. Such election shall be held and conducted and returns thereof made as in the case of the election of city and judicial officers.

Sec. 1579-418.

Criminal and
civil jurisdiction.

SECTION 3. Said municipal court herein established shall have the same jurisdiction in criminal matters and prosecutions for misdemeanors, for violations of ordinances as mayors of cities and any justice of the peace, and in addition thereto shall have ordinary civil jurisdiction within the limits of said city of Massillon and townships of Perry and Tuscarawas, in the county of Stark and state of Ohio, in the following cases:

(1). In all actions and proceedings of which justices of the peace, or such courts as may succeed justice of the peace courts, have or may be given jurisdiction.

(2). In all actions and proceedings at law for the recovery of money and of personal property of which the court of common pleas has or may be given jurisdiction, when the amount claimed by any party, or the appraised value of the personal property sought to be recovered does not exceed one thousand dollars, and in such actions, judgment may be rendered for over one thousand dollars, when the amount over one thousand dollars shall consist of interest or damages, or costs accrued after the commencement of the action.

(3) All actions on contracts express or implied, when the amount claimed by the plaintiff, exclusive of all costs, does not exceed one thousand dollars. When a cause arising out of a contract is pending in the municipal court and when the ends of justice demand that the contract or contracts be reformed or rescinded, the municipal court shall have jurisdiction to decree such reformation or rescission.

(4). All actions or proceedings, whether legal or equitable to enforce the collection of its own judgments.

(5). All actions for the sale of personal property under chattel mortgage, lien or other charges of incumbrance upon personal property, and for marshalling of all liens thereon when the appraised value of such property shall not exceed one thousand dollars.

(6). All actions and proceedings for the sale of personal property under lien of judgment of the municipal court or lien for material or fuel furnished or labor performed and for the marshalling of all liens thereon.

(7). All actions and proceedings in the nature of

creditors' bills in aid of execution, to subject the interest of a debtor in real or personal property to the payment of a judgment of the municipal court.

(8). All actions and proceedings in the nature of interpleader and involving one thousand dollars or less, but parties may interplead as to larger amounts in any action originally instituted, involving one thousand dollars or less.

Sec. 1579-419. SECTION 4. The municipal court shall have jurisdiction within the limits of Stark county. *Jurisdiction within Stark county.*

(1). To compel attendance of witnesses in any pending action or proceeding; also to compel the attendance of witnesses from the township of Sugar Creek, Wayne county, state of Ohio.

(2). To issue execution on its own judgments.

(3). In all actions and proceedings whether legal or equitable to enforce the collection of its own judgments.

(4). In all actions and proceedings where one or more defendants resides or is served with summons in the townships of Perry or Tuscarawas, county of Stark, state of Ohio.

Sec. 1579-420. SECTION 5. In all causes the municipal court shall have jurisdiction in every ancillary and supplemental proceeding, before and after judgment, including attachment of person or property, arrest before judgment, interpleader, aid of execution and the appointment of a receiver, for which authority is now, or may hereafter be conferred upon the court of common pleas, or a judge thereof, or upon justices of the peace. *Ancillary and supplemental proceedings.*

Sec. 1579-421. SECTION 6. The municipal court shall have jurisdiction upon the application of a debtor, to appoint a trustee to receive that portion of the personal earnings of the debtor, which, as against claims for necessaries, is not exempt from execution, attachment, or proceedings in aid of execution, and such additional sums as the debtor may voluntarily pay or assign to said trustee, and to distribute the money pro rata among creditors having claims for necessaries against the debtor at the time of application. *Claims for necessaries; appointment of trustee.*

When a trustee shall be so appointed, no proceeding in attachment, aid of execution or otherwise to subject the personal earnings of the debtor to the payment of claims for necessaries shall be brought or maintained by any creditor having a claim against such debtor at the time of the application herein, before any justice of the peace or in any court, so long as at least fifteen per centum of the personal earnings of such debtor is paid to the trustee at regular intervals, as fixed by the court; provided, however, this provision shall not be construed to prohibit creditors from recovering judgments against the debtor nor to prohibit levy, under a writ of attachment or execution, upon any other property which is not exempt from execution. *When proceeding in attachment may be brought.*

The maintaining of a proceeding in attachment, aid of execution or otherwise, in violation of the foregoing pro- *Writ of prohibition may be employed; when.*

vision, may be prevented by a writ of prohibition, in addi-
·tion to all other remedies provided by law.

Rule for notice to creditors, etc., may be provided.

The municipal court may provide, by rule, for notice to creditors, the authentication and adjudication of claims, the time and manner of payments by the debtor, the distribution of the fund, the bond and the trustee, if required, and for all other matters necessary or proper to carry into effect the jurisdiction conferred by this section. The court shall designate the clerk of the municipal court, trustee, without additional compensation and his official bond shall be construed as conditioned upon the fulfillment of the trust, and no additional bond shall be required.

Sec. 1579-422.

Jurisdiction for violation of ordinance, etc.

SECTION 7. The municipal court shall have jurisdiction of all misdemeanors and of all violations of city ordinances of which police courts or the mayor in municipalities or a justice of the peace now have or may hereafter be given jurisdiction. In felonies the municipal court shall have the power which police courts or the mayor in municipalities or a justice of the peace now have or may hereafter be given.

Sec. 1579-423.

Bastardy and quasi-criminal actions.

SECTION 8. The municipal court shall have jurisdiction of all bastardy and other quasi-criminal actions and proceedings of which a court of a justice of the peace now has or may hereafter be given jurisdiction; and in all such actions the practice and procedure and the powers of the court in relation thereto shall be the same as those which are now or may hereafter be possessed by a court of a justice of the peace.

Sec. 1579-424.

Laws conferring jurisdiction on other courts, applicable.

SECTION 9. In the actions and proceedings of which the municipal court has jurisdiction, all laws conferring jurisdiction upon a court of common pleas, a police court or a justice of the peace or the mayor, giving such court or officer power, to hear and determine such causes, prescribing the force and effect of their judgments, orders or decrees, and authorizing and directing the execution or enforcement thereof, shall be held to extend to the municipal court, unless inconsistent with this act or plainly inapplicable.

Sec. 1579-425.

Excess may be remitted and judgment rendered.

SECTION 10. When the amount due to either party exceeds the sum for which the municipal court is authorized to enter judgment, such party may remit the excess, and judgment may be entered for the residue. Defendant need not remit such excess, and may withhold setting it off. A recovery for the amount set off and allowed, or any part of it, shall not be a bar to his subsequent action for the amount withheld.

Sec. 1579-426.

When proceedings certified to common pleas court.

SECTION 11. Whenever the appraised value of property sought to be recovered or sold (save in the excepted instances heretofore set forth) in any action in the municipal court exceeds one thousand dollars, the judge of the municipal court shall certify the proceedings in the case to the court of common pleas of Stark county and thereupon the clerk of the municipal court shall file the original papers and pleadings together with a certified transcript of the docket and journal entries in the case, in the office of the clerk of said common pleas court. The bailiff shall turn over the property in his possession to the sheriff of Stark county, to be by him held as in like cases originating in the court of common pleas. The case must then proceed as if it had been commenced in said common pleas court.

SECTION 12. Civil actions and proceedings in the municipal court shall be commenced as in the common pleas court, and an action shall be deemed pending so as to carry notice thereof to all persons from the delivery of the summons or writ by the clerk to the bailiff for service.

(1). All writs and process in the municipal court shall be served and returned by the bailiff, or by publication, or in case of foreign service in the same manner as is now, or may hereafter be provided by law for the service and return of writs and process in the court of common pleas. Where the manner of service is not so provided for, service and return may be made in the same manner provided by law for the service and return of process and writs issued by the common pleas court or a police court or mayor or a justice of the peace.

(2). The return day shall be fixed by rule of court and the summons or writs shall, unless accompanied with an order to arrest, be served at least three days before the return day of the summons, writ or process.

(3). In all civil cases in the municipal court, the plaintiff before issuing a summons, shall file a petition setting out his statement of claim, and the defendant shall file an answer setting out a statement of any set-off, counterclaim or defense which he may desire to assert or make. The statement of answer containing a statement of defense shall be filed in such cases, and within such time as may be required by rule of court. In such cases where an answer is required, the summons shall set forth the date when such answer shall be filed, as fixed by rule of court, which shall be not less than seven days, after the return day of the summons, but the court may grant leave for further time to file such answer on good cause shown. The statement shall set forth in plain, direct language the facts constituting the cause of action, set-off, counter-claim or defense.

(4). To expedite the business and promote the ends of justice, said judge may from time to time adopt, publish and revise rules relating to the matter of practice and procedure, classify the causes of action in the court, and prescribe with reference to each class the degree of particularity with which a cause of action, set-off, counterclaim or defense shall be set up. Until otherwise provided by rule of court and except as herein provided, the practice as to pleadings and procedure shall be governed by the civil code of procedure provided for the common pleas court of the state.

Sec. 1579-428.

Practice and procedure.

SECTION 13. In all criminal cases and proceedings the practice and procedure and the mode of bringing and conducting the procedure of defenses and the powers of the court in relation thereto, shall be the same as those which are now, or may hereafter be, possessed by police courts or the mayor in municipalities unless as otherwise provided herein.

Sec. 1579-429.

Annual report to council; contents.

SECTION 14. In addition to the exercise of all other powers of a judge of said court, he shall render a complete annual report to the council of the city of Massillon covering the preceding year, which report shall show the work performed by the court, a summary of all expenses of the civil and criminal branches of the court respectively, a statement of receipts and expenditures, the number of cases heard, decided and settled by the court, the number of decisions of the municipal court reversed or affirmed by a reviewing court, and such other data as a council may require.

Arrangement for both civil and criminal branches.

The conduct of the criminal branch shall be arranged by said judge, and for both the criminal and civil branches of said court he shall prescribe forms, establish a system for the docketing of causes, motions and demurrers, adopt and publish rules governing practice and procedure not otherwise provided for in this act; and designate the mode of keeping and authenticating the records of proceedings had before him.

Summoning jury, taxing costs, etc.

The judge of the court may summon and impanel jurors, tax costs; compel the attendance of witnesses, jurors and parties; issue process; preserve order; punish for contempt; and may exercise all powers which are now, or may hereafter be, conferred upon the court of common pleas or the judge thereof, or upon justices of the peace, or upon police courts of cities or judges thereof, or are necessary for the exercise of the jurisdiction herein conferred and for the enforcement of the judgment and orders of the court.

Sec 1579-430.

When trial shall be by jury; waiver.

SECTION 15. All causes in the municipal court, both civil and criminal, shall be tried to the court unless a jury trial be demanded by a party entitled to the same. The time for making a demand for a jury in civil cases may be fixed and limited by rule of court. In all criminal cases, in which the accused is entitled to a jury trial, a demand for a jury trial must be made by the accused before the court shall proceed to inquire into the merits of the cause, otherwise a jury shall be deemed to be waived and the cause shall be tried by the court. In all civil actions where a jury shall be demanded, except as hereinafter provided, it shall be composed of six men, having qualifications of electors unless the parties agree on a less number; provided, however, that when the amount claimed by any party or the appraised value of the personal property sought to be recovered exceeds the sum of two hundred dollars, either party may demand a jury of twelve men by specifying that number in said written demand. In all actions and proceedings in said municipal court of which police courts in

cities have or may hereinafter be given jurisdiction, where
a jury may be and is demanded, it shall be composed of
twelve men having the qualifications of electors. In all
civil actions a jury shall render a verdict upon the concurrence of three-fourths or more of their number.

Sec. 1579-431.

SECTION 16. In all civil actions and proceedings, when
the amount claimed by any party or the appraised value of
personal property sought to be recovered does not exceed
two hundred dollars, the cost of summoning jurors and the
fees of jurors shall be taxed as part of the costs, and such
costs must be deposited or secured in advance by the party
demanding a jury. In all civil actions and proceedings
where the amount claimed by any party or the appraised
value of the personal property sought to be recovered is in
excess of two hundred dollars, the cost of summoning jurors
and the fees of jurors shall be paid out of the treasury of
Stark county, Ohio, and charged to the appropriate fund
for the payment of jurors serving in the common pleas
court, and shall be collected from the county and distributed
by the clerk of the municipal court; provided, however, that
when the amount claimed by any plaintiff, or by any defendant by way of counterclaim or set-off, shall exceed the
sum of two hundred dollars, and in such cases such claimant shall demand a jury and shall thereafter recover a verdict on his claim of less than fifty dollars, the fees of jurors
shall be taxed against such party so demanding such jury
as a part of the costs, and when collected such jury fees
shall be paid to the county and credited to the appropriate
fund for the payment of jurors serving in the common pleas
court.

Costs when ap-
praised value ex-
ceeds $200.

Sec. 1579-432.

SECTION 17. Jurors in the municipal court shall be
chosen and summoned in accordance with the rules of said
court. Such rules shall provide for a jury wheel similar to
that used for summoning jurors in the common pleas court.
The judge and clerk of the municipal court shall on or before the fifth day of January of each year, appoint two
freehold electors, resident in Perry and Tuscarawas townships, Stark county Ohio, who shall not be of the same
political party, to serve as jury commissioners for the ensuing year, and their duties shall be such as may be prescribed by the rule of court aforesaid. Before entering
upon their duties said commissioners shall take an oath
before the municipal judge similar to that required by jury
commissioners of the common pleas court. Such commissioners shall each receive for his service twenty-five dollars
per year, payable out of the treasury of the city of Massillon. The names of persons who are to serve as jurors shall
be drawn from such jury wheel by the clerk in the presence
of the municipal judge. Jurors in the municipal court
shall be electors of either the township of Perry or the
township of Tuscarawas in the county of Stark, state of
Ohio, and shall be summoned and impaneled in the same
manner and challenged for the same causes as jurors in the

Choosing and
summoning jury;
jury commis-
sioners.

court of common pleas; they shall have the same qualifications as jurors in the court of common pleas and their fees shall be paid as hereinbefore provided. Each juror, when the amount claimed by any party or the appraised value of the personal property sought to be recovered in any suit does not exceed two hundred dollars shall be paid one dollar per day and mileage and when the amount claimed by any party or the appraised value of the personal property sought to be recovered in any suit is in excess of two hundred dollars each juror shall receive two dollars per day and mileage.

Sec. 1579-433.
Setting aside of verdict.

SECTION 18. In all causes the municipal court shall have the same authority to set aside a verdict or a judgment, as is now, or may hereafter be, conferred upon courts of common pleas.

Sec. 1579-434.
Court calendar.

SECTION 19. The calendar of the municipal court shall be divided into four terms of three months each, beginning respectively, on the first of January, April, July and October of each year. The judge of the municipal court may continue the session of any term of said court beyond the time fixed for the commencement of the next term, when such continuance is necessary to finish the trial of any cause, or to receive the verdict or pronounce judgment in any cause, the trial of which has been commenced during the term.

Sec. 1579-435.
Judgment binds property.

SECTION 20. All lands and tenements, including vested interests therein, and permanent leasehold estates, renewable forever, located within the townships of Perry or Tuscarawas in the county of Stark, shall be bound for the satisfaction of any judgment rendered in the municipal court from the first day of the term at which judgment is rendered; but judgments by confession and judgments rendered at the same term at which the action is commenced shall bind such land, tenements, vested interests and permanent leaseholds only from the day on which such judgments are rendered.

Sec. 1579-436.
Transcript of judgment.

SECTION 21. The party in whose favor a judgment is rendered by the municipal court may file a transcript of such judgment in the office of the clerk of the common pleas court in the same manner and under the same conditions as are now, or may hereafter be, provided for filing of transcripts of judgments rendered by justices of the peace; all provisions relative to transcripts of judgments and liens of judgments rendered by justices of the peace, shall, in so far as applicable, be applied to transcripts of judgments and liens of judgments rendered by the municipal court.

Sec. 1579-437.
Enforcement of lien.

SECTION 22. The lien of judgment of the municipal court may be enforced in the court of common pleas in the same manner as the lien of a judgment rendered by the court of common pleas. Execution may be issued on such judgments at any time after a transcript thereof has been filed, as if the judgment had been rendered by the court of common pleas; but all liens shall remain as provided in this act.

Sec. 1579-438.

SECTION 23. The records of the municipal court may be proved by the production of the original records, or by a transcript thereof certified by the clerk of said court under its seal.

Proof of records.

Sec. 1579-439.

SECTION 24. The clerk of the municipal court shall make and maintain an alphabetical index of the names of all plaintiffs and defendants to suits filed in said court.

Index of litigants.

Sec. 1579-440.

SECTION 25. Proceedings in error may be taken to the common pleas court of Stark county from a final judgment or order of the municipal court in the same manner and under the same conditions as provided by law for proceedings in error from the common pleas court, to the court of appeals.

Proceedings in error to common pleas court.

Sec. 1579-441.

SECTION 26. No assignment of error in a review court shall be allowed in any action which shall call in question the decision of the municipal court with reference to any matter pertaining to the practice in said court, provided, however, that the reviewing court may grant relief from error in the municipal court in respect to a matter of practice therein in any case wherein the opinion of the reviewing court such relief is necessary to prevent a failure of justice.

When assignment of error shall not be allowed.

Sec. 1579-442.

SECTION 27. The laws governing the court of common pleas as to security for costs except as herein otherwise provided for, pleadings and procedure, motions for new trials, vacation or modification of judgments before and after terms, the referring of matters to a referee, the issuing of execution and the taking of depositions shall be held to apply so far as applicable to the municipal court. Provided, that a person against whom a judgment has been rendered in the municipal court may stay execution thereon by entering into a bond to the adverse party within ten days after the rendition of such judgment, with sufficient surety, who shall be a freeholder owning real property situated in the county of Stark and state of Ohio, or a corporation authorized to execute surety bonds in this state, approved by the clerk of court, and conditioned for the payment of the amount of such judgment, interest, costs and costs that accrue. Such bonds shall be entered in the docket of the clerk of court and shall be signed by such surety. The giving of such bond shall in no manner impair the lien of judgment against the real estate of said judgment debtor.

Laws governing court of common pleas applicable.

Bond for stay of execution.

The stay of execution hereby authorized shall be graduated as follows:

(1) On a judgment of fifty dollars and under, for thirty days.

(2) On a judgment exceeding fifty dollars but not exceeding five hundred dollars, for ninety days.

(3) On a judgment exceeding five hundred dollars, for one hundred and twenty days.

Sec. 1579-443.

SECTION 28. A clerk for said municipal court shall be elected at the next regular municipal election after the going into effect of this act for a term of four years, com-

Election of clerk; term, salary.

mencing on the first day of January next after said election, and shall hold said office until his successor is duly elected and qualified, and he shall receive an annual salary of fifteen hundred dollars, one thousand dollars of which shall be paid out of the treasury of the city of Massillon in monthly installments, and five hundred dollars to be paid out of the treasury of Stark county in monthly installments.

Deputy clerks.

Such election shall be held and conducted and returns thereof made as in case of the election of city officers. Council shall provide such deputy clerks as may be necessary, and fix their term of office, duties, and compensation. The deputy clerks provided for shall be appointed by the municipal judge.

Sec. 1579-444.

Powers and duties of clerk.

SECTION 29. The clerk of the municipal court shall have power to administer oaths, and take affidavits and acknowledgements and to issue execution upon any judgment rendered in the municipal court, including a judgment for unpaid costs; he shall have power to issue and sign all writs, processes and papers issuing out of the court, and to attach the seal of the court thereto; shall have power to approve all bonds, recognizances and undertakings, fixed by any judge of the court or by law; shall file and safely keep all journals, records, books and papers belonging or appertaining to the court, record its proceedings and perform all other duties which the judge of the court shall prescribe. He shall pay over to the proper parties all moneys received by him as clerk; he shall receive and collect all costs, fines and penalties; he shall pay the same quarterly to the treasurer of the city of Massillon and take his receipt therefor, but money deposited as security for costs shall be retained by him pending the litigation; he shall keep a record showing all receipts and disbursements, which shall be open for public inspection at all times; and shall on the first Monday of each term of court make to the city auditor a report of all receipts and disbursements for the preceding term.

Sec. 1579-445.

Record of moneys deposited and costs; unclaimed costs.

SECTION 30. All money deposited as security for costs, and all other moneys, other than costs, paid into the municipal court, shall be noted on the record of the cause in which they are paid and shall be deposited by the clerk in such banking institutions as shall be designated by council, there to abide the order of the court and to bear interest at the best rate obtainable. On the first Monday in January of each year the clerk shall make a list of the titles of all causes in the municipal court which were finally determined more than one year past, in which there remains unclaimed in the possession of the clerk any of such funds, or any part of a deposit for security for costs not consumed by the costs in the case. The clerk shall give notice of the same to the parties entitled to said moneys, or to their attorneys of record. All such moneys remaining unclaimed on the first day of April of each year shall be paid by the clerk to the city treasurer, provided, however, that any part of such moneys shall be paid by such treasurer at any time to the person having the right thereto upon proper certificate of the clerk of court.

Sec. 1579-446.　SECTION 31. Before entering upon the duties of his office, the clerk of the municipal court shall give a bond to the city of Massillon in the sum of five thousand dollars with suerty to the approval of the municipal judge conditioned upon the faithful performance of his duties as such clerk. The said bond shall be given for the benefit of the city of Massillon, and for the benefit of any person who may suffer loss by reason of a default in any of the conditions of said bond. A vacancy in the office of clerk of the municipal court shall be filled by the judge of said court, by appointment, until his successor is elected and qualified according to law.　Bond of clerk.

Sec. 1579-447.　SECTION 32. The bailiff shall be appointed by the ·judge of such court and hold office during the pleasure of the court, and may be removed at any time by the judge of the municipal court. Every police officer of the city of Massillon shall be ex-officio a deputy bailiff of the municipal court and the chief of police shall assign one or more such police officers from time to time to perform such duties in respect to cases within the jurisdiction within said court as may be required of them by said court or the clerk thereof.　Appointment of bailiff; ex-officio bailiffs.

Sec. 1579-448.　SECTION 33. One bailiff shall be designated as hereinafter provided for in this act. He shall perform for the municipal court, services similar to those usually performed by the sheriff for courts of common pleas and by the constable of courts of justices of the peace. Such bailiff shall receive such compensation not less than six hundred dollars per annum, payable out of the treasury of the city of Massillon in monthly installments as the council may prescribe. Before entering upon his duties, said bailiff shall make and file in the office of the auditor of the city of Massillon, a bond in the amount of not less than two thousand dollars. The terms and sufficiency of said bond shall be subject to the approval of the judge of the court. The said bond shall be given for the benefit of the city of Massillon and of any person who shall suffer loss by reason of the default of any of the conditions of said bond. The bailiff shall receive from the treasury of the city of Massillon, in addition to his compensation, his actual expenses in serving process of the court, not to exceed the sum of twenty dollars per month, payable upon the order of the municipal judge.　Duties of bailiff; bond.

Sec. 1579-449.　SECTION 34. In all actions where the amount claimed by either party or the appraised value of the property sought to be recovered does not exceed two hundred dollars and except as herein provided in all actions where the municipal court has jurisdiction the same as that of a justice of the peace, the fees and costs shall be the same and taxed in the same manner as is now or may hereafter be provided for such actions before a justice of the peace. In all other actions the fees and costs shall be the same and taxed in　Taxing fees and costs.

the same manner as is now or may hereafter be provided for such actions in the court of common pleas. In criminal cases all fees and costs shall be the same as fixed with respect to police courts. The judge of the municipal court may, by rule of court, provide for all cases not covered by this act, a standard of fees and costs not in excess of those provided by general laws. All payments and deposits for costs and jury shall be refunded when the same shall have been paid by the losing party.

Sec. 1579-450.
Accommodations and equipment.

SECTION 35. The council of the city of Massillon shall provide suitable accommodations for the municipal court and its officers, including a private room for said judge and sufficient jury room. The council shall also provide for the use of the court complete sets of the reports of the supreme and inferior courts of Ohio and such other authorities as it shall be deemed necessary and shall provide for the court room the latest edition of the General Code of Ohio' and necessary supplies, including telephone, stationery, furniture, heat and janitor services. The council may also provide for such other ordinary or extraordinary expense as it may deem advisable or necessary for the operation or administration of said court.

Sec. 1579-451.
Seal of court.

SECTION 36. The said municipal court shall have a seal which shall have engraved thereon the coat of arms of the state and shall be approximately one inch in diameter and shall be surrounded by these words, "The Municipal Court of Massillon, Ohio," and shall have no other words or device engraved thereon.

Sec. 1579-452.
Solicitor shall be prosecuting attorney.

SECTION 37. The solicitor for the city of Massillon shall also be prosecuting attorney of the municipal court. He may designate such number of assistant prosecutors as the council of the city of Massillon may authorize. The solicitor or person thus appointed shall receive for their services in city cases such salary as the council may prescribe, and such additional compensation as the county commissioners shall allow. The prosecuting attorney of the municipal court shall prosecute all cases of a criminal nature brought before such court and perform the same duties, so far as they are applicable thereto, as are required of the prosecuting attorney of the county. The council of the city of Massillon, by ordinance, shall provide for one or more official stenographers and fix their compensation, and provide for the payment of the same monthly out of the city treasury and the same shall be appointed by the judge of the municipal court and serve at his pleasure. The court shall regulate the charge for transcripts of testimony and the cost thereof shall be paid to the clerk and by him accounted for.

Sec. 1579-453.
Substitute in case of absence or incapacity.

SECTION 38. Whenever the incumbent of any office created by this act, excepting the municipal judge shall be temporarily absent or incapacitated from acting, the judge shall appoint a substitute who shall have all the qualifications required of the incumbent of the office. Such appointee shall serve until the return of the regular incumbent, or until his incapacity ceases. In case said judge shall be incapacitated from sitting in 'any case, or by reason of absence or inability be unable to attend sessions of said court, the mayor of the city of Massillon may appoint some attorney having the qualifications required by this act, to act in his stead until said judge is able to resume his said position. Such appointments shall be certified by the court or mayor as the case may be and entered upon the record, provided, however, that in the event a member of the bar receives the appointment nothing contained in this act nor in other laws of Ohio shall prevent the acting municipal judge from practicing as an attorney and counselor-at-law in any other court in said state in any and all matters of business not originating or pending in said municipal court.

Sec. 1579-454.

SECTION 39. No justice of the peace in any township in Stark county, other than Perry or Tuscarawas townships, or mayor of any village, in any proceedings, whether civil or criminal, in which any warrant, order of arrest, summons, order of attachment, garnishment or replevin or other process, except subpoena for witnesses, shall have been served upon a citizen or resident of the city of Massillon, Perry or Tuscarawas townships, or a corporation or firm having its principal office therein, shall have jurisdiction, unless such service be actually made by personal service within the township or village in which said proceedings may have been instituted, or in a criminal matter, unless the offense charged in any warrant or order of arrest shall be alleged to have been committed within said township or village. *Limitation of jurisdiction of mayors and justices of the peace.*

Sec. 1579-455.

SECTION 40. All proceedings, judgments, executions, dockets, papers, moneys, property and persons subject to the jurisdiction of the mayor's court of the city of Massillon and the courts of any justice of the peace for Perry and Tuscarawas townships in Stark county on December 31st, 1919, shall be turned over to the municipal court herein created; and thereafter such causes shall proceed in the municipal court as if originally instituted therein, the parties making such amendments to their pleadings as required to conform to the rules of said court. *Proceedings, dockets, moneys, etc., turned over.*

Sec. 1579-456.

SECTION 41. Upon the qualification of the municipal judge, as provided for in section two hereof, the jurisdiction of the mayor of the city of Massillon or any person or officer exercising the jurisdiction of a mayor of the city of Massillon, and of all justices of the peace of Perry and Tuscarawas townships, Stark county, Ohio, in all civil and criminal matters shall cease, and no justice of the peace or constable shall thereafter be elected in said Perry or Tuscarawas townships. *Jurisdiction of mayor and justices shall cease.*

Sec. 1579-457.

SECTION 42. Each section and each subdivision of any section of this act is hereby declared to be independent, and the finding or holding of any section or subdivision of *Each section and part independent.*

any section thereof to be invalid or void shall not be deemed or held to affect the validity of any other section or subdivision.

Sec. 1579-458.

Removal for cause.

SECTION. 43. The judge of the municipal court shall be subject to the same disabilities and may be removed from office for the same causes as the judge of the court of common pleas. The vacancies arising from any cause except as herein provided shall be filled by appointment by the governor of the state.

The sectional numbers on the margin hereof are designated as provided by law. JOHN G. PRICE, Attorney General.

CARL R. KIMBALL,
Speaker of the House of Representatives.
CLARENCE J. BROWN,
President of the Senate.

Passed April 16, 1919.

This bill was presented to the Governor May 7th, 1919, and was not signed or returned to the house in which it originated within ten days after being so presented, exclusive of Sundays and the day said bill was presented, and was filed in the office of the Secretary of State, May 20, 1919.

ROBERT T. CREW,
Veto Clerk.

Filed in the office of the Secretary of State at Columbus, Ohio, on the 20th day of May, A. D. 1919.

161 G.

[House Bill No. 225.]

AN ACT

To amend section 5785 of the General Code, regarding the misbranding of food, drink, flavoring extracts, confectionery and condiment.

Be it enacted by the General Assembly of the State of Ohio:

SECTION 1. That section 5785 of the General Code be amended to read as follows:

What deemed misbranding of food, etc.

Sec. 5785. Food, drink, flavoring extracts, confectionery or condiment shall be misbranded within the meaning of this chapter:

1. If the package fails to bear a statement on the label of the quantity or proportion of morphine, opium, cocaine, heroin, alpha or beta eucaine, chloroform, cannabis indica, chloral hydrate, or acetanilide, or any derivative or preparation of such substances contained therein;

2. If it is labeled or branded so as to deceive or mislead the purchaser, or purport to be a foreign product when not so;

3. If in package form, and the contents are stated in terms of weight or measure, they are not plainly and correctly stated on the outside of the package;

4. In case of a flavoring extract for which no standard exists there is not printed in English, conspicuously, legibly,

and clearly on the label the quantity by volume of alcohol in said extract;

5. If the package containing it or a label thereon bears a statement, design or device regarding it or the ingredients or substances contained therein, which is false or misleading in any particular; provided, that this section shall not apply to mixtures or compounds recognized as ordinary articles or ingredients of articles of food or drink, if each package sold or offered for sale is distinctly labeled in words of the English language as mixtures or compounds, with the name and percentage, in terms of one hundred per cent of each ingredient therein.

The word "compound" or "mixture" shall be printed in letters and figures not smaller in height or width than one-half the largest letter upon any label on the package and the formula shall be printed in letters and figures not smaller in height or width than one-fourth the largest upon any label on the package, and such compound or mixture must not contain any ingredient that is poisonous or injurious to health.

SECTION 2. That said original section 5785 of the General Code be and the same is hereby repealed.

CARL R. KIMBALL,
Speaker of the House of Representatives.
CLARENCE J. BROWN,
President of the Senate.

The sectional number in this act is in conformity to the General Code. JOHN G. PRICE, Attorney General.

Passed April 17, 1919.

This bill was presented to the Governor May 7, 1919, and was not signed or returned to the house in which it originated within ten days after being so presented, exclusive of Sundays and the day said bill was presented, and was filed in the office of the Secretary of State, May 20, 1919.

ROBERT T. CREW,
Veto Clerk.

Filed in the office of the Secretary of State at Columbus, Ohio, on the 20th day of May, A. D. 1919.

162 G.

[House Bill No. 320.]

AN ACT

To establish a municipal court for the city of Portsmouth, Scioto county, Ohio, and fix the jurisdiction thereof, providing for a judge thereof and other necessary officers and define their duties, and to repeal sections 14719 and 14720 of the General Code, relating to the police court of the city of Portsmouth.

Be it enacted by the General Assembly of the State of Ohio:

Sec. 1579-459.

Municipal court of Portsmouth.

SECTION 1. That there be, and hereby is created a court of record for the city of Portsmouth, and the township of Wayne, Scioto county, Ohio, to be styled "The Municipal Court" of the city of Portsmouth, Ohio, with jurisdiction as hereinafter fixed and determined.

Sec. 1579-460.

Election qualification, term and compensation of judge.

SECTION 2. Said municipal court shall be presided over by one judge, designated herein as a "Municipal Judge", and which office is hereby created, and whose term of office shall be for a period of four years. The judge of the municipal court shall receive such compensation, payable out of the treasury of the city of Portsmouth, not less than two thousand dollars per annum, as the council may prescribe, and such further compensation, not less than one thousand dollars per annum, payable in monthly installments out of the county treasury of Scioto county, Ohio, as the county commissioners may prescribe. Said municipal judge, at the time of his election or appointment to said office, shall be a resident and qualified elector of the city of Portsmouth, Ohio, and shall have been admitted to the bar and in the active practice of law in the state of Ohio for a period of not less than five years. Such judge shall be elected at the next regular election after the going into effect of this act, for a term of four years, commencing on the first day of January next thereafter and shall hold office until his successor is elected and duly qualified.

Sec. 1579-461.

Criminal and civil jurisdiction.

SECTION 3. The municipal court herein established shall have the same jurisdiction in criminal matters and prosecutions for misdemeanors, or violation of ordinances, as heretofore had by the police court (mayor's court) of Portsmouth, Ohio, and justices of the peace for Wayne township, and in addition thereto shall have ordinary civil jurisdiction within the limits of said city of Portsmouth, Wayne township, Scioto county, Ohio, in the following cases:

1. In all actions and proceedings of which justices of the peace, or such courts as may succeed justice of the peace courts, have or may be given jurisdiction.

2. In all actions and proceedings for the recovery of money and of personal property of which the court of common pleas has, or may be given jurisdiction, when the amount claimed by any party or the value of the personal property sought to be recovered, does not exceed one thousand dollars, and in such action judgment may be rendered

for over one thousand dollars, when the amount in excess
of said sum shall consist of interest or damages, or costs accrued after the commencement of the action.

3. In all actions or contracts express or implied, when
the amount claimed by the plaintiff, exclusive of all costs
does not exceed the sum of one thousand dollars. When a
course arising out of a contract is pending in the municipal
court, and when the ends of justice demand that the contract be reformed or rescinded the municipal court shall
have jurisdiction to decree such reformation or rescission.

4. In all actions or proceedings whether legal or equitable to enforce the collection of its own judgments.

5. In all actions for the sale of personal property
under chattel mortgage lien or other charge or encumbrance
upon personal property, and for marshaling of all liens
thereon when the appraised value of such property shall not
exceed the sum of three hundred dollars.

6. In all actions and proceedings for the sale of personal property under lien of judgment of the municipal
court, or lien for material or fuel furnished, or labor performed, and for the marshaling of all liens thereon.

7. In all actions and proceedings in the nature of creditor's bills in aid of execution to subject the interest of a
debtor in real or personal property to the payment of a
judgment of the municipal court.

8. In all actions and proceedings in the nature of interpleader and involving three hundred dollars or less, but
parties may interplead as to larger amounts in any action
originally instituted involving three hundred dollars, or less.

Sec. 1579-462. SECTION 4. In all cases the municipal court shall have *Ancillary and supplemental proceedings.*
jurisdiction in every ancillary and supplemental proceeding,
before and after judgment, including attachment of person
or property, arrest before judgment, interpleading, aid of
execution, and the appointment of a receiver for which authority is now, or may hereafter be, conferred upon the court
of common pleas, or a judge thereof, or upon justices of the
peace.

Sec. 1579-463. SECTION 5. The municipal court shall have jurisdic- *Criminal juris-diction.*
tion of all misdemeanors, and all violations of city ordinan-
ces, of which police courts or the mayors in municipalities
now have or may hereafter be given jurisdiction. In felonies the municipal court shall have the powers which police
courts and mayors in municipalities now have or may hereafter be given.

Sec. 1579-464. SECTION 6. In the actions and proceedings of which *Laws governing court in actions and proceedings.*
the municipal court has jurisdiction, all laws conferring
jurisdiction upon a court of common pleas, a police court,
a justice of the peace or a mayor giving such court power to
hear and determine such causes prescribing the force and
effect of their judgments, orders or decrees, shall be held to
extend to the municipal court unless inconsistent with this
act or plainly inapplicable.

Sec. 1579-465.

When amount exceeds authorised judgment.

SECTION 7. When the amount due to either party exceeds the sum for which the municipal court is authorized to enter judgment such party may remit the excess and judgment be entered for the residue. A defendant need not remit such excess, and may withhold setting it off. A recovery for the amount set off and allowed or any part of it, shall be a bar to his subsequent action for the amount withheld.

Sec. 1579-466.

When proceedings certified to common pleas court.

SECTION 8. Whenever the appraised value of property sought to be recovered or sold (save in the excepted cases hereinbefore set forth) in any action in the municipal court exceeds one thousand dollars, the judge thereof shall certify the proceedings in the case to the court of common pleas of Scioto county, and thereupon the clerk of the municipal court shall file the original paper and pleadings, together with a certified transcript of the docket and journal entries in the case, in the office of the clerk of the said court of common pleas. The bailiff shall turn over the property in his possession to the sheriff of Scioto county to be by him held as in like cases originating in the court of common pleas. The case to then proceed as if it had been commenced in the court of common pleas.

Sec. 1579-467.

Commencement of civil actions.

SECTION 9. Civil actions and proceedings in the municipal court shall be commenced as in the common pleas court.

1. All writs and processes in the municipal court shall be served and returned by the bailiff, or by publication in the same manner as they are now, or may hereafter be provided by law, served in the court of common pleas, except that publication shall be complete when published for three consecutive weeks. Where the manner of service is not so provided for, service and return shall be made in the same manner provided by law for the service and return of writs and process issued by police courts, mayors and justices of the peace.

2. The return day shall be fixed by rule of court, and the summons or writs shall, unless accompanied with an order to arrest, be served at least three days before the time of appearance.

3. In all cases in the municipal court the bailiff shall file a statement of claim, and the defendant shall file a like statement of any set-off or counter-claim he may desire to assert. A statement of defense shall be filed in such cases and within such time as may be required by rule of court. In cases where a statement of defense is required the summons shall set forth the date when such statement shall be filed, as fixed by rule of court, which shall not be less than five days after the return day of the summons. The statements shall set forth in plain and direct language the facts constituting the cause of action, set-off, counter-claim or defense.

4. To expedite business and promote the ends of justice the judge may, from time to time, adopt, publish and

revise rules relating to matters of practice and procedure and classify the causes of action in the court.

Sec. 1579-468. SECTION 10. In all criminal cases and proceedings the practice and procedure and mode of bringing and conducting prosecutions for offenses, and the powers of the court in relation thereto, shall be the same as those which are now or may be hereafter possessed by police courts or mayors in municipalities or justices of the peace, unless otherwise herein provided. *Practice and procedure in criminal cases.*

Sec. 1579-469. SECTION 11. In addition to the exercise of the other powers and duties of a judge of said municipal court he shall render a complete annual report to the council of the city of Portsmouth, Ohio, for the preceding year which shall show the work performed by the court, a summary of all the expenses of the civil and criminal branches of the court, respectively, a statement of receipts and expenditures, the number of cases heard, decided and settled, by the court, the number of the decisions of the municipal court reversed and affirmed by a reviewing court, and such other data as the council may require, and said report shall be published for the information of the public. The conduct of the criminal branch of said court shall be determined by the judge, and he shall prescribe forms, establish a system for the docketing of causes, motions and demurrers, adopt and publish rules governing practice and procedure not otherwise provided for in this act; and he shall designate the mode and method of keeping and authenticating the records of proceedings had before him. The judge of the court may summon and impanel jurors, tax costs, compel the attendance of witnesses, jurors and parties, issue process, preserve order, punish for contempt, and may exercise all powers which are now, or may hereafter be conferred upon the court of common pleas or a judge therof, or upon justices of the peace, or upon police courts or the judges thereof, or are necessary for the exercise of the jurisdiction herein conferred, and for the enforcement of the judgments and orders of the municipal court. *Report to council annually.* *Forms and docketing prescribed.* *Summoning jurors, taxing costs, etc.*

Sec. 1579-470. SECTION 12. All causes in the municipal court shall be tried to the court, unless, before the day assigned for the trial of a cause upon its merits, a jury shall be demanded in writing by either party to the action. In all civil actions when a jury is demanded it shall be composed of six jurors having the qualifications of electors, unless the parties agree to a smaller number. Provided, however, that either party may demand a jury of twelve jurors by specifying that number in his written demand. In all actions and proceedings in said municipal court of which police courts in cities have or may hereafter be given jurisdiction where a jury may be and is demanded, it shall be composed of twelve qualified jurors. *When causes shall be tried to jury.*

Sec. 1579-471. SECTION 13. In all civil actions and proceedings the costs of summoning jurors and the fees of jurors shall be *Taxing costs; security.*

taxed as part of the costs of the case, and such costs must be
secured in advance by the party demanding a jury.

Sec. 1579-472.

Summoning and impaneling jury; qualifications.

SECTION 14. Jurors in the municipal court shall be
chosen, summoned and impaneled in the same manner and
challenged for the same causes as jurors in the court of common
pleas, and they shall have the same qualifications and
receive the same fees which shall be paid out of the treasury
of the city of Portsmouth, Ohio. It shall be the duty of the
judge of the municipal court to investigate all jurors summoned
for service in the court as to their qualifications to
act as such, and to reject such persons who do not seem to
possess the legal qualifications of jurors.

Sec. 1579-473.

Setting aside verdict.

SECTION 15. In all causes the municipal court shall
have the same authority to set aside a verdict or a judgment
and grant a new trial, as is now, or may hereafter be conferred
upon courts of common pleas.

Sec. 1579-474.

Court calendar.

SECTION 16. The calendar of the municipal court shall
be divided into four terms of three months each, beginning
respectively, on the first of January, April, July and October
of each year. The judge of the municipal court may
continue the session of any term of said court beyond the
time fixed for the commencement of the next term when
such continuance is necessary to finish the trial of any cause,
or to receive the verdict or pronounce judgment in any
cause the trial of which has been commenced during the
term.

Sec. 1579-475.

Transcript, to court of common pleas.

SECTION 17. The party in whose favor a judgment is
rendered by the municipal court may file a transcript of
such judgment in the office of the clerk of the Scioto county
court of common pleas, and in the same manner and under
the same conditions as are now, or may hereafter be provided
for the filing of transcripts of judgments rendered by
justices of the peace; all provisions relating to transcripts
of judgments, and liens of judgments rendered by justices
of the peace, shall, in so far as applicable, be applied to
transcripts of judgments and liens of judgments rendered
by the municipal court.

Sec. 1579-476.

Enforcement of judgment.

SECTION 18. A judgment of the municipal court may
be enforced in the court of common pleas in the same manner
as a judgment rendered by the court of common pleas.
Execution may be issued on such judgments, at any time
after a transcript thereof has been filed, as if the judgment
had been rendered by the court of common pleas.

Sec. 1579-477.

Proof of records.

SECTION 19. The records of the municipal court may
be proved by the production of the original records, or by a
transcript thereof certified by the clerk of said court under
its seal.

Sec. 1579-478.

Index of cases.

SECTION 20. The clerk of the municipal court shall
make and maintain a direct and reverse alphabetical index
of the names of the plaintiffs and defendants in suits filed in
said court.

Sec. 1579-479.

Proceedings in error.

SECTION 21. Proceedings in error may be taken to the
common pleas court of Scioto county, Ohio, from a final

judgment or order of the municipal court in the same manner and under the same conditions as are or may be provided by law for proceedings in error from the common pleas court to the court of appeals.

Sec. 1579-480. SECTION 22. No assignment of error in a reviewing court shall be allowed in any action which shall call in question the decision of the municipal court in reference to any matter pertaining to the practice in said court; provided, however, that the reviewing court may grant relief from any error of the municipal court in respect to a matter of practice therein in any case where in the opinion of the reviewing court such relief is necessary to prevent a failure of justice. *Practice of court may not be called in question.*

Sec. 1579-481. SECTION 23. The laws governing the court of common pleas as to security for costs except as herein otherwise provided; as to motions for new trials, vacation or modification of judgment before and after terms; the referring of matters to referees; the issuing of execution and orders for stay of execution; and the taking of depositions shall be held to apply so far as applicable to the municipal court. Provided, that a person against whom a judgment has been rendered in the municipal court may stay execution thereon by entering into a bond to the adverse party, within ten days after the rendition of such judgment, with sufficient surety who shall be a freeholder owning real property in the city of Portsmouth, Ohio, or a corporation authorized to execute surety bonds in this state, approved by the court and conditioned for the payment of the amount of such judgment, interest, and all accrued costs. Such bond shall be entered on the docket of the clerk of the court and shall be signed by such surety. When a freeholder of the city of Portsmouth, Ohio, is a surety, said undertaking shall be a lien on his real property situate in the city of Portsmouth, Ohio, from the time of the signing of such undertaking until the judgment and all the costs in the case upon which the stay of execution was granted shall have been paid and satisfied. The stay of execution herein provided for shall be as follows: *Laws governing court of common pleas applicable.* *Stay of execution.*

(1) On a judgment of fifty dollars and under thirty days.

(2) On a judgment for more than fifty dollars, ninety days.

Sec. 1579-482. SECTION 24. A clerk for said municipal court shall be chosen and appointed by the judge thereof to serve as such during his pleasure. The clerk shall give bond to the city of Portsmouth, in such sum as the city council may determine and he shall receive an annual salary, payable monthly, to be fixed by the city council in a sum of not less than ten hundred dollars ($1,000.00) per year. *Appointment of clerk; compensation.*

Sec. 1579-483. SECTION 25. The clerk of the municipal court shall have power to administer oaths, take affidavits and issue executions upon judgments rendered in the municipal court including a judgment for unpaid costs; he shall have power *Powers and duties of clerk.*

to issue and sign all writs, process and papers, issuing out of the court and attach the seal of court thereto; he shall have the power to approve all bonds, recognizances and undertakings, fixed by the court or by law; shall file and safely keep all journals, records, books and papers, belonging to and appertaining to the court, record its proceedings and perform all other duties which the judge of the court may prescribe and authorize. He shall pay to the proper parties all moneys received by him as clerk. All costs, all fines collected for the violation of municipal ordinances of the city of Portsmouth and all fees for marriages shall be paid into the treasury of the city of Portsmouth monthly. All fines collected for violation of state laws shall be paid by said clerk into the treasury of Scioto county monthly. Receipts shall be taken for all moneys disbursed by the clerk. Money deposited as security for costs shall be retained by him pending litigation, and he shall keep a record showing all receipts and disbursements and it shall be open for public inspection at all times; and he shall on the first Monday of each month render to the city auditor a report of all receipts and disbursements for and during the next preceding month.

Sec. 1579-484.

Record of and deposit of moneys; unclaimed costs.

SECTION 26. All moneys deposited as security for costs, and all other moneys, other than costs paid into the municipal court, shall be noted on the record of the cause in which they are paid, and shall be deposited by the clerk in such banking institutions as may have been designated as the depositories of city funds there to be subject to the order of the court and to bear interest at the rate of not less than two (2) per cent per annum. On the first Monday in January in each year the clerk shall make a list of the titles of all causes in the municipal court which were finally determined more than one year last past in which there remains unclaimed in the possession of the clerk any of such funds, or any part of a deposit for costs not consumed by costs in the case. The clerk shall give notice of the same to the parties entitled to said moneys or to their attorneys of record. All such moneys remaining unclaimed on the first day of April of each year shall be paid by the clerk to the city treasurer; provided, however, that any part of such moneys shall be paid by such treasurer at any time to the person having the right thereto upon proper certificate of the clerk of the court.

Sec. 1579-485.

Bailiff and deputies.

SECTION 27. The bailiff shall be a member of the city police force and he shall serve as such during the pleasure of the court. Every police officer of the city of Portsmouth, shall be ex officio a deputy bailiff of the municipal court and the chief of police shall assign one or more such police officers, from time to time, to perform such duties in respect to cases within the jurisdiction of said court as may be required of them by said court or the clerk thereof.

Sec. 1579-486.

Duties of bailiff.

SECTION 28. The bailiff shall perform for the municipal court services similar to those usually performed by sheriffs for the court of common pleas and by constables for courts of justices of the peace.

Sec. 1579-487.

SECTION 29. The costs in said court in civil cases shall Costs. be two dollars ($2.00) in each case, exclusive of witness fees and juror fees and the costs of summoning witnesses and jurors, but in criminal cases they shall be as fixed by law. The fees and costs of summoning jurors and witnesses shall be fixed in the same manner as is now, or may hereafter be, provided in the court of common pleas. The cost of two dollars ($2.00) shall be payable in advance upon the institution of any proceeding unless the party instituting the same shall make an affidavit of inability to pay the said sum or for good cause shown shall be allowed by the judge to institute his action without the payment of such cost. There shall be no advanced costs in any criminal proceeding or in any prosecution under the provisions of the city ordinances.

Sec. 1579-488.

SECTION 30. The council of the city of Portsmouth, Accommodations Ohio, shall provide suitable accommodations for the munic- and equipment. ipal court and its officers including a private room for said judge and sufficient jury room. The council shall also provide for the use of the court the latest edition of the General Code of Ohio, such form books as may be necessary, and necessary supplies, including telephone, stationery, furniture, heat, light and janitor service.

Sec. 1579-489.

SECTION 31. The said municipal court shall have a seal Seal. upon which shall be engraved the coat of arms of the state of Ohio, and shall be one and three-fourths inches in diameter, and shall be surrounded by the words "The Municipal Court of Portsmouth, Scioto Co., O.", and it shall have no other inscription or device thereon.

Sec. 1579-490.

SECTION 32. The solicitor for the city of Portsmouth, Solicitor shall Ohio, shall be the prosecuting attorney of the municipal be prosecuting court, and he may designate such assistants as the city coun- attorney. cil may authorize. The prosecuting attorney of the municipal court shall prosecute all cases of a criminal nature brought before such court and perform the same duties, so far as they are applicable thereto, as are required of the prosecuting attorney of the county. The council of the city of Portsmouth, may provide by ordinance for an official stenographer to be appointed by the judge of the municipal court and to serve as such during his pleasure. The court shall fix and regulate the charge for transcripts of testimony and the cost thereof shall be paid to the clerk and by him accounted for.

Sec. 1579-491.

SECTION 33. Whenever the incumbent of any office Substitute during created by this act shall be temporarily absent, or incapaci- disability. tated from acting as such, the judge shall appoint a qualified substitute and who shall serve during such disability. When said judge shall be incapacitated from presiding in any case, or by reason of absence or inability be unable to attend sessions of the court, the mayor of the city may appoint some attorney-at-law having the required qualifications to act in his stead.

Sec. 1579-492.

Courts superseded.

SECTION 34. The municipal court shall supersede and replace the police (mayor's) court of the city of Portsmouth, and also the courts of the justices of the peace in and for Wayne township, Scioto county, Ohio, and shall have all their powers and authority, and all proceedings, judgments, executions, dockets, papers, moneys, property and persons, subject to the jurisdiction of the said police court and the justices of the peace in and for Wayne township, Scioto county, Ohio, on December 31, 1919, shall be turned over to the municipal court herein created; and thereafter causes shall proceed as though originally instituted therein, the parties making such amendments to their pleadings as shall be required to conform to the rules of the court.

Sec. 1579-493.

Judge shall not practice law.

SECTION 35. The judge shall not, during the term of his office, practice law or give legal advice, or be associated with another in the practice of law.

Sec. 1579-494.

Subject to disabilities.

SECTION 36. The judge of the municipal court, shall be subject to the same disabilities, and may be removed from office for the same causes, as judges of the court of common pleas. The vacancies arising from any cause shall be filled as prescribed for the filling of vacancies in police courts.

Sec. 1579-495.

Police and justices courts abolished.

SECTION 37. Upon the qualification of the "Municipal Judge", as provided in section 2 hereof, the jurisdiction of the police court of the city of Portsmouth, Ohio, and of the justices of the peace in Wayne township, Scioto county, Ohio, shall cease and terminate, and no justice of the peace or constable shall hereafter be elected in said Wayne township.

Sec. 1579-496.

Jurisdiction of mayors and justices outside.

SECTION 38. No justice of the peace in any township, or mayor of any village, in Scioto county, outside of the city of Portsmouth, in any proceeding, civil or criminal, in which any warrant, order of arrest, summons, order of attachment or garnishment, or other process, except subpoena for witness, shall have been served upon a citizen or resident of Portsmouth, or a corporation having its principal office in Portsmouth, shall have jurisdiction, unless such service be actually made by personal service within the township or village in which such proceeding may have been instituted, or in a criminal case, unless the offense charged in any warrant or order of arrest shall be alleged to have been committed within such township or vilage.

Repeals.

SECTION 39. That sections 14719 and 14720 of the General Code be, and the same are hereby repealed.

SECTION 40. This act shall take effect and be in force from and after the earliest period allowed by law.

CARL R. KIMBALL,
Speaker of the House of Representatives.
CLARENCE J. BROWN,
President of the Senate.

Passed April 17, 1919.

This bill was presented to the Governor May 7th, 1919, and was not signed or returned to the house wherein it originated within ten days after being so presented, exclusive of Sundays and the day said bill was presented, and was filed in the office of the Secretary of State May 20, 1919.

ROBERT T. CREW,
Veto Clerk.

Filed in the office of the Secretary of State at Columbus, Ohio, on the 20th day of May, A .D. 1919.

163 G.

[Am. Senate Bill No. 143.]

AN ACT

To amend sections 12603 and 12608 of the General Code of Ohio, to regulate the operation of motor vehicles on the public roads and highways, and to repeal original sections 12603, 12604 and 12608 of the General Code.

Be it enacted by the General Assembly of the State of Ohio:

SECTION 1. That sections 12603 and 12608 of the General Code be amended to read as follows:

Sec. 12603. Whoever operates a motor vehicle or motorcycle on the public roads or highways at a speed greater than is reasonable or proper, having regard for width, traffic, use and the general and usual rules of such road or highway, or so as to endanger the property, life or limb of any person, shall be fined not more than twenty-five dollars, and for a second offense shall be fined not less than twenty-five dollars, nor more than one hundred dollars. *(Operation of motor vehicle at unreasonable speed prohibited.)*

A rate of speed greater than fifteen miles an hour in the business and closely built up portions of a municipality or more than twenty miles an hour in other portions thereof, or more than thirty miles an hour outside of a municipality, shall be presumptive evidence of a rate of speed greater than is reasonable or proper. *(Speed limitations.)*

Sec. 12608. The provisions of section twelve thousand six hundred and three shall not be diminished, restricted or prohibited by an ordinance, rule or regulation of a municipality or other public authority. *(Municipality may not restrict provisions of law.)*

Repeals.

SECTION 2. That said original sections 12603, 12604 and 12608 of the General Code be, and the same are hereby repealed.

CLARENCE J. BROWN,
President of the Senate.
CARL R. KIMBALL,
Speaker of the House of Representatives.

The sectional numbers in this act are in conformity to the General Code. JOHN G. PRICE, *Attorney General.*

Passed April 17, 1919.

This bill was presented to the Governor May 7th, 1919, and was not signed or returned to the house wherein it originated within ten days after being so presented, exclusive of Sundays and the day said bill was presented and was filed in the office of the Secretary of State May 20, 1919.

ROBERT T. CREW,
Veto Clerk.

Filed in the office of the Secretary of State at Columbus, Ohio, on the 20th day of May, A .D. 1919.

164 G.

[Senate Bill No. 128.]

AN ACT

To amend sections 1579-341 and 1579-343 of the General Code, relating to what cases shall be tried by court; what by jury and the summoning and impaneling of jury for the municipal court of the city of Zanesville, Ohio.

Be it enacted by the General Assembly of the State of Ohio:

SECTION 1. That sections 1579-341 and 1579-343 of the General Code be amended so as to read as follows:

When cause shall be tried by jury.

Sec. 1579-341. All cases of the municipal court shall be tried to the court unless jury trial be demanded, in writing, by a party, or unless the judge, in the interest of justice on his own motion orders a trial by jury. The time for making a demand for a jury trial may be fixed and limited by rule of court. In all civil actions, where a jury is demanded, it shall be composed of six lawful men, having the qualifications of electors, unless the parties agree on a less number, provided, however, that any party may demand a jury of twelve men. In all criminal actions, where a jury may be and is demanded, it shall be composed of twelve lawful men having the qualifications of electors. In all civil actions a jury shall render a verdict upon the concurrence of three-fourths or more of their number. Whenever three-fourths of the jury, as herein provided, shall not consist of an integral number, the next highest number shall be construed to represent three-fourths of such number. No venire or summons for jurors shall be issued by the clerk, except when ordered and directed by the court.

Choosing and summoning jury.

Sec. 1579-343. Jurors in the municipal court shall be chosen and summoned in accordance with a rule of said court. Jurors of the municipal court shall be impaneled in the same manner and challenged for the same causes and receive the same fees as jurors in the court of common pleas. Their fees shall be paid out of the treasury of the city of Zanesville.

SECTION 2. That said original sections 1579-341 and 1579-343 of the General Code be and the same are hereby repealed.

CLARENCE J. BROWN,
President of the Senate.
CARL R. KIMBALL,
Speaker of the House of Representatives.

The sectional
numbers in this
act are in con-
formity to the
General Code.
JOHN G. PRICE,
*Attorney
General.*

Passed April 17, 1919.

This bill was presented to the Governor May 10th, 1919, and was not signed or returned to the house wherein it originated within ten days after being so presented, exclusive of Sundays and the day said bill was presented, and was filed in the office of the Secretary of State, May 23rd, 1919.
ROBERT T. CREW,
Veto Clerk.

Filed in the office of the Secretary of State at Columbus, Ohio, on the 23rd day of May, A. D. 1919.
165 G.

[Amended Senate Bill No. 88.]

AN ACT

To amend sections 1558-78 and 1558-83 of the General Code.

Be it enacted by the General Assembly of the State of Ohio:

SECTION 1. That sections 1558-78 and 1558-83 of the General Code be amended to read as follows:

Sec. 1558-78. There shall be a clerk of the municipal court, who shall be nominated and elected for a term of four years in such manner as is or may be provided by charter of the city of Columbus. The first election of clerk shall be held at the regular municipal election in the year 1915, and every four years thereafter a successor shall be elected for a like term. The clerk shall have such powers and shall perform such·duties as are herein given and required. He shall receive an annual salary of thirty-five hundred dollars, twenty-five hundred dollars of which shall be paid out of the treasury of the city of Columbus, and one thousand dollars out of the treasury of Franklin county, payable in monthly installments. *(Election of clerk; term; salary.)*

The term of office of the clerk shall commence on the first day of January next after his election and he shall hold office until a successor is elected and qualified.

The said clerk shall appoint a chief deputy clerk who shall be an elector of the city of Columbus and receive as compensation not less than twenty-four hundred dollars per annum, and six additional deputy clerks, who shall be such electors and shall each receive as compensation not less than *(Chief deputy; compensation.)*

eighteen hundred dollars per annum, payable in semi-monthly installments out of the treasury of-the city of Columbus; however, additional deputies shall be provided for by the council of the city of Columbus on the recommendation of the judges of the municipal court, who shall receive such compensation, not less than fifteen hundred dollars each per annum, payable in semi-monthly installments out of the city treasury of the city of Columbus as the council thereof may prescribe.

Assignment clerk; term; compensation. The judges of the municipal court shall appoint an assignment clerk, who shall assign cases for trial, issue for witnesses and perform such other duties, similar to those performed by the assignment commissioner of the common pleas court of Franklin county as the judges may direct and shall receive as compensation not less than twenty-four hundred dollars per annum payable in semi-monthly installments out of the treasury of the city of Columbus.

The deputy clerks and the assignment clerk shall hold their offices during the pleasure of the appointing power.

Appointment of bailiff and deputies; powers and duties; compensation; bond. Sec. 1558-83. The judges and clerk of the municipal court shall appoint a bailiff. The bailiff shall appoint not exceeding five deputy bailiffs, unless a larger number shall be authorized by the council of the city of Columbus. The bailiff and deputy bailiffs shall hold office during the pleasure of the appointing power, and shall perform for the municipal court service similar to those usually performed by the sheriff and his deputies for the court of common pleas and by constables for the justices of the peace. They shall be governed by all laws pertaining to sheriffs and deputies, and shall serve all process of said court in the manner provided by this act, the laws relating to sheriffs and the rules of the court. The bailiffs shall receive as compensation not less than twenty-four hundred dollars per annum, the deputy bailiffs each not less than fifteen hundred dollars per annum, which compensation of the bailiff and deputy bailiffs shall be payable in semi-monthly installments out of the treasury of the city of Columbus. Before entering upon the duties of their office, the bailiff and deputy bailiffs shall each give bond to the city of Columbus, the bailiff in the sum of two thousand dollars and the deputies each in the sum of one thousand dollars, with surety to the approval of the presiding officer, for the benefit of the city of Columbus and of any person who shall suffer by reason of any default in any of the conditions of such bond. Whenever the bailiff or deputy bailiffs shall give a surety or bonding company bond the premium thereon shall be paid out of the treasury of the city of Columbus.

Execution bailiffs; compensation. In addition to the deputy bailiffs above provided for, there shall be two deputy bailiffs to be known as execution bailiffs, who shall be appointed and dismissed in the manner prescribed for deputy bailiffs and shall have the same powers and give the same bond as other deputy bailiffs; their sole duty shall be to execute the orders, decrees and judg-

ments of the courts. They shall receive as their sole compensation the fees and poundage on the judgments, orders
and decrees that they execute they collect. The same fees
and poundage shall be charged for their work as constables
now are, or hereafter may be, authorized by law to charge
for like services.

Each deputy bailiff and execution bailiff hereinbefore
provided for shall receive from the treasury of the city of
Columbus, in addition to his compensation, not to exceed
the sum of three hundred dollars per annum to cover necessary expenses in serving process of the court, payable
monthly upon the order of the presiding judge.

Additional com-
pensation.

SECTION 2. That said original sections 1558-78 and
1558-83 of the General Code be and the same are hereby repealed.

CLARENCE J. BROWN,
President of the Senate.
CARL R. KIMBALL,
Speaker of the House of Representatives.

The sectional
numbers in this
act are in con-
formity to the
General Code.
JOHN G. PRICE,
Attorney
General.

Passed May 6, 1919.

This bill was presented to the Governor May 10th, 1919,
and was not signed or returned to the house wherein it
originated within ten days after being so presented, exclusive of Sundays and the day said bill was presented, and was
filed in the office of the Secretary of State, May 23rd, 1919.

ROBERT T. CREW,
Veto Clerk.

Filed in the office of the Secretary of State at Columbus,
Ohio, on the 23rd day of May, A. D. 1919.

166 G.

[House Bill No. 551.]

AN ACT

To amend sections 5706, 5751, 6251 and 6254 and to repeal sections
6534, 10801 of the General Code, relative to the rates and pub-
licataion of legal advertising. .

Be it enacted by the General Assembly of the State of Ohio:

SECTION 1. That sections 5706, 5751, 6251 and 6254
of the General Code be amended to read as follows:

Sec. 5706. The publishers of newspapers, for advertising the delinquent and forfeited list of the several counties,
and the notice of sale, shall be entitled to receive a sum not
exceeding the following rates: For the notice of sale, ten dollars; for designating the several school districts, townships,
villages and cities, and the several wards in a city, fifty cents
each; and for each tract of land, city or town lot, or part of
lot, contained in each of such lists, thirty cents. A greater
sum than one-half of the taxes and penalties, due on any
tract, lot or part of lot, shall not be allowed for advertising
such tract, lot or part of lot. Such property shall not be

Fees for publi-
cation of delin-
quent and for-
feited land lists.

· published in a list as delinquent, if the taxes, assessments, and penalty thereon have been paid before the twentieth day of December. Providing, however, newspapers having a circulation of over one hundred thousand shall charge and receive for such advertisements, notices and proclamations, rates charged by them on annual contracts for like amount of space to other advertisers in its general display advertising columns.

Duties of auditor relative to publication and sale. Sec. 5751. The auditor of each county on receiving from the auditor of state such list of lands within his county, if the tax and penalties due thereon have not been paid on or before the fifteenth day of October next ensuing, shall forthwith cause notice thereof to be advertised once a week for four consecutive weeks in two daily newspapers in the English language of opposite politics and of general circulation printed in his county. If there are not two such daily newspapers in the county, then in two weekly newspapers of opposite politics if there be such, if not then publication in one newspaper is required. Such notice shall describe the lands in the manner they are described on the list furnished by the auditor of state and state that if the tax and penalties charged on said list are not paid into the county treasury and the treasurer's receipt produced therefor before the time specified in this chapter for the sale of said lands, which day shall be named therein, that each tract, so delinquent on which the taxes and penalties remain unpaid will be offered for sale on the second Monday of December thereafter, at the court house in such county, in order to satisfy such taxes and penalties, and that such sale will continue from day to day until each of such tracts is sold or offered for sale.

Rates for legal advertising. Sec. 6251. Publishers of newspapers may charge and receive for the publication of advertisements, notices and proclamations required to be published by a public officer of the state, county, city, village, township, school, benevolent or other public institution, or by a trustee, assignee, executor or administrator, the following sums, except where the rate is otherwise fixed by law, to-wit: For the first insertion, one dollar for each square, and for each additional insertion authorized by law or the person ordering the insertion, fifty cents for each square. Fractional squares shall be estimated at a like rate for space occupied. In advertisements containing tabular or rule work fifty per cent may be charged in addition to the foregoing rates. Providing, however, newspapers having a circulation of over one hundred thousand shall charge and receive for such advertisements, notices and proclamations, rates charged on annual contracts by them for like amount of space to other advertisers who advertise in its general display advertising columns.

What constitutes a square; an em. Sec. 6254. A square shall be a space occupied· by two hundred and forty ems of the type used in printing such advertisements. .Legal advertising shall be set up in a compact form, without unnecessary spaces, blanks or headlines and printed in type not smaller than nonpareil. The type of whatever size used must be of such proportions that the body of the capital letter M be no wider than it is high and all other letters and characters in proportion. Except as may be done under sections 1695 to 1697, inclusive, of the General Code, all legal advertisements or notices shall be printed in newspapers published in the English language only.

SECTION 2. That original sections 5706, 5751, 6251, 6254, 6534 and 10801 of the General Code be, and the same are hereby repealed. *Repeals.*

CARL R. KIMBALL,
Speaker of the House of Representatives.
CLARENCE J. BROWN,
President of the Senate.

Passed May 10, 1919.
Approved May 28, 1919.

JAMES M. COX,
Governor.

Filed in the office of the Secretary of State at Columbus, Ohio, on the 28th day of May, A. D. 1919.

167 G.

The sectional numbers in this act are in conformity to the General Code. JOHN G. PRICE, Attorney General.

AN ACT

Making appropriation for necessary improvements in connection with the state fair grounds.

Be it enacted by the General Assembly of the State of Ohio:

SECTION 1. For the purpose of complying with the orders of the Columbus board of health and making other necessary improvements in connection with the state fair grounds, there is hereby appropriated for the use of the Secretary of Agriculture, out of any monies in the state treasury to the credit of the general revenue fund, and not otherwise appropriated, the sum of ten thousand dollars. Such monies so appropriated shall be paid out of the state treasury upon the warrant of the auditor of state upon vouchers approved by the Secretary of Agriculture. *Appropriation for improvement state fair grounds.*

CARL R. KIMBALL,
Speaker of the House of Representatives.
CLARENCE J. BROWN,
President of the Senate.

Passed May 10, 1919.
Approved May 28, 1919.

JAMES M. COX,
Governor.

This act is not of a general and permanent nature and requires no sectional number. JOHN G. PRICE, Attorney General.

Filed in the office of the Secretary of State at Columbus, Ohio, on the 28th day of May, A. D. 1919.

168 L.

[House Bill No. 558.]

AN ACT

To make appropriation for the salaries of members of the House of Representatives and Senate for the calendar year 1920.

Be it enacted by the General Assembly of the State of Ohio:

Appropriation for house and senate.

SECTION 1. The sums set forth in this act are appropriated for the purposes therein specified, namely, one hundred and twenty-four thousand dollars for salaries of members of the House of Representatives for the calendar year 1920 and thirty-three thousand dollars for salaries of the members of the Senate for the same calendar year, which sums are hereby appropriated out of any monies in the state treasury not otherwise appropriated.

This act is not of a general and permanent nature and requires no sectional number. JOHN G. PRICE, Attorney General.

CARL R. KIMBALL,
Speaker of the House of Representatives.
CLARENCE J. BROWN,
President of the Senate.

Passed May 10, 1919.
Approved May 28, 1919.

JAMES M. COX,
Governor.

Filed in the office of the Secretary of State at Columbus, Ohio, on the 28th day of May, A. D. 1919.

169 G.

[House Bill No. 162.]

AN ACT

To amend sections 1178, 1180, 1181, 1184, 1185, 1185-1, 1186, 1187, 1188, 1189, 1201, 1206, 1207, 1208, 1209, 1213-1, 1218, 1218-1, 1221, 1222, 1223, 1224, 1230, 1231-2, 3298-7, 3298-18, 3298-32, 3373, 6912, 6936 and 6956-1 of the General Code, and to enact supplemental sections 1182, 1195-1, 1212-1, 2788-1, 3371-1, 6926-1, 6926-2, 6926-3, 6954, 6956-1a, and 7181-1 of the General Code, relating to a system of highway laws for the state of Ohio, and to enact certain further supplemental provisions relating to the highways of the state.

Be it enacted by the General Assembly of the State of Ohio:

SECTION 1. That sections 1178, 1180, 1181, 1184, 1185, 1185-1, 1186, 1187, 1188, 1189, 1201, 1206, 1207, 1208, 1209, 1213-1, 1218, 1218-1, 1221, 1222, 1223, 1224, 1230, 1231-2, 3298-7, 3298-18, 3298-32, 3373, 6912, 6936 and 6956-1 of the General Code be amended; and supplemental sections 1182, 1195-1, 1212-1, 2788-1, 3371-1, 6926-1, 6926-2, 6926-3, 6954, 6956-1a and 7181-1 of the General Code be added to read as follows:

State highway department; appointment of commissioner; term; qualifications.

Sec. 1178. There shall be a state highway department for the purpose of constructing, improving, maintaining and repairing a state system of highways, co-operating with the federal government in the construction, improvement, maintenance and repair of post roads or other roads designated by the federal authorities, and affording instruction, assistance and co-operation to the counties, townships and other sub-divisions of the state in the construction, improvement, maintenance and repair of the public roads and bridges of the state, under the provisions of this chapter. The governor, with the advice and consent of the senate, shall appoint a state highway commissioner who shall be a competent civil engineer with at least five years experience in the construction and maintenance of highways, and who shall serve for the term of four years, unless sooner removed by the governor. He shall give his whole time and attention to the duties of his office.

Sec. 1180. The state highway commissioner shall be provided with suitable rooms for the use of the department. Such office shall be open at all reasonable times for the transaction of public business and be furnished by the state with necessary stationery, office supplies, fixtures, apparatus for testing material, engineering instruments and supplies. The salary of the state highway commissioner shall be five thousand dollars per annum. In addition to his salary, he shall be allowed his actual and necessary traveling expenses incurred in the discharge of his official duties. *Offices and equipment; salary.*

Sec. 1181. The state highway commissioner shall appoint three deputy highway commissioners, one of whom he shall designate as chief highway engineer and all of whom shall be competent civil engineers and serve during the pleasure of the commissioner. *Three deputies; their qualifications and duties.*

One of these deputy highway commissioners shall be experienced in road construction and improvement, and acting under the direction of the highway commissioner, shall have supervision of all matters pertaining to road construction and improvement as provided for in this chapter. Another of said deputies shall be experienced in road maintenance and repair, and acting under the direction of the state highway commissioner shall have supervision of all matters pertaining to road maintenance and repair. Another of said deputies shall be experienced in the design, construction, maintenance and repair of culverts and bridges, and acting under the direction of the state highway commissioner, shall have supervision of all matters pertaining to the design, construction, maintenance and repair of culverts and bridges. The deputy highway commissioners in addition to performing the duties above assigned to them shall perform such other duties in connection with this department as may be designated by the state highway commissioner.

The salary of each said deputy highway commissioner shall be three thousand three hundred dollars per annum. In addition to their salaries, such deputy highway commissioners shall be paid their actual and necessary traveling *Salary of deputies; bond.*

expenses. The state highway commissioner shall require
each such deputy highway commissioner to give bond in the
sum of five thousand dollars conditioned for the faithful
performance of his duties, with such sureties as the state
highway commissioner approves.

Division engineers; chief clerk and secretary, etc.

Sec. 1182. The state highway commissioner shall also
within the limits of the appropriations made by the general
assembly appoint as many division engineers as may become necessary to carry out the provisions of this chapter.
Each of said division engineers shall be paid a salary of not
more than two thousand seven hundred and fifty dollars
per annum, to be fixed by the state highway commissioner.
Said state highway commissioner may also appoint a chief
clerk, who shall receive a salary of not more than two thousand dollars per annum, to be fixed by the state highway
commissioner, and a secretary who shall receive a salary of
not more than two thousand five hundred dollars per annum, to be fixed by the state highway commissioner. The
state highway commissioner may appoint as many additional clerks or stenographers and such engineers, superintendents, inspectors and other employes, and may purchase,
maintain and operate such equipment within the limits of
appropriations as he may consider necessary to carry out

Salaries of employes.

the provisions of this chapter. Each of said employes shall
be paid a salary to be fixed by the state highway commissioner, within the limits of the appropriations made by
the general assembly. All appointees and employes for
whom provision is made in this and the preceding sections
of this act shall receive their actual and necessary traveling expenses when on official business.

General supervision by commissioner; other powers and duties

Sec. 1184. The state highway commissioner shall have
general supervision of the construction, improvement, maintenance and repair of all inter-county highways and main
market roads, and the bridges and culverts thereon. He
shall aid the county commissioners in establishing, creating
and preparing suitable systems of drainage for all highways within their jurisdiction or control and advise with
them as to the construction, improvement, maintenance and
repair of such highways; and he shall approve the design,
construction, maintenance and repair of all bridges, including superstructure and substructure, and culverts or
other improvements on inter-county or main market roads;
and in the case of bridges and culverts on other roads, when
the estimated cost thereof exceeds ten thousand dollars,
the plans therefor shall be submitted to and approved by
him, before contracts are let therefor. He shall cause plans,
specifications and estimates to be prepared for the construction, maintenance or repair of bridges and culverts
when so requested by the authorities having charge thereof,
and he shall cause to be made surveys, plats, profiles, specifications and estimates for improvement whether upon state,
county or township roads.

He shall make inquiry in regard to systems of road and bridge construction and maintenance wherever he may deem it advisable and conduct investigations and experiments with reference thereto, and make all examinations, in his opinion, advisable, as to materials for road construction or improvement.

Investigations and experiments

Whenever the same will in his judgment facilitate or secure economy in the work of his department, the state highway commissioner may establish branch offices at such times and localities as seem most suitable and designate assistants or other employes to have charge of the same.

Branch offices.

Sec. 1185. The state highway commissioner may, either in person or through a representative of the department, respond to invitations to give addresses and lectures before bodies interested in highway improvements, and he may call public meetings to be held within each county of the state for the purpose of affording instruction in matters pertaining to road and bridge construction, improvement, maintenance and repair. Such called meetings shall be conducted by the state highway commissioner, or his authorized representatives. Upon receipt of notice from the state highway commissioner fixing the date for such meeting, the county surveyor shall notify the county commissioners, township highway superintendents, trustees of each township and ditch superintendents to be present at such meeting. Each of said officials shall be paid in the regular manner his per diem allowance for attending such meetings. The commissioner may prepare, publish and distribute such maps, plans, blueprints, bulletins and reports as he may deem advisable.

Empowered to call and attend public meetings to afford instruction.

Sec. 1185-1. The state highway commissioner is authorized to call the county surveyors together once each year, for the purpose of conducting a conference or school in which the best methods of road building and other matters of interest may be discussed, and at which instructions may be given to said county surveyors pertaining to their work, by the state highway commissioner, or by another person designated by him for that purpose. Nothing herein shall prevent the state highway commissioner from calling any county surveyor into a conference at any time for any purpose connected with his official duties, and such county surveyor shall receive his actual necessary expenses in addition to his salary in attending such school or conference. Instead of a conference or school, the state highway commissioner may hold conferences or schools in various sections of the state for the convenience of the surveyors in such sections.

Call of county surveyors together annually for conference or school.

Sec. 1186. The apparatus and supplies of the college of agriculture and engineering of the Ohio State University, may be used by the state highway commissioner or any of his employes in making investigations concerning the chemical and physical character of road and bridge materials. The college of agriculture and engineering of the

Apparatus and supplies of college of agriculture may be used; college shall conduct experiments, etc.

31—G. & L. L.

Ohio Sta University, when called upon by the state highway cor issioner, shall make investigation and conduct experim ts with reference to road building materials or for the rpose of determining any matters connected with road o. bridge construction. The highway commissioner shall (operate as far as possible with said university in any cc rse offered in highway engineering. The state highway commissioner is hereby authorized to make tests of road building materials for the authorities of any county or municipal corporation, and may employ for that purpose any of the facilities of his department or any of the employes thereof engaged in or qualified to make tests of such materials. When the state highway commissioner makes any such test or tests of such road building materials, he shall collect from such county or municipality a charge sufficient to cover the actual cost of making such tests and the fee so collected shall be paid by him into the state treasury to the credit of the state highway improvement fund. Where such materials so tested are designed for use upon any intercounty highway or main market road, no charge shall be made by the state highway commissioner for testing the same.

Testing materials for county or municipality; fees paid into treasury.

Sec. 1187. The state highway commissioner or chief highway engineer, may call upon the county surveyor, at any time, to furnish a may or maps of the county showing distinctly the location of any rivers, railroads, streams, township lines, cities, villages, public highways and deposits of road material, together with any other information that may be required by said commissioner or engineer. Such information and maps shall be furnished by such surveyor in such form as the state highway commissioner may require. A copy of such maps, plats or other information shall be kept on file in the office of the county surveyor.

Maps by county surveyor showing specific information.

Sec. 1188. The county surveyor shall have the right to call upon the township trustees or township highway superintendents to furnish any part of the information called for by the preceding sections, and such officials when so called upon to furnish such information shall be paid their usual per diem in the regular manner for the time employed in furnishing the same.

Surveyor may require information from trustees.

Sec. 1189. The intercounty highways and the main market roads heretofore established by law, shall continue to be and remain a part of the system of intercounty highways and main market roads of the state unless changed in the manner hereinafter provided. Within one hundred and twenty days after the taking effect of this act the state highway commissioner shall examine into and consider the present main market road system of the state, and if upon such examination and consideration he finds that it would be expedient to vacate or abandon as main market roads any of the highways of the state now so designated, by reason of the fact that such highways are of minor importance

Powers and duties relating to inter-county highways and main market roads; vacation and abandonment.

483

or by reason of the fact that it would be inadvisable for the state to undertake the construction of such highways as main market roads on account of difficulties of construction, character of territory traversed, close proximity of parallel main market roads, or any other similar cause, he shall vacate and abandon such highways as main market roads, and such highways shall cease to be main market roads and shall become and remain inter-county highways and be improved as such. In order to extend the benefits and advantages of the main market road system of the state to every county thereof, the state highway commissioner shall also designate such additional main market roads as are necessary to be established in order that each county in the state shall be traversed by at least one main market road. Such additional main market roads shall be designated over and along the routes of the most important inter-county highways traversing such counties. The state highway commissioner shall also make such minor changes in the routes of existing main market roads, if any are necessary, as to perfect and harmonize the existing system of main market roads. He shall perform the above duties within one hundred and twenty days after the taking effect of this act, and shall file with the governor a report of his action in reference to the foregoing matters. Upon the approval of the governor of such report, the changes and modifications in the main market road system of the state therein reported shall take effect.

In addition to the inter-county highways and main market roads heretofore established under authority of law, or hereafter established under authority of the foregoing provisions, and as shown by the records in the office of the state highway department, and by the reports filed with the governor relating thereto, the state highway commissioner shall, after the execution of the authority hereinbefore conferred, have authority to designate additional intercounty highways or main market roads, or change existing inter-county highways or main market roads after notice and hearing as hereinafter provided.

Before establishing any additional main market roads or inter-county highways, or making any changes in existing inter-county highways or main market roads, the state highway commissioner shall give notice by publication in two newspapers of general circulation in each of the counties in which said inter-county highway or main market road or any part thereof is located, by publication, once each week for two successive weeks. Such notice shall state the time and place of a hearing, which hearing shall be held in the county, or one of the counties, in which said road or some part thereof is situated, and which hearing shall be open to the public, and which notice shall further state the route of the proposed inter-county highway or main market road or the change proposed to be made in an existing inter-county highway or main market road. The state highway commissioner or a deputy highway commissioner designated by him shall attend such hearing and hear any proof offered on such matter. Any changes made in existing inter-county highways or main market roads by the state highway commissioner, or any additional inter-county highways or main market roads established by him following such hearing, shall be certified to the counties interested therein, and a report of such change or addition filed in the office of the governor, and the report of the state highway commissioner making such change or establishing such road shall be placed on file in the office of the department.

In no event shall the main market road mileage of the state be increased under any of the above provisions to exceed three thousand miles.

Distinctive name may be assigned. The state highway commissioner, upon petition of the county commissioners of the counties traversed thereby or upon petition of citizens of such counties, is authorized to officially assign to a main market road a distinctive name commemorative of an historical event or personage, or to officially assign thereto a commonly accepted and appropriate name by which such road is known.

How construction or improvement shall be determined when two or more applications made. Sec. 1195-1. Where applications for state aid in the construction, improvement, maintenance or repair of two or more inter-county highways or main market roads or parts thereof within the same county are received by the state highway commissioner, he shall, in determining which application shall be first granted and which inter-county highway or main market road or part thereof shall be first constructed or improved, look to and consider the relative importance of such inter-county highways or main market roads, the facilities which such road when completed will furnish for through traffic, the location and direction of improvements already constructed, under construction, or projected in adjoining counties, and all other similar factors, and he shall approve such applications in such order and shall proceed with the construction and improvement of such inter-county highways and main market roads in such order as will the most speedily secure the completion throughout the state of a connected system of improved highways. **When commissioner may reject applications and construct, etc. important highway.** If, in the judgment of the state highway commissioner, the county commissioners have applied for state aid in the construction, improvement, maintenance or repair of an inter-county highway or main market road or part thereof of minor importance as compared with other unimproved highways of the same classification within their county, and if, upon request from the state highway commissioner, such county commissioners neglect to make application for state aid in the construction, improvement, maintenance or repair of the most worthy and important unimproved inter-county highways and main market roads within their coutny, the state highway commissioner shall thereupon be authorized to reject all applications for state aid made by such board of county commissioners and forth-

with proceed to co-operate with any board of township
trustees within said county making application for state
aid in the construction, improvement, maintenance or repair of the inter-county highway or main market road or
portion thereof in such county, which in the judgment of
the state highway commissioner should be first constructed
or improved. In default of such application for state aid
from any board of township trustees within such county,
the state highway commissioner shall be authorized to proceed without the co-operation of the county commissioners
or township trustees to construct or improve that inter-
county highway or main market road within such county,
which in his judgment is the most important and should be
first improved, and the construction or improvement of
which will contribute in the largest measure toward the
speedy completion of a connected system of state highways
throughout the state.

Sec. 1201. If the line of the proposed improvement
deviates from the existing highway, or if it is proposed to
change the channel of any stream in the vicinity of such
improvement, the county commissioners or township trustees making application for such improvement must provide the requisite right of way. If the board of county
commissioners or township trustees are unable to agree with
the owner or owners of such land or property as may be
necessary for such change or alteration, or if additional
right of way is required for the same, and the county commissioners or township trustees are unable to agree with
the owner or owners of the land or property in question
then the board of county commissioners or township trustees, as the case may be, may by resolution declare it necessary to condemn and appropriate for public use such land
or property, and shall proceed to fix what they deem to be
the value of such land or property sought to be condemned
or appropriated, together with the damages to the residue,
if any, and deposit the value thereof together with such
damages with the probate court of the county for the use
and benefit of such owner or owners, and thereupon the
board of county commissioners or township trustees shall
be authorized to take immediate possession of and enter
upon said lands for the purpose aforesaid. The probate
judge shall forthwith notify such owner or owners of the
amount of money deposited with him on account of the
land or property sought to be condemned or appropriated
and upon application of such owner or owners he shall
turn over to them the amount of moneys so deposited with
him on account of the land or property sought to be taken.
The probate judge may cause notice of such action to be
served upon such owner or owners by the sheriff or any
other person that he may direct. Proof of service shall be
made by affidavit of the person making such service. In
case the owner or owners are non-residents the probate
judge shall give notice of the deposit of such money by pub-

Requisite right
of way must be
provided; con-
demnation pro-
ceeding when
necessary; pro-
cedure.

lication for one week in some newspaper of general circulation in said county. A copy of such newspaper shall be forthwith mailed to such non-resident owner or owners, if their address is known to the probate court. If the address of such non-resident owner or owners is known the date of mailing shall be considered the date of service, and if the address of such non-resident owner or owners is unknown, the date of publication shall be considered the date of service for the purpose of fixing the time for appeal. If the owner or owners of such land or property are not satisfied with the amount fixed by such county commissioners or township trustees, they shall, within ten days after the service of such notice of the allowance aforesaid, appeal to the probate court of the county in which such land or property, or some part thereof is located, and the probate court upon the filing of such appeal shall fix the appeal bond which shall be furnished within five days after the same is fixed by the court, and thereupon a jury trial shall be had in the manner provided for appeals in road cases.

When change of line of improvement may be made; enforcement of law relating to obstructions.

It shall be the duty of the state highway commissioner in the improvement of inter-county highways and main market roads to change the line of the proposed improvement from that followed by the existing highway whenever such change is practicable and whenever by making such change it is possible to eliminate dangerous curves, sharp angles or steep grades. It shall be the further duty of the state highway department to enforce the statutes relating to obstructions upon a public highway when such highway is or shall become a state road and to cause the removal from all state roads of all fences and other obstructions of every kind and description which interfere in any way with travel or with the proper maintenance of such road and the drainage thereof.

When and how advertisement for bids for improvement shall be made.

Sec. 1206. Upon the receipt of a certified copy of the resolution of the county commissioners or township trustees that such improvement be constructed under the provisions of this chapter, the state highway commissioner shall advertise for bids for two consecutive weeks in two newspapers of general circulation and of the two dominant political parties published in the county or counties in which the improvement, or some part thereof is located, if there be any such papers published in said counties, but if there be no such papers published in said counties then in two newspapers having general circulation in said counties, and such commissioner shall also have authority to advertise for bids in such other publications as he may deem advisable. Such notices shall state that plans and specifications for the improvement are on file in the offices of the state highway commissioner and the county surveyor, and the time within which bids therefor will be received.

Bond shall accompany bid; award of contract.

Each bidder shall be required to file with his bid a bond to the approval of the state highway commissioner in an amount equal to five per cent of the estimated cost, but in no event more than ten thousand dollars, conditioned that in the event he is awarded the contract he will furnish the bond required by section 1208 of the General Code, and enter into a contract for the construction of the work covered by his bid within ten days after he receives notice that the contract has been awarded to him. In lieu of such bond the bidder may file a certified check for an amount equal to five per cent. of the estimated cost, but in no event more than ten thousand dollars, payable to the state highway commissioner, which check shall be forthwith returned to him in case the contract is awarded to another bidder, or in the case of a successful bidder when he has entered into a contract and furnished a bond as required by law. No bidder shall be required to file a signed contract with his bid, or to enter into a contract or furnish the bond required by section 1208 of the General Code until the bids have been opened and he has been notified by the state highway commissioner that he has been awarded the contract.

The state highway commissioner shall award the contract to the lowest and best bidder.

Such award shall be made by the state highway commissioner within ten days after the date on which the bids are opened and the successful bidder shall enter into a contract and furnish a bond as required by law within ten days after he is notified that he has been awarded the contract.

Sec. 1207. No contract for any improvement shall be awarded for a greater sum than the estimated cost thereof. The bids received for an improvement shall be opened at the time stated in the notice and the bids shall conform to such other requirements not inconsistent with the provisions of this chapter as the state highway commissioner may direct. If no acceptable bid is made within the estimate, the state highway commissioner may either readvertise the work at the original estimate or amend the estimate, and certify the same to the county commissioners, and upon their adoption of the amended estimate, again proceed to advertise for bids, and award the contract as provided in the preceding section. The state highway commissioner may, under the provisions of this chapter, contract for the construction or improvement of bridges and culverts or of the grade required in connection with an improvement and may defer making contracts for the remainder of said improvement until such grade has become stable and solid. *Procedure when no bid acceptable.*

Sec. 1208. The state highway commissioner may reject all bids. Before entering into a contract the commissioner shall require a bond with sufficient sureties; conditioned as provided in sections 2365-1 to 2365-4 inclusive of the General Code, and also conditioned that the contractor will perform the work upon the terms proposed, within the time prescribed, and in accordance with the plans and specifications thereof, and that the contractor will indemnify the state, county or township against any damage that may *Rejection of bids; conditions of bond of contractor.*

result by reason of the negligence of the contractor in making said improvement. In no case shall the state be liable for damages sustained in the construction of any improvement under this chapter.

Rights of subcontractors, material men, etc.

The provisions of section 8324 of the General Code and the succeeding sections in favor of subcontractors, material men, laborers and mechanics shall apply to contracts let under the provisions of the preceding sections as fully and to the same extent as in case of counties. The state highway commissioner shall not be required or authorized, however, to retain out of any estimate any sum in excess of the exact amount of any lien filed, and the remainder of any estimate over and above the amount of such lien shall be promptly paid to the contractor.

When surety bond shall be approved; individual surety bond.

If any bond taken under the provisions of this chapter is executed by a surety company, the state highway commissioner shall not be authorized to approve such bond unless there is attached thereto a certificate of the superintendent of insurance that such surety company is authorized to transact business in this state, and the power of attorney of the agent of such company executing such bond. The superintendent of insurance shall upon request issue to any duly licensed agent of such company such certificate without charge. If any bond taken under the provisions of this chapter is executed by a private individual or individuals as sureties, the state highway commissioner shall not be authorized to approve such bond unless there is attached thereto a sworn financial statement of such sureties showing the amount and specific character of their assets and liabilities, or a certificate of the county auditor of the county in which said sureties or one of them reside or have property to the effect that in his judgment such sureties possess the qualifications provided by section 10219 of the General Code. The bond required to be taken under the provisions of this section shall be in an amount equal to one-half of the estimated cost of the work, and to the approval of the state highway commissioner.

Commissioner may complete improvement on failure of contractor and surety.

Sec. 1209. If, in the opinion of the state highway commissioner, the contractor has not commenced his work within a reasonable time, or does not carry the same forward with reasonable progress, or is improperly performing his work, or has abandoned, or fails or refuses to complete a contract entered into under the provisions of this chapter, the state highway commissioner shall make a finding to that effect and so notify the contractor in writing and the right of the contractor to control and supervise the work shall immediately cease. The state highway commissioner shall forthwith give written notice to the surety or sureties on the bond of such contractor of such action. If, within ten days after the receipt of such notice, such surety or sureties or any one or more of them notify the state highway commissioner in writing of their intention to enter upon and complete the work covered by such contract, such

Procedure in terminating contract.

surety or sureties shall be permitted so to do and the state
highway commissioner shall allow them thirty days after
the receipt of such notice in writing from them, within
which to enter upon the work and resume the construction
thereof, unless such time be extended by the state highway
commissioner for good cause shown. If such surety or sureties so entering upon the work do not carry the same forward with reasonable progress or if they improperly perform the work, or abandon, or fail or refuse to complete
the work covered by any such contract, the state highway
commissioner shall complete the same in the manner hereinafter provided. If, after receiving notice of the action
of the state highway commissioner in terminating the control of the contractor over the work covered by his contract,
the surety or sureties on such contractor's bond do not
within ten days give the state highway commissioner the
written notice provided for above, it shall be the duty of
the state highway commissioner to complete the work in the
following manner: He shall first advertise the work for
letting in the manner provided in section 1206 of the General Code, and the estimated cost at which such work shall
be so advertised shall be the difference between the original
contract price therefor and the amount or amounts, theretofore paid to the original contractor, and at such letting
the contract for the completion of the work shall not be let
at a price in excess of such estimate. If no bids to complete
the work for an amount not exceeding such estimate are
received, the state highway commissioner shall cause that
portion of the work still uncompleted to be re-estimated and
shall readvertise the same at the amended estimate in the
manner provided in section 1206 of the General Code, and
relet the work for not more than such estimate. In reletting
uncompleted work in the manner hereinbefore provided,
the contract shall be awarded by the state highway commissioner to the lowest and best bidder. Before entering into
a contract for the completion of any such improvement, the
state highway commissioner shall require a bond with sufficient sureties, conditioned as provided in section 1208 of
the General Code, and in an amount equal to fifty per cent
of the estimated cost of completing the work, and the other
provisions of section 1208 of the General Code, as amended
herein, relating to the bonds of original contractors, shall
apply to such bond. If the cost of completing such work
exceeds the amount set aside or apportioned therefor, the
remainder of the cost shall be paid in the first instance
from any rotary fund or other funds provided for such
purpose by the general assembly, or in default of any such
funds from any appropriations from the state highway improvement fund available for the use of the department
and against which no contractual obligations exist. If the
cost of completing any such improvement exceeds the portion of the contract price remaining unpaid to the contractor at the time of his default, such excess shall be com-

Procedure by
commissioner in
completion of
work.

puted by the state highway commissioner after the completion of the work and it shall thereupon be the duty of the state highway commissioner to certify the facts to the attorney general, who shall proceed to collect such excess cost from the contractor and the surety or sureties upon his bond and the amount so collected shall be paid into the state treasury to the credit of the fund from which the excess cost was originally paid. Where the estimated cost of completing a defaulted contract does not exceed five thousand dollars, the state highway commissioner may complete the same by force account, or by a contract let without advertisement, if, in his judgment a saving can be effected thereby.

Monthly estimates furnished commissioner; verification of estimates; division of state into districts.

Sec. 1212-1. It shall be the duty of the state highway commissioner to so organize his department that the labor performed upon and materials furnished by the contractor in the performance of each contract shall be carefully and promptly estimated at regular intervals of one month. The state highway commissioner shall so organize his department that such estimates shall be regularly and promptly forwarded to the state highway department by the county surveyor or other local engineer designated by the state highway commissioner to have charge of roads and bridges under the control of the state. Such estimates shall be checked and verified as expeditiously as possible and payment made to the contractor of the amount found due. In order to avoid congesting the clerical work of the department at stated monthly intervals and for the further purpose of insuring prompt and regular payment to contractors of estimates earned by them and thereby securing for the department the advantages which inure from the prompt payment of bills due, the state highway commissioner is authorized to divide the state into districts and fix for each district a date upon which all monthly estimates shall be made and forwarded to the state highway department by the county surveyors or other local engineers in charge of state work within such district. Estimates shall not require the approval of the division engineer unless for special reasons the state highway commissioner shall so direct as to specific estimates or contracts.

Where a portion of highway covered by a contract is completed and opened to traffic, all retained percentages held in connection with such portion of highway shall be forthwith released and paid to the contractor.

Counties in which state may assume to pay 90% of improvement.

Sec. 1213-1. In any county in which on the twentieth day of December of any year the aggregate of the tax duplicate for real estate and personal property is twenty-two million dollars or less, and in which county there are at least seven hundred miles of public highways, the state highway commissioner may, if he deems it proper, enter into an agreement with the county commissioners of such county at any time during the ensuing calendar year, by the terms of which agreement the state may assume and pay not more than ninety per cent of the cost of any improvement petitioned for by such county commissioners.

In any county in which on the twentieth day of December of any year the aggregate of the tax duplicate for real estate and personal property is more than twenty-two million dollars and less than thirty million dollars and in which county there are at least seven hundred miles of public highways the state highway commissioner may, if he deems it proper, enter into an agreement with the county commissioners of such county at any time during the ensuing calendar year, by the terms of which agreement the state may assume and pay not more than seventy-five per cent of the cost of any improvement petitioned for by such county commissioners. *Counties in which state may pay 75%.*

In any case in which the authority conferred by this section is exercised by the state highway commissioner, that part of the cost and expense of the improvement assumed in the first instance by the county shall be divided among the county, interested township or townships and property owners in the following proportions: one-half thereof shall be paid by the county, three-tenths thereof shall be paid by the interested township or townships and two-tenths thereof shall be specially assessed. The county commissioners and the trustees of the interested township or townships may, however, agree upon a different division of that part of the cost and expense to be paid by the county and such townships. *Proportions of part cost to be paid by county, township and property owners, etc.*

Sec. 1218. Each contract made by the state highway commissioner under the provisions of this chapter shall be made in the name of the state and executed on its behalf by the state highway commissioner and attested by the secretary of the department. No contract shall be let by the state highway commissioner in a case where the county commissioners or township trustees are to contribute a part of the cost of said improvement, unless the county commissioners of the county in which the improvement is located shall have made a written agreement to assume in the first instance that part of the cost and expense of said improvement over and above the amount to be paid by the state. Where the application for said improvement has been made by township trustees, then such agreement shall be entered into between the state highway commissioner and the township trustees. Such agreement shall be filed in the office of the state highway commissioner with the approval of the attorney general endorsed thereon as to its form and legality. The provisions of section 5660 of the General Code shall apply to such written agreement to be made by the county commissioners or township trustees and a duplicate of the certificate of the county auditor or township clerk made in compliance with the provisions of said section shall be filed in the office of the state highway commissioner. *How and by whom contracts shall be made; agreements filed in office of commissioner.*

The state highway commissioner shall not proceed to the opening of bids for any work to be let by him until *When bids for work may be opened; readvertisement, when.*

the provisions of this section relating to the making of an agreement by the local authorities have been fully complied with, and if at the time fixed for the opening of bids, such provisions have not been fully complied with or if for any other reason the state highway commissioner should at said time find himself without full authority to immediately proceed to determine the lowest and best bidder and to award and enter into a contract, it shall be the duty of the state highway commissioner to forthwith cancel the letting of said work, return all bids unopened and thereafter readvertise the letting of the work at such time as he may be fully authorized to forthwith proceed to determine the lowest and best bidder and award and enter into a contract.

When contract may be awarded to foreign corporation.

Sec. 1218-1. No contract shall be entered into by the state highway commissioner until, if the bidder awarded the contract is a foreign corporation, the secretary of state has certified that such corporation is authorized to do business in this state, and until, if the bidder so awarded the contract is a person or partnership non-resident of the state, such person or partnership has filed with the secretary of state as his or its agent for the purpose of accepting service of summons in any action relating to such contract or brought under the provisions of the highway laws or under the provisions of the workmen's compensation law of this state.

When estimates may be paid to contractor.

No estimate shall be paid to any contractor by the state highway commissioner until the industrial commission of Ohio has certified that such contractor has complied with each and every condition of the act of February 26, 1913, and of all acts amendatory thereof and supplementary thereto and known as the workmen's compensation law. Upon the request of any contractor upon state highway work, or person, firm or corporation intending to engage in contracting upon such work, the industrial commission of Ohio upon the receipt of any premium due shall forthwith forward such certificate to the state highway department. The state highway department, in estimating the cost of work to be let, shall in addition to the other items of cost include an item for the estimated premium which the contractor will be required to pay to the industrial commission of Ohio under the workmen's compensation law, which item shall be separately stated in the estimate and which item shall he computed by applying to the estimated cost of labor on the work the preferred rate then in effect upon such class of work.

Application of state highway improvement fund.

Sec. 1221. The state highway improvement fund produced by the levy hereinafter provided for, shall be applied to the construction, improvement, maintenance and repair of the inter-county and main market road systems as follows:

1. The general assembly may appropriate out of the state highway improvement fund such rotary fund, or funds, or other smiliar funds, as it may deem necessary for the purpose of paying when necessary the federal gov-

ernment's share of any estimate due a contractor, or contractors, on road improvements carried forward by the state highway department in co-operation with the federal government, and to pay when necessary the cost of completing any road improvement carried forward by the state highway department when a contractor has defaulted in his contract or has been removed from his control of the work covered by such contract.

2. Seventy-five per cent of all the remainder of the money paid into the treasury by reason of the levy for the state highway improvement fund shall be used for the construction, improvement, maintenance and repair of the inter-county highways as the same have been heretofore designated or as they may hereafter be established or located by the state highway commissioner in the manner provided by law, and for the maintenance of the state highway department, including the state's portion of the salaries of the county surveyors.

Money appropriated or available for inter-county highways shall be so expended as to produce an equal division among the counties of the state of the moneys so appropriated by the general assembly for each two year period. Nothing herein contained shall be held to require an equal division among the counties of the state of such moneys appropriated for any one year period, but the provision herein contained requiring said moneys to be so expended as to produce an equal division among such counties of the entire appropriation for each two year period shall be held to be mandatory.

3. Twenty-five per cent of all the remainder of the money paid into the treasury of the state by reason of the levy for the state highway improvement fund shall be used for the construction, improvement, maintenance and repair of the main market roads of the state as the same have been heretofore designated or as they may hereafter be established by the state highway commissioner in the manner provided by law. The money to the credit of the state highway improvement fund for use on the main market roads of the state as herein provided shall be so expended as to distribute equitably, as far as practicable, the benefits from such expenditure to the different sections and counties of the state. In the event of the exhaustion of any rotary fund, or funds, or other similar funds, provided by the general assembly, funds appropriated for the construction, improvement, maintenance and repair of main market roads and against which no contractual liabilities have been created may with the approval of any board authorized to transfer funds be used for the purpose or purposes for which such rotary funds were provided.

4. The funds derived by the state highway department from the registration of automobiles shall be used for the maintenance and repair of the inter-county highways and main market roads of the state. The state highway

commissioner may use part of said funds as may be necessary in establishing a system of patrol or gang maintenance on the inter-county highways and main market roads, and for that purpose may employ such patrolmen, laborers and other persons and teams and purchase or lease such oilers, trucks, machinery, tools, material and other equipment and supplies as may be necessary.

Tax levy for county's proportion; application of proceeds; limitations. Sec. 1222. For the purpose of providing a fund for the payment of the county's proportion of the cost and expense of the construction, improvement, maintenance and repair of highways under the provisions of this chapter, the county commissioners are hereby authorized to levy a tax, not exceeding one and one-half mills, upon all the taxable property of the county. Said levy shall be in addition to all other levies authorized by law for county purposes, but subject, however, to the extent of one-half mill thereof, to the limitation upon the combined maximum rate for all taxes now in force. The remaining one mill of said levy so authorized shall be in addition to all other levies made for any purpose or purposes, and the same shall not be construed as limited, restricted or decreased in amount or otherwise by any existing law or laws. The proceeds of such levy shall be used solely for the purpose of paying the county's proportion of the cost and expense of constructing, improving, maintaining and repairing inter-county highways and main market roads or parts thereof in cooperation with the state highway department or the federal government or both; and the funds produced by such levy shall not be subject to transfer to any other fund, either by order of court or otherwise.

The county commissioners of any county in which less than one and one-half mills is levied in any year under the provisions of this section shall within the above limitations determine what part of such levy shall be subject to the limitations upon the combined maximum rate for all taxes now in force and what part of such levy shall be outside such limitation and unrestricted by any existing law or laws.

Tax levy by township trustees or commissioners in townships interested; limitation. For the purpose of providing a fund for the payment of the proportion of the cost and expense to be paid by the interested township or townships for the construction, improvement, maintenance or repair of highways under the provisions of this chapter, the county commissioners or the township trustees are authorized to levy a tax not exceeding two mills upon all taxable property of the township in which such road improvement or some part thereof is situated. Such levy shall be in addition to all other levies authorized by law for township purposes and shall be outside the limitation of two mills for general township purposes, and subject only to the limitation upon the combined maximum rate for all taxes now in force. Where the improvement is made upon the application of the county commissioners said county commissioners shall levy the tax and where the improvement is made upon the application of the township trustees said township trustees shall levy the tax. A county or township may use any moneys lawfully transferred form any fund in place of the taxes provided for under the provisions of this section.

Sec. 1223. The county commissioners, in anticipation of the collection of such taxes and assessments or any part thereof, and whenever such construction, improvement or repair is being done upon their application, may, whenever in their judgment it is deemed necessary sell the bonds of said county in any amount not greater than the aggregate sum necessary to pay the respective shares of the estimated compensation, damages, cost and expense payable by the county, township or townships and the owners of the lands assessed for such improvement, but the aggregate amount of such bonds issued and outstanding at any one time and to be redeemed by a tax levy upon the grand duplicate of the county shall not be in excess of one per cent of the tax duplicate of such county. In computing such one per cent bonds to be redeemed by special assessments or by tax levies upon the interested township or townships shall not be taken into account. Such bonds shall state for what purpose issued and bear interest at a rate not to exceed five per cent per annum, payable semiannually, and in such amounts, and to mature in not more than ten years after their issue, as the county commissioners shall determine. Prior to the issuance of such bonds the county commissioners shall provide for the levying of a tax upon all the taxable property of the county to cover any deficiency in the payment or collection of any special assessments or township taxes anticipated by such bonds. The proceeds of such bonds shall be used exclusively for the payment of the cost and expense of the construction, improvement or repair of the highway for which the bonds are issued. If bids are made for a portion of the proposed issue, the commissioners may accept a combination of bids, if by so doing the bonds will produce the best price to the county, and at the request of the purchaser the bonds may be issued in denominations of one hundred dollars or multiples thereof, notwithstanding any provision of the resolution providing for their issue. Where such construction, improvement or repair is made upon the application of the township trustees such township trustees are hereby authorized to sell the bonds of the interested township in any amount not greater than the estimated compensation, damages, cost and expense of such construction, improvement or repair and under like conditions hereinbefore prescribed for county commissioners.

County bonds in anticipation of tax levies; limitation.

When township trustees shall sell bonds.

Sec. 1224. The state highway commissioner shall maintain and repair to the required standard, and when in his judgment necessary, shall resurface, reconstruct or widen all inter-county highways, main market roads and bridges and culverts constructed by the state, by the aid of state

Powers and duties of commissioner as to maintenance and repair of main market and inter-county highways, contributions.

money or taken over by the state after being constructed.
In repairing inter-county highways and main market roads
the state highway commissioner shall not be limited to the
use of the material with which such inter-county highways
or main market roads were originally constructed, but may
repair such inter-county highways or main market roads
by the use of any material which he deems proper. When
in the repair of an inter-county highway or main market
road the state highway commissioner changes the type of
such road and uses, as the principal material in making
such repair, a material different from that with which the
road was originally constructed, not less than ten per cent
of the cost and expense of such repair shall be assessed
against the property abutting on said road, or within one-
half mile on either side thereof or within one mile on either
side thereof, in the manner hereinbefore provided in the
case of the construction of a road under the supervision of
the state highway department. Nothing in this chapter
shall be construed so as to prohibit a county, township or
municipality or the federal government, or any individual
or corporation from contributing a portion of the cost of the
construction, maintenance and repair of said state highways. When a bridge or culvert on a state highway shall
require renewing, it shall be constructed and the cost apportioned as herein provided for the construction and improvement of bridges and culverts on inter-county highways. The state highway commissioner may enter into a
contract with any individual, firm or corporation which
gives sufficient bond for the faithful performance of said
contract, or with the county commissioners of any county
or the township trustees of any township in which such
highway is situated for the repair and maintenance of such
highway, or any part thereof, according to the plans and
specifications provided by the state commissioner, or for the
furnishing of the material or labor for such repair and
maintenance, or the state highway commissioner may furnish the material or labor or both and supervise the repair
and maintenance. Inter-county highways or main market
roads on which no state aid money has been expended, if
improved with construction equal to that specified by the
state highway commissioner shall be taken over by the
state, and shall thenceforth be maintained as prescribed
herein for inter-county highways and main market roads.
Upon the application of the county commissioners or township trustees the chief highway engineer shall, within sixty
days, specify what changes are required in any portion of
any existing inter-county highways or main market road
to bring it up to the standard required by the state, and
on application, the chief highway engineer shall furnish
specifications for the construction of such road up to the
standard required by the state. The state highway commissioner shall also be authorized to maintain, repair, resurface or reconstruct any inter-county highway or main

market road not originally constructed by the state by the aid of state money or taken over by the state after being constructed. Any such inter-county highway or main market road so maintained, repaired, resurfaced or reconstructed shall not by reason of such operation become a state road unless the work done thereon is of such a character as in the judgment of the state highway commissioner produces an improvement which fully meets the standard prescribed by the state for state roads.

Sec. 1230. There shall be levied annually a tax of five-tenths of one mill on all the taxable property within the state to be collected as are other taxes due the state, and the proceeds of which shall constitute the state highway improvement fund.

State highway fund; tax levy.

Sec. 1231-2. The annual levy of five-tenths of one mill provided for by this act shall be in addition to all other levies made for any purpose or purposes, and the same shall not be construed as limited, restricted or decreased in amount or otherwise by any existing law or laws.

Annual state levy, additional to all other levies.

Sec. 2788-1. The county surveyor shall designate one of his deputies as county maintenance engineer. Such deputy so designated shall be a person experienced in the maintenance and repair of roads and it shall be the duty of such maintenance engineer, acting under the general direction and supervision of the county surveyor, to have charge of all road maintenance and repair work carried forward under the supervision of the county surveyor.

Designation of county maintenance engineer; duties.

The county surveyor, when authorized by the county commissioners, shall appoint a maintenance supervisor or supervisors to have charge of the maintenance of improved highways within a district or districts established by the commissioners and surveyor and containing not less than ten miles of improved county roads. Such maintenance supervisor shall act under the direction of the county surveyor, and the county surveyor, when authorized by the county commissioners, shall establish a patrol or gang system of maintenance under the direct charge of such supervisor. The compensation of such supervisor shall be fixed upon a per diem basis by the county commissioners and shall be paid out of the road repair or county road fund upon the approval of the county surveyor.

Maintenance supervisors authorized; duties.

Sec. 3298-7. Upon the completion of the surveys, plans, profiles, cross-sections, estimates and specifications, for such improvement by the county surveyor, he shall transmit to the township trustees copies of the same; and thereupon, except in cases of reconstruction or repair of roads, where no land or property are taken, the township trustees shall cause to be published in a newspaper, published in the county and of general circulation within such township, if there be any such paper published in the county, but if there be no such paper published in the county then in a newspaper having general circulation in said township, once a week for two consecutive weeks, a no-

Transmission of surveys, plans, specifications to township trustees; publication of notice of improvement.

tice that such improvement is to be made and that copies of the surveys, plans, profiles, cross-sections, estimates and specifications for said improvement are on file with the township trustees for the inspection and examination of all persons interested therein. Such notice shall also state the time and place for hearing objections to said improvement, and for hearing claims for compensation for lands and property to be taken for said improvement or damages sustained on account thereof, and that unless such claims are filed in writing with the township trustees on or before the time fixed for hearing said claims, the same shall be waived, except as to minors and other persons under disability.

Sec. 3298-18. After the annual estimate for each township has been filed with the trustees of the township by the county surveyor they may increase or reduce the amount of any of the items contained in said estimate and at their first meeting after said estimate is filed they shall make their levies for the purposes set forth in the estimate and for the purpose of creating a fund for dragging, maintenance and repair of roads, upon all the taxable property of the township outside of any incorporated village or city, or part thereof therein situated, not exceeding in the aggregate two mills in any one year upon each dollar of the valuation of such taxable property. Such levies shall be in addition to all other levies authorized by law for township purposes and subject only to the limitation upon the combined maximum rate for all taxes now in force. The provisions of this section shall not prevent the expenditure of any portion of the regular levy of two mills for township purposes, but the levies herein provided for are in addition thereto. The board of township trustees of each township shall provide annually by taxation under the provisions of this section or under the provisions of section 3298-15d of the General Code or under both sections an adequate fund for the maintenance and repair of township highways. The maintenance and repair fund so provided shall not be less than one hundred dollars for each mile of improved township highways in the township and twenty dollars for each mile of unimproved township highway within the township. Such levy or levies for maintenance and repair purposes shall be separately set forth in the annual budget of the township trustees presented to the budget commission, and the maintenance and repair levies so made by the township trustees pursuant to the provisions of this section shall be preferred levies as against any other levies made for township road purposes by such trustees. Should the budget commission of any county be unable, by reason of the limitations of law, to allow all of the road levies made by the townhsip trustees, such reductions as are necessary therein shall be first made in levies other than those for maintenance and repair purposes made under the provisions of this section. The fund produced by such levy or levies for maintenance and repair purposes shall not be subject to transfer by order of court or otherwise and shall be used solely for the maintenance and repair of the township roads within the township. The provisions of this section shall not prevent the township trustees from using any other available road funds for the maintenance and repair of township roads.

Sec. 3298-32. Upon the completion of the surveys, plans, profiles, cross-sections, estimates, and specifications, for such improvement by the county surveyor, he shall transmit to the township trustees copies of the same; and thereupon, except in cases of reconstruction or repair of roads, where no lands or property are taken, the township trustees shall cause to be published in a newspaper, published in the county and of general circulation within such district, if there be any such paper published in the county, but if there be no such paper published in the county then a newspaper having general circulation in said district, once a week for two consecutive weeks, a notice that such improvement is to be made and that copies of the surveys, plans, profiles, cross-sections, estimates and specifications for said improvement are on file with the township trustees for the inspection and examination of all persons interested therein. Such notice shall also state the time and place for hearing objections to said improvement, and for hearing claims for compensation for lands and property to be taken for said improvement or damages sustained on account thereof, and that unless such claims are filed in writing with the township trustees on or before the time fixed for hearing said claims, the same shall be waived, except as to minors and other persons under disability.

Transmission of plans, surveys, etc., to trustees; notice of improvement; times for hearing of objections and claims.

Sec. 3371-1. In the maintenance and repair of roads the township trustees and any township highway superintendent, appointed by them, shall be subject to the general supervision and direction of the county surveyor. They shall follow the direction of the county surveyor as to methods to be followed in making repairs and all expenditures made by them for maintenance and repair purposes shall where the amount involved exceeds fifty dollars receive the approval of the county surveyor before payment is made.

County surveyor has supervision of maintenance and repair.

Sec. 3373. In the maintenance and repair of roads the township trustees may proceed either by contract or force account. When they proceed by contract the contract shall, in case the amount involved exceeds two hundred dollars, be let by the township trustees to the lowest responsible bidder after advertisement for bids once not later than two weeks prior to the date fixed for the letting of such contract, in a newspaper published in the county and of general circulation within such township, if there be any such paper published in the county, but if there be no such paper published in the county, then in a newspaper having general circulation in said township. If the amount involved is two hundred dollars or less the contract may be

Trustees may maintain or repair by contract or force account; when contract let by competitive bidding.

let without competitive bidding. Such contract shall be performed under the supervision of a member of the board of township trustees or the township highway superintendent.

Purchase of machinery, tools, etc.; purchase of materials and employment of labor.

Township trustees are hereby authorized to purchase or lease such machinery and tools as may be deemed necessary for use in maintaining and repairing roads and culverts within the township. The township trustees shall provide suitable places for housing and storing machinery and tools owned by the township. They shall have the power to purchase such material and to employ such labor and teams as may be necessary for carrying into effect the provisions of this section, or they may authorize the purchase or employment of the same by one of their number or by the township highway superintendent at a price to be fixed by the township trustees. All payments on account of machinery, tools, material, labor and teams shall be made from the township road fund as provided by law. All purchases of materials, machinery, and tools, shall, where the amount involved exceeds five hundred dollars, be made from the lowest responsible bidder after advertisement made in the manner hereinbefore provided. All force account work shall be done under the direction of a member of the board of township trustees or of the township highway superintendent.

Copies of surveys, plans, estimates, etc., transmitted to commissioners.

Sec. 6912. Upon the completion of the surveys, plans, profiles, cross-sections, estimates and specifications for such improvement by the county surveyor, he shall transmit to the commissioners copies of the same; and thereupon, except in cases of reconstruction or repair of roads, where no lands or property are taken, the county commissioners shall cause to be published in a newspaper published and of general circulation within the county, if there be any such paper published in said county, but if there be no such paper published in said county then in a newspaper having general circulation in said county, once a week for two consecutive weeks, a notice that such improvement is to be made and that copies of the surveys, plans, profiles, cross-sections, estimates and specifications for said improvement are on file in the office of the county commissioners for the inspection and examination of all persons interested therein.

Notice of improvement; time and place of hearing of objections and claims.

Such notice shall also state the time and place for hearing objections to said improvement, and for hearing claims for compensation for lands and property to be taken for said improvement or damage sustained on account thereof, and that unless such claims are filed in writing with the county commissioners on or before the time fixed for hearing said claims the same shall be waived, except as to minors and other persons under disability.

Submission of question of exemption of two mill levy from tax limitations, when and how.

Sec. 6926-1. The county commissioners of any county may, and upon the petition of qualified electors of the county in a number equal to at least five per cent of the number of votes cast therein at the last preceding general election of state and county officers, shall by resolution submit to the electors of such county at the first ensuing November election that occurs more than forty days after the adoption of such resolution, the question of exempting from all tax limitations the levy of two mills provided by section 6926 of the General Code for the purpose of paying the county's proportion of the compensation, damages, costs and expenses of constructing, reconstructing, maintaining and repairing county roads, or the question of so exempting· a part of such levy, such exemption to continue for a definite term of years not exceeding ten. When such question is submitted upon the petition of electors, such petition shall state the portion of the le√y to be so exempted and the number of years during which such exemption shall continue, and these matters set forth in the petition shall also be set forth in like manner in the resolution adopted by the county commissioners pursuant thereto. Where such question is submitted by the commissioners without the filing of a petition by electors, such resolution shall state the portion of the levy to be so exempted and the number of years during which such exemption shall continue. The petition and resolution, or the resolution where the commissioners act without a petition being presented, may also state the part of such levy so to be exempted to be used for constructing and improving county roads and the part of such levy so to be exempted to be used for maintaining and repairing county roads, in which event the proceeds of any such levy exempted by vote of the electors of the county shall be expended in accordance with such division. The board of county commissioners, upon the adoption of such resolution by a majority vote of all the members elected or appointed thereto, shall cause a copy of such resolution to be certified to the deputy state supervisors and inspectors or the deputy state supervisors of elections of the proper county.

Sec. 6926-2. Such proposition shall be submitted to the electors of such county at the first ensuing November election that occurs more than forty days after the adoption of such resolution. The deputy state supervisors and inspectors or deputy state supervisors shall prepare the ballots and make the necessary arrangements for the submission of such question to the electors of such county, and the election shall be governed in all respects by the general election laws of the state and shall be conducted, canvassed and certified in like manner except as otherwise provided by law as regular elections in such county for the election of officers thereof. The county commissioners shall cause to be published for two weeks in two newspapers of general circulation and of the two dominant political parties published in the county if there be any such papers published in such county, but if there be no such papers published in such county, then in two newspapers having general circulation therein, notice of such election, which notice shall state the portion of such levy to be exempted from all tax

Preparation of ballots; notice of election.

limitations, the number of years during which such exemption is to continue in force, the division of such levy between construction and improvement purposes and maintenance and repair purposes, if any, and the time and place of holding the election.

The form of the ballots cast at such election shall be:

Form of ballot.
"For an additional levy of taxes for the purpose of constructing, reconstructing, maintaining and repairing county roads not exceeding ...... mills, for not to exceed .... years. Yes."

"For an additional levy of taxes for the purpose of constructing, reconstructing, maintaining and repairing county roads not exceeding ...... mills, for not to exceed .... years. No."

Result certified by deputy state supervisors.
Sec. 6926-3. The ballots shall be marked as is provided by law with reference to other ballots and the result of such election shall be certified by the deputy state supervisors and inspectors or the deputy state supervisors of elections to the county commissioners of such county. If a majority of the electors voting thereon at such election vote in favor of such levy or levies, it shall be lawful to levy taxes within such county at a rate not to exceed such increased rate for and during the period provided for in such Effect of affirmative vote. resolution, such taxes to be in addition to such other taxes for the same purposes as may be levied subject to any limitation prescribed by law upon the combined maximum rate for all taxes, and the taxes so levied pursuant to such vote of the electors shall be in addition to all other levies made for any purpose or purposes and the same shall not be construed as limited, restricted or decreased in amount or otherwise by any existing law or laws.

Notice of improvement and place of hearing of objections and claims by joint boards.
Sec. 6936. As soon as the county surveyor appointed for that purpose has transmitted to the several boards of county commissioners copies of his surveys, plans, profiles, cross-sections, estimates and specifications for such improvement, the joint board of county commissioners shall, except in cases of reconstruction or repair of roads, where no lands or property are taken, fix a time and place for hearing objections to said improvement and claims for compensation for lands and property to be taken for said improvement, or damages sustained on account thereof. The joint board of county commissioners shall thereupon, except in cases of reconstruction or repair of roads, where no lands or property are taken, cause to be published in a newspaper of general circulation within each of the interested counties, if there be such papers published in said counties, but if there be no such paper published in any of said counties, then in a newspaper having general circulation therein, once a week for two consecutive weeks, a notice that such improvement is to be made and that copies of the surveys, plans, profiles, cross-sections, estimates and specifications therefor are on file in the office of the county commissioners of each interested county for the inspection and examination

of all persons interested therein. Such notice shall also state the time and place for hearing objections to said improvement and for hearing claims for compensation for lands and property to be taken for said improvement or damages sustained on account thereof, and that unless such claims are filed in writing with the joint board of county commissioners at the place fixed for such hearing and on or before the time fixed for hearing said claims, the same shall be waived except as to minors and other persons under disability. In the event that land or property is to be taken for such improvement, such notice shall state whose land or property is to be appropriated and shall be served in the manner provided by section 6913 of the General Code.

Sec. 6954. The board of county commissioners of any county may repair that portion of a county road extending into or through a municipal corporation, or a part of a county road and a city or village street or streets extending into or through a municipal corporation and forming a continuous road improvement, when the consent of the council of said municipal corporation has been first obtained and such consent shall be evidenced by the proper legislation of the council of said municipal corporation entered upon its records. *Improvement through municipality by commissioners; legislation by council.*

Sec. 6956-1. After the annual estimate for the county has been filed with the county commissioners by the county surveyor, and the county commissioners have made such changes and modifications in said estimate as they deem proper, they shall then make their levy for the purposes set forth in said estimate, upon all the taxable property of the county not exceeding in the aggregate two mills upon each dollar of the taxable property of said county. Such levy shall be in addition to all other levies authorized by law for said purposes, but subject, however, to the limitation upon the combined maximum rate for all taxes now in force. The provisions of this section shall not, however, prevent the commissioners from using any surplus in the general funds of the county for the purposes set forth in said estimate. *Annual tax levy by commissioners; additional to other levies.*

Sec. 6956-1a. The board of county commissioners of each county shall provide annually by taxation an adequate fund for the maintenance and repair of improved county highways. Such fund shall be provided by levies made under sections 6926, 6927 and 6956-1 of the General Code and the several sections amendatory thereof or supplementary thereto. The maintenance and repair fund so provided shall not be less than one hundred dollars for each mile of improved county highway within the county. Such levy or levies for maintenance and repair purposes shall be separately set forth in the annual budget of the county commissioners presented to the budget commission, and the maintenance and repair levies so made by the county commissioners pursuant to the provisions of this section shall be preferred levies as against any other levies *Maintenance and repair fund shall be provided; minimum per mile; fund not subject to transfer.*

made by the commissioners for county road purposes. Should the budget commission of any county be unable, by reason of the limitations of law, to allow all of the road levies made by county commissioners, such reductions as are necessary therein shall be first made in levies other than those for maintenance and repair purposes made under the provisions of this section. The fund produced by such levy or levies for maintenance and repair purposes shall not be subject to transfer by order of court or otherwise and shall be used solely for the maintenance and repair of the improved county roads within the county. The provisions of this section shall not prevent the county commissioners from using any other available road funds for the maintenance and repair of improved county roads.

How county line roads reckoned in determining mileage in county; report of mileage to highway commissioner.

Sec. 7181-1. In determining the number of miles of the public roads of the counties of the state the mileage of county line roads shall be reckoned one-half in each county. The number of miles of public roads in each county shall be determined in the first instance by the county surveyor, who shall make a report to the state highway commissioner setting forth the mileage of public roads within his county. The state highway commissioner shall examine such reports and after correcting the same, if necessary, shall approve the reports; and the mileage of public roads in each county, as set forth in such reports as corrected and approved by the state highway commissioner, shall govern in determin-

Salary of surveyor determined by mileage of public roads; report by surveyor.

ing the annual salary of the county surveyor under the provisions of section 7181 of the General Code of Ohio. The county surveyor of each county shall promptly report to the state highway commissioner from time to time any additions to or deductions from the public road mileage of his county by reason of the establishment of any new roads or the vacation of any existing roads. After the state high-

The sectional numbers in this act are in conformity to the General Code. JOHN G. PRICE, *Attorney General.*

way commissioner has examined and approved the report of the county surveyor as to the road mileage of his county, it shall be the duty of the state highway commissioner to certify to the county auditor of said county a copy of such report as approved.

Assessment of compensation and damages against owners of real estate.

Sec. 1214-1. The board of county commissioners of any county or the board of township trustees of any township, authorized to assess all or any part of the compensation, damages, costs and expenses of constructing a road improvement, carried forward by the state highway department or by such board of county commissioners or by such board of township trustees, against the real estate abutting upon said improvement or the real estate situated within one-half mile of either side thereof or the real estate situated within one mile of either side thereof, according to the benefits accruing to such real estate, may in like manner assess such compensation, damages, costs and expenses against the real estate situated within one and one-half miles of either side of such improvement, according to the benefits accruing to such real estate.

505

Sec. 1196-1. It shall be the duty of the state highway department, board of county commissioners or board of township trustees in the making of plans for any road improvement, to cause such plans to be so prepared as to provide for the preservation of all cornerstones and landmarks, set within the limits of the highway to be improved. All such cornerstones and landmarks shall be preserved or reset in their exact locations, and where located within the improved surface of the highway, the plans for the improvement shall be so drawn as to furnish adequate protection to such cornerstones and landmarks and also to furnish by suitable devices or otherwise full opportunity for consulting or referring to the same at any time without destruction to or injury of the surface of the road improvement.

Preservation of cornerstones and landmarks.

Sec. 7201. County commissioners and township trustees, in the purchase of machinery, tools, trucks and other equipment for use in constructing, maintaining and repairing roads, shall be authorized to purchase such machinery, tools, trucks and equipment upon the following terms, to wit: not less than one-third of the purchase price thereof shall be paid in cash, and of the remainder not more than one-third may be paid at any time within one year from the date of purchase and not more than one-third at any time within two years from the date of purchase. Such commissioners or trustees shall be authorized to issue to the purchaser the notes of the county or township, as the case may be, signed by the commissioners or trustees and attested by the signature of the county auditor or township clerk, and covering such deferred payments and payable at the times above provided, which notes may bear interest at not to exceed six per cent per annum. In the legislation under which such notes are authorized, the county commissioners or township trustees shall make provision for levying and collecting annually by taxation an amount sufficient to pay the interest, if any, thereon and to provide a sinking fund for the final redemption of such notes at maturity. The provisions of section 5660 of the General Code shall apply only to such portion of the purchase price of such machinery, tools, trucks or equipment as is to be paid in cash.

Terms authorized in purchase of machinery, tools, etc.; tax levy.

The power herein conferred on township trustees shall be exercised by them only with the consent to and approval of such purchase and the terms thereof by the county commissioners of the county.

SECTION 5. Sections of this act and parts thereof are hereby declared to be independent sections and parts of sections and the holding of any section or part thereof to be unconstitutional, void or ineffective for any cause shall not affect any other section, or sections, or part or parts thereof.

Sections or part void, does not affect others.

SECTION 6. That said original sections 1178, 1180, 1181, 1184, 1185, 1185-1, 1186, 1187, 1188, 1189, 1201, 1206, 1207, 1208, 1209, 1213-1, 1218, 1218-1, 1221, 1222, 1223,

Repeals.

1224, 1230, 1231-2, 3298-7, 3298-18, 3298-32, 3373, 6912, 6936 and 6956-1 of the General Code be, and the same are hereby repealed.

This act shall succeed all acts, and parts of acts, not herein expressly repealed which are inconsistent herewith.

The sectional numbers on the margin hereof are designated as provided by law.
JOHN G. PRICE, Attorney General.

CARL R. KIMBALL,
Speaker of the House of Representatives.
CLARENCE J. BROWN,
President of the Senate.

Passed May 9, 1919.

In the house of representatives passed notwithstanding the objections of the Governor, May 27, 1919.

CARL R. KIMBALL,
Speaker of the House of Representatives.

In the senate passed notwithstanding the objections of the Governor, May 27, 1919.

CLARENCE J. BROWN,
President of the Senate.

Filed in the office of the Secretary of State at Columbus, Ohio, on the 28th day of May, A. D. 1919.

170 G.

[House Bill No. 43.]

AN ACT

To amend section 4715 of the General Code, relating to the compensation of members of boards of education in rural school districts.

Be it enacted by the General Assembly of the State of Ohio:

SECTION 1. That section 4715 of the General Code be amended to read as follows:

Sec. 4715. Each member of the board of education of rural school distrticts, except such districts as contain less than sixteen square miles, shall receive as compensation two dollars for each regular meeting actually attended by such member, and members of such boards in rural school districts containing less than sixteen square miles shall receive one dollar for each meeting, but for not more than ten meetings in any year. The compensation allowed members of the board shall be paid from the contingent fund.

SECTION 2. That original section 4715 of the General ^{Repeal.} Code be, and the same is hereby repealed.

CLARENCE J. BROWN,
President of the Senate.
CARL R. KIMBALL,
Speaker of the House of Representatives.

Passed April 4, 1919.

In the House of Representatives, passed notwithstanding the objection of the Governor, May 29, 1919.

CARL R. KIMBALL,
Speaker of the House of Representatives.

In the Senate, passed notwithstanding the objections of the Governor, May 28, 1919.

CLARENCE J. BROWN,
President of the Senate.

Filed in the office of the Secretary of State of Columbus, Ohio, on the 29th day of May, A. D. 1919.

171 G.

[Amended Senate Bill No. 47.]

AN ACT

To authorize the formation and reorganization of corporations with common stock without par value.

Be it enacted by the General Assembly of the State of Ohio:

Sec. 8728-1.

SECTION 1. Upon the formation of any corporation for profit under the laws of this state, except banking, safe deposit, trust and insurance corporations, or a corporation under the jurisdiction of the public utilities commission, the articles of incorporation required by law may provide for the issuance of the shares of common stock of such corporation, without any nominal or par value, by stating in such articles: *(marginal note: Corporations may issue shares of common stock without nominal value; exceptions.)*

(a) The number of shares that may be issued by the corporation, and if any of such shares be preferred stock, the terms and provisions thereof, as may be authorized by law, and the amount of each share thereof, which shall be five dollars, or some multiple of five dollars, but not more than one hundred dollars. *(marginal note: Statements required in articles.)*

(b) The amount of capital with which the corporation will carry on business, which amount shall be not less than the amount of the preferred capital, if any, authorized to be issued, and in addition thereto as common capital a sum equivalent to five dollars, or to some multiple of five dollars, for each share of common stock to be issued; but in no event shall the amount of common capital be less than five hundred dollars, nor shall the number of shares of preferred stock be more than two-thirds of the total number of shares, common and preferred, authorized to be issued. The secretary of state shall charge and collect for filing such articles of incorporation a fee of ten cents on each share of common *(marginal note: Filing fee)* stock authorized in the articles to be issued without any nominal or par value, and in addition thereto a fee of one-tenth of one per cent of the par value of the preferred stock authorized in the articles, but in no case shall the aggregate amount to be paid to the secretary of state be less than $25.00, and upon any increase of authorized capital stock either common or preferred, or both, such fees shall be charged and collected by the secretary of state.

Statements shall be in lieu of amount of capital stock, etc.

Such statements in the articles of incorporation shall be in lieu of any statements prescribed by law as to the amount of the capital stock, and the number of shares into which the same shall be divided, and the par value of such shares.

What each certificate shall show.

Each share of such common stock without nominal or par value shall be equal to every other share of such stock, subject to the preferences given to the preferred stock, if any, authorized to be issued. Every certificate for such shares without nominal or par value shall have plainly written or printed upon its face the number of such shares which it represents and the number of such shares which the corporation is authorized to issue, and no such certificate shall express any nominal or par value of such shares.

Opening books of subscription; sale of shares; payment of dividends in stock or cash.

Such corporation may receive subscriptions for, and issue and sell its preferred shares, as authorized by law. At the time of opening books of subscription to the capital stock, as required by law, subscriptions may be received for the common shares, without nominal or par value, for such consideration as may be decided upon by the incorporators at the time of ordering books to be opened for subscription; thereafter the corporation may issue and sell its said common shares, from time to time, for such consideration as shall be the fair market value of such shares, or for such consideration as shall be consented to by the holders of a majority in number of the outstanding common shares at a meeting called for that purpose in such manner as shall be prescibed by the code of regulations. The directors may, from time to time, upon payment of the consideration fixed as aforesaid, distribute to the holders of record of the outstanding common shares, proportionately, any authorized unissued common shares of the company, or any part thereof; nothing herein shall prevent a corporation from paying dividends, subject to the limitations of this act, payable in common stock of the company instead of in cash or property. Any and all shares issued as permitted by this section shall be deemed fully paid and non-assessable and the holder of such shares shall not be liable to the corporation or to its creditors in respect thereof.

Sec. 8728-2.

When corporation may begin business.

SECTION 2. No corporation formed pursuant to this act shall begin to carry on business or shall incur any debts until the amount of common capital stock stated in its articles of incorporation, shall have been fully paid to the corporation in money or in property taken at its actual value; and a certificate to that effect signed and acknowledged by at least a majority of the incorporators, before an

officer authorized to administer oaths, shall be filed with the
secretary of state, who shall charge and collect therefor a
fee of $5.00. In case the amount of common capital stated
in its articles of incorporations shall be increased, as hereinafter provided, such corporation shall not increase the
amount of its indebtedness then existing until it shall have
received in money or property, the amount of such increase
of its said stated common capital. The rights of creditors **Rights of creditors and others; limitation of actions.**
and persons dealing with such corporation without knowl-
edge of the failure of the corporation to have complied with
the foregoing provisions, shall not be affected thereby, but
the directors of the corporation assenting to the creation of
any debt in violation of this section, shall be liable jointly
and severally for such debt; but no action shall be brought
under the foregoing provision of this section unless within
one year after the debt shall have been incurred, the creditor shall have served upon the director written notice of
intention to hold him personally liable for such debt. Any **Subrogation of director.**
director, who, because of any such liability under this sec-
tion shall pay any debt of the corporation, shall be subro-
gated to all rights of the creditor in respect thereof against
the corporation and its property, and also shall be entitled
to contribution from all other directors of the corporation
similarly liable for the same debt, and the personal representative of any such director who shall have died before
making such contribution.

No such corporation shall declare or pay any dividend **Payment of dividends.**
out of capital or which shall reduce the amount of its com-
mon capital below the amount stated in the articles of incorporation as the amount of such capital with which the
corporation will carry on business, or from any fund received from the sale or disposition of its capital stock. In
case any such dividend shall be declared or paid the directors in whose administration the same shall have been declared or paid, except those who may have caused their
dissent therefrom to be entered upon the minutes of such
directors at the time, or who were not present when such
action was taken, shall be liable jointly and severally to
such corporation or a creditor thereof, to the full amount of
any loss sustained by such corporation or creditors respectively by reason of such dividend.

The preferred stock, if any, authorized to be issued **When preferred stock may be redeemed.**
shall not be redeemed or purchased by the corporation, as
may be authorized by law, if thereby the property and assets of the corporation will be reduced below the amount
stated in the articles of incorporation or any amendment
thereof, as the common capital with which the corporation
will carry on business; nor shall such preferred stock be redeemed, purchased, or retired, if thereby the property and
assets of the corporation will be reduced below the amount
of its outstanding debts and liabilities.

Corporations formed or reorganized pursuant to this

act shall not be subject to the limitations on borrowing capacity provided for by section 8705.

Sec. 8728-3.
Aggregate amount of capital stock; par value of shares.

SECTION 3. For the purpose of any rule of. law or of any statutory provision (other than as provided for in this act), relating to the amount of the capital stock of a corporation or the amount or par value of its common shares, the aggregate amount of the capital stock of any such corporation formed or reorganized pursuant to this act, shall be deemed to be the aggregate amount, preferred and common respectively, stated in the articles of incorporation or any amendment thereof, or the certificate of reorganization, as the amount of capital with which the corporation will carry on business; and for the same purpose the amount or par value of each share of common stock shall be deemed to be an aliquot part of the aggregate common capital so stated in such articles of incorporation or any amendment thereof, or certificate of reorganization. In any case in which the law requires that the par value of the shares of common stock be stated in any certificate or paper, it shall be stated in respect to such common shares of corporations formed or reorganized under this act, that such common shares are without par value, and the number of such shares shall be given.

Sec. 8728-4.
Increase or decrease of capital stock.

SECTION 4. Any corporation formed or reorganized pursuant to this act may increase or reduce the amount of its stated capital, common and preferred, or either, or may increase its stated capital, by providing for preferred stock, if none theretofore was authorized, or may increase or reduce the number of its shares, in the manner and in accordance with the provisions relating to the amendment of articles of incorporation under the general law.

Amendment to articles.

An amendment cannot be made under this section unless as so amended the articles of incorporation could lawfully have been originally filed under this act. In case of a reduction of the amount of common capital of a corporation, a certificate setting forth the whole amount of the ascertained debts and liabilities of the corporation shall be made, signed and verified by the president or vice-president, and by the secretary or treasurer of the corporation, and filed with the certificate of the reduction, required by law to be filed; and such certificate of debts and liabilities shall have endorsed thereon the certificate of the commissioner of securities that he has received satisfactory proof that the reduced amount of capital is sufficient for the proper purpose of the corporation, and is in excess of its ascertained debts and liabilities; but the rights of creditors shall not be affected thereby.

Sec. 8728-5.
Certificate of reorganization; statements required.

SECTION 5. Any corporation for profit heretofore or hereafter organized under the general incorporation laws of this state, other than corporations belonging to one of the classes specifically excepted by section one of this act, may be reorganized so that such corporation, its officers, directors and stockholders, shall acquire and enjoy all the rights, privileges, powers and exemptions, and become subject to all of the liabilities and obligations imposed by this act, upon the filing and recording in the office of the secretary of state, a certificate of reorganization of the company, pursuant to this act, stating:

First: The name under which the corporation was originally organized, and if it has been changed, the present corporate title.

Second: The date of its articles of incorporation, and all amendments thereof.

Third: The place where it is located or its principal business transacted.

Fourth: The amount of its capital stock, and the number of shares into which it has been divided, and, if classified, the number and par value of the shares included in each class, and the terms and provisions of the preferred stock.

Fifth: The number of shares of each class issued and outstanding.

Sixth: The number of shares that may henceforth be issued by the corporation, which may be either less than, or equal to, or in excess of the number of shares into which the capital stock was previously divided, and all of the matters and things required to be stated in an original certificate of incorporation by subdivision "a" of section one of this act.

Seventh: The amount of capital with which the corporation will carry on business, which shall be in all respects as required by subdivision "b" of section one of this act.

Eighth: The terms upon which the new shares of the reorganized corporation shall be issued in place of the outstanding shares of stock.

Ninth: It may also prescribe the consideration for which the reorganized corporation may issue and sell its authorized shares, or it may authorize the board of directors to issue and sell its authorized shares from time to time, for such consideration, as shall be the fair market value of said shares. The directors may, from time to time, upon payment of the consideration fixed as aforesaid, distribute to the holders of record of the outstanding common shares, proportionately, any authorized unissued common shares of the company, or any part thereof; nothing herein shall prevent a corporation from paying dividends, subject to the limitations of this act, payable in common stock of the company instead of in cash or property. Nothing shall be included in such certificate other than as authorized by this section, and it shall be either:

(a) Signed by every stockholder or record of the corporation, or his duly authorized proxy, and shall have annexed an affidavit of the secretary of the company to the effect that the persons who have executed the certificate, in person or by proxy, constitute the holders of record of all the shares of stock of the corporation, irrespective of class, issued and outstanding, or:

(b) Signed by the president or a vice-president and the secretary or treasurer of the corporation, who shall make and annex an affidavit stating that they have been authorized and directed to execute and file the certificate by the votes, cast in person or by proxy, of the holders of record of two-thirds or more of each class of the outstanding shares of stock, irrespective of any provision of the articles of incorporation purporting to deny voting powers to the holders of any class of stock, at a meeting called and held upon written notice mailed to each stockholder of record at least two weeks before the date set for the meeting and published once a week for at least two successive weeks in a newspaper published and circulating in the county wherein the principal office of the corporation is located; and that such notice did expressly state the purpose of the meeting to be that of reorganizing the corporation pursuant to this act, so as to permit the issuance of shares without par value, and did state the terms upon which the outstanding shares of stock were to be exchanged for the new shares.

Sec. 8728-6.

When affidavit as to debts and liabilities required; endorsement of commissioner.

SECTION 6. If the amount of capital, preferred and common, stated in the certificate of reorganization as that with which the corporation will carry on business, be less than the total amount of the par value of the previously issued and outstanding capital stock, there shall be annexed to such certificate an affidavit of the president or vice-president and the secretary or treasurer of the corporation, setting forth the whole amount of the ascertained debts and liabilities of the corporation; and, in such case, the certificate of reorganization shall have endorsed thereon the approval of the commissioner of securities to the effect that the amount of said capital stated in the certificate as that with which the corporation will carry on business is sufficient for the proper purposes of the corporation and is in excess of its debts and liabilities.

Sec. 8728-7.

Statement by president and treasurer before incurring debts; filing fee; rights of creditors.

SECTION 7. No corporation reorganized under this act shall incur any debts subsequent to the filing of the certificate of reorganization until it shall have assets of an actual value at least equal to the amount of its common capital stated in its certificate of reorganization as that with which it will carry on business, and shall have first filed with the Secretary of State the sworn statement of its president and treasurer of such facts for the filing of which the Secretary of State shall charge and collect a fee of $5.00. The rights of creditors and persons dealing with such corporation without knowledge of the failure of the corporation to have complied with the foregoing provisions shall not be affected thereby, but the directors of a corporation assenting to the creation of a debt in violation of this section shall be jointly and severally liable for such debt in like manner as provided, and subject to the conditions and limitations imposed by section two of this act.

Sec. 8728-8.

SECTION 8. The liability of the corporation, its officers, directors and stockholders for corporate debts contracted or obligations incurred prior to the filing of the certificate of reorganization pursuant to this act shall be unaffected thereby, but for the purpose of enforcing and recovering upon such claims creditors shall have the same right of recourse against the corporation, or against its officers, directors and stockholders individually that they would have had if the corporation had not been reorganized. Except as provided by this section the new shares issued by the reorganized corporation shall be deemed fully paid and nonassessable and the holder of such shares shall not be liable to the corporation or to its creditors in respect thereof. *(Liability unaffected by reorganization.)*

Sec. 8728-9.

SECTION 9. No proceedings taken under section six of this act shall be deemed to work a dissolution, or to create a new corporation or to interrupt in any way the continuity of existence of the corporation affected. *(Proceedings shall not work a dissolution or create new corporation.)*

Sec. 8728-10.

SECTION 10. Every corporation reorganized pursuant to this act and every such reorganized corporation increasing its authorized capital stock shall pay to the secretary of state the same fees provided in section 1 of this act as therein computed; provided, however, that the secretary of state shall charge and collect for the filing of the certificate of reorganizing referred to in section 5 of this act a fee of not less than $25.00. *(Fees to be paid secretary of state.)*

Sec. 8728-11.

SECTION 11. The amount of capital with which a corporation formed or reorganized under this act will carry on business, as stated in its articles of corporation or as thereafter lawfully changed, shall be deemed to be its subscribed or issued and outstanding capital stock for the purpose of sections 5497 and 5498 of the General Code. The amount of capital with which a foreign corporation having shares of capital stock without par value will carry on business, as stated in its articles or certificates of incorporation, or otherwise fixed or as thereafter lawfully changed, shall be deemed to be the authorized capital stock of such foreign corporation for the purposes of sections 180, 183, 184, 185, 5501, 5502 and 5503 of the General Code. *(What deemed subscribed capital stock and authorized capital stock.)*

Sec. 8728-12.

SECTION 12. Nothing in this act shall modify or supersede the jurisdiction of the commissioner of securities over the sale of bonds, stocks and other securities by corporations formed or organized pursuant to this act, under all laws enacted to regulate the sale of bonds, stocks and other securities and to prevent fraud in such sales. Any expenses incurred by the commissioner of securities in the performance of the duties required of him under sections 4 and 6 *(Jurisdiction of commissioner not superseded; expenses paid by corporation under investigation.)*

of this act, shall be paid by the corporation involved in the investigation.

CLARENCE J. BROWN,
President of the Senate.
CARL R. KIMBALL,
Speaker of the House of Representatives.
Passed April 16, 1919.
Approved May 29, 1919.

JAMES M. COX,
Governor.

Filed in the office of the Secretary of State at Columbus, Ohio, on the 2nd day of June, A. D. 1919.

172 G.

[Am. Senate Bill No. 134.]

AN ACT

To amend section 7852 of the General Code, relative to examinations in the German language and to supplement this section by the enactment of sections 7852-1, 7852-2 and 7852-3 of the General Code, relative to an oath or affirmation of allegiance to be taken by all teachers in public, private and parochial schools, or other institutions of learning.

Be it enacted by the General Assembly of the State of Ohio:

SECTION 1. That section 7852 of the General Code be amended and supplemented by the enactment of sections to be known as sections 7852-1, 7852-2 and 7852-3, to read as follows:

Kinds of certificates authorized to be issued apply to city boards.

Sec. 7852. The provisions of this chapter relating to the kinds of certificates authorized to be issued by the county boards of school examiners for teachers in elementary schools, high schools, and for superintendents shall apply to city boards of school examiners; except that city boards, in their discretion, may require teachers in elementary schools to be examined in drawing or music, if such subjects are a part of the regular work of such teachers.

Oath of teachers; form; where filed.

Sec. 7852-1. Any person now holding a certificate and before a certificate is granted to any applicant to teach in any of the public schools of this state, such applicant or teachers shall subscribe to the following oath or affirmation:

"I solemnly swear, or affirm, that I will support the constitution of the United States, the constitution of the state of Ohio, and the laws enacted thereunder, and that I will teach, by precept and example, respect for the flag, reverence for law and order and undivided allegiance to the government of one country, the United States of America."

Said oath or affirmation, duly signed, shall be filed in the office of the examiner issuing such certificate and a copy shall be given the applicant making such oath or affirmation.

Sec. 7852-2. Every teacher in a private or parochial school or in any academy, college, university or other institution of learning in this state, shall, before entering upon the discharge of his duties, take the same oath or affirmation of allegiance as that prescribed for public school teachers in section 7852-1. Such oath or affirmation shall be so taken and subscribed in writing before some officer authorized by the state to administer oaths, a copy of which writing shall be filed with the officer or board of authority in charge or control of such private or parochial school or such academy, college, university or other institution of learning.

Teachers in private or parochial school shall take oath.

Sec. 7852-3. Whoever being in control of any public, private or parochial school, of any academy, college, university or other institution of learning, shall allow or permit any teacher to enter upon the discharge of his duties or to give instruction therein unless such teacher shall have taken and subscribed the oath or affirmation of allegiance as provided for in sections 7852-1 and 7852-2, shall be guilty of a misdemeanor and upon conviction thereof shall be fined in any sum not exceeding one hundred dollars.

Penalty for permitting teachers to enter upon duties without taking oath.

SECTION 2. That said original section 7852 be and the same is hereby repealed.

Repeal.

The sectional numbers in this act are in conformity to the General Code. JOHN G. PRICE, Attorney General.

CLARENCE J. BROWN,
President of the Senate.
CARL R. KIMBALL,
Speaker of the House of Representatives.
Passed April 16, 1919.
Approved June 5, 1919.

JAMES M. COX,
Governor.

Filed in the office of the Secretary of State at Columbus, Ohio, on the 6th day of June, A. D. 1919.

173 G.

[Amended Senate Bill No. 13.]

AN ACT

To establish a municipal court in and for the city of Akron and to repeal an act entitled "An act to establish a police court in the city of Akron, Summit county, Ohio," passed May 10, 1910, and all acts amendatory thereof.

Be it enacted by the General Assembly of the State of Ohio:

Sec. 1579-497. SECTION 1. That there shall be, and hereby is established in and for the city of Akron a municipal court, which shall be a court of record and shall be styled "Municipal Court of Akron", hereinafter designated and referred to as "municipal court" or as "court."

Municipal court of Akron.

Sec. 1579-498. SECTION 2. The calendar of the court shall be divided into four terms of three months each, beginning, respectively, on the first day of January, April, July and October

Calendar of the court; assignment of criminal docket, etc.

of each year. The judges may continue the session of any term of court beyond the time fixed for the commencement of the next term, when such continuance is necessary to finish the trial of any cause or to receive the verdict, or pronounce judgment in any cause, the trial of which has been commenced during the term. The criminal docket shall be assigned to the several judges in rotation, as far as possible, but no judge shall have such criminal docket exclusively for more than two terms in any one year. Any judge may at any time be assigned by the presiding judge to any case, civil or criminal, when not actually engaged in the trial of another case.

Sec. 1579-499.
Seal of the court.

SECTION 3. The court shall have a seal, which shall be one and one-fourth inches in diameter and shall have engraved thereon the coat of arms of the state surrounded by these words: "Municipal Court of Akron, Ohio," and shall have no other words or device thereon.

Sec. 1579-500.
Accommodations and equipment.

SECTION 4. The council of the city of Akron shall provide suitable accommodations for the court and its officers. It shall also provide for the use of the court complete sets of the reports of the supreme and the inferior courts of the state and such other books as the judges from time to time deem necessary, and shall provide for each court room the latest edition of the General Code of Ohio, necessary supplies, including telephones, stationery, furniture and typewriters, and necessary heat, light and janitor service.

Sec. 1579-501.
Number, qualifications and salaries of judges.

SECTION 5. The court shall consist of three judges, all of whom shall be qualified electors and residents of the city of Akron and shall have been admitted to the practice of law in the state of Ohio for at least five years. Each judge shall receive a salary of four thousand five hundred dollars per annum, payable in monthly installments, fifteen hundred dollars of which shall be paid out of the treasury of Summit County and three thousand dollars of which shall be paid out of the treasury of the city of Akron.

Sec. 1579-502.
Nomination and election of judges.

SECTION 6. The judges shall be nominated and elected by the electors of the city of Akron at municipal elections in the same manner as judges of the court of common pleas are nominated and elected. The first election of judges shall be held at the regular municipal election in the year one thousand nine hundred and nineteen. The term of office of each judge shall be four years, commencing on the first day of January next after his election and continuing until his successor is elected and qualified.

Sec. 1579-503.
Presiding judge.

SECTION 7. The judges shall elect a presiding judge from among their number, and in case of absence or disability of the presiding judge, his place shall be temporarily filled by one of the other judges. No judge shall act as presiding judge for more than two terms in any one year.

Sec. 1579-504.
Removal; vacancy.

SECTION 8. The judges shall be subject to the same disabilities, may be removed from office for the same causes and shall be governed by the same provisions of law as judges of the court of common pleas, except as otherwise provided herein. Any vacancy which may occur in the office of judge, other than by temporary absence or disability, shall be filled by appointment by the governor until a successor is elected and qualified. Every such vacancy shall be filled by election at the first general municipal election taking place more than thirty days after the vacancy shall have occurred. The person elected shall fill the office for the unexpired term.

Sec. 1579-505.

SECTION 9. In addition to the other powers of a judge of said court ,the presiding judge shall have the general supervision of the business of the court, and may classify and distribute among the judges the business pending in the court. The judges may sit separately or otherwise; shall meet at least once in each month and at such other times as the presiding judge may determine, for consideration of the business of the court; shall prescribe forms; establish a system for docketing causes, motions and demurrers; and designate the method of keeping the records of the court. The court, or any judge thereof, may summon and impanel jurors, tax costs, compel the attendance of witnesses, jurors and parties, issue process, preserve order, punish for contempts, and exercise all powers which are now, or may hereafter be conferred upon the court of common pleas, or a judge thereof, necessary for the exercise of the jurisdiction herein conferred and for the enforcement of the judgments and orders of the court. Whenever, under the provisions of this act, authority is vested in all the judges constituting the court, such authority shall be exercised in accordance with the decision of the majority of the judges.

Powers of presiding judge and other judges.

Sec. 1579-506.

SECTION 10. The court shall have and exercise original jurisdiction within the limits of the city of Akron as follows:

Original jurisdiction in the city of Akron.

1. In all actions and proceedings of which justices of the peace have or may be given jurisdiction.

2. In all civil actions and proceedings at law for the recovery of money or personal property when the amount claimed by any party, or the appraised value of the personal property sought to be recovered does not exceed one thousand dollars, and in such actions judgment may be rendered for an amount over one thousand dollars when the excess over one thousand dollars consists of interest or costs accrued after the commencement of the action.

3. In all actions arising out of contract when the amount claimed by the plaintiff, exclusive of costs, does not exceed one thousand dollars, the court shall have jurisdiction to decree reformation or cancellation under the ordinary rules and proceedings in equity.

4. In all actions and proceedings at law to enforce the collection of its own judgments or judgments rendered by justices of the peace of Akron township, Summit county, or by the police court of the city of Akron and in all proceedings for the revivor of such judgments.

5. In all actions and proceedings for the sale of personal property under chattel mortgages, liens or other charges or incumbrances thereon and for the marshalling of all liens thereon, when the amount sought to be recovered does not exceed six hundred dollars.

6. In all actions and proceedings in the nature of creditors' bills in aid of execution to subject the interest of a judgment debtor in personal property to the payment of a judgment enforceable by the court.

7. In all actions and proceedings in the nature of interpleader involving amounts not in excess of six hundred dollars.

8. Authority to hear and determine questions of exemptions, upon execution or attachment, upon the application or motion of any officer of the court or of any party to a cause pending or adjudicated in said court.

9. Authority to distribute and control all property levied upon or seized by any legal process issuing from the court, or the proceeds thereof, which may come into the hands of its officers, and to order the immediate sale of any property of a perishable nature which may come into the hands of an officer of the court upon any process issuing from the court, and the money realized therefrom shall be held and retained by the officer until distributed by order of court as herein provided.

10. Within the jurisdiction of the court, authority to make any person a defendant who has or claims an interest in the controversy adverse to the plaintiff, or who is a necessary party to a complete determination or settlement of a question involved therein.

11. Within the jurisdiction of the court, authority to determine any controversy between parties before it, when it can be done without prejudice to the rights of others, or by saving their rights. When such determination cannot be had without the presence of other parties, the court may order them to be brought in or may dismiss the action without prejudice.

Sec. 1579-507.

Power to take acknowledgments and administer oaths.

SECTION 11. The judges shall take acknowledgments of deeds and other instruments, administer oaths, and exercise any other power that now is or that may hereafter be conferred upon justices of the peace.

Sec. 1579-508.

Further jurisdiction in Akron and Summit county.

SECTION 12. The court shall have jurisdiction of all violations of ordinances of the city of Akron, of all misdemeanors committed within the limits of Summit county, and of bastardy complaints arising within Summit county, hear and finally determine the same and impose the prescribed penalty, and in felonies committed within said county the court shall have power to hear the case and to discharge, recognize or commit, and if upon such hearing the court is of the opinion that the offense committed is only a misdemeanor, a plea of guilty may be received and judgment and sentence pronounced.

Sec. 1579-509. SECTION 13. In all causes, the court shall have jurisdiction in the following ancillary and supplemental proceedings, to-wit: Attachment of person or property, arrest before or after judgment, aid of execution and trial of the right of property. The plaintiff shall have an order of attachment, as provided in chapter 2, title II, of part third of the General Code, against the property of the defendant in any civil action of which the court has jurisdiction.

Ancillary and supplemental proceedings.

Sec. 1579-510. SECTION 14. The court shall have jurisdiction within the limits of Summit county:

Jurisdiction within Summit county.

1. To compel the attendance of witnesses in any pending action or proceeding.

2. To issue executions on its own judgments against personal property.

3. In all actions and proceedings to enforce the collection of its own judgments.

4. In all actions and proceedings where one or more defendants reside or are served with summons in the city of Akron.

Sec. 1579-511. SECTION 15. In any action or proceeding of which the court has jurisdiction of the subject matter, when the defendant or one of the defendants resides or is served with summons in the city of Akron, the court shall have jurisdiction to issue summons, writs and process to the sheriff of any county of the state for service by him upon one or more of the defendants.

When process may issue to any sheriff in state.

Sec. 1579-512. SECTION 16. All laws conferring power and jurisdiction upon the court of common pleas, police courts or justices of the peace to hear and determine certain causes and proceedings, prescribing the force and effect of their judgment or orders, and authorizing or directing the execution or enforcement thereof, shall be held to extend to the municipal court, unless inconsistent with the jurisdiction conferred upon said court by this act or clearly inapplicable.

Laws governing other courts applicable.

Sec. 1579-513. SECTION 17. No justice of the peace in any township in Summit county and no mayor of any village in Summit county, in any action or proceeding, whether civil or criminal, in which any warrant, order of arrest, summons, order of attachment or garnishment, or other process, except subpoenas for witnesses, shall have been served upon a resident of the city of Akron or a corporation having its principal office in said city shall have jurisdiction of said resident or corporation unless such service is made by personal service within the township or village in which said proceeding may have been instituted, or, in a criminal matter, unless the offense charged in the warrant or order of arrest is alleged to have been committed within said township or village.

Limitation of jurisdiction of justices and mayors in Summit county.

Sec. 1579-514. SECTION 18. When the amount claimed by the plaintiff exceeds the sum for which the court is authorized to render judgment, he may remit the excess and judgment may be rendered for the residue. A defendant having a counter-claim or set-off which is in excess of such sum, may

When amount exceeds sum court authorized to render judgment for.

assert the same and the court shall have jurisdiction to hear and determine such counter-claim or set-off and render judgment thereon to the amount of six hundred dollars, but such defendant shall not be thereby precluded from setting up the residue of his claim in a separate action. And such defendant may, at his option, withhold setting up such counter-claim or set-off and may make the same the subject of a separate action in a court of competent jurisdiction.

Sec. 1579-515.
When proceedings certified to common pleas.

SECTION 19. Whenever the appraised value of property sought to be recovered in any action in the municipal court exceeds six hundred dollars, the court; or a judge thereof, shall forthwith certify the proceedings in the case to the court of common pleas of Summit county and the clerk of the municipal court shall forthwith file the original papers and pleadings, together with a certified transcript of the docket and journal entries in the case, with the clerk of the court of the common pleas. The bailiff shall forthwith turn over the property in his possession to the sheriff of Summit county, to be by him held as in like cases originating in the court of common pleas. The case shall then proceed as if it had been commenced in the court of common pleas.

Sec. 1579-516.
Commencement of civil actions; summons, etc.

SECTION 20. Civil actions and proceedings in the municipal court shall be commenced by filing a statement of claim, upon which summons or writ shall be issued by the clerk. The form of summons or writ shall be the same as in the court of common pleas, except as hereinafter otherwise provided. In attachment and garnishment proceedings, a true copy of the affidavit shall be served with the summons and order of attachment or garnishment.

1. All writs and process in the municipal court shall be served and returned by the bailiff or a deputy bailiff, or served by publication in the manner which is now or may hereafter be provided by law for service and return of writs and process in the court of common pleas, unless the judges of the municipal court shall provide, by rule of court, for the service of process by mail, in which case service by mail may be made in accordance with such rule of court. In all cases in which service by publication is authorized by law, publication for three consecutive weeks shall be sufficient.

2. The return day of the summons or writ shall be fixed by a rule of court not later than seven days after issuance and the summons or writ shall be served at least three days before the time of appearance, except that in cases in forcible entry and detention or the forcible detention only of real property, the return day shall be as provided by law in such actions before justices of the peace.

3. In all civil cases the plaintiff shall file a statement of claim and the defendant shall file a like statement of any defense, set-off or counter-claim he may have. Such statement of defense, set-off or counter-claim shall be filed within such time as may be required by rule of court, which shall be not less than five days after the return day of the sum-

mons. The statement of the parties shall set forth in plain and direct language the facts constituting the cause of action, set-off, counter-claim or defense.

4. To expedite the business of the court and promote the ends of justice, the judges from time to time shall adopt, publish and revise rules relating to matters of practice and procedure not otherwise provided for in this act.

Sec. 1579-517. SECTION 21. In all criminal cases and proceedings the practice and procedure and mode of bringing and conducting prosecutions for offenses and the power of the court in relation thereto shall be the same as those which are now or may hereafter be conferred upon police courts. *Practice and procedure.*

Sec. 1579-518. SECTION 22. An action shall be deemed to be commenced, within the meaning of this act, as to each defendant, at the date of the summons which is served on him, or on a co-defendant who is a joint contractor or otherwise united in interest with him. When service by publication is proper, the action shall be deemed to be commenced at the date of the first publication. When the summons has been so served or the publication has been so made, the action shall be pending so as to charge third persons with notice of the pendency and while pending no interest can be acquired by third persons in the subject of the action as against the plaintiff's right. *When action deemed commenced.*

Sec. 1579-519. SECTION 23. All civil cases shall be tried to the court unless a trial by jury is demanded by a party or the judge, in the interest of justice, on his own motion, orders a trial by jury. The time for making a demand for trial by jury may be fixed and limited by rule of court. In all civil actions when a jury is demanded, the jury shall be composed of electors of the city of Akron, and the number thereof shall be six, unless a party demand a jury of twelve, in which case the number thereof shall be twelve, provided, that by agreement of the parties the jury may be composed of a less number than either of the numbers aforesaid. In all criminal actions in which the accused is entitled to a trial by jury, trial shall be by jury, unless a jury is waived in writing by the accused and the jury shall be composed of twelve men having the qualifications of electors of Summit county. In civil actions the jury shall render a verdict upon the concurrence of three-fourths or more of their number. No venire or summons for jurors shall be issued by the clerk, except when ordered and directed by the court, or a judge thereof, nor until the party in a civil action demanding a jury shall deposit the sum of $5.00 with the clerk of the court on account of the fees of said jury. *When cases shall be tried by jury.*

Sec. 1579-520. SECTION 24. Jurors shall be chosen and summoned in accordance with a rule of court, shall be impaneled in the same manner and challenged for the same causes as jurors in the court of common pleas, and shall receive as fees for their services, the sum of one dollar and fifty cents each per day, to be paid out of the treasury of the city of Akron, which fees in civil actions shall be taxed as costs. *Summoning and impaneling jury.*

Sec. 1579-521.
Setting aside verdict; new trial.

SECTION 25. In all cases the municipal court shall have the same authority to set aside a verdict or a judgment and grant a new trial as is now or may hereafter be conferred on the court of common pleas.

Sec. 1579-522.
Judgment a lien upon real property.

SECTION 26. A judgment of the municipal court shall be a lien upon real property when the party in whose favor a judgment is rendered by the court files a transcript of such judgment in the office of the clerk of the court of common pleas, in the same manner and under the same conditions as are now or may hereafter be provided for the filing of transcripts of judgments rendered by justices of the peace; and all provisions of law relative to transcripts of judgments rendered by justices of the peace and the enforcement of such judgments and the liens thereof shall apply to transcripts of judgments and liens of judgments rendered by the municipal court.

Sec. 1579-523.
Proof of records.

SECTION 27. The records of the court may be proved by the production of the original records or by a transcript thereof certified by the clerk of the court under its seal, which shall be received as prima facie evidence in any court of this state.

Sec. 1579-524.
Laws governing court of common pleas apply.

SECTION 28. The laws governing the court of common pleas as to security for costs, motions for new trials, vacation and modification of judgments, the issuing of executions against personal property, orders for stay of execution, and the taking of depositions and evidence shall apply to the municipal court.

Sec. 1579-525.
When stay of execution allowed.

SECTION 29. A person against whom a judgment has been rendered may stay execution thereon by entering into a bond to the adverse party, within ten days after the rendition of such judgment, with at least one good and sufficient surety, either a freeholder owning real property situated in the city of Akron, or a corporation authorized to execute surety bonds in this state, to be approved by the clerk of the court, and conditioned for the payment of the amount of such judgment, with interest and costs. Such bond shall be entered on the docket by the clerk of the court and shall be signed by such surety or sureties. The stay of execution hereby authorized shall be as follows: on a judgment of fifty dollars or under, for thirty days; on a judgment exceeding fifty dollars, for ninety days.

Sec. 1579-526.
Judgments in which stay not allowed.

SECTION 30. Stay of execution on the following judgments shall not be allowed:

1. Judgments against sureties or bail for the stay of execution.

2. Judgments rendered in favor of sureties or bail on judicial bonds who have paid money on account of their principal.

3. Judgments rendered against sureties or bail on bonds given in any actions or proceedings in any court.

4. Judgments rendered in favor of any person for wages due for manual labor by him performed.

Sec. 1579-527.

SECTION 31. Proceedings in error may be prosecuted to the court of common pleas of Summit county from a judgment or final order of the municipal court in the same manner and under the same conditions, including proceedings for stay of execution, as provided by law for proceedings in error from the court of common pleas to the court of appeals, except as otherwise provided herein. In such case the clerk and the bailiff of the municipal court shall turn over any moneys or property held by either of them in the action to the clerk and the sheriff respectively of Summit County, to be by them held as in like cases originating in the court of common pleas. *Proceedings in error.*

Sec. 1579-528.

SECTION 32. The bill of exceptions shall be filed with the clerk of the municipal court within fifteen days after the rendition of the judgment or the making of the order complained of. On the filing of such bill of exceptions, the clerk forthwith shall notify the adverse party or his attorney of its filing. Within five days after such notice, any adverse party may file in the cause any objection or amendment he proposes to such bill for its correction. On the expiration of the time fixed for the filing of objections or amendments by the adverse party, or within five days thereafter, or immediately on the filing of the bill, with the consent of the adverse party to such transmission indorsed thereon, the clerk shall transmit it, together with all objections and amendments filed thereto, to the trial judge or judges. The trial judge or judges, on receipt of the bill, shall indorse the date it was received, and within five days thereafter correct it, if necessary, allow and sign it immediately transmit or cause it to be transmitted to the office of the clerk of the court from whom it was received. But if, when such bill is ready for transmission, the trial judge or judges are absent from the City of Akron, the bill, with all objections and amendments, shall be kept by such clerk until the return of the judge or judges, to whom such documents at once must be sent, and who must act thereon as hereinbefore required within five days from the receipt thereof, and thereupon immediately send such documents to the clerk's office . *Bill of exceptions, when filed; notice to adverse party.*

Sec. 1579-529.

SECTION 33. The petition in error shall be filed in the court of common pleas within thirty days after the rendition of the judgment or the making of the order complained of.

Sec. 1579-530.

SECTION 34. In all cases not otherwise specially provided by law, either party may appeal from the final judgment of the municipal court to the court of common pleas of Summit county. Appeals in the following cases shall not be allowed:

1. On judgments rendered on confession of the party or parties.

2. In actions wherein neither party claims in his statement of claim a sum exceeding three hundred dollars.

3. In all actions for forcible entry and detention or the forcible detention only of real property.

4. In actions or proceedings for trial of the right of property levied upon by execution or attached.

5. Upon exemptions determined or fixed by the trial judge or judges.

Sec. 1579-531.

SECTION 35. If any party appealing from a judgment in his favor shall not recover a greater amount than the amount for which such judgment was rendered, besides costs and accrued interest, he shall pay the costs of such appeal.

Sec. 1579-532.

SECTION 36. The party appealing must, within ten days after the rendition of the judgment, enter into a bond to the adverse party with at least one good and sufficient surety, either a freeholder owning real property situated in the city of Akron or a corporation authorized to execute surety bonds in this state, to be approved by the clerk of the court, in a sum not less than fifty dollars in any case nor less than double the amount of the judgment and costs, conditioned that the appellant will prosecute his appeal to effect without unnecessary delay and that if on appeal judgment shall be rendered against him, he will satisfy the judgment and costs.

Sec. 1579-533.

SECTION 37. When a surety in an appeal bond is insufficient or has removed from the state, or the appeal bond is insufficient, in form or amount, on motion, the court of common pleas may order its change or require that a new bond be given, with surety to be approved by the said court or its clerk. If such order is complied with, the cause shall be heard and determined as though the order had not been made, but otherwise the appeal shall be dismissed.

Sec. 1579-534.

Transcript of proceedings; bond.

SECTION 38. The clerk of the municipal court shall make and certify a transcript of the proceedings, including a transcript of the appeal bond, and on demand, after being paid the legal fee therefor, shall deliver the same to the appellant or his agent, who shall deliver the same to the clerk of the court of common pleas of Summit county on or before the thirtieth day from the rendition of the judgment appealed from. The clerk of the municipal court shall also deliver or transmit the statement or statements of claim or claims, the depositions, evidence and all other original papers, if any, used on the trial in the municipal court, to such clerk on or before the thirtieth day from the judgment, and all other proceedings of the municipal court in that case shall cease and be stayed from the time of entering into the appeal bond. In such case the clerk and the bailiff of the municipal court shall turn over any moneys or property held by them in the action to the clerk or sheriff, respectively, of Summit county, to be by them held as in like cases originating in the court of common pleas. If for any reason the cause is not heard and determined by the appellate court, or if the appeal is dismissed by the appellate court or judgment is rendered against the appellant, the surety on the appeal bond shall be liable to the appellee for the whole amount of the debt, costs and damages recovered against the appellant not to exceed the amount of the bond.

Sec. 1579-535.

SECTION 39. There shall be a clerk of the municipal court, who shall be nominated and elected for a term of four years in the manner which is now or may hereafter be provided for the nomination and election of municipal officers of the city of Akron. The first election of clerk shall be held at the regular municipal election in the year one thousand nine hundred and nineteen, and every four years thereafter a successor shall be elected for a like term. The clerk shall receive a salary of two thousand dollars per annum, payable in monthly installments, five hundred dollars of which shall be paid out of the treasury of Summit county and one thousand five hundred dollars of which shall be paid out of the treasury of the city of Akron. The term of office of the clerk shall commence on the first day of January next after his election and shall continue until his successor is elected and qualified. The clerk shall appoint such deputy clerk as the judges shall approve, each of whom shall receive such compensation as may be fixed by the court, not exceeding fifteen hundred dollars per annum, payable in monthly installments out of the treasury of the city of Akron, and they shall have such powers and perform such duties as are herein imposed upon the clerk except the power of appointment.

Election of clerk; term.

Sec. 1579-536.

SECTION 40. The clerk shall have power to administer oaths and take affidavits; and acknowledgments to issue executions upon judgments rendered in the municipal court, including judgments for unpaid costs; to issue and sign all writs, process and papers issuing out of the court and to affix the seal of the court thereto; and to approve all bonds and recognizances required by law or fixed by the court or any judge thereof, except as otherwise provided herein. He shall make, file, and safely keep all journals, records, books and papers belonging or appertaining to the court, including records of its proceedings and shall perform all other duties which the court may require. He shall pay over to the proper parties all moneys received by him as clerk, and shall receive and collect all costs, fees, fines and penalties and, shall pay the same monthly into the treasury of the city of Akron and take a receipt therefor, except as otherwise provided by law, and except that the provisions of section 3056 of the General Code respecting payment to the trustees of law library associations of fines and penalties assessed and collected by police courts for offenses and misdemeanors prosecuted in the name of the state shall be applicable to all fines and penalties assessed and collected by the municipal court in like cases, but money deposited as security for cost shall be retained by him pending litigation. He shall keep a book showing all his receipts and disbursements, which shall be open for public inspection at

Powers and duties of clerk.

all times. He shall, on and after the first day of January 1920, supersede and succeed to, and shall have all the powers and perform all the duties of, the clerk of the police court of the city of Akron and of the clerk of the justices' courts of Akron township, Summit county.

Sec. 1579-537.

Record of costs and moneys; unclaimed costs.

SECTION 41. All money deposited as security for costs and all other moneys other than costs paid into the court shall be noted on the record of the cause in which they are paid and shall be deposited by the clerk daily in such bank or banks in the city of Akron as shall be designated by the judges and shall be paid out and distributed according to law as ordered by the judges. On the first Monday of each January the clerk shall make out a list of the titles of all causes in the court which were finally determined during the preceding year in which there remains unclaimed in the possession of the clerk any funds or any part of a deposit as security for costs not consumed by the costs in the case. The clerk shall give notice of the same to the parties entitled to such moneys or to their attorneys of record. All such money remaining unclaimed on the first day of April of each year shall be paid by the clerk into the city treasury, provided, however, that any part of such money shall be paid by the treasurer of the city of Akron or his successor to the person having the right thereto upon proper certificate of the clerk of the court.

Sec. 1579-538.

Bond of clerk; vacancy.

SECTION 42. Before entering upon the duties of his office, the clerk shall give a bond to the city of Akron in the sum of five thousand dollars, with surety to the approval of the judges, conditioned for the faithful performance of his duties as such clerk. Said bond shall be given for the benefit of the city of Akron and for the benefit of any person who may suffer loss by reason of a default in any of the conditions of said bond. A vacancy in the office of clerk shall be filled by the judges by appointment, until his successor is elected and qualified.

Sec. 1579-539.

Bond of deputy clerk.

SECTION 43. Before entering upon the duties of their respective offices each deputy clerk shall give a bond to the city of Akron in the sum of two thousand five hundred dollars, to be approved by the same authority and conditioned for the same purposes and benefits as required by this act with respect to the bond of the clerk.

Sec. 1579-540.

Appointment of bailiff and deputies; salary; bond.

SECTION 44. The judges shall appoint a bailiff and not to exceed two deputy bailiffs, unless a larger number of deputy bailiffs shall be authorized by the council of the city of Akron. Such bailiff and deputy bailiffs shall perform for the municipal court services similar to those usually performed by the sheriff and his deputies for the court of common pleas and by constables for justices of the peace, with all the powers of such officers, and shall perform such other duties as may be required by rule of court. The salary of the bailiff and deputy bailiffs shall be fixed by the judges, not to exceed one thousand five hundred dollars per annum for the bailiff and one thousand two hundred dollars for each deputy bailiff, payable in monthly installments out of the treasury of the city of Akron. Before entering upon the duties of their offices, the bailiff and deputy bailiffs shall each give bond to the city of Akron, the bailiff in the sum of three thousand dollars and the deputy bailiffs each in the sum of two thousand dollars, with surety to the approval of the judges, conditioned for the faithful performance of their duties as such bailiff and as such deputy bailiffs, respectively. Each of said bonds shall be given for the benefit of the city of Akron and of any person who shall suffer loss by reason of a default in any of the conditions of said bond.

Sec. 1579-541.   SECTION 45. The bailiff and each deputy bailiff shall receive from the treasury of the city of Akron, in addition to his salary, his actual expenses in serving process of the court, not to exceed the sum of fifty dollars per month, payable upon the order of the judges. *Expenses of bailiffs.*

Sec. 1579-542.   SECTION 46. All deputy clerks, the bailiff and all deputy bailiffs shall hold their offices during the pleasure of the appointing power. *Term of office; of deputy clerk and bailiffs.*

Sec. 1579-543.   SECTION 47. Every police officer of the city of Akron shall be ex-officio a deputy bailiff of the municipal court, and the chief of police shall assign one or more such police officers from time to time to perform such duties in respect to cases within the jurisdiction of said court as may be required of them by said court or the clerk thereof. *Ex-officio deputy bailiffs.*

Sec. 1579-544.   SECTION 48. The director of law of the city of Akron shall be the prosecuting attorney of the court. He may detail such of his assistants as he may deem proper to assist in such work. He shall prosecute all criminal cases brought before the court and perform the same duties, as far as they are applicable thereto, as are required of the prosecuting attorney of the county. In addition to the salaries paid such assistants by the city of Akron they shall receive such further compensation payable out of the treasury of Summit county as the county commissioners of said county may allow. *Director of law shall be prosecuting attorney.*

Sec. 1579-545.   SECTION 49. The court in any criminal case may appoint an interpreter, who shall receive as compensation such sum, not exceeding five dollars per day, as the court may fix, payable out of the treasury of the city of Akron, provided, that when members of the police department are designated as interpreters they shall receive no compensation for such services. *Interpreter; compensation.*

Sec. 1579-546.   SECTION 50. Except as otherwise provided in this act, in all civil actions the fees and costs shall be fixed in the same manner and taxed in the same amounts as is now or as may hereafter be provided for such actions before a justice of the peace. In criminal cases all fees and costs shall be the same as is now or as may hereafter be fixed by law for police courts. The judges may by rule of court provide for all cases not covered by this act a schedule of fees and costs, not in excess of those provided by general *Fees and costs.*

laws. Nothing in this act shall be construed so as to prevent a party in any cause from demanding security for costs in a proper case or to prevent the clerk of the court, or a judge thereof, from requiring a deposit of money or a bond as security for costs in a proper case.

Sec. 1579-547.

Section, etc., held void does not affect others.

SECTION 51. Each section and each subdivision of and section of this act hereby is declared to be independent, and the finding or holding of any section or subdivision of any section thereof to be invalid or void shall not be deemed or held to affect the validity of any other section or subdivision thereof.

Sec. 1579-548.

Supersedes police court and justices of the peace.

SECTION 52. The municipal court shall be the successor of the police court of the city of Akron and of the justices of the peace of Akron township, Summit county. The work of such tribunal shall be merged in and continued by the municipal court and all cases and proceedings pending therein on the 31st day of December, 1919, shall be determined and proceed to judgment in the municipal court as though the same had been commenced therein. All moneys, dockets, papers, files and other property belonging to it in the possession of said tribunals or any of the officers thereof shall be transferred to the clerk of the municipal court to be kept and preserved by him in the same manner as like property, papers and records of said municipal court.

Sec. 1579-549.

Abolishment of certain offices.

SECTION 53. On and after the first day of January, 1920, the offices of judge and clerk of the police court of the city of Akron, and the offices of justice of the peace, constable and clerk of the justices' courts of Akron township, Summit county, shall be and the same are hereby abolished.

Repeals.

SECTION 54. An act entitled "An act to establish a police court in the city of Akron, Summit county, Ohio," passed May 10, 1910 (vol. 101 Ohio Laws, page 357 et. seq.) and all acts amendatory thereof are hereby repealed, but this section shall not be in effect until January 1, 1920, providing further that no election shall be held in November, 1919, under said act entitled "An act to establish a police court in the city of Akron, Summit county, Ohio," passed May 10th, 1910 (vol. 101 Ohio Laws, page 357 et seq.).

The sectional numbers on the margin hereof are designated as provided by law. JOHN G. PRICE, Attorney General.

CLARENCE J. BROWN,
President of the Senate.
CARL R. KIMBALL,
Speaker of the House of Representatives.

Passed April 3, 1919.
Approved June 6, 1919.

JAMES M. COX,
Governor.

Filed in the office of the Secretary of State at Columbus, Ohio, on the 6th day of June, A. D. 1919.

174 G.

[House Bill No. 385.]

AN ACT

To amend sections 12600-3 and 12600-5 of the General Code, relating to the construction of theaters and assembly halls.

Be it enacted by the General Assembly of the State of Ohio:
SECTION 1. That sections 12600-3 and 12600-5 of the General Code be amended to read as follows:

Sec. 12600-3. Class of construction. Theaters. The highest point of the main auditorium foyer of any theater shall not be more than three (3) feet above and in no case below the grade line of the buildings at the main entrance. Construction of theaters.

Theaters seating more than one thousand (1000) persons and theaters with one or more balconies shall be of fireproof construction, except the working part of the stage, viz., the stage floor between the jambs of the proscenium opening from the curtain line to the rear wall of the stage which shall be of mill or fireproof construction.

Theaters seating one thousand (1000) persons or less and containing no balcony shall be of fireproof or composite construction, except the working part of the stage floor which shall be of mill construction or better.

No rooms or apartments for any purpose whatsoever shall be placed over a theater seating five hundred (500) persons or more, unless the entire building is of fireproof construction, except that in buildings of substantial construction, seating over three hundred and not more than five hundred persons and where the theater is on the ground floor of the building, rooms in such building may be rented for other purposes, if the floor, ceiling and side walls of such theater are of fireproof construction and all openings communicating with such theater are covered by double standard fire doors.

For air domes and summer theaters see section 40 (G. C. 12600-41).

For minor theaters see section 42 (G. C. 12600-43).

Assembly halls. Assembly halls accommodating more than one thousand (1000) persons and assembly halls with one or more balconies shall be of fireproof construction. Assembly halls.

Assembly halls accommodating one thousand (1000) persons or less, and containing no balcony shall be of fireproof or composite construction.

In the above-mentioned assembly halls the highest point of the main auditorium foyer shall not be more than eight (8) feet above, and in no case below the grade line at the main entrance to the building.

Assembly halls accommodating less than seven hundred and fifty (750) persons, with no balcony, with the highest point of the main auditorium floor not more than four (4) feet above the grade line at the main entrance, and covering not to exceed six thousand (6000) square feet of area; may be built of frame construction, providing all parts below the first floor line are built of composite construction and the building is erected in the "urban" district thirty (30) feet from any other building or structure, or adjoining lot lines, and at least two hundred (200) feet outside of the city fire limits.

Assembly halls accommodating not more than seven hundred (700) persons and with not more than one balcony, may be placed in the second story of a building of fireproof construction, providing the highest point of the main auditorium floors is not more than twenty (20) feet above the grade line at the main entrance to the building.

Assembly halls accommodating not more than four hundred (400) persons and with no balcony, may be placed in the third story of a building of fireproof construction, providing the highest point of the main auditorium floor is not more than thirty-five (35) feet above the grade line at the main entrance to the building.

Assembly halls accommodating not more than four hundred (400) persons and with no balcony, may be placed in the second story of a building of composite construction, providing the highest point of the main auditorium floor is not more than twenty (20) feet above the grade line at the main entrance to the building.

Exceptions. Where an assembly hall is used as a club, lodge, society, dance or banquet hall, the limitations of floor levels shall be as follows:

An assembly hall or lodge room accommodating not to exceed nine hundred (900) persons, with one balcony, may be placed in the second story of a building of fireproof construction providing the main floor level is not more than twenty (20) feet above the grade line at the main entrance to the building.

Assembly halls with a capacity not exceeding five hundred (500) and used as a club, lodge or society hall, may be placed on any floor of buildings of fire proof construction. Banquet halls or ball rooms, not accommodating more than one thousand (1000), may be placed on any floor of buildings of fireproof construction.

An assembly hall or lodge room accommodating not to exceed six hundred persons, with no balcony, may be placed in the second story of a building of composite construction providing the main floor level is not more than twenty (20) feet above the grade line at the main entrance to the building.

An assembly hall or lodge room accommodating not to exceed three hundred (300) persons, with no balcony, may be placed in the third story of a building of composite construction providing the main floor level is not more than thirty-five feet above the grade line at the main entrance to the building.

An assembly hall or lodge room accommodating not to exceed four hundred (400) persons, with no balcony, may be placed in the second story of a building of frame construction, providing such building is located in a strictly rural district, not nearer than one hundred feet to any other structure, and is provided with the proper exits prescribed by law.

Sec. 12600-5. (Sub-divisions and fire stops.) Theaters and assembly halls built in connection with or as a part of a building used for other purposes than a theater or assembly hall, shall have all of its various parts separated from the other (parts of the) building (s) by standard fire walls, or by fireproof walls, ceilings and floors, and all communicating openings between the theater or assembly hall and the other parts of the building shall be covered by double standard fireproof doors, provided that in theaters seating less than three hundred the fireproof ceiling is not required. Subdivisions and fire stops.

If these openings are used or liable to be used as a means of ingress or egress, a standard self-closing firedoor shall be placed on one side of the wall, and either a standard automatic rolling steel shutter or a standard automatic fire door shall be placed on the other side of the wall. The automatic shutters or doors being kept open during the occupancy of the building.

Exceptions. Where an assembly hall is built in connection with and is a necessary adjunct to a church, school building, lodge building, club house, hospital or hotel, and is designed principally for the use of the occupants of such buildings, the above mentioned standard fire walls or fireproof walls, ceilings and floors will not be necessary, providing the construction of the other parts of the building is of the same, or of a better grade than the assembly hall.

No theater or assembly hall shall have any door or window connecting directly with any sleeping or living room of a tenement or dwelling house, and no theater or assembly hall shall be used for living or sleeping purposes.

All exterior and court walls of buildings coming under this classification (except buildings of frame construction) within thirty (30) feet of any other building, structure or lot line, shall be provided with the following fire stops, viz.: walls shall be standard fire walls; all windows shall be standard fireproof windows with automatic attachment and doors shall be standard hinged fire doors without automatic attachment.

SECTION 2. That said original sections 12600-3 and 12600-5 of the General Code be, and the same are hereby repealed.

CARL R. KIMBALL,
Speaker of the House of Representatives.
CLARENCE J. BROWN,
President of the Senate.

Passed May 9, 1919.
Approved June 5, 1919.

JAMES M. COX,
Governor.

Filed in the office of the Secretary of State at Columbus, Ohio, on the 6th day of June, A. D. 1919.

175 G.

[House Bill No. 282.]

AN ACT

To amend sections 12996, 13007-11 and 13007-12 of the General Code relating to the employment of minors.

Be it enacted by the General Assembly of the State of Ohio:
SECTION 1. That sections 12996, 13007-11 and 13007-12 of the General Code be amended to read as follows:

Sec. 12996. No boy under the age of sixteen and no girl under the age of eighteen years shall be employed, permitted or suffered to work in, about or in connection with any establishment or occupation named in section 12993 (1) for more than six days in any one week, (2) or more than forty-eight hours in any one week, (3) nor more than eight hours in any one day, (4) or before the hour of seven o'clock in the morning or after the hour of six o'clock in the evening. The presence of such child in any establishment during working hours shall be prima facie evidence of its employment therein. No boy under the age of eighteen years shall be employed, permitted or suffered to work in, about or in connection with any establishment or occupation named in section 12993 (1) for more than six days in any one week, (2) nor more than fifty-four hours in any week, (3) nor more than ten hours in any one day, (4) or before the hour of six o'clock in the morning or after the hour of ten o'clock in the evening. No girl under the age of twenty-one years shall be employed, permitted or suffered to work in, about or in connection with any establishment or occupation named in section 12993 (1) for more than six days in any one week, (2) nor more than fifty hours in any week, (3) nor more than nine hours in any one day, except Saturday, when the hours of labor in mercantile establishments may be ten hours, (4) or before the hour of six o'clock in the morning or after the hour of ten o'clock in the evening. In estimating such periods, the time spent at different employments or under different employers shall be considered as a whole and not separately.

Sec. 13007-11. Every employer who fails to secure and keep on file employment certificates for all males employed between fifteen and sixteen years of age, and all females employed between sixteen and eighteen years of age, or to return the same as provided by section 12995 of the General Code, or who fails to keep and post lists of the notice, as provided in section 12998 of the General Code, shall be fined not less than twenty-five dollars nor more than one hundred dollars.

Penalty for failure to file certificates, return same, and post lists.

Sec. 13007-12. Any person, firm or corporation, or any manager, foreman, superintendent or agent of the owner or proprietor of any establishment, who (1) hinders or delays any female visitor or district deputy or any other officer charged with the enforcement of any of the provisions of this act in the performance of his or her duties, or (2) refuses to admit or locks out any such inspector or officer from any place where said inspectors or officers are authorized to inspect, or upon request therefor, refuses to give full and complete information regarding any matter proper to be investigated by any such inspector or officer, shall be punished by a fine of not less than twenty-five dollars nor more than two hundred dollars.

Hindrance or delay to visitor or deputy, etc., unlawful.

SECTION 2. That said original sections 12996, 13007-11 and 13007-12 of the General Code be and the same are hereby repealed.

Repeals.

The sectional numbers in this act are in conformity to the General Code.
JOHN G. PRICE,
Attorney
General.

CARL R. KIMBALL,
Speaker of the House of Representatives.
CLARENCE J. BROWN,
President of the Senate.

Passed May 28, 1919.
Approved June 5, 1919.

JAMES M. COX,
Governor.

Filed in the office of the Secretary of State at Columbus, Ohio, on the 6th day of June, A. D. 1919.

176 G.

534

[House Bill No. 493.]   ]

AN ACT

To amend sections 5652, 5652-1, 5652-4, 5652-7, 5652-8, 5652-9, 5652-10, 5652-11, 5652-12, 5652-13, 5652-14, 5652-15, 5653, 5841 and 5845 and that section 5652-1 of the General Code be supplemented by the enactment of section 5652-1a of the General Code, relating to the regulation of dogs and providing compensation for damages done thereby.

Be it enacted by the General Assembly of the State of Ohio:
SECTION 1. That sections 5652, 5652-1, 5652-4, 5652-7, 5652-8, 5652-9, 5652-10, 5652-11, 5652-12, 5652-13, 5652-14, 5652-15, 5653, 5841 and 5845 of the General Code be amended and that section 5652-1 of the General Code be supplemented by the enactment of section 5652-1a to read as follows:

Application for registration; fee. Sec. 5652. Every person who owns, keeps or harbors a dog more than three months of age, annually, before the first day of January of each year, shall file together with a registration fee of one dollar for each male or spayed female dog, and a registration fee of two dollars for each female dog unspayed, in the office of the county auditor of the county in which such dog is kept or harbored, an application for registration for the following year beginning the first day of January of such year, stating the age, sex, color, character of hair, whether short or long, and breed, if known, of such dog, also the name and address of the owner of such dog. Provided that for the calendar year 1920 and thereafter the registration fee for each female dog unspayed shall be three dollars. And provided further that an affidavit shall be made to the county auditor and filed with application for registration of each spayed female dog stating that said female dog has been effectively spayed.

Registration and fee for kennel. Sec. 5652-1. Every owner of a kennel of dogs bred or kept for sale shall in like manner as in section 5652 provided, make application for the registration of such kennel, and pay therewith to the county auditor a registration fee of $10 for such kennel. Provided, however, the owner of such dog kennel shall, in addition to paying such kennel fees, comply with all of the requirements of section 5652 with respect to every dog more than three months of age belonging to such dog kennel not kept constantly confined in such kennel.

Kennel owner defined. Sec. 5652-1a. A kennel owner is hereby defined as being a person, persons, partnership, firm, company or corporation professionally engaged in the business of breeding dogs for hunting or for sale.

Metal tag; form, character and lettering; duplicates. Sec. 5652-4. In addition to the certificate of registration provided for by section 5652-3, the county auditor shall issue to every person making application for the registration of a dog and paying the required fee therefor, a

metal tag for each dog so registered. The form, character
and lettering of such tag shall be prescribed by the state
bureau of inspection and supervision of public offices. If
any such tags be lost, duplicate shall be furnished by the
county auditor upon proper proof of loss and the payment
of twenty-five cents for each diplicate tag so issued.

Sec. 5652-7. County sheriffs shall patrol their respective counties, seize and impound on sight all dogs more
than three months of age, except dogs kept constantly confined in a registered dog kennel found not wearing valid
registration tags. Whenever any person shall make an affidavit before a justice of the peace, mayor or a judge of
the municipal court that a dog more than three months of
age and not kept constantly confined in a registered dog
kennel is not wearing a valid registration tag and is at
large, or is kept or harbored in his jurisdiction, such justice of the peace, mayor or a judge of the municipal court
shall forthwith order the sheriff of the county to seize and
impound such animal. Thereupon such sheriff shall immediately seize and impound such dog so complained of.
Such sheriff shall forthwith give notice to the owner of
such dog if such owner be known to the sheriff, that such
dog has been impounded, and that the same will be sold
or destroyed if not redeemed within three days. If the
owner of such dog be not known to the sheriff, he shall post
a notice in the county court house describing the dog and
place where seized and advising the unknown owner that
such dog will be sold or destroyed if not redeemed within
three days.

Sec. 5652-8. County commissioners shall provide for
the employment of deputy sheriffs necessary to enforce the
provisions of this act, shall provide nets and other suitable
devices for taking dogs in a humane manner, and except as
hereinafter provided, shall also provide a suitable place for
impounding dogs, and make proper provision for feeding
and caring for the same, and shall also provide humane
devices and methods for destroying dogs. Provided, however, that in any county in which there is a society for the
prevention of cruelty to children and animals, incorporated
and organized as provided by law, and having one or more
agents appointed in pursuance to law, and maintaining an
animal shelter suitable for a dog pound and devices for
humanely destroying dogs, county commissioners shall not
be required to furnish a dog pound, but the sheriff shall
deliver all dogs seized by him to such society for the prevention of cruelty to animals and children at its animal
shelter, there to be dealt with in accordance with law, and
the county commissioners shall provide for the payment of
reasonable compensation to such society for its services so
performed out of the dog and kennel fund.

Provided further, that the county commissioners may
with the approval of the sheriff, designate and appoint any
officer regularly employed by any society organized as pro-

Seizing and im-
pounding dogs.

Duties of com-
missioners rela-
tive to impound-
ing dogs.

vided by sections 10062 to 10067, inclusive, of the General Code, to act as deputy sheriff for the purpose of carrying out the provisions of this act, if such society whose agent is so employed, owns or controls a suitable place for keeping and destroying dogs.

Housing and feeding; disposition of dogs.

Sec. 5652-9. Dogs not wearing valid registration tags which have been seized by the sheriff and impounded as hereinbefore provided, shall be kept, housed and fed for three days, at the expiration of which time, unless previously redeemed by the owners thereof, such animals shall either be sold or be humanely destroyed; provided, however, that no dog so sold shall be discharged from such pound until such animal shall have been registered and furnished with a valid registration tag as hereinbefore provided. A record of all dogs impounded, the disposition of the same, the owner's name and address where known, and a statement of costs assessed against such dogs as hereinafter provided, shall be kept by the pound keeper and a transcript thereof by him furnished to the county treasurer quarterly.

Costs assessed.

Sec. 5652-10. Costs shall be assessed against every dog seized and impounded under the provisions of this act as follows:

Filing affidavit and issuing order to sheriff by justice
   of peace, mayor or judge of municipal court... $0.50
Seizing dog and delivering to pound by sheriff..... $2.00
Serving or posting of notice to owner by sheriff.... $0.25
Housing and feeding dog per day.................. $0.50
Selling or destroying dog........................ $0.50

Such costs shall be a valid claim in favor of the county against the owner, keeper or harbourer of a dog seized and impounded under the provisions of this act and not redeemed or sold as hereinafter provided, and such costs shall be recovered by the county treasurer in a civil action against such owner, keeper or harbourer. Justices of the peace or mayor shall be paid from the dog and kennel fund of the county the sum of fifty cents for filing each affidavit and issuing order thereon to the sheriff.

When dog may be redeemed.

Sec. 5652-11. The owner, keeper or harbourer of any dog not wearing a valid registration tag, seized and impounded under the provisions of this act, at any time prior to the expiration of three days from the time such animal is impounded, may redeem the same by paying to the sheriff all of the costs assessed against such animal and providing such animal with a valid registration tag.

Moneys deposited to credit of dog and kennel fund.

Sec. 5652-12. All funds received by the sheriff or pound keeper in connection with the administration of this act shall be deposited in the county treasury and placed to the credit of the dog and kennel fund.

Uses and purposes of fund.

Sec. 5652-13. The registration fees provided for in this act shall constitute a special fund known as the dog and kennel fund which shall be deposited by the county auditor in the county treasury daily as collected and be used for the purpose of defraying the cost of furnishing all blanks, records, tags, nets and other equipment necessary to carry out and enforce the provisions of the laws relating to the registration of dogs, and for the payment of animal claims as provided in sections 5840 to 5849, both inclusive, of the General Code, and in accordance with the provisions of section 5653 of the General Code. Provided, however, that the county commissioners by resolution shall appropriate sufficient funds out of the dog and kennel fund said funds so appropriated not to exceed 35% of the gross receipts of said dog and kennel fund in any calendar year, for the purpose of defraying the necessary expenses of registering, seizing, impounding and destroying dogs in accordance with the provision of section 5652 and supplemental sections of the General Code.

Sec. 5652-14. Whoever, being the owner, keeper or harborer of a dog more than three months of age or being the owner of a dog kennel fails to file the application for registration required by law, or to pay the legal fee therefor, shall be fined not more than twenty-five dollars, and the costs of prosecution. The fine recovered shall be paid by the justice of the peace, mayor or judge of municipal court to the county auditor, who shall immediately pay the same into the county treasury to the credit of the dog and kennel fund. *Penalty for failure to file application.*

Sec. 5652-15. Whoever owns, keeps or harbours a dog wearing a fictitious, altered or invalid registration tag or a registration tag not issued by the county auditor in connection with the registration of such animal, shall be fined not more than one hundred dollars, and the costs of prosecution. *Wearing fictitious or altered tag unlawful.*

All fines collected under the provisions of section 5652-14 and 5652-15 shall be deposited in the county treasury to the credit of the dog and kennel fund. *Deposit of monies.*

Sec. 5653. After paying all horse, sheep, cattle, swine, mule and goat claims at the December session of the county commissioners, if there remain more than one thousand dollars of the dog and kennel fund arising from the registration of dogs and dog kennels for such year the excess at such December session shall be transferred and disposed of as follows: in a county in which there is a society for the prevention of cruelty to children and animals, incorporated and organized as provided by law, which has one or more agents appointed in pursuance of law, or any other society organized as provided by sections 10062 to 10067, inclusive, of the General Code, that owns or controls a suitable dog kennel or place for the keeping and destroying of dogs which has one or more agents appointed and employed in pursuance of law, all such excess as the county commissioners deem necessary for the uses and purposes of such society by order of the commissioners and upon the warrant *Distribution of surplus fund.*

of the county auditor shall be paid to the treasurer of such society, and any surplus not so transferred shall be transferred to the county board of education fund at the direction of the county commissioners.

Proof required of owner.

Sec. 5841. Before any claim shall be allowed by the trustees to the owner of such horses, sheep, cattle, swine, mules or goats, it shall be proved to the satisfaction of the trustees:

(1) That the loss or injury complained of was not caused in whole or in part by a dog or dogs kept or harbored on the owner's premises, or;

(2) If the dog or dogs causing such loss or injury were kept or harbored on such owner's premises, that such dog or dogs were duly registered and that they were destroyed within forty-eight hours from the time of the discovery of the fact that the injury was so caused.

If the owner of the dog or dogs causing such loss or injury is known, it shall be the duty of the trustees to bring an action to recover such damage from the owner of said dog or dogs, if in their judgment said damage could be collected, unless it is shown to said trustees that said dog or dogs were duly registered and that they were destroyed within forty-eight hours after discovery of the fact that the loss was so caused.

Witness fees and mileage.

Sec. 5845. Witnesses not exceeding four in number, as provided in the next preceding section, shall be allowed fifty cents each and mileage at the rate of five cents per mile, going and returning, in each case. The trustees shall administer an oath or affirmation to each claimant or witness. If the horses, sheep, cattle, swine, mules and goats killed or injured, are in the care of an employe or tenant of the owner thereof, the affidavit provided in section 5840, may be made by such employe or tenant, whose testimony may be received in regard to all matters relating thereto to which said owner would be competent to testify.

Affidavit by tenant or employe, when:

Repeals.

SECTION 2. That original sections 5652, 5652-1, 5652-4, 5652-7, 5652-8, 5652-9, 5652-10, 5652-11, 5652-12, 5652-13, 5652-14, 5652-15, 5653, 5841 and 5845 of the General Code be, and the same are hereby repealed.

CARL R. KIMBALL,
Speaker of the House of Representatives.
CLARENCE J. BROWN,
President of the Senate.

The sectional numbers in this act are in conformity to the General Code. JOHN G. PRICE, Attorney General.

Passed May 9, 1919.
Approved June 5, 1919.

JAMES M. COX,
Governor.

Filed in the office of the Secretary of State at Columbus, Ohio, on the 6th day of June, A. D. 1919.

177 G.

[House Bill No. 469.]

AN ACT

To provide for the development of Americanization work and to encourage the patriotic education and assimilation of foreign born residents.

Be it enacted by the General Assembly of the State of Ohio:

SECTION 1. The joint committee on German propaganda of the senate and house of representatives together with the superintendent of public instruction is hereby continued as an Americanization committee for the purpose of carrying on the Americanization and patriotic education work begun by the council of national defense, and of cooperating with the agencies of the federal government in furthering the study and application of Americanization and patriotic education work in this state.

Americanization and patriotic education work; committee continued.

SECTION 2. Such committee shall terminate its existence January 1, 1921. The members shall receive no compensation but shall be allowed their necessary traveling and other expenses while engaged in the work of the committee.

Termination of committee work; expenses.

SECTION 3. It shall be the duty of the Americanization committee to promote such programs for Americanization and patriotic education work as it may formulate; to cooperate with the federal agencies in the promotion of Americanization and patriotic education; to aid in the correlation of aims and work carried on by local bodies and private individuals and organizations; and to study the plans and methods which are proposed or are in use in this work. It shall be the duty of the committee to employ such methods, subject to existing laws as, in its judgment, will tend to bring into sympathetic and mutually helpful relations the state and its residents of foreign origin, to protect immigrants from exploitation and abuse, to stimulate their acquisition and mastery of the English language, to develop their understanding of American government, institutions, and ideals, and, in general, to promote their assimilation and naturalization. For the above purposes, the committee shall have authority to co-operate with other offices, boards, bureaus, commissions, and departments of the state, and with all public agencies, federal, state and municipal.

Duties of committee.

SECTION 4. The committee shall choose its own chairman, shall employ a director and such assistants as may be necessary, shall define their duties and fix their compensation. The expenses of an employe, when traveling in the interest of the committee, shall be paid from the funds hereinafter appropriated. The compensation of director and other assistants and traveling and other expenses shall be paid out on the warrant of the auditor of state on vouchers signed by the director approved by the chairman of the committee.

Organization of committee.

SECTION 5. There is hereby appropriated out of any moneys in the state treasury to the credit of the general revenue fund and not otherwise appropriated, the sum of $25,000 for the purpose of carrying out the provisions of this act.

CARL R. KIMBALL,
Speaker of the House of Representatives.
CLARENCE J. BROWN,
President of the Senate.

Passed May 9, 1919.
Approved June 5, 1919.

JAMES M. COX,
Governor.

Filed in the office of the Secretary of State at Columbus, Ohio, on the 6th day of June, A. D. 1919.

178 G.

[House Bill No. 362.]

AN ACT

To amend section 1008 of the General Code and to supplement section 1008 as amended herein by the enactment of supplemental section 1008-1 and to repeal section 1008 as enacted in Ohio Laws 103, page 555, and to repeal section 13007-6 of the General Code, relative to prohibiting the employment of females in certain occupations.

Be it enacted by the General Assembly of the State of Ohio:
SECTION 1. That section 1008 of the General Code be amended and supplemental section 1008-1 be enacted to read as follows:

Sec. 1008. Every person, partnership or corporation employing females in any factory, workshop, business office, telephone or telegraph office, restaurant, bakery, millinery or dressmaking establishment, mercantile or other establishments shall provide a suitable seat for the use of each female so employed and shall permit the use of such seats when such female employes are not necessarily engaged in the active duties for which they are employed and when the use thereof will not actually and necessarily interfere with the proper discharge of the. duties of such employes, such seat to be constructed, where practicable, with an automatic back support and so adjusted as to be a fixture but not obstruct employes in the performance of duty, and shall further provide a suitable lunch room, separate and apart from the work room, and in establishments where lunch rooms are provided, female employes shall be entitled to no less than thirty minutes for meal time, provided, that in any establishment aforesaid in which it is found impracticable to provide a suitable lunch room, as aforesaid, female

employes shall be entitled to not less than one hour for
meal time during which hour they shall be permitted to
leave the establishment.

Females over eighteen years of age shall not be em- Work hours for females.
ployed or permitted or suffered to work in or in connection
with any factory, workshop, telephone or telegraph office,
millinery or dressmaking establishment, restaurant or in
the distributing or transmission of messages, or in or on
any interurban or street railway car, or as ticket sellers or
elevator operators or in any mercantile establishment located in any city, more than nine hours in any one day,
except Saturday, when the hours of labor in mercantile
establishments may be ten hours, or more than six days, or
more than fifty hours in any one week, but meal time shall
not be included as a part of the work hours of the week or
day, provided, however, that no restriction as to hours of
labor shall apply to canneries or establishments engaged in
preparing for use perishable goods, during the season they
are engaged in canning their products.

Sec. 1008-1. The employment of females in the follow- Occupations in which employment of female prohibited; penalty.
ing occupations or capacities is hereby prohibited, to-wit:
as crossing watchman, section hand, express driver, mould-
er, bell hop, taxi driver, jitney driver, gas or electric meter
reader, ticket seller except between the hours of six o'clock
a. m. and ten o'clock p. m., as workers in blast furnaces,
smelters, mines, quarries except in the offices thereof, shoe
shining parlors, bowling alleys, pool rooms, bar rooms and
saloons or public drinking places which cater to male customers exclusively and in which substitutes for intoxicating
liquors are sold or advertised for sale, in delivery service
on wagons or automobiles, in operating freight or baggage
elevators, in baggage handling, freight handling and truck-
ing of any kind, or in employments requiring frequent or
repeated lifting of weights over twenty-five pounds. Any
violations of the provisions of this section shall be punished
as provided in section 1011 of the General Code.

SECTION 2. That original sections 1008 and 13007-6 Repeal.
of the General Code be, and the same are hereby repealed.

The sectional numbers in this act are in conformity to the General Code. JOHN G. PRICE, Attorney General.

CARL R. KIMBALL,
Speaker of the House of Representatives.
CLARENCE J. BROWN,
President of the Senate.

Passed May 8, 1919.
Approved June 5, 1919.

JAMES M. COX,
Governor.

Filed in the office of the Secretary of State at Columbus,
Ohio, on the 6th day of June, A. D. 1919.

179 G.

542

[Amended Senate Bill No. 140.]

AN ACT

To amend sections 7645 and 7762 of the General Code, relative to the course of study of elementary schools.

Be it enacted by the General Assembly of the State of Ohio:
SECTION 1. That sections 7645 and 7762 of the General Code be amended to read as follows:

Graded course of study shall be provided.

Sec. 7645. Boards of education are required to prescribe a graded course of study for all schools under their control in the branches named in section 7648, subject to the approval of the superintendent of public instruction. The course of study mentioned in this section shall include American government and citizenship in the seventh and eighth grades.

Branches in which children shall be instructed.

Sec. 7762. All parents, guardians and other persons who have care of children, shall instruct them, or cause them to be instructed in reading, spelling, writing, English grammar, geography, arithmetic, United States history, American government and citizenship.

Repeals.

SECTION 2. That original sections 7645 and 7762 of the General Code be, and the same are hereby repealed.

CLARENCE J. BROWN,
President of the Senate.
CARL R. KIMBALL,
Speaker of the House of Representatives.
Passed May 10, 1919.
Approved June 5, 1919.

The sectional numbers in this act are in conformity to the General Code. JOHN G. PRICE, *Attorney General.*

JAMES M. COX,
Governor.

Filed in the office of the Secretary of State at Columbus, Ohio, on the 6th day of June, A. D. 1919.

180 G.

[Amended Senate Bill No. 112.]

AN ACT

To authorize the erection and maintenance of a memorial building, monument, statue or memorial by the trustees of a township or townships to commemorate the services of the soldiers, sailors and marines thereof, and to repeal sections 3410-1 to 3410-13 inclusive of the General Code.

Be it enacted by the General Assembly of the State of Ohio:

Sec. 3410-1.

Authority to build memorial to soldiers, sailors, etc.; petition.

SECTION 1. Whenever there is presented to the trustees of a township, or townships, a petition signed by not less than fifteen per cent of the electors of such township or townships as shown at the last preceding general election held therein, requesting the submission to the electors of such township or townships of the question of issuing bonds in an amount not exceeding $100,000 for the purpose of purchasing a site, if necessary, and erecting and furnishing a memorial building, or erecting a suitable and appropriate monument, statue or memorial to commemorate the services of the soldiers, sailors and marines of such township or townships and of maintaining same, the trustees shall provide by resolution for the submission of such question to the electors of such township or townships at a special or the next general election.

In case the petitions are filed in two or more townships requesting the submission of such question the total amount of bonds estimated for such purpose shall be divided among such townships in proportion to the tax valuation of such townships as shown by the tax duplicate.

c. 3410-2. SECTION 2. The clerk of such township or townships *Copy of petition filed with deputy state supervisors; submission of question.* shall file a certified copy of such resolution with the board of deputy state supervisors of elections or board of deputy state supervisors and inspectors of elections, as the case may be, of the county not less than thirty days before the election at which the question is to be voted upon and shall give notice of the submission of such question to the electors at said election by publication in a paper of general circulation in the township or townships and published in the county, once a week for three weeks before the election, and if there be no such paper, by posting said notice in five public places in the township or townships for three weeks prior to the election. The form of the ballot for such election shall be as follows:

For the issuance of bonds for the erection of a memorial.

Against the issuance of bonds for the erection of a memorial.

3410-3. SECTION 3. The election officers shall forthwith certify *Result certified to township clerk; bond issue; tax levy.* the result of such election to the clerk of the township or townships and the township trustees shall make a record of such result. If a majority of the votes cast on such question be in favor of the issuance of bonds for such purpose, the township trustees shall thereupon issue the bonds of the township in the amount specified in the petition filed as authorized in section one of this act. Such bonds shall be of the denomination and shall run for such period or periods of time as the trustees shall determine. They shall be executed as are other bonds of the township and shall express on their face the purpose for which they are issued, shall bear interest at a rate not to exceed six per cent. per annum, payable semi-annually, and shall be sold for not less than par and accrued interest. Said bonds shall be offered and sold in the manner provided in sections 1465-58, 2294 and 2295 of the General Code. The township trustees shall at the time such bonds are authorized to be issued, provide for levying and collecting annually by taxation an amount sufficient to pay the interest thereon and to create a sinking

544

fund for their redemption at maturity, and shall levy annually a sufficient tax for such purpose.

Sec. 3410-4.

Proceeds shall be
known as "the
memorial fund;"
application of
fund.

SECTION 4. If such improvement is to be made by a single township the proceeds of such bonds, other than any premium and accrued interest which shall be credited to the sinking fund, shall be placed in the township treasury to the credit of a fund to be known as "the memorial fund." If such bonds are issued by two or more townships to build a joint building, the trustees of each township shall select one of their number and the men so selected shall constitute and be known as the memorial trustees. And such memorial trustees shall have full power to do and perform all acts imposed upon the township trustees with reference to a single township memorial, such powers being fully set out in sections 5, 6, 7, 8, 9, 10, and 11 of this act. And wherever the term trustees or township trustees is used in said section with reference to the powers and duties of such trustees as to the construction and maintenance of such memorial building, monument, statue or memorial, the same shall be construed to mean "memorial trustees" in case of a joint building. Such fund shall be paid out upon the order of the township trustees. Upon the completion of the memorial building, monument, statue or memorial, any unexpended balance shall be transferred and placed to the credit of the sinking fund.

Sec. 3410-5.

Employment of
architects, super-
intendents, etc.

SECTION 5. The township trustees shall have authority to appoint such superintendents, architects, clerks, laborers and other employes as they may deem necessary and to fix their compensation; and any of such persons may be removed by a majority of such trustees at any time.

Sec. 3410-6.

Power to acquire
property.

SECTION 6. The township trustees shall have power to acquire by purchase, appropriation or otherwise, any private or public lands which they might deem necessary for their use, and in case of condemnation, the proceedings shall be governed by the provision of law regulating the appropriation of private property by municipal corporations.

Authorized to re-
ceive donations,
legacies, etc.

Said trustees are hereby authorized and empowered to take and to receive donation, legacies or devises in land or money or other property for the general purpose of aiding the objects and purposes of said memorial building, monument, statue or memorial and the endowment thereof. In all cases, however, no matter how the property may be acquired, the title to the same shall be taken in the name of said trustees and their successors in office forever, and shall be free from taxation by state, county or municipality.

Sec. 3410-7.

Powers and
duties of town-
ship trustees.

SECTION 7. The township trustees shall have power to prepare or cause to be prepared plans and specifications and to make contracts for the construction and erection of a memorial building, monument, statue or memorial, for the purposes herein specified and within the amount authorized. In making such contract, the township trustees shall be governed as follows:

First: Contracts for construction shall be based upon detailed plans, specifications, forms of bids and estimates of cost, to be adopted by the township trustees.

Second: The contracts shall be made in writing upon concurrence of a majority of the township trustees, signed by at least two members thereof and by the contractor, after an advertisement in two newspapers published or of general circulation in the township for a period of thirty days.

Third: No contract shall be let except to the lowest and best bidder who shall give a preliminary and a final bond conditioned respectively, that he will enter into the contract if awarded to him and that he will faithfully perform the work and furnish the material agreed upon.

Fourth: When it becomes necessary in the opinion of the township trustees in the prosecution of said work to make alterations or modifications in any contract, such alterations or modifications shall only be made by order of the township trustees and such order shall be of no effect until the price to be paid for the work or materials under such altered or modified contract has been agreed upon in writing and signed by the contractor and at least two of said township trustees.

Fifth: No contract or alteration or modification thereof shall be valid or binding unless made in the manner herein specified.

Sec. 3410-8. SECTION 8. No member of the board of township trustees or any officer or employe thereof shall be interested in any contract entered into by said board; nor shall any trustee or officer or employe of the board be individually liable to any contractor upon any contract made in pursuance of this act, nor to any person on any claims occasioned by any act or default of a contractor or any one employed by such contractor. *Interest in contract, etc., prohibited.*

Sec. 3410-9. SECTION 9. There shall be provided in such memorial building suitable apartments of sufficient dimensions to commemorate the soldiers, sailors and marines of the township who have lost their lives while in the service of the country, and the names of such soldiers, sailors and marines shall be inscribed on suitable tablets in such building or on the monument, statue or memorial erected. *Tablets in suitable apartments provided.*

Sec. 3410-10. SECTION 10. The township trustees shall provide for the maintenance of such memorial building, monument, statue or memorial and shall always keep them in such shape and condition that they will fulfill the purpose for which they were constructed, and are hereby authorized to levy in any year a sufficient tax to create a fund which is to be expended by said township trustees for the maintenance thereof and the making of any necessary improvements thereto. The township trustees may permit the occupancy and use of the memorial building or any part thereof, upon such terms as they deem proper. *Control and maintenance.*

Sec. 3410-11.

Rules and regulations.

SECTION 11. Under such reasonable rules and regulations as the township trustees may prescribe, such memorial building shall be open and free to and for the use of all organizations and allied organizations of present and former soldiers, sailors and marines as a meeting place.

Repeals.

SECTION 12. That sections 3410-1 to 3410-13 inclusive of the General Code be, and the same are hereby repealed.

The sectional numbers on the margin hereof are designated as provided by law. JOHN G. PRICE, Attorney General.

CLARENCE J. BROWN,
President of the Senate.
CARL R. KIMBALL,
Speaker of the House of Representatives.

Passed May 6, 1919.
Approved June 5, 1919.

JAMES M. COX,
Governor.

Filed in the office of the Secretary of State at Columbus, Ohio, on the 6th day of June, A. D. 1919.

181 G.

[Amended Senate Bill No. 133.]

AN ACT

To promote the efficiency of the Ohio national guard to bring the military laws of the state into conformity with the laws of the United States and to amend section 5242 of the General Code.

Be it enacted by the General Assembly of the State of Ohio:

Sec. 5180-1.

Qualifications of staff officers; term of service.

SECTION 1. That hereafter no appointments shall be made of any staff officers (including pay, inspection, subsistence and medical departments) unless such appointees shall have had previous military experience, and they shall hold their appointments until they shall have reached the age of sixty-four (64) years, unless relieved prior to that time by reason of resignation, disability or for cause to be determined by a court-martial legally convened for that purpose. Vacancies among such officers shall hereafter be filled by appointment from the officers of the national guard of this state.

Sec. 5180-2.

Rules and regulations governing appointments.

SECTION 2. The governor of this state is authorized to issue such regulations governing the appointments of officers in the national guard of this state and such other matters pertaining to the national guard as may be necessary in order to conform to the requirements made by congress for participation in federal appropriations for the national guard.

SECTION 3. That section 5242 of the General Code be amended to read as follows:

Sec. 5242. The maximum amount to be expended by the state for the building or purchase of an armory for a single organization, shall not exceed twenty-five thousand dollars, and twelve thousand dollars additional for each organization or headquarters provided for. The adjutant general may allow a sum not to exceed fifteen hundred dollars for the furnishing and equipping of each armory so built or purchased, and in no city shall more than one building be erected or purchased until provisions have been made for all organizations therein. A sum of not to exceed six hundred dollars shall be allowed each organization to cover armory rent, heat, light, water and janitor service.

Sec. 79-1.

SECTION 4. The adjutant general shall give bond in the sum of thirty thousand dollars to the state of Ohio conditioned upon the faithful performance of his duties; the assistant adjutant general shall give like bond in the sum of ten thousand dollars and the assistant quartermaster general shall give a like bond in the sum of twenty thousand dollars. If surety bond be given the premiums therefor shall be paid out of the Maintenance-Ohio national guard fund. Said bonds shall be filed in the office of the auditor of state. All other bonds given by the various officers of the Ohio national guard shall be filed and recorded in the office of the adjutant general.

Sec. 82-1.

SECTION 5. The adjutant general shall cause an inventory to be made of all unexpendable military property of each organization of the national guard which is purchased from state funds or otherwise belongs to the state and a separate inventory of the property received from the federal government. Said inventories shall be kept on file in the office of the adjutant general and shall be open to public inspection during regular office hours. Additions to or deductions from said inventories shall be made from time to time so that each of said inventories shall at all times set forth a correct list of all property owned by or in possession of each organization of the national guard. Whenever deductions are made from such inventories, the time and manner of the disposition of the property shall be entered.

Sec. 274-1.

SECTION 7. The bureau of inspection and supervision of public offices shall have power to inspect and supervise the accounts and reports and verify the inventories of the Ohio National Guard in the same manner as other state officers and to that end the examiners appointed for that purpose shall have all of the powers vested in state examiners as otherwise provided by law. The reports made of such examination shall be filed in the same manner as are reports relative to the expenditure of public money from the state treasury, or to the disposition of property belonging to the state, as provided in section 286 of the General Code.

Nothing in this section shall require the expenses of

Maximum expenditure for armory and each organization or headquarters.

Bond of adjutant general and assistant.

Inventory of state military property kept on file; additions and deductions.

Inspection of accounts and verification of inventories; report.

such inspections or supervisions to be charged to or paid out of the funds of the national guard or units thereof.

Sec. 82-8.

Notice when officer unable to account for money or property; suit to recover.

SECTION 8. Whenever it is ascertained by the adjutant general or the auditor of state that any officer of the national guard is unable to properly account for the property or moneys in his possession he shall give immediate notice thereof to the attorney general for action against such officers and his bondsmen, and the attorney general is hereby authorized and required to bring such action.

SECTION 9. That said original section 5242 of the General Code be, and the same is hereby repealed.

The sectional numbers on the margin hereof are designated as provided by law. JOHN G. PRICE, *Attorney General.*

CLARENCE J. BROWN,
President of the Senate.
CARL R. KIMBALL,
Speaker of the House of Representatives.
Passed April 10, 1919.
Approved June 5, 1919.

JAMES M. COX,
Governor.

Filed in the office of the Secretary of State at Columbus, Ohio, on the 6th day of June, A. D. 1919.

182 G.

[House Bill No. 279.]

AN ACT

To provide for the reimbursement of contractors engaged in the construction of public roads, highways, streets, inter-county highways and main market roads, on account of losses due to government action, and to make an appropriation therefor.

Be it enacted by the General Assembly of the State of Ohio:

Sec. 1208-1.

Reimbursement of contractors for loss on contracts entered into prior to May 25, 1918.

SECTION 1. The claims of road contractors having contracts for the construction, improvement, maintenance or repair of inter-county highways and main market roads let by the state highway department before the twenty-fifth day of May, nineteen hundred and eighteen, for reimbursement to the extent of added freight charges paid by them under and by virtue of the terms of general order number twenty-eight, issued by the United States railroad administration on the twenty-fifth day of May, nineteen hundred and eighteen, or under and by virtue of the terms of any other order issued or promulgated by said United State railroad administration or any other competent public authority on or after said twenty-fifth day of May, nineteen hundred and eighteen, upon materials transported to and used in such work on contracts so let before such twenty-fifth day of May, nineteen hundred and eighteen, are hereby declared to be valid and subsisting obligations of the state of Ohio.

Sec. 1208-2. SECTION 2. For the payment of such obligations there *Appropriation.* is hereby appropriated from the state highway improvement fund the sum of one hundred and eighty thousand dollars.

Sec. 1208-3. SECTION 3. The moneys hereby appropriated shall be *Purposes for which appropriation available.* available for and shall be used to reimburse only those persons, firms and corporations, who on the said twenty-fifth day of May, nineteen hundred and eighteen, had uncompleted contracts with the state of Ohio for the construction, improvement, maintenance or repair of a section or portion of an inter-county highway or main market road within the state, and such contractors shall be reimbursed from the moneys hereby appropriated only to the extent of any increased or extra freight charges paid by them under and by virtue of the terms of said general order number twenty-eight, issued by the United States railroad administration on the twenty-fifth day of May, nineteen hundred and eighteen, or under and by virtue of the terms of any other order issued or promulgated by said United States railroad administration or any other competent public authority on or after said twenty-fifth day of May, nineteen hundred and eighteen. Where anything required to be done or furnished in connection with any such contract has been or shall be performed or furnished by a person, firm or corporation other than the principal contractor, and under and by virtue of a contract entered into by such other person, firm or corporation with the principal contractor prior to the twenty-fifth day of May, nineteen hundred and eighteen, such other person, firm or corporation shall be held to be a contractor within the terms of this act and proof of claim shall be made by and payment made directly to him or it, provided he or it be required by the terms of such contract to pay in the performance thereof extra or added freight charges under said general order number twenty-eight or any order amendatory thereof or supplementary thereto.

The moneys hereby appropriated shall be available for the payment of such excess freight charges only in the event such materials have been or shall be transported to and delivered upon the site of the improvement upon which they are to be used prior to the first day of November, nineteen hundred and nineteen. No part of the moneys hereby appropriated shall be paid to any contractor who has been or who shall be removed from his control of the work covered by his contract under the provisions of section 1209 of the General Code. The term "freight charges" as used herein shall not be held to include demurrage charges.

Sec. 1208-4. SECTION 4. All claims presented for allowance under *Claims filed with state highway commissioner; examination of claims.* the provisions of this act shall be filed with the state highway commissioner on or before the first day of December, nineteen hundred and nineteen. The state highway commissioner shall immediately after such date carefully examine all such claims and the proof offered in support thereof and shall allow thereon such amount as is found

by him to be due under the terms of this act. The amount
to be allowed to each contractor shall be determined by
computing the freight charges which such contractor would
have been required to pay on such materials at the rate in
force and effect on said twenty-fifth day of May, nineteen
hundred and eighteen, and subtracting the amount of such
freight charges so computed from the amount of freight
charges actually paid on such materials by such contractor
under and by virtue of the terms of said general order
number twenty-eight or under and by virtue of the terms
of any other order promulgated by said United States railroad administration or any other lawful authority on or
after the twenty-fifth day of May, nineteen hundred and
eighteen, and the balance or remainder shall constitute the
amount to be allowed. Upon completing his examination

Transmittal of
amounts found
due to sundry
claims board;
payment.
of the claims filed, the state highway commissioner shall
transmit the same, together with his report as to the
amounts found due thereon, to the sundry claims board,
which board shall thereupon examine such claims and the
report of the state highway commissioner in reference thereto and which board may require additional proof as to any
of such claims and shall allow such amounts thereon as are
found to be due. Payment of the amounts so found to be
due shall be made by the warrants of the auditor of state
issued upon the allowance of the sundry claims board, the
same to be paid from the moneys hereby appropriated.
Should the amounts found to be due exceed the amount
hereby appropriated and should no additional allowance
be made according to law, a pro rata distribution of the
amount hereby appropriated shall be made.

Sec. 1208-5.

Subdivisions
authorized to re-
imburse con-
tractor on con-
tract entered into
prior to May 25,
1918.
SECTION 5. The board of county commissioners of
any county, the board of township trustees of any township, or the council of any municipal corporation, or other
corresponding board or officer in the case of a charter city
or village not having a council, is hereby authorized and
empowered to allow and pay to any contractor who has performed or who is engaged in performing any contract entered into with such county, township or municipal corporation or the proper authorities thereof, for the construction, reconstruction, improvement, maintenance or repair of any public road, highway, street, bridge or section
or portion thereof, the increased freight charges paid by
such contractor on materials transported over a railroad
or railroads by him and used in the performance of such
contract, where such materials were transported on and
after the twenty-fifth day of June, nineteen hundred and
eighteen, and such increased freight charges were paid
under and by virtue of the terms of a certain order issued
by the United States railroad administration on the twenty-
fifth day of May, nineteen hundred and eighteen, and
known as general order number twenty-eight, or under and
by virtue of any other order promulgated by said United
States railroad administration or any other lawful author-

ity on or after the twenty-fifth day of May, nineteen hundred and 'eighteen. This authorization shall be effective and such payment shall be made to such contractor only in the event that his said contract was entered into with said county, township or municipal corporation or the proper authorities thereof prior to said twenty-fifth day of May, nineteen hundred and eighteen. The intent and purpose of this section is to fully authorize and empower such county, township or municipal authorities to fully reimburse such contractor for such increased freight charges so paid by him and the amount so authorized to be paid to such contractor shall be determined by computing the freight charges which such contractor would have been required to pay on such materials at the rate in force and effect on said twenty-fifth day of May, nineteen hundred and eighteen, and subtracting the amount of such freight charges so computed from the amount of freight charges actually paid on such materials by such contractor under and by virtue of the terms of said general order number twenty-eight or under and by virtue of the terms of any other order promulgated by said United States railroad administration or any other lawful authority on or after the twenty-fifth day of May, nineteen hundred and eighteen. Where anything required to be done or furnished in connection with any such contract has been or shall be performed or furnished by a person, firm or corporation other than the principal contractor, and under and by virtue of a contract entered into by such other person, firm or corporation with the principal contractor prior to the twenty-fifth day of May, nineteen hundred and eighteen, such other person, firm or corporation shall be held to be a contractor within the terms of this act and proof of claim shall be made by and payment made directly to him or it, provided he or it be required by the terms of such contract to pay in the performance thereof extra or added freight charges under said general order number twenty-eight or any order amendatory thereof or supplementary thereto. Such payments may be made by such county, township or municipal corporation from time to time during the performance of such contract by said contractor, or at the time of the completion of such contract, or at any time thereafter. Payments shall be made from any fund available for the construction, improvement, maintenance or repair of roads, highways, streets or bridges created by general taxation and against which no contractual obligations exist. All bills presented for allowance under the provisions of this section shall be carefully examined before **Examination of claims.** allowance for the purpose of determining that the materials upon which increased freight charges are claimed were actually transported for and employed in the construction of the improvement covered by the contract in question and that the amounts of such increased freight charges are correct.

CARL R. KIMBALL,
Speaker of the House of Representatives.
CLARENCE J. BROWN,
President of the Senate.

Passed May 10, 1919.
Approved June 5, 1919.

JAMES M. COX,
Governor.

Filed in the office of the Secretary of State at Columbus, Ohio, on the 6th day of June, A. D. 1919.

183 G.

[Amended Senate Bill No. 153.]

AN ACT

To amend Chapter 3, Division II, Title V of Part First of the General Code, relating to the institution for the feeble-minded and the commitment and care of feeble-minded persons, and to amend section 1815-12 of the General Code.

Be it enacted by the General Assembly of the State of Ohio:

SECTION 1. That chapter 3, division II, title V of part first of the General Code be entitled institutions for the feeble-minded, and be amended to read as herein provided:

Government and control of institutions for feeble-minded under Ohio board of administration.

Sec. 1891. The Ohio board of administration, hereinafter designated as the board of administration or the board, shall manage and govern the institutions for the feeble-minded and shall have full power and authority hereafter to establish, manage, govern and maintain additional institutions for the feeble-minded whenever the necessary funds therefor have been appropriated by the general assembly and are available for such purpose. The board of administration shall have the power and authority, also, to provide for the custody, supervision, control, care, maintenance and training of feeble-minded persons committed to its custody and care, and to pay, in the manner provided by law, the expense thereof out of any funds available therefor.

Object and purpose of institutions; education and training.

Sec. 1892. The object of the institutions for the feeble-minded shall be to receive, detain, care for and maintain feeble-minded persons committed to the custody and care of the board of administration and to train and educate such of them received as are capable of being trained and educated, so as to render them more comfortable, happy and less burdensome to society. The inmates of the institution shall be furnished such agricultural and mechanical education as they are capable of receiving and as the fa-

cilities furnished by the state will allow. Such other training as the board and the superintendent deem necessary
and useful for the welfare of the inmates, and as tending
to their proper employment, or as contributing to their development, discipline and support, from time to time, may
be added.

Sec. 1893. Feeble-minded persons of any age, whether
public charges or not, shall be admitted to the institutions
for the feeble-minded, provided such persons are of such
inoffensive habits as to make them, in the judgment of the
board of administration, proper subjects for care and discipline. Such persons shall be committed to the board of
adminitsration and admitted to the institutions for the
feeble-minded in the same manner and by like proceedings
as are provided for the commitment and admission of insane persons to the state hospitals for the insane; and the
provisions of chapter 7, division II, title V, part first of
the General Code governing and regulating the admission
and commitment to, and conveyance and escort to and from
the state hospitals for the insane, the clothing, traveling expenses, care and maintenance of persons adjudged insane,
the arrést and return of escaped insane patients, the release
of insane patients from the hospitals for the insane on
habeas corpus, and the record of inquests of lunacy to be
made and kept by the probate judge, shall apply to and
govern the commitment, custody, care, support, maintenance and release of the feeble-minded, and the same fees,
costs and expenses that are allowed and paid in lunacy
cases shall be allowed, taxed and paid for similar services
in all proceedings related to feeble-minded persons. Provided, however, that the medical certificates mentioned in
section 1957 of the General Code shall not, when the same
relate to feeble-minded persons, be void after ten days, as
stated in said section. When they relate to feeble-minded
persons, said certificates shall be valid for an indefinite
period.

Sec. 1894. In the reception of feeble-minded persons
into the institutions for the feeble-minded, preference and
priority, so far as practicable shall be given to feeble-
minded children who are delinquent or dependent, as defined in sections 1644 and 1645, respectively, of the General Code. No prior or separate proceedings under the
juvenile court act as provided in chapter 8, title IV, part·
first of the General Code shall be necessary, however, to the
institution of proceedings and commitment to the board of
administration for admission to the institutions for the
feeble-minded, of a delinquent or dependent feeble-minded
child under the age of eighteen years.

Sec. 1895. If by reason of the incapacity of the institutions for the feeble-minded to receive additional inmates, the board of administration is unable to provide
for the custody and care of any feeble-minded person, said
board shall forthwith notify the judge of the probate court

Who may be ad-
mitted; pro-
cedure in admis-
sion or release;
fees, costs, etc.

What children
given preference.

Disposition of
feeble-minded
when board un-
able to provide
care and cus-
tody.

in which the proceedings for the commitment of such feeble-minded person are pending, of its inability to receive such feeble-minded person. The probate judge shall thereupon take such action and make such order as he may deem necessary and advisable to provide for the detention, supervision, care and maintenance of said feeble-minded person until such time as he may be received in an institution for the feeble-minded.

SECTION 2. That section 1815-12 of the General Code be amended to read as follows:

When county from which inmate came liable for support, etc.

Sec. 1815-12. The county from which an inmate of an institution for the feeble-minded was committed shall be liable for such inmate's support, provided the same is not paid otherwise as provided by this act. The treasurer of each county shall pay to the treasurer of state, upon the warrant of the county auditor, the amount chargeable against such county for the preceding six months for all inmates therefrom not otherwise supported, upon the presentation of the statement thereof. When any person committed to an institution under the control and management of the Ohio board of administration, other than an institution for the feebel-minded, is transferred or removed, as provided by law by said board of administration from such institution to an institution for the feeble-minded, the county from which said person was committed shall be liable for the support of such person while in said institution for the feeble-minded, as hereinabove provided, and to the same extent as if such person had been originally committed from said county to said institution for the feeble-minded.

Repeals.

SECTION 3. That original sections 1891, 1892, 1893, 1894, 1895, 1896, 1897, 1900, 1901, 1902, 1904 and 1815-12 of the General Code be, and the same hereby are, repealed.

The sectional numbers in this act are in conformity to the General Code. JOHN G. PRICE, Attorney General.

CLARENCE J. BROWN,
President of the Senate.

CARL R. KIMBALL,
Speaker of the House of Representatives.

Passed May 6, 1919.
Approved June 5, 1919.

JAMES M. COX,
Governor.

Filed in the office of the Secretary of State at Columbus, Ohio, on the 6th day of June, A. D. 1919.

184 G.

555

[Senate Bill No. 178.]

AN ACT

To authorize the còunty commissioners of Cuyahoga county, Ohio, to pay certain indebtedness.

Be it enacted by the General Assembly of the State of Ohio:

SECTION 1. That the county commissioners of the county of Cuyahoga be, and they are hereby authorized and empowered to pay out of any unappropriated funds in the county treasury of said county an amount not in excess of $14,443.19, and accrued interest thereon to date of payment, for money borrowed by them for the purpose of extending financial aid to farmers and gardeners during the war.

Commissioners of Cuyahoga county authorized to pay certain indebtedness.

This act is not of a general and permanent nature and requires no sectional number.
JOHN G. PRICE, Attorney General.

CARL R. KIMBALL,
Speaker of the House of Representatives.
CLARENCE J. BROWN,
President of the Senate.

Passed May 9, 1919.
Approved June 5, 1919.

JAMES M. COX,
Governor.

Filed in the office of the Secretary of State at Columbus, Ohio, on the 6th day of June, A. D. 1919.

185 L.

[House Bill No. 518.]

AN ACT

To amend section 1465-63 of the General Code, relative to the amount to be contributed to the state insurance fund by school districts.

Be it enacted by the General Assembly of the State of Ohio:

SECTION 1. That section 1465-63 of the General Code be amended to read as follows:

Sec. 1465-63. The amount of money to be contributed by the state itself, and by each county, city, incorporated village or other taxing district of the state shall be, unless otherwise provided by law, a sum equal to one per centum of the amount of money expended by the state and for each county, city, incorporated village or other taxing district respectively during the next preceding fiscal year for the service of persons described in subdivision one of section fourteen hereof, and the amount to be so contributed by any school district shall be equal to one-tenth of one per centum of the amount similarly expended by such dis-

Per centum to be contributed by state and subdivisions.

trict during such preceding fiscal year for the service of persons described as above.

Repeal.

SECTION 2. That said original section 1465-63 of the General Code be, and the same is hereby repealed.

The sectional number in this act is in conformity to the General Code. JOHN G. PRICE, *Attorney General.*

CARL R. KIMBALL,
Speaker of the House of Representatives.
CLARENCE J. BROWN,
President of the Senate.

Passed May 10, 1919.
Approved June 5, 1919.

JAMES M. COX, ·
Governor.

Filed in the office of the Secretary of State at Columbus, Ohio, on the 6th day of June, A. D. 1919.

186 G.

[House Bill No. 169.]

AN ACT

To amend section 13128 of the General Code of Ohio, relative to requiring net weight or content to appear on packages or containers containing commodities offered for sale, regulating charges for such packages or containers and providing penalty for violation of the provisions thereof.

Be it enacted by the General Assembly of the State of Ohio:

SECTION 1. That section 13128 of the General Code be amended to read as follows:

Failure to mark weight or quantity on package; exceptions.

Sec. 13128. Whoever puts up or packs goods or articles sold by weight or count into a sack, bag, barrel, case or package, or whoever puts up or fills a bottle, barrel, keg, drum, can or other container with any commodity sold or offered for sale by liquid measure, shall mark thereon in plain letters and figures the exact quantity of the contents thereof in terms of weight, measure or numerical count; provided, however, that reasonable tolerances and variations and also exemptions as to small packages shall be established by rules made by the secretary of agriculture and shall conform to those of the federal law, and provided, further, that this act shall not apply to such packages or containers, weighed, put up, packed or filled in the presence of the customer.

Transfer of brand, mark or stamp.

Whoever, with intent to defraud, transfers a brand, mark or stamp placed upon a case or package by a manufacturer to another case or package, or with like intent, repacks a case or package so marked, branded or stamped, with goods or articles of quality inferior to those of such manufacturer shall be deemed guilty of a violation of this section.

Any article or commodity packed and sold by weight shall be sold by net weight only, and no wood, paper, burlap, cord, paraffin or other substance used for wrapping or packing, shall be included as a part of the weight of such commodity sold. Wrapping not included as part of weight.

Provided, however, that nothing in this section shall prohibit making a reasonable separate charge for any wrapper or container used in packing or preparing such article or commodity for sale, if such be agreed to by the purchasers of such article or commodity at time of sale. Any person, firm, company, corporation or agent, who fails to comply with any provision of this act, shall be fined not less than twenty-five dollars ($25.00) nor more than five hundred dollars ($500.00). Penalty for failure to comply with law.

SECTION 2. This act shall be in force and take effect at the earliest date allowed by law; provided, however, that prior to June 1, 1920, no penalty or fine shall be enforced for any violations of the provisions of this act as to the markings required by section 1 hereof upon any such package or container weighed, packed, put up or filled prior to the date on which this act takes effect. When act shall take effect.

SECTION 3. That said original section 13128 of the General Code be, and the same is hereby repealed. Repeal.

The sectional number in this act is in conformity to the General Code. JOHN G. PRICE, Attorney General.

CARL R. KIMBALL,
Speaker of the House of Representatives.
CLARENCE J. BROWN,
President of the Senate.

Passed May 10, 1919.
Approved June 5, 1919.

JAMES M. COX,
Governor.

Filed in the office of the Secretary of State at Columbus, Ohio, on the 6th day of June, A. D. 1919.

187 G.

[Am. Senate Bill No. 146.]

AN ACT

To amend sections 5548, 5548-1, 5597, 5609 and 5610 of the General Code, relating to the assessment of property for taxation by the county auditor and the county board of revision and to repeal section 5598 and original sections 5548, 5548-1, 5597, 5609 and 5610 of the General Code.

Be it enacted by the General Assembly of the State of Ohio:

SECTION 1. That sections 5548, 5548-1, 5597, and 5610 of the General Code be amended to read as follows:

Sec. 5548. Each county is made the unit for assessing real estate for taxation purposes. The county auditor in addition to his other duties, shall be the assessor for all the Duties of county auditor in assessment of real estate.

real estate in his county for purposes of taxation, provided
that nothing herein shall affect the power conferred upon
the tax commission of Ohio in the matter of the valuation
and assessment of the property of any public utility. Annually between the first day of January and the first day of
February, the county auditor shall ascertain whether the
real estate in each township, village, ward or city is assessed for taxation in the aggregate at its true value in
money, as the same then appears on the tax duplicate.
If he finds that it is assessed at its true value in money,
in any such township, village, ward, or city, he shall,
subject to the provisions hereinafter made, enter such
valuation upon the tax list and duplicate for the current
year.   In such event, and unless he finds that such
property is not assessed at its true value in money, in each
such subdivision, such assessments shall constitute the valuation for taxation for the current year, subject to the provisions hereinafter made. Said county auditor shall submit his findings concerning the valuation of such real estate
to the board of county commissioners of his county, and
said board shall, at a hearing fixed within not less than
ten nor more than twenty days thereafter, confirm, modify, or set aside the same by order entered on the journal
of said board. Notice of such hearing shall be given by publication in a newspaper of general circulation in the county.
If by such order it be determined that the real estate in any
such subdivision is not on the duplicate at its true value in
money, then such county auditor shall proceed to assess such
real estate in such subdivision or subdivisions. Such assessment shall also be made by him in any such subdivision
upon the filing of a petition therefor with the county auditor signed by not less than twenty-five freeholders in such
subdivision, or by the board of trustees in any such township, or by the council of any such village. Such petition
may be filed at any time between the first day of January
and the first Monday in March in any year. Such assessment shall also be made by him in any such city, village,
township or ward, when the tax commission of Ohio, after
investigation, finds that the aggregate value for taxation of
the real estate therein is not its true value in money and
orders that such assessment be made. The county auditor
shall cause to be made the necessary abstracts from books of
his office, containing such description of real estate in such
subdivisions, together with such plat-books and lists of
transfers of title to land as the county auditor deems necessary in the performance of his duties in valuing such
property for taxation. Such abstracts, plat-books and lists
shall be in such form and detail as the tax commission of
Ohio may prescribe.

Employment of experts, deputies, etc.; salaries and compensation. The county auditor is empowered to appoint and employ such experts, deputies and clerks, or other employes,
as he may deem necessary to the performance of such duties
as such assessor; the amount to be expended in the payment

of their compensation to be fixed and determined by the county commissioners. If, in the opinion of the county auditor the county commissioners shall fail to provide a sufficient amount for their compensation, he may make application to the tax commission of Ohio for an additional allowance, and the additional amount of compensation allowed by such commission, if any, shall be duly certified to the board of county commissioners, and the same shall be final; provided, however, that if the assessment is ordered by the tax commission of Ohio such commission shall in such order prescribe the number of experts, deputies, clerks or employes to be appointed by the county auditor for the purpose of making such assessment, and fix their compensation. The salaries and compensation of such experts, deputies, clerks and employes shall be paid, upon the warrant of the auditor, out of the general fund of the county; and in case the same are, in whole or in part, fixed by the tax commission, they shall constitute a charge against the county, regardless of the amount of money in the county treasury levied or appropriated for such purposes.

Such experts, deputies, clerks and other employes, in addition to their other duties, shall perform such services as the county auditor may direct, in ascertaining such facts, description, location, character, dimensions of buildings and improvements, and such other circumstances reflecting upon the value of such real estate, as will aid the county auditor in fixing its true value in money. Said county auditor may also, if he deem it necessary or advisable, summon and examine any person under oath in respect to any matter pertaining to the value of any real property within the county. *Further duties of experts and deputies.*

Sec. 5548-1. In any year after the year in which an assessment has been made by the county auditor of all the real estate in any subdivision as herein provided, it shall be the duty of such county auditor at any time to revalue and assess any part of the real estate contained in such subdivision where he finds that the same has changed in value, or is not on the duplicate at its true value in money, and in such case he shall determine the true value thereof in money, as herein provided for assessing the entire property in any such subdivision. In such case the county auditor shall notify the owner of such real estate, or the person in whose name the same stands charged on the duplicate of his intention to reassess such real estate and of the change in valuation thereof in such reassessment, and in case the owner of such real estate is not satisfied with such reassessment, the same shall be heard at the next ensuing session of the county board of revision, and such owner shall have the right to appeal therefrom to the tax commission of Ohio as provided in other cases. *Revaluation in subdivision when change in value occurs; notification.*

Sec. 5597. It shall be the duty of the board of revision to hear complaints relating to the valuation or assessment as the same appears upon the tax duplicate of the then current year, of both real and personal property laid *Duty of board of revision.*

before it by the county auditor and it shall investigate all such complaints and may increase or decrease any such valuation or correct any assessment complained of, or it may order a reassessment by the original assessing officer.

Who may file complaint against valuation or assessment. Sec. 5609. Complaint against any valuation or assessment as the same appears upon the tax duplicate of the then current year, may be filed on or before the time limited for payment of taxes for the first half year. Any taxpayer may file such complaint as to the valuation or assessment of his own or another's property, and the county commissioners, the prosecuting attorney, county treasurer, or any board of township trustees, any board of education, mayor or council of any municipal corporation, in the county shall have the right to file such complaint. The county auditor shall lay before the county board of revision all complaints filed with him. **Determination of complaint.** The determination of any such complaint shall relate back to the date when the lien for taxes for the current year attached, or as of which liability for such year was determined, and liability for taxes, and for any penalty for non-payment thereof within the time required by law, shall be based upon the valuation or assessment as finally determined. Each complaint shall state the amount of over-valuation, under-valuation, or illegal valuation, complained of; and the treasurer may accept any amount tendered as taxes upon property concerning which a complaint is then pending, and if such tender is not accepted no penalty shall be assessed because of the non-payment thereof. The acceptance of such tender, however, shall be without prejudice to the claim for taxes upon ·the balance of the valuation or assessment. A like tender may be made, with like effect, in case of the pendency of any proceeding in court based upon an illegal excessive or illegal valuation.

Appeal to tax commission; procedure; hearing. Sec. 5610. An appeal from the decision of a county board of revision may be taken to the tax commission of Ohio, within thirty days after the decision of such board, by the county auditor of any complainant, or any person the valuation of whose property is increased by the county board of revision. Such appeal shall be taken by written notice to that effect, filed with the tax commission, and with the county auditor. Upon receipt of notice of appeal, the county auditor shall notify all parties interested, in the manner provided herein, and shall file proof of such notice with the tax commission of Ohio. The county auditor shall thereupon certify to the commission a copy of the record of the board of revision pertaining to the original complaint, together with the minutes thereof, and all evidence, documentary or otherwise, offered in connection therewith. Such appeal may be heard by the commission in the county where the property is listed for taxation, or the commission may cause one or more of its examiners to be sent to such county, to conduct such hearing, which shall be held not more than thirty days from the notice to such appeal. Such

examiners shall report their findings thereon to the state
tax commission for its affirmation or rejection.

SECTION 2. That section 5598 and original sections Repeals.
5548, 5548-1, 5597, 5609 and 5610 of the General Code be,
and the same are hereby repealed.

CLARENCE J. BROWN,
President of the Senate.
CARL R. KIMBALL,
Speaker of the House of Representatives.

The sectional
numbers in this
act are in con-
formity to the
General Code.
JOHN G. PRICE,
Attorney
General.

Passed April 16, 1919.
Approved June 5, 1919.

JAMES M. COX,
Governor.

Filed in the office of the Secretary of State at Columbus,
Ohio, on the 6th day of June, A. D. 1919.

188 G.

[Amended Senate Bill No. 175.]

AN ACT

Providing for the levy and collection of a tax on all inheritances
and for said purposes amending sections 2624, 2685, 2689, and
5331 to 5348, inclusive, of the General Code, and supplementing
sections 2624, 2685 and 5348 of the General Code by the enactment of sections to be designated as sections 2624-1, 2685-1
and 5348-1 to 5348-14, inclusive, respectively, of the General
Code.

Be it enacted by the General Assembly of the State of Ohio:

SECTION 1. The second subdivision of chapter 2, title "Inheritances."
1, part second, of the General Code heretofore designated
"Collateral Inheritances," and consisting of sections 5331
to 5349 to the General Code, shall be hereafter known and
designated by the title "Inheritances."

SECTION 2. Sections 2624, 2685, 2689 and 5331 to Enactment.
5348, inclusive, of the General Code, are hereby amended to
read as follows; and sections 2624, 2685 and 5348 of the
General Code are hereby supplemented by the enactment of
sections to be known and designated as sections 2624-1,
2685-1, and sections 5348-1 to 5348-14, inclusive, respectively, of the General Code, as follows:

Sec. 2624. On all moneys collected by the county treas- Compensation of auditor.
urer on any tax duplicates of the county, other than the
liquor, inheritance and cigarette duplicates, the county
auditor on settlement semi-annually with the county treasurer and auditor of state, shall be allowed as compensation
for his services the following percentages:

On the first one hundred thousand dollars, one and
one-half per cent.; on the next two million dollars, five-
tenths of one per cent.; on the next two million dollars,

four-tenths of one per cent.; and on all further sums, one-tenth of one per cent. Such compensation shall be apportioned ratably by the county auditor and deducted from the shares or portions of the revenue payable to the state as well as to the county, townships, corporations and school districts.

County treasurer's fees.

Sec. 2685. On settlement semi-annually with the county auditor, the county treasurer shall be allowed as fees on all moneys collected by him on any tax duplicates other than the liquor, inheritance and cigarette duplicates, the following percentages:

On the first one hundred thousand dollars, one and one-half per cent.; on the next two million dollars, five-tenths of one per cent.; on the next two million dollars, four-tenths of one per cent.; and on all further sums, one-tenth of one per cent. Such compensation shall be apportioned ratably by the county auditor and deducted from the shares or portion of the revenue payable to the state as well as to the county, township, corporations and school district; and all moneys collected on liquor, and cigarette duplicate, one per cent., on all moneys collected otherwise than on the said duplicates, except moneys received from the state treasurer or his predecessors in office or his legal representatives or the sureties of such predecessors, and except moneys received from the proceeds of the bonds of the county or of any municipal corporation, five-tenths of one-per cent., on the amount so received, to be paid upon the warrant of the county auditor out of the general fund of the county.

Payments to local treasurers.

Sec. 2689. Immediately after each semi-annual settlement with the county auditor, on demand, and presentation of the warrant of the county auditor therefor, the county treasurer shall pay to the township treasurer, city treasurer, or other proper officer thereof, all moneys in the county treasury belonging to such township, city, village, or school district, except inheritance tax moneys.

Sec. 5331. As used in this subdivision of this chapter:

Definition of terms.

1. The words "estate" and "property" include everything capable of ownership, or any interest therein or income therefrom, whether tangible or intangible, and, except as to real estate, whether within or without this state, which passes to any one person, institution or corporation, from any one person, whether by a single succession or not.

2. "Succession" means the passing of property in possession or enjoyment, present or future.

3. "Within this state," when predicated of tangible property, means physically located within this state; when predicated of intangible property, that the succession thereto is, for any purpose, subject to, or governed by the law of this state.

4. "Decedent" includes a testator, intestate, grantor, assignor, vendor or donor.

5. "Contemplation of death" means that the expec-

tation of death which actuates the mind of a person on the execution of his will.

Sec. 5332. A tax is hereby levied upon the succession to any property passing, in trust or otherwise, to or for the use of a person, institution or corporation, in the following cases:

1. When the succession is by will or by the intestate laws of this state from a person who was a resident of this state at the time of his death.

2. When the succession is by will or by the intestate laws of this state or another state or country, to property within this state, from a person who was not a resident of this state at the time of his death.

3. When the succession is to property from a resident, or to property within this state from a non-resident, by deed, grant, sale, assignment or gift, made without a valuable consideration substantially equivalent in money or money's worth to the full value of such property:

(a) In contemplation of the death of the grantor, vendor, assignor, or donor, or

(b) Intended to take effect in possession or enjoyment at or after such death.

4. Whenever any person or corporation shall exercise a power of appointment derived from any disposition of property heretofore or hereafter made, such appointment when made shall be deemed a succession taxable under the provisions of this subdivision of this chapter in the same manner as if the property to which such appointment relates belonged absolutely to the donee of such power, and had been bequeathed or devised by said donee by will; and whenever any such person or corporation possessing such power of appointment shall omit or fail to exercise the same within the time provided therefor, in whole or in part, a succession taxable under the provisions of this act shall be deemed to take place to the extent of such omission or failure, in the same manner as if the persons, institutions or corporations thereby becoming entitled to the possession or enjoyment of the property to which such power related had succeeded thereto by a will of the donee of the power failing to exercise the same, taking effect at the time of such omission or failure.

5. Whenever property is held by two or more persons jointly, so that upon the death of one of them the survivor or survivors have a right to the immediate ownership or possession and enjoyment of the whole property, the accrual of such right by the death of one of them shall be deemed a succession taxable under the provisions of this subdivision of this chapter in the same manner as if the enhanced value of the whole property belonged absolutely to the decreased person, and had been by him bequeathed to the survivor or survivors by will.

6. When a decedent appoints one or more executors or trustees, and instead of their lawful allowance makes a

bequeath or devise of property to them, which would otherwise be liable to such taxes, or appoints them as residuary legatees, and such bequest, devise or residuary legacy exceeds what would be a reasonable compensation for their services, such excess shall be a succession and liable to such tax, and the probate court having jurisdiction of their accounts shall fix such compensation.

7. When any property shall pass subject to any charge, estate or interest, determinable by the death of any person, or at any period ascertainable only by reference to death, the increase accruing to any person, institution or corporation, on the extinction and determination of such charge, estate or interest, shall be deemed a succession taxable under the provisions of this subdivision of this chapter, in the same manner as if the person, institution or corporation beneficially entitled thereto had then acquired such increase from the person from whom the title to their respective estates or interests is derived.

Such tax shall be upon the excess of the actual market value of such property over and above the exemptions made and at the rates prescribed in this subdivision of this chapter.

When property located outside of state not subject to tax. Sec. 5333. If the succession to property which is not within this state is locally subject in another state or country to a tax of like character and amount to that hereby levied, and if such tax be actually paid or guaranteed or secured in accordance with law in such other state or country, such succession shall not be subject to the tax hereby levied; if locally subject in any state or country to a tax of like character but of less amount than that hereby levied and such tax be actually paid or guaranteed or secured, as aforesaid, such succession shall be taxable under this subdivision of this chapter to the extent of the difference between the taxes actually paid, guaranteed or secured, and the amount for which such succession would otherwise be taxable hereunder.

Property passing to state or other political subdivision not subject to tax; to others taxable above exemptions. Sec. 5334. The succession to any property passing to or for the use of the state of Ohio, or to or for the use of a municipal corporation or other political subdivision thereof for exclusively public purposes, or public institutions of learning, or to or for the use of an institution for purposes only of public charity, carried on in whole or in substantial part within this state, shall not be subject to the provisions of the next preceding section. Successions passing to other persons shall be subject to the provisions of said section to the extent only of the value of the property transferred above the following exemptions:

1. When the property passes to or for the use of the wife or a child of the decedent who is a minor at the death of the decedent, the exemption shall be five thousand dollars.

2. When the property passes to or for the use of the father, mother, husband, adult child, adopted child, or person recognized as an adopted child and made a legal heir

under the provisions of a statute of this or any other state
or country, or the lineal descendants thereof, or a lineal
descendant of an adopted child, the exemption shall be three
thousand five hundred dollars.

3. When the property passes to or for the use of a
brother, or sister, niece, nephew, the wife or widow of a
son, the husband of a daughter of the decedent, or to any
child to whom the decedent, for not less than ten years prior
to the succession stood in the mutually acknowledged relation of a parent, the exemption shall be five hundred dollars.

Sec. 5335. The rates at which such tax is levied are as
follows: Rates of taxa-
tion.

1. On successions passing to any person mentioned
in the first and second sub-paragraphs of the perceding section:

(a) One per centum on the excess of the value of the
property over the exemptions up to and including the sum
of twenty-five thousand dollars.

(b) Two per centum on the next seventy-five thousand
dollars, or any part thereof;

(c) Three per centum on the next one hundred thousand dollars, or any part thereof;

(d) Four per centum on the amount representing the
balance of the value of each individual succession.

2. On successions passing to any person mentioned in
the third sub-paragpraph of the preceding section,

(a) Five per centum on the excess of the value of the
property over the exemptions up to and including twenty-
five thousand dollars;

(b) Six per centum on the next seventy-five thousand dollars, or any part thereof;

(c) Seven per centum on the next one hundred thousand dollars, or any part thereof;

(d) Eight per centum on the amount representing
the balance of the value of each individual succession.

3. On all successions passing to persons other than
those hereinbefore mentioned, or to institutions or corporations:

(a) Seven per centum on the value of the property
up to and including the sum of twenty-five thousand dollars;

(b) Eight per centum on the next seventy-five thousand dollars, or any part thereof;

(c) Nine per centum on the next one hundred thousand dollars, or any part thereof;

(d) Ten per centum on the amount representing the
balance of the value of each individual succession.

Sec. 5336. Taxes levied under this subdivision of this
chapter shall be due and payable at the time of the succession, except as herein otherwise provided, but in no case
prior to the death of the decedent. Taxes upon the suc-
cession to any estate or property, or interest therein lim- When taxes due
and payable.

ited, dependent or determinable upon the happening of any contingency or future event, and not vested at the death of the decedent, by reason of which the actual market value thereof cannot be ascertained at the time of such death, as provided in this subdivision of this chapter, shall accrue and become due and payable when the persons or corporations then beneficially entitled thereto shall come into actual

Tax a lien upon property. possession or enjoyment thereof. Such taxes shall be and remain a lien upon the property passing until paid, and the successor and the executors, of the general estate of the decedent, and the trustees of such property shall be personally liable for all such taxes, with interest as hereina'ter provided, until they shall have been paid as hereinafter directed. Such an administrator, executor or trustee, hav-

Duties of executor, administrator or trustee. ing in charge or in trust for distribution any property the succession to which is subject to such taxes, shall deduct the taxes therefrom, or collect the same from the person entitled thereto. He shall not deliver, or be compelled to deliver, any specific legacy or property, the succession to which is subject to said taxes, to any person, until he shall have collected the taxes thereon. He may sell so much of the estate of the decedent as will enable him to pay said taxes in like manner as he would be empowered to do for the payment of the debts of the decedent.

Tax on legacy shall be retained. Sec. 5337. If a legacy subject to such taxes is charged upon or payable out of real estate, the heir or devisee, before paying it, shall deduct the taxes therefrom and pay such taxes to the executor, administrator or trustee, and the taxes shall remain a charge upon the real estate until it is paid: and the payment thereof shall be enforced by the executor, administrator or trustee, in like manner as the payment of the legacy itself may be enforced, or by the prosecuting attorney as provided in this subdivision of this chapter. If such legacy shall be given in money to a person for a limited period, such administrator, executor or trustee shall retain the tax on the whole amount; and if it be not in money he shall make an application to the court having jurisdiction of his accounts to make an ascertainment, if the case require it, of the sum to be paid into his hands by such legatee on account of the taxes, and for such further order as the case may require.

Tax paid to county treasurer; interest after one year; discount. Sec. 5338. Taxes levied by this subdivision of this chapter shall be paid to the treasurer of the county in which the court having jurisdiction of proceedings under this subdivision of this chapter is held by the person or persons charged with the payment thereof. If such taxes are not paid within one year after the accrual thereof, interest at the rate of eight per centum per annum shall thereafter be charged and collected thereon; unless by reason of claims made upon the estate necessary litigation, or other unavoidable causes of delay, such taxes cannot be determined and paid as hereinbefore provided, in which case interest at the rate of five per centum per annum shall be charged upon such taxes from the accrual thereof until the cause of such delay is removed, after which eight per centum shall be charged. If such taxes are paid before the expiration of one year after the accrual thereof, a discount of one per centum per month for each full month that payment has been made prior to the expiration of the year, shall be allowed on the amount of such taxes.

Sec. 5339. If any debts shall be proven against the general estate of a decedent after the payment of any legacy or distributive share thereof, from which any such tax has been deducted or upon which it has been paid by the person entitled to such legacy or distributive share, and such person is required by order of the probate court having jurisdiction, on notice of the tax commission of Ohio, to refund the amount of such debts, or any part thereof, an equitable proportion of the tax shall be repaid to him by the executor, administrator or trustee, if the tax has not been paid to the county treasurer; or if such tax has been paid to the county treasurer, he shall, on the warrant of the county auditor, refund out of the funds in his hands or custody to the credit of inheritance taxes, such equitable proportion of the tax, without interest, and be credited therewith in his accounts. If after the payment of any tax, in pursuance of an order fixing such tax, made by the probate court having jurisdiction, such order be modified or reversed on due notice to the tax commission of Ohio, the said commission shall, unless further proceedings on appeal or in error are pending or contemplated by order direct the county auditor to refund such amount in the same manner; but no such application for such refunder shall be made after one year from such reversal or modification, by the highest court to which error may be prosecuted. The fees theretofore allowed upon such over-payment shall be adjusted in accordance with such refunder. Where it shall be shown to the satisfaction of the probate court that deductions for debts were erroneously allowed, such probate court may enter an order assessing the taxes upon the amount wrongfully or erroneously deducted.

Sec. 5340. The probate court of any county of the state having jurisdiction to grant letters testamentary or of administration upon the estate of a decedent, on the succession to whose property a tax is levied by this subdivision of this chapter, or to appoint a trustee of such estate, or any part thereof, or to give ancillary letters thereon, shall have jurisdiction to hear and determine the questions arising under the provisions of this subdivision of this chapter, and to do any act in relation thereto authorized by law to be done by a probate court in other matters or proceedings coming within its jurisdiction; and if two or more probate courts shall be entitled to exercise such jurisdiction, the court first acquiring jurisdiction hereunder shall retain the same to the exclusion of every other probate court. Such jurisdiction shall exist not only with respect to suc-

When legatee entitled to refunder; collection where debts erroneously deducted.

Powers and duties of probate court.

cessions in which the jurisdiction of such court would otherwise be invoked, but shall extend to all cases covered by this act, to the end that succession inter vivos, taxable under the provisions of this subdivision of this chapter, may be reached thereby.

Sec. 5341. The county auditor shall be the inheritance tax appraiser for his county. The probate court, upon its own motion may, or upon the application of any interested person, including the tax commission of Ohio, shall by order direct the county auditor to fix the actual market value of any property the succession to which is subject to the tax levied by this subdivision of this chapter. Such auditor shall forthwith give notice by mail to all persons known to him to have a claim or interest in the property to be appraised, including the tax commission of Ohio, and to such persons as the probate court may by order direct, of the time and place when he will appraise such property. He shall at such time and place appraise the same at its actual market value as of the date of the accrual of the tax, except as hereinafter provided, and subject to the rules hereinafter prescribed. Such county auditor for such purpose is hereby authorized to issue subpoenas and to compel the attendance of witnesses and the production of books and papers before him, and to examine such witnesses under oath concerning such property, the value thereof, and the nature and circumstances of the succession. Disobedience of such subpoena, or refusal to testify on such examination shall be punished as a contempt of the probate court. The county auditor shall report his findings in writing, together with the depositions of the witnesses examined, and such other facts in relation thereto as the probate court may order. Such report shall be made in duplicate; one copy thereof shall be filed with the probate court, and the other with the tax commission of Ohio.

The fees of the sheriff or other officer, serving such subpoenas, and the actual and necessary traveling and other expenses incurred by the county auditor in making the appraisement shall be certified by the county auditor on such report. If the probate judge finds such fees and expenses to be correct, he shall allow such fees, and so much of such expenses as he may find to have been reasonable, having regard to the amount of the state's share of the taxes, and certify the amount so allowed for each on the order fixing the taxes. For the purpose of this and succeeding sections of this subdivision of this chapter relating to the assessment of the tax, the entire estate of a decedent, though passing to several persons, institutions or corporations, shall be the subject of inquiry in a single proceeding.

Sec. 5342. The value of a future or limited estate, income, interest or annuity for any life or lives in being, shall be determined by the rule, method and standard of mortality and value employed by the superintendent of insurance in ascertaining the value of annuities for the de-

569

termination óf liabilities of life insurance companies, except that the rate of interest shall be five per centum per
annum. The superintendent of insurance shall, without a
fee, on the application of any probate court or of any
county auditor, determine the value of any such estate, income, interest or annuity, upon the facts contained in any
such application, and other facts to him submitted by such
court or auditor and certify the same in duplicate to such
court or auditor, and his certificate thereof shall be conclusive evidence that the method of computation therein is
correct.

In estimating the value of any estate or interest in
property, to the beneficial enjoyment or possession whereof
there are persons or corporations presently entitled, no allowance shall be made on account of any contingent encumbrance thereon, nor on account of any contingency upon
the happening of which the estate, or some part thereof,
or interest therein, may be abridged, defeated or diminished; but in the event of such encumbrance taking effect
as an actual burden upon the interest of the beneficiary,
or in the event of the abridgement, defeat, or diminution
of such estate, or interest therein, as aforesaid, a refunder
shall be made in the manner provided by section 5339 of the
General Code, to the person properly entitled thereto of a
proportionate amount of such tax on account of the encumbrance when taking effect, or so much as will reduce the
same to the amount which would have been assessed on account of the actual duration or extent of the estate enjoyed.

Sec. 5343. When, upon any succession, the rights, Taxation of esinterests, or estates of the successors are dependent upon tates dependent
contingencies or conditions whereby they may be wholly cies, conditions,
or in part created, defeated, extended or abridged, a tax etc.
shall be imposed upon such successions at the highest rate
which, on the happening of any such contingencies or conditions, would be possible under the provisions of this subdivision of this chapter, and such taxes shall be due and
payable forthwith out of the property passing, and the
probate court shall enter a temporary order determining
the amount of such taxes in accordance with this section;
but on the happening of any contingency whereby the said
property, or any part thereof, passes so that such ultimate
succession would be exempt from taxation under the provisions of this subdivision of this chapter, or taxable at a
rate less than that so imposed and paid, the successor shall
be entitled to a refunder of the difference between the
amount so paid and the amount payable on the ultimate succession under the provisions of this chapter, without interest; and the executor or trustee shall immediately upon
the happening of such contingencies or conditions apply to
the probate court of the proper county, upon a verified petition setting forth all the facts, and giving at least ten
days' notice by mail to all interested parties, for an order
modifying the temporary order of said probate court so as

to provide for a final assessment and determination of the taxes in accordance with such ultimate succession. Such refunder shall be made in the manner provided by section 5339 of the General Code.

Estates in expectancy or held in abeyance.

Sec. 5344. Estates in expectancy which are contingent or defeasible, and in which proceedings for the determination of the taxes have not been taken, or have·been held in abeyance, shall be appraised at their full undiminished value, when the persons entitled thereto shall come into the beneficial enjoyment or possession thereof, without diminution for or on account of any valuation theretofore made of the particular estates for the purpose of this subdivision of this chapter, upon which such estates in expectancy may have been limited. An estate for life or for years which can be divested by the act or omission of the legatee, or devisee, shall be appraised and taxed as if there were no possibility of any such divesting.

Probate court shall find the actual market value, taxes, etc.; notice of order.

Sec. 5345. From the report of appraisal and other evidence relating to any such estate before the probate court, such court shall forthwith upon the filing of such report, by order entered upon the journal thereof, find and determine, as of course, the actual market value of all estates, the amount of taxes to which the succession or successions thereto are liable, the successors and legal representatives liable therefor; and the townships or municipal corporations in which the same originated. Provided, however, that in case no application for appraisement is made the probate court may make and enter such findings and determinations without such appraisement. Thereupon the judge of such court shall immediately give notice of such order to all persons known to be interested therein, and shall immediately forward a copy thereof to the tax commission of Ohio, together with copies of all orders entered by him in relation to or affecting in any way the taxes on such estate, including orders of exemption. If it shall appear at any stage of the proceedings that any of such persons known to be interested in the estate is an infant or of unsound mind, the probate court may if the interest of such person is presently involved and is adverse to that of any of the other persons interested therein, exercise the powers provided for in sections 11249 and 11253, inclusive, of the General Code.

Who may file exceptions; when and where; hearing.

Sec. 5346. The tax commission of Ohio, or any person dissatisfied with the appraisement and determination of taxes, may file exceptions thereto in writing with the probate court within sixty days from the entry of the order, stating the grounds upon which such exceptions are taken. The probate court shall thereupon by order fix a time not less than ten days thereafter for the hearing of such exceptions, and shall give such notice thereof as it may deem necessary; provided, that a copy of such notice and of such exceptions shall be forthwith mailed to the tax commission and the county auditor. Upon the hearing of such exceptions, said court may make such order as to it may seem just and proper in the premises. No costs shall be allowed by the probate court on such exceptions.

Sec. 5347. At the expiration of such period of sixty days if no exceptions be filed, or at any time within such period, on the application of all parties, including the tax commission of Ohio, the probate judge shall make and certify to the county auditor a copy of the order provided for in section 5345 of the General Code. If such exceptions are filed within such period the probate judge shall, within five days after the entry of the final order, make and certify such copy of the original finding and determination, together with any modifications thereof ordered upon the hearing of such exceptions. *When order certified to county auditor.*

The county auditor shall thereupon, on a form to be prescribed for him by the auditor of state, make a charge based upon such order and certify a duplicate thereof to the county treasurer, who shall collect the taxes so charged.

Sec. 5348. An appeal may be taken by any party, including the tax commission of Ohio, from the final order of the probate court under section 5346 of the General Code in the manner provided by law for appeals from orders of the probate court in other cases. An appeal by the tax commission of Ohio may be perfected in the manner provided by section 11209 of the General Code. *Appeal from final order.*

Sec. 2624-1. On all inheritance tax moneys collected by the county treasurer, the county auditor on settlement semi-annually with the auditor of state shall be allowed as compensation for his services under the inheritance tax law the following percentages: *Fees of county auditor.*

Three per cent. on the first fifty thousand dollars; two per cent. on the next fifty thousand dollars, and one-half of one per cent. on all additional sums. Such percentages shall be computed upon the amount collected in a calendar year, and shall be for the use of the fee fund of the county auditor.

Sec. 2685-1. On settlement semi-annually with the county auditor, the county treasurer shall be allowed as fees on all moneys collected by him on inheritance tax duplicates the following percentages: one per cent. on the first fifty thousand dollars, five-tenths of one per cent. on the next fifty thousand dollars, and one-tenth of one per cent. on all additional sums. Such percentages shall be computed upon the amount collected in a calendar year and shall be for the use of the fee fund of the county treasurer. *Fees of county treasurer.*

Sec. 5348-1. Upon the payment to the county treasurer of any tax due under this subdivision of this chapter, such treasurer shall issue a receipt therefor in triplicate. One copy thereof he shall deliver to the person paying such taxes; and the original and one copy thereof he shall immediately send to the auditor of state who shall certify the original and immediately transmit it to the judge of the court fixing the tax. An executor, administrator or trustee shall not be entitled to credits in his accounts, nor *Tax receipts in triplicate; delivery of copies.*

be discharged from liability for such taxes, nor shall the estate under his control be distributed, unless such certified receipt shall have been filed with the court. Any person shall, upon the payment of ten cents to the county treasurer issuing such receipt, be entitled to a duplicate thereof, to be signed and certified in the same manner as the original.

Transfer or delivery of shares, stocks, deposits, etc., not allowed without consent of tax commission; liability for tax.

Sec. 5348-2. No corporation organized or existing under the laws of this state, shall transfer on its books or issue a new certificate for any share or shares of its capital stock belonging to or standing in the name of a decedent or in trust for a decedent, or belonging to or standing in the joint names of a decedent and one or more persons, without the written consent of the tax commission of Ohio. No safe deposit company, trust company, corporation, bank or other institution, person or persons, having in possession or in control or custody, in whole or in part, securities, deposits, assets or property belonging to or standing in the name of a decedent, or belonging to or standing in the joint names of a decedent and one or more persons, including the shares of the capital stock of, or other interest in, such safe deposit company, trust company, corporation, bank or other institution, shall deliver or transfer the same to any person whatsoever whether in a representative capacity or not, or to the survivor or survivors when held in the joint names of a decedent and one or more persons, without retaining a sufficient portion or amount thereof to pay any taxes or interest which would thereafter be assessed thereon under this subdivision of this chapter, and unless notice of the time and place of such delivery or transfer be served upon the tax commission of Ohio and the county auditor at least ten days prior to such delivery or transfer; but the tax commission of Ohio may consent in writing to such delivery or transfer, and such consent shall relieve said safe deposit company, trust company, corporation, bank or other institution, person or persons, from the obligation to give such notice or to retain such portion. The tax commission or the county auditor, personally or by representatives, may examine such securities, deposits or other assets at the time of such delivery or otherwise. Failure to comply with the provisions of this section shall render such safe deposit company, trust company, corporation, bank or other institution, person or persons, liable for the amount of the taxes and interest due under this subdivision of this chapter on the succession to such securities, deposits, assets or property. Such liability may be enforced by action brought by the county treasurer in the name of the state in any court of competent jurisdiction.

Procedure in collection of tax after the expiration of eighteen months.

Sec. 5348-3. If, after the expiration of eighteen months from the accrual of any tax under this subdivision of this chapter, such tax shall remain unpaid, the auditor of state shall notify the prosecuting attorney of the proper county, in writing, of such failure or neglect. If the determination of the tax has been delayed for more than one year after the accrual thereof such notice may be issued at any time after six months from the date of the order determining such tax. Such prosecuting attorney shall thereupon apply to the probate judge in the name of the county auditor on behalf of the state for a transcript of the order fixing the tax. Such transcript shall be filed in the office of the clerk of the common pleas court of the county, and the same proceedings shall be had with respect thereto as are provided by section 11659 of the General Code with respect to transcripts of judgments rendered by justices of the peace and mayors, except that the prosecuting attorney shall not be required to pay the costs thereof accruing at the time of filing the same. Thereupon the same effect shall be given to such transcript for all purposes as is given to such transcripts of judgments of justices of the peace or mayors filed in like manner. Provided, however, that nothing in this section shall be construed to affect the date of the lien of such taxes on the property passing, nor to divest such lien before the payment of such tax in the event of failure to sue out execution within the period prescribed by section 11663 of the General Code.

Sec. 5384-4. The prosecuting attorney shall represent the county auditor of his county in his capacity as inheritance tax appraiser when called upon by him for that purpose. He shall also represent the interests of the state in any and all proceedings under this subdivision of this chapter. The attorney general shall, when requested by the tax commission in writing, appear for the state in any such proceeding. *Prosecuting attorney shall represent the county.*

Sec. 5348-5. The county auditor may, and when directed by the tax commission of Ohio, shall appoint such number of deputies as the tax commission of Ohio may prescribe for him, who shall be qualified to assist him in the performance of his duties as inheritance tax appraiser under the provisions of this subdivision of this chapter. *Appointment of deputies.*

Sec. 5348-6. The tax commission of Ohio may designate such of its examiners, experts, accountants and other assistants as it may deem necessary for the purpose of aiding in the administration of the provisions of this subdivision of this chapter; and such provisions shall be deemed and held to be a law which the tax commission is required to administer for the purposes of sections 1465-9, and 1465-12 to 1465-30, inclusive, section 1465-32, and section 1465-34 of the General Code. It shall be the duty of the tax commission of Ohio in the administration of this subdivision of this chapter to see that the proceedings provided for herein shall be instituted and carried to determination in all cases in which a tax is due hereunder. *Examiners, experts, accountants, etc.*

Sec. 5348-7. Each probate judge shall keep a book, the form thereof shall be prescribed by the auditor of state which shall be a public record, and in which such probate judge shall enter the name of every decedent upon whose estate an application to him has been made for an issue *Record by probate judge; form prescribed by auditor of state.*

of letters of administration, or letters testamentary, or ancillary letters, the date and place of death of said decedent,
the estimated value of his real and personal property, the
names, places of residence and relationship to him of his
heirs at law, the names and places of residence of the legatees or devisees in any will of any such decedent, the
amount of each legacy, and the estimated value of any real
property devised therein, and to whom devised. Such entry shall be made from the data contained in the papers
fil(' on any such application, or in any proceeding relating
to the estate of the decedent. The probate judge shall also
enter in such book the amount of the personal property of
any such decedent, as shown by the inventory thereof when
made and filed in his office, and the returns made by the
county auditor under this subdivision of this chapter, and
the value of annuities, life estates, terms of years and other
property of said decedent, or given by him in his will or
otherwise, as fixed by the probate court, and the taxes assessed thereon, and the township or municipal corporation
in which the same originated, and the amounts of any receipts for payment of any taxes on the estate of such decedent under this subdivision of this chapter, filed with him.
The auditor of state shall also prescribe forms for the reports to be made by each probate judge and county auditor,
which shall correspond with the entries to be made in such
book.

**Semi-annual re-
port by probate
judge to auditor
of state; report
by county re-
corder.** Sec. 5348-8. Each probate judge shall, at the time the
county auditor makes his semi-annual settlement with the
auditor of the state, make a report, upon the form prescribed by the auditor of state, containing all the matters
required to be entered on such book, which shall be immediately forwarded to the auditor of state. The county recorder of each county in the state shall, at the same time
make reports concerning a statement of any deed or other
conveyance filed or recorded in his office, of any property,
which appears to have been made in contemplation of death,
or intended to take effect in possession or enjoyment after
the death of the grantor or vendor, with the name and place
of residence of such grantor or vendor, the name and place
of residence of the grantee or vendee, of the description of
the property transferred, which shall be immediately forwarded to the tax commission of Ohio.

**Account kept by
treasurer; semi-
annual settle-
ment with audi-
tor; allowance
of fees.** Sec. 5348-9. The county treasurer shall keep an account showing the amount of all taxes and interest by him
received under the provisions of this subdivision of this
chapter. On the twenty-fifth day of February and the
twentieth day of August of each year he shall settle with
the county auditor for all such taxes and interest so received at the time of making such settlement, not included
in any preceding settlement, showing for what estate, and
by whom and when paid. At each such settlement the
auditor shall allow to the treasurer and himself on the
moneys so collected and accounted for by him, their re-

spective fees, at the percentages allowed by law. The correctness thereof, together with a statement of the fees allowed at such settlement and the fees and expenses allowed to the probate judge and other officers under this subdivision of this chapter shall be certified by the county auditor.

Sec. 5348-10. Such fees as are allowed by law to the probate judge for services performed under the provisions of this subdivision of this chapter, shall be fixed in each case and certified by him on the order fixing the taxes, together with the fees of the sheriff or other officers and the expenses of the county auditor. The county auditor shall allow such fees and expenses out of said taxes when paid and credit the same to such fee funds, and draw his warrants on the treasurer in favor of the officers personally entitled thereto, payable from such taxes, as the case may require.

Certification and payment of fees of officers.

Sec. 5348-11. Fifty per centum of the gross amount of any taxes levied and paid under the provisions of this subdivision of this chapter shall be for the use of the municipal corporation or township in which the tax originates, and shall be credited, one-half to the sinking fund, if any, of such municipal corporation or township, and the residue to the general revenue fund thereof; the remainder of such taxes, after deducting the fees and costs charged against the proceeds thereof under this subdivision of this chapter, shall be for the use of the state, and shall be paid into the state treasury to the credit of the general revenue fund therein.

Division of tax between state and subdivision.

Sec. 5348-12. At each semi-annual settlement provided for under this subdivision of this chapter, the county auditor shall certify to the auditor of any other county in which may be located in whole or in part, any municipal corporation or township, to which any part of the taxes collected under this subdivision of this chapter, and not previously accounted for, is due, a statement of the amount of such taxes due to each municipal corporation or township in such county entitled to share in the distribution thereof. The amount respectively due upon such settlement to each such municipal corporation or township, and to each municipality and township in the county in which the taxes are collected shall be paid upon the warrant of the county auditor to the treasurer or other proper officer of such municipal corporation or township. The amount of any refunder chargeable against any such municipal corporation or township at the time of making such settlement, shall be adjusted in determining the amount due to such municipal corporation or township at such settlement; provided, however, that if the municipal corporation or township against which such refunder is chargeable is not entitled to share in the fund to be distributed at such settlement, the county auditor shall draw his warrant for the amount thereof in favor of the county treasurer payable from any undivided

Certification to auditor of other county portion of tax due; payment.

general taxes in the possession of such treasurer, unless such municipal corporation or township is located in another county, in which event the county auditor shall issue a certificate for such amount to the auditor of the proper county, who shall draw a like warrant therefor payable from any undivided general taxes in the possession of the treasurer of such county; and in either case at the next semi-annual settlement of such undivided general taxes, the amount of such warrant shall be deducted from the distribution of taxes of such municipal corporation or township and charged against the proceeds of levies for the general revenue fund of such municipal corporation or township.

Where tax deemed to originate on property within the state. Sec. 5348-13. When the property passing is real estate or tangible personal property within this state the tax on the succession thereto shall be deemed to have originated in the municipal corporation or township in which such property is physically located. In case of real estate located in more than one municipal corporation or township the tax on the succession thereto, or to any interest therein, shall be apportioned between the municipal corporation or townships in which it is located in the proportions in which the tract is assessed for general property taxation in such townships or municipal corporations respectively.

Where tax deemed to originate on property not within the state. Sec. 5348-14. The tax on the succession to intangible property or tangible personal property not within this state from a resident of this state shall be deemed to have originated in the municipal corporation or township in which the decedent resided.

Where tax on property of non-resident deemed to have originated; how determined. The municipal corporation or township in which the tax on the succession to the intangible property of a non-resident accruing under the provisions of this subdivision of this chapter, shall be deemed to have originated, shall be determined as follows:

1. In the case of shares of stock in a corporation organized or existing under the laws of this state, such taxes shall be deemed to have originated in the municipal corporation or township in which such corporation has its principal place of business in this state.

2. In case of bonds, notes, or other securities or assets, in the possession or in the control or custody of a corporation, institution or person in this state, such taxes shall be deemed to have originated in the municipal corporation or township in which such corporation, institution or person had the same in possession, control or custody at the time of the succession.

3. In the case of moneys on deposit with any corporation, bank, or other institution, person or persons, such tax shall be deemed to have originated in the municipal corporation or township in which such corporation, bank or other institution had its principal place of business, or in which such person or persons resided at the time of such succession.

SECTION 3. Said original sections 2624, 2685, 2689, **Repeals.**
and 5331 to 5348, inclusive, are hereby repealed.

SECTION 4. This act shall not affect pending proceed- **Pending proceed-**
ings for the assessment and collection of collateral inheri- **ings not affected.**
tance taxes under the original sections hereby amended, nor
the duty to pay, nor the right to collect any such tax which
has accrued prior to the approval of this act, nor the rights
or duties of any officer with respect to the assessment and
collection of such collateral inheritance taxes; nor shall this
act affect successions taking place prior to its approval,
whether the death of the decedent occurred prior to such
approval or not; but all successions occurring subsequently
to the approval of this act shall be affected by and taxable
under it, whether the death of the decedent occurred prior
to its approval or not, unless a tax has already accrued
thereon under the provisions of the original sections hereby
amended.

The sectional numbers in this act are in conformity to the General Code. JOHN G. PRICE Attorney General.

CLARENCE J. BROWN,
President of the Senate.
CARL R. KIMBALL,
Speaker of the House of Representatives.

Passed May 8, 1919.
Approved June 5, 1919.

JAMES M. COX,
Governor.

Filed in the office of the Secretary of State at Columbus,
Ohio, on the 6th day of June, A. D. 1919.

189 G.

[Re-Amended Senate Bill No. 45.]

AN ACT

To codify fish and game laws of Ohio, and to repeal sections of the
General Code relating thereto.

FISH AND GAME.

GENERAL PROVISIONS.

SECTION.
1. Definitions.
2. Taking possession, sale and transportation of
    quadrupeds, fish and birds restricted.
3. Manner of taking game and fish.
4. Transportation.
5. Prohibited sale of certain birds and squirrels.
6. Prima facie evidence.

QUADRUPEDS.

GAME REFUGES, GAME PROPAGATION, TRESPASS.

Be it enacted by the General Assembly of the State of Ohio:

Sec. 1390. SECTION 1. DEFINITIONS. Words and phrases as used in this act shall be construed as follows: *Definition of words and phrases.*

Closed season: That period of time during which hunting, fishing or trapping is prohibited.

Open season: That period of time during which hunting, fishing or trapping is permitted.

Angling or fishing (exclusive of netting): Taking fish by line in hand or rod in hand, with not more than three baited hooks attached thereto, or with lure with not more than three sets of three hooks each attached thereto.

Measurement of fish: Length from end of nose to the longest tip or end of the tail.

Person: Includes company, partnership, corporation or association, also any employe, agent or officer thereof.

Game: Both game quadrupeds and game birds.

Game quadrupeds: Hare or rabbit, gray squirrel, fox squirrel and deer.

Game birds: Ruffed grouse or partridge, woodcock,

pheasant, European partridge, including the so-called Hungarian partridge, black-breasted plover, Wilson or jacksnipe, greater and lesser yellowlegs, rail, coot, gallinule, duck, goose and brant.

Pheasant, or imported pheasant: Hungarian dark-necked pheasant, ring-necked, commonly called English pheasants, Mongolian or Chinese pheasants. Non-game birds; American robin, nuthatch, warbler, flicker, wren, tanager, bobolink, oriole, bluebird, purple martin, swallow, quail or bob-white, turtle or mourning dove, American gold-finch, killdeer, humming bird and all other wild birds not included in the term "game birds."

Quadrupeds: Game quadrupeds and fur-bearing animals.

Fur-bearing animals: Fox, mink, raccoon, skunk, muskrat, opossum.

Whole to include part: Every provision relating to any fish, bird or quadruped shall be deemed to apply to any part thereof with the same force and effect as it applies to the whole.

Sell and sale: Barter, exchange, giving away and offering or exposing for sale.

Possession: Both actual and constructive possession and any control of things referred to.

Transport and transportation: All carrying or moving or causing to be carried or moved.

Take or taking: Includes pursuing, shooting, hunting, killing, trapping, snaring and netting fish, birds and quadrupeds, and all lesser acts, such as wounding, or placing, setting, drawing, or using any net or other device commonly used to take fish, birds or quadrupeds, whether they result in taking or not; includes also every attempt to take and every act of assistance to every other person in taking or attempting to take fish, birds or quadrupeds, provided, that whenever taking is allowed by law, reference is had to taking by lawful means and in a lawful manner.

Hunting: Pursuing, shooting, killing, capturing and trapping game birds or quadrupeds and all other acts such as placing, setting, drawing or using any device commonly used to take game birds or quadrupeds whether they result in taking or not; every attempt to take and every act of assistance to any other person in taking or attempting to take game, fish or quadrupeds.

Bag limit: The number of any kind of game or fish permitted to be taken in a specified time.

Resident: Any citizen of the United States who has lived in the state of Ohio for not less than ninety days next preceding the date of making application for a license.

Non-resident: Any person who is a citizen of the United States and has not resided in the state of Ohio for a period of ninety days or more next preceding the date of making application for license.

Channels and passages: Those narrow bodies of water lying between islands or between an island and the mainland, in Lake Erie. Definition of words and phrases.

Island: A rock or land elevation above the waters of Lake Erie, having an area of five or more acres above water.

Reef: An elevation of rock either broken or in place, or gravel shown by the latest United States chart to be above the common level of the surrounding bottom of the lake, other than the rock bottom or in place forming the base or foundation rock of an island or mainland and sloping from the shore thereof. A reef shall also mean all elevations shown by such chart to be above the common level of such sloping base or foundation rock of an island or mainland, whether running from the shore of an island or parallel with the contour of the shore of an island or in any other way, whether formed by rock, broken or in place, or from gravel.

Interpretation of other words: In the interpretation of this act, words in the present tense include the future tense; words in the masculine gender include the feminine and neuter genders;' words in the singular number include the plural number and in the plural number include the singular number; the word "and" may be read "or" and "or" read "and" if the sense requires it.

Sec. 1391. SECTION 2. OWNERSHIP, RESTRICTIONS, PROHIBITIONS. The ownership of, and the title to all fish, wild birds and quadrupeds in the state of Ohio, not confined and held by private ownership, legally acquired, is hereby declared to be in the state, which holds it in trust for the benefit of all the people, and only in accordance with the terms and provisions of this act shall individual possession be obtained. No person shall at any time of the year take, in any manner, number or quantity, fish, wild quadrupeds or birds protected by law, or buy, sell, offer or expose for sale, the same or any part thereof, transport or have the same in possession, except as permitted by this act; and this prohibition shall be construed as part of each permissive section or part thereof. . A person doing anything prohibited, or neglecting to do anything required by this act, with reference to such fish, quadrupeds or birds, shall be deemed to have violated this section. A person who counsels, aids or assists in the violation of a provision of this act, or knowingly shares in any of the proceeds of such violation by receiving or possessing either a fish, quadruped or bird shall be deemed to have violated this section. Hunting or taking a wild bird or wild game on Sunday is prohibited. Ownership; restrictions; prohibitions.

Sec. 1392. SECTION 3. MANNER OF TAKING. a. Game and birds. A person may take quadrupeds and birds during the open season therefor with the aid of a dog, unless specifically prohibited by this act. No person shall catch, kill, injure or pursue any of the protected wild birds named in this act, with the aid or by the use of any trap, net or Manner of taking game birds.

snare, or disturb or destroy a nest, egg or young thereof, except the eggs of the common tern, or take or pursue a wild duck or other water fowl, with the aid of or by the use of any gun, except a common shoulder gun not larger than ten gauge, or kill or pursue with such intent, any wild bird or wild animal with any gun equipped with any silencer, or with the aid or by the use of any aeroplane or boat, other than a common row boat or punt boat, propelled by oars or punt pole.

Fish. b. Fish. Fish shall be taken only by angling, unless otherwise specifically permitted by this act. In case a fish is unintentionally taken contrary to the prohibitions or restrictions of a provision of this act, such fish shall be immediately liberated and returned to the water without unnecessary injury. Tipups, trot lines, set lines, float lines, spears, grappling hooks, naked hooks, snatch hooks, hook and line with more than three hooks attached, eel weirs, eel pots, and nets of any kind shall not be used to take fish, except as specifically permitted by this act.

Sec. 1393. SECTION 4. TRANSPORTATION. a. General. No common carrier or person in its employ while engaged in **Transportation of fish or game; labeling.** such business as common carrier, shall receive for transportation, transport or cause to be transported any box, package or other receptacle containing wild game, fish or furbearing animals or any part thereof, unless said box, package, or receptacle bears label containing the number and kind of such game, fish or fur-bearing animals or parts thereof, the name of the consignor or consignee, the initial point of billing and the point of destination.

Transportation of squirrel beyond state prohibited. b. Out of State. No person shall receive for transportation, transport, cause to be transported, or have in his possession with intent to transport or secure the transportation of beyond the limits of this state any bird mentioned in this chapter or a squirrel, which has been killed in this state.

Each bird or squirrel taken, etc., constitutes separate offense. Each bird or squirrel killed, taken, had in possession, received for transportation, or transported contrary to the provisions of this section shall constitute a separate offense. The reception by any person within this state of such bird or animal for shipment to a point without the state, shall be prima facie evidence that they were killed within the state for the purpose of conveying them beyond the limits thereof. Provided, however, that such animal if legally taken by a non-resident, may be transported by him from a point within the state to a point out of the state, if the same shall be accompanied by the actual owner thereof, and the said owner shall have first procured a non-resident hunting and trapping license. The prohibition of this section shall not apply to a common carrier into whose possession any of the birds mentioned in this act or any squirrels have come for transportation in the regular course of business, while such birds or squirrels are in transit through this state from a point without, where the killing thereof is lawful.

c. Special. Live game birds for propagation purposes, and fish for propagation purposes, and the plumage or skin of game birds legally taken and possessed may be transported without being marked, as provided in this act, at any time and in any number and quantity.

What game may be taken and transported.

Sec. 1394. SECTION 5. PROHIBITED SALE. No person within this state shall buy, sell, expose for sale, offer for sale, or have in possession for any such purpose, any of the birds named in this act, except as permitted duly authorized game breeders, or any squirrels, whether killed within or without the state, or take, catch, kill or pursue such bird or squirrel, for the purpose of sale within or without the state. Each bird or squirrel bought, sold, exposed for sale, offered for sale, or had in possession for any such purpose, and each bird or squirrel taken, caught or killed contrary to the provisions of this section shall constitute a separate offense.

Buying and selling prohibited.

Sec. 1395. SECTION 6. PRIMA FACIE EVIDENCE. The finding of a gun, net, seine, boat, trap or other device, set, maintained, used or had in possession, in violation of law, shall be prima facie evidence of the guilt of the person owning, using, claiming or possessing such property. The finding of a bird, fish, game or fur-bearing animal, or part thereof, unlawfully in the possession of any person shall be prima facie evidence of the guilt of such person.

What prima facie evidence.

QUADRUPEDS.

Sec. 1396. SECTION 7. HARES OR RABBITS. a. Open season. Hares and rabbits may be taken and possessed from the fifteenth day of November to the first day of January, both inclusive. The owner of lands or his tenants or bona fide employees, may take, except Sunday, and in any number, hares and rabbits which are found doing actual and substantial damage to grain, berries, fruit, vegetables, trees or shrubbery, the property of such owner.

Open season for hares or rabbits.

b. Limit. A person may take in one day and have in his possession at one time, not more than ten hares or rabbits, except as provided in this section, but no person shall catch, kill, injure or pursue with such intent a hare or rabbit, except from one hour before sunrise to one hour after sunset.

Limit that may be taken in one day.

c. Sale. Hares and rabbits may be bought and sold during the open season. When rabbits are brought from without the state they may be bought and sold at any time and in any number.

When buying and selling permitted.

d. Ferrets prohibited. It shall be unlawful for any person to take a hare or rabbit, within the state of Ohio, through the use of a ferret, or to place a ferret in any hole or opening in the ground, or stone wall or log, outside of a building, in which a rabbit might be confined or to be caught in the act of using a ferret in the taking of a rabbit or to

Use of ferrets prohibited.

have a ferret in possession or under control, in either the fields or forests, or to be found possessed of a ferret while hunting; or while going hunting or returning from such hunting to have a ferret either in possession or under control. Each hare or rabbit caught, killed or had in possession, contrary to the provisions of this section, shall constitute a separate offense. Nothing in this section shall prevent the owner of a young fruit orchard, his tenants or bona fide employes from having in his possession a ferret, or using a ferret in any manner to take or kill rabbits or hares when doing actual and substantial damage to his fruit trees.

Sec. 1397.

Open season for squirrel.

Limit in number.

Sale prohibited.

SECTION 8. SQUIRREL. a. Open season. Squirrels may be taken and possessed from the twentieth day of August to the twentieth day of September both inclusive.

b. Limit. A person may take in one day and have in his possession at one time, not more than five squirrels.

c. Sale prohibited. Squirrels whether taken within or without the state shall not be bought or sold at any time. Each squirrel taken or had in possession, contrary to the provisions of this section, shall constitute a separate offense.

Sec. 1398.

Open season for fur-bearing animals.

SECTION 9. FUR-BEARING ANIMALS. a. Open season. Raccoon, skunk, mink and opossum may be taken and possessed only from the first day of November to the first day of February, both inclusive, and muskrat only from the first day of December to the first day of March, and fox only from the second day of October to the first day of January, both inclusive; but groundhog may be taken at any time. The furs of these animals, legally taken, may be possessed, sold and transported in any number, at any time; provided, however, that the same were legally taken. The possession of a skin or pelt of a fox, raccoon, muskrat, skunk, mink or opossum, during the closed season, shall be prima facie evidence that the same was illegally taken, unless such person can show by the original invoice signed by the shipper, that such hide, skin or pelt was shipped from without the state, or furnish satisfactory proof that it was otherwise legally taken. Nothing in this section shall be construed as prohibiting a person from pursuing and killing, at any time, except on Sunday, fur-bearing animals which are injuring property, or which have become a nuisance, or prohibit the owner of a farm or enclosure, used exclusively for the breeding and raising of raccoon, skunk, mink, muskrat or opossum therein, from taking or killing such animals, or any of them, at any time, or having in possession a hide, skin or pelt thereof.

Manner of taking permitted.

b. Manner of taking. No person shall at any time dig out or attempt to dig out, drown out or attempt to drown out, smoke out with fumes or gases, or attempt to smoke out with fumes or gases, any animal protected by this act, or in any manner destroy the house, den or burrow of any such animal. Each roccoon, muskrat, skunk, mink and

opossum, and each hide, skin or pelt of any such animal
taken or had in possession contrary to the provisions of
this section, shall constitute a separate offense.

Sec. 1399.
SECTION 10. TURTLES. Turtles may be taken by _Manner of tak-_
any method, at any time, except they shall not be taken by _ing turtles._
shooting or with nets, the meshes of which are less than
four inches in dimension.

Sec. 1400.
SECTION 11. PETS. Squirrels, rabbits, raccoons and _Game kept as_
deer legally taken, may be possessed alive in enclosures at _pets permitted._
any time as pets.

Sec. 1401.
SECTION 12. DEER. Wild deer may not be taken at _Taking deer pro-_
any time within this state. _hibited._

BIRDS.

Sec. 1402.
SECTION 13. RUFFED GROUSE, HUNGARIAN _Open season for_
PARTRIDGE, PHEASANTS. a. Open season. Ruffed _game birds._
grouse, Hungarian partridge and pheasants may be taken
and possessed only from the fifteenth day of November to
the twenty-fifth day of November, both inclusive.

b. Limit. Cock pheasants only may be taken, and not _Limit to number_
more than three such cock pheasants in any one day, during _of cock pheas-_
the open season, except on Sunday, and except as permitted _ants and grous°._
to game propagators; nor more than three ruffed grouse;
nor more than six Hungarian partridge in any one day
during the open season, except Sunday.

Sec. 1403.
SECTION 14. DUCK, GEESE, COOT, GALLINULE. _Open season for_
a. Open season. Wild geese, brant, coot and wild duck _duck, geese, etc._
(other than wood duck) and gallinules, may be taken only
from the sixteenth day of September to the thirty-first day
of December, both inclusive, and possessed during such additional season as provided for by federal regulations.
Wood duck shall not be taken before September 16, 1922,
or after that date, except from the sixteenth day of September to the thirty-first day of December, both inclusive.
Wild fowl may be taken only during the day from one-
half hour before sunrise until sunset, during the open season, except on Sunday.

b. Limit. A person may take in the open season in _Limit to number_
any one day, except Sunday, not more than twenty-five wild _taken._
ducks of all kinds in the aggregate, and not more than
twenty-five coots and gallinules in the aggregate, and not
more than eight geese in the aggregate, and not more than
eight brant.

Sec. 1404.
SECTION 15. PLOVER, JACKSNIPE, YELLOW- _Open season for_
LEGS. a. Open season. Blackbellied and golden plover, _plover, snipe, etc._
greater and lesser yellowlegs, Wilson snipe or jacksnipe,
may be taken and possessed only from the sixteenth day of
September to the thirty-first of December, both inclusive.

b. Limit. A person may take in any one day, during _Limit to number_
the open season, except Sunday, not to exceed fifteen Wil- _taken._
son snipe or jacksnipe, and not to exceed a total of fifteen

in the aggregate of all kinds of blackbellied and golden plovers, and greater and lesser yellowlegs.

Sec. 1405.

Open season for rail, coot, etc.

SECTION 16. RAIL, GALLINULE. a. Open season. Sora and other rails, except coots and gallinules, may be taken only from the first day of November to the thirty-first day of December, both inclusive.

Limit to number taken.

b. Limit. A person may take in any one day, during the open season, except Sunday, not to exceed twenty-five railbirds in the aggregate of all kinds, except sora, of which thirty-five may be taken.

Sec. 1406.

Open season for woodcock.

SECTION 17. WOODCOCK. a. Open season. Woodcock may be taken and possessed only from the first day of October to the thirtieth day of November, both inclusive.

Limit to number taken.

b. Limit. A person may take a total of not more than six woodcock in any one day, during the open season, except Sunday.

Sec. 1407.

Catching, killing, etc., carrier pigeons prohibited.

SECTION 18. CARRIER PIGEONS. No person, except the owner thereof, shall catch, kill, capture or detain an Antwerp or homing pigeon, commonly called a "carrier" pigeon, which at the time of its capture or detention has the name of its owner stamped upon its wing or tail, or which has upon its leg a band bearing the name or initials of its owner, its number or any other mark designating it as a carrier pigeon.

Sec. 1408.

Catching, killing, etc., other than game birds prohibited.

SECTION 19. NON-GAME BIRDS. No person shall catch, kill, injure, pursue or have in possession, either dead or alive, at any time, or purchase, expose for sale, transport or ship to a point within or without the state, or receive or deliver for transportation any wild bird other than a game bird, nor shall any part of the plumage, skin or body be had in possession, except as specifically permitted by this act, nor shall any person disturb or destroy the eggs, nests or young of such birds; but nothing in this section or act shall prohibit the lawful taking, killing, pursuing or possession of any game bird during the open season for such bird, or the killing of the chicken hawk, blue hawk, Cooper hawk, sharp-shinned hawk, crow, great-horned owl or English sparrow, or the destroying of their nests, or the eggs and nests of the common tern or bass gull, or prohibit the owner or duly authorized agent of the premises from killing blackbirds at any time, except on Sunday, when they are found to be a nuisance or are injuring grain or other property. Each bird or any part thereof taken or had, in possession contrary to the provisions of this section shall constitute a separate offense.

Sec. 1409.

Permit for collections for scientific purposes.

SECTION 20. COLLECTIONS FOR SCIENTIFIC PURPOSES. The secretary of agriculture may issue to any duly accredited person a permit authorizing him to collect any birds, their nests and eggs for scientific purposes only. The applicant for a permit shall present to the secretary the written testimonials of two well-known scientific persons or teachers of science, certifying to the good character and fitness of the applicant and pay the secretary a

587

fee of five dollars. He shall also give bond to the state in the sum of one hundred dollars with two or more sureties approved by the secretary, that he will not kill a bird or take the nest or eggs of a bird for any other purpose than provided herein, which bond shall be kept in the office of the secretary. Each permit shall be in force for one year ·from the date of its issue and shall not be transferable, but upon the forfeiture of a bond of a person his permit shall become void.

Sec. 1410.
SECTION 21. BOUNTIES. A bounty of one dollar shall be allowed and paid in the manner hereinafter provided, for every chicken hawk, American goshawk, blue hawk, Cooper hawk, sharp shinned hawk, duck hawk and great horned owl killed in this state ·by an inhabitant thereof. Any person applying for such bounty shall take such hawk or owl to the clerk of the township in which such hawk ór owl was killed. Such clerk shall issue and deliver to the applicant a certificate stating the bounty to which the applicant is entitled and shall at once destroy all such hawks and owls, but such certificate shall not be issued unless there is a fund in the township treasury out of which such bounty may be paid. Such fund shall be set apart out of the general fund of the township by appropriation therefor by the township trustees, which fund in no year shall exceed the sum of one hundred dollars.

Bounty for hawk, owl, etc.

FISH.

Sec. 1411.
SECTION 22. INLAND AND LAKE ERIE FISHING DISTRICTS DEFINED. The waters of Lake Erie, the waters of Sandusky Bay, as far west as a straight line drawn from the mouth of Tommy Creek to Slate's Point, and as far east as one-fourth of a mile from the mouth of the Clack Channel, and the waters of the Maumee Bay up to a point north of Toledo commonly known as· Presque Isle, are in and shall be known as The Lake Erie Fishing District. All other waters over which the state of Ohio has jurisdiction, whether lakes, rivers, creeks, or reservoirs, or whether natural or artificial, including East Harbor, West Harbor, Middle Harbor, in Ottawa county, and the waters of Ten Mile Creek lying within this state are in and shall be known as the Inland Fishing District.

Inland and Lake Erie fishing districts defined.

Sec. 1412.
SECTION 23. BASS, BLUE GILL AND CRAPPIE. a. Open season. In the inland fishing district of the state black bass may be taken and possessed by angling only from the sixteenth day of June to the thirtieth day of April, both inclusive, and in the Lake Erie fishing district they may be thus taken and possessed only from the fifteenth day of July to the twenty-fourth day of May, both inclusive.

Open season for bass, blue gill and crappie.

b. Method of taking. Black bass, less than eleven inches in length, calico or strawberry bass and crappie less than six inches in length, rock bass and blue gills less than five inches in length may not be taken in either of the fishing districts of this state; but if any of the fish named in this section are caught unintentionally in any net or with hook and line and are released alive in such manner as not to injure them, such taking shall not be considered an offense.

c. Limit. A person shall not take in any one day to exceed twelve black bass, twenty-five rock bass or blue gills, or forty calico or strawberry bass or crappies, nor have in possession at any time more than two days' legal catch of any of the above named varieties.

d. .Sale. No person, firm or corporation, shall buy, sell or offer for sale, barter, give away, or have in possession for any such purpose any fish caught in the inland fishing district of this state, except carp, sheephead, mullet and grass pike, or any black bass, rock bass, calico or strawberry bass, crappie, blue gill or sunfish caught in the Lake Erie fishing district of this state, or outside of the state or have in possession any such fish unlawfully caught, and each fish so bought, sold, offered for sale, exposed for sale, bartered or given away, had in possession unlawfully caught, or for the purpose of sale, or of a less length than herein required shall constitute a separate offense.

Sec. 1413.

Open season for trout and salmon.

SECTION 24. TROUT. a. Open season. Brook trout, speckled trout, Von Bohr or brown trout, land-locked salmon or California salmon may be taken and possessed only from the fifteenth day of April to the fifteenth day of September, both inclusive.

Sec. 1414.

Taking minnows prohibited, except for bait.

SECTION 25. MINNOWS. No person shall take, catch, buy or sell minnows, except for bait, or ship "white bait," except alive, out of the state. In the inland waters of the state no minnows shall be taken or caught with a minnow seine exceeding four feet in depth and eight feet in length and in the Lake Erie fishing district no minnows shall be taken with a minnow seine exceeding thirty feet in length.

Sec. 1415.

Taking by poison or explosive prohibited.

SECTION 26. POISONS AND EXPLOSIVES PROHIBITED. No person shall take, catch, injure or kill fish in any waters over which the state of Ohio has jurisdiction by means of quicklime, electricity, or any kind of explosive or poisonous substance, or place or use quicklime, electricity, explosive or poisonous substances in any such waters, except for engineering purposes and upon the written permission of the secretary of agriculture. Each fish taken, killed or had in possession in violation of this section shall constitute a separate offense.

Sec. 1416.

Obstructions to the transit of fish prohibited.

SECTION 27. OBSTRUCTIONS PROHIBITED. No person shall locate, place or maintain in any of the waters of this state over which the state has jurisdiction, any obstruction to the natural transit of fish. The chief of the division of fish and game, assistant chief, or any fish and game protector or other person, may take up, remove or clear away such obstructions, except mill dams, and if such obstruction is a net or other device used for leading or

catching fish it may be seized and condemned, as provided
in section 60 of this act, but this section shall not apply to
Lake Erie.

Sec. 1417.

SECTION 28. ICE FISHING RESTRICTED. No
person shall take or catch fish in any manner in the inland
fishing district of this state while the waters thereof are
frozen over, covered or partly covered with ice, or through
a fissure, crack or break therein, except through a hole in
the ice not more than two and a half feet in diameter. No
more than two holes shall be used by any one fisherman,
nor shall more than two hooks be used on any one line, and
no fish so caught shall be bartered or sold. Each fish taken,
killed, bartered or sold contrary to the provisions of this
section shall constitute a separate offense.

*Restrictions on
ice fishing.*

Sec. 1418.

SECTION 29. OVERFLOWS AND PRIVATE PONDS
EXEMPTED. Fish may be taken in any manner, in the
ponds or lagoons formed by the receding waters of any
river, when such ponds, or lagoons no longer have any connection with the channels of such streams.

*Exemption of
overflows and
private ponds.*

Sec. 1419.

SECTION 30. CERTAIN NETS EXEMPTED. Noth-
ing in this act shall apply to nets, traps, or other devices
for catching fish, in the posession of the owner of a private
artificial fish pond or privately owned lake for use in such
pond or lake only, or to fish nets, fish traps, or other devices
for catching fish, not otherwise prohibited, to be used in
catching fish in Lake Erie, or in those bays, marshes, estuaries, inlets, bordering on, flowing into or in any manner
connected with Lake Erie, wherein fishing with such devices is permitted, when such fish nets, fish traps, or other
devices are kept within one mile of the waters of the Lake
Erie fishing district. Nothing in this chapter shall apply
to nets, traps, or other devices, in the possession of bona
fide manufacturers, or dealers, when such nets, traps, or
other devices are kept in the regular places of business of
such manufacturers or dealers, or are in course of transportation, or to nets, traps, or other devices in the possession
of common carriers for transportation.

*What nets ex-
empted.*

NETS AND NETTING.

Sec. 1420.

SECTION 31. NET AND LINE PROHIBITION. No
person shall draw, set, place, locate, maintain, or have in
possession, a pound net, crib net, trammel net, fyke net,
set net, seine, bar net, fish trap or any part thereof, throw
or hand line, with more than three hooks attached thereto,
or any other device for catching fish, except a line with not
more than three hooks attached thereto or lure with not
more than three sets of three hooks each in the inland fishing district of this state, except for taking carp, mullet,
sheephead and grass pike as provided in section 32 of this
act, and except as provided in section 29 of this act, or
catch or kill a fish, in such fishing district with what are
known as bob lines, trot lines, float lines, or by grabbing

*Net and line
prohibition.*

with the hands, or by spearing, or shooting, or with any
other device other than by angling; provided, however, that
in the waters of this district, except those lakes, harbors and
reservoirs controlled ·by the state, a trot line may be used
with not more than fifty hooks and no two hooks less than
three feet apart by the owner or person having the owner's
consent in that part of the stream bordering on or running through said owner's lands.

Each fish caught, killed, taken or had in possession contrary to the provisions of this act shall constitute a separate offense.

Sec. 1421.

Provisions as to
carp, mullet and
other fish.

SECTION 32. CARP, MULLET, AND OTHER FISH.
Carp, mullet, grass pike, sheephead and moon-eyed shiners
may be taken in any number, except that they may not be
taken with a net other than a seine having meshes not less
than four inches, stretched mesh, fishing measure, in the
bays, marshes, estuaries, or inlets, bordering upon, flowing
into, or in any manner connected with Lake Erie. They
may, in the same manner be taken in the Ottawa river, no
farther up than the Ann Arbor bridge; in the Maumee
river, no farther up than the terminal bridge above the To-
ledo· Country Club; in Portage river, no farther up than Oak
Harbor bridge; that portion of Sandusky bay and river
west of an imaginary line running from the west point of
Squaw Island across Sandusky River to Teal Pond Point,
thence south to the mainland, in that part of Mud Bay and
Mud Creek west of an imaginary line one-half mile west of
the Mud Creek bridge on Port Clinton road and no farther
up the La Carp Creek, Little Portage River, Tousaint
River, Turtle Creek or Ward's Canal, than the water level
of Lake Erie extends in these streams. In any of the waters
herein described it shall be unlawful to set or leave stationary a seine that will prevent fish from entering or going
from the mouth of any river. In the Lake Erie fishing district a seine of smaller mesh may be used. Nothing in this
section shall be construed to permit the use of any net whatever in any stream flowing into Lake Erie east of Sandusky
Bay, except an eight-foot minnow net.

Sec. 1422.

Netting seasons
in Lake Erie
district.

SECTION 33. LAKE ERIE NETTING SEASONS.
For the Lake Erie fishing district, and in the bays, marshes,
estuaries or inlets bordering upon, flowing into or in any
manner connected with Lake Erie, there shall be two fishing
seasons—the spring fishing season, beginning on the fifteenth day of March and including and closing on the thirty-
first day of August, and the fall fishing season, beginning on
the first day of September and including and closing on the
fifteenth day of December. No person shall draw, set, place,
locate, or maintain a pound net, gill net, bar net, fyke net,
seine, or any fish net whatever in the Lake Erie fishing district of this state, or the bays, marshes, estuaries, or inlets
thereof bordering upon, flowing into or in any manner connected with Lake Erie, between the fifteenth day of De-
·cember and the fourteenth day of March, both inclusive.

Sec. 1423.

SECTION 34. LICENSE AND FEES. No person, License required; schedule of fees.
firm or corporation shall use or operate for the purpose of
catching fish, a boat, net or device other than hook and line
with bait or lure in the Lake Erie fishing district of this
state, or the bays, marshes, estuaries or inlets bordering upon,
flowing into or in any manner connected with Lake Erie,
without a license from the secretary of agriculture. Applications for licenses and all licenses herein required shall be
in such form as the secretary may prescribe. The fees for
license in the Lake Erie fishing district, and in the bays,
marshes, estuaries or inlets bordering upon, flowing into, or
in any manner connected with Lake Erie, where fishing is
permitted with a 4-inch seine, for each fishing season defined in this chapter shall be as follows:

For each rowboat used in fishing with gill nets or bar
nets, four dollars;

For each sailboat used in fishing with gill nets or bar
nets, six dollars;

For each gasoline or other power boat, of five net tons
or under, used in fishing with gill nets or bar nets, twelve
dollars and fifty cents;

For each gasoline or other power boat, of over five net
tons, and for each steamboat used in fishing with gill nets,
twenty dollars;

For each row boat used in fishing with trot lines, one
dollar and fifty cents;

For each seine used in fishing, four dollars;

For each pound net used in fishing, three dollars;

For each net or other device used in fishing, other than
a gill net, bar net, seine, pound net or hook and line, one
dollar and fifty cents.

When a person, firm or corporation applies to the sec- When license issued; must be carried by operator.
retary of agriculture for a license, the secretary, upon re-
ceiving the proper fees as prescribed, shall issue the same.
Such license shall remain in force and entitle the holder
thereof to fish as permitted by law from the date of issue
to and including the last day of the season for which such
license was issued. The license shall be carried by an
operator of boats, net, or other device while being used in
catching fish, and exhibited on demand to any protector,
constable, sheriff, deputy sheriff or other police officer, or the
secretary of agriculture. It shall be unlawful for any
licensee having such license in his possession to refuse to
exhibit it on demand to any proper officer. Each boat, net,
or other device used in catching fish contrary to the provisions of this act, and each net or other device used or
operated without having the metal tag attached thereto, as
provided by law, shall constitute a separate offense.

Sec. 1424.

SECTION 35. REPORTS. Within ten days after the Report by licensee to secretary of agriculture.
expiration of any license, the licensee shall make and deliver
a true and correct report to the secretary of agriculture,
upon blanks furnished by said secretary, of the number and
kinds of nets and of all other devices used in fishing, the

number, kind and size of boats used and the amount, weight and kinds of fish caught by such licensee under such license during the season for which license was issued. Upon the failure of any licensee to comply with the foregoing provisions of this act, the secretary of agriculture shall refuse to issue any new license or to renew license of such licensee until such licensee has made such report and has complied with such provisions.

Sec. 1425.
Metal tag for each net, etc.

SECTION 36. TAGS. The secretary of agriculture shall issue to each person licensed to catch fish in the Lake Erie fishing district, one metal tag for each net or other device allowed by law, other than a gill net, bar net, or hook and line, used by such licensee for catching fish in such district. No licensee shall use such net or other device, other than a gill net, bar net, or hook and line, without attaching such tags thereto, as hereinafter provided, to-wit:

On each crib net a tag shall be attached to the uphaul buoy, which buoy shall be painted red; on each pound net and fyke net a tag shall be attached on the tunnel outhaul stake; and on each seine a tag shall be attached on either brail. If such tags are not attached to such nets as herein required, it shall be prima facie evidence that they have not been lawfully procured, and it shall be unlawful to locate or maintain any crib net in the Lake Erie fishing district of this state, without having a red uphaul buoy attached to the crib thereof, or for any person to fish in the waters of the Lake Erie fishing district with any kind of a net or device other than the following: pound net, gill net, bar net, fyke net, crib net, seine, trot line, minnow net, or hook and line limited to three hooks. The words pound net, fyke net, crib net, shall in each case mean a tarred set net.

Sec. 1426.
"Splashing" for purpose of driving into net, prohibited.

SECTION 37. "SPLASHING" PROHIBITED. No fish shall be driven into any net or device by what is known as "plunging", "splashing", "hammering", or by any noise or other disturbance in or out of the water for such purpose in either of the fishing districts of the state of Ohio, and no net shall be set in less than three feet of water in such districts.

Sec. 1427.
Where nets prohibited.

SECTION 38. NETS, WHERE PROHIBITED. No person shall draw, set, place, locate or maintain any net whatever on any of the reefs of the Lake Erie fishing district, except by permission of the secretary of agriculture, or draw, set, place, locate or maintain any net whatever, in any channel or passage lying between any islands or between any islands and the mainland in such district at a greater distance from the shore of such islands or mainland than one-fourth the distance across such channel or passage; nor set, locate, place or maintain any net or string of nets opposite another net or string of nets in such manner as to close off more than one-fourth the distance across any such channel or passage; nor shall any person draw, set, place, locate or maintain any fish net within a distance of one hundred and twenty-five rods of a line drawn through the

center of Sandusky Bay within a distance of two miles on
either the west or east side of the track of the New York
Central railway crossing such bay. No person shall draw,
set, place, locate or maintain any net whatever within a
radius of one-half mile from a pier or breakwater built or
maintained by the United States government, or at or within
one-half mile from the mouth of any stream flowing into
Lake Erie, or within one-half mile of any embankment, dam
or bridge in any bay or river connected with or flowing into
Lake Erie, or more than one-fourth the distance from shore
across any bay or river whose waters flow into Lake Erie,
or set, place, locate or maintain any net or string of nets opposite another net or string of nets in such manner as to
close off more than one-fourth the distance across such bay
or river.

Sec. 1428.   SECTION 39. NETS, REQUIREMENTS. In the Lake   Requirements in
Erie fishing district the meshes of the back of the crib or   all nets used.
car of all nets used in fishing shall hang squarely and shall
not be less than two and seven-eighths inches, stretched
mesh, fishing measure, except on the edges of the back next
to the corner or side lines for a distance on each side equal
in width to one-third of the width of such back. The mesh
herein specified shall be on the middle of such back, and
extend from the top to the bottom thereof, and hang
squarely. In case of fyke nets, the mesh herein specified
may be placed in the space between the last two hoops
thereof, instead of in the back of the crib or car, such space
to be not less than three feet in width. When such large
mesh is placed in the back of the crib or car, no puckering
back shall be used. A gill net shall not be used or had in
possession in this state, having meshes less than three
inches, stretched mesh, fishing measure.

Sec. 1429.   SECTION 40. LIMITATIONS ON TAKING CER-   Limitations on
TAIN FISH. It shall be unlawful for any person to take   taking certain
or catch a buffalo fish in the Lake Erie fishing district, be-   fish; enumera-
fore March 15, 1924, nor after that date any buffalo fish   tion.
less than fifteen inches in length, or take or catch a sturgeon
in such district after March 15, 1920. No person shall
have in his possession a white fish less than one and three-
quarter pounds in the round, a cat fish less than fifteen
inches in length, a carp less than fifteen inches in length, a
perch, white bass or a bull head less than nine inches in
length, or a blue pike or a sauger or cisco less than eleven
inches in length, or a sheephead less than eleven inches in
length, or a yellowpike or pike perch less than thirteen inches
in length. All such fish caught of a less length or weight than
herein described shall be immediately released alive, while
nets are being lifted or hauled in such manner as not to injure them. It shall be unlawful to release such undersized
fish as herein described into a privately owned pond or lake,
live car or other enclosures. No cat fish or bull head shall
be brought ashore with its head or tail removed, or in such
condition that its length cannot be measured. Nothing

herein shall prohibit the catching or having in possession
such fish when caught with hook and line, and not for
profit; and the having in possession or failure to return to
the water alive in the manner provided a quantity of such
undersized white fish, cisco, cat fish, carp, sheephead, white
bass, perch or bull heads not exceeding in weight three per
cent and not exceeding in weight ten per cent of such undersized yellow pike or pike perch, blue pike or saugers, of
each boatload or part thereof, lot catch, or haul, brought
ashore of each variety of fish shall not be deemed a violation of this section. No person, firm or corporation shall
sell, barter, give away, deliver or ship any package of fish
containing more than three per cent of undersized fish of
the following varieties: White fish, cisco, cat fish, carp,
sheephead, buffalo fish, white bass, perch, bull heads, or
more than ten per cent of undersized pike or pike perch or
saugers. No person shall buy, sell, offer for sale, or have in
his possession a fish caught out of season or in any manner
prohibited, or a fish caught unlawfully outside the state of
Ohio. Fish lawfully taken or caught and confined in a net,
or by a device authorized by law, shall be the property of the
person, firm or corporation operating such net or device,
and it shall be unlawful for any person other than the
owner or person in control of such net or other device, to
take or catch therefrom, or have in possession a fish which is
or has been so confined, and no set net or gill net from one
hour before sunrise to one hour after sunset. Each fish
taken from, caught out of, and each fish had in possession
which was taken from any net legally operated in the Lake
Erie fishing district, by any persons other than the owner or
person in control of such net shall constitute a separate
offense.

HUNTING AND TRAPPING LICENSES.

Sec. 1431.

Hunting and
trapping license;
resident and
non-resident;
fees.

SECTION 41. RESIDENT AND NON-RESIDENT
LICENSE. No person shall hunt, pursue or kill with a
gun any wild bird or wild animal, or take, catch, or kill any
fur-bearing animals, by the aid or use of any trap or other
device, within the state, without first having applied for
and received a hunter's and trapper's license as required
herein. Every applicant for a hunter's and trapper's license, who is a non-resident of the state of Ohio and who is
a citizen of the United States of America, shall pay a fee of
fifteen dollars to the officer issuing same. Every applicant
for hunter's and trapper's license who is a citizen of the
United States of America, and a resident of the state of
Ohio, shall pay a fee of one dollar, but the owner, manager,
tenant or children of the owner, manager or tenant of lands
within this state may hunt and trap upon such lands without a hunter's and trapper's license.

Sec. 1432.

SECTION 42. HOW ISSUED. Hunter's and trapper's license shall be issued by the clerk of the common pleas court, village and township clerks. Every applicant for a hunter's and trapper's license shall make and subscribe an affidavit, setting forth his name, age, weight, occupation, place of residence, personal description and citizenship, and the officer authorized to issue licenses shall charge each applicant a fee of twenty-five cents for taking such affidavit, issuing such license and attaching his seal of office thereto, and clerks of common pleas courts, village and township clerks to whom such application is made are hereby empowered and required to administer the oath and to take and certify the affidavit herein required and to collect and receive the fees therefor as herein provided. The application, license and other blanks required by this act shall be prepared and furnished by the secretary of agriculture and such blanks shall be of different color each year and in such form as such secretary may prescribe to the clerk authorized to issue same, and such license shall be issued applicants by said clerks. The record of licenses kept by said clerk shall be uniform throughout the state and in such form or manner as the state auditor shall prescribe, and be open at all reasonable hours to the inspection of any person. Each such license shall expire on the thirty-first day of December next after its issuance. The secretary of agriculture or the court before whom the case is tried as a part of the punishment shall revoke the license of any person or persons convicted of violating any laws for the protection of birds, game birds, game and fur-bearing animals and the license fee paid by such person shall be forfeited to the state and no license shall be granted to such person until the expiration of one year after the date of his conviction. Persons under sixteen years of age shall not be allowed to hunt with gun under the provisions of this act, unless accompanied by their parents or other adult person instead of parents.

Application for and issue of license; affidavit; expiration; revocation.

Sec. 1433.

SECTION 43. RECORD; APPLICATION OF FEES. Officers authorized to issue licenses shall issue them in consecutive order of their numbers as stamped on the left upper corner of each license with date and exact time of day of issue plainly written thereon and keep a record of such licenses issued and make a report to the board of agriculture quarterly, on March 31st, June 30th, September 30th and December 31st, in such form as the secretary of agriculture shall require, of the number of licenses issued, together with the names and addresses of the persons to whom issued, and shall transmit with such report to the secretary, the moneys received as license fees, other than the amounts paid to the clerks as their fees, which shall be paid into the state treasury to the credit of a fund which is hereby appropriated for the use of the secretary in the preservation and protection of birds, game birds, game and fur-bearing animals. At least fifty per cent of the money arising from all such licenses shall be expended by the secretary for the purchase

Record of licenses; application of fees.

and propagation of game birds and game animals to be used
in re-stocking sections where a scarcity of such birds and
game animals exist, for establishing and purchasing or
otherwise acquiring title to lands for game preserves, and
the secretary is hereby empowered to organize such lands
into state game preserves, under rules and regulations to be
adopted by said secretary, and employ on such preserves one
or more keepers or protectors at such salary and with such
duties, as may be prescribed by the secretary. And it shall
be unlawful for any person, at any time on any such game
preserve, conspicuously posted, or with knowledge that the
same is a game preserve to hunt or trap, kill or pursue any
game birds or game or fur-bearing animal. It shall be unlawful for any person to enter upon any lands owned or
held by the state for purposes of reforestation or for game
preserves with intent to cut growing timber on any such
lands, or otherwise commit waste thereon, or to trap, hunt,
kill, shoot, injure or pursue a game bird or game animal
thereon.

Sec. 1434.

License not transferable nor issued in name of another.

SECTION 44. OTHER PROVISIONS. No hunter's
and trapper's license shall be transferable, and it shall be
an offense for any hunter, or trapper to carry a license issued in the name of another person or which does not contain the seal of the officer issuing the same, and it shall be
unlawful for any person empowered to issue such license
to issue and falsely date a license with a date prior to the

Exhibition of license.

day and date of its issue. Every person shall, while hunting or trapping, carry with him his license and exhibit same
to any game protector, constable, sheriff, deputy sheriff or
police officer, or the owner or person in lawful control of
the land upon which he may be hunting or trapping, or to
any person, and failure and refusal to so carry or exhibit
his license shall constitute an offense under this section.
Nothing in this act shall be construed as allowing any person to hunt or trap on any land without the written con-

Written consent of land owner.

sent of the owner thereof. Each day that any person shall
hunt or trap within the state without having procured the
license herein required shall constitute a separate offense.
The license granted hereunder shall entitle a non-resident
to take with him from this state, game animals killed by

Limitation on number killed by non-resident.

him not to exceed twenty-five of one kind or twenty-five in
the aggregate of all kinds, but he shall not take with him
or transport from the state any game bird killed by him or
in his possession by gift or purchase. Each game bird so
transported shall constitute a separate offense.

GAME REFUGES, GAME PROPAGATION, TRESPASS.

Sec. 1435.

Power of secretary to prohibit or recall the taking of birds, fish or animals upon public lands or waters.

SECTION 45. GAME AND BIRD REFUGES. The
secretary of agriculture may for a specified period of years
prohibit or recall the taking of birds, fish and wild animals,
upon public lands or water set aside with the consent and
approval of the governor, or upon private lands set aside
with the consent of the owner thereof for game refuges. At

least thirty days before such prohibition, rule or regulation shall take effect, a copy of the same shall be filed in the office of the clerk of the township or townships to which they apply. Such game refuges shall be surrounded by at least one wire at the boundary thereof, and notices reading "State Game Refuge; Hunting is unlawful," shall be posted at conspicuous places on said boundary.

1436. SECTION 46. PHEASANT AND WILD DUCK PROPAGATION AND SALE. a. License. It shall be lawful for any citizen of the state of Ohio to engage in the business of raising and selling domesticated English ring neck or Mongolian or Chinese pheasant, mallard or black ducks, on the lands on which he is the owner or lessee. Any citizen desiring to engage in the propagation of the birds herein mentioned, shall make application in writing to the secretary of agriculture for a permit, and when it shall appear that such application is made in good faith, and upon the payment of a fee of five dollars shall be granted a breeder's license, permitting such applicant to breed and raise for commercial purposes the birds above enumerated, under the regulations herein set forth. Such license shall expire on the last day of December of each year at midnight. *Propagation and sale of wild duck and pheasant; license,; fee.*

b. Killing and sale. Any licensee or person having written permission may kill or sell either dead or alive the birds herein enumerated in accordance with the provisions set forth, at any time, and the birds so killed may be bought and sold as hereinafter stated. Before selling any such birds as provided, there shall be securely attached to the leg of each bird, a metal tag bearing the name, initials or registered trade-mark of the licensee producing such bird. Each licensee must have on file with the secretary of agriculture a copy of the trade-mark, name or initials appearing on the metal band, which is required on each bird produced and sold by him, or any person acting under his authority, and it shall be unlawful for any person, firm or corporation to buy, sell, offer for sale, or have in possession for the purpose of sale, any bird named in this section, not bearing the metal tax as herein required. No pheasant, mallard or black duck shall be killed by shooting except during the open season for such birds, or except as provided by this section. No mallard or black duck killed by shooting shall be bought or sold, unless each bird before attaining the age of four weeks shall have had removed from the web of one foot a portion thereof in the form of a V large enough to make a permanent, well-defined mark. which shall be sufficient to identify it as a bird raised in domestication under a written permit. *Killing and sale of birds; permit; attachment of tag.*

c. Report and tags. Every licensee by whom pheasants are sold or shipped under authority of this statute shall, within five days after selling or shipping same, make and file with the secretary of agriculture a written report thereof which report shall contain a statement of the num- *Report to secretary; metal tags with distinctive mark.*

ber and kinds of birds sold or shipped and the name and address of the person, firm or corporation to whom they were sold or shipped and date thereof. Blanks for making the report herein required shall be furnished by the secretary of agriculture to each licensee. The secretary of agriculture shall also, at nominal cost, supply licensee with the necessary metal tags. Such tags shall bear a distinctive mark and it shall be unlawful for any person, firm or corporation to use any other tag than that provided by the secretary of agriculture; it shall be unlawful for any person, firm or corporation, to attach to any birds or fowls mentioned in this bill, or otherwise use a tag belonging to any other licensee.

Marking for transportation.

d. Marking for transportation. It shall be unlawful for any person, firm or corporation, or transportation company to receive for transportation or transport a package, box or other receptacle containing a pheasant, mallard or black duck, unless such package bears a label on the address side, containing the name and address of the owner or consignor and a list showing the number and kinds of birds contained therein.

Sec. 1437.

Hunting without permission, trespass.

SECTION 47. TRESPASS. No person shall hunt or trap upon any lands, pond, lake or private waters of another, except water claimed by riparian right of ownership in adjacent lands, or thereon, shoot, shoot at, catch, kill, injure or pursue a wild bird, wild water fowl or wild animal without obtaining written permission from the owner or his authorized agent.

ORGANIZATION AND POWERS.

Sec. 1438.

Authority and control in secretary of agriculture.

SECTION 48. AUTHORITY OF SECRETARY OF AGRICULTURE. The secretary of agriculture shall have authority and control in all matters pertaining to the protection, preservation and propagation of song and insectivorous and game birds, wild animals and fish within the state and in and upon the waters thereof. He shall enforce by proper legal action or proceeding the laws of the state for the protection, preservation, and propagation of such birds, animals and havens for the propagation of fish and game, and, so far as funds are provided therefor, shall adopt and carry into effect such measures as he deems necessary in the performance of his duties.

Sec. 1439.

Chief of division of fish and game; assistant; supervising protector; term of office.

SECTION 49. APPOINTMENTS. For the purpose of carrying into effect the provisions of the preceding section there shall be appointed a chief of the division of fish and game, and assistant chief, a Lake Erie supervising protector and such number of fish and game protectors and special fish and game protectors as the board of agriculture may prescribe. The chief of the division of fish and game, assistant chief, Lake Erie supervising protector and each fish and game protector shall hold his office for a term of two years, unless sooner removed by the secretary of agriculture. Each special fish and game protector shall have the same powers and perform the same duties as a fish and game protector.

Sec. 1440.

SECTION 50. BONDS. Before entering upon the discharge of the duties of his office, the chief of the division of fish and game shall give bond to the state in the sum of two thousand dollars, the assistant chief and the Lake Erie supervising protector in the sum of one thousand dollars, each fish and game protector in the sum of two hundred dollars, with three sureties approved by the secretary of agriculture, conditioned for the faithful discharge of the duties of his office. Such bond, with the approval of the secretary and the oath of office endorsed thereon, shall be deposited with the secretary and kept in his office.

Bond of chief, assistant, etc., where deposited.

Sec. 1441.

SECTION 51. POWERS AND DUTIES. The chief of the division of fish and game, assistant chief, Lake Erie supervising protector, fish and game protectors and special fish and game protectors shall enforce the provisions of this act and the laws relating to the protection, preservation and propagation of birds, fish, game and fur-bearing animals, and also shall enforce the laws against trespassing on the premises, for the purpose of hunting, without the permission of the owner thereof, and shall have authority to make arrests upon view and without the issuance of a warrant therefor. Under the direction of the secretary of agriculture, the chief of the division of fish and game and assistant chief shall visit all parts of the state and direct and assist fish and game protectors in the discharge of their duties. Each protector, sheriff, deputy sheriff, constable or other police officer, may search any place that he has good reason to believe contains a bird, fish, game or fur-bearing animal, or a skin, hide or pelt thereof, or plumage of a bird killed, taken or had in possession contrary to law, or a gun, boat, net, seine, trap, ferret or device used for taking birds, fish, game or fur-bearing animals had in possession, or used contrary to law and seize each and all of them he may find, so unlawfully taken or possessed. If the owner, or person in charge of the place so searched refuse to permit such search, upon filing an affidavit in accordance with law, before an officer having jurisdiction of the offense, and receiving a search warrant issued thereon, such protector or other police officer may forcibly search the place, and if upon inspection he finds any bird, fish, game or fur-bearing animal, or a skin, hide or pelt thereof or the plumage of a bird, or a gun, net, seine, trap, or ferret, or a device unlawfully in the possession of the person, he shall forthwith seize each and all of them, and arrest the person in whose custody or possession they are found. Such bird, fish, game, fur-bearing animal or the skin, hide or pelt thereof, or the plumage of a bird; or gun, net, seine, trap or ferret, or device unlawfully used in taking such bird, fish, game or fur-bearing animal, so found shall each and all escheat to the state.

Powers and duties of chief, assistant and supervising protector.

Sec. 1442.

SECTION 52. EXECUTION OF WARRANTS; ARRESTS. The chief of the division of fish and game, assistant chief, Lake Erie Supervising protector and protectors may serve and execute warrants and other process of law is-

Execution of warrants; arrests.

sued in the enforcement of any law for the protection, pre-servation, or propagation of birds, fish and game or fur-bearing animals in the same manner as a sheriff or constable may serve and execute a process, and he may arrest on sight and without warrant a person found violating any such law. He shall have the same authority as sheriffs to require aid in executing a process or in making an arrest. He may seize without process, each bird, fish, game or fur-bearing animal and each skin, hide or pelt thereof, or the plumage of each bird when found in possession of such person, to-gether with any gun, net, seine, boat, ferret or device with which they are taken or killed, or used in taking or killing them, and forthwith convey the person so offending before a court or magistrate having jurisdiction of the offense. No person shall interfere with, threaten, abuse, assault, ob-, struct, or in any manner attempt to deter a protector or other police officer from carrying into effect any of the pro-visions of this act, or refuse to accompany a protector or other police officer when placed under arrest. Any game protector shall have the authority to make arrests under the provisions of this section for any such violations. Any pro-tector may enter upon any private lands or waters for the purpose of carrying out the provisions of this act. Arrests may be made on Sunday, in which case the offender shall be taken before a court or magistrate and required to give bond for his appearance at a time fixed for the hearing of the complaint on a week day as soon as practicable after the arrest. If a bond is required for the appearance of the offender and he fails to give it, the court may order him committed to the jail of the county or to some other suitable place until the time set for hearing of the complaint. The jailer or officer in charge of the place designated by the court shall receive the person so committed.

Sec. 1443.
Compensation of chief and others.

SECTION 53. COMPENSATION. The compensation of the chief of the division of fish and game, assistant chief, Lake Erie supervising protector, fish and game protectors and special fish and game protectors shall be fixed and paid in the same manner provided for in section 1087 of the General Code for the compensation of other agents of the secretary of agriculture. There may also be allowed and paid in the manner provided in section 1087 all necessary expenses incurred by them in the performance of their duties.

Sec. 1444.
Who charged with enforce-ment of law.

SECTION 54. SHERIFFS AND CONSTABLES. Sheriffs, deputy sheriffs, constables and other police officers shall enforce the laws for the protection, preservation and propagation of birds, fish, game and fur-bearing animals, and for this purpose they shall have the power conferred upon the fish and game protectors and receive like fees for similar services. Prosecutions by a protector or other pub-lic officer for offenses not committed in his presence shall be instituted only upon the approval of the prosecuting at-

torney of the county in which the offense is committed or
upon the approval of the attorney general.

Sec. 1445.

SECTION 55. RECEIPTS FROM FINES AND LI-
CENSES. All fines, penalties and forfeitures arising from
prosecution, convictions, confiscations, or otherwise under
this act, unless otherwise directed by the secretary of agriculture shall be paid by the officer by whom the fine is collected to the secretary of agriculture and by him paid into
the state treasury to the credit of a fund which shall be appropriated biennially for the use of the secretary of agriculture. All moneys collected as license on nets in the Lake
Erie fishing district under this act shall be paid by the
secretary of agriculture into the state treasury as a special
fund to be used in the betterment and the propagation of
fish therein, or in otherwise propagating fish in such district; and for that purpose such fund shall be appropriated
biennially, and be paid out upon the order of the secretary
of agriculture, but shall not be used or paid out for any
purpose other than the purposes for which such fund is appropriated.

Disposition of receipts from fines and li- censes.

Sec. 1446.

SECTION 56. CONTROL OF STATE WATERS AND
LANDS IN PARKS. All lakes, reservoirs and state lands
dedicated to the use of the public for park and pleasure resort purposes, with respect to the enforcement of all laws
relating to the protection of birds, fish and game, shall be
under the supervision and control of the secretary of agriculture. All laws for the protection of fish in inland rivers
and streams of the state, and all laws for the protection of
birds, fish and game and fur-bearing animals, shall apply
to all such state reservoirs and lakes. No person shall disturb, injure or destroy a tree, plant, lawn, embankment,
decoration or other property, or kill, injure or disturb a
waterfowl, water animal, bird or game, or fur-bearing animal, kept as a semi-domestic pet upon an island or within
the boundary lines of Buckeye Lake, Indian Lake, Portage
Lake, Lake St. Marys, Loramie reservoir, or any other territory over which the state has jurisdiction or an embankment or state land adjacent thereto, or take or disturb fish
in any lagoon or any other portion of any of the waters over
which the state has jurisdiction and which have been set
aside by the secretary of agriculture for the purpose of
propagation of fish.

Supervision and control by secre- tary of agricul- ture.

Sec. 1447.

SECTION 57. POWER TO TAKE FISH AND
SPAWN. Nothing in this act shall prevent the secretary
of agriculture, his agents and employes from taking fish at
any time or place or in any manner for the maintenance or
cultivation of fish in hatcheries or for the purpose of stock-
ing ponds, lakes, or rivers, or from exterminating carp in
any waters or from setting aside any portion of such waters
for the propagation of fish or water fowls. For the purpose of obtaining spawn for the fish hatcheries, the secretary
of agriculture may place his agents in any boat used in
taking fish and pay for such spawn such amount as he may

Power of secre- tary to take fish and spawn.

fix. No person engaged in fishing shall refuse to take such agents in such boat owned by him or under his control or refuse to afford them opportunity to take spawn or refuse to assist them in the performance of such duty.

PROSECUTIONS.

Sec. 1448.

Courts having final jurisdiction.

SECTION 58. JURISDICTION OF COURTS. A justice of the peace, mayor or police judge shall have final jurisdiction within his county in a prosecution for violation of any provision of the laws relating to the protection, preservation or propagation of birds, fish, game and fur-bearing animals and shall have like jurisdiction in a proceeding for the condemnation and forfeiture of property used in the violation of any such law.

Sec. 1449.

Service on corporations.

SECTION 59. SERVICE OF SUMMONS ON CORPORATIONS. When an affidavit is filed and a warrant issued against a corporation for a violation of any provision of this act, a summons shall be issued directed to the sheriff, constable or protector, commanding him to notify the accused thereof, and returnable on or before the tenth day after its date. The summons together with a copy of the warrant, shall be served and returned in the manner provided for the service of summons upon corporations in civil actions. On or before the return day, the corporation may appear by one of its officers or by council and answer the warrant by motion, demurrer or plea, but upon failure to make appearance and answer, a plea of not guilty shall be entered. Upon such appearance or plea the corporation shall be deemed present in court until the cause is finally disposed of.

Sec. 1450.

Forfeiture of illegal devices; proceedings.

SECTION 60. FORFEITURE OF ILLEGAL DEVICES. Any gun, net, seine, trap or other device used in the unlawful taking, catching or killing of a bird, fish, game or fur-bearing animal is a public nuisance. Each protector or other police officer shall seize and safely keep such property, including the illegal results thereof, and unless otherwise ordered by the secretary of agriculture, shall institute, within five days, proceedings in a proper court of the county for its forfeiture as provided by law. A writ of replevin shall not lie to take the property from his custody or from the custody or jurisdiction of the court in which such proceeding is instituted, nor shall such proceeding affect a criminal prosecution for the unlawful use of such property. An action for the forfeiture of any such property shall be commenced by the filing of an affidavit describing the property seized, and stating the unlawful use made of it, the time and place of seizure, the name of the person owning or using it at the time of seizure if known, and if unknown such fact shall be stated. Upon filing the affidavit the court shall issue a summons setting forth the facts stated in the affidavit and fixing a time and place for the hearing of the complaint. A copy of the summons shall be served on the owner or person using the property at the time of its seizure, if he is known, or by leaving a copy thereof at his usual residence, or place of business in the county, at least three days before the time fixed for the hearing of the complaint. If the owner or user is unknown or a non-resident of the county or cannot be found therein, a copy of the summons shall be posted at a suitable place nearest the place of seizure, but if his address is known a copy of the summons shall be mailed to him at least three days before the time fixed for the hearing of the complaint. On the date fixed for the hearing the officer making such service shall make a return of the time and manner of making the service. Upon proper cause shown, the court may postpone the hearing. If the owner or person unlawfully using such property at the time of its seizure is arrested, pleads guilty and confesses that the property at the time of the seizure was being used by him in violation of law, no proceedings of forfeiture shall be instituted, but the court in imposing sentence shall order the property so seized forfeited to the state, to be disposed of thereafter as the secretary of agriculture may direct.

Sec. 1451.

SECTION 61. TRIAL BY JURY. If the defendant in a proceeding for forfeiture or condemnation under this act demands a jury, the court shall issue a venire to a fish and game protector or constable of the county containing the names of sixteen persons to serve as jurors therein, who must be electors of the township, city or village for which such judge or magistrate was chosen. Such officer shall promptly execute and make return of the venire. If it be exhausted without obtaining the required number of jurors, the court may direct the officer to summon bystanders or other person. If the defendant consents in writing and such consent is entered on record, the cause may be heard by a jury composed of six persons in which case the venire shall not contain the names of more than ten electors. Each party shall be entitled to two peremptory challenges of jurors and such challenges for cause as in civil cases in the court of common pleas. A petition in error to the court of common pleas, court of appeals or supreme court may be prosecuted by the officer or person filing the complaint or by the owner or user of the property seized, to review the judgment and order of the court in forfeiting the property or in ordering its release. Such petition shall be governed by the provisions governing petitions in error in felony cases tried in the court of common pleas.

When trial shall be by jury; summoning and impaneling.

Sec. 1452.

SECTION 62. COSTS IN PROSECUTIONS. A person authorized by law to prosecute a case under the provisions of this act shall not be required to advance or secure costs therein. If the defendant be acquitted or discharged from custody, or if he be convicted and committed in default of payment of fine and costs, such costs shall be certified, under oath by the justice of the peace or other magistrate to the county auditor who shall correct all errors

Costs in prosecutions.

therein and issue his warrant on the county treasurer payable to the person or persons entitled.

Sec. 1453.

Judgment a lien on property; exemption not allowed.

SECTION 63. JUDGMENTS. If the defendant in a prosecution or condemnation proceeding under the provisions of this act is convicted, judgment shall be rendered against him for the costs in addition to the fine imposed or forfeiture declared. The judgment shall be the first lien upon his property and no exemption shall be claimed or allowed against such lien. If he fails to pay the fine and costs imposed or execution issued is returned unsatisfied, the person convicted shall be committed to the jail of the county or to a workhouse and there confined one day for each dollar of fine and costs adjudged against him. He shall not be discharged or paroled therefrom by any board or officer except upon payment of the fine and costs remaining unpaid or upon the order of the secretary of agriculture.

PENALTIES.

Sec. 1454.

Penalties for violations of law.

SECTION 64. FINES; IMPRISONMENT. Whoever violates the provisions of section 47 of this act shall be fined not less than ten dollars nor more than fifteen dollars, and for each subsequent offense shall be fined not less than fifteen dollars nor more than fifty dollars. Whoever violates the provisions of sections 26 and 52 of this act shall be fined not less than one hundred dollars nor more than five hundred dollars, and the costs of prosecution. Whoever violates any of the other provisions of this act shall be fined not less than twenty-five dollars nor more than two hundred dollars and the cost of prosecution, and upon default of payment of fine and costs assessed for any violation of this act he shall be committed to the jail of the county or to some workhouse, and there confined one day for each dollar of the fine imposed and the costs assessed. He shall not be discharged, paroled or released therefrom by any board or officers, except upon payment of the fine and costs or that portion of the fine and costs remaining unpaid or except upon the order of the secretary of agriculture.

Repeals.

SECTION 65. That sections of the General Code, 1390, 1391, 1392, 1393, 1394, 1395, 1396, 1397, 1398, 1399, 1400, 1401, 1402, 1403, 1404, 1405, 1406, 1407, 1408, 1409, 1410, 1411, 1412, 1412-1, 1412-2, 1412-3, 1412-4, 1412-5, 1413, 1414, 1415, 1415-1, 1416, 1416-1, 1417, 1418, 1419, 1420, 1421, 1422, 1423, 1424, 1425, 1426, 1427, 1428, 1429, 1430, 1431, 1432, 1433, 1434, 1435, 1436, 1437, 1437-1, 1437-2, 1438, 1439, 1440, 1441, 1442, 1443, 1444, 1445, 1446, 1447, 1448, 1449, 1450, 1451, 1452, 1453, 1454, 1455, 1456, 1457, 1458, 1459, 1460, 1461, 1462, 1463, 1464, 1465, 485, 12521,

605 .

12523, 5831-1, 5831-2, 5831-3, be, and the same are hereby repealed.

CLARENCE J. BROWN,
President of the Senate.
CARL R. KIMBALL,
Speaker of the House of Representatives.

Passed May 10, 1919.
Approved June 5, 1919.

JAMES M. COX,
Governor.

Filed in the office of the Secretary of State at Columbus, Ohio, on the 6th day of June, A. D. 1919.

190 G.

[House Bill No. 363.]

AN ACT

To supplement section 7766 of the General Code by the enactment of section 7766-1 of the General Code, making it a misdemeanor to fail or refuse to issue schooling certificate.

Be it enacted by the General Assembly of the State of Ohio:

SECTION 1. That section 7766 of the General Code be supplemented by the addition of a supplemental section to be known as section 7766-1, to read as follows:

Sec. 7766-1. Any officer or person charged by law with issuance of age and schooling certificates, who fails or refuses, upon request, to issue such certificate, in conformity to law, or who issues any such certificate contrary to any of the provisions of the law relating to the issuance of age and schooling certificates, shall be fined not less than twenty-five dollars nor more than one hundred dollars.

CARL R. KIMBALL,
Speaker of the House of Representatives.
CLARENCE J. BROWN,
President of the Senate.

Passed May 10, 1919.
Approved June 5, 1919.

JAMES M. COX,
Governor.

Filed in the office of the Secretary of State at Columbus, Ohio, on the 6th day of June, A. D. 1919.

191 G.

606

[House Bill No. 63.]

AN ACT

To amend section 7998 of the General Code, relative to the property rights of husband and wife.

Be it enacted by the General Assembly of the State of Ohio:
SECTION 1. That section 7998 of the General Code be amended to read as follows:

Interest in the property of the other.

Sec. 7998. Neither husband nor wife has any interest in the property of the other, except as mentioned in the next preceding section, the right to dower and to remain in the mansion house after the death of either, as provided by law; and neither can be excluded from the other's dwelling, except upon a decree or order of injunction made by a court of competent jurisdiction.

Repeal.

SECTION 2. That said original section 7998 of the General Code be, and the same is hereby repealed.

The sectional number in this act is in conformity to the General Code. JOHN G. PRICE, Attorney General.

CARL R. KIMBALL,
Speaker of the House of Representatives.
CLARENCE J. BROWN,
President of the Senate.

Passed May 9, 1919.
Approved June 5, 1919.

JAMES M. COX,
Governor.

Filed in the office of the Secretary of State at Columbus, Ohio, on the 6th day of June, A. D. 1919.
192 G.

[Amended Senate Bill No. 82.]

AN ACT

To amend section 5564 of the General Code, to enable the county auditor to determine the value of buildings and improvements.

Be it enacted by the General Assembly of the State of Ohio:
SECTION 1. That section 5564 of the General Code be amended to read as follows:

Notice to county auditor of building or improvement costing over $200,000.

Sec. 5564. For the purpose of enabling the county auditor to determine the value and location of buildings and other improvements every individual, partnership, incorporated company, or otherwise, except railroads and public utilities whose property is valued for taxation by the state tax commission, who shall erect or construct any building or other improvement costing over two hundred ($200.00) dollars upon any lot or land within any of the various townships, villages or municipalities not having and requiring a system of building registration and inspection shall within sixty days after said building or other improvement shall have been commenced, notify the auditor of the county within which such land or lot is located, that said building or improvement has been completed or is in process of construction. Said notice shall be in writing and contain an estimate of the cost of said building or improvement and such description of the lot or land and ownership thereof as will identify the lot or tract of land on said auditor's duplicate. Upon failure to give notice as herein provided, and upon said improvement not being returned for taxation as otherwise provided by law, and upon the discovery of such building or improvement by the county auditor after the same has been erected or constructed, the said building or improvement shall be appraised by the county auditor at its true value in money and placed upon the duplicate together with a tax penalty of fifty per cent for each of the years from the date of the erection or construction to the date of discovery. Said county auditor may enter, by himself, or deputy, within reasonable hours, and fully examine all buildings and structures of every kind, which are by this title either liable to or exempt from taxation.

Penalty for failure to give notice; appraisement by county auditor.

Examinations.

SECTION 2. That original section 5564 of the General Code be and the same is hereby repealed.

Repeals.

The sectional number in this act is in conformity to the General Code. JOHN G. PRICE, Attorney General.

CLARENCE J. BROWN,
President of the Senate.
CARL R. KIMBALL,
Speaker of the House of Representatives.
Passed May 9, 1919.
Approved June 5, 1919.

JAMES M. COX,
Governor.

Filed in the office of the Secretary of State at Columbus, Ohio, on the 6th day of June, A. D. 1919.
193 G.

[House Bill No. 544.]

AN ACT

To amend section 10150 of the General Code, regulating chambers of commerce.

Be it enacted by the General Assembly of the State of Ohio:
SECTION 1. That section 10150 of the General Code be amended to read as follows:

Sec. 10150. Such an incorporated association may purchase or lease suitable grounds and erect thereon such buildings as the board of directors may deem proper, for its interest. It may lease any portion of such building, that is not occupied by or needed for its immediate use. Such association, by a two-thirds favorable vote of its board of

Purchase or lease of grounds and erection of buildings; authority to sell and convey.

directors, may sell and convey its real estate and may borrow money and execute and sell or otherwise dispose of its bonds or obligations secured by a mortgage of its property or otherwise. The president and secretary of such association, when so authorized, shall sign all obligations and conveyances.

Repeal.

The sectional number in this act is in conformity to the General Code. JOHN G. PRICE, *Attorney General.*

SECTION 2. That said original section 10150 of the General Code be, and the same is hereby repealed.

CARL R. KIMBALL,
Speaker of the House of Representatives.
CLARENCE J. BROWN,
President of the Senate.

Passed May 10, 1919.
Approved June 5, 1919.

JAMES M. COX,
Governor.

Filed in the office of the Secretary of State at Columbus, Ohio, on the 6th day of June, A. D. 1919.

194 G.

[Senate Bill No. 111.]

AN ACT

To amend section 14203-23 of the General Code, relating to the abandonment of that portion of the Ohio Canal between the Aqueduct of said canal over Raccoon Creek and the village of Hebron, Licking county, Ohio.

Be it enacted by the General Assembly of the State of Ohio:

SECTION 1. That section 14203-23 of the General Code be amended to read as follows:

Appraisement, sale and lease of lands.

Sec. 14203-23. As soon as surveys and plats of said abandoned canal lands have been completed, the superintendent of public works shall proceed to appraise, sell or lease said lands, subject to the approval of the governor and attorney general, in strict conformity with the various provisions of the General Code relating to the selling and leasing of state canal lands, (section 13971 G. C.) except that the term of such leases shall not be for less than fifteen, nor more than twenty-five years, and that the bed and banks of such canal may be included in any lease of such abandoned canal lands, and in case of a sale of such land, the fee simple title thereto shall be conveyed.

Notice of sale or lease.

Before proceeding to sell or lease any of said abandoned Ohio Canal lands, except to the owners of existing leases, the superintendent of public works, shall give at least thirty days notice by publication in two newspapers of opposite politics and of general circulation in the county where said lands are located, that he will on and after the date of publication and for ninety days thereafter receive applications for the purchase or lease of said abandoned canal lands, and after the expiration of said period, leases and sales of said abandoned canal lands may be made in accordance with the provisions of this act.

SECTION 2. That said original section 14203-23 of the General Code be, and the same is hereby repealed.

Repeal.

CLARENCE J. BROWN,
President of the Senate.
CARL R. KIMBALL,
Speaker of the House of Representatives.

Passed May 8, 1919.
Approved June 5, 1919.

JAMES M. COX,
Governor.

Filed in the office of the Secretary of State at Columbus, Ohio, on the 6th day of June, A. D. 1919.

195 G.

[Senate Bill No. 135.]

AN ACT

To aid in defraying the expenses of maintaining permanent headquarters for the department of Ohio, United Spanish War Veterans, at Columbus, Ohio.

Be it enacted by the General Assembly of the State of Ohio:

Sec. 14875-3.

SECTION 1. That the General Assembly shall assist, by appropriations of money, in defraying the expense in maintaining a permanent headquarters of the department of Ohio, United Spanish War Veterans, in the city of Columbus, Ohio.

Headquarters of O. U. S. war veterans in Columbus.

Sec. 14875-4.

SECTION 2. That, for the purpose set forth in section 1 of this act, there is hereby appropriated from the general revenue fund of the state, not otherwise appropriated, the sum of fifteen hundred dollars for the fiscal year ending June 30, 1920, and fifteen hundred dollars for the fiscal year ending June 30, 1921. The expenditure of this money shall be on vouchers drawn on the auditor of state and signed by the department commander, attested by the adjutant, department of Ohio, United Spanish War Veterans.

Appropriation.

CLARENCE J, BROWN,
President of the Senate.
CARL R. KIMBALL,
Speaker of the House of Representatives.

Passed April 9, 1919.
Approved June 5, 1919.

JAMES M. COX,
Governor.

Filed in the office of the Secretary of State at Columbus, Ohio, on the 6th day of June, A. D. 1919.

196 G.

[House Bill No. 537.]

AN ACT

Giving to councils power and authority to permit the use of a reasonable portion of any public park in any city for Chautauqua Assembly purposes, and regulating matters connected therewith.

Be it enacted by the General Assembly of the State of Ohio:

Sec. 5893-1.

Council may permit public park to be used by Chautauqua.

SECTION 1. That councils of all cities of this state having a population of not more than 13,388 by the federal census of 1910, shall have power and authority to permit the use of a reasonable portion of any public park in such cities for a period not to exceed thirty days in any one year for Chautauqua assembly purposes, and shall have power and authority to permit the persons so using any portion of any public park for Chautauqua assembly purposes to temporarily enclose such portion of any such public park so used and to charge an entrance fee to such park so temporarily enclosed as aforesaid. Provided, however, that any person or persons so permitted to use any portion of any public park for the purposes aforesaid, shall be required to restore such portion of such park so used to the same condition it was in before such use; and, provided, further, that all funds derived from such use of such park after paying the expenses of any such Chautauqua assembly shall be used for park improvements or charitable purposes in such city.

SECTION 2. This act shall take effect and be in force at the earliest period allowed by law.

The sectional number on the margin hereof is designated as provided by law.
JOHN G. PRICE,
Attorney
General.

CARL R. KIMBALL,
Speaker of the House of Representatives.
CLARENCE J. BROWN,
President of the Senate.

Passed May 10, 1919.
Approved June 5, 1919.

JAMES M. COX,
Governor.

Filed in the office of the Secretary of State at Columbus, Ohio, on the 6th day of June, A. D. 1919.

197 G.

[Senate Bill No. 167.]

AN ACT

To amend sections 2068, 1815-13 and 1815-14 of the General Code, relating to the admission of persons into the Ohio State Sanatorium, and payment for their support.

Be it enacted by the General Assembly of the State of Ohio:
SECTION 1. That sections 2068, 1815-13, 1815-14 of the General Code be amended to read as follows:

Sec. 2068. Any citizen of this state of more than seven years of age, suffering from pulmonary tuberculosis in the incipient or early stage, as determined by the superintendent, may be admitted to the sanatorium upon payment in advance of a sum to be fixed by the superintendent, said sum to be not less than five dollars nor more than twenty-five dollars each week, according to the financial condition and ability to pay of the person applying for admittance or any other person legally liable for the care and support of said applicant. Said sum, so fixed, shall fully cover all expenses for medical treatment, medicine, nursing, board, lodging and laundry. The superintendent shall make such investigation as is necessary to determine such financial condition and ability to pay, and may at any time increase or decrease the amount within the limits herein prescribed upon the approval of the Ohio board of administration. Payment for the support of patients in the sanatorium shall be made in accordance with the provisions of sections 1815-13, 1815-14 and 1815-15 of the General Code. *(Who entitled to admission; payment for support.)*

Sec. 1815-13. It shall be the duty of the board of state charities to make collections for the support of patients at the Ohio state sanatorium.. When the superintendent of the Ohio state sanatorium shall report to the board of state charities that an applicant for admission to or an inmate of that institution or any person legally responsible for his support is not financially able to pay the minimum amount fixed by section 2068 of the General Code, it shall be the duty of the state board of charities by its authorized agents to make a thorough investigation as is provided by law for such investigations in other institutions. *(Collections for support; investigations.)*

Sec. 1815-14. If after the investigation provided in the next preceding section it shall be found that said applicant or inmate or any person legally responsible for his support is unable to pay the minimum amount fixed by law, said board of state charities shall determine what amount, if any, said applicant or inmate or any person legally responsible for his support shall pay. The difference between the amount so determined and the minimum amount fixed by section 2068 of the General Code shall be paid by the county in which said applicant or patient has a legal residence. The amount so determined to be paid by the county shall be paid from the poor fund on the order of the county commissioners. *(When county shall pay for support of patients.)*

SECTION 2. That said original sections 2068, 1815-13 and 1815-14 of the General Code be, and the same hereby are repealed.

CLARENCE J. BROWN,
President of the Senate.
CARL R. KIMBALL,
Speaker of the House of Representatives.
Passed May 9, 1919.
Approved June 5, 1919.

JAMES M. COX,
Governor.

Filed in the office of the Secretary of State at Columbus, Ohio, on the 6th day of June, A. D. 1919.

198 G.

[House Bill No. 255.]

AN ACT

To amend section 5330 of the General Code, so as to provide a definite rule for valuation of school and ministerial lands held under perpetual lease.

Be it enacted by the General Assembly of the State of Ohio:
SECTION 1. That section 5330 of the General Code be amended to read as follows:

Sec. 5330. Whenever lands belonging to the state, a municipal corporation, religious, scientific or benevolent society or institution, whether incorporated or unincorporated, or to trustees for free education only, or held by the state in trust, are held under lease for a term of years renewable forever and not subject to revaluation, such lands shall be considered, for all purposes of taxation, as the property of the lessees and shall be assessed in their names. Whenever school and ministerial lands are held under perpetual lease subject to revaluation, the interest of such lessees in such lands shall be subject to taxation. In determining the value for purposes of taxation of such leasehold interest, the true value in money of the land shall be ascertained, the annual rent reserved in the lease shall be capitalized on a six per centum basis and that sum deducted from the true value of the land in money; the result so obtained plus the value of all of the improvements upon such land shall be the appraised taxable value of such leasehold interest.

Whenever such school or ministerial lands are held under lease for terms of years renewable forever, whether subject to revaluation or not, such lands shall for all purposes of special assessment for improvements benefiting such land be considered as the property of the lessee. Whenever such lands are held on leases for terms not renewable forever, such lands shall be subject to special assessments benefiting such lands, which shall be paid out of the annual rents accruing to the trust.

Whenever it appears that the net annual rents or earnings accruing from such lands will be insufficient to pay the sum of such assessment as the same becomes payable, the state supervisor of school and ministerial lands, upon the request of the trustees in local charge of such lands shall issue and sell notes for the sum so required, payable in such number of years as will be required for the net rents to meet the whole sum of such assessment, and bearing interest at not more than five per centum per annum as the state supervisor shall determine. But such notes shall not be sold for less than par. Such notes and interest thereon shall be a lien upon the rents or earnings of the proceeds of any sale of such lands so assessed, and the sum of such notes and interest shall be paid out of such rents or earnings or proceeds of such sale by the state supervisor. *When notes shall be issued to pay assessment.*

SECTION 2. That said original section 5330 of the General Code be, and the same is hereby repealed. *Repeal.*

he sectional number in this ct is in conformity to the General Code.
OHN G. PRICE,
ttorney
General.

CARL R. KIMBALL,
Speaker of the House of Representatives.
CLARENCE J. BROWN,
President of the Senate.

Passed May 6, 1919.
Approved June 5, 1919.

JAMES M. COX,
Governor.

Filed in the office of the Secretary of State at Columbus, Ohio, on the 6th day of June, A. D. 1919.

199 G.

[House Bill No. 408.]

AN ACT

To amend section 7642 of the General Cole, relating to school libraries.

Be it enacted by the General Assembly of the State of Ohio:

SECTION 1. That section 7642 of the General Code be amended to read as follows:

Sec. 7642. The board of education of any school district of the state, in which there is not a public library operated under public authority and free to all the residents of such district annually may appropriate not to exceed two hundred and fifty dollars from its contingent fund for the purchase of books, other than school books, for the use and improvement of the teachers and pupils of such school district. And whenever the board of education of such district receives donations or bequests for the purposes aforesaid *School library may be provided.*

the board of education shall appropriate from its tuition or contingent funds or both a like amount, but not to exceed one hundred dollars in any one year for any particular school in such district. The books so purchased shall constitute a school library, the control and management of which shall be vested in the board of education, which may receive donations and bequests of money or property therefor.

Repeal.

SECTION 2. That original section 7642 of the General Code be, and the same is hereby repealed.

CARL R. KIMBALL,
Speaker of the House of Representatives.
CLARENCE J. BROWN,
President of the Senate.

The sectional number in this act is in conformity to the General Code. JOHN G. PRICE, Attorney General.

Passed May 10, 1919.
Approved June 5, 1919.

JAMES M. COX,
Governor.

Filed in the office of the Secretary of State at Columbus, Ohio, on the 6th day of June, A. D. 1919.

200 G.

[Amended Senate Bill No. 137.]

AN ACT

To supplement section 7762 of the General Code, by the addition of supplemental sections to be known as sections 7762-1, 7762-2, 7762-3 and 7762-4, and to repeal section 7729, concerning elementary, private and parochial schools and providing that instruction shall be in the English language.

Be it enacted by the General Assembly of the State of Ohio:

SECTION 1. That section 7762 be supplemented by sections 7762-1, 7762-2, 7762-3 and 7762-4 to read as follows:

Branches in elementary schools shall be taught in English only.

Sec. 7762-1. That all subjects and branches taught in the elementary schools of the state of Ohio below the eighth grade shall be taught in the English language only. The board of education, trustees, directors and such other officers as may be in control, shall cause to be taught in the elementary schools all the branches named in section 7648 of the General Code. Provided, that the German language shall not be taught below the eighth grade in any of the elementary schools of this state.

Pupils in private parochial schools, etc., shall be taught in English only.

Sec. 7762-2. All private and parochial schools and all schools maintained in connection with benevolent and correctional institutions within this state which instruct pupils who have not completed a course of study equivalent to that prescribed for the first seven grades of the elementary schools of this state, shall be taught in the English language only, and the person or persons, trustees or officers in control shall cause to be taught in them such branches of learning as prescribed in section 7648 of the General Code or such as the advancement of pupils may require, and the persons or officers in control direct; provided that the German language shall not be taught below the eighth grade in any such schools within this state.

Sec. 7762-3. Any person or persons violating the provisions of this act shall be guilty of a misdemeanor and shall be fined in any sum not less than twenty-five dollars nor more than one hundred dollars, and each separate day in which such act shall be violated shall constitute a separate offense. *Penalty for violations of law.*

Sec. 7762-4. In case any section or sections of this act shall be held to be unconstitutional by the supreme court of Ohio such decision shall not affect the validity of the remaining sections. *Section held unconstitutional shall not affect others.*

SECTION 2. That section 7729 of the General Code be, and the same is hereby repealed.

The sectional numbers in this act are in conformity to the General Code. JOHN G. PRICE, Attorney General.

CLARENCE J. BROWN,
President of the Senate.
CARL R. KIMBALL,
Speaker of the House of Representatives.

Passed May 8, 1919.
Approved June 5, 1919.

JAMES M. COX,
Governor.

Filed in the office of the Secretary of State at Columbus, Ohio, on the 6th day of June, A. D. 1919.

201 G.

[House Bill No. 352.]

AN ACT

To empower board of state charities to appoint voluntary investigators.

Be it enacted by the General Assembly of the State of Ohio:

Sec. 1359.

SECTION 1. The board of state charities is hereby empowered to appoint and commission any competent agency or person, willing to do so without compensation, as a special agent, investigator or representative to perform a designated duty for and in behalf of such board. Specific credentials shall be given by such board to each person so designated, and each credential shall state the name; agency with which connected, if any; purpose of appointment; date *Appointment of special agent or investigator authorized; credentials.*

616

of expiration of appointment, and such other information as such board may deem proper.

The sectional number on the margin hereof is designated as provided by law.
JOHN G. PRICE, Attorney General.

CARL R. KIMBALL,
Speaker of the House of Representatives.
CLARENCE J. BROWN,
President of the Senate.

Passed May 6, 1919.
Approved June 5, 1919.

JAMES M. COX,
Governor.

Filed in the office of the Secretary of State at Columbus, Ohio, on the 6th day of June, A. D. 1919.

202 G.

[House Bill No. 540.]

AN ACT

To amend section 12805 of the General Code, to provide penalty for disorderly conduct at militia encampment and military cantonment.

Be it enacted by the General Assembly of the State of Ohio:

SECTION 1. That section 12805 of the General Code be amended to read as follows:

Penalty for entering camp or cantonment without permission.

Sec. 12805. Whoever enters an encampment of the national guard, or a camp or cantonment of any military organization of the United States, when forbidden so to do, or, having been permitted to enter therein, conducts himself in a disorderly manner or resists a sentry or guard acting under orders to prevent such entry or disorderly conduct, shall be fined not more than one hundred dollars and be committed until such fines and costs are paid.

Repeal.

SECTION 2. That said original section 12805 of the General Code be, and the same is hereby repealed.

The sectional number in this act is in conformity to the General Code.
JOHN G. PRICE, Attorney General.

CARL R. KIMBALL,
Speaker of the House of Representatives.
CLARENCE J. BROWN,
President of the Senate.

Passed May 7, 1919.
Approved June 5, 1919.

JAMES M. COX,
Governor.

Filed in the office of the Secretary of State at Columbus, Ohio, on the 6th day of June, A. D. 1919.

203 G.

617

[Amended Senate Bill No. 141.]

AN ACT

To amend section 1946 of the General Code, relative to the officers and employes of the Ohio Soldiers' and Sailors' Orphans' Home.

Be it enacted by the General Assembly of the State of Ohio:
SECTION 1. That section 1946 of the General Code be, and the same is hereby amended to read as follows:

Sec. 1946. The compensation of the officers and employes of the home shall be fixed by the board of trustees. No person, unless he shall have been in the actual military or naval service of the United States and shall have received an honorable discharge therefrom, shall be eligible to hold the position or office of superintendent. Provided, however, that the provisions of this section shall not affect the tenure of the position or office of the present superintendent.

Compensation of officers and employes.

SECTION 2. That original section 1946 of the General Code be, and the same is hereby repealed.

The sectional number in this act is in conformity to the General Code.
JOHN G. PRICE, Attorney General.

CLARENCE J. BROWN,
President of the Senate.
CARL R. KIMBALL,
Speaker of the House of Representatives.

Passed May 10, 1919.
Approved June 5, 1919.

JAMES M. COX,
Governor.

Filed in the office of the Secretary of State at Columbus, Ohio, on the 6th day of June, A. D. 1919.

204 G.

[House Bill No. 538.]

AN ACT

For the relief of John J. Boyle, county treasurer of Cuyahoga county.

Be it enacted by the General Assembly of the State of Ohio:
SECTION 1. That the county commissioners of Cuyahoga county be and are hereby authorized to pay to John J. Boyle, county treasurer of Cuyahoga county one hundred and ninety-five dollars and fifty-four cents ($195.54) in full payment for postage purchased from the postmaster of

Authority to pay John J. Boyle, Cuyahoga county.

Cleveland on February 12th, and February 25th, 1919, such payment to be made in the usual manner prescribed by law.

CARL R. KIMBALL,
Speaker of the House of Representatives.
CLARENCE J. BROWN,
President of the Senate.

Passed May 10, 1919.
Approved June 5, 1919.

JAMES M. COX,
Governor.

Filed in the office of the Secretary of State at Columbus, Ohio, on the 6th day of June, A. D. 1919.

205 G.

[House Bill No. 407.]

AN ÁCT

To amend sections 3197, 3199, 3203-5, 3203-8, 3203-21 and 3203-35 and to supplement sections 3193, 3203-2, 3203-4, 3203-12 and 3203-21 by the enactment respectively of sections 3193-1, 3203-2a, 3203-4a, 3203-12a and 3203-21a of the General Code, relating to school and ministerial lands.

Be it enacted by the General Assembly of the State of Ohio:
SECTION 1. That sections 3197, 3199, 3203-5, 3203-8, 3203-21 and 3203-35 of the General Code be amended and that sections 3193, 3203-2, 3203-4, 3203-12 and 3203-21 be supplemented respectively by the enactment of sections to be known as sections 3193-1, 3203-2a, 3203-4a, 3203-12a and 3203-21a of the General Code, to read as follows:

Bonds of officers. Sec. 3197. The duties herein devolved upon the township trustees, clerk and treasurer shall be in addition to the duties otherwise devolving upon them by law, and the bonds of each, executed pursuant to sections 3269, 3270, 3300, 3310 and 3311 of the General Code, shall be liable for the faithful performance of their several duties under this act, and the faithful accounting for all property and moneys that may come into their hands pursuant to the provisions of this act, or under color of office. The state supervisor may,
State supervisor may require increase of bond. however, require that the bonds required by the aforementioned sections of the General Code shall be increased in such sum as in his opinion will be necessary to fully protect the school and ministerial land trust. If the state supervisor appoints an agent in the stead of a relieved and discharged township officer, such agent shall give bond, payable to the state of Ohio, with sureties approved by the state supervisor, in such sum as the state supervisor shall prescribe, conditioned on the faithful performance of his duties as such agent, and that he will fully account for all property and moneys that may come into his hands as such agent pur-

suant to law or under color of his office. Such bonds required of agents shall be filed with the state supervisor. The cost of such bonds required of agents and the cost of such increased sum of the bonds of township officers shall be paid out of any funds derived from the rents of the school or ministerial lands.

Sec. 3199. If the state supervisor finds upon investigation that any such township officer is not satisfactorily administering such trust, or fails to properly perform any duty or act herein required of him, or if any township officer requests to be relieved of duties relating to the school or ministerial lands, the state supervisor may relieve and discharge such officer from the performance of all duties imposed upon him in the administration of the school and ministerial land trust under this act. The state supervisor may thereupon select and appoint in the stead of such discharged and relieved township officer an agent, which agent shall perform all and singular the duties devolved by law upon such relieved and discharged township officer, and shall give bond as required by law. The release and discharge of such township officer shall not otherwise affect him or operate to relieve him from his duties otherwise devolving upon him as such township officer. The agent so appointed may be appointed to act in the stead of more than one township officer. Removal of officer; appointment of agent.

Sec. 3203-8. The rent reserved in such leases shall in all cases be such bonus as may be bid therefor together with five per centum per annum on the appraised value. Rent.

Sec. 3203-21. At any time within three years next following June 29, 1917, any lessee, holding under a lease renewable forever, may make application to the state supervisor setting forth a description of the lands for which he desires a title in fee simple, the quantity thereof, the date of his lease or assignment of lease under which he claims title, the price per acre and the total price which he desires to pay for such title in fee simple, and such further information that may be required by the state supervisor. The state supervisor thereupon shall make such investigation of the title of such applicant, and of the history of the tract of land in question, as he shall deem necessary to make a determination of the price which such applicant shall be required to pay for such title in fee simple. In making such determination the state supervisor may take into consideration the amount of taxes for state, county and other purposes which have been charged upon such lands and paid, the moral obligation which may rest upon the state because of the neglect of its administrative officers to administer the trust and the terms of the trust as defined in the acts of congress relating thereto; but nothing herein shall be construed as creating any legal obligation against the state arising from the payment of such taxes or such neglect of its administrative agencies. The state supervisor shall determine what price the applicant shall pay for the fee simple title to such lands and the manner of payment, and How lessee may obtain title in fee simple.

whenever the applicant or his assigns shall have paid the said purchase money in full into the state treasury, the auditor of state shall prepare a deed for such lands conveying the same in fee simple to such applicant or his assigns, and shall deliver such deed to the governor of the state, together with his certificate that all papers required by law have been properly filed and that all conditions precedent to the execution of such deed have been complied with. When signed by the governor, countersigned by the secretary of state and sealed with the great seal of the state of Ohio, such deed shall be returned to the state supervisor who shall transmit it to the applicant or his assigns.

Apportionment by county auditor.

Sec. 3203-35. Money received by the county treasurer under sections 3203-33 and 3203-34 of the General Code, derived from the rents of lands appropriated for the use of common schools, shall be apportioned by the county auditor at the time he makes the apportionment of the interest on the common school fund upon the basis of the enumeration of youth of school age in each school district or part of a school district lying within the original survey township or other district of county to which such money belongs.

Fees of trustees and clerk.

Sec. 3193-1. Whenever the trustees meet for the purpose of making distribution of the ministerial trust fund, they shall each receive a fee of ten per centum of the sum to be distributed, but in no case to exceed one dollar and fifty cents each, and the township clerk shall receive a fee of fifty cents for recording the action of the trustees and writing the orders on the county auditor.

When new appraisement may be directed; report to supervisor.

Sec. 3203-2a. If the lessees or the trustees fail within thirty days after notice from the state supervisor to make and report to the state supervisor the name and address of such arbitrator, or if the arbitrators fail to meet at the time and place designated by the state supervisor, the state supervisor may direct a new appraisement to be made by two householders of the township in which the lands lie. The report of such householders shall be filed with the state supervisor and a copy posted at the usual meeting place of the township trustees, and any person affected by such appraisal may, within thirty days after the receipt of such report by the state supervisor, file with the state supervisor a protest against the same. Should the state supervisor, on hearing, find that the protest is just, he may set aside such last appraisal and direct a new appraisal by two householders of the county in which such lands lie.

Resurvey and lease.

Sec. 3203-4a. Whenever lands are to be leased and the lessee in possession has no option of acceptance pursuant to section 3203-12, the state supervisor may cause such lands to be resurveyed and leased in separate tracts of not less than ten acres, nor more than one hundred and sixty acres.

Publication of intended lease or sale of lease; acceptance of proposals.

Sec. 3203-5. In all cases where such lands are to be leased, the state supervisor shall cause pubication thereof to be made in such newspapers as he shall direct, or by posting notices thereof in at least five public places within such township. Such publication shall be for such time and made in such manner as he shall direct, and shall advertise the appraised value of each tract of land, the time when proposals will be received or the sale of such leases had, and such other facts as in the opinion of the state supervisor shall be made known. If the state supervisor determines that it is for the best interest of the trust he may provide for the sale of such lease or leases by public auction held upon or in the vicinity of such lands; otherwise he shall require the filing of sealed proposals. He shall give preference to and accept only the proposal for each tract so to be leased which offers the best terms for the trust. He may refuse to accept any or all proposals. The state supervisor may require the lessee of such lands, at the time of the execution of the lease therefor, to execute notes for the payment of the rents reserved, with or without security to his approval.

Sec. 3203-12a. If upon the advice of the township trustees the state supervisor is of the opinion that any tract of land can yield the best gain by leasing the same upon a contract providing for the farming of the same on shares in lieu of a cash rent, the state supervisor may enter into such a lease and contract. Whenever the state supervisor finds that it is for the best interest of the trust he shall advertise the sale of such a contract and lease, publishing the time and place where sealed bids will be received, or the sale of such lease had, the fact that a lease and contract will be executed in the manner aforesaid and a pertinent description of the land. Such advertisement shall be in such form and manner as the state supervisor shall determine. On the day so advertised such sale shall be had or all bids shall be opened, and the bidder who offers the best terms for the trust shall be awarded such lease and contract. The term of such lease and contract shall be governed by the provisions of section 3203-6 of the General Code. *Lease upon contract providing shares in lieu of cash.*

Sec. 3203-21a. All deeds heretofore executed pursuant to section 3203-21 of the General Code for any lands for which the full purchase price as determined pursuant to said section 3203-21 of the General Code has been paid into the state treasury, and the sales of which lands are evidenced by such deeds, are hereby confirmed, and the filing of an application, the determination of a price by the state supervisor and the payment in full into the state treasury of the price so determined shall be held to be a sufficient compliance with the law, though otherwise the conditions precedent to the execution and delivery of such deed have not been complied with, and the purchasers and their assigns and heirs at law shall hold the said lands by a title as good and valid as though the proceedings for such sale had been in complete conformance with section 3203-21 of the General Code. *What deemed compliance with law in conveyances.*

SECTION 2. That original sections 3197, 3199, 3203-5, 3203-8, 3203-21 and 3203-35 of the General Code be, and the same are hereby repealed.

CARL R. KIMBALL,
Speaker of the House of Representatives.
CLARENCE J. BROWN,
President of the Senate.

Passed May 7, 1919.
Approved June 5, 1919.

JAMES M. COX,
Governor.

Filed in the office of the Secretary of State at Columbus, Ohio, on the 6th day of June, A. D. 1919.

206 G.

[Senate Bill No. 44.]

AN ACT

To further supplement sections 7823 and 7807 and to supplement section 7831 by the enactment of supplemental sections 7823-2, 7807-9 and 7831-1 of the General Code, to provide for the certification of teachers of classes supported with federal aid under supervision of the state board of education.

Be it enacted by the General Assembly of the State of Ohio:

SECTION 1. That supplementary sections 7823-2, 7807-9 and 7831-1 of the General Code be added to read as follows:

Qualifications and examination of teachers to give vocational instruction.

Sec. 7823-2. Applicants for certificates to teach vocational agriculture, home economics, specific industrial vocational subjects, or other subjects taught in classes supported with federal aid and under the supervision of the state board of education, must possess such qualifications. certified to the board of examiners by the superintendent of public instruction and must pass such examination, as may be determined by the superintendent of public instruction with the approval of the state board of education.

Provisional certificates valid for four years shall be granted; fee.

Sec. 7807-9. State provisional certificates valid for four years to teach vocational agriculture, home economics, specific industrial vocational subjects, or other subjects, taught in classes supported with federal aid and under the supervision of the state board of education, shall be granted by the superintendent of public instruction upon formal application and the payment of a fee of one dollar, to those who have completed such requirements for the particular certificates as shall have been established by the superintendent of public instruction with the approval of the state board of education.

Teacher must have certificate of character and qualifications.

Sec. 7831-1. No person shall be employed or enter upon the performance of his duties as teacher of a class supported with federal aid under the supervision of the state board of education in any school district who has not obtained from a certificating authority having legal jurisdiction a certificate certifying to his good moral character and to the qualifications to teach such class which may be prescribed by the superintendent of public instruction with the approval of the state board of education.

CLARENCE J. BROWN,
President of the Senate.
CARL R. KIMBALL,
Speaker of the House of Representatives.
Passed May 10, 1919.
Approved June 5, 1919.

JAMES M. COX,
Governor.

Filed in the office of the Secretary of State at Columbus, Ohio, on the 6th day of June, A. D. 1919.
207 G.

[House Bill No. 473.]

AN ACT

To amend section 2503 of the General Code, relative to Memorial Day.

Be it enacted by the General Assembly of the State of Ohio:
SECTION 1. That section 2503 of the General Code be amended to read as follows:

Sec. 2503. The commissioners of a county, annually, upon request of the officials thereof, may appropriate to each post of the Grand Army of the Republic, to each camp of Spanish war veterans, and to each camp or post of any organization of veterans of the world war against the Central Powers of Europe, in the county, the sum of fifty dollars to aid in defraying the expenses of Memorial day, and whenever any post or camp is combined with another post or camp, or when a post or camp is now composed of two or more posts or camps combined, then such appropriation to each post or camp shall be made to include an amount for each original post or camp the same as before they were so combined. The township trustees may, on or before the 15th day of May in each year appropriate a sum not to exceed twenty-five dollars from the general expense fund of the township for the purpose of properly observing Memorial day within the township, and if any post or camp of any organization of veterans who have served in any war in the service of the United States, is located within such township, such appropriation shall be made to such post or camp. Any municipality located within a township may cooperate with such township or with the county in observing Memorial day, and the council thereof may make the necessary appropriation therefor.

Memorial day appropriations

SECTION 2. That original section 2503 of the General Code be, and the same is hereby repealed.

The sectional number in this act is in conformity to the General Code. JOHN G. PRICE, Attorney General.

CARL R. KIMBALL,
Speaker of the House of Representatives.
CLARENCE J. BROWN,
President of the Senate.

Passed May 10, 1919.
Approved June 5, 1919.

JAMES M. COX,
Governor.

Filed in the office of the Secretary of State at Columbus, Ohio, on the 6th day of June, A. D. 1919.

208 G.

[House Bill No. 507.]

AN ACT

To amend section 1683-9 of the General Code relating to mothers' pensions.

Be it enacted by the General Assembly of the State of Ohio.

SECTION 1. That section 1683-9 of the General Code be amended to read as follows:

Provisions for mothers' pensions; tax levy.

Sec. 1683-9. It is hereby made the duty of the county commissioners to provide out of the money in the county treasury such sum each year thereafter as will meet the requirements of the court in these proceedings. To provide the same they shall levy a tax not to exceed one-fifth of a mill on the dollar valuation of the taxable property of the county. Such levy shall be subject to all the limitations provided by law upon the aggregate amount, rate, maximum rate and combined maximum rate of taxation. The county auditor shall issue a warrant upon the county treasurer for the payment of such allowance as may be ordered by the juvenile judge.

Repeal.

SECTION 2. That said original section 1683-9 of the General Code be, and the same is hereby repealed.

The sectional number in this act is in conformity to the General Code. JOHN G. PRICE, Attorney General.

CARL R. KIMBALL,
Speaker of the House of Representatives.
CLARENCE J. BROWN,
President of the Senate.

Passed May 10, 1919.
Approved June 5, 1919.

JAMES M. COX,
Governor.

Filed in the office of the Secretary of State at Columbus, Ohio, on the 6th day of June, A. D. 1919.

209 G.

[Senate Bill No. 132.]

AN ACT

To amend section 10494 of the General Code of Ohio, relative to the jurisdiction of the probate courts in certain counties.

Be it enacted by the General Assembly of the State of Ohio:

SECTION 1. That section 10494 of the General Code be amended to read as follows:

Sec. 10494. In the counties of Pickaway, Licking, Richland, Perry, Defiance, Henry, Fayette and Coshocton, the Probate Court shall have concurrent jurisdiction with the court of Common Pleas in all proceedings in divorce, alimony, partition, and foreclosure of mortgages. In such suits or proceedings in the probate courts of such counties, it shall have jurisdiction to make, and enter any finding, order, judgment or decree, which the common pleas could make, and enter in such suits or proceedings. *Concurrent jurisdiction with common pleas.*

SECTION 2. That said original section 10494 be, and the same hereby is repealed. *Repeal.*

CLARENCE J. BROWN,
President of the Senate.
CARL R. KIMBALL,
Speaker of the House of Representatives.

The sectional number in this act is in conformity to the General Code. JOHN G. PRICE, Attorney General.

Passed May 9, 1919.
Approved June 5, 1919.

JAMES M. COX,
Governor.

Filed in the office of the Secretary of State at Columbus, Ohio, on the 6th day of June, A. D. 1919.

210 G.

[Amended Senate Bill No. 132.]

AN ACT

To amend section 1921 of the General Code, and enact supplemental section 1921-1 of the General Code, providing for further admissions to the Madison Home.

Be it enacted by the General Assembly of the State of Ohio:

SECTION 1. That section 1921 of the General Code be amended to read as follows:

Sec. 1921. Subject to the provision that preference be given to those who served in Ohio military organizations, the following persons may be admitted to the Madison homes: All honorably discharged soldiers, sailors and marines, who served the United States government in the Civil war, from eighteen hundred sixty-one to eighteen hundred sixty-five, who are citizens of Ohio, and who are not able to support themselves; their wives, to whom such soldiers, *Who entitled to admission to Madison home.*

sailors, and marines were married at any time prior to June first, nineteen hundred five; their widows, to whom such soldiers, sailors and marines were married prior to June first, nineteen hundred five; and the dependent mothers of such soldiers, sailors and marines; residents of Ohio; in case of death of such soldier, sailor or marine, his surviving wife may live in and be supported by the home.

Limitation as to widows, mothers or nurses of the war with Spain. SECTION 1921-1. Subject to the provisions of Sec. 1921 there may be admitted to the Madison home, not to exceed five widows, mothers or nurses of the war with Spain.

SECTION 3. That original section 1921 of the General Code be, and the same is hereby repealed.

The sectional numbers in this act are in conformity to the General Code. JOHN G. PRICE, Attorney General.

CLARENCE J. BROWN,
President of the Senate.
CARL R. KIMBALL,
Speaker of the House of Representatives.
Passed April 9, 1919.
Approved June 5, 1919.

JAMES M. COX,
Governor.

Filed in the office of the Secretary of State at Columbus, Ohio, on the 6th day of June, A. D. 1919.

211 G.

[Amended Senate Bill No. 136.]

AN ACT

To amend section 2250 of the General Code, relating to the annual salaries of appointive state officers and employes, and to repeal said original section 2250 of the General Code.

Be it enacted by the General Assembly of the State of Ohio:

Salaries of appointive state officers. SECTION 1. That section 2250 of the General Code be amended to read as follows:

Sec. 2250. The annual salaries of the appointive state officers and employes herein enumerated shall be as follows:

Superintendent of insurance, four thousand five hundred dollars;

Superintendent of banks, seventy-five hundred dollars.

Supervisor of public printing, two thousand dollars.

State librarian, three thousand dollars; assistant state librarian, one thousand and five hundred dollars.

Commissioner of soldiers' claims, two thousand five hundred dollars.

Secretary of state board of health, three thousand five hundred dollars.

SECTION 2. That said original section 2250 of the General Code be and the same 'is hereby repealed. *Repeal.*

CLARENCE J. BROWN,
President of the Senate.
CARL R. KIMBALL,
Speaker of the House of Representatives.
Passed May 9, 1919.
Approved June 5, 1919.

JAMES M. COX,
Governor.

Filed in the office of the Secretary of State at Columbus, Ohio, on the 6th day of June, A. D. 1919.

212 G.

[House Bill No. 463.]

AN ACT

To amend sections 2433, 2434 and 2446 of the General Code relating to the requirement of land for public buildings by county commissioners.

Be it enacted by the General Assembly of the State of Ohio:

SECTION 1. That sections 2433, 2434 and 2446 of the General Code be amended to read as follows:

Sec. 2433. When, in their opinion, it is necessary, the commissioners may purchase a site for a court house, or jail, or land for an infirmary or a detention home, public market place, or market house, or additional land for an infirmary or county children's home at such price and upon such terms of payment, as are agreed upon between them and the owner or owners of the property. The title to such real estate shall be conveyed in fee simple to the county. *Purchase of site for court house, etc.*

Sec. 2434. For the execution of the objects stated in the preceding section, or for the purpose of erecting or acquiring a building in memory of Ohio soldiers, or for a court house, county offices, jail, county infirmary, detention home, public market house, or additional land for an infirmary or county children's home or other necessary buildings or bridges, or for the purpose of enlarging, repairing, improving, or rebuilding thereof, or for the relief or support of the poor, the commissioners may borrow such sum or sums of money as they deem necessary, at a rate of interest not to exceed six per cent, per annum, and issue the bonds of the county to secure the payment of the principal and interest thereof. *Authority to borrow money.*

Provided, that if the judge designated to transact the business arising under the jurisdiction provided for in section 1639 of the General Code of the state of Ohio, shall advise and recommend in writing to the county commissioners of any county the purchase of land for and the erection of a place to be known as a detention home, or additional land *Purchase of land for certain purposes.*

Submission of
question; tax
levy.
for an infirmary or county children's home, the commissioners without first submitting the question to the vote of the county may levy a tax for either or both of such purposes in an amount not to exceed in any one year two-tenths of one mill for every dollar of taxable property on the tax duplicate of said county.

For what purposes may appropriate land.
Sec. 2446. When in the opinion of the commissioners it is necessary to procure real estate, or the right of way, or easement for a court house, jail, or public offices, or for a bridge and the approaches thereto, or other lawful structure, or public market place or market house, and they and the owner or owners thereof are unable to agree upon its purchase and sale, or the amount of damages to be awarded therefor, the commissioners may appropriate such real estate, right of way or easement, and for this purpose they shall cause an accurate survey and description to be made of the parcel of land needed for such purpose, or in case of a bridge, or the right of way and easement required and shall file it with the probate judge. Thereupon the same proceedings shall be had, as are provided for the appropriation of private property by municipal corporations.

Repeals.
SECTION 2. That said original sections 2433, 2434 and 2446 of the General Code be, and the same are hereby repealed.

The sectional
numbers in this
act are in conformity to the
General Code.
JOHN G. PRICE,
Attorney
General.

CARL R. KIMBALL,
Speaker of the House of Representatives.
CLARENCE J. BROWN,
President of the Senate.

Passed May 8, 1919.
Approved June 5, 1919.

JAMES M. COX,
Governor.

Filed in the office of the Secretary of State at Columbus, Ohio, on the 6th day of June, A. D. 1919.

213 G.

[Senate Bill No. 181.]

AN ACT

To amend sections 5612 and 5613 of the General Code requiring each county auditor to prepare and transmit to the tax commission of Ohio, annually, an abstract of the aggregate amount and assessed valuation of real and personal property in his county and the taxing districts therein, and requiring the tax commission of Ohio to equalize the assessed valuation of such real and personal property, and fixing the time when the same shall be done.

Be it enacted by the General Assembly of the State of Ohio:
SECTION 1. That sections 5612 and 5613 of the General Code be amended to read as follows:

Sec. 5612. Annually on or before the first day of September, each county auditor shall make out and transmit to the Tax Commission of Ohio an abstract of the real and personal property of each taxing district in his county, in which he shall set forth the aggregate amount and valuation of each class of real and personal property in such county, and in each taxing district therein, as it appears on his tax list, or on the statements and returns on file in his office. *Abstract of real and personal property transmitted to tax commission.*

Sec. 5613. The Tax Commission of Ohio annually, at a meeting to be held at its office in Columbus, on the second Monday in September, or on such date thereafter to which such meeting may be adjourned, shall determine whether the real and personal property, and the various classes thereof, in the several counties, cities, villages and taxing districts in the state, have been assessed at the true value thereof in money, and if it finds that the real or personal property, or any class of real or personal property, in any county, city, village or taxing district 'in the state as reported by the several county auditors to it, is not listed at its true value in money, it may increase or decrease the aggregate value of the real property or of the personal property, or any class of real or personal property, in any such county, township, city, village, or taxing district, or in any ward or division of a municipal corporation, by such rate per cent., or by such amount as will place such property on the tax list at its true value in money, to the end that each and every class of real and personal property shall be listed and valued for taxation by an equal and uniform rule at its true value in money. *Increase or decrease of aggregate value of real or personal property.*

SECTION 2. That sections 5612 and 5613 of the General Code be, and the same are hereby repealed. *Repeal.*

The sectional numbers in this act are in conformity to the General Code. JOHN G. PRICE, Attorney General.

CLARENCE J. BROWN,
President of the Senate.
CARL R. KIMBALL,
Speaker of the House of Representatives.

Passed May 9, 1919.
Approved June 5, 1919.

JAMES M. COX,
Governor.

Filed in the office of the Secretary of State at Columbus, Ohio, on the 6th day of June, A. D. 1919.

214 G.

630

[Amended Senate Bill No. 119.]

AN ACT

To amend section 464 and to supplement section 13916 by sections 13916-1, 13916-2, 13916-3 and 13916-4 of the General Code, relative to authorizing the attorney general and the superintendent of public works to investigate the title of swamp and marsh lands and recover the same for the state.

Be it enacted by the General Assembly of the State of Ohio:

SECTION 1. That section 464 of the General Code be amended and supplemental sections 13916-1, 13916-2, 13916-3 and 13916-4 be added to read as follows:

Powers and duties of canal commission conferred on superintendent of public works.

Sec. 464. In addition to the powers and duties herein conferred upon the superintendent of public works, said superintendent shall exercise all of the powers and duties heretofore conferred by law upon the Ohio canal commission and the board of public works with respect to the lease and sale of canal or other state lands, the location, ascertainment, perfection and recording of title to all swamp, marsh, overflow lands and all other lands within the state, to which the state has or should have title, and all other powers and duties now conferred by law upon said canal commission or board of public works, but no land lease, or sale of canal or other state lands, shall be made except upon the written approval of the governor and the attorney general.

Power to administer oaths and take testimony.

Sec. 13916-1. In the discharge of his duties under sections 464 and 13916 of the General Code, the superintendent of public works, the agent of canal lands, the secretary of public works and the attorney general, or such special counsel as may be assigned as hereinafter provided, shall each have the power to administer oaths and affirmations and to take testimony relative to any matter of the location, title or possession of any of the public lands referred to in section 13916 of the General Code, or other provisions of law relating to the public lands of Ohio.

The superintendent of public works shall have power to subpoena and require the attendance in this state of witnesses and the production thereby of books and papers pertinent to the investigations and inquiries concerning said lands. Fees shall be allowed the witnesses, and on the certificate of said superintendent of public works, duly admitted, the same shall be paid by the state treasurer, for attendance and traveling, as provided in section 3012 of the General Code for witnesses in courts of record.

Attachment proceedings in case of refusal.

In case of disobedience thereto, or neglect by any person of any subpoena issued by said superintendent of public works, or the refusal of any witness to testify to any matter regarding which he may lawfully be interrogated, it shall be the duty of the court of common pleas of any county, or any judge thereof where such disobedience, neglect or refusal occurs, on application of said superintendent of public works, to compel obedience by attachment proceedings for

contempt, as in the case of disobedience of the requirements
of a subpoena issued from such court or a refusal to testify
therein.

Sec. 13916-2. In the discharge of his duties under the
two preceding sections, the superintendent of public works
may require the counsel and assistance of the attorney general
and may employ a stenographer to transcribe records,
testimony of investigations, and such other evidences of
title as he may require, and said superintendent of public
works and his authorized agents or employes, and said attorney
general, or such special counsel as he may assign to
the service of such superintendent of public works, shall receive
their necessary expenses incurred in the discharge of
their duties herein, which with all other expenses incurred
by said superintendent of public works or his authorized
agents or employes under this and the two preceding sections
shall be paid as hereinafter provided. *(margin: Counsel and stenographers; expenses.)*

Sec. 13916-3. Upon the ascertainment, location and
recording of the title of the state to any swamp, marsh or
overflow lands within the state, said superintendent of public
works, subject to the approval of the governor and attorney
general, may lease said swamp, marsh or overflow
lands to the fish and game commission of Ohio, for the term
of ninety-nine years, renewable forever, for fish and game
preserves, upon such terms as he may deem for the best interests
of the citizens of the state of Ohio, or to such other
officer or board performing the duties of such commission
for the protection, preservation and propagation of birds,
animals and fish described in section 1390 of the General
Code. *(margin: Lease of swamp, marsh or overflow lands.)*

Upon the recording of such lease in the state department
of public works as required in the leasing of other
state lands, for the term therein stated, said swamp, marsh
and overflow lands, leased as aforesaid, and the waters adjacent
thereto, shall forever be open to the public as state
parks and pleasure resorts, as provided in sections 469 to
486-1 inclusive, of the General Code. *(margin: Open as state parks and pleasure resorts.)*

Sec. 13916-4. The actual expenses of said superintendent
of public works or his authorized agents or employes,
and the attorney general, or special counsel assigned
by him as aforesaid, shall be paid by the state treasurer
upon the warrant of the state auditor, out of the fund referred
to by section 1423 of the General Code, and shall be
deemed as an expenditure therein authorized for the propagation
of game birds and game animals, and to establish
and acquire game preserves. *(margin: Expenses paid from state treasury.)*

Repeal.

The sectional numbers in this act are in conformity to the General Code. JOHN G. PRICE, *Attorney General.*

SECTION 2. That original section 464 of the General Code be and the same is hereby repealed.

CLARENCE J. BROWN,
President of the Senate.
CARL R. KIMBALL,
Speaker of the House of Representatives.

Passed April 14, 1919.
Approved June 5, 1919.

JAMES M. COX,
Governor.

Filed in the office of the Secretary of State at Columbus, Ohio, on the 6th day of June, A. D. 1919.

215 G.

[House Bill No. 217.]

AN ACT

To amend sections 151, 153 and 154 of the General Code, relative to appointment, duties and salaries of day and night policemen and visitors' attendants in the State House.

Be it enacted by the General Assembly of the State of Ohio:
SECTION 1. That sections 151, 153 and 154 of the General Code be amended to read as follows:

Policemen and attendants.

Sec. 151. The adjutant general shall appoint two day policemen, two night policemen and two visitors' attendants.

Duties of policemen and attendants.

Sec. 153. The policemen shall protect the state house and offices therein and prevent improper conduct and tresspassing in and about the buildings and grounds. The visitors' attendants shall attend those visiting the capitol and care for the building and premises in the absence of the policemen. The policemen and visitors' attendants shall so arrange that the building and grounds of the capitol shall be at all times under police protection.

Salary of policemen and attendants.

Sec. 154. The day policemen and visitors' attendants shall each receive an annual salary of eight hundred dollars and night policemen shall each receive an annual salary of eight hundred and forty dollars.

Repeals.

SECTION 2. That said original sections 151, 153 and 154 of the General Code be, and the same are hereby repealed.

The sectional numbers in this act are in conformity to the General Code. JOHN G. PRICE, *Attorney General.*

CARL R. KIMBALL,
Speaker of the House of Representatives.
CLARENCE J. BROWN,
President of the Senate.

Passed May 10, 1919.
Approved June 5, 1919.

JAMES M. COX,
Governor.

Filed in the office of the Secretary of State at Columbus, Ohio, on the 6th day of June, A. D. 1919.

216 G.

[House Bill No. 508.]

AN ACT

To amend section 2934 of the General Code, relative to the extension of soldiers' relief to indigent veterans of the war with Germany.

Be it enacted by the General Assembly of the State of Ohio:

SECTION 1. That section 2934 of the General Code be amended to read as follows:

Sec. 2934. Each township and ward soldiers' relief committee, shall receive all applications for relief under these provisions, from applicants residing in such township or ward, examine carefully into the case of each applicant and on the first Monday in May in each year make a list of the names of all indigent soldiers, sailors and marines, and of their indigent parents, wives, widows and minor children, including widows of soldiers, sailors and marines who have remarried, but again have become indigent widows, who reside in such township or ward, and including the soldiers, sailors and marines of the Spanish-American war, and the war with Germany, and their wives, widows, indigent parents, minor children and wards, who have been bona fide residents of the state one year, and of the county six months, next prior to such first Monday in May, and who, in the opinion of such relief committee, require aid, and are entitled to relief under these provisions. *(margin: Lists of persons entitled to relief made by committee annually.)*

SECTION 2. That original section 2934 of the General Code be, and the same is hereby repealed. *(margin: Repeal.)*

CARL R. KIMBALL,
Speaker of the House of Representatives.
CLARENCE J. BROWN,
President of the Senate.

(margin: The sectional number in this act is in conformity to the General Code. JOHN G. PRICE, Attorney General.)

Passed May 10, 1919.
Approved June 5, 1919.

JAMES M. COX,
Governor.

Filed in the office of the Secretary of State at Columbus, Ohio, on the 6th day of June, A. D. 1919.

217 G.

634

[Amended Senate Bill No. 144.]

AN ACT

Providing that licensed embalmers who entered the military service
of the United States shall be reinstated without further examination.

Be it enacted by the General Assembly of the State of Ohio:
SECTION 1. That section 1343 of the General Code be
supplemented by the enactment of supplemental section
1343a of the General Code to read as follows:

Reinstatement of
those who en-
tered military
service.

SECTION 1343a. All persons duly licensed to practice
embalming by the state board of embalming examiners who
entered the military service of the United States in the war
with the Central Powers of Europe, shall upon application
to the board of embalming examiners, accompanied by the
proper credentials of service or honorable discharge, and
the payment of a fee of one dollar, be reinstated by such
board without examination. Such application, however,
shall be made within six months after the taking effect of
this act, or within six months after discharge from military
service.

The sectional
number in this
act is in con-
formity to the
General Code.
JOHN G. PRICE,
*Attorney
General.*

CLARENCE J. BROWN,
President of the Senate.
CARL R. KIMBALL,
Speaker of the House of Representatives.
Passed May 9, 1919.
Approved June 6, 1919.

JAMES M. COX,
Governor.

Filed in the office of the Secretary of State at Columbus,
Ohio, on the 7th day of June, A. D. 1919.

218 G.

[Amended Senate Bill No. 66.]

AN ACT

To prevent and correct the pollution of streams, to provide for the
collection and disposal of sewage and other liquid wastes, and
for the development of district water supplies, to authorize the
organization of sewerage and sanitation and water supply
districts.

Be it enacted by the General Assembly of the State of Ohio:

I. SHORT TITLE AND INTERPRETATION.

Sec. 6602-54.

"Sanitary dis-
trict of Ohio."
Definition of
terms used.

SECTION 1. Terms Defined. This act may be known
and cited as the "Sanitary District Act of Ohio"; the bonds
which may be issued hereunder may be briefly called "Sanitary District Bonds", and shall be so engraved or printed

on their face; the districts created hereunder shall be briefly termed "Sanitary Districts";the tax books and records provided for hereunder shall be termed "Sanitary District Books" or "Sanitary District Records," and such titles shall be printed, stamped or written thereon.

Wherever the term "publication" is used in this act and no manner specified therefor, it shall be taken to mean once a week for three consecutive weeks in each of two newspapers of different political affiliations (if such newspapers there be) and of general circulation in the county or counties wherein such publication is to be made. It shall not be necessary that publication shall be made on the same day of the week in each of the three weeks; but not less than fourteen days, (excluding the day of first publication), shall intervene between the first publication and the last publication, and publication shall be complete on the date of the last publication.

Wherever the term "person" is used in this act, and not otherwise specified, it shall be taken to mean person, firm, copartnership, association or corporation, other than county, township, city, village or other political subdivision. Similarly, the words "public corporation" shall be taken to mean counties, townships, cities, villages, school districts, road districts, ditch districts, park districts, levee districts, and all other governmental agencies clothed with the power of levying general or special taxes.

Wherever the term "court" is used, and not otherwise specified, it shall be taken to mean the court of common pleas wherein the petition for the organization of the district was filed and granted. In case of a district lying in more than one county, the term "court", when not otherwise specified, shall be taken to mean the court comprised of one common pleas judge from each county as hereinafter provided.

Wherever the terms "land" or "property" are used in this act they shall, unless otherwise specified, be held to mean real property, as the words "real property" are used in and defined by the laws of the State of Ohio, and shall embrace all railroads, tramroads, roads, electric railroads, street and interurban railroads, streets and street improvements, telephones, telegraph, and transmission lines, gas, sewerage and water systems, pipe lines and rights of way of public service corporations, and all other real property whether public or private.

Wherever the term "board of directors" or term "directors" is used in this act said term or terms shall be taken to apply to the duties of one director in a district lying wholly within one county.

II. ORGANIZATION OF DISTRICT.

Sec. 6602-35.

Organization of district by court of common pleas.

SECTION 2. Court of Common Pleas to Organize Districts. The court of common pleas of any county in this state, is hereby vested with jurisdiction, power and authority, when the conditions stated in the third section of this act are found to exist, to establish sanitary districts, within the county in which said court is located. Districts partly within and partly without such county may also be established by a court comprising one common pleas judge from each county having area within the district, as hereinafter provided.

In the event there are but two common pleas judges, who sit as court under the provisions of section 2, and the said judges find themselves unable to agree as to the establishment of such sanitary district, or upon any other question left for their decision, then, and in such event a third common pleas judge from a disinterested county shall be appointed by the chief justice of the supreme court of the state of Ohio, which said judge shall sit with the other two judges, and the decisions of a majority of said judges shall be final. Compensation for said judge shall be fixed by the appointing judge. Such sanitary districts may be established for all or any of these purposes:

Purposes for which districts may be established.

(a) To prevent and correct the pollution of streams;

(b) To clean and improve stream channels for sanitary purposes;

(c) To regulate the flow of streams for sanitary purposes;

(d) To provide for the collection and disposal of sewage and other liquid wastes produced within the district;

(e) To provide a water supply for domestic, municipal and public use within the district, and incident to such purposes and to enable their accomplishment, to construct reservoirs, trunk sewers, intercepting sewers, siphons, pumping stations, wells, intakes, pipe lines, purification works, treatment and disposal works; to maintain, operate and repair the same, and do all other things necessary for the fulfillment of the purposes of this act.

Sec. 6602-36.

Petition; who may sign.

SECTION 3. Petition. Before any court shall establish a district as outlined in section 2, a petition shall be filed in the office of the clerk of said court, signed by five hundred freeholders, or by a majority of the freeholders, or by the owners of more than half of the property, in either acreage or value, within the limits of the territory proposed to be organized into a district. Such a petition may be signed by the governing body of any public corporation lying wholly or partly within the proposed district, in such manner as it may prescribe, and when so signed by such governing body such a petition on the part of said governing body shall fill all the requirements of representation upon such petition of the freeholders of such public corporation, as they appear upon the tax duplicate; and thereafter it shall not be necessary for individuals within said public corporation to sign such a petition. Such a petition may also be signed by railroads and other corporations owning lands. And such petition may also be filed by any city or cities interested in some degree in the improvement, upon proper action by their governing bodies. However, property in each political subdivision wholly or partly included in the proposed district shall be represented by the signers of the petition provided for by this section. And provided: That the petition for the establishment of a district for the purpose of providing a water supply for domestic, municipal and public use shall be signed by the governing body of each municipality, or part thereof included in the proposed district, or by a majority of the freeholders of political subdivisions or parts thereof included in the proposed district and lying outside of municipalities, and shall also be signed by the public service corporation which may be supplying water to the inhabitants of such political subdivisions under franchise granted by the governing bodies thereof.

The petition shall set forth: What shall be set forth in petition.

First: The proposed name of said district.

Second: The necessity for the proposed work and that it will be conducive to the public health, safety, comfort, convenience or welfare.

Third: A general description of the purpose of the contemplated improvement, and of the territory to be included in the proposed district. Said description need not be given by metes and bounds or by legal subdivisions, but it shall be sufficient if a generally accurate description is given of the territory to be organized as a district. Said territory shall include two or more political subdivisions or portions thereof and, except as a subdistrict provided for by section 62 of this act, shall not be included wholly within the limits of a single municipality. Said territory need not be contiguous, provided it be so situated that the public health, safety, comfort, convenience or welfare will be promoted by the organization as a single district of the territory described.

Fourth: Said petition shall pray for the organization of the district by the name proposed.

No petition with the requisite signature shall be declared null and void on account of alleged defects, but the court may at any time permit the petition to be amended in form and substance to conform to the facts, by correcting any errors in the description of the territory, or in any other particular. Several similar petitions or duplicate copies of the same petition for the organization of the same district may be filed and shall together be regarded as one petition. All such petitions filed prior to the hearing on said petition shall be considered by the court the same as though filed with the first petition placed on file. Amendment and correction of errors.

In determining when a majority of land owners have signed the petition the court shall be governed by the names as they appear upon the tax duplicate, which shall be prima facie evidence of such ownership.

SECTION 4. Bond of Petitioners. At the time of filing the petition, or at any time subsequent thereto and prior to the time of the hearing on said petition, a bond shall be filed, with security approved by the court, sufficient to pay all the expenses connected with the proceedings in case the court refuses to organize the distrtict. If at any time during the proceeding the court shall be satisfied that the bond first executed is insufficient in amount, it may require the execution of an additional bond within a time to be fixed to be not less than ten days distant, and upon failure of the petitioners to execute the same the petition shall be dismissed. ·

SECTION 5. Notice of Hearing on Petition. Immediately after the filing of such petition, the clerk of the court with whom such petition is filed shall cause notice by publication, (form 1, schedule), to be made of the pendency of the petition and of the time and place of the hearing thereon.

And further, he shall also cause such notices to be served personally upon the clerk of each political subdivision within the proposed district.

The court of common pleas of the county in which the petition was filed shall thereafter, for all purposes of this act, except as hereinafter otherwise provided, maintain and have original and exclusive jurisdiction co-extensive with the boundaries and limits of said district and of lands and other property proposed to be included in said district or affected by said district, without regard to the usual limits of its jurisdiction.

SECTION 6. Hearing on Petition.—Organization of District. Any owner of real property in said proposed district who individually may not have signed such a petition and who wishes to object to the organization and incorporation of said district shall, on or before the date set for the cause to be heard, file his objections why such district should not be organized and incorporated. Such objections shall be limited to a denial of the statements in the petition, and shall be heard by the court as an advanced case without unnecessary delay.

Upon the said hearing, if it shall appear that the purposes of this act would be subserved by the creation of a sanitary district, the court shall, after disposing of all objections as justice and equity require, by its findings, duly entered of record, adjudicate all questions of jurisdiction, declare the district organized and give it a corporate name, by which in all proceedings it shall thereafter be known, and thereupon the district shall be a political subdivision of the State of Ohio, a body corporate with all the powers of a corporation, shall have perpetual existence, with power to sue and be sued, to incur debts, liabilities and obligations; to exercise the right to eminent domain and of taxation and assessment as herein provided; to issue bonds and to do and perform all acts herein expressly authorized and all acts necessary and proper for the carrying out of the purposes for which the district was created, and for executing the powers with which it is invested.

In such decree the court shall designate the place where the office or principal place of business of the district shall be located, which shall be within the corporate limits of the district if practicable, and which may be changed by order of court from time to time. The regular meetings of the board of directors shall be held at such office or place of business, but for cause may be adjourned to any other convenient place. The official records and files of the district shall be kept at the office so established. *Designation of place of business.*

If the court finds that the property set out in said petition should not be incorporated into a district, it shall dismiss said proceedings, and adjudge the costs against the signers of the petition, in the proportion of the interest represented by them. *When proceedings dismissed.*

After an order is entered establishing the district, such order shall be deemed final and binding upon the real property within the district and shall finally and conclusively establish the regular organization of the said district against all persons except the State of Ohio upon suit commenced by the attorney general. Any such suit must be commenced within three months after said decree declaring such distrtict organized as herein provided, and not otherwise. The organization of said district shall not be directly or collaterally questioned in any suit, action or proceeding except as herein expressly authorized. *Order establishing district binding upon real property.*

In case of a district lying in more than one county, one common pleas judge of each of the counties having land in the district shall sit as a court in the court house where the original petition was filed, to make the findings required by this section and by section 13 herein. The majority of said judges shall be necessary to render a decision. *Establishing district lying in more than one county.*

Sec. 6602-40.

SECTION 7. Decree of Incorporation Filed. Within thirty days after the said district has been declared a corporation by the court, the clerk of the court shall transmit to the secretary of state, and to the county recorder in each of the counties having lands in said district, copies of the findings and the decree of the court incorporating said district. The same shall be filed and recorded in the office of the secretary of state in the same manner as articles of incorporation are now required to be filed and recorded under the general law concerning corporations, and copies shall also be filed in the office of the county recorder of each county in which a part of the district may be, where they shall become permanent records; and the recorder in each county shall receive a fee of one dollar for filing and preserving the same, and the secretary of state shall receive for filing and for recording said copies such fees as now *Decree of incorporation filed with secretary of state and county recorder.*

are or hereafter may be provided by law for like services in similar cases.

III. ORGANIZATION OF BOARD—ITS POWERS AND DUTIES.

Sec. 6602-41.

SECTION 8.

Appointment of director; qualifications; vacancy.

APPOINTMENT OF DIRECTORS.

Within thirty days after entering the decree incorporating said district, providing said district is wholly within one county, the court shall appoint one person who shall be a resident freeholder within the district as a director of the district for a term of five years from the date of his appointment. Provided further that in case said district is composed of more than one county, or part thereof, then each county shall be entitled to one director who shall be a resident freeholder of such county. In no event shall there be more than one director for each county. The court shall fill all vacancies which may occur in the office of director or directors.

Sec. 6602-42.

SECTION 9.

DIRECTOR OR BOARD OF DIRECTORS TO ORGANIZE.

Bond and oath of office.

Each director before entering upon his official duties shall take and subscribe to an oath, before an officer duly authorized to administer oaths that he will honestly, faithfully and impartially perform the duties of his office, and that he will not be interested directly or indirectly in any contract let for the purpose of carrying out any of the provisions of this act; and said oath shall be filed in the office of the clerk of courts of the county from which he was appointed.

Each director shall give a good and sufficient bond for the faithful and honest performance of his duties.

Organization; Appointment of secretary; oath; seal.

In the event there is but one director, upon taking oath, he shall select some suitable person as secretary; in the event there is more than one director, they shall, upon taking oath, choose one of their number as president of the board and shall select some suitable person as secretary, who may or may not be a member of said board. Such director or board shall adopt a seal, and shall keep in a well bound book a record of all proceedings, minutes of all meetings, certificates, contracts, bonds given by employes and all corporate acts, which shall be open to the inspection of all owners of property in the district as well as all other interested parties or persons. In the event that the district is composed of an even number of counties or parts thereof and the directors of said district find themselves unable to agree on any question pertaining to or in connection with

their op·ration or management of said district then, and
in such event at the request of any director, another person
from within or without the district shall be appointed director temporarily by the court of the district as organized
under section 2 of this act; and such temporary director
shall serve as a member of such board of directors until the
question in dispute has been satisfactorily adjusted. Compensation for said director shall be fixed by the appointing
court.

Sec. 6602-43. SECTION 10. Quorum. A majority of the directors **Quorum.**
shall constitute a quorum, and a concurrence of the ma-
jority in any matter within their duties shall be sufficient
for its determination. All actions by the directors shall be
by. resolution.

Sec. 6602-44. SECTION 11. May 'Employ Agents. The secretary **Duties of secre-**
shall be the custodian of the records of the district and of **tary.**
its corporate seal and shall assist the board in such particulars as it may direct in the performance of its duties. It
shall be the duty of the secretary to attest, under the corporate seal of the district, all certified copies of the official
records and files of the district that may be required of him
by the provisions of this act, or by any person ordering the
same and paying the reasonable cost of transcription. And
any portion of the record so certified and attested shall
prima facie import verity. The secretary shall serve also as
treasurer of the district, unless a treasurer is otherwise provided for by the board. The board may also employ a chief **Employment of**
engineer who may be an individual, copartnership or cor- **engineer, attor-**
poration; an attorney; and such other engineers, attorneys **ney, etc.**
and other agents and assistants as may be needful; and may
provide for their compensation, and maintain. furnish and
equip an office or offices, and purchase such office supplies,
equipment, apparatus, appliances, instruments and tools
as are necessary, which, with all other necessary expenditures, shall be taken as a part of the cost of the improvement. The employment of the secretary, treasurer, chief engineer and attorney for the district shall be evidenced by
agreements in writing, which, so far as possible. shall specify
the amounts to be paid for their services. The chief en-
gineer shall be superintendent of all the works and improve- **Annual. report.**
ments, and shall make a full report to the board each year.
or oftener if required. and may make such suggestions and
recommendations to the board as he may deem proper.

Sec. 6602-45. SECTION 12. To Approve Plans for Sewerage Improve- **Approval of**
ments Within District. If a district is established for pur- **plans for sewage**
poses other than the provision of a water supply for domes- **improvement.**
tic, municipal, and public use after the establishment of the
district and the organization of the board no public corporation or person shall install within such district any outlet
for discharge of sewage or other liquid waste, treatment or
disposal works, until the plans therefor have been submitted
to and received approval of the directors.

32—6. A L A

SECTION 13. To Prepare Plans. Upon their qualification, the board shall prepare or cause to be prepared a plan for the improvements for which the district was created. Such plan shall include such maps, profiles, plans and other data and descriptions as may be necessary to set forth properly the location and character of the work, and of the property benefited or taken or damaged, with estimates of cost.

In the preparation of the plan, the board may recognize the necessity of future extensions and enlargements which may result from enlargements of the area of the district, in order that the district improvements may be designed to meet properly such increased demands. The plan for a water supply for domestic, municipal and public use shall be prepared with recognition of an equitable apportionment of the available supply to each political subdivision within the district. In case the purposes for which the district was established include both improved sanitation and improved water supply a plan shall be prepared for each purpose.

In case the board of directors finds that any former survey made by any other district or in any other manner is useful for the purposes of the district, the board of directors may take over the data secured by such survey, or such other proceedings as may be useful to it, and may pay therefor an amount equal to the value of such data to said district.

Upon the completion of such plan the board shall submit it to the state department of health for approval. If the state department of health should reject such plan, the said board shall proceed as in the first instance under this section to prepare another plan. If the state department of health should refer back said plan for amendment, the board shall prepare and submit to the state department of health an amended plan. If the state department of health should approve said plan, a copy of the action of said state department of health shall be filed with the secretary of the board of directors and by him incorporated into the records of the district.

Upon the approval of such plan by the state department of health, the board shall cause notice by publication to be given as provided in section 1 herein in each county of said district, of such completion of said plan, and shall permit the inspection thereof at their office by all persons interested. Said notice shall fix the time and place for the hearing of all objections to said plan not less than twenty days nor more than thirty days after the last publication of said notice. All objections to said plan shall be in writing and filed with the secretary of said board at his office not more than ten days after the last publication of said notice. After said hearing before the board of directors, the said board shall adopt the plan as the official plan of the said district. If, however, any person or persons object to said official plan, so adopted, then such person or persons may, within ten days, from the adoption of said official plan, file their objections in writing, specifying the features of the plan to which they object, in the original case establishing the district in the office of the clerk of said court, and he shall fix a day for the hearing thereof before the court, not less than twenty days nor more than thirty days after the time fixed for filing objections, at which time the judges, sitting as a court as provided for in section 6 herein, for the organization of the district, shall meet at the court house of the county where said original case is pending, and hear said objections and adopt, reject or refer back said plan to said board of directors. A majority of the judges shall control. If said court should reject said plan, then said board shall proceed as in the first instance under this section to prepare another plan. If the court should refer back said plan to said board for amendment, then the court shall continue the hearing to a day certain without publication of notice. If the said court should approve said plan as the official plan of said district, then a certified copy of said journal of said court shall be filed with the secretary of the board of directors, and by him incorporated into the records of the district. The official plan may be altered in detail from time to time until the assessment roll is filed, and of all such alterations the appraisers shall take notice. But after the assessment roll has been fil l in court no alterations of the official plan shall be made except as in section 36 hereof provided.

Sec. 6602-47.

SECTION 14. To Execute Works. The board of directors shall have full power and authority to devise, prepare for, execute, maintain and operate any or all works or improvements necessary or desirable to complete, maintain, operate and protect the official plan. They may secure and use men and equipment under the supervision of the chief engineer or other agents, or they may in their discretion let contracts for such works, either as a whole or in parts.

Power to execute, maintain and operate improvement.

Sec. 6602-48.

SECTION 15. May Enter Upon Lands. The board of directors of any district organized under this act, or their employees or agents, including contractors and their employees, and the members of the board of appraisers and their assistants, may enter upon lands within or without the district in order to make surveys and examinations to accomplish the necessary preliminary purposes of the district, or to have access to the work, being liable, however, for actual damage done, but no unnecessary damage shall be done. Any person or corporation preventing such entrance shall be guilty of a misdemeanor, punishable by a fine not exceeding fifty dollars.

Right to enter upon lands.

Sec. 6602-49.

SECTION 16. General Powers. The powers of the board shall not include construction and maintenance of lateral sewers, sewerage systems, water mains and distributing systems or other related improvements for local service

General powers of the board.

within the political subdivisions forming the district, and
such improvements shall in every case be provided by the
public corporations or persons served by the works of the
district; and the powers of the board shall be limited to
the construction and maintenance of such works as are necessary to carry out the purposes of the district in improvement of sanitation and water supply as set forth in section
2 of this act. This act shall not limit or interfere with the
right of public corporations to install, maintain and operate
sewerage systems and water works systems as otherwise
permitted by law. However, this act shall give to the
board of directors full power and authority in the construction and maintenance of improvements for the purposes of the district to serve the area included within the
district, and the board shall have power to require the use
of the improvements of the district by public corporations
and persons included within the district and for which the
improvements were installed. In order to effect the proper
collection and disposal of sewage and other liquid wastes
produced within the district, to provide a water supply for
domestic, municipal and public use within the district, to
promote the public health, comfort, convenience and welfare, and to accomplish all other purposes of the district,
the board of directors is authorized to clean out, straighten,
alter, deepen, or otherwise improve any stream, watercourse, or body of water receiving sewage or other liquid
wastes and located in or out of said district; to fill up any
abandoned or altered stream, water-course, or body of water
located in or out of said district; to construct and maintain
trunk sewers, intercepting sewers, siphons, pumping stations, wells, intakes, pipe lines, purification works, treatment
and disposal works, reservoirs and any other works and
improvements deemed necessary to accomplish the purposes
of the district and to construct, preserve, operate or maintain such works in or out of said district; to construct connections to the works of the district for the delivery thereto
of sewage and other liquid wastes; to construct connections
for the delivery of a water supply from the works of the
district to public corporations and persons within the district; to incorporate with the works of the district or otherwise utilize any public sewers, drains or other sewerage and
water supply improvements either without modification or
with such repairs, modifications or changes as are deemed
necessary; to construct any and all of said works and improvements across or through any public or private property in or out of said district; and to hold, encumber, control, acquire by donation, purchase or condemnation, construct, own, lease, use and sell any real or personal property,
or easement necessary for right of way or location for the
works and improvements of the district, or for any necessary purpose, or for obtaining or storing material to be
used in constructing and maintaining said works and improvements. In case a district or subdistrict is organized

for the purpose of providing ·a water supply for domestic, municipal and public use within such district or subdistrict the board of directors shall proceed to prepare a plan for such improvements and the proceedings in reference to the improvement shall in all matters conform to the provisions of this act; except that in the issuance of bonds, in the levying of assessments or taxes, and in all other matters affecting only the improvements of the district for water supply for domestic, municipal and public use all proceedings and records thereof shall be kept separate from and shall not be amalgamated with the proceedings and records of the district in case it is also organized for other purposes, and provided, that no maintenance assessments shall be levied upon the property of the district for the purpose of maintaining a water supply for domestic, municipal and public use and the maintenance fund for such purpose shall be obtained from the sale of water to public corporations and persons within the district. The board shall determine the rates of compensation for such water which rates shall be reasonable, and may require bond to be given to secure the payment for such use. Upon the determination of any rate, or rates, the board shall make a report of its determination to the court. The court shall thereupon cause personal notice by summons to be given to the parties interested, stating that such a determination of rate has been made, that a hearing before the court will be had thereon on a certain day, and that objection may be made at such time to such determination of rates. A hearing may be had before the court, and objections may be made in the same manner as in case of the appraisal of benefits. Upon the final determination of the matter by the court, the determination of such rates of compensation shall be conclusive and binding for the term and under the conditions specified in the lease or other agreement. In case of failure of any user to pay for use in the manner specified by order of the court, the board may compel payment, and may enjoin further use until such payment is made. The rights under any lease or sale shall not extend to a change of use, or of place, time or manner of use, except in so far as is specifically stated in the lease or other agreement. The compensation for the use of water furnished by the district, may be made by payment according to a unit price per cubic foot of water used, or in any other reasonable measurement of value received. All money received as compensation under the provisions of this paragraph shall be added to the maintenance funds of the district for water supply purposes.

SECTION 17. To Advertise and Let Contracts. When it is determined to let the work by contract, contracts in amounts to exceed ten thousand dollars shall be advertised after notice calling for bids shall have been published, once a week for five consecutive weeks completed on date of last publication, in at least one newspaper of general circulation within said district, where the work is to be done, and the board may let said contract to the lowest or best bidder who shall give a good and approved bond, with ample security, conditioned on the carrying out of the contract, and the payment for all labor and material. Such contract shall be in writing, and shall be accompanied by or shall refer to plans and specifications for the work to be done, prepared by the chief engineer. The plans and specifications shall at all times be made and considered a part of the contract. Said contract shall be approved by the board of directors and signéd by the president of the board and by the contractor, and shall be executed in duplicate. Provided, that in case of emergency the advertising of contracts may be waived upon the consent of the board of directors, with the approval of the court or judge in vacation.

Sec. 6602-51.

Dominant right of eminent domain.

SECTION 18. Dominant Right of Eminent Domain. Said board, where necessary for the purposes of this act, shall have a dominant right of eminent domain over the right of eminent domain of railroad, telegraph, telephone, gas, water power and other companies and corporations, and over townships, villages, counties and cities.

In the exercise of this right due care shall be taken to do no unnecessary damage to other public utilities, and, in case of failure to agree upon the mode and terms of interference, not to interfere with their operation or usefulness beyond the actual necessities of the case, due regard being paid to the other public interests involved.

Sec. 6602-52.

Power to appropriate land.

SECTION 19. May Condemn Under General Law. Said board shall also have the right to condemn for the use of the district, any land or property within or without said district not acquired or condemned by the court on the report of the appraisers, according to the procedure provided by law for the appropriation of land or other property taken for telegraph, telephone and railroad rights of way, instead of having appraisals and assessments made by the board of appraisers.

Sec. 6602-53.

Regulations for protection of improvement.

SECTION 20. May Make Regulations to Protect Works. Where necessary, in order to secure the best results from the construction, operation and maintenance of the works and improvements of the district and to prevent damage to the same from misuse, the board of directors may make and enforce regulations pertaining to the use by public corporations and persons of the works and improvements of the district, and by such regulations may prescribe the design, construction and use of sewers within the district, the manner in which connections to trunk sewers, intercepting sewers, pipe lines and to other works of the district shall be made, may prescribe the permissible uses of the water supply of the district, the manner of its distribution and may prevent the pollution or unnecessary waste of the supply, and may prohibit discharge into such sewers of any liquid or solid wastes deemed detrimental to the works and improvements of the district. Provided, however, that such regulations shall have no effect until they have been approved by the state department of health. The district board may recover by civil action from any person or public corporation violating such regulations, for each offense, in any sum not less than five hundred dollars nor more than one thousand dollars together with costs. The directors shall have authority to enforce by mandamus or otherwise all necessary regulations made by them and authorized by this act, and may remove any improper construction or may close any connection made improperly or in violation of said regulations, and they are authorized to bring such suits in mandamus in the court of appeals in the first instance, if deemed advisable by them. Any public corporation or person wilfully failing to comply with such regulations shall be liable for damages caused by such failures and for the cost of renewing any construction damaged or destroyed.

ec. 6602-54. SECTION 21. May Remove Obstructions. All public corporations or persons having buildings, structures, works, conduits, mains, pipes, tracks or other physical obstructions in, over or upon the public streets, lanes, alleys or highways, which shall interfere with or impede the progress of construction, maintenance or repair of the works of the district shall upon reasonable notice from the board promptly so shift, adjust, accommodate or remove the same, as fully to meet the exigencies occasioning such action. Upon failure of any public corporation or person to make such changes the board may do so. Unless otherwise mutually agreed to the cost and expense of such changes shall be met by the district.

Removal of obstructions; procedure.

ec. 6602-55. SECTION 22. May Make Surveys and Investigations. The board of directors shall also have the right to establish and maintain stream gages and rain gages, and may make such surveys and examinations of rainfall, stream flow, and other scientific and engineering subjects as are necessary and proper for the purposes of the district, and they may issue reports of their findings.

Surveys and investigations.

ec. 6602-56. SECTION 23. May Co-operate with U. S. Government or Other Agencies—Outlets in Other States. The board of directors shall also have the right and authority to enter into contracts or other arrangements with the United States government or any department thereof, with persons, railroads or other corporations, with public corporations, and the state government of this or other states, with sewerage, drainage, conservation, conservancy, or other improvement districts, in this or other states, for co-operation or assistance in constructing, maintaining, using and operating the works of the district or the waters thereof, not in violation of Article VIII of the Constitution; or for making surveys and investigations or reports thereon; and may purchase, lease or acquire land or other property in adjoining states in order to secure outlets or for other purposes of this act, and may let contracts or spend money for securing such outlets or other works in adjoining states.

Board may co-operate with U. S. government and other agencies.

64

Sec. 6603-57.
Procedure when
cemetery taken
or damaged.

SECTION 24. Cemeteries. Whenever it may be necessary for the purposes of a district to take or damage any cemetery, the appraisers of the district shall appraise the cost of such taking or easement in the same manner as appraisals are made for other property.

Said directors shall have the same powers in case of the removal of a cemetery to agree with the authorities owning or controlling the said cemetery in the same manner that township trustees are authorized by section 3465 of the General Code; and in case of agreement the directors may purchase the necessary land, and remove or contract for the removal of those buried, together with all monuments. They may also contract for an easement therein if removal is not desired.

All proceedings in regard to such cemeteries shall be in conformity with the order of the court. In case condemnation proceedings are necessary they shall be instituted and conducted according to law in the county where such cemeteries are located.

IV. APPRAISALS OF BENEFITS.

Sec. 6602-58.
Appointment of
appraisers; quali-
fications, powers
and duties.

SECTION 25. Appointment of Appraisers. At the time of making its order organizing the district or at any suitable time thereafter, either in term or in vacation, the court or judge shall appoint three appraisers, who shall in every case where appraisers are appointed under this act be recommended by the board of directors, and whose duty it shall be to appraise the lands or other property within and without the district to be acquired for rights of way, reservoirs and other works of the district, and to appraise all benefits and damages accruing to all lands within or without the district by reason of the execution of the official plan. Said appraisers shall be freeholders residing within the State of Ohio, who may or may not own lands within said district. Provided further that no two of said appraisers shall be residents of the same county. Each of the appraisers shall, before taking up his duties, take and subscribe to an oath that he will faithfully and impartially discharge his duties as such appraiser, and that he will make a true report of such work done by him. The said appraisers shall at their first meeting elect one of their own number chairman, and the secretary of the board of directors or his deputy shall be ex officio secretary of said board of appraisers during their continuance in office. A majority of the appraisers shall constitute a quorum, and a concurrence of the majority in any matter within their duties shall be sufficient for its determination. Said appraisers shall continue to hold their offices until excused by the court, and the court shall fill all vacancies in the board of appraisers, or may appoint a new board for subsequent appraisals, as occasion may require. Such new board, if appointed, shall fill all the requirements of the board of appraisers of the district, and perform its duties.

SECTION 26. Appraisals. During the preparation of the official plan, the board of appraisers shall examine and become acquainted with the nature of plans for the improvement and of the lands and other property affected thereby, in order that they may be better prepared to make appraisals.

When the official plan is filed with the secretary of the district he shall at once notify the board of appraisers, and they shall thereupon proceed to appraise the benefits of. every kind to all real property within or without the district, which will result from the organization of said district and the execution of the official plan; and also to appraise the damages sustained and the value of the land and other property necessary to be taken by the district for which settlement has not been made by the board of directors. In the progress of their work, they shall have the assistance of the attorney, engineers, secretary and other agents and employees of the board of directors.

The board of appraisers shall also appraise the benefits and damages, if any, accruing to cities, villages, counties, townships and other public corporations, as political entities, and to the State of Ohio.

Before appraisals of compensation and damages are made, the directors of the district may report to the appraisers the parcels of land or other property they may wish to purchase and for which they may wish appraisals to be made, both for easement and for purchase in fee simple. The board may, if it deems best, specify in case of any property the particular purpose for which and the extent to which an easement in the same is desired, describing definitely such purpose and extent. The appraisers shall appraise all damages which may, because of the execution of the official plan, accrue to real or other property either within or without the district, which damages shall also represent easements acquired by the district for all of the purposes of the district, unless otherwise specifically stated. Wherever instructed to do so by the board of directors, they shall appraise lands or other property which it may be necessary or desirable for the district to own, and when instructed by the directors to do so they shall appraise both the total value of the land, and also the damages due to an easement for the purposes of the district. Upon such appraisals being confirmed by the court, the directors of the district shall have the option of paying the entire appraised value of the property and acquiring full title to it (in fee simple), or of paying only the costs of such easement for the purposes of the district. The appraisers in appraising benefits and damages shall consider only the effect of the execution of the official plan. The appraisers may give consideration to benefits resulting from the provision of improved sewage and sewage disposal, improved water supply for domestic, municipal and public use, the improvement of conditions affecting health, comfort, convenience and welfare, and other benefits deemed proper to recognize. The appraisers in making appraisals shall give due consideration and credit to any other works or systems already constructed, or under construction, which form a useful part of the work of the district according to the official plan. Where the appraisers return no appraisal of damages to any property, it shall be deemed a finding by them that no damages will be sustained.

Sec. 6602-60.

Appraisement of benefits and damages to lands outside district.

SECTION 27. Land Affected Outside District. If the appraisers find that lands or other property not embraced within the boundaries of the district will be affected by the proposed improvement, or should be included in the district, they shall appraise the benefits and damages to such land, and shall file notice, in the court, of the appraisal which they have made upon the lands beyond the boundaries of the district, and to the land which in their opinion should be included in the district. The appraisers shall also report to the court any lands which in their opinion should be eliminated from the district.

Sec. 6602-61.

Notice of hearing on land excluded from or taken into district.

SECTION 28. Notice of Hearing on Land Excluded From or Taken into District. If the report of the board of appraisers includes recommendations that other lands be included in the district, or that certain lands be excluded from the district, it shall be the duty of the clerk of the court before which the proceeding is pending to give notice to the owners of such property by publication to be made as provided in this act for a hearing on the petition for the creation of the district. Such notice to those owners whose lands are to be added to the district may be substantially as shown in the schedule herein. The time and place of the hearing may be the same as those of the hearing on appraisals. To the owners of property to be excluded from the district it will be sufficient to notify them of that fact.

Sec. 6602-62.

Report of appraisers to be known as sanitary district appraisal record; what record shall show.

SECTION 29. Board Shall Make Report. The board of appraisers shall prepare a report of its findings which shall be arranged in tabular form and bound in book form, and which shall be known as the sanitary district appraisal record. In case the purposes of the district include both improved sanitation and improved water supply, the appraisers shall prepare a separate report for each purpose. Such record shall contain the name of the owner of property appraised as it may appear on the tax duplicate or the deed records, a description of the property appraised, the amount of benefits appraised, the amount of damages appraised, and the appraised value of land or other property which may be taken for the purposes of the district. They shall also report any other benefits or damages or any other matter which in their opinion should be brought to the attention of the court. No error in the names of the owners of real property or in the descriptions thereof shall invalidate said appraisal or the levy of assessments or taxes based thereon, if sufficient description is given to identify such real property. When their report is completed, it shall be signed by at least a majority of the appraisers and deposited with the clerk of the court who shall file it in the original case. At the same time copies of that part of the report giving the appraisal of benefits and appraisals of land to be taken and of damages, in any county shall be made, certified to, and filed with the clerk of the court of common pleas of such county.

ec. 6602-63.   SECTION 30. Notice of Hearing on Appraisals. Upon the filing of the report of the appraisers, the clerk of the court shall give notice thereof, as provided in this act, in each county in the district. Said notice shall be substantially as in form 6 of the schedules hereto attached. It shall not be necessary for said clerk to name the parties interested. It shall not be necessary to describe separate lots or tracts of land in giving said notice, but it shall be sufficient to give such descriptions as will enable the owner to determine whether or not his land is covered by such description. For instance, it will be sufficient to state "All land lying in the .... ward of the city of ....," or "All land abutting on .... street in the city of ....," or "All land lying west of .... river and east of .... railroad in .... township," or any other general description pointing out the lands involved. Where lands in different counties are mentioned in said report, it shall not be necessary to publish a description of all the lands in the district in each county, but only of that part of the said lands situate in the county in which publication is made.

(margin: Notice of hearing on appraisals.)

Sec. 6602-64.   SECTION 31. Hearing on Appraisals. Any property owner may accept the appraisals in his favor of benefits and of damages and of lands to be taken made by the appraisers, or may acquiesce in their failure to appraise damages in his favor, and shall be construed to have done so unless he shall within ten days after the last publication provided for in the preceding section file exceptions to said report or to any appraisal of either benefits or damages or of land to be taken which may be appropriated. All exceptions shall be heard by the court beginning not less than twenty nor more than thirty days after the last publication provided for herein, and determined in advance of other business so as to carry out, liberally, the purposes and needs of the district. The court may, if it deem necessary, return the report to the board of appraisers for their further consideration and amendment, and enter its order to that effect. If, however, the appraisal roll as a whole is referred back to the appraisers, the court shall not resume the hearing thereof without new notice, as for an original hearing thereon. But the court may, without losing jurisdiction over the roll, order the appraisers to recast the roll when the order of the court specifies the precise character of the changes thereof.

(margin: Hearing on appraisals; filing exceptions.)

Sec. 6602-65.   SECTION 32. Decree on Appraisals. If it appears to the satisfaction of the court after having heard and deter-

(margin: Decree on appraisals.)

mined all said exceptions that the estimated cost of constructing the improvement contemplated in the official plan is less than the benefits appraised, then the court shall approve and confirm said appraisers' report as so modified and amended, and such findings and appraisals shall be final and incontestable. In considering the appraisals made by the board of appraisers, the court shall take cognizance of the official plan and of the degree to which it is effective for the purposes of the district. In case the court shall find that the estimated benefits appraised are less than the total costs of the execution of the official plan, exclusive of interest on deferred payments, or that the official plan is not suited to the requirements of the district, it may at its discretion return said official plan to the directors of the district with the order for them to prepare new or amended plans, or it may disorganize the district after having provided for the payment of all expenditures.

Sec. 6602-66.
Appeal from award.

SECTION 33. Appeal From Award. Any person, or public or private corporation desiring to appeal from an award as to compensation or damages, shall within ten days from the judgment of the court confirming the report of the appraisers, file with the clerk of the court a written notice making demand for a jury trial. He shall at the same time file a bond with good and sufficient security to be approved by the clerk in the sum of not more than two hundred dollars to the effect that if the appellant does not recover more by the verdict of the jury than the sum awarded him by the appraisers or if the verdict is not more favorable to him, he will pay the costs of the appeal. He shall state definitely from what part of the order he appeals.

The appeal shall be from the award of compensation or damages, or both of them, but from no other part of the decree of the court.

In case more than one appeal is entered from the awards as to compensations or damages in the same county, the court may, upon a showing that the same may be consolidated without injury to the interests of any one, consolidate and try the same together.

Upon demand for a jury the court shall order the directors to at once begin condemnation proceedings, according to law, in the county in which the lands are situated which are sought to be condemned or appraised in the court of common pleas of such county, which suit shall be proceeded with in accordance with the statute regulating appropriation by other than municipal corporations. And said court shall have full jurisdiction to act.

Sec. 6602-67.
Possession after verdict and deposit of award.

SECTION 34. Entry After Deposit of Award. No property shall be taken under this act until compensation has been paid according to law. But where a trial is had by jury, and a verdict has been rendered which has been confirmed by the court, the board of directors may pay the amount allowed into court in money with the costs, and thereupon the court shall make an order admitting the said corporation into possession of the property and confirming its title thereto, although the owner may take steps to take the case to a higher court. And thereupon the board of directors may enter into undisturbed possession of the property and rights involved.

SECTION 35. Filing Decree. Upon the entry of the order of the court approving the report of the appraisers, as provided for in this act, the clerk of said court in which the same is entered shall transmit a certified copy of the said decree, and of the appraisals as confirmed by the court, except those parts from which appeals have been perfected but not determined, to the secretary of the district. When any appeal has been finally determined, the clerk of that court shall certify the amount of each item of the judgment to the clerk of the court having the original case, who shall file the same therein and thereupon transmit certified copies of the same as in this section above provided.

Transmittal of certified copy of decree and appraisals to secretary of district.

SECTION 36. Change of Official Plan. The board of directors may at any time, when necessary to fulfill the objects for which the district was created, alter or add to the official plan, and when such alterations or additions are formally approved by the board, by the state department of health, and by the court, and are filed with the secretary, they shall become parts of the official plan for all purposes of this act. Where such alterations or additions in the judgment of the court neither materially modify the general character of the work, nor materially increase resulting damages for which the board is not able to make amicable settlement, nor increase the cost more than ten per cent, no action other than a resolution of the board of directors and approval by the state department of health shall be necessary for the approval of such alterations or additions. In case the proposed alterations or additions materially modify the general character of the work or materially modify the resulting damages or materially reduce the benefits, for which the board is not able to make amicable settlement, or materially increase the benefits in such a manner as to require a new appraisal, or increase the cost more than ten per cent, the court shall direct the board of appraisers (which may be the original board, or a new board appointed by the court on petition of the board of directors or otherwise), to appraise the property to be taken, benefited or damaged, by the proposed alterations or additions. Upon the completion of the report by the board of appraisers, notice shall be given and a hearing had on their report in the same manner as in the case of the original report of the board of appraisers, and the same right of appeal to a jury shall exist. Provided: That where few land owners are affected, the clerk of the court may, on order of the court, if found to be more economical and convenient, give personal notice of the pendency of the report of said appraisers, instead of notice by publication; and Provided: That when the only question at issue is additional damages or re-

Power to alter or add to official plan; procedure.

duction of benefits to property, due to modifications or additions to the plans, the board of directors may, if they find it practicable, make settlements with the owners of the property damaged, instead of having appraisals made by the board of appraisers. In case such settlements are made, notice and hearing need not be had. After bonds have been sold, in order that their security may not be impaired, no reduction shall be made in the amount of benefits appraised against property in the district, but in lieu of such reductions of benefits, if any are made, the amount shall be paid to the party in cash. This provision shall apply to all changes in appraisals under this act.

Sec. 6602-70.

Appeal shall not delay proceedings; waiver.

SECTION 37. Appeals Not to Delay Proceedings. No appeal under this act shall be permitted to interrupt or delay any action or the prosecution of any work under this act, except where the party appealing is entitled to a jury under the constitution of the state, and such jury trial has not been had; in which case, only so much of the work shall be interrupted or delayed as would constitute a taking of or a damaging of the property of the appellant. The board of directors of any district organized under the terms of this act shall have the right to appeal from any order of the court of common pleas made in any proceedings under this act, not requiring the intervention of a jury. The failure to appeal from any order of the court in any proceedings under this act within the time specified herein shall constitute a waiver of any irregularity in the proceedings, and the remedies provided for in this act shall exclude all other remedies except as herein provided.

Sec. 6602-71.

Lands exempt and later liable to assessment; appraisement.

SECTION 38. Lands Exempt and Later Liable to Assessment. If any lands in any district organized under this act are not liable for taxation or assessment at the time of the execution of the work, but afterwards, during the period when such work is being paid for, become liable to taxation or assessment by reason of some change in condition, benefit or ownership, such lands shall thereupon be appraised and assessed as other lands in said district receiving equal benefits.

Sec. 6602-72.

Subsequent appraisements authorized.

SECTION 39. Subsequent Appraisals. In case any real property within or without any district is benefited which for any reason was not appraised in the original proceedings, or was not appraised to the extent of benefits received, or in case any individual, corporation, municipality, political subdivision, or other district shall make use of or profit by the works of any district organized under this act to a degree not compensated for in the original appraisal, or in case the directors of the district find it necessary, subsequent to the time when the first appraisals are made, to take or damage any additional property, the directors of said district at any time such condition becomes evident, shall direct the board of appraisers to appraise the benefits or the enhanced benefits received by such property, or such damages or value of property taken, and proceedings outlined in this act for appraising lands not at first included with the boundaries of the district shall in all matters be conformed with, including notice to the party or parties. Or the board may, at its discretion, make any suitable settlement with such individual or other district, corporation county or municipality for such use, benefit, damage or property taken.

Sec. 6609-73. SECTION 40. Proceedings Not Invalid. No fault in any notice or other proceedings shall affect the validity of any proceeding under this act except to the extent to which it can be shown that such fault resulted in a material denial of justice to the property owner complaining of such fault. In case it is found upon a hearing that by reason of some irregularity or defect in the proceedings the appraisal has not been properly made, the court may nevertheless, on having proof that expense has been incurred which is a proper charge against the property of the complainant, render a finding as to the amount of benefits to said property, and appraise the proper benefits accordingly, where the party is entitled thereto, and thereupon said land shall be assessed as other land equally benefited. In the event that at any time either before or after the issuance of bonds pursuant to the provisions of this act, the appraisal of benefits, either as a whole or in part, be declared by any court of competent jurisdiction to be invalid by reason of any defect or irregularity in the proceedings therefor, whether jurisdictional or otherwise, the said court of common pleas is hereby authorized and directed on the application of the board of directors of the said district or on the application of any holder of any bonds which may have been issued pursuant hereto, promptly and without delay to remedy all defects or irregularities as the case may require, by directing and causing to be made in the manner hereinbefore provided, a new appraisal of the amount of benefits against the whole or any part of the lands in the said district as the case may require.

Proceedings not invalid except where fault results in denial of justice.

V. FINANCIAL ADMINISTRATION.

Sec. 6609-74. SECTION 41. Funds. The moneys of every sanitary district organized hereunder shall consist of three separate funds: (1) Preliminary Fund, by which is meant the proceeds of the ad volorem tax authorized by this act and such advancements as may be made from the general county funds as provided in section 42 of this act; (2) Bond Fund, by which is meant the proceeds of levies made against the special assessments of benefits equalized and confirmed under the provisions of this act; and (3) Maintenance Fund, which is a special assessment to be levied annually for the purpose of upkeep, administration and current expenses as hereinafter provided. Except that the maintenance fund for improved water supply for domestic, municipal, and public use shall be derived from the sale of water

Funds into which moneys of district divided; how provided.

as hereinafter provided. Except that the maintenance fund for improved water supply for domestic, municipal, and public use, shall be derived from the sale of water as hereinafter provided. It is intended that the cost of preparing the official plan, the appraisal (except as paid out of the preliminary fund) and the entire cost of construction and superintendence, including all charges incidental thereto, and the cost of administration during the period of construction, shall be paid out of the bond fund. No vouchers shall be drawn against the preliminary fund (except for advances from the general county funds) or against the maintenance fund provided for purposes other than improved water supply for domestic, municipal, and public use, until a tax-levying resolution shall have been properly passed by the board of directors, and duly entered upon its records; no bonds shall be issued against the bond fund until an assessment-levying resolution shall have been properly passed by the board of directors and duly entered upon its records, and until the property owners shall have been given an opportunity for a period of not less than thirty days to pay the assessments so levied against their respective properties. In case the purposes of the district include both improved sanitation and improved water supply, the funds for these purposes shall be kept separate.

Sec. 6602-75.

Payment of preliminary expenses.

SECTION. 42. Preliminary Expenses.—How Paid. After the filing of a petition under this act, and before the district shall be organized, the costs of publication and other official costs of the proceedings shall be paid out of the general funds of the county in which the petition is pending. Such payment shall be made on the warrant of the auditor on the order of the court. In case the district is organized, such cost shall be repaid to the county out of the first funds received by the district through levying of taxes or assessments or selling of bonds, or the borrowing of money. If the district is not organized, then the cost shall be collected from the petitioners or their bondsmen. Upon the organization of the district, the court shall make an order indicating a preliminary division of the preliminary expenses between the counties included in the district in approximately the proportions of interest of the various counties as may be estimated by said court. And the court shall issue an order to the auditor of each county to issue his warrant upon the treasurer of his county to reimburse the county having paid the total cost.

Payment of expense after organization.

Expenses incurred thereafter prior to the receipt of money by the district from taxes or assessments, bond sales, or otherwise, shall be paid from the general funds of the counties upon the order of the court and upon certification of the clerk of the court of such order specifying the amount and purpose of the levy, to the auditor of each county, who shall thereupon at once issue his warrant to the treasurer of his county, said payments to be made in proportion of the order outlined by the court aforesaid. Upon

receipt of funds by the district from the sale of bonds or
by taxation or assessment the funds so advanced by the
counties shall be repaid.

As soon as any district shall have been organized under
this act, and a board of directors shall have been appointed
and qualified, such board of directors shall have the power
and authority to levy upon the property of the district not
to exceed three-tenths of a mill on the assessed valuation
thereof as a level rate to be used for the purpose of paying
expenses of organization, for surveys and plans, and for
other incidental expenses which may be necessary up to the
time money is received from the sale of bonds or otherwise.
This tax shall be certified to the auditors of the various
counties and by them to the respective treasurers of their
counties. If such items of expense have already been paid
in whole or in part from other sources, they may be repaid
from the receipts of such levy, and such levy may be made
although the work proposed may have been found impracticable or for other reasons is abandoned. The collection of
such tax levy shall conform in all matters to the collection
of taxes and assessments for the district outlined in this act,
and the same provisions concerning the non-payment of
taxes shall apply. The board may borrow money in any
manner provided for in this act, and may pledge the receipts from such taxes for its repayment, the information
collected by the necessary surveys, the appraisal of benefits
and damages, and other information and data being of real
value and constituting benefits for which said tax may be
levied. In case a district is disbanded for any cause whatever before the work is constructed, the data, plans and estimates which have been secured shall be filed with the
clerk of the court before which the district was organized
and shall be matters of public record available to any person interested.

Sec. 6602-76. SECTION 43. May Borrow Money. In order to facilitate the preliminary work, the board may borrow money at
a rate of interest not exceeding six per cent per annum, may
issue and sell or pay to contractors or others, negotiable evidence of debt (herein called warrants) therefor signed by
the members of the board, and may pledge (after it has
been levied) the preliminary tax of not exceeding three-
tenths of a mill for the repayment thereof. If any warrant
issued by the board of directors is presented for payment
and is not paid for want of funds in the treasury, that
fact with the date of refusal shall be endorsed on the back
of such warrant, and said warrant shall thereafter draw
interest at the rate of six per cent until such time as there
is money on hand sufficient to pay the amount of said
warrant with interest.

Sec. 6602-77. SECTION 44. Board of Directors to Levy Assessment
for Bond Fund.—Additional Levies. After the list of real
property, with the appraised benefits as approved by the
court, or that part thereof from which no appeal is pending,

has been filed with the secretary of the district, then from time to time, as the affairs of the district demand it, the board of directors shall levy on all real property, upon which benefits have been appraised, an assessment of such portion of said benefits as may be found necessary by said board to pay the cost of the execution of the official plan including superintendence of construction and administration, plus ten per cent of said total, to be added for contingencies, but not to exceed, in the total of principal, the appraised benefits so adjudicated. The said assessment shall

be apportioned to and levied on each tract of land or other property in said district in proportion to the benefits appraised, and not in excess thereof, and in case bonds are issued as provided herein and hereafter, then the amount of interest, which will accrue on such bonds, as estimated by said board of directors, shall be included in and added to the said assessment, but the interest to accrue on account of the issuing of said bonds shall not be construed as a part of the cost of construction in determining whether or not the expenses and costs of making said improvement are or

are not equal to or in excess of the benefits appraised. As soon as said assessment is levied, the secretary of the board of directors, at the expense of the district, shall prepare in duplicate an assessment record of the district. It shall be in a well-bound book endorsed and named, "Sanitary District Assessment Record of .... District." A separate record shall be preserved in case the purposes of the district include both improved sanitation and improved water supply. It shall contain in tabular form a notation of the items of property appraised, the total amount of benefits appraised against each item, and the total assessment levied against each item. Where successive levies of assessment are made for the bond fund, the sanitary district assessment record shall contain suitable notation to show the number of levies and the amount of each, to the end that the sanitary distrtict assessment record may disclose the aggregate of all levies for the bond fund up to that time. Upon the completion of such record it shall be signed and certified by the president and secretary of the board of directors, attested by the seal of the district, and the same shall thereafter become a permanent record in the office of said dis-

trict. A copy of that part of the sanitary district assessment record affecting lands in any county shall be filed with the auditor of such county. If it should be found at any time that the total amount of assessment levied is insufficient to pay the cost of works set out in the official plan or of additional work done, the board of directors may make an additional levy to provide funds to complete the work, provided the total of all levies of such assessment exclusive of

interest does not exceed the total benefits appraised. In no event shall the total of all levies of such assessments during any ten-year period exceed three per cent of the appraised valuation of the property within the district as listed and assessed for taxation, and provided further, that in no event shall the levy exceed in or for any one year, five-tenths of one per cent of said appraised valuation.

SECTION 45. Property Owners May Pay Assessment in Full. When the assessment roll is placed on file in the office of the district, notice by publication shall be given to property owners that they may pay their assessments. Any owner of real property assessed for the execution of the official plan under the provisions of this act shall have the privilege of paying such assessment to the treasurer of the board of directors within thirty days from the time such assessment is placed on file in the office of the district, and the amount to be paid shall be the full amount of the assessment less any amount added thereto to meet interest. When such assessment has been paid, the secretary of the board shall enter upon the said assessment record opposite each tract for which payment is made the words "Paid in Full," and such assessment shall be deemed satisfied. The payment of such assessment shall not relieve the land owner from the necessity for the payment of a maintenance assessment nor for payment of any further assessment which may be necessary as herein provided. Any property-owner failing to pay assessments in full as provided for herein shall be deemed to have consented to the issuance of bonds as provided for in this act, and to payment of interest thereon.

Property owners may pay assessment in full.

After the expiration of the period of thirty days within which the property owners may pay their respective assessments, as limited herein, the treasurer of the district shall certify to the board of directors the aggregate of the amount so paid, and thereupon the board of directors shall pass and spread upon their records a bonding resolution in which shall be stated the amount of the assessment, and the amount thereof paid as aforesaid, and thereupon the board shall in the same resolution apportion the uncollected assessment into installments or levies, provide for the collection of interest upon the unpaid installments, and they may order the issuance of bonds (in an amount not exceeding ninety per cent of the levy) in anticipation of the collection of said installments. The residue of the tax so levied (not less than ten per cent) shall constitute a contingent account to protect the bonds from casual default, and any part thereof in excess of ten per cent of the next installment of maturing bond principal, together with the next two installments of semi-annual interest, if not needed for this purpose, may be transferred from time to time to the maintenance fund of the district.

SECTION 46. Board of Directors May Issue Bonds.— How Paid.—Funds.—How to Be Used. The board of directors may, if in their judgment it seems best, issue bonds not to exceed ninety per cent of the total amount of the assessments, exclusive of interest, levied under the provisions of this act, in denomination of not less than one hundred dollars bearing interest from date at a rate not to ex-

Issue of bonds authorized.

ceed six per cent per annum, payable semi-annually, to mature at annual intervals within thirty years, commencing not later than five years, to be determined by the board of directors, both principal and interest payable at the office of the treasurer of the State of Ohio. Said bonds shall be signed by the president of the board of directors, attested with the seal of said district and by the signature of the secretary of the said board, and shall be registered by the treasurer of the State of Ohio. In case any of the officers whose signatures, counter-signatures or certificates appearing upon bonds or coupons issued pursuant to this act, shall cease to be such officer before the delivery of such bonds to the purchaser, such signatures, or counter-signatures and certificates shall nevertheless be valid and sufficient for all purposes, the same as if they had remained in office until the delivery of the bonds. All of said bonds shall be executed and delivered to the treasurer of said district, who shall sell the same in such quantities and at such dates as the board of directors may deem necessary to meet the payments for the works and improvements of the district. Said bonds, if bearing less than six per cent interest, may be sold below par, but they shall be sold at such a price that the total payment of principal and interest shall not be greater than would have been required, if the bonds had borne six per cent interest and had sold for par and accrued interest. They shall show on their face the purpose for which they are issued, and shall be payable out of money derived from the bond fund. A sufficient amount of the assessment shall be appropriated by the board of directors for the purpose of paying the principal and interest of bonds and the same shall, when collected, be set apart in a separate fund for that purpose and no other. All bonds and coupons not paid at maturity shall bear interest at the rate of six per cent per annum from maturity until paid, or until sufficient funds have been deposited at the place of payment. Any expenses incurred in paying said bonds and interest thereon and reasonable compensation to the state treasurer for registering and paying same, shall be paid out of the other funds in the hands of the district treasurer and collected for the purpose of meeting the expenses of administration.

Provisions for payment of bonds.

It shall be the duty of said board of directors in making the annual assessment levy, as heretofore provided, to take into account the maturing bonds and interest on all bonds, and to make ample provision in advance for the payment thereof. In case the proceeds of the original tax assessment made under the provisions of this act are not sufficient to pay the principal and interest of all bonds issued, then the board of directors shall make such additional levy or levies as are necessary for this purpose, and under no circumstances shall any assessment levies be made that will in any manner or to any extent impair the security of said bonds or the fund available for the payment of the principal and interest of the same. Said district treasurer shall, at the time of taking office, execute and deliver to the president of the board of directors of the said district, a bond with good and sufficient sureties, to be approved by the said board of directors, conditioned that he shall account for and pay over as required by law, and as ordered by said board of directors, any and all money received by him on the sale of such bonds, or any of them, or from any other source, and that he will only sell and deliver such bonds to the purchaser or purchasers thereof under and according to the terms herein prescribed, and that he will, when ordered by said board so to do, return to said board, duly cancelled, any and all bonds not sold, which said bonds shall remain in the custody of the said president of said board of directors, who shall produce the same for inspection or for use as evidence whenever and wherever legally requested so to do. The said treasurer shall promptly report all sales of bonds to the board of directors, and the board shall issue warrants at the proper time for the payment of the maturing bonds so sold and the interest payments coming due on all bonds sold, and the said treasurer shall place sufficient funds at the place of payment to pay the same. In case proper warrants are not issued by the board of directors as herein provided, then the treasurer shall of his own accord place funds at the place of payment and the cancelled bonds and coupons and the receipts of the state treasurer shall be accepted in lieu of warrants. The successor in office of any such district treasurer shall not be entitled to said bonds or the proceeds thereof until he shall have complied with all the foregoing provisions applicable to his predecessor in office; Provided, if it should be deemed more expedient to the board of directors, as to moneys derived from the sale of bonds issued or from any other source, said board may by resolution, select some suitable bank or banks or other depository, which depository shall give good and sufficient bond, as temporary or assistant treasurer or treasurers, to hold and disburse said moneys on the orders of the board as the work progresses, until such fund is exhausted or transferred to the treasurer by order of the said board of directors. For such deposits the district shall receive not less than two nor more than four per cent interest per annum. The funds derived from the sale of said bonds or any of them shall be used for the purpose of paying the cost of the works and improvements and such costs, expenses, fees and salaries as may be authorized by law and shall be used for no other purpose.

If at the time the bonds are ready to be issued, the board shall be of the opinion that such bonds cannot advantageously be issued and sold in whole or in part, the board may sell parts only of the entire issue or may pledge all or part of said issue as collateral to a loan, but no partial sale or pledge shall be made without the order of the board made and entered of record, and no pledge shall be made at a greater margin than at the rate of one hundred

[marginal note: Bond of district treasurer, sale of bonds by; report.]

[marginal note: May designate depository; interest on deposits.]

[marginal note: May sell part or pledge part of issue on order of board.]

dollars of bond principal for ninety dollars of loan. The district may secure the payment of loans from the United States government in the same manner as it may secure the payment of bonds, and the board of directors may make any necessary regulations to provide for such payment. A party who has not sought a remedy against any proceeding under this act until after bonds have been sold or the work constructed, cannot for any cause have an injunction against the collection of taxes or assessments for the payment of said bonds.

This act shall, without reference to any other act of the general assembly of Ohio, be full authority for the issuance and sale of the bonds in this act authorized, which bonds shall have all the qualities of negotiable paper under the law merchant, and when executed and sealed and registered in the office of the state treasurer in conformity with the provisions of this act, and when sold in the manner prescribed herein and the consideration therefor received by the district, shall not be invalid for any irregularity or defect in the proceedings for the issue and sale thereof, and shall be incontestable in the hands of bona fide purchasers or holders thereof for value. No proceedings in respect to the issuance of any such bonds shall be necessary except such as are required by this act. Whenever the owner of any coupon bond issued pursuant to the provisions of this act shall present such bond to the treasurer of the district with a request for the conversion of such bond into a registered bond, the said treasurer shall cut off and cancel the coupons of any such coupon bond so presented and shall stamp, print or write upon such coupon bond so presented either upon the back or the face thereof, as may be convenient, a statement to the effect that the said bond is registered in the name of the owner and that thereafter the interest and principal of said bond are payable to the registered owner. Thereafter and from time to time, such bond may be transferred by such registered owner in person or by attorney duly authorized on presentation of such bond to the treasurer of the district and the bond again registered as before, a similar statement being stamped, printed or written thereon. Such statement stamped, printed or written upon any such bond may be substantially in the following form:

(Date, giving month, year and day)

This bond is registered pursuant to the statutes in such case made and provided, in the name of (here insert name of owner), and the interest and principal thereof are hereafter payable to such owner.

Treasurer .... Sanitary District.

If any bond shall be registered as aforesaid, the principal and interest of such bond shall be payable to the registered owner. The treasurer of the district shall enter in a register of said bonds to be kept by him or in a separate book, the fact of the registration of such bond and the name

Owner may register bond; transfer; payment.

of the registered owner thereof, so that said register or book shall at all times show what bonds are registered and the name of the registered owner thereof.

Sec. 6602-80.

SECTION 47. Board of Directors May Levy Maintenance Assessment. To maintain, operate and preserve the reservoirs, sewers, pumping stations, treatment and disposal works, or other improvements made pursuant to this act other than those connected with the development of a water supply for the district and to strengthen, repair and restore the same, when needed, and for the purpose of defraying the current expenses of the district, other than those expenses connected with the water supply of the district, the board of directors may upon the substantial completion of said improvements and on or before the first day of September in each year thereafter, levy an assessment upon each tract or parcel of land and upon corporate property within the district, subject to assessments under this act, to be known as a "Sanitary District Maintenance Assessment." Said maintenance assessment shall be apportioned upon the basis of the total appraisal of benefits accruing for original and subsequent construction, shall not exceed one per cent thereof in any one year unless the court shall by its order authorize an assessment of a larger percentage, and shall be certified in duplicate to the auditor of each county in which lands of said district are situate, in the same book but in a separate column, or in a separate book kept for that purpose, in like manner and at the same time as the annual installment tax is credited, under the heading "Maintenance Assessment." Said auditor shall certify the same to the treasurer of the county at the same time that he certifies the annual installment of the bond fund, and the sum of the installments of both funds for any tract may be certified as a single item. The treasurer shall demand and collect the maintenance assessment and make return thereof, and shall be liable for the same penalties for failure or neglect so to do, as may be provided herein for the annual installment of the assessment. The amount of the maintenance tax paid by any parcel of land shall not be credited against the benefits assessed against such parcel of land; but the maintenance tax shall be in addition to any tax that has been or can be levied against the benefit assessment.

Maintenance assessment levy authorized; apportionment; certification of duplicate to county auditor; collection.

To maintain, operate and preserve the improvements of the district made in connection with the development of the water supply for domestic, municipal and public use within the distrtict, and to strengthen, repair and restore the same, and to defray the current expense of the district for this purpose, the board of directors may use moneys from the maintenance fund for this purpose which shall be derived from the sale of water to public corporations and persons within the district. The rates to be charged for such water shall be uniform and shall be fixed and adjusted from time to time at intervals of not less than one year

Use of maintenance fund.

by the board of directors so that the income thus produced
will be adequate to provide a maintenance fund sufficient
for the purpose of the district, and contracts for supplying
water to public corporations and persons shall be entered
into before such service is rendered by the district and such
contracts shall specify the maximum quantity of water
which will be furnished to the public corporation or person and this quantity shall be fixed so as to distribute the
supply with an equitable apportionment. Preference shall
be given to water supply furnished to public corporations
for domestic, municipal and public use. Bills for water
supplied to a public corporation shall be rendered to the
proper managing officers of such corporation at monthly
intervals and shall be paid from the funds of the water
works department of such public corporation; and if such
department is unable to pay such indebtedness, the governing or taxing body of such public corporation shall provide
the necessary funds for the payment of the same by borrowing money, levying taxes, or in other manner permitted by
law.

Sec. 6602-81.
Petition for re-
adjustment of
maintenance as-
sessment; hear-
ing; appraise-
ment.

SECTION 48. Petition for Readjustment of Maintenance Assessments. Whenever the owners or representatives
of twenty-five per cent or more of the acreage or value of
the lands in the district shall file a petition with the clerk of
the court in whose office the petition was filed, stating that
there has been a material change in the values of the property in the district since the last previous appraisal of
benefits, and paying for a readjustment of the appraisal
of benefits for the purpose of making a more equitable
basis for the levy of the maintenance assessment, the said
clerk shall give notice of the filing and hearing of said petition in the manner hereinbefore provided. Upon hearing of
said petition if said court shall find there has been a material
change in the value of property in said district since the
last previous appraisal of benefits, the court shall order that
there be a readjustment of the appraisal of benefits for the
purpose of providing a basis upon which to levy the maintenance assessment of said district. Thereupon the court
shall direct the appraisers of the sanitary district to make
such readjustment of appraisal in the manner provided in
this act, and said appraisers shall make their report; and
the same proceedings shall be had thereon, as nearly as
may be, as are herein provided for the appraisal of benefits
accruing for original construction: Provided, that in making the readjustment of the appraisal of the benefits said
appraisals shall not be limited to the aggregate amount of
the original or any previous appraisal of benefits, and that
after the making of such readjustment the limitation of
the annual maintenance assessment to one per cent of the
total appraised benefits shall apply to the amount of the
benefits as readjusted; and provided, further, that there
shall be no such readjustment of benefits oftener than once
in eight years.

SECTION 49. Annual Levy. The board of directors shall each year thereafter determine, order and levy the part of the total assessments levied under this act, which shall become due and be collected during each year at the same time that state and county taxes are due and collected, which annual levy shall be evidenced and certified by said board not later than September first each year to the auditor of each county in which the real property of said district is situate. The certificate of said annual levy shall be substantially as in the schedule herein. Then shall follow a table or schedule showing in properly ruled columns: 1. The names of the owners of said property, which may be as they appeared in the decree of the court confirming the appraisals. In case of a city, county, village or township, the names of individual owners need not be given, but only the name of the city, county, village or township. 2. The descriptions of the property opposite the names of the said owners. 3. The total amount of the said annual installment of all assessments on each piece of property for the account of all funds. 4. A blank column in which the auditor shall record the several amounts as collected by him. 5. A blank column in which the auditor shall record the date of payment of the different sums. 6. A blank column in which the auditor shall report the names of the person or persons paying the several amounts. The said certificate and report shall be prepared in triplicate in a well-bound book which shall be endorsed and named "Sanitary District Assessment Book of .... Distrtict, ... County, Ohio," which endorsement shall also be printed at the top of each page in said book. A separate record shall be maintained in case the purposes of the district include both improved sanitation and improved water supply.

Two copies of that part of such triplicate affecting lands in any county shall be forwarded to the county auditor of such county, one for his use and one for the county treasurer, to whom the auditor shall certify one copy. It shall be the duty of the auditor of each county to receive the same as a tax book, and to certify the same as other tax records of the county treasurer of his county, whose duty it shall be to collect the same according to law. And such tax book or assessment book shall be the treasurer's warrant and authority to demand and receive the assessments due in his county as found in the same. In the event of any failure or neglect of the board of directors of the district to determine and order an annual levy for the purpose of paying the interest and principal of any bonds pursuant to this act, it shall be the duty of the auditor of the county in which the lands subject to such assessments are situated, to make and complete a levy of the taxes or special assessments necessary for the said purpose against the lands in the said district, and each piece of property therein against which benefits shall have been appraised; any assessment so made and completed by the county auditor shall be made and completed by him in the manner hereinbefore provided for the making and completion of an assessment by the board of directors of the district, and shall have the same force and effect as a levy of assessments determined and ordered by the board of directors.

Sec. 6602-83.
Duties of county officers.

SECTION 50. Duties of County Officers. The county treasurer of each county in which lands of the district lie, shall make due report to the auditor of the county of the sums collected by him, and it shall be the duty of the auditor to issue his warrant payable to the treasurer of the district for all sums of money in the hands of the treasurer of the county, according to his report as aforesaid. Said auditor shall, as soon as the books for collection are closed by the county treasurer according to law, make report to the treasurer of the said district of the sums collected, and of the assessments not collected, as returned to him by the treasurer of the county.

Delinquent list certified by secretary to county auditor; penalty.

The secretary of the board of directors shall thereupon provide a certified delinquent tax or assessment list, and forward the same in duplicate to the auditor of said county, who shall add the penalty fixed by law and transmit one copy to the treasurer of the county, who shall forthwith proceed to collect the said tax or levy or assessment and penalty, according to law. All assessments or taxes provided for in this act, remaining unpaid after they become due and collectable, shall be delinquent and bear a penalty of two per cent a month from the date of closing the county treasurer's books until paid. The return of the auditor shall be verified by affidavit.

Sec. 6602-84.
Bond of county treasurer.

SECTION 51. Bond of County Treasurer. Before receiving the aforesaid "assessment book" the treasurer of each county in which lands or other property of the district are located, shall execute to the board of directors of the district a bond with at least two good and sufficient sureties or a surety company, and which shall be paid for by the district in a sum not less than the probable amount of any annual levy of said assessment to be collected by him during any one year, conditioned that said treasurer shall pay over and account for all assessments so collected by him according to law. Said bond after approval by said board of directors shall be deposited with the secretary of the board of directors who shall be custodian thereof and who shall produce same for inspection and use as evidence whenever and wherever lawfully requested so to do.

Sec. 6602-85.
Sanitary district assessment a lien; how evidenced.

SECTION 52. Sanitary District Assessment to Constitute a Lien.—How Evidenced. All sanitary district assessments and taxes provided for in this act, together with all penalties for default in payment of the same, all costs in collecting the same, including a reasonable attorney's fee, to be fixed by the court and taxed as costs in the action brought to enforce payment, shall, from date of filing the certificate herein described in the office of the auditor for the county wherein the lands and properties are situate, until paid, constitute a lien, to which only the lien of the state for general state, county, city, village, school and road taxes shall be paramount, upon all the lands and other property against which such taxes shall be levied as is provided in this act. Such lien may be evidenced by a certificate substantially in the form in the schedule herein. The certificate and tables shall be prepared in a well-bound book by the secretary of the board of directors at the expense of the district. Unless expressly declared to the contrary, no warranty in any warranty deed or in any deed made pursuant to a judicial sale shall warrant against any portion of any assessment or assessments levied hereunder except past and current installments payable in the year which such deed or deeds bear date.

Sec. 6602-86.

SECTION 53. Assessment Book to be Prima Facie Evidence.—Suits for Assessments and Taxes.—How Brought. The "Delinquent Sanitary District Assessment Book" of the district shall be prima facie evidence in all courts of all matters therein contained. The liens established and declared in the preceding sections may be enforced at the option of the board of directors by an action on delinquent tax bills or assessment bills, made and certified by the county auditor, which action shall be instituted in the court of common pleas without regard to the amount of the claim, within six months after December thirty-first of the year for which said assessments were levied. The suit shall be brought in the corporate name of the district by its attorney against the land or lands, property or properties, on which such tax or assessment has not been paid. In the event of any default in the payment of the interest or principal of any bonds issued pursuant to this act, and if the said district or its proper officers shall fail or neglect to enforce the payment of any unpaid tax or assessment, the holder of such bonds may, for himself and for the benefit of all others similarly situated, enforce the said liens by suit or action against the land or lands, property or properties, on which such tax or assessment has not been paid, and against the said district, and the court shall have full power, jurisdiction and authority to apply the said tax when collected in the payment of the interest or principal upon the said bonds as justice and equity may require. The suit shall be brought in the county in which the property is situate, except when the tract of property sued upon be in more than one county, in which event the suit may be brought on the whole tract, parcel or property, in any county in which any portion thereof may be situate. The pleadings, process, proceedings, practice and sales, in cases arising under this act shall, except as herein provided, be the same as in an action for the enforcement of the state's lien for delinquent general taxes upon real estate. All sales of lands made under this section shall be by the sheriff, as is now provided under the general law. All sheriff's deeds executed and delivered pursuant to this act shall have the same probative force as other deeds executed by a

sheriff. Abbreviations shall not defeat the action. The
title acqu:red through any sale of lands or other property
under the aforesaid proceedings shall be subject to the
lien of all subsequent annual installments of distrtict tax or
assessment. In all suits for the collection of delinquent
taxes or assessments, the judgment for said delinquent
taxes or assessments and penalty shall also include all costs
of suit and a reasonable attorney's fee to be fixed by the
court, recoverable the same as the delinquent tax and in
the same suit. The proceeds of sales made under and by
virtue of this act shall be paid at once to the aforesaid
county treasurer and shall be properly credited and accounted for by him the same as other district taxes and assessments. If any assessments made pursuant to the provisions of this act shall prove invalid, the board of directors shall by subsequent or amended acts or proceedings
promptly and without delay remedy all defects or irregularities as the case may require by making and providing
for the collection of new assessments or otherwise.

Sec. 6602-87.

**Duties of officers
relating to as-
sessments.**

SECTION 54. Duties of Officers as to Assessments.
Whenever under the provisions of this act, an assessment
is made or a tax levied against a county, city, village, or
township, it shall be the duty of the governing or taxing
body of such political subdivision, upon receipt of the order
of the court which established the district, confirming the
appraisal of benefits and the assessment based thereon, to
receive and file the said order, and to immediately take all
the legal and necessary steps to collect the same. It shall
be the duty of the said governing or taxing body or persons
to levy and assess a tax, by a uniform rate upon all the
taxable property within the political subdivision, to make
out the proper duplicate, certify the same to the auditor of
the county in which such subdivision is, whose duty it shall
be to receive the same, certify the same for collection to
the treasurer of the county, whose duty it shall be to collect
the same for the benefit of the sanitary district, all of said
officers above named being authorized and directed to take
all the necessary steps for the levying, collection and distribution of such tax. Nothing in this section shall prevent
the assessment of the real estate of other corporations or
persons situated within such political subdivision, which
may be subject to assessment for special benefits to be received. In the event of any dissolution or disincorporation
of any sanitary district organized pursuant to the provisions of this act, such dissolution or disincorporation shall
not affect the lien of any assessment for benefits imposed
pursuant to the provisions of this act, or the liability of any
land or lands in such district to the levy of any future assessments for the purpose of paying the principal and interest of any bonds issued hereunder, and in that event, or
in the event of any failure on the part of the officers of any
district to qualify and act, or in the event of any resigna-
tions or vacancies in the office, which shall prevent action

by the said district or by its proper officers, it shall be the duty of the county auditor and of all other officers charged in any manner with the duty of assessing, levying and collecting taxes for public purposes in any county, municipality or political subdivision in which such lands shall be situated, to do and perform all acts which may be necessary and requisite to the collection of any such assessment which may have been imposed and to the levying, imposing and collecting of any assessment which it may be necessary to make for the purpose of paying the principal and interest of the said bonds. Any holder of any bonds issued pursuant to the provisions of this act or any person or officers being a party in interest, may either at law or in equity by suit, action or mandamus, enforce and compel performance of the duties required by this act of any of the officers or persons mentioned in this act.

ec. 6602-88. SECTION 55. Penalty for Failure of Treasurer to Pay Over Tax. If any county treasurer or other person entrusted with the collection of these assessments refuses, fails or neglects to make prompt payment of the tax or any part thereof collected under this act to the treasurer of said district upon his presentation of a proper demand, then he shall pay a penalty of ten per cent on the amount of his delinquency; such penalty shall at once become due and payable and both he and his securities shall be liable therefor on his official bond. The said county treasurer shall retain for his services one per cent of the amount he collects on delinquent taxes.

Penalty for failure of treasurer to pay over tax.

sec. 6602-89. SECTION 56. Surplus Funds and Annual Reports. Any surplus funds in the treasury of the district may be used for retiring bonds, reducing the rate of assessment or for accomplishing any other of the legitimate objects of the district. At least once a year, or oftener if the court shall so order, the board of directors shall make a report to the court of its proceedings and an accounting of receipts and disbursements to that date which shall be filed with the clerk of the court.

Surplus fund and annual reports; inspection of accounts and reports.

The bureau of inspection and supervision of public offices shall inspect and supervise the accounts and reports of the district and all laws pertaining to said bureau shall be applicable to such inspection and supervision.

Said accounts shall also be audited at least once a year by the department of the auditor of state.

sec. 6602-90. SECTION 57. Compensation of Officials Under This Act. The members of the board of directors and the board of appraisers shall receive proper compensation to be fixed by the court in accordance with the time actually employed in performance of duties and shall also receive necessary expenses incurred in performance of duties. Before any duties devolve upon a county auditor or a county treasurer under this act, the board of directors of the district shall consult them and agree upon the salaries for the extra clerical force, if any, required in their respective offices to carry

Compensation of officials.

out the requirements of the law by reason of the establishment of said district, and the said board of directors shall provide for and pay said salaries to said clerk or clerks, while engaged on the work of the district, which clerks shall be selected and appointed by each of said county officers for their respective offices. In case of disagreement as to the compensation of such extra clerical force, the matter shall be referred to the court for its determination.

VI. INTERCORPORATE RELATIONS AND CONFLICT IN JURISDICTION.

Sec. 6602-91.

When lands may be included in more than one district.

SECTION 58. Lands in More That One District. The same land, if conducive to public health, safety, convenience or welfare, may be included in more than one district and be subject to the provisions of this act for each and every district in which it may be included, provided, that no district shall be organized under this act in whole or in part within the territory of a district already organized under this act until the court or courts determine whether the public health, safety, convenience or welfare demand the organization of an additional district, whether it demand that the territory proposed to be organized into an additional district shall be added to the existing district; and in case the proceedings concerning two or more such districts are before the court of common pleas of two or more counties, such determination shall be as provided in the next section.

Sec. 6602-92.

Jurisdiction where district partly within and partly without the same territory.

SECTION 59. Jurisdiction. In case any district or districts are being organized within, or partly within and partly without, the same territory in which some other district or distrticts have been or are being organized, one common pleas judge of each county in which such distrticts have been or are being organized shall confer at the earliest convenient moment after they ascertain the possibility of a conflict in jurisdiction, the sitting to be had in the county having the largest assessed valuation in the proposed district or distrticts. At such conference, the several judges shall determine to what extent the several districts should be consolidated or to what extent the boundaries should be adjusted in order to most fully carry out the purposes of this act; and they shall by suitable orders make such determination effective. In event notices have been issued or jurisdiction acquired in any proceeding concerning territory which is transferred to the court of common pleas of another county such notice shall not become void and jurisdiction so acquired shall not be lost; but in each case the court acquiring jurisdiction over such transferred territory shall hold the same without further notice, as if originally embraced in said district. At such conferences, the decision of the majority of the judges shall be final. The provisions of this and of the preceding section shall not operate to delay or to interrupt any proceeding under this act until the question of jurisdiction has been finally determined.

SECTION 60. Union of Districts. In case two or more districts have been organized under this act in a territory, which, in the opinion of the directors of either of the districts, should constitute but one distrtict, the board of directors of any of the districts may petition the court for an order uniting said districts into a single distrtict. Said petition shall be filed in the office of the clerk of that county which has the greatest valuation of real property within the districts sought to be included, as shown by the tax duplicates of the respective counties. Said petition shall set forth the necessity for such union of the two or more districts and that the union of said districts would be conducive to the public health, convenience, safety or welfare, and to the economical execution of the purposes for which the districts were organized. Upon receipt of said petition, the clerk of said court shall give notice by publication, or by personal service, to the board of directors or boards of directors of the district or districts which it is desired to unite with the district of the petitioners. Such notice shall contain the time and place where the hearing on the petition will be had and the purpose of the same. Such hearing shall be had in accordance with the provisions of this act in original hearing. After the hearing should the court find that the averments of the petition are true and that the said districts, or any of them should be united, it shall so order, and thereafter such districts shall be united into one and proceed as such. The court shall designate the corporate name of such united district, and such further proceedings shall be taken as provided for in this act. The court shall direct in such order who shall be the directors of such united district, who shall thereafter have such powers and be subject to such regulations as are provided for directors in districts created in the first instance. All legal proceedings already instituted by or against any of such constituent districts may be revived and continued against such united distrtict by an order of court substituting the name of such united district for such constituent district and such proceedings shall then proceed as herein provided.

Instead of organizing a new district from such constituent districts the court may, in its discretion, direct that one or more of such districts described in the petition be included into another of said districts which other shall continue under its original corporate name and organization, or it may direct that the district or districts so obsorbed shall be represented on the board of directors of the original district, designating what members of the board of directors of the original district shall be retired from the new board and what members representing the included district or districts shall take their places; or it may direct that the included district or districts shall become subdistricts of the main district. In case the districts sought to be united were organized in different counties, then the court to determine the question involved shall consist of one judge from each of the counties in the court of which one of the districts was organized, and the decision of the majority of the judges shall be final. No action under the provisions of this section shall operate to interrupt or delay any proceeding under this act until the questions involved were finally determined.

Sec. 6602-94.

Remedy for injury by district.

SECTION 61. Remedy for Injury by District. In case any person or public corporation, within or without any district organized under this act, shall consider itself injuriously affected in any manner whatsoever by any act performed by any official or agent of such district, or by the execution, maintenance or operation of the official plan, and in case no other method of relief is offered under this act, the remedy shall be as follows: The person or public corporation considering itself to be injuriously affected shall petition the court before which said district was organized for an appraisal of damages sufficient to compensate for such injuries. The court shall thereupon direct the board of appraisers of the district to appraise said damages and injuries, and to make a report to the court on or before the time named in the order of the court. Upon the filing of said report of said board of appraisers, the court shall cause notice to be given to the petitioner and to the directors of the district, of a hearing on said report. At the time of such hearing, the court shall consider said report of said appraisers, and may ratify said report or amend it as the court may deem equitable, or may return it to the said board of appraisers and require them to prepare a new report. Upon the filing of an order of the court approving said report of said appraisers, with such modifications as it may have made, said order shall constitute a final adjudication of the matter unless it shall be appealed from within twenty days. Appeal to a jury from said order may be had as provided in the general appropriation statute by the petitioner, by the directors of the district, or by any person or corporation who has been assessed for the costs of the district. No damages shall be allowed under this section which would not otherwise be allowed in law.

Sec. 6602-95.

Organization of subdistricts authorised.

SECTION 62. Subdistricts. Whenever it is desired to construct improvements wholly within or partly within and partly without any district organized under this act, which improvements will affect only a part of said district, for the purpose of accomplishing such work, subdistricts may be organized upon petition of the owners of real property, within or partly within and partly without the district. which petition shall fulfill the same requirements concerning the subdistricts as the petition outlined in section 3 of this act is required to fulfill concerning the organization of the main district, and shall be filed with the clerk of the same court of common pleas, and shall be accompanied by a bond as provided for in section 4 of this act. All proceedings relating to the organization of such subdistricts shall conform in all things to the provisions of this act relating to the organization of districts. Whenever the court shall by its order duly entered of record declare and decree such subdistricts to be organized, the clerk of said court shall thereupon give notice of such order to the directors of the district, who shall thereupon act also as directors of the subdistrict. Thereafter, the proceedings in reference to the subdistrict shall in all matters conform to the provisions of this act; except that in appraisal of benefits and damages for the purposes of such subdistricts, in the issuance of bonds, in the levying of assessments or taxes, and in all other matters affecting only the subdistrict, the provisions of this act shall apply to this subdistrict as though it were an independent district, and it shall not, in these things, be amalgamated with the main district. The board of directors, board of appraisers, chief engineer, attorney, secretary and other officers, agents and employees of the district shall, so far as it may be necessary, serve in the same capacities for such subdistricts, and contracts and agreements between the main district and the subdistrict may be made in the same manner as contracts and agreements between two districts. The distrtibution of administrative expense between the main district and subdistrict shall be in proportion to the interests involved and the amount of service rendered, such division to be made by the board of directors with an appeal to the court establishing the district. This section shall not be held to prevent the organization of independent districts for local improvements under other laws within the limits of a district organized under this act, as provided in sections 58 and 59 of this act.

VII. POLICE POWERS AND REGULATIONS.

Sec. 6602-96.

SECTION 63. May Police District. The board of directors shall have the right to police the works of the district, and in times of great emergency may compel assistance in the protection of such works, and shall, also, have the right to prevent persons, vehicles or live stock from passing over the works of the district in any manner which would result in damage thereto.
Authority to police districts.

Sec. 6602-97.

SECTION 64. Injury to Survey Marks Prohibited. The wilful destruction, injury or removal of any bench marks, witness marks, stakes or other reference marks, placed by the surveyors or engineers of the district or by contractors in constructing the works of the district, shall be a misdemeanor, punishable by fine not exceeding one hundred dollars.
Injury to survey marks prohibited.

Sec. 6602-98.

SECTION 65. Owners Liable for Damage to District. All persons and corporations shall be liable for damage done to works of the district by themselves, their agents, their employes, or by their live stock. All persons guilty of wilful damage shall be guilty of a misdemeanor, and shall be fined not to exceed five hundred dollars and costs, and
Owners liable for damage to district; penalty.

shall be liable for all damages and costs. The board of directors shall have authority to repair such damage at the expense of the person or corporation committing it.

Sec. 6602-99.

Penalty for fraud.

SECTION 66. Penalty for Fraud. The making of profit, directly or indirectly, by any officer of any district organized under this act, or by any other public officer within the state, out of any contracts entered into by the district, or use of any money belonging to district by loaning it or otherwise using it, or by depositing the same in any manner, contrary to law, or by removal of any money by any such officer or by his consent and placing it elsewhere than is prescribed either by law or by the official acts of the board of directors, for the purpose of profit, shall constitute a felony, and on conviction thereof shall subject such officer to imprisonment in the state penitentiary for a term not exceeding two years, or a fine not exceeding five thousand dollars, or both fine and imprisonment, and the officer offending shall be liable personally and upon his official bond for all losses to such district and for all profits realized by such unlawful use of moneys.

Removal of officers.

Officials Removed for or Without Cause. Any director, appraiser or other officer or employee of any district organized under this act may be removed for or without cause, at any time by the authority appointing him or them.

Sec. 6602-100.

Proceedings to compel performance.

SECTION 68. Performance of Duties Enforced by Mandamus. The performance of all duties prescribed in this act concerning the organization and administration or operation of the district may be enforced against any officer or against any person or corporation refusing to comply with any order of the board by mandamus at the instance of the board or of any person or corporation interested in any way in such district or proposed district. And the board may institute such proceedings in the court of appeals in the first instance.

VIII. CONSTRUCTION AND INTERPRETATION.

Sec. 6602-101.

Faulty notice, how corrected.

SECTION 69. Faulty Notice.—How Corrected. In any and every case where a notice is provided for in this act, if the court finds for any reason that due notice was not given, the court shall not thereby lose jurisdiction, and the proceeding in question shall not thereby be void; but the court shall in that case order due notice to be given, and shall continue the hearing until such time as such notice shall be properly given, and thereupon shall proceed as though notice had been properly given in the first instance. In case any individual appraisal or appraisals, assessment or assessments, or levy or levies, shall be held void for want of legal notice or in case the board may determine that any notice with reference to any land or lands may be faulty, then the board may file a motion in the original cause asking that the court order notice to the owner of such land or lands given and set a time for hearing as provided in this act.

And in case the original notice as a whole was sufficient, and was faulty only with reference to publication as to certain tracts, only the owners of and persons interested in those particular tracts need be notified by such subsequent notice. And if the publication of any notice in any county was defective or not made in time, publication of the defective notice need be had only in the county in which the defect occurred.

ec. 6602-102. SECTION 70. Question of Validity Advanced in Courts. All cases in which there arises a question of the validity of the organization of sanitary districts shall be advanced as a matter of immediate public interest and concern, and heard in all courts at the earliest practicable moment. The court shall be open at all times for the purposes of this act.

ec. 6602-103. SECTION 71. If Part Declared Unconstitutional. In case any section or sections or part of any section of this act shall be found to be unconstitutional, the remainder of this act shall not thereby be invalidated, but shall remain in full force and effect.

ec. 6602-104. SECTION 72. What Other Acts are Repealed. All acts or parts of acts conflicting in any way with any of the provisions of this act, in regard to improvements of this or a similar character or regulating or limiting power of taxation or assessment, or otherwise interfering with the execution of this law according to its terms, are hereby declared inoperative and ineffective as to this act, as if they did not exist, but all such laws and parts of laws shall not be in any other way affected by this law. This act shall not repeal the act or any part thereof passed February 5, 1914, and approved February 17, 1914, known as the Conservancy Act of Ohio, Volume 104, Page 13, Ohio Laws.

ec. 6602-105. SECTION 73. Short Forms and Abbreviations. For the sake of convenience:

(a) In any orders of court the words "The court now here finds that it hath jurisdiction of the parties to and of the subject matter of this proceeding" shall be equivalent to a finding that each jurisdictional fact necessary to confer plenary jurisdiction upon the court, beginning with the proper signing and filing of the initial petition to the date of the order to meet every legal requirement imposed by this act.

(b) No other or further evidence of the legal hypothecation of the special tax to the payment of the bonds shall be required than the passage of a bonding resolution by the board of directors and the issuance of bonds in accordance therewith.

(c) In the preparation of any assessment or appraisal roll the usual abbreviations employed by engineers, surveyors and abstractors may be used.

(d) Where properly to describe any parcel of land, it would be necessary to use a long description, the appraisers after locating the land generally, may refer to the book and page of the public record of any instrument in which the

land is described, which reference shall suffice to identify for
all the purposes of that act the land described in the public
record so referred to.

(e) It shall not be necessary in any notice required
by this act to be published to specify the names of the
owners of the lands or of the persons interested therein;
but any such notice may be addressed "To All Persons Interested" with like effect as though such notice named by
name every owner, of any lands within the territory specified in the notice and every person interested therein, and
every lienor, actual or inchoate.

(f) Every district declared upon hearing to be a
sanitary district shall thereupon become a political subdivision and a public corporation of the State of Ohio, invested with all the powers and privileges conferred upon
such districts by this act.

IX. SCHEDULE.

Sec. 6602-106.

Forms and sug-
gestions in pro
cedure under act.

SECTION 74. Forms and Suggestions. The following
forms may suffice to illustrate the character of the procedure contemplated by this act; and if substantially complied
with, those things being changed which (to meet the requirements of the particular case) should be changed, such
procedure shall be held to meet the requirements of this act.

1. Form of Notice of Hearing on the Petition: To
All Persons Interested:

Public Notice is Hereby Given:

1. That on the ..... day of ...., 19....,
pursuant to the provisions of The Sanitary District Act of
Ohio, there was filed in the office of the Clerk of the Court
of Common Pleas of .... County, Ohio, the petition of .... and others for the establishment of a Sanitary District to be known as ....
Sanitary District. (Here insert the purposes.)

2. That the lands sought to be included in said District comprise lands in .... and ....,
Counties, Ohio, described substantially as follows:

Beginning on the north line of .... County
at its point of intersection with the west bank of the......
...... River; thence west along the north line of ....
County to the high bluffs facing said .... River
on the west; thence following the base of the line of said
bluffs to the north line of the right of way of the ....
.... Railroad; thence west along the north right of way
line of said railroad to the center line of ....
avenue in the village of ....; thence south along
the center line of .... avenue to the......
.... Pike; thence southeasterly along the ....
Pike to the southeasterly line of the right of way of the
.... Railroad; thence southeasterly along said
right of way line to the corporate limits of the City of......
........; thence with said corporation line southerly, east-

erly and northerly to the southerly right of way line of the main track of the .... Railroad; thence easterly along said last named right of way line to the boundary line between .... Counties; thence north along said County line to the southerly line of .... County; thence easterly along the dividing line between .... Counties to the easterly line of the right of way of the .... Railroad; thence northerly along said right of way line to its intersection with the .... Pike; thence westerly along said Pike to the center line of the bridge over .... Creek; thence up said Creek and along the center line thereof to the north line of .... County; thence west to the place of beginning.

Or, if found more convenient, the lands sought to be included in the District may be described as follows:

All of Township .... in Range .... between the .... Railroad and the .... River; the following lands in .... Township and .... Range; Section .... and the .... half of Section ......; also all lands within the corporate limits of the City of .... etc., etc., etc.

3. That a public hearing on said petition will be had in said court on .... the .... day of .... at the hour of .... o'clock .... M. by the Court of Common Pleas of .... County, at the Court House in the City of ...., ... County, Ohio.

All persons and public corporations owning or interested in real estate within the territory hereinbefore described will be given the opportunity to be heard at the time and place above specified.

....
Clerk of the Court of Common Pleas
of .... County, Ohio.
Dated ...., Ohio, ..., 19....

2. Form of Finding on Hearing:
State of Ohio,
.... County
ss.
In the Court of Common Pleas .... County.
In Matter of
.... Sanitary District:

FINDINGS AND DECREE ON HEARING.

On this .... day of ...., 19...., this cause coming on for hearing on the petition of .... and others, for the organization of a sanitary district under the Sanitary District Act of the State of Ohio, the Court, after a full hearing now here find:

1. That it hath jurisdiction of the parties to, and the subject matter of this proceeding.

Forms and suggestions in procedure under act. 2. That the purposes for which said district is established are:

(Insert the purposes.)

And that it is a public necessity.

3. That the public safety, health, convenience and welfare will be promoted by the organization of a sanitary district substantially as prayed in said petition, (if additional lands are added by petition) except, that the following additional lands at the petition of the owners thereof should be, and hereby are included in said district:

(Here insert additional lands.)

4. That the boundaries of said district as modified by the last finding herein are as follows:

(Here insert corrected boundaries of district.)

5. That the said territory last above described should be erected into and created a sanitary district under the Sanitary District Act of the State of Ohio under the corporate name of .... Sanitary District.

Wherefore, it is by the Court ordered, adjudged, and decreed:

That the territory as above described be, and the same hereby is erected into and created a sanitary district under the Sanitary District Act of Ohio under the corporate name of .... Sanitary District, with its office or principal place of business at ...., in ......
.... County, Ohio. (If directors are appointed at the sametime.) And the following persons are hereby appointed directors of said sanitary district:

.... for the term of three years,
.... for the term of five years,
.... for the term of seven years,

who are hereby directed to qualify and proceed according to law.

6. For consideration of other matters herein, this cause is retained on the docket.

.... Judge.

3. Form of Notice to Property Owners to Pay Assessment:

.... Sanitary District.

To All Persons Interested:

Public Notice is Hereby Given:

1. That on the .... day of ...., 19....,
the Board of Directors of .... Sanitary District duly levied for the account of the Bond Fund of said District an assessment upon all the property in said District in the aggregate sum of ...., has caused the same to be extended upon the assessment duplicate of said District, and that said assessment duplicate is now in collection by the County Treasurer of the County in which the lands are situated.

2. That the entire assessment against any parcel of land may be paid at any time on or prior to ....,
19...., without costs and without interest.

3. That as soon after the .... day of ....
...... 19...., as conveniently may be, the Board of Directors of said District will divide the uncollected portion of said assessment into convenient installments and will issue bonds bearing interest not exceeding six per cent per annum in anticipation of the collection of the several installments of said assessment, pursuant to the Sanitary District Act of the State of Ohio.

....
President.

....
Secretary.

4. Form of Bond, and of Coupon.

(Form of Bond.)

No... $...

UNITED STATES OF AMERICA

State of Ohio

.... Sanitary District.

Sanitary District Bond.

Know All Men by These Presents that ....
sanitary district, a legally organized sanitary district of the State of Ohio, acknowledges itself to owe and for value received hereby promises to pay to bearer .... dollars ($.....) on the first day ...., 19...., with interest thereon from the date hereof until paid at the rate of .... per cent. per annum, payable ...., 19...., and semi-annually thereafter on the first day of .... and of .... in each year on presentation and surrender of the annexed interest coupons as they severally become due. Both principal and interest of this bond are hereby made payable in lawful money of the United States of America, at the office of the Treasurer of the State of Ohio, in the city of Columbus, Ohio.

This bond is one of a series of bonds issued by .... sanitary district for the purpose of paying the cost of constructing a system of trunk sewers (or for other works) for said district and in anticipation of the collection of the several installments of an assessment duly levied upon lands within said district and benefited by said improvement in strict compliance with the sanitary district act of Ohio, and pursuant to an order of the board of directors of said district duly made and entered of record.

And it is hereby certified and recited that all acts, conditions and things required to be done in locating and establishing said district and in equalizing appraisals of benefits and in levying assessments against lands benefited thereby, and in authorizing, executing and issuing this bond,

Forms and sug-
gestions in pro
cedure under act. have been legally had, done and performed in due form of
law; that the total amount of bonds issued by said district
does not exceed ninety (90) per cent of the assessments so
levied and unpaid at the time said bonds are issued or any
legal limitation thereof.

And for the performance of all the covenants and stipu-
lations of this bond and of the duties imposed by law upon
said district for the collection of the principal and interest
of said assessments and the application thereof to the payment of this bond and the interest thereon, and for the
levying of such other and further assessments as are authorized by law and as may be required for the prompt payment of this bond and the interest thereon, the full faith,
credit and resources of said .... sanitary district are hereby irrevocably pledged.

In Testimony Whereof the Board of Directors of ....
.... Sanitary District has caused this bond to be
signed by its President and sealed with the corporate seal
of said District, attested by its Secretary, and registered by
the State Treasurer of the State of Ohio, and the coupons
hereto annexed to be executed by the fac-simile signatures
of said President and Secretary, as of the .... day of
.............., 19.....

....
President.

Attest:

....
Secretary.

(Form of Coupon.)

$........

On the first day of " .... " 19..............
....
Sanitary District promises to pay to bearer............,.....
Dollars ($........) lawful money of the United States of
America, at the office of the Treasurer of the State of Ohio,
in the City of Columbus, Ohio, being semi-annual interest
due on that date on its Sanitary District Bond dated ......
........, 19....

No........

....
President.

....
Secretary.

5. Form of Notice of Enlargement of District:
State of Ohio,
ss.
County of ....

In the Court of Common Pleas,
.... County, Ohio.

In the Matter of
.... Sanitary District.

NOTICE OF ENLARGEMENT OF DISTRICT.

Forms and suggestions in procedure under act.

To All Persons (and Public Corporations, if any) Interested:

Public Notice is Hereby Given:

1. That heretofore on the .... day of ...., 19...., the Court of Common Pleas of .... County, Ohio, duly entered a final decree erecting and creating .... Sanitary District and appointing a Board of Directors therefor.

2. That thereafter this Court duly appointed
....
....
....
to be the Board of Appraisers for said District. That said Board of Appraisers on the .... day of ...., 19..., filed their report recommending that the following described lands, not originally included in the District, be added thereto:
(Here describe generally the lands which the report of the Board of Appraisers recommends should be added to the District.)

3. That on ...., the ...... day of ...., 19..., (or as soon thereafter as the convenience of the Court will permit) at the Court House in .... of ...., Ohio, the Court of Common Pleas of .... County, Ohio, will hear all persons and public corporations, who are owners of or interested in the property described in this notice upon the question whether said lands should be added to and included in said...... ....Sanitary District.

....
Clerk of the Court of Common Pleas
of .... County, Ohio.

6. Form of Notice of Hearing on Appraisals:
State of Ohio,
ss.
County of ....
In the Court of Common Pleas,
.... County, Ohio.
"In the Matter of
" ....
Sanitary District

NOTICE OF HEARING ON APPRAISALS.

To All Persons and Public Corporations Interested:
Public Notice is Hereby Given:
1. That heretofore on the ...... day of..........., 19..., the Court of Common Pleas of ....

County, Ohio, duly entered a decree, erecting and creating
.... Sanitary District and appointing a
Board of Directors therefor.

2. That thereafter this Court duly appointed

....

....

....

the Board of Appraisers for said District. That said Board
of Appraisers on the ...... day of ...., 19...,
filed their Appraisal of Benefits and Damages and of land
to be taken as follows: (Here insert general description
of land appraised.)

The said appraisal of benefits and damages and of land
to be taken is now on file in the office of the clerk of this
court.

3. All public corporations and all persons, owners of
or interested in the property described in said Report,
whether as benefited property or as property taken and
damaged (whether said taken or damaged property lies
within or without said district), desiring to contest the
appraisals as made and returned by the Board of Appraisers, must file their objections in said court on or before the
...... day of ...., 19..., (here insert a date
ten (10) days after the last publication of the notice) and
a hearing on said appraisal will be had on the ...... day of
.............., 19..., (here insert a date not less than
twenty (20), nor more than thirty (30), days after the
date of the last publication of this notice, as fixed by the
court) in the City of ...., Ohio, at
which time an opportunity will be afforded all objectors to
be heard upon their several objections.

....
Clerk of the Court of Common Pleas
of ....County, Ohio.

Dated at the City of ...., Ohio,
this ...... day of ...., 19....

7. Form of Certificate of Levy of Assessments:

State of Ohio,

ss.

County of ....

To the Auditor of .... County, Ohio:

This is to certify that by virtue and under the authority of the Sanitary District Act of Ohio, the Board of
Directors of .... Sanitary District have
and do hereby levy the sum of .... Dollars
for the account of the Bond Fund of said District, which
said assessment bears interest as provided by law and is
payable in installments as follows: (Here insert.)

You are further notified that for the account of the
Maintenance Fund for the year 19..., this Board has
levied the sum of .... Dollars.

The amounts of the said levies upon the several parcels
of land upon which the same are imposed are set forth

683

upon the schedule hereunto attached, marked ....
.... Sanitary District Assessment Book. The said
assessments shall be collectable and payable the present
year in the sums therein specified at the same time that the
state and county taxes are due and collectable, and you
are directed and ordered to require the Treasurer of ......
.... County, Ohio, to demand and collect such assessments at the time that he demands and collects the state
and county taxes due on the same lands, and this Sanitary
District Assessment Book shall be your authority and the
authority of the Treasurer to make such collection.

Witness the signature of the President of said Board
of Directors, attested by the seal of said corporation, and
the signature of its Secretary, this ...... day of ....
........, 19....

....
President.

....
Secretary.

CARL R. KIMBALL,
Speaker of the House of Representatives.
CLARENCE J. BROWN,
President of the Senate.

Passed May 7, 1919.
Approved June 6, 1919.

JAMES M. COX,
Governor.
Filed in the office of the Secretary of State at Columbus,
Ohio, on the 7th day of June A. D., 1919.
219 G.

[House Bill No. 317.]

AN ACT

To amend sections 7807-1, 7807-2, 7824, 7826, 7830, 7831, 7832-2, 7832-3, 7840, 7847 and 7852 of the General Code, and to enact supplemental sections 7807-10, 7823-3, 7831-3, 7847-1, 7848 and 7852-1 of the General Code, relating to life certificates, and temporary certificates and to provide kindergarten primary certificates.

Be it enacted by the General Assembly of the State of Ohio:
SECTION 1. That sections 7807-1, 7807-2, 7824, 7826, 7830, 7831, 7832-2, 7832-3, 7840, 7847 and 7852 of the General Code be amended, and that supplemental sections 7807-10, 7823-3, 7831-3, 7847-1, 7848, 7852-1 be added to the General Code to read as follows:
Sec. 7807-1. Applicants for elementary life certificates and special life certificates, not provided for in sections 7807-6 or 7807-8 shall have completed fifty months of successful teaching experience, a four year high school course

The sectional numbers on the margin hereof are designated as provided by law. JOHN G. PRICE, Attorney General.

Forms and suggestions in procedure under act.

Experience and professional training for elementary life certificates.

or the equivalent, and college or normal credit aggregating one year, including one half year of professional training, and shall complete such additional requirements and tests as are prescribed by the state board of school examiners.

Experience and training for high school life certificates.
Sec. 7807-2. Applicants for high school life certificates shall have completed fifty months of successful teaching experience, a four year high school course or the equivalent, and college or normal credit aggregating two years, including one half year of professional training, and unless applying under section 7807-6 or 7807-7 shall complete such additional requirements and tests as are prescribed by the state board of school examiners.

Provisional certificates, in kindergarten, first and second grades.
Sec. 7807-10. State provisional certificates valid for four years to teach in kindergarten and first and second grades of elementary schools shall be granted by the superintendent of public instruction upon formal application and the payment of a fee of one dollar, to those who have completed a four year high school course or the equivalent and at least a two year course in an approved school for the training of teachers, provided the course as conducted is approved by the superintendent of public instruction for the specific purpose.

Training determined by superintendent; issue of certificates.
Sec. 7823-3. The amount of training completed by a prospective applicant for a teacher's certificate shall be determined by the superintendent of public instruction after an inspection of the credits held by the prospective applicant. He shall issue certificates of professional training which shall state the total number of multiples of six-weeks' training completed by the prospective applicant. The superintendent of public instruction shall have power equitably to estimate extension or other credits not regularly earned by full attendance at an institution but which might apply on courses in approved institutions for training teachers and include them in the training which is certified. These certificates issued by the superintendent of public instruction shall be required by boards of examiners as evidence of the training required by law.

When certificates may be issued without formal examination.
Sec. 7824. Boards of school examiners at their discretion may issue certificates without formal examinations to holders of certificates granted by other county and city boards of school examiners in Ohio, and, with the approval in each case of the superintendent of public instruction, to holders of certificates granted by certificating authorities in other states. Such certificates may be renewed under regulations provided by the superintendent of public instruction.

Temporary certificates may be issued, when.
Sec. 7826. Between regular examinations boards of examiners under such conditions as may from time to time be prescribed by the superintendent of public instruction may issue temporary certificates which shall be valid only until the next regular examination held by such boards after the issue of such certificate, and at any regular examination such board, upon proper application being made,

subject to the same rules and laws as apply to the granting of regular certificates, may issue temporary certificates valid from the date of issue to the first day of September following.

Sec. 7830. No person shall be employed or enter upon the performance of his duties as teacher in any elementary school supported wholly or in part by the state in any school district who has not obtained from a certificating authority having legal jurisdiction a certificate of good moral character; that he is qualified to teach orthography, reading, writing, arithmetic, English grammar and composition, geography, history of the United States, physiology, including narcotics, literature, and elementary agriculture, and that he possesses an adequate knowledge of the principles of teaching; except as provided in sections 7807-9, 7807-10, 7807-6, 7852 and 7831-1. *Elementary certificate; branches qualified to teach.*

Sec. 7831. No person shall be employed or enter upon the performance of his duties as a teacher in any recognized high school supported wholly or in part by the state, except as provided for teachers in classes supported with federal aid under the supervision of the state board of education, in any school district or act as superintendent of schools in such district, who has not obtained from a certificating authority having legal jurisdiction a certificate of good moral character and such knowledge of subject matter and ability to teach as may be necessary for the performance of his duties; and no such certificate shall be issued by such authority except on the specific conditions provided by the statutes. *High school certificate.*

Sec. 7831-2. Every applicant for high school certificate by examination shall be examined in English and in the principles of teaching and in addition in five branches selected from the following: literature, general history, modern history, algebra, physics, physiology, Latin, French, Spanish, civics, geometry, physical geography, botany, chemistry, high school agriculture, economics, sociology, manual training, home economics. *Branches in which applicant for high school certificate examined.*

Sec. 7832-2. The county board of school examiners shall grant elementary certificates valid for one year to graduates of first grade high schools or those with equivalent preparation as determined by the superintendent of public instruction, who have completed in addition a one year normal course approved by the superintendent of public instruction. Such certificates may be renewed twice for one year and three times for three years. *To whom one year elementary certificates granted.*

Sec. 7832-3. The county board of school examiners prior to January 1, 1924, may grant one year elementary certificates to applicants who have completed a one year normal course approved by the superintendent of public instruction, provided, after January 1, 1921, that such applicants have completed two years of high school credit or the equivalent as determined by the superintendent of *To whom one year elementary certificates granted.*

public instruction. Such certificates may be renewed twice for one year and three times for three years.

Standard of qualification prior to and after year 1924.

Sec. 7840. Each city board of school examiners shall prior to the year 1924 determine the standard of qualifications necessary for admission of applicants to examination to receive certificates, excepting applicants for certificates to teach in classes supported with federal aid under the supervision of the state board of education; after January 1, 1924, the qualifications shall be equivalent to and determined in like manner as those prescribed for applicants for county certificates.

To whom law applies.

Sec. 7847. All provisions of preceding and following sections pertaining to county school examiners and applicants for county teachers' certificates shall apply also to city examiners and applicants for city teachers' certificates unless there are specific provisions of law applying to the latter.

Questions for examinations.

Sec. 7847-1. City boards of examiners shall provide the questions used in the respective city examinations but may arrange to use questions prepared for county examinations as provided in section 7819, or questions prepared for city examinations under the directions of the superintendent of public instruction for such dates as may be arranged.

Substitute for practical teaching test.

Sec. 7848. City and county boards of examiners at their discretion may substitute for the practical teaching test provided by section 7825 such an investigation of the teaching of the applicant as they deem best, and any member of the board of examiners may examine any school in the district when such examination is deemed necessary to ascertain a teacher's qualifications.

Discretion of city boards in branches.

Sec. 7852. City boards of examiners at their discretion may require teachers in elementary schools to be examined in drawing, music or physical training if such subjects are a part of the regular work of such teachers: they may also at their discretion relieve applicants for elementary certificates from examination in agriculture or substitute general science or nature study therefor.

Certificates to teach special classes.

Sec. 7852-1. City and county boards of examiners may upon proper examination issues certificates valid to teach special classes for the deaf, feeble-minded, backward, and the like, but such applicants must have all necessary and legal qualifications for elementary teachers and in addition such qualifications in such special studies as may be prescribed by the superintendent of public instruction.

SECTION 2. That original sections of the General Code 7807-1, 7807-2, 7824, 7826, 7830, 7831, 7832-2, 7832-3, 7840, 7847 and 7852 be and the same are hereby repealed. _{Repeals.}

CARL R. KIMBALL,
Speaker of the House of Representatives.
CLARENCE J. BROWN,
President of the Senate.

Passed May 10, 1919.
Approved June 5, 1919.

JAMES M. COX,
Governor.

Filed in the office of the Secretary of State at Columbus, Ohio, on the 7th day of June. A. D., 1919.

220 G.

[Senate Bill No. 28.]

AN ACT

To amend section 12556 of the General Code, requiring railroads to employ full crews for through freight trains and light engines, and the penalty for violation thereof.

Be it enacted by the General Assembly of the State of Ohio:

SECTION 1. That section 12556 of the General Code, be amended to read as follows:

Sec. 12556. Whoever, being a superintendent or other employee of a railroad company, sends or causes to be sent out on main track, a through freight train with less than one engineer, one fireman, one conductor and two brakemen, or a light engine without cars, to a point more than three miles distant from original starting point, with less than one engineer, one fireman and one conductor or flagman, shall be fined not less than one hundred dollars for each offense. _{Penalty for sending train out more than three miles with less than specified crew.}

Sec. 12556-1. SECTION 2. The Public Utilities Commission shall be empowered to enforce the foregoing sections and prosecute any violations thereof. _{Enforcement of law.}

SECTION 3. That said original section 12556 of the General Code be, and the same is hereby repealed. _{Repeal.}

CLARENCE J. BROWN,
President of the Senate.
CARL R. KIMBALL,
Speaker of the House of Representatives.

Passed May 7, 1919.

This bill was presented to the Governor May 27, 1919, and was not signed or returned to the house wherein it originated within ten days after being so presented exclusive of Sundays, and the day said bill was presented, and was filed in the office of the Secretary of State, June 9, 1919.

ROBERT T. CREW,
Veto Clerk.

Filed in the office of the Secretary of State at Columbus, Ohio, on the 9th day of June, A. D. 1919.

221 G.

688

[Amended Senate Bill No. 55.]

AN ACT

To supplement section 9485 by the addition of supplemental section 9485-1 of the General Code, to provide for the further regulation of fraternal benefit societies.

Be it enacted by the General Assembly of the State of Ohio:

SECTION 1. That section 9485 be repealed and that there be enacted sections 9485, 9485-1 of the General Code to read as follows:

Maintenance of financial condition at each triennial valuation; proceedings to dissolve on failure.

SECTION 9485. If the valuation of the certificates, as hereinbefore provided, on December 31, 1920, shall show that the present value of future net contributions, together with the admitted assets, is less than the present value of the promised benefit and accrued liabilities, such society shall thereafter maintain said financial condition at each succeeding triennial valuation in respect of the degree of deficiency as shown in the valuation as of December 31, 1920. If at any succeeding triennial valuation such society does not show at least the same condition, the superintendent shall direct that it thereafter comply with the requirements herein specified. If the next succeeding triennial valuation after the receipt of such notice shall show that the society has failed to maintain the conditions required herein, the superintendent may, in the absence of good cause shown for such failure, institute proceedings for the dissolution of such society, in accordance with the provision of section 9486 of this act, or in the case of a foreign society, its license may be cancelled in the manner provided in this act.

Any such society, shown by any triennial valuation, subsequent to December 31st, 1920, not to have maintained the condition herein required, shall within two years thereafter, make such improvement as to show a percentage of deficiency not greater than as of December 31st, 1920, or thereafter, as to all new members admitted, be subject, so far as stated rates of contribution are concerned, to the provisions of section 9473 of this act, applicable in the organization of new societies; provided that the net mortuary or beneficiary contributions and funds of such new members shall be kept separate and apart from the other funds of the society. If such required improvement is not shown by the succeeding triennial valuation, then the said new members may be placed in a separate class and their certificates valued as an independent society in respect to contributions and funds.

Charge for cost of insurance.

SECTION 9485-1. In lieu of the requirements of sections 9484 and 9485, any society accepting in its laws the provisions of this section may value its certificates on a basis, herein designated "accumulation basis," by crediting each member with the net amount contributed for each year and with interest at approximately the net rate earned and by charging him with his share of the losses for each year, herein designated "cost of insurance" and carrying the balance, if any, to his credit. The charge for the cost of insurance may be according to the actual experience of the society applied to a table of mortality recognized by the law of this state, and shall take into consideration the amount at risk during each year, which shall be the amount payable at death less the credit to the member. Except as specifically provided in its articles or laws or contracts, no charge shall be carried forward from the first valuation hereunder against any member for any past share of losses exceeding the contributions and credit. If, after the first valuation, any member's share of losses for any year exceeds his credit, including the contribution for the year, the contribution shall be increased to cover his share of the losses, and, if the credit at the time any benefit becomes payable during the lifetime of the member, including any available funds does not equal such benefit, the contributions to be made by him or on his behalf shall be increased by the difference. Any such excess share of losses chargeable to any member may be paid out of a fund or contributions especially created or required for such purpose.

Any member may transfer to any plan adopted by the society with net rates on which tabular reserves are maintained, and on such transfer shall be entitled to make such application of his credit as provided in the laws of the society. *Provisions for transfer.*

Certificates issued, rerated or readjusted on a basis providing for adequate reserves to mature such certificates upon assumptions for mortality and interest recognized by law of this state shall be valued on such basis, herein designated the "tabular basis," provided that if on the first valuation under this section a deficiency in reserve shall be shown for any such certificate, the same shall be valued on the accumulation basis. *Valuation of certificates on tabular basis.*

Whenever in any society having members upon the tabular basis and upon the accumulation basis, the total of all costs of insurance provided for any year shall be insufficient to meet the actual death and disability losses for the year, the deficiency shall be met for the year from the available funds after setting aside all credits in the reserve; or from increased contributions or by an increase in the number of assessments applied to the society as a whole or to classes of members as may be specified in its laws. Savings from a lower amount of death losses may be returned in like manner as may be specified in its laws. *How deficiencies met.*

If the laws of the society so provide, the assets representing the reserves of any separate class of members may be carried separately for such class as if in an independent society, and the required reserve accumulation of such class so set apart shall not thereafter be mingled with the assets of other classes of the society. *When assets carried separately for a class.*

Table of rates and credits filed with annual report.

A table showing the rates being paid by and the credits to individual members at each age and year of entry, and showing opposite each credit the tabular rates and the tabular reserve required, or at the option of the society the required reserve on a level rate equivalent to that being paid, according to assumption of mortality and interest recognized by the laws of this state and adopted by the society, and, in either case, including any benefit payable at a specified age or on account of old age disability shall be filed by the society with each annual report and also be furnished to each member before July first of each year.

In lieu of the aforesaid statement there may be furnished to each member within the same time a statement giving the data aforesaid for such member. No table or statement need be made or furnished when the reserves are maintained on the tabular basis.

For this purpose, individual bookkeeping accounts for each member shall not be required and all calculations may be made by actuarial methods.

Surplus may be maintained over credits and reserve.

Nothing herein contained shall prevent the maintenance of such surplus over and above the credits on the accumulation basis and the reserves on the tabular basis as the society may provide by or pursuant to its laws; nor be construed as giving to the individual member any right or claim to any such reserve or credit other than in manner as expressed in the contract and its laws; nor as making any such reserve or credits a liability in determining the legal solvency of the society.

The sectional numbers in this act are in conformity to the General Code. JOHN G. PRICE, Attorney General.

CLARENCE J. BROWN,
President of the Senate.
CARL R. KIMBALL,
Speaker of the House of Representatives.

Passed May 6, 1919.

This bill was presented to the Governor May 27th, 1919, and was not signed or returned to the house wherein it originated within ten days after being so presented, exclusive of Sundays and the day said bill was presented, and was filed in the office of the Secretary of State June 9, 1919.
ROBERT T. CREW,
Veto Clerk.

Filed in the office of the Secretary of State at Columbus, Ohio, on the 9th day of June, A. D. 1919.

222 G.

[House Bill No. 502.]

An ACT

. To authorize the city of Nelsonville, Athens county, Ohio, to enter
upon, improve and occupy a portion of the Hocking Canal as
a public highway and for sewerage and water purposes.

Be it enacted by the General Assembly of the State of Ohio:

SECTION 1. That the portion of the Hocking canal
situate within the corporate limits of the city of Nelsonville,
Athens county, Ohio, be, and the same is hereby, vacated
and abandoned for canal purposes.

SECTION 2. That there is hereby granted to said city
of Nelsonville, the authority and permission to enter upon,
improve and occupy forever as a public highway and for
sewerage and water purposes, that portion of the Hocking
canal situate within the corporate limits of said city.

Provided, however, said city shall have the right to
dispose of the width of any portion of the canal in excess
of sixty feet, the street to be defined by straight lines as
nearly as possible, and that no portion of the canal property in the sixty feet reserved for street purposes herein
described, shall ever be used for any purpose or purposes
other than for streets and avenues, parking purposes, sewerage and water purposes, and provided further that any
portion of the said abandoned canal property that is not
so occupied and used at the end of ten years from the date
of the passage of this act, shall immediately revert to the
state of Ohio; and provided further that if at any time the
state of Ohio shall have an opportunity to lease a right-of-
way over the abandoned Hocking canal property between
Lancaster and Nelsonville, it may include a right-of-way
over the canal property herein conveyed, even though the
same is improved as a street or highway.

SECTION 3. That whatever title and interest remains
to the state of Ohio in that part of the Hocking canal vacated and abandoned by section 1 of this act, are hereby re-
linquished and transferred to said city of Nelsonville.

CARL R. KIMBALL,
Speaker of the House of Representatives.
CLARENCE J. BROWN,
President of the Senate.

Passed May 8, 1919.

This bill was presented to the Governor May 27, 1919,
and was not signed or returned to the house wherein it
originated within ten days after being so presented, exclusive of Sundays and the day said bill was presented, and
was filed in the office of Secretary of State June 9, 1919.

ROBERT T. CREW,
Veto Clerk.

Filed in the office of the Secretary of State at Columbus,
Ohio, on the 9th day of June, A. D. 1919.

223 G.

Portion of canal,
Nelsonville, va-
cated for canal
purposes.

Nelsonville au-
thorized to im-
prove.

Title transferred
to Nelsonville.

This act is not
of a general and
permanent na-
ture and requires
no sectional
number.
JOHN G. PRICE,
Attorney
General.

[House Bill No. 373.]

An ACT

To amend section 1662 of the General Code (as amended 1ⁿ7 O. L., 19) relating to probation officers, their appointment : nd compensation.

Be it enacted by the General Assembly of the State of Ohio:

SECTION 1. That section 1662 of the General Code be amended to read as follows:

Probation officers, appointment, compensation; chief probation officer.

Sec. 1662. The judge designated to exercise jurisdiction may appoint one or more discreet persons of good moral character, one or more of whom may be a woman, to serve as probation officers, during the pleasure of the judge. One of such officers shall be known as chief probation officer and there may be one or more assistants. Such chief probation officer and assistants shall receive such compensation as the judge appointing them may designate at the time of the appointment, but the compensation of the chief probation officer shall not exceed three thousand dollars per annum and that of the assistants shall not exceed eighteen hundred dollars per annum. The judge may appoint other probation officers, with or without compensation, when the interests of the county require it.

The compensation of the probation officers shall be paid by the county treasurer from the county treasury upon the warrant of the county auditor, which shall be issued upon itemized vouchers sworn to by the probation officers and certified to by the judge of the juvenile court. The county auditor shall issue his warrant upon the treasury and the treasurer shall honor and pay the same, for all salaries, compensation and expenses provided for in this act, in the order in which proper vouchers therefor are presented to him.

SECTION 2. That said original section 1662 of the General Code (as amended 107 O. L. 19) be, and the same is hereby repealed.

The sectional number in this act is in conformity to the General Code. JOHN G. PRICE, *Attorney General.*

CLARENCE J. BROWN,
President of the Senate.
CARL R. KIMBALL,
Speaker of the House of Representatives.
Passed May 10, 1919.

This bill was presented to the Governor May 27, 1919, and was not signed or returned to the house wherein it originated within ten days after being so presented, exclusive of Sundays and the day said bill was presented, and was filed in the office of the Secretary of State June 9, 1919.

ROBERT T. CREW,
Veto Clerk.

Filed in the office of the Secretary of State at Columbus, Ohio, on the 9th day of June, A. D. 1919.

224 G.

[Amended Senate Bill No. 125.]

AN ACT

To amend sections 5123-1 and 5123-3 of the General Code, relative to the submission of proposed amendments to the constitution to the electors.

Be it enacted by the General Assembly of the State of Ohio:

SECTION 1. Sections 5123-1; and 5123-3 of the General Code are hereby amended to read as follows:

Sec. 5123-1. Amendments to the constitution which have been or may hereafter be proposed to be submitted to the electors, may be submitted at any regular election or at a special election, as prescribed by the general assembly in the resolution proposing such amendment, and the judges and clerks of election in each township, ward and precinct, shall, in addition to the returns provided by law for any other election held therein on the same day, at the same time make return to the deputy state supervisors of elections of the vote cast for or against any proposed amendments to the constitution of Ohio that may be submitted to the voters of the state for adoption or rejection at such election. *Return of votes cast for and against constitutional amendments.*

Sec. 5123-3. The secretary of state shall cause amendments to the constitution proposed by the general assembly to be published once a week for five consecutive weeks preceding such election, in at least one newspaper in each county of the state, where a newspaper is published. *Publication of proposed amendments.*

SECTION 2. Original sections 5123-1 and 5123-3 of the General Code are hereby repealed. *Repeal.*

The sectional numbers in this act are in conformity to the General Code. JOHN G. PRICE, Attorney General.

CLARENCE J. BROWN,
President of the Senate.
CARL R. KIMBALL,
Speaker of the House of Representatives.

Passed April 15, 1919.

This bill was presented to the Governor, May 27, 1919, and was not signed or returned to the house wherein it originated within ten days after being so presented exclusive of Sundays and the day said bill was presented, and was filed in the office of the Secretary of State, June 9, 1919.

ROBERT T. CREW,
Veto Clerk.

Filed in the office of the Secretary of State at Columbus, Ohio, on the 9th day of June, A. D. 1919.

225 G.

[Amended Senate Bill No. 185.]

AN ACT

To authorize the taxing authorities of counties, municipal corporations, townships and school districts to fund deficiencies in operating revenues for the year 1919, and to levy taxes in addition to all other taxes for such purpose.

Be it enacted by the General Assembly of the State of Ohio:

SECTION 1. For the purposes of this act:

"Subdivision" defined.

"Subdivision" means a county, a municipal corporation, a township or a school district.

"Taxing authorities" means the board of county commissioners of a county, the council or other legislative body of a municipal corporation, the trustees of a township or the board of education of a school district.

"Deficiency" defined.

"Deficiency" means the aggregate sum of the following:

1. The unfunded obligations of a subdivision created prior to and outstanding on July 1, 1919, and due on or before said date, or to become due thereafter during the current fiscal year of the subdivision, for the payment of which sufficient funds are not in the treasury thereof on July 1, 1919, or estimated to come into such treasury thereafter during the then current fiscal year from taxes and other sources of revenue, to the extent of the excess of such obligations over and above such funds on hand and estimated future receipts applicable to the payment thereof and not needed to pay the fixed charges against the appropriate funds and the current expenses payable therefrom for the remainder of such fiscal year.

2. The excess, if any, of the estimated aggregate fixed charges and current expenses of such subdivision for the remainder of such fiscal year over and above the revenues from taxes and other sources estimated to come into such treasury after July 1, 1919, and applicable to such fixed charges and current expenses.

"Fixed charges" defined.

"Fixed charges" include salaries, wages, payments on contracts for fixed or regular services, as for light, heat, power, water or gas, tuition and transportation of school pupils, and charges by law made payable from any such treasury without action by the legislative or other taxing authorities thereof, election expenses, and contributions to libraries, universities, hospitals and pension funds. It excludes funded debt service, expenditures for permanent improvements, and such ordinary expenses as are included within the scope of "current expenses" as hereinafter defined.

Said term "fixed charges" means expenses of the character indicated by the foregoing enumeration for the purposes provided, and at rates and quantities not in excess of those provided by laws, ordinances, resolutions and contracts in force on January 1, 1919, by ordinances and reso-

lutions of municipal corporations passed prior to such date
and not effective thereon for want of due publication, or
pending the expiration of a referendum period, and by
laws passed after such date, or ordinances or resolutions
adopted in compliance with such laws; it being the intention of this act that no increase in the fixed charges of any
subdivision beyond those established on January 1, 1919,
shall enter into a deficiency except as herein expressly provided. But in case a substantial increase in the enrollment
of school pupils in a school district is estimated for the
school year commencing on the first day of September,
1919, the fixed charges of such district may include the
salaries of a sufficient number of teachers to provide for
such additional pupils during the fiscal year of such district
as defined in section 9 hereof.

"Current expenses" include such items of expense as
the repair and maintenance of streets, roads, highways and
bridges, other than such as may be provided for by special
proceedings under sections 6906 to 6953, inclusive, of the
General Code, and sections 1191 to 1219, inclusive, of the
General Code; the repair and maintenance of other public
property, the purchase of supplies and equipment of a consumable character, other than such as are herein referred to
as fixed charges, and salaries and wages incidental thereto.
It excludes funded debt service, expenditures for permanent
improvements, and such expenses as are included within the
scope of "fixed charges" as hereinbefore defined.

The foregoing enumeration of expenses as fixed charges
and current expenses, is descriptive, and not exclusive or
definitive; and matters and things similar in nature to those
mentioned under each heading and not expressly excluded
from either, shall be included within the scope of said terms.

SECTION 2. The taxing authorities of a subdivision, by
resolution passed not later than the fourth Monday in September, 1919, may direct the accounting officer of the subdivision to make up a financial statement of such subdivision as of the first day of July, 1919. Such accounting
officer shall immediately examine the records, books and
accounts of his office, and shall make up and file such statement in the office of the clerk of the taxing authorities not
later than the fifth Monday in September, 1919. Such
statement shall contain:

1. The balance standing to the credit or debit of the
several funds, excepting sinking funds, on the books of the
subdivision on July 1, 1919.

2. A showing in detail of the outstanding unfunded
indebtedness of the several funds of such subdivision on
July 1, 1919, whether represented by certificates of indebtedness, accounts payable, or otherwise, with the dates of
maturity thereof.

3. An estimate of the amount necessary to provide for
the fixed charges and current expenses of the subdivision
for the remainder of the then current fiscal year, including

"Current ex-
penses" defined.

Statement by ac-
counting officer
filed with taxing
authorities; con-
tents of state-
ment.

obligations for such fixed charges or current expenses incurred prior to July 1, 1919, and payable within the then current fiscal year.

4. The amount of taxes estimated to come into the treasury of such subdivision to the credit of such funds during the remainder of the then current fiscal year, and applicable to the purposes of such year.

5. An estimate of the amount which will be received by such subdivision during the remainder of the current fiscal year from sources of revenue other than taxation, and credited to such funds.

If such accounting officer finds that a deficiency exists in such funds of the subdivision, he shall certify the amount thereof, together with the various funds affected, under oath, on such statement.

How deficiency determined.

SECTION. 3 Thereupon the taxing authorities, by resolution passed by an affirmative vote of a majority of all their members elected or appointed, not later than the first Monday in October, 1919, shall determine whether or not such deficiency exists and the amount thereof, which shall not be greater than that certified to it by the accounting officer. If such amount does not exceed five thousand dollars, the taxing authorities may by such resolution issue and sell bonds of the subdivision in the amount so determined for the purpose of funding the deficiency of the subdivision. If such amount exceeds five thousand dollars the taxing authorities in such resolution may declare it necessary to issue and sell bonds of the subdivision for the purpose of funding the deficiency of the subdivision, if any, in the amount so determined; and in such event, such resolution shall also specify the number of years which such bonds shall run, not exceeding five, and the estimated rate of taxes required to pay the interest thereon and retire the principal thereof, and shall order that the question of issuing bonds and levying taxes for such purposes shall be submitted to the electors of the subdivision. A resolution substantially in the following form shall be sufficient:

Resolution for sale of bonds; submission of question.

Be it resolved by the .... of the .... that a deficiency exists in the .... funds of the .... in the amount of .... dollars ($........) and it is hereby declared necessary to issue and sell bonds of the .... in said amount for the purpose of funding said deficiency. Said bonds shall run for a period of .... years. It is hereby estimated that it will require a rate of .... mills annually on the taxable property in said .... on the grand duplicate to pay the interest thereon and retire the principal thereof. The question of issuing bonds and levying taxes for such purpose shall on Tuesday, the fourth day of November, 1919, be submitted to the electors of the said ....

Such resolution shall go into immediate effect, without publication and without being subject to a referendum.

SECTION 4. A copy of such resolution shall be certified to the deputy state supervisors of elections of the county or counties in which the subdivision is situated. The deputy state supervisors shall prepare the ballots and make the necessary arrangements for the submission of such question to the electors of such subdivision at the general election to be held on the fourth day of November, 1919. The result of the election shall be certified and canvassed in like manner as regular elections of such subdivisions for the election of officers thereof. Notice of such election for not less than ten days shall be given by the deputy state supervisors in one or more newspapers printed in the subdivision, once a week on the same day of the week for two consecutive times prior thereto. If no newspaper is printed therein such notice shall be posted for ten days prior to the election in five conspicuous places in the subdivision, and published as aforesaid in a newspaper of general circulation in such subdivision. A notice substantially in the following form shall be sufficient:

[margin note: Copy certified to deputy state supervisors; notice of election.]

NOTICE OF ELECTION.

Notice is hereby given that at the general election to be held in the .... Ohio, on Tuesday, the fourth day of November, 1919, the question whether or not bonds of said .... shall be issued in the amount of $.......... for the purpose of funding a deficiency in the revenue of said .... and the levy of an additional tax of approximately .... mills for .... years shall be made to retire said bonds, will be submitted to the voters of said ....
The expense of giving such notice shall be certified by the deputy state supervisors to the accounting officer of the subdivision and shall be paid as expenses of notices of elections in such subdivisions are paid.

SECTION 5. The ballots used at such election shall indicate the name of the subdivision, and further shall be in form as follows:

[margin note: Form of ballot.]

"For additional tax levy of approximately .... mills, for .... years to retire bonds in the amount of $........ for the purpose of funding deficiencies in current revenues. Yes.

"For additional tax levy of approximately .... mills, for .... years to retire bonds in the amount of $.......... for the purpose of funding deficiencies in current revenues. No."

SECTION 6. If a majority of the electors voting on the proposition so submitted vote in favor thereof. upon the certification and canvass of such result the taxing authorities shall issue the bonds in an amount not to exceed the

[margin note: Execution and sale of bonds.]

amount determined by the preliminary resolution to run
for the period fixed thereby. All bonds issued under the
authority of this act shall be in denominations to be determined by the taxing authorities. They shall be executed
as are other bonds of the subdivision, shall express on their
face the purpose for which they are issued, shall bear interest at a rate not to exceed 6 per cent per annum, payable
semi-annually, and shall be sold for not less than par and
accrued interest. Such provisions of sections 2294, 2295,
3295, 3922 to 3924, inclusive, 3926, 3927, 7619 and 1465-58
of the General Code, as relate to the sale of bonds of the
subdivision shall apply to the sale of such bonds.

Tax levy for re-demption.
SECTION 7. For the payment of the interest on such
bonds and to provide a sinking fund for their redemption
at maturity the proper levying authorities of the subdivision
shall annually levy a sufficient tax. Such levy shall not be
subject to any limitation on tax rates, and shall be in addition to all other taxes; provided, however, that the entire
proceeds of any inheritance tax accruing to such subdivision
in any fiscal year within the period which such bonds shall
have to run shall, to the extent necessary to provide for the
payment of the entire amount thereof at maturity and the
interest to accrue thereon, not otherwise provided for, be
credited to the sinking fund of the subdivision and be there
held and used for the purpose of paying such interest as it
accrues and the principal thereof at maturity, and for no
other purpose, anything in the inheritance tax law of this
state to the contrary notwithstanding; and in case any such
inheritance taxes shall so accrue, any levy or levies required
by this section to be made thereafter in such subdivision
shall be exonerated or reduced accordingly and limited to
such amount as shall be necessary to meet the interest and
sinking fund requirements of the net indebtedness on account of such bonds thereafter remaining. If any such inheritance tax accrues to such subdivision in an amount in
excess of that necessary to accomplish the foregoing purpose, the surplus thereof shall be credited to funds of the
subdivision in the proportions provided by such inheritance
tax law as now or hereafter in force. Such bonds shall not
be counted in ascertaining any of the limitations prescribed
by law upon the creation of bonded indebtedness or the total
amount of outstanding bonded indebtedness of such subdivision.

Application of proceeds.
SECTION 8. The proceeds of such bonds shall be credited to the proper funds of the subdivision in the several
accounts in which deficiencies exist in accordance with the
respective amounts of such deficiencies, shall then be deemed
appropriated and made available for expenditure for the
purposes with respect to which said deficiencies exist, and
shall not be used for any other purpose.

"Current fiscal year" in this act defined.
SECTION 9. As to school districts the term "current
fiscal year" as used in this act shall include the remainder

of the present school year and the part of the ensuing school
year ending on the first day of March, 1920.

CLARENCE J. BROWN,
President of the Senate.
CARL R. KIMBALL,
Speaker of the House of Representatives.
Passed May 28, 1919.

This act is not
of a general or
permanent na-
ture and re-
quires no sec-
tional number.
JOHN G. PRICE,
*Attorney
General.*

In the house of representatives passed notwithstanding
the objections of the Governor, three-fifths of the members
concurring therein. Passed June 17, 1919.
CARL R. KIMBALL,
Speaker of the House of Representatives.

Passed by the senate notwithstanding the objections of
the Governor, three-fifths of the members concurring therein. Passed June 17, 1919.
CLARENCE J. BROWN,
President of the Senate.

Filed in the office of the Secretary of State at Columbus, Ohio, on the 18th day of June, A. D. 1919.
226 G.

[House Bill No. 9.]

AN ACT

To amend sections 4862 and 4940 of the General Code, to provide
that women may vote and be voted for for presidential electors.

Be it enacted by the General Assembly of the State of Ohio:
SECTION 1. That sections 4862 and 4940 of the General Code be amended to read as follows:

Sec. 4862. Every woman, born in the United States
or who is the wife or daughter of a citizen of the United
States, who is over twenty-one years of age and possesses
the necessary qualifications in regard to residence hereinafter provided for men shall be entitled to vote and be
voted for for member of the board of education and presidential elector and upon no other question.

Offices for which
women entitled
to vote and be
voted for:

Sec. 4940. The provisions of this chapter relating to
registration shall apply to women upon whom the right to
vote for member of the board of education or presidential
elector is conferred by law, but the names of such women
may be placed on a separate list.

Registration of
women.

700

SECTION 2. That said original sections 4862 and 4940 of the General Code be and the same are hereby repealed.

CARL R. KIMBALL,
Speaker of the House of Representatives.
CLARENCE J. BROWN,
President of the Senate.

Passed June 16, 1919.
Approved June 18, 1919.

JAMES M. COX,
Governor.

Filed in the office of the Secretary of State at Columbus, Ohio, on the 18th day of June, A. D. 1919.

227 G.

[House Bill No. 442.]

AN ACT

To create boards of trustees of the sinking fund in the several counties of the state, define the powers and duties of said boards and repeal sections 2609 to 2614 inclusive, and the act approved March 5, 1919 (House Bill No. 116).

Be it enacted by the General Assembly of the State of Ohio:

Sec. 2976-18.

County board of trustees of sinking fund.

SECTION 1. In each county owing a bonded debt, there shall be a board designated as the trustees of the sinking fund, to be composed of the prosecuting attorney, the county auditor and the county treasurer. The prosecuting attorney shall be the president of such board and the county auditor shall be the secretary thereof.

Sec. 2976-19.

Duties of board of trustees.

SECTION 2. The trustees of the sinking fund shall provide for the payment of all bonds issued by the county and the interest maturing thereon. All taxes, assessments and other moneys collected for such purposes, or held in the county treasury to the credit of the sinking fund, shall be subject to investment and disbursement by them in the manner provided by law. For the satisfaction of any obligation under their supervision, the trustees of the sinking fund may sell or use any of the securities in their possession or disburse any of the money under their control.

Sec. 2976-20.

Report by auditor to trustees semi-annually.

SECTION 3. Immediately after each semi-annual settlement of taxes and assessments the county auditor shall report to the trustees the amount in the treasury of the county to the credit of the sinking fund.

Sec. 2976-21.

Investment of funds.

SECTION 4. The trustees of the sinking fund shall invest all monies subject to their control in bonds of the United States, the state of Ohio, or of a municipal corporation, school district, township or county of the state, and hold in reserve in cash only such sums as may be needed for effecting the purposes of this act.

SECTION 5. The meetings of the trustees shall be open to the public, and all questions relating to the purchase or sale of securities or the payment of bonds or interest shall be decided by a yea and nay vote, which shall be recorded on their journal.

SECTION 6. Money shall be drawn from the county treasury for investment or disbursement by the trustees of the sinking fund by the issuance of a voucher signed by all the members of the board and directed to the county auditor, on which a warrant shall be drawn on the county treasurer, payable from the proper fund. All moneys received by such trustees shall be paid into the county treasury to the credit of the proper fund on the certificate of the county auditor. All securities held by such trustees shall be deposited with the county treasurer. When so deposited they shall be withdrawn only upon the written application of all the members of the board and in the presence of two of them.

SECTION 7. The trustees of the sinking fund shall keep a full and complete record of their transactions, a complete record of the funded debt of the county specifying the dates, purposes, amounts, numbers, maturities and rates and maturities of interest installments thereof, and where payable, and an account exhibiting the amount held in the sinking fund for the payment thereof.

SECTION 8. Before they become valid in the hands of any purchaser, all bonds issued by the county shall be recorded in the office of the trustees of the sinking fund, and shall bear a stamp containing the words "Recorded in the office of the sinking fund trustees" signed by the secretary.

SECTION 9. On or before the first Monday in May of each year, the trustees of the sinking fund shall certify to the board of county commissioners the rate of tax necessary to provide a sinking fund for the payment at maturity of bonds issued by the county and for the payment of interest on bonded indebtedness. The amount so certified shall be set forth in the annual budget of the county commissioners without diminution.

SECTION 10. When the county commissioners issue bonds, they shall first offer them at par and accrued interest to the trustees of the sinking fund, who may take any or all of them at such price, if they have moneys available in the sinking fund therefor.

SECTION 11. Sections 2609 to 2614, inclusive, of the General Code, and an act entitled "An act authorizing county commissioners to invest sinking funds in bonds of the United States, the state of Ohio or of any municipal corporation, school township or county bonds in this state." (H. B. No. 116) passed February 27th, 1919, and approved March 5th, 1919, are hereby repealed.

SECTION 12. Immediately upon the taking effect of this act, the county auditor shall make, for the use of the trustees of the sinking fund, a full and detailed statement of the outstanding indebtedness of the county for bonds issued, and the money in the county treasury to the credit of the sinking fund or funded debt account.

CARL R. KIMBALL,
Speaker of the House of Representatives.
CLARENCE J. BROWN,
President of the Senate.

Passed May 28, 1919.
Approved June 18, 1919.

JAMES M. COX,
Governor.

Filed in the office of the Secretary of State at Columbus, Ohio, on the 19th day of June, A. D. 1919.
228 G.

The sectional numbers on the margin hereof are designated as provided by law. JOHN G. PRICE, Attorney General.

[Amended Senate Bill No. 174.]

AN ACT

To amend section 871-47 of the General Code, relative to the compensation of members of the Ohio Board of Censors.

Be it enacted by the General Assembly of the State of Ohio:
SECTION 1. That section 871-47 of the General Code be amended to read as follows:

Sec. 871-47. The industrial commission shall furnish the board of censors with suitable office rooms and with sufficient equipment to properly carry out the provisions of this act. The board of censors may organize by electing one of its members as president. The secretary of the industrial commission shall act as secretary of the board. Each member of the board of censors shall receive an annual salary of two thousand dollars per year. Such salary and expenses shall in no case exceed the fees paid to the Ohio board of censors for examination and approval of motion picture films.

The members of the board shall be considered as employes of the industrial commission and shall be paid as other employes of such commission are paid. The industrial commission shall appoint such other assistant as may be necessary to carry on the work of the board.

Rooms and equipment; organization; salary.

SECTION 2. That original section 871-47 of the General Code be, and the same is hereby repealed.

Repeal.

CLARENCE J. BROWN,
President of the Senate.
CARL R. KIMBALL,
Speaker of the House of Representatives.

Passed May 6, 1919.
Approved June 18, 1919.

JAMES M. COX,
Governor.

Filed in the office of the Secretary of State at Columbus, Ohio, on the 19th day of June, A. D. 1919.
229 G.

The sectional number in this act is in conformity to the General Code. JOHN G. PRICE, Attorney General.

[House Bill No. 451.]

AN ACT

To amend section 10697 of the General Code, relative to the sale of personal property by executors and administrators.

Be it enacted by the General Assembly of the State of Ohio:
SECTION 1. That section 10697 of the General Code be amended to read as follows:

Sec. 10697. Within three months after the date of his bond, the executor or administrator shall sell the whole of the personal property belonging to the estate, which is liable for payment of debts and is assets in his hands to be administered, except promissory notes, unless as otherwise provided herein, and claims, demands, and rights in action which can be collected by him, and bonds and stocks when the sale thereof is not necessary to pay debts; and also except the following:

(1) Such as the widow desires to take at the valuation by the appraisers, she securing payment therefor to the executor or administrator as other purchasers;

(2) Property specifically bequeathed, until the residue of the personal estate is sold, and found to be insufficient to pay the debts of the estate;

(3) The executor or administrator may defer the sale of the emblements or annual crops raised by labor, not severed from the land of deceased at the time of his death, beyond the three months herein prescribed for the sale of the assets. These may be sold before or after they are severed from the land at his discretion, in the mode prescribed for the sale of other goods and chattels. If by the terms of a last will the testator expresses a wish that no sale of his personal property be made, the court admitting it to probate at its discretion, may direct its omission. At a later period, on application of a party interested, the court may, and for good cause shall require, such sale to be made.

(4) The executor or administrator may sell and transfer, without recourse, any promissory notes secured by mortgage and the mortgage securing the same at not less than the face value thereof with accrued interest.

(5) The executor or administrator within one year after his appointment, unless for good cause shown further time is granted by the probate court, and unless he has made or is able to make distribution in kind to the parties who are entitled to their respective portions of the estate in his hands, may sell either at public or private sale, any promissory notes, claims, demands, rights in action, bonds and stocks by first obtaining an order of the probate court therefor. The probate court may order said executor or administrator to sell at public or private sale and shall fix the price for which any of said property may be sold, and the same shall not be sold for less than the price so fixed.

(margin note: Personal property, executor or administrator may sell.*)*

Provided, further, that if said property shall not be sold on the first application, the executor or administrator shall report his proceedings to the probate court, and the court may make such further orders as he in his judgment may deem best.

SECTION 2. That original section 10697 of the General Code be, and the same is hereby repealed.

CARL R. KIMBALL,
Speaker of the House of Representatives.
CLARENCE J. BROWN,
President of the Senate.

Passed May 26, 1919.
Approved June 18, 1919.

JAMES M. COX,
Governor.

Filed in the office of the Secretary of State at Columbus, Ohio, on the 19th day of June, A. D. 1919.

230 G.

[House Bill No. 348.]

AN ACT

To amend sections 4688, 4688-1, 4696, 4714, 4729, 4730, 4731, 4732, 4734, 4736, 4744-1, 4747-1, 4782, 7730 and 7731-1 of the General Code, to correct errors in various sections of the General Code, which are also a part of the school laws of the state of Ohio, and in certain instances to clarify said sections and add thereto.

Be it enacted by the General Assembly of the State of Ohio:

SECTION 1. That sections 4688, 4688-1, 4696, 4714, 4729, 4730, 4731, 4732, 4734, 4736, 4744-1, 4747-1, 4782, 7730 and 7731-1, of the General Code be amended to read as follows:

What village districts may become exempt from supervision of county board.

Sec. 4688. The board of education of any village school district containing a village which according to the last census had a population of three thousand or more, may by a majority vote of the full membership thereof decide to be exempted from the supervision of the county board of education. Such village school district by notifying the county board of education of such decision before May first in any year, shall be exempt from the supervision of the county board of education for the following school year which begins September first thereafter. The village once so exempted shall remain so until the board of education thereof by a majority vote of the full membership determines that it desires to be supervised by the county board of education and notifies the county board of education on or before May first in any year to that effect.

When a census of the village district may be taken; return; notice.

Sec. 4688-1. The board of education of a village school district shall, upon the petition of one hundred or more electors of such district, or upon its own motion, duly passed by a majority vote of the entire board, order a census to be taken of the population of such district. One or more persons may be appointed by the board to take such census. Each person so appointed shall take an oath or affirmation to take such census accurately. He shall make his return under oath to the clerk of the board, and certified copies of such return shall be sent to the county auditor and superintendent of public instruction. If the census shows a population of three thousand or more in the village school district, and such census is approved by the superintendent of public instruction, such district shall be exempted from the supervision of the county board of education after due notice is given as is provided in section 4688.

Sec. 4696. A county board of education may transfer a part or all of a school district of the county school district to an adjoining exempted village school district or city school district or to another county school district upon the petition of a majority of the freeholders residing in the territory to be transferred and make an equitable division of the funds and indebtedness between said districts; and a county board of education may accept a transfer of territory from an adjoining exempted village school district, city school district or another county school district and annex same to a school district of the county school district. When territory is to be transferred from an exempted village school district, city school district or another county school district, the board of education of the district from which such territory is to be transferred shall pass a resolution by a majority vote of the full membership of such board asking for such transfer, and file the same with the county board of education of the county school district to which such territory is to be transferred. Such transfer shall not be complete until the county board of education of the county in which such transfer is to be made shall pass a resolution by a majority vote of the full membership of such board, accepting such transferred territory and such county board shall make an equitable distribution of the funds and the indebtedness between the district from which and to which such territory is transferred; nor shall any transfer mentioned in this section be complete until a map shall be filed with the county auditor of the county or auditors of the counties affected by such transfer. When territory is so transferred the legal title of the school property, both real and personal shall become vested in the board of education of the school district to which such territory is transferred. *[Apportionment of funds and indebtedness when territory transferred.]*

Sec. 4714. Electors residing in a rural school district may vote for school officers and on school questions at their regular voting places at all general elections, but if a special election is called by the board of education of a rural district the board may designate a convenient place in such district for the holding of such election and the board of deputy state supervisors of elections of the county in which *[Where electors shall vote for officers and on questions.]*

such rural district is located shall provide for the holding of such special election in like manner as other special elections are held. Notice of such election shall be had as is provided in section 4839.

When and how members of county board elected; term of office; per diem and mileage for presidents.

Sec. 4729. On the second Saturday after the first Monday in January, 1920, and each year thereafter, the presidents of the various village and rural school districts in each county school district shall meet and elect one member of the county board of education for a term of five years, such term to begin on the third Saturday of January of the year of such election. The presidents of the various boards of education within the county school district shall be paid three dollars and mileage one way at the rate of ten cents a mile to cover their necessary and actual expenses incurred while meeting for the purpose of electing members of the county board of education. Such expenses shall be allowed by the county auditor and paid out of the county treasury upon the order of the chairman and clerk of the meeting.

Call for meeting; election of member; qualification; certification.

Sec. 4730. The call for the meeting provided for in section 4729 shall be issued by the county superintendent. The meeting shall organize by electing a chairman and clerk. The vote of a majority of the members present shall be necessary to elect a member of the county board. The member of the county board so elected, may or may not be a member or officer of any village or rural board of education. The result of the election of the member of the county board of education shall be certified to the county auditor by the chairman and clerk of the meeting, and a certificate of election signed by such chairman and clerk shall be mailed to the member so elected on the same day the meeting is held.

Oath of office; vacancy.

Sec. 4731. Each member of the county board of education shall before entering upon the duties of his office, take an oath that he will faithfully perform the duties of his office. Such oath may be taken before any one authorized by law to administer oaths. If any person so elected shall fail to take such oath before the beginning of his term, the office to which he was elected shall be considered vacant. Any vacancy on the board shall be filled in the same manner as is provided in section 4748 of the General Code.

Meetings of county board; organization; record.

Sec. 4732. Each county board of education shall meet on the third Saturday of January of each year, and shall organize by electing one of its members president and another vice-president, both of whom shall serve for one year. The county superintendent shall act as secretary of the board. The secretary shall keep a full record of the proceedings of the board, properly indexed, in a book provided for that purpose. Each motion, with the name of the person making it and the vote thereon, shall be entered on the record.

Sec. 4734. Each member of the county board of education shall be paid three dollars a day and mileage at the rate of ten cents a mile one way, to cover his actual and necessary expenses incurred during his attendance upon any meeting of the board. Such expenses, and the expenses of the county superintendent, itemized and verified shall be paid from the county board of education fund upon vouchers signed by the president of the board. **Per diem and mileage for members.**

Sec. 4736. The county board of education may create a school district from one or more school districts or parts thereof, and in so doing shall make an equitable division of the funds or indebtedness between the newly created district and any districts from which any portion of such newly created district is taken. Such action of the county board of education shall not take effect if a majority of the qualified electors residing in the territory affected by such order shall within thirty days from the time such action is taken file with the county board of education a written remonstrance against it. Members of the board of education of the newly created district shall be appointed by the county board of education and shall hold their office until the first election for members of a board of education held in such district after such appointment, at which said first election two members shall be elected for two years and three members shall be elected for four years, and thereafter their successors shall be elected in the same manner and for the term as is provided by section 4712 of the General Code. The board so appointed by the county board of education shall organize on the second Monday after their appointment. **Power to create school district.** **Appointment of board in new district; election.**

Sec. 4744-1. The salary of the county superintendent shall be fixed by the county board of education to be not less than twelve hundred dollars per year, and shall be paid out of the county board of education fund on vouchers signed by the president of the county board. Half of such salary up to the amount of two thousand dollars shall be paid by the state and the balance by the county school district. In no case shall the amount paid by the state be more than one thousand dollars. The county board may also allow the county superintendent a sum not to exceed three hundred dollars per annum for traveling expenses and may employ an efficient stenographer or clerk for such superintendent. The part of all salaries and expenses paid by the county school district shall be prorated among the village and rural school districts in the county in proportion to the number of teachers employed in each district, but the county board of education must take into consideration and use any funds secured from the county dog and kennel fund or from any other source and which is not already appropriated before the amount is prorated to the various rural and village districts. **Salary of county superintendent; how paid.**

Annual meeting of all members for discussion of school matters.

Sec. 4747-1. Once each year all the members of the boards of education of the various village and rural school districts within any county school district shall hold a meeting for the purpose of discussing matters relating to the schools of such county school district. The county superintendent shall arrange for the time and place of holding such a meeting and shall act as chairman thereof. Each member of a rural and village board of education may receive the amount of two dollars for attending said meeting upon filing a certificate for attendance thereof with the board of which he is a member, this to be in addition to the allowance made rural board of education members under authority of section 4715.

When treasurer of school fund dispensed with.

Sec. 4782. When a depository has been provided for the school moneys of a district, as authorized by law, the board of education of the district shall dispense with a treasurer of the school moneys belonging to such school district. The clerk of the board of education of such district shall perform all the services, discharge all the duties and be subject to all the obligations required by law of the treasurer of such school district.

When and how rural or village school suspended.

Sec. 7730. The board of education of any rural or village school district may suspend temporarily or permanently any or all schools in such village or rural school district because of disadvantageous location or any other cause. Whenever the average daily attendance of any school in the school district for the preceding year has been below ten the county board of education shall direct the suspension and thereupon the board of education of the village or rural school district shall suspend such school. Whenever any school is suspended the board of education of the district shall provide for the transfer of the pupils residing within the territory of the suspended school to other schools. Upon such suspension the board of education of such village or rural district shall provide for the conveyance of all pupils of legal school age who reside in the territory of the suspended district and who live more than two miles from the school to which they have been assigned, to a public school in the rural or village district or to a public school in another district. Notice of such suspension shall be posted in five conspicuous places within such village or rural school district by the board of education within ten days after the resolution providing for such suspension is adopted. Wherever such suspension is had on the direction of the county board of education, then upon the direction of such county board, and in other cases upon the finding by the board of education ordering such suspension that such school ought to be re-established, such school shall be re-established. If at any time it appears that the average daily attendance of enrolled pupils residing within the territory of the suspended school as it was prior to such suspension is twelve or more then, upon a petition asking for re-establishment signed by a majority of the voters of the said territory, the board of education may re-establish such school.

Sec. 7731-1. The boards of education of city, village or rural school districts may by resolution designate certain places as depots from which to gather children for transportation to school, when such districts provide transportation. The places designated as depots shall be provided with a shelter and be made comfortable during cold and stormy weather. Such depots shall in no case be more than one-half mile from the residence or the private entrance to such residence of pupils who are compelled to use such depots. *Depots for school children where transportation provided.*

SECTION 2. That said original sections 4688, 4688-1, 4696, 4714, 4729, 4730, 4731, 4732, 4734, 4736, 4744-1, 4747-1, 4782, 7730 and 7731-1 of the General Code be, and the same are hereby repealed. *Repeals.*

The sectional numbers in this act are in conformity to the General Code. JOHN G. PRICE, Attorney General.

CARL R. KIMBALL,
Speaker of the House of Representatives.
CLARENCE J. BROWN,
President of the Senate.

Passed May 28, 1919.
Approved June 21, 1919.

JAMES M. COX,
Governor.

Filed in the office of the Secretary of State at Columbus, Ohio, on the 23rd day of June, A. D. 1919.

231 G.

[House Bill No. 567.]

AN ACT

To authorize the taxing authorities of counties, municipal corporations, townships and school districts to fund deficiencies in operating revenues for the year 1919, issue bonds and to levy taxes for such purposes.

Be it enacted by the General Assembly of the State of Ohio:

SECTION 1. For the purpose of this act:

"Subdivision" means a county, a municipal corporation, a township or a school district. *"Subdivision" defined.*

"Taxing authorities" means the board of county commissioners of a county, the council or other legislative body of a municipal corporation, the trustees of a township or the board of education of a school district. *"Taxing authorities" defined.*

"Deficiency" means the aggregate sum of the following: *"Deficiencies" defined.*

1. The unfunded obligations of a subdivision created prior to and outstanding on July 1, 1919, and due on or before said date, or to become due thereafter during the then current fiscal year of the subdivision, for the payment of which sufficient funds are not in the treasury thereof on

July 1, 1919, or estimated to come into such treasury thereafter during such fiscal year from taxes and other sources of revenue, to the extent of the excess of such obligations over and above such funds on hand and estimated future receipts applicable to the payment thereof and not needed to pay the fixed charges against the appropriate funds and the current expenses payable therefrom for·the remainder of such fiscal year.

2. The excess, if any, of the estimated aggregate fixed charges and current expenses of such subdivision for the remainder of such fiscal year over and above the revenues from taxes and other sources estimated to come into such treasury after July 1, 1919, and applicable to such fixed charges and current expenses.

"Fixed charges" defined.

"Fixed charges" include salaries, wages, payments on contracts for fixed or regular services, as for light, heat, power, water or gas, tuition and transportation of school pupils, and charges by law made payable from any such treasury without action by the legislative or other taxing authorities thereof, election expenses, and contributions to libraries, universities, hospitals and pension funds. It excludes funded debt service, expenditures for permanent improvements, and such ordinary expenses as are included within the scope of "current expenses" as hereinafter defined.

Said term "fixed charges" means expenses of the character indicated by the foregoing enumeration for the purposes provided, and, except as to number and salaries of school teachers, at rates and quantities not in excess of those provided by laws, ordinances, resolutions and contracts in force on January 1, 1919, by ordinances and resolutions of municipal corporations passed prior to such date and not effective thereon for want of due publication, or pending the expiration of a referendum period, and by laws passed after such date, or ordinances or resolutions adopted in compliance with such laws; it being the intention of this act that no increase in the fixed charges of any subdivision beyond those established on January·1, 1919, shall enter into a deficiency except as herein expressly provided.

"Current expenses" defined.

"Current expenses" include such items of expense as the repair and maintenance of streets, roads, highways and bridges, other than such as may be provided for by special proceedings under sections 6906 to 6953, inclusive, of the General Code, and sections 1191 to 1219 inclusive, of the General Code; the repair and maintenance of other public property, the purchase of supplies and equipment of a consumable character, other than such as are herein referred to as fixed charges, and salaries and wages incidental thereto. It excludes funded debt service, expenditures for permanent improvements, and such expenses as are included within the scope of "fixed charges" as hereinbefore defined.

The foregoing enumeration of expenses as fixed charges and current expenses, is descriptive, and not exclusive or definitive; and matters and things similar in nature to those mentioned under each heading and not expressly excluded from either, shall be included within the scope of said terms.

SECTION 2. The taxing authorities of a subdivision, by resolution passed not later than the first Monday in October, 1919, may direct the accounting officer of the subdivision to make up a financial statement of such subdivision as of the first day of July, 1919. Such accounting officer shall immediately examine the records, books and accounts of his office, and shall make up and file such statement in the office of the clerk of the taxing authorities. Such statement shall contain:

1. The balance outstanding to the credit or debit of the several funds, except sinking funds, on the books of the subdivision on July 1, 1919.

2. A showing in detail of the outstanding unfunded indebtedness of the several funds of such subdivision on July 1, 1919, whether represented by certificates of indebtedness, accounts payable, or otherwise, with the dates of maturity thereof.

3. An estimate of the amount necessary to provide for the fixed charges and current expenses of the subdivision for the remainder of the then current fiscal year, including obligations for such fixed charges or current expenses incurred prior to July 1, 1919, and payable within the then current fiscal year.

4. The amount of taxes estimated to come into the treasury of such subdivision to the credit of such funds during the remainder of the then current fiscal year, and applicable to the purposes of such year.

5. An estimate of the amount which will be received by such subdivision during the remainder of the current fiscal year from sources of revenue other than taxation, and credited to such funds.

If such accounting officer finds that a deficiency exists in such funds of the subdivision, he shall certify the amount thereof, together with the various funds affected, under oath, on such statement.

SECTION 3. Thereupon the taxing authorities, by resolution passed by an affirmative vote of two-thirds of all their members elected or appointed, shall determine whether or not such deficiency exists and the amount thereof, which shall not be greater than that certified to it by the accounting officer, and may issue and sell bonds of the subdivision in the amount so determined for the purpose of funding the deficiency of the subdivision.

Such resolution shall go into immediate effect without publication and without being subject to referendum.

Statement by accounting officer filed with taxing authorities; contents of statement.

Determining deficiency; sale of bonds.

Execution of
bonds; rate of
interest; exempt
from certain
provisions.

SECTION 4. All bonds issued under the authority of
this act shall be in denominations to be determined by
the taxing authorities and shall run for a period not exceeding eight years. They shall be executed as are other
bonds of the subdivision, shall express on their face the
purpose for which they are issued, shall bear interest at a
rate not to exceed six per cent. per annum, payable semi-
annually, and shall be sold for not less than par and accrued interest. Such provisions of sections 2294, 2295,
3295, 3922 to 3924, inclusive, 3926, 3927, 7619 and 1465-58
of the General Code, as relate to the sale of bonds of the
subdivision shall apply to the sale of such bonds.

Tax levy for in-
terest and re-
demption.

SECTION 5. For the payment of the interest on such
bonds and to provide a sinking fund for their redemption
at maturity the proper levying authorities of the subdivision shall annually levy a sufficient tax. Such levy shall
be subject only to the limitation on the combined maximum
rate for all taxes levied in the subdivision, and shall be in
addition to all other taxes for the purposes of such subdivision; provided, however, that the entire proceeds of any
inheritance tax distributed to such subdivision in any fiscal
year within the period which such bonds have to run, ex-

Application of
inheritance tax.

cept as hereinafter provided, shall, to the extent necessary
to provide for the payment of the entire amount thereof
at maturity and the interest to accrue thereon, not otherwise provided for be credited to the sinking fund of the
subdivision and be there held and used for the purpose
of paying such interest as it accrues and the principal
thereof at maturity, and for no other purpose, anything in
section 5348-11 of the General Code, or former section 5331
of the General Code to the contrary notwithstanding; and
in case any such inheritance taxes shall be so distributed
any levy or levies required by this section to be made thereafter in such subdivision shall be exonerated or reduced
accordingly and limited to such amount as shall be necessary to meet the interest and sinking fund requirements
of the net indebtedness on account of such bonds thereafter
remaining. If any such inheritance tax is distributed to
such subdivision in an amount in excess of that necessary
to accomplish the foregoing purpose, the surplus thereof
shall be credited to funds of the subdivision in the proportions provided by the inheritance tax law as now or hereafter in force. Such bonds shall not be counted in ascertaining any of the limitations prescribed by law upon
the creation of bonded indebtedness or the total amount of
outstanding bonded indebtedness of such subdivision.

Financial state-
ment to tax com-
mission by tax-
ing authorities.

SECTION 6. At the time of making up their annual
budget in the year 1920 as to boards of education, or in
the year 1921 as to all others, the taxing authorities may
determine whether or not the revenues of the subdivision
from all existing sources, including inheritance and income
taxes, are sufficient to meet all other needs of the subdivision without exempting the levies required to be made by

section 5 hereof from the limitation on the combined maximum rate for all taxes levied in the subdivision during the remainder of the period within which they are to be made, if any. For this purpose they shall cause to be made up and filed with the tax commission of Ohio, on forms prescribed by it, a financial statement under oath of the financial officer of the subdivision, showing the facts and information referred to in section 2 of this act, as of the first day of July, 1920, as to school districts, or as of the first day of July, 1921, as to all others, and relating to the remainder of the period within which levies are required to be made by section 5 hereof, together with such other facts and information as may be required by the tax commission in the forms prescribed by it, provided, however, that the limitation on the amount of the fixed charges of the subdivision prescribed by said section 2 shall not apply for the purpose of such financial statement. The tax commission shall investigate such statement and shall afford to the taxing authorities an opportunity to be heard publicly thereon. If the commission finds that the facts given in such statement are true and that the estimates of future needs and revenues are reasonable, it shall certify its findings to the taxing authorities not later than the second Monday in September, 1920, as to boards of education, or 1921 as to all others. If the tax commission finds otherwise, it shall revise such statement and certify its findings in like manner not later than such date.

SECTION 7. Upon receipt of the tax commission's certificate, the taxing authorities shall determine whether or not it is necessary to make the levy required by section 5 of this act outside of the limitation on tax levies. If they so determine by a majority vote of all their members elected or appointed, they shall by resolution so passed, declare such necessity and order that the question of exempting such levies from the limitation on the combined maximum rate shall be submitted to the electors of the subdivision. Such resolution shall specify the estimated rate of such levy and the number of years during which it is to be levied. *Resolution for submission of question of exemption of tax levy from limitations.*

SECTION 8. A copy of such resolution shall be certified to the deputy state supervisors of elections of the county or counties in which the subdivision is situated. The deputy state supervisors shall prepare the ballots and make the necessary arrangements for the submission of such question to the electors of such subdivision at the regular election in November, 1920, as to school districts, or 1921 as to all others. The result of the election shall be certified and canvassed in like manner as regular elections of such subdivisions for the election of officers thereof. Notice of such election for not less than ten days shall be given by the deputy state supervisors in one or more newspapers printed in the subdivision, once a week on the same day of the week for two consecutive times prior thereto. If no news- *Submission of question.* *Notice of election.*

paper is printed therein such notice shall be posted for ten days prior to the election in five conspicuous places in the subdivision and published as aforesaid in a newspaper of general circulation in such subdivision. A notice substantially in the following form shall be sufficient:

NOTICE OF ELECTION.

Notice is hereby given that at the regular election to be held on the Tuesday after the first Monday in November ......, there will be submitted to the electors of .... the question whether or not an additional tax levy of approximately .... mills for ...... years shall be made to complete the retirement of the special 1919 deficiency bonds of said ....

The expense of giving such notice shall be certified by the deputy state supervisors to the accounting officer of the subdivision and shall be paid as expenses of notices of elections in such subdivisions are paid.

Form of ballot. SECTION 9. The ballots used at such election shall indicate the name of the subdivision and further shall be in form as follows:

"For addition tax levy of approximately .... mills for .... years to complete the retirement of bonds issued for the purpose of funding deficiencies in 1919 current revenues. Yes.

"For an additional tax levy of approximately .... mills, for .... years to complete the retirement of bonds issued for the purpose of funding deficiencies in 1919 current revenues. No."

Duties of budget commission and county auditor. SECTION 10. If a majority of the electors voting on the proposition so submitted vote in favor thereof, upon the certification and canvass of such result the budget commission and county auditor (to whom the canvass shall be certified) shall readjust the levies in such subdivision accordingly and thereafter, beginning with the duplicate of 1920, as to school districts, or 1921, as to all others the tax levies required to be made in such subdivision by section 5 hereof shall not be subject to any limitation on tax rates; and, after the beginning of the next ensuing fiscal year, the inheritance taxes distributed to such subdivision shall no longer be applied exclusively to the interest and sinking fund purposes thereof on account of such bonds, but shall be distributed in accordance with the provisions of the general law respecting inheritance taxes.

Application of proceeds. SECTION 11. The proceeds of such bonds shall be credited to the proper funds of the subdivision in the several accounts in which deficiencies exist in accordance with the respective amounts of such deficiencies, shall then be deemed appropriated and made available for expenditure for the purposes with respect to which said deficiencies exist, and shall not be used for any other purpose.

SECTION 12. As to school districts the term "current fiscal year" as used in this act shall include the remainder of the present school year, the whole of the ensuing school year, and the part of the school year ending on the first day of March 1921.

SECTION 13. The act entitled "An act to authorize the taxing authorities of counties, municipal corporations, townships and school districts to fund deficiencies in operating revenues for the year 1919, issue bonds and to levy taxes for such purpose," passed June 17, 1919, is hereby repealed.

SECTION 14. This act is hereby declared to be an emergency law necessary for the immediate preservation of the public peace, health and safety. Such necessity arises from the fact that under existing limitations on tax levies deficiencies exist in many of the subdivisions of the state, arising largely from the recent abnormal increase of operating expenses, and the anticipated loss of revenue from the liquor tax; and by reason thereof such subdivisions, unless immediately afforded extraordinary means of extinguishing such deficiencies and meeting fixed charges and current expenses will be unable to carry on the ordinary operations of government until permanent revenues can be provided and made available. Therefore, this act shall take effect immediately.

CARL R. KIMBALL,
Speaker of the House of Representatives.
CLARENCE J. BROWN,
President of the Senate.

This act is not of a general and permanent nature and requires no sectional number.
JOHN G. PRICE, Attorney General.

Passed June 18, 1919.
Approved June 21, 1919.

JAMES M. COX,
Governor.

Filed in the office of the Secretary of State at Columbus, Ohio, on the 23rd day of June, A. D. 1919.

232 G.

[House Bill No. 527.]

AN ACT

To provide for the enforcement of laws and the constitutional amendment prohibiting the manufacture and sale of intoxicating liquors as a beverage, and to repeal the provisions of an act to provide for license to, traffic in intoxicating liquors as found in Volume 103, Ohio Laws, at pages 216-243, being sections 1261-16 to 1261-73 inclusive, of the General Code, and to repeal all other sections of the General Code inconsistent herewith.

Be it enacted by the General Assembly of the State of Ohio:

Sec. 6212-107.

When warrant shall issue to search and seize liquors and equipment.

SECTION 1. If a person makes a sworn complaint or affidavit before a mayor, justice of the peace, judge of the court of common pleas, probate court or a municipal or police court, that he has reason to believe and does believe that intoxicating liquors are manufactured, sold, furnished or given away as a beverage or kept for the purpose of being sold, furnished or given away as a beverage in violation of any law or constitutional amendment prohibiting the manufacture, sale, furnishing or giving away of intoxicating liquors as a beverage, such magistrate or judge shall issue his warrant directed to any officer designated by the complainant, having power to serve criminal process, commanding him to search the premises described and designated in such complaint and warrant and, if such liquors are found, to seize them with the vessels in which they are contained and all implements and furniture used or kept for such illegal manufacturing, selling, furnishing, or giving away of intoxicating liquors, safely keep them and forthwith make return on such warrant.

Sec. 6212-108.

Liquors and articles used as evidence.

SECTION 2. The liquors, furniture and implements used for such manufacture or sale shall be held subject to the order of the court or magistrate to be used as evidence in the prosecution of any case for the violation of any law or constitutional amendment prohibiting the manufacture and sale of intoxicating liquor as a beverage.

Sec. 6212-109.

Who shall file affidavit charging violation of law.

SECTION 3. When such intoxicating liquor or implements, vessels, or furniture used for the manufacture, sale, furnishing or giving away of intoxicating liquors as a beverage are seized as hereinbefore provided, the officer serving the warrant shall forthwith file an affidavit charging the violation of the law or constitutional amendment prohibiting the manufacture and sale of intoxicating liquor as a beverage, which the evidence in the case justifies. If such officer refuses or neglects to file such affidavit, the person filing the affidavit for a search warrant or any other person may file it, but nothing herein contained shall prevent any person or officer filing such affidavit before the search warrant is issued or served.

Sec. 6212-110.

What used as evidence.

SECTION 4. All intoxicating liquors, vessels, furniture and implements seized as hereinbefore provided, may be used as evidence at the trial or hearing based upon such affidavit or complaint charging the violation of any law or constitutional amendment prohibiting the manufacture and sale of intoxicating liquor as a beverage.

Sec. 6212-111.   SECTION 5. A warrant for search shall not be issued When search warrant shall issue. until there has been filed with the magistrate an affidavit of at least two persons particularly describing the house or place to be searched, the things to be searched for, and alleging substantially the offense in relation thereto and that affiant believes and has good cause to believe that such liquor is there concealed. Such warrant for search shall be directed to the proper officer and shall show by a copy of the affidavit inserted therein or annexed and referred to, or recite, all of the material facts alleged in the affidavit, and particularly describe the thing to be searched for and the place to be searched.

Sec. 6212-112.   SECTION 6. A warrant for search substantially in the Form of warrant. following form shall be sufficient:

"State of Ohio   ⎱
                        ⎰Greeting:
.... County⎱

WHEREAS, there has been filed with the under-signed an affidavit of which the following is a copy: (Here copy affidavit).

These are therefore to command you in the name of the state of Ohio together with the necessary and proper assistance to enter into (here describe the house or place in the affidavit) of the said .... situated in the .... of .... in the county aforesaid and there diligently search for the said intoxicating liquors and implements, to wit: (here describe the articles as in the affidavit) and that you bring them or any part thereof found in such search forthwith before me to be disposed of and dealt with according to law.

Given under my hand this .... day of .... A. D.

....

Sec. 6212-113.   SECTION 7. Fluids poured out or otherwise destroyed Fluids poured out prima facie evidence. by a tenant, assistant or other person when the premises are searched, or to be searched, manifestly for the purpose of preventing their seizure by officers authorized to make such search and seizure, shall be prima facie intoxicating liquor and intended for unlawful sale.

Sec. 6212-114.   SECTION 8. When liquors are seized as provided in Statement by officer making seizure. this act, the officer making such seizure, in his return upon the warrant, shall make a statement setting forth their seizure and place of detention and they shall be held by such officer subject to the order of the court. Upon final judgment of the court on the affidavit or complaint pro-vided in this act, such intoxicating liquors shall be returned to the lawful owner thereof in case of acquittal, or shall be destroyed or be otherwise disposed of according to law in case of conviction.

Sec. 6212-115.

Liquor not returned because of insufficient description; hearing.

SECTION 9. Such liquors having been seized by virtue of such warrant, shall not be discharged or returned to a person claiming them by reason of an alleged insufficiency of the description, in the complaint or warrant, of the liquor or place, but such person shall be entitled to a hearing when the case is tried on the affidavit provided in section sixty-one hundred and seventy-one, or at the hearing provided in section sixty-one hundred and seventy-eight.

Sec. 6212-116.

Procedure when no person found in possession; hearing.

SECTION 10. If no person is found in possession of the premises where such liquors are found, the officer taking such liquors shall post in a conspicuous place on such building or premises a copy of his warrant, take possession of such liquors and vessels containing them and hold them subject to the order of the court or magistrate issuing the warrant· and make return of his proceedings thereon. Thereupon such magistrate shall fix a time for hearing and determine the purpose for which such liquors are kept and issue notice thereof to such officer who shall post a copy thereof on such building or premises. If at the time fixed for such hearing, or within thirty days thereafter, no persons appear to claim such liquors and implements for their sale or distribution, such magistrate or court shall order them destroyed.

Sec. 6212-117.

Residence not subject to search.

SECTION 11. A warrant shall not be issued to search a private residence, occupied as such, unless it, or some part thereof, is used as a store, shop, hotel or boarding house, or unless such residence is a place of public resort.

Sec. 6212-118.

Affiant or agent may accompany officer.

SECTION 12. A person making the affidavit for the warrant to search a place where intoxicating liquor is disposed of contrary to law or constitutional amendment, or his agent may accompany the officer serving the warrant, enter the place with the officer and give information and assistance to the officer in searching the place for intoxicating liquors as hereinbefore described.

Sec. 6212-119.

Liquors, etc., shall not be taken from officer by replevin or other process.

SECTION 13. Liquors seized, as hereinbefore provided, and the vessels containing them, shall not be taken from the custody of the officer by writ of replevin or other process while the proceedings herein provided are pending. Final judgment of conviction in such proceedings is in all cases a bar to all suits for the recovery of liquors seized or their value, or for damages alleged to arise by seizure and detention thereof.

Sec. 6212-120.

What officers shall search without warrant.

SECTION 14. A marshal, deputy marshal, sheriff, constable or other officer having power to serve criminal process, if he has personal information that intoxicating liquors are kept with the intention to sell, furnish or give them away as a beverage, when prohibited by a law or constitutional amendment prohibiting the manufacture and sale of intoxicating liquor as a beverage, or are manufactured, sold, furnished or given away in a place contrary to law or con-

stitutional amendment, shall search such place without a
warrant or an affidavit being filed.

Sec. 6212-121.

SECTION 15. If such officer finds intoxicating liquors kept in a place contrary to law or constitutional amendment for the purposes provided in the next preceding section, he shall seize them and any persons in charge thereof or aiding in any way in carrying on the business conducted in such place. As soon as may be convenient he shall take such persons with the liquor seized before a court or magistrate having jurisdiction to try cases for violation of the laws or constitutional amendment prohibiting the manufacture and sale of intoxicating liquors as a beverage, and make a written complaint under oath, subscribed by him, to such court or magistrate that intoxicating liquors were manufactured, sold, furnished or given away as a beverage or such place was kept for the manufacturing, furnishing, sale or giving away of intoxicating liquor as a beverage.

Seizure of liquors and persons in charge; complaint.

SECTION 16. That the provisions of an act to provide for license to traffic in intoxicating liquors as found in volume 103, Ohio Laws, pages 216-243, known as sections 1261-16, 1261-17, 1261-18, 1261-19, 1261-20, 1261-21, 1261-22, 1261-23, 1261-24, 1261-25, 1261-26, 1261-27, 1261-28, 1261-29, 1261-30, 1261-31, 1261-32, 1261-33, 1261-34, 1261-35, 1261-36, 1261-37, 1261-38, 1261-39, 1261-40, 1261-41, 1261-42, 1261-43, 1261-44, 1261-45, 1261-46, 1261-47, 1261-48, 1261-49, 1261-50, 1261-51, 1261-52, 1261-53, 1261-54, 1261-55, 1261-56, 1261-57, 1261-58, 1261-59, 1261-60, 1261-61, 1261-62, 1261-63, 1261-64, 1261-65, 1261-66, 1261-67, 1261-68, 1261-69, 1261-70, 1261-71, 1261-72 and 1261-73 of the General Code and any amendment thereto, and all other sections of the General Code inconsistent with this act be and the same are hereby repealed.

Repeals.

CARL R. KIMBALL,
Speaker of the House of Representatives.
CLARENCE J. BROWN,
President of the Senate.

The sectional numbers on the margin hereof are designated as provided by law.
JOHN G. PRICE,
Attorney General.

Approved June 21, 1919.
Passed June 17, 1919.

JAMES M. COX,
Governor.

Filed in the office of the Secretary of State at Columbus, Ohio, on the 23rd day of June, A. D. 1919.

233 G.

[House Bill No. 526.]

AN ACT

To provide against the manufacture and sale of intoxicating liquors as a beverage and to repeal the provisions of an act to provide for license to traffic in intoxicating liquors as found in Volume 103, Ohio Laws, at pages 216-243, being sections 1261-16 to 1261-73 inclusive, of the General Code, and to repeal all other sections of the General Code inconsistent herewith.

Be it enacted by the General Assembly of the State of Ohio:

Sec. 6212-85.

Penalty for keeping place for sale, selling, manufacturing, etc., of intoxicating liquors.

SECTION 1. Whoever keeps a place where intoxicating liquors are manufactured, sold, furnished or given away in violation of law or constitutional amendment, or whoever manufactures, sells, furnishes or gives away intoxicating liquor as a beverage except as herein provided, shall be fined not less than one hundred dollars nor more than five hundred dollars, and, for each subsequent offense shall be fined not less than two hundred dollars nor more than five hundred dollars. The court, on conviction for a second or subsequent offense for keeping such place, shall order the place where such liquor is manufactured, sold, furnished or given away in violation of law or constitutional amendment, to be abated as a nuisance, or shall order the person convicted for such offense to give bond to the state of Ohio in the sum of one thousand dollars, with sureties to the acceptance of the court, that such person will not manufacture, sell, furnish or give away intoxicating liquor in violation of law or constitutional amendment, and will pay all fines, costs and damages assessed against him for violation of the laws and constitutional amendment relating to the manufacture and sale of intoxicating liquors. The giving away of intoxicating liquors, or other shift or device to evade the provisions of this section, shall be unlawful selling.

Sec. 6212-86.

What "liquor" or "intoxicating liquor" shall include.

SECTION 2. That the word "liquor" or the phrase "intoxicating liquor" used in this act shall be construed to include any distilled, malt, spiritous, vinous, fermented, or alcoholic liquor containing more than one-half of one per centum alcohol by volume, and all alcoholic liquids and compounds, whether medicated, proprietary, patented, or not, and by whatever name called, which are potable or capable of being used as a beverage.

To whom act does not apply.

Provided, that the provisions of this act shall not be construed to apply to the manufacture, importation, exportation or sale of flavoring extracts, perfumes, toilet preparations, or patent or proprietary medicines sold in good faith for culinary, flavoring, toilet or medicinal purposes which contain no more alcohol than is necessary for the purpose of extraction, solution or preservation.

Sec. 6212-87.

"Giving away" defined.

SECTION 3. The phrase "giving away" as used in this act and other statutes of this state relating to the manufacture and sale of intoxicating liquor, shall not apply to the giving away of intoxicating liquor by a person in his private dwelling, unless such private dwelling is a place of public resort.

Sec. 6212-88. SECTION 4. The payment of the United States special tax as manufacturer of, or retail dealer in, intoxicating liquor, except by a regular druggist, shall be prima facie evidence that the person paying such tax is violating the law and constitutional amendment prohibiting the manufacture and sale of intoxicating liquor as a beverage. Payment of U. S. tax prima facie evidence.

Sec. 6212-89. SECTION 5. A notice, or sign, on or about a place indicating that intoxicating liquor is there manufactured, sold, kept for sale or given away, shall be prima facie evidence that the person, firm or corporation, displaying such notice or sign is violating the law and constitutional amendment prohibiting the manufacture and sale of intoxicating liquor as a beverage. Certain sign unlawful and prima facie evidence.

Sec. 6212-90. SECTION 6. The keeping of intoxicating liquor in a room, building or other place, except in a regular drug store or wholesale drug store, in a manufactory of alcohol or wine for purposes permitted herein, or in a bona fide private residence, shall be prima facie evidence that such liquor is kept for unlawful sale, furnishing or giving away. Keeping liquor in certain rooms unlawful.

Sec. 6212-91. SECTION 7. No provision of this act shall prevent the sale of alcohol or wine at retail by a regular druggist for exclusively known medical, mechanical, pharmaceutical, scientific or sacramental purposes; nor in addition thereto, shall it prevent the manufacture and sale of cider and fruit juices for vinegar or, when not intoxicating as defined herein, for use and sale, nor the manufacture of alcohol or wine for purposes permitted herein, nor the sale thereof for such purposes in quantities of not less than a gallon, by a manufacturer thereof or wholesale druggist, provided that such manufacturer or wholesale druggist obtains a permit therefor; and provided, further, that the same record of such sale is kept as is required of a druggist in section 9 of this act; except that the signed order of the purchaser may be filed in the record book in lieu of his siganture; nor shall it prevent the transportation of intoxicating liquors to places outside the state for purposes not prohibited at the point of destination. What sale and manufacture lawful.

Sec. 6212-92. SECTION 8. When alcohol or wine is sold for medicinal purposes, it shall be done only in good faith upon a written prescription issued, signed and dated in good faith by a reputable physician in active practice and in conformity with the provisions of this act. Such prescription shall be used but once and must contain the name and quantity of liquor prescribed, the name of the person for whom prescribed, the date on which the prescription is written and directions for the use of the liquor therein so prescribed. Sale of alcohol and wine for medicinal purposes.

Sec. 6212-93. SECTION 9. A book shall be kept by each retail druggist and pharmacist in which shall be entered, at the time Record of sales; form of record.

of each sale of alcohol or wine, the date thereof, the name of the purchaser, who shall sign his name in such book as part of such entry, the kind, quantity and price of such liquor, the purpose for which it was sold and the residence by street and number, if there be such, of such purchaser. When such sale is for medicinal purposes, such book shall also contain the name of the physician issuing the prescription. Such prescription shall be cancelled by writing on it the word "cancelled" and the date on which it was presented and filled. Such book shall be in form substantially as follows:

Date—Name of Purchaser—Residence — Kind and Quantity—Purpose and Use—Price—Name of Physician—Signature of Purchaser.

Sec.-6212-94.

File and record of prescriptions open to inspection of officers.

SECTION 10. Such prescription shall be kept on file and such book and prescription shall be open to the inspection of any county, police or city prosecutor, mayor, justice of the peace, judge of the court of common pleas, probate court, or any municipal or police court or any sheriff, constable, marshal, or other police officer or by any person holding any order from such officer to inspect such records, books and prescriptions.

Sec. 6212-95.

Fines, etc., a lien upon real property.

SECTION 11. Fines and forfeited bonds resulting from the violation of this act shall attach and operate as a lien upon the real property on or in which such unlawful act or act in violation of the constitutional amendment was committed.

Sec. 6212-96.

Penalty for violations by common carrier, agent, etc.

SECTION 12. Whoever violates any provision of this section shall be fined not less than fifty dollars nor more than two hundred dollars, and for each subsequent offense shall be fined not less than two hundred dollars nor more than five hundred dollars. No railroad or common carrier, or agent thereof, drayman or other person, corporation or firm, shall ship, receive, transport, carry or handle intoxicating liquor under a false or fictitious name or title, or unless there appears in a conspicuous place on the outside of the package containing such intoxicating liquor a statement clearly legible in the English language as to the kind and quantity of liquor contained therein. The carriage, transportation, possession, removal, delivery or acceptance with knowledge thereof, of any such liquor under a false or fictitious name or title or without labeling the package containing such liquor as provided herein, shall work its forfeiture. The books and waybills used in handling such liquor may be examined by any public officer at any time to trace such liquor to shipper or receiver.

Sec. 6212-97.

Violation by druggist prohibited from sale, for two years.

SECTION 13. Whoever, being a druggist or pharmacist convicted of selling intoxicating liquor as a beverage contrary to a law or constitutional amendment, sells intoxicating liquor for any purpose, personally or by agent, within two years thereafter in this state shall be fined not less than two hundred and fifty dollars nor more than five hundred dollars, and, for each subsequent offense shall be fined not less than five hundred dollars nor more than one thousand dollars.

Sec. 6212-98. SECTION 14. Upon a second conviction for a violation of the next preceding section, the certificate to practice pharmacy of such druggist or pharmacist shall be revoked and the judge or officer convicting him shall so order and send a copy of such order to the secretary of the state board of pharmacy, upon receipt of which such certificate shall forthwith be revoked by such board. *Revocation of certificate on second offense.*

Sec. 6212-99. SECTION 15. A certified transcript from the docket of the mayor or other officer, before whom a druggist, or pharmacist was convicted under the next preceding section, or before whom a physician was convicted under section thirteen thousand two hundred and seventeen or thirteen thousand two hundred and eighteen, shall be sufficient evidence of such conviction. *Transcript sufficient evidence.*

Sec. 6212-100. SECTION 16. Whoever, being a retail druggist or pharmacist, wholesale druggist or manufacturer of alcohol or wine fails to keep the book required by law in which is entered at the time of each sale of alcohol or wine, the date thereof, the name and signature of the purchaser, or if a manufacturer of alcohol or wine or wholesale druggist, the signed order referred to in section 7 of this act, the kind, quantity and price of such liquor, the purpose for which it was sold, and the residence by street and number of such purchaser, if there be such residence, or fails, if such sale is for medicinal purposes, to enter the name of the physician issuing the prescription, and cancel such prescription by writing the word "cancelled" thereon, and the date on which it was presented and filled or fails or refuses to make any entry in such books required by law, or destroys, alters, or changes an entry therein or such prescription, or sells alcohol or wine for medicinal purposes except on written prescription, shall be fined not less than fifty dollars nor more than five hundred dollars. *Penalty for failure to keep record required by law.*

Sec. 6212-101. SECTION 17. When a prosecution is commenced before a court or magistrate for the violation of a law or constitutional amendment prohibiting the manufacture and sale of intoxicating liquors as a beverage and the liquors seized by virtue thereof are to be used as evidence in such trial, such trial must take place in not more than thirty days. If at the time appointed for such trial, the returns have not been properly made, or for other sufficient cause, the trial is postponed to a further date, it shall not be continued more than fifteen days beyond such thirty days. *When trial must be had; limitation of continuance.*

Sec. 6212-102. SECTION 18. Any justice of the peace, police justice, mayor, police judge, municipal judge or common pleas or probate judge with whom an affidavit is filed charging the violation of a law or constitutional amendment prohibiting the manufacture and sale of intoxicating liquors as a beverage, when the offense is alleged to have been committed in the county in which such judge or other officer or magistrate may be sitting, shall have final jurisdiction to try *Courts having final jurisdiction; trial without jury, when.*

such case upon such affidavit without a jury unless imprisonment is a part of the penalty.

Sec. 6212-103.

Information or indictment not necessary.

SECTION 19. In cases under this act, it shall not be necessary that information be filed by the prosecuting attorney or that an indictment be found by the grand jury.

Sec. 6212-104.

Petition in error; procedure.

SECTION 20. A petition in error shall not be filed in a court to reverse a conviction for violation of a law or constitutional amendment prohibiting the manufacture and sale of intoxicating liquors or to reverse a judgment affirming such conviction except after leave granted by the reviewing court. Such leave shall not be granted except for good cause shown at a hearing of which counsel for the complainant in the original case shall have had actual and reasonable notice. Such petition in error must be filed not more than thirty days after the judgment complained of, and the case shall be heard by such reviewing court within thirty court days from such filing. When a reviewing court is not in session within the time provided for, the motion for leave to file a petition in error and the petition in error may be filed with and heard by such reviewing court within ten days after it is in session. This section shall not confer a right of review in such cases in addition to that which is now provided by law.

Sec. 6212-105.

Disposition of fines, etc.

SECTION 21. Fines and forfeited bonds collected under this act, if enforced in the county court, shall be paid into the county treasury, and, if enforced in municipal courts, shall be paid into the treasury of the municipal corporation in which the cause was tried, and, if enforced in the court of a justice of the peace, shall be paid into the treasury of the township in which said justice of the peace was elected.

Sec. 6212-106.

How costs taxed.

SECTION 22. Costs arising as a result of an affidavit duly filed and warrant issued under this act or any law relating to the manufacture and sale of intoxicating liquors, whereby liquors, vessels, and furniture are seized, shall be taxed with the costs in the trial for the violation of the law or constitution amendment prohibiting the manufacture and sale of intoxicating liquors.

Repeals.

SECTION 23. That the provisions of an act to provide for license to traffic in intoxicating liquors as found in volume 103, Ohio Laws, at pages 216-243, known as section 1261-16, 1261-17, 1261-18, 1261-19, 1261-20, 1261-21, 1261-22, 1261-23, 1261-24, 1261-25, 1261-26, 1261-27, 1261-28, 1261-29, 1261-30, 1261-31, 1261-32, 1261-33, 1261-34, 1261-35, 1261-36, 1261-37, 1261-38, 1261-39, 1261-40, 1261-41, 1261-42, 1261-43, 1261-44, 1261-45, 1261-46, 1261-47, 1261-48, 1261-49, 1261-50, 1261-51, 1261-52, 1261-53, 1261-54, 1261-55, 1261-56, 1261-57, 1261-58, 1261-59, 1261-60, 1261-61, 1261-62, 1261-63, 1261-64, 1261-65, 1261-66, 1261-67, 1261-68, 1261-69, 1261-70, 1261-71, 1261-72 and 1261-73 of the General Code and any amendments thereto, and all other sections of the General Code inconsistent with this act, be and the same are hereby repealed.

The sectional numbers on the margin hereof are designated as provided by law.
JOHN G. PRICE, Attorney General.

CARL R. KIMBALL, ·
Speaker of the House of Representatives.
CLARENCE J. BROWN,
President of the Senate.

Passed June 17, 1919.
Approved June 21, 1919.

JAMES M. COX,
Governor.

Filed in the office of the Secretary of State at Columbus, Ohio, on the 23rd day of June, A. D. 1919.

234 G.

[Amended Senate Bill No. 162.]

AN ACT

To provide for the appointment of a commissioner of prohibition of Ohio and assistants to secure the enforcement of laws prohibiting the liquor traffic and to prescribe their powers and duties and to fix their compensation.

Be it enacted by the General Assembly of the State of Ohio:

Sec. 6212-122.   SECTION 1. An officer to be known as the commissioner of prohibition of Ohio shall be appointed as hereinafter provided, who shall be an elector of the state. The attorney general of Ohio, upon assuming office, shall appoint such commissioner by and with the consent of the senate, and the term of such commissioner shall coincide with that of the attorney general; provided, that the term of the commissioner first appointed hereunder shall begin on the day next following that on which this act shall take effect and continue until the second Monday of January, 1921. Such commissioner shall take the constitutional oath of office, and his salary shall be five thousand dollars per year, and he shall be allowed and paid his necessary expenses. He shall devote his entire time and attention to the duties of his office. 〔Commissioner of prohibition; appointment, term, oath, removal.〕

The attorney general shall at any time have the power to remove said commissioner for immoral conduct, inefficiency or neglect of duty, giving to said commissioner a copy of the charges against him and an opportunity to be heard thereon. If such commissioner shall be removed, the attorney general shall file in the office of the secretary of state a statement of all charges made against such commissioner, and his findings thereon, and his decision therein shall be final.

Sec. 6212-123.   SECTION 2. The commissioner of prohibition shall appoint, with the approval of the attorney general, one deputy commissioner for each of the four districts created by this 〔Deputy commissioners; salary, powers and duties.〕

act. The deputy for the Columbus district shall have all the powers and perform all the duties of the commissioner during the absence or the disability of the commissioner. All of said deputies shall be under the direction and control of said commissioner, and shall hold their office at the pleasure of said commissioner. Such deputies shall devote their entire time to the duties of the office, and each shall receive an annual salary of thirty-six hundred dollars and shall be allowed and paid their actual and necessary expenses.

Inspectors; appointment, salary.

The commissioner of prohibition shall have authority to appoint not to exceed sixteen regular inspectors, who shall hold office at the pleasure of the commissioner, and who shall have the powers and authority herein provided. They shall be under the control of said commissioner and shall exercise the powers herein provided, as directed by said commissioner. Each of said inspectors shall receive a salary of not less than fifteen hundred dollars nor more than two thousand dollars per annum, as determined by the commissioner, and be allowed and paid his actual and necessary expenses.

Temporary inspectors; compensation.

The commissioner may appoint such temporary inspectors as emergency demands, who shall hold office at the pleasure of the commissioner, and who shall have only the powers and authority delegated to them in their appointment and not inconsistent with this act. The number of such temporary inspectors shall not exceed that fixed by the attorney general. They shall be under the control of said commissioner, and shall receive such compensation as may be fixed by him, not exceeding ten dollars per day, when actually employed, and shall be allowed and paid their actual and necessary expenses. They shall perform such duties as are assigned by the commissioner.

Appointees in unclassified service.

Said commissioner, deputies and inspectors shall be included in the unclassified civil service of the state and shall not be included in the classified civil service thereof.

Sec. 6212-124.

Designated districts; how composed.

SECTION 3. The state shall be divided into four districts, designated as the Columbus district, Cleveland district, Cincinnati district and Toledo district. Such districts shall be composed of the following counties respectively:

1. COLUMBUS DISTRICT.

Montgomery, Greene, Clark, Fayette, Madison, Union, Delaware, Franklin, Pickaway, Ross, Vinton, Hocking, Fairfield, Perry, Licking, Knox, Holmes, Coshocton, Muskingum, Morgan, Athens, Meigs, Washington, Noble, Monroe, Guernsey, Belmont, Jefferson, Harrison, Tuscarawas, Carroll.

2. CLEVELAND DISTRICT.

Ashtabula, Trumbull, Mahoning, Columbiana, Stark, Portage, Geauga, Lake, Cuyahoga, Summit, Wayne, Medina, Lorain, Ashland.

3. TOLEDO DISTRICT.

Williams, Defiance, Paulding, Van Wert, Mercer, Darke, Miami, Shelby, Auglaize, Allen, Putnam, Henry, Fulton, Lucas, Wood, Hancock, Hardin, Logan, Champaign, Marion, Wyandot, Morrow, Crawford, Seneca, Sandusky, Ottawa, Erie, Huron, Richland.

4. CINCINNATI DISTRICT.

Preble, Butler, Hamilton, Warren, Clermont, Clinton, Brown, Highland, Adams, Pike, Scioto, Jackson, Gallia, Lawrence.

Sec. 6212-125. SECTION 4. The office of the commissioner shall be in the city of Columbus, and each district shall have an office in charge of a deputy assigned by the commissioner. The district offices shall be respectively at Columbus, Cleveland, Toledo and Cincinnati, and the commissioner of prohibition and the deputy for the Columbus district shall occupy the same office quarters. Provision shall be made by the commissioner for suitable office rooms, furniture, stationery and other facilities for transacting the business of each state and district office; and such clerical and other assistance may be employed at each office as the needs of such office demand. *Place of office of commissioner; district offices.*

Sec. 6212-126. SECTION 5. It shall be the duty of said commissioner, deputies and inspectors diligently to enforce the laws of the state having to do with the prohibition of the liquor traffic and exercise all powers herein conferred, provided, however, that nothing in this act contained shall in any manner relieve any officer from responsibility for the enforcement of such laws. *General duties of commissioner, deputies and inspectors.*

Any person who hinders, obstructs, or interferes with said commissioner, or any of his deputies and inspectors herein provided for, or with any other officer whose duty it is to enforce the laws of this state, relating to intoxicating liquors, in their efforts to enforce the same, or who fails to render aid to any of said officers when lawfully called on to do so, shall be deemed guilty of a misdemeanor and on conviction thereof shall be fined not less than twenty-five dollars nor more than one hundred dollars, together with the costs of prosecution. In default of payment of such fine and costs he shall be confined in the county jail until such fine and costs are paid or secured to be paid or he be otherwise discharged according to law. *Hindering, interfering, etc., with officers; penalty.*

Sec. 6212-127. SECTION 6. Upon securing evidence of violations in any county of laws relating to intoxicating liquors, said commissioner shall personally, or through his deputies, make or cause to be made complaints against violators, and institute such other proceedings as may be authorized by law, but in such cases no bond or security for costs shall be required. When the commissioner shall deem it expedient, *Filing complaints; supervising prosecutions.*

he shall appear in person, or by deputy, and supervise such prosecutions.

Sec. 6212-128.

Powers of commissioner, deputies and inspectors.

SECTION 7. In cases arising under the laws prohibiting the liquor traffic, said commissioner, deputies and inspectors shall have the same power to serve criminal and other process and papers as is now or may hereafter be conferred by law upon sheriffs and shall have the same rights as sheriffs to require aid in executing such process; but nothing in this act shall in any way relieve state, county, township or municipal officers of the duties devolving upon them by virtue of the law governing such duties. There shall be taxed in the several courts of the state for such commissioner, his deputies and inspectors, in the bills of cost in any case in which they perform any such service, the same fees as sheriffs are entitled to receive, which shall be paid promptly into the state treasury.

Sec. 6212-129.

Who empowered to administer oaths and examine witnesses.

SECTION 8. The said attorney general, his lawfully appointed and qualified assistants, the commissioner, deputies and inspectors, shall each have authority to administer oaths to and examine any persons they may know or suspect to have knowledge of any violations of the laws relating to intoxicating liquors wherever they may find such person. Any person or persons giving testimony before such attorney general, his assistants, the commissioner, deputy or inspector, shall on written request of such officer sign under oath a transcript of such testimony, or a correct abstract thereof, and a refusal to sign such transcript or abstract,

Witness refusing to sign transcript a misdemeanor.

or the making of a false statement therein or on said examination, or a refusal to answer any question or questions relating to violations or alleged or suspected violations of the laws relating to intoxicating liquors, or a failure to obey any lawful process, shall be deemed a misdemeanor and such person, upon conviction thereof, shall be punished by a fine not to exceed one hundred dollars and costs of prosecution. Such witness or persons so examined shall not be subject to prosecution for violation of the laws relating to intoxicating liquors as to any matter disclosed by his statement or testimony; nor shall such statement be used against him in any civil action, or criminal, quasi-criminal or statutory prosecution except in prosecutions for perjury.

Attendance of witnesses, production of books, etc.

In the performance of the duties imposed upon them by law, the attorney general, his assistants, the commissioner, deputies and inspectors may summon and compel the attendance of persons before them for examination and may require the production of any book, paper, document or other thing under the control of such person. Subpoenas for such persons may be served by any of the officers mentioned herein, and upon the request of any of such officers, by the sheriff, constable or other police officer in the county where such person resides. Each person summoned for examination, as aforesaid, shall receive the same fees as witnesses before justices of the peace. Such sheriff, constable or other police officer for their services shall receive the same fees as provided by law for sheriffs for like services.

In the performance of the duties imposed upon them by law, the commissioner, deputies and inspectors, for the purpose of examination, may at all reasonable hours, enter into or upon all buildings, places and things, excepting such buildings, places or things or parts thereof as are used exclusively for bona fide private residence purposes. Right of entry upon and into buildings, etc.

Sec. 6212-130.   SECTION 9. Said commissioner, deputies and inspectors may arrest without a warrant any person found by them violating the laws relating to the liquor traffic, and take such person before a justice of the peace, or other officer, or tribunal having jurisdiction in such proceeding, and take such further action as the law provides. Arrest without warrant.

Sec. 6212-131.   SECTION 10. The attorney general and any of the persons appointed by him under sections 334 and 336 of the General Code, shall have authority, and are hereby authorized to exercise in any part of the state all the statutory powers of prosecuting attorneys in their respective counties, in any matter connected with the violation of the liquor laws of the state of Ohio, and as to such matters shall have all the rights, privileges and powers conferred by section 13560 General Code upon prosecuting attorneys. Powers of attorney general and appointees in prosecutions in counties.

Sec. 6212-132.   SECTION 11. Justices of the peace, mayors, municipal courts and police courts, shall have final jurisdiction within their respective counties, of all misdemeanors arising under laws relating to intoxicating liquors or for the enforcement of such laws. Courts having final jurisdiction.

Sec. 6212-133.   SECTION 12. The commissioner shall make annual report to the attorney general on or about the first day of June of each year, a copy of which report shall be by the attorney general filed with the governor. The annual report shall be printed and published on or before the first day of September next thereafter. Said report shall cover the administration of the liquor laws for the preceding year, and shall, among other things, show the number of places inspected, the number of specimens analyzed, number of complaints against persons for violating the laws, the number of convictions had and the amount of fines imposed therefor, and such other information as the commissioner deems valuable in securing the enforcement of the liquor prohibitory laws, together with such recommendations relative to the status thereof as his experience may justify. Annual report to attorney general; contents of report.

Sec. 6212-134.   SECTION 13. Said commissioner, his deputies and regular inspectors shall, before entering upon the duties of their office, subscribe to and file in the office of the secretary of state an oath of office as prescribed by the constitution of this state, and said commissioner shall give bond in the sum of ten thousand dollars, each of said deputies in the sum of five thousand dollars and each regular inspector in the sum of two thousand dollars, payable to the state of Ohio, conditioned upon the faithful performance of their duties. All of said bonds shall be approved by the attorney Bond and oath of commissioner and deputies.

general. When on duty, said commissioner, deputies and regular and temporary inspectors shall have the same authority to go armed as is extended to sheriffs by section 12819, General Code.

Sec. 6212-135.

Salaries and expenses paid from general revenue fund.

SECTION 14. All salaries provided in this act, and all expenses and fees incurred in carrying out its provisions, shall be paid out of the general revenue fund of the state upon proper voucher signed by the commissioner.

Sec. 6212-136.

Section or part held void shall not affect others.

SECTION 15. Each section of this act, and every part thereof, is hereby declared to be an independent section and part of section, and the holding of any section or part thereof to be void or ineffective for any cause shall not be deemed to affect any other section or part thereof.

The sectional numbers on the margin hereof are designated as provided by law. JOHN G. PRICE, Attorney General.

CLARENCE J. BROWN,
President of the Senate.
CARL R. KIMBALL,
Speaker of the House of Representatives.

Passed June 16, 1919.
Approved June 21, 1919.

JAMES M. COX,
Governor.

Filed in the office of the Secretary of State at Columbus, Ohio, on the 23rd day of June, A. D. 1919.

235 G.

[House Bill No. 350.]

AN ACT

To further supplement section 13031 of the General Code by the enactment of sections to be known as sections 13031.13, 13031-14, 13031-15, 13031-16, 13031-17, 13031-18 and 13031-19, providing for the suppression of prostitution.

Be it enacted by the General Assembly of the State of Ohio:

SECTION 1. That section 13031 of the General Code be further supplemented by the enactment of supplemental sections 13031-13, 13031-14, 13031-15, 13031-16, 13031-17, 13031-18 and 13031-19, to read as follows:

Keeping, maintaining, occupying, permitting, etc., a place for prostitution, prohibited.

Sec. 13031-13. From and after the passage of this act it shall be unlawful to keep, set up, maintain or operate any place, structure, building or conveyance for the purpose of prostitution, lewdness or assignation; or to occupy any place, structure, building or conveyance for the purpose of prostitution, lewdness or assignation or for any person to permit any place, structure, building or conveyance owned by him or under his control to be used for the purpose of prostitution, lewdness or assignation, with knowledge or reasonable cause to know that the same is, or is to be, used for such purpose; or to receive or to offer or agree to receive any person into any place, structure, building or conveyance for the purpose of prostitution, lewdness or assignation or to permit any person to remain there for such purpose; or to direct, take or transport, or to offer or agree to take or transport, any person to any place, structure or building or to any other person with knowledge or reasonable cause to know that the purpose of such directing, taking or transporting is prostitution, lewdness or assignation; or to procure or to solicit or to offer to procure or solicit for the purpose of prostitution, lewdness or assignation; or to reside in, enter or remain in any place, structure or building, or to enter or remain in any conveyance, for the purpose of prostitution, lewdness or assignation; or to engage in prostitution, lewdness or assignation or to aid or abet prostitution, lewdness or assignation by any means whatsoever.

Sec. 13031-14. The term "prostitution" shall be construed to include the offering or receiving of the body for sexual intercourse for hire, and, shall also be construed to include the offering or receiving of the body for indiscriminate sexual intercourse without hire. The term "lewdness" shall be construed to include any indecent or obscene act. The term "assignation" shall be construed to include the making of any appointment or engagement for prostitution or lewdness or any act in furtherance of such appointment or engagement. *Terms "prostitution," "lewdness" and "assignation" defined.*

Sec. 13031-15. In the trial of any person, charged with a violation of any of the provisions of section 13031-13 of the General Code, testimony of a prior conviction, or testimony concerning the reputation of any place, structure or building and of the person or persons who reside in or frequent the same and of the defendant shall be admissible in evidence in support of the charge. *Prior conviction and testimony admissible evidence.*

Sec. 13031-16. Whoever shall be found to have committed two or more violations of any of the provisions of section 13031-13 of the General Code within a period of one year next preceding the date named in an indictment, information or charge of violating any of the provisions of section 13031-13 of the General Code, shall be deemed guilty in the first degree. Whoever shall be found to have committed a single violation of any of the provisions of this act shall be deemed guilty in the second degree. *First and second degree guilt, defined.*

Sec. 13031-17. (a) Whoever shall be found guilty in the first degree, as set forth in section 13031-16, shall be subject to imprisonment in, or commitment to, any penal or reformatory institution in this state for not less than one nor more than three years; provided, that in case of a commitment to a reformatory institution the commitment shall be made for an indeterminate period of time of not less than one nor more than three years in duration, and the board of managers or directors of the reformatory institution, or other officer, board or commission vested with such powers, shall have authority to discharge or to place on parole any person so committed after the service of the minimum term, *Penalty for guilt in first degree.*

or any part thereof, and to require the return to the said institution for the balance of the maximum term of any person who shall violate the terms or conditions of the parole.

(b) Whoever shall be found guilty in the second degree, as set forth in section 13031-16, shall be subject to imprisonment for not more than one year; provided; that the sentence imposed, or any part thereof, may be suspended, and provided further that the defendant may be placed' on probation in the care of a probation officer designated by law or theretofore appointed by the court upon the recommendation of five responsible citizens.

(c) Any person charged with a violation of section 13031-13 of the General Code, shall, upon the order of the court having jurisdiction of such case, be subjected to examination to determine if such person is infected with a venereal disease. Such examination shall be made by the physician employed to render medical service to persons confined or detained by the municipality or county, or by some physician designated by the court or by the board of health to make such examination. Any such person found to have a venereal disease in the infective stage shall receive medical treatment therefor and shall pay for such treatment if able to do so. If not able to pay, such medical treatment shall be at the expense of the municipality or county. No person charged with a violation of section 13031-13 of the General Code shall be discharged from custody, paroled or placed on probation if he or she has a venereal disease in an infective stage unless the court having jurisdiction shall be assured that such person will continue medical treatment until cured or rendered non-infectious.

(d) No girl or woman who shall be convicted under this act shall be placed on probation or on parole in the care or charge of any person except a woman probation officer.

Sec. 13031-18. The declaration by the courts of any of the provisions of this act as being in violation of the constitution of this state shall not invalidate the remaining provisions.

CARL R. KIMBALL,
Speaker of the House of Representatives.
CLARENCE J. BROWN,
President of the Senate.

Passed June 17, 1919.
Approved June 21, 1919.

JAMES M. COX,
Governor.

Filed in the office of the Secretary of State at Columbus, Ohio, on the 23rd day of June, A. D. 1919.

236 G.

[House Bill No. 586.]

AN ACT

To make general appropriations.

Be it enacted by the General Assembly of the State of Ohio:

SECTION 1. The sums set forth in sections 2 and 3 of this act in the columns therein designated "Appropriations" for the purposes therein specified, are hereby appropriated out of any monies in the state treasury not otherwise appropriated. Appropriations enumerated in such sections for departments, boards, commissions, bureaus, institutions, and offices, for the uses and purposes of which, or of any activity or function thereof, specific funds in the state treasury are provided by law, are hereby made from such specific funds, insofar as such funds are subject by law to appropriation and expenditure for the purposes therein mentioned, and to the extent that the monies to the credit of such specific funds on July 1st, 1919, or which may be credited thereto prior to June 30th, 1921, shall be sufficient to satisfy such appropriation. Any sums necessary to supply the balance of such appropriations are hereby appropriated out of any monies in the state treasury to the credit of the general revenue fund, but no monies shall be taken from the general revenue fund to support the highway department, or the fish and game division of the board of agriculture.

SECTION 2. The following sums shall not be expended to pay liabilities or deficiencies existing prior to July 1st, 1919, or incurred subsequent to June 30th, 1921:

STATE BOARD OF ACCOUNTANCY.

(a)	Items	Appropriations
Personal Service—		
A 2 Wages—		
Per diem 3 members of board........	$200 00	
Stenographic service..	65 00	
Total personal service...............		$265 00
Maintenance—		
C Supplies—		
C 4 Office	$50 00	
E Equipment—		
E 1 Office.........	$100 00	
F Contract and Open Order Service—		
F 6 Traveling expense	$100 00	
F 7 Communication	10 00	
F 9 General plant..	100 00	
Total	$316 00	

	Items.	Appropriations.
H Fixed Charges and Contributions—		
H 8 Contributions .	5 00	
Total maintenance..........		365 00
Total		$630 00

ADJUTANT GENERAL.

Personal Service—		
A 1 Salaries—		
Adjutant general....	$3,500 00	
Assistant adjutant general	2,000 00	
Assistant quartermaster general......	2,000 00	
Grade II bookkeeper.	1,860 00	
Chief clerk..........	1,600 00	
Grade III clerk......	1,200 00	
Roster clerk.........	1,200 00	
Grade III stenographer	1,200 00	
Commission clerk....	1,200 00	
2 Quartermaster clerks.	2,400 00	
2 Grade III stenographers	1,800 00	
Grade II typist......	840 00	
Messenger	840 00	
Total personal service........		$21,640 00
Maintenance—		
C Supplies—		
C 4 Office	$900 00	
E Equipment—		
E 1 Office	$150 00	
E 6 Motor vehicles.	300 00	
Total	$450 00	
F Contract and Open Order Service—		
F 1 Repairs—		
Repairs to state buildings	$5,000 00	
F 6 Traveling expense	300 00	
F 7 Communication	575 00	
Total	$5,875 00	
Total maintenance..........		7,225 00
Total		$28,865 00

General appropriations. 1919-1920.

	Items.	Appropriations.
A Personal Service—		
A 1 Salaries—		
Superintendent of laborers	$1,100 00	
11 Laborers	9,900 00	
2 Night policemen.....	1,680 00	
2 Day policemen.......	1,680 00	
2 Visitors' attendants..	1,680 00	
Carpenter	1,300 00	
Chief Engineer......	1,400 00	
Electrician	1,200 00	
2 Engineer helpers....	2,400 00	
Fireman	1,080 00	
2 Elevator attendants..	2,040 00	
Caretaker rest room..	600 00	
Total personal service.........		$26,060 00
Maintenance—		
C Supplies—		
C 2 Forage	$50 00	
C 3 Fuel	6,000 00	
C 6 Cleaning	300 00	
C 9 Agricultural .	165 00	
C 11 General Plant.	200 00	
Total	$6,715 00	
D Materials—		
D 3 General plant..	$500 00	
E Equipment—		
E 9 General plant..	$2,000 00	
F Contract and Open Order Service—		
F 1 Repairs	$600 00	
F 3 Water	500 00	
F 4 Light, heat and power	10,000 00	
F 5 Freight, express and drayage....	100 00	
F 7 Communication.	60 00	
F 9 General Plant—		
To comply with the provisions of senate Joint Resolution No. 33......	250 00	
Total	$11,510 00	
Total maintenance..........		20,725 00
Total		$46,785 00

WYANDOTTE BUILDING.

	Items.	Appropriations.
Personal Service—		
A 1 Salaries—		
Engineer	$1,400 00	
Assistant engineer...	1,000 00	
Fireman a n d watch-man	1,000 00	
Head janitor	1,000 00	
2 Elevator attendants..	1,800 00	
6 Janitors	5,400 00	
Total personal service		$11,600 00
Maintenance—		
C Supplies—		
C 3 Fuel	$1,400 00	
C 6 Cleaning	600 00	
C 11 General plant.	425 00	
Total	$2,425 00	
E Equipment—		
E 9 General plant..	$500 00	
F Contract and Open Order Service—		
F 1 Repairs	$5,000 00	
F 3 Water	400 00	
F 4 Light, heat and power	2,000 00	
F 5 Freight, express and drayage	150 00	
Total	$7,550 00	
Total maintenance		10,475 00
Total		$22,075 00

OHIO BOARD OF ADMINISTRATION.

Personal Service—	
A 1 Salaries—	
4 Members	$16,000 00
Fiscal supervisor-secretary	3,600 00
Purchasing agent	5,000 00
Chief agriculturist...	3,600 00
Horticulturist	2,500 00
Assistant superintendent of construction	1,500 00
Mechanical engineer.	2,500 00

	Items.	Appropriations.	General appropriations. 1919-1920.
Grade II engineer...	3,000 00		
Grade IV engineer .	1,800 00		
Grade V engineer....	1,200 00		
3 Grade III bookkeepers	4,140 00		
Grade IV bookkeeper.	840 00		
Executive clerk......	2,400 00		
Grade I clerk......	1,680 00		
Grade II clerk.......	1,200 00		
Grade III clerk......	900 00		
Grade IV clerk......	1,260 00		
2 Grade II stenographers	2,400 00		
6 Grade III stenographers	5,400 00		
Grade I telephone operator	780 00		
Grade III engineer...	2,400 00		
Architectural draftsman	1,500 00		
Employes bureau of juvenile research.	25,000 00		
21 managing officers....	52,200 00		
Minor officers and employes	1,690,000 00		
Total ....$	1,832,800 00		
A 2 Wages	5,000 00		
A 3 Unclassified—			
Prisoners' compensation	100,000 00		
Total personal service........		$1,937,800 00	

Maintenance—

C Supplies—

		Items.
C 1	Food ....$	1,750,000 00
C 2	Forage	150,000 00
C 3	Fuel	475,000 00
C 4	Office	19,000 00
C 5	Medical	35,000 00
C 6	Cleaning	60,000 00
C 8	Educational ..	4,000 00
C 9	Agricultural .	25,000 00
C 11	General plant.	90,000 00
	Total ....$	2,608,000 00

D Materials—

D 2	Building	$150,000 00
D 3	General plant..	275,000 00
	Total	$425,000 00

Items.　　Appropriations.

E Equipment—

E 1	Office	$1,000 00
E 2	Household	85,000 00
E 3	Surgical	4,000 00
E 4	Live stock.....	40,000 00
E 5	Agricultural ..	1,600 00
E 6	Motor vehicle..	7,500 00
E 7	Wearing apparel	225,000 00
E 8	Educational ...	5,000 00
E 9	General plant..	75,000 00

Total $444,100 00

F Contract and Open Order Service—

F 1	Repairs	$100,000 00
F 3	Water	21,000 00
F 4	Light, heat and power	32,000 00
F 5	Freight, express and drayage.....	2,000 00
F 6	Traveling expense	10,000 00
F 7	Communication	9,000 00
F 9	General plant..	30,000 00
	Advertising sale of cattle	2,000 00

Total $206,000 00

H Fixed Charges and Contributions—

H 6	Rent	$8,900 00
H 7	Insurance	1,017 50
H 8	Contributions .	12,000 00

Total $21,917 50

I Rotary Funds—
Manufacturing and sales central warehouse ......
Total maintenance.......... 3,705,017 50

Total $5,642,817 50

BOARD OF AGRICULTURE OF OHIO.

Personal Service—
A 1 Salaries—
Secretary $4,000 00

	Items.	Appropriations.	General appropriations. 1919-1920.
Chief bureau of fair administration ..	2,600 00		
Publicity specialist...	1,600 00		
Superintendent of fair grounds....	1,300 00		
Chief bureau of horticulture	3,000 00		
8 Deputy inspectors nurseries and orchards	11,200 00		
Chief bureau of markets	2,500 00		
Deputy inspector bureau of markets.	1,500 00		
Chief bureau of feeds and fertilizers...	1,900 00		
4 Deputy inspectors feeds and fertilizers	4,800 00		
State veterinarian...	3,600 00		
Assistant state veterinarian	2,100 00		
Pathologist	2,400 00		
Assistant pathologist.	1,800 00		
Bacteriologist	1,600 00		
14 Field veterinarians...	25,200 00		
Local veterinarian in charge	2,000 00		
Grade III bookkeeper	1,380 00		
Confidential secretary	1,380 00		
Grade II clerk.......	1,260 00		
3 Grade III clerks.....	3,560 00		
Grade IV clerk......	600 00		
3 Grade II stenographers	3,360 00		
4 Grade III stenographers	3,540 00		
2 Grade II typists.....	1,800 00		
Telephone operator..	780 00		
5 Laborers serum plant.	4,500 00		
Chief bureau of agricultural statistics	600 00		
Messenger and janitor	1,020 00		
Seed analyst.........	1,800 00		
3 Assistant seed analists	2,700 00		
Stenographer	840 00		
Total	$102,220 00		
A 2 Wages	17,000 00		
A 3 Unclassified	1,200 00		
Total personal service........		$120,420 00	

General
appropriations.
1919-1920.

Maintenance—

C Supplies—

C 2	Forage		$6,000 00
C 3	Fuel		1,500 00
C 4	Office		6,500 00
C 5	Medical		500 00
C 6	Cleaning		90 00
C 9	Agricultural .		750 00
C 11	General Plant—		
Pigs for serum tests..			70,000 00
Other			1,400 00
	Total		$86,740 00

D Materials—

D 2	Building		$2,450 00
D 3	General plant..		4,400 00
	Total		$6,850 00

E Equipment—

E 1	Office		$400 00
E 3	Surgical		100 00
E 7	Wearing apparel		50 00
E 9	General plant..		1,000 00
	Total		$1,550 00

F Contract and Open Order Service—

F 1	Repairs		$600 00
Repairs buildings state fair grounds			10,000 00
F 3	Water		700 00
F 4	Light, heat and power		600 00
F 5	Freight, express and drayage.....		600 00
F 6	Traveling expense		30,000 00
F 7	Communication.		1,650 00
F 9	General Plant—		
Uses and purposes of state fair.......			110,000 00
Experimental work diseases of animals ....,			2,500 00
Apple and fruit shows			1,500 00
Other			1,733 00
	Total		$159,883 00

	Items.	Appropriations.	General appropriations. 1919-1920.

H Fixed Charges and Contributions—

| H 6 Rent .... | $20 00 | | |
| H 7 Insurance .... | 25 00 | | |

H 8 Contributions—

State share of pay due owners of tubercular cattle killed according to law..	60,000 00		
State share of pay due owners of glandered horses killed according to law..	18,000 00		
Other	25 00		

| Total .... | $78,070 00 | | |
| Total maintenance........... | | 333,093 00 | |

| Total .... | | $453,513 00 | |

DAIRY AND FOOD DIVISION.

Personal Service—

A 1 Salaries—

Chief of division.....	$2,000 00		
Chief inspector weights and measures	1,500 00		
Inspector weights and measures	1,350 00		
5 Dairy inspectors.....	6,750 00		
4 Drug inspectors.....	5,400 00		
9 Food inspectors......	13,500 00		
Cannery inspector...	1,350 00		
Chief narcotic inspector	1,650 00		
Narcotic inspector...	1,350 00		
Grade II clerk......	1,200 00		
Grade III clerk.....	900 00		
Grade III stenographer	1,000 00		
Messenger and janitor	840 00		

| Total .... | $38,790 00 | | |
| A 3 Unclassified .... | 1,700 00 | | |

| Total personal service........ | | $40,490 00 | |

General appropriations, 1919-1920.	Maintenance—	Items.	Appropriations.
	C Supplies—		
	C 4 Office	$265 00	
	C 11 General plant.	·35 00	
	Total	$300 00	
	E Equipment—		
	E 1 Office	$100 00	
	E 9 General plant..	50 00	
	Total	$150 00	
	F Contract and Open Order Service—		
	F 5 Freight, express and drayage.....	$100 00	
	F 6 Traveling expense	22,000 00	
	F 7 Communication.	25 00	
	F 9 General plant..	150 00	
	Total	$22,275 00	
	Total maintenance............		$22,725 00
	Total		$63,215 00

FISH AND GAME DIVISION.

Personal Service—		
A 1 Salaries—		
Chief warden........	$3,000 00	
Assistant chief warden	1,800 00	
3 Grade III clerks.....	3,840 00	
Grade II stenographer	1,200 00	
2 Grade III stenographers	1,740 00	
30 Wardens	36,000 00	
20 Wardens	18,000 00	
Supervisor Lake Erie district	1,600 00	
Superintendent Lake hatchery	1,200 00	
Assistant Lake Erie hatchery	1,080 00	
Fireman Lake Erie hatchery	840 00	
Captain patrol boat..	1,200 00	
Engineer patrol boat.	1,080 00	
Fireman patrol boat.	900 00	
Deck hand patrol boat	900 00	

	Items.	Appropriations.	General Appropriations. 1919-1920.

Superintendent London hatchery.... 1,080 00

4 Superintendents of hatcheries 4,020 00

Superintendent Wellington game farm 1,800 00

Gamekeeper London.. 1,200 00

Farmer 720 00

4 Laborers 3,000 00

Total $86,200 00

A 2 Wages—

Extra game wardens. $8,000 00

Laborers Lake Erie.. 2,000 00

Laborers inland fish hatcheries 1,000 00

Total $11,000 00

A 3 Unclassified—

Securing game fish for inland distribution $6,000 00

Total personal service........ $103,200 00

Maintenance—

C Supplies—

C 2 Forage $2,500 00

C 3 Fuel 2,500 00

C 4 Office 600 00

C 9 Agricultural .. 1,000 00

C 11 General plant. 4,000 00

Total $10,600 00

D Materials—

D 2 Building $500 00

D 3 General plant.. 1,000 00

Total $1,500 00

E Equipment—

E 4 Livestock—

Purchase of fish spawn $5,000 00

Purchase of pheasant eggs, game birds and hens... 15,000 00

E 5 Agricultural .. 280 00

E 5 Agricultural .. 280 00

E 6 Motor vehicle.. 500 00

E 9 General plant.. 150 00

Total $20,930 00

	Items.	Appropriations.
F Contract and Open Order Service—		
F 1 Repairs	$100 00	
F 3 Water	450 00	
F 5 Freight, express and drayage.....	3,850 00	
F 6 Traveling expense	24,000 00	
F 7 Communication	700 00	
F 9 General plant—		
Printing game laws	5,000 00	
Fish propagation and distribution.	17,000 00	
Total	$51,100 00	
H Fixed Charges and Contributions—		
H 6 Rent	$637 40	
Total maintenance..........		84,767 40
Total		$187,967 40

ARCHAEOLOGICAL AND HISTORICAL SOCIETY.

Personal Service—	
A 1 Salaries—	
Curator	$2,500 00
Assistant curator....	1,700 00
Secretary	1,000 00
2 Assistant librarians..	1,340 00
Stenographer	720 00
Superintendent of building	900 00
2 Janitors	1,420 00 ·
Caretaker Fort Ancient park......	360 00
Caretaker Serpent Mound park.....	240 00
Caretaker Logan Elm park	25 00
Caretaker Spiegel Grove park.....	720 00
Bookkeeper	150 00
Treasurer	300 00
Clerk Historical Commission of Ohio..	840 00
Binder	900 00
Author "Ohio in Civil War"	1,200 00
Total	$14,315 00

	Items.	Appropriations.	General appropriations, 1919-1920.

A 2 Wages—
    W o r k m e n Spiegel
        Grove park..... $100 00

        Total personal service............. $14,415 00

Maintenance—
  C Supplies—
    C 4 Office $300 00
    C 11 General plant. 175 00

        Total $475 00

  F Contract and Open Or-
      der Service—
    F 1 Repairs $900 00
    F 3 Water 90 00
    F 4 Light, heat and
        power 900 00
    F 5 Freight, express
        and drayage..... 150 00
    F 6 T r a v eling ex-
        pense 250 00
    F 7 Communication. 93 00
    F 8 Contingencies . 50 00
    F 9 General Plant—
        Publications ...... ·3,000 00
        E x p l orations and
        field work...... 500 00
        Republishing arch-
        a e o l ogical a n d
        historical reports
        —To be pro-rated
        among the legis-
        lative districts of
        the state and to
        be distributed to
        schools and libra-
        ries designated by
        the g e n e r a l as-
        sembly 13,000 00

        Total $18,933 00
        Total maintenance.......... ·19,408 00

        Total $33,823 00

ATTORNEY GENERAL.

Personal Service—
  A 1 Salaries—
    Attorney general.... $6,500 00

	Items.	Appropriations.
1st assistant attorney general	4,000 00	
2nd assistant attorney general	2,500 00	
Chief clerk..........	1,500 00	
Grade I clerk........	2,000 00	
Grade I clerk.......	1,500 00	
8 Grade II stenographers	10,380 00	
Clerk	840 00	
Total	$29,220 00	
A 2 Wages—		
Extra stenographic work	$1,500 00	
A 3 Unclassified—		
Special counsel......	55,000 00	
Expense of investigation	2,500 00	
Costs in cases........	3,500 00	
Total	$61,000 00	
Total personal service........		$91,720 00
Maintenance—		
C Supplies—		
C 4 Office	$1,612 00	
D Materials—		
D 3 General plant..	100 00	
E Equipment—		
E 1 Office	$496 06	
E 9 General plant..	300 00	
Total	$796 06	
F Contract and Open Order Service—		
F 1 Repairs	$100 00	
F 5 Freight, express and drayage.....	50 00	
F 6 Traveling expense	4,000 00	
F 7 Communication.	1,000 00	
F 9 General plant..	100 00	
Total	$5,250 00	
Total maintenance...........		7,758 06
Total		$99,478 06

AUDITOR OF STATE.

	Items.	Appropriations.
Personal Service—		
A 1 Salaries—		
Auditor	$6,500 00	
Deputy auditor......	3,000 00	
Chief clerk..........	2,400 00	
Deputy supervisor school lands.....	2,500 00	
Secretary	2,000 00	
Statistician	2,000 00	
Grade II clerk......	1,500 00	
Janitor and mailing clerk	640 00	
Examiner	2,800 00	
Grade I examiner....	3,000 00	
4 Grade II examiners..	7,500 00	
2 Grade II examiners..	3,200 00	
Grade I stenographer.	1,500 00	
Grade I accountant..	2,600 00	
2 Grade II accountants.	4,500 00	
Grade III accountant	1,500 00	
2 Grade II examiners..	3,600 00	
Grade III bookkeeper	1,950 00	
2 Grade III bookkeepers	2,400 00	
3 Grade I typists......	2,760 00	
2 Grade III clerks.....	2,400 00	
Grade IV clerk......	1,000 00	
Grade II clerk......	1,500 00	
Grade III stenographer	1,200 00	
Total	$63,950 00	
A 3 Unclassified—		
Investigation school and ministerial lands	$3,000 00	
Total personal service........		$66,950 00
Maintenance—		
C Supplies—		
C 4 Office ......'.....	$1,000 00	
E Equipment—		
E 1 Office	$600 00	
F Contract and Open Order Service—		
F 1 Repairs	$75 00	

		Items.	Appropriations.
F 6	Traveling expense	1,200 00	
F 7	Communication.	400 00	
F 8	Contingencies .	1,000 00	
F 9	General plant..	200 00	
	Total	$2,875 00	
	Total maintenance..........		4,475 00
	Total		$71,425 00

BUREAU OF INSPECTION AND SUPERVISION OF PUBLIC OFFICES.

Personal Service—
A 1 Salaries—

	Items.	Appropriations.
2 Deputy inspectors....	$5,000 00	
Statistician	1,800 00	
Grade I clerk.......	1,800 00	
Grade I stenographer	1,500 00	
Grade II clerk.......	1,140 00	
2 Grade II stenographers	2,400 00	
Janitor	360 00	
Total personal service........		$14,000 00

Maintenance—
C Supplies—

C 4 Office	$1,200 00

E Equipment—

E-1 Office	$250 00

F Contract and Open Order Service—

F 1	Repairs	$25 00	
F 6	Traveling expense	200 00	
F 7	Communication.	275 00	
F 8	Contingencies .	1,500 00	
F 9	General plant..	25 00	
	Total	$2,025 00	
	Total maintenance..........		3,475 00
	Total		$17,475 00

DEPARTMENT OF BANKS AND BANKING.

General appropriations. 1919-1920.

	Items	Appropriations
Personal Service—		
A 1 Salaries—		
Superintendent	$5,000 00	
Assistant superintendent	3,300 00	
Secretary	1,500 00	
Attorney	3,300 00	
2 Grade I examiners	6,900 00	
13 Examiners	32,800 00	
4 Assistant examiners	6,900 00	
Grade III statistician	1,380 00	
Grade III bookkeeper	1,380 00	
4 Grade II stenographers	4,560 00	
Total	$67,020 00	
A 3 Unclassified	200 00	
Foreign exchange inspection	3,500 00	
Total	$3,700 00	
Total personal service		$70,720 00
Maintenance—		
C Supplies—		
C 4 Office	$1,800 00	
E Equipment—		
E 1 Office	$356 00	
F Contract and Open Order Service—		
F 1 Repairs	$20 00	
F 5 Freight, express and drayage	50 00	
F 6 Traveling expense	23,500 00	
F 7 Communication	700 00	
F 9 General plant	292 00	
Printing	3,000 00	
Total	$27,562 00	
H Fixed Charges and Contributions—		
H 6 Rent	$722 00	
H 7 Insurance	700 00	
H 8 Contributions	20 00	
Total	$1,442 00	
Total maintenance		31,160 00
Total		$101,880 00

General
appropriations.
1919-1920.

OHIO COMMISSION FOR THE BLIND.

	Items.	Appropriations.
A 1 Salaries—		
Executive secretary..	$2,500 00	
Chief clerk..........	1,000 00	
Grade III stenographer	900 00	
Grade III bookkeeper	1,260 00	
Publicity man.......	200 00	
Supervisor of inspectors	1,500 00	
6 Inspectors	7,800 00	
Supervisor of women's work.......	900 00	
Grade III stenographer	900 00	
Home teacher.......	900 00	
7 Home teachers......	2,940 0C	
Foreman and instructor	600 00	
Assistant foreman...	780 00	
Telephone operator and typist.;.....	660 00	
Total	$22,840 00	
A 3 Unclassified—		
Laundry and dry cleaning	$25 00	
Janitor service......	260 00	
Total	$285 00	
Total personal service........		$23,125 00
Maintenance—		
C Supplies—		
C 4 Office	$200 00	
C 5 Medical	50 00	
C 6 Cleaning	50 00	
C 8 Educational ..	100 00	
C 11 General plant.	100 00	
Total	$500 00	
E Equipment—		
E 1 Office	$200 00	
E 3 Surgical	50 00	
E 9 General plant..	150 00	
Total	$400 00	

	Items.	Appropriations.	General appropriations, 1919-1920.
F Contract and Open Order Service—			
F 1 Repairs	$100 00		
F 3 Water	15 00		
F 4 Light, heat and power	175 00		
F 5 Freight, express and drayage....	25 00		
F 6 Traveling expense	9,800 00		
F 7 Communication.	160 00		
F 9 General plant..	100 00		
Total	$10,375 00		
H Fixed Charges and Contributions—			
H 6 Rent	$750 00		
H 8 Contributions	2,200 00		
To be transferred to the rotary fund at the discretion of the controlling board.......	25,000 00		
Total	$27,950 00		
Total maintenance...............		39,225 00	
Total		$62,350 00	

BUREAU OF BUILDING AND LOAN ASSOCIATIONS.

Personal Service—		
A 1 Salaries—		
Inspector	$3,600 00	
Deputy inspector....	2,000 00	
Assistant deputy inspector	1,800 00	
12 Examiners	21,600 00	
Grade II accountant..	1,500 00	
Grade III statistician	1,500 00	
Correspondence clerk.	1,200 00	
Total personal service........		$33,200 00
Maintenance—		
C Supplies—		
C 4 Office	$600 00	
E Equipment—		
E 1 Office	$400 00	

	Items.	Appropriations.

F Contract and Open Order Service—

F 1 Repairs $25 00
F 5 Freight, express and drayage 25 00
F 6 Traveling expense 10,000 00
F 7 Communication. 200 00
F 9 General plant.. 20 00

Total $10,270 00
Total maintenance.......... 11,270 00

Total $44,470 00

BOARD OF STATE CHARITIES.

Personal Service—
A 1 Salaries—

Secretary $3,000 00
Social investigator..: 1,800 00
Agent 1,800 00
3 Assistant agents.... 4,500 00
Grade III clerk...... 1,200 00
Director of children's welfare 3,000 00
Assistant director of children's welfare 1,560 00
Grade IV bookkeeper 900 00
3 Institution inspectors. 3,600 00
Supervisor of child placing 1,800 00
2 District superintendents 3,600 00
Supervisor of boarding home........ 1,200 00
Assistant supervisor of boarding home 900 00
16 Field agents........ 19,900 00
Special nurse....... 900 00
6 Grade III stenographers 5,340 00
2 Grade II stenographers 2,280 00
Grade I typist....... 1,020 00
Telephone operator... 660 00
Matron 600 00
Housekeeper 480 00

Total $60,040 00

		Items.	Appropriations.	General appropriations, 1919-1920.

A 3 Unclassified—
Examination and treatment of minor wards of board $900 00
To provide medical and surgical treatment for crippled children 5,000 00

Total $5,900 00
Total personal service......... $65,940 00

Maintenance—
C Supplies—
C 1 Food $1,500 00
C 3 Fuel 500 00
C 4 Office 1,500 00
C 5 Medical 175 00
C 6 Cleaning 50 00
C 11 General plant. 250 00

Total $3,975 00

E Equipment—
E 1 Office $500 00
E 2 Household 100 00

Total $600 00

F Contract and Open Order Service—
F 1 Repairs $300 00
F 3 Water 15 00
F 4 Light, heat and power 50 00
F 5 Freight, express and drayage..... 50 00
F 6 Traveling expense 22,000 00
F 7 Communication. 450 00
F 9 General plant.. 350 00

Total $23,215 00

H Fixed Charges and Contributions—
H 6 Rent—Office .. $1,812 00
Receiving home...... 1,500 00

Total $3,312 00

I Rotary fund........... $3,000 00
Total maintenance........... $34,102 00

Total $100,042 00

STATE CIVIL SERVICE COMMISSION.

		Items.	Appropriations.
Personal Service—			
A 1 Salaries—			
2 Commissioners		$8,000 00	
Secretary		3,000 00	
Assistant chief examiner		3,000 00	
4 Examiners		7,400 00	
Efficiency examiner..		2,400 00	
Assistant efficiency examiner		1,560 00	
Grade I clerk........		1,800 00	
4 Grade II clerks......		4,680 00	
2 Grade III clerks.....		1,800 00	
Grade IV clerks.....		660 00	
Publicity clerk......		720 00	
Grade II stenographer		1,200 00	
Grade III stenographer		1,200 00	
3 Grade III stenographers		2,700 00	
Total		$40,120 00	
A 2 Wages—			
Special examiners, extra clerks and stenographers ...		$600 00	
Total personal service........			$40,720 00
Maintenance—			
C Supplies—			
C 4 Office		$2,300 00	
E Equipment—			
E 1 Office		$300 00	
F Contract and Open Order Service—			
F 5 Freight, express and drayage.....		$10 00	
F 6 Traveling expense		1,700 00	
F 7 Communication		425 00	
F 9 General plant..		200 00	
Total		$2,335 00	
Total maintenance...........			4,935 00
Total			$45,655 00

OHIO BOARD OF CLEMENCY.

	Items.	Appropriations.
Personal Service—		
A 1 Salaries—		
2 members of board..	$7,200 00	
Secretary	1,500 00	
Total personal service........		$8,700 00
Maintenance—		
C Supplies—		
C 4 Office	$110 00	
E Equipment—		
E 1 Office	$50 00	
F Contract and Open Or-		
der Service—		
F 6 T r a v e l i n g ex-		
pense	$200 00	
F 7 Communication.	85 00	
F 9 General plant..	15 00	
Total	$300 00	
H F i x e d Charges a n d		
Contributions—		
H 7 Insurance	$25 00	
Total maintenance..........		485 00
Total		$9,185 00

STATE DENTAL BOARD.

	Items.	Appropriations.
Personal Service—		
A 1 Salaries—		
Secretary	$1,200 00	
Stenographer	225 00	
Total	$1,425 00	
A 2 Wages—		
Per diem 5 members		
of board.......	$2,000 00	
Total personal service........		$3,425 00
Maintenance—		
C Supplies—		
C 4 Office	$150 00	

	Items.	Appropriations.
F Contract and Open Order Service—		
F 5 Freight, express and drayage	10 00	
F 6 Traveling expense	850 00	
F 7 Communication.	10 00	
Total	$870 00	
Total maintenance..........		1,020 00
Total		$4,445 00

STATE BOARD OF EDUCATION.

Maintenance—
F Contract and Open Order Service—
F 9 General Plant—
Co-operative work with federal government in vocational education in accordance with provisions of the Smith-Hughes law....... $152,428 90

STATE BOARD OF EMBALMING EXAMINERS.

	Items.	Appropriations.
Personal Service—		
A 1 Salaries—		
Secretary	$1,200 00	
A 2 Wages—		
A 2 Wages—		
Per diem 2 members of board........	600 00	
Total personal service..........		$1,800 00
Maintenance—		
C Supplies—		
C 4 Office	$400 00	
C II General Plant—		
Cadavers	150 00	
Total	$550 00	
F Contract and Open Order Service—		
F 6 Traveling expense	$600 00	
F 9 General plant..	150 00	
Total	$750 00	
Total maintenance..........		1,300 00
Total		$3,100 00

EXECUTIVE DEPARTMENT.

		Items.	Appropriations.
Personal Service—			
A 1 Salaries—			
	Governor	$10,000 00	
	Secretary to the governor	5,000 00	
	Executive clerk......	3,000 00	
	Correspondence clerk.	2,000 00	
	Commission clerk....	1,800 00	
	Stenographer	1,400 00	
	Messenger	1,200 00	
	Total personal service.......		$24,400 00
Maintenance—			
C Supplies—			
C 3	Fuel	$25 00	
C 4	Office ....:	1,000 00	
	Total	$1,025 00	
E Equipment—			
E 1	Office	$500 00	
F Contract and Open Order Service—			
F 1	Repairs	$100 00	
F 6	Traveling expense	250 00	
F 7	Communication.	1,200 00	
F 8	Contingencies .	6,000 00	
F 9	General Plant— Maintenance of governor's mansion	5,000 00	
	Total	$12,550 00	
	Total maintenance..............		14,075 00
	Total		$38,475 00

BUDGET COMMISSIONER.

		Items.	Appropriations.
Personal Service—			
A 1 Salaries—			
	Commissioner	$4,000 00	
	Assistant commissioner	1,800 00	
	Secretary	1,680 00	
	Messenger	300 00	
	Total	$7,780 00	
A 2	Wages	1,200 00	
	Total personal service........		$8,980 00

Maintenance—
  C Supplies—
    C 4 Office $150 00

  E Equipment—
    E 1 Office $150 00

  F Contract and Open Or-
    der Service—
    F 1 Repairs $15 00
    F 5 Freight, ex-
      press and drayage   10 00
    F 6 Traveling ex-
      pense 600 00
    F 7 Communication.   200 00
    F 9 General plant..   100 00

    Total $925 00
    Total maintenance..........   1,225 00

    Total $10,205 00

OHIO AGRICULTURAL EXPERIMENT STATION.

Personal Service—
  A 1 Salaries—
    Director $4,000 00
    Director—Soils and
      research 2,500 00
    8 Deputy chiefs—
      Agronomy, bot-
      any, chemistry,
      dairying, ento-
      mology, forestry,
      horticulture,
      farm manage-
      ment 20,000 00
    Bursar 2,200 00
    4 Associates 8,400 00
    32 Assistants 45,500 00
    Editor 1,800 00
    Librarian 1,300 00
    Photographer 780 00
    4 Office assistants......   3,730 00
    4 Field assistants......   4,450 00
    2 Engineers 2,100 00
    Mechanic 900 00
    Printer 960 00
    Mailing clerk........   780 00
    3 Farm managers......   3,150 00
    2 Herdsmen 1,800 00
    Shepherd 840 00
    5 Foremen 4,320 00

		Items.	Appropriations.	General appropriations. 1919-1920.
	Assistant foreman....	960 00		
	Stenographer	660 00		
2	Clerks	1,380 00		
4	Superintendents of county experiment farms......	7,200 00		
	Total	$119,710 00		
A 2	Wages	50,000 00		
A 3	Unclassified— Fees, etc...........	200 00		
	Total personal service........		$169,910 00	

Maintenance—
C Supplies—

		Items.
C 1	Food	$10 00
C 2	Forage	8,000 00
C 3	Fuel	7,000 00
C 4	Office	2,000 00
C 6	Cleaning	200 00
C 9	Agricultural .	2,500 00
C 11	General plant.	7,000 00
	Total	$26,710 00

D Materials—

D 2	Building	$1,200 00
D 3	General plant	3,000 00
	Total	$4,200 00

E 1	Office	$200 00
E 4	Livestock	500 00
E 5	Agricultural ..	1,000 00
E 7	Wearing apparel	15 00
E 8	Educational ...	700 00
E 9	General plant..	8,000 00
	Total	$10,415 00

F Contract and Open Order Service—

F 1	Repairs	$2,000 00
F 4	Light, heat and power	200 00
F 5	Freight, express and drayage	2,000 00
F 6	Traveling expense..	14,000 00
F 6	Traveling expense	14,000 00

	Items.	Appropriations.
F 7 Communication.	500 00	
F 9 General plant..	1,200 00	

All monies appropriated by the U. S. government which are now in the Adams-Hatch fund or which may be credited to such fund prior to July 1, 1921.

Total	$19,900 00	
H Fixed Charges and Contributions—		
H 6 Rent	$1,500 00	
H 7 Insurance	100 00	
H 8 Contributions .	50 00	
Total	$1,650 00	

I Rotary—
Animal husbandry, cost-feeding experimental work, dairying ....

Total maintenance..........		,62,875 00
Total		$232,785 00

STATE FIRE MARSHAL.

Personal Service—
A 1 Salaries—

Marshal	$4,500 00
2 Deputy marshals....	4,000 00
Chief assistant.......	2,400 00
Chief inspector......	1,800 00
Statistician	1,200 00
27 Assistants	40,500 00
Electrical inspector..	1,500 00
Water supply engineer	1,600 00
Grade I clerk.......	1,800 00
Clerk	900 00
6 Grade III stenographers	5,400 00
2 Grade II stenographers	2,160 00
Record clerk.......	1,080 00
Total	$68,840 00

A 2   Wages—
Assistants 2,000 00

A 3   Unclassified—
Fees, m i l e a g e and maintenance, fire chiefs, m a y o r s, township c l e r k s and w i t n e s s e s, s p e c i a l stenographers, l e g a l fees, court costs.   2,250 00

Total personal service........ $73,090 00

Maintenance—
C Supplies—
C   4   Office $4,800 00
C 11   General plant.   500 00

Total $5,300 00

E Equipment—
E   1   Office $500 00

F Contract and Open Or-
der Service—
F   4   Light, heat and power $72 00
F   5   Freight, express and drayage.....   25 00
F   6   T r a v e ling expense 20,000 00
F   7   Communication.   1,200 00
F   9   General plant..   2,000 00

Total $23,297 00

H Fixed C h a r g e s and Contributions—
H   6   Rent $1,788 00

I Rotary—
For tearing down and r e p airing buildings, c o r r ecting or removing hazardous conditions according to pro- v i s i o n s of Sec. 836-2 G. C...... $1,000 00

Total maintenance..........   31,885 00

Total $104,975 00

GEOLOGICAL SURVEY.

	Items.	Appropriations.
Personal Service—		
A 1 Salaries—		
State geologist.......	$1,500 00	
Assistant geologist....	2,000 00	
Grade II stenographer	1,080 00	
Total	$4,580 00	
A 2 Wages—		
5 Assistant geologists.	$1,875 00	
Student assistants....	50 00	
Total	$1,925 00	
Total personal service........		$6,505 00
Maintenance—		
C Supplies—		
C 4 Office	$150 00	
C 11 General plant.	100 00	
Total	$250 00	
E Equipment—		
E 1 Office	$25 00	
E 9 General plant..	100 00	
Total	$125 00	
F Contract and Open Order Service—		
F 1 Repairs	$30 00	
F 5 Freight, express and drayage	150 00	
F 6 Traveling expense	1,700 00	
F 7 Communication.	30·00	
F 9 General plant..	100 00	
Total	$2,010 00	
Total maintenance...........		2,385 00
Total		$8,890 00

HEADQUARTERS OHIO G. A. R.

Personal Service—		
A 1 Salaries—		
Assistant adjutant general	$1,200 00	
Clerk	750 00	
Total personal service........		$1,950 00

	Items.	Appropriations	General appropriations, 1919-1920.

Maintenance—
F Contract and Open Order Service—
F 9   General plant.. $500 00

Total maintenance.......... 500 00

Total ....:. $2,450 00

STATE DEPARTMENT OF HEALTH.

Personal Service—
A 1   Salaries—

Commissioner of health	$6,000 00	
Deputy commissioner.	4,000 00	
Publicity director....	1,700 00	
2 Grade II clerks......	2,340 00	
3 Grade III clerks.....	2,760 00	
Grade IV clerk......	840 00	
2 Grade II stenographers	2,160 00	
11 Grade III stenographers	9,660 00	
Grade I telephone operator ·.........	720 00	
Janitor	900 00	
Grade I engineer.....	4,000 00	
3 Grade III engineers..	6,480 00	
Grade IV engineer...	1,440 00	
Plumbing inspector..	2,200 00	
2 Deputy plumbing inspectors	3,200 00	
Director of laboratories	3,000 00	
Bacteriologist	2,100 00	
Chemist	2,200 00	
2 Laboratory assistants.	3,240 00	
4 Laboratory assistants.	5,860 00	
4 Laboratory helpers...	3,000 00	
Janitor	840 00	
Director division of communicable diseases	3,000 00	
Epidemiologist .	2,400 00	
Statistician	1,200 00	
Director division of public health education and tuberculosis	3,000 00	
Director hospital division	2,000 00	

		Items.	Appropriations.
	Chief of nursing service	1,600 00	
3	Public health nurses..	3,900 00	
	Director division of industrial hygiene	3,000 00	
	Assistant director division industrial hygiene	1,600 00	
	Division division of child hygiene....	2,400 00	
4	Inspectors	4,800 00	
8	District health supervisors	20,000 00	
	Total salaries....	$117,540 00	

A 2 Wages—

	Items.	Appropriations.
Per diem members public health council	$500 00	
Emergency nurses...	1,000 00	
Emergency physicians	100 00	
Total wages.....	$1,600 00	

A 3 Unclassified—

	Items.	Appropriations.
Referees fees........	$300 00	
Reporting fees.......	500 00	
Operation of trachoma clinics and hospitals in co-operation with United States public health service, counties and municipalities	10,000 00	
Total	$10,800 00	
Total personal service.........		$129,940 00

Maintenance—

C Supplies—

		Items.	Appropriations.
C 2	Forage	$250 00	
C 4	Office	3,500 00	
C 5	Medical	2,500 00	
C 11	General plant.	1,700 00	
	Total	$7,950 00	

E Equipment—

		Items.	Appropriations.
E 1	Office	$500 00	
E 3	Surgical	3,300 00	
E 4	Livestock	200 00	

765

	Items.	Appropriations.
E 7 Wearing apparel	50 00	
E 8 Educational	1,200 00	
E 9 General plant	900 00	
Total	$6,150 00	
F Contract and Open Order Service—		
F 1 Repairs	$2,500 00	
F 4 Light, heat and power	1,000 00	
F 5 Freight, express and drayage	1,000 00	
F 6 Traveling expense	21,000 00	
F 7 Communication	1,000 00	
F 9 General plant	2,000 00	
All monies appropriated by the U. S. government under the Chamberlain-Kahn act and	25,000 00	
Total	$53,500 00	
Total maintenance		67,600 00
Total		$197,540 00

HIGHWAY DEPARTMENT.

Personal Service—
A 1 Salaries—

Commissioner	$5,000 00	
3 Deputy commissioners	9,900 00	
17 Grade III engineers	46,750 00	
5 Grade IV engineers	8,640 00	
Testing engineer	2,400 00	
2 Assistant engineers	3,240 00	
Chief clerk	2,000 00	
Secretary	2,500 00	
2 Grade III bookkeepers	2,640 00	
6 Grade II clerks	8,280 00	
Grade IV clerk	660 00	
2 Grade II stenographers	2,160 00	
8 Grade III stenographers	7,200 00	
Grade III typist	900 00	

General appropriations, 1919-1920.

			Items.	Appropriations.
	Chauffeur and mechanician		1,200 00	
		Total	$103,470 00	
A 2	Wages		3,500 00	
A 3	Unclassified		5,000 00	
		Total personal service........		$111,970 00

Maintenance—

C Supplies—

C 3	Fuel		$2,100 00	
C 4	Office		3,000 00	
C 11	General plant.		2,275 00	
	Total		$7,375 00	

D Materials—

D 3	General plant..		$500 00

E Equipment—

E 1	Office		$800 00
E 6	Motor vehicles.		7,000 00
E 9	General plant..		500 00
	Total		$8,300 00

F Contract and Open Order Service—

F 1 Repairs—

To police, patrol and maintain highways as provided in Sec. 6309 G. C......$2,250,000 00

Other 3,500 00

F 5 Freight, express and drayage..:.. 1,000 00

F 6 Traveling expense 16,000 00

F 7 Communication. 2,000 00

F 9 General Plant—

All monies appropriated by the U. S. government and allotted to the state of Ohio for highway improvement which shall be received prior to July 1, 1921, and 6,000 00

Total $2,278,500 00

	Items.	Appropriations.	General appropriations. 1919-1920.

H Fixed Charges and
Contributions—
H 6   Rent $5,075 00
H 7   Insurance 400 00
                        _____
      Total $5,475 00

I Rotáry Fund—
To pay when neces-
sary the federal
g o v e r n m e n t's
share of any esti-
mates due con-
tractors on road
i m p r o vements,
and to pay when
necessary the cost
of completing any
r o a d improve-
ment upon which
t h e contractor
s h a l l h a v e
defaulted subse-
quent ot July 1,
1919, or f r o m
which such con-
t r a c t o r s h a l l
h a v e been re-
m o v e d subse-
quent to July 1,
1919 .... $200,000 00
To pay the cost of
completing all im-
provements upon
which contractors
shall h a v e de-
faulted prior to
May 1, 1919, or
from which con-
tractors have been
removed prior to
May 1, 1919, re-
g a r d l e s s of
whether such im-
provements shall
be completed by
m e a n s of new
contracts or by
the highway de-
partment by force
account 306,000 00

General
appropriations.
1919-1920.

Items.   Appropriations.

Provided, however,
that all monies
which may be col-
lected from such
defaulting c o n-
tractors or from
the sureties of the
same shall not be
credited to any
rotary fund of
the highway de-
p a r t m e n t but
shall be credited
to the highway
i m p r o v e m e n t
fund.

The appropriations
herein made to
the rotary funds
of t h e highway
d e p a rtment are
hereby made from
monies provided
by sections 6924
et seq G. C., sec-
tion 1221 G. C. to
the contrary not-
withstanding.

Total maintenance........ 2,806,150 00

Total $2,918,120 00

INDUSTRIAL COMMISSION OF OHIO.

EXECUTIVE.

Personal Service—
  A 1 Salaries—
    3 Commissioners $14,000 00
      Secretary 3,000 00
      Assistant secretary...   2,000 00
      Grade I bookkeeper..   2,200 00
    2 Grade III bookkeepers   2,760 00
    2 Grade I clerks.......   3,240 00
      Grade II clerk.......   1,200 00
    2 Grade III clerks.....   1,860 00
    2 Grade IV clerks......   1,320 00
      Librarian 900 00
      Telephone operator...   660 00
    5 Grade II s t e n o g-
        raphers 5,880 00

	Items.	Appropriations.	General appropriations 1919 1920.

5 Grade III stenog-
raphers 4,380 00
5 Grade II examiners
c o m p e n s ation
claims 9,000 00
Grade II examiner
c o m p e n s ation
claims 1,200 00

WORKMEN'S COMPENSATION.

	Auditor	$2,400 00
27	Payroll auditors.....	36,450 00
	Actuary	4,000 00
	Assistant actuary....	2,400 00
	Codifier	1,140 00
	Rating actuary......	2,200 00
3	Grade IV statisticians	3,000 00
	Director of claims...	2,400 00
	Deputy director ·of claims	2,000 00
3	Reviewers of claims..	5,600 00
14	Claim examiners.....	17,100 00
3	Claims referees......	6,600 00
7	Claims investigators..	9,750 00
	Chief medical exam- iner	3,500 00
4	Assistant medical ex- aminers	10,000 00
3	Special medical exam- iners	7,500 00
2	Grade IV bookkeepers	1,800 00
3	Grade I clerks.......	4,680 00
27	Grade II clerks......	32,220 00
40	Grade II clerks......	34,440 00
4	Grade IV clerks.....	2,910 00
10	Grade II stenog- raphers	11,160 00
23	Grade III stenog- raphers	19,800 00
6	Grade I typists......	5,760 00
23	Grade II typists.....	19,680 00
2	Claim sheet clerks...	1,860 00
	Branch office deputy.	1,800 00
	Claim investigator...	1,200 00

STATISTICS.

	Chief statistician....	$3,000 00
	Assistant statistician.	1,800 00
	Statistical clerk......	1,500 00
4	Special investigators.	5,100 00

25—G. & L. A.

		Items.
4	Grade III clerks.....	3,600 00
	Grade II stenog-rapher	1,080 00
4	Grade III stenog-raphers	3,660 00
	Salaries free employ-ment agencies...	40,000 00

WORKSHOPS AND FACTORIES.

	Chief deputy........	$3,000 00
	Assistant chief deputy	2,500 00
	Deputy	2,000 00
	Director of safety....	3,000 00
6	Deputy safety direc-tors	12,000 00
2	Inspectors power and hydraulic piping.	3,600 00
22	District inspectors...	33,000 00
8	Lady visitors........	9,600 00
	High explosive in-spector	1,800 00
	Grade I clerk.......	1,800 00
	Grade III clerk......	900 00
	Grade II stenographer	1,080 00
4	Grade III stenog-raphers	3,480 00

MINING DEPARTMENT.

	Chief deputy........	$3,000 00
12	District deputies.....	21,600 00
	Caretaker mine res-cue car.........	1,200 00
	Grade I clerk.......	1,560 00
2	Grade I typists......	1,980 00
	Grade II typist......	900 00
	Grade II stenog-rapher	900 00

EXAMINER OF STEAM ENGINEERS.

	Chief deputy........	$3,000 00
	Assistant deputy.....	2,000 00
10	District deputies.....	17,000 00
	Grade II clerk......	1,700 00
	Grade III clerk......	1,200 00

BOILER INSPECTION.

	Chief deputy........	$3,000 00
	Assistant chief deputy	2,300 00

	Items.	Appropriations.	General appropriations, 1919-1920.
8 District deputies.....	16,000 00		
Grade IV bookkeepers	1,200 00		
Grade I clerk.......	1,800 00		
Grade III stenographer	900 00		
Grade I typist.......	1,200 00		
2 Grade II typists.....	2,040 00		

FILM CENSORSHIP.

	Items.		
3 Members of board....	$6,000 00		
2 Operators	2,400 00		
Grade II clerk......:	1,200 00		
2 Grade III clerks.....	1,740 00		
4 Grade III stenographers	3,480 00		
Total	$543,750 00		
A 2 Wages	750 00		
A 3 Unclassified—			
Local and special medical examinations	$2,000 00		
Witness fees........	600 00		
Miscellaneous	500 00		
Total	$3,100 00		
Total personal service........		$547,600 00	

Maintenance—
C Supplies—

	Items.		
C 1 Food	$100 00		
C 3 Fuel	100 00		
C 4 Office	37,000 00		
C 5 Medical	25 00		
C 11 General Plant—			
Leaders	2,000 00		
Other ....:.....	1,000 00		
Total	$40,225 00		

E Equipment—

	Items.		
E 1 Office	$5,000 00		
E 3 Surgical	100 00		
E 9 General plant..	2,500 00		
Total	$7,600 00		

F Contract and Open Order Service—

	Items.		
F 1 Repairs	$1,800 00		

		Items.	Appropriations.
F 4	Light, heat and power	900 00	
F 5	Freight, express and drayage.....	1,000 00	
F 6	Traveling expense	74,000 00	
F 7	Communication.	3,700 00	
F 9	General plant..	5,000 00	
	Total	$86,400 00	

II Fixed Charges and Contributions—

H 6	Rent	$38,792 00	
II 7	Insurance	300 00	
	Total	$39,092 00	
	Total maintenance..........		173,317 00
	Total		$720,917 00

DEPARTMENT OF PUBLIC INSTRUCTION.

Personal Service—
A 1 Salaries—

Superintendent	$4,000 00	
Assistant superintendent	2,500 00	
Examination clerk...	1,800 00	
Chief clerk..........	2,000 00	
Statistician	2,200 00	
2 High school inspectors	4,000 00	
6 Half time high school inspectors	6,000 00	
Grade IV clerk......	1,000 00	
2 Grade II stenographers	2,400 00	
3 Grade III stenographers	2,700 00	
Inspector of teacher training	2,500 00	
Total	$31,100 00	

A 2 Wages—

Per diem state board school examiners.	$1,000 00	
Extra stenographic work	200 00	
Total	$1,200 00	
Total personal service........		$32,300 00

	Items.	Appropriations.	General appropriations. 1919-1920.

Maintenance—
C Supplies—
    C 4   Office $2,400 00

E Equipment—
    E 1   Office $200 00

F Contract and Open Order Service—
    F 1   Repairs $20 00
    F 6   T r a v e ling ex-
        pense 8,000 00
    F 7   Communication.   350 00
    F 9   General plant..   200 00

        Total $8,570 00

H F i x e d Charges a n d Contributions—
    H 8   Contributions—
    State c o n tribution
        toward salaries of
        county superin-
        tendents $88,000 00
    State c o n tribution
        toward salaries of
        district s u perin-
        tendents 200,000 00
    State c o ntribution
        to districts with
        county n o r m a l
        schools 50,000 00
    Model rural schools   6,000 00

        Total $344,000 00
        Total maintenance.......... $355,170 00

        Total $387,470 00

SUPERINTENDENT OF INSURANCE.

Personal Service—
    A 1   Salaries—
    Superintendent $4,500 00
    Deputy s u perintend-
        ent 3,000 00
    Grade II clerk.......   1,980 00
    Grade III statistician.   1,680 00
    Secretary 1,560 00
    Bookkeeper 2,100 00
    Assistant bookkeeper.   1,140 00
    Warden 2,400 00
    Chief examiner......   3,000 00

		Items.	Appropriations.
5	Examiners	9,600 00	
5	Assistant examiners..	7,860 00	
	Chief actuary.......	4,000 00	
	1st assistant actuary.	1,800 00	
3	Assistant actuaries...	4,020 00	
2	Grade II clerks......	2,280 00	
2	License clerks.......	3,360 00	
	Rating clerk........	3,000 00	
	Grade II stenographer	1,140 00	
	Grade III stenog-		
	Grade IV clerk......	600 00	
	Total	$59,920 00	

A 2 Wages—
6 Extra clerks...... $1,350 00

Total personal service........ $61,270 00

Maintenance—
C Supplies—
C 4 Office $2,200 00

E Equipment—
E 1 Office $300 00

F Contract and Open Order Service—

F 1	Repairs	$25 00	
F 5	Freight, express and drayage.....	50 00	
F 6	Traveling expense	11,000 00	
F 7	Communication.	370 00	
F 9	General plant..	100 00	
	Total	$11,545 00	

H Fixed Charges and Contributions—

H 6	Rent	$2,980 00	
H 8	Contributions .	252 00	
	Total	$3,232 00	
	Total maintenance...........		$17,277 00

Total $78,547 00

THE JUDICIARY.

	Items.	Appropriations.
Personal Service—		
A 1 Salaries—		
127 Judges common pleas	$381,000 00	
24 Judges court of appeals	144,000 00	
6 Justices supreme court	39,000 00	
Chief justice supreme court	7,000 00	
3 Judges superior court	9,000 00	
8 Stenographers	14,400 00	
Total personal service........		$594,400 00
Maintenance—		
F Contract and Open Order Service—		
F 6 Traveling expense	$13,800 00	
Chief justice supreme court	200 00	
Total	$14,000 00	
Total maintenance..........		$14,000 00
Total		$608,400 00

LEGISLATIVE REFERENCE DEPARTMENT.

	Items.	Appropriations.
Personal Service—		
A 1 Salaries—		
Assistant director....	$1,800 00	
Librarian	1,020 00	
Secretary	1,140 00	
Research assistant....	720 00	
Total personal service........		$4,680 00
Maintenance—		
C Supplies—		
C 4 Office	$100 00	
C 11 General plant.	100 00	
Total	$200 00	
E Equipment—		
E 1 Office	$100 00	
E 9 General plant..	250 00	
Total	$350 00	

General
appropriations.
1919-1920.

		Items.	Appropriations.
F Contract and Open Order Service—			
F 1	Repairs	$10 00	
F 7	Communication.	135 00	
F 9	General plant..	50 00	
	Total	$195 00	
	Total maintenance..........		745 00
	Total		$5,425 00

STATE LIBRARY.

Personal Service—
A 1 Salaries—

		Items.	Appropriations.
	Librarian	$3,000 00	
	Assistant librarian...	1,500 00	
	Assistant secretary...	900 00	
	Document librarian..	1,100 00	
8 Assistants		7,380 00	
	Stenographer	720 00	
	Messenger	900 00	
	Total	$15,500 00	

A 2 Wages—

	Laborer	$400 00	
	Total personal service........		$15,900 00

Maintenance—
C Supplies—

C 4	Office	$550 00	
C 11	General plant.	50 00	
	Total	$600 00	

E Equipment—

E 1	Office	$200 00	
E 9	General plant..	3,500 00	
	Total	$3,700 00	

F Contract and Open Order Service—

F 1	Repairs	$200 00	
F 6	Traveling expense	400 00	
F 7	Communication.	225 00	
F 9	General plant..	200 00	
	Total	$1,025 00	
	Total maintenance..........		$5,325 00
	Total		$21,225 00

LIBRARY ORGANIZATION.

General appropriations. 1919-1920.

	Items.	Appropriations.
Personal Service—		
A 1 Salaries—		
Library organizer....	$1,500 00	
Office assistant	720 00	
Total personal service........		$2,220 00
Maintenance—		
C Supplies—		
C 4 Office	$300 00	
F Contract and Open Order Servcie—		
F 6 Traveling expense	700 00	
F 7 Communication.	95 00	
Total	$795 00	
Total maintenance		$1,095 00
Total		$3,315 00

TRAVELING LIBRARY.

	Items.	Appropriations.
Personal Service—		
A 1 Salaries—		
Superintendent	$1,200 00	
4 Assistants	3,600 00	
Stenographer	840 00	
Janitor	780 00	
Total personal service........		$6,420 00
Maintenance—		
C Supplies—		
C 4 Office	$350 00	
E Equipment—		
E 1 Office	150 00	
E 9 General plant..	1,500 00	
Total	$1,650 00	
F Contract and Open Order Service—		
F 1 Repairs	$25 00	
F 4 Light, heat and power	80 00	
F 5 Freight, express and drayage.....	175 00	
F 7 Communication.	100 00	
F 9 General plant..	50 00	
Total	$430 00	

	Items.	Appropriations.
H Fixed Charges and Contributions—		
H 6 Rent	$2,062 44	
Total maintenance		4,492 44
Total		$10,912 44

STATE MEDICAL BOARD.

Personal Service—
  A 1 Salaries—

	Items.	Appropriations.
Secretary	$3,000 00	
Entrance examiner...	450 00	
Clerk-stenographer ..	1,200 00	
Grade II stenographer	1,200 00	
Inspector	1,200 00	
Total	$7,050 00	

A 2 Wages—

	Items.	Appropriations.
Per diem board members	$2,250 00	
Osteopathic examining committee...	200 00	
Special examiners....	200 00	
Total	$2,650 00	

	Items.	Appropriations.
A 3 Unclassified	1,200 00	
Total personal service........		$10,900 00

Maintenance—
  C Supplies—

	Items.	Appropriations.
C 4 Office	$700 00	
C 6 Cleaning	35 00	
Total	$735 00	

E Equipment—

	Items.	Appropriations.
E 1 Office	$155 50	
E 9 General plant..	10 00	
Total	$165 50	

F Contract and Open Order Service—

	Items.	Appropriations.
F 1 Repairs	$50 00	
F 5 Freight, express and drayage.....	20 00	
F 6 Traveling expense	2,600 00	

		Items.	Appropriations.	General appropriations, 1919-1920.
F 7	Communication.	110 00		
F 9	General plant..	160 00		
	Total	$2,940 00		
H	Fixed Charges and Contributions—			
H 6	Rent	$92 00		
H 7	Insurance	12 50		
H 8	Contributions..	25 00		
	Total	$129 50		
	Total maintenance.............		3,970 00	
	Total	$14,870 00		

NURSE REGISTRATION.

		Items.	Appropriations.	General appropriations, 1919-1920.
Personal Service—				
A 1	Salaries—			
	Secretary	$1,200 00		
	Entrance examiner...	850 00		
	Chief examiner......	2,000 00		
	Grade III stenographer	900 00		
	Total	$4,950 00		
A 2	Wages—			
	Per diem nurses' examination committee	1,900 00		
A 3	Unclassified—			
	Engrossing certificates	100 00		
	Reading entrance examination papers	50 00		
	Witness fees and mileage	35 00		
	Other	80 00		
	Total	$265 00		
	Total personal service........		$7,115 00	
Maintenance—				
C Supplies—				
C 4	Office	$375 00		
C 6	Cleaning	17 50		
	Total	$392 50		

	Items.	Appropriations.
E Equipment—		
E 1 Office	$18 00	
F Contract and Open Order Service—		
F 1 Repairs	$5 00	
F 5 Freight, express and drayage.....	5 00	
F 6 Traveling expense	800 00	
F 7 Commuincation.	80 00	
F 9 General plant..	113 00	
Total	$1,003 00	
H Fixed Charges and Contributions—		
H 6 Rent	$100 00	
Total maintenace...........		$1,513 50
Total		$8,628 50

MISCELLANEOUS BUDGET.

CONTROLLING BOARD.

Maintenance—
  F Contract and Open Order Service—
    F 8 Contingencies $12,000 00

EMERGENCY BOARD.

Maintenance—
  F Contract and Open Order Service—
    F 8 Contingencies—Uses and purposes $250,000 00
    To be used only in case the Ohio national guard is called into active service in connection with floods, fires and riots.....   150,000 00
    To be available for food and fuel only 150,000 00

IRREDUCIBLE DEBT.

Maintenance—
  H Fixed Charges and Contributions—
    H 8 Contributions $262,000 00

COMMON SCHOOLS.

Maintenance—
  H Fixed Charges and Contributions—
    H 8 Contributions $2,735,000 00

STATE AID TO WEAK SCHOOLS.

Items. Appropriations.

Maintenance—
H Fixed Charges and Contributions—
  H 8 Contributions $600,000 00

SCHOOLS FOR DEAF, BLIND AND CRIPPLED CHILDREN.

Maintenance—
H Fixed Charges and Contributions—
  H 8 Contributions $140,000 00

CITY OF COLUMBUS PAVING.

Maintenance—
H Fixed Charges and Contributions—
  H 8 Contributions—To pay for
state's share of paving—Third
street from Broad street to
State street — Parsons avenue
from Main street to Bryden
alley; Eleventh avenue side-
walks adjacent to state fair
grounds $18,000 00

OHIO BOARD OF ADMINISTRATION.

Maintenance—
H Fixed Charges and Contributions—
  H 8 Contributions—
    Improvement of road from pike
      to institution of Ohio
      state sanatorium, Mt.
      Vernon $20,000 00
    Provided, however, that the
      board of county commis-
      sioners of Knox county
      shall pay the cost of said
      road above said sum of
      $20,000.00.

MIAMI UNIVERSITY.

Maintenance—
H Fixed Charges and Contributions—
  H 8 Contributions—
    To pay for state's share of
      paving High street, Oxford $22,000 00
    To pay for state's share of pav-
      ing Patterson avenue, Ox-
      ford 8,000 00

HEADQUARTERS SPANISH-AMERICAN WAR VETERANS.

	Items.	Appropriations.

Maintenance—
  F Contract and Open Order Service—
    F 9 General plant.............. $1,500 00

LEGISLATIVE JOINT COMMITTEE.

Maintenance—
  F Contract and Open Order Service—
    F 9 General Plant—
      To carry out provisions of senate joint resolution 36.... $30,000 00

OHIO NATIONAL GUARD.

Personal Service—
  A 1 Salaries—

Superintendent state arsenal	$1,800 00	
Clerk state arsenal...	960 00	
Machinist state arsenal	1,200 00	
Stockkeeper state arsenal	1,200 00	
4 Laborers state arsenal	4,000 00	
Total	$9,160 00	

OHIO NATIONAL GUARD.

A 2 Wages—

Drill pay...........	$20,000 00
Camp pay..........	40,000 00
Total	$60,000 00

A 3 Unclassified—

Inspections and examinations	$12,000 00	
Other	15,000 00	
Total	$27,000 00	
Total personal service........		$96,160 00

Maintenance—

C Supplies and subsistence	$43,000 00
E Equipment and uniforms	14,500 00
F Contract and Open Order Service—	
F 5 Freight, express and drayage	5,000 00

	Items.	Appropriations.	General appropriations. 1919-1920.
F 6 Traveling expense	35,000 00		
F 9 General Plant—Incidental expense military companies	31,287 10		
Horse hire........	5,000 00		
Incidental camp expenses	10,000 00		
Expenses Camp Perry	10,000 00		
Promotion rifle practice	10,000 00		
Other	15,000 00		
Essex Ship Company	3,000 00		
Dorothea Ship Company	3,000 00		
Total	$127,287 10		
Total maintenance..........		$184,787 10	

ARMORY FUND.

	Items.	Appropriations.	
Personal Service— A 1 Salaries— Architect	$3,000 00		
Clerk state armories	1,200 00		
Total personal service........		$4,200 00	
Maintenance— F Contract and Open Order Service— F 9 General plant..	$20,000 00		
Maintenance of armories	14,800 00		
Total	$34,800 00		
H Fixed Charges and Contributions— H 6 Rent	$26,765 00		
Total maintenance..........		61,565 00	
Total		$346,712 10	

STATE INSPECTOR OF OILS.

	Items.	
Personal Service— A 1 Salaries— Inspector	$3,500 00	

General
appropriations,
1919-1920.

		Items.	Appropriations.
	Chief clerk..........	1,500 00	
42	Deputy inspectors...	48,000 00	
	Total personal service........		$53,000 00

Maintenance—
C Supplies—
  C 4 Office $200 00

E Equipment—
  E 1 Office $25 00
  E 9 General plant..   100 00

    Total $125 00

F Contract and Open Or-
    der Service—
  F 1 Repairs $25 00
  F 6 T r a v eling ex-
    pense 11,000 00
  F 7 Communication.   200 00
  F 9 General plant..   200 00

    Total $11,425 00

H Fixed C h a r g e s and
    Contributions—
  H 7 Insurance $200 00
    Total maintenance...........   11,950 00

    Total $64,950 00

STATE BOARD OF OPTOMETRY.

Personal Service—
A 1 Salaries—
  Secretary $500 00
  Clerk 840 00

    Total $1,340 00

A 2 Wages—
  Per diem 5 members
    of board......... $2,000 00
  Extra help..........   500 00

    Total $2,500 00
    Total personal service........ $3,840 00
Maintenance—
C Supplies—
  C 4 Office $250 00
  C 11 General plant.   25 00

    Total $275 00

E Equipment—
  E 1   Office $300 00
F Contract and Open Or-
       der Service—
  F 6   T r a v e l i n g   ex-
       pense $500 00
  F 7   Communication.   100 00
  F 9   General plant..   75 00

         Total $675 00

H Fixed C h a r g e s and
       Contributions—
  H 6   Rent $300 00

         Total maintenance...........   1,550 00

         Total $5,390 00

OHIO PENITENTIARY COMMISSION.

Maintenance—
F Contract and Open Order Service—
  F 9   General plant.............. $750 00

STATE BOARD OF PHARMACY.

Personal Service—
  A 1   Salaries—
       Secretary $2,000 00
       Stenographer 900 00
       Inspector 1,200 00
       Entrance examiner...   200 00

         Total $4,300 00

  A 2   Wages—
       Per diem 5 members
         of board........ $1,500 00
       Janitor 15 00

         Total $1,515 00
         Total personal service....... $5,815 00
Maintenance—
  C Supplies—
    C 4   Office $650 00

  E Equipment—
    E 1   Office 50 00

  F Contract and Open Or-
       der Service—
    ·F 1   Repairs $10 00

	Items.	Appropriations.
F 6 Traveling expense	2,500 00	
F 7 Communication.	125 00	
F 9 General plant..	25 00	
Total	$2,660 00	

H Fixed Charges and Contributions—
H 8 Contributions . $25 00

Total maintenance.......... 3,385 00

Total $9,200 00

COMMISSIONER OF PUBLIC PRINTING.

Personal Service—
A 1 Salaries—
Secretary $500 00

Total personal service........ $500 00

Maintenance—
D Materials—
D 3 General Plant—
Printing paper.. $100,000 00
Printing paper for experiment station 1,500 00

Total $101,500 00
Total maintenance.......... 101,500 00

Total $102,000 00

SUPERVISOR OF PUBLIC PRINTING.

Personal Service—
A 1 Salaries—
Supervisor $2,000 00
Secretary 900 00

Total personal service........ $2,900 00

Maintenance—
C Supplies—
C 4 Office $125 00

F Contract and Open Order Service—
F 7 Communication. 140 00

	Items.	Appropriations.	General appropriations, 1919-1920.
F 9 General plant— state printing....	95,000 00		
Total	$95,140 00		
Total maintenance..........		$95,265 00	
Total		$98,165 00	

STATE BINDERY.

Personal Service—
A 1 Salaries—

	Items.	Appropriations.
Superintendent	$1,900 00 .	
Stenographer and bookkeeper	960 00	
Forelady	762 00	
Bindery workers.....	6,882 00	
2 Rulers	2,580 00	
Stamper	1,290 00	
Job forwarder.......	1,290 00	
Machinist ....,	1,290 00	
Blank book forwarder	1,290 00	
Finisher	1,290 00	
Folding machine operator	1,200 00	
10 Edition forwarders...	12,060 00	
Messenger	1,090 00	
Elevator operator....	810 00	
Janitor	810 00	
Total personal service........		$35,504 00

Maintenance—
C Supplies—

	Items.	Appropriations.
C 4 Office	$75 00	
C 6 Cleaning	39 00	
C 11 General plant.	12,000 00	
Total	$12,114 00	

F Contract and Open Order Service—

	Items.	Appropriations.
F 1 Repairs	$350 00	
F 4 Light, heat and power	280 00	
F 5 Freight, express and drayage	135 00	
F 7 Communication.	135 00	
F 9 General plant..	400 00	
Total	$1,300 00	

		Items.	Appropriations.
H Fixed Charges and Contributions—			
H 6 Rent		$4,100 00	
Total maintenance...........			$17,514 00
Total			$53,018 00

PROSECUTION AND TRANSPORTATION OF CONVICTS.

Maintenance—
F   Contract and Open Or-
der Service—
F 9   General Plant—
Fees, costs, mileage
and other ex-
penses provided
by statute................... $170,000 00

HOUSE OF REPRESENTATIVES.

Personal Service—
A 1   Salaries—

Clerk	$3,000 00	
Deputy clerk........	1,800 00	
Clerk-stenographer ..	1,800 00	
Cust dian	1,800 00	
Porte.	900 00	
Total	$9,300 00	

A 3 · Unclassified—

Labor	$50 00	
Author legislative his-tory	3,900 00	
Total	$3,950 00	
Total personal service............		$13,250 00

Maintenance—
C   Supplies—

C 4 Office	$120 00	
C 6 Cleaning	200 00	
C 11 General Plant.	100 00	
Total	$420 00	

E   Equipment—

E 1 Office	$250 00	
E 9 General Plant—Carpet for house of representatives	1,500 00	

	Items.	Appropriations.	General appropriations. 1919-1920.
Other	500 00		
Total	$2,250 00		

F Contract and Open Or-
   der Service—

	Items.		
F 1 Repairs	$1,000 00		
F 5 Freight, express and drayage.....	50 00		
F 7 Communication.	180 00		
F 8 Contingencies .	500 00		
F 9 General Plant —Expense legislative committees.	3,000 00		
Total	$4,730 00		

H Fixed Charges and
   Contributions—

H 8 Contributions .	50 00		
Total maintenance...........		$7,450 00	
Total		$20,700 00	

SENATE.

Personal Service—
  A 1 Salaries—

	Items.	Appropriations.	
Lieutenant governor..	$1,500 00		
Clerk	3,000 00		
Assistant clerk......	1,800 00		
Recording clerk......	1,800 00		
Custodian	1,800 00		
Porter	900 00		
Stenographer	1,200 00		
Stenographer for lieutenant governor and senators....	1,200 00		
Total personal service........		$13,200 00	

Maintenance—
  C Supplies—

	Items.		
C 4 Office	$200 00		
C 6 Cleaning	100 00		
Total	$300 00		

E Equipment—

	Items.		
E 1 Office	$100 00		

	Items.	Appropriations.
F Contract and Open Order Service—		
F 1 Repairs	$2,500 00	
F 5 Freight, express and drayage	200 00	
F 7 Communication.	150 00	
F 8 Contingencies .	150 00	
F 9 General Plant—		
Expense legislative committees	2,500 00	
Expense joint committees	3,500 00	
Other	150 00	
Total	$9,150 00	
H Fixed Charges and Contributions—		
H 8 Contributions—		
Painting lieutenant governor's picture	$500 00	
Picture of members	100 00	
Total	$600 00	
Total maintenance...........		$10,150 00
Total		$23,350 00

SECRETARY OF STATE.

Personal Service—
A 1 Salaries—

Secretary of state....	$6,500 00
Assistant secretary of state	3,000 00
Corporation advisor..	2,200 00
Statistician	2,800 00
Superintendent of distribution	1,500 00
Stockman	1,500 00
Cashier	2,000 00
Grade III clerk......	1,500 00
Assistant recording clerk	1,500 00
Grade II clerk......	1,350 00
Special statistician...	2,000 00
Grade II stenographer	1,080 00
Grade III stenographer	1,080 00
2 Grade I typists......	2,160 00
Stenographer	1,200 00

	Items.	Appropriations.	General appropriations, 1919-1920.
Janitor and messenger	700 00		
Total personal service........		$31,570 00	

Maintenance—
 C Supplies—
   C 4   Office $1,500 00

 E Equipment—

	Items.		
E 1 Office	$175 00		
E 9 General plant..	200 00		
Total	$375 00		

 F Contract and Open Order Service—

	Items.		
F 1 Repairs	$50 00		
F 6 Traveling expense	35 00		
F 7 Communication.	600 00		
F 8 Contingencies— Absent voters' fund	$1,000 00		
F 9 General Plant— Distribution of books	3,000 00		
Printing and distributing constitutional amendments	30,000 00		
Total	$34,685 00		
Total maintenance..........		36,560 00	
Total		$68,130 00	

AUTOMOBILE DEPARTMENT.

Personal Service—
 A 1   Salaries—

	Items.		
Registrar	$3,000 00		
Grade I clerk........	1,980 00		
Cashier	1,980 00		
Grade I clerk........	1,800 00		
3 Grade II lcerks......	3,420 00		
3 Grade III clerks.....	2,580 00		
2 Grade II stenographers	2,160 00		
4 Grade II typists.....	3,600 00		
Grade II typist......	840 00		
2 Inspectors	2,400 00		
Janitor and messenger	900 00		
Total	$24,660 00		

	Items.	Appropriations.

A 2 Wages—
  10 Extra clerks and ste-
     nographers $4,200 00
   3 Extra clerks and ste-
     nographers 1,800 00

        Total $6,000 00
        Total personal service........ $30,660 00

Maintenance— . .
  C Supplies—
      C 4   Office $33,500 00
      C 11   General Plant—
             Automobile a n d
               motorcycle tags 90,000 00

        Total $123,500 00

  D Materials—
      D 3 General Plant—
           Print paper..... $3,000 00

  F Contract and Open Or-
      der Service—
      F 6   T r a v eling ex-
             pense .... ·1,800 00
      F 7   Communication. 250 00
      F 9   General plant.. 14,000 00

        Total $16,050 00
        Total maintenance.......... 142,550 00

        Total $173,210 00

STATE PURCHASING AGENT.

Personal Service—
  A 1 Salaries—
      Purchasing agent.... $3,000 00
      Grade II clerk...... 1,140 00
      G r a d e III stenog-
        rapher 960 00
      Bookkeeper-typist ... 840 00
      Grade III clerk...... 900 00
      Clerk 1,200 00

        Total personal service........ $8,040 00

Maintenance—
  C Supplies—
      C 4 Office $350 00

  E Equipment—
      E 1 Office $200 00

	Items.	Appropriations.	General appropriations. 1919-1920.
F Contract and Open Order Service—			
F 1 Repairs	$100 00		
F 7 Communication.	200 00		
F 9 General plant.	1,000 00		
Total	$1,300 00		
Total maintenance..........		1,850 00	
Total		$9,890 00	

BUREAU OF VITAL STATISTICS.

	Items.	Appropriations.
Personal Service—		
A 1 Salaries—		
Registrar	$2,000 00	
Grade II clerk.......	1,500 00	
Chief inspector......	1,500 00	
Statistician	1,500 00	
Grade III clerk......	1,200 00	
12 Grade III clerks.....	10,800 00	
Grade II stenographer	1,080 00	
4 Grade III stenographers	3,600 00	
2 Grade I typists......	2,040 00	
Total personal service........		$25,220 00
Maintenance—		
C Supplies—		
C 4 Office	$3,000 00	
E Equipment—		
E 1 Office	$300 00	
F Contract and Open Order Service—		
F 5 Freight, express and drayage	100 00	
F 6 Traveling expense	1,100 00	
F 7 Communication.	250 00	
F 9 General plant..	50 00	
Total	$1,500 00	
H Fixed Charges and Contributions—		
H 6 Rent	$240 00	
Total maintenance..........		$5,040 00
Total		$30,260 00

SECURITIES DEPARTMENT.

	Items.	Appropriations.
Personal Service—		
A 1 Salaries—		
Commissioner	$4,000 00	
Deputy commissioner.	3,000 00	
Stenographer	1,320 00	
2 Grade III stenog-		
raphers	1,800 00	
Grade III clerk......	900 00	
Grade III bookkeeper.	1,800 00	
Chief examiner......	2,750 00	
7 Examiners	14,000 00	
Accountant	2,000 00	
Chief examiner chat-		
tel loan.........	2,500 00	
Examiner	2,000 00	
Examiner	1,600 00	
2 Assistant examiners..	3,000 00	
Grade III stenog-		
rapher	900 00	
Total	$41,570 00	
A 2 Wages—		
Extra help..........	$125 00	
A 3 Unclassified	100 00	
Total personal service........		$41,795 00
Maintenance—		
C Supplies—		
C 4 Office	$900 00	
E Equipment—		
E 1 Office	75 00	
E 9 General plant..	25 00	
Total	$100 00	
F Contract and Open Or-		
der Service—		
F 1 Repairs	$20 00	
F 6 Traveling		
expense	11,500 00	
F 7 Communication.	500 00	
F 9 General plant..	100 00	
Total	$12,120 00	
H Fixed Charges and		
Contributions—		
H 6 Rent	$1,620 00	

		Items.	Appropriations.	General appropriations. 1919-1920.
H 7	Insurance	225 00		
H 8	Contributions .	200 00		

Total	$2,045 00		
Total maintenance..........		$15,165 00	

Total		$56,960 00

COMMISSIONER OF SOLDIERS' CLAIMS.

Personal Service—
  A 1 Salaries—

Commissioner	$2,500 00	
Chief clerk..........	1,140 00	
Notarial clerk......	420 00	

Total personal service........	$4,060 00

Maintenance—
  C Supplies—
    C 4 Office $125 00

F Contract and Open Or-
    der Service—
    F 7 Communication.   40 00

Total maintenance..........	165 00

Total	$4,225 00

OHIO SOLDIERS' AND SAILORS' ORPHANS' HOME

Personal Service—
  A 1 Salaries—

Superintendent	$2,100 00	
Chief matron........	720 00	
Bookkeeper	780 00	
Storekeeper	900 00	
Assistant storekeeper.	900 00	
Physician	1,500 00	
Dentist	540 00	
Superintendent of schools.......	1,500 00	
36 Matrons	18,960 00	
28 Teachers	13,690 00	
Minor officers and employees	48,630 00	

Total	$89,620 00

A 2	Wages	2,800 00
A 3	Unclassified	500 00

Total personal service.......	$92,920 00

				Items.	Appropriations.

Maintenance—

C Supplies—

C	1	Food	$75,000	00
C	2	Forage	4,000	00
C	3	Fuel	18,500	00
C	4	Office	350	00
C	5	Medical	500	00
C	6	Cleaning	3,000	00
C	8	Educational	675	00
C	9	Agricultural	550	00
C	11	General plant.	2,100	00
		Total	$104,675	00

D Materials—

D	2	Buliding	$2,000	00
D	3	General plant..	21,000	00
		Total	$23,000	00

E Equipment—

E	1	Office	$100	00
E	2	Household	5,000	00
E	3	Medical	250	00
E	4	Livestock	200	00
E	5	Agricultural	300	00
E	6	Motor vehicle..	250	00
E	7	Wearing apparel	2,000	00
E	8	Educational	1,000	00
E	9	General plant..	2,000	00
		Total	$12,100	00

F Contract and Open Order Service—

F	1	Repairs	$9,500	00
F	5	Freight, express and drayage	500	00
F	6	Traveling expense	2,000	00
F	7	Communication.	275	00
F	9	General plant..	1,300	00
		Total	$13,575	00

H Fixed Charges and Contributions—

| H | 6 | Rent | $415 | 00 |
| H | 7 | Insurance | 112 | 50 |

		Items.	Appropriations.	General appropriations. 1919-1920.
H 8	Contributions— P r e s e n t s to dis- charged pupils...	2,000 00		
	Total	$2,527 50		
I	Rotary fund..........	$400 00		
	Total maintenance...........		$156,277 50	
	Total		$249,197 50	

SUPREME COURT AND LAW LIBRARY.

		Items.	Appropriations.
Personal Service—			
A 1	Salaries—		
	M a r s h a l and law librarian	$2,500 00	
	A s s i s tant librarian and chief clerk..	2,000 00	
2	Assistant librarians..	2,700 00	
	1st deputy marshal..	1,500 00	
	.2nd deputy marshal..	1,200 00	
	3rd deputy marshal..	1,200 00	
	Secretary	1,500 00	
3	Secretaries	5,140 00	
3	Porters	3,060 00	
	Total	$20,800 00	
A 2	Wages	130 00	
	Total personal service........		$20,930 00
Maintenance—			
C	Supplies—		
C 4	Office	$506 00	
C 6	Cleaning	85 00	
C 11	General plant.	100 00	
	Total	$691 00	
D	Materials—		
D 3	General plant..	$76 00	
E	Equipment—		
E 1	Office	$265 00	
E 8	Educational— Books and legal pe- riodicals	2,900 00	
E 9	General plant..	50 00	
	Total	$3,215 00	

		Items.	Appropriations.
F	Contract and Open Order Service—		
F 1	Repairs	$100 00	
F 5	Freight, express and drayage	90 00	
F 6	Traveling expense	50 00	
F 7	Communication.	1,150 00	
F 8	Contingencies ·..	75 00	
F 9	General plant..	196 00	
	Total	$1,661 00	
H	Fixed Charges and Contributions—		
H 6	Rent	$20 00	
	Total maintenance...........		5,663 00
	Total .....•...............		$26,593 00

CLERK SUPREME COURT.

Personal Service—			
A 1	Salaries—		
	Clerk	$4,000 00	
	1st deputy clerk.....	2,100 00	
	2nd deputy clerk....	1,800 00	
	Correspondence clerk.	1,500 00	
	Messenger	900 00	
	Total personal service........		$10,300 00
Maintenance—			
C	Supplies—		
C 4	Office	$400 00	
E	Equipment—		
E 1	Office	$192 10	
F	Contract and Open Order Service—		
F 1	Repairs	$10 00	
F 5	Freight, express and drayage.....	3 00	
F 7	Communication.	144 00	
F 9	General plant..	15 00	
	Total	$172 00	
	Total maintenance...........		764 10
	Total ....·....		$11,064 10

SUPREME COURT REPORTER.

	Items.	Appropriations.
Personal Service—		
A 1 Salaries—		
Reporter	$3,000 00	
2 Assistant reporters...	4,000 00	
Clerk	1,600 00	
Total personal service........		$8,600 00
Maintenance—		
C Supplies—		
C 4 Office	$110 00	
E Equipment—		
E 1 Office	$100 00	
F Contract and Open Or-		
Service—		
F 7 Communication.	$90 00	
F 8 Contingencies ..	75 00	
F 9 General plant..	50 00	
Total	$215 00	
Total maintenance..........		425 00
Total ....:......		$9,025 00

TAX COMMISSION OF OHIO.

	Items.	
Personal Service—		
A 1 Salaries—		
3 Commissioners	$12,000 00	
Secretary	3,000 00	
Auditor	3,600 00	
Special accountant...	3,000 00	
Corporation ac-		
countant	2,700 00	
2 Special examiners....	4,800 00	
2 Grande II accountants	4,400 00	
Grade II accountant..	1,800 00	
Junior accountant...	1,200 00	
Grade III stenog-		
rapher	1,080 00	
3 Grade II stenog-		
raphers	3,480 00	
Grade III stenog-		
rapher	840 00	
Stenographer	1,200 00	
Grade II typist......	1,200 00	
Total	$44,300 00	

	Items.	Appropriations.
A 2 Wages—		
Extra stenographic work	250 00	
A 3 Unclassified	500 00	
Total personal service		$45,050 00

Maintenance—
  C Supplies—

C 4 Office	$2,000 00	

E Equipment—

E 1 Office	$200 00	

F Contract and Open Order Service—

F 1 Repairs	$30 00	
F 6 Traveling expense	3,500 00	
F 7 Communication.	500 00	
F 9 General plant..	500 00	
Total	$4,530 00	
Total maintenance		6,730 00
Total		$51,780 00

TREASURER OF STATE.

Personal Service—
  A 1 Salaries—

Treasurer	$6,500 00	
Cashier	3,400 00	
Chief clerk	2,400 00	
Grade I bookkeeper..	2,100 00	
Grade II bookkeeper.	1,740 00	
Bookkeeper	1,800 00	
Bond clerk	2,100 00	
Correspondence clerk.	1,200 00	
3 Grade II clerks	4,860 00	
2 Grade III clerks	1,800 00	
Janitor and messenger	960 00	
Total personal service		$28,860 00

Maintenance—
  C Supplies—

C 4 Office	$4,000 00	

E Equipment—

E 1 Office	$625 00	

		Items.	Appropriations.	General appropriations. 1919-1920.
F	Contract and Open Order Service—			
F 7	Communication.	$300 00		
F 9	General plant..	150 00		
	Total	$450 00		
H	Fixed Charges and Contributions—			
H 7	Insurance—			
	Premium on treasurer's bond	1,800 00		
	Premium on cashier's bond...	300 00		
	Total	$2,100 00		
	Total maintenance..........		7,175 00	
	Total		$36,035 00	

PUBLIC UTILITIES COMMISSION.

	Items.	
Personal Service—		
A 1 Salaries—		
3 Commissioners	$13,500 00	
Engine and boiler inspector	2,000 00	
Inspector automatic couplers	1,750 00	
Secretary	3,000 00	
Assistant secretary...	2,400 00	
Attorney	4,000 00	
Superintendent bureau of rates and service	4,000 00	
Auditor and statistician	3,000 00	
Inspector in charge..	1,750 00	
5 Inspectors	8,750 00	
Grade I engineer....	4,500 00	
2 Grade II engineers...	6,000 00	
2 Grade III engineers..	4,320 00	
2 Grade I clerks.......	3,480 00	
2 Grade II clerks.....	2,520 00	
4 Grade II stenographers	4,800 00	
Grade I telephone operator	720 00	
Grade I typist.......	1,400 00	
Total	$71,890 00	

	Items.	Appropriations.

A 3 Unclassified—
  Investigation issues of
    securities $2,500 00
  Reporting hearings
    and transcribing
    testimony 3,300 00

  Total $5,800 00

  Total personal service....... $77,690 00

Maintenance—
  C Supplies—
    C 4 Office $1,200 00

  E Equipment—
    E 1 Office $1,000 00

  F Contract and Open Or-
      der Service—
    F 1 Repairs $50 00
    F 5 Freight, express
        and drayage..... 100 0C
    F 6 Traveling
        expense 10,000 C0
    F 7 Communication. 1,600 00
    F 9 General plant.. 150 00

    Total $11,900 00

  H Fixed Charges and
      Contributions—
    H 7 Insurance 60 00

    Total maintenance.......... 14,160 00

    Total $91,850 00

PHYSICAL VALUATION—PUBLIC UTILITIES.

Personal Service—
  A 1 Salaries—
    2 Grade III engineers.. $3,840 00
    18 Grade IV engineers.. 32,460 00
    10 Grade II clerks...... 14,410 00
    Grade II stenog-
      rapher 1,080 00

    Total $51,790 00

  A 3 Unclassified—
    Additional help $2,000 00

    Total personal service........ $53,790 00

	Items.	Appropriations.	General appropriations. 1919-1920.
Maintenance—			
C Supplies—			
C 4 Office	$150 00		
C 11 General plant..	25 00		
Total	$175 00		
E Equipment—			
E 1 Office	$200 00		
E 9 General plant..	100 00		
Total	$300 00		
F Contract and Open Order Service—			
F 1 Repairs	$25 00		
F 5 Freight, express and drayage	25 00		
F 6 Traveling expense	12,000 00		
F 7 Communication.	200 00		
F 9 General plant..	50 00		
Total	$12,300 00		
H Fixed Charges and Contributions—			
H 6 Rent	$200 00		
Total maintenance..........		12,975 00	
Total		$66,765 00	

DEPARTMENT OF PUBLIC WORKS.

	Items.		
Personal Service—			
A 1 Salaries—			
Superintendent	$4,000 00		
Assistant superintendent	2,500 00		
Secretary	2,000 00		
Grade IV engineer...	2,400 00		
Grade IV engineer...	1,800 00		
Grade IV engineer...	1,620 00		
Grade V engineer....	1,500 00		
Clerk-stenographer ..	1,200 00		
2 Grade III stenographers	1,920 00		
Grade IV clerk......	840 00		
8 Foremen	9,660 00		
39 Patrolmen	11,430 00		

General
appropriations.
1919-1920.

		Items.	Appropriations.
4 Policemen		3,420 00	
Total		$44,290 00	
A 2 Wages		30,000 00	
Total personal service........			$74,290 00

Maintenance—
C Supplies—

C 3 Fuel	$1,800 00
C 4 Office	600 00
C 11 General plant.	1,000 00
Total	$3,400 00

D Materials—

| D 3 General plant.. | $2,500 00 |

E Equipment—

E 1 Office	$100 00
E 9 General plant..	500 00
Total	$600 00

F Contract and Open Order Service—

F 1 Repairs	75 00
F 4 Light, heat and power	60 00
F 5 Freight, express and drayage	500 00
F 6 Traveling expense	3,500 00
F 7 Communication.	800 00
F 9 General plant..	600 00
Total	$5,535 00

| Total maintenance.......... | 12,035 00 |
| Total .... | $86,325 00 |

BOWLING GREEN STATE NORMAL SCHOOL.

Personal Service—
A 1 Salaries—

President	$4,300 00
Dean	2,750 00
Dean of women — 12 months	1,600 00
Financial clerk......	1,500 00
Clerk	1,000 00
Stenographer	720 00
2 Janitors	1,680 00
Janitress ....,.....	500 00

	Items.	Appropriations.	General appropriations. 1919-1920.
Superintendent of buildings and grounds	900 00		
Chief engineer......	1,080 00		
2 Firemen	1,800 00		
Night watchman.....	780 00		
2 Librarians	1,600 00		
2 Extension lecturers..	4,000 00		
High school inspector.	1,000 00		
Professors, instructors and other employes	49,250 00		
Total	$74,460 00		

A 2 Wages—

	Items.		
Extra labor.........	$1,400 00		
Extra clerk hire.....	500 00		
Student assistants....	1,152 00		
Critic teacher part time	1,500 00		
Summer school......	10,500 00		
Total	$15,052 00		
A 3 Unclassified	140 00		
Total personal service........		$89,652 00	

Maintenance—

C Supplies—

			Items.		
	1	Food	$150 00		
	3	Fuel	8,000 00		
	4	Office	600 00		
	6	Cleaning	150 00		
	8	Educational ..	1,600 00		
C	9	Agricultural .	300 00		
C	11	General plant.	1,200 00		
		Total	$12,000 00		

D Materials—

		Items.		
D 3	General plant..	$600 00		

E Equipment—

		Items.		
E 1	Office	$200 00		
E 8	Educational ...	1,000 00		
E 9	General plant..	566 00		
	Total	$1,766 00		

F Contract and Open Order Service—

		Items.		
F 1	Repairs	$600 00		

		Items.	Appropriations.
F 3	Water	600 00	
F 4	Light, heat and power	800 00	
F 5	Freight, express and drayage	300 00	
F 6	Traveling expense	1,700 00	
F 7	Communication.	150 00	
F 9	General plant..	1,500 00	
	Total	$5,650 00	
	Total maintenance...........		20,016 00
	Total		$109,668 00

KENT STATE NORMAL SCHOOL.

Personal Service—

A 1 Salaries—

	Items.
President	$4,500 00
Assistant to president —12 months....	1,800 00
Dean of women—12 months	1,600 00
2 Extension teachers...	4,000 00
Professor of Agriculture	2,500 00
High school inspector.	1,000 00
2 Assistant librarians..	1,600 00
Clerk	1,050 00
Financial clerk......	1,500 00
Custodian	1,200 00
Engineer	1,080 00
2 Firemen	1,860 00
Night watchman.....	780 00
Superintendent of grounds	780 00
Mechanician	960 00
Teamster	720 00
3 Janitors	2,340 00
Professors, instructors and other employes	59,850 00
Total	$89,120 00

A 2 Wages—

Student assistants....	$1,152 00
Labor	900 00
Summer school.......	16,000 00
Total	$18,052 00

			Items.	Appropriations.	General appropriations, 1919-1920.
A 3	Unclassified		140 00		
	Total personal service........			$107,312 00	

Maintenance—
C Supplies—

			Items.		
C	1	Food	$200 00		
C	3	Fuel	11,600 00		
C	4	Office	500 00		
C	6	Cleaning	300 00		
C	8	Educational ..	1,600 00		
C	9	Agricultural .	300 00		
C	11	General plant.	1,200 00		
		Total	$15,700 00		

D Material—

D	2	Building	$400 00		
D	3	General plant..	600 00		
		Total	$1,000 00		

E Equipment—

E	1	Office	$305 00		
E	8	Educational ...	1,000 00		
E	9	General plant..	600 00		
		Total	$1,905 00		

F Contract and Open Order Service—

F	1	Repairs	$600 00		
		Painting Merrill hall.	2,100 00		
F	3	Water	710 00		
F	4	Light, heat and power	700 00		
F	5	Freight, express and drayage	300 00		
F	6	Traveling expense	1,700 00		
F	7	Communication.	240 00		
F	9	General plant..	2,000 00		
		Total	$8,350 00		
		Total maintenance...........		$26,955 00	
		Total		$134,267 00	

808

MIAMI UNIVERSITY.

		Items.	Appropriations.
Personal Service—			
A 1 Salaries—			
	President	$5,000 00	
	Secretary to board of trustees	2,400 00	
	Secretary to the president	1,250 00	
	Secretary to dean teachers' college and field agent..	1,200 00	
2	Stenographers	1,680 00	
2	Bookkeepers	2,080 00	
	Cashier	1,020 00	
	Registrar	400 00	
	Assistant registrar...	900 00	
	Dean of women......	1,400 00	
	Assistant to dean of women	200 00	
	Librarian	2,200 00	
3	Assistant librarians..	2,760 00	
	Chief engineer.......	1,620 00	
2	Engineers	2,100 00	
2	Firemen	910 00	
	Night watchman.....	900 00	
8	Janitors	5,580 00	
	Truck driver........	450 00	
	Carpenter	1,080 00	
3	Deans	9,000 00	
	High school inspector	1,000 00	
2	Extension lecturers..	4,000 00	
	Professors, instructors and other employes	118,225 00	
	Total	$167,355 00	
A 2 Wages—			
	Summer school......	$14,000 00	
	Student assistants, labor and clerical help	7,000 00	
	Total	$21,000 00	
A 3 Unclassified—			
	Commencement speaker	$100 00	
	Total personal service........		$188,455 00

	Items.	Appropriations.	General appropriations, 1919-1920.

Maintenance—
C Supplies—

C 1	Food	$300 00	
C 3	Fuel	10,500 00	
C 4	Office	2,400 00	
C 6	Cleaning	200 00	
C 8	Educational ..	1,100 00	
C 9	Agricultural .	150 00	
C 11	General plant.	875 00	
	Total	$15,525 00	

D Materials—

D 3	General plant..	$1,000 00	

E Equipment—

E 1	Office	$200 00	
E 8	Educational ..	7,000 00	
E 9	General plant..	700 00	
	Total	$7,900 00	

F Contract and Open Order Service—

F 1	Repairs	$4,450 00	
F 3	Water	2,100 00	
F 4	Light, heat and power	800 00	
F 5	Freight, express and drayage	75 00	
F 6	Traveling expense	3,000 00	
F 7	Communication.	500 00	
F 9	General Plant— All endowment monies due Miami university on account of rent and taxes, in Oxford, Milford and Hanover townships, and......	$3,700 00	
	Total	$14,625 00	

H Fixed Charges and Contributions—

H 7	Insurance	$825 00	
H 8	Contributions .	385 00	
	Total	$1,210 00	
	Total maintenance..........		40,260 00
	Total		$228,715 00

OHIO UNIVERSITY.

	Items.	Appropriations.
Personal Service—		
A 1 Salaries—		
President	$6,000 00	
2 Deans	6,000 00	
Dean of women......	2,000 00	
Registrar	2,000 00	
Librarian	1,600 00	
Treasurer a n d busi-		
ness manager....	2,500 00	
Secretary-auditor ...	600 00	
High school inspector	1,000 00	
2 Extension lecturers..	4,000 00	
Library assistants...	2,000 00	
4 Engineers	5,100 00	
3 Firemen	3,060 00	
9 Janitors	7,560 00	
2 Stenographers	1,620 00	
2 Bookkeepers	2,040 00	
Carpenter	1,200 00	
Plumber	1,100 00	
Painter	900 00	
Night watchman.....	840 00	
Professors, instructors		
and o t h e r em-		
ployes	135,500 00	
Total	$186,620 00	
A 2 Wages—		
Extra clerks and, la-		
borers	$4,000 00	
Spring term........	1,000 00	
Summer term.......	16,000 00	
Total	$21,000 00	
Total personal service............		$207,620 00
Maintenance—		
C Supplies—		
C 1 Food	$300 00	
C 2 Forage	150 00	
C. 3 Fuel	11,500 00	
C 4 Office	1,200 00	
C 6 Cleaning	200 00	
C 8 Educational .	1,100 00	
C 9 Agricultural .	150 00	
C 11 General plant.	1,000 00	
Total	$15,600 00	

	Items.	Appropriations.	General appropriations, 1919-1920.

D Materials—
    D 3 General plant.. $3,000 00

E Equipment—
    E 1 Office $200 00
    E 8 Educational ... 7,000 00
    E 9 General plant.. 700 00

        Total $7,900 00

F Contract and Open Or-
    der Service—
    F 1 Repairs $2,350 00
    F 3 Water 2,200 00
    F 4 Light, heat and
        power 1,100 00
    F 5 F r e i g h t, ex-
        press and drayage 100 00
    F 6 T r a v eling ex-
        pense 3,000 00
    F 7 Communication. 500 00

    F 9 General Plant—
    All e n d o w m e n t
    monies d u e Ohio
    university on ac-
    count of rents and
    taxes in Athens
    and A l e x ander
    townships, and... 3,700 00

        Total $12,950 00

H Fixed Ch a r g e s and
    Contributions—
    H 7 Insurance $900 00

        Total maintenance.......... 40,350 00

        Total $247,970 00

OHIO STATE UNIVERSITY.

Personal Service—
    A 1 Salaries—
        President $7,000 00
        Secretary and busi-
        ness manager.... 5,000 00
        Registrar ,.......... 2,500 00
        Purchasing agent.... 2,500 00
        Secretary to entrance
        board 2,400 00
        Dean of women...... 2,400 00

	Items.	Appropriations.
Professors, instructors and o t h e r employes	1,025,820 00	
Total	$1,047,120 00	
A 2 Wages—		
Labor	$50,000 00	
Prison labor.........	4,000 00	
Summer session......	25,405 00	
Summer law school...	1,800 00	
Total	$81,205 00	
A 3 Unclassified	15,000 00	
Total personal service........		$1,143,325 00

Maintenance—

C Supplies—

		Items.	Appropriations.
C	1	Food	$1,500 00
C	2	Forage	10,000 00
C	3	Fuel	51,000 00
C	4	Office	9,500 00
C	5	Medical	1,600 00
C	6	Cleaning	2,000 00
C	8	Educational ..	40,000 00
C	9	Agricultural ..	1,500 00
C	11	General plant.	4,000 00
		Total	$121,100 00

D Material—

			Items.
D	2	Building	$1,000 00
D	3	General plant..	15,000 00
		Total	$16,000 00

E Equipment—

			Items.
E	1	Office	$3,000 00
E	3	Medical	1,000 00
E	4	Livestock	3,800 00
E	5	Agricultural ..	250 00
E	8	Educational—	
		Library books.....	15,000 00
		Law library books..	2,500 00
		Medical library books	2,000 00
		Other	40,000 00
E	9	General plant..	5,000 00
		Total	$72,550 00

	Items.	Appropriations.	General appropriations, 1919-1920.

F Contract and Open Order Service—

F 1 Repairs	$12,000 00	
F 3 Water	10,000 00	
F 4 Light, heat and power	1,100 00	
F 5 Freight, express and drayage	2,000 00	
F 6 Traveling expense ....:.....	2,000 00	
F 7 Communication.	5,000 00	
F 9 General plant..	25,000 00	
Engineering experiment station...:..	10,000 00	
Fiftieth anniversary celebration	10,000 00	

All monies appropriated by the U. S. government under the Morrill act of 1890, and the Nelson amendment of 1907, and the Smith-Lever agricultural act, which may be received prior to July 1, 1921.

Total	$77,100 00	

H Fixed Charges and Contributions—

H 6 Rent	$1,830 00	
H 7 Insurance	125 00	
Total	$1,955 00	

I Rotary Fund—

Total maintenance...........	288,705 00
Total	$1,432,030 00

AGRICULTURAL EXTENSION.

Personal Service—

A 1 Salaries—		
Director	$3,600 00	
Secretary and assistant	2,300 00	
7 Stenographers	5,760 00	
Agricultural editor...	3,000 00	

	Items.	Appropriations.
Assistant agricultural editor	2,100 00	
State leader boys' and girls' club work..	750 00	
2 Assistant leaders boys' and girls' club work	820 00	
4 Professors	10,250 00	
5 Assistant professors..	11,000 00	
10 Instructors	12,750 00	
3 Professors part time..	1,833 33	
3 Assistant professors part time........	2,208 00	
Assistant	1,200 00	
County agent leader.	1,100 00	
Assistant county agent leader.........	1,000 00	
Assistant in county agent work	1,600 00	
County agents.......	44,950 00	
Farmers' institutes...	3,780 00	
Total	$110,001 33	

A 2 Wages—

Farmers' institute speakers	$7,000 00	
Other	1,000 00	
Total	$8,000 00	

A 3 Unclassified—

Farmers' week speakers	$750 00	
Total personal service.........		$118,751 33

Maintenance—
C Supplies—

C 4 Office	$2,000 00	
C 8 Educational ...	300 00	
Total	$2,300 00	

D Material—

D 3 General plant..	$100 00	

E Equipment—

E 1 Office	$300 00	
E 8 Educational ...	2,500 00	
Total	$2,800 00	

	Items.	Appropriations.	General appropriations, 1919-1920.

F Contract and Open Order Service—

F 1 Repairs	$50 00		
F 6 Traveling expense	23,600 00		
F 7 Communication.	500 00		
F 9 General plant..	3,000 00		
Total	$27,150 00		
Total maintenance..........		$32,350 00	
Total		$151,101 33	

COMBINED NORMAL AND INDUSTRIAL DEPARTMENT OF WILBERFORCE UNIVERSITY.

Personal Service—
A 1 Salaries—

Superintendent	$3,000 00	
Executive clerk......	1,200 00	
Custodian	1,080 00	
Record clerk and storekeeper	1,200 00	
Farm manager......	600 00	
2 Engineers	1,920 00	
Night watchman.....	600 00	
2 Matrons	1,200 00	
Stewardess	480 00	
Attendant purification plant	480 00	
Farm hand..........	480 00	
Student janitors.....	2,000 00	
Instructors and other minor employes..	33,700 00	
Total	$47,940 00	

A 2 Wages—

Extra labor........,.	$3,800 00	
A 3 Unclassified	200 00	
Extension teaching...	2,000 00	
Total	$2,200 00	
Total personal service..........		$53,940 00

Maintenance—
C Supplies—

C 1 Food	$125 00	
C 2 Forage	400 00	
C 3 Fuel	12,000 00	
C 4 Office	400 00	
C 5 Medical	75 00	

			Items.	Appropriations
C	6	Cleaning	250 00	
C	8	Educational ..	1,800 00	
C	9	Agricultural .	400 00	
C	11	General plant.	1,000 00	

Total $16,450 00

D Materials—

| D 2 | Building ..... | $2,000 00 |
| D 3 | General plant.. | 1,500 00 |

Total $3,500 00

E Equipment—

E 1	Office	$100 00
E 2	Household	800 00
E 5	Agricultural ..	150 00
E 8	Educational ...	2,000 00
E 9	General plant..	350 00
Linoleum for boys' dormitory		1,250 00

Total $4,650 00

F Contract and Open Order Service—

F 1	Repairs	$2,000 00
F 5	Freight, express and drayage	300 00
F 6	Traveling expense	850 00
F 7	Communication.	320 00
F 9	General plant..	600 00
Teaching service Wilberforce university		5,000 00

Total $9,070 00

H Fixed Charges and Contributions—

| H 6 | Rent .... | $8 00 |
| H 8 | Contributions . | 125 00 |

Total $133 00

I Rotary Fund—

Total maintenance........... 33,803 00

Total $87,743 00

(b) The monies herein appropriated shall not be expended prior to July 1st, 1920, nor to pay liabilities incurred subsequent to June 30th, 1921. General appropriations. 1920-1921.

STATE BOARD OF ACCOUNTANCY.

	Items.	Appropriations.
Personal Service—		
A 2 Wages—		
Per diem three members of board....	$200 00	
Stenographic service..	65 00	
Total personal service......		$265 00
Maintenance—		
C Supplies—		
C 4 Office	$50 00	
E Equipment—		
E 1 Office	$100 00	
F Contract and Open Order Service—		
F 6 Traveling expense	$100 00	
F 7 Communication.	10 00	
F 9 General plant..	100 00	
Total	$210 00	
H Fixed Charges and Contributions—		
H 8 Contributions .	$5 00	
Total maintenance...........		365 00
Total		$630 00

ADJUTANT GENERAL.

Personal Service—		
A 1 Salaries—		
Adjutant General....	$3,500 00	
Assistant adjutant general.....	2,000 00	
Assistant quartermaster general......	2,000 00	
Grade II bookkeeper.	1,860 00	
Chief clerk..........	1,600 00	
Grade III clerk......	1,200 00	
Roster clerk.........	1,200 00	

	Items.	Appropriations.
Grade III s te n o g-rapher	1,200 00	
Commission clerk....	1,200 00	
2 Quartermaster clerks.	2,400 00	
2 Grade III s te n o g-raphers	1,800 00	
Grade II typist.....	840 00	
Messenger	840 00	
Total personal service........		$21,640 00

Maintenance—
C Supplies—

C 4 Office	$900 00	

E Equipment—

E 1 Office	$150 00	
E 6 Motor vehicle..	300 00	
Total	$450 00	

F Contract and Open Or-der Service—
F 1 Repairs—

Repairs to s t a t e buildings	$5,000 00	
F 6 T r a v e l i n g expense	300 00	
F 7 Communication.	575 00	
Total	$5,875 00	
Total maintenance.........		7,225 00
Total		$28,865 00

STATE HOUSE AND GROUNDS.

Personal Service—
A 1 Salaries—

Superintendent of laborers	$1,100 00	
11 Laborers	9,900 00	
2 Night policemen.....	1,680 00	
2 Day policemen......	1,680 00	
2 Visitors' attendants..	1,680 00	
Carpenter	1,080 00	
Chief engineer.......	1,400 00	
Electrician	1,200 00	
2 Engineer helpers.....	2,400 00	
Fireman	1,080 00	
2 Elevator attendants...	2,040 00	

	Items.	Appropriations.	General appropriations, 1920-1921.
Caretaker rest room..	600 00		
Total personal service.......		$26,060 00	

Maintenance—
C Supplies—

		Items.		
C 2	Forage	$50 00		
C 3	Fuel	6,000 00		
C 6	Cleaning	300 00		
C 9	Agricultural ..	165 00		
C 11	General plant.	200 00		
	Total	$6,715 00		

D Material—
    D 3 General plant.. $500 00

E Equipment—
    E 9 General plant.. $2,000 00

F Contract and Open Order Service—

		Items.		
F 1	Repairs	$600 00		
F 3	Water	500 00		
F 4	Light, heat and power	10,000 00		
F 5	Freight, express and drayage	100 00		
F 7	Communication.	60 00		
	Total	$11,260 00		

Total maintenance..........		20,475 00
Total		$46,535 00

WYANDOTTE BUILDING.

Personal Service—
A 1 Salaries—

	Items.	Appropriations.
Engineer	$1,400 00	
Assistant engineer...	1,000 00	
Fireman and watchman	1,000 00	
Head janitor	1,000 00	
2 Elevator attendents...	1,800 00	
6 Janitors	5,400 00	
Total personal service........		$11,600 00

Maintenance—	Items.	Appropriations.
C Supplies—		
C 3 Fuel	$1,400 00	
C 6 Cleaning	600 00	
C 11 General plant.	425 00	
Total	$2,425 00	
E Equipment—		
E 9 General plant..	$500 00	
F Contract and Open Order Service—		
F 1 Repairs	$1,000 00	
F 3 Water	400 00	
F 4 Light, heat and power	2,000 00	
F 5 Freight, express and drayage	150 00	
Total	$3,550 00	
Total maintenance...........		6,475 00
Total		$18,075 00

OHIO BOARD OF ADMINISTRATION.

Personal Service—	
A 1 Salaries—	
4 Members	$16,000 00
Fiscal supervisor-secretary	3,600 00
Purchasing agent....	5,000 00
Chief agriculturist...	3,600 00
Horticulturist	2,500 00
Assistant superintendent of construction	1,500 00
Mechanical engineer..	2,500 00
Grade II engineer....	3,000 00
Grade IV engineer...	1,800 00
Grade V engineer....	1,200 00
3 Grade III bookkeepers	4,140 00
Grade IV bookkeeper.	840 00
Executive clerk......	2,400 00
Grade I clerk.......	1,680 00
Grade II clerk......	1,200 00
Grade III clerk.....	900 00
Grade IV clerk.....	1,260 00

	Items.	Appropriations.	General appropriations, 1920-1921.
2 Grade II stenographers	2,400 00		
6 Grade III stenographers	5,400 00		
Grade I telephone operator	780 00		
Grade III engineer....	2,400 00		
Architectural draftsman	1,500 00		
Employes Bureau of Juvenile Research	35,000 00		
21 Managing officers....	52,200 00		
Minor officers and employes	1,690,000 00		
Total $1,842,800 00			

A 2 Wages	5,000 00	
A 3 Unclassified—		
Prisoners' compensation	100,000 00	
Total personal service........		$1,947,800 00

Maintenance—

C	1	Food $1,750,000 00	
C	2	Forage	150,000 00
C	3	Fuel	475,000 00
C	4	Office	19,000 00
C	5	Medical	35,000 00
C	6	Cleaning	60,000 00
C	8	Educational ..	4,000 00
C	9	Agricultural ..	25,000 00
C	11	General plant.	75,000 00
		Total $2,593,000 00	

D   Material—

D	2	Buildings	$150,000 00
D	3	General plant..	275,000 00
		Total	$425,000 00

E   Equipment—

E	1	Office	$1,000 00
E	2	Household	85,000 00
E	3	Surgical	4,000 00
E	4	Livestock	40,000 00
E	5	Agricultural ..	1,600 00
E	6	Motor vehicle..	7,000 00

General
appropriations,
1930-1931.

	Items.	Appropriations.
E 7 Wearing apparel ...:.......	225,000 00	
E 8 Educational ..	5,000 00	
E 9 General plant..	75,000 00	
Total	$444,100 00	
F Contract and Open Order Service—		
F 1 Repairs	$150,000 00	
F 3 Water	21,000 00	
F 4 Light, heat and power	32,000 00	
F 5 Freight, express and drayage	2,000 00	
F 6 Traveling expense	10,000 00	
F 7 Communication.	9,000 00	
F 9 General plant..	30,000 00	
Advertising sale of cattle	1,000 00	
Total	$255,000 00	
H Fixed Charges and Contributions—		
H 6 Rent	$8,900 00	
H 7 Insurance	1,017 50	
H 8 Contributions..	12,000 00	
Total	$21,917 50	
Total maintenance..........		3,739,017 50
Total		$5,686,817 50

BOARD OF AGRICULTURE OF OHIO.

Personal Service—	
A 1 Salaries—	
Secretary	$4,000 00
Chief bureau of fair administration ..	2,600 00
Publicity specialist...	1,600 00
Superintendent of fair grounds....	1,300 00
Chief bureau of horticulture	3,000 00
8 Deputy inspectors nurseries and orchards	11,200 00

		Items.	Appropriations.	General appropriations 1920-1921.
	Chief bureau of markets	2,500 00		
	Deputy inspector bureau markets....	1,500 00		
	Chief bureau of feeds and fertilizers...	1,900 00		
4	Deputy inspectors feeds and fertilizers	4,800 00		
	State veterinarian....	3,600 00		
	Assistant state veterinarian	2,100 00		
	Pathologist	2,400 00		
	Assistant pathologist.	1,800 00		
	Bacteriologist	1,600 00		
14	Field veterinarians...	25,200 00		
	Local veterinarian in charge	2,000 00		
	Grade III bookkeeper	1,380 00		
	Confidential secretary	1,380 00		
	Grade II clerk.......	1,260 00		
3	Grade III clerks.....	3,560 00		
	Grade IV clerk......	600 00		
3	Grade II stenographers	3,360 00		
4	Grade III stenographers	3,540 00		
2	Grade II typists.....	1,800 00		
	Telephone operator...	780 00		
5	Laborers serum plant.	4,500 00		
	Chief bureau agricultural statistics...	600 00		
	Messenger and janitor	1,020 00		
	Seed analyst........	2,700 00		
3	Assistant seed analysts	2,700 00		
	Stenographer	900 00		
	Total	$103,180 00		
A 2	Wages	17,000 00		
A 3	Unclassified	1,200 00		
	Total personal service........		$121,380 00	

Maintenance—
  C Supplies—

	C	2	Forage	$6,000 00
		3	Fuel	1,500 00
		4	Office	6,500 00
		5	Medical	500 00
	C	6	Cleaning	90 00
	C	9	Agricultural .	750 00

	Items.	Appropriations.
C 11 General Plant—		
Pigs for serum tests..	70,000 00	
Other	1,400 00	
Total	$86,740 00	
D Materials—		
D 2 Building	$2,450 00	
D 3 General plant..	4,400 00	
Total	$6,850 00	
E Equipment—		
E 1 Office	$400 00	
E 3 Surgical	100 00	
E 7 Wearing apparel	50 00	
E 9 General plant..	1,000 00	
.Total	$1,550 00	
F Contract and Open Order Service—		
F 1 Repairs	$600 00	
F 3 Water	700 00	
F 4 Light, heat and power	600 00	
F 5 Freight, express and drayage	600 00	
F 6 Traveling expense	30,000 00	
F 7 Communication.	1,650 00	
F 9 General Plant—		
Uses and purposes of state fair.......	110,000 00	
Experimental work diseases of animals	2,500 00	
Apple and fruit shows	1,500 00	
Other	1,733 00	
Total	$149,883 00	
H Fixed Charges and Contributions—		
H 6 Rent	$20 00	
H 7 Insurance	.25 00	
H 8 Contributions—		
State share of pay due owners of tubercular cattle killed according to law.	60,000 00	

	Items.	Appropriations.	General appropriations, 1919-1921.
State share of pay due owners of g l a n- d e r e d h o r s e s killed according to law..........	18,000 00		
Other	25 00		
Total	$78,070 00		
Total maintenance..........		323,093 00	
Total		$444,473 00	

DAIRY AND FOOD DIVISION.

Personal Service—
  A 1   Salaries—

Chief of division.....	$2,000 00	
Chief inspector weights and meas- ures	1,500 00	
Inspector weights and measures	1,350 00	
5 Dairy inspectors.....	6,750 00	
4 Drug inspectors......	5,400 00	
9 Food inspectors......	13,500 00	
Cannery inspector...	1,350 00	
Chief narcotic inspec- tor	1,650 00	
Narcotic inspector...	1,350 00	
Grade II clerk.......	1,200 00	
Grade III clerk......	900 00	
Grade III stenog- rapher	1,000 00	
Messenger	840 00	
Total	$38,790 00	
A 3 Unclassified	1,700 00	
Total personal service........		$40,490 00

Maintenance—
  C Supplies—

C 4 Office	$265 00	
C 11 General plant.	35 00	
Total	$300 00	

  E Equipment—

E 1 Office	$100 00	
E 9 General plant..	50 00	
Total	$150 00	

	Items.	Appropriations.
F Contract and Open Or-		
der Service—		
F 5 Freight, ex-		
press and drayage	$100 00	
F 6 Traveling ex-		
pense	22,000 00	
F 7 Communication.	25 00	
F 9 General plant..	150 00	
Total	$22,275 00	
Total maintenance..........		22,725 00
Total		$63,215 00

FISH AND GAME DIVISION.

Personal Service—	
A 1 Salaries—	
Chief warden........	$3,000 00
Assistant chief war-	
den	1,800 00
3 Grade III clerks.....	3,840 00
Grade II stenog-	
rapher	1,200 00
2 Grade III stenog-	
raphers	1,740 00
30 Wardens	36,000 00
20 Wardens	18,000 00
Supervisor Lake Erie	
district	1,600 00
Superintendent Lake	
Erie hatchery...	1,200 00
Assistant Lake Erie	
hatchery	1,080 00
Firemen Lake Erie	
hatchery	840 00
Captain patrol boat..	1,200 00
Engineer patrol boat.	1,080 00
Fireman patrol boat.	900 00
Deckhand patrol boat	900 00
Superintendent Lon-	
don hatchery....	1,080 00
4 Superintendents of	
hatcheries	4,020 00
Superintendent Well-	
ington game farm	1,800 00
Gamekeeper, London.	1,800 00
Farmer	720 00
4 Laborers	3,000 00
Total	$86,800 00

A 2 Wages—
Extra game wardens. $8,000 00
Laborers, Lake Erie..   2,000 00
Laborers, inland fish
   hatchery 1,000 00

    Total $11,000 00

A 3 Unclassified—
Securing g a m e fish
  for inland distri-
  bution $6,000 00

    Total personal service........ $103,800 00

Maintenance—
C Supplies—
  C 2   Forage $2,500 00
  C 3   Fuel 2,500 00
  C 4   Office ...,....   600 00
  C 9   Agricultural .   1,000 00
  C 11   General plant.   4,000 00

    Total $10,600 00

D Materials—
  D 2   Building $500 00
  D 3   General plant..   1,000 00

    Total $1,500 00

E Equipment—
  E 4   Livestock—
Purchase of fish
  spawn $5,000 00
Purchase of pheasant
  eggs, game birds
  and hens........   15,000 00
  E 6   Motor vehicle..   500 00
  E 9   General palnt..   150 00

    Total $20,650 00
F Contract and Open Or-
  der Service—
  F 1   Repairs $100 00
  F 3   Water 450 00
  F 5   F r e i g h t, ex-
    press and drayage   3,850 00
  F 6   T r a v eling ex-
    pense 24,000 00
  F 7   Communicatio.n   700 00

	Items.	Appropriations.
F 9 General Plant—		
Printing game laws..	5,000 00	
Fish propagation and distribution	17,000 00	
Total	$51,100 00	
H Fixed C h a r g e s and Contributions—		
H 6 Rent	$637 40	
Total maintenance...........		84,437 40
Total		$188,287 40

ARCHAEOLOGICAL AND HISTORICAL SOCIETY.

Personal Service—		
A 1 Salaries—		
Curator	$2,500 00	
Assistant curator....	1,700 00	
Secretary	1,000 00	
2 Assistant librarians ..	1,340 00	
Stenographer	720 00	
Superintendent of buildings	900 00	
2 Janitors	1,420 00	
Caretaker Fort Ancient park......	360 00	
Caretaker S e r p e n t Mound park.....	240 00	
Caretaker Logan Elm park	25 00	
C a r e t a k e r Spiegel Grove park.....	720 00	
Bookkeeper	150 00	
Clerk, Historical commission of Ohio..	840 00	
Treasurer	300 00	
Binder	900 00	
A u t h o r "Ohio in Civil W a r"—t o complete	1,200 00	
Total	$14,315 00	
A 2 Wages—		
Workmen S p i e g e l Grove park.....	$100 00	
Total personal service........		$14,415 00

	Items.	Appropriations.	General appropriations. 1919-1921.
Maintenance—			
C Supplies—			
C 4 Office	$300 00		
C 11 General plant.	175 00		
Total	$475 00		
F Contract and Open Order Service—			
F 1 Repairs	$900 00		
F 3 Water	90 00		
F 4 Light, heat and power	900 00		
F 5 Freight, express and drayage	150 00		
F 6 Traveling expense	150 00		
F 7 Communication.	93 00		
F 8 Contingencies .	50 00		
F 9 General Plant— Publications	$3,000 00		
Exploration and field work	500 00		
Total	$5,833 00		
Total maintenance..........		6,308 00	
Total		$20,723 00	

ATTORNEY GENERAL.

	Items.		
Personal Service—			
A 1 Salaries—			
Attorney general....	$6,500 00		
1st assistant attorney general	4,000 00		
2nd assistant attorney general	2,500 00		
Chief clerk..........	1,500 00		
Grade I clerk.......	2,000 00		
Grade I clerk.......	1,500 00		
8 Grade II stenographers	10,380 00		
Clerk	840 00		
Total	$29,220 00		
A 2 Wages—			
Extra stenographic work	$1,500 00		

		Items.	Appropriations.
A 3	Unclassified—		
	Special counsel......	$55,000 00	
	Expense of investiga-tion	2,500 00	
	Costs in cases.......	3,500 00	
	Total	$61,000 00	
	Total personal service........		$91,720 00

Maintenance—
C Supplies—

		Items.	Appropriations.
C 4	Office	$1,612 00	

D Materials—

D 3	General plant..	$100 00	

E Equipment—

E 1	Office	$496 06	
E 9	General plant..	300 00	
	Total	$796 06	

F Contract and Open Or-der Service—

F 1	Repairs	$100 00	
F 5	Freight, ex-press and drayage	50 00	
F 6	Traveling ex-pense	4,000 00	
F 7	Communication.	1,000 00	
F 9	General plant..	100 00	
	Total	$5,250 00	
	Total maintenance...........		7,758 06
	Total		$99,478 06

AUDITOR OF STATE.

Personal Service—
A 1 Salaries—

	Items.
Auditor	$6,500 00
Deputy auditor......	3,000 00
Chief clerk..........	2,400 00
Deputy supervisor school lands.....	2,500 00
Secretary	2,000 00
Statistician	2,000 00
Grade II clerk.......	1,500 00
Janitor and mailing clerk	640 00
Examiner	2,800 00

	Items.	Appropriations.	General appropriations, 1920-1921.
Grade I examiner....	3,000 00		
4 Grade II examiners..	7,500 00		
2 Grade II examiners..	3,200 00		
Grade I stenographer	1,500 00		
Grade I accountant..	2,600 00		
2 Grade II accountants.	4,500 00		
Grade III accountant.	1,500 00		
2 Grade II examiners..	3,600 00		
Grade III bookkeeper	1,950 00		
2 Grade III bookkeepers	2,400 00		
3 Grade I typists......	2,760 00		
2 Grade III clerks.....	2,400 00		
Grade IV clerk......	1,000 00		
Grade II clerk......	1,500 00		
Grade III stenographer	1,200 00		
Total	$63,950 00		

A 3 Unclassified—
Investigation school and ministerial lands $3,000 00

Total personal service........ $66,950 00

Maintenance—
C Supplies—
C 4 Office $1,000 00

E Equipment—
E 1 Office $600 00

F Contract and Open Order Service—

F 1	Repairs	$75 00
F 6	Traveling expense	1,200 00
F 7	Communication.	400 00
F 8	Contingencies .	1,000 00
F 9	General plant..	200 00

Total $2,875 00
Total maintenance.......... $4,475 00

Total $71,425 00

BUREAU OF INSPECTION AND SUPERVISION OF PUBLIC OFFICES.

	Items.	Appropriations.
Personal Service—		
A 1 Salaries—		
2 Deputy inspectors...	$5,000 00	
Statistician	1,800 00	
Grade I clerk.......	1,800 00	
Grade I stenographer.	1,500 00	
Grade II clerk.......	1,140 00	
2 Grade II stenographers	2,400 00	
Janitor	360 00	
Total personal service.........		$14,000 00
Maintenance—		
C Supplies—		
C 4 Office	$1,200 00	
E Equipment—		
E 1 Office	$250 00	
F Contract and Open Order Service—		
F 1 Repairs	$25 00	
R 6 Traveling expense	200 00	
F 7 Communication.	275 00	
F 8 Contingencies .	1,500 00	
F 9 General plant..	25 00	
Total	$2,025 00	
Total maintenance..........		$3,475 00
Total		$17,475 00

DEPARTMENT OF BANKS AND BANKING.

Personal Service—		
A 1 Salaries—		
Superintendent	$7,500 00	
Assistant superintendent	3,300 00	
Secretary	1,500 00	
Attorney	3,300 00	
2 Grade I examiners...	6,900 00	
13 Examiners	32,800 00	
4 Assistant examiners..	6,900 00	
Grade III statistician	1,380 00	
Grade III bookkeeper	1,380 00	
4 Grade II stenographers	4,560 00	
Total	$69,520 00	

	Items.	Appropriations.	General appropriations. 1930-1931.
A 3 Unclassified	$200 00		
Foreign exchange inspection ..,....	3,500 00		
Total	$3,700 00		
Total personal service........		$73,220 00	

Maintenance—
  C Supplies—
    C 4   Office $1,800 00

  E Equipment—
    E ·1   Office $356 00

  F Contract and Open Order Service—
    F 1   Repairs....... $20 00
    F 5   Freight, express and drayage 50 00
    F 6   Traveling expense 23,500 00
    F 7   Communication. 700 00
    F 9   General plant.. 292 00
    Printing 3,000 00

    Total $27,562 00

  H Fixed Charges and Contributions—
    H 6   Rent $722 00
    H 7   Insurance 700 00
    H 8   Contributions . 20 00

    Total $1,442 00
    Total maintenance.......... 31,160 00

    Total $104,380 00

OHIO COMMISSION FOR THE BLIND.

Personal Service—
  A 1   Salaries—
    Executive secretary.. $2,500 00
    Chief clerk......... 1,000 00
    Grade III stenographer 900 00
    Grade III bookkeeper 1,260 00
    Publicity man....... 200 00
    Supervisor of inspectors 1,500 00
    6 Inspectors 7,800 00

		Items.	Appropriations.
	Supervisor of women's work	900 00	
	Grade III stenographer	900 00	
	Home Teacher	900 00	
7	Home teachers	2,940 00	
	Foreman and instructor	600 00	
	Assistant foreman	780 00	
	Telephone operator and typist	660 00	
	Total	**$22,840 00**	

A 3 Unclassified—

		Items.	Appropriations.
	Laundry and dry cleaning	$25 00	
	Janitor service	260 00	
	Total	**$285 00**	
	Total personal service		$23,125 00

Maintenance—
C Supplies—

		Items.	
C 4	Office	$200 00	
C 5	Medical	50 00	
6	Cleaning	50 00	
C 8	Educational	100 00	
C 11	General plant.	100 00	
	Total	**$500 00**	

E Equipment—

		Items.	
E 1	Office	$200 00	
E 3	Surgical	50 00	
E 9	General plant.	150 00	
	Total	**$400 00**	

F Contract and Open Order Service—

		Items.	
F 1	Repairs	$100 00	
F 3	Water	15 00	
F 4	Light, heat and power	175 00	
F 5	Freight, express and drayage	25 00	
F 6	Traveling expense	9,800 00	
F 7	Communication.	160 00	

	Items.	Appropriations.	General appropriations, 1920-1921.
F 9 General plant..	100 00		
Total	$10,375 00		
H Fixed Charges and Contributions—			
H 6 Rent	$750 00		
H 8 Contributions . To be transferred to the rotary fund at the discretion of the cotnrolling board	2,200 00 25,000 00		
Total	$27,950 00		
Total maintenance...............		39,225 00	
Total		$62,350 00	

BUREAU OF BUILDING AND LOAN ASSOCIATIONS.

Personal Service—		
A 1 Salaries—		
Inspector	$3,600 00	
Deputy inspector....	2,000 00	
Assistant deputy inspector	1,800 00	
12 Examiners	21,600 00	
Grade II accountant.	1,500 00	
Grade III statistician.	1,500 00	
Correspondence clerk.	1,200 00	
Total personal service........		$33,200 00
Maintenance—		
C Supplies—		
C 4 Office	$600 00	
E Equipment—		
E 1 Office	$100 00	
F Contract and Open Order Service—		
F 1 Repairs	$25 00	
F 5 Freight, express and drayage	25 00	
F 6 Traveling expense	10,000 00	
F 7 Communication.	200 00	

	Items.	Appropriations.
F 9 General plant..	20 00	
Total	$10,270 00	
Total maintenance...........		$10,970 00
Total		$44,170 00

BOARD OF STATE CHARITIES.

Personal Service—
  A 1 Salaries—

Secretary	$3,000 00	
Social investigator...	1,800 00	
Agent	1,800 00	
3 Assistant agents.....	4,500 00	
Grade III clerk......	1,200 00	
Director of children's welfare	3,000 00	
Assistant director of children's welfare	1,560 00	
Grade IV bookkeeper.	900 00	
3 Institution inspectors	3,600 00	
Supervisor of child placing	1,800 00	
2 District superintendents	3,600 00	
Supervisor of boarding home.......	1,200 00	
Assistant supervisor of boarding home	900 00	
16 Field agents.........	19,900 00	
Special nurse........	900 00	
6 Grade III stenographers	5,340 00	
Telephone operator..	660 00	
2 Grade II stenographers	2,280 00	
Grade I typist	1,020 00	
Matron	600 00	
Housekeeper	480 00	
Total	$60,040 00	

  A 3 Unclassified—

Examination and treatment of minor wards of board	$900 00	
To provide medical and surgical treatment for		

	Items.	Appropriations.	General appropriations, 1920-1921.
crippled children	10,000 00		
Total	$10,900 00		
Total personal service........		$70,940 00	

Maintenance—

C Supplies—

		Items.		
C 1	Food	$1,500 00		
C 3	Fuel	500 00		
C 4	Office	1,500 00		
C 5	Medical	175 00		
C 6	Cleaning	50 00		
C 11	General plant.	250 00		
	Total	$3,975 00		

E Equipment—

E 1	Office	$500 00		
E 2	Household	100 00		
	Total	$600 00		

F Contract and Open Order Service—

F 1	Repairs	$300 00		
F 3	Water	15 00		
F 4	Light, heat and power	50 00		
F 5	Freight, express and drayage	50 00		
F 6	Traveling expense	22,000 00		
F 7	Communication.	450 00		
F 9	General plant..	350 00		
	Total	$23,215 00		

H Fixed Charges and Contributions—

H 6	Rent—Office ..	$1,812 00		
	Receiving home......	1,500 00		
	Total	$3,312 00		
	Total maintenance...........		31,102 00	
	Total		$102,042 00	

STATE CIVIL SERVICE COMMISSION.

	Items.	Appropriations.
Personal Service—		
A 1 Salaries—		
2 Commissioners	$8,000 00	
Secretary	3,000 00	
Assistant chief examiner	3,000 00	
4 Examiners	7,400 00	
Efficiency examiner..	2,400 00	
Assistant efficiency examiner	1,560 00	
Grade I clerk........	1,800 00	
4 Grade II clerks......	4,680 00	
2 Grade III clerks.....	1,800 00	
Grade IV clerk......	660 00	
Publicity clerk......	720 00	
Grade II stenographer	1,200 00	
Grade III stenographer	1,200 00	
3 Grade III stenographers	2,700 00	
Total	$40,120 00	
A 2 Wages—		
Special examiners, extra clerks and stenographers ...	$600 00	
Total personal service........		$40,720 00
Maintenance—		
C Supplies—		
C 4 Office	$2,300 00	
E Equipment—		
E 1 Office	$300 00	
F Contract and Open Order Service—		
F 5 Freight, express and drayage	$10 00	
F 6 Traveling expense	1,700 00	
F 7 Communication.	425 00	
F 9 General plant..	200 00	
Total	$2,335 00	
Total maintenance		4,935 00
Total		$45,655 00

OHIO BOARD OF CLEMENCY.

	Items.	Appropriations.
Personal Service—		
A 1 Salaries—		
2 Members of board.	$7,200 00	
Secretary	1,500 00	
Total personal service........		$8,700 00
Maintenance—		
C Supplies—		
C 4 Office	$110 00	
E Equipment—		
E 1 Office	$50 00	
F Contract and Open Or-		
der Service—		
F 6 T r a v eling ex-		
pense	$200 00	
F 7 Communication.	85 00	
F 9 General plant..	15 00	
Total	$300 00	
H Fixed C h a r g e s and		
Contributions—		
H 7 Insurance	$25 00	
Total maintenance..........		485 00
Total		$9,185 00

STATE DENTAL BOARD.

	Items.	Appropriations.
Personal Service—		
A 1 Salaries—		
Secretary ....:.	$1,200 00	
Stenographer	225 00	
Total	$1,425 00	
A 2 Wages—		
Per diem 5 members		
of board........	2,000 00	
Total personal service........		$3,425 00
Maintenance—		
C Supplies—		
C 4 Office	$150 00	

	Items.	Appropriations.
F Contract and Open Order Service—		
F 5 Freight, express and drayage	$10 00	
F 6 Traveling expense	850 00	
F 7 Communication.	10 00	
Total	$870 00	
Total maintenance..........		$1,020 00
Total		$4,445 00

STATE BOARD OF EDUCATION.

Maintenance—
F Contract and Open Order Service—
F 9 General Plant—
Co-operative work with federal government in vocational education in accordance with provisions of the Smith-Hughes law............. $195,000 00

STATE BOARD OF EMBALMING EXAMINERS.

	Items.	Appropriations.
Personal Service—		
A 1 Salaries—		
Secretary	$1,200 00	
A 2 Wages—		
Per diem 2 members of board.......	600 00	
Total personal service.......		$1,800 00
Maintenance—		
C Supplies—		
C 4 Office	$400 00	
C 11 General Plant—		
Cadavers	150 00	
Total	$550 00	
F Contract and Open Order Service—		
F 6 Traveling expense	$600 00	
F 9 General plant..	150 00	
Total	$750 00	
Total maintenance..........		1,300 00
Total		$3,100 00

EXECUTIVE DEPARTMENT.

	Items.	Appropriations.
Personal Service—		
A 1 Salaries—		
Governor	$10,000 00	
Secretary to the governor	5,000 00	
Executive clerk......	3,000 00	
Correspondence clerk.	2,000 00	
Commission clerk....	1,800 00	
Stenographer	1,400 00	
Messenger	1,200 00	
Total personal service........		$24,400 00
Maintenance—		
C Supplies—		
C 3 Fuel	$25 00	
C 4 Office	1,000 00	
Total	$1,025 00	
E Equipment—		
E 1 Office	$500 00	
F Contract and Open Order Service—		
F 1 Repairs	$100 00	
F 6 T r a v eling expense	250 00	
F 7 Communication.	1,200 00	
F 8 Contingencies .	6,000 00	
F 9 General Plant—		
Maintenance of governor's mansion.	5,000 00	
Total	$12,550 00	
Total maintenance..........		14,075 00
Total		$38,475 00

BUDGET COMMISSIONER.

	Items.	Appropriations.
Personal Service—		
A 1 Salaries—		
Commissioner	$4,000 00	
Assistant commissioner	1,800 00	
Secretary	1,680 00	
Messenger	300 00	
Total	$7,780 00	
A 2 Wages	1,200 00	
Total personal service........		$8,980 00

	Items.	Appropriations.

Maintenance—
  C Supplies—
    C 4 Office $150 00

  E Equipment—
    E 1 Office $150 00

  F Contract and Open Or-
      der Service—
    F 1 Repairs $15 00
    F 5 F r e i g h t, ex-
        press and dray-
        age 10 00
    F 6 T r a v eling ex-
        pense 600 00
    F 7 Communication. 200 00
    F 9 General plant.. 100 00

        Total $925 00
        Total maintenance........... 1,225 00

        Total $10,205 00

OHIO AGRICULTURAL EXPERIMENT STATION.

Personal Service—
  A 1 Salaries—
    Director $4,000 00
    Director—Soils a n d
      research 2,500 00
    8 Deputy Chiefs—
      Agronomy, botany,
        chemistry, dairy-
        ing, e n tomology,
        forestry, horticul-
        ture, farm man-
        agement 20,000 00
    Bursar 2,200 00
  4 Associates 8,400 00
  32 Assistants 45,500 00
    Editor ....,.. 1,800 00
    Librarian 1,300 00
    Photographer 780 00
  4 Office assistants...... 3,730 00
  4 Field assistants...... 4,450 00
  2 Engineers 2,100 00
    Mechanic 900 00
    Printer 960 00
    Mailing clerk........ 780 00
  3 Farm managers...... 3,150 00
  2 Herdsmen 1,800 00
    Shepherd ...·........ 840 00

	Items.	Appropriations.	General appropriations, 1920-1921.

	Items.
5 Foremen	4,320 00
Assistant foreman...	960 00
Stenographer	660 00
2 Clerks..............	1,380 00
4 Superintendents of county experiment farms.....	7,200 00
Total	$119,710 00
A 2 Wages	50,000 00
A 3 Unclassified— Fees, etc............	200 00

Total personal service........ $169,910 00

Maintenance—
C Supplies—

	Items.
C 1 Food	$10 00
C 2 Forage	8,000 00
C 3 Fuel	7,000 00
C 4 Office	2,000 00
C 6 Cleaning	200 00
C 9 Agricultural .	2,500 00
C 11 General plant.	7,000 00
Total	$26,710 00

D Materials—

	Items.
D 2 Building	$1,200 00
D 3 General plant..	3,000 00
Total	$4,200 00

E Equipment—

	Items.
E 1 Office	$200 00
E 4 Livestock	500 00
E 5 Agricultural ..	1,000 00
E 7 Wearing apparel	15 00
E 8 Educational ...	700 00
E 9 General plant..	8,000 00
Total	$10,415 00

F Contract and Open Order Service—

	Items.
F 1 Repairs	$2,000 00
F 4 Light, heat and power	200 00
F 5 Freight, express and drayage	2,000 00

	Items.	Appropriations.
F 6 Traveling expense	14,000 00	
F 7 Communication.	500 00	
F 9 General plant service	1,200 00	
All monies appropriated by the U. S. government which are now in the Adams-Hatch fund or which may be credited to such fund prior to July 1, 1921.		
Total	$19,900 00	
H Fixed Charges and Contributions—		
H 6 Rent	$1,500 00	
H 7 Insurance	100 00	
H 8 Contributions .	50 00	
Total	$1,650 00	
I Rotary Fund— Animal husbandry cost-feeding experimental work, dairying— Total maintenance...........		62,875 00
Total		$232,785 00

STATE FIRE MARSHAL.

Personal Service— A 1 Salaries—	
Marshal	$4,500 00
2 Deputy marshals....	4,000 00
Chief assistant........	2,400 00
Chief inspector......	1,800 00
Statistician	1,200 00
27 Assistants	40,500 00
Electrical inspector..	1,500 00
Water supply engineer	1,600 00
Grade I clerk........	1,800 00
Clerk	900 00
6 Grade III stenographers	5,400 00
2 Grade II stenographers	2,160 00

	Items.	Appropriations.	General appropriations, 1920-1921.
Record clerk........	1,080 00		

		Items.	Appropriations.
	Total	$68,840 00	

Record clerk........   1,080 00

Total $68,840 00

A 2   Wages—
Assistants 2,000 00

A 3   Unclassified—
Fees, m i l e a g e and m a intenance fire chiefs, m a y o rs, township c l e rks and w i t n e sses, s p e c i al stenog- r a p h e r s, legal fees, court costs.   2,250 00

Total personal service........ $73,090 00

Maintenance—
C Supplies—
C 4   Office $4,800 00
C 11   General plant.   500 00

Total $5,300 00

E Equipment—
E 1   Office $300 00

F Contract and Open Or- der Service—
F 4   Light, heat and power $72 00
F 5   F r e i g h t, ex- press a n d dray- age 25 00
F 6   T r a veling ex- pense 20,000 00
F 7   Communication.   1,200 00
F 9   General palnt..   2,000 00

Total $23,297 00

H Fixed C h a r g e s and Contributions—
H 6   Rent $1,788 00

Total maintenance...........   30,685 00

Total $103,775 00

GEOLOGICAL SURVEY.

	Items.	Appropriations.
Personal Service—		
A 1 Salaries—		
State geologist......	$1,500 00	
Assistant geologist...	2,000 00	
Grade II stenographer	1,080 00	
Total	$4,580 00	
A 2 Wages—		
5 Assistant geologists	$1,875 00	
Student assistants...	50 00	
Total	$1,925 00	
Total personal service.......		$6,505 00
Maintenance—		
C Supplies—		
C 4 Office	$150 00	
C 11 General plant.	100 00	
Total	$250 00	
E Equipment—		
E 1 Office	$25 00	
E 9 General plant..	100 00	
Total	$125 00	
F Contract and Open Order Service—		
F 1 Repairs	$30 00	
F 5 Freight, express and drayage	150 00	
F 6 Traveling expense	1,700 00	
F 7 Communication.	30 00	
F 9 General plant..	100 00	
Total	$2,010 00	
Total maintenance..........		2,385 00
Total		$8,890 00

HEADQUARTERS OHIO G. A. R.

Personal Service—		
A 1 Salaries—		
Assistant adjutant general	$1,200 00	

	Items.	Appropriations.	General appropriations. 1920-1921.
Clerk	750 00		
Total personal service........		$1,950 00	

Maintenance—
F Contract and Open Or-
    der Service—
    F 9 General plant.. $500 00

Total maintenance..........	500 00
Total	$2,450 00

STATE DEPARTMENT OF HEALTH.

Personal Service—
  A 1 Salaries—

Commissioner of health	$6,000 00
Deputy commissioner	4,000 00
Publicity director....	1,700 00
2 Grade II clerks......	2,340 00
3 Grade III clerks.....	2,760 00
Grade IV clerk......	840 00
2 Grade II stenographers	2,160 00
11 Grade III stenographers	9,660 00
Grade I telephone operator	720 00
Janitor	900 00
Grade I engineer....	4,000 00
3 Grade III engineers..	6,480 00
Grade IV engineer...	1,440 00
Plumbing inspector..	2,200 00
2 Deputy plumbing inspectors	3,200 00
Director of laboratories	3,000 00
Bacteriologist	2,100 00
Chemist	2,200 00
2 Laboratory assistants.	3,240 00
4 Laboratory assistants.	5,860 00
4 Laboratory helpers...	3,000 00
Janitor	840 00
Director division of communicable diseases	3,000 00
Epidemiologist	2,400 00
Statistician	1,200 00

	Items.	Appropriations.
Director division of public health education and tuberculosis	3,000 00	
Director hospital division	2,000 00	
Chief of nursing service	1,600 00	
3 Public health nurses.	3,900 00	
Director division of industrial hygiene	3,000 00	
Assistant director director division of industrial hygiene	1,600 00	
Director division of child hygiene....	2,400 00	
4 Inspectors	4,800 00	
8 District health supervisors	20,000 00	
Total	$117,540 00	

A 2 Wages—

	Items.	Appropriations.
Per diem members public health council	$500 00	
Emergency nurses...	1,000 00	
Emergency physicians	100 00	
Total	$1,600 00	

A 3 Unclassified—

	Items.	Appropriations.
Referee fees.........	$300 00	
Reporting fees.......	500 00	
Operation of trachoma clinics and hospitals in co-operation with United States public health service, counties and municipalities	10,000 00	
Total	$10,800 00	
Total personal service........		$129,940 00

Maintenance—
C Supplies—

	Items.
C 2 Forage	$250 00
C 4 Office	3,500 00

		Items.
C 5	Medical	2,500 00
C 11	General plant.	1,700 00
	Total	$7,950 00

E Equipment—

E 1	Office	$500 00
E 3	Surgical	3,300 00
E 4	Livestock	200 00
E 7	Wearing apparel	50 00
E 8	Educational ...	1,200 00
E 9	General plant..	900 00
	Total	$6,150 00

F Contract and Open Order Service—

F 1	Repairs	$600 00
F 4	Light, heat and power	1,000 00
F 5	Freight, express and drayage	1,000 00
F 6	Traveling expense	21,000 00
F 7	Communication.	1,000 00
F 9	General plant..	2,000 00
	All moneys appropriated by the U. S. government under the Chamberlain-Kahn act and	25,000 00
	Total	$51,600 00
	Total maintenance...........	65,700 00
	Total	$195,640 00

HIGHWAY DEPARTMENT.

Personal Service—

A 1	Salaries—	
	Commissioner	$5,000 00
3	Deputy commissioners	9,900 00
17	Grade III engineers..	46,750 00
5	Grade IV engineers..	8,640 00
	Testing engineer.....	2,400 00
2	Assisting engineers..	3,240 00

	Items.	Appropriations.
Chief clerk..........	2,000 00	
Secretary	2,500 00	
2 Grade III bookkeepers	2,640 00	
6 Grade II clerks......	8,280 00	
Grade IV clerk......	660 00	
2 Grade II stenog-		
raphers	2,160 00	
8 Grade III stenog-		
raphers	7,200 00	
Grade III typist.....	900 00	
Chauffeur and mech-		
anician	1,200 00	
Total	$103,470 00	
A 2 Wages	3,500 00	
A 3 Unclassified	5,000 00	
Total personal service........		$111,970 00

Maintenance—
C Supplies—

C 3 Fuel	$2,100 00	
C 4 Office	3,000 00	
C 11 General plant.	2,275 00	
Total	$7,375 00	

D Materials—

D 3 General plant..	$500 00	

E Equipment—

E 1 Office	$800 00	
E 6 Motor vehicles.	7,000 00	
E 9 General plant..	500 00	
Total	$8,300 00	

F Contract and Open Or-
der Service—
F 1 Repairs—
To police, patrol
and maintain
highways as pro-
vided in Sec.
6309 G. C......$3,000,000 00
Other 3,500 00
F 5 Freight, ex-
press and dray-
age 1,000 00
F 6 Traveling ex-
pense 16,000 00
F 7 Communication. 2,000 00

	Items.	Appropriations.	General appropriations, 1920-1921.
F 9 General plant..	6,000 00		

Total $3,028,500 00

H Fixed Charges and
Contributions—
| H 6 Rent .... | $5,075 00 | |
| H 7 Insurance .... | 400 00 | |

Total $5,475 00
Total maintenance.......... 3,050,150 00

Total $3,162,120 00

INDUSTRIAL COMMISSION OF OHIO.

EXECUTIVE.

Personal Service—
A 1 Salaries—
3 Commissioners	$14,000 00
Secretary	3,000 00
Assistant secretary...	2,000 00
Grade I bookkeeper..	2,200 00
2 Grade III bookkeepers	2,760 00
2 Grade I clerks.......	3,240 00
Grade II clerk......	1,200 00
2 Grade III clerks.....	1,860 00
2 Grade IV clerks.....	1,320 00
Librarian	900 00
Telephone operator...	660 00
5 Grade II stenographers	5,880 00
5 Grade III stenographers	4,380 00
5 Grade II examiners compensation claims	9,000 00
Grade II examiner compensation claims	1,200 00

WORKMEN'S COMPENSATION

Auditor	$2,400 00
27 Payroll auditors.....	36,450 00
Actuary	4,000 00
Assistant actuary....	2,400 00
Codifier	1,140 00
Rating actuary......	2,200 00
3 Grade IV statisticians	3,000 00
Director of claims ...	2,400 00

	Items.	Appropriations.
Deputy director of claims	2,000 00	
3 Reviewers of claims..	5,600 00	
14 Claims examiners....	17,100 00	
3 Claims referees......	6,600 00	
7 Claims investigators..	9,750 00	
Chief medical examiner	3,500 00	
4 Assistant medical examiners	10,000 00	
3 Special medical examiners	7,500 00	
2 Grade IV bookkeepers	1,800 00	
3 Grade I clerks.......'	4,680 00	
27 Grade II clerks......	32,220 00	
40 Grade II clerks......	34,440 00	
4 Grade IV clerks.....	2,910 00	
10 Grade II stenographers	11,160 00	
23 Grade III stenographers	19,800 00	
6 Grade I typists......	5,760 00	
23 Grade II typists.....	19,680 00	
2 Claim sheet clerks....	1,800 00	
Branch office deputy.	1,800 00	
Claim investigator...	1,200 00	

STATISTICS.

Chief statistician....	$3,000 00	
Assistant statistician.	1,800 00	
Statistical clerk......	1,500 00	
4 Special investigators.	5,100 00	
4 Grade III clerks.....	3,600 00	
Grade II stenographer	1,080 00	
4 Grade III stenographers	3,660 00	
Salaries free employment agencies...	40,000 00	

WORKSHOPS AND FACTORIES.

Chief deputy........	$3,000 00	
Assistant chief deputy	2,500 00	
Deputy	2,000 00	
Director of safety....	3,000 00	
6 Deputy safety directors	12,000 00	
2 Inspectors power and hydraulic piping.	3,600 00	
22 District inspectors...	33,000 00	
8 Lady visitors........	9,600 00	

High explosive inspector	1,800	00
Grade I clerk.......	1,800	00
Grade III clerk......	900	00
Grade II stenographers	1,080	00
4 Grade III stenographers	3,480	00

MINING DEPARTMENT.

Chief deputy........	$3,000	00
12 District deputies.....	21,600	00
Caretaker mine rescue car	1,200	00
Grade I clerk.......	1,560	00
2 Grade I typists......	1,980	00
Grade II typist......	900	00
Grade II stenographer	900	00

EXAMINER OF STEAM ENGINES.

Chief deputy........	$3,000	00
Assistant deputy.....	2,000	00
10 District deputies.....	17,000	00
Grade II clerk.......	1,700	00
Grade III clerk......	1,200	00

BOILER INSPECTION.

Chief deputy........	$3,000	00
Assistant chief deputy	2,300	00
8 District deputies.....	16,000	00
Grade IV bookkeeper.	1,200	00
Grade I clerk.......	1,800	00
Grade III stenographer	900	00
Grade I typist.......	1,200	00
2 Grade II typists.....	2,040	00

FILM CENSORSHIP.

3 Members of board...	$6,000	00
2 Operators	2,400	00
Grade II clerk......	1,200	00
2 Grade III clerks.....	1,740	00
4 Grade III stenographers	3,480	00
Total	$543,750	00
A 2 Wages	750	00

854

General
appropriations.
1930-1931.

	Items.	Appropriations.
A 3 Unclassified—		
Local and special medical examination.	$2,000 00	
Witness fees.......	600 00	
Miscellaneous	500 00	
Total	$3,100 00	
Total personal service........		$547,600 00
Maintenance—		
C Supplies—		
C 1 Food	$100 00	
C 3 Fuel	100 00	
C 4 Office	37,000 00	
C 5 Medical	25 00	
C 11 General Plant—		
Leaders	2,000 00	
Other	1,000 00	
Total	$40,225 00	
E Equipment—		
E 1 Office	$5,000 00	
E 3 Surgical	100 00	
E 9 General plant..	2,500 00	
Total	$7,600 00	
F Contract and Open Order Service—		
F 1 Repairs	$1,000 00	
F 4 Light, heat and power	900 00	
F 5 Freight, express and drayage	1,000 00	
F 6 Traveling expense	74,000 00	
F 7 Communication.	3,700 00	
F 9 General plant..	5,000 00	
Total	$85,600 00	
H Fixed Charges and Contributions—		
H 6 Rent	$38,792 00	
H 7 Insurance	300 00	
Total	$39,092 00	
Total maintenance...........		172,517 00
Total		$720,117 00

DEPARTMENT OF PUBLIC INSTRUCTION.

	Items.	Appropriations.
Personal Service—		
A 1 Salaries—		
Superintendent	$4,000 00	
Assistant superintendent	2,500 00	
Examination clerk...	1,800 00	
Chief clerk..........	2,000 00	
Statistician	2,200 00	
2 High school inspectors	4,000 00	
6 Half time high school inspectors	6,000 00	
Grade IV clerk......	1,000 00	
2 Grade II stenographers	2,400 00	
3 Grade II stenographers	2,700 00	
Inspector of teacher training	2,500 00	
Total	$31,100 00	
A 2 Wages—		
Per diem state board school examiners.	$1,000 00	
Extra stenographic work	200 00	
Total	$1,200 00	
Total personal service........		$32,300 00
Maintenance—		
C Supplies—		
C 4 Office	$2,400 00	
E Equipment—		
E 1 Office	$200 00	
F Contract and Open Order Service—		
F 1 Repairs	$20 00	
F 6 Traveling expense	8,000 00	
F 7 Communication.	350 00	
F 9 General plant..	200 00	
Total	$8,570 00	

General appropriations. 1920-1921.	H Fixed Charges and Contributions—	Items.	Appropriations.

H Fixed Charges and Contributions—
  H 8 Contributions—
    State contribution toward salaries of county superintendents $88,000 00
    State contribution toward salaries of district superintendents 200,000 00
    State contribution to districts with county normal schools 50,000 00
    Model rural schools 6,000 00

    Total $344,000 00
    Total maintenance........... 355,170 00

    Total $387,470 00

SUPERINTENDENT OF INSURANCE.

Personal Service—
  A 1 Salaries—
    Superintendent $4,500 00
    Deputy superintendent 3,000 00
    Grade II clerk....... 1,980 00
    Grade III statistician 1,680 00
    Secretary 1,560 00
    Bookkeeper 2,100 00
    Assistant bookkeeper. 1,140 00
    Warden 2,400 00
    Chief examiner...... 3,000 00
    5 Examiners 9,600 00
    5 Assistant examiners.. 7,860 00
    Chief actuary....... 4,000 00
    1st assistant actuary. 1,800 00
    3 Assistant actuaries... 4,020 00
    2 Grade II clerks...... 2,280 00
    2 License clerks....... 3,360 00
    Rating clerk........ 3,000 00
    Grade II stenographer 1,140 00
    Grade III stenographer 900 00
    Grade IV clerk...... 600 00

    Total $59,920 00

	Items.	Appropriations.	General appropriations, 1920-1921.

A 2 Wages—
  6 Extra clerks....... 1,350 00

Total personal service........ $61,270 00

Maintenance—
C Supplies—
  C 4 Office $2,200 00

E Equipment—
  E 1 Office $300 00

F Contract and Open Order Service—
  F 1 Repairs $25 00
  F 5 Freight, express and drayage 50 00
  F 6 Traveling expense 11,000 00
  F 7 Communication. 370 00
  F 9 General plant.. 100 00

Total $11,545 00

H Fixed Charges and Contributions—
  H 6 Rent $2,980 00
  H 8 Contributions.. 252 00

Total $3,232 00

Total maintenance 17,277 00

Total $78,547 00

THE JUDICIARY.

Personal Service—
A 1 Salaries—
  127 Judges common pleas $381,000 00
  24 Judges court of appeals 144,000 00
  6 Justices supreme court 39,000 00
  Chief justice supreme court 7,000 00
  3 Judges superior court 9,000 00
  8 Stenographers 14,400 00

Total personal service......... $594,400 00

		Items.	Appropriations.
Maintenance—			
F Contract and Open Or- der Service—			
F 6 Traveling expense		$13,800 00	
Chief justice su- preme court.		200 00	
Total		$14,000 00	
Total maintenance			14,000 00
Total			$608,400 00

LEGISLATIVE REFERENCE DEPARTMENT.

		Items.	Appropriations.
Personal Service—			
A 1 Salaries—			
Assistant director....		$1,800 00	
Librarian		1,020 00	
Secretary		1,140 00	
Research assistant....		720 00	
Total		$4,680 00	
A 2 Wages		1,200 00	
A 3 Unclassified		300 00	
Total personal service........			$6,180 00
Maintenance—			
C Supplies—			
C 4 Office		$200 00	
C 11 General plant.		150 00	
Total		$350 00	
E Equipment—			
E 1 Office		$125 00	
E 9 General plant..		300 00	
Total		$425 00	
F Contract and Open Or- der Servcie—			
F 1 Repairs		$10 00	
F 7 Communication.		200 00	
F 9 General plant..		200 00	
Total		$410 00	
Total maintenance			1,185 00
Total			$7,365 00

859

STATE LIBRARY.

General
appropriations,
1920-1921.

	Items.	Appropriations.
Personal Service—		
A 1 Salaries—		
Librarian	$3,000 00	
Assistant librarian	1,500 00	
Assistant secretary	900 00	
Document librarian	1,100 00	
8 Assistants	7,380 00	
Stenographer	720 00	
Messenger	900 00	
Total	$15,500 00	
A 2 Wages—		
Laborer	400 00	
Total personal service		$15,900 00
Maintenance—		
C Supplies—		
C 4 Office	$550 00	
C 11 General plant.	50 00	
Total	$600 00	
E Equipment—		
E 1 Office	$200 00	
E 9 General plant..	3,500 00	
Total	$3,700 00	
F Contract and Open Order Service—		
F 1 Repairs	$200 00	
F 6 Traveling expense	400 00	
F 7 Communication.	225 00	
F 9 General plant..	200 00	
Total	$1,025 00	
Total maintenance		5,325 00
Total		$21,225 00

LIBRARY ORGANIZATION.

	Items.	Appropriations.
Personal Service—		
A 1 Salaries—		
Library organizer	$1,500 00	
Office assistant	720 00	
Total personal service		$2,200 00

		Items.	Appropriations.

Maintenance—
C Supplies—
  C 4 Office $300 00

F Contract nad Open Or-
   der Service—
   F 6 T r a v e l i n g
     expense $700 00
   F 7 Communication. 95 00

   Total $795 00

   Total maintenance 1,095 00

   Total $3,315 00

TRAVELING LIBRARY.

Personal Service—
A 1 Salaries—
  Superintendent $1,200 00
  4 Assistants 3,600 00
  Stenographer 840 00
  Janitor 780 00

  Total personal service........ $6,420 00

Maintenance—
C Supplies—
  C 4 Office $350 00

E Equipment—
  E 1 Office 150 00
  E 9 General plant.. 1,500 00

  Total $1,650 00

F Contract and Open Or-
   der Service—
   F 1 Repairs $25 00
   F 4 Light, heat and
     power 80 00
   F 5 Freight, express
     and drayage 175 00
   F 7 Communication. 100 00
   F 9 General plant.. 50 00

   Total $430 00

	Items.	Appropriations.	General appropriations. 1920-1921.

H Fixed Charges and Contributions—
H 6 Rent 2,062 44

Total maintenance 4,492 44

Total $10,912 44

STATE MEDICAL BOARD.

Personal Service—
A 1 Salaries—
Secretary $3,000 00
Entrance examiner... 450 00
Clerk-stenographer .. 1,200 00
Grade II stenog-
rapher 1,200 00
Inspector 1,200 00

Total $7,050 00

A 2 Wages—
Per diem board mem-
bers $2,250 00
Osteopathic examining
committee 200 00
Special examiners.... 200 00

Total $2,650 00

A 3 Unclassified 1,200 00

Total personal service........ $10,900 00

Maintenance—
C Supplies—
C 4 Office $700 00
C 6 Cleaning 35 00

Total $735 00

E Equipment—
E 1 Office $155 50
E 9 General plant.. 10 00

Total $165 50

F Contract and Open Or-
der Service—
F 1 Repairs $50 00
F 5 Freight, express
and drayage 20 00

	Items.	Appropriations.
F 6 Traveling expense	2,600 00	
F 7 Communication.	110 00	
F 9 General plant..	160 00	
Total	$2,940 00	
H Fixed Charges and Contributions—		
H 6 Rent	$92 00	
H 7 Insurance	12 50	
H 8 Contributions..	25 00	
Total	$129 50	
Total maintenance		3,970 00
Total		$14,870 00

NURSE REGISTRATION.

	Items.	Appropriations.
Personal Service—		
A 1 Salaries—		
Secretary	$1,200 00	
Entrance examiner...	850 00	
Chief examiner......	2,000 00	
Grade III stenographer	900 00	
Total	$4,950 00	
A 2 Wages—		
Per diem nurses' examination committee	1,900 00	
A 3 Unclassified—		
Engrossed certificates.	100 00	
Reading entrance examination papers.	50 00	
Witness fees and mileage	35 00	
Other	80 00	
Total	$265 00	
Total personal service........		$7,115 00
Maintenance—		
C Supplies—		
C 4 Office	$375 00	
C 6 Cleaning	71 50	
Total	$392 50	

		Items.	Appropriations.	General appropriations. 1920-1921.

E Equipment—
 E 1 Office $18 00

F Contract and Open Or-
  der Service—
 F 1 Repairs 5 00
 F 5 Freight, express
  and drayage 5 00
 F 6 T r a v e l i n g
  expense 800 00
 F 7 Communication. 80 00
 F 9 General plant.. 113 00

  Total $1,003 00

H Fixed Charges and
  Contributions—
 ·H 6 Rent $100 00

  Total maintenance 1,513 50

  Total $8,628 50

MISCELLANEOUS BUDGET.

CONTROLLING BOARD.

Maintenance—
 F Contract and Open Order Service—
  F 8 Contingencies—Uses and pur-
   poses $12,000 00

EMERGENCY BOARD.

Maintenance—
 F Contract and Open Order Service—
  F 8 Contingencies, Uses and pur-
   poses $250,000 00

IRREDUCIBLE DEBT.

Maintenance—
 H Fixed Charges and Contributions—
  H 8 Contributions $262,000 00

COMMON SCHOOLS.

Maintenance—
 H Fixed Charges and Contributions—
  H 8 Contributions $2,775,000 00

STATE AID TO WEAK SCHOOLS.

	Items.	Appropriations.

Maintenance—
H   Fixed Charges and Contributions—
    H 8   Contributions $600,000 00

SCHOOL FOR DEAF, BLIND AND CRIPPLED CHILDREN.

Maintenance—
H   Fixed Charges and Contributions—
    H 8   Contributions $160,000 00

HEADQUARTERS SPANISH-AMERICAN WAR VETERANS.

Maintenance—
F   Contract and Open Order Service—
    F 9   General plant.............. $1,500 00

OHIO NATIONAL GUARD.

Personal Service—
A 1   Salaries—
    Superintendent state
        arsenal $1,800 00
    Clerk state arsenal...   960 00
    Machinist state
        arsenal 1,200 00
    Stockkeeper state
        arsenal 1,200 00
    4 Laborers state arsenal.   4,000 00

        Total $9,160 00

A 2   Wages—
    Drill pay $40,000 00
    Camp pay 60,000 00

        Total $100,000 00

A 3   Unclassified—
    Inspections and ex-
        aminations $16,000 00
    Other 15,000 00

        Total $31,000 00

        Total personal service........ $140,160 00

Maintenance—
C   Supplies and subsist-
        ence $43,000 00

		Items.	Appropriations.	General appropriations, 1920-1921.

E Equipment and uniforms 14,500 00

F Contract and Open Order Service—
    F 5 Freight, express and drayage $5,000 00
    F 6 Traveling expense 45,000 00
    F 9 General Plant—
    Incidental expense military companies 31,287 10
    Horse hire........   15,000 00
    Incidental camp expenses 10,000 00
    Expenses Camp Perry.   10,000 00
    Promotion rifle practiice 20,000 00
    Other 15,000 00
    Essex Ship Company 6,000 00
    Dorothea Shpi Company 6,000 00

        Total $163,287 10

        Total maintenance $220,787 10

Armory Fund.

Personal Service—
  A 1 Salaries—
    Architect $3,000 00
    Clerk state armories..   1,200 00

        Total personal service........ $4,200 00

Maintenance—
  F Contract and Open Order Service—
    F 9 General plant.. $46,765 00
    Maintenance of armories 14,800 00

        Total $61,565 00

  H Fixed Charges and Contributions—
    H 6 Rent 50,000 00

        Total maintenance 111,565 00

        Total $476,712 10

General
appropriations,
1920-1921.

STATE INSPECTOR OF OILS.

	Items.	Appropriations.
Personal Service—		
A 1 Salaries—		
Inspector	$3,500 00	
Chief clerk..........	1,500 00	
42 Deputy inspectors....	48,000 00	
Total personal service........		$53,000 00
Maintenance—		
C Supplies—		
C 4 Office	$200 00	
E Equipment—		
E 1 Office	$25 00	
E 9 General plant..	100 00	
Total	$125 00	
F Contract and Open Order Service—		
F 1 Repairs	$25 00	
F 6 Traveling expense	11,000 00	
F 7 Communication.	200 00	
F 9 General plant..	200 00	
Total	$11,425 00	
H Fixed Charges and Contribuions—		
H 7 Insurance	200 00	
Total maintenance		11,950 00
Total		$64,950 00

STATE BOARD OF OPTOMETRY.

	Items.	
Personal Service—		
A 1 Salaries—		
Secretary	$500 00	
Clerk	840 00	
Total	$1,340 00	
A 2 Wages—		
Per diem five members of board	$2,000 00	

	Items.	Appropriations.	General appropriations, 1920-1921.
Extra help	500 00		
Total	$2,500 00		
Total personal service........		$3,840 00	

Maintenance—
C Supplies—

C 4 Office	$250 00	
C 11 General plant.	25 00	
Total	$275 00	

E Equipment—

E 1 Office	$100 00	

F Contract and Open Order Service—

F 6 Traveling expense	$500 00	
F 7 Communication.	100 00	
F 9 General plant..	75 00	
Total	$675 00	

H Fixed Charges and Contributions—

H 6 Rent	$300 00	
Total maintenance		1,350 00
Total		$5,190 00

OHIO PENITENTIARY COMMISSION.

Maintenance—
F Contract and Open Order Service—

F 9 General plant	$750 00

STATE BOARD OF PHARMACY.

Personal Service—
A 1 Salaries—

Secretary	$2,000 00
Stenographer	900 00
Inspector	1,200 00
Entrance examiner...	200 00
Total	$4,300 00

		Items.	Appropriations.
A 2 Wages—			
Per diem five members of board........		$1,500 00	
Janitor		15 00	
Total		$1,515 00	
Total personal service........			$5,815 00
Maintenance—			
C Supplies—			
C 4 Office		$650 00	
E Equipment—			
E 1 Office		$50 00	
F Contract and Open Order Service—			
F 1 Repairs		$10 00	
F 6 Traveling expense		2,500 00	
F 7 Communication.		125 00	
F 9 General plant..		25 00	
Total		$2,660 00	
H Fixed Charges and Contributions—			
H 8 Contributions .		$25 00	
Total maintenance			3,385 00 .
Total			$9,200 00

COMMISSIONERS OF PUBLIC PRINTING

		Items.	Appropriations.
Personal Service—			
A 1 Salaries—			
Secretary		$500 00	
Total personal service........			$500 00
Maintenance—			
D Materials—			
D 3 General Plant—			
Printing paper		$90,000 00	
Printing paper for experiment station		1,500 00	
Total		$91,500 00	
Total maintenance...........			91,500 00
Total			$92,000 00

SUPERVISOR OF PUBLIC PRINTING.

	Items.	Appropriations.
Personal Service—		
A 1 Salaries—		
Supervisor	$2,000 00	
Secretary	900 00	
Total personal service........		$2,900 00
Maintenance—		
C Supplies—		
C 4 Office	$125 00	
F Contract and Open Order Service—		
F 7 Communication.	$140 00	
F 9 General Plant—		
State printing...	95,000 00	
Total	$95,140 00	
Total maintenance..........		95,265 00
Total		$98,165 00

STATE BINDERY.

	Items.	Appropriations.
Personal Service—		
A 1 Salaries—		
Superintendent	$1,900 00	
Stenographer and bookkeeper	960 00	
Forelady	762 00	
Bindery workers.....	6,882 00	
2 Rulers	2,580 00	
Stamper	1,290 00	
Job forwarder.......	1,290 00	
Machinist	1,290 00	
Blank book forwarder	1,290 00	
Finisher	1,290 00	
Folding machine operator	1,200 00	
10 Edition forwarders..	12,060 00	
Messenger	1,090 00	
Elevator operator....	810 00	
Janitor	810 00	
Total personal service........		$35,504 00
Maintenance—		
C Supplies—		
C 4 Office	$75 00	
C 6 Cleaning	39 00	
C 11 General plant.	12,000 00	
Total	$12,114 00	

	Items.	Appropriations.

F Contract and Open Order Service—

F 1 Repairs	$350 00	
F 4 Light, heat and power	280 00	
F 5 Freight, express and drayage	135 00	
F 7 Communication.	135 00	
F 9 General plant..	400 00	
Total	$1,300 00	

H Fixed Charges and Contributions—

H 6 Rent	$4,100 00	
Total maintenance...........		17,514 00
Total		$53,018 00

PROSECUTION AND TRANSPORTATION OF CONVICTS.

Maintenance—
F Contract and Open Order Service—
F 9 General Plant—
Fees, costs, mileage and other expenses provided by statute.. $170,000 00

HOUSE OF REPRESENTATIVES.

Personal Service—
A 1 Salaries—

125 Members	$125,000 00
Clerk	3,000 00
Deputy clerk........	1,800 00
Clerk-stenographer ..	1,800 00
Custodian	1,800 00
Porter	900 00
Total	$134,300 00

A 2 Wages—

10 Assistant clerks......	$6,000 00
Superintendent of stenographers ...	600 00
10 Stenographers	6,000 00
4 Sergeants-at-arms ...	2,400 00
Assistant postmaster.	600 00
2 Telephone attendants.	960 00
2 Cloak room attendants	840 00

	Items.	Appropriations.	General appropriations. 1920-1921.
5 Doorkeepers	2,100 00		
5 Committee room attendants	2,100 00		
5 Porters	2,100 00		
10 Pages	3,000 00		
Total	$26,700 00		
A 3 Unclassified—			
Chaplain	$200 00		
Labor	100 00		
Total	$300 00		
Total personal service........		$161,300 00	
Maintenance—			
C Supplies—			
C 4 Office	$1,500 00		
C 5 Cleaning	300 00		
C 11 General plant.	50 00		
Total	$1,850 00		
E Equipment—			
E 1 Office	$200 00		
E 9 General plant..	500 00		
Total	$700 00		
F Contract and Open Order Service—			
F 1 Repairs	$500 00		
F 5 Freight, express and drayage	100 00		
F 6 Traveling expense	15,000 00		
F 7 Communication.	1,500 00		
F 9 General Plant—			
Expense legislative committees	3,000 00		
Printing enrolled bills	3,500 00		
Total	$23,600 00		
H Fixed Charges and Contributions—			
H 6 Rent	$300 00		
H 8 Contributions .	400 00		
Total	$700 00		
Total maintenance...........		26,850 00	
Total		$188,150 00	

SENATE.

	Items.	Appropriations.

Personal Service—
  A 1 Salaries—

37 Senators	$37,000 00	
Lieutenant governor.	1,500 00	
Clerk	3,000 00	
Assistant clerk......	1,800 00	
Recording clerk......	1,800 00	
Custodian	1,800 00	
Porter	900 00	
Stenographer for lieutenant governor and senators....	1,200 00	
Stenographer	1,200 00	
Total	$50,200 00	

  A 2 Wages—

5 Clerks	$3,000 00	
4 Assistant sergeant-at-arms	2,400 00	
3 Doorkeepers	1,260 00	
4 Committee room attendants	1,680 00	
2 Custodians of cloak room	840 00	
2 Telephone attendants.	840 00	
Assistant postmaster.	600 00	
Assistant bill clerk...	600 00	
7 Stenographers	4,200 00	
4 Pages	1,200 00	
2 Porters	840 00	
Total	$17,460 00	
Total personal service.........		$67,660 00

Maintenance—
  C Supplies—

C 4 Office	$1,000 00	
C 6 Cleaning	150 00	
Total	$1,150 00	

  E Equipment—

E 1 Office	$100 00	

  F Contract and Open Order Service—

F 1 Repairs	$100 00	

	Items.	Appropriations.	General appropriations. 1920-1921.
F 6 Traveling Expense—			
Mileage of members	2,500 00		
Other	100 00		
F 7 Communication.	1,000 00		
F 8 Contingencies .	500 00		
F 9 General Plant—			
Expense legislative committees	4,000 00		
Expense joint committees	1,500 00		
.Printing enrolled bills	3,000 00		
Total	$12,700 00		
H Fixed Charges and Contributions—			
H 6 Rent	$150 00		
Total maintenance...........		14,100 00	
Total		$81,760 00	

SECRETARY OF STATE.

	Items.	Appropriations.
Personal Service—		
A 1 Salaries—		
Secretary of state....	$6,500 00	
Assistant secretary of state	3,000 00	
Corporation adviser..	2,200 00	
Statistician	2,300 00	
Superintendent of distribution	1,500 00	
Stockman	1,500 00	
Cashier	2,000 00	
Grade III clerk, ...	1,500 00	
Assistant recording clerk	1,500 00	
Grade II clerk......	1,350 00	
Special statistician...	2,000 00	
Grade II stenographer	1,080 00	
Grade III stenographer	1,080 00	
2 Grade I typists......	2,160 00	
Stenographer	1,200 00	
Janitor and messenger	700 00	
Total personal service........		$31,570 00

		Items.	Appropriations.
Maintenance—			
C Supplies—			
C 4 Office		$1,500 00	
E Equipment—			
E 1 Office		$175 00	
F Contract and Open Order Service—			
F 1 Repairs		$50 00	
F 6 Traveling expense		35 00	
F 7 Communication.		600 00	
F 8 Contingencies—			
Absent voters' fund		1,000 00	
F 9 General Plant—			
Distribution of books		3,000 00	
Printing and distributing constitutional amendments		30,000 00	
Total		$34,685 00	
Total maintenance...........			36,360 00
Total			$67,930 00

AUTOMOBILE DEPARTMENT.

		Items.	Appropriations.
Personal Service—			
A 1 Salaries—			
Registrar		$3,000 00	
Grade I clerk........		1,980 00	
Cashier		1,980 00	
Grade I clerk........		1,800 00	
3 Grade II clerks......		3,420 00	
3 Grade III clerks.....		2,580 00	
2 Grade II stenographers		2,160 00	
4 Grade II typists.....		3,600 00	
Grade II typist......		840 00	
2 Inspectors		2,400 00	
Janitor and messenger		900 00	
Total		$24,660 00	
A 2 Wages—			
10 Extra clerks and stenographers ...		$4,200 00	

	Items.	Appropriations.	General appropriations. 1920-1921.
3 Extra clerks and stenographers ...	1,800 00		
Total	$6,000 00		
Total personal service........		$30,660 00	

Maintenance—
 C Supplies—

C 4 Office	$33,500 00		
C 11 General Plant—Automobile and motorcycle tags....	90,000 00		
Total	$123,500 00		

D Materials—

D 3 General Plant—Print paper.......	$3,000 00		

F Contract and Open Order Service—

F 6 Traveling expense	$1,800 00		
F 7 Communication.	250 00		
F 9 General plant..	14,000 00		
Total	$16,050 00		
Total maintenance..........		142,550 00	
Total		$173,210 00	

STATE PURCHASING AGENT.

Personal Service—
 A 1 Salaries—

Purchasing agent.....	$3,000 00		
Grade II clerk.......	1,140 00		
Grade III stenographer	960 00		
Bookkeeper-typist ...	840 00		
Grade III clerk......	900 00		
Clerk	1,200 00		
Total personal service........		$8,040 00	

Maintenance—
 C Supplies—

C 4 Office	$350 00		

E Equipment—

E 1 Office	$200 00		

	Items.	Appropriations.
F Contract and Open Order Service—		
F 1 Repairs	$100 00	
F 7 Communication.	200 00	
F 9 General plant..	1,000 00	
Total	$1,300 00	
Total maintenance..........		1,850 00
Total		$9,890 00

BUREAU OF VITAL STATISTICS.

	Items.	Appropriations.
Personal Service—		
A 1 Salaries—		
Registrar	$2,000 00	
Grade II clerk......	1,500 00	
Chief inspector......	1,500 00	
Statistician	1,500 00	
Grade III clerk......	1,200 00	
12 Grade III clerks.....	10,800 00	
Grade II stenographer	1,080 00	
4 Grade III stenographers	3,600 00	
2 Grade I typists......	2,040 00	
Total personal service........		$25,220 00
Maintenance—		
C Supplies—		
C 4 Office	$3,000 00	
E Equipment—		
E 1 Office	$300 00	
F Contract and Open Order Service—		
F 5 Freight, express and drayage	$100 00	
F 6 Traveling expense	1,100 00	
F 7 Communication.	250 00	
F 9 General plant..	50 00	
Total	$1,500 00	
H Fixed Charges and Contributions—		
H 6 Rent	$240 00	
Total maintenance..........		5,040 00
Total		$30,260 00

SECURITIES DEPARTMENT.

	Items.	Appropriations.
Personal Service—		
A 1 Salaries—		
Commissioner	$4,000 00	
Deputy commissioner.	3,000 00	
Stenographer	1,320 00	
2 Grade III stenographers	1,800 00	
Grade III clerk......	900 00	
Grade III bookkeeper	1,800 00	
Chief examiner......	2,750 00	
7 Examiners	14,000 00	
Accountant	2,000 00	
Chief examiner chattel loans........	2,500 00	
Examiner	2,000 00	
Examiner	1,600 00	
2 Assistant examiners..	3,000 00	
Grade III stenographer	900 00	
Total	$41,570 00	
A 2 Wages—		
Extra help..........	$125 00	
A 3 Unclassified	100 00	
Total personal service........		$41,795 00
Maintenance—		
C Supplies—		
C 4 Office	$900 00	
E Equipment—		
E 1 Office	$75 00	
E 9 General plant..	25 00	
Total	$100 00	
F Contract and Open Order Service—		
F 1 Repairs	$20 00	
F 6 Traveling expense	11,500 00	
F 7 Communication.	500 00	
F 9 General plant..	100 00	
Total	$12,120 00	

H Fixed Charges and Contributions—	Items.	Appropriations.
H 6 Rent	$1,620 00	
H 7 Insurance	225 00	
H 8 Contributions .	200 00	
Total	$2,045 00	
Total maintenance...........		15,165 00
Total		$56,960 00

COMMISSIONER OF SOLDIERS' CLAIMS.

Personal Service— A 1 Salaries—		
Commissioner	$2,500 00	
Chief clerk.........	1,140 00	
Notarial clerk.......	420 00	
Total personal service........		$4,060 00

Maintenance— C Supplies—		
C 4 Office	$125 00	
F Contract and Open Order Service—		
F 7 Communication.	$40 00	
Total maintenance...........		165 00
Total		$4,225 00

OHIO SOLDIERS' & SAILORS' ORPHANS' HOME.

Personal Service— A 1 Salaries—		
Superintendent	$2,100 00	
Chief matron........	720 00	
Bookkeeper	780 00	
Storekeeper	900 00	
Assistant storekeeper.	300 00	
Physician	1,500 00	
Dentist	540 00	
Superintendent of schools	1,500 00	
36 Matrons	18,960 00	
28 Teachers	13,690 00	
Minor officers and employes	48,630 00	
Total	$89,620 00	

		Items.	Appropriations.	General Appropriations. 1920-1921.
A 2	Wages	2,800 00		
A 3	Unclassified	500 00		
	Total personal service........		$92,920 00	

Maintenance—
C Supplies—

			Items.
C	1	Food	$75,000 00
C	2	Forage	4,000 00
C	3	Fuel	18,500 00
C	4	Office	350 00
C	5	Medical	500 00
C	6	Cleaning	3,000 00
C	8	Educational ..	675 00
C	9	Agricultural .	550 00
C	11	General plant.	2,100 00
		Total	$104,675 00

D Materials—

D	2	Building	$2,000 00
D	2	General plant..	20,000 00
		Total	$22,000 00

E Equipment—

E	1	Office	$61 50
E	2	Household	2,000 00
E	3	Medical	250 00
E	4	Livestock	50 00
E	5	Agricultural ..	100 00
E	6	Motor vehicle..	200 00
E	7	Wearing apparel	2,000 00
E	8	Educational ...	1,000 00
E	9	General plant..	3,000 00
		Total	$8,661 50

F Contract and Open Order Service—

F	1	Repairs	$1,000 00
F	5	Freight, express and drayage	500 00
F	6	Traveling expense	2,000 00
F	7	Communication.	275 00
F	9	General plant..	1,300 00
		Total	$5,075 00

		Items.	Appropriations.
H Fixed Charges and Contributions—			
H 6	Rent	$415 00	
H 7	Insurance	112 50	
H 8	Contributions—		
	Presents to discharged pupils	2,000 00	
	Total	$2,527 50	
	Total maintenance..........		142,939 00
	Total		$235,859 00

SUPREME COURT AND LAW LIBRARY.

Personal Service—			
A 1 Salaries—			
	Marshal and law librarian	$2,500 00	
	Assistant librarian and chief clerk..	2,000 00	
2	Assistant librarians..	2,700 00	
	1st deputy marshal..	1,500 00	
	2nd deputy marshal..	1,200 00	
	3rd deputy marshal..	1,200 00	
	Secretary	1,500 00	
3	Secretaries	5,140 00	
3	Porters	3,060 00	
	Total	$20,800 00	
A 2	Wages	130 00	
	Total personal service........		$20,930 00

Maintenance—			
C Supplies—			
C 4	Office	$506 00	
C 6	Cleaning	85 00	
C 11	General plant.	100 00	
	Total	$691 00	
D Materials—			
D 3	General plant..	$76 00	
E Equipment—			
E 1	Office	$265 00	
E 8	Educational— Books and legal periodicals	2,900 00	
E 9	General plant..	50 00	
	Total	$3,215 00	

	Items.	Appropriations.	General appropriations. 1920-1921.
F Contract and Open Order Service—			
F 1 Repairs	$100 00		
F 5 Freight, express and drayage	90 00		
F 6 Traveling expense	50 00		
F 7 Communication.	1,150 00		
F 8 Contingencies .	75 00		
F 9 General plant..	196 00		
Total	$1,661 00		
H Fixed Charges and Contributions—			
H 6 Rent	$20 00		
Total maintenance..........		5,663 00	
Total		$26,593 00	

CLERK SUPREME COURT.

	Items.	Appropriations.	
Personal Service—			
A 1 Salaries—			
Clerk	$4,000 00		
1st deputy clerk.....	2,100 00		
2nd deputy clerk.....	1,800 00		
Correspondence clerk.	1,500 00		
Messenger	900 00		
Total personal service..........		$10,300 00	
Maintenance—			
C Supplies—			
C 4 Office	$400 00		
E Equipment—			
E 1 Office	$50 00		
F Contract and Open Order Service—			
F 1 Repairs	$10 00		
F 5 Freight, express and drayage	3 00		
F 7 Communication.	144 00		
F 9 General plant..	15 00		
Total	$172 00		
Total maintenance..........		622 00	
Total		$10,922 00	

SUPREME COURT REPORTER.

	Items.	Appropriations.
Personal Service—		
A 1 Salaries—		
Reporter	$3,000 00	
2 Assistant reporters...	4,000 00	
Clerk	1,600 00	
Total personal service........		$8,600 00
Maintenance—		
C Supplies—		
C 4 Office	$110 00	
E Equipment—		
E 1 Office	$100 00	
F Contract and Open Or- der Service—		
F 7 Communication.	$90 00	
F 8 Contingencies .	75 00	
F 9 General plant..	50 00	
Total	$215 00	
Total maintenance..........		425 00
Total		$9,025 00

TAX COMMISSSION OF OHIO.

	Items.	
Personal Service—		
A 1 Salaries—		
3 Commissioners	$12,000 00	
Secretary	3,000 00	
Auditor	3,600 00	
Special accountant...	3,000 00	
Corporation account- ant	2,700 00	
2 Special examiners....	4,800 00	
2 Grade II accountants.	4,400 00	
Grade II accountant..	1,800 00	
Junior accountant...	1,200 00	
Grade III stenog- rapher	1,080 00	
3 Grade II stenog- raphers	3,480 00	
Grade III stenog- rapher	900 00	
Stenographer	1,200 00	
Grade II typist......	1,200 00	
Total	$44,300 00	

	Items.	Appropriations.	General appropriations, 1920-1921.

A 2 Wages—
    Extra stenographic
      work 250 00
A 3 Unclassified 500 00

        Total personal service........ $45,050 00

Maintenance—
  C Supplies—
    C 4 Office $2,000 00

  E Equipment—
    E 1 Office $200 00

  F Contract and Open Order Service—

    F 1 Repairs $30 00
    F 6 Traveling expense 3,500 00
    F 7 Communication. 500 00
    F 9 General plant.. 500 00

      Total $4,530 00
      Total maintenance.......... 6,730 00

      Total $51,840 00

TREASURER OF STATE.

Personal Service—
  A 1 Salaries—
    Treasurer $6,500 00
    Cashier 3,400 00
    Chief clerk.......... 2,400 00
    Grade I bookkeeper.. 2,100 00
    Grade II bookkeeper. 1,740 00
    Bookkeeper 1,800 00
    Bond clerk.......... 2,100 00
    Correspondence clerk 1,200 00
    3 Grade II clerks...... 4,860 00
    2 Grade III clerks..... 1,800 00
    Janitor and messenger 960 00

      Total personal service........ $28,860 00

Maintenance—
  C Supplies—
    C 4 Office $4,000 00

  E Equipment—
    E 1 Office $400 00

	Items.	Appropriations.
F Contract and Open Order Service—		
F 7 Communication.	$300 00	
F 9 General plant..	150 00	
Total	$450 00	
H Fixed Charges and Contributions—		
H 7 Insurance—		
Premium on treasurer's bond.....	$1,800 00	
Premium on cashier's bond	300 00	
Total	$2,100 00	
Total maintenance..........		6,950 00
Total		$35,810 00

PUBLIC UTILITIES COMMISSION.

Personal Service—		
A 1 Salaries—		
3 Commissioners	$13,500 00	
Engine and boiler inspector	2,000 00	
Inspector automatic couplers	1,750 00	
Secretary	3,000 00	
Assistant secretary...	2,400 00	
Attorney	4,000 00	
Superintendent bureau of rates and service	4,000 00	
Auditor and statistician	3,000 00	
Inspector in charge..	1,750 00	
5 Inspectors	8,750 00	
Grade I engineer....	4,500 00	
2 Grade II engineers...	6,000 00	
2 Grade III engineers..	4,320 00	
2 Grade I clerks.......	3,480 00	
2 Grade II clerks......	2,520 00	
4 Grade II stenographers	4,800 00	
Grade I telephone operator	720 00	
Grade I typist......	1,400 00	
Total	$71,890 00	

	Items.	Appropriations.	General appropriations. 1920-1921.
A 3 Unclassified—			
Investigating issues of securities	$2,500 00		
Reporting h e a r i n g s and transcribing testimony	3,300 00		
Total	$5,800 00		
Total personal service........		$77,690 00	

Maintenance—
C Supplies—

C 4 Office	$1,200 00		

E Equipment—

E 1 Office	$1,000 00		

F Contract and Open Order Service—

F 1 Repairs	$50 00		
F 5 F r e i g h t, express a n d drayage	100 00		
F 6 T r a v eling expense	10,000 00		
F 7 Communication.	1,600 00		
F 9 General plant.	150 00		
Total	$11,900 00		

H Fixed C h a r g e s and Contributions—

H 7 Insurance	$60 00		
Total maintenance..........		14,160 00	
Total		$91,850 00	

PHYSICAL VALUATION—PUBLIC UTILITIES.

Personal Service—
A 1 Salaries—

2 Grade III engineers.	$3,840 00		
18 Grade IV engineers..	32,460 00		
10 Grade II clerks......	14,410 00		
Grade II s t e n o gographer	1,080 00		
Total	$51,790 00		
A 3 Unclassified—			
Additional help......	2,000 00		
Total personal service........		$53,790 00	

	Items.	Appropriations.
Maintenance—		
C Supplies—		
C 4 Office	$150 00	
C 11 General plant.	25 00	
Total	$175 00	
E Equipment—		
E 1 Office	$200 00	
E 9 General plant..	100 00	
Total	$300 00	
F Contract and Open Order Service—		
F 1 Repairs	$25 00	
F 5 Freight, express and drayage	25 00	
F 6 Traveling expense	12,000 00	
F 7 Communication.	200 00	
F 9 General plant..	50 00	
Total	$12,300 00	
H Fixed Charges and Contributions—		
H 6 Rent	$200 00	
Total maintenance..........		12,975 00
Total		$66,765 00

DEPARTMENT OF PUBLIC WORKS.

	Items.	
Personal Service—		
A 1 Salaries—		
Superintendent	$4,000 00	
Assistant superintendent	2,500 00	
Secretary	2,000 00	
Grade IV engineer...	2,400 00	
Grade IV engineer...	1,800 00	
Grade IV engineer...	1,620 00	
Grade V engineer....	1,500 00	
Clerk-stenographer ..	1,200 00	
2 Grade III stenographers	1,920 00	
Grade IV clerk......	840 00	
8 Foremen	9,660 00	
39 Patrolmen	11,430 00	

	Items.	Appropriations.	General appropriations. 1920-1921.
4 Policemen	3,420 00		
Total	$44,290 00		
A 2 Wages	30,000 00		
Total personal service........		$74,290 00	

Maintenance—
  C Supplies—

		Items.		
C 3	Fuel	$1,800 00		
C 4	Office	600 00		
C 11	General plant.	1,000 00		
	Total	$3,400 00		

D Materials—

D 3	General plant..	$2,500 00

E Equipment—

E 1	Office	$100 00
E 9	General plant...	500 00
	Total	$600 00

F Contract and Open Order Service—

F 1	Repairs	$75 00		
F 4	Light, heat and power	60 00		
F 5	Freight, express and drayage	500 00		
F 6	Traveling expense	3,500 00		
F 7	Communication.	800 00		
F 9	General plant..	600 00		
	Total	$5,535 00		
	Total maintenance..........		12,035 00	
	Total		$86,325 00	

BOWLING GREEN STATE NORMAL SCHOOL.

Personal Service—
  A 1 Salaries—

President	$4,300 00
Dean	2,750 00
Dean of women—12 months	1,600 00
Financial clerk......	1,500 00
Clerk	1,000 00

	Items.	Appropriations.
Stenographer	720 00	
2 Janitors	1,680 00	
Janitress	500 00	
Superintendent of buildings and grounds	900 00	
Chief engineer.......	1,080 00	
2 Firemen	1,800 00	
Night watchman.....	780 00	
2 Librarians	1,600 00	
2 Extension lecturers..	4,000 00	
High school inspector.	1,000 00	
Professors, instructors and other employes	49,250 00	
Total	$74,460 00	

A 2 Wages—

Extra labor.........	$1,400 00	
Extra clerk hire.....	500 00	
Student assistants....	1,152 00	
Critic teachers—Part time	1,500 00	
Summer school..	10,500 00	
Total	$15,052 00	
A 3 Unclassified	140 00	
Total personal service........		$89,652 00

Maintenance—

C Supplies—

C 1	Food	$150 00	
C 3	Fuel	8,000 00	
C 4	Office	600 00	
C 6	Cleaning	150 00	
C 8	Educational ..	1,600 00	
C 9	Agricultural .	300 00	
C 11	General plant.	1,200 00	
	Total	$12,000 00	

D Materials—

D 3	General plant..	$600 00

E Equipment—

E 1	Office	$200 00
E 8	Educational ..	1,000 00
E 9	General plant..	566 00
	Total	$1,766 00

	Items.	Appropriations.	General appropriations 1920-1921.
F Contract and Open Order Service—			
F 1 Repairs	$600 00		
F 3 Water	600 00		
F 4 Light, heat and power	800 00		
F 5 Freight, express and drayage	300 00		
F 6 Transportation.	1,700 00		
F 7 Communication.	150 00		
F 9 General plant..	1,500 00		
Total	$5,650 00		
Total maintenance...........		20,016 00	
Total		$109,668 00	

KENT STATE NORMAL SCHOOL.

	Items.	
Personal Service—		
A 1 Salaries—		
President	$4,500 00	
Assistant to president—12 months.	1,800 00	
Dean of women—12 months	1,600 00	
2 Extension teachers...	4,000 00	
Professor of agriculture	2,500 00	
High school inspector	1,000 00	
2 Assistant librarians..	1,600 00	
Clerk	1,050 00	
Financial clerk......	1,500 00	
Custodian	1,200 00	
Engineer	1,080 00	
2 Firemen	1,860 00	
Night watchman.....	780 00	
Superintendent of grounds	780 00	
Teamster	720 00	
Mechanician	960 00	
3 Janitors	2,340 00	
Professors, instructors and other employes	59,850 00	
Total	$89,120 00	
A 2 Wages—		
Student assistants...	$1,152 00	
Labor	900 00	

		Items.		Appropriations.
Summer school......		16,000	00	
	Total	$18,052	00	
A 3 Unclassified		140	00	
	Total personal service.......			$107,312 00

Maintenance—
C Supplies—

C 1	Food	$200	00
C 3	Fuel	11,600	00
C 4	Office	500	00
C 6	Cleaning	300	00
C 8	Educational ..	1,600	00
C 9	Agricultural ..	300	00
C 11	General plant.	1,200	00
	Total	$15,700	00

D Materials—

D 2	Building	$400	00
D 3	General plant..	600	00
	Total	$1,000	00

E Equipment—

E 1	Office	$305	00
E 8	Educational ...	1,000	00
E 9	General plant..	600	00
	Total	$1,905	00

F Contract and Open Order Service—

F 1	Repairs	$600	00
F 3	Water	710	00
F 4	Light, heat and power	700	00
F 5	Freight, express and drayage	300	00
F 6	Traveling expense	1,700	00
F 7	Communication.	240	00
F 9	General plant..	2,000	00
	Total	$6,250	00
	Total maintenance..........			24,855 00
	Total			$132,167 00

MIAMI UNIVERSITY.

	Items.	Appropriations.
Personal Service—		
A 1 Salaries—		
President	$5,000 00	
Secretary to board of trustees	2,400 00	
Secretary to the president	1,250 00	
Secretary to dean teachers' college and field agent..	1,200 00	
2 Stenographers	1,680 00	
2 Bookkeepers	2,080 00	
Cashier	1,020 00	
Registrar	400 00	
Assistant registrar...	900 00	
Dean of women......	1,400 00	
Assistant to dean of women	200 00	
Librarian	2,200 00	
3 Assistant librarians..	2,760 00	
Chief engineer......	1,620 00	
2 Engineers	2,100 00	
2 Firemen	910 00	
Night watchman.....	900 00	
8 Janitors	5,580 00	
Truck driver........	450 00	
Carpenter	1,080 00	
3 Deans	9,000 00	
High school inspector.	1,000 00	
2 Extension lecturers..	4,000 00	
Professors, instructors and other employes	118,225 00	
Total	$167,355 00	
A 2 Wages—		
Summer school......	$14,000 00	
Student assistants, labor and clerical help........	7,000 00	
Total	$21,000 00	
A 3 Unclassified—		
Commencement speaker	$100 00	
Total personal service........		$188,455 00

			Items.	Appropriations.
Maintenance—				
C Supplies—				
C	1	Food	$300 00	
C	3	Fuel	10,500 00	
C	4	Office	2,400 00	
C	6	Cleaning	200 00	
C	8	Educational ..	1,100 00	
C	9	Agricultural .	150 00	
C	11	General plant.	875 00	
		Total	$15,525 00	
D Materials—				
D	3	General plant..	$1,000 00	
E Equipment—				
E	1	Office	$200 00	
E	8	Educational ...	7,000 00	
E	9	General plant..	700 00	
		Total	$7,900 00	
F Contract and Open Order Service—				
F	1	Repairs	$4,450 00	
F	3	Water	2,100 00 ·	
F	4	Light, heat and power	800 00	
F	5	Freight, express and drayage	75 00	
F	6	Traveling expense	3,000 00 ·	
F	7	Communication.	500 00	
F	9	General Plant— All endownment monies due Miami University on account of rent and taxes in Oxford, Milford and Hanover townships and	3,700 00	
		Total	$14,625 00	
H Fixed Charges and Contributions—				
H	7	Insurance	$825 00	
H	8	Contributions .	385 00	
		Total	$1,210 00	
		Total maintenance...........		40,260 00
		Total		$228,715 00

OHIO UNIVERSITY.

	Items.	Appropriations.
Personal Service—		
A 1 Salaries—		
President	$6,000 00	
2 Deans	6,000 00	
Dean of women	2,000 00	
Registrar	2,000 00	
Librarian	1,600 00	
Treasurer and business manager	2,500 00	
Secretary-auditor	600 00	
High school inspector	1,000 00	
2 Extension lecturers	4,000 00	
Library assistants	2,000 00	
4 Engineers	5,100 00	
3 Firemen	3,060 00	
9 Janitors	7,560 00	
2 Stenographers	1,620 00	
2 Bookkeepers	2,040 00	
Carpenter	1,200 00	
Plumber	1,100 00	
Painter	900 00	
Night watchman	840 00	
Professors, instructors and other employes	135,500 00	
Total	$186,620 00	
A 2 Wages—		
Extra clerks and laborers	$4,000 00	
Spring term	1,000 00	
Summer term	16,000 00	
Total	$21,000 00	
Total personal service		$207,620 00
Maintenance—		
C Supplies—		
C 1 Food	$300 00	
C 2 Forage	150 00	
C 3 Fuel	11,500 00	
C 4 Office	1,200 00	
C 6 Cleaning	200 00	
C 8 Educational	1,100 00	
C 9 Agricultural	150 00	
C 11 General plant.	1,000 00	
Total	$15,600 00	

			Items.	Appropriations.
D	Materials—			
	D 3	General plant..	$3,000 00	
E	Equipment—			
	E 1	Office	$200 00	
	E 8	Educational ...	7,000 00	
	E 9	General plant..	700 00	
		Total	$7,900 00	
F	Contract and Open Order Service—			
	F 1	Repairs	$2,350 00	
	F 3	Water	2,200 00	
	F 4	Light, heat and power	1,100 00	
	F 5	Freight, express and drayage.....	100 00	
	F 6	Traveling expense	3,000 00	
	F 7	Communication.	500 00	
	F 9	General Plant— All endowment monies due Ohio University on account of rents and taxes in Athens and Alexander townships and	3,700 00	
		Total	$12,950 00	
H	Fixed Charges and Contributions—			
	H 7	Insurance	$900 00	
		Total maintenance		40,350 00
		Total		$247,970 00

OHIO STATE UNIVERSITY.

			Items.
Personal Service—			
A 1	Salaries—		
	President		$7,000 00
	Secretary and business manager		5,000 00
	Registrar		2,500 00
	Purchasing agent....		2,500 00
	Secretary to entrance board		2,400 00
	Dean of women.....		2,400 00

Professors, instructors and other employes 1,025,320 00

Total $1,047,120 00

A 2 Wages—
Labor $50,000 00
Prison labor 4,000 00
Summer session 25,405 00

Total $79,405 00

A 3 Unclassified 15,000 00

Total personal service $1,141,525 00

Maintenance—
C Supplies—

			Items	
C	1	Food	$1,500	00
C	2	Forage	10,000	00
C	3	Fuel	51,000	00
C	4	Office	9,500	00
C	5	Medical	1,600	00
C	6	Cleaning	2,000	00
C	8	Educational	40,000	00
C	9	Agricultural	1,500	00
C	11	General plant.	4,000	00

Total $121,100 00

D Materials—
D 2 Building $1,000 00
D 3 General plant. . 15,000 00

Total $16,000 00

E Equipment—
E 1 Office $3,000 00
E 3 Medical 1,000 00
E 4 Livestock 3,800 00
E 5 Agricultural . . 250 00
E 8 Educational—
Library books . . . 15,000 00
Law library books 2,500 00
Medical library books 2,000 00
Other 40,000 00
E 9 General plant. . 5,000 00

Total $72,550 00

		Items.	Appropriations.
F	Contract and Open Order Service—		
	F 1 Repairs	$12,000 00	
	F 3 Water	10,000 00	
	F 4 Light, heat and and power	1,100 00	
	F 5 Freight, express and drayage.....	2,000 00	
	F 6 Traveling expense	2,000 00	
	F 7 Communication.	5,000 00	
	F 9 General plant..	40,000 00	
	Engineering experiment station	10,000 00	
	Total	$82,000 00	
H	Fixed Charges and Contributions—		
	H 6 Rent	$1,830 00	
	H 7 Insurance	125 00	
	Total	$1,955 00	
I	Rotary Fund—		
	Total maintenance		293,705 00
	Total ....•.................		$1,435,230 00

AGRICULTURAL EXTENSION.

		Items.	
Personal Service—			
A 1 Salaries—			
	Director	$3,600 00	
	Director and assistant	2,300 00	
7	Stenographers	5,760 00	
	Agricultural editor...	3,000 00	
	Assistant·agricultural editor	2,100 00	
	State leader boys and girls club work...	750 00	
2	Assistant leaders boys and girls club work	820 00	
4	Professors	10,250 00	
5	Assistant professors.	11,000 00	
10	Instructors	12,750 00	
3	Professors part time..	1,833 33	
3	Assistant professors part time	2,208 00	

	Items.	Appropriations.	General appropriations 1920 1921.
Assistant	1,200 00		
County agent leader.	1,100 00		
Assistant county agent leader	1,000 00		
Assistant in county agent work	1,600 00		
County agents.......	63,850 00		
Farmers institutes...	3,780 00		
Total	$128,901 33		

A 2 Wages—
Farmers institute speakers	$7,000 00		
Other	1,000 00		
Total	$8,000 00		

A 3 Unclassified—
Farmers week speakers	$750 00		
Total personal service........		$137,651 33	

Maintenance—
C Supplies—
C 4 Office	$2,000 00		
C 8 Educational ...	300 00		
Total	$2,300 00		

D Materials—
D 3 General plant..	$100 00		

E Equipment—
E 1 Office	$300 00		
E 8 Educational ...	2,500 00		
Total	$2,800 00		

F Contract and Open Order Service—
F 1 Repairs	$50 00		
F 6 Traveling expense	23,600 00		
F 7 Communication.	500 00		
F 9 General plant..	3,000 00		
Total	$27,150 00		
Total maintenance		32,350 00	
Total		$170,001 33	

29—G. & L. A.

COMBINED NORMAL AND INDUSTRIAL DEPART-
MENT OF WILBERFORCE UNIVERSITY.

		Items.	Appropriations.
Personal Service—			
A 1 Salaries—			
	Superintendent	$3,000 00	
	Executive clerk	1,200 00	
	Custodian	1,080 00	
	Record clerk and storekeeper	1,200 00	
	Farm manager......	600 00	
	2 Engineers	1,920 00	
	Night watchman.....	600 00	
	2 Matrons	1,200 00	
	Stewardess	480 00	
	Attendant purification plant.......	480 00	
	Farm hand	480 00	
	Student janitors.....	2,000 00	
	Instructors and other minor employes..	33,700 00	
	Total	$47,940 00	
A 2 Wages—			
	Extra labor.........	$3,800 00	
A 3 Unclassified		$200 00	
	Extension teaching...	2,000 00	
	Total	$2,200 00	
	Total personal service........		$53,940 00
Maintenance—			
C Supplies—			
C 1	Food	$125 00	
C 2	Forage	400 00	
C 3	Fuel	12,000 00	
C 4	Office	400 00	
C 5	Medical	75 00	
C 6	Cleaning	250 00	
C 8	Educational ..	1,800 00	
C 9	Agricultural ..	400 00	
C 11	General plant...	1,000 00	
	Total	$16,450 00	
D Materials—			
D 2	Building	$2,000 00	
D 3	General plant..	1,500 00	
	Total	$3,500 00	

		Items.	Appropriations.	General appropriations, 1920-1921.

E Equipment—

		Items.
E 1	Office	$100 00
E 2	Household	800 00
E 5	Agricultural ...	150 00
E 8	Educational ...	2,000 00
E 9	General plant..	350 00

Total $3,400 00

F Contract and Open Order Service—

		Items.
F 1	Repairs	$2,000 00
F 5	Freight, express and drayage	300 00
F 6	Traveling expense	850 00
F 7	Communication.	320 00
F 9	General plant..	600 00
	Teaching service Wilberforce University..	5,000 00

Total $9,070 00

H Fixed Charges and Contributions—

		Items.
H 6	Rent	$8 00
H 8	Contributions ..	125 00

Total $133 00

I Rotary Fund—

Total maintenance 32,553 00

Total $86,493 00

SECTION 3. The following sums shall not be expended to pay liabilities or deficiencies incurred prior to July 1st, 1919:

OHIO BOARD OF ADMINISTRATION.

G Additions and Betterments—

G 1 Lands $76,500 00

G 2 Buldings—

ATHENS STATE HOSPITAL.

Tubercular cottage. $20,000 00

General
appropriations,
1920-1921.

BOYS' INDUSTRIAL SCHOOL.

	Items.	Appropriations
G 2 Buildings—		
Wing for contagion hospital	$25,000 00	

COLUMBUS STATE HOSPITAL.

Wagon sheds and hog houses	$1,000 00	

DAYTON STATE HOSPITAL.

Remodeling House —Assistant physician	$1,500 00	
Garden house	1,000 00	
Hog feeding building ....:....	1,000 00	
Bull pens........	1,000 00	

OHIO HOSPITAL FOR EPILEPTICS.

2 Cottages—240 patients	$88,000 00	
6 Porches	12,000 00	
Milking barn......	6,000 00	

INSTITUTION FOR FEEBLE-MINDED.

5 Cottages—600 patients	$220,000 00	
Cold storage and storeroom— Orient	20,000 00	
Drying and canning building and equipment	3,500 00	

BUREAU OF JUVENILE RESEARCH.

Hospital	$25,000 00	

MASSILLON STATE HOSPITAL.

Tubercular cottage.	$20,000 00	
Improvement to barn	1,000 00	

NEW PRISON FARM.

	Items.	Appropriations.
To be available toward construction of new penitentiary after July 1st, 1920...	$200,000 00	
2 Silos	2,500 00	
Slaughter house...	1,000 00	
Hog houses........	2,500 00	

TOLEDO STATE HOSPITAL.

Wing to dairy barn	$5,000 00	
G 3 Miscellaneous—		

ATHENS STATE HOSPITAL.

G 31 Capital Equipment—		
Dental equipment..	$500 00	
Equipment for tubercular cottages.	3,000 00	
Generator set.....	7,000 00	
G 32 Other Capital Outlay—		
Fencing	$1,500 00	

STATE SCHOOL FOR THE BLIND.

G 31 Capital Equipment—		
2 250 H. P. boilers with equipment..	$25,000 00	

BOYS' INDUSTRIAL SCHOOL.

G 31 Capital Equipment—		
Dental department.	$500 00	
Generating set....	7,000 00	

CLEVELAND STATE HOSPITAL.

G 31 Capital Equipment—		
Hydrotherapeutic equipment	$6,000 00	
Dental equipment..	500 00	

Items.   Appropriations.

G 32 Other Capital
  Outlay—
  Brick road around
    main building... $4,500 00
  Concrete walks.....   500 00

COLUMBUS STATE HOSPITAL.

G 31 Capital Equip-
  ment—
  Dental equipment.. $500 00
  X-Ray equipment.   1,000 00

DAYTON STATE HOSPITAL.

G 31 Capital Equip-
  ment—
  Dental equipment.. $500 00
  X-Ray equipment.. 2,000 00

G 32 Other Capital
  Outlay—
  Fencing $1,000 00

STATE SCHOOL FOR THE DEAF.

G 31 Capital Equip-
  ment—
  Water heater $3,000 00
  Dental equipment..   500 00

OHIO HOSPITAL FOR EPILEPTICS.

G 31 Capital Equip-
  ment—
  Equipment two
    cottages $10,000 00
  Bakery equpiment..   5,000 00
  Laundry equipment 15,000 00
  Heating System—
    Hillside cottages.. 10,000 00
  X-ray equipment...   2,500 00
  Dental equipment..   500 00
  Equipment two
    cottages 18,000 00
  Light truck.......   800 00

INSTITUTION FOR FEEBLE-MINDED.

G 31 Capital Equip-
  ment—
  Boiler with stokers. $10,000 00

	Items.	Appropriations.	General appropriations 1920-1921.
Direct engine type unit	7,500 00		
Feed water heater..	4,000 00		
Auto dump truck..	4,000 00		
Equipment cottages	21,000 00		
Dental equipment..	500 00		
Equipment carpenter shop	250 00		

G 32 Other Capital
Outlay—

Sidewalks to new cottages	1,500 00	
Water softener at Orient	5,000 00	
Drainage, tiling, etc.	750 00	
Fencing	1,000 00	
Tractor	1,250 00	
Dredging and dyke.	5,000 00	

GIRLS' INDUSTRIAL SCHOOL.

G 31 Capital Equipment—
Dental equipment.. $500 00

BUREAU OF JUVENILE RESEARCH.

G 31 Capital Equipment—
Miscellaneous $10,000 00

LIMA STATE HOSPITAL.

G 31 Capital Equipment—
Dental equipment.. $500 00

LONGVIEW HOSPITAL.

G 31 Capital Equipment—

Dental equipment..	$500 00
Laundry machniery	15,000 00
Two trucks........	6,000 00

MASSILLON STATE HOSPITAL.

G 31 Capital Equipment—
Hydrotherapeutic
equipment $4,500 00

General
appropriations.
1920-1921.

	Items.	Appropriations.
Motor truck.......	750 00	
2 250 H. P. boilers and equipment..	43,000 00	
Improving water supply	5,000 00	
Dental equipment..	500 00	

G 32 Other Capital Outlay—

Fencing	$300 00	
Drainage	2,500 00	
Roads	250 00	

OHIO STATE REFORMATORY.

G 31 Capital Equipment—

| 2-250 H. P. boilers and equipment.. | $20,000 00 | |

OHIO REFORMATORY FOR WOMEN.

G 32 Other Capital Outlay—

| Fencing .... | $300 00 | |
| Drainage .... | 500 00 | |

OHIO STATE SANATORIUM.

G 31 Capital Equipment—

Water heaters and purifiers	$5,000 00	
Equipment for machine shop......	200 00	
Fluoroscope	1,000 00	

G 32 Other Capital Outlay—

2-inch steam line to kitchen	$500 00	
Drainage	500 00	
Improvement to spring	1,500 00	

TOLEDO STATE HOSPITAL.

G 31 Capital Equipment—

Dental equipment..	$500 00	
Truck	2,500 00	
2-250 H. P. boilers and equipment..	43,000 00	

	Items.	Appropriations.	General appropriations. 1920-1921.

G 32 Other Capital
Outlay—
Fencing $500 00

Total $1,086,850 00

BOARD OF AGRICULTURE.

G Additions and Betterments—
G 2 Buildings—
Waiting station, se-
rum plant....... $300 00

G 3 Miscellaneous—
G 31 Capital Equip-
ment—
Miscellaneous $1,225 00
G 32 Other Capital
Outlay—
Covered walks state
fair grounds.... $4,000 00
Stuccoing g r a n d .
stand state f a i r
grounds 3,500 00
Reduction plant, se-
rum plant......   3,500 00
Electrical e q u i p-
ment state fair
grounds 7,450 00

Total $19,975 00

FISH AND GAME DIVISION.

G A d d i t i o n s and Better-
ments—
G 2 Buildings—
House for game farm,
Wellington $3,000 00
Storage house, Well-
ington 500 00
Outbuildings, W e l l-
ington 1,500 00
G 3 Miscellaneous—
G 32 Other C a pital
Outlay—
Fencing farm, Well-
ington 1,500 00
Tiling farm, Well-
ington 200 00

Total $6,700 00

ATTORNEY GENERAL.

	Items.	Appropriations.
G Additions and Betterments—		
G 3 Miscellaneous—		
G 31 Capital Equipment—		
Filing cases..................		$200 00

ARCHAEOLOGICAL AND HISTORICAL SOCIETY.

G Additions and Betterments—		
G 2 Buildings—		
To complete shelter house Serpent mound	$200 00	
G 3 Miscellaneous—		
G 31 Capital Equipment—		
Books, maps, manuscripts and engravings	500 00	
Museum collections.	500 00	
Exhibition cases...	200 00	
G 32 Other Capital Outlay—		
Miscellaneous	300 00	
Total		$1,700 00

BANKS AND BANKING.

G Additions and Betterments—		
G 3 Miscellaneous—		
G 31 Capital Equipment—		
Desks, rugs, chairs, steel file cases		$600 00

STATE BOARD OF CHARITIES.

G Additions and Betterments—		
G 3 Miscellaneous—		
G 31 Capital Equipment—		
Miscellaneous		$950 00

OHIO AGRICULTURAL EXPERIMENT STATION.

G Additions and Betterments—		
G 1 Land—		
200 Acres Fry tract..	$25,000 00	
26½ Acres Thompson tract	3,100 00	
G 3 Miscellaneous—		
G 31 Capital Equipment—		
150 H. P. boiler...	3,000 00	

	Items.	Appropriations.	General appropriations. 1920-1921.

G 32 Other Capital
  Outlay—
    Fencing 1,000 00

      Total $32,100 00

STATE HIGHWAY DEPARTMENT.

G 3 Miscellaneous—
  G 32   Other Capital Out-
    lay—
      To construct, improve,
        maintain and re-
        pair main market
        roads $2,255,500 00
      To construct, improve,
        maintain and re-
        pair intercounty
        highways 6,466,500 00

      Total $8,722,000 00

INDUSTRIAL COMMISSION OF OHIO.

G Additions and Betterments—
  G 3   Miscellaneous—
    G 31   Capital Equipment—
      Miscellaneous $12,000 00

SUPERINTENDENT OF INSURANCE.

G Additions and Betterments—
  G 3   Miscellaneous—
    G 31   Capital Equipment—
      Miscellaneous $1,000 00

NURSE REGISTRATION.

G Additions and Betterments—
  G 3   Miscellaneous—
    G 31   Capital Equipment—
      2 Files $136 00

OHIO NATIONAL GUARD.

G 2 Buildings—
    To construct and equip an armory
      building in the city of Youngs-
      town, Ohio................. $100,000 00
    Provided, however, that above shall
      not be available until the citi-
      zens of Youngstown shall have
      deeded to the state of Ohio a lot
      suitable for a site for such ar-

Items. Appropriations.

mory, and until the adjutant
general of Ohio shall have accepted the same; and, provided,
further, that the above amount
shall not be available until the
citizens of Youngstown shall
have contributed $100,000 00
toward the construction and
equipment of such armory.

To construct and equip an armory
at New Lexington, Ohio...... 30,000 00

Provided, however, that the same
shall not be available until the
citizens of New Lexington shall
have deeded to the state of
Ohio a lot suitable for a site for
such armory; and, provided,
further that the citizens of New
Lexington shall furnish all
equipment not needed for military purposes.

HOUSE OF REPRESENTATIVES.

G Additions and Betterments—
  G 3 Miscellaneous—
    G 31 Capital Equipment—
      General Codes and supplements $600 00

OHIO PENITENTIARY COMMISSION.

G 32 Other Capital Outlay—
  Drainage, roads, railway spur, etc...... $50,000 00

SECRETARY OF STATE.

G Additions and Betterments—
  G 3 Miscellaneous—
    G 31 Capital Equipment—
      File cases.................. $500 00

AUTOMOBILE DEPARTMENT.

G Additions and Betterments—
  G 3 Miscellaneous—
    G 31 Capital Equipment—

Filing cases.....	$500 00	
Typewriters	600 00	
Typewriter tables	300 00	
Total		$1,130 00

General
appropriations,
1920-1921.

	Items.	Appropriations.

G Additions and Betterments—
  G 3   Miscellaneous—
    G 31   Capital Equipment—
      Miscellaneous $300 00

OHIO SOLDIERS' AND SAILORS' ORPHANS' HOME.

G Additions and Betterments—
  G 3   Miscellaneous—
    G 32   Other Capital
      Outlay—

	Items.	Appropriations.
Completion of wells	$1,000 00	
Fencing	700 00	
Lighting premises..	100 00	
New supports for tunnel	3,500 00	
I n t e r communicating telephone system	1,000 00	
Total		$6,300 00

SUPREME COURT AND LAW LIBRARY.

G Additions and Betterments—
  G 31   Capital equipment............. $100 00

PUBLIC UTILITIES COMMISSION.

G Additions and Betterments—
  G 31   Capital equipment............. $100 00

PUBLIC UTILITIES COMMISSION.

G Additions and Betterments—
  G 3   Miscellaneous—
    G 31   Capital Equipment—
      Legal plblications............ $300 00

PHYSICAL VALUATION—PUBLIC UTILITIES COMMISSION.

G Additions and Betterments—
  G 3   Miscellaneous—
    G 31   Capital Equipment—
      Miscellaneous $300 00

PUBLIC WORKS.

G Additions and Betterments—
  G 1   Land—
    Tracts south shore
    Loramie reservoir $500 00

General appropriations, 1920-1921.

	Items.	Appropriations
Tracts north shore Buckeye lake....	500 00	
G 2 Buildings—		
Boat house and office, Buckeye lake....	500 00	
G 3 Miscellaneous—		
G 32 Other Capital Outlay—		
Piling at Rudolph landing, St. Marys	500 00	
Culvert,, M. & E. canal, Spencerville	1,500 00	
Repair walls Buckeye lake........	1,000 00	
Culvert, Spencerville	925 00	
Culvert, Lock 14, near St. Marys..	765 00	
For widening and deepening the channel in Buckeye lake from Thornport to Avondale lake and for dredging a channel from Avondale lake to Cranberry lake..	4,000 00	
Total		$10,190 00

BOWLING GREEN STATE NORMAL SCHOOL.

	Items.	Appropriations
G Additions and Betterments—		
G 3 Miscellaneous—		
G 31 Capital Equipment—		
200 H. P. boiler...	$6,000 00	
Miscellaneous educational equipment	1,500 00	
Library books.....	1,500 00	
G 32 Other Capital Outlay—		
Drainage, fencing and landscape improvements	5,000 00	
Total		$14,000 00

KENT STATE NORMAL SCHOOL.

	Items.	Appropriations.
G Additions and Betterments—		
G 2 Buildings—		
Connecting corridors.	$25,000 00	
G 3 Miscellaneous—.		
G 31 Capital Equipment—		
Library books.....	1,500 00	
Educational equipment	5,000 00	
G 32 Other Capital Outlay—		
Drainage, grading, fencing, etc......	5,000 00	
Total		$36,500 00

MIAMI UNIVERSITY.

	Items.	Appropriations.
G Additions and Betterments—		
G 3 Miscellaneous—		
G 31 Capital Equipment—		
Library stacks....	$3,000 00	
Equipment home economics department	300 00	
G 32 Other Capital Outlay—		
Cement walks and gutters	1,750 00	
Grading	500 00	
Total		$5,550 00

OHIO UNIVERSITY.

	Items.	Appropriations.
G Additions and Betterments—		
G 3 Miscellaneous—		
G 31 Capital Equipment—		
Boiler feed pump..	$500 00	
G 32 Other Capital Outlay—		
Wire cable for electric current.....	745 00	
Installation of hot water system at gymnasium	1,500 00	
Total		$2,745 00

OHIO STATE UNIVERSITY.

	Items.	Appropriations.
G Additions and Betterments—		
G 2 Buildings—		
Addition to chemistry building	$30,000 00	
Hog building	10,000 00	
Sheep building	15,000 00	
Artillery horse stable.	10,000 00	
G 3 Miscellaneous—		
G 31 Capital Equipment—		
Miscellaneous	500 00	
G 32 Other Capital Outlay—		
Tiling and drainage	2,000 00	
Total		$67,500 00

COMBINED NORMAL AND INDUSTRIAL DEPARTMENT OF WILBERFORCE UNIVERSITY.

	Items.	Appropriations.
G Additions and Betterments—		
G 3 Miscellaneous—		
G 31 Capital Equipment—		
Delivery truck	$1,800 00	
G 32 Other Capital Outlay—		
Fencing	280 00	
Sewer line	360 00	
Soft water line	195 00	
Roads	300 00	
Walks	400 00	
Total		$3,335 00

SECTION 4. The sums set forth in the columns designated "items" in sections 2 and 3 of this act, opposite the several classifications of detailed purposes, shall not be expended for any other purposes except as herein provided.

Authority to expend the monies appropriated in sections 2 and 3 of this act otherwise than in accordance with such classifications of detailed purposes, but within the purpose for which appropriation is made, may be granted to any department, institution, board or commission for which appropriations are made in said sections, by a board to be known as the "Controlling Board," consisting of the governor, or the budget commissioner, if appointed by the governor for such purpose, the chairman of the finance committee of the house of representatives and of the senate, respectively, the attorney general and the auditor of state. The present chairmen of said finance committees shall continue to serve as members of said controlling board not-withstanding the expiration of their respective terms of office as members of the general assembly, until the senate and the house of representatives of the succeeding general assembly shall have organized and the chairmen of the respective finance committees thereof have been selected. The governor or the budget commissioner shall be president, and the auditor of state shall be secretary of the board.

Application for such authority shall be made to the president of the controlling board in writing, and the consent of not less than four members of the controlling board shall be required for the granting of such authority. Said board may authorize the expenditure of monies appropriated in said sections 2 and 3 of this act within the purpose for which the appropriation is made, whether included in the detailed purposes for which such appropriations are distributed by "items" in said section, or not. *Application.*

The secretary shall make a complete record of authority so granted, and shall certify a copy of the record of each action of the board to the president thereof. All meetings of the board shall be open to the public. The necessary expenses of the chairmen of the finance committees of the house of representatives and the senate, when engaged in their duties as members of said board, shall be paid from any funds appropriated for the expenses of legislative committees, upon itemized vouchers approved by the president and secretary of the board. *Record of proceedings.*

In case of any variance between the several specified sums in the columns designated "appropriations" and the aggregate amount of said sums in such column, the respective specified sums shall be deemed to have been appropriated; and in case of any variance between the amount of any appropriation and the aggregate amount of the "items" thereof, the controlling board shall, with the advice and assistance of the department, institution or board affected thereby, adjust the "items" so as to correspond in the aggregate with the proper appropriation.

SECTION 5. The term "rotary fund" as used in this act means a fund set aside to enable a department or institution to carry on a function or an activity, self-sustaining in its nature, the receipts from which are to be used for the function or activity for which the rotary fund is established. *"Rotary fund" defined.*

Money obtained from the function or activity for which a rotary fund is provided shall be turned into the treasury, and such monies so turned into the treasury between July 1, 1919, and June 30, 1921, both inclusive, are hereby appropriated for the purpose for which such rotary fund is herein established.

All monies to the credit of existing rotary funds are hereby appropriated and all existing rotary funds are hereby continued in effect for the full period named in this section.

SECTION 6. If the order and invoice drawn against any appropriation herein is made for labor and material furnished or for commodities purchased, it shall show that the same was furnished or purchased pursuant to competitive bidding and that the lowest bidder was awarded the contract, unless the controlling board shall have authorized the furnishing of such labor or material or the purchase of such commodity without competitive bidding.

Whenever in the judgment of the department, board, commission or institution affected, it seems desirable and in the interests of economy to construct or repair any building or make any other improvement herein provided by force account and the controlling board consents to such method and certifies such consent in writing to the auditor of state, sections 2314 to 2330 inclusive of the General Code, shall be deemed not to apply to that part of such work to be done by force account. It shall be the duty of the auditor of state to see that these provisions are complied with.

SECTION 7. A transfer, in whole or in part, of the functions of any existing department, board or commission, for the uses and purposes of which appropriations are made in sections 2 and 3 of this act, to any other department, board or commission by a law which takes effect after the date on which this act shall become effective, shall not affect the availability of any such appropriations except as hereinafter provided. On and after the date on which any such law shall become effective such appropriations shall be available for the proper uses and purposes of the department, board or commission to which such functions are thereby transferred, and such department, board or commission shall on and after such date have the exclusive power and authority to incur liabilities against such appropriations and to draw orders and invoices on account thereof as provided in section 4 hereof, to the extent only, however, of the balances then remaining to the credit of such appropriations in excess of the amount of contingent liabilities theretofore incurred, which shall be considered the net balances thereof for the purposes of this section. In the event that any department, board or commission, for the uses and purposes of which an appropriation is made in sections 2 and 3 of this act, is abolished by any such law, and any function of such department, board or commission so abolished is not transferred to any other department, board or commission by the provisions of such law, the net balances of appropriations available for the uses and purposes of such abolished department, board or commission in the discharge of such function shall, on the date on which such law shall become effective, lapse into the fund from which they were appropriated.

If any appropriation account, whether for personal service or otherwise, created by sections 2 and 3 of this act for the uses and purposes of a department, board or commission which is abolished, or any function, or functions, of which are transferred to any other department, board,

or commission by the provisions of any law so taking effect
as aforesaid is primarily available in the discharge of all
or several of the functions of such first department, board
or commission, the controlling board, immediately upon the
taking effect of such law, at a meeting open to the public,
and after consultation with each of the departments, boards
or commissions to be effected by its action, shall ascertain
and determine the proportion of the net balance of any
such appropriation account which will be needed in the discharge of each of the functions or group of functions so
transferred to a single department, board or commission,
or the proportion thereof which will no longer be needed by
reason of the abolition of any such functions. The board
shall determine the amount of the net balance of such appropriation account attributable to each of the functions
for which the original appropriation was made, and the
auditor of state shall divide the appropriation accounts on
the books of his office in accordance therewith, and in the
event of the abolition of a function shall lapse the appropriation or the net balance of such appropriation account
determined by the board to be attributable to each abolished
function, into the fund from which the original appropriation was taken.

SECTION 8. Each department, board or commission for
which an appropriation is made in this act for the salaries
of a specified number of employes where salaries are not
fixed by law, shall, not less than ten days prior to the date
on which such appropriation becomes effective, apportion
such appropriation account and file the same with the president of the controlling board. Said board may change such
apportionment and shall certify such apportionment with
any modifications it may make to the auditor of state, with
the approval of the board endorsed thereon.

SECTION 9. So much of the appropriation herein made
for personal service as pertains to the compensation of employes in the following groups and grades of the classified
civil service of the state, save and except employes in such
groups and grades in the state universities and the universities receiving state aid, normal schools, institutions under
the control of the Ohio board of administration, the Ohio
agricultural experiment station and the Ohio soldiers' and
sailors' orphans' home, may be expended only in accordance with the classification and rules of the state civil service commission and at the following rates of annual salaries for the respective groups and grades,

ENGINEERING GROUP.

Grade I.   Rates   C
                   $4,500 00 and up.
Grade II.   Rates   C   B   A
                   $2,700 00 $3,000 00 $3,300 00
Grade III.   Rates   C   B   A
                   $1,920 00 $2,160 00 $2,400 00

Grade IV. Rates	C	B	A
	$1,440 00	$1,620 00	$1,800 00
Grade V. Rates	C	B	A
	$960 00	$1,080 00	$1,200 00
Grade VI. Rates	C	B	A
	$720 00	$780 00	$840 00

CLERICAL SERVICE.

BOOKKEEPER GROUP.

Grade I. Rates	C		
	$2,100 00 and up.		
Grade II. Rates	C	B	A
	$1,740 00	$1,860 00	$1,980 00
Grade III. Rates	C	B	A
	$1,140 00	$1,260 00	$1,380 00
Grade IV. Rates	C	B	A
	$840 00	$900 00	$960 00

CLERK GROUP.

Grade I. Rates D	C	B	A
$1,560 00	$1,680 00	$1,800 00	$1,980 00
Grade II. Rates	C	B	A
	$1,140 00	$1,260 00	$1,380 00
Grade III. Rates		B	A
		$840 00	$900 00
Grade IV. Rates	C	B	A
	$600 00	$660 00	$720 00

STENOGRAPHER GROUP.

Grade I. Rates	C	B	A
	$1,260 00	$1,320 00	$1,380 00
Grade II. Rates	C	B	A
	$1,080 00	$1,140 00	$1,200 00
Grade III. Rates		B	A
		$840 00	$900 00

TELEPHONE OPERATOR GROUP.

Grade I. Rates	C	B	A
	$660 00	$720 00	$780 00

TYPIST GROUP.

Grade I. Rates	C	B	A
	$960 00	$1,020 00	$1,080 00
Grade II. Rates		B	A
		$840 00	$900 00

provided, however, that rates of compensation of persons now employed in the foregoing groups and grades of the

classified civil service of the state, which on the date of the
passage of this act may exceed the uniform rate fixed herein
for the service, group and grade of their positions, as so
classified, shall not be affected by the provisions of this section; but such rates of compensation as fixed on said date
for such positions shall be the rates at which the appropriations herein made may be expended for the compensation of such persons while holding such positions.

In case any personal service appropriation made in section 2 of this act is insufficient in amount to enable the department, institution, board or commission, for which the
same is made to comply with the provisions of this section
in the payment of the compensation of its employes, the
controlling board may from the appropriation made to such
controlling board, allot to such department, institu'ion,
t oard or commission a sum sufficient to enable such department, institution, bcard or commission to comply with
this section. Such allotment shall be made on application
and all the provision of section 4 of this act, so far as consistent herewith, shall apply. A written order signed by
the president and secretary of the controlling board and
specifying the amount of such allotment, shall be issued to
the auditor of state, who shall thereupon deduct the amount
of such allotment from the appropriation made to such
controlling board, and add the same to the amount available to such department, institution, board or commission
for personal service.

SECTION 10. Unexpended balances of all appropria- Re-appropriation
tions, made by the eighty-second general assembly, against of unexpended
which contingent liabilities have been lawfully incurred,
are to the extent of such liabilities only, and whether the
same have been lapsed prior to the taking effect of this act
with respect thereto or not, hereby appropriated and made
available for the purpose of discharging such contingent
liabilities and for no other purpose. Provided, that, should
no contingent liabilities have been incurred against the appropriation made in house bill 452, eighty-second general
assembly, or against the appropriations for the use of the
Ohio State University, "G 2. Structures and parts," under
the item "Addition Chemistry Building" or the item, "G 2
Buildings—

To supplement appropriation made in H.
  B. No. 452 (107 O. L. 51) for wom-
    en's building $150,000 00;..........   90 000 00

made in house bill 276 in an act filed in the office of the
secretary of state, March 20, 1919, then and in that event,
there is hereby appropriated out of any monies in the state
treasury to the credit of the general revenue fund not otherwise appropriated, the following amounts for the following
purposes,

Ohio State University.

G 2   Buildings—
  Women's building, to carry out the pro-
    vision of said H. B. 452............   150,000 00
  Addition to chemistry building........   85,000 00

Charge of expenses against farm operated; sa e of commodities; account.

SECTION 11.   There shall be charged to each farm operated by the Ohio board of administration all the expense incurred in such operation, and any and all commodities produced by such farms and furnished to any institution under the control of said board, including the institution under which the farm is operated, shall be paid for by such institution at the prevailing market price, on voucher against the proper appropriation; and any warrant issued on account of such vouchers shall be paid into the state treasury as a receipt from the farm on which the commodity so paid for, was produced, to the credit of the Ohio board of administration as a supplement to either, as the case may be, the Maintenance C-1 food or C-2 forage appropriations hereinbefore made to said board.

Profits shown in annual report.

The profits accruing from the operation of any farm, for the year covered, shall be shown in the annual report of the board of administration as a proper reduction of the expense of the institution under which the farm is operated, or in case such farm is operated at a loss, such loss shall be shown as an addition to the expense of such institution.

Normal school extension fund, h w expended.

SECTION 12.   Monies appropriated herein to the various normal schools for extension teaching shall be expended only upon the approval of the state superintendent of public instruction; such approval to consist in the approval of the course of study and the location of each extension center.

SECTION 13.   This act shall not take effect until July 1, 1919.

This act is not of a general and permanent nature and requires no sectional number. JOHN G. PRICE, Attorney General.

CARL R. KIMBALL,
Speaker of the House of Representatives.
CLARENCE J. BROWN,
President of the Senate.

Passed May 28, 1919.

This bill was presented to the Governor June 17, 1919, and was not signed or returned to the house wherein it originated within ten days after being so presented, exclusive of Sundays and the day said bill was presented, and was filed in the office of the Secretary of State June 30, 1919.

ROBERT T. CREW,
Veto Clerk.

Filed in the office of the Secretary of State at Columbus, Ohio, on the 30th day of June, A. D. 1919.

237 G.

[House Bill No. 569.]

AN ACT

To make appropriation for the payment of salaries of the employes of the House of Representatives and counsel for the joint committee on taxation.

Be it enacted by the General Assembly of the State of Ohio:
SECTION 1. The sums set forth in this act are hereby appropriated out of any moneys in the state treasury not otherwise appropriated:

HOUSE OF REPRESENTATIVES.

Personal Service—
A 2. Wages—

10 assistant clerks	$1,150 00
11 stenographers	1,265 00
4 sergeants-at-arms	460 00
1 assistant postmaster	115 00
2 telephone attendants	207 00
2 cloak room attendants	184 00
5 committee room attendants	460 00
5 doorkeepers	460 00
5 porters	460 00
7 pages	483 00
C. D. Laylin	2,000 00
L. D. Johnson	2,000 00

CARL R. KIMBALL,
Speaker of the House of Representatives.
CLARENCE J. BROWN,
President of the Senate.

Passed June 19, 1919.
Approved June 30, 1919.

JAMES M. COX,
Governor.

Filed in the office of the Secretary of State at Columbus, Ohio, on the 30th day of June, A. D. 1919.

238.

[Senate Bill No. 189.]

AN ACT

To authorize and empower the commissioners of Franklin county to sell and convey the Franklin County Children's Home and to purchase grounds and erect a children's home for Franklin county, and to repeal an act passed April 9, 1919, and approved May 6, 1919, entitled "An act to authorize and empower the commissioners of Franklin county to sell and convey the Franklin County Children's Home and to purchase grounds and erect a children's home for Franklin county."

WHEREAS, Prior to the year 1878 the board of county commissioners of Franklin county, Ohio, pursuant to law

erected a children's home for said Franklin county, and
have since and are still maintaining and using said home
as a children's home for said county; and

WHEREAS, By reason of the increase of population in
said Franklin county, said children's home is not of sufficient size nor suitable to accommodate and care for the
children entitled to its care under the law; and

WHEREAS, By reason of the growth of the city of
Columbus and the extension of its corporate limits, said city
has grown to and around and wholly encloses said children's
home, thereby rendering it unsuitable for the purpose of a
children's home; and

WHEREAS, By reason of the growth of said city of
Columbus, the price of adjoining and contiguous lands has
increased in value until it is impracticable to purchase lands
suitable for the enlargement of said present children's
home, now, therefore,

Be it enacted by the General Assembly of the State of Ohio:

Authority to sell and convey Franklin county children's home. SECTION 1. The board of county commissioners of
Franklin county, Ohio, are hereby authorized and em-
powered to sell and convey the present Franklin county
children's home. Said sale to be made after four weeks'
advertisement in two newspapers of general circulation in
Franklin county, Ohio, and that said sale shall be made to
the highest and best bidders, and said board of county
commissioners may at said bidding, reject any and all bids
and re-advertise the same, as herein provided for the sale
of said premises.

Application of proceeds in purchase of land, erection and equipment of children's home. The commissioners of said county are hereby also
authorized and directed to use the amount of money de-
rived from the sale of the present children's home in the
purchase of farm lands and the erection thereon of suitable buildings and equipment for said children's home. The
commissioners are hereby authorized and directed to cause
estimates to be made of the probable cost thereof and in
order to defray the expenses of the same, the commissioners
are authorized and directed to cause to be levied a tax
Tax levy; bond issue. upon all the taxable property in said county, and to issue
the notes or bonds of the county in anticipation of the col-
lection of the same for a sum of money not exceeding two
hundred and fifty thousand dollars; that the county auditor
and county treasurer be, and they are hereby authorized
and directed to place said tax upon the duplicate of the
taxable property of Franklin county for the purpose of the
redemption of said notes or bonds of the county, as issued
by said commissioners, and for the maintenance of the said
institution as now provided by law. Said notes or bonds
may be issued when, and in such amounts, as may be needed,
and be redeemable at such period, as may be decided upon
by said county commissioners; but in no case shall said
bonds or notes be payable at a period longer than ten years
from date of issue, and at a rate of interest no greater than
six per centum per annum.

SECTION 3. The county commissioners of said county are hereby authorized to exercise the powers herein conferred without submitting to the voters of said county the question of either selling said present site of said children's home, or the purchase of another site therefor, and the erection of new buildings thereon. Said commissioners of said county shall also exercise all the powers herein conferred without reference to Chapter 1, Title IX, of the General Code of Ohio, pertaining to public buildings regulations. Authorized to exercise powers without submission of question.

SECTION 4. That an act entitled "An act to authorize and empower the commissioners of Franklin county to sell and convey the Franklin county children's home and to purchase grounds and erect a children's home for Franklin county," passed April 9. Repeal of former act.

SECTION 5. That it is necessary for the immediate preservation of the public safety that the provisions of this act become effective at once because of the immediate necessity of providing housing facilities for the children enclosed in this children's home, free from the dangers of fire and disaster, and therefore an emergency is hereby declared to exist and this act shall take effect and be in full force and effect from and after its passage and approval. Emergency measure.

CLARENCE J. BROWN,
President of the Senate.
CARL R. KIMBALL,
Speaker of the House of Representatives.
Passed June 18, 1919.
Approved June 30, 1919.

JAMES M. COX,
Governor.

Filed in the office of the Secretary of State at Columbus, Ohio, on the 30th day of June, A. D. 1919.

239 L.

act is not general and ment na- ind requires ctional er. r G. PRICE, ney General.

[Amended Senate Bill No. 114.]

An ACT

To amend section 270-6 of the General Code, relative to the sundry claims board.

Be it enacted by the General Assembly of the State of Ohio:
SECTION 1. That section 270-6 of the General Code be amended to read as follows:

Sec. 270-6. There is hereby created a board ·to be known as the "sundry claims board" to consist of the major appointee authorized by section 270-5 of the General Code, commonly known as the "budget commissioner" who shall be president, the auditor of state who shall be secretary, the attorney general, the chairman of the senate finance committee, and the chairman of the finance committee of the "Sundry claims board;" how composed; powers and duties.

house of representatives. In addition to any other duties that may by law devolve upon such board, it is hereby authorized and empowered to receive original papers representing claims against the state of Ohio for the payment of which no monies have been appropriated. Such claims shall be filed and properly designated either by number or short title or both. All such claims shall be carefully investigated by such board. The president of the sundry claims board shall, for the purposes contemplated by this section, have power to administer oaths, compel the attendance of witnesses, and the production of books and papers, and to punish for disobedience of subpoena, refusal to be sworn, or to answer as a witness, or to produce books and papers, as is conferred upon officers authorized to take depositions. After such investigation the board shall either approve, approve with conditions and limitations or disapprove of each such claim, and append to the original papers heretofore mentioned representing each claim, a concise statement of facts brought out in such investigation upon which its approval or disapproval is based. Such original papers and appended statements shall be filed in the office of the president of such board, and delivered to the chairman of the finance committee of the house of representatives of the next general assembly promptly upon the appointment of such chairman. A copy of the above-mentioned appended statement shall be kept on file in the office of the president of such board and, together with the original papers representing such claim and any other matters pertaining thereto, shall constitute a permanent claims' record.

Per diem and expenses for members.

A per diem of ten dollars for each day actually spent by the chairman of the finance committee of the senate and house respectively, while in the performance of the duties herein enumerated, and upon the summons of the president of the board, together with their necessary expenses, shall be paid from the funds appropriated for the expense of legislative committees upon vouchers approved by the president and secretary of the board herein created; provided, however, that the provisions of this act shall not be construed to conflict with section 15 of the General Code.

SECTION 2. That original section 270-6 of the General Code be, and the same is hereby repealed.

The sectional number in this act is in conformity to the General Code. JOHN G. PRICE, Attorney General.

CLARENCE J. BROWN,
President of the Senate.
CARL R. KIMBALL,
Speaker of the House of Representatives.

Passed June 18, 1919.
Approved July 1, 1919.

JAMES M. COX,
Governor.

Filed in the office of the Secretary of State at Columbus, Ohio, on the 2nd day of July, A. D. 1919.

240 G.

923

[House Bill No. 209.]

AN ACT

To provide a license for angling in Ohio.

Be it enacted by the General Assembly of the State of Ohio:

1430.   SECTION 1. Fishing License. No non-resident shall take
or catch any fish by angling in any of the waters of the
state of Ohio, or engage in fishing in such waters without
first having procured a license so to do. Said license shall
be procured in the manner provided for taking out hunting
and trapping licenses. The applicants shall pay to the
clerk having authority to issue such license, the sum of two
dollars, together with the sum of twenty-five cents, as a fee
to the clerk; provided, however, that any person under the
age of sixteen years, may take or catch fish by angling,
without a license. The provisions of the hunting and
trapping license section of this state in so far as the same
are applicable to licenses shall apply to all licenses issued
under this section.

sectional
ber on the
fin. hereof
signated as
lded by law.
N G. PRICE,
rney
   General.

CLARENCE J. BROWN,
President of the Senate.
CARL R. KIMBALL,
Speaker of the House of Representatives.
Passed April 14, 1919.
Approved July 2, 1919.

JAMES M. COX,
Governor.

Filed in the office of the Secretary of State at Columbus,
Ohio, on the 2nd day of July, A. D. 1919.

241 G.

[House Bill No. 191.]

AN ACT

To amend section 905 of the General Code, relative to the compensation of the district inspectors of mines.

Be it enacted by the General Assembly of the State of Ohio:

SECTION 1. That section 905 of the General Code be
amended to read as follows:

Sec. 905. The chief inspector of mines shall receive
three thousand dollars per annum and each district inspector of mines shall receive two thousand one hundred
dollars per annum. The chief inspector of mines, and each
district inspector of mines, shall receive, in addition to the
salaries herein provided for, all necessary and legitimate
expenses incurred by them in the discharge of their duties,
to be approved by the chief inspector of mines, itemized
statements of which expenses shall be filed with the auditor

Compensation of
chief and district mine inspectors.

of state. Provided, however, that any public officer who knowingly accepts any payment from any mine inspector for political purposes shall forfeit his office, and any person who accepts any contribution of money or anything of value from any mine inspector for use in any political campaign, or for any campaign purpose, shall be guilty of a misdemeanor.

SECTION 2. That original section 905 of the General Code be, and the same is hereby repealed.

CARL R. KIMBALL,
Speaker of the House of Representatives.
CLARENCE J. BROWN,
President of the Senate.

Passed June 18, 1919.

This bill was presented to the Governor on June 23rd, 1919, and was not signed or returned to the house wherein it originated within ten days after being so presented, exclusive of Sundays and the day said bill was presented, and was filed in the office of the Secretary of State July 7th, 1919.

The sectional number in this act is in conformity to the General Code. JOHN G. PRICE, Attorney General.

ROBERT T. CREW,
Veto Clerk.

Filed in the office of the Secretary of State at Columbus, Ohio, on the 7th day of July, A. D. 1919.

242 G.

[Senate Bill No. 187.]

AN ACT

To authorize boards of education to levy taxes outside of all limitations for the purpose of meeting deficiencies in current revenues.

Be it enacted by the General Assembly of the State of Ohio:

Tax levy authorized to meet deficiencies in current revenues.

SECTION 1. In addition to all other means provided by law for meeting deficiencies in the current revenues of school districts, the board of education of any such district may levy in the year 1919 not to exceed two mills for any and all purposes for which such boards may levy taxes, upon securing the approval of the electors of such district in the following manner:

Copy of resolution certified to deputy state supervisors of elections.

By resolution passed by an affirmative vote of a majority of all its members elected or appointed, such board may order that the question of levying such tax, at a rate to be fixed therein, shall be submitted to the electors of the district at a special election to be held therein on Tuesday the twelfth day of August, 1919. A copy of such resolution shall be certified to the deputy state supervisors of elections of the county or counties in which the district is situated. The deputy state supervisors shall prepare the ballots and make the necessary arrangements for the submission of such question. The result of the election shall be certified and canvassed in like manner as all regular elections for the election of members of boards of education. Notice of such election for not less than ten days shall be given by the deputy state supervisors of elections in one or more newspapers printed in the district, once a week on the same day of the week for two consecutive times prior thereto. If no newspaper is printed therein such notice shall be posted for ten days prior to the election in five conspicuous places in the district, and published as aforesaid in a newspaper of general circulation therein. A notice substantially in the following form shall be sufficient: *Notice of election.*

NOTICE OF SPECIAL ELECTION.

Notice is hereby given that a special election will be held in the .... school district, Ohio, on Tuesday the twelfth day of August, 1919, to determine whether an additional tax levy of ...... mills, outside of all limitations, for the year 1919-20, shall be made for school purposes in such district.

The expense of giving such notice shall be certified by the deputy state supervisors to the clerk of the board of education and shall be paid as expenses of notices of school elections are paid.

SECTION 2. The ballots used at such election shall indicate the name of the school district and, further shall be in form as follows: *Form of ballot.*

"For additional tax levy of .... mills for the year 1919-1920, for school purposes. Yes.

"For additional tax levy of .... mills for the year 1919-20, for school purposes. No."

SECTION 3. If a majority of the electors voting on the proposition so submitted vote in favor thereof, upon the certification and canvass of such result it shall be lawful for such board of education to levy taxes at the aggregate rate so authorized for such purposes in addition to all other taxes for like purposes. Such levy shall be certified to the county auditor, who shall place it on the tax duplicate; it shall not be subject to any limitation on tax rates now in force, and shall not be subject to the control of the budget commission, nor shall such budget commission reduce the amount of other levies made by any board below the amount allowed such board for the preceding year. *Certification of result; of tax levy to county auditor.*

SECTION 4. This act is hereby declared to be an emergency law necessary for the immediate preservation of the public peace and safety. The necessity therefor lies in the fact that in many school districts of the state, under the limitations on tax levies provided by law, deficiencies exist in operating revenues, arising from the abnormal increase of operating expenses and the desirability of increasing the compensation of school teachers: so that unless afforded extraordinary means of raising revenues the boards of edu- *Emergency act.*

cation of such district will be unable to carry on the function of public education until permanent revenues can be provided. Therefore this act shall go into immediate effect.

This act is not of a general and permanent nature and requires no sectional number.
J. HY G. PRICE, Attorney General.

CLARENCE J. BROWN,
President of the Senate.
CARL R. KIMBALL,
Speaker of the House of Representatives.

Passed June 18, 1919.

This bill was presented to the Governor on June 23rd. 1919, and was not signed or returned to the house wherein it originated within ten days after being so presented, exclusive of Sundays and the day said bill was presented, and was filed in' the office of the Secretary of State July 7th, 1919.

ROBERT T. CREW,
Veto Clerk.

Filed in the office of the Secretary of State at Columbus, Ohio, on the 7th day of July, A. D. 1919.

243 G.

An ACT

[Amended Senate Bill No. 100.]
To codify, consolidate, and clarify the ditch laws of the state according to the report of the commission aappointed therefor. under an act passed March 21, 1917 (O. L. 107 V. 611), to amend sections 3001. 6564, 6565 of the General Code and to repeal all sections of the General Code superseded by, or in conflict with such reported codified consolidation.

Be it enacted by the General Assembly of the State of Ohio:
SECTION 1. That sections 3386, 3387. 3388, 3389, 3390, 6442, 6443, 6444, 6445, 6446, 6447, 6448, 6449, 6450, 6451, 6452, 6453, 6454, 6455, 6456, 6457, 6458, 6459, 6460, 6461. 6462, 6463, 6464, 6465, 6566, 6467, 6468, 6969, 6470, 6471, 6472, 6473, 6474, 6475, 6476, 6477, 6478, 6479, 6480, 6481. 6482, 6483, 6484, 6485, 6486, 6487, 6488, 6489, 6490, 6491. 6492, 6493, 6494, 6495, 6496, 6497, 6498, 6499, 6500, 6501. 6502, 6503, 6504, 6505, 6506, 6507, 6508, 6509, 6510, 6511. 6512, 6513. 6514, 6515, 6516, 6517, 6518. 6519, 6520, 6521, 6522, 6523. 6524, 6525, 6526, 6527, 6528, 6529, 6530, 6531, 6532, 6533, 6534, 6535, 6535-1, 6535-2,· 6535-3, 6535-4. 6535-5, 6535-6, 6535-7, 6535-8, 6535-9, 6535-10, 6535-11, 6535-12, 6535-13, 6535-14, 6535-15, 6535-16, 6535-17, 6535-18, 6535-19, 6535-20, 6535-21, 6535-22, 6535-23, 6535-24. 6535-25, 6536, 6537, 6538, 6539, 6540, 6541, 6542, 6543, 6544, 6545, 6546, 6547, 6548, 6549, 6550, 6551, 6552, 6553, 6554, 6555, 6556, 6557, 6558, 6559, 6560, 6561. 6562. 6563, 6563-1. 6563-2, 6563-3, 6563-4. 6563-5. 6563-6, 6563-7, 6563-8. 6563-9, 6563-10, 6563-11, 6563-12, 6563-13, 6563-14, 6563-15, 6563-16, 6563-17, 6563-18, 6563-19. 6563-20, 6563-21, 6563-22, 6563-23, 6563-24, 6563-25, 6563-26.

6563-27, 6563-28, 6563-29, 6563-30, 6563-31, 6563-32,
6563-33, 6563-34, 6563-35, 6563-36, 6563-37, 6563-38,
6563-39, 6563-40, 6563-41, 6563-42, 6563-43, 6563-44,
6563-45, 6563-46, 6563-47, 6563-48, 6603, 6604, 6605, 6606,
6607, 6608, 6609, 6610, 6611, 6612, 6613, 6614, 6615, 6616,
6617, 6618, 6619, 6620, 6621, 6622, 6623, 6624, 6625, 6626,
6627, 6628, 6629, 6630, 6631, 6632, 6633, 6634, 6635, 6636,
6637, 6638, 6639, 6640, 6641, 6642, 6643, 6644, 6645, 6646,
6647, 6648, 6649, 6650, 6651, 6652, 6653, 6654, 6655, 6656,
6657, 6658, 6659, 6660, 6661, 6662, 6663, 6664, 6665, 6666,
6667, 6668, 6669, 6670, 6671, 6672, 6673, 6674, 6675, 6676,
6677, 6678, 6679, 6680, 6681, 6682, 6683, 6684, 6685, 6686,
6687, 6688, 6689, 6690, 6691, 6692, 6693, 6694, 6695, 6696,
6697, 6698, 6699, 6700, 6701, 6702, 6703, 6704, 6705, 6706,
6707, 6708, 6709, 6710, 6711, 6712, 6713, 6714, 6715, 6716,
6717, 6718, 6719, 6720, 6721, 6722, 6723, 6724, 6725, 6726,
6726-1, 6726-2, 6726-3, 6726-4, 6777, 6778, 6779, 6780, 6781,
6782, 6783, 6784, 6785, 6786, 6791, 6792, 6793, 6795, 6806,
6807, 6808, 6809, 6810, 6818, 6819, 6820, 6821, 6822, of the
General Code be consolidated, clarified, supplemented and
re-codified and that sections 3001, 6564 and 6565 of the
General Code be amended, to read as follows:

2.   SECTION 1. DEFINITIONS. The words "ditch or   Definition of
drain" as used in this chapter shall include any open or   terms.
covered artificial trench or drainage channel, artificial
watercourse or natural watercourse constructed, or improved and used for the purpose of the irrigation or drainage of lands for agricultural or other industrial purposes;
and where the subject matter and sense require it, the word
"ditch" or "drain" in the singular shall be read as in the
plural and shall be deemed to include a side lateral, spur,
branch ditch, or watercourse discharging into a main ditch
or drain and constituting a part of an improvement.

The word "outlet" as used in this chapter shall be
deemed to be any place of discharge provided or existing
for the discharge of any ditch or drain as above defined;
and shall include, when so used, any larger or main ditch
or drain, any natural or artificial watercourse, river, lake
or underground stream; or any artificially constructed
basin or filtration plant provided for the disposal of drainage mentioned in this chapter; or any sink hole, fissure,
break or opening in the earth or rock into which drainage
is discharged.

The word "improvement" as used in this chapter, shall
include and cover the construction or reconstruction, widening, deepening, straightening, boxing, tiling, filling, walling,
or arching with brick or other material any ditch or drain
or outlet as above defined, or any alteration in such ditch
or drain or outlet already constructed, or any part thereof;
or any change in the alinement or location of a ditch, drain
or outlet, or of a river, creek, or watercourse; or the enlarging, deepening, closing and filling of any sink hole,
fissure, break, or opening in the earth or rock used or to be
used or abandoned as an outlet to a ditch or drain; or the

necessary preparation incident to the location or construction of a ditch, drain, or outlet, as by removing from the line or location thereof or adjacent lands, timber, brush, trees, rock or other substances necessary either to construction or successful operation after construction. And said word improvement shall also include creeks and rivers, the construction of any necessary works for the discharge of water from submerged lands, as by pumping, or the disposition or treatment of any drainage for sanitary purposes, as by filtration plants or other means, or the construction of any levee, dike, embankment wall, breakwater or any other artificial retainer to protect lands from overflow, or to otherwise salvage any lands against water to make them suitable for agricultural or healthful for residential purposes, or to substantially increase the value thereof for the purpose of public taxation.

The word "levee" as used in this chapter shall embrace and include any wall, embankment, jetty, breakwater or other structure for the protection of lands from overflow from any stream, lake, pond, fissure or other opening in the earth or rock, or for the protection of any outlet; and when used in a petition for a main levee shall be deemed to include any side lateral, or spur levee necessary to secure the object and purpose for which the main levee may be made.

The words "benefit" and "benefits" as used in this chapter, in directing the assessment of lands therefor, shall be deemed to cover any advantage to the owner of the land or lands by reason of the improvement, as above defined, either by making the same more healthful or increasing the productivity or value thereof to him, or by reclamation and increase of market value adding to the taxable value for the purpose of public taxation or increasing the healthfulness of the vicinity.

The word "person" as used in this chapter shall, when the sense requires it to make the provision in which it is used uniform in operation be deemed to include corporations public or private, partnerships or other associations of persons joined in interest, townships, counties, boards, commissioners or trustees of public institutions of whatever nature and by whatever name the controlling officers of the same are officially designated.

The words "county engineer" shall be deemed to refer to and include an elected or legally appointed county surveyor, and any legally appointed engineer in charge of any improvement provided for in this chapter; and also any duly appointed deputy of such county surveyor or engineer in charge of work, providing such appointment has been approved by the county commissioners, or court; as in this chapter provided.

The words "railway company" shall be deemed to include a company owning or operating a railway using steam, electricity or other power for the propulsion of its rolling stock; "right of way" shall be deemed to be the right of way used by any such company.

The word "contractor" shall include any person, partnership, corporation, or association of persons undertaking or engaging to do any work upon or furnish any material for any improvement under this chapter.

All words in the singular number shall be read in the plural when the sense requires it, and words in the masculine gender shall be construed as feminine in any case where the application of any provision requires it.

Any reference herein to any existing office or officer, whether by title or designation as now fixed by statute, or by any ex-officio designation or title in this act provided, shall be deemed to refer to the provisions of this act only, and the statute designation and ex-official title shall be deemed synonymous.

6443. SECTION 2. Whenever any owner or owners of any separate or distinct tracts of land, not lying within the corporate limits of a municipality, the trustees of a township, the board of education of any public school district, any public board having charge and control of any roads or lands of a township or district, not within the corporate limits of a municipality, the board of county commissioners, the council of a city or village, or the trustees of any state, county or municipal public institution desire to provide drainage for such tracts of land, public highways, or the grounds of a public school; and whenever the council of any city or village, the board of education of any public school district, or the trustees of any state, county or municipal public institution find it necessary for the successful drainage of any public streets, highways or grounds located within a municipal corporation to drain the same either by an open ditch or tiled drain or other improvement, and the drainage thereof cannot be accomplished in the best and cheapest manner without affecting the lands of others not within such municipality, such owner or owners, township trustees, board of education, municipal council, board of county commissioners or trustees of any state, county or municipal public institution may file a petition with the county auditor of the county wherein all or the greater part of the land affected by such proposed drainage lies, setting forth the desire for, the necessity of and the believed benefits of such drainage, with the beginning, route and termini of the needed ditch or drain, or other improvement, including the necessary branches thereof. The petition shall also state the nature of the lands or places to be drained, as whether at present agricultural lands, submerged or overflowed lands, marsh lands, sink holes, or other lands to be benefited, and shall give the approximate acreage and the method by which in the opinion of the petitioner the object of the petition should be accomplished, as by open or tiled drain, diking, pumping, or other means. Such petition shall also contain the names of the persons and corporations, public or private, including any munici-

pal corporation into or through which the improvement will
pass, with the address, if known, whose lands, in the opinion
of the petitioner or petitioners, will in any way be benefited
by the proposed drainage, or damaged by the construction
of the improvement. Such petitioner or petitioners shall
also file with the county auditor at the time such petition is
filed a bond in the minimum penal sum of one hundred
dollars and a maximum of fifty dollars additional for each
mile, or fraction thereof, of said improvement above one
mile of length, with at least two sureties who are freeholders
of the county. But in lieu of such personal sureties, a
surety company authorized to do business in Ohio may be
substituted. Such bond shall be made payable to the state
of Ohio and conditioned for the payment of all costs if the
prayer of the petition is not granted, or said petition is for
any cause dismissed. But if said petition be filed by a board
of education of any public school district, the council of a
municipality, the board of county commissioners of any
county or the trustees of any state, county or municipal
public institution, no bond shall be required.

Sec. 6444.

Notice of filing
petition.

SECTION 3. If such petition be filed by any party other
than a board of county commissioners the county auditor
shall give notice of the filing of such petition to the board
of county commissioners of his county at their next meeting; and if a municipality be named as affected he shall at
the same time notify the mayor thereof by mail; and if any
building or ground under the control of any board of education or the trustees of any state, county, township or municipal public institution be named as affected, he shall at
the same time notify by mail the president of the board of
education or trustees of such institution named. If any
private institution be named as affected he shall at the same
time notify by mail the president of the board of trustees
of such institution. And if the petition be filed by the
county commissioners, or if they be one of the petitioners,
then such notice shall be given by the auditor to the clerk
of the common pleas court of his county and the petition
shall be filed with him, who shall docket the same as: "In
the matter of the petition of the county commissioners of
..........Co. for ditch improvement No. ......" And
when the petition is filed by the county commissioners of
a county, all subsequent filings shall be in, and all original
proceedings before, the court of common pleas of such
county in the same manner, and under all the provisions
of this chapter, as provided for proceedings before the
county commissioners. And the judge of the common pleas
court, when the county commissioners are a petitioner, shall
have and exercise the same jurisdiction therein, that the
county commissioners exercise in the case of other petitioners. Upon such notice being received, the county commissioners or the common pleas court, shall order the county
engineer to visit within thirty days the proposed location
of such ditch or drain or other improvement and make any
necessary survey thereof, both of the line proposed in said

petition and any other line appearing to him more feasible, if such there be, to accomplish the purpose of said petition, and to prepare suitable maps and profiles of such location or locations and surveys, including necessary branches, and make an estimate of the probable cost and expense of the construction of such improvement and its proposed branches, if any, on the lines deemed by him best to accomplish the object of the petition. And if upon the line of the improvement the construction shall require the construction, removal and replacing of any bridge or culvert of any railroad, interurban railroad, street railroad, or other corporation of the county or township, for any other cause than the insufficient elevation or insufficient waterway thereof, said engineer shall estimate separately the cost of the construction, removal and replacing of such bridge, and report the same as a probable claim for damages by the owner thereof with other matters herein required to be reported, and shall file with said county auditor, or clerk of court, within said thirty days a report of his proceedings with maps, profiles, and preliminary estimate of the probable cost and also to report if in his judgment there are highways or other lands that will be beneficially affected by such improvement other than those mentioned in the petition, with the names of the owners thereof and the address of each so far as the same can reasonably be ascertained by him. And he shall also report whether or not in his judgment there are lands or property, including public highways, bridges, culverts and the like, that would be damaged by the construction of said improvement and indicate the nature of such damage. And he shall file therewith a statement of the actual cost and expenses of his proceedings and report, including the time of any assistants, at its actual cost to the county, but not to exceed the rate regularly paid to the chief deputy of the county engineer.

Maps and profiles of locations and surveys; estimate of cost.

If said thirty days shall not be sufficient for said engineer to complete said work and report, or for any other good cause, the time therefor may be extended by said county commissioners or by said common pleas court as may be necessary.

Extension of time.

SECTION 4. If the proposed improvement is a ditch or drain, and the county engineer by his surveys finds that the proposed drainage can be effected as well in connection with a ditch or drain necessary or advantageous for the improvement of a public highway already established, or such as may be thereafter required, he shall report that fact and any change of route from that named in the petition necessary to accomplish such object, and if upon the hearing of the petition in this act provided, the commissioners or court find the fact to be as reported such change of route shall be made.

§ 6445.

When change of route may be made.

And if the route proposed in the petition is upon a line or subdivision line of a section where a public highway will probably be required, and in all cases where the proposed location of a ditch, drain, or watercourse is along highways already established, the improvement shall be located at a sufficient distance to one side of such line or from the center of such highway to admit of the highway construction and maintenance along such central line

So far as practicable regarding economy of construction and availability for use, the commissioners shall avoid locating ditches and drains diagonally across sections or parts of sections of land, and shall locate them within the boundaries of the public highways.

Sec. 6446.
Date of hearing; notice.

SECTION 5. Upon the filing of such report, the board of county commissioners, or the court of common pleas, shall fix a date within a period of time not less than twenty days or more than thirty days, when a hearing upon said petition shall be had. Upon such day being fixed, the county auditor, or the clerk of court, if before the common pleas court, shall prepare and mail, in a five day return addressed envelope, to each person signing or named in the petition and to each other person named in the engineer's report as affected by said improvement, whose mail address is given, a written notice of the date and time of such hearing. Such notice shall contain the name of the first signed petitioner, the nature of the improvement asked for, and the general location of the same and also the statement that it is claimed that the improvement will affect property owned by them. And if the residence of any persons named in the petition or report cannot be ascertained, or if any mailed notice be returned undelivered, such auditor or clerk of court, shall publish such notice to all such persons in a newspaper of general circulation in the county by publishing the same in two successive weekly issues thereof, but on the same day of the week if it be a daily paper. The last publication shall be made at least five days before the date of hearing. The receipt of such notice by the owner of land or property affected or the due publication of the same if residence is unknown shall be deemed to have the same effect as a summons in a civil action and to enter the appearance of the party to the proceedings; and if the mailed notice be not returned undelivered it shall be prima facie service of the same.

Sec. 6447.
Hour for hearing; postponement.

SECTION 6. The hearing on the day set shall be held at ten o'clock A. M., at the office of the county commissioners, or in the common pleas court as the case may be, but either said commissioners, or court, may on good cause shown therefor, or the then occupation of the board or court in other matters postpone said hearing to another hour or day, but not more than twenty days. And, provided, if at the time of filing of said engineer's report, any of said persons affected by said improvement have in writing waived service of notice of hearing, and such waiver is filed with the auditor or clerk of court, no notice shall be served upon them. Proof of published notice shall be made by affidavit of the printer or other person knowing the fact and filed in said proceeding. And the auditor or clerk shall certify the persons served by mail.

48.

SECTION 7. On the day fixed for said hearing and at the hour of ten A. M., or such other hour and day to which the matter may be lawfully postponed, the county commissioners shall meet at their office, or the common pleas court shall sit, and shall conduct said hearing by causing the petition to be publicly read with the report of the engineer as to the feasibility of the line or method he deems more feasible to accomplish the object of the petition, and the estimated probable cost thereof, and any estimated damage to any property by the construction thereof, including highways, bridges, culverts, whether of private or public ownership, or other public property. And after such public reading, any person, corporation, public official, board or other interested party, may, if they desire, file in writing their objections and the grounds thereof to the allowance of said petition, and in person or by counsel be orally heard thereon; and if facts involved in the petition or the report of the engineer be put in issue by such objection, then, or at some time to be fixed by the commissioners, or the court, proof shall be heard upon such controverted facts by oral or documentary evidence according to the rules of evidence in civil cases in Ohio. And also it may be shown if there are others than those named in the petition or the engineer's report who will be benefited or damaged by the proposed improvement and have not been notified of the hearing.

Procedure on day of hearing; filing objections; hearing objections.

1449.

SECTION 8. If upon such hearing, and before deciding upon the necessity of such improvement, or the validity of any objection thereto, the county commissioners, or the court, find that all the parties necessary have not been notified as provided for in this act, or if they, or it, deem it necessary to personally inspect and view the location of the improvement proposed by the petition, or reported more feasible by the engineer, the hearing shall be adjourned, but not for a longer period than twenty days, to give time to notify necessary parties or for such inspection. If the postponement be for inspection, it shall be made before the adjourned date of hearing, and the actual cost thereof shall be included with the other cost of said improvement. If the commissioners, or the court, find for the improvement they shall fix a day for the hearing of claims for the appropriation of land taken therefor and the damages to be sustained by any person affected by it, which claims shall be filed in writing with the auditor, or the clerk, on or before the day set for their hearing.

Adjournment of hearing; causes.

Upon the day fixed for the hearing of claims for damages or compensation, the county commissioners, shall hear any competent evidence offered by any of the interested parties upon any claims filed as provided, and also the testimony of the county engineer, and upon consideration of all the evidence they shall find and by resolution adopted by a majority shall determine the amount of damage, if any, to which any property owner is entitled, and the fair value of any property taken for said improvement, and by such resolution authorize the auditor of the county to issue

Hearing of claims for damages and compensation.

his warrants upon the treasurer payable from the general ditch improvement fund to such claimants for such amounts, at the time that contracts for such improvement may be made, or any time thereafter on demand.

Hearing when proceedings commenced in common pleas court. But if the proceedings for an improvement be commenced in the court of common pleas by the petition of the county commissioners, then if the petition be granted and the improvement be located by the decision and order of the court, if any party to such proceeding or any person affected thereby, shall file claim for damage to property affected or for compensation for property taken therefor, if any party to said proceeding resists the claim as made, the court shall, unless trial by jury be waived by claimant and contestant submit the same at the earliest convenient day to a jury for determination, as in an action for a money demand, and render its judgment as to such claim upon the jury verdict, as in other jury trials in which trial, and to which verdict the respective parties may save exceptions, file motion for new trial and prosecute error to the court of appeals as in ordinary actions at law. The verdict of the jury in such case shall fix the amount to be paid as damage or compensation, and costs of such trial shall be taxed as in trials for condemnation of property under the provisions of law. Upon rendition of judgment the court shall authorize the payment of the same as is above provided in case of determination by the commissioners.

But where in the opinion of the county commissioners, or the court, the damage that will be sustained by any person by the construction of the improvement cannot be readily ascertained until after the completion of the improvement, the hearing thereon may be postponed to a day not more than ninety days after the completion of the same.

Should no claims be filed for damages or compensation, but should the report of the engineer contain an estimate of such, then the amount so estimated shall be set apart from the general ditch improvement fund and held as security for the benefit of any claimant of damages or compensation until it be determined whether any legal claim exists therefor.

Sec. 6450.

Report by officer upon receipt of notice; resolution concurring in or opposing improvement. SECTION 9. Upon receipt of either the notice of the filing of the petition, or of the time set by the county commissioners, or the court, by the mayor of any municipality, president of any board of education or president of any board of trustees of any state, county, township or municipal public institution he shall either report the fact to the council, board of education or trustees of the institution for its action by resolution in said matter, which may provide for concurrence in said proposed improvement, defense against it or such other action as in their discretion is proper to protect the municipal interest therein; or the mayor may upon his own discretion appoint the city or village solicitor and city or village engineer, if the municipality have such officers or employees, to act with himself as a committee to represent the municipality in the proceedings of such improvement, but if he so act and appoint without order by the council by resolution, it shall be without expense to the municipality other than the regular salary or per diem of such officers or employees. And the mayor or said committee shall not be authorized to employ legal counsel in said matter without authority given by the council.

451. SECTION 10. The county commissioners, or the court, may hear and determine, at the same time and under the same petition, the necessity or advantage of locating a new ditch or drain, or a ditch or drain partly old and partly new, or a ditch or drain partly open and party tiled, or of deepening, widening, straightening, tiling, or altering in any manner an old ditch or drain; or for connecting together into a single system two or more old ditches or drains for the purpose of a common outlet. And the county commissioners, or the court, may, on application of parties, or in their discretion, consolidate and treat as a petition for one improvement petitions pending at the same time for separate ditches, drains, outlets, or other improvements incident thereto, where the same will serve common territory, or readily combine into one system with a common outlet. And in case of such consolidation, the county commissioners shall cause entry to be made upon their journal of their action, and if necessary, on their order, the county engineer shall re-estimate said consolidated improvement as one improvement.

Hearing as to new location, system, deepening, widening, etc., at same time under same petition.

5452. SECTION 11. If the county commissioners, or the court, find an improvement by ditch or drain or other means is necessary, and grant the petition therefor, either for the line set forth in the petition, or upon one which in their judgment is more feasible to accomplish the object of the petition, all the cost and expense connected with their proceedings, as well as the cost and expense of construction of the improvement shall be assessed upon the property affected beneficially by such improvement, including any highways or other public grounds, according to the benefit derived therefrom and in proportion thereto. And as a part of such cost and expenses, to be so assessed, shall be included such portion of the expense of enlarging any waterway through a public highway or constructing, altering or reconstructing any bridge over such waterway, as may be determined by the county commissioners, or the court, and such portion of such expense shall be paid by the county from its bridge fund.

Assessment of cost and expense when petition granted.

5453. SECTION 12. If the county commissioners, or the court, shall find that the improvement petitioned for is not necessary and will not confer benefit upon the lands of the petitioners, and will not be conducive to the public welfare; or that if conferring some benefit to the lands of the petitioners or conducive to some extent to the advantage and welfare of the public that the inconvenience thereof to others, or the probable cost and expense thereof will be disproportionate to such benefit to petitioner, or advantage

Costs and expense when petition dismissed.

and welfare to the public, said commissioners, or the court, shall dismiss the petition and proceedings at the cost of the petitioners. Such costs shall be itemized by the auditor, or the clerk of court, and approved by the county commissioners, or the court, and ordered paid by the petitioners and bondsmen within a period to be fixed in such order, which shall not exceed thirty days; and such dismissal and order as to costs shall be entered on record on the journal of the county commissioners, or the court, as are final orders; and such order of dismissal shall contain a statement of the finding of facts on which the order is based, but such order shall be suspended by an appeal as in this chapter provided.

When petitioner and bondsmen released from costs

But if the county commissioners, or the court, shall grant the petition and no appeal therefrom be taken. then all the said costs with other costs of construction and any award for damages to, or compensation for property taken shall be assessed upon the benefited property as in this chapter provided, and the petitioner and bondsmen shall from such finding and expiration of the time fixed for appeal be released from all obligation for said costs and under said bond therefor.

Sec. 6454.

Duties of engineer when finding is for improvement.

SECTION 13. If the county commissioners, or the court, find for the improvement. and the preliminary survey provided for in this act and reported by the engineer is not sufficient for the construction of the improvement, the county engineer shall be directed to complete such survey, upon the plan and line or lines decided upon, set proper construction stakes and if the improvement be a ditch, drain, watercourse or levee, number them at every one hundred feet from the head of the improvement down stream to its end; and if not done in said preliminary survey, the engineer shall note the intersection of the line of the improvement with the land boundaries of separate owners, township and county lines, natural land marks, road crossings, or other lines or marks and take and note any necessary levels off the line of the improvement for contour purposes to determine the area of the land of any owner subject to drainage or special benefit by its construction. He shall also at intervals of not less than one in each mile of the main line and at least one upon every improvement, establish in the most practicable permanent form, and in locations where destruction or disturbance is improbable, bench marks from which the original levels of the improvement can be established. Such bench marks and all levels of such improvements shall be based upon some established elevation of the Geological Survey of the United States, if any, in the county, and the relation of any assumed elevation used by the county engineer, in his work and levels upon any improvement, to said elevation established by said geological survey, shall be accurately stated in the record of levels in this chapter provided to be kept. In connection with his said surveys, the county engineer shall complete or make a permanent record of such surveys and levels in his office. And he shall make a schedule containing the name of each land owner, with a description of the land believed by him to be benefited by the improvement, and the approximate number of acres so benefited, and the relative per cent of benefit thereto as in his opinion the same may be, based on his said surveys and contours, and the location of the land relative to the improvement and feasibility and probable expense of making the same available. Such record shall include: the name and number of the improvement; accurate field notes of the line, if it be a ditch or watercourse or levee of any kind, with witness points accurately located, by angular and distance data, at all angles in such line, at the discretion of the county engineer, and the elevation of the grade line at such angles and at the junction of any side branch or spur; the location and nature of all permanent bench marks, and their actual elevation above or below the base elevation used from said geological survey of the United States; and such other data as in the judgment of the county engineer will aid in retracing lines, levels, or other features of said improvements at any time, or will in the future aid in mapping the surface or topography of the county. And to such record, the county engineer may add any statements as to the nature of the excavation and location of special features such as quicksand, rock, and the like.

The engineer shall prepare proper working specifications and detail drawings for the construction of said improvement, including culverts, bridges, catch basins, manholes, wells, embankments and like features, unless standard specifications and drawings for any part have been adopted for county work by the county commissioners, in which case the same shall become a part of any contract given for the construction of the portion of the work covered thereby, unless for good cause a different plan shall be adopted. The engineer shall also estimate the number of cubic yards of earth and other material to be removed in the construction of the improvement, and if it be a ditch or watercourse, for each section of one hundred feet, and the aggregate amount for each working section proposed to be under separate constructive contracts. If the improvement be a levee, dike, embankment, or other work requiring the furnishing and placing of material such as masonry, concrete, stone, earth and the like, the county engineer shall in like manner compute the number of cubic yards or feet of each separate substance required to comply with the plans and specifications and all amounts of material to be placed or removed shall be appropriately inserted in the specifications, which amount shall be an essential element and part of any contract for such placing or removal. And he shall also return an estimate of the cost of all work and material necessary in the improvement with the separate items thereof. The county engineer, who for the purpose shall have the counsel and aid of the prosecuting attorney, shall prepare forms for contracts with bidders for said work and material,

(marginal note: Specifications and detail drawings for construction.)

(marginal note: Estimate of cost of work and material; forms of contracts and bonds.)

and proper forms of bonds to secure the performance of such contracts.

Sec. 6455.

Record of plans and specifications; letting contract.

SECTION 14. Such plans and specifications when finished shall be submitted by the county engineer to the county commissioners, or the court, who, when they find the same to conform to their previous order, shall approve them by order upon their journal record of the proceeding, and upon such approval they shall fix a time within thirty days and not less than two weeks, for letting the contract or contracts for the construction of the improvement and the furnishing of necessary material, unless an appeal from the finding of the commissioners, or the court, has been taken against the location and construction of the improvement as in this chapter provided, in which case the letting of the contract shall be suspended until final order or judgment on such appeal is rendered.

Sec. 6456.

Notice of letting contract.

SECTION 15. When the commissioners, or the court, have set a day for the letting of contracts for construction, of any improvement under this chapter, it shall be the duty of the county engineer to give at least two weeks' public notice of the time when and place where bids will be received for furnishing any material therefor, or constructing all or any part thereof. Such notice shall indicate concisely, the nature of the improvement and location, and the character of the material and work required. Such notice may be given by posting at the front door of the county court house, unless the estimated cost of the construction and material required in said improvement exceeds one thousand dollars in which case advertisement shall also be made at least once in a newspaper printed in the county and having a general circulation therein, if there be one. And in case manufactured material is required, the county commissioners, or the court, may direct the engineer to send copies of the notice by mail to such dealers or manufacturers as they may designate.

Sec. 6457.

Receiving bids; deposit by bidder required.

SECTION 16. At the time and place so advertised, the county engineer, or a deputy designated by him, shall attend and receive all bids submitted, which bids shall be in writing on a form to be furnished by the county engineer, and which shall by reference coincide with and cover the specifications for the construction of the improvement or furnishing of material, as the case may be, for which the bid is asked. All bids shall be sealed except as otherwise provided and accompanied with either a deposit of money, or a certified check on some bank or a bill of current commercial exchange in an amount of three per cent of the bid, but in no case less than ten dollars, as a guaranty that, if the bid is accepted, the bidder will sign the contract for the performance of the work or furnishing of the material bid upon, and will furnish such bond to the county for the performance of the contract signed as may be required by law. Such contract shall in all cases be deemed to include the plans and specifications of the improvement, the bid of

939

the contractor and all provisions of law governing the subject matter of the contract.

All such deposits and checks of unsuccessful bidders shall on rejection of bids be at once returned, and the deposit or check of the successful bidder shall be held until the contract is signed and bond given when it shall be returned. Should a bidder after his bid is accepted refuse, or for five days neglect to sign said contract or furnish said bond, the county commissioners, or the court, may declare such deposit or check forfeited, and shall so declare, unless for good cause shown further time be allowed to the bidder to comply herewith. Any action of the commissioners, or the court, forfeiting the bidder's deposit or check, shall be entered on their journal as other matters of record of the improvement. Any forfeited sum hereunder shall be paid into the general ditch improvement fund. *Return of deposit, when; forfeit of deposit.*

458. SECTION 17. In all cases where the improvement requires both labor and material which is used in and remains as a part of the completed improvement, the bids shall state separately the bidder's offer upon each, and for each kind of material required. And if the specifications do not name a specific grade, quality, kind or size of any material, of which different standard grades, qualities, kinds or sizes are in use, then the bid shall specify the grade, quality, kind or size proposed to be furnished; and unless the specifications otherwise provide, all bids for material shall be deemed to be for delivery at the location of the improvement, and at such place as may be designated by the engineer in charge of the work, except that tile or conduit pipe of any kind shall be along the line of the improvement, and where the same are by the plans and specifications to be used, providing such location is accessible. *Statements required in bids.*

Any bidder may submit a bid for any portion of the improvement that is the subject of a separate estimate, whether of construction or material, providing it be for work or material that can be done or furnished independent of other work or material.

1459. SECTION 18. When the time has passed for the receiving of bids, the engineer shall as soon as is practicable open, canvass, and tabulate them and report the same to the county commissioners, or the court, as received by him, with his recommendation of which bid or combination of bids in all respects is the best. The commissioners, or the court, shall accept the bid or bids they deem best, and may accept any combination of bids of different bidders for different parts of the work, or for furnishing different materials, that they find will be more economical or advantageous than the aggregate bid of a single bidder; but no bid shall be accepted for any part or thing that exceeds the estimate of the engineer, unless only by such acceptance can contract for completion of the entire improvement be let within the aggregate estimate reported by him. *Canvass of bids and report to commissioners or court; acceptance.*

Should it be found that all bids for work and material, or all bids for any separate part or parts of work and *When re-advertisement may be ordered.*

material are in excess of the estimates reported by the
county engineer, the commissioners may in their discretion
order the re-advertisement of the same or any part thereof,
for which the bids are in excess, and they may direct the
county engineer to re-estimate the work, material or the
necessary part thereof and re-advertise the same for bids
on such new estimate.

Sec. 6460.

When contract may be let by competitive bidding at public outcry.

SECTION 19. When the estimated total cost for labor
and material in any improvement is less than three hundred dollars, a contract for the entire improvement including work and material may be let at competitive bidding
at public outcry, by the engineer; and if the improvement
consists only of an open or tiled ditch or drain, or one partly
open and party tiled, with incident catch basins, culverts
and retaining walls, and the estimate of the engineer shows
the total cost of material and construction not to exceed
eight thousand dollars, and no single class of work or material to exceed seventy-five per cent of the total cost, the
bids therefor may be received in competition at public outcry, instead of sealed bids; but such bids shall be separately taken for work and material, except that if the estimate of material, and construction of catch basins, culverts and retaining walls is not more than ten per cent of
the aggregate estimate, or the furnishing of material and
labor for the construction of the catch basins, culverts and
retaining walls does not exceed seventy-five dollars, such
material and their construction may be included in a bid
for construction of the improvement; and if the estimated
cost thereof be not more than five per cent of the aggregate, they may be awarded at their estimate to the successful bidder for construction. Bids taken and contracts let
by public outcry shall be subject to all provisions covering
sealed bids, applicable thereto. Authority to receive bids
by public outcry shall be given by the commissioners or
court and entered on the journal.

Sec. 6461.

Rejection of bids: collusion among bidders effects forfeiture.

SECTION 20. Any and all bids may be rejected, and
if the commissioners, or the court, believe there has been
collusion among the bidders, shall be rejected, in which
case the work shall be readvertised, and no bid shall on such
readvertising be received or considered from any person
found to have been in collusion in the earlier bidding; nor
shall such collusive bidder become a subcontractor of work
or furnisher of material directly or indirectly to any successful bidder. And any successful bidder knowingly employing such collusive bidder, or subcontracting to, or purchasing from him work or material for use in said improvement shall forfeit all compensation for such portion
of work, or for such material. But the labor employed by
him, or material used, not done or furnished by such collusion, shall be protected by the bond of such guilty contractor.

6462. SECTION 21. If in the progress of work of excavation upon any improvement, there occur, hardpan or quicksand not noted in the engineer's report, and necessary to be removed or controlled in performance of the required work, the same may be done by the contractor under the direction and supervision of the engineer in charge, and the actual expense thereof, with five per cent allowance to the contractor shall be paid as extra compensation, on the certificate of the engineer, as a part of the cost of the improvement. *When extra compensation may be allowed contractor.*

6463. SECTION 22. Upon the acceptance of any bid for all or any portion of a drainage improvement under this chapter, the bidder shall within five days enter into a contract in writing to perform the work or furnish the material bid for, as prepared by the engineer. And unless a different time be fixed by order of the commissioners, or the court, such work shall be done and material furnished within a period of one hundred and twenty days from the date of the contract. But if an improvement require both labor and material, and contracts be given therefor to different persons, the time of furnishing such material shall correspond with the time provided for its use in the progress of the work. *Contract in writing.*

6464. SECTION 23. During the execution of the work contracted, as the same may be necessary, the county engineer shall give sufficient notice in writing, not less than twenty days, to any owner of a bridge, culvert, fence or floodgate other than the county, where the removal or alteration of the same is necessary to the progress of the work of the improvement, to remove or make such alteration as the county engineer finds necessary; and when the completion of the improvement requires a change in elevation of such bridge, or removal of any fence or floodgate, or an increase in the width of the waterway beneath the same, which has been designated in the report of the engineer, he shall give like notice to such owner to make said change within the time limited for the completion of the improvement. And the cost of such removal and replacement and cost of any alteration made necessary by such improvement, which cost shall in no case exceed the value of such bridge, culvert, fence or floodgate when such improvement was made, shall be determined and paid as are other damages to property as a part of the cost of improvement, except that if the alteration by change of width of waterway or elevation of any bridge or culvert is necessary because the owner, in its original construction, obstructed or unduly contracted the natural and normal channel of a public watercourse, then such part of the expense of the alteration as is made necessary by such obstruction or contraction shall not be deemed to be a damage to property or paid for as such. *Notice to owner when removal or alteration necessary.* *Cost of removal or replacement.*

6465. SECTION 24. The time fixed in a contract for the performance of any work, or the furnishing of any material, on good cause shown, the case to be specifically set forth by affidavit, and if required by the commissioners, or the *Extension of time; how obtained.*

court, supported by the affidavits of 'others having personal knowledge of the facts, may be extended by said commissioners, or court, for any definite period they may find reasonably necessary under all the circumstances to complete the work or furnish the material under such contract; and in case of such extension the contractor's bond, and sureties thereon, shall remain liable, as if such extended time had been originally named in said bond. But the commissioners, or the court, shall not extend the contract time of furnishing any material to be used by an independent contractor, unless by consent of such using contractor the time for performance of his contract is correspondingly extended. Any action or order extending or refusing to extend contract time hereunder, shall be by resolution spread on the journal of the commissioners, or the record of the court, and the evidence on which such action is taken preserved in the files of the case. The authority herein given to extend the time of performance of a contract shall include all contracts heretofore made and not fully performed at the passage and taking effect of this act.

Sec. 6466.

Amount of bond; signatures; conditions.

SECTION 25. The bond provided to be given for the enforcement of a contract for work or material used in the construction of an improvement under this chapter, shall be in the penal sum of the engineer's estimated cost of the work or material covered by the bid and contract. It shall in terms be made payable to the state of Ohio for the benefit of the county, and any person having a right of action thereon as in this act provided. It shall be signed by the contractor as principal with two sureties neither of whom are contractors on the same improvement and be approved by the county commissioners, or the court, or in lieu of two personal sureties, the bond may be signed by a surety company qualified by the laws of the state to do business therein. If personal sureties are offered, they shall be residents of one of the counties wherein the improvement is located, or if non-residents, the bond shall have endorsed thereon the signed statement of each surety under oath, that he is worth double the amount of the bond in tangible property above all exemptions and encumbrances. The bond shall in terms be conditioned—

First: To save the county or counties interested harmless from any loss caused by delay in completing the work or furnishing the material within the time and in the manner expressed in the contract bid and specifications;

Second: For the payment of all labor and material furnished to the contractor or hired and used by him under the contract;

Third: For the payment of claims of any person arising out of the unlawful acts or negligence of the contractor in the performance of his contract, including personal injuries.

Priority of claims.

And said sureties shall not be otherwise obligated upon said bond. In case of claims under two or more of the said classes, they shall have priority in the order herein stated,

provided such priority shall only be given for six months
after the expiration of the time, or any extension of time
given, for performance of the contract. After said period
of six months, all persons having rights of action shall have
priority in order of the commencement of action in a court
having jurisdiction. The contractor shall at all times remain personally liable for his acts or omissions as to any
person aggrieved as if no bond were required.

147.

SECTION 26. All work upon any improvement to be
done, and all material furnished for use therein, shall be
subject to and under the supervision and inspection of the
county engineer, or some deputy appointed for the purpose
by him. All material furnished under specification and
contract for said work by contractors, or material men, shall
be inspected by the county engineer, or his deputy, before
use and within sixty days from the time the same is delivered and placed upon the line of the improvement, or
such other place as may be designated. And when, and if,
the same corresponds to the specifications, and otherwise
complies with the terms of the contract, the county engineer shall give a certificate thereof to the contractor, or
person furnishing the same, which certificate shall show the
amount furnished and accepted, the contract price thereof,
and the person by whom the same is furnished. The contractor, or person so furnishing said material, unless it be a
person or company regularly engaged in the manufacture
and sale thereof to the public, and given such certificate,
may file the same with the county auditor and shall file
therewith a sworn statement that the material so furnished
and accepted has been by him paid for in full, or if not
paid for in full, the name of the person having a claim
therefor and the amount of the same. And when not less
than one-fourth of the portion of the work included in a
contract of more than one thousand dollars and not more
than five thousand dollars or fifteen per cent of any larger
contract is completed in accordance with the specifications
and the terms thereof, the county engineer shall upon demand and within a reasonable time give a certificate to the
contractor for such work showing the proportion of the
work completed and accepted and the contract price thereof.
And the contractor receiving such certificate may file the
same with the county auditor and shall therewith file an
affidavit containing a complete statement of his payroll, of
labor-used upon said work and upon oath show either that
said labor is paid in full, or the amounts that are due and
the persons to whom are due any unpaid sums for labor.
When such certificates and affidavits are filed, the county
auditor shall draw his warrant upon the treasurer of the
county in the case of material for the full contract price of
such material, if all material under the contract has been
furnished, and if material is still to be furnished under
said contract, then for seventy-five per cent of the amount
called for by said certificate as furnished, but such war-

Supervision and inspection of work and material; certificate of engineer.

Filing certificate and statement with county auditor.

When county auditor may issue warrant for material or work.

rants shall be less any unpaid amount to any person therefor, unless a written release by such person be filed by the contractor. And in like manner, upon the certificate of any contractor for work upon said improvement the auditor shall draw his warrant for the full amount, if the work required by the contract be entirely completed and accepted. But if said work be not entirely completed, then for seventy-five per cent of the contract price of the amount certified completed, but in either case, less any sum shown by his affidavit to be due to workmen, or others employed thereon, unless he shall furnish signed releases of such persons. And the said auditor upon the application of any person shown by the affidavit of contractors to be unpaid for material or work shall draw his warrant to them, upon their application for the same, for the amount shown to be due them in such affidavit, and charge such payments to the contractor.

Payment of warrants. The treasurer of the county shall pay said warrants out of any funds in the treasury applicable for such purpose. And if the county commissioners have determined to issue bonds for the construction of said improvement, and the contractor, material man, or laborer consents thereto, he may pay said warrants in the bonds of the county for said imporvement; providing no bonds shall be paid in fractional sums, nor in less amounts than one hundred dollars.

Sec. 6468.
When assessments shall be paid. SECTION 27. At the time of granting the petition for any improvement under this chapter, the commissioners, or the court shall determine how long a period of time, in semi-annual installments, as taxes are paid, shall be given to owners of lands benefited to pay the assessments that may be made therefor; and whether bonds shall be issued and sold in anticipation of such payments or not, and if bonds are to be issued, the rate of interest they shall bear. But if the estimated cost of the improvement, as reported by the county engineer does not exceed one thousand dollars, not more than two years' time, in four semi-annual installments, shall be given; and no bonds in such case shall be issued or sold unless the county has no funds available in its general ditch improvement fund from which payment in anticipation of collection of assessments can be made. Nor shall more than five years' time, in ten semi-annual installments, be given in any case for any assessment for benefits for any improvement under this chapter.

If bonds be not issued, but the improvement be paid for from the general ditch improvement fund, there shall be included in any installment when paid, interest on all unpaid intsallments at the rate of five per cent per annum, payable semi-annually. And when bonds are issued and sold the rate of interest on such bonds shall in like manner be included in the assessment for their redemption, and paid semi-annually with the current installment.

169.

SECTION 28. After the granting of the petition for any improvement under this chapter, and the letting of contracts for work and material, and the ascertainment and determination of all known claims for compensation for property taken, or damages to property from the construction of the improvement, the total cost thereof including the preliminary cost, and the actual or estimated cost of supervision and any known costs of litigation taxed against the county shall be assessed proportionally, according to special benefits conferred, upon all the lots and parcels of land specially benefited thereby, the owners of which have, as in this chapter provided, had notice of the proceedings for such improvement, whether such lots and parcels of land abut on the improvement or not. Such assessment shall be made as well against the lands of any railway company, township, county, municipality, school district or board of education, or any other public board, as against privately owned property, for the benefit to the premises owned or controlled by such public corporation or body.

And in arriving at the amount of benefit to any piece of property due regard shall be had to any conditions that would require precedent expense before the benefit from the improvement would be available, and to any conditions that would permanently affect the degree of benefit that could be derived.

Provided that the county commissioners, or the court, if, and when, it is found that the improvement will benefit the public health, convenience and welfare, or the result will increase to a practicable degree the valuation of property for public taxation, may order such an amount of such total cost, not exceeding ten per cent, paid from the general ditch improvement fund, or if there be not sufficient unappropriated in such fund, from any unappropriated money of the general fund of the county. And the balance shall be assessed according to benefits as herein provided.

6470.

SECTION 29. In making the assessment for benefits provided for in the preceding section, the county engineer shall prepare a schedule of the lands shown by his surveys, or otherwise known to him to receive benefit from the improvement, and whose owners have had notice of its proposed construction, and shall show in such schedule the number of acres believed by him to be benefited and the percentage of such benefit, on the basis of one hundred per cent benefit to the land or lands subject to assessment and receiving the highest benefit from the improvement at the least probable additional cost to make it available. And he shall in such schedule, based on such acreage, percentage, and total amount to be assessed show the amount of assessment on each separate description of land, and the owner's name, if known.

But when the council of a municipal corporation, board of education or trustees of a state, county, township or municipal public institution is a petitioner for an improvement under this chapter, or named and notified as one of the parties affected thereby, and such improvement equally benefits the whole territory, or any defined portion thereof, within the limits of such municipal corporation, whether any part of the improvement lie within such limits or not, the engineer, county commissioners, court or jury having the duty of determining what portion of the cost and expense shall be assessed upon lands within such municipal limits for such benefit, may consider and treat such territory as a single parcel of land, and the sum so assessed shall be apportioned to all the lots and lands within the municipality or the benefited portion, by the county auditor according to the valuation of the separate parcels therein for taxation.

Sec. 6471.

Filing and publication of schedule of lands and assessments; objections.

SECTION 30. The county engineer shall file his schedule of lands and assessments with the county auditor and the county auditor shall within ten days from such filing, make publication of the fact of the filing of the same, and that it is subject to public inspection and the filing of objections by any owner for twenty days from the date of first publication. Such publication shall give the name and number of the improvement and the name of the first signed petitioner, or if it be a consolidated improvement the fact shall be stated and the name of the first signer of each petition in the consolidation shall be given. Said publications shall be made for two weeks, once each week, on the same day of the week, if in a daily paper, and in two papers representing in politics the two dominant political parties in the county, if there be two such papers printed and published in the county. If there be not such two papers available, then publication shall be made in one, if there be one, and by posting such notice at the front door of the court house of the county for said period, and if there be no paper published in the county notice by said posting shall be sufficient.

Sec. 6472.

Confirmation of assessment; duplicate furnished treasurer; collection.

SECTION 31. If no objection to said assessment as made by the county engineer be filed with the county auditor within twenty days after the date of first publication provided for, then the county commissioners, or the court, shall by order confirm said assessment and direct the auditor to make and furnish to the treasurer of the county a special duplicate with the assessment arranged thereon, as required by their order. The auditor shall retain a copy thereof in his office. All assessments shall be collected and accounted for by the treasurer as are taxes. If any objections are filed, then at the first regular meeting of the commissioners following the expiration of time for filing objections, or at some later date at such meeting fixed, the commissioners shall hear said objections, and all evidence offered by any interested party pertaining thereto and make such modification in the reported assessment as justice requires, and as so modified confirm the same, and so return it to the auditor. When an assessment remains unpaid for one year after it is placed upon the special duplicate, unless otherwise ordered by the commissioners, it shall be placed on the general duplicate for collection, together with a penalty of not less than six per cent annually, as county ditch taxes, and the amount of delinquent tax thus placed on the general duplicate shall be charged respectively to the several ditches on account of which such assessment has been made as a transfer from the general ditch improvement fund. And all collections of said assessments and interest penalties shall be paid into the said fund.

73.   SECTION 32. The finding of a board of county commissioners, or the court, for or against any improvement petitioned for under this chapter, and the decision or judgment of either upon any claim for compensation for property taken or damage to property by reason of the construction of an improvement or the confirmation of any assessment for benefit to property shall be deemed to be a final order of the date on which such finding or decision is made. And the same shall be entered as of such date on the journal record of proceedings of said improvement. *What deemed a final order; journal entry.*

74.   SECTION 33. Any interested party to an improvement proceeding under this act, or any number jointly interested, may appeal from any final decision or order made therein, by a board of county commissioners, to the common pleas court of the county wherein the proceeding was instituted. And if the county commissioners of any county be a party, and the proceeding was commenced orinigally in the common pleas court, then any interested party may appeal from any final order or judgment of such common pleas court granting, refusing or locating the improvement petitioned for, to the superintendent of public works as the drainage commissioner provided for in a subsequent section of this act. *Appeal from final order; notice.*

Notice of appeals herein provided for may be given at the time the decision, order or judgment is made or rendered, and noted by the commissioners or court on their minutes or docket; or written notice of such appeal may be filed in writing within three days from the date of the decision, order or judgment, with the county auditor, or clerk of court, as the case may be. But if the decision be rendered in the absence of parties interested, notice of appeal shall be entered for them as a matter of course, by the county commissioners or court.

475.   SECTION 34. To perfect appeal, the appellant shall within ten days from the date of the final order appealed from, file with the county auditor, if the appeal be from the decision or order of the county commissioners, and with the clerk of the common pleas court, if it be from the decision, order or judgment of the court, an appeal bond, with surety to be approved by the auditor or clerk, as the case may be, conditioned to pay all costs on appeal if the decision, order or judgment appealed from be sustained on the hearing or trial thereof. Within said ten days the ap- *Procedure to perfect appeal.*

pellant shall also file in the court or with the drainage commissioners, to whichever the appeal is taken, (wherein it shall be docketed as are other civil cases, and entitled in the matter of the improvement known as—giving by name and number, if it have one —), a concise statement of the decision, order or judgment appealed from, and the grounds of such decision, order or judgment as entered of record, and the claims of the appellant as to the error or injustice thereof; and on default of such bond and pleading being filed within said ten days said appeal shall be without effect and shall be dismissed at the cost of the appellant.

Sec. 6476.
Transcript.

SECTION 35. If said appeal be perfected, the auditor or clerk, as the case may be, shall within ten days from the filing of the appeal bond and statement, make and file in the appellate court or with the drainage commissioner, a full transcript of the journal entry containing the finding and decision appealed from, with the original petition and engineer's report, assessment or such other original papers as are pertinent to the appelled issue. The issue for hearing or trial shall be deemed to be made by the original petition, the said statement of the appellant and the entry of the decision appealed from, and all parties to the proceeding not joining with the appellant in the appeal shall be considered defendants, and prima facie opposed thereto. No answer need be filed by any defendant. But after appeal has been perfected by any party, any other interested party may by motion made in person, or by counsel, oral or written, in session or at chambers, be entered on the record and considered as joined in interest with the appellant, and in such case, shall, with the appellant, be bound for costs, if the decision, order or judgment appealed from be sustained.

Sec. 6477.
Hearing; precedence over other matters.

SECTION 36. Trial or hearing of said appeal on the issue made shall be had under the rules of law for civil cases, so far as the same are applicable, the appellants being considered as plaintiffs having the affirmative, and being required to produce the preponderance of evidence to reverse or modily the decision, order or judgment appealed from. If the appeal be from a decision or order for or against the location or construction of an improvement, or an assessment for benefits, the same shall be heard by the court as a case in equity; but if the decision, order or judgment appealed from be for the payemnt of, or the refusal to pay, a sum of money in compensation for property taken for such improvement, or as to damages to property affected thereby, the trial shall be to a jury as for a money demand.

If the appeal be from a court of common pleas to the drainage commissioner, the same shall be heard and decided by said drainage commissioner, or his official board of appeal, if he summon the same, as in this act provided, as are equity cases in courts having such jurisdiction. ·

So far as consistent with the rights of others, appeal under this act, shall by the trial court, or drainage commissioner, be given precedence over other matters. The common pleas court, when the case is triable by jury, may at the request of plaintiffs or defendants, under rules as in other civil cases, 'have the jury view the location of the improvement, and the expense of such view shall be taxed as are other costs upon the appeal.

178.

SECTION 37. The sheriff, or his deputy, and the surveyor or engineer who surveyed, leveled, apportioned, and platted the improvement, in case a view be directed, may accompany the jury, and point out its location and route; but no other person shall give any information to the jurors in the discharge of their duty. After the jury has fully examined the premises, and returned to court, either party may be heard, in person or by counsel, and offer evidence to the jury under the direction of the court, upon any matter given it specially in charge as in other civil trials. *View of location and route by jury.*

479.

SECTION 38. The jury shall, upon the case being submitted to it, under the proper charge of the court, and upon a form provided by the court, return its verdict determining the matter in issue appealed from, upon which judgment shall be rendered by the court as in other cases. The verdict shall be signed by the jury as is provided by law, and by at least nine of the panel to make the same effective. The amount of the compensation or damage to be paid, if any, is the issue to be determined by the jury, and it may sustain the award that has been appealed from, or if it does not find such amount to agree with justice and equity determine the amount which upon the facts put in evidence does so accord. In case such amount differs from the award appealed from, the difference shall be pro-rated by addition or deduction from the assessments, if assessments have been made, upon the property assessed for such improvement. *Verdict.*

If in jury trials there are more than one appellant, and with separate claims and issues as to different properties, the court may in its discretion submit all the several claims and issues to the same jury together, or it may direct separate trials for the separate claims and issues or any number of them. In case of such joint submission, the jury shall be approximately charged, and provided with a form to return the compensation or damage separately as to each property and appellant. Also if one appellant shall have appealed from an award as to each compensation for property taken and damages to property caused by the improvement the verdict of the jury shall separately state its findings as to each issue in controversy. In finding its verdict for compensation for property taken, or for damages to a property by an improvement, the jury shall not consider, or deduct, the value of any benefit that it will receive from the construction of such improvement.

If the appeal be upon both court issues and jury issues as in this act defined, the court shall appropriately separate the same for hearing and trial, and render its order or decree upon the court issues, and its judgment upon the verdict of the jury.

Sec. 6480.

Judgment; taxing costs.

SECTION 39. The court trying such appeal shall receive the verdict, and if no motion for new trial thereof be filed within three days, which motion may be filed as in other civil cases at law and for like causes; or if such motion be overruled, it shall render judgment according to said verdict, and for or against the plaintiffs separately, if there be more than one. And the court shall tax the costs on appeal in favor of the prevailing party or parties. If the plaintiffs prevail, then their costs shall be taxed against the county, and the county commissioners shall pay the same from the general ditch improvement fund, and add the same to the costs and expense of the improvement to be assessed upon all benefited property. If the plaintiffs shall not prevail, then the costs on appeal shall be taxed against and collected from them on their bond as in other civil cases. If more than one matter is appealed from, and plaintiff prevails as to one, and loses as to another, then the court shall determine how much of the costs each party shall pay and tax the same accordingly against and collected from them or their bond as in other civil cases. plaintiff, and costs be taxed against them, the court shall apportion and tax the costs to be paid by the plaintiffs equitably among them.

Sec. 6481.

Transcript after judgment certified to county auditor; journal entry.

SECTION 40. After the final judgment, decree or order upon an appeal is rendered by the appellate court, the clerk thereof shall within ten days make a transcript of the same, and certify and transmit it with all original papers in the case and the taxed bill of costs to the county auditor, or the court from which it came on appeal. The auditor, or clerk of court, receiving such transcript and papers shall forthwith notify the county commissioners, or court, of such receipt and the judgment, decree or order shall be entered on their journal, and thereupon such commissioners or court shall proceed with said improvement proceedings in compliance with such final judgment, decree or order, from the point at which they were terminated by such appeal, as if the same had not been taken. And if costs have been taxed against the plaintiffs, and are not paid before the assessment for the improvement is placed upon the property, such costs may be added to the amount of the assessment of such plaintiffs, and certified to the county treasurer for collection and collected with the assessment for benefit, and upon collection paid to the proper court for distribution to the persons, or fund, to which they belong. And any such costs belonging to the county shall be paid into the general ditch improvement fund.

Sec. 6482.

Proceedings in error.

SECTION 41. In addition to the right of appeal in the preceding sections of this act provided for, error may be prosecuted to the court of appeals from a final order or a judgment rendered by a court of common pleas upon either proceeding in the matter of a petition originally filed therein, or heard or tried therein on an appeal from a final order of a board of county commissioners. Proceedings in error hereunder and the costs thereof shall be governed by the provisions of law now or hereafter in force in civil cases.

If the plaintiff or plaintiffs in error be not a board of county commissioners, or joint board of county commissioners, it shall be sufficient to make the board or joint board of county commissioners which originally rendered the decision complained of, or is opposed in interest, defendant in error, and such board or joint board shall be deemed to represent those opposed in interest to the plaintiff in error; and if the plaintiff or plaintiffs in error are a board or joint board of county commissioners, it shall be sufficient to make the petitioners for the improvement defendants in error. All parties to said proceeding in the court of common pleas affected by said proceeding in error shall be deemed to be parties defendant in error, and opposed to the contention of the plaintiffs in error, unless by motion therefor they be admitted and joined with plaintiffs in error in interest.

183. SECTION 42. No appeal, nor any proceeding in error allowed or provided for the parties to an improvement proceeding under this chapter, except an appeal from a final order granting a petition for an improvement, shall operate to suspend or defer any of the proceedings provided for the surveying and estimating the cost of any improvement, or the letting of the contract for and the construction of it, all of which shall proceed as if no appeal had been taken or error had been prosecuted. *Proceedings shall not suspend construction.*

1484. SECTION 43. Any owner of land affected by an improvement as defined in this chapter, who has not received notice thereof, and had opportunity to be heard as in this act provided, may bring an action in the common pleas court of the county wherein the improvement is located, against the county commissioners in their official capacity to recover any tax or assessment therefor, if paid, or to enjoin any tax, assessment or levy therefor upon his lands, or to recover for any damages sustained, or for compensation for any property taken, and his rights and remedies in such action shall be as for any like demand arising from any other cause. But in such action, it shall be competent for the defendant to plead and prove the value of any actual benefit, or increase of value of the premises affected by the improvement by reason thereof in mitigation of any claim for damage or compensation that may be pleaded by the plaintiff. *When owner may recover tax or assessment or enjoin collection.*

.6485. SECTION 44. The court in which a proceeding is brought to recover a tax or assessment paid, or to declare void the proceedings to locate or construct an improvement, or to enjoin a tax or assessment, levied or ordered to be levied to pay the costs and expense thereof, if there is manifest error in the proceedings, whether the same be before the court on appeal, or by action brought as in this act pro- *Evidence in action to recover tax or assessment.*

952

vided, shall allow the plaintiff in the action to show that he
has been injured thereby: and the court in its discretion
upon application of either party may direct and cause any
necessary survey of the premises affected to be made by a
competent disinterested engineer, who shall upon oath report his findings by his survey upon the matters covered by
the court's order, and such report shall be received and
considered by court and jury as is other competent evidence upon the issue to be determined. And the court shall
allow oral testimony that any acts required by law for an
improvement hereunder have been substantially complied
with, notwithstanding the record required to be kept, or
kept by any board or officer. And in case of claimed want
of notice as by this act required, any evidence may be offered that the plaintiff had knowledge of the proceedings
for said improvement and actual opportunity to appear
therein and be heard, which also may be considered upon
the issues. And if said cause is tried before the construction of said improvement is let by contract, then oral evidence may be offered for and against the necessity of the
same, and whether it be conducive to public health, con-·
venience and welfare as defined in this chapter.

Judgment and order.

Upon such trial to the court or jury, the court shall
upon its findings, or upon the verdict of the jury, render
such judgment or make such order as will be equitable, and
may order any tax or assessment to remain on the duplicate
for collection, or order it to be levied, or perpetually enjoin
it or any part thereof as to the plaintiff, or if it has been in
whole or part paid under protest or without knowledge,
order the whole or such part as is just and equitable to be
refunded. And if said improvement is not constructed, and
would irreparably injure the plaintiff if constructed so that
his damage could not be measured by money recovery, the
court may perpetually enjoin such construction. And upon
a partial recovery by the plaintiff the court may apportion
the costs equitably between the parties.

Sec. 6486.

Improvement may not be per-petually enjoined nor proceedings declared void for error.

SECTION 45. Neither the location or construction of
an improvement,·nor the taxes or assessments levied or ordered to be levied to provide for the cost and expense thereof shall be perpetually enjoined, nor the proceedings therefor declared void in consequence of an error committed by
the engineer, the county auditor, county commissioners or
other officer, in the location, construction or record thereof; nor shall such error if not materially affecting the rights
of any interested party, or causing actual damage to property, be a defense to the collection of any tax or assessment
therefor levied thereon, if such tax assessment or levy was
made or done within the jurisdiction conferred by law on
the board or taxing officer making or levying the same.

Sec. 6487.

Appointment of engineer; com-pensation.

SECTION 46. The county commissioners shall have authority, in case the county does not have an elected county
engineer, or in case of his inability for any cause to do the
work required to be done by an engineer, in this act, to
appoint a competent civil engineer to perform the duties

required upon any improvement under this chapter; and in case of such appointment to fix the compensation to be paid to him for his service and the amount of a bond which such engineer shall give with good and sufficient surety to be approved by the commissioners, or court, conditioned for the faithful performance of his duties hereunder. And in case of any default by such engineer, an action may be brought on such bond by a person aggrieved, in the name of such person; and recovery may be had for his use and benefit. If the county engineer be in charge of the work, he shall be liable on his official bond for the faithful performance of all duties required of him in this act.

5488. SECTION 47. The county commissioners of any county, on a petition therefor being filed, and a bond given as provided for the location and construction of an improvement, and under the same proceedings of notice to interested parties for a hearing upon such petition, may determine whether any ditch or drain or other improvement described in such petition has ceased to be a public utility, and whether the public health, convenience or welfare longer demands the maintenance thereof and if its abandonment will be to the advantage of the public convenience or health. If they find such facts to exist, they may declare the same to be vacated and abandoned and its location and establishment held for naught, and may under the petition as a petition for an improvement cause the same to be filed and the cost and expense assessed on the property benefited. But the private rights of persons acquired by reason of the location and establishment of such ditch or drain shall not be interferred with, nor impaired thereby without due compensation be made therefor, to be assessed on property benefited thereby as in this chapter provided. *(Abandonment of improvement; procedure.)*

.6489. SECTION 48. When an improvement which consists of a ditch, drain, or watercourse and which has become the outlet of agricultural drainage has been established and constructed for the public health, convenience or welfare, and such ditch, drain or waterway has been so used for seven years or more, it shall be deemed to be a public watercourse notwithstanding error, defects, or irregularities in the location, establishment or construction thereof. And the public shall have and possess in and to such watercourse the rights and privileges which relate and pertain to natural watercourses; but the same shall be subject to any improvement upon petition as in this chapter provided. *(When ditch, drain, etc., becomes public watercourse.)*

t.6490. SECTION 49. The county commissioners of each county, if the same is not already done, shall provide and establish a permanent fund to be known as the general ditch improvement fund, and which shall be used as a sinking fund for all bonds issued under the provisions of this chapter. Said fund in any county shall consist of all funds in any ditch fund it has at the taking effect of this act that are not then specifically appropriated; of any taxes then or thereafter levied and collected for ditch and drainage pur- *(General ditch improvement fund.)*

poses under county, township and municipal levies not by law otherwise disposed of; the proceeds of all bonds issued and sold under this chapter; the collections from all special assessments for benefits to property in this act provided for and such other funds as by law are or may be provided to be paid therein.

Sec. 6491.
Payments from ditch fund.

SECTION 50. From the general ditch improvement fund, except as otherwise by law provided, all costs and expenses of improvements under this chapter shall be paid including damages, compensation, contract prices of construction, engineering expense, except the salary of the county engineer, costs and expenses of litigation, except the services of the prosecuting attorney and of any other county officer, deputy or employee for whose services, fees or costs are by law collected, which go into the county fee fund for payment of the same.

But no warrants shall be drawn to be paid from said fund unless it contain a sufficient amount not otherwise specifically appropriated to pay the same, and the letting and approving of any contract for an improvement or any award or judgment for compensation, damages or refund of assessments shall be deemed to be a specific appropriation of the amount of such obligation, and such amount shall be set apart for the purpose of such payment and contingently charged against said fund. If at any time said fund contains the proceeds of bonds issued and sold under this chapter, then said fund shall not be depleted below the obligation incurred by such bond issue or issues unless assessments or levies have been made or ordered made and in sufficient amount to redeem the same as they fall due. In case at any time obligations legally incurred exceed the amount of said improvement fund, an amount of the general revenue fund in the county treasury, if otherwise unappropriated, equal to the deficiency, may by resolution of the board of county commissioners be transferred to the general ditch improvement fund.

Sec. 6492.
Tax levy by commissioners.

SECTION 51. The county commissioners of each county in the state, if necessary, annually, at their March session, shall levy upon the grand duplicate of the county, a tax not to exceed five-tenths of one mill on the dollar, sufficient to pay for the location and construction of such portions of the respective improvements located by them, or by the commissioners of two or more counties, as may be apportioned to the county, or which under the provisions of this chapter they have determined to pay, which levy when collected shall be credited to the general ditch improvement fund.

Sec. 6493.
Tax levy by township trustees.

SECTION 52. The trustees of a township to which is apportioned by the county commissioners, or court, under the provisions of this chapter, a portion of the expenses of the construction of one or more improvements, shall levy annually, upon the grand duplicate of the township, a tax sufficient, in their judgment, to pay such apportionments, but not to exceed five-tenths of one mill on the dollar, and certify to the county auditor on or before the fifteenth day of May in each year until all installments are provided for.

494. SECTION 53. If a party to an improvement proceeding under this chapter, the board of education of a district interested in land granted by congress for the support of common schools, unless such lands have been permanently leased, and of a district owning or holding other land for school purposes, when an assessment is made upon such land, or part thereof, under the provisions of this chapter, shall pay such assessment out of the contingent fund of the district, and, if necessary for that purpose, may increase the levy for such fund otherwise authorized by law. *Tax levy by board of education.*

495. SECTION 54. If one or more commissioners of a county are petitioners or own lands shown to be affected by an improvement petition, the auditor shall notify the judge of the common pleas court of the county, who shall within five days ·appoint as many disinterested freeholders of the county as may be necessary to take the place of such interested members. Such appointees shall not be related by blood or affinity to either of the interested commissioners. They shall before acting be sworn to faithfully and impartially perform the duties of commissioner in the matter of said improvement, which oath shall be signed by them and the officer before whom the same is taken and filed with the auditor of the county. Upon appointment on qualification, such appointees shall in the proceeding upon the petition and improvement perform all the duties of the disqualified commissioners, and shall receive, to be paid from the general ditch improvement fund five dollars per day for their services therein as shown by the record of the matter, for which sum the auditor shall draw a proper warrant. *Appointees when commissioners petitioner or land owner affected.*

6496. SECTION 55. In any case where the county commissioners have determined to issue and sell bonds in anticipation of the payments of assessments for benefits or any portion thereof, they shall so declare by resolution, and fix the rate of interest such bonds shall bear, dates of maturity, and denomination and number of bonds. Such bonds shall express upon their face the purpose for which they are issued, with the date of the resolution authorizing the issue, the rate of interest, which shall not exceed six per cent per annum payable semi-annually, the date of maturity, the name and number of the improvement for which they are issued, and any other proper descriptive matter. They may be made subject to registration and have proper interest coupons attached thereto. *Resolution to sell bonds in anticipation of assessments.*

The bonds upon issue shall be signed by the chairman of the county commissioners and countersigned by the auditor, as shall also interest coupons, if attached thereto.

Said bonds may he sold upon popular subscription for par and accrued interest in any quantities without advertisement, or at such value paid to any contractor upon accepted work and material, or the commissioners may cause them to be sold to the highest bidder therefor, under sealed *Sale of bonds.*

bids, for which sale advertisement shall be made for thirty days in at least one, and may be made in two papers printed and of general circulation in the county, but no bid for less than par and accrued interest shall be accepted.

In case of failure to sell said bonds by popular subscription or on advertisement, the bonds or any portion thereof may be sold by the county commissioners at private sale at not less than par and accrued interest, or failing of sale by any of said methods for four months or more, they may, or any unsold portion may be withdrawn by resolution of said county commissioners, and if necessary, a new issue under a new resolution may be substituted therefor.

Sec. 6497.

When refunding bonds may be issued.

SECTION 56. If in any case delinquency in payment of assessments or other cause prevents the accumulation of funds to meet bonds issued in anticipation of assessments under this chapter at their maturity, the county commissioners shall, if no other funds are available to retire them, issue refunding bonds under the same provisions as for the original issue, for any outstanding unredeemed amounts, but such refunding bonds shall not be given a maturity date more than five years from the maturity of the original issue.

Sec. 6498.

Per diem for commissioner in addition to salary.

SECTION 57. In addition to the regular salary provided by law for the county commissioners, each county commissioner shall receive five dollars per day for 'each day he is actually engaged on improvements under this act, but in no case shall any commissioner receive an aggregate of more than twenty-five dollars for services on one improvement, nor shall they receive pay for two separate improvements on the same day. Such amounts shall be paid by warrants issued by the county auditor upon the county treasurer, upon the filing in his cffice of an itemized statement by the commissioner of such service; provided, however, that the aggregate compensation paid a county commissioner under this section for said service shall not exceed in one year five hundred dollars.

Sec. 6499.

Disposition of fees collected.

SECTION 58. The fees that shall be charged and collected for services required of any public officer under this chapter, if not specifically otherwise designated, shall be the fees allowed for like service in the office to which he was elected or appointed, and if he be an officer receiving a salary, and his collection of fees go to the county, then such fees collected hereunder shall be in like manner accounted for.

Legal rate for publication.

Publication of notices, and service by publication in this chapter required, shall be paid at the legal rate provided for publication of like matter originating in the common pleas court.

Sec. 6500.

Books and records furnished engineer and auditor.

SECTION 59. The county commissioners shall provide the auditor and county engineer with suitable books to make and preserve permanent records of all improvements constructed under this chapter, including a book to be kept by the auditor in which shall be recorded an accurate ac-

count of the amount assessed against any tract of land with
a description sufficient to identify the same for the purpose
of the assessment of any repairs to said improvement in the
future. Such books of record shall also contain by name
and number of improvement an accurate account of all cost
and expense of the same with the principal items thereof,
and all receipts from assessments, sale of bonds, and other
sources, so that such amount will show its debtor or credit
balance to the general ditch improvement fund of the
county.

And the provisions of this section shall apply in cases
of improvements under this act located in or affecting more
than one county so far as the expense thereof is apportioned to any county.

01. SECTION 60. Should any contractor of work or ma- *Sworn statement*
terial, upon any improvement under this chapter, inten- *by creditor in*
tionally or by oversight omit from his sworn statement of *case of omission*
or mistake;
his indebtedness for labor or material provided to be filed *notice.*
with his certificate of work completed or material furnished, the name and amount due any person from him
for labor or material used by him upon such improvement;
or should he in such statement give a less amount than in
fact is due, the person so omitted, or whose claim is incor-
rectly stated may file with the auditor a sworn statement
of his credit as he claims it to be with his address, and give
written notice to said contractor, or to the person or agent
having charge of the work of said contractor at said improvement, or to a person, agent, or clerk having charge of
an office of such contractor, of the filing of such claim with
the auditor and the amount claimed. If said contractor
personally, or by some one having personal knowledge of
the facts does not within five days from the giving of such
notice file an affidavit with the auditor denying such claim,
it shall stand as admitted by such contractor and by the
auditor be paid when and as other acknowledged claims
against him are paid.

502. SECTION 61. Should the claims acknowledged by a con- *Procedure when*
tractor upon any improvement, with claims filed against *claims exceed*
amount due con-
him for work and material, exceed the amount due him *tractor.*
upon such contract after any claim or set-off the county
may have against him is deducted, the county auditor shall
give notice by mail thereof to all such claimants, (the cost
of which notice shall be charged against such fund), of
such fact, and the amount of the apparent fund and the
claims against it. Unless within thirty days after such notice is mailed some claimant or said contractor commences
action in a court of competent jurisdiction, claiming a
preference in said fund or the exclusion of some claimant
or claimants from participation therein, the auditor shall
pay the same pro rata to those whose claims are filed against
it with him, and such payment shall release the county from
all obligation thereon to said contractor or claimants.

But the failure of the contractor to contest any claim

by affidavit, or the failure of either claimant or contractor to commence any action to determine the validity of a claim within said thirty days shall not be deemed to waive or in any manner abrogate or affect any right of action thereon or pertaining thereto that under the laws of the state either of them may have against the other, but the fund only and the county shall be released.

Sec. 6503.

When claim denied by affidavit.

SECTION 62. Should a filed claim be denied by affidavit of the contractor, or a person in his behalf having personal knowledge of the facts out of which the claim arises, the claimant shall within thirty days commence action against such contractor in a court of competent jurisdiction to determine the controversy, or his claim shall be deemed to be abandoned, and payment may be made to said contractor or other claimants whose claims are not denied.

Sec. 6504.

Auditor shall retain fund in controversy; rights of others not postponed.

SECTION 63. In case of the action provided for in either of the two preceding sections being commenced, and notice thereof being served on the auditor, he shall retain the fund involved in such controversy until final judgment in said cause, and as against the contractor sufficient to pay the costs of action. But the rights of other claimants to their portion of such fund shall not be postponed, nor any amount retained therefrom in anticipation of any costs that may be taxed against such contractor. On final judgment, unappealed from, or bond not given in proceedings in error, the auditor shall by warrant, pay said fund retained according to the order of the court rendering the judgment.

Sec. 6505.

Estimate and report by engineer when cleaning, repair, etc. necessary.

SECTION 64. In all cases, except as herein provided, when cleaning, repair, or replacement is found by the county commissioners to be necessary upon any improvement, before the same shall be done, the county engineer, upon the order of the county commissioners, shall make an estimate of the probable cost and expense of material and labor therefor, and report the same to the county commissioners in writing. When such report shows the probable cost to be less than three hundred dollars in the aggregate, the same at the discretion of the county commissioners, may be let by contract made by the engineer with the approval of the county commissioners without public bidding and without petition or other proceedings. But if the estimate of said cost and expense in its entirety exceeds the sum of three hundred dollars except in case of an emergency, the same shall be done by public letting of contract as provided for the original construction of improvements under this chapter.

Sec. 6506.

Emergency repairs.

SECTION 65. In case of an emergency, and when the county commissioners shall by resolution entered on their journal find such emergency to exist, and that the necessary delay for estimate and letting by contract by notice, as above provided, will cause greater loss and damage, the county commissioners may order the county engineer to proceed at once to make said cleaning, repair, or replacement, in temporary or permanent form as the emergency may demand, either by contract for the necessary work and material or by purchase of material and hiring of labor as the circumstances may demand. But upon a contract let for emergency purposes hereunder, no margin of profit shall be allowed above 10 per cent of the actual cost of labor and material used.

SECTION 66. If the estimated cost of material for any necessary repair or replacement of an improvement does not exceed the amount of twenty-five dollars, and the property owner or owners to be benefited thereby, or any of them, are willing to do the necessary labor without expense to the county to properly make such repair or replacement, the county commissioners shall, in their discretion, furnish the material and allow the work to be so done, with such order to the engineer as to supervision as they deem necessary. And such material shall be paid for from the general ditch improvement fund, and no special assessment be made therefor.

When property owner may make repair, etc.

SECTION 67. The actual cost of the cleaning, repair, or replacement of any improvement constructed after the passage of this act shall be distributed and charged to the lands, including township and county, originally assessed for the construction of the same, in the ratio of such assessment, and the auditor shall add such amounts to the taxes otherwise levied on such lands and certify the same to the county treasurer to be collected as are other taxes with the next semi-annual installment. When such taxes are paid they shall be credited to the general ditch improvement fund in this act provided.

Ratio of distribution and charge of assessment; collection.

The actual cost of the cleaning, repair, or replacement of any drainage improvement constructed prior to the passage of this act, of which there is a record of the assessment of the original cost according to benefits and the lands on which it was assessed, shall be distributed and charged to such lands in the manner provided herein for the cost of cleaning, repair and replacement of improvements constructed since the passage hereof. But if no such record has been preserved, or such a record as will accurately disclose such facts, then such cost shall be assessed according to benefits as on the construction of an original improvement, and by like proceedings, and after notice, placed by the auditor on the tax duplicate; but in all cases there shall be a right of appeal by any interested party as is provided from assessment on an original improvement.

SECTION 68. When an owner of land requiring drainage and whose natural and only practicable outlet requires the construction of a drain across the land of another, and such owners cannot agree upon a location, size of tile or other material condition, or the compensation that shall be paid for the privilege of crossing such other lands, the upper owner may give a written notice to the lower owner specifying the general course of the location desired to reach the outlet, the size of the tile proposed to be used and the approximate depth they are to be laid, and offer such lower

Procedure when improvement required by one owner crosses land of another.

owner any sum he deems just for the privilege of such drain and the right to maintain it. If such offer is refused, and no compromise can be reached by said owners, the proposer may file with the trustees of the township in which the lands of the lower owner lie, a copy of his proposition.

The trustees shall fix a time, within ten days, to meet the owners at the proposed location, of which date and hour the proposer shall give the lower owner notice. At the time fixed, the trustees shall meet said owners and adjust the matter between them by agreement if possible, but if they will not agree, then such trustees shall fix and determine the location of such drain, the size and depth of tile to be used, and sum that the upper owner shall pay the lower owner for the privilege of maintaining such drain. The sum awarded shall be paid or tendered before the construction of said drain is commenced. And besides the sum paid for such privilege the upper owner shall also give bond, with a surety approved by the trustees to compensate the lower owner for any damage to crops or fences caused by the construction of said drain.

If such lower owner is not satisfied with the sum awarded by the trustees, he may bring action before the justice of the peace in the township where the proposer resides within thirty days from the payment or tender of the sum awarded, or within thirty days of the meeting if no sum is awarded, for any further sum he may believe himself entitled to and pursue such case to judgment and execution as other actions for money, the costs to be paid by the defeated party.

After the construction of such drain if use is desired to be made of it by the lower owner for drainage of his land, he shall make any necessary enlargement at his own expense so that damage from such use shall not be caused to the upper land, unless by the agreement entered into provision for such use was made and defined.

Sec. 6510.

Ex-officio drainage commissioner.

SECTION 69. By this act, the superintendent of public works is constituted ex-officio drainage commissioner. He shall receive no additional salary or fees as such officer, but shall receive the necessary traveling and other incidental expenses incurred in the discharge of his official duties as such commissioner.

Sec. 6511.

Bond; supplies for drainage commissioner.

SECTION 70. The official bond of the superintendent of public works shall cover and be liable for the performance of all his official duties and obligations as drainage commissioner in like manner as for his duties and obligations in the office of superintendent of public works. As drainage commissioner the office of the superintendent of public works shall be furnished with all necessary additional furniture, stationery, office supplies, apparatus and fixtures for the performance of the duties in this act provided.

Sec. 6512.

Employment of assistants; compensation.

SECTION 71. In the performance of his duties a drainage commissioner, the superintendent of public works shall employ any necessary office assistants, who in addition to any salary or compensation received shall be entitled to receive their actual necessary expenses incurred in the performance of any duty. The compensation of any assistant employed by the drainage commissioner shall be such as the general assembly may provide.

§13.

SECTION 72. The drainage commissioner·shall carry into operation the provisions herein relating to his office and all other laws providing for the assistance, co-operation or arbitration with local, state or federal authorities in the construction, improvement or altering of rivers, drains, creeks, ditches or ·waterways for drainage purposes. He shall make inquiry into the needs for the improvement of ditches, rivers or drains used as general outlets for the purpose of reclaiming land, and offer such assistance as may be necessary in the proper procedure of local or state authorities in procuring the same. He may collect data on all rivers, streams, creeks, or ditches affecting three or more counties relative to drainage area, surface spill, maximum discharge in flood period, and average discharge at low water at points not exceeding ten miles apart beginning at the source.

He shall on application assist county engineers and commissioners in the best methods of assessment according to benefits, ascertaining damages to property and keeping of systematic records. The commissioners shall furnish to township trustees, village and city councils, boards of county commissioners, the state agricultural department, state game warden, and state department of public health any information they may want relative to the feasibility of flood prevention, reclamation of agricultural lands, purification of the water of streams made uninhabitable for fish by sewer or factory disposal, and drainage of marshes. He shall also hear and determine all appeals provided in this act to be made to him under its provisions, and all other things by its provisions required. The drainage commissioner shall do all other things provided in this chapter to be done by him; and shall annually report to the governor upon such matters as he deems to be of general public interest, and as to all matters of apportionment of assessments between counties in joint improvements.

Duties of drainage commissioner.

6514.

SECTION 73. The superintendent of public works as drainage commissioner in all matters of appeal to him, provided by this act shall have the right to, and if requested in writing by any of the parties in interest, shall call to his aid the state highway commissioner and the dean of the engineering department of the Ohio State University, who in such case shall with the drainage commissioner constitute an official board of appeals, and by a majority vote determine all issues to be determined upon matters appealed to the drainage commissioner under this act.

Official board of appeal.

6515.

SECTION 74. When the improvement proposed is located in, or affects lands in two or more counties, and neither county is a petitioner, the proceedings in this chap-

When proceedings conducted by joint board of commissioners.

ter shall be conducted by a joint board of county commissioners, consisting of the members of the boards of commissioners of the several counties; and in such case the auditor of the county with whom the petition is filed shall give notice of such filing with a copy of the petition to the auditor or auditors of the several other counties interested, who shall forthwith notify the boards of commissioners of each county in which lands are by the petition shown to be affected by the improvement petitioned for; and in such notice, the auditor shall call a joint meeting of said boards at one of the county seats at a date not less than ten, nor more than twenty days from the date of the notice. On the date so fixed, said boards shall meet and organize a joint board, by electing one of their number president and one clerk, but president and clerk shall not be from the same county, if the commissioners of two or more counties attend; and so organized they shall have and exercise, as a joint board, the same jurisdiction and authority that in this chapter is conferred on single boards of county commissioners. A quorum of such joint board at each meeting thereof shall consist of such of the commissioners in office in all said counties as may attend such meeting, and all its decisions shall be by a numerical majority of those present at its sessions, except as herein otherwise provided, and its actions, except for adjournments and dates of meetings shall be by a recorded individual vote upon motion or resolution.

Sec. 6516.
General powers and duties of joint board.

SECTION 75. At its first meeting, the joint board of county commissioners shall direct the county engineers of the several counties interested to either each make in his own county the preliminary surveys and estimates necessary and perform the other duties provided for in this act for the county engineer or the joint board may agree on one or more of the several county engineers to make all necessary surveys in all the interested counties, or with the consent of the joint board the several county engineers may delegate one or more of their number to act for all in making such preliminary surveys and estimates, or the joint board may employ a competent disinterested engineer regardless of his residence to perform all or any of the duties of the county engineer upon the improvement before them.

Sec. 6517.
Reports of engineers; approval and rejection.

SECTION 76. If one or more of the county engineers make said surveys, or each county engineer makes the surveys in his own county, the work of each said engineer shall be submitted to and approved or disapproved by the engineers of the other interested counties, and if disapproved, the reasons therefor given. And in any case any board of county commissioners for its better information may cause its county engineer to make the preliminary surveys in this act provided of the portion of the improvement located in his county, or any, or all of the counties, but at the expense and cost of its county alone. Any surveys made prior to the passage of this act may be used if deemed sufficiently accurate by the engineer or engineers in charge.

18.

SECTION 77. The report of the preliminary survey Filing pre-liminary survey; notice; hearing; when made shall be filed with the auditor of the county in which the petition for the improvement was filed. And upon being filed, notice of such filing shall be forthwith given by such auditor to the president of the joint board of commissioners, who shall then fix a date for the hearing of the petition and said report, and notify said auditor of the same. Thereupon the auditor shall give notice as provided in single county improvements as shown by the petition and engineer's report, and for those whose residences are unknown, he shall make publication in some paper in the county in which their land is situated as is provided in case of single county improvements, and make return of the persons served and manner of service to the joint board of county commissioners, which return shall be entered on the record of the case.

19.

SECTION 78. In case the joint board of county commissioners upon hearing dismiss the petition, the costs of Costs when petition dismissed; sworn statements. each county, itemized, shall be by the auditors of the several interested counties certified to the auditor of the county where the petition was filed, to whom the same shall be paid by the petitioners or their sureties, as provided in case of single county improvements. Such costs shall include the actual expenses of each of the commissioners and engineers of the counties, statements of which itemized and sworn to shall be filed with their county auditors, and attached to their cost bills, and the engineers of the respective counties shall likewise furnish itemized statements of all sums paid or to be paid to assistants upon said preliminary surveys verifying the same, and which shall be included in said auditor's statement of costs.

120.

SECTION 79. If a petition is granted by a joint board Proceedings when petition granted. of county commissioners, such board shall proceed under the provisions of this act for single boards of county commissioners to complete necessary surveys, schedules and records, make awards of damages to property or compensation for property taken, and ascertain the entire cost of the joint county improvement.

121.

SECTION 80. When the total cost and expense of a Apportionment of cost, etc., to each county. joint county improvement is ascertained, and the proceedings have reached the point where assessment of the same upon property benefited should be made, the joint board of commissioners shall, upon the call of its president, meet and apportion to each county the share of such cost and expense which shall be provided and paid by each county as its portion, according to benefit, for the improvement. Such apportionment as to each county shall be made by a majority vote of the joint board of commissioners and by the concurrence of at least two of the commissioners of the particular county to the amount apportioned to their county.

In case said joint board of commissioners cannot determine said apportionment as herein provided, then their When apportionment certified to superintendent of public works; decision final. failure so to agree shall be certified by the clerk and president to the superintendent of public works, who shall at a time to be fixed by him, and at the county seat of one of the counties interested, meet said joint board and investigate the matter and make such apportionment as he deems just and equitable between the counties affected, which apportionment shall be final. And to the amount so apportioned, there shall be added one per cent which additional sum the counties affected shall pay to the state treasurer, the same to be held and used for the expenses of the superintendent of public works as in this act provided.

Should the superintendent of public works find it necessary he may cause any additional surveys to be made and the cost thereof shall be added to the cost of the improvement.

SECTION 81. When the apportionment between the several counties has been made, either by the agreement of the counties, or by the superintendent of public works, then in each county the apportionment to such county shall be assessed on all the premises affected, including any portion of a municipality as an entirety, under the proceedings and by the officers provided for assessing the cost of single county improvements, and subject to the same right to appeal for assessments as to benefits conferred as thereby allowed.

SECTION 82. An appeal may be taken by any interested party from a final order of a joint board of county commissioners for or against the location or construction of any improvement that passes into or through two or more counties, to the superintendent of public works, in the same manner, and to be perfected by the same proceedings and in the same time as are appeals in single county improvements. But the statement of the decision appealed from and the appeal bond in such cases may be filed with the auditor of any of the interested counties; and the bond submitted may be approved by him. The auditor shall endorse the date of such filing, retain the bond in his official custody and forthwith forward the statement of appeal to the clerk of the joint board of county commissioners, who, within the time fixed for the filing of transcripts in single county improvement appeals, shall forward said statement with transcripts and papers, as in appeals in single county improvements, to the superintendent of public works at the state capitol.

SECTION 83. When the appeal is so perfected and filed with said superintendent of public works, he shall fix a date within thirty days, at one of the county seats of the counties interested, where he shall attend and hear the same, and notify the clerk of the joint board of such date and place. The clerk of the joint board whose decision is appealed from shall upon receipt of such date and place forthwith notify all parties to said proceeding by a short published notice in some paper printed in each county interested and any non-resident, whose address is known, by mail. But every party to the proceedings who shall have been in any manner previously made aware of the petition and proceedings for the improvement shall be deemed to have notice of proceedings therein on appeal.

15.

SECTION 84. Upon the hearing of said appeal either the superintendent of public works, or the appeal board provided for in this act, any two members of which shall be a quorum to proceed if the other cannot for any reason attend, shall have and exercise the jurisdiction given to the court of common pleas in case of appeals upon single county improvements from the granting or dismissal of a petition for an improvement, and shall in determining said matter find whether or not under the definitions in this act provided the improvement in question will be conducive to public health, convenience, and welfare, and a benefit to lands in the petition described. If the hearing be by two members of such appeal board and they do not agree, they shall adjourn the matter to some day when the third member can sit with them, when the questions at issue shall be decided by a majority vote of the board. *Judgment; certification to commissioner.*

The finding and decision of the superintendent of public works, or of said board, shall be final, and be certified to the joint board of county commissioners from which it came who shall upon such mandate according to the decision proceed with the improvement or dismiss the petition.

26.

SECTION 85. An appeal from any award made or a refusal to make an award for damages to property, or compensation for property taken, by a joint board of county commissioners may be taken and perfected to the court of common pleas of any of the counties interested in the same manner as provided for appeals in the case of awards in single county improvements, and the proceedings on such appeal shall be governed by all the provisions therefor. *Appeal from award for damages, etc.*

27.

SECTION 86. All the provisions for the relief of an owner of land who has not had notice and an opportunity to be heard in a proceeding for a single county improvement shall apply to any such owner of lands affected by a joint county improvement. *Relief to owner who has had no notice.*

28.

SECTION 87. In the matter of an improvement under this chapter there shall be included as a portion of the costs and expenses to be paid by the petitioners if the petition be dismissed, or assessed if it be granted, the actual expenses of the members of the joint board of county commissioners while in the performance of their duty at places other than at their county seat. *Expense of members of joint board.*

29.

SECTION 88. The joint board of county commissioners shall by resolution designate at which county seat the letting of contracts for the work and material for the joint improvement shall take place. The auditor and treasurer of such county shall ex officio become the fiscal agents of all the counties interested. Each other county shall on ascertainment of its apportionment of any cost or expense of such joint improvement pay to the treasurer of the desig- *Where contracts for joint improvement let; fiscal agents.*

nated county from time to time such sums as may be necessary to meet its share of expense, and said treasurer shall disburse the same on the warrant of the auditor. The treasurer and auditor with their bondsmen shall be liable upon their official bonds for any misappropriation of such funds.

All the provisions as to filing and paying of claims for labor and material provided in this act with the duties of the auditor shall apply in joint improvements as in single county improvements, but such filing shall be with the auditor of the said designated county.

Provision applicable to joint improvement.

All of the provisions for the issuing and sale of bonds in anticipation of assessments for benefits in case of single county improvements shall apply in like manner in case of joint county improvements; but the county commissioners of each county forming the joint board of county commissioners in the matter of determining whether to issue and sell bonds, or to make payment from the general ditch improvement fund of their respective counties shall act individually and for their own county only. For this purpose, and in anticipation of the apportionment of the cost of expense of the joint improvement to the several counties, the commissioners of any county may estimate the probable apportionment to their county and base their bond issues on such estimate; and if the same be less than the apportionment finally determined upon, they may at their discretion make a supplemenetary bond issue to meet the deficiency, or may pay the excess of the apportionment from their general ditch improvement fund.

Sec. 6530.

Repair or replacement affecting lands in two or more counties.

SECTION 89. If the cleaning, repair, or replacement of an improvement, constructed since or before the passage of this act, affects lands in more than one county, the commissioners of either county may by resolution refer the matter to all other interested counties with a specification of the work deemed necessary, and a request that such county or counties join in such cleaning, repair, or replacement. The county commissioners of whom such request is made shall, within thirty days from its receipt, decide and determine whether they will voluntarily join in such work or not and notify the requesting board of county commissioners whether they will or will not join, or such counties, or any of them, may request a conference of all the boards of county commissioners interested and set a date therefor not more than 20 days from the date of request for such conference. Such conference shall be held at the office of the board from whom the request to join originated. At such conference, the commissioners of each board, acting independently and not as a joint board, shall determine whether they will or will not join, and if the determination be to join on what terms as to the apportionment of the expense of the work undertaken. If all the interested boards agree, they shall by resolution, to be entered on their several journals, record such agreement, and the share of expense that each county shall assume and bear as its portion. If no agreement is reached at said meeting, the board of commissioners from which the request originated may at its election proceed with such cleaning, repair and replacement, as herein provided when one county only is interested, and may make, upon the ascertainment of the entire cost, a demand on such counties as they deem benefited for their shares of the total expense, but not exceeding such proportion of the cost of cleaning, repair or replacement as each county paid of the original cost of construction of the same improvement, if the same can be ascertained. If the county commissioners of the non-joining county or counties, on such demand, refuse payment, action may be brought in the common pleas court and any disinterested county, nearest adjoining the counties interested, for such sum as a demand for money, and the same shall be tried as are other actions for money, and the plaintiff county shall be entitled to recover any sum not exceeding the sum demanded nor the benefit conferred on the lands of the defendant county by the cleaning, repair or replacement made.

If a county to which a request is sent refuse to join, or if no reply be made to the request to join within the time limited therefor by the county to which it is sent, such silence shall be deemed to be a refusal, and the requesting county may proceed as in case of an unsuccessful conference.

§31.   SECTION 90. When the final ascertainment of apportionment among the counties interested is concluded by conference or judgment, the commissioners of each county shall assess the apportionment to their county on the lands benefited in the manner and to the extent provided for assessing such cleaning, repair, or replacement, as if affecting one county only. *Assessment of apportionment in each county.*

§32.   SECTION 91. When one or more boards of county commissioners are petitioners for an improvement that will affect a body of land in one or more counties, and in the opinion of the petitioning board or boards, the construction of such improvement will materially increase the value of the lands affected thereby for general taxation, they may state such fact in the petition with the percentage of increase in value in the aggregate they deem will be effected by such construction to the lands served thereby, and when in the course of proceedings upon the petition as in this chapter provided in the report of the county engineer has been made, showing the location, line, and other data, with the estimated cost of the improvement and the lands affected thereby, the board or boards of commissioners of any county or counties so affected may apply to the superintendent of public works for state aid in the construction of such improvement. In such case, if upon investigation the superintendent of public works find the claim in the petition as to such increased value for purposes of taxation to be true, and that such increase will be material and will beneficially affect the said counties interested and the state of Ohio, the *Proceedings when one or more boards are petitioners; state aid.*

superintendent of public works may grant such per cent
of estimated cost of the same as in its judgment shall be
commensurate with the advantage that will accrue to the
state within ten years by reason of such improvement, if
constructed, but not in any case to exceed twenty-five per
cent of such estimated cost. But if such aid be given, it
shall be upon the condition that the said counties interested shall in the proportion of the aggregate portions of
the assessment upon the lands within their boundaries benefited by the improvement pay toward the construction of
such improvement from their general funds at least one-
half the amount that may be given by the state. Such aid
so determined and provided by the superintendent of public
works shall be paid upon his certificate by the state treasurer from any funds available for the purpose and shall
be paid to the treasurers of the separate counties to be used
with the amounts paid by such counties for said purpose.
But such payment by the state shall not be made to any
county until the conditions herein have been complied with
by such county by the appropriation of its share toward
such construction, and not before the work proposed in the
petition has been contracted for.

Sec. 6533.
Tax on excess value paid into state treasury.

SECTION 92. Whenever any state aid has been thus
estimated, the lands assessed as benefited by the improvement shall be placed upon the tax duplicate of the county
by the county auditor or the taxing officer having authority
for the time being at their true value in money after said
improvement is completed. And the general tax levied on
any increase of value in excess of the valuation which such
lands had for taxation prior to the improvement, shall be
paid into the state treasury from year to year until the aid
given by the state has been fully repaid with interest at
four per cent per annum. Such payments shall be made to
the state at the times and in the manner of other tax payments to it as provided by law.

Sec. 6534.
Oath administered to witnesses.

SECTION 93. In any hearing in this chapter provided
for, before a board of county commissioners, joint board of
county commissioners, the superintendent of public works,
or a court where testimony to determine any fact is to be
received and considered an oath, as in trials in the courts
of the state, shall be administered to all witnesses before
they testify. Such oath may be administered by the presiding officer or any member of such trial body, or its clerk.
False testimony given under such oath shall be perjury,
and shall be punished under the provisions of law upon
indictment and conviction thereof.

Sec. 6535.
Penalty for false oath or statement.

SECTION 94. Whoever shall knowingly make a false
oath to any statement required by the provisions of this act
to be made upon oath, except in testimony as a witness,
shall upon conviction thereof be punished by a fine of not
less than one hundred dollars nor more than five hundred
dollars, or by imprisonment in the county jail, or workhouse used by the county, for not less than thirty days nor

more than six months, or by both such fine and imprisonment in the discretion of the court.

Any contractor who shall knowingly by himself or his agents or employees, do and conceal any work under his contract in violation of the terms and specifications therefor, or knowingly use and conceal in his work material defective under, or not in conformity to the specifications therefor, or otherwise violate the conditions of his contract in the performance of work or furnishing the material upon any improvement to the damage of the county or counties interested therein shall, in addition to any civil liability be deemed to be guilty of a misdemeanor, and upon conviction thereof be punished by a fine of not less than one hundred dollars nor more than five hundred dollars, or by imprisonment in the county jail, or workhouse used by the county, for not less than thirty days nor more than six months, or by both such fine and imprisonment in the discretion of the court.

onal on the weoof nated as by law. PRICE, Ieneral.

SECTION 95. That sections 3001, 6564 and 6565 be amended to read as follows:

SECTION 3001. The annual compensation of each county commissioner shall be determined as follows:

In each county in which on the twentieth day of December, 1909, the aggregate of the tax duplicate for real estate and personal property is five million dollars or less, such compensation shall be seven hundred and fifty dollars, and in addition thereto, in each county in which such aggregate is more than five million dollars, three dollars on each full one hundred thousand dollars of the amount of such duplicate in excess of five million dollars. That the compensation of each county commissioner for the year 1912, and each year thereafter, shall not in the aggregate exceed 115 per cent of the compensation paid to each county commissioner for the official year ending on the third Monday of September, 1911.

Such compensation shall be in equal monthly installments from the county treasury upon the warrant of the county auditor.

Sec. 6564. Where the board of county commissioners of one or more counties have been notified that a petition for the improvement of a ditch or drain has been regularly filed with the auditor thereof, then said commissioners shall proceed as in single county ditches, if lands affected by said improvement lie wholly in one county, and as in joint-county procedure if two or more counties are affected, and shall order the county engineer, or engineers, or disinterested engineers, of such county or counties, in addition to the preliminary survey as provided for in other cases, to consult with the proper official, or officials of the county or counties of an adjoining state through which the route of the improvement would pass.

Sec. 6565. Upon the filing of the engineer's report with the auditor or auditors of the county or counties affected in this state, the county auditor of the county or counties in which the petition was filed, shall notify, in writing, of the filing of said report the proper official of the county of the adjoining state. A copy of the petition and bond shall be attached thereto. The notice shall state the time and place of meeting for the purpose of organizing.

Repeals.

SECTION 96. That said original sections viz.: 3386, 3387, 3388, 3389, 3390, 6442, 6443, 6444, 6445, 6446, 6447, 6448, 6449, 6450, 6451, 6452, 6453, 6454, 6455, 6456, 6457, 6458, 6459, 6460, 6461, 6462, 6463, 6464, 6465, 6466, 6467, 6468, 6469, 6470, 6471, 6472, 6473, 6474, 6475, 6476, 6477, 6478, 6479, 6480, 6481, 6482, 6483, 6484, 6485, 6486, 6487, 6488, 6489, 6490, 6491, 6492, 6493, 6494, 6495, 6496, 6497, 6498, 6499, 6500, 6501, 6502, 6503, 6504, 6505, 6506, 6507, 6508, 6509, 6510, 6511, 6512, 6513, 6514, 6515, 6516, 6517, 6518, 6519, 6520, 6521, 6522, 6523, 6524, 6525, 6526, 6527, 6528, 6529, 6530, 6531, 6532, 6533, 6534, 6535, 6535-1, 6535-2, 6535-3, 6535-4, 6535-5, 6535-6, 6535-7, 6535-8, 6535-9, 6535-10, 6535-11, 6535-12, 6535-13, 6535-14, 6535-15, 6535-16, 6535-17, 6535-18, 6535-19, 6535-20, 6535-21, 6535-22, 6535-23, 6535-24, 6536, 6537, 6538, 6539, 6540, 6541, 6542, 6543, 6544, 6545, 6546, 6547, 6548, 6549, 6550, 6551, 6552, 6553, 6554, 6555, 6556, 6557, 6558, 6559, 6560, 6561, 6562, 6563, 6563-1, 6563-2, 6563-3, 6563-4, 6563-5, 6563-6, 6563-7, 6563-8, 6563-9, 6563-10, 6563-11, 6563-12, 6563-13, 6563-14, 6563-15, 6563-16, 6563-17, 6563-18, 6563-19, 6563-20, 6563-21, 6563-22, 6563-23, 6563-24, 6563-25, 6563-26, 6563-27, 6563-28, 6563-29, 6563-30, 6563-31, 6563-32, 6563-33, 6563-34, 6563-35, 6563-36, 6563-37, 6563-38, 6563-39, 6563-40, 6563-41, 6563-42, 6563-43, 6563-44, 6563-45, 6563-46, 6463-47, 6563-48, 6603, 6604, 6605, 6606, 6607, 6608, 6609, 6610, 6611, 6612, 6613, 6614, 6615, 6616, 6617, 6618, 6619, 6620, 6621, 6622, 6623, 6624, 6625, 6626, 6627, 6628, 6629, 6630, 6631, 6632, 6633, 6634, 6635, 6636, 6637, 6638, 6639, 6640, 6641, 6642, 6643, 6644, 6645, 6646, 6647, 6648, 6649, 6650, 6651, 6652, 6653, 6654, 6655, 6656, 6657, 6658, 6659, 6660, 6661, 6662, 6663, 6664, 6665, 6666, 6667, 6668, 6669, 6670, 6671, 6672, 6673, 6674, 6675, 6676, 6677, 6678, 6679, 6680, 6681, 6682, 6683, 6684, 6685, 6686, 6687, 6688, 6689, 6690, 6691, 6692, 6693, 6694, 6695, 6696, 6697, 6698, 6699, 6700, 6701, 6702, 6703, 6704, 6705, 6706, 6707, 6708, 6709, 6710, 6711, 6712, 6713, 6714, 6715, 6716, 6717, 6718, 6719, 6720, 6721, 6722, 6723, 6724, 6725, 6726, 6726-1, 6726-2, 6726-3, 6726-4, 6777, 6778, 6779, 6780, 6781, 6782, 6783, 6784, 6785, 6786, 6791, 6792, 6793, 6795, 6806, 6807, 6808, 6809, 6810, 6818, 6819, 6820, 6821, 6822, and original sections 3001,

6564, 6565 and all other sections of the General Code that may be found to be in conflict with this act so far as they pertain to matters specifically covered by the provisions of this act be and the same are hereby repealed.

The sectional numbers in this act are in conformity to the General Code.
JOHN G. PRICE,
Attorney General.

CLARENCE J. BROWN,
President of the Senate.
CARL R. KIMBALL,
Speaker of the House of Representatives.

Passed June 19, 1919.

This bill was presented to the Governor on June 28, 1919, and was not signed or returned to the house wherein it originated within ten days after being so presented, and was filed in the office of the Secretary of State, July 11, 1919.

ROBERT T. CREW,
Veto Clerk.

Filed in the office of the Secretary of State at Columbus, Ohio, on the 11th day of July, A. D. 1919.

244 G.

(972)

TIMES FOR HOLDING THE COURTS OF APPEALS AND COURTS OF COMMON PLEAS IN OHIO IN 1919.

Counties.	County Seats.	Appellate District.	Courts of Appeals.	Courts of Common Pleas.
Adams	West Union	4	May 13, October 28	February 3, May 5, Oct. 6.
Allen	Lima	3	January 6, September 8	January 6, April 7, Sept. 8.
Ashland	Ashland	5	April 14, October 13	February 3, May 5, Sept. 8
Ashtabula	Jefferson	7	January 27, September 8	January 6, April 7, Sept. 29.
Athens	Athens	4	January 16, October 9	February 10, May 5, Nov. 10.
Auglaize	Wapakoneta	3	January 6, September 8	January 2, May 5, Oct. 1.
Belmont	St. Clairsville	7	May 12, December 8	January 7, March 25, Sept. 23.
Brown	Georgetown	4	May 14, October 29	January 14, April 15, Oct. 14.
Butler	Hamilton	1	April 14, October 13	January 6, May 5, Oct. 6.
Carroll	Carrollton	7	April 14, November 10	February 3, May 26, Oct. 20.
Champaign	Urbana	2	April 9, October 22	January 6, May 5, Oct. 6.
Clark	Springfield	2	May 19, November 24	January 6, May 5, Oct. 6.
Clermont	Batavia	1	April 7, October 6	January 6, April 8, Oct. 7.
Clinton	Wilmington	1	April 30, October 31	January 6, April 7, Oct. 6.
Columbiana	Lisbon	7	April 7, November 3	January 6, April 21, Sept. 15.
Coshocton	Coshocton	5	May 19, November 24	January 6, April 7, Sept. 8.
Crawford	Bucyrus	3	January 6, September 8	January 6, April 7, Sept. 8.
Cuyahoga	Cleveland	8	January 6, October 6	January 6, April 7, July 7, Sept. 8.
Darke	Greenville	2	May 5, November 10	January 6, May 5, Oct. 6.
Defiance	Defiance	3	January 6, September 8	January 13, April 7, Oct. 6.
Delaware	Delaware	5	May 13, December 2	January 6, April 7, Sept. 15.
Erie	Sandusky	6	April 7, September 22	January 6, April 14, Sept. 15.
Fairfield	Lancaster	5	March 25, September 16	January 13, April 28, Oct. 27.
Fayette	Washington C. H.	2	May 12, November 17	January 6, May 5, Oct. 6.
Franklin	Columbus	2	January 6, September 15	January 6, April 14, Sept. 15.
Fulton	Wauseon	6	May 12, October 27	January 6, March 31, Oct. 13.
Gallia	Gallipolis	4	February 4, October 21	January 1, May 1, Sept. 1.
Geauga	Chardon	7	February 5, September 17	January 6, April 7, Sept. 29.
Greene	Xenia	2	March 31, October 13	January 6, May 5, Oct. 6.
Guernsey	Cambridge	7	April 21, November 17	January 6, May 5, Oct. 6.
Hamilton	Cincinnati	1	January 6, November 10	1st Monday Jan., April, July & Oct.
Hancock	Findlay	3	January 6, September 8	January 6, April 7, Sept. 8.
Hardin	Kenton	3	January 6, September 8	January 6, April 7, Sept. 22.
Harrison	Cadiz	7	May 5, December 1	January 6, March 10, Sept. 22.
Henry	Napoleon	3	January 6, September 8	January 6, May 5, Sept. 8.
Highland	Hillsboro	4	April 10, December 11	January 6, April 7, Oct. 6.
Hocking	Logan	4	January 22, October 15	January 12, April 6, Oct. 12.
Holmes	Millersburg	5	April 7, October 27	February 10, May 26, Nov. 10.
Huron	Norwalk	6	April 14, September 29	January 6, April 21, Oct. 6.
Jackson	Jackson	4	April 2, December 3	January 6, May 19, Oct. 6.
Jefferson	Steubenville	7	May 19, December 15	January 6, April 7, Sept. 8.
Knox	Mt. Vernon	5	March 31, October 20	January 6, May 5, Oct. 6.
Lake	Painesville	7	February 5, September 15	January 6, April 7, Sept. 22.
Lawrence	Ironton	4	March 4, November 11	January 6, April 7, Oct. 20.
Licking	Newark	5	March 4, October 7	January 6, April 7, Sept. 8.
Logan	Bellefontaine	3	January 6, September 8	January 6, May 5, Sept. 15.
Lorain	Elyria	8	April 28, September 22	January 6, April 7, Sept. 29.
Lucas	Toledo	6	January 6, November 3	January 6, April 7, Sept. 8.
Madison	London	2	April 7, October 20	January 6, April 7, Oct. 6.
Mahoning	Youngstown	7	February 24, October 6	January 6, May 12, Sept. 15.
Marion	Marion	3	January 6, September 8	January 20, April 28, Sept. 22.
Medina	Medina	8	April 21, October 1	January 20, April 21, Sept. 15.
Meigs	Pomeroy	4	February 5, October 22	January 6, May 5, Sept. 22.
Mercer	Celina	3	January 6, September 8	January 6, April 7, Oct. 6.
Miami	Troy	2	April 14, October 27	January 6, May 5, Oct. 6.
Monroe	Woodsfield	7	April 29, November 25	January 27, May 26, Sept. 29.
Montgomery	Dayton	2	May 26, December 1	January 6, April 7, Oct. 6.
Morgan	McConnelsville	2	May 6, November 13	January 7, April 1, Oct. 7.
Morrow	Mt. Gilead	5	May 27, December 9	January 6, May 5, Oct. 6.
Muskingum	Zanesville	5	April 29, November 5	January 6, April 7, Sept. 22.
Noble	Caldwell	7	April 28, November 24	January 6, May 5, Oct. 6.
Ottawa	Port Clinton	6	April 28, October 13	January 6, May 5, Oct. 20.
Paulding	Paulding	3	January 6, September 8	January 13, April 14, Oct. 13.
Perry	New Lexington	5	April 22, November 18	February 24, May 19, Oct. 27.
Pickaway	Circleville	4	April 22, December 16	January 6, April 7, Oct. 6.
Pike	Waverly	4	April 1, December 2	January 6, May 5, Oct. 6.
Portage	Ravenna	7	February 17, September 29	January 13, March 31, Sept. 22.
Preble	Eaton	2	April 30, November 5	January 6, May 5, Oct. 6.
Putnam	Ottawa	3	January 6, September 8	January 7, May 6, Oct. 14.
Richland	Mansfield	5	January 6, September 2	January 6, April 21, Sept. 15.
Ross	Chillicothe	4	April 8, December 9	January 6, April 14, Oct. 6.
Sandusky	Fremont	6	April 21, October 6	January 6, April 7, Oct. 13.
Scioto	Portsmouth	4	March 11, November 18	February 10, April 14, Sept. 8.
Seneca	Tiffin	3	January 6, September 8	January 13, April 14, Oct. 6.
Shelby	Sidney	2	April 28, November 3	January 6, April 7, Oct. 6.
Stark	Canton	5	February 4, September 23	January 6, May 5, Sept. 22.
Summit	Akron	8	April 7, September 8	January 1, April 7, July 7, Oct. 6.

TIMES FOR HOLDING THE COURTS OF APPEALS AND COURTS OF
COMMON PLEAS IN OHIO IN 1919—Concluded. .

Counties.	County Seat.	Appellate District.	Courts of Appeals.	Courts of Common Pleas.
Trumbull	Warren	7	February 10, September 22	January 20, April 21, Sept. 22.
Tuscarawas	New Philadelphia	5	June 3, December 16	January 6, April 7, Sept. 22.
Union	Marysville	3	January 6, September 8	January 6, April 7, Sept. 8.
Van Wert	Van Wert	3	January 6, September 8	anuĒry 20, April 21, Oct. 13.
Vinton	McArthur	4	January 21, October 14	January 13, May 26, Oct. 20.
Warren	Lebanon	1	April 28, October 27	January 6, April 7, Oct. 13.
Washington	Marietta	4	January 14, October 7	January 6, April 7, Oct. 6.
Wayne	Wooster	5	January 27, September 8	January 6, April 28, Sept. 15.
Williams	Bryan	6	May 5, October 20	January 13, May 5, Oct. 6.
Wood	Bowling Green	6	May 5, October 20	January 6, April 7, Sept. 15.
Wyandot	Upper Sandusky	3	January 0, September 8	January 6, April 7, Sept. 8.

·Index to Laws

979

GENERAL CODE—

Table of sections amended, enacted, repealed, etc.

Section.		Page.	Section.		Page.
50.	Am.	262	1185-1.	Am.	478
79-1.	En.	547	1186 to 1189.	Am.	478
82-1.	En.	547	1195-1.	En.	478
82-2.	En.	548	1196-1.	En.	503
151.	Am.	632	1201.	Am.	478
153.	Am.	632	1206 to 1209.	Am.	478
154.	Am.	632	1208-1 to 1208-5.	En.	548
190-1.	En.	44	1212-1.	En.	478
218-1.	En.	71	1213-1.	Am.	478
270-6.	Am.	921	1214-1.	En.	504
274-1.	En.	547	1218 to 1218-1.	Am.	478
276.	Am.	262	1221-1224.	Am.	478
290 to 295.	Re.	129	1230.	Am.	478
367-2.	Am.	356	1231-2.	Am.	478
367-5.	Am.	356	1232-1.	En.	148
367-6.	Am.	356	1233-1.	En.	148
464.	Am.	630	1234-1.	En.	148
479, Rule 3.	Am.	137	1236-6.	En.	46
412-1 to 412-15.	En.	219	1245-1246.	Am.	236
485.	Re.	604	1249-1259.	Am.	297
504-2 to 504-3.	Am.	372	1258-1 to 1258-8.	En.	297
660.	Am.	420	1259-1.	Am.	297
614-44.	Am.	428	1260-1261.	Am.	297
710.	Re.	129			418
710-1 to 710-189.	En.	80	1261-16 to 1261-73.	Re.	719
711 to 736.	Re.	129			724
736-1 to 736-2.	Re.	129	1261-16 to 1261-43.	Reen.	236
737 to 742.	Re.	129	1286-2.	En.	131
742-1 to 742-16.	Re.	129	1288.	Am.	160
743.	Re.	129	1295-5.	Am.	48
744-1 to 744-13	Re.	129	1295-6.	Am.	48
840.	Am.	292	1295-21 to 1295-35.	En.	73
843.	Am.	288	1302.	Am.	254
843-1 to 843-18.	En.	288	1303.	Am.	254
843-19 to 843-53.	En.	306	1303-1.	Am.	254
871-1.	Am.	58	1306 1 to 1306-2.	En.	14
871-47.	Am.	702	1343a.	En.	634
886 to 896.	Re & Reen	349	1352.	Am.	46
896-1 to 896-16.	En.	351	1352-6.	En.	140
905.	Am.	923	1352-8 to 1352-11.	En.	134
934-1.	En.	60	1356 to 1357.	Am.	427
991-992.	Am.	347	1359.	En.	615
1008.	Am.	540	1390 to 1429.	Re & Reen	579
1008-1.	En.	540	1412-1 to 1412-5.	Re.	604
1069-3 to 1069-16.	En.	325	1415-1.	Re.	604
1090 to 1090-21.	En.	330	1416-1.	Re.	604
1122 to 1136.	Re & Reen	358	1430.	Re.	604
1136-1.	Re.	358	1430.	En.	923
1137 to 1140.	Re & Reen	358	1431 to 1454.	Re & Reen	579
1140-1 to 1140-6.	En.	358	1437-1 to 1437-2.	Re.	604
1141.	En.	287	1455 to 1465.	Re.	604
1177-60 to 1177-70.	En.	164	1465-45.	Am.	313
1178.	Am.	478	1465-47 to 1465-49	Am.	313
1180 to 1181.	Am.	478	1465-53 to 1465-55.	Am.	313
1182.	En.	478	1465-58a.	En.	277
1184 to 1185.	Am.	478	1465-60 to 1465-61.	Am.	313

GENERAL CODE—Continued.

Section.		Page.	Section.		Page.
1465-63	Am.	555	1815-13 to 1815-14	Am.	611
1465-69	Am.	313	1891 to 1895	Am.	552
1465-72a	En.	313	1896 to 1897	Re.	554
1465-79 to 1465-80	Am.	313	1900-1902	Re.	554
1465-82 to 1465-83	Am.	313	1904	Re.	554
1465-90	Am.	313	1904-1 to 1904-3	En.	430
1465-93 to 1465-95	Am.	313	1921	Am.	625
1483	Am.	276	1921-1	En.	625
1488	Am.	276	1946	Am.	617
1520	Am.	276	1981	Am.	262
1558-78	Am.	473	2068	Am.	611
1558-83	Am.	473	2250	Am.	626
1579-6	Am.	166	2251-1	Am.	188
1579-8	Am.	166	2253	Am.	374
1579-16	Am.	166	2394	Am.	266
1579-20	Am.	166	2412	Am.	251
1579-26	Am.	166	2419	Am.	387
1579-36	Am.	166	2419-3	En.	268
1579-39	Am.	166	2421-1	En.	259
1579-91	Am.	149	2433	Am.	627
1579-92	Am.	149	2434	Am.	627
1579-92a to 1579-92c	En.	149	2446	Am.	627
1579-93	Am.	149	2502	Re.	62
1579-97	Am.	149	2503	Am.	623
1579-102	Am.	149	2506	Am.	40
1579-111a	Am.	149	2522 to 2523	Am.	266
1579-119	Am.	149	2526	Am.	266
1579-126a	En.	149	2528	Am.	266
1579-197 to 1579-198	Am.	153	2532	Am.	266
1579-204	Am.	153	2533	Re.	266
1579-207	Am.	153	2534	Re.	266
1579-220	Am.	153	2535	Am.	266
1579-224	Am.	153	2542	Am.	266
1579-226	Am.	153	2544	Am.	266
1579-229	Am.	153	2545	Re.	266
1579-282	Am.	436	2546	Am.	266
1579-286	Am.	436	2548 to 2550	Am.	266
1579-288	Am.	436	2551	Re.	266
1579-293	Am.	436	2552	Re.	266
1579-295 to 1579-296	Am.	436	2553 to 2556	Am.	266
1579-297	Am.	436	2557	Re.	266
1579-301	Am.	436	2572	Am.	266
1579-307 to 1579-308	Am.	436	2573	Am.	282
1579-311 to 1579-314	Am.	436	2609 to 2614	Re.	700
1579-318 to 1579-322	Am.	436	2614-1	En.	19
1579-324	Am.	436	2614-1	Re.	700
1579-326	Am.	436	2624	Am.	561
1579-341	Am.	472	2624-1	En.	561
1579-343	Am.	472	2685	Am.	561
1579-367 to 1579-415	En.	171	2685-1	En.	561
1579-416 to 1579-458	En.	447	2689	Am.	561
1579-459 to 1579-496	En.	462	2766-1	En.	163
1579-497 to 1579-549	En.	515	2768	Am.	282
1643	Am.	260	2788-1	En.	478
1662	Am.	692	2934	Am.	633
1672	Am.	260	2950	Am.	34
1683-9	Am.	624	2967 to 2968	Am.	421
1683-12 to 1683-19	Re.	380	2976-18, 2976-27	En.	700
1693	Am.	162	2980-1	Am.	62
1701-1	En.	67	3001	Am.	926
1815-12	Am.	554	3002	Re.	266

GENERAL CODE—Continued.

Section.		Page.	Section.		Page.
3061	Am.	70	4736	Am.	704
3082-1	En.	79	4744-1	Am.	704
3092	Am.	51	4744-2	Am.	233
3093	Am.	260	4747-1	Am.	704
3107-1	En.	79	4782	Am.	704
3128	Am.	255	4862	Am.	699
3130 to 3134	Am.	255	4940	Am.	699
3136 to 3137	Am.	255	5123-1	Am.	693
3138-1	Am.	62	5123-3	Am.	693
3141-1	En.	230	5180-1 to 5180-2	En.	546
3147	Am.	230	5242	Am.	547
3148	Am.	252	5243	Am.	130
3148-1 to 3148-3	En.	253	5330	Am.	612
3153-1, 3153-3	Am.	230	5331 to 5348	Am.	561
3153-6	Am.	230	5348-1 to 5348-14	En.	561
3193-1	En.	618	5366	Am.	138
3197	Am.	618	5366-1	Am.	131
3199	Am.	618	5404-1	En.	131
3203-2a	En.	618	5449 to 5451	Am.	141
3203-4a	En.	618	5458	Am.	141
3203-5	Am.	618	5470	Am.	141
3203-8	Am.	618	5473-1	Am.	141
3203-12a	En.	618	5474	Am.	141
3203-21	Am.	618	5548 to 5548-1	Am.	557
3203-21a	En.	618	5564	Am.	606
3203-35	Am.	618	5597	Am.	557
3285-1	En.	281	5598	Re.	557
3298-7	Am.	478	5609 to 5610	Am.	557
3298-18	Am.	478	5612 to 5613	Am.	628
3298-32	Am.	478	5652 to 5652-1	Am.	534
3371-1	En.	478	5652-1a	En.	534
3373	Am.	478	5652-4	Am.	534
3386 to 3390	Re.	926	5652-7 to 5652-15	Am.	534
3391 to 3394	Re.	236	5653	Am.	534
3410-1 to 3410-11	Re & Reen	542	5704	Am.	50
3410-12 to 3410-13	Re.	542	5706	Am.	475
3476	Am.	266	5751	Am.	475
3479	Am.	266	5777 to 5778	Am.	15
3481 to 3484	Am.	266	5584	Am.	15
3492 to 3495	Am.	266	5785	Am.	460
3618-1	Am.	184	5805-1 to 5805-12	Re & Reen	52
3812-2 to 3812-3	En.	215	5805-13 to 5805-14	En.	52
4228	Am.	43	5831-1 to 5831-3	Re.	605
4250	Am.	45	5841	Am.	534
4404 to 4405	Am.	236	5845	Am.	534
4406 to 4410	Am.	236	5893-1	En.	610
4411	Am.	11	5903 to 5907	Re.	347
4413	Am.	236	5903-1 to 5903-26	En.	334
4429 to 4430	Am.	236	5966	Am.	218
4436 to 4437	Am.	236	6064 to 6066	Re.	418
4476	Am.	236	6070	Re.	418
4688	Am.	704	6083 to 6084	Re.	418
4688-1	Am.	704	6087 to 6089	Re.	418
4696	Am.	704	6091	Re.	418
4698 to 4699	Am.	192	6102 to 6106	Re.	418
4701	Am.	192	6106 to 6120	Re.	418
4714	Am.	704	6122	Re.	418
4715	Am.	506	6125	Re.	418
4727	Am.	235	6127 to 6128	Re.	418
4729 to 4732	Am.	704	6130	Re.	418
4734	Am.	704	6132	Re.	418

GENERAL CODE—Continued.

Station.		Page.	Section.		Page.
6134 to 6138	Re.	418	7645	Am.	542
6140	Re.	418	7654–1 to 7654–5	Am.	233
6142 to 6152	Re.	418	7729	Re.	614
6155 to 6157	Re.	418	7730	Am.	431
6159	Re.	418	7730	Am.	704
6161 to 6168	Re.	418	7731–1	Am.	704
6187 to 6192	Re.	418	7762	Am.	542
6212–13 to 6212–85	En.	388	7762–1 to 7762–4	En.	624
6212–85 to 6212–106	En.	720	7776–1	En.	605
6212–107 to 6212–121	En.	716	7807–1 to 7807–2	Am.	683
6212–122 to 6212–136	En.	725	7807–9	En.	622
6251	Am.	475	7807–10	En.	683
6253	Re.	34	7817	Am.	66
6254	Am.	475	7823–2	En.	622
6257 to 6258	Re.	46	7823–3	En.	683
6259	Am.	46	7824	Am.	683
6262	Am.	46	7826	Am.	683
6422–1 to 6422–10	En.	292	7830 to 7831	Am.	683
6442 to 6535	Re & Reen	926	7831–1	En.	622
6534 (void)	Re.	477	7831–3	En.	683
6535–1 to 6535–21	Re.	926	7832–2 to 7832–3	Am.	683
6536 to 6563	Re.	926	7840	Am.	683
6563–1 to 6563–48	Re.	926	7847	Am.	683
6564 to 6565	Am.	926	7847–1	En.	683
6602–1	Am.	368	7848	En.	683
6602–4	Am.	368	7852	Am.	514
6602–8b	Am.	368	7852	Am.	683
6602–8h	Am.	368	7852–1	En.	514
6602–17	Am.	375	7852–1	En.	683
6602–20	Am.	375	7852–2 to 7852–3	En.	514
6602–26	Am.	375	7896–1, 7896–63	En.	195
6602–32	Am.	375	7998	Am.	606
6602–34 to 6602–106	En.	634	8301	Am.	132
6603 to 6726	Re.	927	8565–1 to 8565–2	En.	13
6726–1 to 6726–4	Re.	927	8574	Am.	69
6777 to 6786	Re.	927	8728–1 to 8728–12	En.	507
6791 to 6793	Re.	927	9156	Am.	136
6795	Re.	927	9485	Re & Reen	688
6806 to 6810	Re.	927	9485–1	En.	688
6818 to 6822	Re.	927	9510–3 to 9510–4	En.	385
6859–3a	En.	426	9618	Am.	72
6912	Am.	478	9676 to 9750	Re.	129
6926–1 to 6926–3	En.	478	9752	Re.	129
6936	Am.	478	9752–1 to 9752–2	Re.	129
6954	En.	478	9753 to 9790	Re.	129
6956–1	Am.	478	9790–1	Re.	129
6956–1a	En.	478	9791 to 9796	Re.	129
6957 to 6964	En.	304	9796–1 to 9796–3	Re.	129
7146	Reen.	232	9797 to 9849	Re.	129
7150 to 7153	Reen.	232	9856	Re.	129
7181–1	En.	478	9880	Am.	381
7201	En.	505	9880–1	Am.	381
7491	Am.	65	9881 to 9882	Am.	381
7594–1	En.	431	9883	Re.	381
7595–1 to 7595–2	Am.	431	9884	Am.	381
7595–3 to 7595–5	En.	431	9884–1 to 9884–4	En.	381
7604	Am.	20	9894	Am.	381
7620	Am.	187	9809	Am.	381
7621	Am.	133	9911	Re.	381
7621–1	En.	133	9914 to 9915	Re.	381
7642	Am.	613	9921–6	En.	364

GENERAL CODE—Concluded.

Section.		Page.	Section.		Page.
10150	Am.	607	12805	Am.	616
10494	Am.	625	12815	Am.	136
10605	Am.	275	12898 to 12899	Re.	129
10697	Am.	703	12906–1	En.	133
10801	Re.	477	12996	Am.	532
10933	Am.	366	13007–6	Re.	541
10989	Am.	387	13007–11 to 13007–12	Am.	532
11186	Am.	12	13031–13 to 13031–18	En.	730
11198–1	En.	12	13108	Re.	292
11273	Am.	49	13128	Am.	556
11683 to 11684	Re.	34	13163–1	En.	64
11710 to 11711	Am.	10	13182 to 13187	Re.	129
12398–1 to 12398–2	En.	57	13193–1	Re.	129
12473	Re.	129	13403–1	En.	61
12512–1	En.	187	13421–23 to 13421–26	En.	189
12521	Re.	604	13423	Am.	40
12523	Re.	605	13555	Am.	42
12533 to 12537	Re.	347	13560	Am.	4
12537–1	Re.	347	13560	Am.	158
12538 to 12541	Re .	347	13698	Am.	18
12556	Am.	687	13700	Am.	18
12556–1	En.	687	13702 to 13703	Am.	18
12600–3	Am.	529	13706	Am.	144
12600–5	Am.	529	13755	Am.	36
12603	Am.	471	13916–1 to 13916–4	En.	630
12604	Re.	472	14203–23	Am.	608
12608	Am.	471	14719 to 14720	Re.	470
12694	Am.	40	14867–2 to 14867–8	En.	285
12708	Am.	427	14867–9 to 14867–15	En.	348
12785	Am.	236	14875–3 to 14875–4	En.	609
12788	Am.	161	15301–1 to 15301–9	En.	284
12798–6	En.	419			

1037

Lightning Source UK Ltd.
Milton Keynes UK
UKHW031320271218
334537UK00006B/109/P